GO!
Premium Media Site

Improve your grade with hands-on tools and resources!

- Master *Key Terms* to expand your vocabulary.
- Assess your knowledge with fun *Crossword Puzzles* and *Flipboards*, which let you flip through the definitions of the key terms and match them with the correct term.
- Prepare for exams by taking practice quizzes in the *Online Chapter Review*.
- Download *Student Data Files* for the application projects in each chapter.
- Answer matching and multiple choice questions to test what you learned in each chapter.

And for even more tools, you can access the following Premium Resources using your Access Code. Register now to get the most out of *GO!*.

- *Student Training Videos* for each Objective have been created by the author - a real instructor teaching the same types of courses that you take.*
- *GO! to Work* videos are short interviews with workers showing how they use Office in their job.*
- *GO! for Job Success* videos related to the projects in the chapter cover such important topics as Dressing for Success, Time Management, and Making Ethical Choices.*

*Access code required for these premium resources

Your Access Code is:

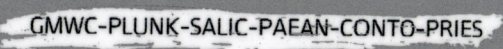

GMWC-PLUNK-SALIC-PAEAN-CONTO-PRIES

Note: If there is no silver foil covering the access code, it may already have been redeemed, and therefore may no longer be valid. In that case, you can purchase online access using a major credit card or PayPal account. To do so, go to **www.pearsonhighered.com/go**, select your book cover, click on "Buy Access" and follow the on-screen instructions.

To Register:

- To start you will need a valid email address and this access code.
- Go to **www.pearsonhighered.com/go** and scroll to find your text book.
- Once you've selected your text, on the Home Page for the book, click the link to access the Student Premium Content.
- Click the Register button and follow the on-screen instructions.
- After you register, you can sign in any time via the log-in area on the same screen.

System Requirements

Windows 7 Ultimate Edition; IE 8
Windows Vista Ultimate Edition SP1; IE 8
Windows XP Professional SP3; IE 7
Windows XP Professional SP3; Firefox 3.6.4
Mac OS 10.5.7; Firefox 3.6.4
Mac OS 10.6; Safari 5

Technical Support

http://247pearsoned.custhelp.com

Word 2013

Comprehensive

GO!

with Microsoft®

Word 2013
Comprehensive

Shelley Gaskin, Alicia Vargas, and Carol Martin

PEARSON

Boston   Columbus   Indianapolis   New York   San Francisco   Upper Saddle River
Amsterdam   Cape Town   Dubai   London   Madrid   Milan   Munich   Paris   Montréal   Toronto
Delhi   Mexico City   São Paulo   Sydney   Hong Kong   Seoul   Singapore   Taipei   Tokyo

Editor in Chief: Michael Payne
Executive Acquisitions Editor: Jenifer Niles
Editorial Project Manager: Carly Prakapas
Product Development Manager: Laura Burgess
Development Editor: Shannon LeMay-Finn
Editorial Assistant: Andra Skaalrud
Director of Marketing: Maggie Leen
Marketing Manager: Brad Forrester
Marketing Coordinator: Susan Osterlitz
Marketing Assistant: Darshika Vyas
Managing Editor: Camille Trentacoste
Senior Production Project Manager: Rhonda Aversa

Operations Specialist: Maura Zaldivar-Garcia
Senior Art Director: Jonathan Boylan
Cover Photo: © photobar/Fotolia
Associate Director of Design: Blair Brown
Director of Media Development: Taylor Ragan
Media Project Manager, Production: Renata Butera
Full-Service Project Management: PreMediaGlobal
Composition: PreMediaGlobal
Printer/Binder: R. R. Donnelley
Cover Printer: Lehigh-Phoenix Color/Hagerstown
Text Font: MinionPro

Library of Congress data on file

5 6 7 8 9 10 20 19 18 17 16 15

ISBN 10: 0-13-341746-8
ISBN 13: 978-0-13-341746-3

Brief Contents

Table of Contents

Office

Word Introduction to Microsoft Word 2013   49

Chapter 1   Creating Documents with Microsoft Word 2013.........51

Chapter 2   Using Tables and Templates to Create Resumes and Cover Letters 109

Chapter 9 Creating Standardized Forms and Managing Documents

Chapter 12 Integrating Word with PowerPoint and Modifying Document Components 641

Glossary G-1

Index I-1

About the Authors

Shelley Gaskin, Series Editor, is a professor in the Business and Computer Technology Division at Pasadena City College in Pasadena, California. She holds a bachelor's degree in Business Administration from Robert Morris College (Pennsylvania), a master's degree in Business from Northern Illinois University, and a doctorate in Adult and Community Education from Ball State University (Indiana). Before joining Pasadena City College, she spent 12 years in the computer industry, where she was a systems analyst, sales representative, and director of Customer Education with Unisys Corporation. She also worked for Ernst & Young on the development of large systems applications for their clients. She has written and developed training materials for custom systems applications in both the public and private sector, and has also written and edited numerous computer application textbooks.

This book is dedicated to my students, who inspire me every day.

Alicia Vargas is a faculty member in Business Information Technology at Pasadena City College. She holds a master's and a bachelor's degree in business education from California State University, Los Angeles, and has authored several textbooks and training manuals on Microsoft Word, Microsoft Excel, and Microsoft PowerPoint.

This book is dedicated with all my love to my husband Vic, who makes everything possible; and to my children Victor, Phil, and Emmy, who are an unending source of inspiration and who make everything worthwhile.

Carol L. Martin is recently retired from the faculty at Harrisburg (Pennsylvania) Area Community College. She holds a bachelor's degree in Secondary Education—Mathematics from Millersville (Pennsylvania) University and a master's degree in Training and Development from Pennsylvania State University. For over 40 years, she has instructed public school students and educators in the use of various computer applications. She has written and edited a variety of textbooks dealing with Microsoft Office applications and has co-authored several training manuals for use in Pennsylvania Department of Education in-service courses.

This book is dedicated to my husband Ron—a constant source of encouragement and technical support; and to my delightful grandsons, Tony and Josh, who keep me young at heart.

GO! with Word 2013

GO! with Word 2013 is the right solution for you and your students in today's fast-moving, mobile environment. The GO! Series content focuses on the real-world job skills students need to succeed in the workforce. They learn Office by working step-by-step through practical job-related projects that put the core functionality of Office in context. And as has always been true of the GO! Series, students learn the important concepts when they need them, and they never get lost in instruction, because the GO! Series uses Microsoft procedural syntax. Students learn how and learn why—at the teachable moment.

After completing the instructional projects, students are ready to apply the skills in a wide variety of progressively challenging projects that require them to solve problems, think critically, and create projects on their own. And, for those who want to go beyond the classroom and become certified, GO! provides clear MOS preparation guidelines so students know what is needed to ace the Core exam!

What's New

New Design reflects the look of Windows 8 and Office 2013 and enhances readability.

Enhanced Chapter Opener now includes a deeper introduction to the A and B instructional projects and more highly-defined chapter Objectives and Learning Outcomes.

New Application Introductions provide a brief overview of the application and put the chapters in context for students.

Coverage of New Features of Office 2013 ensures that students are learning the skills they need to work in today's job market.

New Application Capstone Projects ensure that students are ready to move on to the next set of chapters. Each Application Capstone Project can be found on the Instructor Resource Center and is also a Grader project in MyITLab.

More Grader Projects based on the E, F, and G mastering-level projects, both homework and assessment versions! These projects are written by our GO! authors, who are all instructors in colleges like yours!

New Training and Assessment Simulations are now written by the authors to match the book one-to-one!

New MOS Map on the Instructor Resource Site and in the Annotated Instructor's Edition indicates clearly where each required MOS Objective is covered.

Three Types of Videos help students understand and succeed in the real world:

- *Student Training Videos* are broken down by Objective and created by the author—a real instructor teaching the same types of courses that you do. Real personal instruction.
- *GO! to Work* videos are short interviews with workers showing how they use Office in their jobs.
- *GO! for Job Success* videos relate to the projects in the chapter and cover important career topics such as *Dressing for Success*, *Time Management*, and *Making Ethical Choices*. **Available for Chapters 1–3 only.**

New GO! Learn It Online section at the end of the chapter indicates where various student learning activities can be found, including multiple choice and matching activities.

New Styles for In-Text Boxed Content: Another Way, Notes, More Knowledge, Alerts, and **new *By Touch* instructions** are included in line with the instruction and not in the margins so that the student is more likely to read this information.

Clearly Indicated Build from Scratch Projects: GO! has always had many projects that begin "from scratch," and now we have an icon to really call them out!

New Visual Summary focuses on the four key concepts to remember from each chapter.

New Review and Assessment Guide summarizes the end-of-chapter assessments for a quick overview of the different types and levels of assignments and assessments for each chapter.

New Skills and Procedures Summary Chart (online at the Instructor Resource Center) summarizes all of the shortcuts and commands covered in the chapter.

New End-of-Chapter Key Term Glossary with Definitions for each chapter, plus a comprehensive end-of-book glossary.

New Flipboards and Crossword Puzzles enable students to review the concepts and key terms learned in each chapter by completing online challenges.

Teach the Course You Want in Less Time

A Microsoft® Office textbook designed for student success!

- **Project-Based –** Students learn by creating projects that they will use in the real world.

- **Microsoft Procedural Syntax –** Steps are written to put students in the right place at the right time.

- **Teachable Moment –** Expository text is woven into the steps—at the moment students need to know it—not chunked together in a block of text that will go unread.

- **Sequential Pagination –** Students have actual page numbers instead of confusing letters and abbreviations.

New Feature

Student Outcomes and Learning Objectives – Objectives are clustered around projects that result in student outcomes.

New Design – Provides a more visually appealing and concise display of important content.

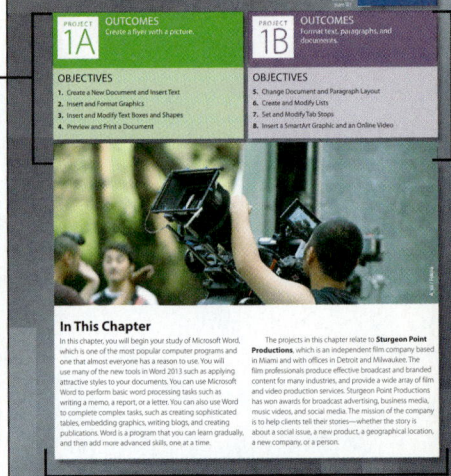

New Application Introductions – Provide an overview of the application to prepare students for the upcoming chapters.

Simulation Training and Assessment – Give your students the most realistic Office 2013 experience with open, realistic, high-fidelity simulations.

Scenario – Each chapter opens with a job-related scenario that sets the stage for the projects the student will create.

Project Activities – A project summary stated clearly and quickly.

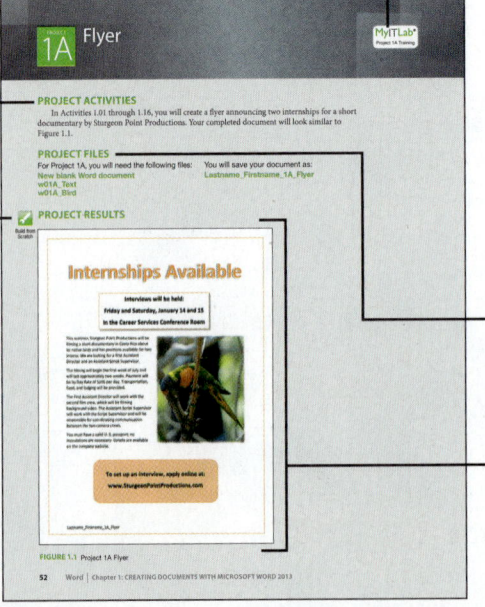

Project Files – Clearly shows students which files are needed for the project and the names they will use to save their documents.

New Build from Scratch Icons – Enable you to easily see all the projects that the student builds from scratch.

Project Results – Shows students what successful completion looks like.

In-Text Features
Another Way, Notes, More Knowledge, Alerts, and By Touch Instructions

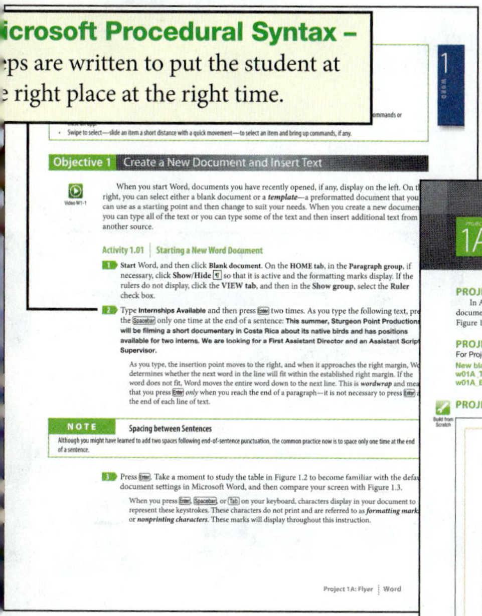

Microsoft Procedural Syntax – eps are written to put the student at e right place at the right time.

Color Coding – Each chapter has two instructional projects, which is less overwhelming for students than one large chapter project. The two projects are differentiated by different colored numbering and headings.

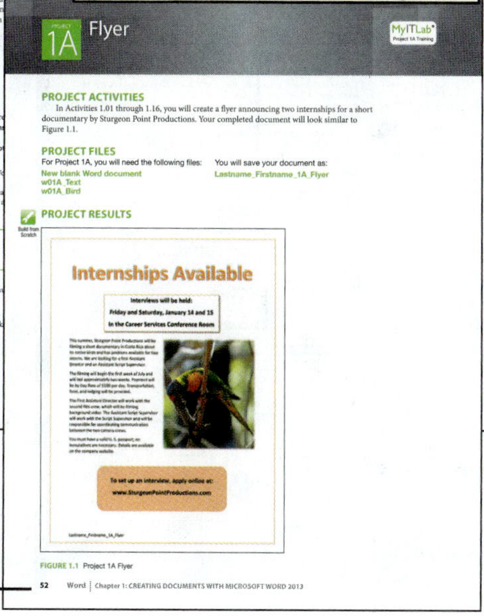

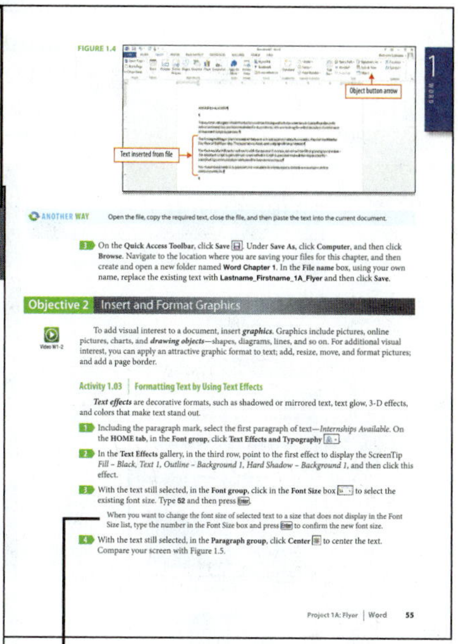

Sequential Pagination – Students are given actual page numbers to navigate through the textbook instead of confusing letters and abbreviations.

Teachable Moment – Expository text is woven into the steps—at the moment students need to know it—not chunked together in a block of text that will go unread.

End-of-Chapter
Content-Based Assessments – Assessments with defined solutions.

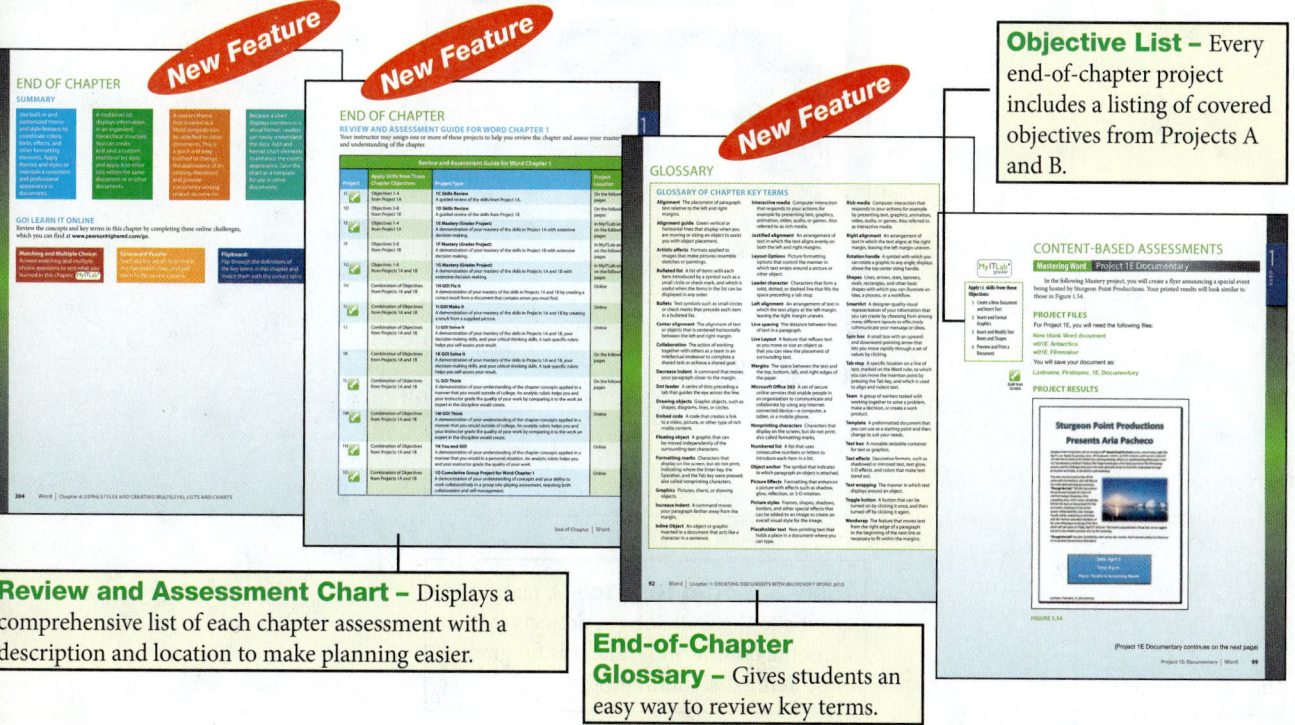

Objective List – Every end-of-chapter project includes a listing of covered objectives from Projects A and B.

Review and Assessment Chart – Displays a comprehensive list of each chapter assessment with a description and location to make planning easier.

End-of-Chapter Glossary – Gives students an easy way to review key terms.

End-of-Chapter

Content-Based Assessments – Assessments with defined solutions. (continued)

Grader Projects – Each chapter has six MyITLab Grader projects—three homework and three assessment—clearly indicated by the MyITLab logo.

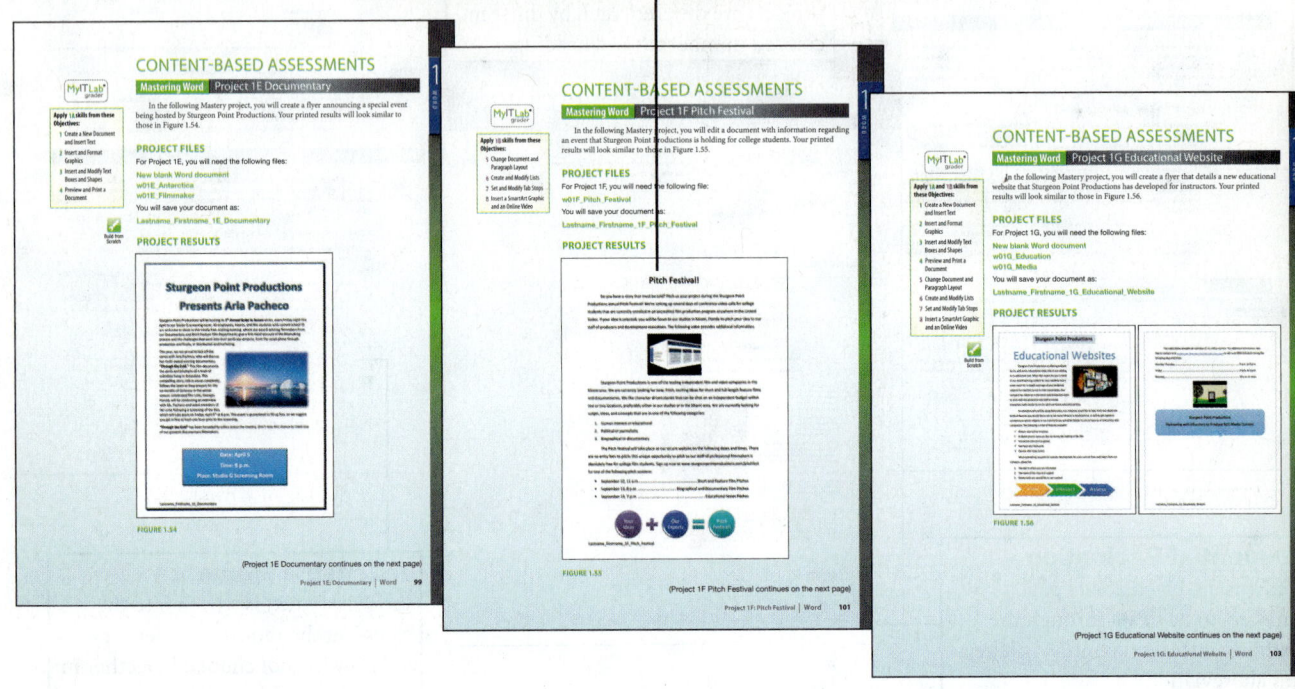

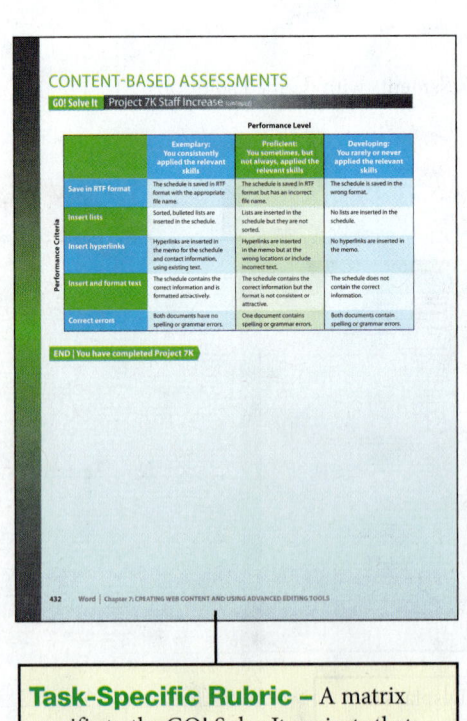

Task-Specific Rubric – A matrix specific to the GO! Solve It projects that states the criteria and standards for grading these defined-solution projects.

End-of-Chapter

Outcomes-Based Assessments – Assessments with open-ended solutions.

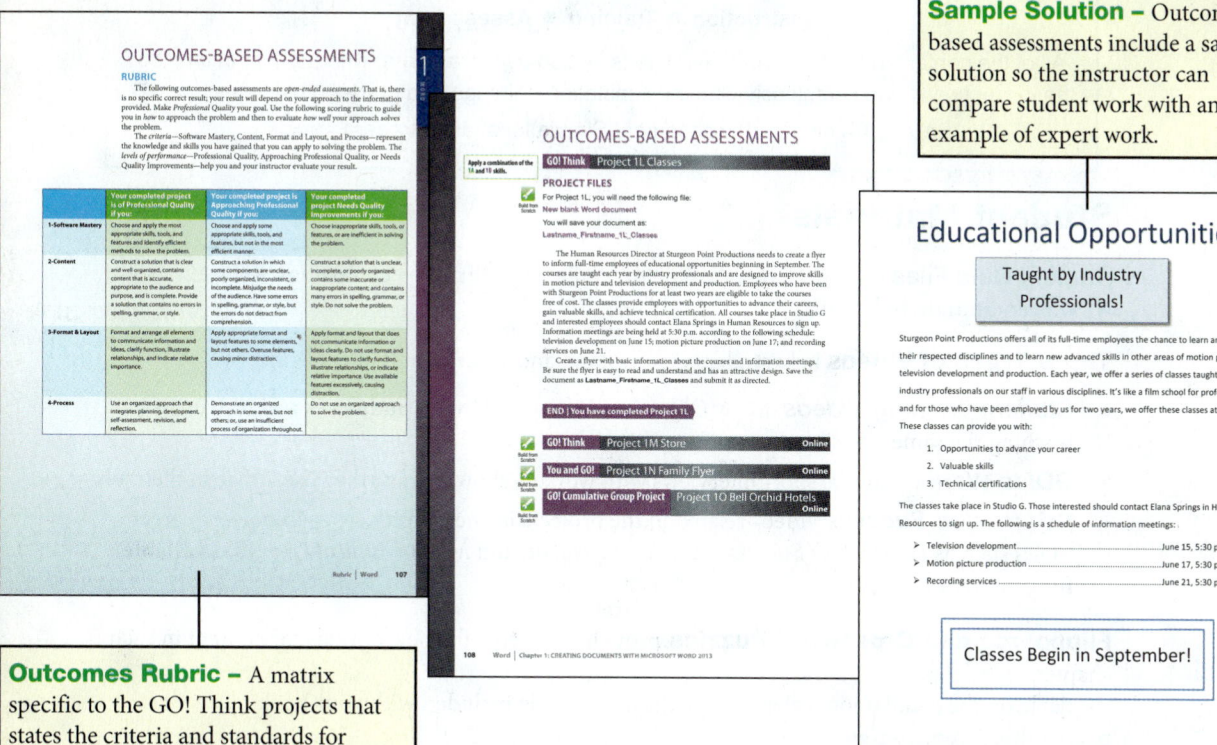

Sample Solution – Outcomes-based assessments include a sample solution so the instructor can compare student work with an example of expert work.

Outcomes Rubric – A matrix specific to the GO! Think projects that states the criteria and standards for grading these open-ended assessments.

GO! with Microsoft Office 365 – A collaboration project for each chapter teaches students how to use the cloud-based tools of Office 365 to communicate and collaborate from any device, anywhere. **Available for Chapters 1–3 only.**

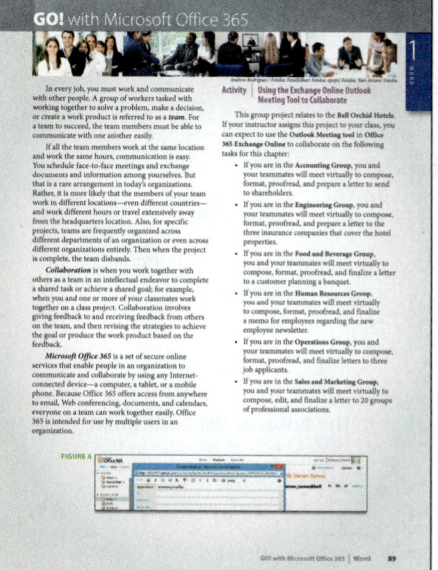

Office Online (formerly Web Apps) – For each instructional project, students can create the same or similar result in the corresponding Office Online application - 24 projects in all! **Available for Chapters 1–3 only.**

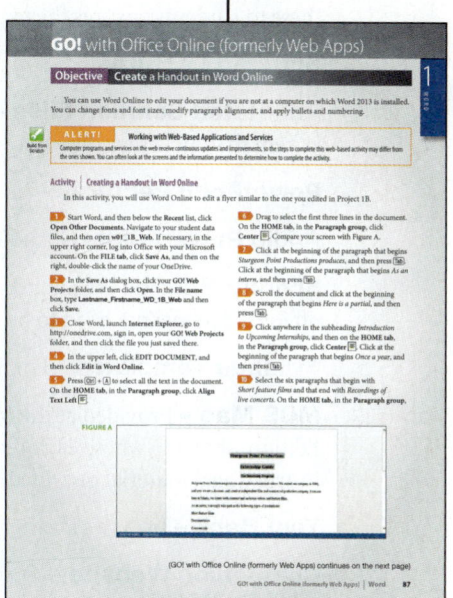

Student Materials

Student Data Files – All student data files are available to all on the companion website: www.pearsonhighered.com/go.

Three Types of Videos help students understand and succeed in the real world:

- *Student Training Videos* are by Objective and created by the author—a real instructor teaching the same types of courses that you teach.
- *GO! to Work* videos are short interviews with workers showing how they use Office in their job.
- *GO! for Job Success* videos related to the projects in the chapter cover important career topics such as *Dressing for Success*, *Time Management*, and *Making Ethical Choices*. **Available for Chapters 1–3 only.**

Flipboards and Crossword Puzzles provide a variety of review options for content in each chapter.
Available on the companion website using the access code included with your book.
pearsonhighered.com/go.

All Instructor and Student materials available at pearsonhighered.com/go

Instructor Materials

Annotated Instructor Edition – An instructor tool includes a full copy of the student textbook and a guide to implementing your course in three different ways, depending on the emphasis you want to place on digital engagement. Also included are teaching tips, discussion topics, and other useful pieces for teaching each chapter.

Student Assignment Tracker (previously called Assignment Sheets) **–** Lists all the assignments for the chapter. Just add the course information, due dates, and points. Providing these to students ensures they will know what is due and when.

Scripted Lectures – A script to guide your classroom lecture of each instructional project.

Annotated Solution Files – Coupled with the scorecards, these create a grading and scoring system that makes grading easy and efficient.

PowerPoint Lectures – PowerPoint presentations for each chapter.

Audio PowerPoints – Audio versions of the PowerPoint presentations for each chapter.

Scoring Rubrics – Can be used either by students to check their work or by you as a quick check-off for the items that need to be corrected.

Syllabus Templates – For 8-week, 12-week, and 16-week courses.

MOS Map – Provided at the Instructor Resource Center site and in the Annotated Instructor's Edition, showing where each required MOS Objective is covered either in the book or via additional instructional material provided.

Test Bank – Includes a variety of test questions for each chapter.

Companion Website – Online content such as the Online Chapter Review, Glossary, and Student Data Files are all at www.pearsonhighered.com/go.

Reviewers

GO! Focus Group Participants

Kenneth Mayer	Heald College
Carolyn Borne	Louisiana State University
Toribio Matamoros	Miami Dade College
Lynn Keane	University of South Carolina
Terri Hayes	Broward College
Michelle Carter	Paradise Valley Community College

GO! Reviewers

Abul Sheikh	Abraham Baldwin Agricultural College
John Percy	Atlantic Cape Community College
Janette Hicks	Binghamton University
Shannon Ogden	Black River Technical College
Karen May	Blinn College
Susan Fry	Boise State University
Chigurupati Rani	Borough of Manhattan Community College / CUNY
Ellen Glazer	Broward College
Kate LeGrand	Broward College
Mike Puopolo	Bunker Hill Community College
Nicole Lytle-Kosola	California State University, San Bernardino
Nisheeth Agrawal	Calhoun Community College
Pedro Diaz-Gomez	Cameron
Linda Friedel	Central Arizona College
Gregg Smith	Central Community College
Norm Cregger	Central Michigan University
Lisa LaCaria	Central Piedmont Community College
Steve Siedschlag	Chaffey College
Terri Helfand	Chaffey College
Susan Mills	Chambersburg
Mandy Reininger	Chemeketa Community College
Connie Crossley	Cincinnati State Technical and Community College
Marjorie Deutsch	City University of New York - Queensborough Community College
Mary Ann Zlotow	College of DuPage
Christine Bohnsak	College of Lake County
Gertrude Brier	College of Staten Island
Sharon Brown	College of The Albemarle
Terry Rigsby	Columbia College
Vicki Brooks	Columbia College
Donald Hames	Delgado Community College
Kristen King	Eastern Kentucky University
Kathie Richer	Edmonds Community College
Gary Smith	Elmhurst College
Wendi Kappersw	Embry-Riddle Aeronautical University
Nancy Woolridge	Fullerton College
Abigail Miller	Gateway Community & Technical College
Deep Ramanayake	Gateway Community & Technical College
Gwen White	Gateway Community & Technical College
Debbie Glinert	Gloria K School
Dana Smith	Golf Academy of America
Mary Locke	Greenville Technical College
Diane Marie Roselli	Harrisburg Area Community College
Linda Arnold	Harrisburg Area Community College - Lebanon
Daniel Schoedel	Harrisburg Area Community College - York Campus
Ken Mayer	Heald College
Xiaodong Qiao	Heald College
Donna Lamprecht	Hopkinsville Community College
Kristen Lancaster	Hopkinsville Community College
Johnny Hurley	Iowa Lakes Community College
Linda Halverson	Iowa Lakes Community College
Sarah Kilgo	Isothermal Community College
Chris DeGeare	Jefferson College
David McNair	Jefferson College
Diane Santurri	Johnson & Wales University
Roland Sparks	Johnson & Wales University
Ram Raghuraman	Joliet Junior College
Eduardo Suniga	Lansing Community College
Kenneth A. Hyatt	Lone Star College - Kingwood
Glenn Gray	Lone Star College - North Harris
Gene Carbonaro	Long Beach City College
Betty Pearman	Los Medanos College
Diane Kosharek	Madison College
Peter Meggison	Massasoit Community College
George Gabb	Miami Dade College
Lennie Alice Cooper	Miami Dade College
Richard Mabjish	Miami Dade College
Victor Giol	Miami Dade College
John Meir	Midlands Technical College
Greg Pauley	Moberly Area Community College
Catherine Glod	Mohawk Valley Community College
Robert Huyck	Mohawk Valley Community College
Kevin Engellant	Montana Western
Philip Lee	Nashville State Community College
Ruth Neal	Navarro College
Sharron Jordan	Navarro College
Richard Dale	New Mexico State University
Lori Townsend	Niagara County Community College
Judson Curry	North Park University
Mary Zegarski	Northampton Community College
Neal Stenlund	Northern Virginia Community College
Michael Goeken	Northwest Vista College
Mary Beth Tarver	Northwestern State University
Amy Rutledge	Oakland University
Marcia Braddock	Okefenokee Technical College
Richard Stocke	Oklahoma State University - OKC
Jane Stam	Onondaga Community College
Mike Michaelson	Palomar College
Kungwen (Dave) Chu	Purdue University Calumet
Wendy Ford	City University of New York - Queensborough Community College
Lewis Hall	Riverside City College
Karen Acree	San Juan College
Tim Ellis	Schoolcraft College
Dan Combellick	Scottsdale Community College
Pat Serrano	Scottsdale Community College
Rose Hendrickson	Sheridan College
Kit Carson	South Georgia College
Rebecca Futch	South Georgia State College
Brad Hagy	Southern Illinois University Carbondale
Mimi Spain	Southern Maine Community College
David Parker	Southern Oregon University
Madeline Baugher	Southwestern Oklahoma State University
Brian Holbert	St. Johns River State College
Bunny Howard	St. Johns River State College
Stephanie Cook	State College of Florida
Sharon Wavle	Tompkins Cortland Community College
George Fiori	Tri-County Technical College
Steve St. John	Tulsa Community College
Karen Thessing	University of Central Arkansas
Richard McMahon	University of Houston-Downtown
Shohreh Hashemi	University of Houston-Downtown
Donna Petty	Wallace Community College
Julia Bell	Walters State Community College
Ruby Kowaney	West Los Angeles College
Casey Thompson	Wiregrass Georgia Technical College
DeAnnia Clements	Wiregrass Georgia Technical College

Introduction to Microsoft Office 2013 Features

PROJECT 1A

OUTCOMES
Create, save, and print a Microsoft Office 2013 document.

OBJECTIVES

1. Use File Explorer to Download, Extract, and Locate Files and Folders
2. Use Start Search to Locate and Start a Microsoft Office 2013 Desktop App
3. Enter, Edit, and Check the Spelling of Text in an Office 2013 Program
4. Perform Commands from a Dialog Box
5. Create a Folder and Name and Save a File
6. Insert a Footer, Add Document Properties, Print a File, and Close a Desktop App

---

PROJECT 1B

OUTCOMES
Use the ribbon and dialog boxes to perform commands in Microsoft Office 2013.

OBJECTIVES

7. Open an Existing File and Save It with a New Name
8. Sign In to Office and Explore Options for a Microsoft Office Desktop App
9. Perform Commands from the Ribbon and Quick Access Toolbar
10. Apply Formatting in Office Programs
11. Compress Files and Use the Microsoft Office 2013 Help System
12. Install Apps for Office and Create a Microsoft Account

etse1112/Fotolia

In This Chapter

In this chapter, you will use File Explorer to navigate the Windows folder structure, create a folder, and save files in Microsoft Office 2013 programs. You will also practice using features in Microsoft Office 2013 that work similarly across Word, Excel, Access, and PowerPoint. These features include managing files, performing commands, adding document properties, signing in to Office, applying formatting, and using Help. You will also practice compressing files and installing Apps for Office from the Office Store. In this chapter, you will also learn how to set up a free Microsoft account so that you can use OneDrive.

The projects in this chapter relate to **Skyline Metro Grill**, which is a chain of 25 casual, full-service restaurants based in Boston. The Skyline Metro Grill owners are planning an aggressive expansion program. To expand by 15 additional restaurants in Chicago, San Francisco, and Los Angeles by 2018, the company must attract new investors, develop new menus, develop new marketing strategies, and recruit new employees, all while adhering to the company's quality guidelines and maintaining its reputation for excellent service. To succeed, the company plans to build on its past success and maintain its quality elements.

PROJECT

1A Note Form

MyITLab®
Project 1A Training

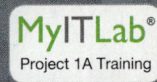

PROJECT ACTIVITIES

In Activities 1.01 through 1.09, you will create a note form using Microsoft Word, save it in a folder that you create by using File Explorer, and then print the note form or submit it electronically as directed by your instructor. Your completed note form will look similar to Figure 1.1.

PROJECT FILES

For Project 1A, you will need the following file:
New blank Word document

You will save your file as:
Lastname_Firstname_1A_Note_Form

PROJECT RESULTS

Build from Scratch

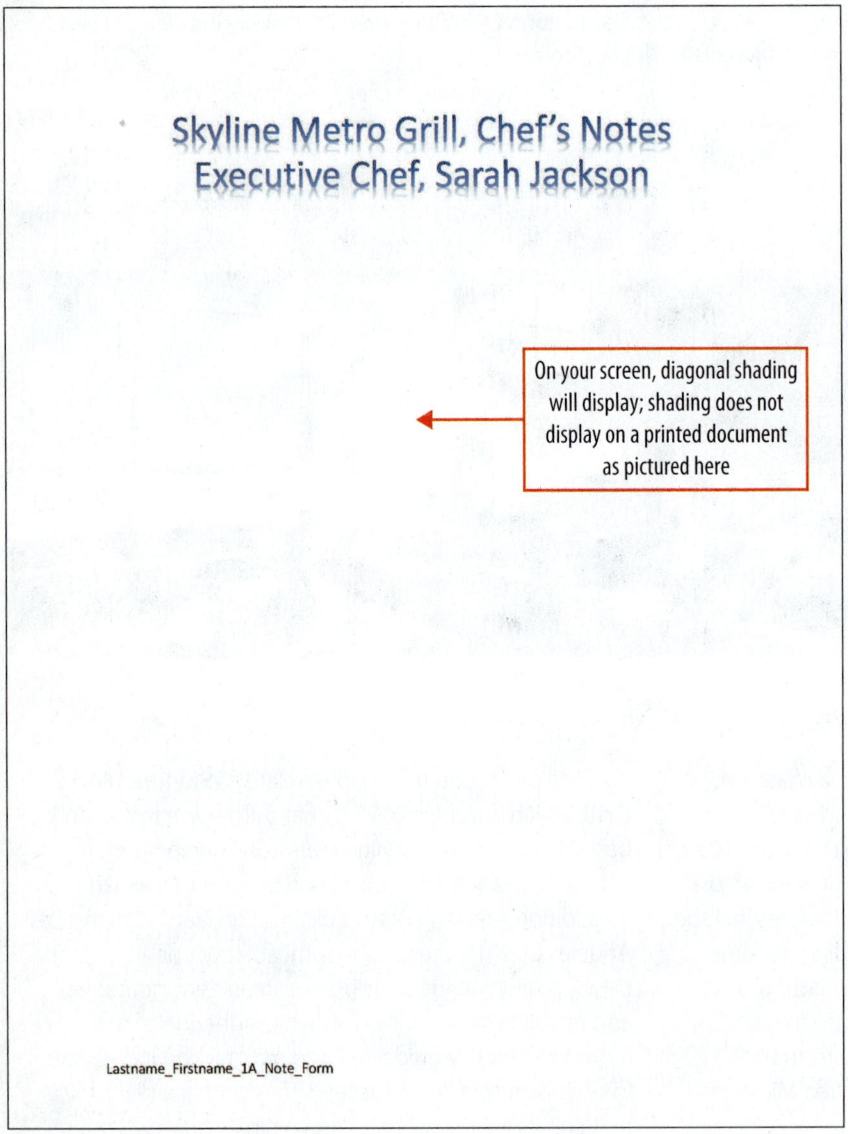
Skyline Metro Grill, Chef's Notes
Executive Chef, Sarah Jackson

Lastname_Firstname_1A_Note_Form

On your screen, diagonal shading will display; shading does not display on a printed document as pictured here

FIGURE 1.1 Project 1A Note Form

Objective 1   Use File Explorer to Download, Extract, and Locate Files and Folders

Video OF1-1

A *file* is a collection of information stored on a computer under a single name, for example, a Word document or a PowerPoint presentation. A file is stored in a *folder*—a container in which you store files—or a *subfolder*, which is a folder within a folder. The Windows operating system stores and organizes your files and folders, which is a primary task of an operating system.

You *navigate*—explore within the organizing structure of Windows—to create, save, and find your files and folders by using the *File Explorer* program. File Explorer displays the files and folders on your computer and is at work anytime you are viewing the contents of files and folders in a *window*. A window is a rectangular area on a computer screen in which programs and content appear; a window can be moved, resized, minimized, or closed.

Activity 1.01   Using File Explorer to Download, Extract, and Locate Files and Folders

> **ALERT!** You Will Need a USB Flash Drive
>
> You will need a USB flash drive for this activity to download the Student Data Files for this chapter. If your instructor is providing the files to you, for example by placing the files at your learning management system, be sure you have downloaded them to a location where you can access the files and then skip to Activity 1.02.

> **NOTE** Creating a Microsoft Account
>
> Use a free Microsoft account to sign in to Windows 8 and Office 2013 so that you can work on different PCs and use your OneDrive. You need not use the Microsoft account as your primary email address unless you want to do so. To create a Microsoft account, go to **www.outlook.com**.

1 Sign in to Windows 8 with your Microsoft account—or the account provided by your instructor—to display the Windows 8 **Start screen**, and then click the **Desktop** tile. Insert a **USB flash drive** in your computer; **Close** [x] any messages or windows that display.

The *desktop* is the screen in Windows that simulates your work area. A *USB flash drive* is a small data storage device that plugs into a computer USB port.

2 On the taskbar, click **Internet Explorer** [e]. Click in the **address bar** to select the existing text, type **www.pearsonhighered.com/go** and press [Enter]. Locate and click the name of this textbook, and then click the **STUDENT DATA FILES tab**.

The *taskbar* is the area along the lower edge of the desktop that displays buttons representing programs—also referred to as desktop apps. In the desktop version of Internet Explorer 10, the *address bar* is the area at the top of the Internet Explorer window that displays, and where you can type, a *URL—Uniform Resource Locator*—which is an address that uniquely identifies a location on the Internet.

3 On the list of files, move your mouse pointer over—*point* to—**Office Features Chapter 1** and then *click*—press the left button on your mouse pointing device one time.

4 In the **Windows Internet Explorer** dialog box, click **Save As**.

A *dialog box* is a small window that contains options for completing a task.

5 In the **Save As** dialog box, on the left, locate the **navigation pane**, and point to the vertical **scroll bar**.

The Save As dialog box is an example of a *common dialog box*; that is, this dialog box looks the same in Excel and in PowerPoint and in most other Windows-based desktop applications—also referred to as programs.

Use the *navigation pane* on the left side of the Save As dialog box to navigate to, open, and display favorites, libraries, folders, saved searches, and an expandable list of drives. A *pane* is a separate area of a window.

A *scroll bar* displays when a window, or a pane within a window, has information that is not in view. You can click the up or down scroll arrows—or the left and right scroll arrows in a horizontal scroll bar—to scroll the contents up and down or left and right in small increments.

You can also drag the *scroll box*—the box within the scroll bar—to scroll the window or pane in either direction.

This is a *compressed folder*—also called a *zipped folder*—which is a folder containing one or more files that have been reduced in size. A compressed folder takes up less storage space and can be transferred to other computers faster.

N O T E | **Comparing Your Screen with the Figures in This Textbook**

Your screen will match the figures shown in this textbook if you set your screen resolution to 1280 × 768. At other resolutions, your screen will closely resemble, but not match, the figures shown. To view your screen's resolution, on the desktop, right-click in a blank area, and then click Screen resolution.

---

6 In the **navigation pane**, if necessary, on the scroll bar click ⌄ to scroll down. If necessary, to the left of **Computer**, click ▷ to expand the list. Then click the name of your **USB flash drive**.

7 With *Office_Features* displayed in the **File name** box, in the lower right corner click **Save**.

At the bottom of your screen, the *Notification bar* displays information about pending downloads, security issues, add-ons, and other issues related to the operation of your computer.

8 In the **Notification bar**, when the download is complete, click **Open folder** to display the folder window for your **USB flash drive**.

A *folder window* displays the contents of the current location—folder, library, or drive—and contains helpful parts so that you can navigate within the file organizing structure of Windows.

9 With the compressed **Office_Features** folder selected, on the ribbon, click the **Extract tab** to display the **Compressed Folder Tools**, and then click **Extract all**.

The *ribbon* is a user interface in both Office 2013 and Windows 8 that groups the commands for performing related tasks on tabs across the upper portion of a window.

In the dialog box, you can *extract*—decompress or pull out—files from a compressed folder.

You can navigate to some other location by clicking the Browse button and navigating within your storage locations.

10 In the **Extract Compressed (Zipped) Folders** dialog box, click to the right of the selected text, and then press ⟨Backspace⟩ until only the drive letter of your USB and the colon following it display—for example G:—and then click **Extract**. Notice that a progress bar indicates the progress of the extract process, and that when the extract is complete, the **Office_Features** folder displays on the file list of your **USB flash drive**.

In a dialog box or taskbar button, a **progress bar** indicates visually the progress of a task such as a download or file transfer.

The **address bar** in File Explorer displays your current location in the folder structure as a series of links separated by arrows, which is referred to as the **path**—a sequence of folders that leads to a specific file or folder.

By pressing ⟨Backspace⟩ in the Extract dialog box, you avoid creating an unneeded folder level.

11 Because you no longer need the compressed (zipped) version of the folder, be sure it is selected, click the **Home tab**, and then click **Delete**. In the upper right corner of the **USB drive** folder window, click **Close** ☒. **Close** ☒ the **Internet Explorer** window and in the Internet Explorer message, click **Close all tabs**.

Your desktop redisplays.

<table><tr><td>**Objective 2**</td><td>Use Start Search to Locate and Start a Microsoft Office 2013 Desktop App</td></tr></table>

Video OF1-2

The term **desktop app** commonly refers to a computer program that is installed on your computer and requires a computer operating system such as Microsoft Windows or Apple OS to run. The programs in Microsoft Office 2013 are considered to be desktop apps. Apps that run from the *device software* on a smartphone or a tablet computer—for example, iOS, Android, or Windows Phone—or apps that run from *browser software* such as Internet Explorer, Safari, Firefox, or Chrome on a desktop PC or laptop PC are referred to simply as **apps**.

Activity 1.02 | Using Start Search to Locate and Start a Microsoft Office 2013 Desktop App

The easiest and fastest way to search for an app is to use the **Start search** feature—simply display the Windows 8 Start screen and start typing. By default, Windows 8 searches for apps; you can change it to search for files or settings.

1 With your desktop displayed, press ⟨⊞⟩ to display the Windows 8 **Start screen**, and then type **word 2013** With *word 2013* bordered in white in the search results, press ⟨Enter⟩ to return to the desktop and open Word. If you want to do so, in the upper right corner, sign in with your Microsoft account, and then compare your screen with Figure 1.2.

Documents that you have recently opened, if any, display on the left. On the right, you can select either a blank document or a **template**—a preformatted document that you can use as a starting point and then change to suit your needs.

 **BY TOUCH** Swipe from the right edge of the screen to display the charms, and then tap Search. Tap in the Apps box, and then use the onscreen keyboard that displays to type *word 2013*. Tap the selected Word 2013 app name to open Word.

FIGURE 1.2

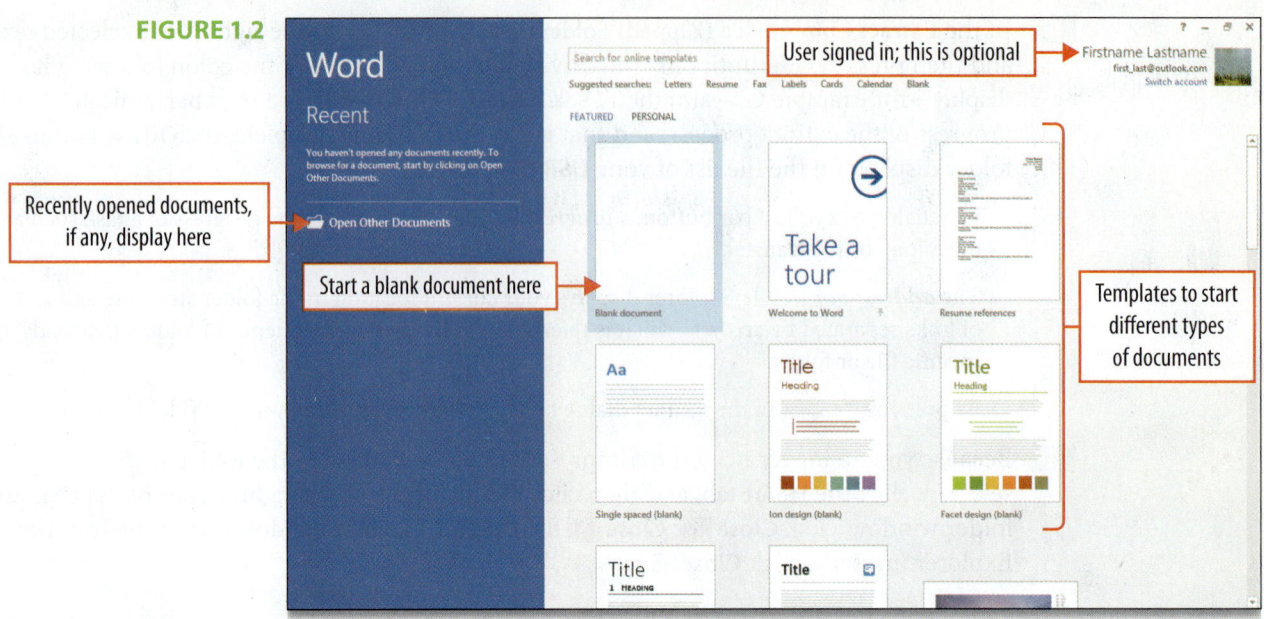

Recently opened documents, if any, display here

Start a blank document here

User signed in; this is optional

Templates to start different types of documents

2 ▶ Click **Blank document**. Compare your screen with Figure 1.3, and then take a moment to study the description of these screen elements in the table in Figure 1.4.

N O T E | **Displaying the Full Ribbon**

If your full ribbon does not display, click any tab, and then at the right end of the ribbon, click ⊡ to pin the ribbon to keep it open while you work.

FIGURE 1.3

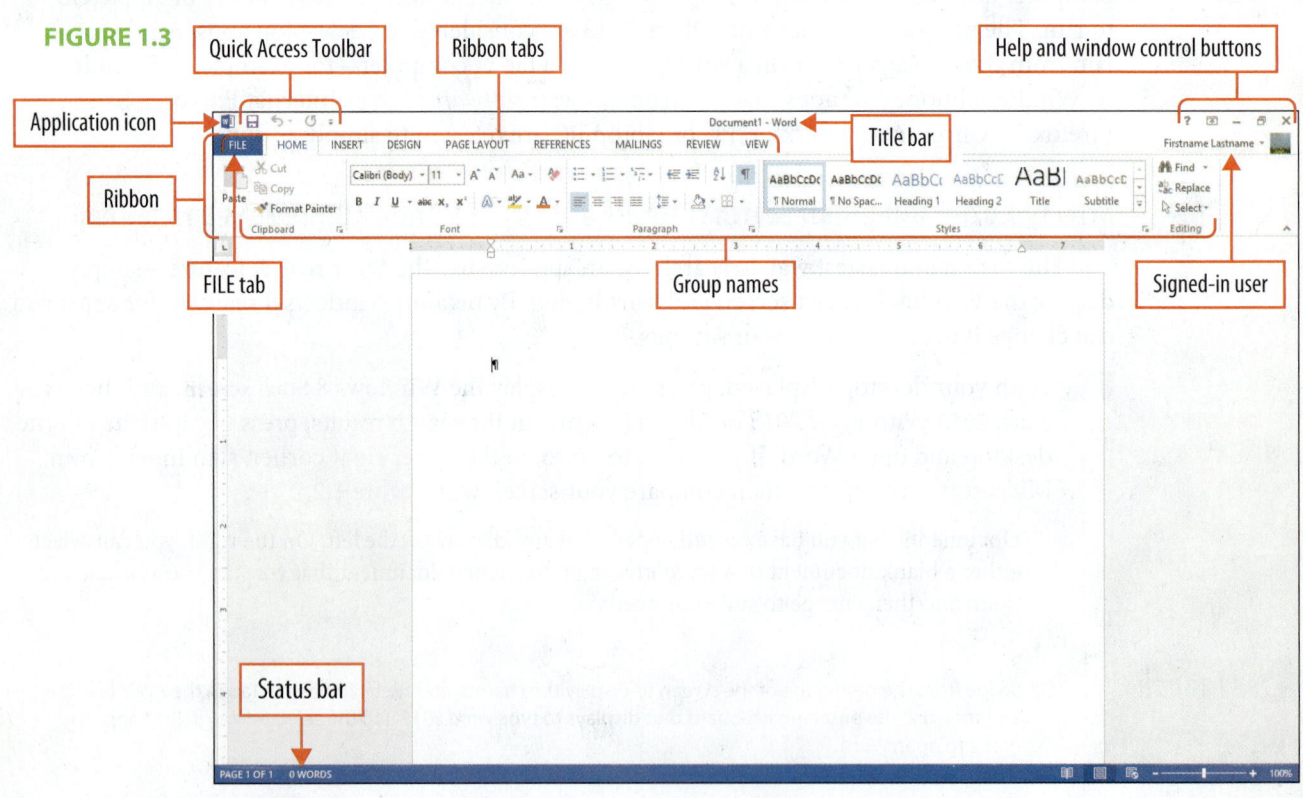

Quick Access Toolbar

Ribbon tabs

Help and window control buttons

Application icon

Ribbon

FILE tab

Title bar

Group names

Signed-in user

Status bar

FIGURE 1.4

MICROSOFT OFFICE SCREEN ELEMENTS	
SCREEN ELEMENT	**DESCRIPTION**
FILE tab	Displays Microsoft Office Backstage view, which is a centralized space for all of your file management tasks such as opening, saving, printing, publishing, or sharing a file—all the things you can do *with* a file.
Group names	Indicate the names of the groups of related commands on the displayed tab.
Help and window control buttons	Display Word Help and Full Screen Mode and enable you to Minimize, Restore Down, or Close the window.
Application icon	When clicked, displays a menu of window control commands including Restore, Minimize, and Close.
Quick Access Toolbar	Displays buttons to perform frequently used commands and use resources with a single click. The default commands include Save, Undo, and Redo. You can add and delete buttons to customize the Quick Access Toolbar for your convenience.
Ribbon	Displays a group of task-oriented tabs that contain the commands, styles, and resources you need to work in an Office 2013 desktop app. The look of your ribbon depends on your screen resolution. A high resolution will display more individual items and button names on the ribbon.
Ribbon tabs	Display the names of the task-oriented tabs relevant to the open program.
Status bar	Displays file information on the left; on the right displays buttons for Read Mode, Print Layout, and Web Layout views; on the far right displays Zoom controls.
Title bar	Displays the name of the file and the name of the program. The Help and window control buttons are grouped on the right side of the title bar.
Signed-in user	Name of the Windows 8 signed-in user.

Objective 3 Enter, Edit, and Check the Spelling of Text in an Office 2013 Program

Video OF1-3

All of the programs in Office 2013 require some typed text. Your keyboard is still the primary method of entering information into your computer. Techniques to enter text and to *edit*—make changes to—text are similar among all of the Office 2013 programs.

Activity 1.03 | Entering and Editing Text in an Office 2013 Program

1 On the ribbon, on the HOME tab, in the Paragraph group, if necessary, click Show/Hide ¶ so that it is active—shaded. If necessary, on the VIEW tab, in the Show group, select the Ruler check box so that rulers display below the ribbon and on the left side of your window.

The *insertion point*—a blinking vertical line that indicates where text or graphics will be inserted—displays. In Office 2013 programs, the mouse *pointer*—any symbol that displays on your screen in response to moving your mouse device—displays in different shapes depending on the task you are performing and the area of the screen to which you are pointing.

When you press Enter, Spacebar, or Tab on your keyboard, characters display to represent these keystrokes. These screen characters do not print and are referred to as *formatting marks* or *nonprinting characters*.

2 Type **Skyline Grille Info** and notice how the insertion point moves to the right as you type. Point slightly to the right of the letter *e* in *Grille* and click to place the insertion point there. Compare your screen with Figure 1.5.

A *paragraph symbol* (¶) indicates the end of a paragraph and displays each time you press Enter. This is a type of formatting mark and does not print.

FIGURE 1.5

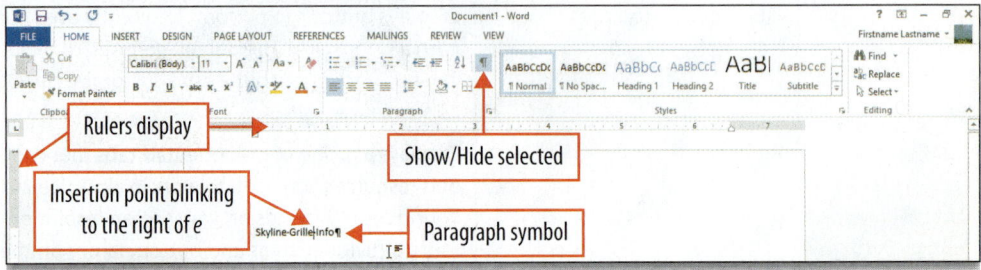

3 On your keyboard, locate and then press the Backspace key to delete the letter *e*.

Pressing Backspace removes a character to the left of the insertion point.

4 Press → one time to place the insertion point to the left of the *I* in *Info*. Type **Chef's** and then press Spacebar one time.

By *default*, when you type text in an Office program, existing text moves to the right to make space for new typing. Default refers to the current selection or setting that is automatically used by a program unless you specify otherwise.

5 Press Del four times to delete *Info* and then type **Notes**

Pressing Del removes a character to the right of the insertion point.

6 With your insertion point blinking after the word *Notes*, on your keyboard, hold down the Ctrl key. While holding down Ctrl, press ← three times to move the insertion point to the beginning of the word *Grill*.

This is a *keyboard shortcut*—a key or combination of keys that performs a task that would otherwise require a mouse. This keyboard shortcut moves the insertion point to the beginning of the previous word.

A keyboard shortcut is commonly indicated as Ctrl + ← (or some other combination of keys) to indicate that you hold down the first key while pressing the second key. A keyboard shortcut can also include three keys, in which case you hold down the first two and then press the third. For example, Ctrl + Shift + ← selects one word to the left.

7 With the insertion point blinking at the beginning of the word *Grill*, type **Metro** and press Spacebar.

8 Press Ctrl + End to place the insertion point after the letter *s* in *Notes*, and then press Enter one time. With the insertion point blinking, type the following and include the spelling error: **Exective Chef, Madison Dunham**

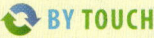 **9** With your mouse, point slightly to the left of the *M* in *Madison*, hold down the left mouse button, and then *drag*—hold down the left mouse button while moving your mouse—to the right to select the text *Madison Dunham* but not the paragraph mark following it, and then release the mouse button. Compare your screen with Figure 1.6.

> The *mini toolbar* displays commands that are commonly used with the selected object, which places common commands close to your pointer. When you move the pointer away from the mini toolbar, it fades from view.

> *Selecting* refers to highlighting, by dragging or clicking with your mouse, areas of text or data or graphics so that the selection can be edited, formatted, copied, or moved. The action of dragging includes releasing the left mouse button at the end of the area you want to select.

> The Office programs recognize a selected area as one unit to which you can make changes. Selecting text may require some practice. If you are not satisfied with your result, click anywhere outside of the selection, and then begin again.

FIGURE 1.6

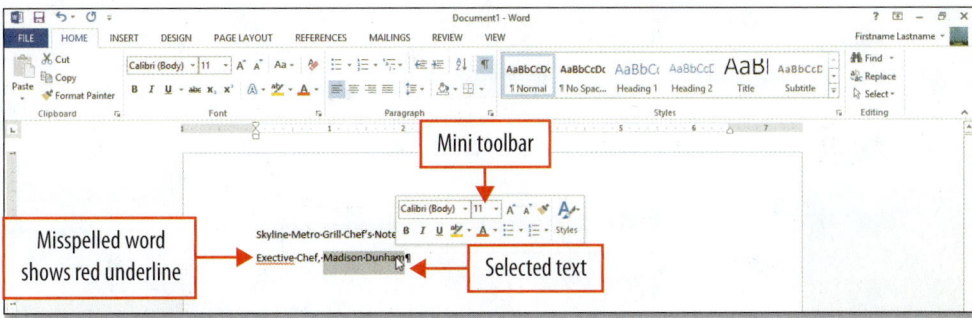

10 With the text *Madison Dunham* selected, type **Sarah Jackson**

> In any Windows-based program, such as the Microsoft Office 2013 programs, selected text is deleted and then replaced when you begin to type new text. You will save time by developing good techniques for selecting and then editing or replacing selected text, which is easier than pressing the [Del] key numerous times to delete text.

Activity 1.04 | Checking Spelling

Office 2013 has a dictionary of words against which all entered text is checked. In Word and PowerPoint, words that are not in the dictionary display a wavy red line, indicating a possible misspelled word or a proper name or an unusual word—none of which are in the Office 2013 dictionary.

In Excel and Access, you can initiate a check of the spelling, but red underlines do not display.

1 Notice that the misspelled word *Exective* displays with a wavy red underline.

2 Point to *Exective* and then *right-click*—click your right mouse button one time.

> A *shortcut menu* displays, which displays commands and options relevant to the selected text or object. These are *context-sensitive commands* because they relate to the item you right-clicked. These types of menus are also referred to as *context menus*. Here, the shortcut menu displays commands related to the misspelled word.

3 Press [Esc] to cancel the shortcut menu, and then in the lower left corner of your screen, on the **status bar**, click the **Proofing** icon [icon], which displays an *X* because some errors are detected. Compare your screen with Figure 1.7.

> The Spelling pane displays on the right. Here you have many more options for checking spelling than you have on the shortcut menu. The suggested correct word, *Executive*, is highlighted.
>
> You can click the speaker icon to hear the pronunciation of the selected word. You can also see some synonyms for *Executive*. Finally, if you have not already installed a dictionary, you can click *Get a Dictionary*—if you are signed in to Office with a Microsoft account—to find and install one from the online Office store; or if you have a dictionary app installed, it will display here and you can search it for more information.
>
> In the Spelling pane, you can ignore the word one time or in all occurrences, change the word to the suggested word, select a different suggestion, or add a word to the dictionary against which Word checks.

FIGURE 1.7

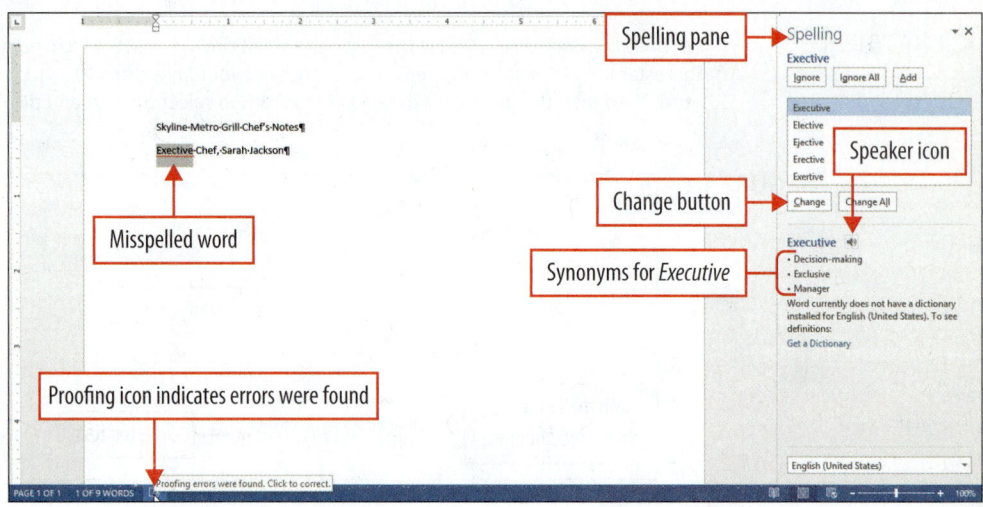

 **ANOTHER WAY**   Press [F7] to display the Spelling pane; or, on the Review tab, in the Proofing group, click Spelling & Grammar.

4 In the **Spelling** pane, click **Change** to change the spelling to *Executive*. In the message box that displays, click **OK**.

Objective 4 | Perform Commands from a Dialog Box

Video OF1-4

In a dialog box, you make decisions about an individual object or topic. In some dialog boxes, you can make multiple decisions in one place.

Activity 1.05 | Performing Commands from a Dialog Box

1 On the ribbon, click the **DESIGN tab**, and then in the **Page Background group**, click **Page Color**.

2 At the bottom of the menu, notice the command **Fill Effects** followed by an **ellipsis** (…). Compare your screen with Figure 1.8.

> An *ellipsis* is a set of three dots indicating incompleteness. An ellipsis following a command name indicates that a dialog box will display when you click the command.

FIGURE 1.8

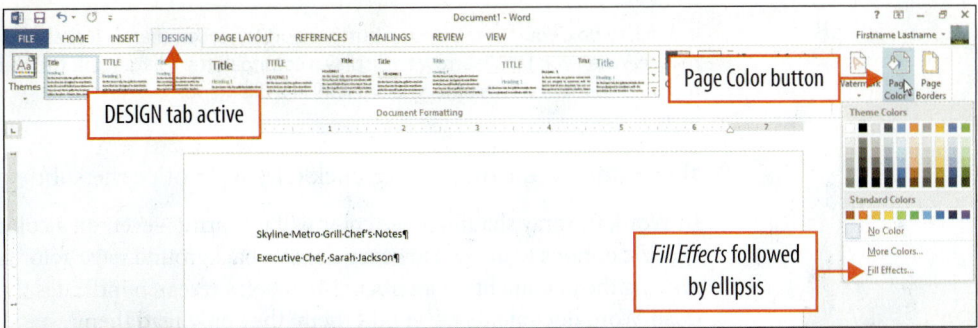

3 ▶ Click **Fill Effects** to display the **Fill Effects** dialog box. Compare your screen with Figure 1.9.

Fill is the inside color of a page or object. The Gradient tab is active. In a *gradient fill*, one color fades into another. Here, the dialog box displays a set of tabs across the top from which you can display different sets of options. Some dialog boxes display the option group names on the left.

FIGURE 1.9

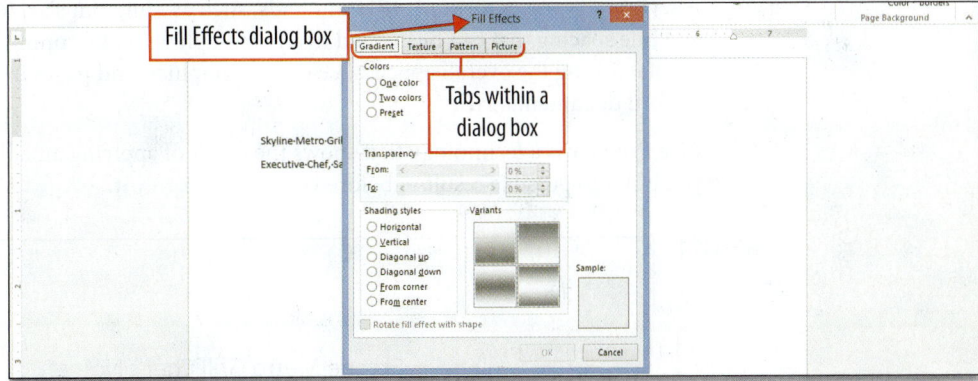

4 ▶ Under **Colors**, click the **One color** option button.

The dialog box displays settings related to the One color option. An *option button* is a round button that enables you to make one choice among two or more options.

5 ▶ Click the **Color 1 arrow**—the arrow under the text *Color 1*—and then in the third column, point to the second color to display the ScreenTip *Gray-25%, Background 2, Darker 10%*.

A *ScreenTip* displays useful information about mouse actions, such as pointing to screen elements or dragging.

6 ▶ Click **Gray-25%, Background 2, Darker 10%**, and then notice that the fill color displays in the **Color 1** box. In the **Dark Light** bar, click the **Light arrow** as many times as necessary until the scroll box is all the way to right. Under **Shading styles**, click the **Diagonal down** option button. Under **Variants**, click the upper right variant. Compare your screen with Figure 1.10.

FIGURE 1.10

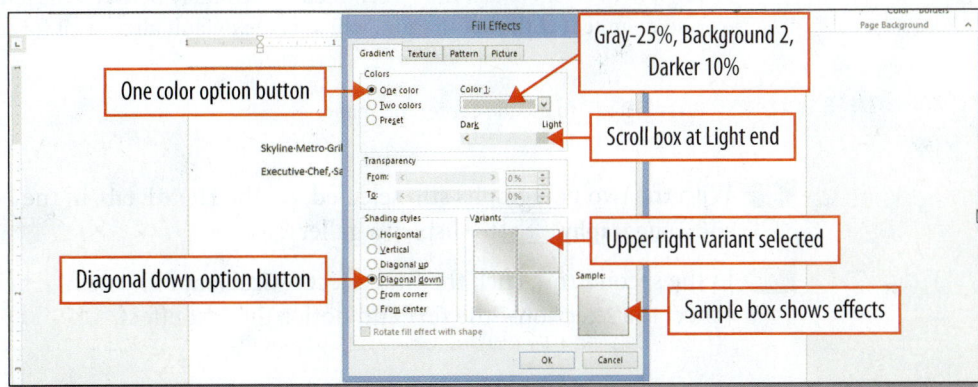

7 At the bottom of the dialog box, click **OK**, and notice the subtle page color.

In Word, the gray shading page color will not print—even on a color printer—unless you set specific options to do so. However a subtle background page color is effective if people will be reading the document on a screen. Microsoft's research indicates that two-thirds of people who open Word documents never edit them; they only read them.

Activity 1.06 | Using Undo

1 Point to the *S* in *Skyline*, and then drag down and to the right to select both paragraphs of text and include the paragraph marks. On the mini toolbar, click **Styles**, and then *point to* but do not click **Title**. Compare your screen with Figure 1.11.

A *style* is a group of *formatting* commands, such as font, font size, font color, paragraph alignment, and line spacing that can be applied to a paragraph with one command. Formatting is the process of establishing the overall appearance of text, graphics, and pages in an Office file—for example, in a Word document.

Live Preview is a technology that shows the result of applying an editing or formatting change as you point to possible results—before you actually apply it.

FIGURE 1.11

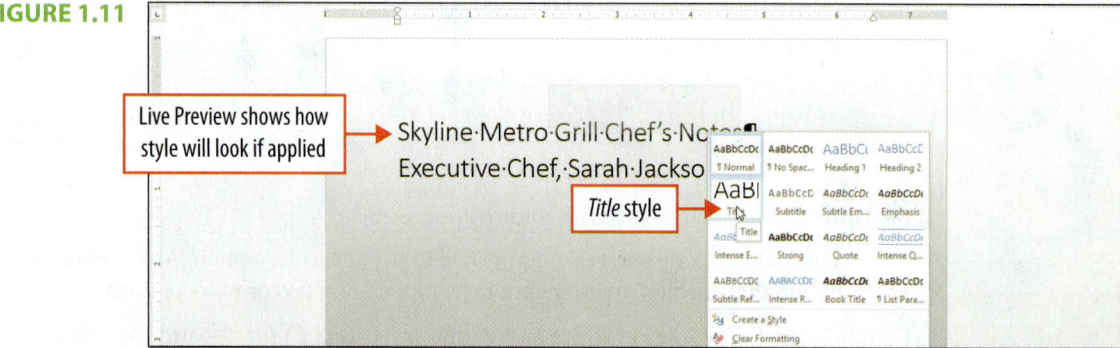

2 In the **Styles** gallery, click **Title**.

A *gallery* is an Office feature that displays a list of potential results.

3 On the ribbon, on the **HOME tab**, in the **Paragraph group**, click **Center** to center the two paragraphs.

Alignment refers to the placement of paragraph text relative to the left and right margins. *Center alignment* refers to text that is centered horizontally between the left and right margins. You can also align text at the left margin, which is the default alignment for text in Word, or at the right.

4 With the two paragraphs still selected, on the **HOME tab**, in the **Font Group**, click **Text Effects and Typography** to display a gallery.

5 In the second row, click the first effect—**Gradient Fill – Gray**. Click anywhere to *deselect*—cancel the selection—the text and notice the text effect.

6 Because this effect might be difficult to read, in the upper left corner of your screen, on the **Quick Access Toolbar**, click **Undo** [Undo].

The **Undo** command reverses your last action.

ANOTHER WAY Press Ctrl + Z as the keyboard shortcut for the Undo command.

7 Display the **Text Effects and Typography** gallery again, and then in the second row, click the second effect—**Gradient Fill – Blue, Accent 1, Reflection**. Click anywhere to deselect the text and notice the text effect. Compare your screen with Figure 1.12.

As you progress in your study of Microsoft Office, you will practice using many dialog boxes and applying interesting effects such as this to your Word documents, Excel worksheets, Access database objects, and PowerPoint slides.

FIGURE 1.12

Text formatted with blue reflective text effect
Skyline·Metro·Grill·Chef's·Notes¶
Executive·Chef,·Sarah·Jackson¶
Gray page fill effects

Objective 5 Create a Folder and Name and Save a File

Video OF1-5

A ***location*** is any disk drive, folder, or other place in which you can store files and folders. Where you store your files depends on how and where you use your data. For example, for your college classes, you might decide to store on a removable USB flash drive so that you can carry your files to different locations and access your files on different computers.

If you do most of your work on a single computer, for example your home desktop system or your laptop computer that you take with you to school or work, then you can store your files in one of the Libraries—Documents, Music, Pictures, or Videos—that the Windows 8 operating system creates on your hard drive.

The best place to store files if you want them to be available anytime, anywhere, from almost any device is on your ***OneDrive***, which is Microsoft's free ***cloud storage*** for anyone with a free Microsoft account. Cloud storage refers to online storage of data so that you can access your data from different places and devices. ***Cloud computing*** refers to applications and services that are accessed over the Internet, rather than to applications that are installed on your local computer.

Because many people now have multiple computing devices—desktop, laptop, tablet, smartphone—it is common to store data *in the cloud* so that it is always available. ***Synchronization***, also called ***syncing***—pronounced SINK-ing—is the process of updating computer files that are in two or more locations according to specific rules. So if you create and save a Word document on your OneDrive using your laptop, you can open and edit that document on your tablet. And then when you close the document again, the file is properly updated to reflect your changes.

You need not be connected to the Internet to access documents stored on OneDrive because an up-to-date version of your content is synched to your local system and available on OneDrive. You must, however, be connected to the Internet for the syncing to occur. Saving to OneDrive will keep the local copy on your computer and the copy in the cloud synchronized for as long as you need it. If you open and edit on a different computer, log into the OneDrive website, and then edit using Office 2013, Office 2010, or *Office Online*, you can save any changes back to OneDrive. Office Online is the free online companion to Microsoft Word, Excel, PowerPoint, Access, and OneNote. These changes will be synchronized back to any of your computers that run the OneDrive for Windows application, which you get for free simply by logging in with your Microsoft account at onedrive.com.

The Windows operating system helps you to create and maintain a logical folder structure, so always take the time to name your files and folders consistently.

Activity 1.07 | Creating a Folder and Naming and Saving a File

A Word document is an example of a file. In this activity, you will create a folder on your USB flash drive in which to store your files. If you prefer to store on your OneDrive or in the Documents library on your hard drive, you can use similar steps.

1 If necessary, insert your **USB flash drive** into your computer.

As the first step in saving a file, determine where you want to save the file, and if necessary, insert a storage device.

2 At the top of your screen, in the title bar, notice that *Document1 – Word* displays.

The Blank option on the opening screen of an Office 2013 program displays a new unsaved file with a default name—*Document1, Presentation1*, and so on. As you create your file, your work is temporarily stored in the computer's memory until you initiate a Save command, at which time you must choose a file name and a location in which to save your file.

3 In the upper left corner of your screen, click the **FILE tab** to display **Backstage** view. Compare your screen with Figure 1.13.

Backstage view is a centralized space that groups commands related to *file* management; that is why the tab is labeled *FILE*. File management commands include opening, saving, printing, publishing, or sharing a file. The *Backstage tabs*—*Info, New, Open, Save, Save As, Print, Share, Export,* and *Close*—display along the left side. The tabs group file-related tasks together.

Here, the *Info tab* displays information—*info*—about the current file, and file management commands display under Info. For example, if you click the Protect Document button, a list of options that you can set for this file that relate to who can open or edit the document displays.

On the right, you can also examine the *document properties*. Document properties, also known as *metadata*, are details about a file that describe or identify it, such as the title, author name, subject, and keywords that identify the document's topic or contents. To close Backstage view and return to the document, you can click ⬅ in the upper left corner or press Esc.

FIGURE 1.13

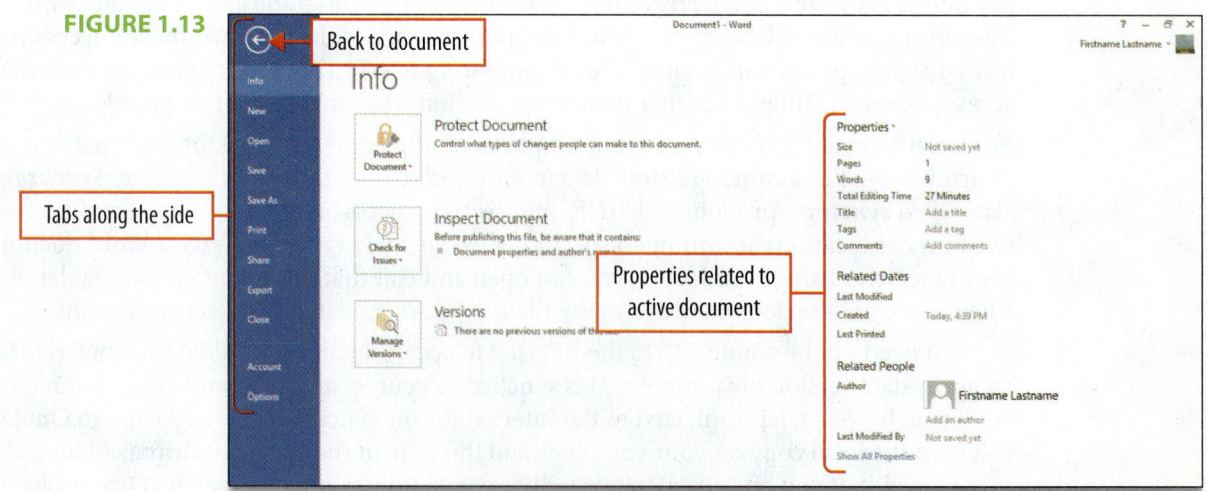

4 On the left, click **Save As**, and notice that the default location for storing Office files is your **OneDrive**—if you are signed in. Compare your screen with Figure 1.14.

> When you are saving something for the first time, for example a new Word document, the Save and Save As commands are identical. That is, the Save As commands will display if you click Save or if you click Save As.

FIGURE 1.14

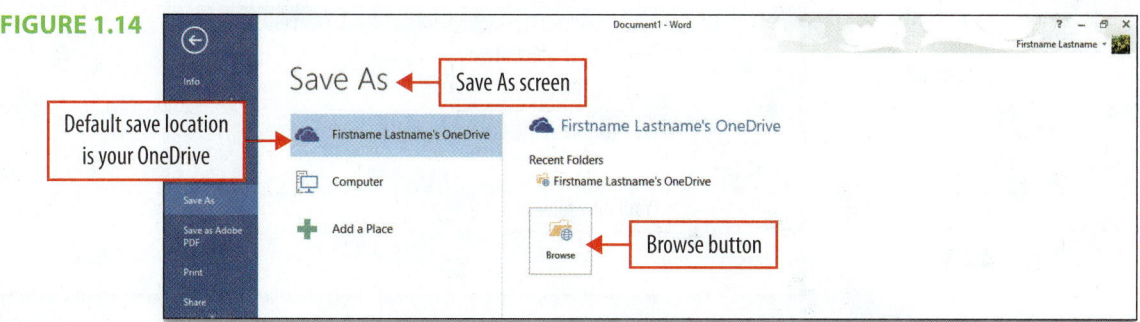

---

5 To store your Word file on your **USB flash drive**—instead of your OneDrive—click the **Browse** button to display the **Save As** dialog box. On the left, in the navigation pane, scroll down, and then under **Computer**, click the name of your **USB flash drive**. Compare your screen with Figure 1.15.

> In the Save As dialog box, you must indicate the name you want for the file and the location where you want to save the file. When working with your own data, it is good practice to pause at this point and determine the logical name and location for your file.

> In the Save As dialog box, a *toolbar* displays. This is a row, column, or block of buttons or icons, that usually displays across the top of a window and that contains commands for tasks you perform with a single click.

FIGURE 1.15

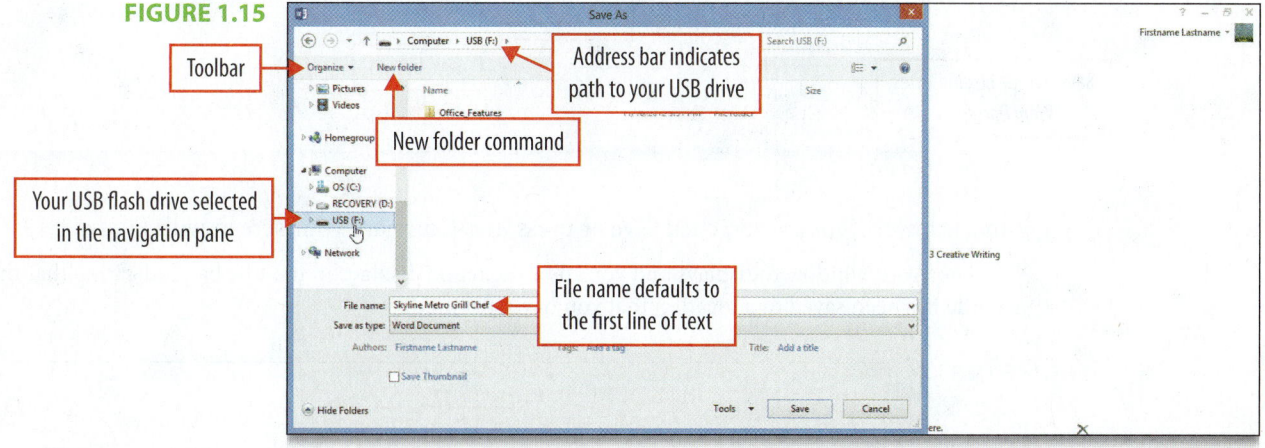

6 ▶ On the toolbar, click **New folder**.

In the file list, Word creates a new folder, and the text *New folder* is selected.

7 ▶ Type **Office Features Chapter 1** and press Enter. Compare your screen with Figure 1.16.

In Windows-based programs, the Enter key confirms an action.

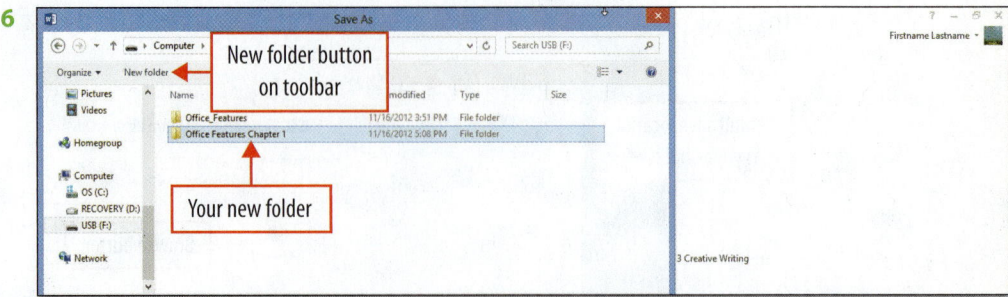

8 ▶ In the **file list**, double-click the name of your new folder to open it and display its name in the **address bar**.

9 ▶ In the lower portion of the dialog box, click in the **File name** box to select the existing text. Notice that Office inserts the text at the beginning of the document as a suggested file name.

10 ▶ On your keyboard, locate the hyphen ⸺ key. Notice that the Shift of this key produces the underscore character. With the text still selected and using your own name, type **Lastname_Firstname_1A_Note_Form** and then compare your screen with Figure 1.17.

You can use spaces in file names, however, some people prefer not to use spaces. Some programs, especially when transferring files over the Internet, may insert the extra characters *%20* in place of a space. This can happen in *SharePoint*, so using underscores instead of spaces can be a good habit to adopt. SharePoint is Microsoft's collaboration software with which people in an organization can set up team sites to share information, manage documents, and publish reports for others to see. In general, however, unless you encounter a problem, it is OK to use spaces. In this textbook, underscores are used instead of spaces in file names.

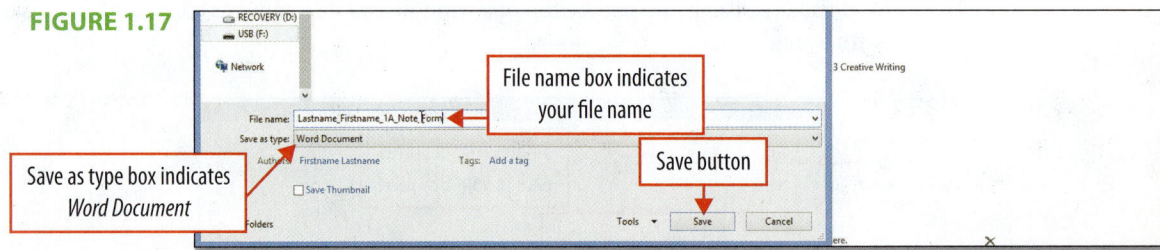

11 ▶ In the lower right corner, click **Save** or press Enter. Compare your screen with Figure 1.18.

The Word window redisplays and your new file name displays in the title bar, indicating that the file has been saved to a location that you have specified.

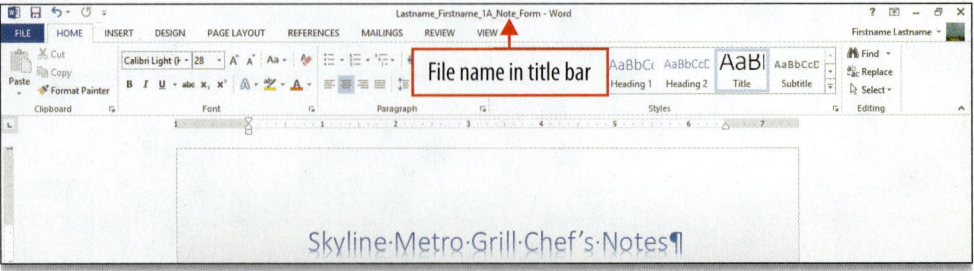

12 In the first paragraph, click to place the insertion point after the word *Grill* and type , (a comma). In the upper left corner of your screen, on the **Quick Access Toolbar**, click **Save** 🖫.

After a document is named and saved in a location, you can save any changes you have made since the last Save operation by using the Save command on the Quick Access Toolbar. When working on a document, it is good practice to save your changes from time to time.

Video OF1-6

For most of your files, especially in a workplace setting, it is useful to add identifying information to help in finding files later. You might also want to print your file on paper or create an electronic printout. The process of printing a file is similar in all of the Office applications.

Activity 1.08 | **Inserting a Footer, Inserting Document Info, and Adding Document Properties**

> **NOTE** | **Are You Printing or Submitting Your Files Electronically?**
>
> In this activity, you can either produce a paper printout or create an electronic file to submit to your instructor if required.

1 On the ribbon, click the **INSERT tab**, and then in the **Header & Footer group**, click **Footer**.

2 At the bottom of the list, click **Edit Footer**. On the ribbon, notice that the **HEADER & FOOTER TOOLS** display.

The *Header & Footer Tools Design* tab displays on the ribbon. The ribbon adapts to your work and will display additional tabs like this one—referred to as ***contextual tabs***—when you need them.

A ***footer*** is a reserved area for text or graphics that displays at the bottom of each page in a document. Likewise, a ***header*** is a reserved area for text or graphics that displays at the top of each page in a document. When the footer (or header) area is active, the document area is dimmed, indicating it is unavailable.

3 On the ribbon, under **HEADER & FOOTER TOOLS**, on the **DESIGN tab**, in the **Insert group**, click **Document Info**, and then click **File Name** to insert the name of your file in the footer, which is a common business practice. Compare your screen with Figure 1.19.

Ribbon commands that display ▼ will, when clicked, display a list of options for the command.

FIGURE 1.19

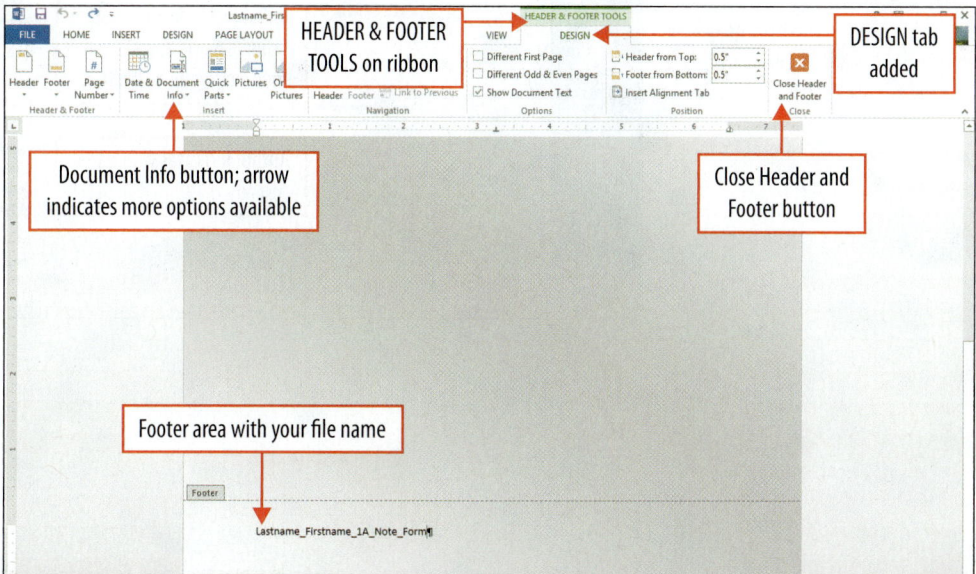

> **4** At the right end of the ribbon, click **Close Header and Footer**.

🔄 **ANOTHER WAY**   Double-click anywhere in the dimmed document to close the footer.

> **5** Click the **FILE tab** to display **Backstage** view. On the right, at the bottom of the **Properties** list, click **Show All Properties**.

🔄 **ANOTHER WAY**   Click the arrow to the right of Properties, and then click Show Document Panel to show and edit properties at the top of your document window.

> **6** On the list of **Properties**, click to the right of **Tags** to display an empty box, and then type **chef, notes, form**

> *Tags*, also referred to as ***keywords***, are custom file properties in the form of words that you associate with a document to give an indication of the document's content. Adding tags to your documents makes it easier to search for and locate files in File Explorer and in systems such as Microsoft SharePoint document libraries.

🔄 **BY TOUCH**   Tap to the right of Tags to display the Tags box and the onscreen keyboard.

> **7** Click to the right of **Subject** to display an empty box, and then type your course name and section #; for example *CIS 10, #5543*.

> **8** Under **Related People**, be sure that your name displays as the author. If necessary, right-click the author name, click Edit Property, type your name, click outside of the Edit person dialog box, and then click OK. Compare your screen with Figure 1.20.

FIGURE 1.20

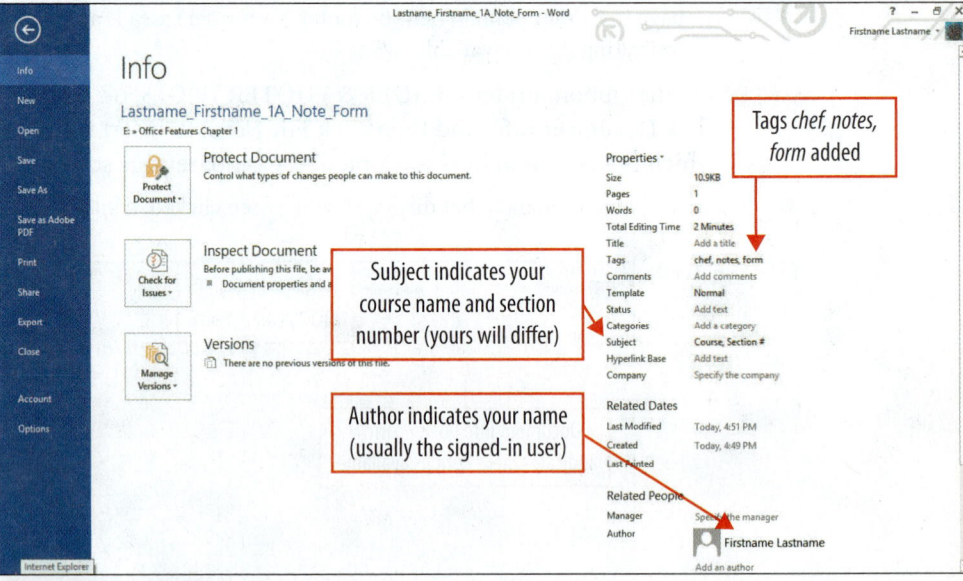

Activity 1.09 | Printing a File and Closing a Desktop App

1 On the left, click **Print**, and then compare your screen with Figure 1.21.

> Here you can select any printer connected to your system and adjust the settings related to how you want to print. On the right, the **Print Preview** displays, which is a view of a document as it will appear on paper when you print it.
>
> At the bottom of the Print Preview area, in the center, the number of pages and page navigation arrows with which you can move among the pages in Print Preview display. On the right, the Zoom slider enables you to shrink or enlarge the Print Preview. **Zoom** is the action of increasing or decreasing the viewing area of the screen.

ANOTHER WAY   From the document screen, press [Ctrl] + [P] or [Ctrl] + [F2] to display Print in Backstage view.

FIGURE 1.21

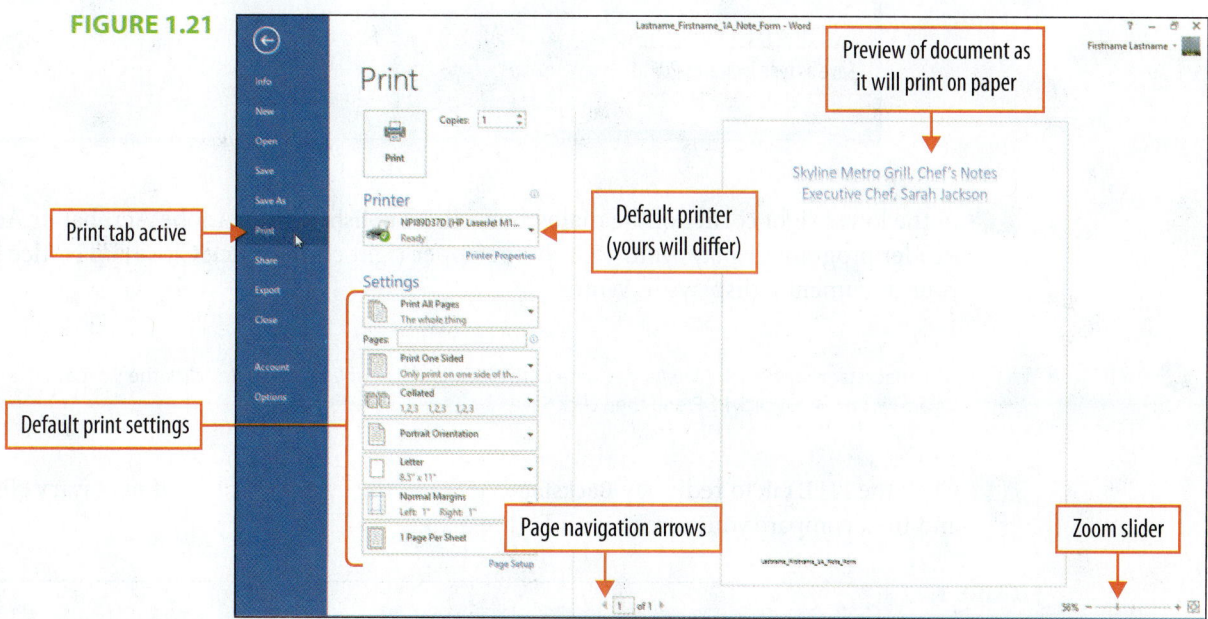

Print tab active

Default printer (yours will differ)

Default print settings

Preview of document as it will print on paper

Page navigation arrows

Zoom slider

2 To submit your file electronically, skip this step and continue to Step 3. To print your document on paper using the default printer on your system, in the upper left portion of the screen, click the **Print** button.

> The document will print on your default printer; if you do not have a color printer, the blue text will print in shades of gray. The gray page color you applied to the document does not display in Print Preview nor does it print unless you specifically adjust some of Word's options. Backstage view closes and your file redisplays in the Word window.

3 To create an electronic file, on the left click **Export**. On the right, click the **Create PDF/XPS** button to display the **Publish as PDF or XPS** dialog box.

> **PDF** stands for **Portable Document Format**, which is a technology that creates an image that preserves the look of your file. This is a popular format for sending documents electronically, because the document will display on most computers.
>
> **XPS** stands for **XML Paper Specification**—a Microsoft file format that also creates an image of your document and that opens in the XPS viewer.

4 ▶ On the left in the **navigation pane**, if necessary expand ▷ Computer, and then navigate to your **Office Features Chapter 1** folder on your **USB flash drive**. Compare your screen with Figure 1.22.

FIGURE 1.22

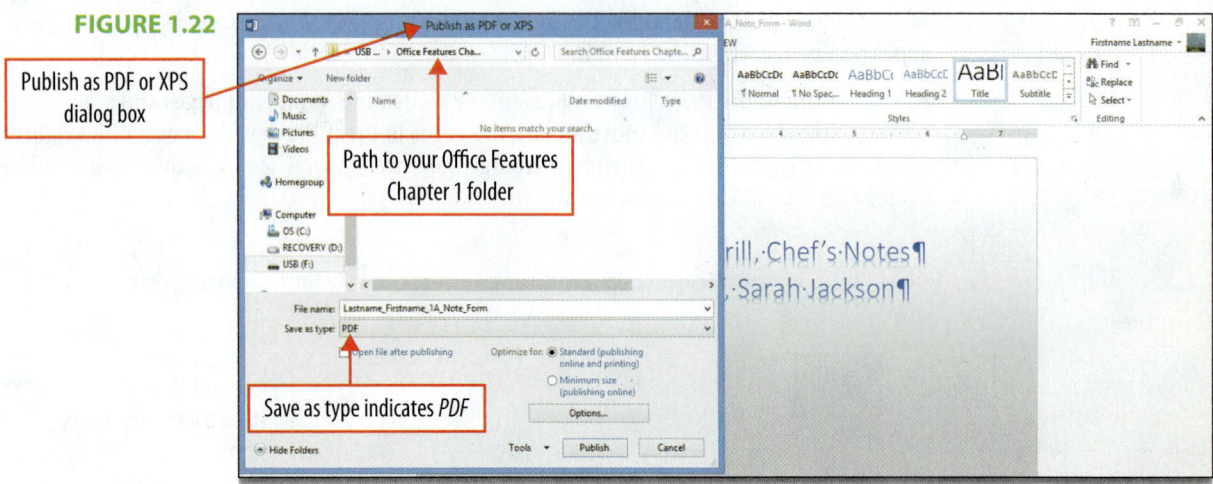

Publish as PDF or XPS dialog box

Path to your Office Features Chapter 1 folder

Save as type indicates *PDF*

5 ▶ In the lower right corner of the dialog box, click **Publish**; if your Adobe Acrobat or Adobe Reader program displays your PDF, in the upper right corner, click Close 🅇. Notice that your document redisplays in Word.

 **ANOTHER WAY**   In Backstage view, click Save As, navigate to the location of your Chapter folder, click the Save as type arrow, on the list click PDF, and then click Save.

6 ▶ Click the **FILE tab** to redisplay **Backstage** view. On the left, click **Close**, if necessary click Save, and then compare your screen with Figure 1.23.

FIGURE 1.23

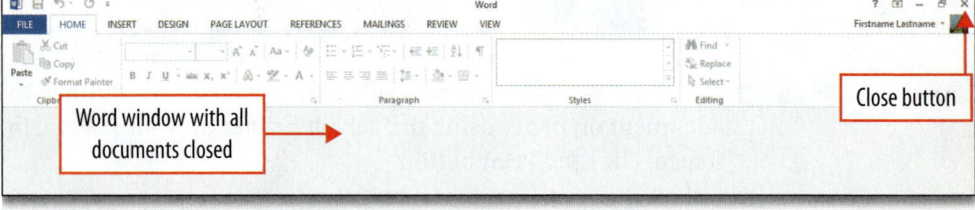

Word window with all documents closed

Close button

7 ▶ In the upper right corner of the Word window, click **Close** ⟨ × ⟩. If directed by your instructor to do so, submit your paper or electronic file.

END | You have completed Project 1A

PROJECT ACTIVITIES

In Activities 1.10 through 1.21, you will open, edit, and then compress a Word file. You will also use the Office Help system and install an app for Office. Your completed document will look similar to Figure 1.24.

PROJECT FILES

For Project 1B, you will need the following file:

of01B_Rehearsal_Dinner

You will save your file as:

Lastname_Firstname_1B_Rehearsal_Dinner

PROJECT RESULTS

Skyline Metro Grill

TO:	Sarah Jackson, Executive Chef
FROM:	Laura Mabry Hernandez, General Manager
DATE:	February 17, 2016
SUBJECT:	Wedding Rehearsal Dinners

In the spring and summer months, wedding rehearsal dinners provide a new marketing opportunity for Skyline Metro Grill at all of our locations. A rehearsal dinner is an informal meal following a wedding rehearsal at which the bride and groom typically thank those who have helped them make their wedding a special event.

Our smaller private dining rooms with sweeping city views are an ideal location for a rehearsal dinner. At each of our locations, I have directed the Sales and Marketing Coordinator to partner with local wedding planners to promote Skyline Metro Grill as a relaxed yet sophisticated venue for rehearsal dinners. The typical rehearsal dinner includes the wedding party, the immediate family of the bride and groom, and out-of-town guests.

Please develop six menus—in varying price ranges—to present to local wedding planners so that they can easily promote Skyline Metro Grill to couples who are planning a rehearsal dinner. In addition to a traditional dinner, we should also include options for a buffet-style dinner and a family-style dinner.

This marketing effort will require extensive communication with our Sales and Marketing Coordinators and with local wedding planners. Let's meet to discuss the details and the marketing challenges, and to create a promotional piece that begins something like this:

Skyline Metro Grill for Your Rehearsal Dinner

Lastname_Firstname_1B_Rehearsal_Dinner

FIGURE 1.24 Project 1B Memo

Video OF1-7

In any Office program, you can display the *Open dialog box*, from which you can navigate to and then open an existing file that was created in that same program.

The Open dialog box, along with the Save and Save As dialog boxes, is a common dialog box. These dialog boxes, which are provided by the Windows programming interface, display in all Office programs in the same manner. So the Open, Save, and Save As dialog boxes will all look and perform the same regardless of the Office program in which you are working.

Activity 1.10 | Opening an Existing File and Saving It with a New Name

In this activity, you will display the Open dialog box, open an existing Word document, and then save it in your storage location with a new name.

1 Sign in to your computer, and then on the Windows 8 Start screen, type **word 2013** Press Enter to open Word on your desktop. If you want to do so, on the taskbar, right-click the **Word icon**, and then click **Pin this program to taskbar** to keep the Word program available from your desktop.

2 On Word's opening screen, on the left, click **Open Other Documents**. Under **Open**, click **Computer**, and then on the right click **Browse**.

3 In the **Open** dialog box, on the left in the **navigation pane**, scroll down, if necessary expand ▷ Computer, and then click the name of your **USB flash drive**. In the **file list**, double-click the **Office_Features** folder that you downloaded.

4 Double-click **of01B_Rehearsal_Dinner**. If **PROTECTED VIEW** displays at the top of your screen, in the center click **Enable Editing**.

In Office 2013, a file will open in *Protected View* if the file appears to be from a potentially risky location, such as the Internet. Protected View is a security feature in Office 2013 that protects your computer from malicious files by opening them in a restricted environment until you enable them. *Trusted Documents* is another security feature that remembers which files you have already enabled.

You might encounter these security features if you open a file from an email or download files from the Internet; for example, from your college's learning management system or from the Pearson website. So long as you trust the source of the file, click Enable Editing or Enable Content—depending on the type of file you receive—and then go ahead and work with the file.

5 With the document displayed in the Word window, be sure that **Show/Hide** is active; if necessary, on the HOME tab, in the Paragraph group, click Show/Hide to activate it. Compare your screen with Figure 1.25.

FIGURE 1.25

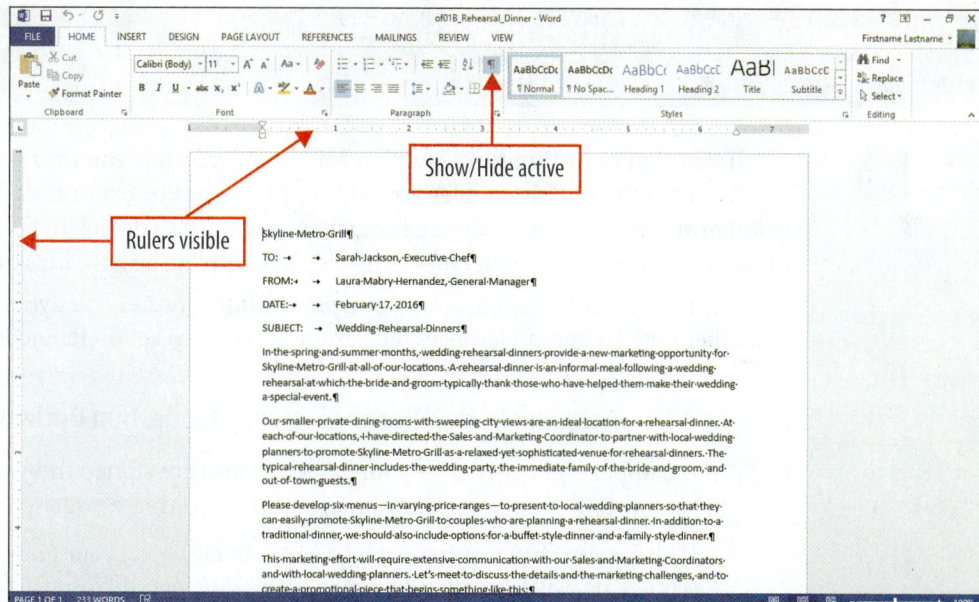

6 Click the **FILE tab** to display **Backstage** view, and then on the left, click **Save As**. On the right, click the folder under **Current Folder** to open the **Save As** dialog box. Notice that the current folder is the **Office_Features** folder you downloaded.

 **ANOTHER WAY**　　　Press F12 to display the Save As dialog box.

7 In the upper left corner of the **Save As** dialog box, click the **Up** button ↑ to move up one level in the File Explorer hierarchy. In the **file list**, double-click your **Office Features Chapter 1** folder to open it.

8 Click in the **File name** box to select the existing text, and then, using your own name, type **Lastname_Firstname_1B_Rehearsal_Dinner** Compare your screen with Figure 1.26.

FIGURE 1.26

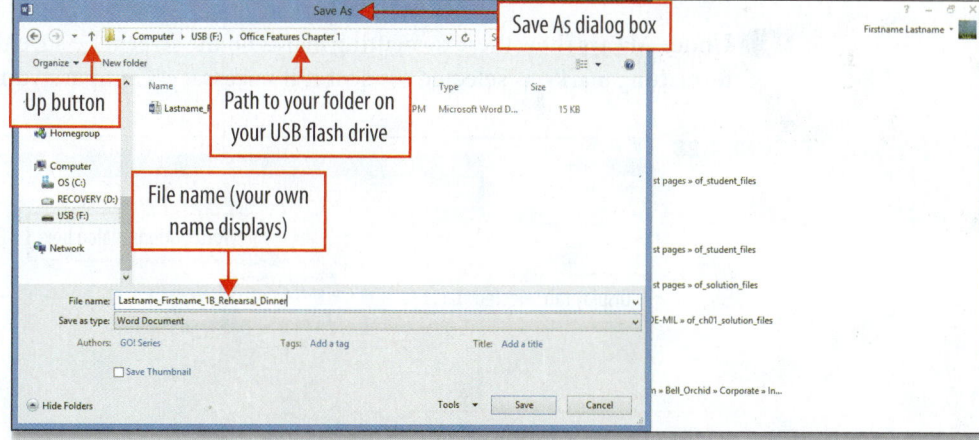

9 Click **Save** or press Enter; notice that your new file name displays in the title bar.

The original document closes, and your new document, based on the original, displays with the name in the title bar.

More Knowledge　　**Read-Only**

Some files might display *Read-Only* in the title bar, which is a property assigned to a file that prevents the file from being modified or deleted; it indicates that you cannot save any changes to the displayed document unless you first save it with a new name.

Video OF1-8

If you sign in to Windows 8 with a Microsoft account, you may notice that you are also signed in to Office. This enables you to save files to and retrieve files from your OneDrive and to *collaborate* with others on Office files when you want to do so. To collaborate means to work with others as a team in an intellectual endeavor to complete a shared task or to achieve a shared goal.

Within each Office application, an ***Options dialog box*** enables you to select program settings and other options and preferences. For example, you can set preferences for viewing and editing files.

Activity 1.11 | Signing In to Office and Viewing Application Options

1▶ In the upper right corner of your screen, if you are signed in with a Microsoft account, click the arrow to the right of your name, and then compare your screen with Figure 1.27.

Here you can change your photo, go to About me to edit your profile, examine your Account settings, or switch accounts to sign in with a different Microsoft account.

FIGURE 1.27

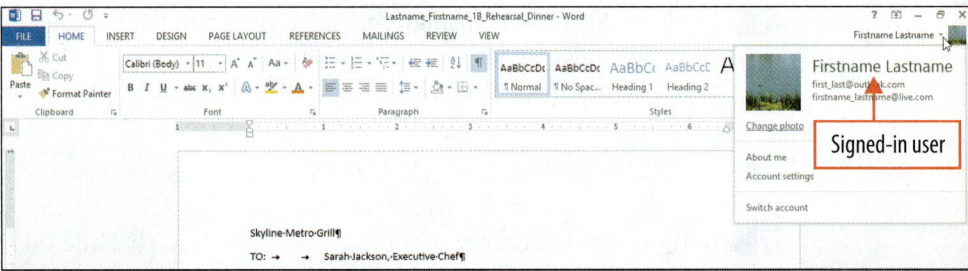

2▶ Click the **FILE tab** to display **Backstage** view. On the left, click the last tab—**Options**.

3▶ In the **Word Options** dialog box, on the left, click **Display**, and then on the right, locate the information under **Always show these formatting marks on the screen**.

4▶ Under **Always show these formatting marks on the screen**, be sure the last check box, **Show all formatting marks**, is selected—select it if necessary. Compare your screen with Figure 1.28.

FIGURE 1.28

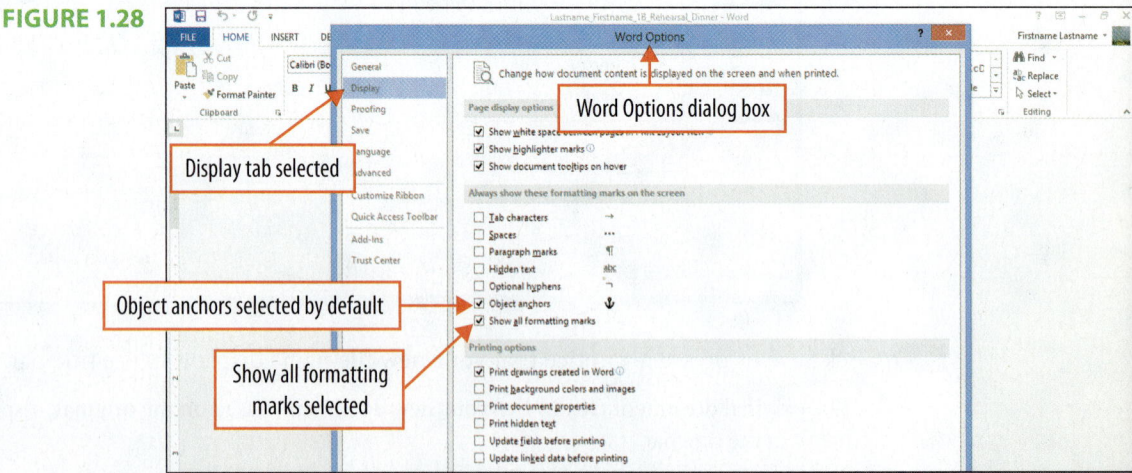

5▶ In the lower right corner of the dialog box, click **OK**.

Objective 9 | Perform Commands from the Ribbon and Quick Access Toolbar

Video OF1-9

The ribbon that displays across the top of the program window groups commands in a manner that you would most logically use them. The ribbon in each Office program is slightly different, but all contain the same three elements: *tabs*, *groups*, and *commands*.

Tabs display across the top of the ribbon, and each tab relates to a type of activity; for example, laying out a page. Groups are sets of related commands for specific tasks. Commands—instructions to computer programs—are arranged in groups and might display as a button, a menu, or a box in which you type information.

You can also minimize the ribbon so only the tab names display, which is useful when working on a smaller screen such as a tablet computer where you want to maximize your screen viewing area.

Activity 1.12 | Performing Commands from and Customizing the Ribbon and the Quick Access Toolbar

1 Take a moment to examine the document on your screen. If necessary, on the ribbon, click the VIEW tab, and then in the Show group, click to place a check mark in the Ruler check box. Compare your screen with Figure 1.29.

This document is a memo from the General Manager to the Executive Chef regarding a new restaurant promotion for wedding rehearsal dinners.

When working in Word, display the rulers so that you can see how margin settings affect your document and how text and objects align. Additionally, if you set a tab stop or an indent, its location is visible on the ruler.

FIGURE 1.29

Ruler checkbox selected

VIEW tab active

Show group

Rulers display

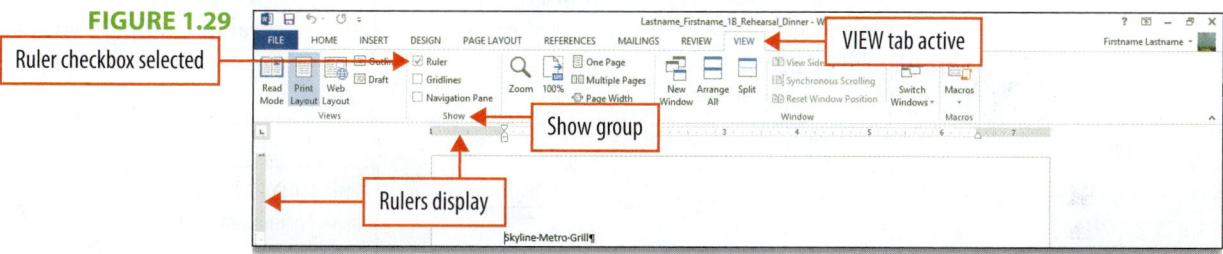

2 In the upper left corner of your screen, above the ribbon, locate the **Quick Access Toolbar**.

Recall that the Quick Access Toolbar contains commands that you use frequently. By default, only the commands Save, Undo, and Redo display, but you can add and delete commands to suit your needs. Possibly the computer at which you are working already has additional commands added to the Quick Access Toolbar.

3 At the end of the **Quick Access Toolbar**, click the **Customize Quick Access Toolbar** button ⬇, and then compare your screen with Figure 1.30.

A list of commands that Office users commonly add to their Quick Access Toolbar displays, including New, Open, Email, Quick Print, and Print Preview and Print. Commands already on the Quick Access Toolbar display a check mark. Commands that you add to the Quick Access Toolbar are always just one click away.

Here you can also display the More Commands dialog box, from which you can select any command from any tab on the ribbon to add to the Quick Access Toolbar.

 **BY TOUCH**   Tap once on Quick Access Toolbar commands.

FIGURE 1.30

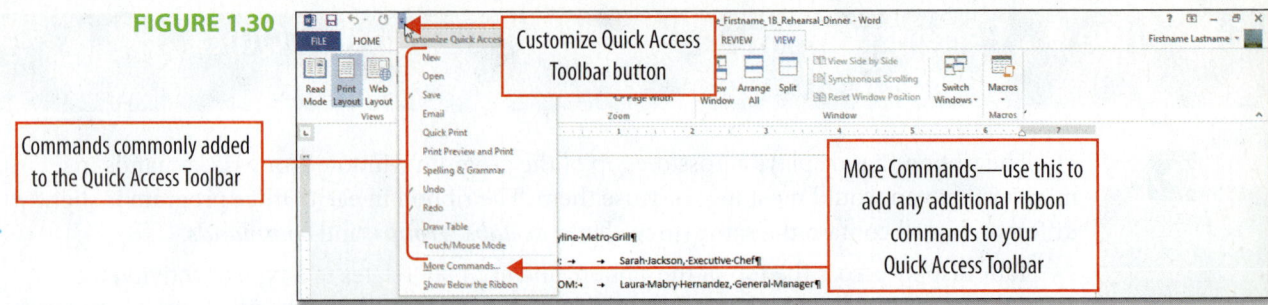

Commands commonly added to the Quick Access Toolbar

Customize Quick Access Toolbar button

More Commands—use this to add any additional ribbon commands to your Quick Access Toolbar

4 ▶ On the list, click **Print Preview and Print**, and then notice that the icon is added to the **Quick Access Toolbar**. Compare your screen with Figure 1.31.

The icon that represents the Print Preview command displays on the Quick Access Toolbar. Because this is a command that you will use frequently while building Office documents, you might decide to have this command remain on your Quick Access Toolbar.

ANOTHER WAY   Right-click any command on the ribbon, and then on the shortcut menu, click Add to Quick Access Toolbar.

FIGURE 1.31

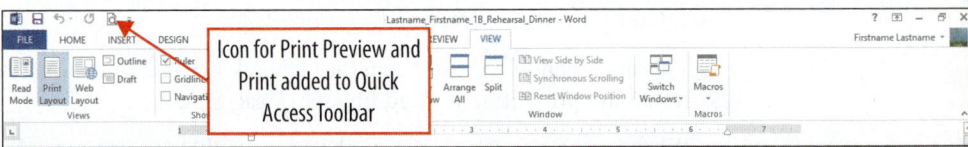

Icon for Print Preview and Print added to Quick Access Toolbar

5 ▶ In the first line of the document, if necessary, click to the left of the *S* in *Skyline* to position the insertion point there, and then press Enter one time to insert a blank paragraph. Press ↑ one time to position the insertion point in the new blank paragraph. Compare your screen with Figure 1.32.

FIGURE 1.32

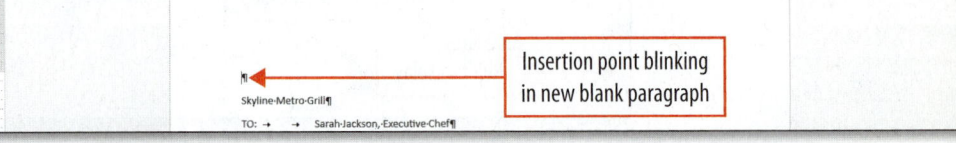

Insertion point blinking in new blank paragraph

6 ▶ On the ribbon, click the **INSERT tab**. In the **Illustrations group**, *point* to the **Online Pictures** button to display its ScreenTip.

Many buttons on the ribbon have this type of *enhanced ScreenTip*, which displays useful descriptive information about the command.

7 ▶ Click **Online Pictures**, and then compare your screen with Figure 1.33.

Here you can also search for images using the Bing search engine, and if you are signed in with your Microsoft account, you can also find images on your SkyDrive or on your computer by clicking Browse.

FIGURE 1.33

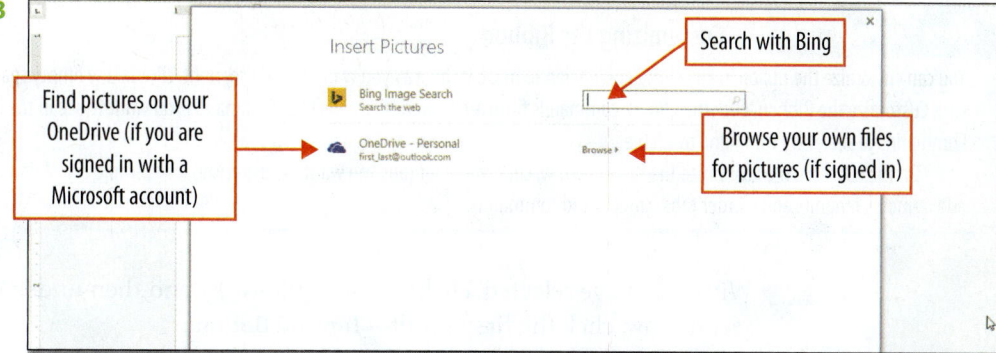

Find pictures on your OneDrive (if you are signed in with a Microsoft account)

Search with Bing

Browse your own files for pictures (if signed in)

8 ▸ Click in the **Search Bing** box. Type **salad in a bowl** as shown in Figure 1.34.

You can use various keywords to find images that is appropriate for your documents.

FIGURE 1.34

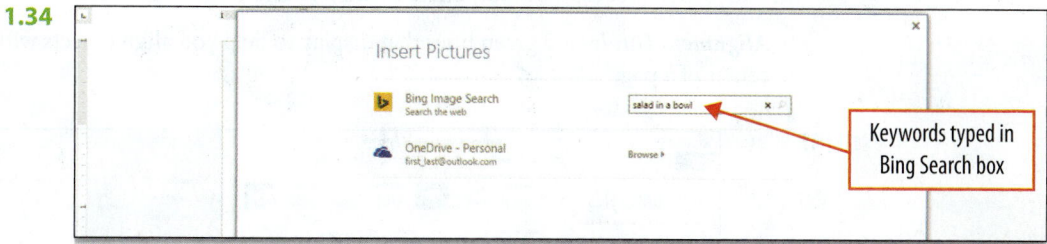

Keywords typed in Bing Search box

9 ▸ Press [Enter] to display several images. Choose an appropriate image and then in the lower right corner, click **Insert**. In the upper right corner of the picture, point to the **Layout Options** button [icon] to display its ScreenTip, and then compare your screen with Figure 1.35. If you cannot find the image, select a similar image, and then drag one of the corner sizing handles to match the approximate size shown in the figure.

Inserted pictures anchor—attach to—the paragraph at the insertion point location—as indicated by the anchor symbol. *Layout Options* enable you to choose how the *object*—in this instance an inserted picture—interacts with the surrounding text. An object is a picture or other graphic such as a chart or table that you can select and then move and resize.

When a picture is selected, the PICTURE TOOLS become available on the ribbon. Additionally, *sizing handles*—small squares that indicate an object is selected—surround the selected picture.

FIGURE 1.35

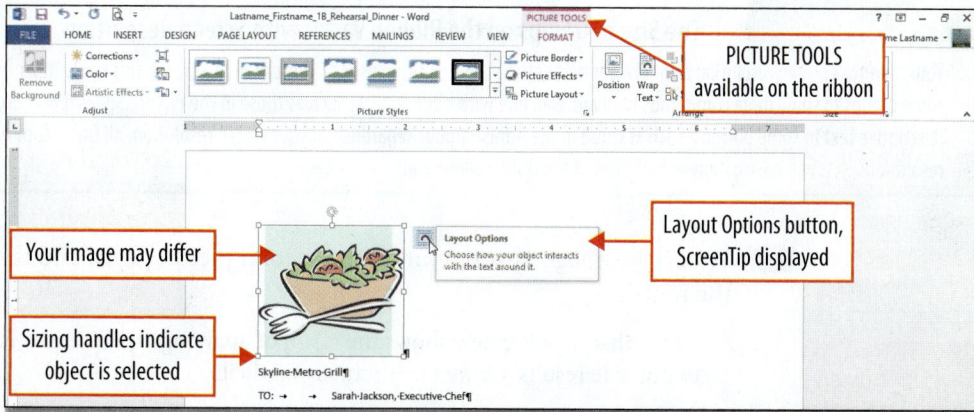

PICTURE TOOLS available on the ribbon

Layout Options button, ScreenTip displayed

Your image may differ

Sizing handles indicate object is selected

10 ▶ With the image selected, click **Layout Options** 🖼, and then under **With Text Wrapping**, in the second row, click the first layout—**Top and Bottom**.

11 ▶ Point to the image to display the 🔆 pointer, hold down the left mouse button to display a green line at the left margin, and then drag the image to the right and slightly upward until a green line displays in the center of the image and at the top of the image, as shown in Figure 1.36, and then release the left mouse button. If you are not satisfied with your result, on the Quick Access Toolbar, click Undo ↩ and begin again.

> *Alignment Guides* are green lines that display to help you align objects with margins or at the center of a page.

FIGURE 1.36

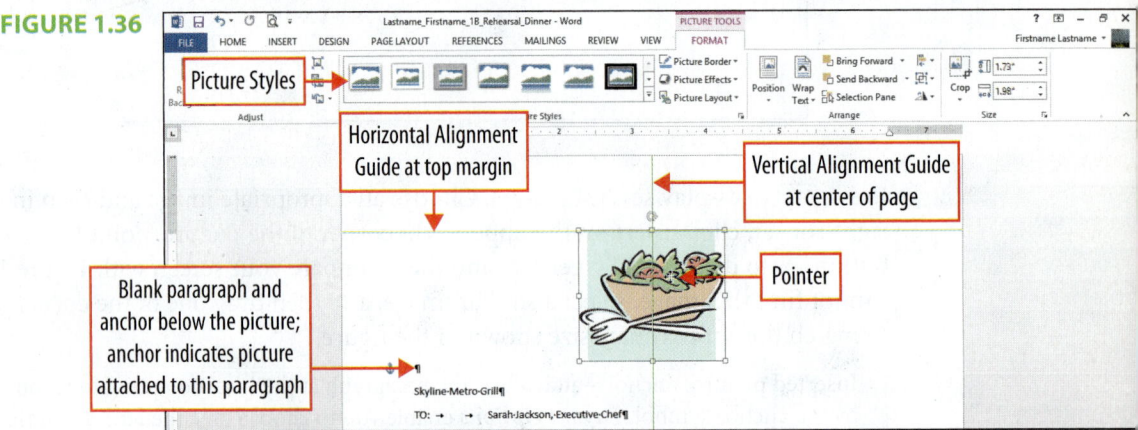

12 ▶ On the ribbon, in the **Picture Styles group**, point to the first style to display the ScreenTip *Simple Frame, White*, and notice that the image displays with a white frame.

NOTE   The Size of Groups on the Ribbon Varies with Screen Resolution

Your monitor's screen resolution might be set higher than the resolution used to capture the figures in this book. At a higher resolution, the ribbon expands some groups to show more commands than are available with a single click, such as those in the Picture Styles group. Or, the group expands to add descriptive text to some buttons, such as those in the Adjust group. Regardless of your screen resolution, all Office commands are available to you. In higher resolutions, you will have a more robust view of the ribbon commands.

13 ▶ Watch the image as you point to the second picture style, and then to the third, and then to the fourth.

> Recall that Live Preview shows the result of applying an editing or formatting change as you point to possible results—*before* you actually apply it.

14 In the **Picture Styles group**, click the second style—**Beveled Matte, White**—and then click anywhere outside of the image to deselect it. Notice that the *PICTURE TOOLS* no longer display on the ribbon. Compare your screen with Figure 1.37.

Contextual tabs on the ribbon display only when you need them.

FIGURE 1.37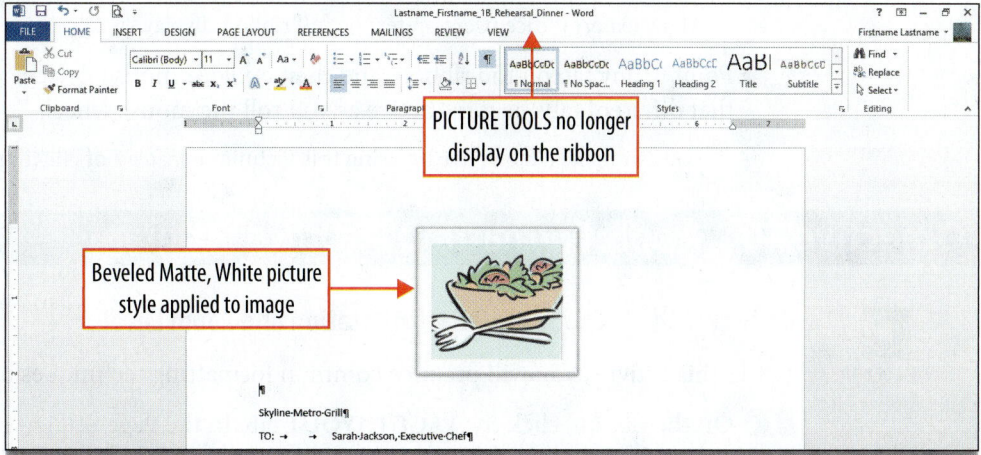

PICTURE TOOLS no longer display on the ribbon

Beveled Matte, White picture style applied to image

15 On the **Quick Access Toolbar**, click **Save** to save the changes you have made.

Activity 1.13 | Minimizing and Using the Keyboard to Control the Ribbon

Instead of a mouse, some individuals prefer to navigate the ribbon by using keys on the keyboard.

1 On your keyboard, press Alt, and then on the ribbon, notice that small labels display. Press N to activate the commands on the **INSERT tab**, and then compare your screen with Figure 1.38.

Each label represents a *KeyTip*—an indication of the key that you can press to activate the command. For example, on the INSERT tab, you can press F to open the Online Pictures dialog box.

FIGURE 1.38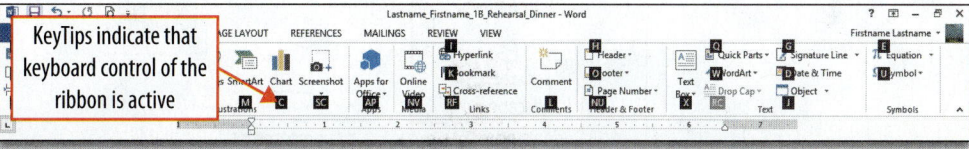

KeyTips indicate that keyboard control of the ribbon is active

2 Press Esc to redisplay the KeyTips for the tabs. Then, press Alt or Esc again to turn off keyboard control of the ribbon.

3 Point to any tab on the ribbon and right-click to display a shortcut menu.

Here you can choose to display the Quick Access Toolbar below the ribbon or collapse the ribbon to maximize screen space. You can also customize the ribbon by adding, removing, renaming, or reordering tabs, groups, and commands, although this is not recommended until you become an expert Office user.

4 ▸ Click **Collapse the Ribbon**. Notice that only the ribbon tabs display. Click the **HOME tab** to display the commands. Click anywhere in the document, and notice that the ribbon goes back to the collapsed display.

5 ▸ Right-click any ribbon tab, and then click **Collapse the Ribbon** again to remove the check mark from this command.

Many expert Office users prefer the full ribbon display.

6 ▸ Point to any tab on the ribbon, and then on your mouse device, roll the mouse wheel. Notice that different tabs become active as you roll the mouse wheel.

You can make a tab active by using this technique instead of clicking the tab.

Objective 10 | Apply Formatting in Office Programs

Video OF1-10

Activity 1.14 | Changing Page Orientation and Zoom Level

In this activity, you will practice common formatting techniques used in Office applications.

1 ▸ On the ribbon, click the **PAGE LAYOUT tab**. In the **Page Setup group**, click **Orientation**, and notice that two orientations display—*Portrait* and *Landscape*. Click **Landscape**.

In *portrait orientation*, the paper is taller than it is wide. In *landscape orientation*, the paper is wider than it is tall.

2 ▸ In the lower right corner of the screen, locate the **Zoom slider** ⊟———┃——⊞ .

Recall that to zoom means to increase or decrease the viewing area. You can zoom in to look closely at a section of a document, and then zoom out to see an entire page on the screen. You can also zoom to view multiple pages on the screen.

3 ▸ Drag the **Zoom slider** ⊟————┃——⊞ to the left until you have zoomed to approximately *60%*. Compare your screen with Figure 1.39.

FIGURE 1.39

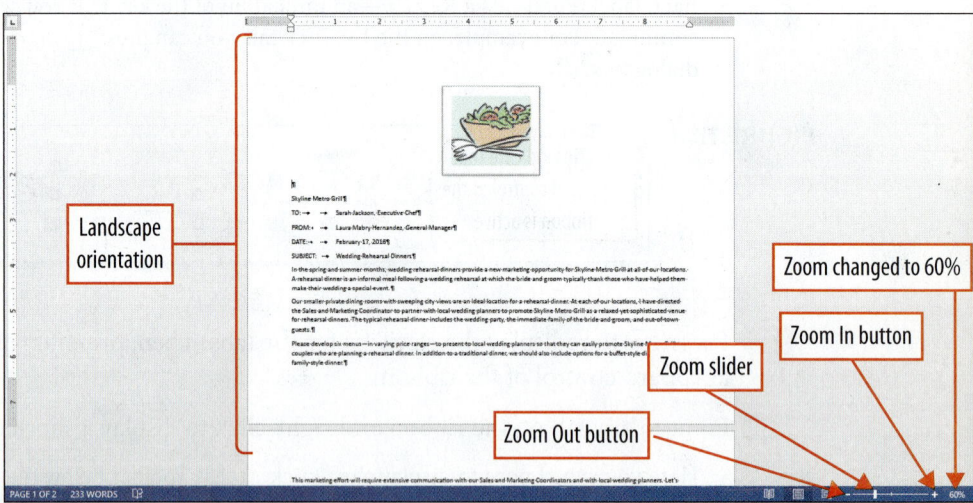

> BY TOUCH   Drag the Zoom slider with your finger.

4 ▸ Use the technique you just practiced to change the **Orientation** back to **Portrait**.

The default orientation in Word is Portrait, which is commonly used for business documents such as letters and memos.

5 In the lower right corner, click the **Zoom In** button + as many times as necessary to return to the **100%** zoom setting.

Use the zoom feature to adjust the view of your document for editing and for your viewing comfort.

 **ANOTHER WAY**   You can also control Zoom from the ribbon. On the VIEW tab, in the Zoom group, you can control the Zoom level and also zoom to view multiple pages.

6 On the **Quick Access Toolbar**, click **Save** 🖫.

More Knowledge   **Zooming to Page Width**

Some Office users prefer Page Width, which zooms the document so that the width of the page matches the width of the window. Find this command on the VIEW tab, in the Zoom group.

Activity 1.15 | Formatting Text by Using Fonts, Alignment, Font Colors, and Font Styles

1 If necessary, on the right side of your screen, drag the vertical scroll box to the top of the scroll bar. To the left of *Skyline Metro Grill*, point in the margin area to display the 🔏 pointer and click one time to select the entire paragraph. Compare your screen with Figure 1.40.

Use this technique to select complete paragraphs from the margin area—drag downward to select multiple-line paragraphs—which is faster and more efficient than dragging through text.

FIGURE 1.40

2 On the ribbon, click the **HOME tab**, and then in the **Paragraph group**, click **Center** ☰ to center the paragraph.

3 On the **HOME tab**, in the **Font group**, click the **Font button arrow** Calibri (Body) ▾. On the alphabetical list of font names, scroll down and then locate and *point to* **Cambria**.

A *font* is a set of characters with the same design and shape. The default font in a Word document is Calibri, which is a *sans serif* font—a font design with no lines or extensions on the ends of characters.

The Cambria font is a *serif font*—a font design that includes small line extensions on the ends of the letters to guide the eye in reading from left to right.

The list of fonts displays as a gallery showing potential results. For example, in the Font gallery, you can point to see the actual design and format of each font as it would look if applied to text.

4 Point to several other fonts and observe the effect on the selected text. Then, scroll back to the top of the **Font** gallery. Under **Theme Fonts**, click **Calibri Light**.

A *theme* is a predesigned combination of colors, fonts, line, and fill effects that look good together and is applied to an entire document by a single selection. A theme combines two sets of fonts—one for text and one for headings. In the default Office theme, Calibri Light is the suggested font for headings.

5 With the paragraph *Skyline Metro Grill* still selected, on the **HOME tab**, in the **Font group**, click the **Font Size button arrow** 11 ▾, point to **36**, and then notice how Live Preview displays the text in the font size to which you are pointing. Compare your screen with Figure 1.41.

FIGURE 1.41

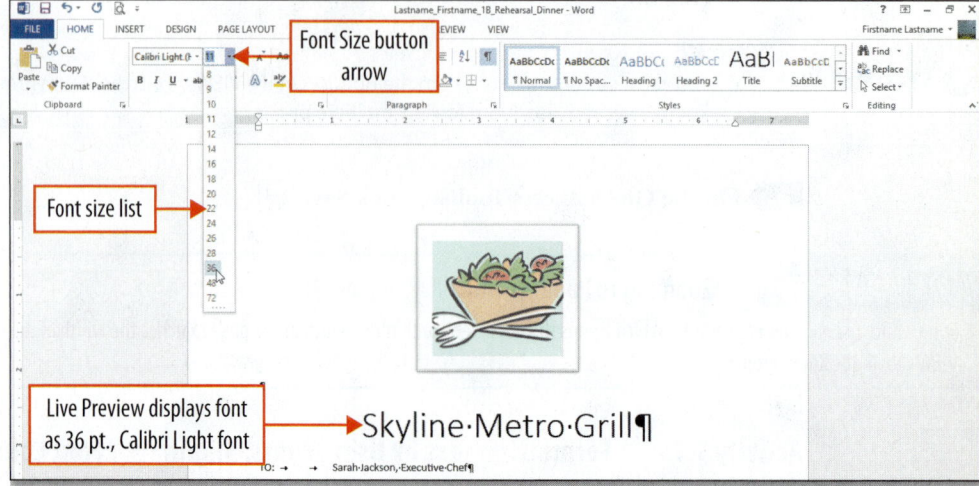

6 On the list of font sizes, click **20**.

Fonts are measured in *points*, with one point equal to 1/72 of an inch. A higher point size indicates a larger font size. Headings and titles are often formatted by using a larger font size. The word *point* is abbreviated as *pt*.

7 With *Skyline Metro Grill* still selected, on the **HOME tab**, in the **Font group**, click the **Font Color button arrow** ▾. Under **Theme Colors**, in the last column, click the last color—**Green, Accent 6, Darker 50%**. Click anywhere to deselect the text.

8 To the left of *TO:*, point in the left margin area to display the ⌐ pointer, hold down the left mouse button, and then drag down to select the four memo headings. Compare your screen with Figure 1.42.

Use this technique to select complete paragraphs from the margin area—drag downward to select multiple paragraphs—which is faster and more efficient than dragging through text.

 **BY TOUCH** Tap once on TO: to display the gripper, then with your finger, drag to the right and down to select the four paragraphs.

FIGURE 1.42

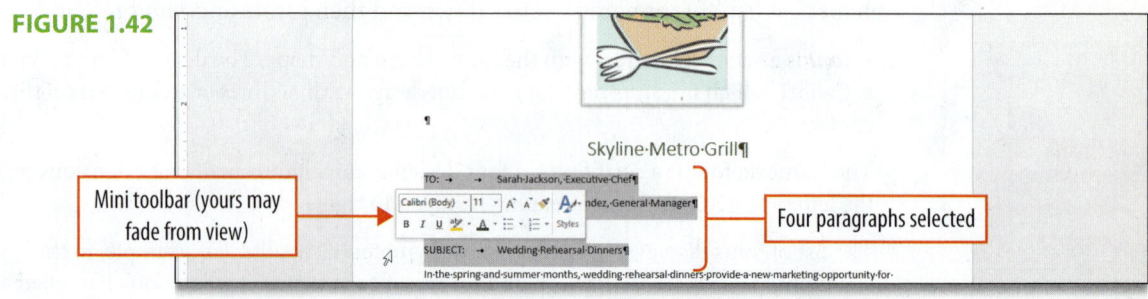

9 With the four paragraphs selected, on the mini toolbar, click the **Font Color** button ![A], and notice that the text color of the four paragraphs changes.

> The font color button retains its most recently used color—Green, Accent 6, Darker 50%. As you progress in your study of Microsoft Office, you will use other buttons that behave in this manner; that is, they retain their most recently used format. This is commonly referred to as *MRU*—most recently used.

> Recall that the mini toolbar places commands that are commonly used for the selected text or object close by so that you reduce the distance that you must move your mouse to access a command. If you are using a touchscreen device, most commands that you need are close and easy to touch.

10 On the right, drag the vertical scroll box down slightly to position more of the text on the screen. Click anywhere in the paragraph that begins *In the spring*, and then *triple-click*—click the left mouse button three times—to select the entire paragraph. If the entire paragraph is not selected, click in the paragraph and begin again.

11 With the entire paragraph selected, on the mini toolbar, click the **Font Color button arrow** ![A], and then under **Theme Colors**, in the sixth column, click the last color— **Orange, Accent 2, Darker 50%.**

12 In the memo headings, select the guide word *TO:* and then on the mini toolbar, click **Bold** ![B] and **Italic** ![I].

> *Font styles* include bold, italic, and underline. Font styles emphasize text and are a visual cue to draw the reader's eye to important text.

13 On the mini toolbar, click **Italic** ![I] again to turn off the Italic formatting.

> A *toggle button* is a button that can be turned on by clicking it once, and then turned off by clicking it again.

Activity 1.16 | Using Format Painter

Use the Format Painter to copy the formatting of specific text or of a paragraph and then apply it in other locations in your document.

1 With *TO:* still selected, on the mini toolbar, click **Format Painter** ![brush]. Then, move your mouse under the word *Sarah*, and notice the ![pointer] mouse pointer. Compare your screen with Figure 1.43.

> The pointer takes the shape of a paintbrush, and contains the formatting information from the paragraph where the insertion point is positioned. Information about the Format Painter and how to turn it off displays in the status bar.

FIGURE 1.43

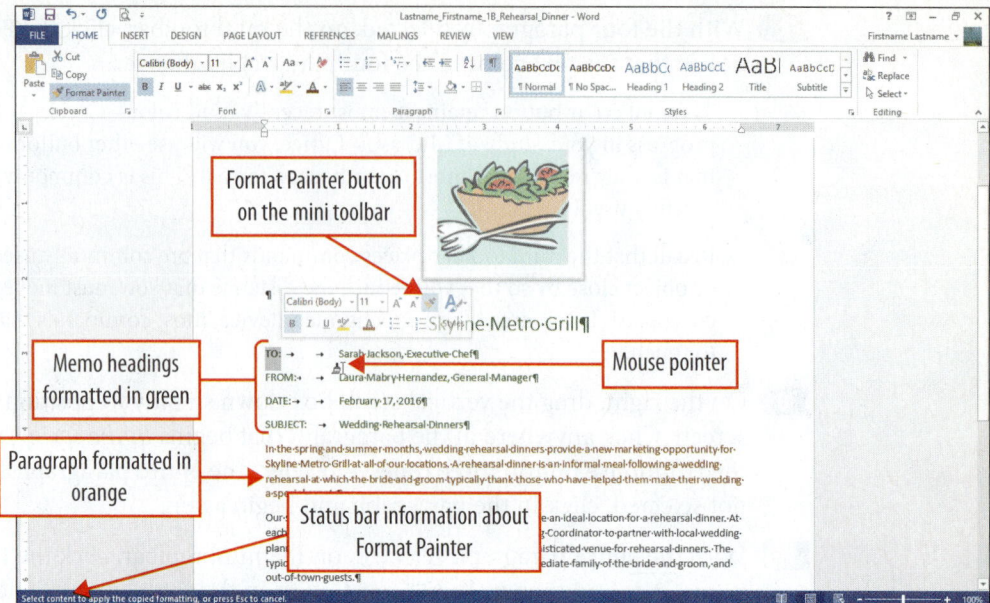

2 With the ⌶ pointer, drag to select the guide word *FROM:* and notice that Bold formatting is applied. Then, point to the selected text *FROM:* and on the mini toolbar, *double-click* **Format Painter** ⌗.

3 Select the guide word *DATE:* to copy the Bold formatting, and notice that the pointer retains the ⌶ shape.

When you *double-click* the Format Painter button, the Format Painter feature remains active until you either click the Format Painter button again, or press ⌷Esc⌷ to cancel it—as indicated on the status bar.

4 With Format Painter still active, select the guide word *SUBJECT:*, and then on the ribbon, on the **HOME tab**, in the **Clipboard group**, notice that **Format Painter** ⌗ is selected, indicating that it is active. Compare your screen with Figure 1.44.

FIGURE 1.44

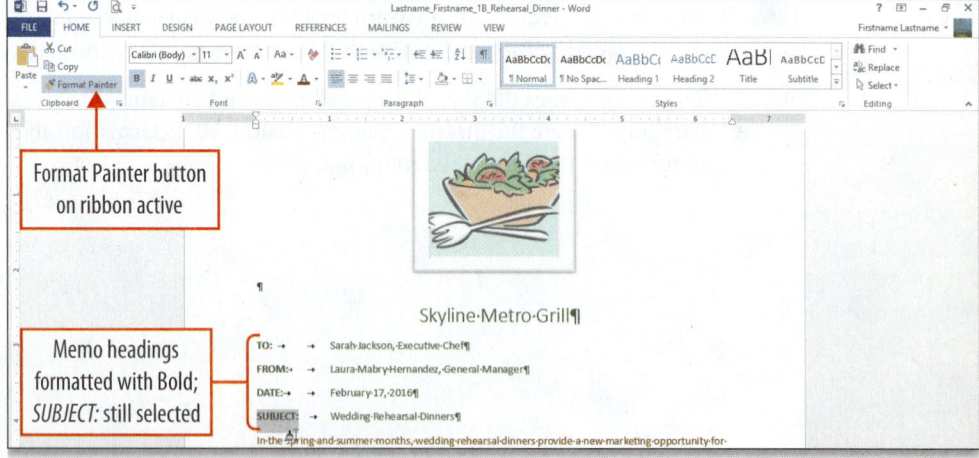

5 On the ribbon, click **Format Painter** ⌗ to turn the command off.

 **ANOTHER WAY** Press ⌷Esc⌷ to turn off Format Painter.

6 In the paragraph that begins *In the spring*, triple-click again to select the entire paragraph. On the mini toolbar, click **Bold** B and **Italic** I . Click anywhere to deselect.

7 On the **Quick Access Toolbar**, click **Save** 🖫 to save the changes you have made to your document.

Activity 1.17 | Using Keyboard Shortcuts and Using the Clipboard to Copy, Cut, and Paste

The *Clipboard* is a temporary storage area that holds text or graphics that you select and then cut or copy. When you *copy* text or graphics, a copy is placed on the Clipboard and the original text or graphic remains in place. When you *cut* text or graphics, a copy is placed on the Clipboard, and the original text or graphic is removed—cut—from the document.

After copying or cutting, the contents of the Clipboard are available for you to *paste*—insert—in a new location in the current document, or into another Office file.

1 Hold down Ctrl and press Home to move to the beginning of your document, and then take a moment to study the table in Figure 1.45, which describes similar keyboard shortcuts with which you can navigate quickly in a document.

FIGURE 1.45

KEYBOARD SHORTCUTS TO NAVIGATE IN A DOCUMENT	
TO MOVE	**PRESS**
To the beginning of a document	Ctrl + Home
To the end of a document	Ctrl + End
To the beginning of a line	Home
To the end of a line	End
To the beginning of the previous word	Ctrl + ←
To the beginning of the next word	Ctrl + →
To the beginning of the current word (if insertion point is in the middle of a word)	Ctrl + ←
To the beginning of the previous paragraph	Ctrl + ↑
To the beginning of the next paragraph	Ctrl + ↓
To the beginning of the current paragraph (if insertion point is in the middle of a paragraph)	Ctrl + ↑
Up one screen	PgUp
Down one screen	PgDn

2 To the left of *Skyline Metro Grill*, point in the left margin area to display the pointer, and then click one time to select the entire paragraph. On the **HOME tab**, in the **Clipboard group**, click **Copy** 🖺 .

Because anything that you select and then copy—or cut—is placed on the Clipboard, the Copy command and the Cut command display in the Clipboard group of commands on the ribbon. There is no visible indication that your copied selection has been placed on the Clipboard.

🔄 **ANOTHER WAY**   Right-click the selection, and then click Copy on the shortcut menu; or, use the keyboard shortcut Ctrl + C.

3 On the **HOME tab**, in the **Clipboard group**, to the right of the group name *Clipboard*, click the **Dialog Box Launcher** button 🔲, and then compare your screen with Figure 1.46.

> The Clipboard pane displays with your copied text. In any ribbon group, the *Dialog Box Launcher* displays either a dialog box or a pane related to the group of commands. It is not necessary to display the Clipboard in this manner, although sometimes it is useful to do so.

FIGURE 1.46

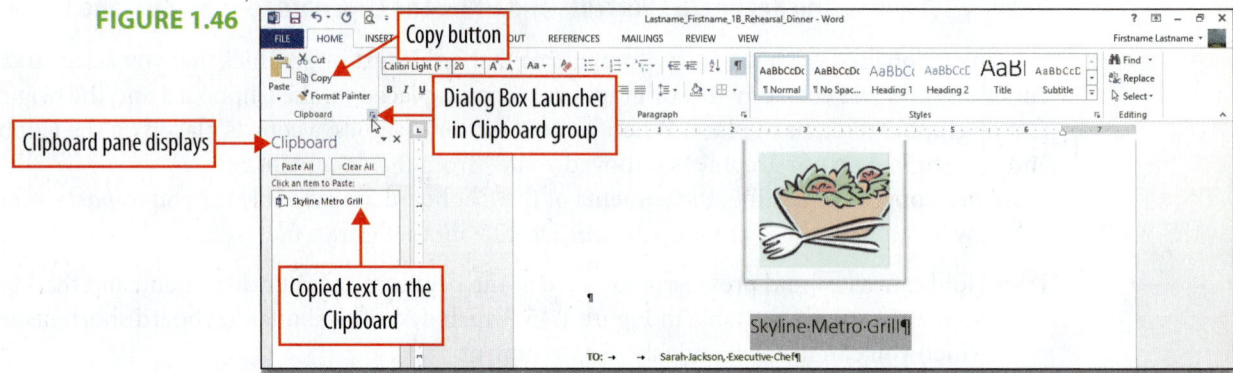

4 In the upper right corner of the **Clipboard** pane, click **Close** ✖.

5 Press Ctrl + End to move to the end of your document. Press Enter one time to create a new blank paragraph. On the **HOME tab**, in the **Clipboard group**, point to **Paste**, and then click the *upper* portion of this split button.

> The Paste command pastes the most recently copied item on the Clipboard at the insertion point location. If you click the lower portion of the Paste button, a gallery of Paste Options displays. A *split button* is divided into two parts; clicking the main part of the button performs a command, and clicking the arrow displays a list or gallery with choices.

🔄 **ANOTHER WAY**   Right-click, on the shortcut menu under Paste Options, click the desired option button; or, press Ctrl + V.

6 Below the pasted text, click **Paste Options** 📋 as shown in Figure 1.47.

> Here you can view and apply various formatting options for pasting your copied or cut text. Typically you will click Paste on the ribbon and paste the item in its original format. If you want some other format for the pasted item, you can choose another format from the *Paste Options gallery*.

> The Paste Options gallery provides a Live Preview of the various options for changing the format of the pasted item with a single click. The Paste Options gallery is available in three places: on the ribbon by clicking the lower portion of the Paste button—the Paste button arrow; from the Paste Options button that displays below the pasted item following the paste operation; or on the shortcut menu if you right-click the pasted item.

FIGURE 1.47

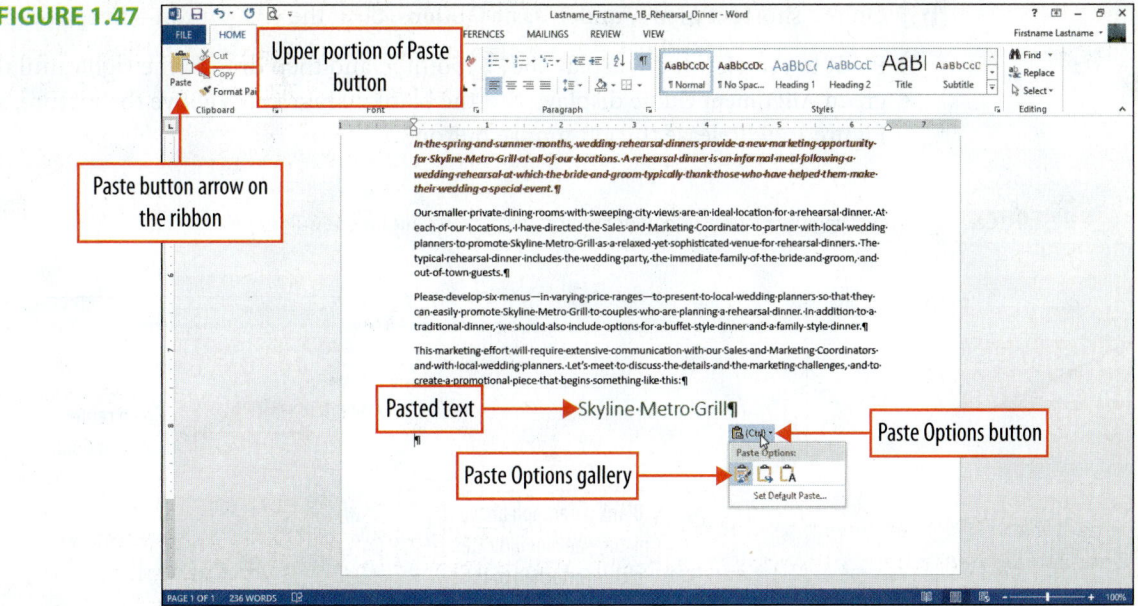

7 In the **Paste Options** gallery, *point* to each option to see the Live Preview of the format that would be applied if you clicked the button.

The contents of the Paste Options gallery are contextual; that is, they change based on what you copied and where you are pasting.

8 Press Esc to close the gallery; the button will remain displayed until you take some other screen action.

9 Press Ctrl + Home to move to the top of the document, and then click the **salad image** one time to select it. While pointing to the selected image, right-click, and then on the shortcut menu, click **Cut**.

Recall that the Cut command cuts—removes—the selection from the document and places it on the Clipboard.

 **ANOTHER WAY**   On the HOME tab, in the Clipboard group, click the Cut button; or, use the keyboard shortcut Ctrl + X.

10 Press Del one time to remove the blank paragraph from the top of the document, and then press Ctrl + End to move to the end of the document.

11 With the insertion point blinking in the blank paragraph at the end of the document, right-click, and notice that the **Paste Options** gallery displays on the shortcut menu. Compare your screen with Figure 1.48.

FIGURE 1.48

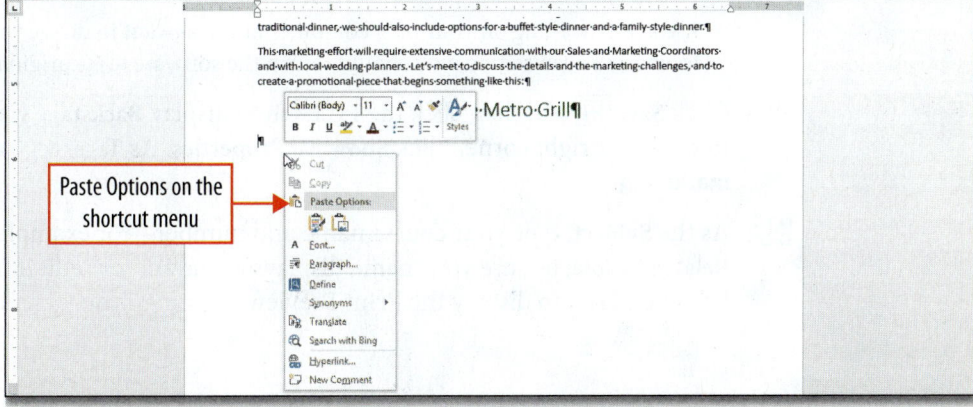

12 On the shortcut menu, under **Paste Options**, click the first button—**Keep Source Formatting**.

13 Point to the picture to display the  pointer, and then drag to the right until the center green **Alignment Guide** displays and the blank paragraph is above the picture, as shown in Figure 1.49. Release the left mouse button.

🔄 **BY TOUCH**   Drag the picture with your finger to display the Alignment Guide.

FIGURE 1.49

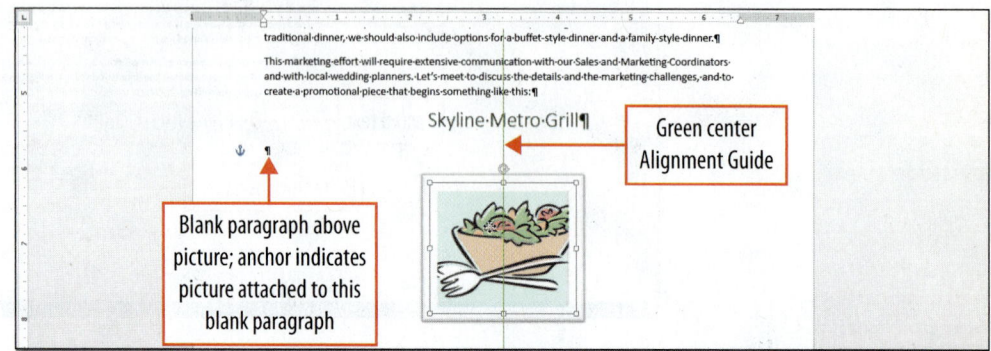

14 Above the picture, click to position the insertion point at the end of the word *Grill*, press [Spacebar] one time, type **for Your Rehearsal Dinner** and then **Save** 🔲 your document. Compare your screen with Figure 1.50.

FIGURE 1.50

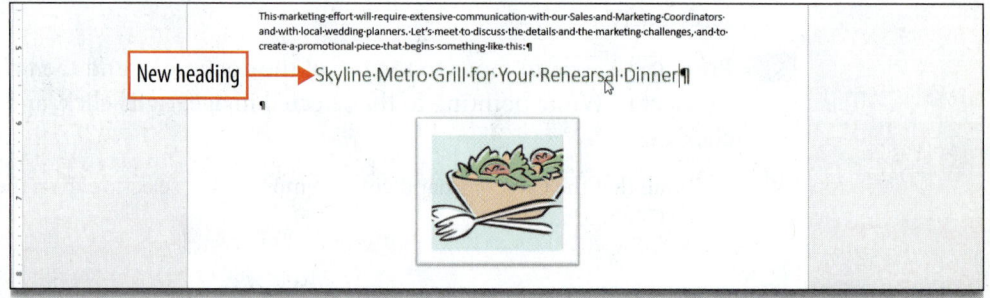

15 On the **INSERT tab**, in the **Header & Footer group**, click **Footer**. At the bottom of the list, click **Edit Footer**, and then with the **HEADER & FOOTER Design tab** active, in the **Insert group**, click **Document Info**. Click **File Name** to add the file name to the footer.

16 On the right end of the ribbon, click **Close Header and Footer**.

17 On the **Quick Access Toolbar**, point to the **Print Preview and Print icon** 🔍 you placed there, right-click, and then click **Remove from Quick Access Toolbar**.

If you are working on your own computer and you want to do so, you can leave the icon on the toolbar; in a lab setting, you should return the software to its original settings.

18 Click **Save** 🔲 and then click the **FILE tab** to display **Backstage** view. With the **Info tab** active, in the lower right corner click **Show All Properties**. As **Tags**, type **weddings, rehearsal dinners, marketing**

19 As the **Subject**, type your course name and number—for example *CIS 10, #5543*. Under **Related People**, be sure your name displays as the author (edit it if necessary), and then on the left, click **Print** to display the Print Preview. Compare your screen with Figure 1.51.

FIGURE 1.51

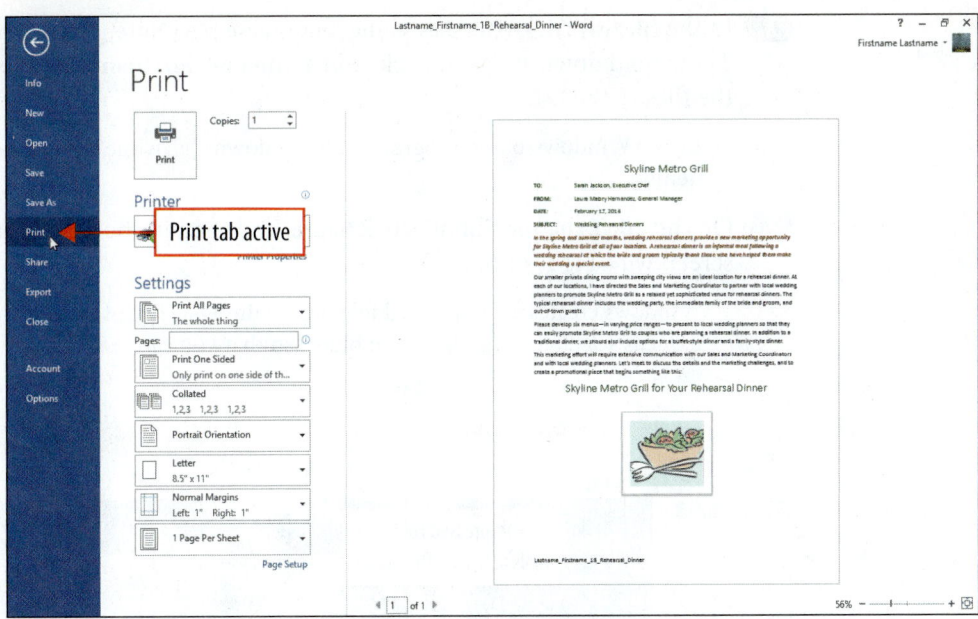

20 On the left side of **Backstage** view, click **Save**. As directed by your instructor, print or submit your file electronically as described in Project 1A, and then in the upper right corner of the Word window, click **Close** ☒.

21 If a message indicates *Would you like to keep the last item you copied?* click **No**.

This message displays if you have copied some type of image to the Clipboard. If you click Yes, the items on the Clipboard will remain for you to use in another program or document.

Objective 11 | Compress Files and Use the Microsoft Office 2013 Help System

Video OF1-11

A *compressed file* is a file that has been reduced in size. Compressed files take up less storage space and can be transferred to other computers faster than uncompressed files. You can also combine a group of files into one compressed folder, which makes it easier to share a group of files.

Within each Office program, the Help feature provides information about all of the program's features and displays step-by-step instructions for performing many tasks.

Activity 1.18 | Compressing Files

In this activity, you will combine the two files you created in this chapter into one compressed file.

1 On the Windows taskbar, click **File Explorer** 📁. On the left, in the **navigation pane**, navigate to your **USB flash drive**, and then open your **Office Features Chapter 1** folder. Compare your screen with Figure 1.52.

FIGURE 1.52

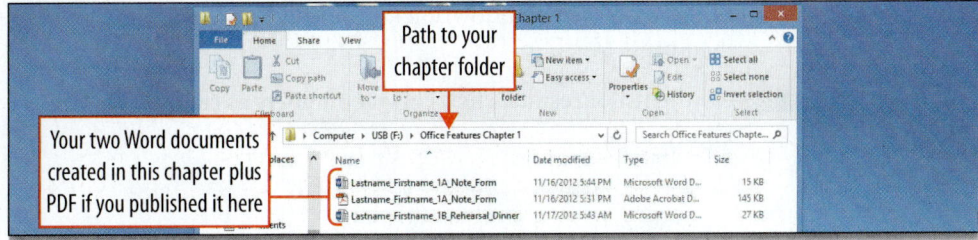

2 In the **file list**, click your **Lastname_Firstname_1A_Note_Form** Word file one time to select it. Then, hold down Ctrl, and click your **Lastname_Firstname_1B_Rehearsal_Dinner** file to select the files in the list.

> In any Windows-based program, holding down Ctrl while selecting enables you to select multiple items.

3 On the **File Explorer** ribbon, click **Share**, and then in the **Send group**, click **Zip**. Compare your screen with Figure 1.53.

> Windows creates a compressed folder containing a *copy* of each of the selected files. The folder name is selected—highlighted in blue—so that you can rename it.

🔄 **BY TOUCH**   Tap the ribbon commands.

FIGURE 1.53

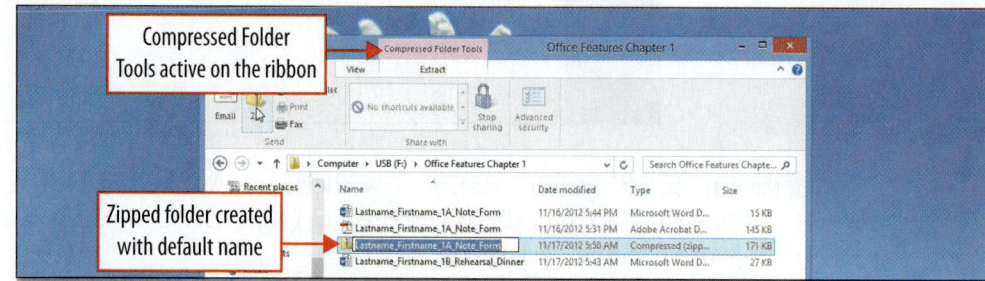

🔄 **ANOTHER WAY**   Point to the selected files in the File List, right-click, point to Send to, and then click Compressed (zipped) folder.

4 Using your own name, type **Lastname_Firstname_Office_Features_Chapter_1** and press Enter.

> The compressed folder is ready to attach to an email or share in some other format.

5 In the upper right corner of the folder window, click **Close** ⊠.

Activity 1.19 | Using the Microsoft Office 2013 Help System in Excel

In this activity, you will use the Microsoft Help feature to find information about formatting numbers in Excel.

1 Press ⊞ to display the Windows 8 **Start screen**, and then type **excel 2013** Press Enter to open the Excel desktop app.

2 On Excel's opening screen, click **Blank workbook**, and then in the upper right corner, click **Microsoft Excel Help** ❓.

🔄 **ANOTHER WAY**   Press F1 to display Help in any Office program.

3 In the **Excel Help** window, click in the **Search online help** box, type **formatting numbers** and then press Enter.

4 On the list of results, click **Format numbers as currency**. Compare your screen with Figure 1.54.

FIGURE 1.54

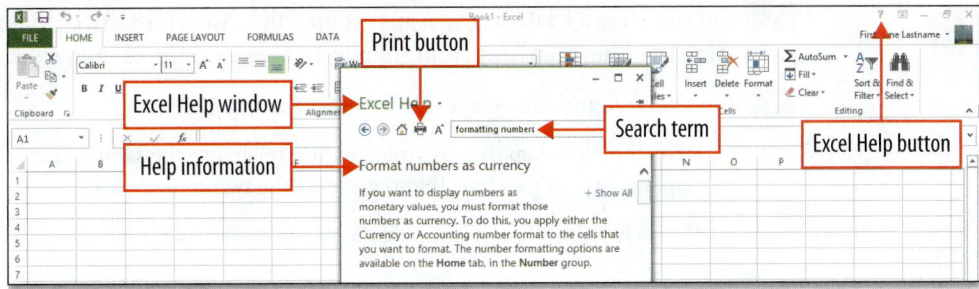

> **5** If you want to do so, at the top of the **Excel Help** window, click Print 🖨 to print a copy of this information for your reference.

> **6** In the upper right corner of the Help window, click **Close** ☒.

> **7** Leave Excel open for the next activity.

Objective 12 | Install Apps for Office and Create a Microsoft Account

ALERT! **Working with Web-Based Applications and Services**

Computer programs and services on the web receive continuous updates and improvements. Thus, the steps to complete the following web-based activities may differ from the ones shown. You can often look at the screens and the information presented to determine how to complete the activity.

Video OF1-12

Apps for Office 2013 and SharePoint 2013 are a collection of downloadable apps that enable you to create and view information within your familiar Office programs. Some of these apps are developed by Microsoft, but many more are developed by specialists in different fields. As new apps are developed, they will be available from the online Office Store.

An *app for Office* is a webpage that works within one of the Office applications, such as Excel, that you download from the Office Store. Office apps combine cloud services and web technologies within the user interface of Office and SharePoint. For example, in Excel, you can use an app to look up and gather search results for a new apartment by placing the information in an Excel worksheet, and then use maps to determine the distance of each apartment to work and to family members.

Activity 1.20 | Installing Apps for Office

ALERT! **You Must Be Signed In to Office with a Microsoft Account to Complete This Activity**

To download an Office app, you must be signed in to Office with a free Microsoft account. If you do not have a Microsoft account, refer to the next activity to create one by using Microsoft's outlook.com email service, which includes free OneDrive cloud storage.

> **1** On the Excel ribbon, click the **INSERT tab**. In the **Apps group**, click the **Apps for Office** arrow, and then click **See All**.

> **2** Click **FEATURED APPS**, and then on the right, click in the **Search for apps on the Office Store** box, type **Bing Maps** and press Enter.

> **3** Click the **Bing logo**, and then click the **Add** button, and then if necessary, click Continue.

> **4** **Close** ☒ Internet Explorer, and then **Close** ☒ the **Apps for Office** box.

5 On the **INSERT tab**, in the **Apps group**, click **Apps for Office**, click **See All**, click **MY APPS**, click the **Bing Maps** app, and then in the lower right corner, click **Insert**.

6 On the Welcome message, click **Insert Sample Data**.

Here, the Bing map displays information related to the sample data. Each state in the sample data displays a small pie chart that represents the two sets of data. Compare your screen with Figure 1.55.

This is just one example of many apps downloadable from the Office store.

FIGURE 1.55

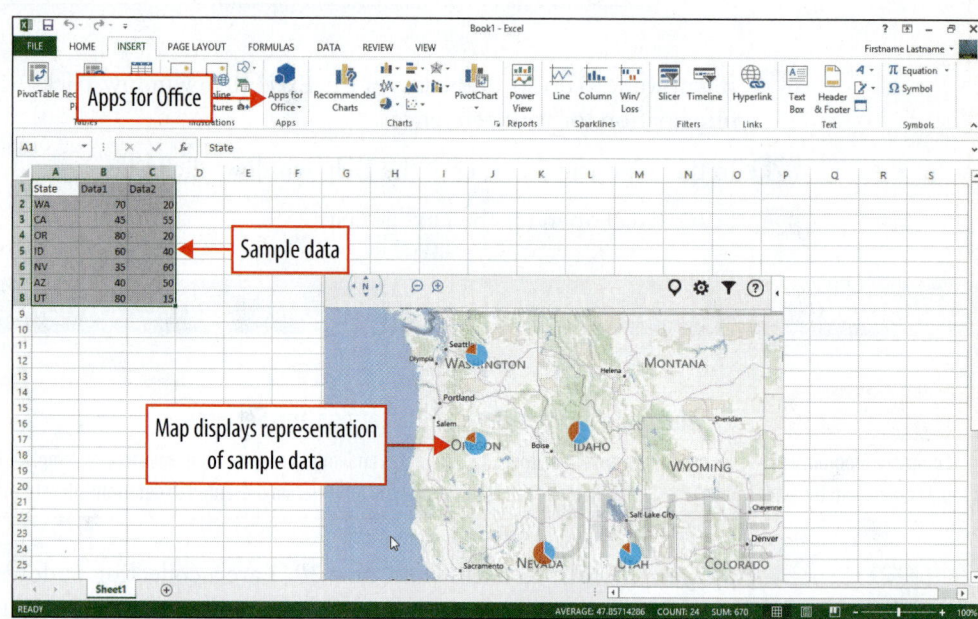

7 **Close** ☒ Excel without saving.

Activity 1.21 | Creating a Microsoft Account

In Windows 8, you can create a Microsoft account, and then use that account to sign in to *any* Windows 8 PC. Signing in with a Microsoft account is recommended because you can:

- Download Windows 8 apps from the Windows Store.
- Get your online content—email, social network updates, updated news—automatically displayed in an app on the Windows 8 Start screen when you sign in.
- Synch settings online to make every Windows 8 computer you use look and feel the same.
- Sign in to Office so that you can store documents on your OneDrive and download Office apps.

1 Open Internet Explorer 🅔, and then go to **www.outlook.com**

2 Locate and click **Sign up now** to display a screen similar to Figure 1.56. Complete the form to create your account.

FIGURE 1.56

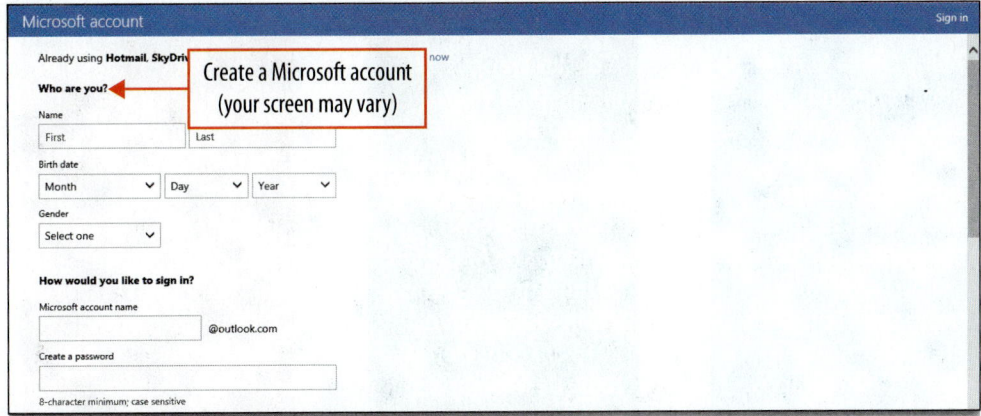

3 Close ⊠ Internet Explorer.

END | You have completed Project 1B

END OF CHAPTER

SUMMARY

Many Office features and commands, such as the Open and Save As dialog boxes, performing commands from the ribbon and from dialog boxes, and using the Clipboard are the same in all Office desktop apps.

A desktop app is installed on your computer and requires a computer operating system such as Microsoft Windows or Apple OS to run. The programs in Microsoft Office 2013 are considered to be desktop apps.

Apps that run on a smartphone or tablet computer—for example, iOS, Android, or Windows Phone—or apps that run from browser software such as Internet Explorer or Chrome on a PC, are referred to as apps.

Within each Office app, you can install additional Apps for Office from the Office Store. You must have a Microsoft account, which includes free OneDrive storage, to download Windows 8 or Office apps.

GO! LEARN IT ONLINE

Review the concepts and key terms in this chapter by completing these online challenges, which you can find at **www.pearsonhighered.com/go**.

Matching and Multiple Choice: Answer matching and multiple choice questions to test what you learned in this chapter. MyITLab®

Crossword Puzzle: Spell out the words that match the numbered clues, and put them in the puzzle squares.

Flipboard: Flip through the definitions of the key terms in this chapter and match them with the correct term.

GLOSSARY

GLOSSARY OF CHAPTER KEY TERMS

Address bar (Internet Explorer) The area at the top of the Internet Explorer window that displays, and where you can type, a URL—Uniform Resource Locator—which is an address that uniquely identifies a location on the Internet.

Address bar (Windows) The bar at the top of a folder window with which you can navigate to a different folder or library, or go back to a previous one.

Alignment The placement of text or objects relative to the left and right margins.

Alignment guides Green lines that display when you move an object to assist in alignment.

App The term that commonly refers to computer programs that run from the device software on a smartphone or a tablet computer—for example, iOS, Android, or Windows Phone—or computer programs that run from the browser software on a desktop PC or laptop PC—for example Internet Explorer, Safari, Firefox, or Chrome.

App for Office A webpage that works within one of the Office applications, such as Excel, and that you download from the Office Store.

Apps for Office 2013 and SharePoint 2013 A collection of downloadable apps that enable you to create and view information within your familiar Office programs.

Backstage tabs The area along the left side of Backstage view with tabs to display screens with related groups of commands.

Backstage view A centralized space for file management tasks; for example, opening, saving, printing, publishing, or sharing a file. A navigation pane displays along the left side with tabs that group file-related tasks together.

Center alignment The alignment of text or objects that is centered horizontally between the left and right margins.

Click The action of pressing and releasing the left button on a mouse pointing device one time.

Clipboard A temporary storage area that holds text or graphics that you select and then cut or copy.

Cloud computing Refers to applications and services that are accessed over the Internet, rather than to applications that are installed on your local computer.

Cloud storage Online storage of data so that you can access your data from different places and devices.

Collaborate To work with others as a team in an intellectual endeavor to complete a shared task or to achieve a shared goal.

Commands An instruction to a computer program that causes an action to be carried out.

Common dialog boxes The set of dialog boxes that includes Open, Save, and Save As, which are provided by the Windows programming interface, and which display and operate in all of the Office programs in the same manner.

Compressed file A file that has been reduced in size and thus takes up less storage space and can be transferred to other computers quickly.

Compressed folder A folder that has been reduced in size and thus takes up less storage space and can be transferred to other computers quickly; also called a *zipped* folder.

Context menus Menus that display commands and options relevant to the selected text or object; also called *shortcut menus*.

Context-sensitive commands Commands that display on a shortcut menu that relate to the object or text that you right-clicked.

Contextual tabs Tabs that are added to the ribbon automatically when a specific object, such as a picture, is selected, and that contain commands relevant to the selected object.

Copy A command that duplicates a selection and places it on the Clipboard.

Cut A command that removes a selection and places it on the Clipboard.

Default The term that refers to the current selection or setting that is automatically used by a computer program unless you specify otherwise.

Deselect The action of canceling the selection of an object or block of text by clicking outside of the selection.

Desktop In Windows, the screen that simulates your work area.

Desktop app The term that commonly refers to a computer program that is installed on your computer and requires a computer operating system like Microsoft Windows or Apple OS to run.

Dialog box A small window that contains options for completing a task.

Dialog Box Launcher A small icon that displays to the right of some group names on the ribbon, and which opens a related dialog box or pane providing additional options and commands related to that group.

Document properties Details about a file that describe or identify it, including the title, author name, subject, and keywords that identify the document's topic or contents; also known as *metadata*.

Drag The action of holding down the left mouse button while moving your mouse.

Edit The process of making changes to text or graphics in an Office file.

Ellipsis A set of three dots indicating incompleteness; an ellipsis following a command name indicates that a dialog box will display if you click the command.

Enhanced ScreenTip A ScreenTip that displays more descriptive text than a normal ScreenTip.

Extract To decompress, or pull out, files from a compressed form.

File A collection of information stored on a computer under a single name, for example, a Word document or a PowerPoint presentation.

File Explorer The program that displays the files and folders on your computer, and which is at work anytime you are viewing the contents of files and folders in a window.

Fill The inside color of an object.

Folder A container in which you store files.

Folder window In Windows, a window that displays the contents of the current folder, library, or device, and contains helpful parts so that you can navigate the Windows file structure.

Font A set of characters with the same design and shape.

Font styles Formatting emphasis such as bold, italic, and underline.

Footer A reserved area for text or graphics that displays at the bottom of each page in a document.

Formatting The process of establishing the overall appearance of text, graphics, and pages in an Office file—for example, in a Word document.

Formatting marks Characters that display on the screen, but do not print, indicating where the Enter key, the Spacebar, and the Tab key were pressed; also called *nonprinting characters*.

Gallery An Office feature that displays a list of potential results instead of just the command name.

Gradient fill A fill effect in which one color fades into another.

Groups On the Office ribbon, the sets of related commands that you might need for a specific type of task.

Header A reserved area for text or graphics that displays at the top of each page in a document.

Info tab The tab in Backstage view that displays information about the current file.

Insertion point A blinking vertical line that indicates where text or graphics will be inserted.

Keyboard shortcut A combination of two or more keyboard keys, used to perform a task that would otherwise require a mouse.

KeyTip The letter that displays on a command in the ribbon and that indicates the key you can press to activate the command when keyboard control of the ribbon is activated.

Keywords Custom file properties in the form of words that you associate with a document to give an indication of the document's content; used to help find and organize files. Also called *tags*.

Landscape orientation A page orientation in which the paper is wider than it is tall.

Layout Options A button that displays when an object is selected and that has commands to choose how the object interacts with surrounding text.

Live Preview A technology that shows the result of applying an editing or formatting change as you point to possible results—*before* you actually apply it.

Location Any disk drive, folder, or other place in which you can store files and folders.

Metadata Details about a file that describe or identify it, including the title, author name, subject, and keywords that identify the document's topic or contents; also known as *document properties*.

Mini toolbar A small toolbar containing frequently used formatting commands that displays as a result of selecting text or objects.

MRU Acronym for *most recently used*, which refers to the state of some commands that retain the characteristic most recently applied; for example, the Font Color button retains the most recently used color until a new color is chosen.

Navigate The process of exploring within the organizing structure of Windows.

Navigation pane In a folder window, the area on the left in which you can navigate to, open, and display favorites, libraries, folders, saved searches, and an expandable list of drives.

Nonprinting characters Characters that display on the screen, but do not print, indicating where the Enter key, the Spacebar, and the Tab key were pressed; also called *formatting marks*.

Notification bar An area at the bottom of an Internet Explorer window that displays information about pending downloads, security issues, add-ons, and other issues related to the operation of your computer.

Object A text box, picture, table, or shape that you can select and then move and resize.

Office Online The free online companion to Microsoft Word, Excel, PowerPoint, Access, and OneNote.

OneDrive Microsoft's free cloud storage for anyone with a free Microsoft account.

Open dialog box A dialog box from which you can navigate to, and then open on your screen, an existing file that was created in that same program.

Option button In a dialog box, a round button that enables you to make one choice among two or more options.

Options dialog box A dialog box within each Office application where you can select program settings and other options and preferences.

Pane A separate area of a window.

Paragraph symbol The symbol ¶ that represents the end of a paragraph.

Paste The action of placing text or objects that have been copied or cut from one location to another location.

Paste Options gallery A gallery of buttons that provides a Live Preview of all the Paste options available in the current context.

Path A sequence of folders that leads to a specific file or folder.

PDF The acronym for Portable Document Format, which is a file format that creates an image that preserves the look of your file; this is a popular format for sending documents electronically because the document will display on most computers.

Point The action of moving your mouse pointer over something on your screen.

Pointer Any symbol that displays on your screen in response to moving your mouse.

Points A measurement of the size of a font; there are 72 points in an inch.

Portable Document Format A file format that creates an image that preserves the look of your file, but that cannot be easily changed; a popular format for sending documents electronically, because the document will display on most computers.

Portrait orientation A page orientation in which the paper is taller than it is wide.

Print Preview A view of a document as it will appear when you print it.

Progress bar In a dialog box or taskbar button, a bar that indicates visually the progress of a task such as a download or file transfer.

Protected View A security feature in Office 2013 that protects your computer from malicious files by opening them in a restricted environment until you enable them; you might encounter this feature if you open a file from an email or download files from the Internet.

pt The abbreviation for *point*; for example, when referring to a font size.

Quick Access Toolbar In an Office program window, the small row of buttons in the upper left corner of the screen from which you can perform frequently used commands.

Read-Only A property assigned to a file that prevents the file from being modified or deleted; it indicates that you cannot save any changes to the displayed document unless you first save it with a new name.

Ribbon A user interface in both Office 2013 and File Explorer that groups the commands for performing related tasks on tabs across the upper portion of the program window.

Right-click The action of clicking the right mouse button one time.

Sans serif font A font design with no lines or extensions on the ends of characters.

ScreenTip A small box that that displays useful information when you perform various mouse actions such as pointing to screen elements or dragging.

Scroll bar A vertical or horizontal bar in a window or a pane to assist in bringing an area into view, and which contains a scroll box and scroll arrows.

Scroll box The box in the vertical and horizontal scroll bars that can be dragged to reposition the contents of a window or pane on the screen.

Selecting Highlighting, by dragging with your mouse, areas of text or data or graphics, so that the selection can be edited, formatted, copied, or moved.

Serif font A font design that includes small line extensions on the ends of the letters to guide the eye in reading from left to right.

SharePoint Collaboration software with which people in an organization can set up team sites to share information, manage documents, and publish reports for others to see.

Shortcut menu A menu that displays commands and options relevant to the selected text or object; also called a *context menu*.

Sizing handles Small squares that indicate a picture or object is selected.

Split button A button divided into two parts and in which clicking the main part of the button performs a command and clicking the arrow opens a menu with choices.

Start search The search feature in Windows 8 in which, from the Start screen, you can begin to type and by default, Windows 8 searches for apps; you can adjust the search to search for files or settings.

Status bar The area along the lower edge of an Office program window that displays file information on the left and buttons to control how the window looks on the right.

Style A group of formatting commands, such as font, font size, font color, paragraph alignment, and line spacing that can be applied to a paragraph with one command.

Subfolder A folder within a folder.

Synchronization The process of updating computer files that are in two or more locations according to specific rules—also called *syncing*.

Syncing The process of updating computer files that are in two or more locations according to specific rules—also called *synchronization*.

Tabs (ribbon) On the Office ribbon, the name of each activity area.

Tags Custom file properties in the form of words that you associate with a document to give an indication of the document's content; used to help find and organize files. Also called *keywords*.

Taskbar The area along the lower edge of the desktop that displays buttons representing programs.

Template A preformatted document that you can use as a starting point and then change to suit your needs.

Theme A predesigned combination of colors, fonts, and effects that look good together and is applied to an entire document by a single selection.

Title bar The bar at the top edge of the program window that indicates the name of the current file and the program name.

Toggle button A button that can be turned on by clicking it once, and then turned off by clicking it again.

Toolbar In a folder window, a row of buttons with which you can perform common tasks, such as changing the view of your files and folders or burning files to a CD.

Triple-click The action of clicking the left mouse button three times in rapid succession.

Trusted Documents A security feature in Office that remembers which files you have already enabled; you might encounter this feature if you open a file from an email or download files from the Internet.

Uniform Resource Locator An address that uniquely identifies a location on the Internet.

URL The acronym for Uniform Resource Locator, which is an address that uniquely identifies a location on the Internet.

USB flash drive A small data storage device that plugs into a computer USB port.

Window A rectangular area on a computer screen in which programs and content appear, and which can be moved, resized, minimized, or closed.

XML Paper Specification A Microsoft file format that creates an image of your document and that opens in the XPS viewer.

XPS The acronym for XML Paper Specification—a Microsoft file format that creates an image of your document and that opens in the XPS viewer.

Zipped folder A folder that has been reduced in size and thus takes up less storage space and can be transferred to other computers quickly; also called a *compressed* folder.

Zoom The action of increasing or decreasing the size of the viewing area on the screen.

Introduction to Microsoft Word 2013

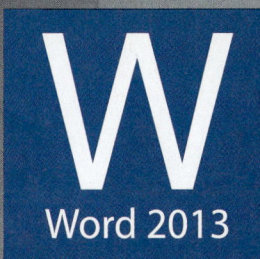

W Word 2013

Fotowerk / Fotolia

Word 2013: Introduction

Video WA

Content! Defined by Merriam-Webster's online dictionary as "the topic or matter treated in a written work" and also as "the principal substance (as written matter, illustrations, or music) offered by a World Wide Web site," content is what you consume when you read on paper or online, when you watch video, or when you listen to any kind of music—live or recorded.

Content is what you *create* when your own words or performances are recorded in some form. For creating content in the form of words, Microsoft Office 2013 is a great choice. Rather than just a tool for word processing, Word is now a tool for you to communicate and collaborate with others. When you want to communicate with pictures or images in your Word document, Office 2013 has many new features to help you do so. Microsoft Word 2013 works best on a Windows 8 PC—desktop, laptop, or tablet—because if your PC is touch-enabled, you will be able to use your fingers to work with Word. For example, the ribbon expands to make it easy to tap commands and you can resize images by moving your fingers on the screen.

Best of all, Microsoft Word 2013 is integrated into the cloud. If you save your documents to your OneDrive that comes with any free Microsoft account, such as one you can create at outlook.com, you can retrieve them from any device and continue to work with and share your documents. Enjoy learning Word 2013!

Creating Documents with Microsoft Word 2013

GO! to Work
Video W1

PROJECT 1A

OUTCOMES
Create a flyer with a picture.

OBJECTIVES

1. Create a New Document and Insert Text
2. Insert and Format Graphics
3. Insert and Modify Text Boxes and Shapes
4. Preview and Print a Document

PROJECT 1B

OUTCOMES
Format text, paragraphs, and documents.

OBJECTIVES

5. Change Document and Paragraph Layout
6. Create and Modify Lists
7. Set and Modify Tab Stops
8. Insert a SmartArt Graphic and an Online Video

A. ya / Fotolia

In This Chapter

In this chapter, you will begin your study of Microsoft Word, which is one of the most popular computer programs and one that almost everyone has a reason to use. You will use many of the new tools in Word 2013 such as applying attractive styles to your documents. You can use Microsoft Word to perform basic word processing tasks such as writing a memo, a report, or a letter. You can also use Word to complete complex tasks, such as creating sophisticated tables, embedding graphics, writing blogs, and creating publications. Word is a program that you can learn gradually, and then add more advanced skills, one at a time.

The projects in this chapter relate to **Sturgeon Point Productions**, which is an independent film company based in Miami and with offices in Detroit and Milwaukee. The film professionals produce effective broadcast and branded content for many industries, and provide a wide array of film and video production services. Sturgeon Point Productions has won awards for broadcast advertising, business media, music videos, and social media. The mission of the company is to help clients tell their stories—whether the story is about a social issue, a new product, a geographical location, a new company, or a person.

Flyer

PROJECT ACTIVITIES

In Activities 1.01 through 1.16, you will create a flyer announcing two internships for a short documentary by Sturgeon Point Productions. Your completed document will look similar to Figure 1.1.

PROJECT FILES

For Project 1A, you will need the following files: You will save your document as:

New blank Word document   **Lastname_Firstname_1A_Flyer**
w01A_Text
w01A_Bird

PROJECT RESULTS

Build from Scratch

Internships Available

Interviews will be held:

Friday and Saturday, January 14 and 15

In the Career Services Conference Room

This summer, Sturgeon Point Productions will be filming a short documentary in Costa Rica about its native birds and has positions available for two interns. We are looking for a first Assistant Director and an Assistant Script Supervisor.

The filming will begin the first week of July and will last approximately two weeks. Payment will be by Day Rate of $100 per day. Transportation, food, and lodging will be provided.

The First Assistant Director will work with the second film crew, which will be filming background video. The Assistant Script Supervisor will work with the Script Supervisor and will be responsible for coordinating communication between the two camera crews.

You must have a valid U. S. passport; no inoculations are necessary. Details are available on the company website.

To set up an interview, apply online at:

www.SturgeonPointProductions.com

Lastname_Firstname_1A_Flyer

FIGURE 1.1 Project 1A Flyer

Objective 1   Create a New Document and Insert Text

Video W1-1

When you start Word, documents you have recently opened, if any, display on the left. On the right, you can select either a blank document or a ***template***—a preformatted document that you can use as a starting point and then change to suit your needs. When you create a new document, you can type all of the text or you can type some of the text and then insert additional text from another source.

Activity 1.01 │ Starting a New Word Document

1 **Start** Word, and then click **Blank document**. On the **HOME tab**, in the **Paragraph group**, if necessary, click **Show/Hide** ¶ so that it is active and the formatting marks display. If the rulers do not display, click the **VIEW tab**, and then in the **Show group**, select the **Ruler** check box.

2 Type **Internships Available** and then press Enter two times. As you type the following text, press the Spacebar only one time at the end of a sentence: **This summer, Sturgeon Point Productions will be filming a short documentary in Costa Rica about its native birds and has positions available for two interns. We are looking for a First Assistant Director and an Assistant Script Supervisor.**

As you type, the insertion point moves to the right, and when it approaches the right margin, Word determines whether the next word in the line will fit within the established right margin. If the word does not fit, Word moves the entire word down to the next line. This is ***wordwrap*** and means that you press Enter *only* when you reach the end of a paragraph—it is not necessary to press Enter at the end of each line of text.

N O T E   **Spacing between Sentences**

Although you might have learned to add two spaces following end-of-sentence punctuation, the common practice now is to space only one time at the end of a sentence.

3 Press Enter. Take a moment to study the table in Figure 1.2 to become familiar with the default document settings in Microsoft Word, and then compare your screen with Figure 1.3.

When you press Enter, Spacebar, or Tab on your keyboard, characters display in your document to represent these keystrokes. These characters do not print and are referred to as ***formatting marks*** or ***nonprinting characters***. These marks will display throughout this instruction.

FIGURE 1.2

DEFAULT DOCUMENT SETTINGS IN A NEW WORD DOCUMENT	
SETTING	**DEFAULT FORMAT**
Font and font size	The default font is Calibri and the default font size is 11 points.
Margins	The default left, right, top, and bottom page margins are 1 inch.
Line spacing	The default line spacing is 1.08, which provides slightly more space between lines than single spacing does.
Paragraph spacing	The default spacing after a paragraph is 8 points, which is slightly less than the height of one blank line of text.
View	The default view is Print Layout view, which displays the page borders and displays the document as it will appear when printed.

FIGURE 1.3

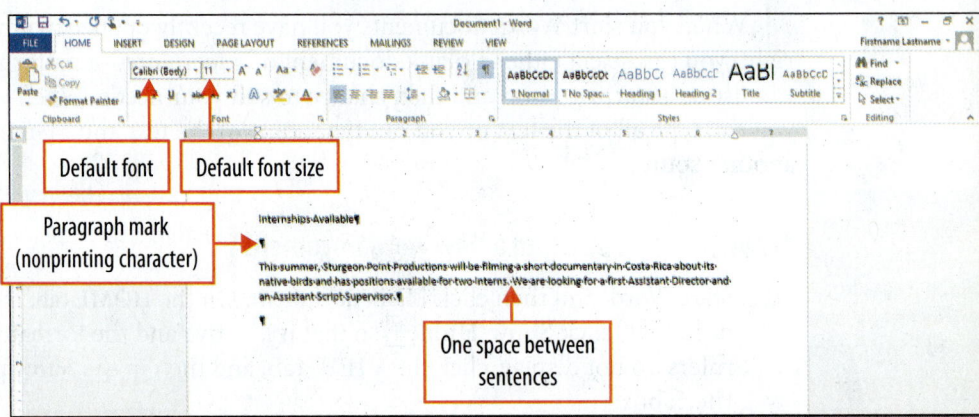

More Knowledge — Word's Default Settings Are Easier to Read Online

Until just a few years ago, word processing programs used single spacing, an extra blank paragraph to separate paragraphs, and 12 pt Times New Roman as the default formats. Now, studies show that individuals find the Word default formats described in Figure 1.2 to be easier to read online, where many documents are now viewed and read.

Activity 1.02 | Inserting Text from Another Document

1 On the ribbon, click the **INSERT tab**. In the **Text group**, click the **Object button arrow**, and then click **Text from File**.

ALERT! — Does the Object Dialog Box Display?

If the Object dialog box displays, you probably clicked the Object *button* instead of the Object *button arrow*. Close the Object dialog box, and then in the Text group, click the Object button arrow, as shown in Figure 1.4. Click *Text from File*, and then continue with Step 2.

2 In the **Insert File** dialog box, navigate to the student files that accompany this textbook, locate and select **w01A_Text**, and then click **Insert**. Compare your screen with Figure 1.4.

A *copy* of the text from the w01A_Text file displays at the insertion point location; the text is not removed from the original file.

FIGURE 1.4

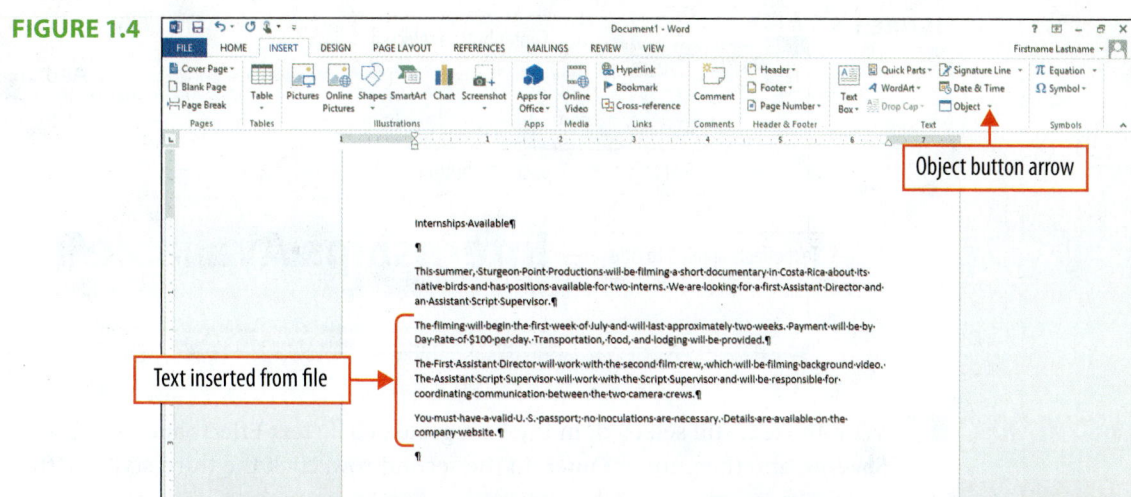

Object button arrow

Text inserted from file

 **ANOTHER WAY**   Open the file, copy the required text, close the file, and then paste the text into the current document.

3 On the **Quick Access Toolbar**, click **Save** 🖫. Under **Save As**, click **Computer**, and then click **Browse**. Navigate to the location where you are saving your files for this chapter, and then create and open a new folder named **Word Chapter 1**. In the **File name** box, using your own name, replace the existing text with **Lastname_Firstname_1A_Flyer** and then click **Save**.

Objective 2   Insert and Format Graphics

▶ Video W1-2

To add visual interest to a document, insert *graphics*. Graphics include pictures, online pictures, charts, and *drawing objects*—shapes, diagrams, lines, and so on. For additional visual interest, you can apply an attractive graphic format to text; add, resize, move, and format pictures; and add a page border.

Activity 1.03 | Formatting Text by Using Text Effects

Text effects are decorative formats, such as shadowed or mirrored text, text glow, 3-D effects, and colors that make text stand out.

1 Including the paragraph mark, select the first paragraph of text—*Internships Available*. On the **HOME tab**, in the **Font group**, click **Text Effects and Typography** 🅐▾.

2 In the **Text Effects** gallery, in the third row, point to the first effect to display the ScreenTip *Fill – Black, Text 1, Outline – Background 1, Hard Shadow – Background 1*, and then click this effect.

3 With the text still selected, in the **Font group**, click in the **Font Size** box 11 ▾ to select the existing font size. Type **52** and then press Enter.

   When you want to change the font size of selected text to a size that does not display in the Font Size list, type the number in the Font Size box and press Enter to confirm the new font size.

4 With the text still selected, in the **Paragraph group**, click **Center** ≡ to center the text. Compare your screen with Figure 1.5.

FIGURE 1.5

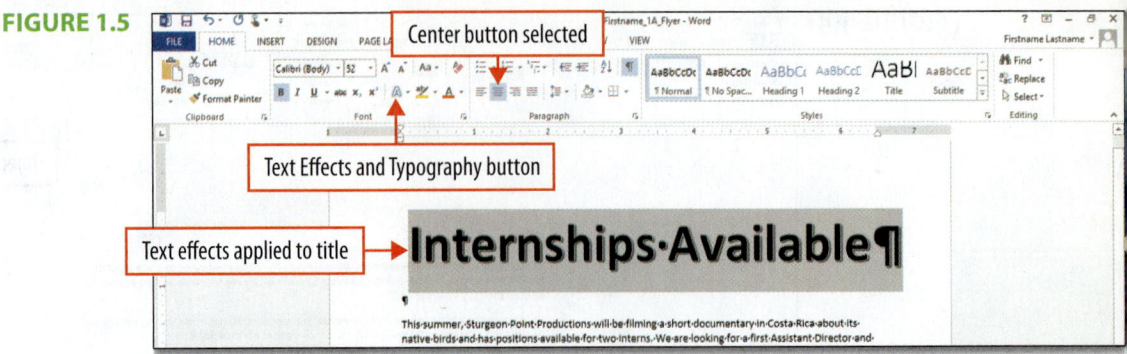

5 With the text still selected, in the **Font group**, click **Text Effects and Typography** [A ▼]. Point to **Shadow**, and then under **Outer**, in the second row, click the third style—**Offset Left**.

6 With the text still selected, in the **Font group**, click the **Font Color button arrow** [A ▼]. Under **Theme Colors**, in the sixth column, click the first color—**Orange, Accent 2**.

7 Click anywhere in the document to deselect the text, click **Save** [💾], and then compare your screen with Figure 1.6.

FIGURE 1.6

> **More Knowledge** | **Clear Existing Formatting**
>
> If you do not like your text effect, you can remove all formatting from any selected text. To do so, on the HOME tab, in the Font group, click Clear All Formatting [◊].

Activity 1.04 | Inserting Pictures

1 In the paragraph that begins *This summer*, click to position the insertion point at the beginning of the paragraph.

2 On the **INSERT tab**, in the **Illustrations group**, click **Pictures**. In the **Insert Picture** dialog box, navigate to your student data files, locate and click **w01A_Bird**, and then click **Insert**.

> Word inserts the picture as an ***inline object***; that is, the picture is positioned directly in the text at the insertion point, just like a character in a sentence. The Layout Options button displays to the right of the picture. You can change the ***Layout Options*** to control the manner in which text wraps around a picture or other object. Sizing handles surround the picture indicating it is selected.

3 Notice the square sizing handles around the border of the selected picture, as shown in Figure 1.7.

> The corner sizing handles resize the graphic proportionally. The center sizing handles resize a graphic vertically or horizontally only; however, sizing with these will distort the graphic. A ***rotation handle***, with which you can rotate the graphic to any angle, displays above the top center sizing handle.

FIGURE 1.7

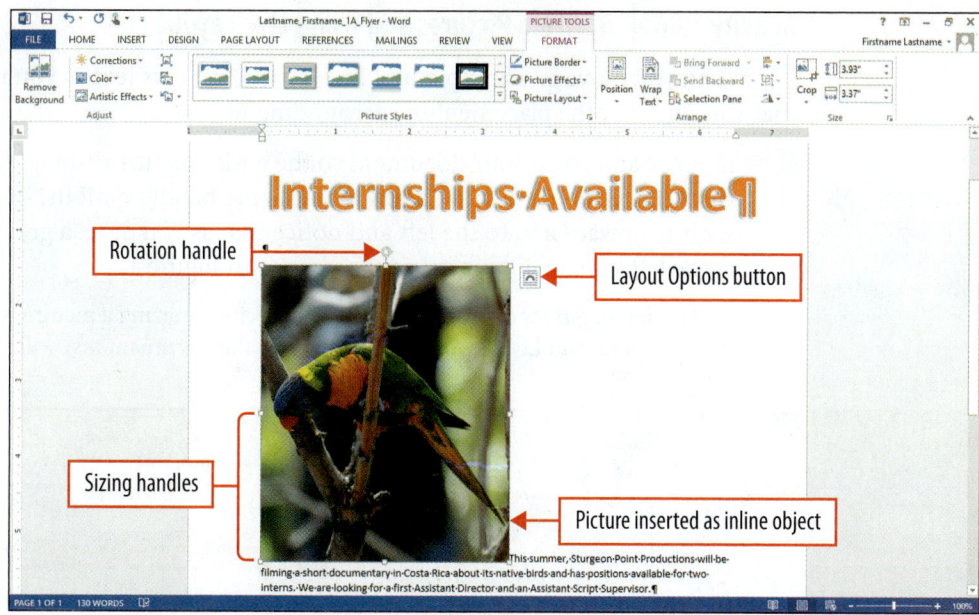

Rotation handle

Layout Options button

Sizing handles

Picture inserted as inline object

Activity 1.05 | Wrapping Text around a Picture Using Layout Options

Recall that Layout Options enable you to control *text wrapping*—the manner in which text displays around an object.

1 Be sure the picture is selected—you know it is selected if the sizing handles display.

2 To the right of the picture, click **Layout Options** to display a gallery of text wrapping arrangements. Point to each layout option icon to view its ScreenTip.

Each icon visually depicts how text will wrap around an object.

 **ANOTHER WAY**   On the FORMAT tab, in the Arrange group, click Wrap Text.

3 From the gallery, under **With Text Wrapping**, click the first layout—**Square**. Compare your screen with Figure 1.8.

Select Square text wrapping when you want to wrap the text to the left or right of an image. To the left of the picture, an *object anchor* displays indicating that the selected object is anchored to the text at this location in the document.

FIGURE 1.8

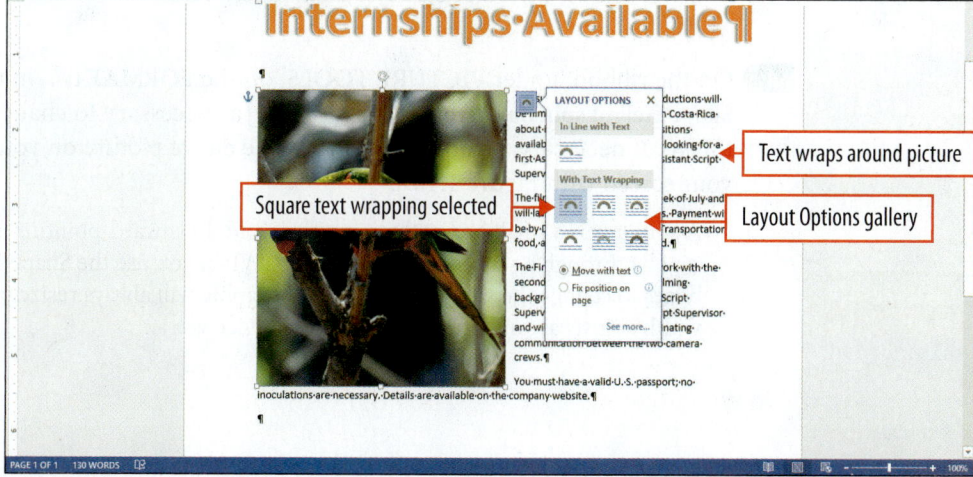

Text wraps around picture

Square text wrapping selected

Layout Options gallery

4 **Close** the **Layout Options**, and then **Save** your document.

Activity 1.06 | Resizing Pictures and Using Live Layout

When you move or size a picture, *Live Layout* reflows text as you move or size an object so that you can view the placement of surrounding text.

1 If necessary, scroll your document so the entire picture displays on the screen. At the lower right corner of the picture, point to the sizing handle until the ⬚ pointer displays. Drag slightly upward and to the left and notice that as you drag, a green alignment guide displays at the left margin. Compare your screen with Figure 1.9.

> *Alignment guides* display when you are moving or sizing a picture to help you with object placement, and Live Layout shows you how the document text will flow and display on the page.

FIGURE 1.9

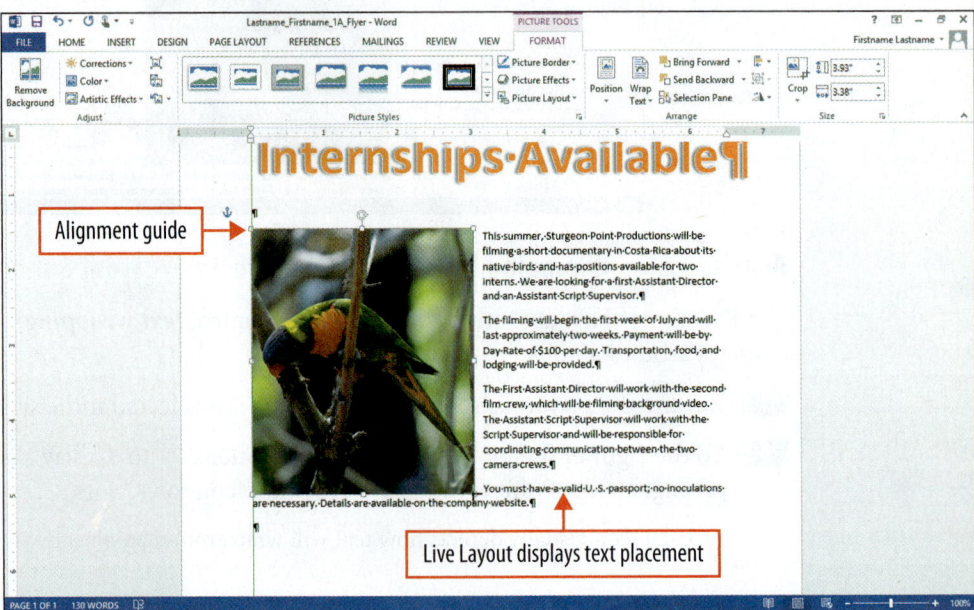

2 Continue to drag up and to the left until the bottom of the graphic is aligned at approximately **4 inches on the vertical ruler** and notice that the graphic is proportionally resized.

3 On the **Quick Access Toolbar**, click **Undo** ↺ to restore the picture to its original size.

🔄 **ANOTHER WAY**   On the FORMAT tab, in the Adjust group, click Reset Picture.

---

4 On the ribbon, under **PICTURE TOOLS**, on the **FORMAT tab**, in the **Size group**, click the **Shape Height spin box arrows** 🔲 Height: 0.19″ ⬍ as necessary to change the height of the picture to **3.8″**. If necessary, scroll down to view the entire picture on your screen, and then compare your screen with Figure 1.10.

> A *spin box* is a small box with an upward- and downward-pointing arrow that lets you move rapidly through a set of values by clicking. When you use the Shape Height and Shape Width spin boxes to change the size of a graphic, the graphic will always resize proportionally; that is, the width adjusts as you change the height and vice versa.

FIGURE 1.10

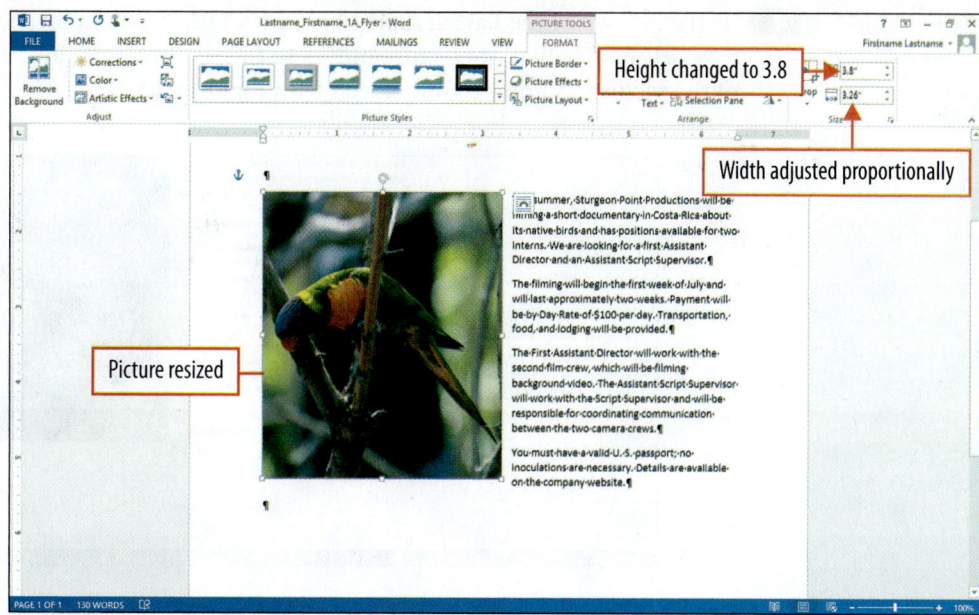

Height changed to 3.8

Width adjusted proportionally

Picture resized

5 Save 🖫 your document.

Activity 1.07 | Moving a Picture

There are two ways to move a picture in a document. You can point to the picture and then drag it to a new position. You can also change the picture settings in a dialog box, which gives you more precise control over the picture location.

1 Be sure the picture is selected. On the ribbon, click the **FORMAT tab**. In the **Arrange group**, click **Position**, and then click **More Layout Options**.

2 In the **Layout** dialog box, be sure the **Position tab** is selected. Under **Horizontal**, click the **Alignment** option button. To the right of **Alignment**, click the **arrow**, and then click **Right**. To the right of **relative to**, click the **arrow**, and then click **Margin**.

3 Under **Vertical**, click the **Alignment** option button. Change the **Alignment** options to **Top relative to Line**. Compare your screen with Figure 1.11.

With these alignment settings, the picture will move to the right margin of the page and the top edge will align with the top of the first line of the paragraph to which it is anchored.

FIGURE 1.11

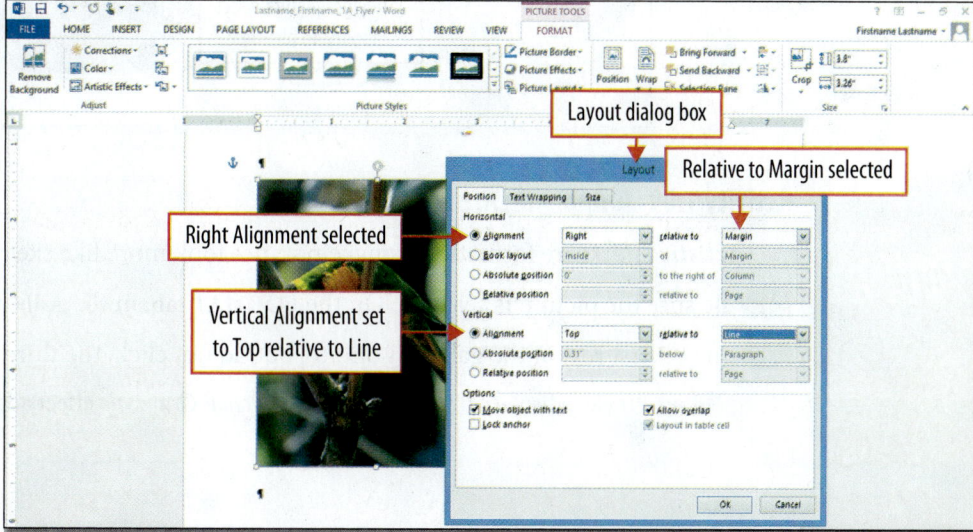

Layout dialog box

Relative to Margin selected

Right Alignment selected

Vertical Alignment set to Top relative to Line

4 At the bottom of the **Layout** dialog box, click **OK**, and then on the **Quick Access Toolbar**, click **Save** 🔲. Notice that the picture moves to the right margin, and the text wraps on the left side of the picture. Compare your screen with Figure 1.12.

FIGURE 1.12

Activity 1.08 | Applying Picture Effects

Picture styles include shapes, shadows, frames, borders, and other special effects with which you can stylize an image. *Picture Effects* enhance a picture with effects such as shadow, glow, reflection, or 3-D rotation.

1 Be sure the picture is selected. On the **FORMAT tab**, in the **Picture Styles group**, click **Picture Effects**.

2 Point to **Soft Edges**, and then click **5 Point**.

The Soft Edges feature fades the edges of the picture. The number of points you choose determines how far the fade goes inward from the edges of the picture.

3 Compare your screen with Figure 1.13, and then **Save** 🔲 your document.

FIGURE 1.13

Activity 1.09 | Applying Artistic Effects

Artistic effects are formats that make pictures look more like sketches or paintings.

1 Be sure the picture is selected. On the **FORMAT tab**, in the **Adjust group**, click **Artistic Effects**.

2 In the first row of the gallery, point to, but do not click, the third effect—**Pencil Grayscale**.

Live Preview displays the picture with the *Pencil Grayscale* effect added.

3 In the second row of the gallery, click the third effect—**Paint Brush. Save** 🔲 your document, and then notice that the picture looks more like a painting than a photograph. Compare your screen with Figure 1.14.

FIGURE 1.14

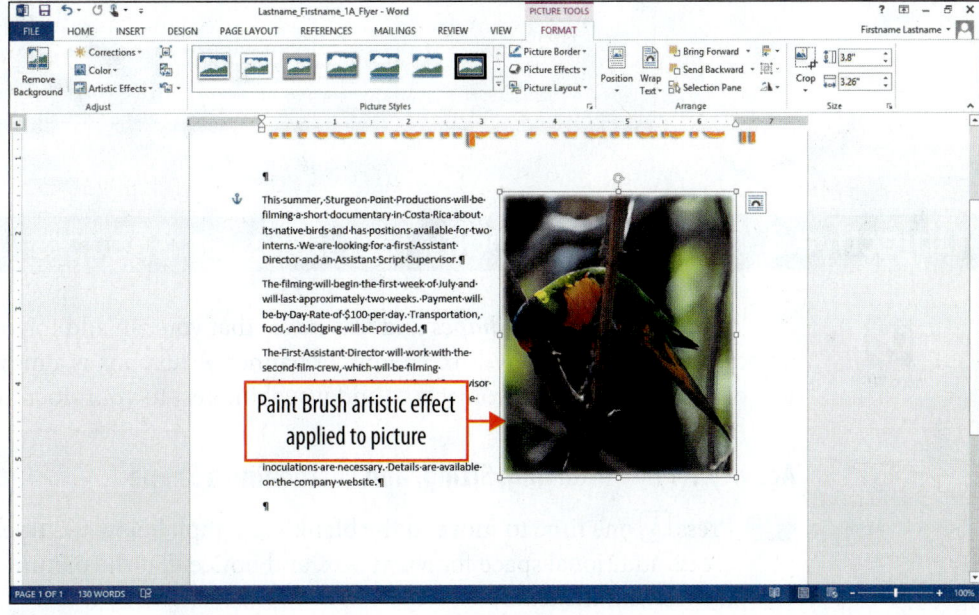

Activity 1.10 │ Adding a Page Border

Page borders frame a page and help to focus the information on the page.

1 Click anywhere outside the picture to deselect it. On the **DESIGN tab**, in the **Page Background group**, click **Page Borders**.

2 In the **Borders and Shading** dialog box, on the **Page Border tab**, under **Setting**, click **Box**. Under **Style**, scroll the list and click the seventh style—double lines.

3 Click the **Color arrow**, and then in the sixth column, click the first color—**Orange, Accent 2**.

4 Under **Apply to**, be sure **Whole document** is selected, and then compare your screen with Figure 1.15.

FIGURE 1.15

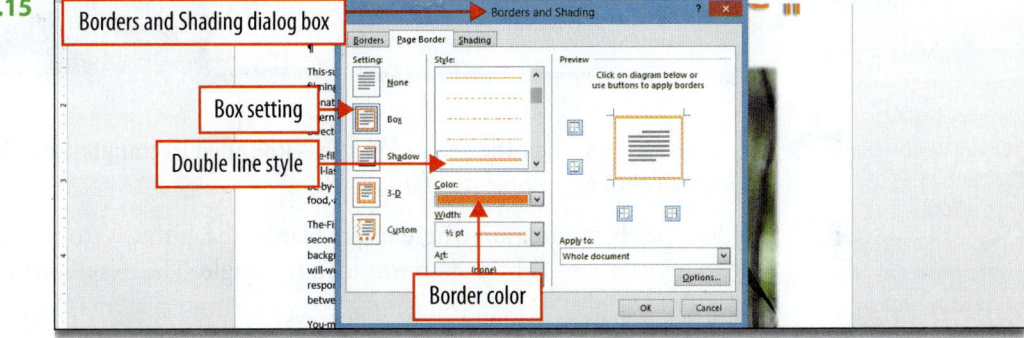

5 At the bottom of the **Borders and Shading** dialog box, click **OK**.

6 Press Ctrl + Home to move to the top of the document, click **Save** 🔲, and then compare your screen with Figure 1.16.

FIGURE 1.16

Page border applied to document

Objective 3 Insert and Modify Text Boxes and Shapes

Video W1-3

Word has predefined **shapes** and **text boxes** that you can add to your documents. A shape is an object such as a line, arrow, box, callout, or banner. A text box is a movable, resizable container for text or graphics. Use these objects to add visual interest to your document.

Activity 1.11 | Inserting, Sizing, and Positioning a Shape

1 Press ↓ one time to move to the blank paragraph below the title. Press Enter four times to create additional space for a text box, and notice that the picture anchored to the paragraph moves with the text.

2 Press Ctrl + End to move to the bottom of the document, and notice that your insertion point is positioned in the empty paragraph at the end of the document. Press Delete to remove the blank paragraph.

3 Click the **INSERT tab**, and then in the **Illustrations group**, click **Shapes** to display the gallery. Compare your screen with Figure 1.17.

FIGURE 1.17

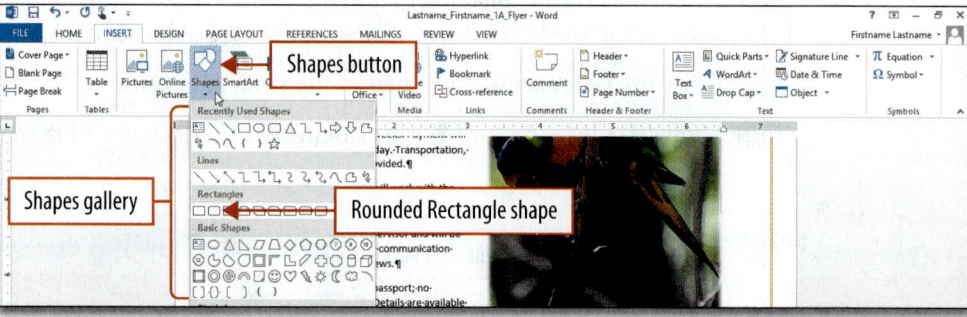

4 Under **Rectangles**, click the second shape—**Rounded Rectangle**, and then move your pointer. Notice that the ➕ pointer displays.

5 Position the ➕ pointer anywhere in the blank area at the bottom of the document. Click one time to insert a 1-inch by 1-inch rounded rectangle. The exact location is not important.

A blue rectangle with rounded edges displays.

6 To the right of the rectangle object, click **Layout Options** 🔲, and then at the bottom of the gallery, click **See more** to display the **Layout** dialog box.

 **ANOTHER WAY**   On the FORMAT tab, in the Arrange group, click Position.

7 In the **Layout** dialog box, under **Horizontal**, click **Alignment**. To the right of **Alignment**, click the **arrow**, and then click **Centered**. To the right of **relative to**, click the **arrow**, and then click **Page**. Under **Vertical**, click in the **Absolute position** box to select the existing number, and then type **1** To the right of **below**, be sure that **Paragraph** displays. Click **OK**.

> This action centers the rectangle on the page and positions the rectangle one inch below the last paragraph.

8 On the **FORMAT tab**, click in the **Shape Height** box ⬍ Height: 0.19" ▲▼ to select the existing text. Type **1.5** and then click in the **Shape Width** box 🔲 Width: 6.49" ▲▼. Type **4.5** and then press Enter.

9 Compare your screen with Figure 1.18, and then **Save** 💾 your document.

FIGURE 1.18

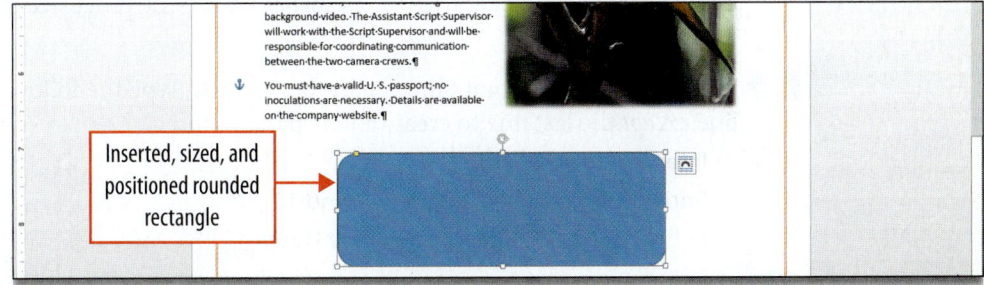

Inserted, sized, and positioned rounded rectangle

Activity 1.12 | Typing Text in a Shape and Formatting a Shape

1 If necessary, select the rectangle shape. Type **To set up an interview, apply online at:** and then press Enter. Type **www.SturgeonPointProductions.com**

2 Press Ctrl + A to select the text you just typed. Right-click over the selected text to display the mini toolbar, and then click **Bold** B. With the text still selected, click **Increase Font Size** A^ three times to increase the font size to **16 pt**.

> The keyboard shortcut Ctrl + A is convenient to select all of the text in a text box.

3 With the text still selected, on the mini toolbar, click the **Font Color button arrow**. Under **Theme Colors**, click **Black, Text 1**.

4 Click outside the shape to deselect the text. Click the border of the shape to select the shape but not the text. On the **FORMAT tab**, in the **Shape Styles group**, click **Shape Fill**. In the sixth column, click the fourth color—**Orange, Accent 2, Lighter 40%**.

5 With the shape still selected, in the **Shape Styles group**, click **Shape Outline**. In the sixth column, click the first color—**Orange, Accent 2**. Compare your screen with Figure 1.19, and then **Save** 💾 your document.

FIGURE 1.19

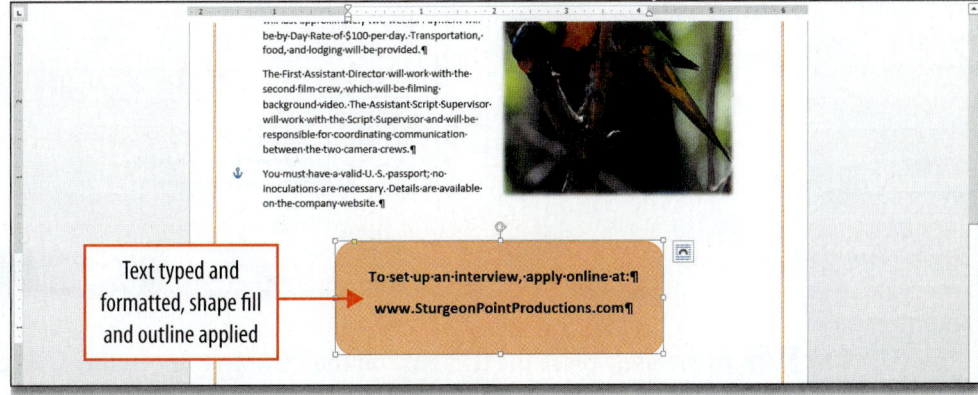

Text typed and formatted, shape fill and outline applied

Activity 1.13 | Inserting a Text Box

A text box is useful to differentiate portions of text from other text on the page. Because it is a *floating object*—a graphic that can be moved independently of the surrounding text characters—you can place a text box anywhere on the page.

1 Press Ctrl + Home to move to the top of the document.

2 On the **INSERT tab**, in the **Text group**, click **Text Box**. At the bottom of the gallery, click **Draw Text Box**.

3 Position the ✛ pointer over the first blank paragraph—aligned with the left margin and at approximately **1 inch on the vertical ruler**. Drag down and to the right to create a text box approximately **1.5 inches** high and **4 inches** wide—the exact size and location need not be precise.

4 With the insertion point blinking in the text box, type the following, pressing Enter after each line *except* the last line to create a new paragraph:

> **Interviews will be held:**
>
> **Friday and Saturday, January 14 and 15**
>
> **In the Career Services Conference Room**

5 Compare your screen with Figure 1.20, and then **Save** 💾 your document

FIGURE 1.20

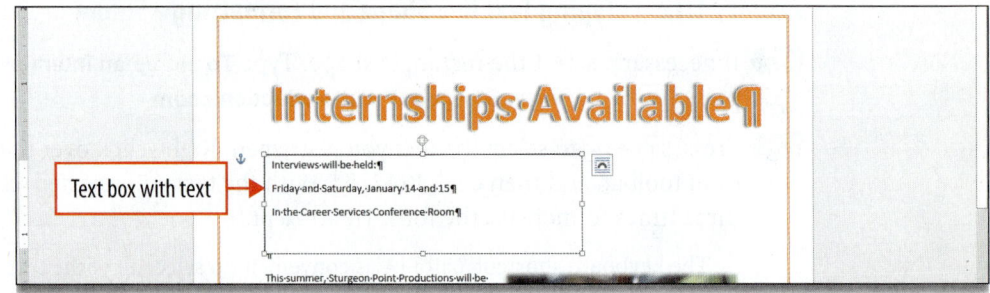

Activity 1.14 | Sizing and Positioning a Text Box and Formatting a Text Box Using Shape Styles

1 Point to the text box border to display the 🔧 pointer. In the space below the *Internships Available* title, by dragging, move the text box until a horizontal green alignment guide displays above the first blank paragraph mark and a vertical green alignment guide displays in the center of the page as shown in Figure 1.21.

FIGURE 1.21

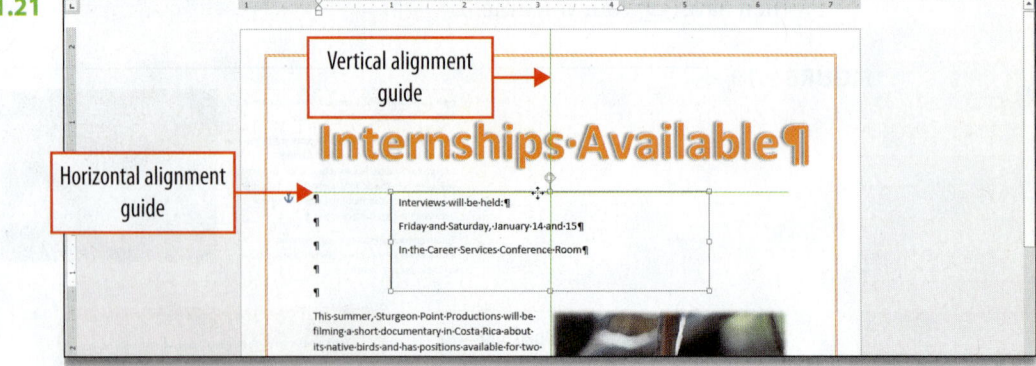

2 To precisely place the text box, on the **FORMAT tab**, in the **Arrange group**, click **Position**, and then click **More Layout Options**.

3 In the **Layout** dialog box, under **Horizontal**, click **Alignment**. To the right of **Alignment**, click the **arrow**, and then click **Centered**. To the right of **relative to**, click the **arrow**, and then click **Page**.

4 Under **Vertical**, click in the **Absolute position** box, select the existing number, and then type **1.25** To the right of **below**, click the **arrow**, and then click **Margin**.

5 In the **Layout** dialog box, click the **Size tab**. Under **Height**, select the number in the **Absolute** box. Type **1.25** and then under **Width**, select the number in the **Absolute** box. Type **4** and then click **OK**.

> The text box is sized correctly, centered horizontally, and the top edge is positioned 1.25 inches below the top margin of the document.

6 Click in the text box, and then press Ctrl + A to select all of the text. Right-click over the selected text to display the mini toolbar, change the **Font Size** to **16** and apply **Bold** B. Press Ctrl + E to center the text.

> Ctrl + E is the keyboard shortcut to center text in a document or object.

7 On the ribbon, under **DRAWING TOOLS**, click the **FORMAT tab**. In the **Shape Styles group**, click **More**, and then in the first row, click the third style—**Colored Outline – Orange, Accent 2**.

8 On the **FORMAT tab**, in the **Shape Styles group**, click **Shape Effects**. Point to **Shadow**, and then under **Outer**, in the first row, click the first effect—**Offset Diagonal Bottom Right**.

9 Click anywhere in the document to deselect the text box. Compare your screen with Figure 1.22, and then **Save** your document.

FIGURE 1.22

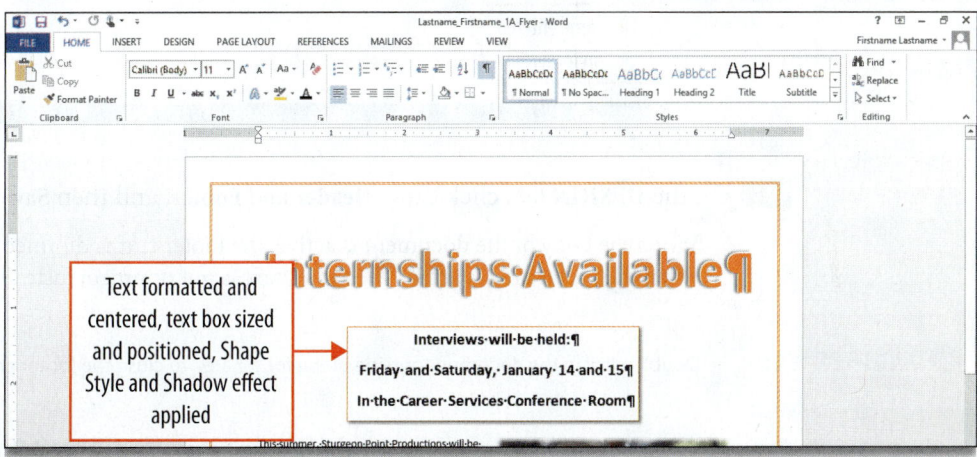

Text formatted and centered, text box sized and positioned, Shape Style and Shadow effect applied

---

Objective 4   Preview and Print a Document

Video W1-4

While you are creating your document, it is useful to preview your document periodically to be sure that you are getting the result you want. Then, before printing, make a final preview to be sure the document layout is what you intend.

Activity 1.15 | Adding a File Name to the Footer by Inserting a Field

Information in headers and footers helps to identify a document when it is printed or displayed electronically. Recall that a header is information that prints at the top of every page; a footer is information that prints at the bottom of every page. In this textbook, you will insert the file name in the footer of every Word document.

> **1** Click the **INSERT tab**, and then in the **Header & Footer group**, click **Footer**.

> **2** At the bottom of the gallery, click **Edit Footer**.

> The footer area displays with the insertion point blinking at the left edge, and on the ribbon, the Header & Footer Tools display.

🔁 **ANOTHER WAY**   At the bottom edge of the page, right-click, and then on the shortcut menu, click Edit Footer.

> **3** On the ribbon, under the **HEADER & FOOTER TOOLS**, on the **DESIGN tab**, in the **Insert group**, click **Document Info**, and then click **File Name**. Compare your screen with Figure 1.23.

FIGURE 1.23

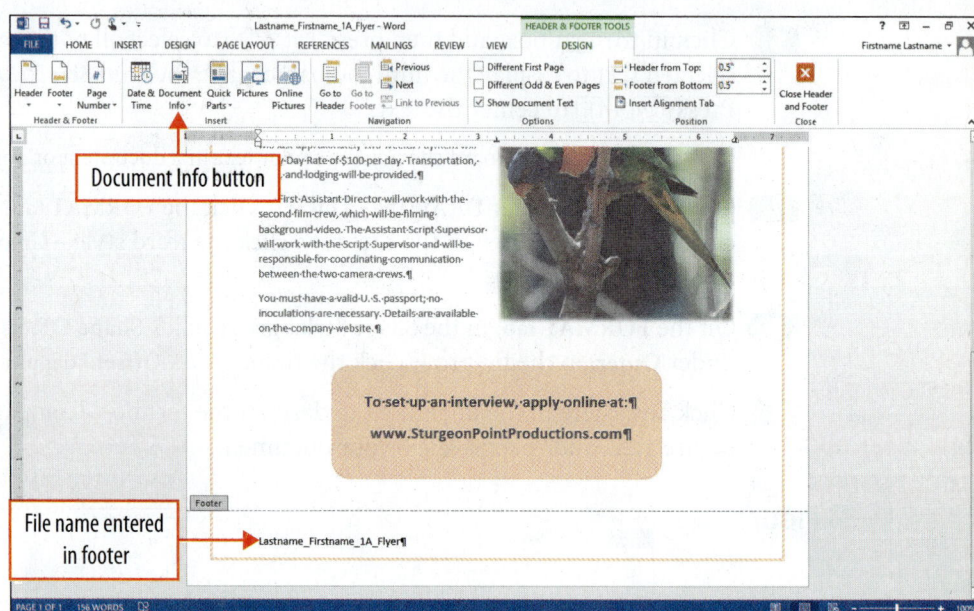

Document Info button

File name entered in footer

> **4** On the **DESIGN tab**, click **Close Header and Footer**, and then **Save** 🖫 your document.

> When the body of the document is active, the footer text is dimmed—displays in gray. Conversely, when the footer area is active, the footer text is not dimmed; instead, the document text is dimmed.

🔁 **ANOTHER WAY**   Double-click in the document outside of the footer area to close the footer and return to the document.

Activity 1.16 | Adding Document Properties and Previewing and Printing a Document

> **1** Press `Ctrl` + `Home` to move the insertion point to the top of the document. In the upper left corner of your screen, click the **FILE tab** to display **Backstage** view. On the right, at the bottom of the **Properties** list, click **Show All Properties**.

> **2** On the list of **Properties**, click to the right of **Tags** to display an empty box, and then type **internship, documentary**

> **3** Click to the right of **Subject** to display an empty box, and then type your course name and section number. Under **Related People**, be sure that your name displays as the author. If necessary, right-click the author name, click **Edit Property**, type your name, press `Enter` and click **OK**.

4 On the left, click **Print** to display the **Print Preview**. Compare your screen with Figure 1.24.

Here you can select any printer connected to your system and adjust the settings related to how you want to print. On the right, Print Preview displays your document exactly as it will print; the formatting marks do not display. At the bottom of the Print Preview area, in the center, the number of pages and arrows with which you can move among the pages in Print Preview display. On the right, Zoom settings enable you to shrink or enlarge the Print Preview.

FIGURE 1.24

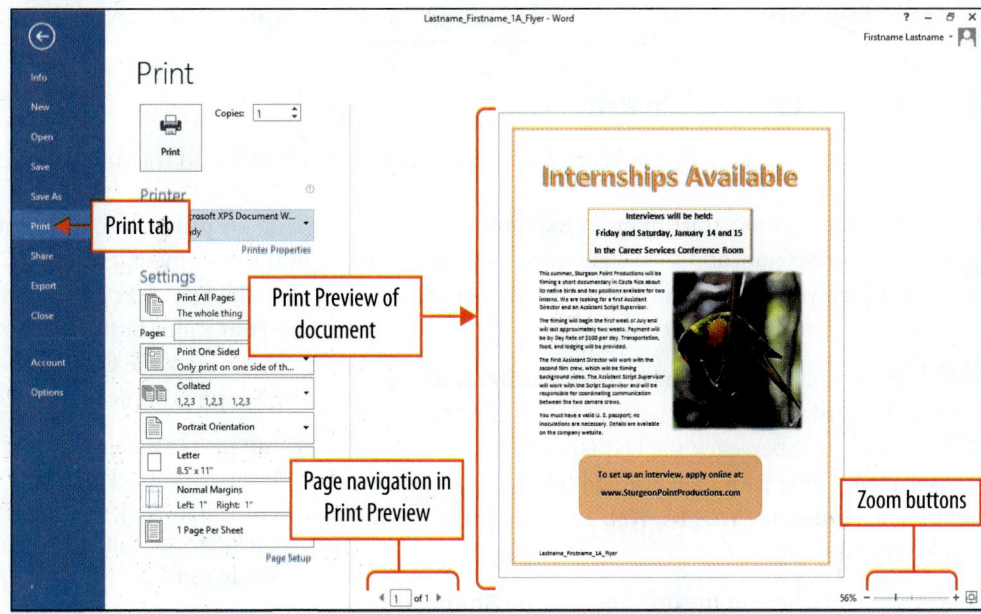

5 In the lower right corner of the window, click **Zoom In** ⊕ several times to view the document at a larger size, and notice that a larger preview is easier to read. Click **Zoom to Page** ▣ to view the entire page.

6 To submit your file electronically, skip this step and move to Step 7. To print your document on paper using the default printer on your system, in the upper left portion of the screen, click **Print**.

The document will print on your default printer; if you do not have a color printer, colors will print in shades of gray. Backstage view closes and your file redisplays in the Word window.

7 To create an electronic printout, on the left, click **Export**. On the right, click **Create PDF/XPS**. In the **Publish as PDF or XPS** dialog box, navigate to your **Word Chapter 1** folder, and then click **Publish**. If your Adobe Acrobat or Adobe Reader program displays your PDF, in the upper right corner, click **Close** ⊠.

8 **Save** 🖫 your document. In the upper right corner of the Word window, click **Close** ⊠. If directed by your instructor to do so, submit your paper or electronic printout or your Word file.

END | You have completed Project 1A

GO! with Office Online (formerly Web Apps)

Build from Scratch

ALERT! **Working with Web-Based Applications and Services**

Computer programs and services on the web receive continuous updates and improvements, so the steps to complete this web-based activity may differ from the ones shown. You can often look at the screens and the information presented to determine how to complete the activity.

Activity | Creating a Flyer in Word Online

In this activity, you will use Word Online to create a flyer similar to the one you created in Project 1A.

1 From the desktop, start Internet Explorer. Navigate to **http://onedrive.com**, and then sign in to your Microsoft account. Open your **GO! Web Projects** folder—or create and then open this folder if necessary.

2 On the OneDrive menu bar, click **Create**, and then click **Word document**. In the middle of the blue, Word Online title bar, click the text **Document1** so that it is selected. Using your own last and first name, type **Lastname_Firstname_WD_1A_Web** and then press Enter to change the file name.

3 Click anywhere in the document. Type **Sturgeon Point Productions** and then press Enter.

4 Type the following four lines of text, pressing Enter after each line *except* for the last line:

Internships Available for a Costa Rica
Native Birds Documentary
Interviews on Friday, January 14
Filming Begins the First Week of July

5 By using your [I] pointer, drag to select the first line in the document. On the **HOME tab**, in the **Font group**, click the **Font Size button arrow**, and then click **36**. Click the **Font Color button arrow**, and then in the fourth column, click the first color—**Blue Gray, Text 2**. In the **Paragraph group**, click **Center**.

In Word Online, you must drag to select text—triple-clicking a line will not select the line, nor will moving the pointer into the left margin and clicking. You can, however, double-click to select a single word.

6 Select the remaining text in the document, and then on the **HOME tab** in the **Font group**, click **Bold**. Click the **Font Size button arrow**, and then click **24**. In the **Paragraph group**, click **Center**. Compare your screen with Figure A.

FIGURE A

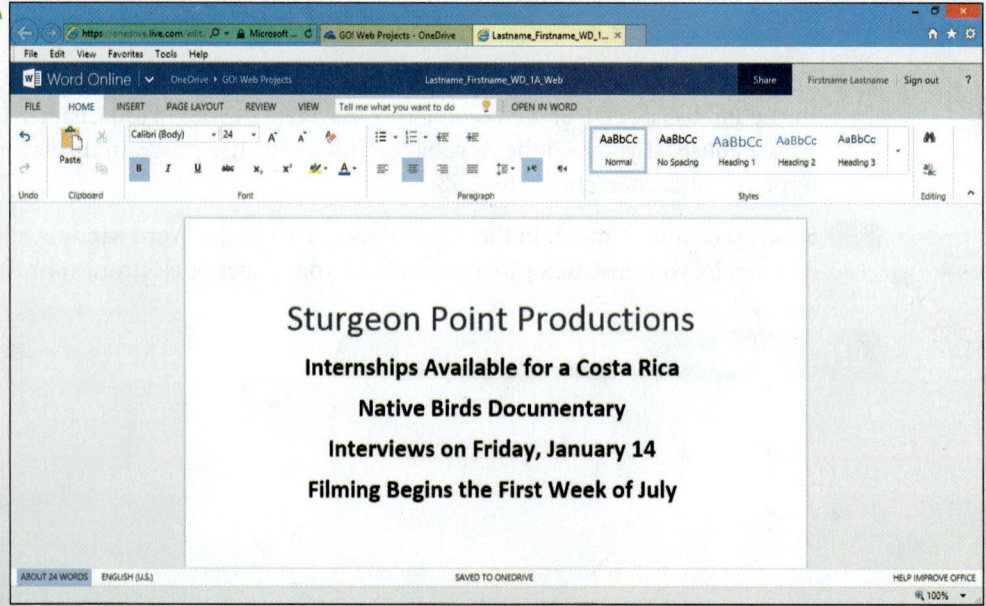

(GO! with Office Online (formerly Web Apps) continues on the next page)

7 Click at the end of the line *Interviews on Friday, January 14*, and then press [Enter] to insert a blank line.

8 On the **INSERT tab**, in the **Pictures group**, click **Picture**. Navigate to the location where your student data files are stored, and then click **w01A_Bird**. Click **Open**. Notice that the picture is dimmed, indicating that it is selected.

9 Under **PICTURE TOOLS**, click the **FORMAT tab**, and then in the **Image Size group**, click **Shrink** several times until the **Scale** box displays **40.48%**. If the box does not display this exact number, select the number in the **Scale** box, type **40.48%** and then press [Enter].

10 With the picture still selected, on the **FORMAT tab**, in the **Picture Styles group**, click the sixth style—**Soft Edge Rectangle**.

11 Click anywhere in a blank area of the document so that the picture is not selected, and then compare your screen with Figure B.

12 Submit your file as directed by your instructor. If you are instructed to submit an electronic printout of your file, create a PDF as indicated in the Note box that follows. Sign out of your OneDrive and close Internet Explorer.

> **NOTE** **Creating a PDF from Word Online**
>
> Click the FILE tab, click Save As, and then click Download as PDF. In the Microsoft Word Online message box, click Click here to view the PDF of your document. In the message bar at the bottom of your screen, click the Save arrow, and then click Save as. In the Save As dialog box, navigate to your Word Chapter 1 folder, and then save the file.

FIGURE B

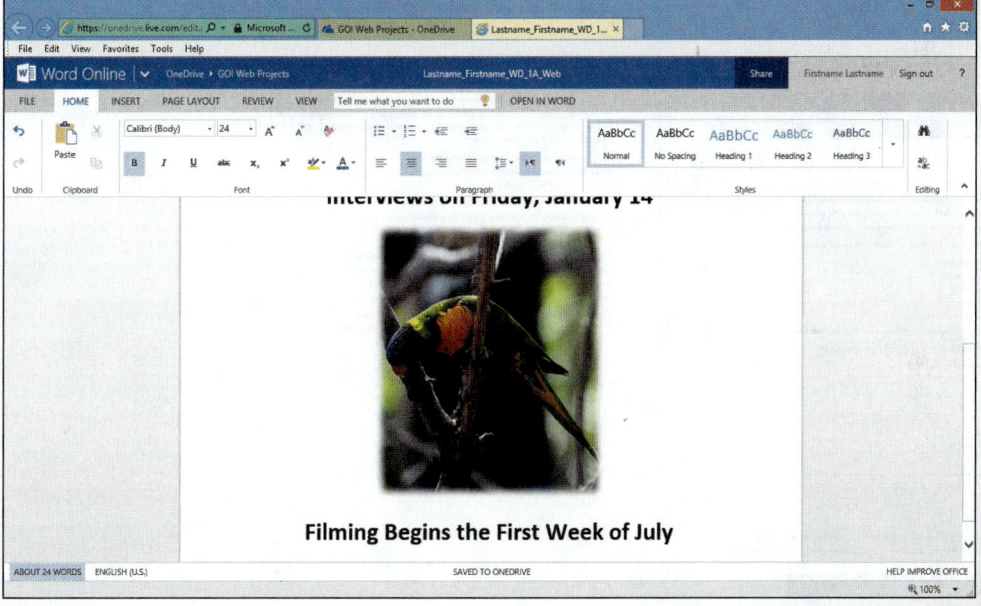

PROJECT ACTIVITIES

In Activities 1.17 through 1.29, you will format an information handout from Sturgeon Point Productions that describes internships available to students. Your completed document will look similar to Figure 1.25.

PROJECT FILES

For Project 1B, you will need the following files: You will save your document as:

w01B_Programs
w01B_Web

Lastname_Firstname_1B_Programs

PROJECT RESULTS

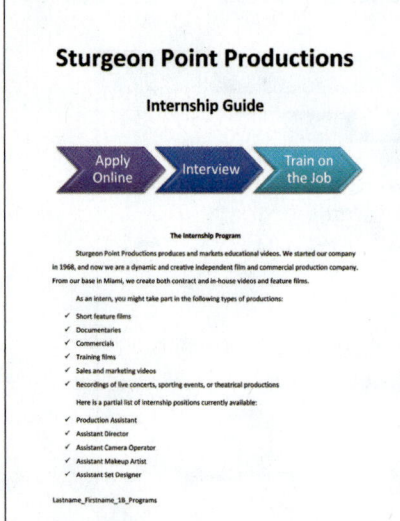
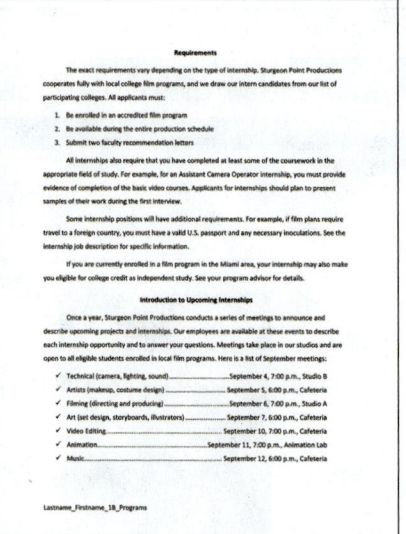
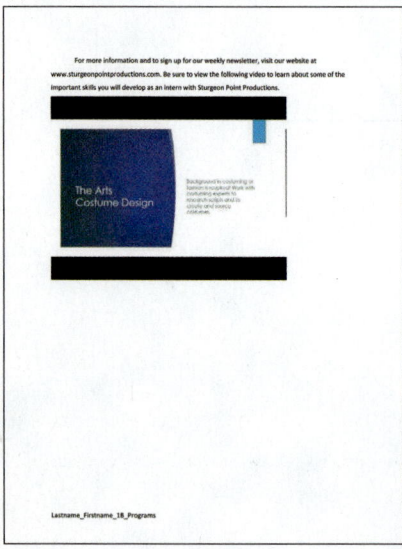

FIGURE 1.25 Project 1B Information Handout

Video W1-5

Document layout includes *margins*—the space between the text and the top, bottom, left, and right edges of the paper. Paragraph layout includes line spacing, indents, and tabs. In Word, the information about paragraph formats is stored in the paragraph mark at the end of a paragraph. When you press Enter, the new paragraph mark contains the formatting of the previous paragraph, unless you take steps to change it.

Activity 1.17 | Setting Margins

1 Start Word, and then click **Open Other Documents**. Navigate to the student files that accompany this textbook, and then open the document **w01B_Programs**. On the **HOME tab**, in the **Paragraph group**, be sure **Show/Hide** ¶ is active so that you can view the formatting marks.

2 Click the **FILE tab**, and then click **Save As**. Navigate to your **Word Chapter 1** folder, and then using your own name, **Save** the document as **Lastname_Firstname_1B_Programs**

3 Click the **PAGE LAYOUT tab**. In the **Page Setup group**, click **Margins**, and then take a moment to study the settings in the Margins gallery.

If you have recently used custom margins settings, they will display at the top of this gallery. Other commonly used settings also display.

4 At the bottom of the **Margins** gallery, click the command followed by an ellipsis—**Custom Margins** to display the **Page Setup** dialog box.

5 In the **Page Setup** dialog box, under **Margins**, press Tab as necessary to select the value in the **Left** box, and then, with *1.25"* selected, type **1**

This action will change the left margin to 1 inch on all pages of the document. You do not need to type the inch (") mark.

6 Press Tab to select the margin in the **Right** box, and then type **1** At the bottom of the dialog box, notice that the new margins will apply to the **Whole document**. Compare your screen with Figure 1.26.

FIGURE 1.26

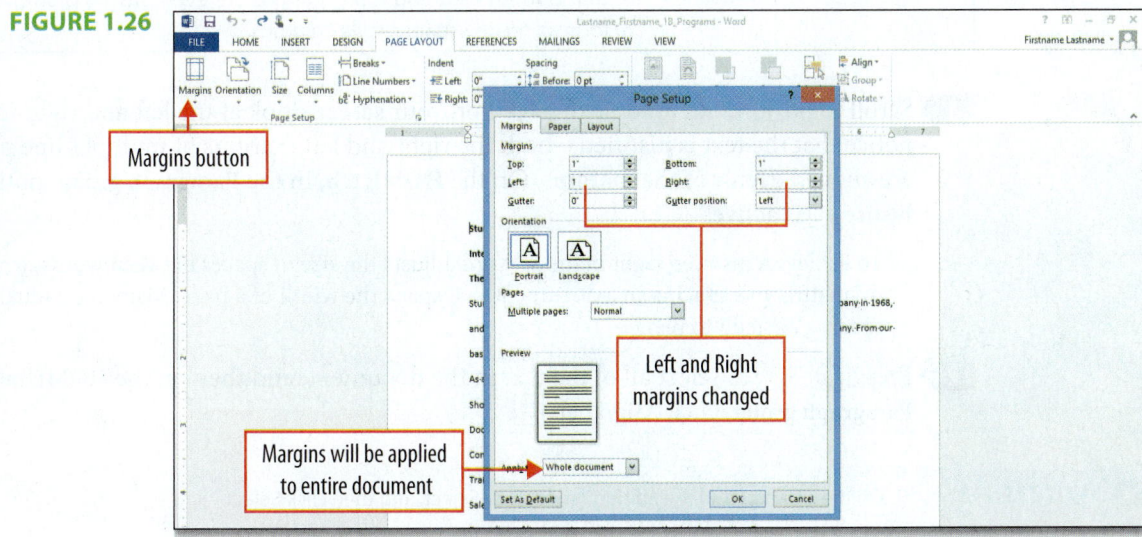

Margins button

Left and Right margins changed

Margins will be applied to entire document

7 ▶ Click **OK** to apply the new margins and close the dialog box. If the ruler below the ribbon is not displayed, on the **VIEW** tab, in the **Show group**, select the **Ruler** check box.

8 ▶ Scroll to position the bottom of **Page 1** and the top of **Page 2** on your screen. Notice that the page edges display, and the page number and total number of pages display on the left side of the status bar.

9 ▶ Near the bottom edge of **Page 1**, point anywhere in the bottom margin area, right-click, and then click **Edit Footer** to display the footer area.

10 ▶ On the ribbon, under the **HEADER & FOOTER TOOLS**, on the **DESIGN tab**, in the **Insert group**, click **Document Info**, and then click **File Name**.

11 ▶ Double-click anywhere in the document to close the footer area, and then **Save** 🖫 your document.

Activity 1.18 | Aligning Text

Alignment refers to the placement of paragraph text relative to the left and right margins. Most paragraph text uses *left alignment*—aligned at the left margin, leaving the right margin uneven. Three other types of paragraph alignment are: *center alignment*—centered between the left and right margins; *right alignment*—aligned at the right margin with an uneven left margin; and *justified alignment*—text aligned evenly at both the left and right margins. The table in Figure 1.27 shows examples of these alignment types.

FIGURE 1.27

TYPES OF PARAGRAPH ALIGNMENT		
ALIGNMENT	**BUTTON**	**DESCRIPTION AND EXAMPLE**
Align Left	☰	Align Left is the default paragraph alignment in Word. Text in the paragraph aligns at the left margin, and the right margin is uneven.
Center	☰	Center alignment aligns text in the paragraph so that it is centered between the left and right margins.
Align Right	☰	Align Right aligns text at the right margin. Using Align Right, the left margin, which is normally even, is uneven.
Justify	☰	The Justify alignment option adds additional space between words so that both the left and right margins are even. Justify is often used when formatting newspaper-style columns.

1 ▶ Scroll to position the middle of **Page 2** on your screen, look at the left and right margins, and notice that the text is justified—both the right and left margins of multiple-line paragraphs are aligned evenly at the margins. On the **HOME tab**, in the **Paragraph group**, notice that **Justify** ☰ is active.

To achieve a justified right margin, Word adjusts the size of spaces between words, which can result in unattractive spacing in a document that spans the width of a page. Many individuals find such spacing difficult to read.

2 ▶ Press Ctrl + A to select all of the text in the document, and then on the **HOME tab**, in the **Paragraph group**, click **Align Left** ☰.

 **ANOTHER WAY**   On the HOME tab, in the Editing group, click Select, and then click Select All.

3 Press `Ctrl` + `Home` to move to the beginning of the document. In the left margin area, point to the left of the first paragraph—*Sturgeon Point Productions*—until the  pointer displays, and then click one time to select the paragraph.

Use this technique to select entire lines of text.

4 On the mini toolbar, in the **Font Size** box, select the existing number, type **40** and then press `Enter`.

Use this technique to change the font size to a size that is not available on the Font Size list.

5 Select the second paragraph—*Internship Guide*—and then on the mini toolbar, change the **Font Size** to **26 pt**. Point to the left of the first paragraph—*Sturgeon Point Productions*—to display the  pointer again, and then drag down to select the first two paragraphs, which form the title and subtitle of the document.

6 On the **HOME tab**, in the **Paragraph group**, click **Center** ≡ to center the title and subtitle between the left and right margins, and then compare your screen with Figure 1.28.

FIGURE 1.28

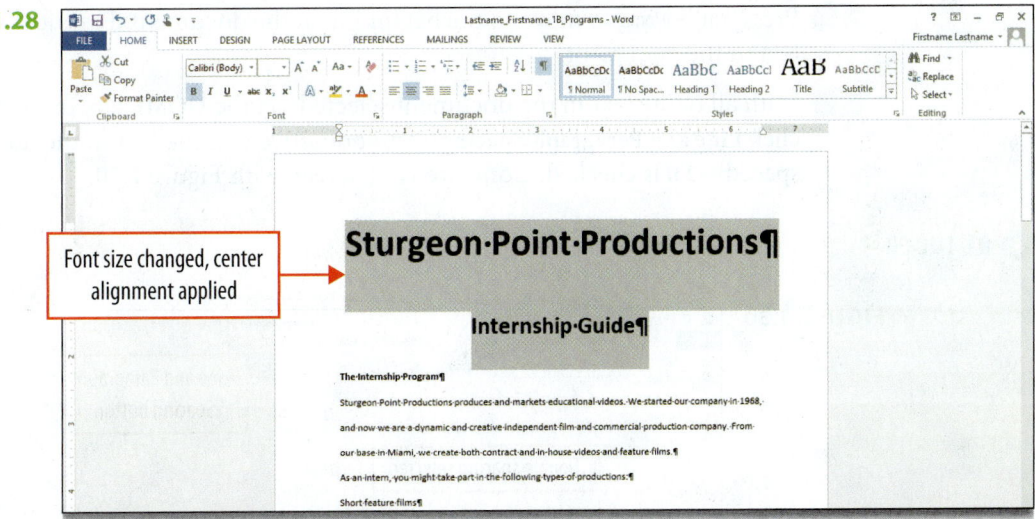

Font size changed, center alignment applied

7 Near the top of **Page 1**, locate the first bold subheading—*The Internship Program*. Point to the left of the paragraph to display the  pointer, and then click one time to select this text.

8 With *The Internship Program* selected, use your mouse wheel or the vertical scroll bar to bring the bottom portion of **Page 1** into view. Locate the subheading *Requirements*. Move the pointer to the left of the paragraph to display the  pointer, hold down `Ctrl`, and then click one time. Scroll to the middle of **Page 2**, and then use the same technique to select the third subheading—*Introduction to Upcoming Internships*.

Three subheadings are selected; in Windows-based programs, you can hold down `Ctrl` to select multiple items.

9 Click **Center** ≡ to center all three subheadings, and then click **Save** 🖫.

Activity 1.19 | Changing Line Spacing

Line spacing is the distance between lines of text in a paragraph. Three of the most commonly used line spacing options are shown in the table in Figure 1.29.

FIGURE 1.29

LINE SPACING OPTIONS	
ALIGNMENT	**DESCRIPTION, EXAMPLE, AND INFORMATION**
Single spacing	**This text in this example uses single spacing**. Single spacing was once the most commonly used spacing in business documents. Now, because so many documents are read on a computer screen rather than on paper, single spacing is becoming less popular.
Multiple 1.08 spacing	**This text in this example uses multiple 1.08 spacing**. The default line spacing in Microsoft Word 2013 is 1.08, which is slightly more than single spacing to make the text easier to read on a computer screen. Many individuals now prefer this spacing, even on paper, because the lines of text appear less crowded.
Double spacing	**This text in this example uses double spacing**. College research papers and draft documents that need space for notes are commonly double-spaced; there is space for a full line of text between each document line.

1 ▸ Press Ctrl + Home to move to the beginning of the document. Press Ctrl + A to select all of the text in the document.

2 ▸ With all of the text in the document selected, on the **HOME tab**, in the **Paragraph group**, click **Line and Paragraph Spacing**, and notice that the text in the document is double spaced—**2.0** is checked. Compare your screen with Figure 1.30.

🔄 **BY TOUCH** Tap the ribbon commands.

FIGURE 1.30

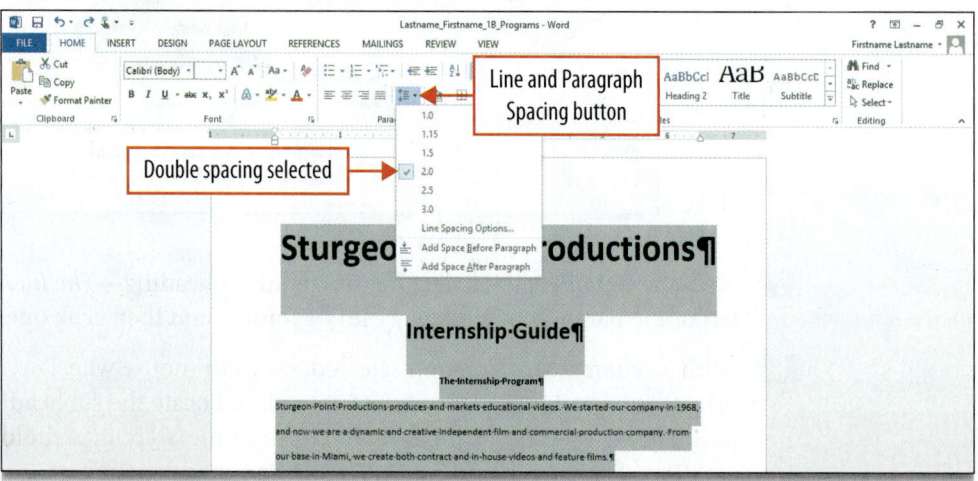

3 ▸ On the **Line Spacing** menu, click the *third* setting—**1.5**—and then click anywhere in the document to deselect the text. Compare your screen with Figure 1.31, and then **Save** your document.

FIGURE 1.31

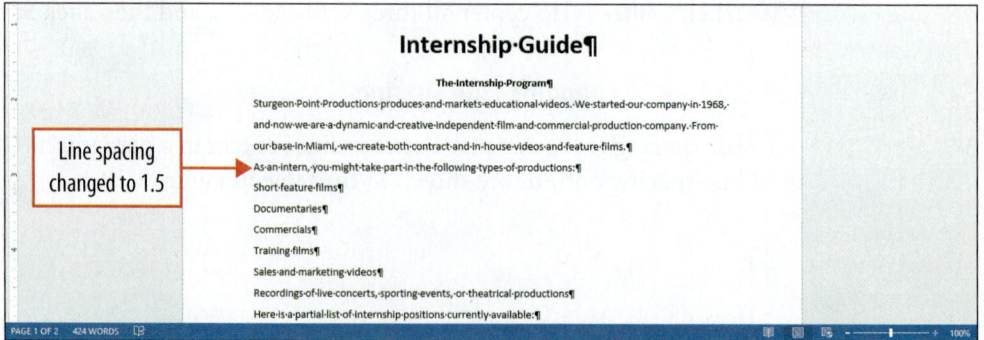

Activity 1.20 | Indenting Text

Indenting the first line of each paragraph is a common technique to distinguish paragraphs.

1 Below the title and subtitle of the document, click anywhere in the paragraph that begins *Sturgeon Point Productions produces*.

2 On the **HOME tab**, in the **Paragraph group**, click the **Dialog Box Launcher**.

3 In the **Paragraph** dialog box, on the **Indents and Spacing tab**, under **Indentation**, click the **Special arrow**, and then click **First line** to indent the first line by 0.5", which is the default indent setting. Compare your screen with Figure 1.32.

FIGURE 1.32

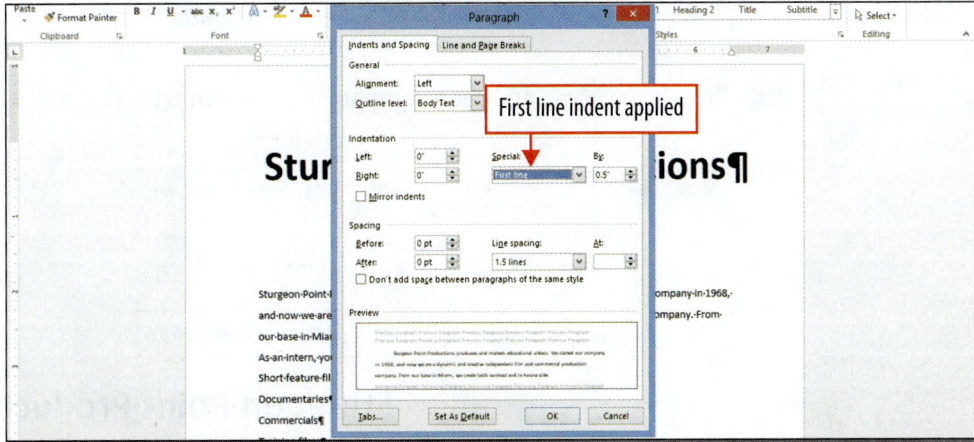

4 Click **OK**, and then click anywhere in the next paragraph, which begins *As an intern*. On the ruler under the ribbon, drag the **First Line Indent** marker to **0.5 inches on the horizontal ruler**, and then compare your screen with Figure 1.33.

FIGURE 1.33

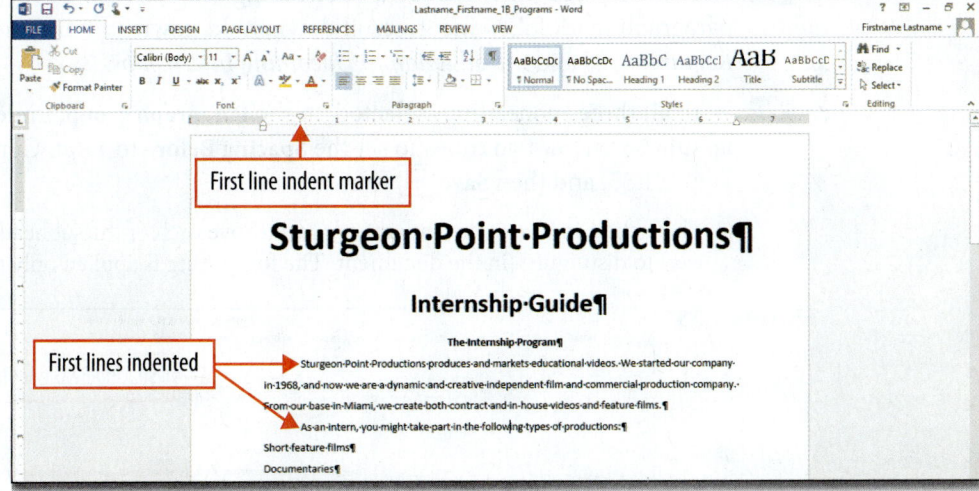

5 By using either of the techniques you just practiced, or by using the **Format Painter**, apply a first line indent of **0.5"** in the paragraph that begins *Here is a partial* to match the indent of the remaining paragraphs in the document.

6 Save your document.

Activity 1.21 | Adding Space Before and After Paragraphs

Adding space after each paragraph is another technique to differentiate paragraphs.

1 ▸ Press [Ctrl] + [A] to select all of the text in the document. Click the **PAGE LAYOUT tab**, and then in the **Paragraph group**, under **Spacing**, click the **After spin box up arrow** one time to change the value to **6 pt**.

To change the value in the box, you can also select the existing number, type a new number, and then press [Enter]. This document will use 6 pt spacing after paragraphs to add space.

🔄 **ANOTHER WAY**   On either the HOME tab or the PAGE LAYOUT tab, display the Paragraph dialog box from the Paragraph group, and then under Spacing, click the spin box arrows as necessary.

2 ▸ Press [Ctrl] + [Home], and then compare your screen with Figure 1.34.

FIGURE 1.34

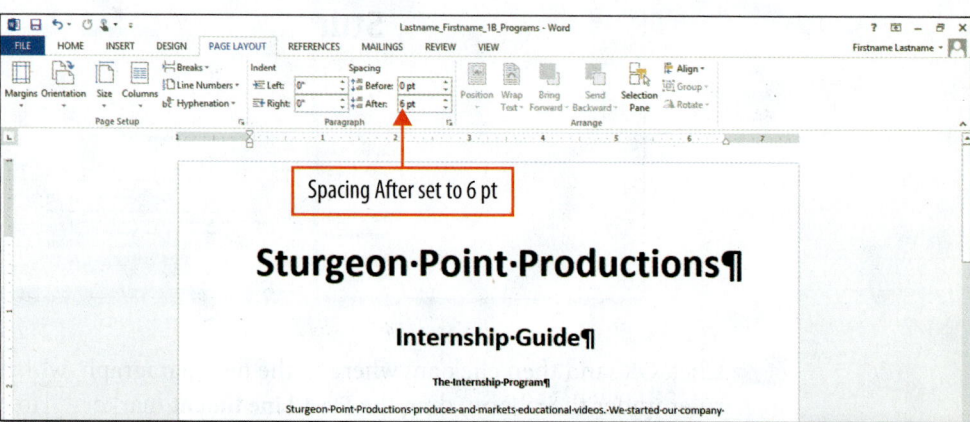

3 ▸ Near the top of **Page 1**, select the subheading *The Internship Program*, including the paragraph mark following it, scroll down, hold down [Ctrl], and then select the subheadings *Requirements* and *Introduction to Upcoming Internships*.

4 ▸ With all three subheadings selected, in the **Paragraph group**, under **Spacing**, click the **Before up spin box arrow** two times to set the **Spacing Before** to **12 pt**. Compare your screen with Figure 1.35, and then **Save** 💾 your document.

This action increases the amount of space above each of the subheadings, which will make them easy to distinguish in the document. The formatting is applied only to the selected paragraphs.

FIGURE 1.35

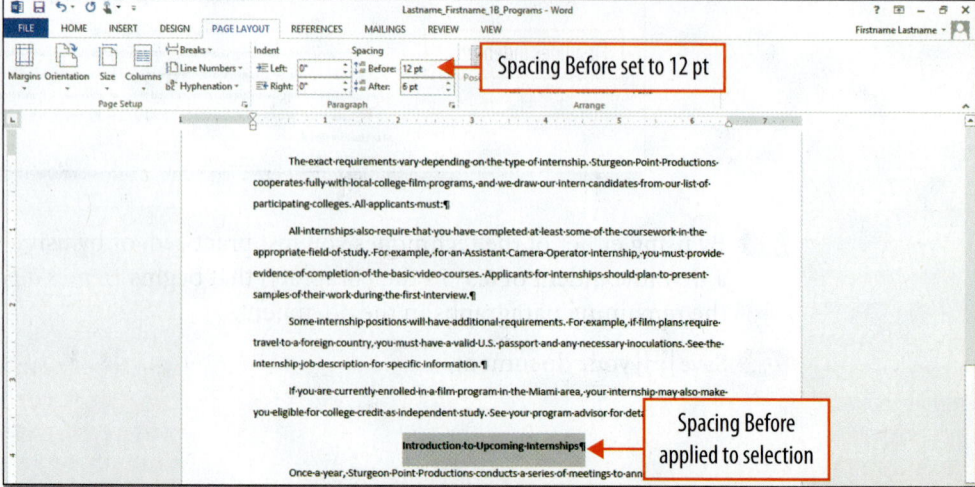

Objective 6 Create and Modify Lists

To display a list of information, you can choose a **bulleted list**, which uses **bullets**—text symbols such as small circles or check marks—to introduce each item in a list. You can also choose a **numbered list**, which uses consecutive numbers or letters to introduce each item in a list.

Use a bulleted list if the items in the list can be introduced in any order; use a numbered list for items that have definite steps, a sequence of actions, or are in chronological order.

Video W1-6

Activity 1.22 | Creating a Bulleted List

1 In the upper portion of **Page 1**, locate the paragraph *Short feature films*, and then point to this paragraph from the left margin area to display the pointer. Drag down to select this paragraph and the next five paragraphs.

2 On the **HOME tab**, in the **Paragraph group**, click **Bullets** to change the selected text to a bulleted list.

> The spacing between each of the bulleted points changes to the spacing between lines in a paragraph—in this instance, 1.5 line spacing. The 6 pt. spacing after each paragraph is eliminated with the exception of the last item in the list. Each bulleted item is automatically indented.

3 On the ruler, point to **First Line Indent** and read the ScreenTip, and then point to **Hanging Indent** . Compare your screen with Figure 1.36.

> By default, Word formats bulleted items with a first line indent of 0.25" and adds a Hanging Indent at 0.5". The hanging indent maintains the alignment of text when a bulleted item is more than one line.

> You can modify the list indentation by using Decrease Indent or Increase Indent . **Decrease Indent** moves your paragraph closer to the margin. **Increase Indent** moves your paragraph farther away from the margin.

FIGURE 1.36

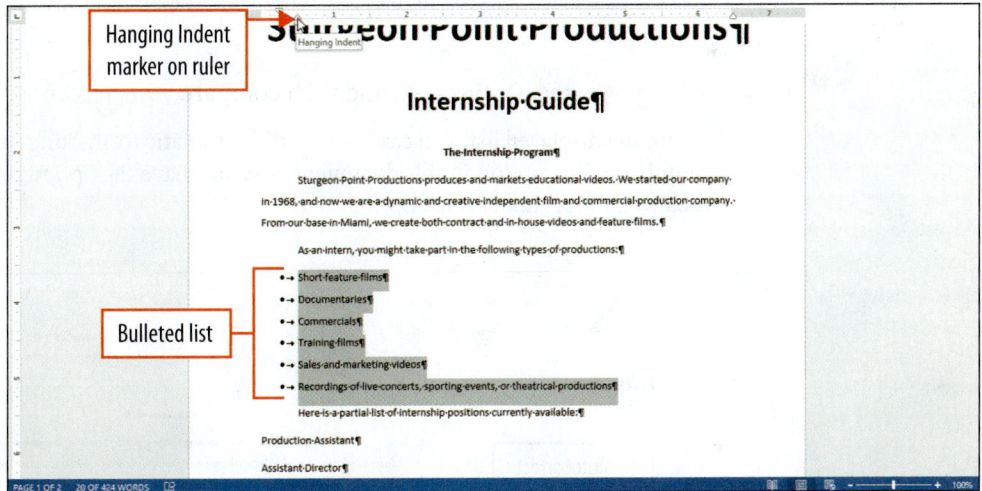

4 Scroll down slightly, and then by using the pointer from the left margin area, select the five internship positions, beginning with *Production Assistant* and ending with *Assistant Set Designer*. In the **Paragraph group**, click **Bullets** .

5 Scroll down to view **Page 2**. Apply bullets to all of the paragraphs that indicate the September meetings and meeting dates, beginning with *Technical* and ending with *Music*. **Save** your document.

Activity 1.23 | Creating a Numbered List

1 Under the subheading *Requirements*, in the paragraph that begins *The exact requirements*, click to position the insertion point at the *end* of the paragraph, following the colon. Press [Enter] to create a blank paragraph. Notice that the paragraph is indented, because the First Line Indent from the previous paragraph carried over to the new paragraph.

2 To change the indent formatting for this paragraph, on the ruler, drag the **First Line Indent** marker ▽ to the left so that it is positioned directly above the lower button.

3 Being sure to include the period, type **1.** and press [Spacebar]. Compare your screen with Figure 1.37.

> Word determines that this paragraph is the first item in a numbered list and formats the new paragraph accordingly, indenting the list in the same manner as the bulleted list. The space after the number changes to a tab, and the AutoCorrect Options button displays to the left of the list item. The tab is indicated by a right arrow formatting mark.

FIGURE 1.37

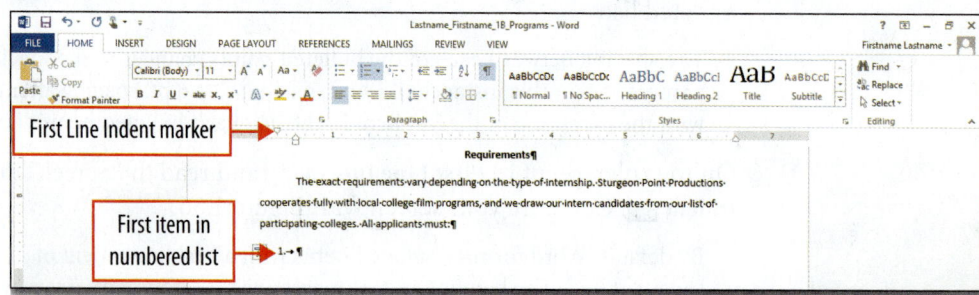

A L E R T !	**Activating Automatic Numbered Lists**

If a numbered list does not begin automatically, click the FILE tab, and then click the Options tab. On the left side of the Word Options dialog box, click Proofing. Under AutoCorrect options, click the AutoCorrect Options button. In the AutoCorrect dialog box, click the AutoFormat As You Type tab. Under *Apply as you type*, select the *Automatic numbered lists* check box, and then click OK two times to close both dialog boxes.

---

4 Click **AutoCorrect Options** 🖅, and then compare your screen with Figure 1.38.

> From the displayed list, you can remove the automatic formatting here, or stop using the automatic numbered lists option in this document. You also have the option to open the AutoCorrect dialog box to *Control AutoFormat Options*.

FIGURE 1.38

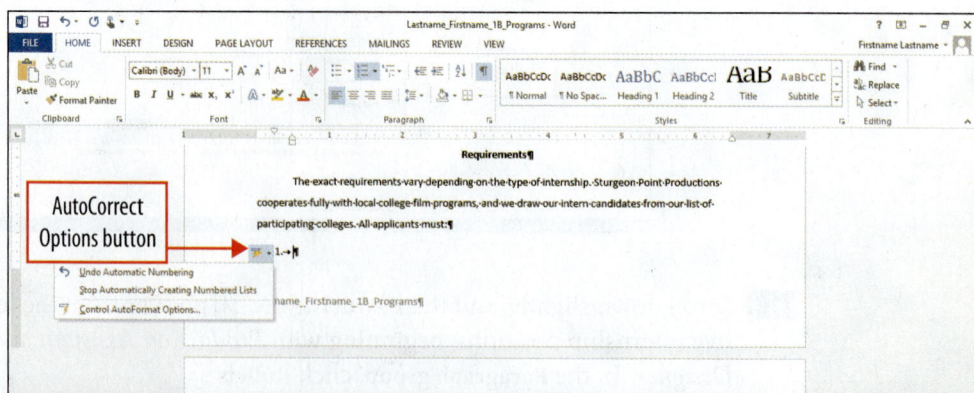

5 Click **AutoCorrect Options** 🖅 again to close the menu without selecting any of the commands. Type **Be enrolled in an accredited film program** and press [Enter]. Notice that the second number and a tab are added to the next line.

6 Type **Be available during the entire production schedule** and press Enter. Type **Submit two faculty recommendation letters** Compare your screen with Figure 1.39, and then **Save** your document.

FIGURE 1.39

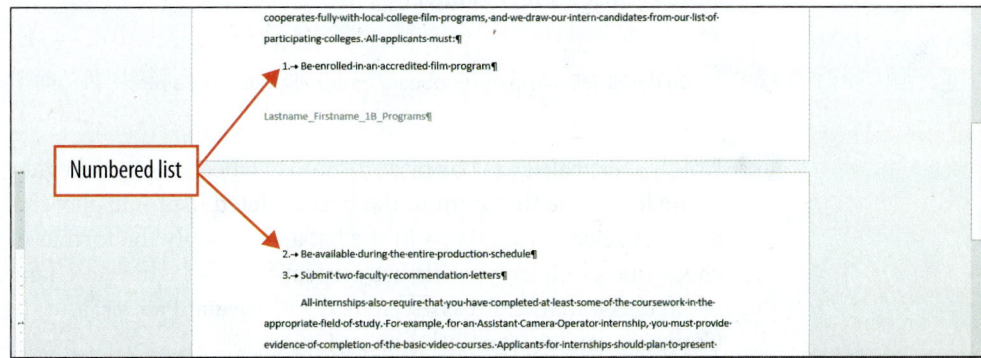

Numbered list

> **More Knowledge** | **To End a List**
>
> To turn a list off, you can press Backspace, click the Numbering or Bullets button, or press Enter two times. Both list buttons—Numbering and Bullets—act as **toggle buttons**; that is, clicking the button one time turns the feature on, and clicking the button again turns the feature off.

Activity 1.24 | Customizing Bullets

You can use any symbol from any font for your bullet characters.

1 Press Ctrl + End to move to the end of the document, and then scroll up as necessary to display the bulleted list containing the list of meetings.

2 Point to the left of the first list item to display the ⚲ pointer, and then drag down to select all six meetings in the list—the bullet symbols are not highlighted.

3 On the mini toolbar, click the **Bullets button arrow** ⬛ to display the **Bullet Library**, and then compare your screen with Figure 1.40.

FIGURE 1.40

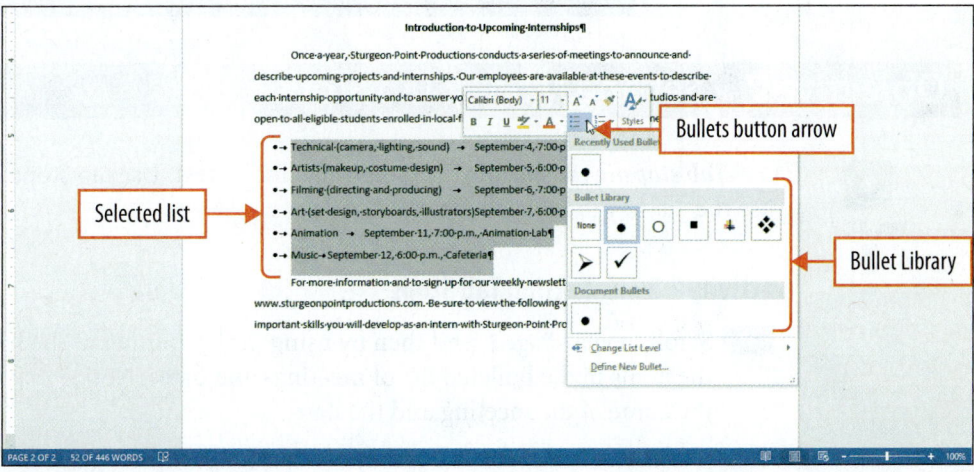

Selected list

Bullets button arrow

Bullet Library

> **A L E R T !** | **Did Your Bullet Symbols Disappear?**
>
> If the bullet symbols no longer display, then you clicked the Bullets button. The Bullets button is a toggle button that turns the bullet symbols on and off. Click Undo to reapply the bullets, and then repeat Step 3, making sure that you click the Bullets button arrow.

4 ▸ Under **Bullet Library**, click the **check mark** symbol. If the check mark is not available, choose another bullet symbol.

5 ▸ With the bulleted list still selected, right-click over the list, and then on the mini toolbar, double-click **Format Painter** 💅.

🔄 **ANOTHER WAY**   On the HOME tab, in the Clipboard group, click Format Painter.

6 ▸ Use the vertical scroll bar or your mouse wheel to scroll to view **Page 1**. Move the pointer to the left of the first item in the first bulleted list to display the 🔊 pointer, and then drag down to select all six items in the list and to apply the format of the third bulleted list—the check mark bullets—to this list. Repeat this procedure to change the bullets in the second list to check marks. Press [Esc] to turn off **Format Painter**, and then **Save** 💾 your document. Compare your screen with Figure 1.41.

FIGURE 1.41

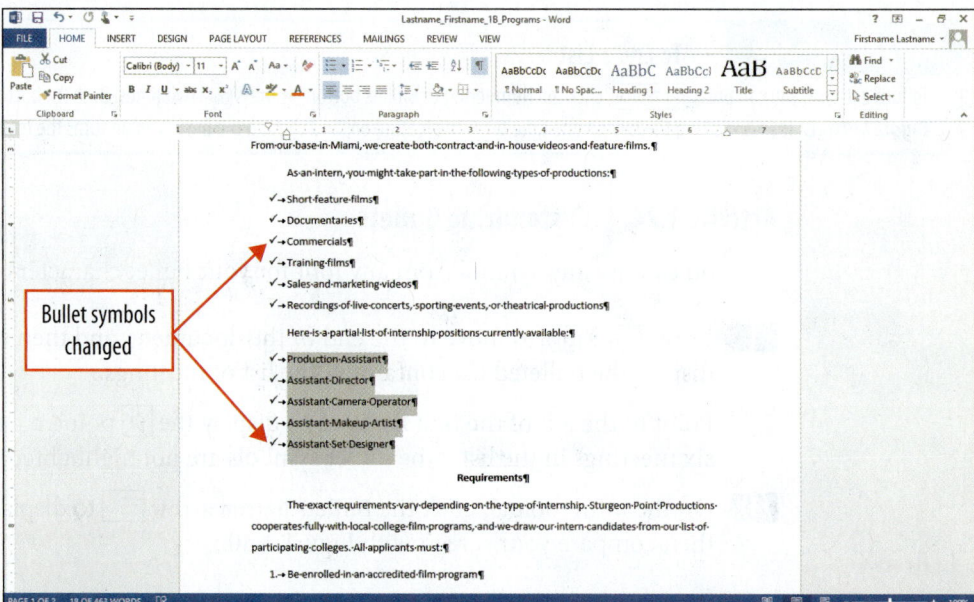

Bullet symbols changed

Objective 7   Set and Modify Tab Stops

Video W1-7

Tab stops mark specific locations on a line of text. Use tab stops to indent and align text, and use the [Tab] key to move to tab stops.

Activity 1.25   Setting Tab Stops

1 ▸ Scroll to view **Page 2**, and then by using the 🔊 pointer at the left of the first item, select all of the items in the bulleted list of meetings and dates. Notice that there is a tab mark between the name of the meeting and the date.

The arrow that indicates a tab is a nonprinting formatting mark.

2 ▸ To the left of the horizontal ruler, point to **Tab Alignment** 🔲 to display the *Left Tab* ScreenTip, and then compare your screen with Figure 1.42.

FIGURE 1.42

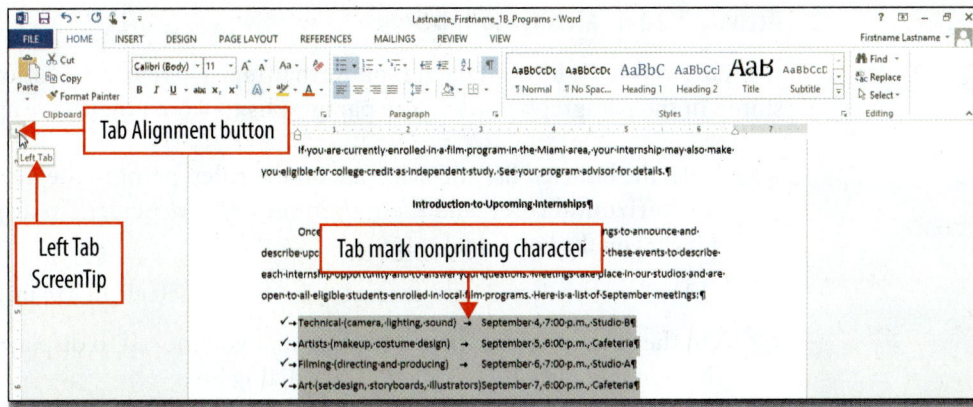

3 Click **Tab Alignment** ⬜ several times to view the tab alignment options shown in the table in Figure 1.43.

FIGURE 1.43

TAB ALIGNMENT OPTIONS		
TYPE	**TAB ALIGNMENT BUTTON DISPLAYS THIS MARKER**	**RESULT OF TAB ALIGNMENT**
Left	⬜	Text is left aligned at the tab stop and extends to the right.
Center	⬜	Text is centered around the tab stop.
Right	⬜	Text is right aligned at the tab stop and extends to the left.
Decimal	⬜	The decimal point aligns at the tab stop.
Bar	⬜	A vertical bar displays at the tab stop.
First Line Indent	▽	Text in the first line of a paragraph indents.
Hanging Indent	⬠	Text in all lines except the first line in the paragraph indents.

4 Display **Left Tab** ⬜. Along the lower edge of the horizontal ruler, point to and then click at **3.5 inches on the horizontal ruler**. Notice that all of the dates left align at the new tab stop location, and the right edge of the column is uneven.

5 Compare your screen with Figure 1.44, and then **Save** 💾 your document.

FIGURE 1.44

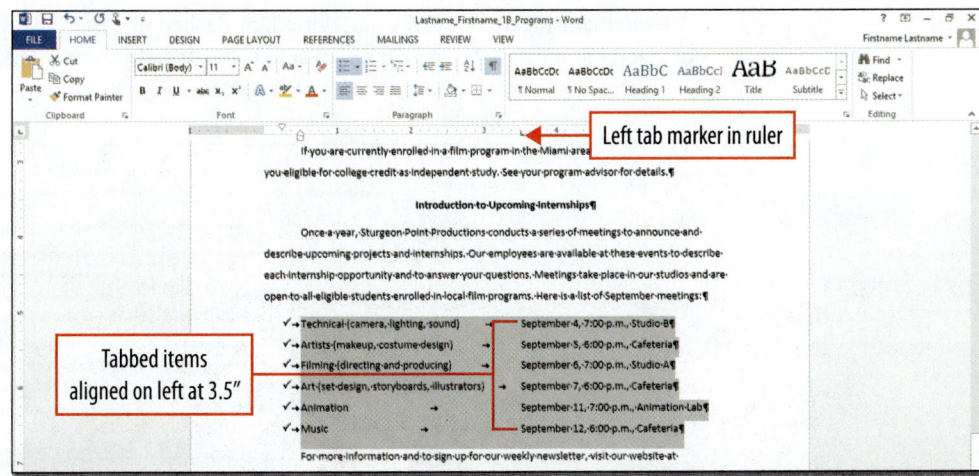

Activity 1.26 | Modifying Tab Stops

Tab stops are a form of paragraph formatting. Therefore, the information about tab stops is stored in the paragraph mark in the paragraphs to which they were applied.

1 With the bulleted list still selected, on the ruler, point to the new tab marker at **3.5 inches on the horizontal ruler**, and then when the *Left Tab* ScreenTip displays, drag the tab marker to **4 inches on the horizontal ruler**.

In all of the selected lines, the text at the tab stop left aligns at 4 inches.

2 On the ruler, point to the tab marker that you moved to display the *Left Tab* ScreenTip, and then double-click to display the **Tabs** dialog box.

 **ANOTHER WAY** On the HOME tab, in the Paragraph group, click the Dialog Box Launcher. At the bottom of the Paragraph dialog box, click the Tabs button.

3 In the **Tabs** dialog box, under **Tab stop position**, if necessary, select *4"* and then type **6**

4 Under **Alignment**, click the **Right** option button. Under **Leader**, click the **2** option button. Near the bottom of the **Tabs** dialog box, click **Set**.

Because the Right tab will be used to align the items in the list, the tab stop at 4" is no longer necessary.

5 In the **Tabs** dialog box, in the **Tab stop position** box, click **4"** to select this tab stop, and then in the lower portion of the **Tabs** dialog box, click the **Clear** button to delete this tab stop, which is no longer necessary. Compare your screen with Figure 1.45.

FIGURE 1.45

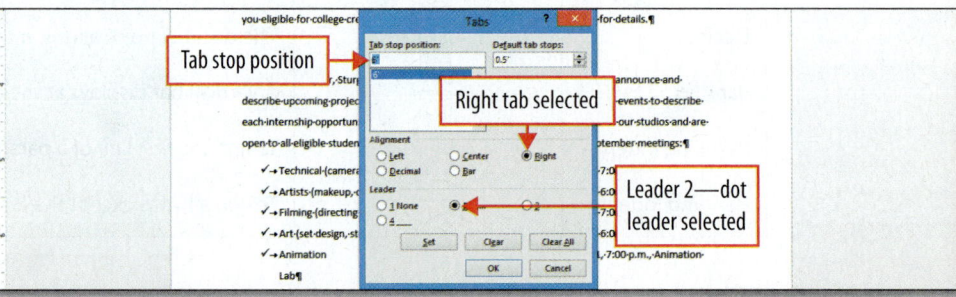

6 Click **OK**. On the ruler, notice that the left tab marker at *4"* no longer displays, a right tab marker displays at *6"*, and a series of dots—a **dot leader**—displays between the columns of the list. Notice also that the right edge of the column is even. Compare your screen with Figure 1.46.

A **leader character** creates a solid, dotted, or dashed line that fills the space to the left of a tab character and draws the reader's eyes across the page from one item to the next. When the character used for the leader is a dot, it is commonly referred to as a dot leader.

FIGURE 1.46

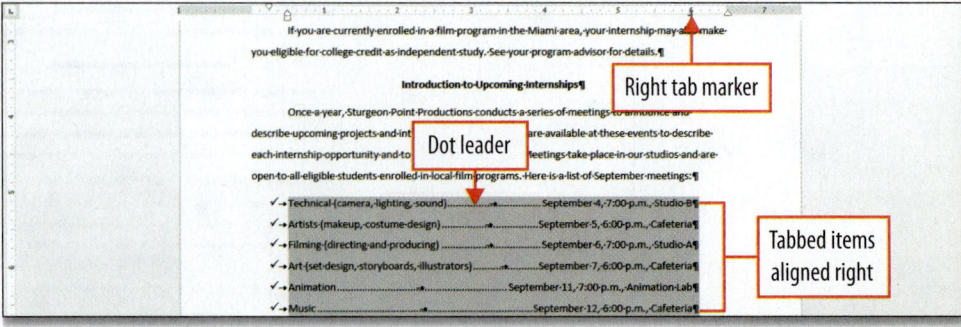

7 In the bulleted list that uses dot leaders, locate the *Art* meeting, and then click to position the insertion point at the end of that line, after the word *Cafeteria*. Press Enter to create a new blank bullet item.

8 Type **Video Editing** and press Tab. Notice that a dot leader fills the space to the tab marker location.

9 Type **September 10, 7:00 p.m., Cafeteria** and notice that the text moves to the left to maintain the right alignment of the tab stop.

10 **Save** 💾 your document.

Objective 8 | Insert a SmartArt Graphic and an Online Video

Video W1-8

SmartArt graphics are designer-quality visual representations of information, and Word provides many different layouts from which you can choose. You can also insert a link to an online video from a variety of online sources, thus enabling the reader to view the video when connected to the Internet. SmartArt graphics and videos can communicate your messages or ideas more effectively than plain text and these objects add visual interest to a document or webpage.

Activity 1.27 | Inserting a SmartArt Graphic

1 Press Ctrl + Home to move to the top of the document, and then click to the right of the subtitle *Internship Guide*.

2 Click the **INSERT tab**, and then in the **Illustrations group**, point to **SmartArt** to display its ScreenTip. Read the ScreenTip, and then click **SmartArt**.

3 In the center portion of the **Choose a SmartArt Graphic** dialog box, scroll down and examine the numerous types of SmartArt graphics available.

4 On the left, click **Process**, and then by using the ScreenTips, locate and click **Basic Chevron Process**. Compare your screen with Figure 1.47.

At the right of the dialog box, a preview and description of the SmartArt displays.

FIGURE 1.47

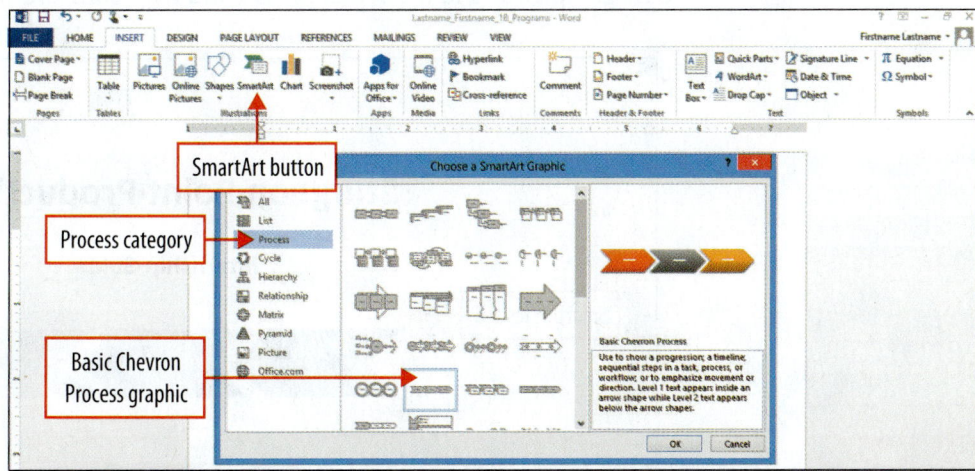

5 Click **OK** to insert the SmartArt graphic.

To the left of the inserted SmartArt graphic the text pane may display. The text pane provides one method for entering text into your SmartArt graphic. If you choose not to use the text pane to enter text, you can close it.

6 ▶ On the ribbon under **SMARTART TOOLS**, on the **DESIGN tab**, in the **Create Graphic group**, notice the **Text Pane** button. If the Text Pane button is selected, click **Text Pane** to close the pane.

7 ▶ In the SmartArt graphic, in the first blue arrow, click *[Text]*, and notice that *[Text]* is replaced by a blinking insertion point.

The word *[Text]* is called ***placeholder text***, which is non-printing text that indicates where you can type.

8 ▶ Type **Apply Online**

9 ▶ Click the placeholder text in the middle arrow. Type **Interview** and then click the placeholder text in the third arrow. Type **Train on the Job** and then compare your screen with Figure 1.48.

FIGURE 1.48

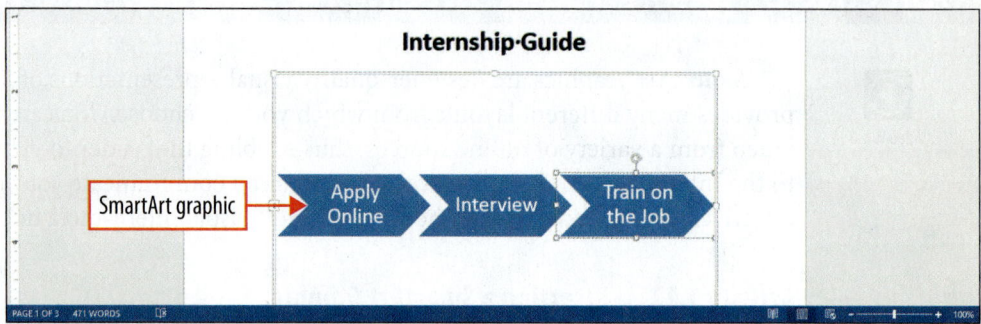

10 ▶ Save 🖫 your document.

Activity 1.28 | Sizing and Formatting a SmartArt Graphic

1 ▶ Click the SmartArt graphic border to select it. Be sure that none of the arrows have sizing handles around their border, which would indicate the arrow was selected, not the entire graphic.

2 ▶ Click the **FORMAT tab**, and then in the **Size group**, if necessary, click **Size** to display the **Shape Height** and **Shape Width** boxes.

3 ▶ Set the **Height** to **1.75"** and the **Width** to **6.5"**, and then compare your screen with Figure 1.49.

FIGURE 1.49

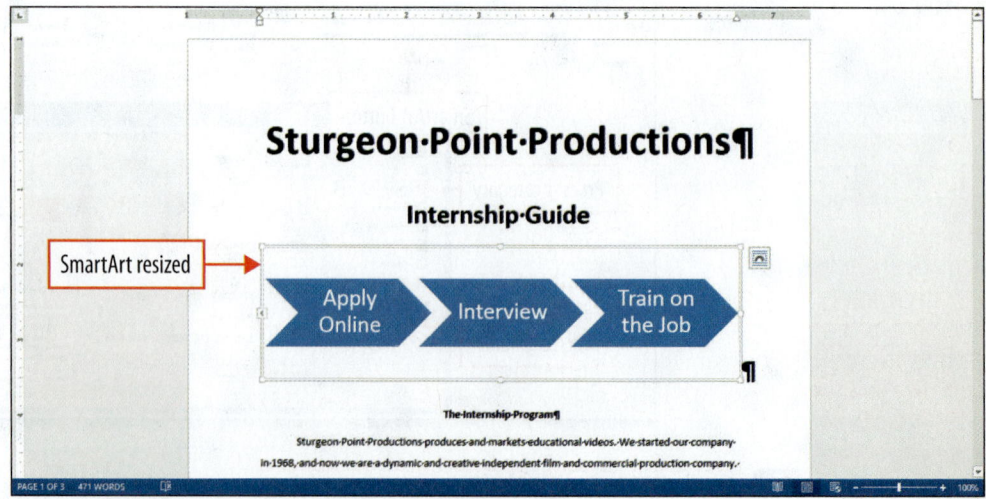

4 With the SmartArt graphic still selected, click the **SMARTART TOOLS DESIGN tab**, and then in the **SmartArt Styles group**, click **Change Colors**. Under **Colorful**, click the fourth style— **Colorful Range–Accent Colors 4 to 5**.

5 On the **SMARTART TOOLS DESIGN tab**, in the **SmartArt Styles group**, click **More** ⊡. Under **3-D**, click the second style—**Inset**. Click **Save** 🖫, and then compare your screen with Figure 1.50.

FIGURE 1.50

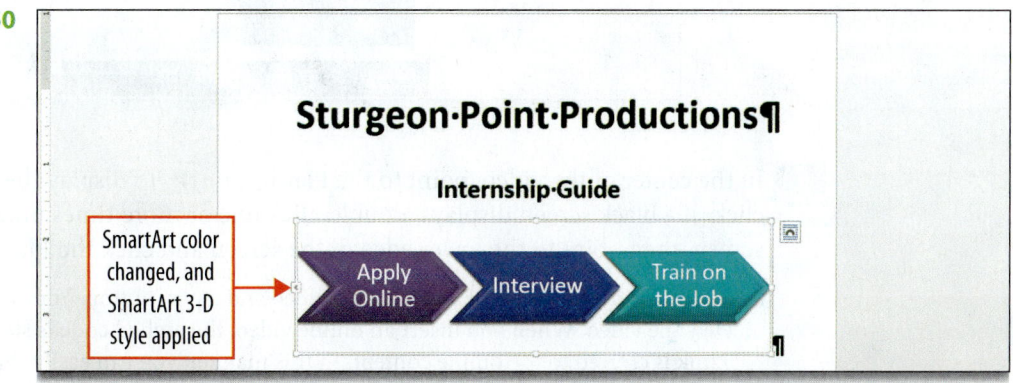

Activity 1.29 | Inserting an Online Video

Microsoft's research indicates that two-thirds of people who open Word documents never edit them; they only read them. So with more and more documents being read online—and not on paper—it makes sense that you may want to include videos in your Word documents.

1 Press Ctrl + End to move to the end of the document.

2 On the **INSERT tab**, in the **Media group**, click **Online Video**. If the YouTube search box does not display, in the lower left corner of the Insert Video window, under Also insert from: click YouTube.

Here you can search the web for an online video, search YouTube, or enter an *embed code* to insert a link to a video from a website. An embed code is a code that creates a link to a video, picture, or other type of *rich media* content. Rich media, also called *interactive media*, refers to computer interaction that responds to your actions; for example by presenting text, graphics, animation, video, audio, or games.

3 In the **Search YouTube** box, being sure to include the quotation marks, type **"Go 2013 1B Video"** and then press Enter.

4 Point to the displayed thumbnail and notice the ScreenTip. Click the **1B video**, and then click **Insert**. Compare your screen with Figure 1.51.

FIGURE 1.51

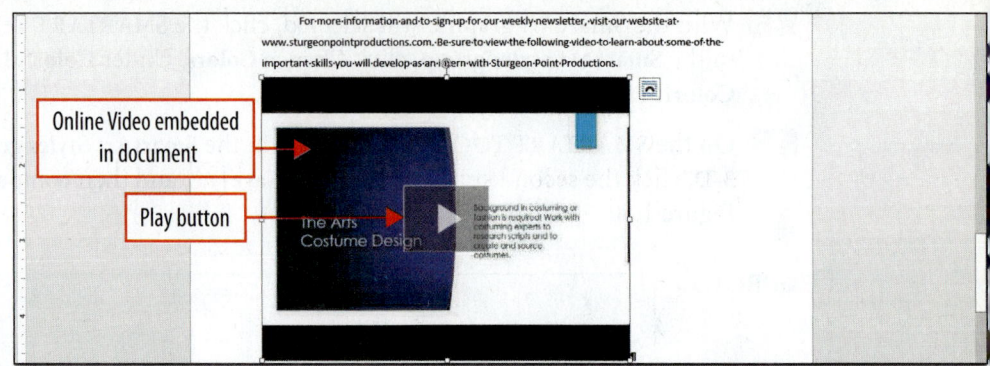

Online Video embedded in document

Play button

5 ▶ In the center of the video, point to the **Play** button ▶ to display the 🖑 pointer, and then click. If a black screen displays, double-click one or more times until you see text on the screen, then point to the lower edge of the screen and click the Play button.

A new window opens that contains the video and a play button. You can click the play button to view the video. When you insert an online video, the embed code is stored with the document and a link is created to the online content. In this manner, you can easily share video content that is relevant to the document without increasing the file size of the document.

6 ▶ View a few seconds of the video—more if you want—and then press Esc to return to your document.

7 ▶ Click **Save** 🖫, and then press Ctrl + Home to move to the top of your document.

8 ▶ Click the **FILE tab**, and then in the lower right portion of the screen, click **Show All Properties**. In the **Tags** box, type **internship** and in the **Subject** box, type your course name and section number. In the **Author** box, be sure your name displays; edit if necessary.

9 ▶ On the left, click **Print** to display **Print Preview**. At the bottom of the preview, click the **Previous Page** ◀ and **Next Page** ▶ buttons to move between pages. If necessary, return to the document and make any necessary changes.

10 ▶ As directed by your instructor, print your document or submit it electronically. **Save** 🖫 your document and **Close** ☒ Word.

END | You have completed Project 1B

Objective	Create a Handout in Word Online

You can use Word Online to edit your document if you are not at a computer on which Word 2013 is installed. You can change fonts and font sizes, modify paragraph alignment, and apply bullets and numbering.

> **ALERT!** **Working with Web-Based Applications and Services**
>
> Computer programs and services on the web receive continuous updates and improvements, so the steps to complete this web-based activity may differ from the ones shown. You can often look at the screens and the information presented to determine how to complete the activity.

Activity | Creating a Handout in Word Online

In this activity, you will use Word Online to edit a flyer similar to the one you edited in Project 1B.

1 Start Word, and then below the **Recent** list, click **Open Other Documents**. Navigate to your student data files, and then open **w01_1B_Web**. If necessary, in the upper right corner, log into Office with your Microsoft account. On the **FILE tab**, click **Save As**, and then on the right, double-click the name of your OneDrive.

2 In the **Save As** dialog box, click your **GO! Web Projects** folder, and then click **Open**. In the **File name** box, type **Lastname_Firstname_WD_1B_Web** and then click **Save**.

3 Close Word, launch **Internet Explorer**, go to http://onedrive.com, sign in, open your **GO! Web Projects** folder, and then click the file you just saved there.

4 In the upper left, click **EDIT DOCUMENT**, and then click **Edit in Word Online**.

5 Press Ctrl + A to select all the text in the document. On the **HOME tab**, in the **Paragraph group**, click **Align Text Left**.

6 Drag to select the first three lines in the document. On the **HOME tab**, in the **Paragraph group**, click **Center**. Compare your screen with Figure A.

7 Click at the beginning of the paragraph that begins *Sturgeon Point Productions produces*, and then press Tab. Click at the beginning of the paragraph that begins *As an intern*, and then press Tab.

8 Scroll the document and click at the beginning of the paragraph that begins *Here is a partial*, and then press Tab.

9 Click anywhere in the subheading *Introduction to Upcoming Internships*, and then on the **HOME tab**, in the **Paragraph group**, click **Center**. Click at the beginning of the paragraph that begins *Once a year*, and then press Tab.

10 Select the six paragraphs that begin with *Short feature films* and that end with *Recordings of live concerts*. On the **HOME tab**, in the **Paragraph group**,

FIGURE A

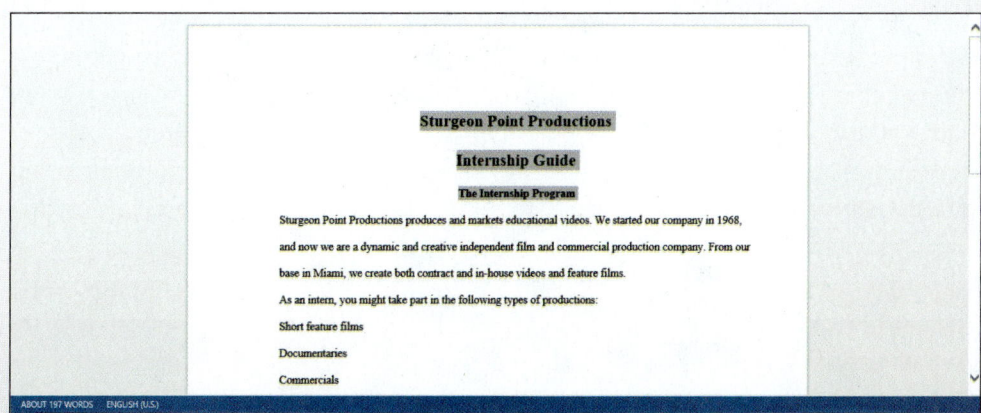

(GO! with Office Online (formerly Web Apps) continues on the next page)

click **Bullets** 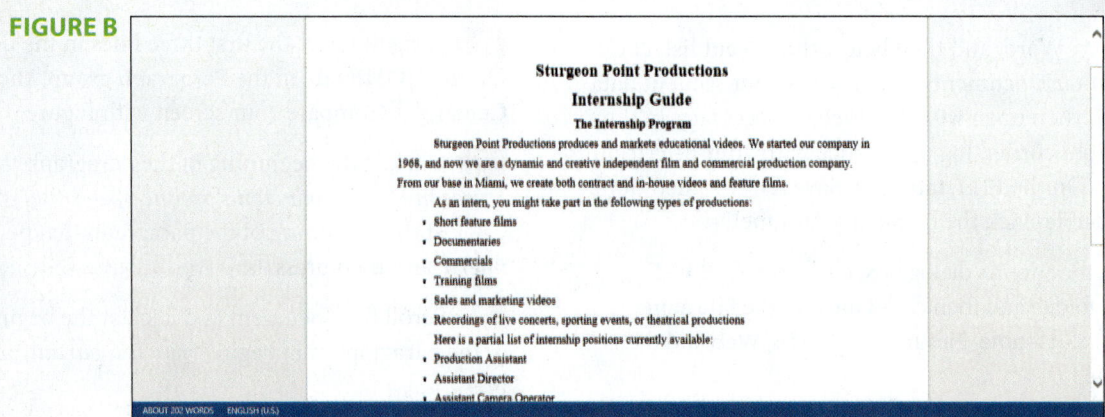 to apply round, filled bullets to the selection.

11 ▸ Select the list that begins with *Production Assistant* and ends with *Assistant Set Designer*, and then click **Bullets** to apply bullets to the selection.

12 ▸ Select the first list to which you applied bullets. On the **HOME tab**, in the **Paragraph group**, click the **Bullets button arrow**, and then click **Square Bullet**. Notice that the same bullet style is applied to the second list.

13 ▸ Scroll the document and then select the list that begins with *Artists* and ends with *Music*. On the **HOME**

tab, in the **Paragraph group**, click **Numbering** to apply numbers to the list.

14 ▸ Press [Ctrl] + [A] to select the entire document. On the **HOME tab**, in the **Paragraph group**, click **Line Spacing**, and then click **1.5** to change the line spacing for the entire document. Press [Ctrl] + [Home] to move to the top of the document and then compare your screen with Figure B.

15 ▸ Submit your file as directed by your instructor. Sign out of your OneDrive and close Internet Explorer.

FIGURE B

In every job, you must work and communicate with other people. A group of workers tasked with working together to solve a problem, make a decision, or create a work product is referred to as a *team*. For a team to succeed, the team members must be able to communicate with one another easily.

If all the team members work at the same location and work the same hours, communication is easy. You schedule face-to-face meetings and exchange documents and information among yourselves. But that is a rare arrangement in today's organizations. Rather, it is more likely that the members of your team work in different locations—even different countries— and work different hours or travel extensively away from the headquarters location. Also, for specific projects, teams are frequently organized across different departments of an organization or even across different organizations entirely. Then when the project is complete, the team disbands.

Collaboration is when you work together with others as a team in an intellectual endeavor to complete a shared task or achieve a shared goal; for example, when you and one or more of your classmates work together on a class project. Collaboration involves giving feedback to and receiving feedback from others on the team, and then revising the strategies to achieve the goal or produce the work product based on the feedback.

Microsoft Office 365 is a set of secure online services that enable people in an organization to communicate and collaborate by using any Internet-connected device—a computer, a tablet, or a mobile phone. Because Office 365 offers access from anywhere to email, Web conferencing, documents, and calendars, everyone on a team can work together easily. Office 365 is intended for use by multiple users in an organization.

Activity | Using the Exchange Online Outlook Meeting Tool to Collaborate

This group project relates to the **Bell Orchid Hotels**. If your instructor assigns this project to your class, you can expect to use the **Outlook Meeting tool** in **Office 365 Exchange Online** to collaborate on the following tasks for this chapter:

- If you are in the **Accounting Group**, you and your teammates will meet virtually to compose, format, proofread, and prepare a letter to send to shareholders.

- If you are in the **Engineering Group**, you and your teammates will meet virtually to compose, format, proofread, and prepare a letter to the three insurance companies that cover the hotel properties.

- If you are in the **Food and Beverage Group**, you and your teammates will meet virtually to compose, format, proofread, and finalize a letter to a customer planning a banquet.

- If you are in the **Human Resources Group**, you and your teammates will meet virtually to compose, format, proofread, and finalize a memo for employees regarding the new employee newsletter.

- If you are in the **Operations Group**, you and your teammates will meet virtually to compose, format, proofread, and finalize letters to three job applicants.

- If you are in the **Sales and Marketing Group**, you and your teammates will meet virtually to compose, edit, and finalize a letter to 20 groups of professional associations.

FIGURE A

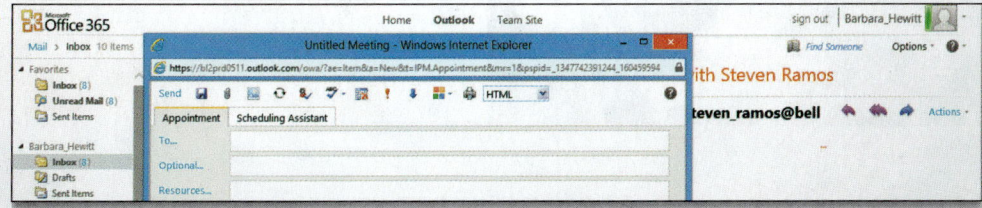

END OF CHAPTER

SUMMARY

In a document, you can type all of the text, or you can type some of the text and then insert additional text from another source such as another Word document. As you type, word wrap determines the line endings.

Graphics include pictures, shapes, and text boxes. Use graphics, text effects, and pictures to add visual appeal. When you insert pictures, Word provides many ways to position and format the pictures on the page.

SmartArt graphics visually represent your ideas and there are many SmartArt graphics from which to choose. You can also use online videos in your documents to provide visual information to the reader.

Word documents can be formatted to display your information attractively. You can add a page border, add bulleted and numbered lists, change margins and tabs, and modify paragraph and line spacing.

GO! LEARN IT ONLINE

Review the concepts and key terms in this chapter by completing these online challenges, which you can find at **www.pearsonhighered.com/go.**

Matching and Multiple Choice:
Answer matching and multiple choice questions to test what you learned in this chapter. MyITLab®

Crossword Puzzle:
Spell out the words that match the numbered clues, and put them in the puzzle squares.

Flipboard:
Flip through the definitions of the key terms in this chapter and match them with the correct term.

GO! FOR JOB SUCCESS

Video: Personal Branding

Your instructor may assign this video to your class, and then ask you to think about, or discuss with your classmates, these questions:

FotolEdhar / Fotolia

How do you suggest job seekers communicate their unique value—their *personal brand*—to potential employers online?

What are the best ways to network online and offline?

What are some of the biggest pitfalls in using social media to communicate a personal brand?

END OF CHAPTER

REVIEW AND ASSESSMENT GUIDE FOR WORD CHAPTER 1

Your instructor may assign one or more of these projects to help you review the chapter and assess your mastery and understanding of the chapter.

	Review and Assessment Guide for Word Chapter 1		
Project	**Apply Skills from These Chapter Objectives**	**Project Type**	**Project Location**
1C	Objectives 1-4 from Project 1A	**1C Skills Review** A guided review of the skills from Project 1A.	On the following pages
1D	Objectives 5-8 from Project 1B	**1D Skills Review** A guided review of the skills from Project 1B.	On the following pages
1E	Objectives 1-4 from Project 1A	**1E Mastery (Grader Project)** A demonstration of your mastery of the skills in Project 1A with extensive decision making.	In MyITLab and on the following pages
1F	Objectives 5-8 from Project 1B	**1F Mastery (Grader Project)** A demonstration of your mastery of the skills in Project 1B with extensive decision making.	In MyITLab and on the following pages
1G	Objectives 1-8 from Projects 1A and 1B	**1G Mastery (Grader Project)** A demonstration of your mastery of the skills in Projects 1A and 1B with extensive decision making.	In MyITLab and on the following pages
1H	Combination of Objectives from Projects 1A and 1B	**1H GO! Fix It** A demonstration of your mastery of the skills in Projects 1A and 1B by creating a correct result from a document that contains errors you must find.	Online
1I	Combination of Objectives from Projects 1A and 1B	**1I GO! Make It** A demonstration of your mastery of the skills in Projects 1A and 1B by creating a result from a supplied picture.	Online
1J	Combination of Objectives from Projects 1A and 1B	**1J GO! Solve It** A demonstration of your mastery of the skills in Projects 1A and 1B, your decision-making skills, and your critical thinking skills. A task-specific rubric helps you self-assess your result.	Online
1K	Combination of Objectives from Projects 1A and 1B	**1K GO! Solve It** A demonstration of your mastery of the skills in Projects 1A and 1B, your decision-making skills, and your critical thinking skills. A task-specific rubric helps you self-assess your result.	On the following pages
1L	Combination of Objectives from Projects 1A and 1B	**1L GO! Think** A demonstration of your understanding of the chapter concepts applied in a manner that you would outside of college. An analytic rubric helps you and your instructor grade the quality of your work by comparing it to the work an expert in the discipline would create.	On the following pages
1M	Combination of Objectives from Projects 1A and 1B	**1M GO! Think** A demonstration of your understanding of the chapter concepts applied in a manner that you would outside of college. An analytic rubric helps you and your instructor grade the quality of your work by comparing it to the work an expert in the discipline would create.	Online
1N	Combination of Objectives from Projects 1A and 1B	**1N You and GO!** A demonstration of your understanding of the chapter concepts applied in a manner that you would in a personal situation. An analytic rubric helps you and your instructor grade the quality of your work.	Online
1O	Combination of Objectives from Projects 1A and 1B	**1O Cumulative Group Project for Word Chapter 1** A demonstration of your understanding of concepts and your ability to work collaboratively in a group role-playing assessment, requiring both collaboration and self-management.	Online

GLOSSARY

GLOSSARY OF CHAPTER KEY TERMS

Alignment The placement of paragraph text relative to the left and right margins.

Alignment guide Green vertical or horizontal lines that display when you are moving or sizing an object to assist you with object placement.

Artistic effects Formats applied to images that make pictures resemble sketches or paintings.

Bulleted list A list of items with each item introduced by a symbol such as a small circle or check mark, and which is useful when the items in the list can be displayed in any order.

Bullets Text symbols such as small circles or check marks that precede each item in a bulleted list.

Center alignment The alignment of text or objects that is centered horizontally between the left and right margin.

Collaboration The action of working together with others as a team in an intellectual endeavor to complete a shared task or achieve a shared goal.

Decrease Indent A command that moves your paragraph closer to the margin.

Dot leader A series of dots preceding a tab that guides the eye across the line.

Drawing objects Graphic objects, such as shapes, diagrams, lines, or circles.

Embed code A code that creates a link to a video, picture, or other type of rich media content.

Floating object A graphic that can be moved independently of the surrounding text characters.

Formatting marks Characters that display on the screen, but do not print, indicating where the Enter key, the Spacebar, and the Tab key were pressed; also called nonprinting characters.

Graphics Pictures, charts, or drawing objects.

Increase Indent A command moves your paragraph farther away from the margin.

Inline Object An object or graphic inserted in a document that acts like a character in a sentence.

Interactive media Computer interaction that responds to your actions; for example by presenting text, graphics, animation, video, audio, or games. Also referred to as rich media.

Justified alignment An arrangement of text in which the text aligns evenly on both the left and right margins.

Layout Options Picture formatting options that control the manner in which text wraps around a picture or other object.

Leader character Characters that form a solid, dotted, or dashed line that fills the space preceding a tab stop.

Left alignment An arrangement of text in which the text aligns at the left margin, leaving the right margin uneven.

Line spacing The distance between lines of text in a paragraph.

Live Layout A feature that reflows text as you move or size an object so that you can view the placement of surrounding text.

Margins The space between the text and the top, bottom, left, and right edges of the paper.

Microsoft Office 365 A set of secure online services that enable people in an organization to communicate and collaborate by using any Internet-connected device—a computer, a tablet, or a mobile phone.

Nonprinting characters Characters that display on the screen, but do not print; also called formatting marks.

Numbered list A list that uses consecutive numbers or letters to introduce each item in a list.

Object anchor The symbol that indicates to which paragraph an object is attached.

Picture Effects Formatting that enhances a picture with effects such as shadow, glow, reflection, or 3-D rotation.

Picture styles Frames, shapes, shadows, borders, and other special effects that can be added to an image to create an overall visual style for the image.

Placeholder text Non-printing text that holds a place in a document where you can type.

Rich media Computer interaction that responds to your actions; for example by presenting text, graphics, animation, video, audio, or games. Also referred to as interactive media.

Right alignment An arrangement of text in which the text aligns at the right margin, leaving the left margin uneven.

Rotation handle A symbol with which you can rotate a graphic to any angle; displays above the top center sizing handle.

Shapes Lines, arrows, stars, banners, ovals, rectangles, and other basic shapes with which you can illustrate an idea, a process, or a workflow.

SmartArt A designer-quality visual representation of your information that you can create by choosing from among many different layouts to effectively communicate your message or ideas.

Spin box A small box with an upward- and downward-pointing arrow that lets you move rapidly through a set of values by clicking.

Tab stop A specific location on a line of text, marked on the Word ruler, to which you can move the insertion point by pressing the Tab key, and which is used to align and indent text.

Team A group of workers tasked with working together to solve a problem, make a decision, or create a work product.

Template A preformatted document that you can use as a starting point and then change to suit your needs.

Text box A movable resizable container for text or graphics.

Text effects Decorative formats, such as shadowed or mirrored text, text glow, 3-D effects, and colors that make text stand out.

Text wrapping The manner in which text displays around an object.

Toggle button A button that can be turned on by clicking it once, and then turned off by clicking it again.

Wordwrap The feature that moves text from the right edge of a paragraph to the beginning of the next line as necessary to fit within the margins.

CHAPTER REVIEW

Skills Review | Project 1C Photography

Apply 1A skills from these Objectives:

1 Create a New Document and Insert Text
2 Insert and Format Graphics
3 Insert and Modify Text Boxes and Shapes
4 Preview and Print a Document

Build from Scratch

In the following Skills Review, you will create a flyer announcing a photography internship with Sturgeon Point Productions. Your completed document will look similar to Figure 1.52.

PROJECT FILES

For Project 1C, you will need the following files:

New blank Word document
w01C_Building
w01C_Photographer

You will save your document as:

Lastname_Firstname_1C_Photography

PROJECT RESULTS

FIGURE 1.52

(Project 1C Photography continues on the next page)

CHAPTER REVIEW

1 Start Word and then click **Blank document**. On the **HOME tab**, in the **Paragraph group**, if necessary, click **Show/Hide** to display the formatting marks. If the rulers do not display, click the **VIEW tab**, and then in the **Show group**, select the **Ruler** check box.

a. Type **Internship Available for Still Photographer** and then press Enter two times. Type the following text: **This fall, Sturgeon Point Productions will film a documentary on the historic architecture in and around Milwaukee, Wisconsin.** Press Enter.

b. On the ribbon, click the **INSERT tab**. In the **Text group**, click the **Object button arrow**, and then click **Text from File**. In the **Insert File** dialog box, navigate to the student files that accompany this textbook, locate and select **w01C_Photographer**, and then click **Insert**. Delete the blank paragraph at the end of the document.

c. Including the paragraph mark, select the first paragraph of text—*Internship Available for Still Photographer*. On the **HOME tab**, in the **Font group**, click **Text Effects and Typography**. In the **Text Effects** gallery, in the first row, click the fourth effect—**Fill – White, Outline – Accent 1, Shadow**.

d. With the text still selected, in the **Font group**, click in the **Font Size** box to select the existing font size. Type **44** and then press Enter. In the **Font group**, click the **Font Color button arrow**. Under **Theme Colors**, in the fourth column, click the first color—**Blue-Gray, Text 2**.

e. With the text still selected, in the **Font group**, click **Text Effects and Typography**. Point to **Shadow**, and then under **Outer**, in the second row, click the third style—**Offset Left**. In the **Paragraph group**, click **Center**.

f. On the **Quick Access Toolbar**, click **Save**. Under **Places**, click **Computer**, and then click **Browse**. Navigate to your **Word Chapter 1** folder. In the **File name** box, replace the existing text with **Lastname_Firstname_1C_Photography** and then click **Save**.

2 In the paragraph that begins *The filming*, click to position the insertion point at the beginning of the paragraph. On the **INSERT tab**, in the **Illustrations group**, click **Pictures**. In the **Insert Picture** dialog box, navigate to your student data files, locate and click **w01C_Building**, and then click **Insert**.

a. To the right of the selected picture, click the **Layout Options** button, and then under **With Text Wrapping**, click the first option—**Square**. **Close** the **Layout Options**.

b. On the **FORMAT tab**, in the **Size group**, click the **Shape Height spin box down arrow** as necessary to change the height of the picture to **2.7"**.

c. With the picture selected, on the **FORMAT tab**, in the **Arrange group**, click **Position**, and then click **More Layout Options**. In the **Layout** dialog box, on the **Position tab**, in the middle of the dialog box, under **Vertical**, click the **Alignment** option button. To the right of **Alignment**, click the arrow, and then click **Top**. To the right of **relative to**, click the arrow, and then click **Line**. Click **OK**.

d. On the **FORMAT tab**, in the **Picture Styles group**, click **Picture Effects**. Point to **Soft Edges**, and then click **5 Point**. On the **FORMAT tab**, in the **Adjust group**, click **Artistic Effects**. In the fourth row, click the third effect—**Crisscross Etching**.

e. Click anywhere outside the picture to deselect it. On the **DESIGN tab**, in the **Page Background group**, click **Page Borders**. In the **Borders and Shading** dialog box, on the **Page Border tab**, under **Setting**, click **Box**. Under **Style**, scroll the list and then click the third style from the bottom—a black line that fades to gray.

f. Click the **Color arrow**, and then in the next to last column, click the first color—**Blue, Accent 5**. Under **Apply to**, be sure **Whole document** is selected, and then click **OK**. Click **Save**.

3 Click the **INSERT tab**, and then in the **Illustrations group**, click **Shapes** to display the gallery. Under **Basic Shapes**, in the second row, click the fifth shape—**Frame**.

a. Position the ✛ pointer anywhere in the blank area at the bottom of the document. Click one time to insert a 1" by 1" frame. The exact location need not be precise. To the right of the shape, click the **Layout Options** button, and at the bottom click **See more**.

b. In the **Layout** dialog box, under **Horizontal**, click the **Alignment** option button. To the right of **Alignment**, click the arrow, and then click **Centered**. To the right of **relative to**, click the arrow, and then click **Page**. Under **Vertical**, click the **Absolute position**

(Project 1C Photography continues on the next page)

option button. In the **Absolute position** box, select the existing number, and then type **1** To the right of **below**, click the arrow, and then click **Paragraph**. Click **OK**.

c. On the **FORMAT tab**, click in the **Shape Height** box. Type **1.5** and then click in the **Shape Width** box. Type **5.5** and then press Enter.

d. If necessary, select the frame shape. On the **FORMAT tab**, in the **Shape Styles group**, click **More** ⬇. In the **Shape Styles** gallery, in the first row, click the sixth style—**Colored Outline - Blue, Accent 5**. Type **Submit Your Application by June 30!** Select the text you just typed, and then on the mini toolbar, change the **Font Size** to **22**.

4 Click outside of the frame to deselect, and then press Ctrl + Home to move to the top of the document. Press ↓ two times to move to the blank paragraph below the title. Press Enter four times to make space for a text box.

a. On the **INSERT tab**, in the **Text group**, click **Text Box**. At the bottom of the gallery, click **Draw Text Box**. Position the ➕ pointer over the first blank paragraph at the left margin. Drag down and to the right to create a text box approximately 1.5 inches high and 4 inches wide—the exact size and location need not be precise.

b. With the insertion point blinking in the text box, type the following, pressing Enter after the first two lines to create a new paragraph; do *not* press Enter after the last line:

This position requires skill in the use of:

Professional full-frame DSLR cameras

Tilt-shift lenses for tall buildings

c. To precisely place the text box, on the **FORMAT tab**, in the **Arrange group**, click **Position**, and then click **More Layout Options**. In the **Layout** dialog box, under **Horizontal**, click the **Alignment** button. To the right of **Alignment**, click the arrow, and then click **Centered**. To the right of *relative to*, click the arrow, and then click **Page**.

d. Under **Vertical**, click the **Absolute position** button. In the **Absolute position** box, select the existing number. Type **2** To the right of **below**, click the **arrow**, and then click **Margin**.

e. In the **Layout** dialog box, click the **Size tab**. Under **Height**, select the number in the **Absolute** box. Type **1** and then under **Width**, select the number in the **Absolute** box. Type **3.75** and then click **OK**.

f. In the text box, select all of the text. If necessary, right-click over the selected text to display the mini toolbar. Change the **Font Size** to **12**, apply **Bold**, and then press Ctrl + E to **Center** the text.

g. On the **FORMAT tab**, in the **Shape Styles group**, click **Shape Effects**. Point to **Shadow**, and then under **Outer**, in the first row, click the first style—**Offset Diagonal Bottom Right**.

h. In the **Shape Styles group**, click **Shape Outline**. In the fifth column, click the first color—**Blue, Accent 1** to change the color of the text box border. Click **Shape Fill**, and then in the fifth column, click the second color—**Blue, Accent 1, Lighter 80%**. Click **Save**.

5 Click the **INSERT tab**, and then in the **Header & Footer group**, click **Footer**. At the bottom of the menu, click **Edit Footer**. On the **HEADER & FOOTER TOOLS DESIGN tab**, in the **Insert group**, click **Document Info**, and then click **File Name**. Double-click in the document outside of the footer area to close the footer and return to the document.

a. Press Ctrl + Home to move the insertion point to the top of the document. In the upper left corner of your screen, click the **FILE** tab to display **Backstage** view. On the right, at the bottom of the **Properties list**, click **Show All Properties**.

b. On the list of Properties, click to the right of **Tags** to display an empty box, and then type **internship, photographer** Click to the right of **Subject** to display an empty box, and then type your course name and section #. Under **Related People**, be sure that your name displays as the author. If necessary, edit the author name.

c. **Save** your file and submit as directed by your instructor. **Close** Word.

END | You have completed Project 1C

CHAPTER REVIEW

Skills Review Project 1D Internships

In the following Skills Review, you will edit an information handout regarding production and development internships with Sturgeon Point Productions. Your completed document will look similar to Figure 1.53.

PROJECT FILES

For Project 1D, you will need the following file:

w01D_Internship

You will save your document as:

Lastname_Firstname_1D_Internship

PROJECT RESULTS

STURGEON POINT PRODUCTIONS

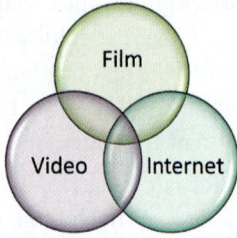

Sturgeon Point Productions is a full service film and video production facility located in Miami, Florida. Celebrating over 45 years of producing top quality commercial and independent film, our projects range from award winning documentaries and live action short features, to live concert and sporting events, to popular educational and training series of videos for schools, businesses, trade shows and multi-media presentations. We currently offer internships to film students in participating local colleges and universities, in both our development and production departments.

In-House Office Internships

Sturgeon Point Productions is looking for story analysts, research, post production and production assistants to work in our offices. We offer college credit as independent study at participating schools for one semester, which can be repeated for up to one year from the start date of the internship. To receive credit, interns must:

1. Be enrolled as a film major at a participating local college or university
2. Maintain a 3.0 GPA
3. Receive satisfactory monthly progress reports from their direct supervisor

Lastname_Firstname_1D_Internship

Following is a list of departments in our Miami office, currently seeking development and production interns:

✓ Development Department .... Researcher
✓ Development Department ....Asst. to Producer
✓ Development Department ....Writer's Assistant
✓ Post Production...Asst. Editor
✓ Post Production...Asst. Sound Editor
✓ Production...Asst. Office Manager

Additional Information

For more information and to sign up for our weekly newsletter, visit our website at www.sturgeonpointproductions.com. Be sure to view the following video to learn about some of the important skills you will develop as an intern with Sturgeon Point Productions.

The Arts Costume Design

Background in costuming or fashion is required. Work with costuming experts to research scripts and to create and source costumes.

Lastname_Firstname_1D_Internship

FIGURE 1.53

(Project 1D Internships continues on the next page)

CHAPTER REVIEW

1 Start Word, and then click **Open Other Documents**. Click **Computer**, and then click **Browse**. Navigate to your student files, and then open **w01D_Internship**. On the **HOME tab**, in the **Paragraph group**, be sure **Show/Hide** is active. Click the **FILE tab**, and then click **Save As**. Navigate to your **Word Chapter 1** folder, and then **Save** the document as **Lastname_Firstname_1D_Internship**

a. Click the **PAGE LAYOUT tab**. In the **Page Setup group**, click **Margins**, and then click **Custom Margins**. In the **Page Setup** dialog box, press Tab as necessary to select the value in the **Left** box. Type **1** and then press Tab to select the value in the **Right** box. Type **1** and then click **OK**.

b. Scroll down to view the bottom of **Page 1**, point anywhere in the bottom margin area, right-click, and then click **Edit Footer** to display the footer area. On the **HEADER & FOOTER TOOLS DESIGN tab**, in the **Insert group**, click **Document Info**, and then click **File Name**. Double-click anywhere in the document to close the footer area.

c. Press Ctrl + A to select all of the text in the document, and then on the **HOME tab**, in the **Paragraph group**, click **Align Left**.

d. Press Ctrl + Home. Select the document title, and then on the **HOME tab**, in the **Paragraph group**, click **Center**.

e. Locate the first bold subheading—*In-House Office Internships*. Point to the left of the paragraph to display the pointer, and then click one time to select the text. With *In-House Office Internships* selected, locate the subheading *Additional Information*. Move the pointer to the left of the paragraph to display the pointer, hold down Ctrl, and then click one time to select both paragraphs. In the **Paragraph group**, click **Center**.

f. Press Ctrl + A to select all of the text in the document. On the **HOME tab**, in the **Paragraph group**, click **Line and Paragraph Spacing**, and then click **1.5**.

2 Below the title of the document, click anywhere in the paragraph that begins *Sturgeon Point Productions is a full service*. On the **HOME tab**, in the **Paragraph group**, click the **Dialog Box Launcher**.

a. In the **Paragraph** dialog box, on the **Indents and Spacing tab**, under **Indentation**, click the **Special**

arrow, and then click **First line** to indent the first line by 0.5". Click **OK**, and then click anywhere in the paragraph that begins *Sturgeon Point Productions is looking for*. On the ruler under the ribbon, drag the **First Line Indent** marker to **0.5 inches on the horizontal ruler**.

b. Press Ctrl + A to select all of the text in the document. Click the **PAGE LAYOUT tab**, and then in the **Paragraph group**, under **Spacing**, click the **After spin box up arrow** one time to change the value to **6 pt**.

c. Select the subheading *In-House Office Internships*, including the paragraph mark following it. Scroll down, hold down Ctrl, and then select the subheading *Additional Information*. With both subheadings selected, in the **Paragraph group**, under **Spacing**, click the **Before up spin box arrow** two times to set the **Spacing Before** to **12 pt**. **Save** your document.

3 Locate the first paragraph that begins *Development Department*, and then point to this paragraph from the left margin area to display the pointer. Drag down to select this paragraph and the next five paragraphs so that six paragraphs are selected. On the **HOME tab**, in the **Paragraph group**, click **Bullets** to change the selected text to a bulleted list.

a. Under the subheading *In-House Office Internships*, in the paragraph that begins *Sturgeon Point Productions*, click to position the insertion point at the *end* of the paragraph, following the colon. Press Enter to create a blank paragraph. On the ruler, drag the **First Line Indent** marker to the left so that it is positioned directly above the lower button. Being sure to include the period, type **1.** and then press Spacebar to create the first item in a numbered list.

b. Type **Be enrolled as a film major at a participating local college or university** and then press Enter. Type **Maintain a 3.0 GPA** and then press Enter. Type **Receive satisfactory monthly progress reports from their direct supervisor**

c. Scroll down to view the bulleted list of departments, and then select all six bulleted items in the list. On the mini toolbar, click the **Bullets button arrow**, and then under **Bullet Library**, click the **check mark symbol**. If the check mark is not available, choose another bullet symbol.

(Project 1D Internships continues on the next page)

CHAPTER REVIEW

4 With the list selected, move the pointer to the horizontal ruler, and then point to and click at **3.5 inches on the horizontal ruler** to insert a tab and align the job titles at the tab mark.

a. With the bulleted list still selected, on the ruler, point to the new tab marker at **3.5 inches on the horizontal ruler**, and then when the *Left Tab* ScreenTip displays, drag the tab marker to **4 inches on the horizontal ruler**.

b. On the ruler, point to the tab marker that you moved to display the *Left Tab* ScreenTip, and then double-click to display the **Tabs** dialog box.

c. In the **Tabs** dialog box, under **Tab stop position**, if necessary select *4"*, and then type **6** Under **Alignment**, click the **Right** option button. Under **Leader**, click the **2** option button. Near the bottom of the **Tabs** dialog box, click **Set**.

d. Under **Tab stop position**, select **4"**, and then click **Clear** to delete the tab stop. Click **OK**. **Save** your document.

5 Press Ctrl + Home to move to the top of the document, and then in the title, click to the right of the *S* in *PRODUCTIONS*.

a. Click the **INSERT tab**, and then in the **Illustrations group**, click **SmartArt**. On the left, click **Relationship**, and then scroll the list to the bottom. Locate and then click **Basic Venn**. Click **OK** to insert the SmartArt graphic. If necessary, close the Text Pane.

b. In the SmartArt graphic, click on *[Text]* in the top circle shape. Type **Film** and then click on the placeholder *[Text]* in the lower left shape. Type **Video** In the third circle, type **Internet**

c. Click the SmartArt graphic border to select it. Click the **FORMAT tab**, and then in the **Size group**, if necessary click **Size** to display the **Shape Height** and **Shape Width** boxes. Set the **Height** to 3" and the **Width** to 6.5".

d. With the SmartArt graphic still selected, on the ribbon, under **SMARTART TOOLS**, click the **DESIGN tab**, and then in the **SmartArt Styles group**, click **Change Colors**. Under **Colorful**, click the third style—**Colorful Range–Accent Colors 3 to 4**. On the **DESIGN tab**, in the **SmartArt Styles group**, click **More** ⬇. Under **3-D**, in the first row, click the third style—**Cartoon**. Click **Save**.

6 Hold down Ctrl and then press End to move to the end of the document. On the **INSERT tab**, in the **Media group**, click **Online Video**. If necessary, in the lower left corner of the Insert Video window, click YouTube. Click in the **Search YouTube** box. Including the quotation marks, type **"Go 2013 1B video"** and then press Enter. In the first row, click the first video, and then click **Insert**.

a. Click the **FILE tab**, and then on the right, click **Show All Properties**. In the **Tags** box, type **internship** and in the **Subject** box, type your course name and section number. Be sure that your name displays as the author. Click **Save**.

b. Click the **FILE tab** to display **Backstage** view. Click **Print** to display **Print Preview**. At the bottom of the preview, click the **Next Page** and **Previous Page** buttons to move between pages. If necessary, return to the document and make any necessary changes.

c. As directed by your instructor, print your document or submit it electronically. **Close** Word.

END | You have completed Project 1D

CONTENT-BASED ASSESSMENTS

Mastering Word   Project 1E Documentary

In the following Mastery project, you will create a flyer announcing a special event being hosted by Sturgeon Point Productions. Your printed results will look similar to those in Figure 1.54.

Apply **1A** skills from these Objectives:

1 Create a New Document and Insert Text
2 Insert and Format Graphics
3 Insert and Modify Text Boxes and Shapes
4 Preview and Print a Document

PROJECT FILES

For Project 1E, you will need the following files:

New blank Word document
w01E_Antarctica
w01E_Filmmaker

You will save your document as:

Lastname_Firstname_1E_Documentary

Build from Scratch

PROJECT RESULTS

FIGURE 1.54

(Project 1E Documentary continues on the next page)

CONTENT-BASED ASSESSMENTS

1 **Start** Word and display a **Blank document** with the ruler and formatting marks displayed. Type **Sturgeon Point Productions Presents Aria Pacheco** and then press Enter. From your student data files, insert the text file **w01E_Filmmaker**. Using your own name, **Save** the document in your **Word Chapter 1** folder as **Lastname_Firstname_1E_Documentary**

2 To the document title, apply the **Fill – White, Outline – Accent 1, Glow – Accent 1** text effect, and then change the **Font Size** to **36**. Change the **Font Color** to **Blue-Gray, Text 2**—in the fourth column, the first color. Apply an **Outer Shadow** using **Offset Left**—in the second row, the third style. **Center** the title.

3 Position the insertion point at the beginning of the paragraph that begins with *This year*, and then from your student data files, insert the picture **w01E_Antarctica**. Change the **Layout Options** to **Square** and then change the **Height** of the picture to **2.5**

4 Using the **Position** command, display the **Layout** dialog box, and then change the **Horizontal Alignment** to **Right relative to** the **Margin**. Apply a **10 Point Soft Edges** picture effect to the image, and then display the **Artistic Effects** gallery. In the third row, apply the fourth effect—**Mosaic Bubbles**.

5 Deselect the picture. Apply a **Page Border** to the document using the **Shadow** setting. Select the first style, and change the **Color** to **Blue-Gray, Text 2**. Change the **Width** to **3 pt**.

6 Below the last paragraph, draw a **Text Box** that is approximately 1.5 inches high and 4 inches wide—the exact size and location need not be precise. In the text box, type the following text:

> **Date: April 5**
>
> **Time: 8 p.m.**
>
> **Place: Studio G Screening Room**

7 Change the **Height** of the text box to **1.5** and the **Width** to **4.5** and then change the font size to **18**. Apply **Bold** and **Center**. To precisely place the text box, display the **Layout** dialog box. Change the **Horizontal Alignment** to **Centered**, **relative to** the **Page**, and then change the **Vertical Absolute position** to **0.5** below the **Paragraph**.

8 Apply a **Shape Style** to the text box—in the last row, select the second style—**Intense Effect – Blue, Accent 1**. Change the **Shape Outline** to **Black, Text 1**.

9 Insert the **File Name** in the footer, and then display the document properties. As the **Tags**, type **documentary, interview** As the **Subject**, type your course and section #. Be sure your name is indicated as the **Author**. **Save** your file.

10 Display the **Print Preview** and if necessary, return to the document and make any necessary changes. As directed by your instructor, print your document or submit it electronically. **Close** Word.

END | You have completed Project 1E

CONTENT-BASED ASSESSMENTS

Mastering Word | Project 1F Pitch Festival

Apply 1B skills from these Objectives:

5 Change Document and Paragraph Layout

6 Create and Modify Lists

7 Set and Modify Tab Stops

8 Insert a SmartArt Graphic and an Online Video

In the following Mastery project, you will edit a document with information regarding an event that Sturgeon Point Productions is holding for college students. Your printed results will look similar to those in Figure 1.55.

PROJECT FILES

For Project 1F, you will need the following file:

w01F_Pitch_Festival

You will save your document as:

Lastname_Firstname_1F_Pitch_Festival

PROJECT RESULTS

Pitch Festival!

Do you have a story that must be told? Pitch us your project during the Sturgeon Point Productions annual Pitch Festival! We're setting up several days of conference video calls for college students that are currently enrolled in an accredited film production program anywhere in the United States. If your idea is selected, you will be flown to our studios in Miami, Florida to pitch your idea to our staff of producers and development executives. The following video provides additional information:

Sturgeon Point Productions is one of the leading independent film and video companies in the Miami area. We are currently looking for new, fresh, exciting ideas for short and full-length feature films and documentaries. We like character driven stories that can be shot on an independent budget within one or two locations, preferably either in our studios or in the Miami area. We are currently looking for scripts, ideas, and concepts that are in one of the following categories:

1. Human interest or educational
2. Political or journalistic
3. Biographical or documentary

The Pitch Festival will take place at our secure website on the following dates and times. There are no entry fees to pitch; this unique opportunity to pitch to our staff of professional filmmakers is absolutely free for college film students. Sign up now at www.sturgeonpointproductions.com/pitchfest for one of the following pitch sessions:

- September 12, 11 a.m...Short and Feature Film Pitches
- September 13, 8 p.m. ....Biographical and Documentary Film Pitches
- September 14, 7 p.m. ....Educational Series Pitches

Lastname_Firstname_1F_Pitch_Festival

FIGURE 1.55

(Project 1F Pitch Festival continues on the next page)

1 Start Word, and then from your student files, open **w01F_Pitch_Festival**. Display formatting marks, and then **Save** the file in your **Word Chapter 1** folder as **Lastname_Firstname_1F_Pitch_Festival**

2 Insert the **File Name** in the footer. Select all the document text, and then change the **Line Spacing** for the entire document to **1.5**. **Center** the document title, and then change the title font size to **24**. Change the **Top** and **Bottom** margins to **0.5**

3 Select the three paragraphs below the title, and then apply a **First line** indent of 0.5". Select the entire document, and then change the **Spacing Before** to **6 pt** and the **Spacing After** to **6 pt**.

4 Select the last three paragraphs containing the dates, and then apply filled square bullets. If the bullets are not available, choose another bullet style. With the bulleted list selected, set a **Right** tab with **dot leaders** at 6".

5 Locate the paragraph that begins *Sturgeon Point Productions*, and then click at the end of the paragraph, after the colon. Press [Enter]. Create a numbered list with the following three numbered items; be sure to remove the first line indent before creating the numbered list:

Human interest or educational

Political or journalistic

Biographical or documentary

6 Position the insertion point at the end of the document after the word *Pitches*. Do *not* insert a blank line. Insert a **SmartArt** graphic from the **Process** category. Toward the bottom of the gallery, select the **Equation** SmartArt. Select the outside border of the SmartArt, and then change the **Height** of the SmartArt to **1** and the **Width** to **6.5**

7 With the SmartArt selected, change the layout to **Square**, and change the **Horizontal Alignment** to **Centered relative to** the **Page**. Change the **Vertical Alignment** to **Bottom relative to** the **Margin**.

8 In the first circle type **Your Ideas** and in the second circle type **Our Experts** In the third circle type **Pitch Festival!** Change the SmartArt color to **Colorful Range – Accent Colors 4 to 5**. Apply the **3-D Polished** style.

9 Click at the end of the paragraph below the title. Press [Enter], remove the first line indent, and then center the blank line. Insert an **Online Video**. In the **Search YouTube** box, type, including the quotations marks, **"Go 2013 1F Video"** and then insert the video with the cube on a black background. Change the height of the video to **1.5**.

10 Display the document properties. In the **Tags** box, type **pitch festival** and in the **Subject** box, type your course name and section number. Be sure your name displays as the author.

11 Display the **Print Preview** and if necessary, return to the document and make any necessary changes. As directed by your instructor, print your document or submit it electronically. **Close** Word.

END | You have completed Project 1F

CONTENT-BASED ASSESSMENTS

Mastering Word | Project 1G Educational Website

In the following Mastery project, you will create a flyer that details a new educational website that Sturgeon Point Productions has developed for instructors. Your printed results will look similar to those in Figure 1.56.

Apply 1A and 1B skills from these Objectives:

1. Create a New Document and Insert Text
2. Insert and Format Graphics
3. Insert and Modify Text Boxes and Shapes
4. Preview and Print a Document
5. Change Document and Paragraph Layout
6. Create and Modify Lists
7. Set and Modify Tab Stops
8. Insert a SmartArt Graphic and an Online Video

Build from Scratch

PROJECT FILES

For Project 1G, you will need the following files:

New blank Word document
w01G_Education
w01G_Media

You will save your document as:

Lastname_Firstname_1G_Educational_Website

PROJECT RESULTS

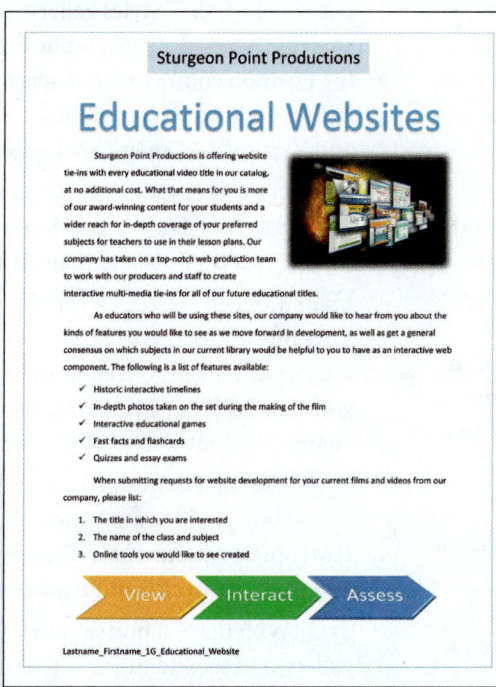

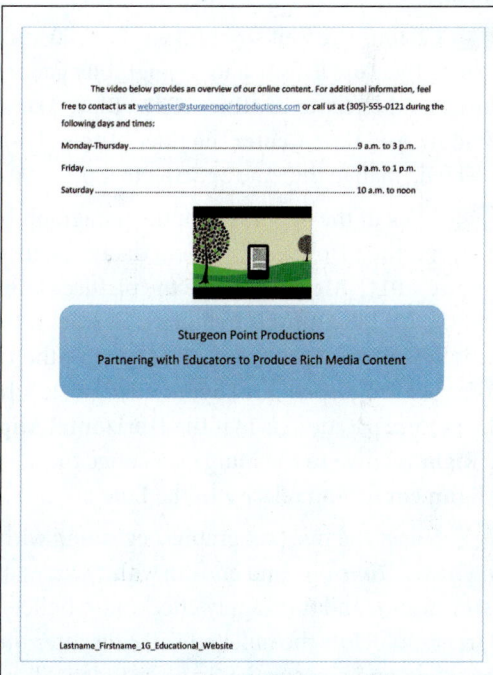

FIGURE 1.56

(Project 1G Educational Website continues on the next page)

CONTENT-BASED ASSESSMENTS

1 ▶ Start Word and display a blank document. Display formatting marks and the ruler. Type **Educational Websites** and then press Enter. Type **Sturgeon Point Productions is offering website tie-ins with every educational video title in our catalog, at no additional cost.** Press Spacebar, and then **Save** the document in your **Word Chapter 1** folder as **Lastname_Firstname_1G_Educational_Website**

2 ▶ With the insertion point positioned at the end of the sentence that you typed, insert the text from your student data file **w01G_Education**. Change the **Line Spacing** for the entire document to **1.5** and the spacing **After** to **6 pt**. To each of the four paragraphs that begin *Sturgeon Point Productions, As educators, When submitting*, and *The video*, apply a **First Line** indent of **0.5"**.

3 ▶ Change the font size of the title to **50** and then display the **Text Effects and Typography** gallery. Apply the second effect to the title—**Fill – Blue, Accent 1, Shadow**, and then **Center** the title. With only the title selected, change the **Line Spacing** to **1.0**.

4 ▶ Click at the beginning of the paragraph below the title, and then from your student data files, insert the picture **w01G_Media**. Change the picture **Height** to **2** and the **Layout Options** to **Square**. Format the picture with **Soft Edges** in **10 Point**, and then use the **Position** command to display the **Layout** dialog box. Change the picture position so that the **Horizontal Alignment** is **Right relative to** the **Margin**. Change the **Vertical Alignment** to **Top relative to** the **Line**.

5 ▶ Select the five paragraphs beginning with *Historic interactive timelines* and ending with *Quizzes and essay exams*, and then apply checkmark bullets. In the paragraph below the bulleted list, click after the colon. Press Enter and remove the first line indent. Type a numbered list with the following three numbered items:

   The title in which you are interested

   The name of the class and subject

   Online tools you would like to see created

6 ▶ With the insertion point located at the end of the numbered list, insert a **SmartArt** graphic. In the **Process** category, locate and select the **Basic Chevron Process**. In the first shape type **View** In the second shape type **Interact** and in the third shape type **Assess**

7 ▶ Change the SmartArt color to **Colorful Range – Accent Colors 4 to 5**, and then apply the **3-D Flat Scene** style. Change the **Height** of the SmartArt to **1** and the **Width** to **6.5** Change the **Layout Options** to **Square**, the **Horizontal Alignment** to **Centered relative to** the **Page**, and the **Vertical Alignment** to **Bottom relative to** the **Margin**.

8 ▶ Select the days and times at the end of the document, and then set a **Right** tab with **dot leaders** at **6"**. Click in the blank line below the tabbed list, and **Center** the line. Insert an **Online Video**. In the **Search YouTube** box, type **Pearson Higher Education Learning**, and then insert the first video that displays. Change the video **Height** to **1.5**

9 ▶ In the space below the video, insert a **Rounded Rectangle** shape. The exact location need not be precise. Change the **Shape Height** to **1.5** and the **Shape Width** to **6.5** Display the **Shape Styles** gallery, and then in the fourth row, apply the second style—**Subtle Effect - Blue, Accent 1**. Use the **Position** command to display the **Layout** dialog box, and then change the position so that both the **Horizontal** and **Vertical Alignment** are **Centered relative to** the **Margin**.

10 ▶ In the rectangle, type **Sturgeon Point Productions** and then press Enter. Type **Partnering with Educators to Produce Rich Media Content** and then change the font size to **16**.

11 ▶ Move to the top of the document and insert a **Text Box** above the title. The exact location need not be precise. Change the **Height** of the text box to **0.5** and the width to **3.7** Type **Sturgeon Point Productions** and then change the font size to **22 Center** the text.

12 ▶ Use the **Position** command to display the **Layout** dialog box, and then position the text box so that the **Horizontal Alignment** is **Centered relative to** the **Page** and the **Vertical Absolute position** is **0.5 below** the **Page**.

13 ▶ With the text box selected, display the **Shape Fill** gallery, and then in the next to last column, select the second color—**Blue, Accent 5, Lighter 80%**. Change the **Shape Outline** to the same color—**Blue, Accent 5, Lighter 80%**.

14 ▶ Deselect the text box. Apply a **Page Border** to the document. Use the **Box** setting, and choose the first style. Change the **Color** to **Blue, Accent 5**. Change the **Top** margin to **1.25** and insert the **File Name** in the footer.

15 ▶ Display the document properties. As the **Tags** type **website** and as the **Subject** type your course and section #. Be sure your name displays in the **Author** box, and then **Save** your file. Submit your document as directed.

END | You have completed Project 1G

CONTENT-BASED ASSESSMENTS

Apply a combination of the 1A and 1B skills.

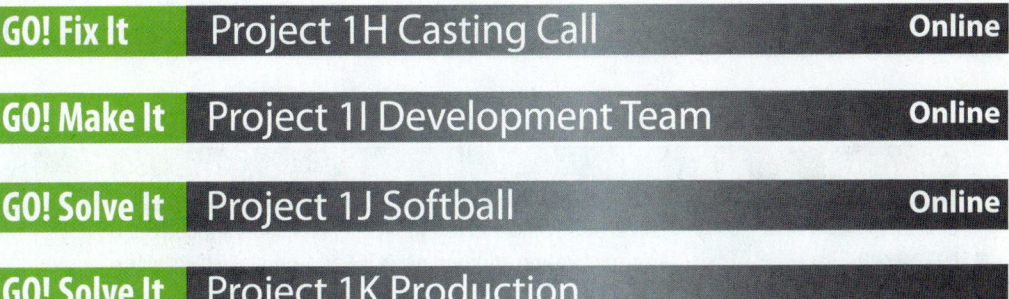

Build from Scratch

GO! Fix It	Project 1H Casting Call	Online
GO! Make It	Project 1I Development Team	Online
GO! Solve It	Project 1J Softball	Online
GO! Solve It	Project 1K Production	

PROJECT FILES

For Project 1K, you will need the following files:

w01K_Production
w01K_Studio

You will save your document as:

Lastname_Firstname_1K_Production

The Marketing Director for Sturgeon Point Productions is developing marketing materials aimed at filmmakers. Use the following information to format a flyer that uses text effects, an appropriately placed picture with an artistic effect and text wrapping applied, and an appropriately formatted SmartArt graphic.

From the student files that accompany this textbook, locate and open the file w01K_Production. Format the document using techniques you learned in this chapter. From your student data files, insert the picture w01K_Studio, and then format the picture with an artistic effect. Insert a **SmartArt** graphic that illustrates two or three important points about the company. Be sure the flyer is easy to read and understand and has an attractive design. Save the file in your **Word Chapter 1** folder as **Lastname_Firstname_1K_Production** and submit it as directed.

(Project 1K Production continues on the next page)

CONTENT-BASED ASSESSMENTS

Performance Level

Performance Criteria		Exemplary	Proficient	Developing
	Use text effects	Text effects applied to text in an attractive and appropriate manner.	Text effects applied but do not appropriately display text.	Text effects not used.
	Insert and format a picture	The picture is inserted and positioned correctly; text wrapping and an artistic effect are applied.	The picture is inserted but not formatted properly.	No picture is inserted in the document.
	Insert and format SmartArt	The SmartArt is inserted and appropriately formatted.	The SmartArt is inserted but no formatting is applied.	No SmartArt is inserted in the document.

END | You have completed Project 1K

OUTCOMES-BASED ASSESSMENTS

RUBRIC

The following outcomes-based assessments are *open-ended assessments*. That is, there is no specific correct result; your result will depend on your approach to the information provided. Make *Professional Quality* your goal. Use the following scoring rubric to guide you in *how* to approach the problem and then to evaluate *how well* your approach solves the problem.

The *criteria*—Software Mastery, Content, Format and Layout, and Process—represent the knowledge and skills you have gained that you can apply to solving the problem. The *levels of performance*—Professional Quality, Approaching Professional Quality, or Needs Quality Improvements—help you and your instructor evaluate your result.

	Your completed project is of Professional Quality if you:	Your completed project is Approaching Professional Quality if you:	Your completed project Needs Quality Improvements if you:
1-Software Mastery	Choose and apply the most appropriate skills, tools, and features and identify efficient methods to solve the problem.	Choose and apply some appropriate skills, tools, and features, but not in the most efficient manner.	Choose inappropriate skills, tools, or features, or are inefficient in solving the problem.
2-Content	Construct a solution that is clear and well organized, contains content that is accurate, appropriate to the audience and purpose, and is complete. Provide a solution that contains no errors in spelling, grammar, or style.	Construct a solution in which some components are unclear, poorly organized, inconsistent, or incomplete. Misjudge the needs of the audience. Have some errors in spelling, grammar, or style, but the errors do not detract from comprehension.	Construct a solution that is unclear, incomplete, or poorly organized; contains some inaccurate or inappropriate content; and contains many errors in spelling, grammar, or style. Do not solve the problem.
3-Format & Layout	Format and arrange all elements to communicate information and ideas, clarify function, illustrate relationships, and indicate relative importance.	Apply appropriate format and layout features to some elements, but not others. Overuse features, causing minor distraction.	Apply format and layout that does not communicate information or ideas clearly. Do not use format and layout features to clarify function, illustrate relationships, or indicate relative importance. Use available features excessively, causing distraction.
4-Process	Use an organized approach that integrates planning, development, self-assessment, revision, and reflection.	Demonstrate an organized approach in some areas, but not others; or, use an insufficient process of organization throughout.	Do not use an organized approach to solve the problem.

OUTCOMES-BASED ASSESSMENTS

Apply a combination of the **1A** and **1B** skills.

GO! Think Project 1L Classes

Build from
Scratch

PROJECT FILES

For Project 1L, you will need the following file:

New blank Word document

You will save your document as:

Lastname_Firstname_1L_Classes

The Human Resources Director at Sturgeon Point Productions needs to create a flyer to inform full-time employees of educational opportunities beginning in September. The courses are taught each year by industry professionals and are designed to improve skills in motion picture and television development and production. Employees who have been with Sturgeon Point Productions for at least two years are eligible to take the courses free of cost. The classes provide employees with opportunities to advance their careers, gain valuable skills, and achieve technical certification. All courses take place in Studio G and interested employees should contact Elana Springs in Human Resources to sign up. Information meetings are being held at 5:30 p.m. according to the following schedule: television development on June 15; motion picture production on June 17; and recording services on June 21.

Create a flyer with basic information about the courses and information meetings. Be sure the flyer is easy to read and understand and has an attractive design. Save the document as **Lastname_Firstname_1L_Classes** and submit it as directed.

END | You have completed Project 1L

Build from
Scratch

GO! Think Project 1M Store   Online

Build from
Scratch

You and GO! Project 1N Family Flyer   Online

Build from
Scratch

GO! Cumulative Group Project Project 1O Bell Orchid Hotels
                                                                        Online

Using Tables and Templates to Create Resumes and Cover Letters

GO! to Work
Video W2

PROJECT 2A	**OUTCOMES** Write a resume by using a Word table.

OBJECTIVES

1. Create a Table
2. Format a Table
3. Present a Word Document Online

PROJECT 2B	**OUTCOMES** Write a cover letter and use a template to create a cover sheet.

OBJECTIVES

4. Create a Custom Word Template
5. Correct and Reorganize Text
6. Use the Proofing Options and Print an Envelope
7. Create a Document Using a Predesigned Microsoft Template

onewordphoto / Fotolia

In This Chapter

Tables are useful for organizing and presenting data. Because a table is so easy to use, many individuals prefer to arrange tabular information in a Word table rather than setting a series of tabs. For example, you can use a table when you want to present rows and columns of information or to create a format for a document such as a resume.

When using Word to write business or personal letters, use a commonly approved letter format, and always use a clear writing style. You will make a good impression on prospective employers if you use a standard business letter style when you are writing a cover letter for a resume.

The projects in this chapter relate to the **College Career Center at Florida Port Community College** in St. Petersburg, Florida, a coastal port city near the Florida High Tech Corridor. With 60 percent of Florida's high tech companies and a third of the state's manufacturing companies located in the St. Petersburg and Tampa Bay areas, the college partners with businesses to play a vital role in providing a skilled workforce. The College Career Center assists students in exploring careers, finding internships, and applying for jobs. The Center offers workshops for resume and cover letter writing and for practice interviews.

Resume

PROJECT ACTIVITIES

In Activities 2.01 through 2.11, you will create a table to use as the format for a resume. The director of the Career Center, Mary Walker-Huelsman, will use this model when assisting students with building their resumes. Your completed document will look similar to Figure 2.1.

PROJECT FILES

For Project 2A, you will need the following files:

New blank Word document
w02A_Experience

You will save your document as:

Lastname_Firstname_2A_Resume

Build from
Scratch

PROJECT RESULTS

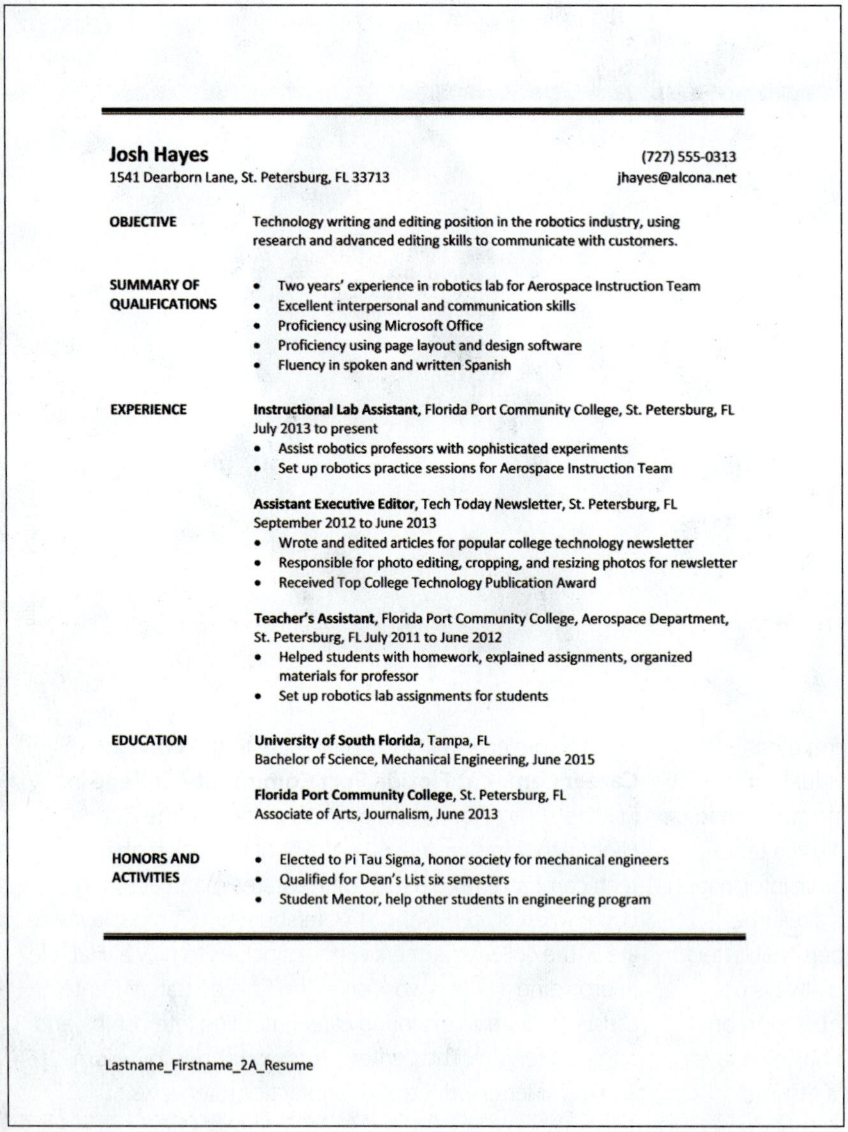

Josh Hayes
1541 Dearborn Lane, St. Petersburg, FL 33713

(727) 555-0313
jhayes@alcona.net

OBJECTIVE	Technology writing and editing position in the robotics industry, using research and advanced editing skills to communicate with customers.
SUMMARY OF QUALIFICATIONS	• Two years' experience in robotics lab for Aerospace Instruction Team • Excellent interpersonal and communication skills • Proficiency using Microsoft Office • Proficiency using page layout and design software • Fluency in spoken and written Spanish
EXPERIENCE	**Instructional Lab Assistant**, Florida Port Community College, St. Petersburg, FL July 2013 to present • Assist robotics professors with sophisticated experiments • Set up robotics practice sessions for Aerospace Instruction Team **Assistant Executive Editor**, Tech Today Newsletter, St. Petersburg, FL September 2012 to June 2013 • Wrote and edited articles for popular college technology newsletter • Responsible for photo editing, cropping, and resizing photos for newsletter • Received Top College Technology Publication Award **Teacher's Assistant**, Florida Port Community College, Aerospace Department, St. Petersburg, FL July 2011 to June 2012 • Helped students with homework, explained assignments, organized materials for professor • Set up robotics lab assignments for students
EDUCATION	**University of South Florida**, Tampa, FL Bachelor of Science, Mechanical Engineering, June 2015 **Florida Port Community College**, St. Petersburg, FL Associate of Arts, Journalism, June 2013
HONORS AND ACTIVITIES	• Elected to Pi Tau Sigma, honor society for mechanical engineers • Qualified for Dean's List six semesters • Student Mentor, help other students in engineering program

Lastname_Firstname_2A_Resume

FIGURE 2.1 Project 2A Resume

Video W2-1

A *table* is an arrangement of information organized into rows and columns. The intersection of a row and a column in a table creates a box called a *cell* into which you can type. Tables are useful to present information in a logical and orderly format.

Activity 2.01 | Creating a Table by Defining Table Dimensions

1 **Start** Word and then click **Blank document**. On the **HOME tab**, in the **Paragraph group**, if necessary click **Show/Hide** to display the formatting marks. If the rulers do not display, click the **VIEW tab**, and then in the **Show group**, select the **Ruler check box**.

2 Click the **FILE tab**, and then in **Backstage** view, click **Save As**. In the **Save As** dialog box, navigate to the location where you are storing your projects for this chapter. Create a new folder named **Word Chapter 2**

3 **Save** the file in the **Word Chapter 2** folder as **Lastname_Firstname_2A_Resume**

4 On the **INSERT tab**, in the **Header & Footer group**, click **Footer**, and then at the bottom of the list, click **Edit Footer**. On the ribbon, in the **Insert group**, click **Document Info**, click **File Name**, and then at the right end of the ribbon, click **Close Header and Footer**.

5 On the **INSERT tab**, in the **Tables group**, click **Table**. In the **Insert Table** grid, in the fourth row, point to the second square, and notice that the cells are bordered in orange and *2x4 Table* displays at the top of the grid. Compare your screen with Figure 2.2.

FIGURE 2.2

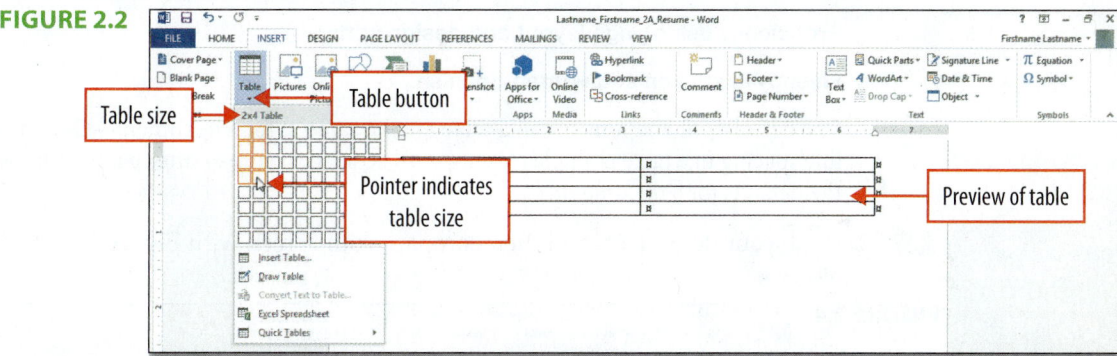

6 Click one time to create the table. Notice that formatting marks in each cell indicate the end of the contents of each cell; the mark to the right of each *row* indicates the row end. **Save** your document, and then compare your screen with Figure 2.3.

A table with four rows and two columns displays at the insertion point location, and the insertion point displays in the upper left cell. The table fills the width of the page, from the left margin to the right margin. On the ribbon, TABLE TOOLS and two additional tabs—*DESIGN* and *LAYOUT*—display. Borders display around each cell in the table.

FIGURE 2.3

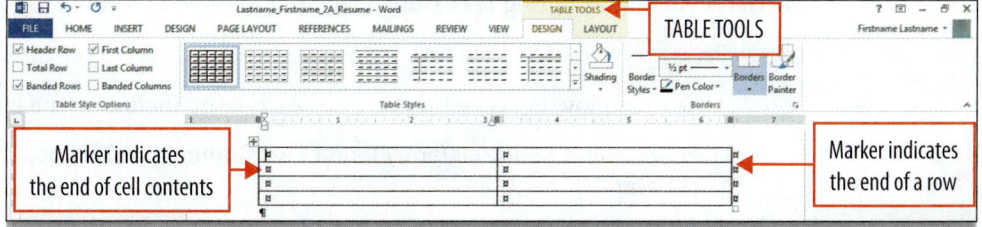

Activity 2.02 | Typing Text in a Table

In a Word table, each cell behaves similarly to a document. For example, as you type in a cell, when you reach the right border of the cell, wordwrap moves the text to the next line. When you press Enter, the insertion point moves down to a new paragraph in the same cell. You can also insert text from another document into a table cell.

There are numerous acceptable formats for resumes, many of which can be found in Business Communications textbooks. The layout used in this project is suitable for a recent college graduate and places topics in the left column and details in the right column.

1 With the insertion point blinking in the first cell in the first row, type **OBJECTIVE** and then press Tab.

> Pressing Tab moves the insertion point to the next cell in the row, or, if the insertion point is already in the last cell in the row, pressing Tab moves the insertion point to the first cell in the next row.

2 Type **Technology writing and editing position in the robotics industry, using research and advanced editing skills to communicate with customers.** Notice that the text wraps in the cell and the height of the row adjusts to fit the text.

3 Press Tab to move to the first cell in the second row. Type **SUMMARY OF QUALIFICATIONS** and then press Tab. Type the following, pressing Enter at the end of each line *except* the last line:

Two years' experience in robotics lab for Aerospace Instruction Team

Excellent interpersonal and communication skills

Proficiency using Microsoft Office

Proficiency using page layout and design software

Fluency in spoken and written Spanish

> The default font and font size in a table are the same as for a document—Calibri 11 pt. The default line spacing in a table is single spacing with no space before or after paragraphs, which differs from the defaults for a document.

4 Save your document, and then compare your screen with Figure 2.4.

FIGURE 2.4

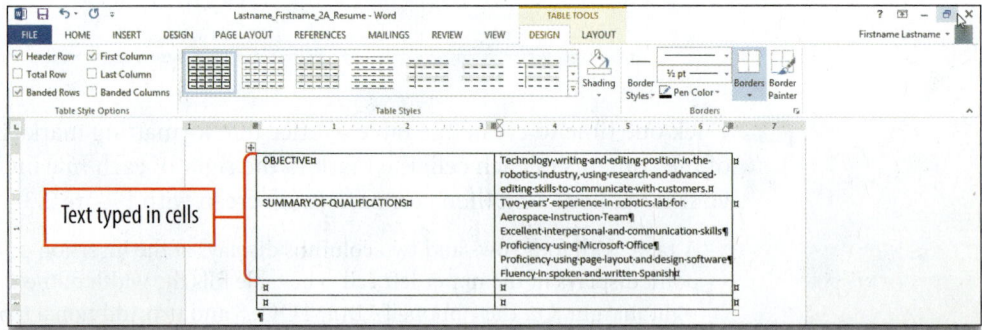

Text typed in cells

Activity 2.03 | Inserting Text from a File and Removing Blank Paragraphs

1 Press Tab to move to the first cell in the third row. Type **EXPERIENCE** and then press Tab.

2 Type the following, pressing Enter after each item, including the last item:

Instructional Lab Assistant, Florida Port Community College, St. Petersburg, FL July 2013 to present

Assist robotics professors with sophisticated experiments

Set up robotics practice sessions for Aerospace Instruction Team

3 Be sure your insertion point is positioned in the second column to the left of the cell marker below *Instruction Team*. Compare your screen with Figure 2.5.

FIGURE 2.5

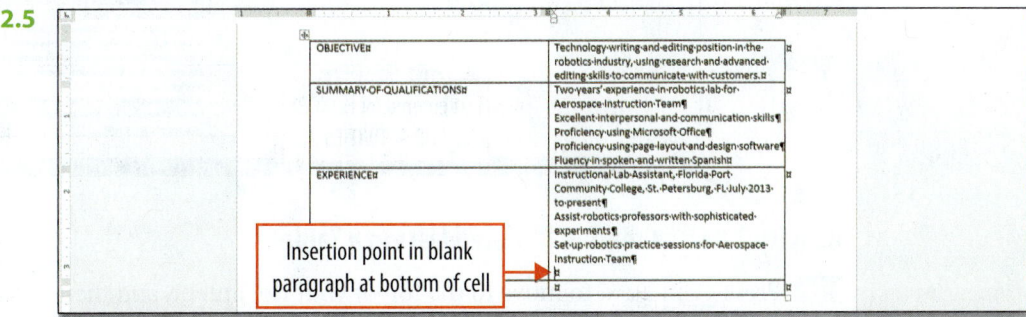

Insertion point in blank paragraph at bottom of cell

4 On the **INSERT tab**, in the **Text group**, click the **Object button arrow**, and then click **Text from File**. Navigate to your student files, select **w02A_Experience**, and then click **Insert**.

All of the text from the w02A_Experience document is added to the document at the insertion point.

ANOTHER WAY   Open the second document and select the text you want. Copy the text, and then paste at the desired location.

5 Press Backspace one time to remove the blank paragraph at the end of the inserted text, and then compare your screen with Figure 2.6.

FIGURE 2.6

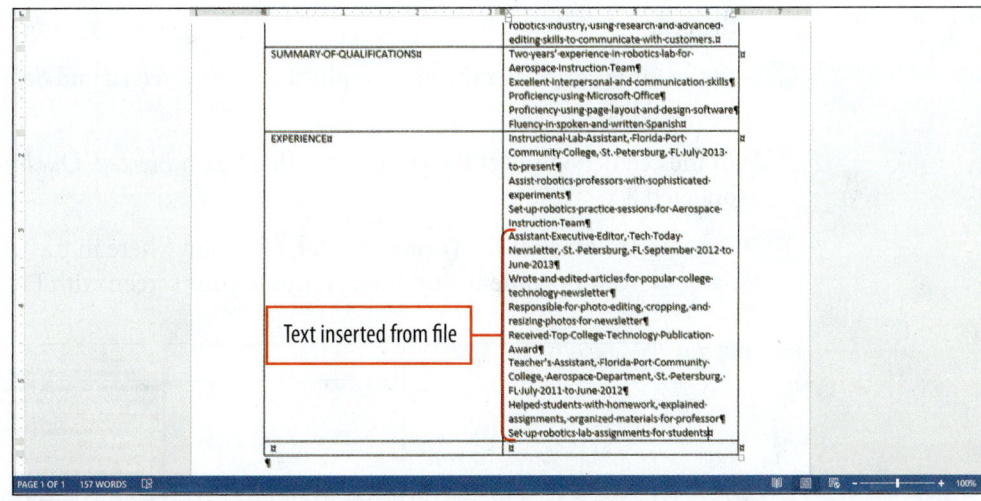

Text inserted from file

6 Press Tab to move to the first cell in the fourth row. Type **HONORS AND ACTIVITIES** and then press Tab.

7 Type the following, pressing Enter at the end of each item *except* the last one:

Elected to Pi Tau Sigma, honor society for mechanical engineers

Qualified for Dean's List, six semesters

Student Mentor, help other students in engineering program

8 Save your document, and then compare your screen with Figure 2.7.

FIGURE 2.7

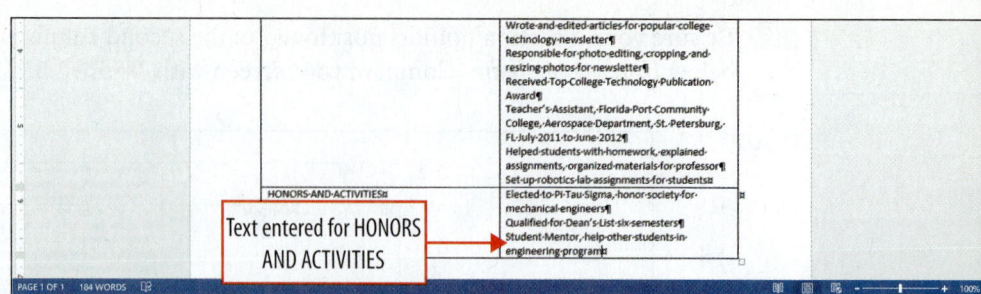

Text entered for HONORS AND ACTIVITIES

Activity 2.04 | Creating Bulleted Lists in a Table

1 Press [Ctrl] + [Home] to move to the top of your document, and then in the cell to the right of *SUMMARY OF QUALIFICATIONS*, select all of the text.

2 On the **HOME tab**, in the **Paragraph group**, click **Bullets** .

The selected text displays as a bulleted list to make each qualification more distinctive.

3 In the **Paragraph group**, click **Decrease Indent** one time to align the bullets at the left edge of the cell.

4 Scroll as necessary so that you can view the entire *EXPERIENCE* and *HONORS AND ACTIVITIES* sections on your screen. With the bulleted text still selected, in the **Clipboard group**, double-click **Format Painter**.

5 In the cell to the right of EXPERIENCE, select the second and third paragraphs—beginning *Assist* and *Set up*—to create the same style of bulleted list as you did in the previous step.

6 In the same cell, under *Assistant Executive Editor*, select the three paragraphs that begin *Wrote* and *Responsible* and *Received* to create another bulleted list aligned at the left edge of the cell.

7 In the same cell, select the paragraphs that begin *Helped* and *Set up* to create the same type of bulleted list.

8 In the cell below, select the paragraphs that begin *Elected*, *Qualified*, and *Student* to create a bulleted list.

9 Press [Esc] to turn off the **Format Painter**. Click anywhere in the table to deselect the text, **Save** your document, and then compare your screen with Figure 2.8.

FIGURE 2.8

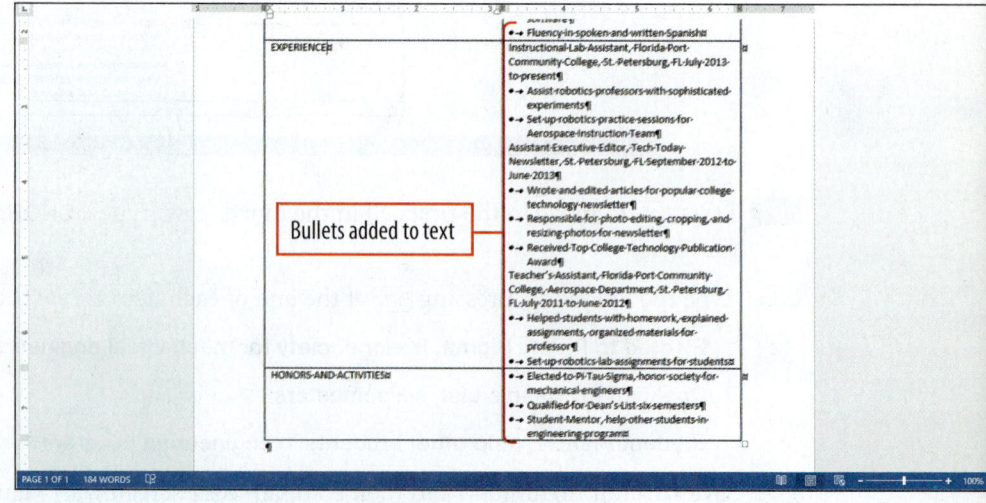

Bullets added to text

Video W2-2

Use Word's formatting tools to make your tables attractive and easy to read. Types of formatting you can add to a table include changing the row height and the column width, removing or adding borders, increasing or decreasing the paragraph or line spacing, and enhancing the text.

Activity 2.05 | Changing the Width of Table Columns and Using AutoFit

When you create a table, all of the columns are of equal width. In this activity, you will change the width of the columns.

1 Press Ctrl + Home. Click anywhere in the first column, and then on the ribbon, under **TABLE TOOLS**, click the **LAYOUT tab**. In the **Cell Size group**, notice the **Width** box, which displays the width of the active column.

2 Look at the horizontal ruler and locate the **1.5-inch mark**. Then, in the table, in any row, point to the vertical border between the two columns to display the ✛ pointer.

3 Hold down the left mouse button and drag the column border to the left until the white arrow on the ruler is at approximately **1.5 inches on the horizontal ruler** and then release the left mouse button.

4 In the **Cell Size group**, click the **Width box down spin arrow** as necessary to set the column width to **1.4"** and notice that the right border of the table moves to the right.

Adjusting column width by dragging a column border adjusts only the width of the column; adjusting column width with the Width box simultaneously adjusts the right border of the table.

5 In the **Cell Size group**, click **AutoFit**, and then click **AutoFit Window** to stretch the table across the page within the margins so that the right border of the table is at the right margin. **Save** 🖫 and then compare your screen with Figure 2.9.

 **ANOTHER WAY**
You can adjust column widths by dragging the Move Table Column markers on the ruler. To maintain the right border of the table at the right margin, hold down Shift while dragging. To display measurements on the ruler, hold down Alt while dragging the marker.

FIGURE 2.9

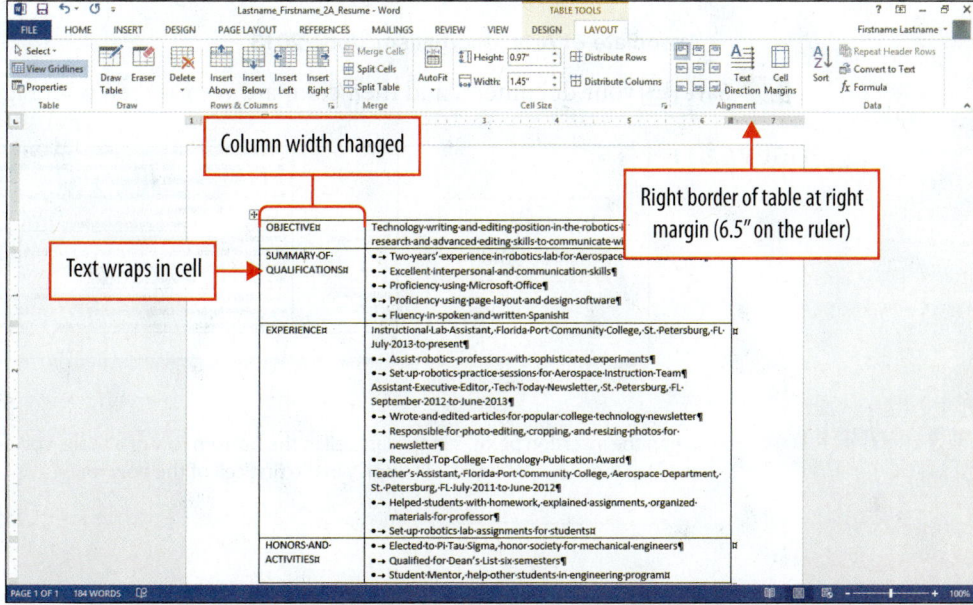

Activity 2.06 | Using One-Click Row/Column Insertion to Modify Table Dimensions

One of the most common actions you will take in a table is adding another row or another column. By using *One-click Row/Column Insertion* you can do so in context by pointing to the left or top edge where you want the row or column to appear and then clicking the ⊕ button to add it.

1 ▶ Scroll to view the lower portion of the table. On the left border of the table, *point* to the upper left corner of the cell containing the text *HONORS AND ACTIVITIES* to display the **One-click Row/Column Insertion** button ⊕. Compare your screen with Figure 2.10.

FIGURE 2.10

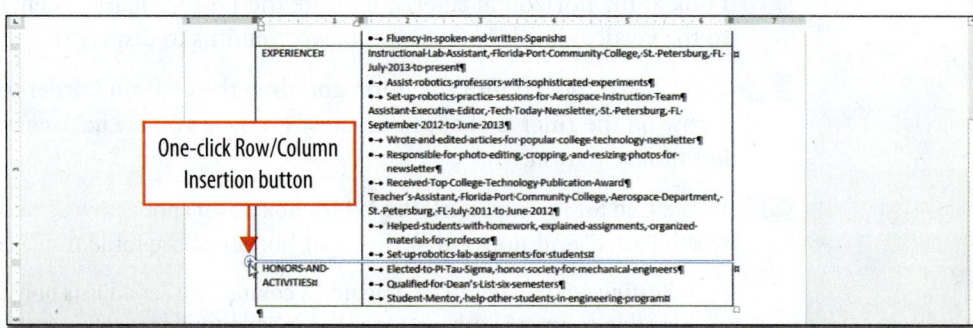

2 ▶ Click ⊕ one time to insert a new row above the HONORS AND ACTIVITIES row.

3 ▶ Click in the left cell of the new row, type **EDUCATION** and then press Tab.

4 ▶ Type the following, pressing Enter at the end of each item *except* the last one:

University of South Florida, Tampa, FL

Bachelor of Science, Mechanical Engineering, June 2015

Florida Port Community College, St. Petersburg, FL

Associate of Arts, Journalism, June 2013

5 ▶ **Save** 🖫 your document, and then compare your screen with Figure 2.11.

FIGURE 2.11

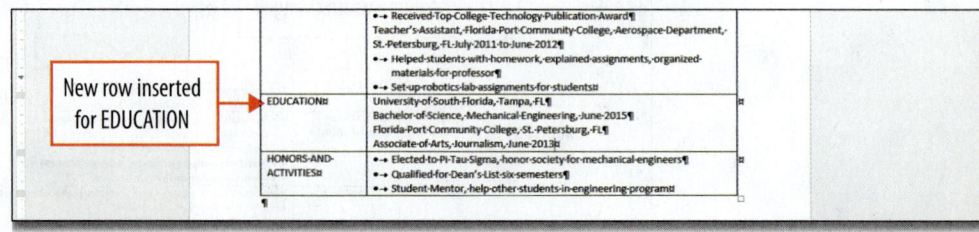

 **ANOTHER WAY**   When the insertion point is in the last cell in the bottom row of a table, you can add a row by pressing the Tab key; the insertion point will display in the first cell of the new row.

Activity 2.07 | Merging Table Cells

The title of a table typically spans all of the columns. In this activity, you will merge cells so that you can position the personal information across both columns.

1 ▸ Press Ctrl + Home to move to the top of your document, and then click anywhere in the top row of the table.

2 ▸ On the **LAYOUT tab**, in the **Rows & Columns group**, click **Insert Above**.

A new row displays above the row that contained the insertion point, and the new row is selected. This is another method to insert rows and columns in a table; use this method to insert a new row at the top of a table.

ANOTHER WAY   Right-click in the top row, point to Insert, and then click Insert Rows Above.

3 ▸ Be sure the two cells in the top row are selected; if necessary, drag across both cells to select them.

4 ▸ On the **LAYOUT tab**, in the **Merge group**, click **Merge Cells**.

The cell border between the two cells no longer displays.

ANOTHER WAY   Right-click the selected row and click Merge Cells on the shortcut menu.

Activity 2.08 | Setting Tabs in a Table

1 ▸ With the merged cell still selected, on the **HOME tab**, in the **Paragraph group**, click the **Dialog Box Launcher** to display the **Paragraph** dialog box.

2 ▸ On the **Indents and Spacing tab**, in the lower left corner, click **Tabs** to display the **Tabs** dialog box.

3 ▸ Under **Tab stop position**, type **6.5** and then under **Alignment**, click the **Right** option button. Click **Set**, and then click **OK** to close the dialog box.

4 ▸ Type **Josh Hayes** Hold down Ctrl and then press Tab. Notice that the insertion point moves to the right-aligned tab stop at 6.5".

In a Word table, you must use Ctrl + Tab to move to a tab stop, because pressing Tab is reserved for moving the insertion point from cell to cell.

5 ▸ Type **(727) 555-0313** and then press Enter.

6 ▸ Type **1541 Dearborn Lane, St. Petersburg, FL 33713** Hold down Ctrl and then press Tab.

7 ▸ Type **jhayes@alcona.net** Save your document, and then compare your screen with Figure 2.12.

FIGURE 2.12

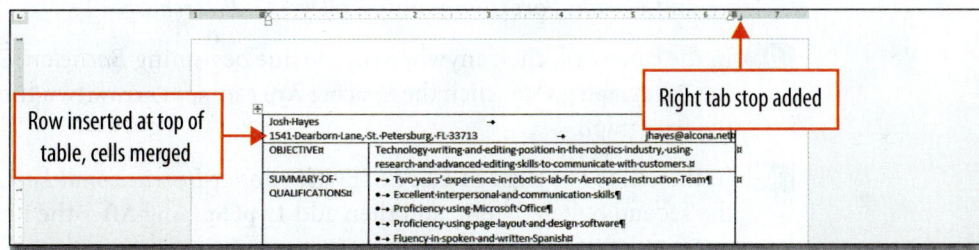

Row inserted at top of table, cells merged

Right tab stop added

Activity 2.09 | Modifying Fonts in a Table and Using Spacing After

1 In the first row of the table, select the name *Josh Hayes*, and then on the mini toolbar, apply **Bold** B and change the **Font Size** to **16**.

2 Under *Josh Hayes*, click anywhere in the second line of text, which contains the address and email address.

3 On the **PAGE LAYOUT tab**, in the **Paragraph group**, click the **Spacing After up spin arrow** three times to add **18 pt** spacing between the first row of the table and the second row. Compare your screen with Figure 2.13.

This action separates the personal information from the body of the resume and adds focus to the name.

FIGURE 2.13

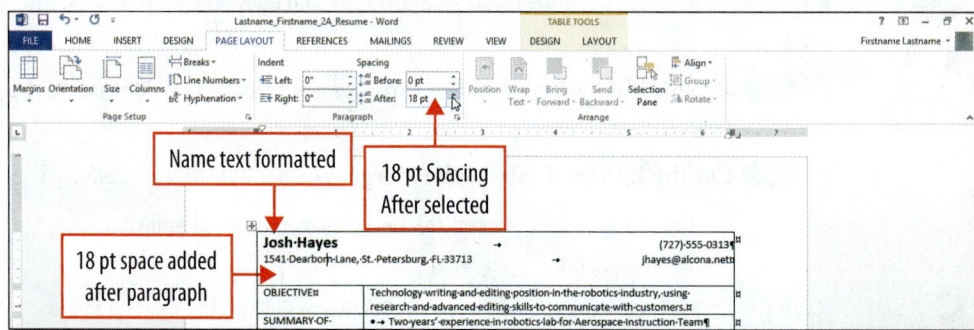

4 Using the technique you just practiced, in the second column, click in the last paragraph of *every cell* and add **18 pt Spacing After** including the last row; a border will be added to the bottom of the table, and spacing will be needed between the last row and the border.

5 In the second row, point to the word *OBJECTIVE*, hold down the left mouse button, and then drag downward in the first column to select all the headings in uppercase letters. On the mini toolbar, click **Bold** B .

> ### NOTE | Selecting Only One Column
>
> When you drag downward to select the first column, a fast mouse might also begin to select the second column when you reach the bottom. If this happens, drag upward slightly to deselect the second column and select only the first column.

---

6 In the cell to the right of *EXPERIENCE*, without selecting the following comma, select *Instructional Lab Assistant* and then on the mini toolbar, click **Bold** B .

7 In the same cell, apply **Bold** B to the other job titles—*Assistant Executive Editor* and *Teacher's Assistant*.

8 In the cell to the right of *EDUCATION*, apply **Bold** B to *University of South Florida, Tampa, FL* and *Florida Port Community College, St. Petersburg, FL*.

9 In the same cell, click anywhere in the line beginning *Bachelor*. On the **PAGE LAYOUT tab**, in the **Paragraph group**, click the **Spacing After up spin arrow** two times to add **12 pt** spacing after the paragraph.

10 In the cell to the right of *EXPERIENCE*, under *Instructional Lab Assistant*, click anywhere in the second bulleted item, and then add **12 pt Spacing After** the item.

11 In the same cell, repeat this process for the last bulleted item under *Assistant Executive Editor*.

12 Scroll to view the top of your document, **Save** 🖫 your document, and then compare your screen with Figure 2.14.

FIGURE 2.14

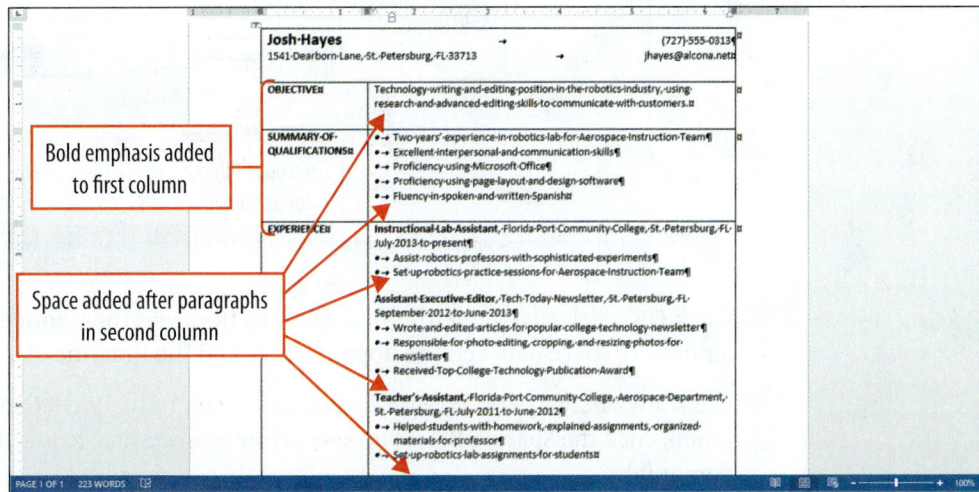

Bold emphasis added to first column

Space added after paragraphs in second column

Activity 2.10 | Modifying Table Borders and Using Spacing Before

When you create a table, all of the cells have black 1/2-point, single-line, solid-line borders that print unless you remove them. Most resumes do not display any cell borders. A border at the top and bottom of the resume, however, is attractive and adds a professional look to the document.

1 Scroll as necessary to view the top margin area above the table, and then point slightly outside of the upper left corner of the table to display the **table move handle** ⊞.

2 With the 🏃 pointer, click one time to select the entire table, and notice that the row markers at the end of each row are also selected.

> Shaded row markers indicate that the entire row is selected. Use this technique to select the entire table.

3 On the ribbon, under **TABLE TOOLS**, click the **DESIGN tab**. In the **Borders group**, click the **Borders button arrow**, and then click **No Border**.

> The black borders no longer display.

4 Press Ctrl + P, which is the keyboard shortcut to view the Print Preview, and notice that no borders display in the preview. Then, press **Back** ← to return to your document.

5 With the table still selected, on the **DESIGN tab**, in the **Borders group**, click the **Borders button arrow**, and then at the bottom of the **Borders** gallery, click **Borders and Shading**.

6 In the **Borders and Shading** dialog box, on the **Borders tab**, under **Setting**, click **Custom**. Under **Style**, scroll down about one-third of the way, and then click the style with a **thick upper line and a thin lower line**.

7 In the **Preview** box at the right, point to the *top* border of the small preview and click one time.

🔄 **ANOTHER WAY** Click the top border button, which is one of the buttons that surround the Preview.

8 Under **Style**, scroll down if necessary, click the opposite style—with the **thin upper line and the thick lower line**, and then in the **Preview** box, click the *bottom* border of the preview. Compare your screen with Figure 2.15.

FIGURE 2.15

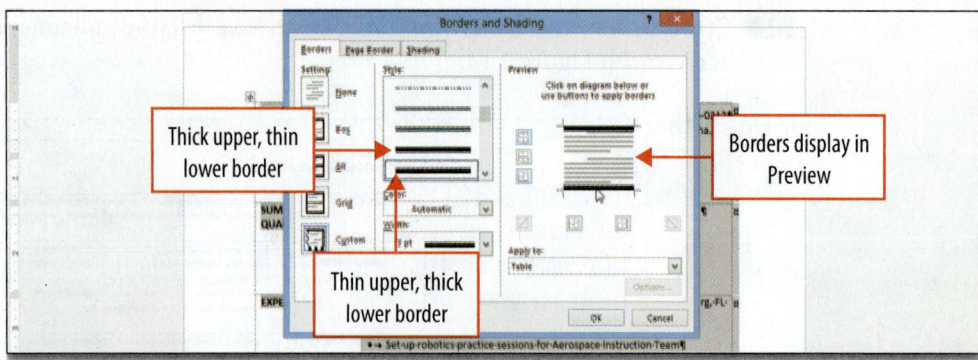

9 Click **OK**, click anywhere to cancel the selection, and then notice that there is only a small amount of space between the upper border and the first line of text.

10 Click anywhere in the text *Josh Hayes*, and then on the **PAGE LAYOUT tab**, in the **Paragraph group**, click the **Spacing Before up spin arrow** as necessary to add **18 pt** spacing before the first paragraph.

11 Press Ctrl + P to display **Print Preview**. Compare your screen with Figure 2.16.

FIGURE 2.16

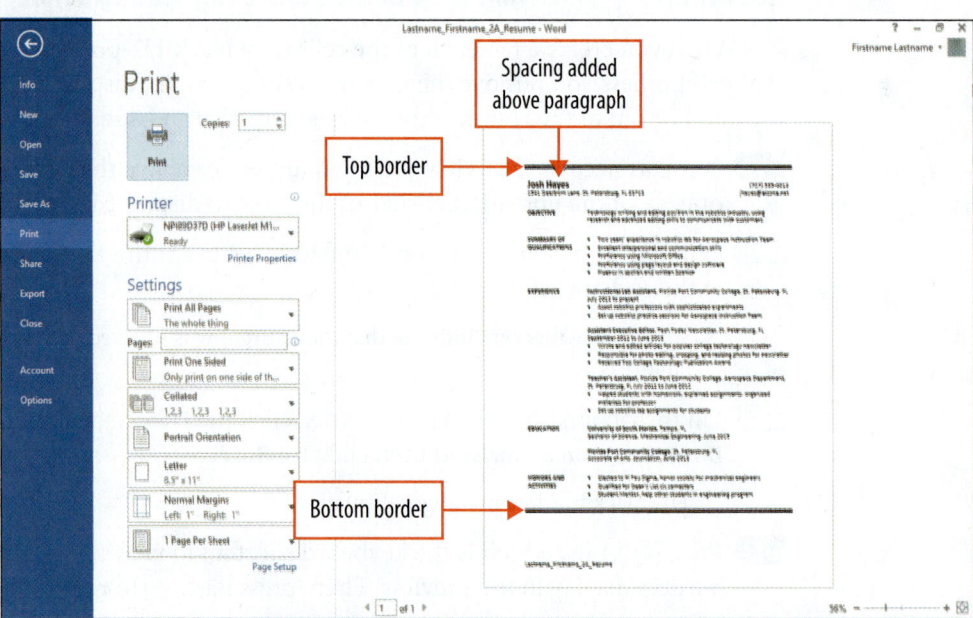

12 Press **Back** to return to your document, and then on the Quick Access Toolbar, click **Save**.

More Knowledge   **View Gridlines in a Table**

After you remove borders from a table, you can still view nonprinting gridlines, which show the cell boundaries of a table whenever the table does not have borders applied. Some people find this a useful visual aid. If you cannot see the gridlines, on the ribbon, under TABLE TOOLS, on the DESIGN tab, in the Borders group, click the Borders button arrow, and then click View Gridlines.

More Knowledge   **Convert Text to a Table**

To convert paragraphs or lists to a table, insert separator characters such as commas or tabs to show where to divide the text into columns. Then insert paragraph marks (press ENTER) to show where to begin the rows. Select the text, and then on the INSERT tab, in the Table group, click Convert Text to Table. In the Convert Text to Table dialog box, choose the options you want, and then click OK.

Video W2-3

Office Presentation Service enables you to present your Word document to others who can watch in a web browser. No preliminary setup is necessary; Word creates a link to your document that you can share with others via email or instant message. Anyone to whom you send the link can see your document while you are presenting online.

Individuals watching your presentation can navigate within the document independently of you or others in the presentation, so they can use a mouse, keyboard, or touch input to move around in the document while you are presenting it. If an individual is viewing a different portion of the document than the presenter, an alert displays on his or her screen. To return to the portion of the document that the presenter is showing, a Follow Presenter button displays.

While you are presenting, you can make minor edits to the document. If you want to share a copy of the document to the presentation attendees, you can select *Enable remote viewers to download the document* when you start the presentation. You can also share any meeting notes that you or others created in OneNote.

Activity 2.11 | Presenting a Word Document Online

If you are creating your own resume, it will be valuable to get feedback from your friends, instructors, or Career Center advisors before you submit your resume for a job application. In this Activity, you will present the resume document online for others to look at.

N O T E   **You May Be Asked to Sign in with Your Microsoft Account**

You may be asked to sign in with your Microsoft account, even if you are already signed in, to present your document online.

---

1 With your resume document displayed, click **Save** 🖫 .

2 Click the **FILE tab**, on the left click **Share**, and then under **Share**, click **Present Online**.

3 On the right, under **Present Online**, be sure **Office Presentation Service** displays; if necessary, click the arrow on the right to select it. Click the **Present Online** button. Wait a moment for the service to connect, and then compare your screen with Figure 2.17.

There are several methods to send your meeting invitation to others. You can click Copy Link to copy and paste the hyperlink; for example, you could copy the link into a *Skype* window. Skype is a Microsoft product with which you can make voice calls, make video calls, transfer files, or send messages—including instant messages and text messages—over the Internet.

You can also select Send in Email, which will open your Outlook email window if you use Outlook as your mail client.

N O T E   **Other Presentation Services May Display**

Under Present Online, you might have other services displayed. For example, if you are using Office 365, Microsoft Lync may display as the default presentation service.

FIGURE 2.17

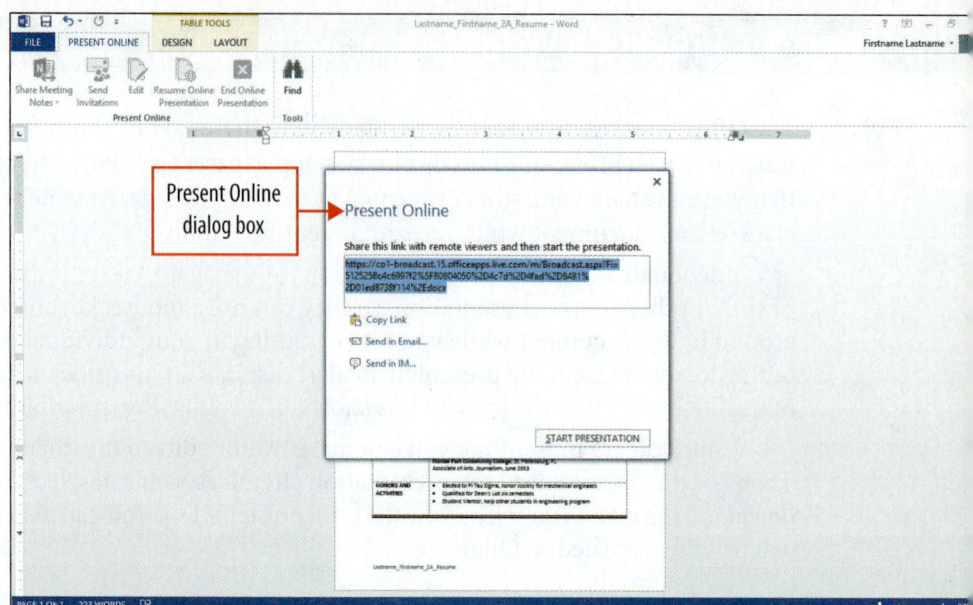

Present Online dialog box

4 If you want to do so, identify a classmate or friend who is at a computer and available to view your presentation, select one of the methods to share, click **START PRESENTATION**, and when you are finished, on the ribbon, click **End Online Presentation**. Otherwise, **Close** ☒ the **Present Online** dialog box.

   If you present online, you will need to initiate voice communication using Skype or by simply phoning the other person.

5 Be sure you have closed the **Present Online** dialog box. On the ribbon, on the **PRESENT ONLINE tab**, click **End Online Presentation**, and then in the message, click **End Online Presentation**.

6 Press Ctrl + Home to move to the top of your document. In the lower right corner, click **Zoom In** ⊞ as necessary to set the Zoom level to **100%**. If necessary, on the **HOME tab**, redisplay the formatting marks by clicking **Show/Hide**.

7 Click the **FILE tab**, and then in the lower right portion of the screen, click **Show All Propertie** In the **Tags** box, type **resume, Word table** and in the **Subject** box, type your course name and section number. In the **Author** box, be sure your name is indicated and edit if necessary.

8 On the left, click **Print** to display **Print Preview**. If necessary, return to the document and make any necessary changes.

9 As directed by your instructor, print your document or submit it electronically. **Save** 🖫 you document and **Close** ☒ Word.

More **Knowledge**   **Convert a Table to Text**

To convert a table to text, select the rows or table you want to convert to paragraphs, and then on the LAYOUT tab, in the Data group, click Convert to Text. In the Convert to Text dialog box, under Separate text at, click the separator character to use in place of the column boundaries, and then click OK.

END | You have completed Project 2A

Objective   Edit a Resume in Word Online

You can create and edit tables in Word Online if you are not at a computer on which Word 2013 is installed.

Activity | Editing a Resume in Word Online

In this activity, you will use Word Online to edit a Word table containing a resume similar to the resume you created in Project 1A.

1 From the desktop, start Internet Explorer. Navigate to **http://onedrive.com** and then sign in to your Microsoft account. Click your **GO! Web Projects** folder to open it— or create and then open this folder if necessary.

2 On the OneDrive menu bar, click **Upload**. In the **Choose File to Upload** dialog box, navigate to your student data files, click **w02_2A_Web**, and then click **Open**.

3 Point to the uploaded file **w02_2A_Web**, and then right-click. On the shortcut menu, scroll down as necessary and then click **Rename**. Using your own last name and first name, type **Lastname_Firstname_WD_2A_Web** and then press Enter to rename the file.

4 Click the file that you just renamed, and then in the upper left, click **EDIT DOCUMENT**. On the list, click **Edit in Word Online**.

5 If necessary, click to place the insertion point in the cell *OBJECTIVE*. On the ribbon, under **TABLE TOOLS**, click the **LAYOUT tab**, and then in the **Insert group**, click **Insert Above**.

6 In the first cell of the new row, type **Daniela Frank** press Enter, select the text you just typed, and then on the

HOME tab, in the **Styles group**, click the **More Styles arrow**, and then click **Title**. With the text selected, change the **Font** to **Calibri (Body)**.

7 Click in the second cell of the new row, and then type **1343 Siena Lane, Deerfield, WI 53531** and press Enter. Type **(608) 555-0588** and press Enter. Type **dfrank@alcona.net** and press Enter. Right-click the email address, and then click **Remove Link**. Select all the text in the second cell that you just typed, and then on the **HOME tab**, in the **Paragraph group**, click **Align Text Right**. Click anywhere to deselect, and then compare your screen with Figure A.

8 Scroll down and click anywhere in the *EXPERIENCE* cell. On the ribbon, under **TABLE TOOLS**, click the **LAYOUT tab**, and then in the **Insert group**, click **Insert Below**. In the first cell of the new row, press Backspace one time to move the insertion point to the left edge of the cell. Type **EDUCATION** Select the text you just typed, and then if necessary, from the **HOME tab**, apply **Bold** B.

9 Press Tab to move to the second cell in the new row, press Backspace one time to move to the left edge of the cell,

FIGURE A

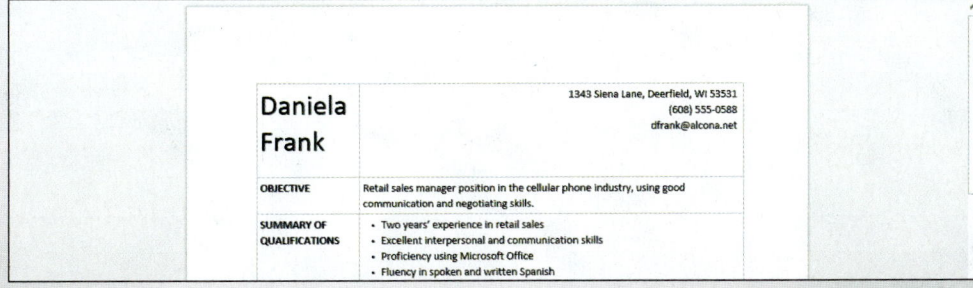

(GO! with Office Online (formerly Web Apps) continues on the next page)

and then type **Madison Area Technical College, Madison, WI** and press Enter.

10 Type **Associate of Arts in Information Systems, June 2014** and press Enter. Select the line of text you just typed, and then press Ctrl + B to remove **Bold**. Click

anywhere to deselect, and then compare your screen with Figure B.

11 Submit the file as directed by your instructor. Sign out of your OneDrive and close Internet Explorer.

FIGURE B

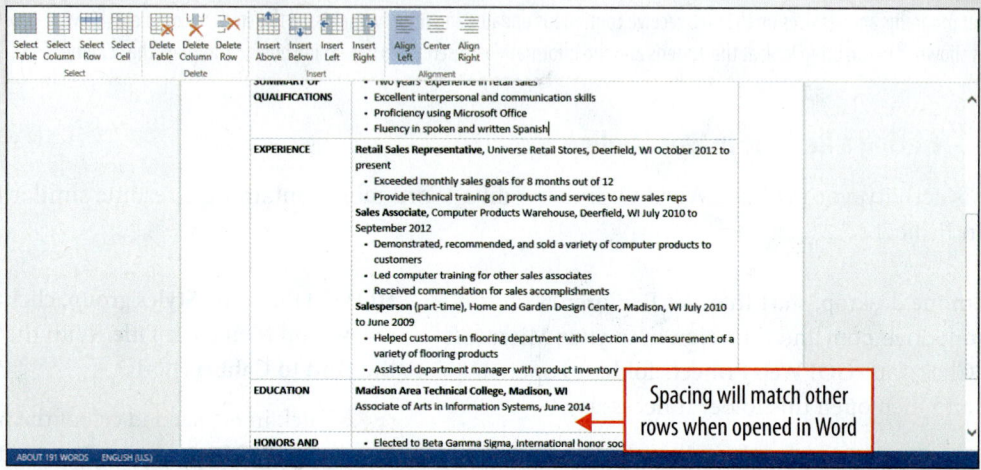

Spacing will match other rows when opened in Word

Cover Letter, Reference List, and Envelope

PROJECT ACTIVITIES

In Activities 2.12 through 2.24, you will create a letterhead, save the letterhead as a custom Word template, and then use the letterhead to create a cover letter to accompany a resume. You will also create a list of references from a Microsoft predesigned template and, if you have an envelope and printer available, format and print an envelope. Your completed documents will look similar to Figure 2.18.

PROJECT FILES

For Project 2B, you will need the following files:

New blank Word document
w02B_Cover_Letter_Text

You will save your documents as:

Lastname_Firstname_2B_Cover_Letter
Lastname_Firstname_2B_Reference_List

PROJECT RESULTS

Jennifer Garcia

1776 Bay Cliff Drive, Tampa, FL 33602
(727) 555-0347 jgarcia@alcona.net

January 8, 2013

Ms. Mary Walker-Huelsman, Director
Florida Port Community College Career Center
2745 Oakland Avenue
St. Petersburg, FL 33713

Dear Ms. Walker-Huelsman:

I am seeking a position in which I can use my computer and communications skills. My education and experience, outlined on the enclosed resume, includes a Business Software Applications Specialist certificate from Florida Port Community College.

With a permanent position as my ultimate goal, I hope to use the Florida Port Community College Career Center to secure a temporary job. I can be available for a flexible number of hours or days and am willing to work in a variety of businesses or organizations.

As my resume illustrates, I have excellent computer skills. I am an honor student at Florida Port Community College and have outstanding references. In addition, I have part-time work experience as a software tester, where I perform the following computer activities:

Microsoft Access	Test database queries
Microsoft Excel	Enter software test data
Microsoft Word	Create and mail form letters

You can contact me by email at jgarcia@alcona.net or by telephone at (727) 555-0347. I am available for an interview at your convenience.

Sincerely,

Jennifer Garcia

Enclosure

Lastname_Firstname_2B_Cover_Letter

Jennifer Garcia
1776 Bay Cliff Drive
Tampa, FL 33602
(727) 555-0347
jgarcia@alcona.net

REFERENCES:

Dr. Tracey Scott
Professor
Florida Port Community College
2745 Oakland Avenue
St. Petersburg, FL 33713
(727) 555-0974
tscott@fpcc-science.edu

Relationship: Professor at Florida Port Community College from July 2012 to July 2013

Mr. James Johnson
Systems Manager
Tampa Tech Group
Two Tech Plaza
Tampa, FL 33602
(727) 555-0144
jjohnson@tech-pro.net

Relationship: Supervisor at Tampa Tech Group from July 2013 to present

Lastname_Firstname_2B_Reference_List

FIGURE 2.18 Project 2B Cover Letter and Reference List

Video W2-4

A *template* is a file you use as a starting point for a *new* document. A template has a predefined document structure and defined settings, such as font, margins, and available styles. On Word's opening screen, you can select from among many different templates—or you can create your own custom template.

When you open a template as the starting point for a new document, the template file opens a copy of itself, unnamed, and then you use the structure—and possibly some content, such as headings—as the starting point for a new document.

All documents are based on a template. When you create a new blank document, it is based on Word's *Normal template*, which serves as the starting point for all blank Word documents.

Activity 2.12 | Changing the Document Style Set for Paragraph Spacing and Applying a Bottom Border to a Paragraph

A *letterhead* is the personal or company information that displays at the top of a letter, and which commonly includes a name, address, and contact information. The term also refers to a piece of paper imprinted with such information at the top. In this activity, you will create a custom template for a personal letterhead.

1 Start Word and display a blank document; be sure that formatting marks and rulers display.

2 On the **DESIGN tab**, in the **Document Formatting group**, click **Paragraph Spacing**.

The Paragraph Spacing command offers various options for setting the line and paragraph spacing of your entire document. A gallery of predefined values displays; or you can create your own custom paragraph spacing.

3 On the list *point* to **Default** and notice the settings in the ScreenTip.

Recall that the default spacing for a new Word document is 0 points of blank space before a paragraph, 8 points of blank space following a paragraph, and line spacing of 1.08.

4 Point to **No Paragraph Space** and notice the settings in the ScreenTip.

The *No Paragraph Space* style inserts *no* extra space before or after a paragraph and uses line spacing of 1. This is the same format used for the line spacing commonly referred to as *single spacing*.

5 Click **No Paragraph Space**.

By using the No Paragraph Space style, you will be able to follow the prescribed format of a letter, which Business Communications texts commonly describe in terms of single spacing.

ANOTHER WAY

On Word's opening screen, select the Single spaced (blank) document; or, in a blank document, select the entire document, and then on the HOME tab, in the Styles group, click No Spacing. Also, so long as you leave an appropriate amount of space between the elements of the letter, you can use Word's default spacing. Finally, you could use one of Word's predesigned templates for a cover letter and observe all spacing requirements for a letter.

6 Type **Jennifer Garcia** and then press Enter.

7 Type **1776 Bay Cliff Drive, Tampa, FL 33602** and then press Enter.

8 Type **(727) 555-0347 jgarcia@alcona.net** and then press Enter. If the web address changes to blue text, right-click the web address, and then, click **Remove Hyperlink**.

9 Select the first paragraph—*Jennifer Garcia*—and then on the mini toolbar, apply **Bold** B and change the **Font Size** to **16**.

10 ▶ Select the second and third paragraphs. On the mini toolbar, apply **Bold** [B] and change the **Font Size** to **12**.

11 ▶ With the two paragraphs still selected, on the **HOME tab**, in the **Paragraph group**, click **Align Right** [≡].

🔄 **ANOTHER WAY**   Press [Ctrl] + [R] to align text to the right.

12 ▶ Click anywhere in the first paragraph—*Jennifer Garcia*. In the **Paragraph group**, click the **Borders button arrow** [⊞ ▾], and then at the bottom, click **Borders and Shading**.

13 ▶ In the **Borders and Shading** dialog box, on the **Borders tab**, under **Style**, be sure the first style—a single solid line—is selected.

14 ▶ Click the **Width arrow**, and then click **3 pt**. To the right, under **Preview**, click the bottom border of the diagram. Under **Apply to**, be sure *Paragraph* displays. Compare your screen with Figure 2.19.

FIGURE 2.19

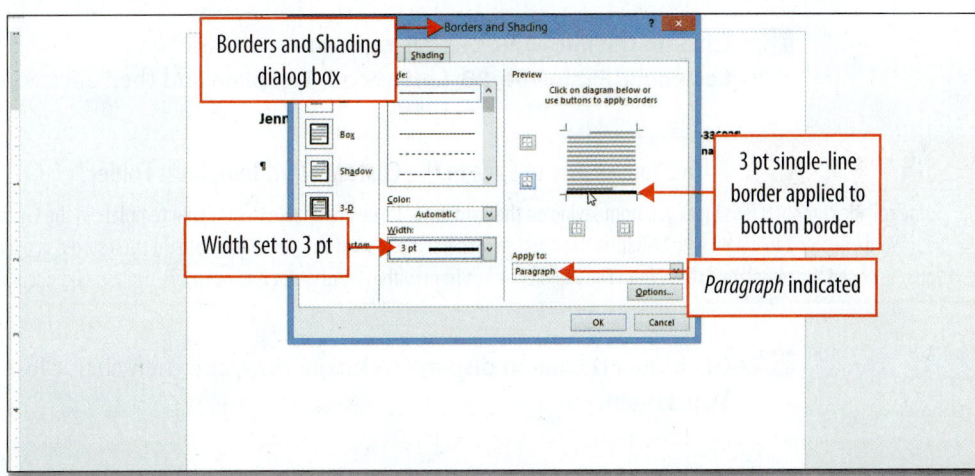

🔄 **ANOTHER WAY**   Alternatively, under Preview, click the bottom border button [⊞ ▾].

15 ▶ Click **OK** to display a 3 pt line below *Jennifer Garcia*, which extends from the left margin to the right margin.

> The border is a paragraph command and uses the same margins of the paragraph to which it is applied.

Activity 2.13 | Saving a Document as a Custom Word Template

After you create a document format that you like and will use again, for example, a letterhead for personal letters during a job search, you can save it as a template and then use it as the starting point for any letter.

1 ▶ Press [F12] to display the **Save As** dialog box. In the lower portion of the dialog box, in the **Save as type** box, at the right edge, click the arrow, and then click **Word Template**.

ALERT!   **Are You Using a Laptop Computer?**

On some laptop computers, you might have to hold down the key labeled FN while pressing the F12 key in order to display the Save As dialog box.

2 ▶ At the top of the **Save As** dialog box, notice the path, and then compare your screen with Figure 2.20.

By default, Word stores template files on your hard drive in your user folder, in a folder named Custom Word Templates. By doing so, the template is available to you from the Word opening screen.

FIGURE 2.20

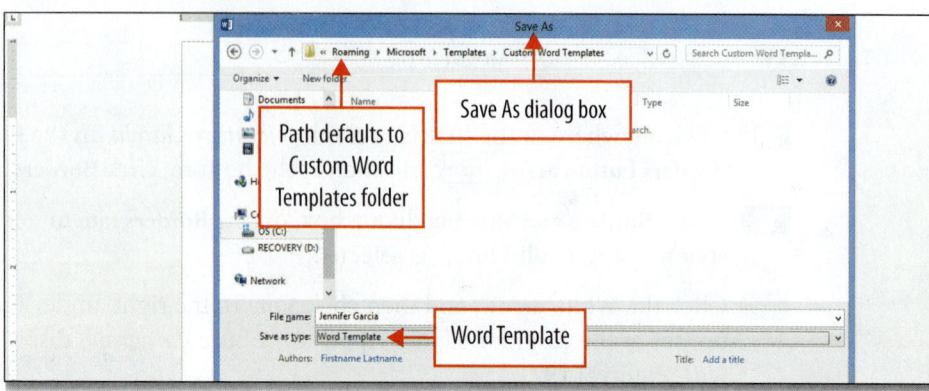

3 ▶ Click in the **File name** box, using your own name, type **Lastname_Firstname_2B_Letterhead_Template** and then click **Save**.

4 ▶ Click the **FILE tab** to display **Backstage** view, and then click **Close** to close the file but leave Word open.

Activity 2.14 | Creating a Cover Letter from a Custom Word Template

A *cover letter* is a document that you send with your resume to provide additional information about your skills and experience. An effective cover letter includes specific information about why you are qualified for the job for which you are applying. Use the cover letter to explain your interest in the position and the organization.

1 ▶ With Word open but no documents displayed, click the **FILE tab** to display **Backstage** view, and then click **New** to display the new document options. Compare your screen with Figure 2.21.

Here you can create a new document from a blank document or from one of Word's many built-in or online templates.

FIGURE 2.21

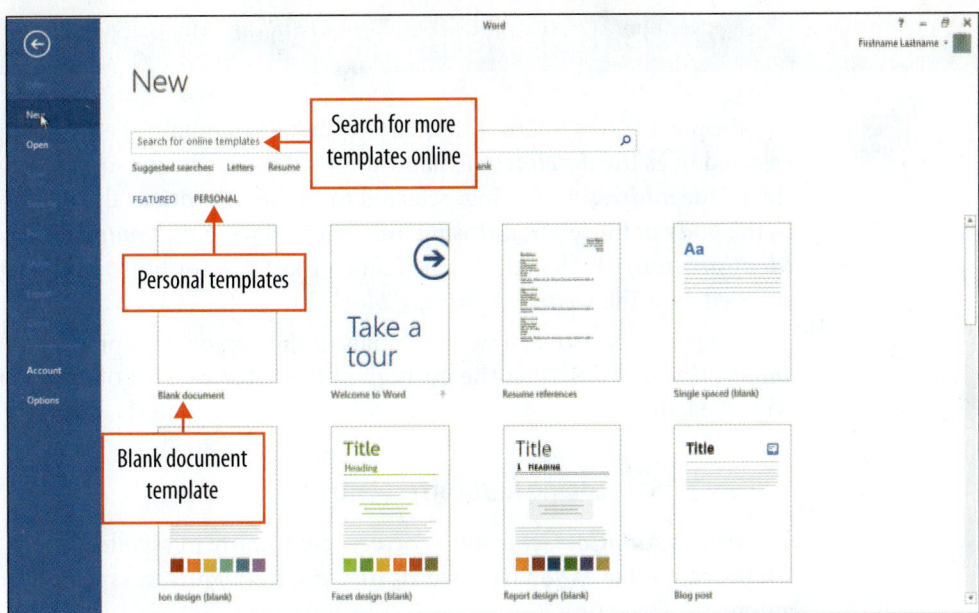

2 Under **Suggested searches**, click **PERSONAL**, *point* to the name of your letterhead template, and then compare your screen with Figure 2.22.

> Custom templates that you create and that are stored in the Custom Word Templates folder on your hard drive are accessible to you here whenever you want to create a new document from your stored template.

FIGURE 2.22

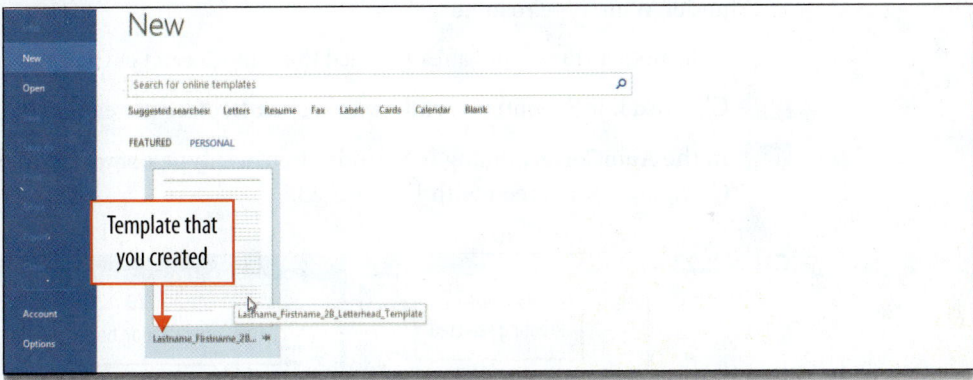

3 Click your letterhead template.

> Word opens a copy of your 2B_Letterhead_Template in the form of a new Word document—the title bar indicates *Document* followed by a number. You are not opening the original template file, and changes that you make to this new document will not affect the contents of your 2B_Letterhead_Template file.

4 Press F12 to display the **Save As** dialog box, and then navigate to your **Word Chapter 2** folder. **Save** the file as **Lastname_Firstname_2B_Cover_Letter**

5 On the **INSERT tab**, in the **Header & Footer** group, click **Footer**, click **Edit Footer**, and then in the **Insert group**, click **Document Info**. Click **File Name**, and then click **Close Header and Footer**.

6 Save 🖫 your document.

Video W2-5

Business letters follow a standard format and contain the following parts: the current date, referred to as the *dateline*; the name and address of the person receiving the letter, referred to as the *inside address*; a greeting, referred to as the *salutation*; the text of the letter, usually referred to as the *body* of the letter; a closing line, referred to as the *complimentary closing*; and the *writer's identification*, which includes the name or job title (or both) of the writer and which is also referred to as the *writer's signature block*.

Some letters also include the initials of the person who prepared the letter, an optional *subject line* that describes the purpose of the letter, or a list of *enclosures*—documents included with the letter.

Activity 2.15 │ Adding AutoCorrect Entries

Word's *AutoCorrect* feature corrects commonly misspelled words automatically; for example *teh* instead of *the*. If you have words that you frequently misspell, you can add them to the list for automatic correction.

1 Click the **FILE tab** to display **Backstage** view. On the left, click **Options** to display the **Word Options** dialog box.

2 On the left side of the **Word Options** dialog box, click **Proofing**, and then under **AutoCorrect options**, click the **AutoCorrect Options** button.

3 In the **AutoCorrect** dialog box, click the **AutoCorrect tab**. Under **Replace**, type **resumee** and under **With**, type **resume**

   If another student has already added this AutoCorrect entry, a Replace button will display.

4 Click **Add**. If the entry already exists, click **Replace** instead, and then click **Yes**.

5 In the **AutoCorrect** dialog box, under **Replace**, type **computr** and under **With**, type **computer** Compare your screen with Figure 2.23.

FIGURE 2.23

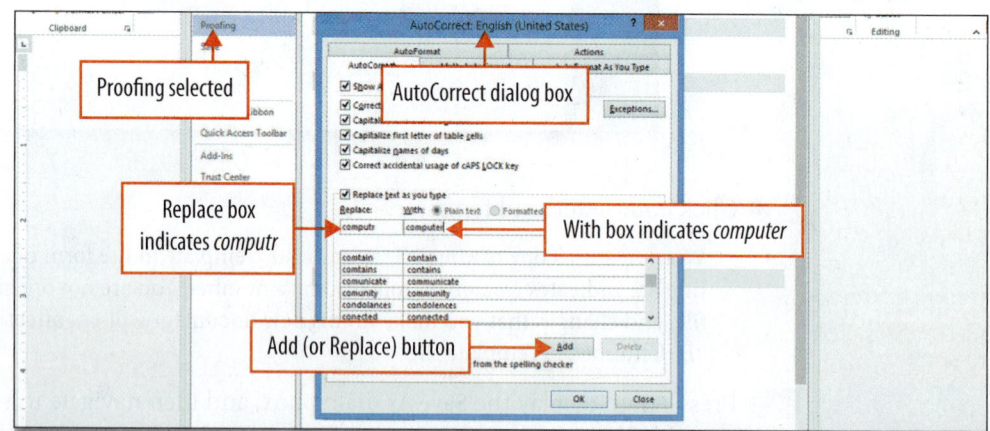

6 Click **Add** (or **Replace**) and then click **OK** two times to close the dialog boxes.

Activity 2.16 | Inserting the Current Date and Creating a Cover Letter

By using the *Date & Time* command, you can select from a variety of formats to insert the current date and time in a document.

For cover letters, there are a variety of accepted letter formats that you will see in reference manuals and Business Communications texts. The one used in this chapter is a block style cover letter following the style in Courtland Bovee and John Thill, *Business Communication Today*, Eleventh Edition, Pearson Prentice Hall, 2012, p. A-2.

1 Press `Ctrl` + `End` to move the insertion point to the blank line below the letterhead, and then press `Enter` three times.

2 On the **INSERT tab**, in the **Text group**, click **Date & Time**, and then click the third date format. Click **OK** to create the dateline.

> Most Business Communication texts recommend that the dateline be positioned at least 0.5 inch (3 blank lines) below the letterhead; or, position the dateline approximately 2 inches from the top edge of the paper.

3 Press `Enter` four times, which leaves three blank lines. Type the following inside address on four lines, but do *not* press `Enter` following the last line:

Ms. Mary Walker-Huelsman, Director

Florida Port Community College Career Center

2745 Oakland Avenue

St. Petersburg, FL 33713

The recommended space between the dateline and inside address varies slightly among experts in Business Communication texts and office reference manuals. However, all indicate that the space can be from 1 to 10 blank lines depending on the length of your letter.

4 Press `Enter` two times to leave one blank line, and then compare your screen with Figure 2.24.

FIGURE 2.24

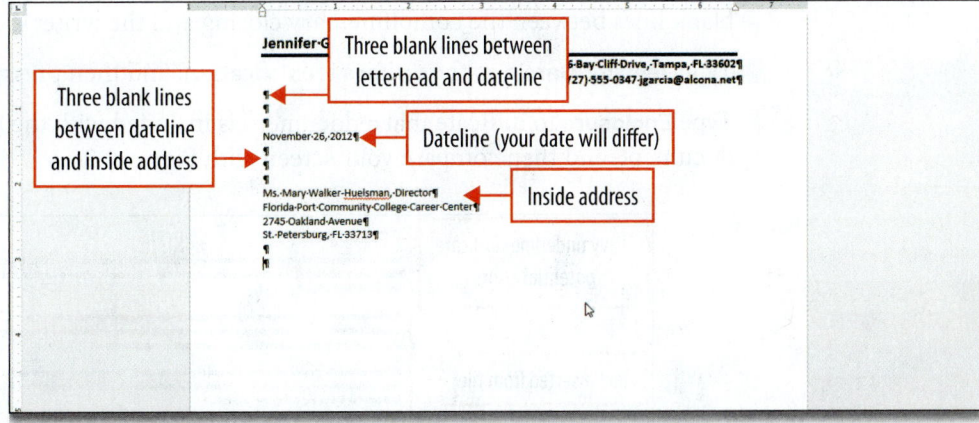

5 Type the salutation **Dear Ms. Walker-Huelsman:** and then press `Enter` two times.

> Always leave one blank line above and below the salutation.

6 Type, exactly as shown, the following opening paragraph that includes an intentional word usage error: **I am seeking a position in witch I can use my** and press `Spacebar`. Type, exactly as shown, **computr** and then watch *computr* as you press `Spacebar`.

> The AutoCorrect feature recognizes the misspelled word, and then changes *computr* to *computer* when you press `Spacebar`, `Enter`, or a punctuation mark.

7 Type the following, including the misspelled last word: **and communication skills. My education and experience, outlined on the enclosed resumee** and then type **,** (a comma). Notice that when you type the comma, AutoCorrect replaces *resumee* with *resume*.

8 Press [Spacebar], and then complete the paragraph by typing **includes a Business Software Applications Specialist certificate from FPCC.** Compare your screen with Figure 2.25.

FIGURE 2.25

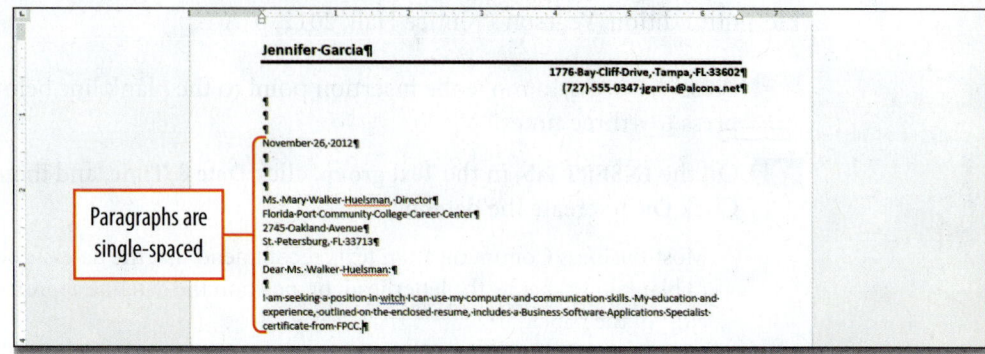

Jennifer Garcia¶

1776 Bay Cliff Drive, Tampa, FL 33602¶
(727) 555-0347 jgarcia@alcona.net¶

November 26, 2012¶

Ms. Mary Walker Huelsman, Director¶
Florida Port Community College Career Center¶
2745 Oakland Avenue¶
St. Petersburg, FL 33713¶

Dear Ms. Walker Huelsman:¶

I am seeking a position in witch I can use my computer and communication skills. My education and experience, outlined on the enclosed resume, includes a Business Software Applications Specialist certificate from FPCC.

Paragraphs are single-spaced

9 Press [Enter] two times. On the **INSERT tab**, in the **Text group**, click the **Object button arrow**, and then click **Text from File**. From your student files, locate and **Insert** the file **w02B_Cover_Letter_Text**.

Some of the words in the cover letter text display red or blue wavy underlines. These indicate potential spelling, grammar, or word usage errors, and will be addressed before the end of this project.

10 Scroll as necessary to display the lower half of the letter on your screen, and be sure your insertion point is positioned in the blank paragraph at the end of the document.

11 Press [Enter] one time to leave one blank line between the last paragraph of the letter and the complimentary closing.

12 Type **Sincerely,** as the complimentary closing, and then press [Enter] four times to leave three blank lines between the complimentary closing and the writer's identification.

13 Type **Jennifer Garcia** as the writer's identification, and then press [Enter] two times.

14 Type **Enclosure** to indicate that a document is included with the letter. **Save** 🖫 your document, and then compare your screen with Figure 2.26.

FIGURE 2.26

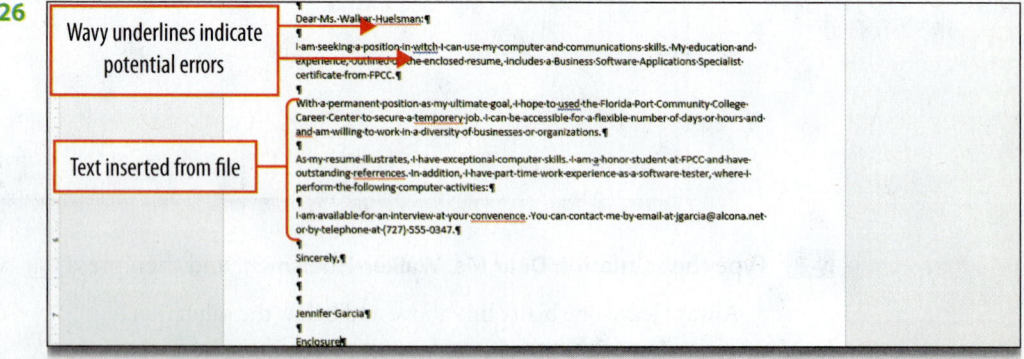

Wavy underlines indicate potential errors

Dear Ms. Walker Huelsman:¶

I am seeking a position in witch I can use my computer and communications skills. My education and experience, outlined on the enclosed resume, includes a Business Software Applications Specialist certificate from FPCC.¶

With a permanent position as my ultimate goal, I hope to used the Florida Port Community College Career Center to secure a temporary job. I can be accessible for a flexible number of days or hours and and am willing to work in a diversity of businesses or organizations.¶

As my resume illustrates, I have exceptional computer skills. I am a honor student at FPCC and have outstanding references. In addition, I have part-time work experience as a software tester, where I perform the following computer activities:¶

I am available for an interview at your convenence. You can contact me by email at jgarcia@alcona.net or by telephone at (727) 555-0347.¶

Sincerely,¶

Jennifer Garcia¶

Enclosure¶

Text inserted from file

Activity 2.17 | Finding and Replacing Text

Use the Find command to locate text in a document quickly. Use the Find and Replace command to make the same change, or to make more than one change at a time, in a document.

1 Press Ctrl + Home to position the insertion point at the beginning of the document.

Because a find operation—or a find and replace operation—begins from the location of the insertion point and proceeds to the end of the document, it is good practice to position the insertion point at the beginning of the document before initiating the command.

2 On the **HOME tab**, in the **Editing group**, click **Find**.

The navigation pane displays on the left side of the screen with a search box at the top of the pane.

ANOTHER WAY Hold down Ctrl and press F.

3 In the **navigation** pane, in the search box, type **ac** If necessary, scroll down slightly in your document to view the entire body text of the letter, and then compare your screen with Figure 2.27.

In the document, the search letters *ac* are selected and highlighted in yellow for both words that begin with the letters *ac* and also for the word *contact* which contains this letter combination. In the navigation pane, the three instances are shown in context—*ac* displays in bold.

FIGURE 2.27

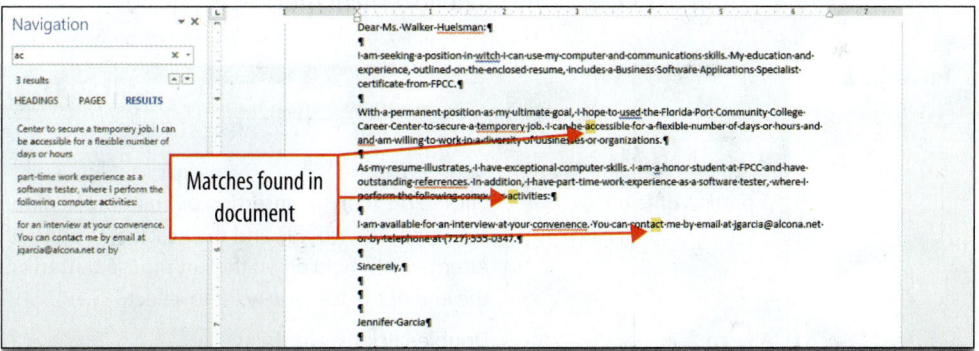

4 Click in the search box again, and type as necessary to display the word *accessible* in the search box.

One match for the search term displays in context in the navigation pane and is highlighted in the document.

5 In the document, double-click the yellow highlighted word *accessible*, and then type **available** to replace the word.

6 Close ✕ the **navigation** pane, and then on the **HOME tab**, in the **Editing group**, click **Replace**.

7 In the **Find and Replace** dialog box, in the **Find what** box, replace the existing text by typing **FPCC** and in the **Replace with** box, type **Florida Port Community College** and then compare your screen with Figure 2.28.

FIGURE 2.28

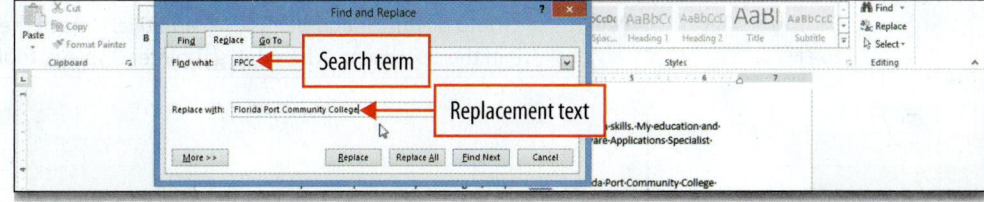

8 In the lower left corner of the dialog box, click **More** to expand the dialog box, and then under **Search Options**, select the **Match case** check box.

The acronym *FPCC* appears in the document two times. In a formal letter, the reader may not know what the acronym means, so you should include the full text instead of an acronym. In this instance, you must select the *Match case* check box so that the replaced text will match the case you typed in the Replace with box, and *not* display in all uppercase letters in the manner of *FPCC*.

9 In the **Find and Replace** dialog box, click **Replace All** to replace both instances of *FPCC*. Click **OK** to close the message box.

10 In the **Find and Replace** dialog box, clear the **Match case** check box, click **Less**, and then **Close** the dialog box. **Save** 🖫 your document.

The Find and Replace dialog box opens with the settings used the last time it was open. Therefore, it is good practice to reset this dialog box to its default settings each time you use it.

Activity 2.18 | Selecting and Moving Text to a New Location

By using Word's ***drag-and-drop*** feature, you can use the mouse to drag selected text from one location to another. This method is most useful when the text you are moving is on the same screen as the destination location.

1 Take a moment to study the table in Figure 2.29 to become familiar with the techniques you can use to select text in a document quickly.

FIGURE 2.29

SELECTING TEXT IN A DOCUMENT	
TO SELECT THIS:	**DO THIS:**
A portion of text	Click to position the insertion point at the beginning of the text you want to select, hold down Shift, and then click at the end of the text you want to select. Alternatively, hold down the left mouse button and drag from the beginning to the end of the text you want to select.
A word	Double-click the word.
A sentence	Hold down Ctrl and click anywhere in the sentence.
A paragraph	Triple-click anywhere in the paragraph; or, move the pointer to the left of the line, into the margin area. When the 𝄢 pointer displays, double-click.
A line	Point to the left of the line. When the 𝄢 pointer displays, click one time.
One character at a time	Position the insertion point to the left of the first character, hold down Shift, and press ← or → as many times as desired.
A string of words	Position the insertion point to the left of the first word, hold down Shift and Ctrl, and then press ← or → as many times as desired.
Consecutive lines	Position the insertion point to the left of the first word, hold down Shift and press ↑ or ↓.
Consecutive paragraphs	Position the insertion point to the left of the first word, hold down Shift and Ctrl and press ↑ or ↓.
The entire document	Hold down Ctrl and press A. Alternatively, move the pointer to the left of any line in the document. When the 𝄢 pointer displays, triple-click.

2 Be sure you can view the entire body of the letter on your screen. In the paragraph that begins *With a permanent position*, in the second line, locate and double-click *days*.

3 Point to the selected word to display the 🔾 pointer.

4 Drag to the right until the dotted vertical line that floats next to the pointer is positioned to the right of the word *hours* in the same line, as shown in Figure 2.30.

FIGURE 2.30

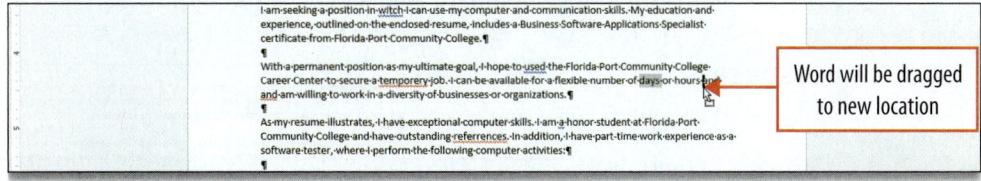

I·am·seeking·a·position·in·witch·I·can·use·my·computer·and·communication·skills.·My·education·and· experience,·outlined·on·the·enclosed·resume,·includes·a·Business·Software·Applications·Specialist· certificate·from·Florida·Port·Community·College.¶
¶
With·a·permanent·position·as·my·ultimate·goal,·I·hope·to·used·the·Florida·Port·Community·College· Career·Center·to·secure·a·temporery·job.·I·can·be·available·for·a·flexible·number·of·days·or·hours·and· and·am·willing·to·work·in·a·diversity·of·businesses·or·organizations.¶
¶
As·my·resume·illustrates,·I·have·exceptional·computer·skills.·I·am·a·honor·student·at·Florida·Port· Community·College·and·have·outstanding·refrrences.·In·addition,·I·have·part·time·work·experience·as·a· software·tester,·where·I·perform·the·following·computer·activities:¶
¶

> Word will be dragged to new location

5 Release the mouse button to move the text. Select *hours* and drag it to the left of the word *or*—the previous location of the word *days*. Click anywhere to deselect the text.

6 Examine the text that you moved, and add or remove spaces as necessary.

7 Hold down [Ctrl], and then in the paragraph that begins *I am available*, click anywhere in the first sentence to select the entire sentence.

8 Drag the selected sentence to the end of the paragraph by positioning the small vertical line that floats with the pointer to the left of the paragraph mark. **Save** 🖫 your document, and then compare your screen with Figure 2.31.

FIGURE 2.31

> Sentence moved to end of paragraph

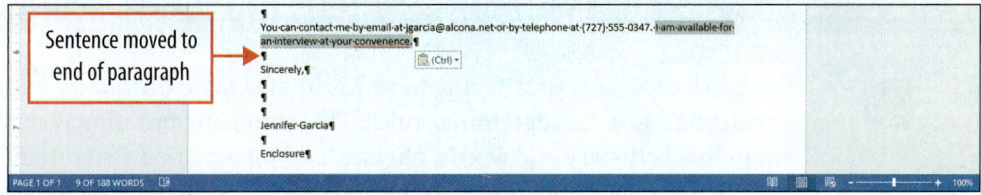

¶
You·can·contact·me·by·email·at·jgarcia@alcona.net·or·by·telephone·at·(727)·555-0347.·I·am·available·for· an·interview·at·your·convenence.¶
¶   🗐 (Ctrl) ▾
Sincerely,¶
¶
¶
Jennifer·Garcia¶
¶
Enclosure¶

Activity 2.19 | Inserting a Table into a Document and Applying a Table Style

1 Locate the paragraph that begins *You can contact me*, and then click to position the insertion point in the blank line above that paragraph. Press [Enter] one time.

2 On the **INSERT tab**, in the **Tables group**, click **Table**. In the **Table** grid, in the third row, click the second square to insert a 2 × 3 table.

3 In the first cell of the table, type **Microsoft Access** and then press [Tab]. Type **Test database queries** and then press [Tab]. Complete the table using the following information:

Microsoft Excel	Enter software test data
Microsoft Word	Create and mail form letters

4 Point slightly outside of the upper left corner of the table to display the **table move handle** button ⊞. With the 🡵 pointer, click one time to select the entire table.

5 On the **LAYOUT tab**, in the **Cell Size group**, click **AutoFit**, and then click **AutoFit Contents** to have Word choose the best column widths for the two columns based on the text you entered.

6 With the table still selected, on the **DESIGN tab**, in the **Table Styles group**, click **More** ⏷.
Under **Plain Tables**, click the second style—**Table Grid Light**.

> Use Table Styles to change the visual style of a table.

7 With the table still selected, on the **HOME tab**, in the **Paragraph group**, click **Center** ▤ to
center the table between the left and right margins. Click anywhere to deselect the table.

8 **Save** ▤ and then compare your screen with Figure 2.32.

FIGURE 2.32

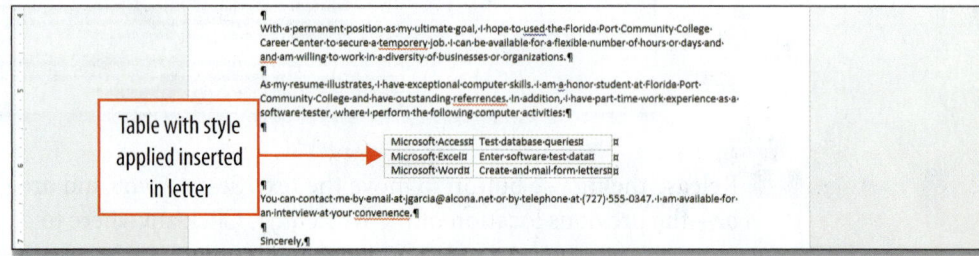

More Knowledge | **Configure Cell Margins in a Table**

You can modify the margins of a cell to increase or decrease the distance between the cell border and the text in the cell. To do so, on the LAYOUT tab, in the
Alignment group, click Cell Margins, and then enter the new margins.

Objective 6 | Use the Proofing Options and Print an Envelope

Video W2-6

Word compares your typing to words in the Office dictionary and compares your phrases and
punctuation to a list of grammar rules. This automatic proofing is set by default. Words that are
not in the dictionary and words, phrases, and punctuation that differ from the grammar rules are
marked with wavy underlines; for example, the misuse of *their*, *there*, and *they're*.

Word will not flag the word *sign* as misspelled even though you intended to type *sing a
song* rather than *sign a song*, because both are words contained within Word's dictionary. Your
own knowledge and proofreading skills are still required, even when using a sophisticated word
processing program like Word.

Activity 2.20 | Checking for Spelling and Grammar Errors

There are two ways to respond to spelling and grammar errors flagged by Word. You can
right-click a flagged word or phrase, and then from the shortcut menu choose a correction
or action. Or, you can initiate the Spelling & Grammar command to display the Spelling and
Grammar pane, which provides more options than the shortcut menus.

ALERT! | **Activating Spelling and Grammar Checking**

If you do not see any wavy red or blue lines under words, the automatic spelling or grammar checking has been turned off on your system. To activate the
spelling and grammar checking, display Backstage view, click Options, click Proofing, and then under *When correcting spelling in Microsoft Office programs*,
select the first four check boxes. Under *When correcting spelling and grammar in Word*, select the first four check boxes, and then click the Writing Style arrow
and click Grammar Only. Under *Exceptions for*, clear both check boxes. To display the flagged spelling and grammar errors, click the Recheck Document button,
and then close the dialog box.

1 Position the body of the letter on your screen, and then examine the text to locate wavy underlines.

> A list of grammar rules applied by a computer program like Word can never be exact, and a computer dictionary cannot contain all known words and proper names. Therefore, you will need to check any words flagged by Word with wavy underlines, and you will also need to proofread for content errors.

2 In the lower left corner of your screen, in the status bar, locate and point to the ⬚ icon to display the ScreenTip *Proofing errors were found. Click to correct.* Compare your screen with Figure 2.33.

> If this button displays, you know there are potential errors identified in the document.

FIGURE 2.33

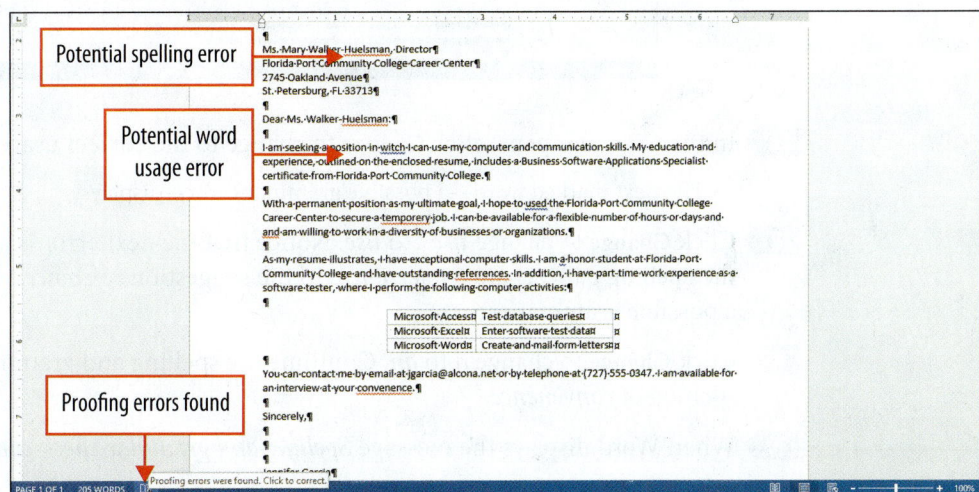

3 In the paragraph that begins *With a permanent*, in the second line, locate the word *temporery* with the wavy red underline. Point to the word and right-click, and then click **temporary** to correct the spelling error.

4 In the next line, locate the word *and* that displays with a wavy red underline, point to the word and right-click, and then on the shortcut menu, click **Delete Repeated Word** to delete the duplicate word.

5 Press Ctrl + Home to move the insertion point to the beginning of the document. Click the **REVIEW tab**, and then in the **Proofing group**, click **Spelling & Grammar** to check the spelling and grammar of the text in the document.

> The Spelling pane displays on the right, and the proper name *Huelsman* is flagged. Word's dictionary contains only very common proper names—unusual names like this one will typically be flagged as a potential spelling error. If this is a name that you frequently type, consider adding it to the dictionary.

↻ ANOTHER WAY   Press F7 to start the Spelling & Grammar command.

6 In the **Spelling** pane, click **Ignore All**. Compare your screen with Figure 2.34.

> The word *witch* is highlighted as a grammar error, and in the Grammar pane, *which* is suggested.

FIGURE 2.34

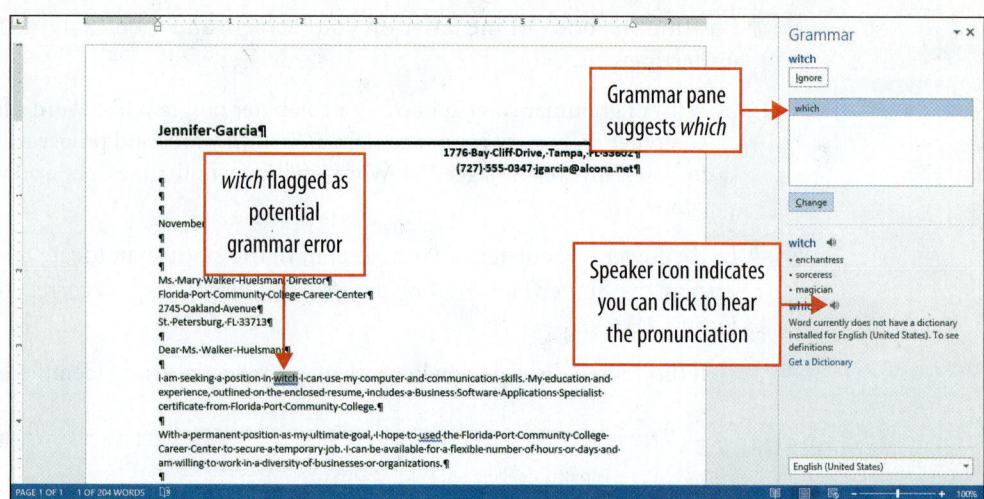

Jennifer-Garcia¶

1776-Bay-Cliff-Drive,-Tampa,-FL-33602-¶
(727)-555-0347-jgarcia@alcona.net¶

witch flagged as potential grammar error

Grammar pane suggests *which*

Speaker icon indicates you can click to hear the pronunciation

7 ▶ In the **Grammar** pane, click **Change** to change to the correct usage *which*.

> The next marked word—a possible grammar error—displays.

8 ▶ Click **Change** to change *used* to *use*. Notice that the next error is a potential spelling error. In the **Spelling** pane, change *referrences* to the suggestion *references*. Notice that the next error is a possible grammar error.

9 ▶ Click **Change** to change *a* to *an*. Continue the spelling and grammar check and correct the spelling of *convenence*.

10 ▶ When Word displays the message *Spelling and grammar check complete*, click **OK**.

11 ▶ **Save** 🖫 your document.

Activity 2.21 | Using the Thesaurus

A **thesaurus** is a research tool that lists **synonyms**—words that have the same or similar meaning to the word you selected.

1 ▶ Scroll so that you can view the body of the letter. In the paragraph that begins *With a permanent*, double-click to select the word *diversity*, and then in the **Proofing** group, click **Thesaurus**.

> The Thesaurus pane displays on the right a list of synonyms; the list will vary in length depending on the selected word.

🔁 **ANOTHER WAY** Right-click the word, on the shortcut menu, point to Synonyms, and then click Thesaurus.

2 ▶ In the **Thesaurus** pane, point to the word *variety*, and then click the arrow that displays. Click **Insert** to change *diversity* to *variety*.

3 ▶ In the paragraph that begins *As my resume*, double-click the word *exceptional*, and then on the ribbon, click **Thesaurus** again.

4 ▶ In the **Thesaurus** pane, point to *excellent*, click the **arrow**, and then click **Insert**. Compare your screen with Figure 2.35.

FIGURE 2.35

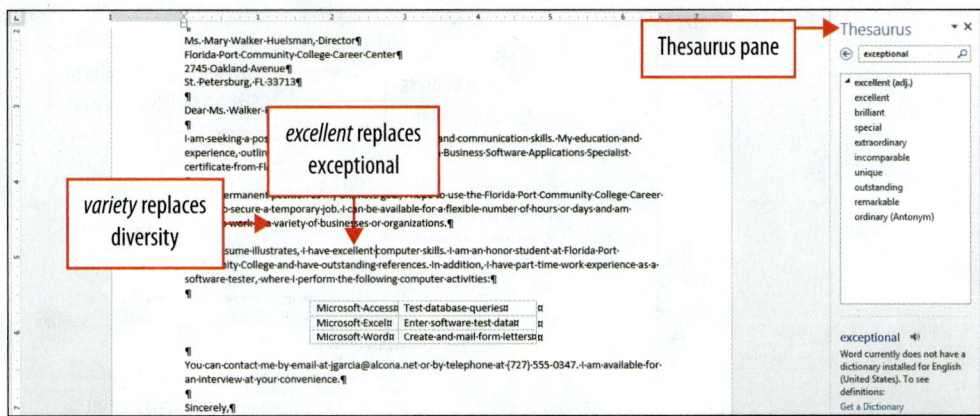

5 ▶ **Close** ✕ the **Thesaurus** pane.

6 ▶ Click the **FILE tab** to display **Backstage** view, and then on the **Info tab**, in the lower right portion of the screen, click **Show All Properties**. If you used your template, notice that it is indicated to the right of *Template*.

7 ▶ In the **Tags** box, type **cover letter** and in the **Subject** box, type your course name and section number. In the **Author** box, be sure your name is indicated and edit if necessary.

8 ▶ On the left, click **Print** to display **Print Preview**. If necessary, return to the document and make any necessary changes.

9 ▶ As directed by your instructor, print your document or submit it electronically. **Save** 🖫 your document and **Close** ✕ Word.

Activity 2.22 | Addressing and Printing an Envelope

Use Word's Envelopes command on the Mailings label to format and print an envelope.

N O T E   **This Is an Optional Activity**

This activity is optional. If you do not have an envelope and printer, or do not want to complete the activity at this time, move to Activity 2.23.

---

1 ▶ Display your **2B_Cover_Letter**, and then select the four lines that comprise the inside address.

2 ▶ On the **MAILINGS tab**, in the **Create group**, click **Envelopes**. Notice that the **Delivery address** contains the selected inside address.

3 ▶ Click in the **Return address** box, and then type **Jennifer Garcia** and press ⏎. Type **1776 Bay Cliff Drive** and then press ⏎. Type **Tampa, FL 33602**

4 ▶ In the lower portion of the **Envelopes and Labels** dialog box, click **Options**, and then compare your screen with Figure 2.36.

The default envelope size is a standard business envelope referred to as a Size 10.

FIGURE 2.36

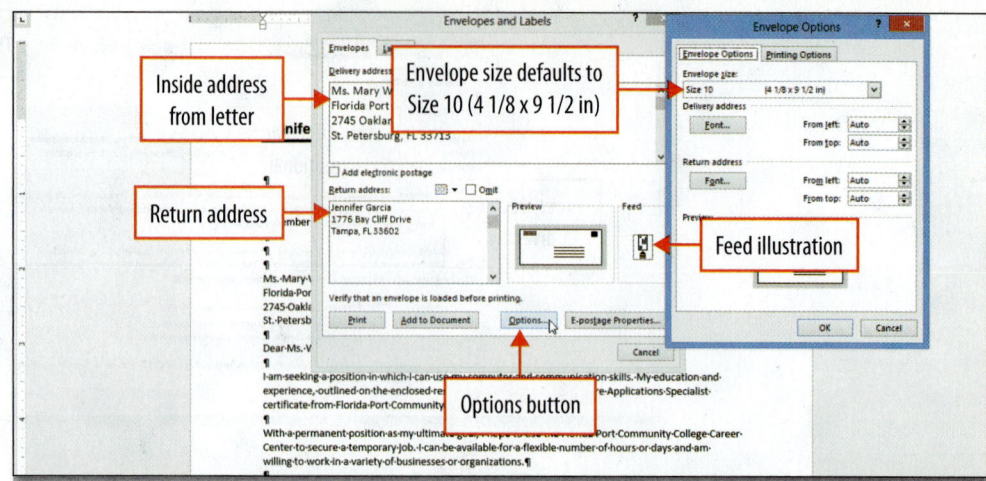

Labels in figure:
- Inside address from letter
- Envelope size defaults to Size 10 (4 1/8 x 9 1/2 in)
- Return address
- Feed illustration
- Options button

5 ▸ Click **OK** to close the **Envelope Options** dialog box. As shown under **Feed**, insert an envelope in your printer and then click **Print**.

Depending on the type and brand of printer you are using, your feed area may vary.

6 ▸ Close your **2B_Cover_Letter**, and then **Close** Word.

Objective 7 Create a Document Using a Predesigned Microsoft Template

Video W2-7

Microsoft provides predesigned templates for letters, calendars, invoices, and other types of documents. Recall that when you open a template, it opens unnamed so that you can reuse it as often as you need to do so.

Activity 2.23 │ Locating and Opening a Template

In this activity, you will use a predesigned template to create a list of references to accompany a resume. References are not included on a resume, because you want to use the resume space for personal information. Most employers do not check references until after the first interview and when they have decided to consider you for a position. Be sure that you have already notified these individuals, asked their permission to use their name as a reference, and then contact them to tell them that a specific employer may be contacting them.

1 ▸ **Start** Word, and then on the opening screen, in the **Search for online templates** box, type **resume references** and press Enter.

2 ▸ Locate the reference list that contains three left-aligned reference items as shown in Figure 2.37.

FIGURE 2.37

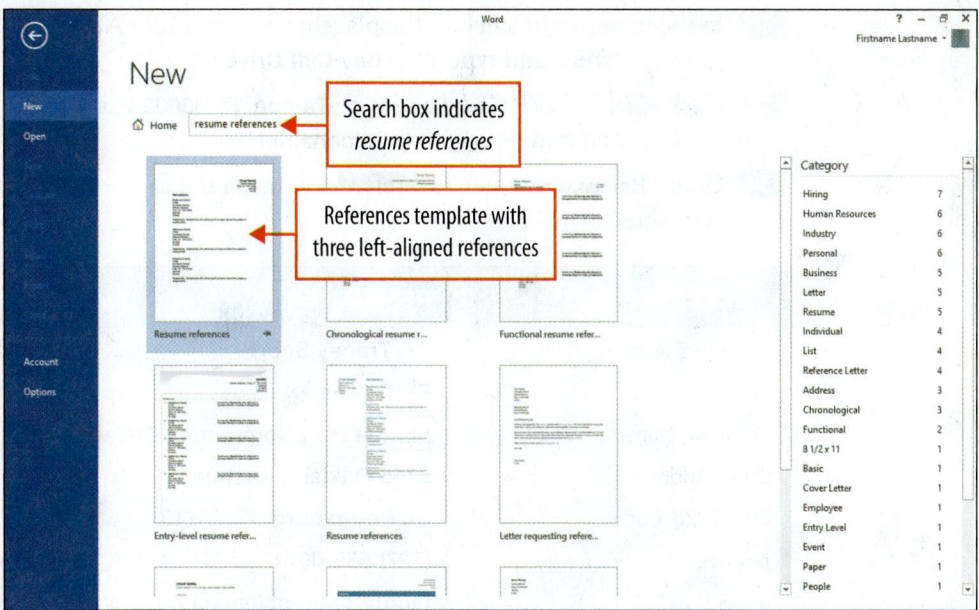

3 ▶ Click the three-item reference template, and then click **Create**. Compare your screen with Figure 2.38.

> The template opens a copy of itself in the form of a new Word document—the title bar indicates *Document* followed by a number. Recall that you are not opening the template itself, and that changes you make to this new document will not affect the contents of the template file.

FIGURE 2.38

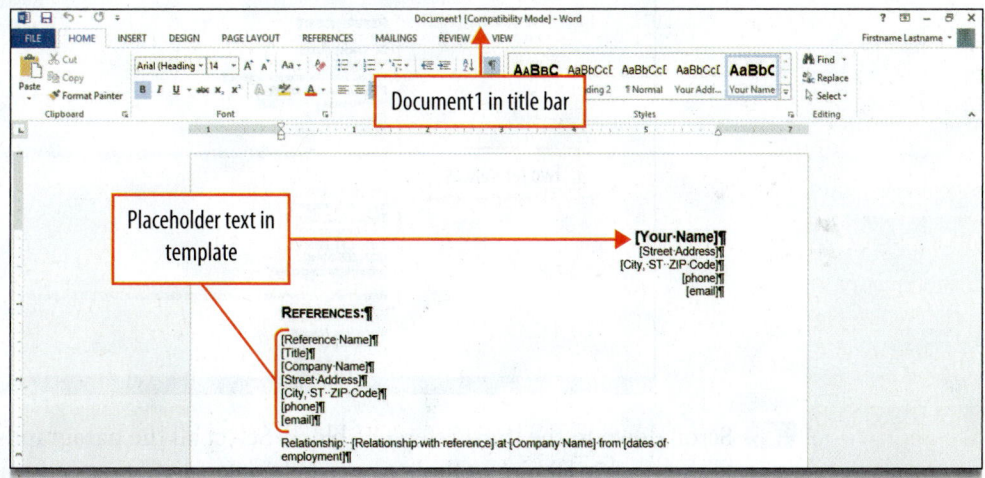

4 ▶ Press F12 to display the **Save As** dialog box. **Save** the document in your **Word Chapter 2** folder as **Lastname_Firstname_2B_Reference_List** and click **Save**. If a message indicates that you will be upgraded to the newest file format, click **OK**.

5 ▶ Add the file name to the footer, and then **Save** 🖫 your document.

Activity 2.24 | Replacing Template Placeholder Text and Removing Controls

After you save the template file as a Word document, you can begin to substitute your own information in the indicated locations. *Placeholder text* is text that indicates the type of information to be entered. Text surrounded by brackets is called a *content control*. There are several different types of content controls, including date, picture, and *text controls*. All of the controls in this template are text controls.

1 In the upper right, click in the placeholder text *[Your Name]* and type **Jennifer Garcia** Click *[Street Address]* and type **1776 Bay Cliff Drive**

2 Click *[City, ST ZIP Code]* and type **Tampa, FL 33602** Click *[phone]* and type **(727) 555-0347** Click *[email]* and type **jgarcia@alcona.net**

3 Under **References**, enter two references using the following information, and then compare your screen with Figure 2.39.

TEMPLATE FIELD	REFERENCE 1	REFERENCE 2
Reference Name	**Dr. Tracey Scott**	**Mr. James Johnson**
Title	**Professor**	**Systems Manager**
Company Name	**Florida Port Community College**	**Tampa Tech Group**
Street Address	**2745 Oakland Avenue**	**Two Tech Plaza**
City, ST ZIP Code	**St. Petersburg, FL 33713**	**Tampa, FL 33602**
phone	**(727) 555-0974**	**(727) 555-0144**
email	**tscott@fpcc-science.edu**	**jjohnson@tech-pro.net**
Relationship with reference	**Professor**	**Supervisor**
Company Name	**Florida Port Community College**	**Tampa Tech Group**
dates of employment	**July 2012 to July 2013**	**July 2013 to present**

FIGURE 2.39

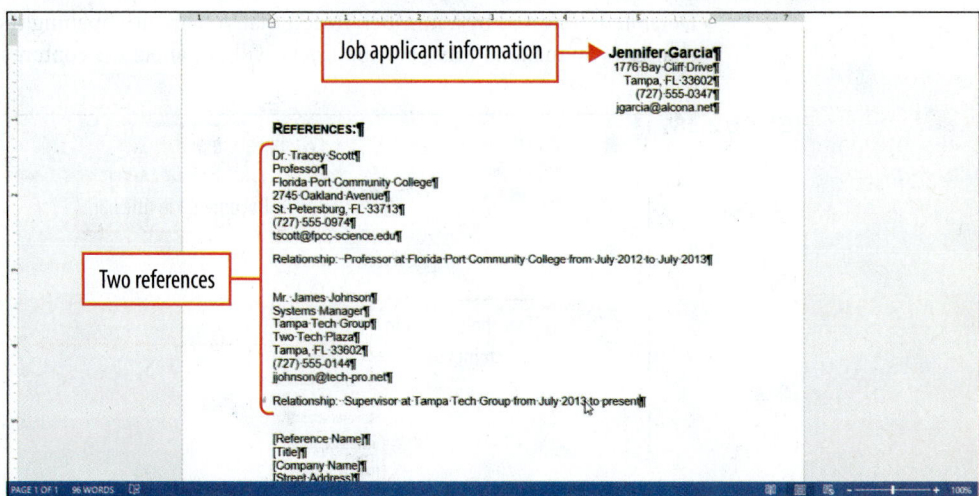

4 Scroll down to the third reference block. Select all the paragraphs of placeholder text, and then press [Del] to delete these unneeded controls; this list will contain only two references.

🔄 **ANOTHER WAY**   Point to a content control, right-click, and then on the shortcut menu, click Remove Content Control.

5 Click **Save** 🖫. Click the **FILE tab**, and then in the lower right portion of the screen, click **Show All Properties**. In the **Tags** box, type **reference list** and in the **Subject** box, type your course name and section number. In the **Author** box, be sure your name is indicated and edit if necessary.

6 On the left, click **Print** to display **Print Preview**. If necessary, return to the document and make any necessary changes.

7 As directed by your instructor, print your document or submit it electronically. **Save** 🖫 your document and **Close** ☒ Word.

END | You have completed Project 2B

Objective | Create a Table in Word Online

You can create and edit tables in Word Online if you are not at a computer on which Word 2013 is installed.

Activity | Creating a Table in Word Online

In this activity, you will use Word Online to create a Word table within a document similar to Project 2B.

1 From the desktop, start Internet Explorer. Navigate to **http://onedrive.com** and then sign in to your Microsoft account. Open your **GO! Web Projects** folder—or create and then open this folder if necessary.

2 On the OneDrive menu bar, click **Upload**. In the **Choose File to Upload** dialog box, navigate to your student data files, click **w02_2B_Web**, and then click **Open**.

3 Point to the uploaded file **w02_2B_Web**, and then right-click. On the shortcut menu, scroll down as necessary and then click **Rename**. Using your own last name and first name, type **Lastname_Firstname_WD_2B_Web** and then press Enter to rename the file.

4 Click the file that you just renamed, and then in the upper left, click **EDIT DOCUMENT**. On the list, click **Edit in Word Online**.

5 Press Ctrl + End to move to the end of the document, and then press Enter.

6 On the **INSERT tab**, in the **Tables group**, click **Table**, and then insert a **3 × 4 Table**.

7 Type **Position** and press Tab. Type **Type** and press Tab. Type **Location** and press Tab.

8 In the second row type **Paralegal** and press Tab. Type **Part-time** and press Tab. Type **Tampa** and press Tab. Compare your screen with Figure A.

9 Type **Legal Records Clerk** and press Tab. Type **Full-time, 2 months** and press Tab. Type **North Tampa** and press Tab.

10 On the ribbon, under **TABLE TOOLS**, click the **LAYOUT tab**, and then in the **Delete group**, click **Delete Row**.

FIGURE A

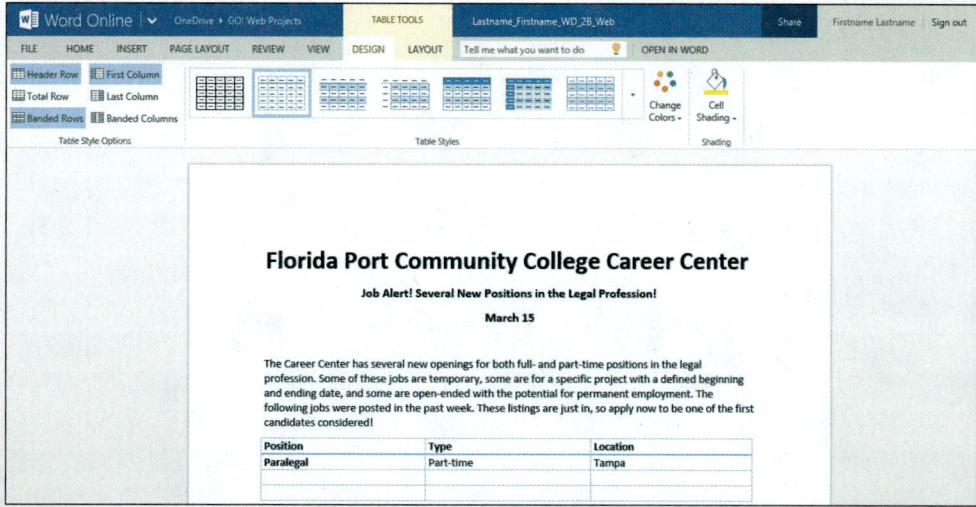

(GO! with Office Online (formerly Web Apps) continues on the next page)

11 Drag to select all the cells in the first row, and then on the **HOME tab**, in the **Styles group**, click **Heading 1**. With the three column titles still selected, in the **Paragraph group**, click **Center** ▤. In the **Font group**, change the Font Color to **Black, Text 1**. Compare your screen with Figure B.

12 Submit the file as directed by your instructor. Sign out of your OneDrive and close Internet Explorer.

FIGURE B

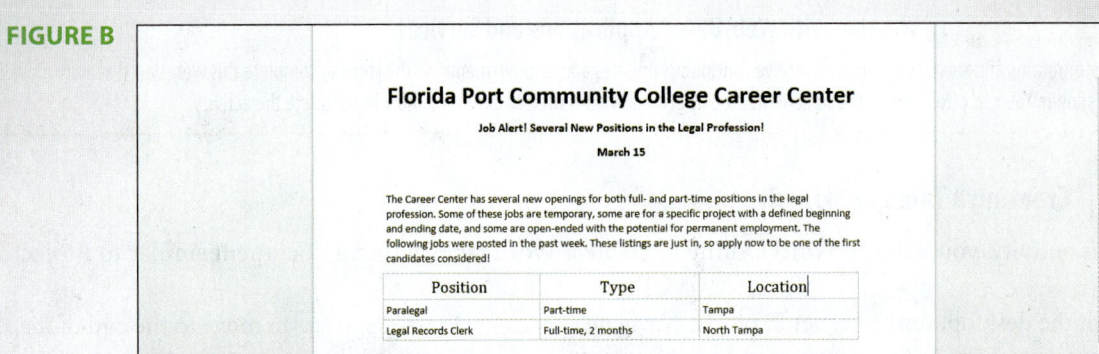

Andrew Rodriguez / Fotolia; FotolEdhar/ Fotolia; apops/ Fotolia; Yuri Arcurs/ Fotolia

Office 365 combines tools for collaboration and productivity and delivers them to multiple users in an organization by using *cloud computing*—applications and services that are accessed over the Internet with multiple devices. For example, one cloud service with which you might be familiar is *OneDrive*, a free web-based application with which you can save, store, organize, and share files online. This cloud service is available for anyone that has a free Microsoft account.

Another cloud service from Microsoft is *Office Online*. These are the online companions to the desktop versions of Microsoft Office Word, Excel, PowerPoint, and OneNote that enable you to create, access, share, and perform light editing on Microsoft Office documents from any device that connects to the Internet and uses a supported *web browser*. A web browser is software, such as Internet Explorer, Firefox, Safari, or Chrome, that displays web pages.

For an organization, cloud computing enables the addition of services without investing in additional hardware and software. For you as a team member, you can simply use your web browser to access, edit, store, and share files. You do not need to have a full version of Office installed on your computer to do this. You have all the tools and security that large organizations have!

When you use using Office 365, your email and storage servers are hosted by Microsoft. Your organization gets business-class security from Microsoft—a large, well-established company. Sophisticated security and data management features are built into Office 365 so that you can control *permissions*—access rights that define the ability of an individual or group to view or make changes to documents—and provide secure email and communications.

Activity | Using Lync to Collaborate by Using a Video Call

This group project relates to the **Bell Orchid Hotels**. If your instructor assigns this project to your class, you can expect to use **Lync** in **Office 365** to collaborate on the following tasks for this chapter:

- If you are in the **Accounting Group**, you and your teammates will conduct a video call to discuss and agree on the letter that will be sent to shareholders.

- If you are in the **Engineering Group**, you and your teammates will conduct a video call to discuss and agree on the letter that will be sent to the three insurance companies that cover the hotel properties.

- If you are in the **Food and Beverage Group**, you and your teammates will conduct a video call to discuss and agree on the letter that will be sent to a customer planning a banquet.

- If you are in the **Human Resources Group**, you and your teammates will conduct a video call to discuss and agree on the memo for employees regarding the new employee newsletter.

- If you are in the **Operations Group**, you and your teammates will conduct a video call to discuss and agree on the letter that will be sent to three job applicants.

- If you are in the **Sales and Marking Group**, you and your teammates will conduct a video call to discuss and agree on the letter that will be sent to 20 groups of professional associations.

FIGURE A

END OF CHAPTER

SUMMARY

Word tables enable you to present information in a logical and orderly format. Each cell in a Word table behaves like a document; as you type in a cell, wordwrap moves text to the next line.

A good source of information for resume formats is a business communications textbook. A simple two-column table created in Word is suitable to create an appropriate resume for a recent college graduate.

Use Word's Office Presentation Service to present a Word document to others who can watch in a web browser. Word automatically creates a link to your document that you can share with others via email.

A template is useful because it has a predefined document structure and defined settings such as font, margins, and available styles. On Word's opening screen, you can select from thousands of templates.

GO! LEARN IT ONLINE

Review the concepts and key terms in this chapter by completing these online challenges, which you can find at **www.pearsonhighered.com/go**.

Matching and Multiple Choice: Answer matching and multiple choice questions to test what you learned in this chapter. MyITLab®

Crossword Puzzle: Spell out the words that match the numbered clues, and put them in the puzzle squares.

Flipboard: Flip through the definitions of the key terms in this chapter and match them with the correct term.

GO! FOR JOB SUCCESS

Video: Cover Letter and Resume Tips

Your instructor may assign this video to your class, and then ask you to think about, or discuss with your classmates, these questions:

FotolEdhar / Fotolia

A cover letter should contain different but complimentary information than the facts on your resume and be tailored to the specific job you are applying for. Name two different things that you could mention in a cover letter.

What type of information belongs in the Career Objective portion of your resume?

When is it best to use a chronological resume layout, and when is it appropriate to use a functional resume layout?

END OF CHAPTER

REVIEW AND ASSESSMENT GUIDE FOR WORD CHAPTER 2

Your instructor may assign one or more of these projects to help you review the chapter and assess your mastery and understanding of the chapter.

Project	Apply Skills from These Chapter Objectives	Project Type	Project Location
Review and Assessment Guide for Word Chapter 2			
2C	Objectives 1-3 from Project 2A	**2C Skills Review** A guided review of the skills from Project 2A.	On the following pages
2D	Objectives 4-7 from Project 2B	**2D Skills Review** A guided review of the skills from Project 2B.	On the following pages
2E	Objectives 1-3 from Project 2A	**2E Mastery (Grader Project)** A demonstration of your mastery of the skills in Project 2A with extensive decision making.	In MyITLab and on the following pages
2F	Objectives 4-7 from Project 2B	**2F Mastery (Grader Project)** A demonstration of your mastery of the skills in Project 2B with extensive decision making.	In MyITLab and on the following pages
2G	Objectives 1-7 from Projects 2A and 2B	**2G Mastery (Grader Project)** A demonstration of your mastery of the skills in Projects 2A and 2B with extensive decision making.	In MyITLab and on the following pages
2H	Combination of Objectives from Projects 2A and 2B	**2H GO! Fix It** A demonstration of your mastery of the skills in Projects 2A and 2B by creating a correct result from a document that contains errors you must find.	Online
2I	Combination of Objectives from Projects 2A and 2B	**2I GO! Make It** A demonstration of your mastery of the skills in Projects 2A and 2B by creating a result from a supplied picture.	Online
2J	Combination of Objectives from Projects 2A and 2B	**2J GO! Solve It** A demonstration of your mastery of the skills in Projects 2A and 2B, your decision-making skills, and your critical thinking skills. A task-specific rubric helps you self-assess your result.	Online
2K	Combination of Objectives from Projects 2A and 2B	**2K GO! Solve It** A demonstration of your mastery of the skills in Projects 2A and 2B, your decision-making skills, and your critical thinking skills. A task-specific rubric helps you self-assess your result.	On the following pages
2L	Combination of Objectives from Projects 2A and 2B	**2L GO! Think** A demonstration of your understanding of the chapter concepts applied in a manner that you would outside of college. An analytic rubric helps you and your instructor grade the quality of your work by comparing it to the work an expert in the discipline would create.	On the following pages
2M	Combination of Objectives from Projects 2A and 2B	**2M GO! Think** A demonstration of your understanding of the chapter concepts applied in a manner that you would outside of college. An analytic rubric helps you and your instructor grade the quality of your work by comparing it to the work an expert in the discipline would create.	Online
2N	Combination of Objectives from Projects 2A and 2B	**2N You and GO!** A demonstration of your understanding of the chapter concepts applied in a manner that you would in a personal situation. An analytic rubric helps you and your instructor grade the quality of your work.	Online
2O	Combination of Objectives from Projects 2A and 2B	**2O Cumulative Group Project for Word Chapter 2** A demonstration of your understanding of concepts and your ability to work collaboratively in a group role-playing assessment, requiring both collaboration and self-management.	Online

GLOSSARY

GLOSSARY OF CHAPTER KEY TERMS

AutoCorrect A feature that corrects common typing and spelling errors as you type, for example changing *teh* to *the*.

Body The text of a letter.

Cell The box at the intersection of a row and column in a Word table.

Cloud computing Applications and services that are accessed over the Internet with multiple devices.

Complimentary closing A parting farewell in a business letter.

Content control In a template, an area indicated by placeholder text that can be used to add text, pictures, dates, or lists.

Cover letter A document that you send with your resume to provide additional information about your skills and experience.

Date & Time A command with which you can automatically insert the current date and time into a document in a variety of formats.

Dateline The first line in a business letter that contains the current date and which is positioned just below the letterhead if a letterhead is used.

Drag-and-drop A technique by which you can move, by dragging, selected text from one location in a document to another.

Enclosures Additional documents included with a business letter.

Inside address The name and address of the person receiving the letter and positioned below the date line.

Letterhead The personal or company information that displays at the top of a letter.

No Paragraph Style The built-in paragraph style—available from the Paragraph Spacing command—that inserts *no* extra space before or after a paragraph and uses line spacing of 1.

Normal template The template that serves as a basis for all Word documents.

Office Presentation Service A Word feature to present your Word document to others who can watch in a web browser.

One-click Row/Column Insertion A Word table feature with which you can insert a new row or column by pointing to the desired location and then clicking.

Placeholder text The text in a content control that indicates the type of information to be entered in a specific location.

Salutation The greeting line of a business letter.

Single spacing The common name for line spacing in which there is *no* extra space before or after a paragraph and that uses line spacing of 1.

Skype A Microsoft product with which you can make voice calls, make video calls, transfer files, or send messages— including instant message and text messages—over the Internet.

Subject line The optional line following the inside address in a business letter that states the purpose of the letter.

Synonyms Words with the same or similar meaning.

Table An arrangement of information organized into rows and columns.

Template An existing document that you use as a starting point for a new document; it opens a copy of itself, unnamed, and then you use the structure—and possibly some content, such as headings—as the starting point for a new document.

Text control A content control that accepts only a text entry.

Thesaurus A research tool that provides a list of synonyms.

Writer's identification The name and title of the author of a letter, placed near the bottom of the letter under the complimentary closing—also referred to as the *writer's signature block*.

Writer's signature block The name and title of the author of a letter, placed near the bottom of the letter, under the complimentary closing—also referred to as the *writer's identification*.

CHAPTER REVIEW

Skills Review | Project 2C Student Resume

Apply 2A skills from these Objectives:

1 Create a Table
2 Format a Table
3 Present a Word Document Online

In the following Skills Review, you will use a table to create a resume for Ashley Kent. Your completed resume will look similar to the one shown in Figure 2.40.

PROJECT FILES

Build from Scratch

For Project 2C, you will need the following files:

New blank Word document
w02C_Skills
w02C_Experience

You will save your document as:

Lastname_Firstname_2C_Student_Resume

PROJECT RESULTS

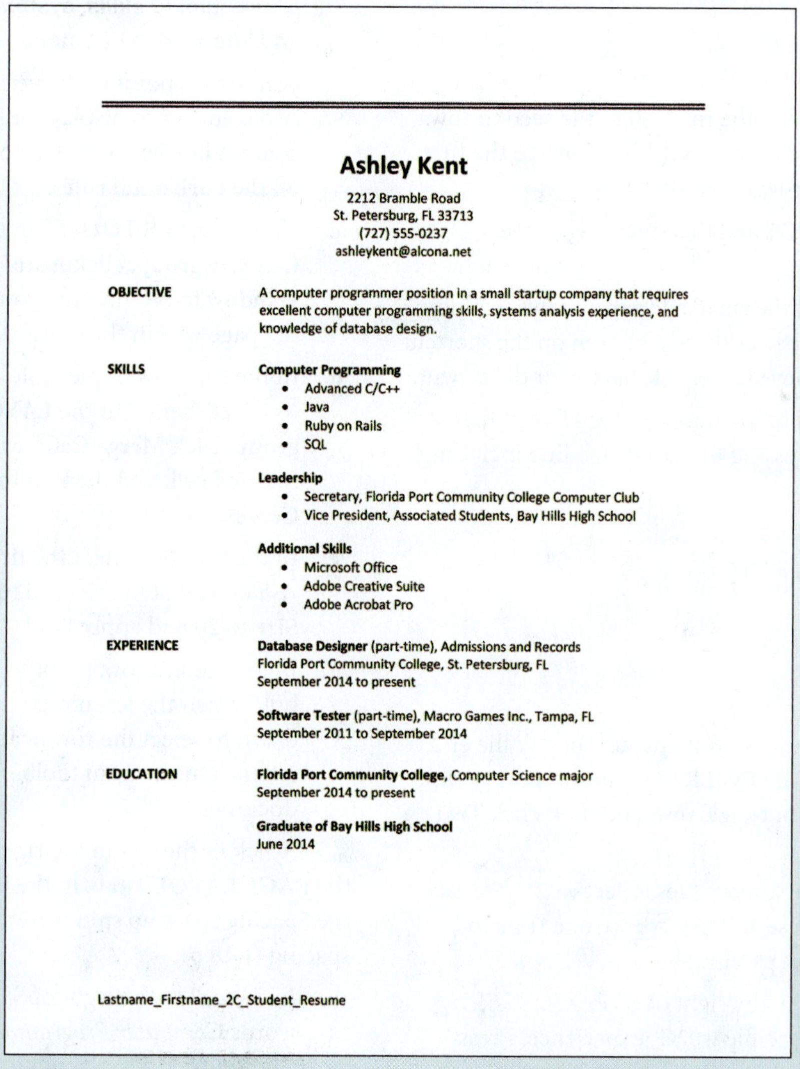

Ashley Kent

2212 Bramble Road
St. Petersburg, FL 33713
(727) 555-0237
ashleykent@alcona.net

OBJECTIVE   A computer programmer position in a small startup company that requires excellent computer programming skills, systems analysis experience, and knowledge of database design.

SKILLS   **Computer Programming**
- Advanced C/C++
- Java
- Ruby on Rails
- SQL

Leadership
- Secretary, Florida Port Community College Computer Club
- Vice President, Associated Students, Bay Hills High School

Additional Skills
- Microsoft Office
- Adobe Creative Suite
- Adobe Acrobat Pro

EXPERIENCE   **Database Designer** (part-time), Admissions and Records
Florida Port Community College, St. Petersburg, FL
September 2014 to present

Software Tester (part-time), Macro Games Inc., Tampa, FL
September 2011 to September 2014

EDUCATION   **Florida Port Community College**, Computer Science major
September 2014 to present

Graduate of Bay Hills High School
June 2014

Lastname_Firstname_2C_Student_Resume

FIGURE 2.40

(Project 2C Student Resume continues on the next page)

CHAPTER REVIEW

1 **Start** Word and display a blank document. Be sure that formatting marks and rulers display. **Save** the document in your **Word Chapter 2** folder as Lastname_Firstname_2C_Student_Resume

a. Add the file name to the footer, and then close the footer area. Click the **INSERT tab**, and then in the **Tables group**, click **Table**. In the **Table** grid, in the fourth row, click the second square to insert a **2 × 4** table.

b. In the first cell of the table, type **Ashley Kent** and then press Enter. Type the following text, pressing Enter after each line *except* the last line:

2212 Bramble Road

St. Petersburg, FL 33713

(727) 555-0237

ashleykent@alcona.net

c. Press ↓ to move to the first cell in the second row. Type **SKILLS** and then press ↓ to move to the first cell in the third row.

d. Type **EXPERIENCE** and then press ↓. Type **EDUCATION**

e. In the first cell, if the email address displays in blue, right-click the email address, and then on the shortcut menu, click **Remove Hyperlink**. **Save** your document.

2 Click in the cell to the right of *SKILLS*, and then type the following, pressing Enter after each line including the last line:

Computer Programming

Advanced C/C++

Java

Ruby on Rails

SQL

a. With the insertion point in the new line at the end of the cell, click the **INSERT tab**. In the **Text group**, click the **Object button arrow**, and then click **Text from File**.

b. Navigate to your student files, select **w02C_Skills**, and then click **Insert**. Press Backspace one time to remove the blank paragraph.

c. Click in the cell to the right of *EXPERIENCE*, and then insert the file **w02C_Experience**. Press Backspace one time to remove the blank line.

d. Click in the cell to the right of *EDUCATION*, and then type the following, pressing Enter after all lines *except* the last line:

Florida Port Community College, Computer Science major

September 2014 to present

Graduate of Bay Hills High School

June 2014

3 Point to the upper left corner of the *SKILLS* cell, and then click the **Row Insertion** button. In the first cell of the new row, type **OBJECTIVE** and then press Tab.

a. Type **A computer programmer position in a small startup company that requires excellent computer programming skills, systems analysis experience, and knowledge of database design.**

b. In any row, point to the vertical border between the two columns to display the ✛ pointer. Drag the column border to the left to approximately **1.5 inches on the horizontal ruler**.

c. Under **TABLE TOOLS**, on the **LAYOUT tab**, in the **Cell Size group**, click **AutoFit**, and then click **AutoFit Window** to be sure that your table stretches across the page within the margins.

d. In the first row of the table, drag across both cells to select them. On the **LAYOUT tab**, in the **Merge group**, click **Merge Cells**. Right-click over the selected cell, and then on the mini toolbar, click **Center**.

e. In the top row, select the first paragraph of text— *Ashley Kent*. On the mini toolbar, increase the **Font Size** to **20** and apply **Bold**.

f. In the second row, point to the word *OBJECTIVE*, hold down the left mouse button, and then drag down to select the row headings in uppercase letters. On the mini toolbar, click **Bold**. **Save** your document.

4 Click in the cell to the right of *OBJECTIVE*. On the **PAGE LAYOUT tab**, in the **Paragraph group**, click the **Spacing After up spin arrow** three times to change the spacing to **18 pt**.

a. In the cell to the right of *SKILLS*, apply **Bold** to the words *Computer Programming, Leadership,* and *Additional Skills*. Then, under each bold heading in

(Project 2C Student Resume continues on the next page)

the cell, select the lines of text, and create a bulleted list.

b. In the first two bulleted lists, click in the last bullet item, and then on the **PAGE LAYOUT tab**, in the **Paragraph group**, set the **Spacing After** to **12 pt**.

c. In the last bulleted list, click in the last bullet item, and then set the **Spacing After** to **18 pt**.

d. In the cell to the right of *EXPERIENCE*, apply **Bold** to *Database Designer* and *Software Tester*. Click in the line *September 2014 to present* and apply **Spacing After** of **12 pt**. Click in the line *September 2011 to September 2014* and apply **Spacing After** of **18 pt**.

e. In the cell to the right of *EDUCATION*, apply **Bold** to *Florida Port Community College* and *Graduate of Bay Hills High School*.

f. In the same cell, click in the line *September 2014 to present* and apply **Spacing After** of **12 pt**.

g. In the first row, click in the last line—*ashleykent@ alcona.net*—and then change the **Spacing After** to **18 pt**. Click in the first line—*Ashley Kent*—and set the **Spacing Before** to **30 pt** and the **Spacing After** to **6 pt**.

5 Point to the upper left corner of the table, and then click the **table move handle** ⊞ to select the entire table. Under **TABLE TOOLS**, on the **DESIGN tab**, in the **Table**

Styles group, click the **Borders button arrow**, and then click **No Border**.

a. In the **Table Styles group**, click the **Borders button arrow** again, and then at the bottom of the gallery, click **Borders and Shading**. In the **Borders and Shading** dialog box, under **Setting**, click **Custom**. Under **Style**, scroll down slightly, and then click the style with two equal lines.

b. Click the **Width arrow**, and then click **1 1/2 pt**. Under **Preview**, click the top border of the preview box, and then click **OK**.

c. Click the **FILE tab** to display **Backstage** view, and then in the lower right portion of the screen, click **Show All Properties**. In the **Tags** box, type **resume, table** and in the **Subject** box, type your course name and section number. In the **Author** box, be sure your name is indicated and edit if necessary.

d. On the left, click **Print** to display **Print Preview**. If necessary, return to the document and make any necessary changes.

e. **Save** 💾 your document, and then if you want to do so, present your document online to a fellow classmate. Then as directed by your instructor, print your document or submit it electronically. **Close** Word.

> **END | You have completed Project 2C**

CHAPTER REVIEW

Skills Review   Project 2D Cover Letter and Reference List

In the following Skills Review, you will create a letterhead, save the letterhead as a custom Word template, and then use the letterhead to create a cover letter to accompany a resume. You will also create a list of references from a Microsoft predesigned template and, if you have an envelope and printer available, format and print an envelope. Your completed documents will look similar to Figure 2.41.

PROJECT FILES

Build from Scratch

For Project 2D, you will need the following files:

New blank Word document
w02D_Cover_Letter_Text

You will save your documents as:

Lastname_Firstname_2D_Cover_Letter
Lastname_Firstname_2D_Reference_List

PROJECT RESULTS

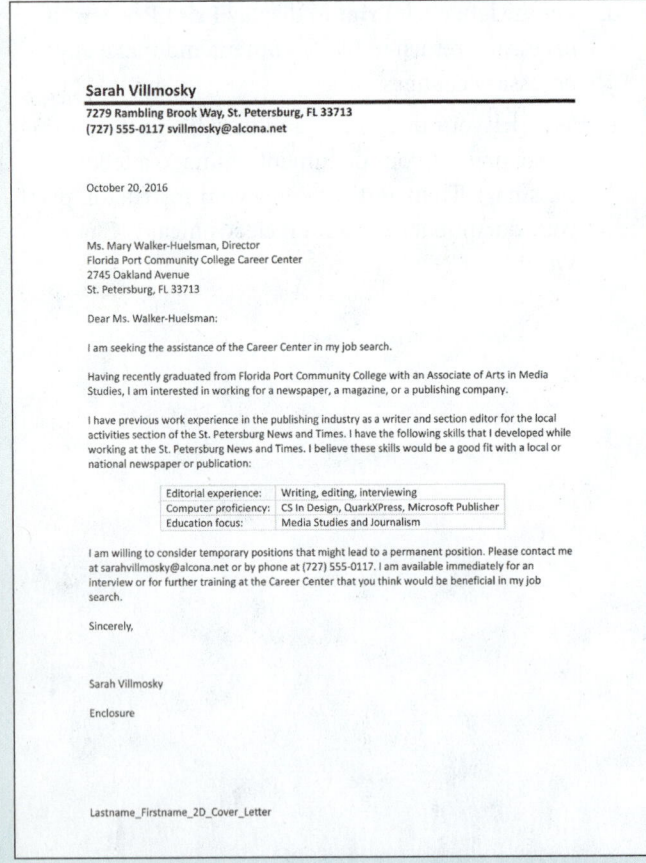

FIGURE 2.41

(Project 2D Cover Letter and Reference List continues on the next page)

CHAPTER REVIEW

1 **Start** Word and display a blank document; be sure that formatting marks and rulers display. On the **DESIGN tab**, in the **Document Formatting group**, click **Paragraph Spacing**, and then click **No Paragraph Space**.

a. Type **Sarah Villmosky** and then press Enter. Type **7279 Rambling Brook Way, St. Petersburg, FL 33713** and then press Enter.

b. Type **(727) 555-0117 svillmosky@alcona.net** and then press Enter. If the web address changes to blue text, right-click the web address, and then click **Remove Hyperlink**.

c. Select the first paragraph—*Sarah Villmosky*—and then on the mini toolbar, apply **Bold**, and change the **Font Size** to **16**.

d. Select the second and third paragraphs, and then on the mini toolbar, apply **Bold**, and change the **Font Size** to **12**.

e. Click anywhere in the first paragraph—*Sarah Villmosky*. On the **HOME tab**, in the **Paragraph group**, click the **Borders button arrow**, and then click **Borders and Shading**. Under **Style**, click the first style—a single solid line. Click the **Width arrow**, and then click **3 pt**. In the **Preview** area, click the bottom border, and then click **OK**.

f. Press F12 to display the **Save As** dialog box. In the lower portion of the dialog box, in the **Save as type** box, click the arrow, and then click **Word Template**. In the **File name** box, type **Lastname_Firstname_2D_Letterhead_Template** and then click **Save** to save the custom Word template in the default path, which is the Templates folder on the hard drive of your computer.

g. Click the **FILE tab** to display **Backstage** view, and then click **Close** to close the file but leave Word open.

h. With Word open but no documents displayed, click the **FILE tab**, and then click **New**. Under **Suggested searches**, click **PERSONAL**, and then locate and click the letterhead template that you just created.

i. Press F12 to display the **Save As** dialog box, navigate to your **Word Chapter 2** folder, and then **Save** the file as **Lastname_Firstname_2D_Cover_Letter**

j. On the **INSERT tab**, in the **Header & Footer group**, click **Footer**, click **Edit Footer**, and then in the **Insert**

group, click **Document Info**. Click **File Name**, and then click **Close Header and Footer**. Click **Save**.

2 Click the **FILE tab**. On the left, click **Options**. On the left side of the **Word Options** dialog box, click **Proofing**, and then under **AutoCorrect options**, click the **AutoCorrect Options** button.

a. In the **AutoCorrect** dialog box, click the **AutoCorrect tab**. Under **Replace**, type the misspelled word **assistence** and under **With**, type **assistance** Click **Add**. If the entry already exists, click **Replace instead**, and then click **Yes**. Click **OK** two times to close the dialog boxes.

b. Press Ctrl + End, and then press Enter three times. On the **INSERT tab**, in the **Text group**, click **Date & Time**, and then click the third date format. Click **OK**.

c. Press Enter four times. Type the following inside address using four lines, but do *not* press Enter after the last line:

Ms. Mary Walker-Huelsman, Director

Florida Port Community College Career Center

2745 Oakland Avenue

St. Petersburg, FL 33713

d. Press Enter two times, type **Dear Ms. Walker-Huelsman:** and then press Enter two times. Type, exactly as shown with the intentional misspelling, and then watch *assistence* as you press Spacebar: **I am seeking the assistence**

e. Type **of the Career Center in my job search.** Press Enter two times.

f. On the **INSERT tab**, in the **Text Group**, click the **Object button arrow**, and then click **Text from File**. From your student files, locate and insert the file **w02D_Cover_Letter_Text**.

g. Scroll to view the lower portion of the page, and be sure your insertion point is in the empty paragraph mark at the end. Press Enter, type **Sincerely,** and then press Enter four times. Type **Sarah Villmosky** and press Enter two times. Type **Enclosure** and then **Save** your document.

h. Press Ctrl + Home. On the **HOME tab**, in the **Editing group**, click **Find**. In the **navigation** pane, click in the search box, and then type **journalism** In the letter,

(Project 2D Cover Letter and Reference List continues on the next page)

CHAPTER REVIEW

double-click the yellow highlighted word *Journalism* and type **Media Studies**

i. **Close** the **navigation** pane, and then on the **HOME tab**, in the **Editing group**, click **Replace**. In the **Find and Replace** dialog box, in the **Find what** box, replace the existing text by typing **SPNT** In the **Replace with** box, type **St. Petersburg News and Times** Click **More** to expand the dialog box, select the **Match case** check box, click **Replace All**, and then click **OK**. **Close** the **Find and Replace** dialog box.

j. In the paragraph that begins *I am available*, hold down Ctrl, and then click anywhere in the first sentence. Drag the selected sentence to the end of the paragraph by positioning the small vertical line that floats with the point to the left of the paragraph mark.

3 ▸ Below the paragraph that begins *I have previous*, click to position the insertion point in the blank paragraph, and then press Enter one time. On the **INSERT tab**, in the **Tables group**, click **Table**. In the **Table grid**, in the third row, click the second square to insert a 2 × 3 table. Type the following information in the table:

Editorial experience:	Writing, editing, interviewing
Computer proficiency:	CS In Design, QuarkXPress, Microsoft Publisher
Education focus:	Media Studies and Journalism

a. Point outside of the upper left corner of the table and click the **table move handle** button to select the entire table. On the **LAYOUT tab**, in the **Cell Size group**, click **AutoFit**, and then click **AutoFit Contents**.

b. With the table selected, on the **DESIGN tab**, in the **Table Styles group**, click **More** ▾. Under **Plain Tables**, click the second style—**Table Grid Light**.

c. With the table still selected, on the **HOME tab**, in the **Paragraphs group**, click **Center**. **Save** your document.

4 ▸ Press Ctrl + Home. On the **REVIEW tab**, in the **Proofing group**, click **Spelling & Grammar**. For the spelling of *Villmosky*, in the **Spelling** pane, click **Ignore All**. For the spelling of *Huelsman*, click **Ignore All**.

a. For the grammar error *a*, click **Change**. Click **Change** to correct the misspelling of *intrested*. Click **Delete** to delete the duplicated word *for*. Change *activitys* to *activities*. Change *benificial* to *beneficial*. Click **OK** when the Spelling & Grammar check is complete.

b. In the paragraph that begins *I am willing*, in the third line, double-click the word *preparation*. In the **Proofing group**, click **Thesaurus**.

c. In the **Thesaurus** pane, point to *training*, click the arrow, and then click **Insert**. **Close** the **Thesaurus** pane.

d. Click **FILE tab**, and then in the lower right portion of the screen, click **Show All Properties**. In the **Tags** box, type **cover letter** and in the **Subject** box, type your course name and section number.

e. In the **Author** box, be sure your name is indicated and edit if necessary. On the left, click **Print**. If necessary, return to the document and make any necessary changes. **Save** your document, and then **Close** Word.

5 ▸ **Start** Word, and then on the opening screen, in the **Search online templates** box, type **resume references** and press Enter. Click the reference list that contains three left-aligned reference items, and then click **Create**.

a. Press F12 to display the **Save As** dialog box. **Save** the document in your **Word Chapter 2** folder as **Lastname_Firstname_2D_Reference_List** A message may indicate that the file will be upgraded to the newest file format.

b. Add the file name to the footer.

c. In the upper right, click in the placeholder text *[Your Name]* and type **Sarah Villmosky** Click *[Street Address]* and type **7279 Rambling Brook Way**

d. Click *[City, ST ZIP Code]* and type **St. Petersburg, FL 33713** Click *[phone]* and type **(727) 555-0177** Click *[email]* and type **svillmosky@alcona.net**

(Project 2D Cover Letter and Reference List continues on the next page)

CHAPTER REVIEW

6 Under **References**, enter two references using the information in Table 1:

a. Delete the remaining template controls.

b. Click the **FILE tab**, click **Show All Properties**, and then in the **Tags** box, type **reference list** and in the **Subject** box type your course name and section number. In the **Author** box, be sure your name is indicated and edit if necessary.

c. On the left, click **Print**. If necessary, return to the document and make any changes. Click **Save**. As directed by your instructor, print or submit electronically the two documents that are the results of this project. **Close** Word.

TABLE 1

Template Field	Reference 1	Reference 2
Reference Name	**Dr. Thomas Robins**	**Ms. Janice Nguyen**
Title	**Professor**	**Editor**
Company Name	**Florida Port Community College**	**St. Petersburg News and Times**
Street Address	**2745 Oakland Avenue**	**One Gateway Center**
City, ST ZIP Code	**St. Petersburg, FL 33713**	**St. Petersburg, FL 33713**
phone	**(727) 555-0902**	**(727) 555-0932**
email	**trobins@fpcc-english.edu**	**jnguyen@spnt-editorial.net**
Relationship with reference	**Professor**	**Editor**
Company Name	**Florida Port Community College**	**St. Petersburg News and Times**
dates of employment	**July 2012 to July 2013**	**July 2013 to present**

END | You have completed Project 2D

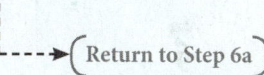

Return to Step 6a

CONTENT-BASED ASSESSMENTS

Apply 2A skills from these Objectives:

1 Create a Table
2 Format a Table
3 Present a Word Document Online

Build from Scratch

In the following Mastering Word project, you will create an announcement for new job postings at the Career Center. Your completed document will look similar to Figure 2.42.

PROJECT FILES

For Project 2E, you will need the following files:

New blank Word document
w02E_New_Jobs

You will save your document as:

Lastname_Firstname_2E_Job_Listings

PROJECT RESULTS

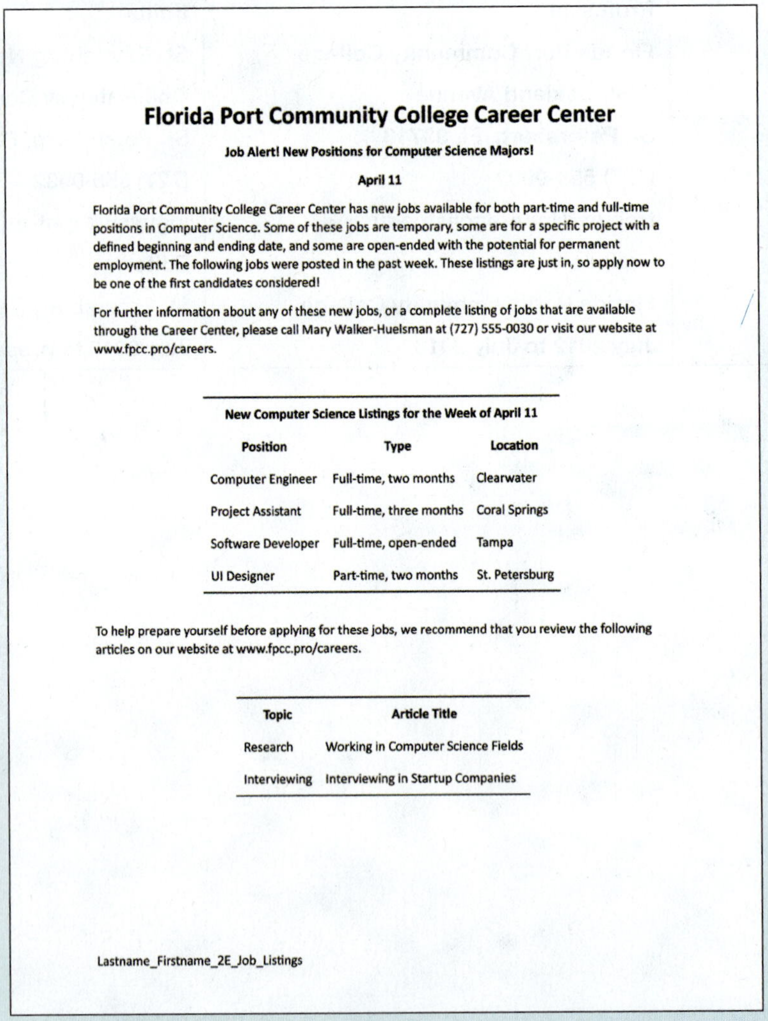

Florida Port Community College Career Center

Job Alert! New Positions for Computer Science Majors!

April 11

Florida Port Community College Career Center has new jobs available for both part-time and full-time positions in Computer Science. Some of these jobs are temporary, some are for a specific project with a defined beginning and ending date, and some are open-ended with the potential for permanent employment. The following jobs were posted in the past week. These listings are just in, so apply now to be one of the first candidates considered!

For further information about any of these new jobs, or a complete listing of jobs that are available through the Career Center, please call Mary Walker-Huelsman at (727) 555-0030 or visit our website at www.fpcc.pro/careers.

New Computer Science Listings for the Week of April 11		
Position	**Type**	**Location**
Computer Engineer	Full-time, two months	Clearwater
Project Assistant	Full-time, three months	Coral Springs
Software Developer	Full-time, open-ended	Tampa
UI Designer	Part-time, two months	St. Petersburg

To help prepare yourself before applying for these jobs, we recommend that you review the following articles on our website at www.fpcc.pro/careers.

Topic	**Article Title**
Research	Working in Computer Science Fields
Interviewing	Interviewing in Startup Companies

Lastname_Firstname_2E_Job_Listings

FIGURE 2.42

(Project 2E Table of Job Listings continues on the next page)

CONTENT-BASED ASSESSMENTS

1 **Start** Word and display a blank document; display formatting marks and rulers. **Save** the document in your **Word Chapter 2** folder as **Lastname_Firstname_2E_Job_Listings** and then add the file name to the footer.

2 Type **Florida Port Community College Career Center** and press Enter. Type **Job Alert! New Positions for Computer Science Majors!** and press Enter. Type **April 11** and press Enter. **Insert** the file **w02E_New_Jobs**.

3 At the top of the document, select and **Center** the three title lines. Select the title *Florida Port Community College Career Center*, change the **Font Size** to **20 pt** and apply **Bold**. Apply **Bold** to the second and third title lines. Locate the paragraph that begins *For further*, and then below that paragraph, position the insertion point in the second blank paragraph. **Insert** a 3 × 4 table. Enter the following in the table:

Position	Type	Location
Computer Engineer	Full-time, two months	Clearwater
Software Developer	Full-time, open-ended	Tampa
UI Designer	Part-time, two months	St. Petersburg

4 In the table, point to upper left corner of the cell *Software Developer* to display the **Row Insertion** button, and then click to insert a new row. In the new row, type the following information so that the job titles remain in alphabetic order:

Project Assistant	Full-time, three months	Coral Springs

5 Select the entire table. On the **LAYOUT tab**, in the **Cell Size group**, click **AutoFit**, and then click **AutoFit Contents**. With the table still selected, on the **HOME tab**, **Center** the table. With the table still selected, on the **PAGE LAYOUT tab**, add **6 pt Spacing Before** and **6 pt Spacing After**.

6 With the table still selected, remove all table borders, and then add a **Custom 1 pt** solid line top border and bottom border. Select all three cells in the first row, apply **Bold**, and then **Center** the text. Click anywhere in the first row, and then on the **LAYOUT tab**, in the **Rows & Columns group**, insert a row above. Merge the three cells in the new top row, and then type **New Computer Science Listings for the Week of April 11** Notice that the new row keeps the formatting of the row from which it was created.

7 At the bottom of the document, **Insert** a 2 × 3 table. Enter the following:

Topic	Article Title
Research	Working in Computer Science Fields
Interviewing	Interviewing in Startup Companies

8 Select the entire table. On the **LAYOUT tab**, in the **Cell Size group**, use the **AutoFit** button to **AutoFit Contents**. On the **HOME tab**, **Center** the table. On the **PAGE LAYOUT tab**, add **6 pt Spacing Before** and **6 pt Spacing After**. With the table still selected, remove all table borders, and then add a **Custom 1 pt** solid line top border and bottom border. Select the cells in the first row, apply **Bold**, and then **Center** the text.

9 Click the **FILE tab** to display **Backstage** view, and then in the lower right portion of the screen, click **Show All Properties**. In the **Tags** box, type **new listings, computer science** and in the **Subject** box, type your course name and section number. In the **Author** box, be sure your name is indicated and edit if necessary.

10 On the left, click **Print** to display **Print Preview**. If necessary, return to the document and make any necessary changes. **Save** your document, and then if you want to do so, present your document online to a fellow classmate. Then as directed by your instructor, print your document or submit it electronically. **Close** Word.

END | You have completed Project 2E

CONTENT-BASED ASSESSMENTS

Mastering Word | Project 2F Career Tips Memo and Fax Cover Sheet

In the following Mastering Word project, you will create a memo and fax cover sheet that includes job tips for students and graduates using the services of the Florida Port Community College Career Center. Your completed documents will look similar to Figure 2.43.

Apply 2B skills from these Objectives:

4 Create a Custom Word Template

5 Correct and Reorganize Text

6 Use the Proofing Options and Print an Envelope

7 Create a Document Using a Predesigned Microsoft Template

PROJECT FILES

For Project 2F, you will need the following files:

w02F_Memo_Template
w02F_Memo_Text
Equity Fax template from Microsoft's installed templates

You will save your documents as:

Lastname_Firstname_2F_Career_Tips
Lastname_Firstname_2F_Fax

PROJECT RESULTS

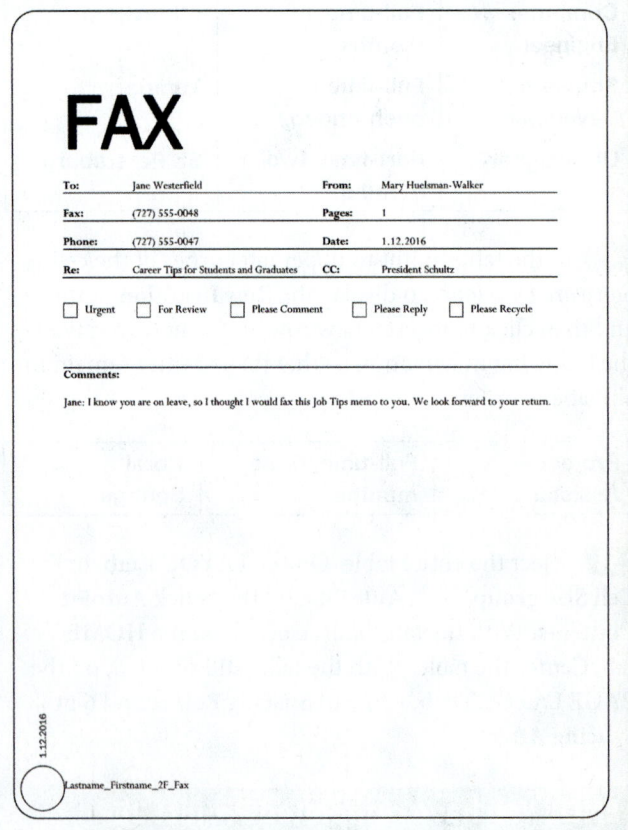

FIGURE 2.43

(Project 2F Career Tips Memo and Fax Cover Sheet continues on the next page)

1 Be sure that Word is *closed*. On the taskbar, click **File Explorer**. Navigate to your student files and open **w02F_Memo_Template**. Notice that *Document1* displays in the title bar. (Recall that custom templates stored in a location other than the Templates folder on your hard drive must be opened directly from File Explorer in order for you to create and open a new document based on the template.)

2 Press F12. Navigate to your **Word Chapter 2** folder, and then in the **File name** box, using your own name, type **Lastname_Firstname_2F_Career_Tips**

3 Add the file name to the footer. At the top of your document, in the *DATE* paragraph, click to the right of the tab formatting mark, and then type **January 12, 2016** Use a similar technique to add the following information:

TO:	Florida Port Community College Students and Graduates
FROM:	Mary Huelsman-Walker, Director
SUBJECT:	Using the CC

4 Position the insertion point in the blank paragraph below the memo heading. **Insert** the file **w02F_Memo_Text**, and then press Backspace one time to remove the blank line at the end of the inserted text.

5 Select and **Center** the title *Tips for Students and Recent Graduates of Florida Port Community College*. By using either the **Spelling & Grammar** command on the **REVIEW** tab or by right-clicking words that display blue or red wavy underlines, correct or ignore words flagged as spelling, grammar, or word usage errors. Note: If you are checking an entire document, it is usually preferable to move to the top of the document, and then use the **Spelling & Grammar** command so that you do not overlook any flagged words.

6 In the paragraph that begins *Treat every job*, in the second line of the paragraph, locate and double-click *donate*. On the **REVIEW tab**, in the **Proofing group**, click **Thesaurus**, and then from the **Thesaurus** pane, change the word to *contribute*. In the last line of the same paragraph, point to *fundamentals*, right-click, point to **Synonyms**, and then click *basics*.

7 Using Match Case, replace all instances of *CC* with *Career Center*, and then in the paragraph that begins *An Associate degree*, move the first sentence to the end of the paragraph.

8 At the end of the paragraph that begins *Treat every job*, create a blank paragraph. **Insert** a 2 × 4 table, and then type the following information:

Job Item	Tip for Success
Time Management	Show up on time and don't hurry to leave
Attire	Dress appropriately for the job
Work Area	Keep your work area neat and organized

9 Select the entire table. **AutoFit Contents**, and then apply the **Grid Table 1 Light – Accent 1** table style—under **Grid Tables**, in the first row, the second style. **Center** the table.

10 Click the **FILE tab**, and then click **Show All Properties**. As the **Tags**, type **memo, job tips** and as the **Subject**, type your course name and section number. Be sure your name is indicated as the **Author**, and edit if necessary. **Save** and **Close** the document but leave Word open. Hold this file until you complete this project.

11 With Word open but no documents displayed, click the **FILE tab**, and then click **New**. In the **Search for online templates** box, type **fax (equity)** and press Enter, and then click the first **Fax (Equity theme)** template. Click **Create**. Press F12. Save the document in your **Word Chapter 2** folder, using your own name, as **Lastname_Firstname_2F_Fax** and then insert the file name in the footer. You may see a message indicating that the file will be upgraded to the newest format.

12 Use the following information to type in each control:

To:	Jane Westerfield
From:	Mary Huelsman-Walker
Fax:	(727) 555-0048
Pages:	1
Phone:	(727) 555-0047
Date:	1/12/2016
Re:	Career Tips for Students and Graduates
CC:	President Schultz
COMMENTS:	Jane: I know you are on leave, so I thought I would fax this Job Tips memo to you. We look forward to your return.

(Project 2F Career Tips Memo and Fax Cover Sheet continues on the next page)

CONTENT-BASED ASSESSMENTS

13 Click the **FILE tab**, and then click **Show All Properties**. As the **Tags**, type **memo, job tips** and as the **Subject**, type your course name and section number. The author will indicate *Mary Huelsman-Walker*. **Save** and

Close the document. As directed by your instructor, print or submit electronically the two files that are the results of this project. **Close** Word.

END | You have completed Project 2F

CONTENT-BASED ASSESSMENTS

Mastering Word | Project 2G Application Letter, Resume, and Fax Cover Sheet

In the following Mastering Word project, you will create a letter from a custom template, a resume, and a fax cover sheet from a Microsoft predesigned template. Your completed documents will look similar to Figure 2.44.

Apply 2A and 2B skills from these Objectives:

1 Create a Table
2 Format a Table
3 Present a Word Document Online
4 Create a Custom Word Template
5 Correct and Reorganize Text
6 Use the Proofing Options and Print an Envelope
7 Create a Document Using a Predesigned Microsoft Template

PROJECT FILES

For Project 2G, you will need the following files:

w02G_Letter_Text
w02G_Letterhead_Template
w02G_Resume
Equity Fax template from Microsoft's installed templates

You will save your documents as:

Lastname_Firstname_2G_Letter
Lastname_Firstname_2G_Resume
Lastname_Firstname_2G_Fax

PROJECT RESULTS

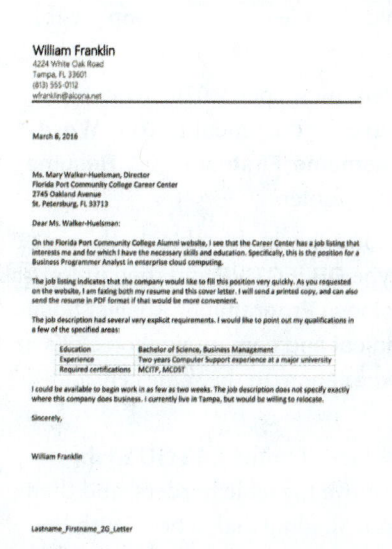

FIGURE 2.44

(Project 2G Application Letter, Resume, and Fax Cover Sheet continues on the next page)

1 Be sure that Word is *closed*. On the taskbar, click **File Explorer**. Navigate to your student files and open **w02G_Letterhead_Template**. Notice that *Document1* displays in the title bar. (Recall that custom templates stored in a location other than the Templates folder on your hard drive must be opened directly from File Explorer in order for you to create and open a new document based on the template.)

2 Press F12. Navigate to your **Word Chapter 2** folder, and then in the **File name** box, using your own name, type **Lastname_Firstname_2G_Letter**

3 Add the file name to the footer. Be sure that rulers and formatting marks display. Move to the end of the document, and then press Enter three times. Use the **Date & Time** command to insert the current date using the third format, and then press Enter four times. Type the following:

> **Ms. Mary Walker-Huelsman, Director**
>
> **Florida Port Community College Career Center**
>
> **2745 Oakland Avenue**
>
> **St. Petersburg, FL 33713**

4 Press Enter two times, type **Dear Ms. Walker-Huelsman:** and press Enter two times. **Insert** the text from the file **w02G_Letter_Text** and press Backspace one time to remove the blank paragraph at the bottom of the selected text.

5 By using either the **Spelling & Grammar** command on the **REVIEW tab** or by right-clicking words that display blue or red wavy underlines, correct or ignore words flagged as spelling, grammar, or word usage errors. Hint: If you are checking an entire document, it is usually preferable to move to the top of the document, and then use the **Spelling & Grammar** command so that you do not overlook any flagged words.

6 Replace all instances of **posting** with **listing**. In the paragraph that begins *The job description*, use the **Thesaurus** pane or the **Synonyms** command on the shortcut menu to change *specific* to *explicit* and *credentials* to *qualifications*.

7 In the paragraph that begins *I currently live in Tampa*, select the first sentence of the paragraph and drag it to the end of the same paragraph. Click in the blank paragraph below the paragraph that begins *The job*

description, and then press Enter one time. **Insert** a **2 X 3** table, and then type the text shown in Table 1.

TABLE 1

Education	Bachelor of Science, Business Management
Experience	Two years Computer Support experience at a major university
Required Certifications	MCITP, MCDST

8 Select the entire table. **AutoFit Contents**, and then apply the **Table Grid Light** table style—under **Plain Tables**, in the first row, the first style. **Center** the table.

9 Click the **FILE tab**, and then click **Show All Properties**. As the **Tags**, type **letter, alumni website** and as the **Subject**, type your course name and section number. Be sure your name is indicated as the **Author**, and edit if necessary. **Save** and **Close** the document but leave Word open. Hold this file until you complete this project.

10 From your student files, open **w02G_Resume**. Press F12, and then **Save** the document in your **Word Chapter 2** folder as **Lastname_Firstname_2G_Resume** Add the file name to the footer.

11 **Insert** a new second row in the table. In the first cell of the new row, type **OBJECTIVE** and then press Tab. Type **To obtain a Business Programmer Analyst position that will use my technical and communication skills and computer support experience.** In the same cell, add **12 pt Spacing After**.

12 Select the entire table. On the **LAYOUT tab**, **AutoFit Contents**. Remove the table borders, and then display the **Borders and Shading** dialog box. With the table selected, create a **Custom** single solid line **1 1/2 pt** top border.

13 In the first row of the table, select both cells and then **Merge Cells**. **Center** the five lines and apply **Bold**. In the first row, select *William Franklin* and change the **Font Size** to **20 pt** and add **24 pt Spacing Before**. In the email address at the bottom of the first row, add **24 pt Spacing After**.

14 In the first column, apply **Bold** to the four headings. In the cell to the right of *EDUCATION*, apply **Bold** to the

(Project 2G Application Letter, Resume, and Fax Cover Sheet continues on the next page)

name and address of the two colleges. Add **12 pt Spacing After** to the two lines that begin *September*. In the cell to the right of *RELEVANT EXPERIENCE*, apply **Bold** to the names of the two jobs—*IT Analyst* and *Computer Technician*. In the same cell, below the line that begins *January 2014*, apply bullets to the six lines that comprise the job duties. Create a similar bulleted list for the duties as a Computer Technician. Add **12 pt Spacing After** to the last line of each of the bulleted lists.

15 In the cell to the right of *CERTIFICATIONS*, select all four lines and create a bulleted list. Click the **FILE tab**, and then click **Show All Properties**. As the **Tags**, type **resume, business programmer analyst** and as the **Subject**, type your course name and section number. Be sure your name is indicated as the **Author**, and edit if necessary. **Save** and **Close** the document but leave Word open. Hold this file until you complete this project.

16 In Word's templates, search for **personal fax** and then select the second (shorter) template named **Fax cover sheet (informal)**. Click **Create**. **Save** the document in your **Word Chapter 2** folder as **Lastname_Firstname_2G_Fax** and then add the file name to the footer.

17 Type the text shown in Table 2 for the content controls.

TABLE 2

Subject:	**Application for Job Listing on Alumni Website**
Date:	**March 6, 2016**
To:	**Mary Walker-Huelsman**
From:	**William Franklin**
Phone number:	**(727) 555-0056**
Phone number:	**(813) 555-0122**
Fax number:	**(727) 555-0057**
No. of Pages	**1**
Comments:	**Two pages to follow that include my resume and a cover letter for the position of Business Programmer Analyst.**

18 Click the **FILE tab**, and then click **Show All Properties**. As the **Tags**, type **fax cover page** and as the **Subject**, type your course name and section number. Be sure your name is indicated as the **Author**, and edit if necessary. Click **Save**. As directed by your instructor, print or submit electronically the three files that are the results of this project. **Close** Word.

END | You have completed Project 2G

CONTENT-BASED ASSESSMENTS

Apply a combination of the **2A** and **2B** skills.

Build from Scratch

Build from Scratch

Build from Scratch

GO! Fix It	Project 2H New Jobs	Online

GO! Make It	Project 2I Training	Online

GO! Solve It	Project 2J Job Postings	Online

GO! Solve It	Project 2K Agenda	

PROJECT FILES

For Project 2K, you will need the following file:

Agenda template from Word's Online templates

You will save your document as:

Lastname_Firstname_2K_Agenda

On Word's opening screen, search for an online template using the search term **formal meeting agenda**. Create the agenda and then save it in your Word Chapter 2 folder as **Lastname_Firstname_2K_Agenda** Use the following information to prepare an agenda for an FPCC Career Center meeting.

The meeting will be chaired by Mary Walker-Huelsman. It will be the monthly meeting of the Career Center's staff—Kevin Rau, Marilyn Kelly, André Randolph, Susan Nguyen, and Charles James. The meeting will be held on March 15, 2016, at 3:00 p.m. The old business agenda items (open issues) include (1) seeking more job listings related to the printing and food service industries, (2) expanding the alumni website, and (3) the addition of a part-time trainer. The new business agenda items will include (1) writing a grant so the center can serve more students and alumni, (2) expanding the training area with 20 additional workstations, (3) purchase of new computers for the training room, and (4) renewal of printing service contract.

Add the file name to the footer, add your name, your course name, the section number, and then add the keywords **agenda, monthly staff meeting** to the Properties area. Submit as directed.

Performance Level

Performance Criteria	Exemplary: You consistently applied the relevant skills	Proficient: You sometimes, but not always, applied the relevant skills	Developing: You rarely or never applied the relevant skills
Select an agenda template	Agenda template is appropriate for the information provided for the meeting.	Agenda template is used, but does not fit the information provided.	No template is used for the agenda.
Add appropriate information to the template	All information is inserted in the appropriate places.	All information is included, but not in the appropriate places.	Information is missing.
Format template information	All text in the template is properly aligned and formatted.	All text is included, but alignment or formatting is inconsistent.	No additional formatting has been added.

END | You have completed Project 2K

OUTCOMES-BASED ASSESSMENTS

RUBRIC

The following outcomes-based assessments are *open-ended assessments*. That is, there is no specific correct result; your result will depend on your approach to the information provided. Make *Professional Quality* your goal. Use the following scoring rubric to guide you in *how* to approach the problem and then to evaluate *how well* your approach solves the problem.

The *criteria*—Software Mastery, Content, Format and Layout, and Process—represent the knowledge and skills you have gained that you can apply to solving the problem. The *levels of performance*—Professional Quality, Approaching Professional Quality, or Needs Quality Improvements—help you and your instructor evaluate your result.

	Your completed project is of Professional Quality if you:	Your completed project is Approaching Professional Quality if you:	Your completed project Needs Quality Improvements if you:
1-Software Mastery	Choose and apply the most appropriate skills, tools, and features and identify efficient methods to solve the problem.	Choose and apply some appropriate skills, tools, and features, but not in the most efficient manner.	Choose inappropriate skills, tools, or features, or are inefficient in solving the problem.
2-Content	Construct a solution that is clear and well organized, contains content that is accurate, appropriate to the audience and purpose, and is complete. Provide a solution that contains no errors in spelling, grammar, or style.	Construct a solution in which some components are unclear, poorly organized, inconsistent, or incomplete. Misjudge the needs of the audience. Have some errors in spelling, grammar, or style, but the errors do not detract from comprehension.	Construct a solution that is unclear, incomplete, or poorly organized; contains some inaccurate or inappropriate content; and contains many errors in spelling, grammar, or style. Do not solve the problem.
3-Format & Layout	Format and arrange all elements to communicate information and ideas, clarify function, illustrate relationships, and indicate relative importance.	Apply appropriate format and layout features to some elements, but not others. Overuse features, causing minor distraction.	Apply format and layout that does not communicate information or ideas clearly. Do not use format and layout features to clarify function, illustrate relationships, or indicate relative importance. Use available features excessively, causing distraction.
4-Process	Use an organized approach that integrates planning, development, self-assessment, revision, and reflection.	Demonstrate an organized approach in some areas, but not others; or, use an insufficient process of organization throughout.	Do not use an organized approach to solve the problem.

OUTCOMES-BASED ASSESSMENTS

Apply a combination of the **2A** and **2B** skills.

Build from
Scratch

GO! Think Project 2L Workshops

PROJECT FILES

For Project 2L, you will need the following files:

New blank Word document
w02L_Workshop_Information

You will save your document as:

Lastname_Firstname_2L_Workshops

The Florida Port Community College Career Center offers a series of workshops for both students and alumni. Any eligible student or graduate can attend the workshops, and there is no fee. Currently, the Career Center offers a three-session workshop covering Excel and Word, a two-session workshop covering Business Communication, and a one-session workshop covering Creating a Resume.

Print the w02L_Workshop_Information file and use the information to complete this project. Create an announcement with a title, an introductory paragraph, and a table listing the workshops and the topics covered in each workshop. Use the file w02L_Workshop_Information for help with the topics covered in each workshop. Format the table cells appropriately. Add an appropriate footer and document properties. Save the document as **Lastname_Firstname_2L_Workshops** and submit it as directed.

END | You have completed Project 2L

Build from
Scratch

GO! Think! Project 2M Planner **Online**

Build from
Scratch

You and GO! Project 2N Personal Resume **Online**

Build from
Scratch

GO! Cumulative Group Project Project 2O Bell Orchid Hotels **Online**

Creating Research Papers, Newsletters, and Merged Mailing Labels

GO! to Work
Video W3

PROJECT 3A

OUTCOMES
Create a research paper that includes citations and a bibliography.

OBJECTIVES
1. Create a Research Paper
2. Insert Footnotes in a Research Paper
3. Create Citations and a Bibliography in a Research Paper
4. Use Read Mode and PDF Reflow

PROJECT 3B

OUTCOMES
Create a multiple-column newsletter and merged mailing labels.

OBJECTIVES
5. Format a Multiple-Column Newsletter
6. Use Special Character and Paragraph Formatting
7. Create Mailing Labels Using Mail Merge

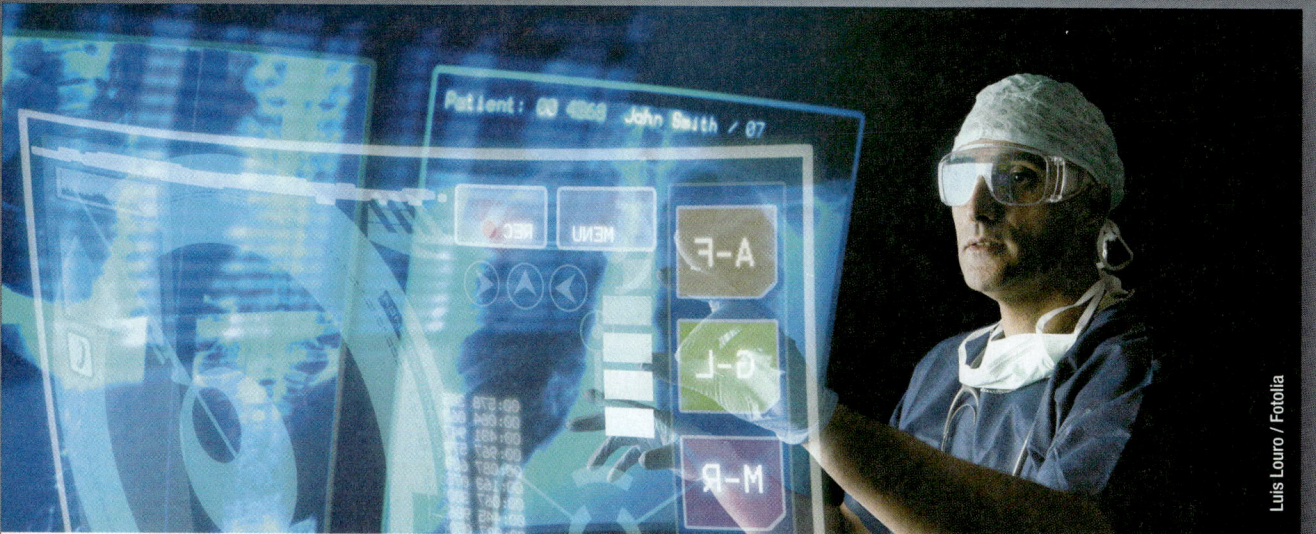

Luis Louro / Fotolia

In This Chapter

Microsoft Word provides many tools for creating complex documents. For example, Word has tools that enable you to create a research paper that includes citations, footnotes, and a bibliography. You can also create multiple-column newsletters, format the nameplate at the top of the newsletter, use special character formatting to create distinctive title text, and add borders and shading to paragraphs to highlight important information.

In this chapter, you will edit and format a research paper, create a two-column newsletter, and then create a set of mailing labels to mail the newsletter to multiple recipients.

The projects in this chapter relate to **University Medical Center**, which is a patient-care and research institution serving the metropolitan area of Memphis, Tennessee. Because of its outstanding reputation in the medical community and around the world, University Medical Center is able to attract top physicians, scientists, and researchers in all fields of medicine and achieve a level of funding that allows it to build and operate state-of-the-art facilities. A program in biomedical research was recently added. Individuals throughout the eastern United States travel to University Medical Center for diagnosis and care.

Research Paper

PROJECT ACTIVITIES

In Activities 3.01 through 3.14, you will edit and format a research paper that contains an overview of a new area of study. This paper was created by Gerard Foster, a medical intern at University Medical Center, for distribution to his classmates studying various physiologic monitoring devices. Your completed document will look similar to Figure 3.1.

PROJECT FILES

For Project 3A, you will need the following file:

w03A_Quantitative_Technology

You will save your document as:

Lastname_Firstname_3A_Quantitative_Technology

PROJECT RESULTS

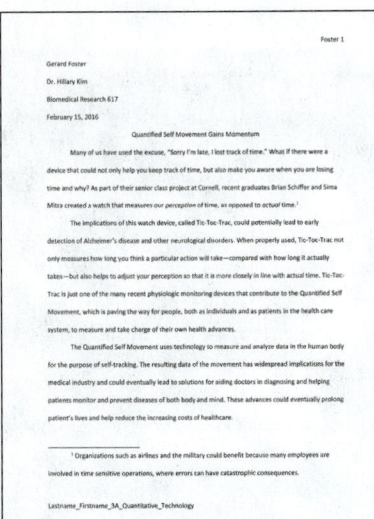

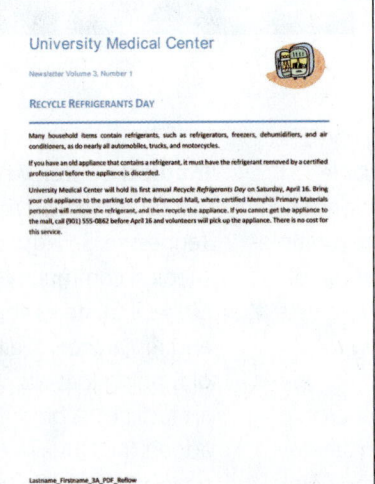

FIGURE 3.1 Project 3A Research Paper

Video W3-1

When you write a research paper or a report for college or business, follow a format prescribed by one of the standard *style guides*—a manual that contains standards for the design and writing of documents. The two most commonly used styles for research papers are those created by the ***Modern Language Association (MLA)*** and the ***American Psychological Association (APA)***; there are several others.

NOTE | **If You Are Using a Touchscreen**

- Tap an item to click it.
- Press and hold for a few seconds to right-click; release when the information or commands displays.
- Touch the screen with two or more fingers and then pinch together to zoom in or stretch your fingers apart to zoom out.
- Slide your finger on the screen to scroll—slide left to scroll right and slide right to scroll left.
- Slide to rearrange—similar to dragging with a mouse.
- Swipe from edge: from right to display charms; from left to expose open apps, snap apps, or close apps; from top or bottom to show commands or close an app.
- Swipe to select—slide an item a short distance with a quick movement—to select an item and bring up commands, if any.

Activity 3.01 | Formatting the Spacing and First-Page Information for a Research Paper

When formatting the text for your research paper, refer to the standards for the style guide that you have chosen. In this activity, you will create a research paper using the MLA style. The MLA style uses 1-inch margins, a 0.5" first line indent, and double spacing throughout the body of the document with no extra space above or below paragraphs.

1 Start Word. From your student files, locate and **Open** the document **w03A_Quantitative_Technology**. If necessary, display the formatting marks and rulers. In the location where you are storing your projects for this chapter, create a new folder named **Word Chapter 3** and then **Save** the file in the folder as **Lastname_Firstname_3A_Quantitative_Technology**

2 Press [Ctrl] + [A] to select the entire document. On the **HOME tab**, in the **Paragraph group**, click **Line and Paragraph Spacing** [icon], and then change the line spacing to **2.0**. On the **PAGE LAYOUT tab**, in the **Paragraph group**, change the **Spacing After** to **0 pt**.

3 Press [Ctrl] + [Home] to deselect and move to the top of the document. Press [Enter] one time to create a blank line at the top of the document, and then click to position the insertion point in the blank line. Type **Gerard Foster** and press [Enter].

4 Type **Dr. Hillary Kim** and press [Enter]. Type **Biomedical Research 617** and press [Enter]. Type **February 15, 2016** and press [Enter].

5 Type **Quantified Self Movement Gains Momentum** and then press [Ctrl] + [E], which is the keyboard shortcut to center a paragraph of text. Click **Save** [icon], and then compare your screen with Figure 3.2.

***More* Knowledge** | **Creating a Document Heading for a Research Paper**

On the first page of an MLA-style research paper, on the first line, type the report author. On the second line, type the person for whom the report is prepared—for example, your professor or supervisor. On the third line, type the name of the class or business. On the fourth line, type the date. On the fifth line, type the report title and center it.

FIGURE 3.2

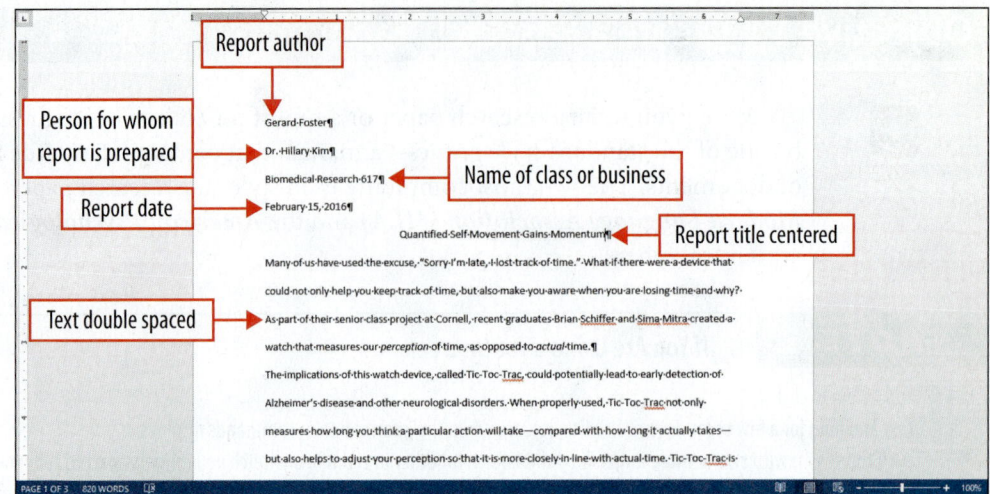

Report author

Person for whom report is prepared

Name of class or business

Report date

Report title centered

Text double spaced

Creating a Bookmark

In a document, you can mark a place you want to find again easily. Select the content to which you want to assign the bookmark. On the INSERT tab, in the Links group, click Bookmark, and assign a name. To go to the bookmark, press CTRL + G, select Bookmark, and then click the bookmark name.

Activity 3.02 | Formatting the Page Numbering and Paragraph Indents for a Research Paper

1 On the **INSERT tab**, in the **Header & Footer group**, click **Header**, and then at the bottom of the list, click **Edit Header**.

2 Type **Foster** and then press Spacebar.

Recall that the text you insert into a header or footer displays on every page of a document. Within a header or footer, you can insert many different types of information; for example, automatic page numbers, the date, the time, the file name, or pictures.

3 Under **HEADER & FOOTER TOOLS**, on the **DESIGN tab**, in the **Header & Footer group**, click **Page Number**, and then point to **Current Position**. In the gallery, under **Simple**, click **Plain Number**. Compare your screen with Figure 3.3.

Word will automatically number the pages using this number format.

FIGURE 3.3

Last name of report author and page number field added to header

4 On the **HOME tab**, in the **Paragraph group**, click **Align Right**. Double-click anywhere in the document to close the Header area.

5 Near the top of **Page 1**, locate the paragraph beginning *Many of us*, and then click to position the insertion point at the beginning of the paragraph. By moving the vertical scroll bar, scroll to the end of the document, hold down Shift, and then click to the right of the last paragraph mark to select all of the text from the insertion point to the end of the document. Release Shift.

6 With the text selected, in the **Paragraph group**, click the **Dialog Box Launcher** button 🔲 to display the **Paragraph** dialog box.

7 On the **INDENTS and SPACING tab**, under **Indentation**, click the **Special arrow**, and then click **First line**. In the **By** box, be sure **0.5"** displays. Click **OK**. Compare your screen with Figure 3.4.

The MLA style uses 0.5-inch indents at the beginning of the first line of every paragraph. *Indenting*—moving the beginning of the first line of a paragraph to the right or left of the rest of the paragraph—provides visual cues to the reader to help divide the document text and make it easier to read.

FIGURE 3.4

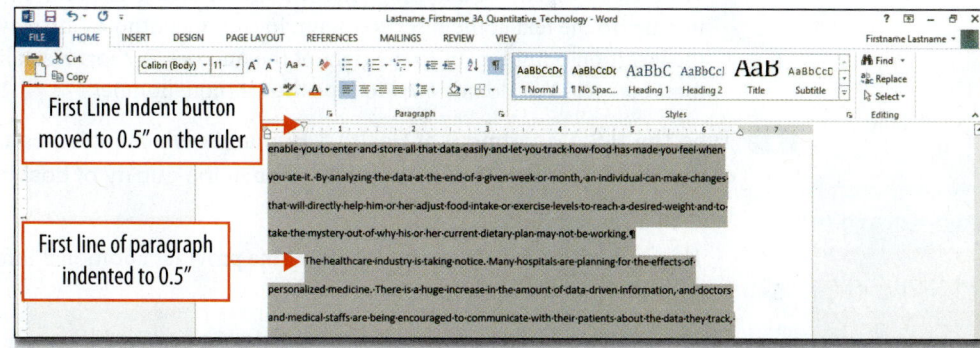

⟳ ANOTHER WAY   On the ruler, point to the First Line Indent button 🔽, and then drag the button to 0.5" on the horizontal ruler.

8 Press Ctrl + Home to deselect and move to the top of the document. On the **INSERT tab**, in **the Header & Footer group**, click **Footer**, and then at the bottom of the list click **Edit Footer**.

9 In the **Insert group**, click **Document Info**, and then click **File Name**. On the ribbon, click **Close Header and Footer**.

The file name in the footer is *not* part of the research report format, but it is included in projects in this textbook so that you and your instructor can identify your work.

10 Save 🔲 your document.

> **More Knowledge**   **Suppressing the Page Number on the First Page of a Document**
>
> Some style guidelines require that the page number and other header and footer information on the first page be hidden from view—***suppressed***. To hide the information contained in the header and footer areas on Page 1 of a document, double-click in the header or footer area. Then, under HEADER & FOOTER TOOLS, on the DESIGN tab, in the Options group, select the Different First Page check box.

Objective 2   Insert Footnotes in a Research Paper

Video W3-2

Reports and research papers typically include information that you find in other sources, and these must be credited. Within report text, numbers mark the location of *notes*—information that expands on the topic being discussed but that does not fit well in the document text. The numbers refer to *footnotes*—notes placed at the bottom of the page containing the note, or to *endnotes*—notes placed at the end of a document or chapter.

Activity 3.03 | Inserting Footnotes

You can add footnotes as you type your document or after your document is complete. Word renumbers the footnotes automatically, so footnotes need not be entered in order, and if one footnote is removed, the remaining footnotes automatically renumber.

1 Scroll to view the upper portion of **Page 2**, and then locate the paragraph that begins *Accurate records*. In the third line of the paragraph, click to position the insertion point to the right of the period after *infancy*.

2 On the **REFERENCES tab**, in the **Footnotes group**, click **Insert Footnote**.

Word creates space for a footnote in the footnote area at the bottom of the page and adds a footnote number to the text at the insertion point location. Footnote *1* displays in the footnote area, and the insertion point moves to the right of the number. A short black line is added just above the footnote area. You do not need to type the footnote number.

3 Type **The U.S. Department of Health & Human Services indicates that the widespread use of Health Information Technology will improve the quality of health care and prevent medical errors.**

This is an explanatory footnote; the footnote provides additional information that does not fit well in the body of the report.

4 Click the **HOME tab**, and then examine the font size and line spacing settings. Notice that the new footnote displays in 10 pt font size and is single-spaced, even though the font size of the document text is 11 pt and the text is double-spaced, as shown in Figure 3.5.

FIGURE 3.5

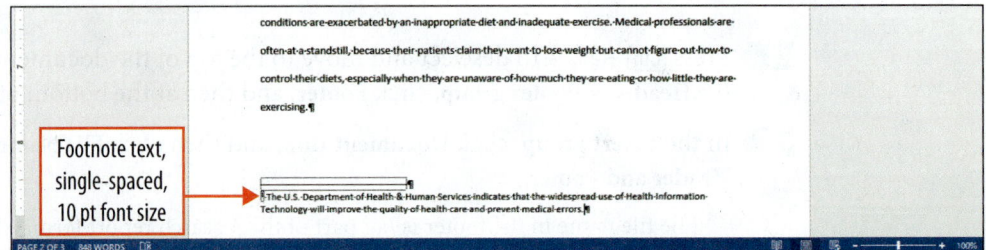

Footnote text, single-spaced, 10 pt font size

5 Scroll to view the top of **Page 1**, and then locate the paragraph that begins *Many of us*. At the end of the paragraph, click to position the insertion point to the right of the period following *time*.

6 On the **REFERENCES tab**, in the **Footnotes group**, click **Insert Footnote**. Type **Organizations such as airlines and the military could benefit because many employees are involved in time-sensitive operations, where errors can have catastrophic consequences.** Notice that the footnote you just added becomes the new footnote *1*. Click **Save**, and then compare your screen with Figure 3.6.

The first footnote that you typed, which is on Page 2 and begins *The U.S. Department of Health*, is renumbered as footnote *2*.

FIGURE 3.6

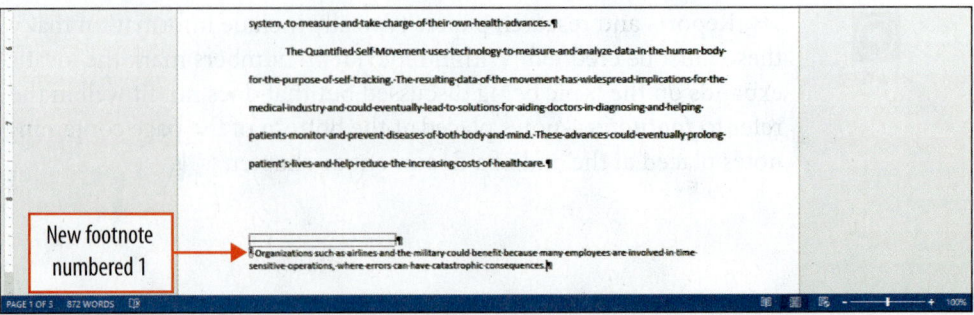

New footnote numbered 1

Activity 3.04 | Modifying a Footnote Style

Microsoft Word contains built-in paragraph formats called *styles*—groups of formatting commands, such as font, font size, font color, paragraph alignment, and line spacing—that can be applied to a paragraph with one command.

The default style for footnote text is a single-spaced paragraph that uses a 10-point Calibri font and no paragraph indents. MLA style specifies double-spaced text in all areas of a research paper—including footnotes. According to the MLA style, first lines of footnotes must also be indented 0.5 inch and use the same font size as the report text.

1 ▶ At the bottom of **Page 1**, point anywhere in the footnote text you just typed, right-click, and then on the shortcut menu, click **Style**. Compare your screen with Figure 3.7.

> The Style dialog box displays, listing the styles currently in use in the document, in addition to some of the word processing elements that come with special built-in styles. Because you right-clicked on the footnote text, the selected style is the Footnote Text style.

FIGURE 3.7

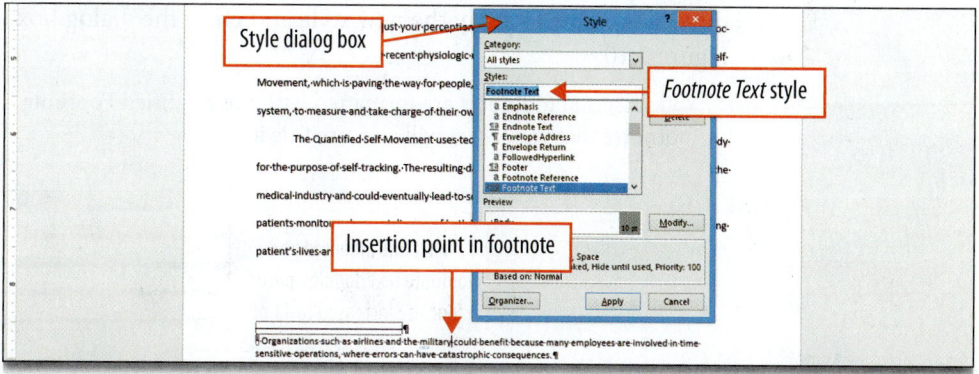

2 ▶ In the **Style** dialog box, click **Modify**, and then in the **Modify Style** dialog box, locate the small **Formatting** toolbar in the center of the dialog box. Click the **Font Size button arrow**, click **11**, and then compare your screen with Figure 3.8.

FIGURE 3.8

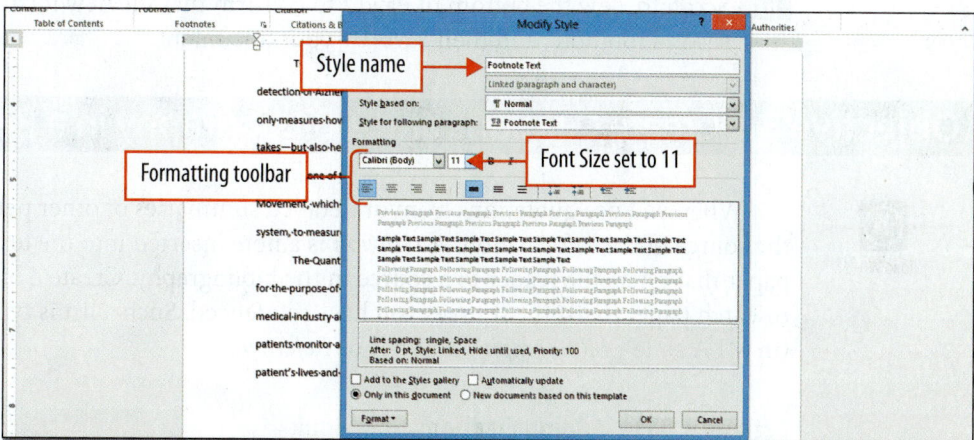

3 In the lower left corner of the dialog box, click **Format**, and then click **Paragraph**. In the **Paragraph** dialog box, on the **Indents and Spacing tab**, under **Indentation**, click the **Special arrow**, and then click **First line**.

4 Under **Spacing**, click the **Line spacing arrow**, and then click **Double**. Compare your dialog box with Figure 3.9.

FIGURE 3.9

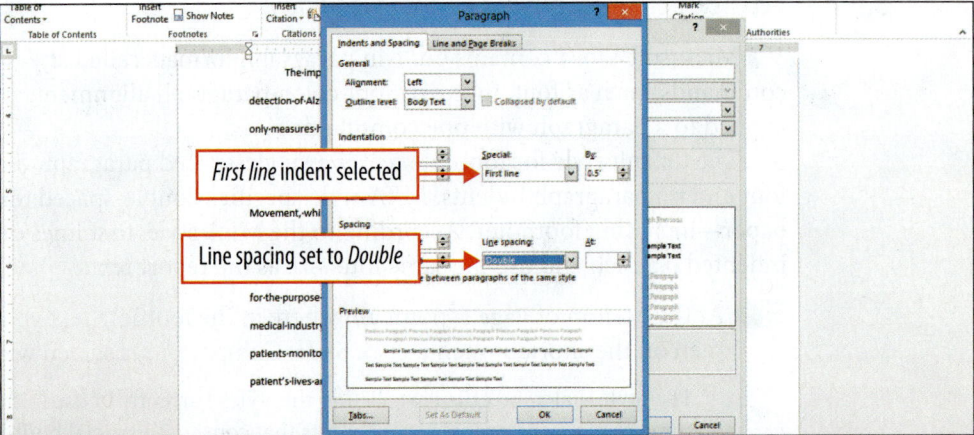

First line indent selected
Line spacing set to *Double*

5 Click **OK** to close the **Paragraph** dialog box, click **OK** to close the **Modify Style** dialog box, and then click **Apply** to apply the new style and **close** the dialog box. Compare your screen with Figure 3.10.

Your inserted footnotes are formatted with the modified Footnote Text paragraph style; any new footnotes that you insert will also use this format.

FIGURE 3.10

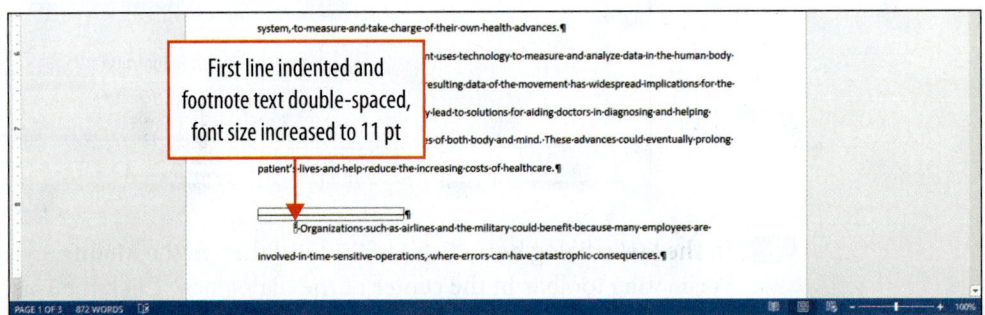

First line indented and footnote text double-spaced, font size increased to 11 pt

6 Scroll to view the bottom of **Page 2** to confirm that the new format was also applied to the second footnote, and then **Save** your document.

Objective 3 | Create Citations and a Bibliography in a Research Paper

Video W3-3

When you use quotations from or detailed summaries of other people's work, you must specify the source of the information. A ***citation*** is a note inserted into the text of a report or research paper that refers the reader to a source in the bibliography. Create a ***bibliography*** at the end of a research paper to list the sources you have referenced. Such a list is typically titled ***Works Cited*** (in MLA style), *Bibliography*, *Sources*, or *References*.

Activity 3.05 | Adding Citations for a Book

When writing a long research paper, you will likely reference numerous books, articles, and websites. Some of your research sources may be referenced many times, others only one time.

References to sources within the text of your research paper are indicated in an *abbreviated* manner. However, as you enter a citation for the first time, you can also enter the *complete* information about the source. Then, when you have finished your paper, you will be able to automatically generate the list of sources that must be included at the end of your research paper.

1 Scroll to view the middle of **Page 2**. In the paragraph that begins *Accurate records*, at the end of the paragraph, click to position the insertion point to the right of the quotation mark.

The citation in the document points to the full source information in the bibliography, which typically includes the name of the author, the full title of the work, the year of publication, and other publication information.

2 On the **REFERENCES tab**, in the **Citations & Bibliography group**, click the **Style button arrow**, and then click **MLA** to insert a reference using MLA bibliography style.

3 Click **Insert Citation**, and then click **Add New Source**. Click the **Type of Source arrow**, and then click **Book**. Add the following information, and then compare your screen with Figure 3.11:

Author:	Sopol, Eric J.
Title:	The Creative Destruction of Medicine
Year:	2012
City:	New York
Publisher:	Basic Books
Medium	Print

FIGURE 3.11

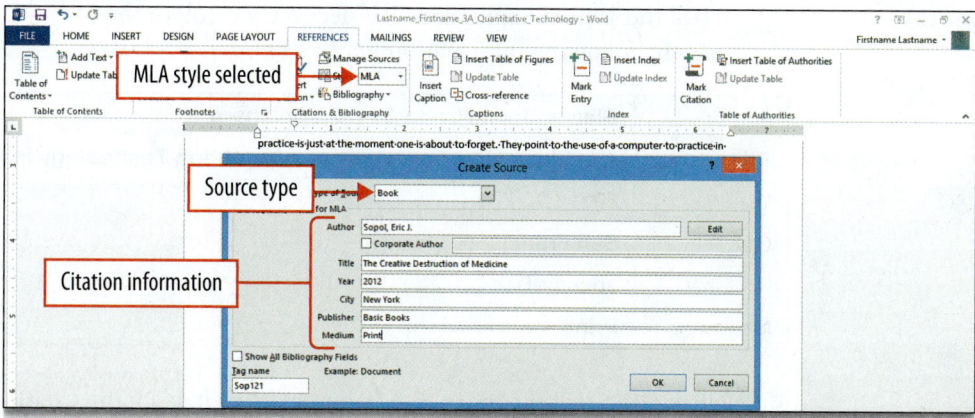

> **NOTE** **Citing Corporate Authors and Indicating the Medium**
>
> If the author of a document is only identified as the name of an organization, select the Corporate Author check box and type the name of the organization in the Corporate Author box.
>
> In the Seventh edition of the *MLA Handbook for Writers of Research Papers*, the category Medium was added and must be included for any item on the Works Cited page. Entries for this category can include Print, Web, Performance, and Photograph, among many others.

4 Click **OK** to insert the citation. Point to *(Sopol)* and click one time to select the citation.

In the MLA style, citations that refer to items on the *Works Cited* page are placed in parentheses and are referred to as ***parenthetical references***—references that include the last name of the author or authors and the page number in the referenced source, which you add to the reference. No year is indicated, and there is no comma between the name and the page number.

5 Save the document.

Activity 3.06 | Editing Citations

1 In the lower right corner of the box that surrounds the reference, point to the small arrow to display the ScreenTip *Citation Options*. Click this **Citation Options arrow**, and then on the list of options, click **Edit Citation**.

2 In the **Edit Citation** dialog box, under **Add**, in the **Pages** box, type **5** to indicate that you are citing from Page 5 of this source. Compare your screen with Figure 3.12.

FIGURE 3.12

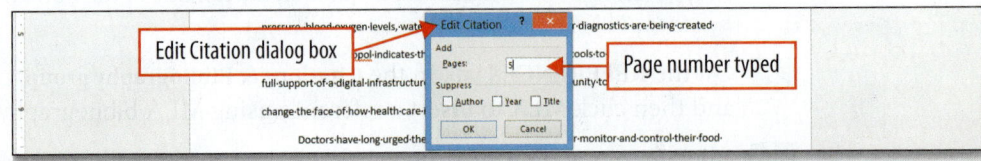

3 Click **OK** to display the page number of the citation. Click outside of the citation box to deselect it. Then type a period to the right of the citation, and delete the period to the left of the quotation mark.

> In the MLA style, if the reference occurs at the end of a sentence, the parenthetical reference always displays to the left of the punctuation mark that ends the sentence.

4 Press Ctrl + End to move to the end of the document, and then click to position the insertion point after the letter *e* in *disease* and to the left of the period.

5 In the **Citations & Bibliography group**, click **Insert Citation**, and then click **Add New Source**. Click the **Type of Source arrow**, if necessary scroll to the top of the list, click **Book**, and then add the following information:

Author:	Glaser, John P. and Claudia Salzberg
Title:	The Strategic Application of Information Technology in Health Care Organizations
Year:	2011
City:	San Francisco
Publisher:	Jossey-Bass
Medium:	Print

6 Click **OK**. Click the inserted citation to select it, click the **Citation Options arrow**, and then click **Edit Citation**.

7 In the **Edit Citation** dialog box, under **Add**, in the **Pages** box, type **28** to indicate that you are citing from page 28 of this source. Click **OK**.

8 On the **REFERENCES tab**, in the **Citations & Bibliography group**, click **Manage Sources**, and then compare your screen with Figure 3.13.

> The Source Manager dialog box displays. Other citations on your computer display in the Master List box. The citations for the current document display in the Current List box. Word maintains the Master List so that if you use the same sources regularly, you can copy sources from your Master List to the current document. A preview of the bibliography entry also displays at the bottom of the dialog box.

FIGURE 3.13

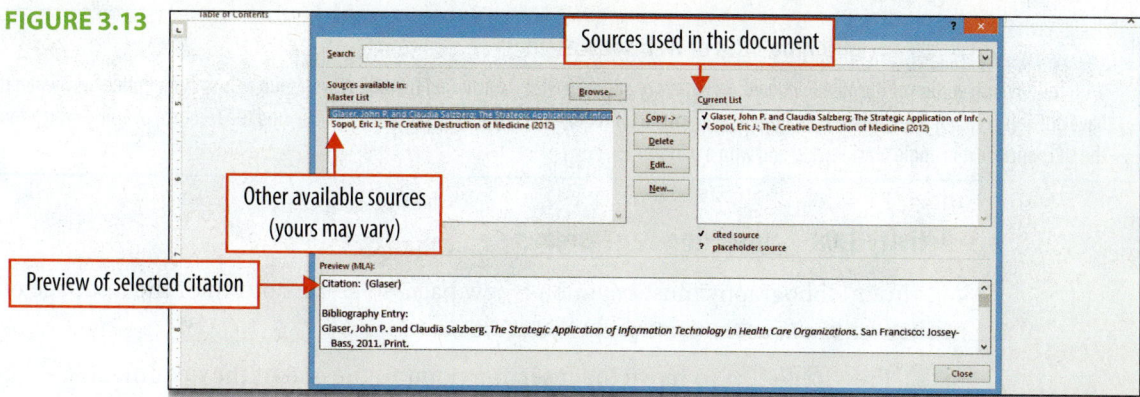

9 At the bottom of the **Source Manager** dialog box, click **Close**. Click anywhere in the document to deselect the parenthetical reference, and then **Save** 🖫 your document.

Activity 3.07 │ Adding Citations for a Website

1 In the lower portion of **Page 2**, in the paragraph that begins *Doctors have long*, in the third line, click to position the insertion point after the s in *States* and to the left of the period.

2 In the **Citations & Bibliography group**, click **Insert Citation**, and then click **Add New Source**. Click the **Type of Source arrow**, scroll down as necessary, and then click **Web site**. Type the following information:

Author:	Ogden, Cynthia L., Margaret D. Carroll, Brian K. Kit, and Katherine M. Flegal.
Name of Web Page:	NCHS Data Brief Number 82
Year:	2012
Month:	January
Day:	15
Year Accessed:	2016
Month Accessed:	January
Day Accessed:	17
Medium	Web

3 Click **OK**. Save 🖫, and then compare your screen with Figure 3.14.

A parenthetical reference is added. Because the cited web page has no page numbers, only the author name is used in the parenthetical reference.

FIGURE 3.14

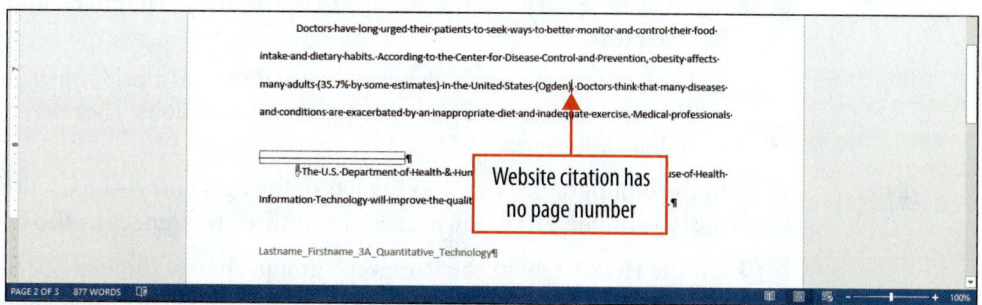

Activity 3.08 | Inserting Page Breaks

Your bibliography must begin on a new page, so at the bottom of the last page of your report, you must insert a manual page break.

1 Press Ctrl + End to move the insertion point to the end of the document.

If there is a footnote on the last page, the insertion point will display at the end of the final paragraph, but above the footnote—a footnote is always associated with the page that contains the citation.

2 Press Ctrl + Enter to insert a manual page break.

A *manual page break* forces a page to end at the insertion point location, and then places any subsequent text at the top of the next page. Recall that the new paragraph retains the formatting of the previous paragraph, so in this instance the first line is indented.

A *page break indicator*, which shows where a manual page break was inserted, displays at the bottom of Page 3.

3 On the **HOME tab**, in the **Paragraph group**, click the **Dialog Box Launcher** button 🔲 to display the **Paragraph** dialog box.

4 On the **Indents and Spacing tab**, under **Indentation**, click the **Special arrow**, and then click **(none)**. Click **OK**, and then **Save** 💾 your document.

 **ANOTHER WAY**   On the ruler, point to the First Line Indent button 🔽, and then drag the button to 0" on the horizontal ruler.

Activity 3.09 | Creating a Reference Page

At the end of a report or research paper, include a list of each source referenced. *Works Cited* is the reference page heading used in the MLA style guidelines. Other styles may refer to this page as a *Bibliography* (Business Style) or *References* (APA Style). Always display this information on a separate page.

1 With the insertion point blinking in the first line of **Page 4**, type **Works Cited** and then press Enter. On the **REFERENCES tab**, in the **Citations & Bibliography group**, in the **Style** box, be sure *MLA* displays.

2 In the **Citations & Bibliography group**, click **Bibliography**, and then near the bottom of the list, click **Insert Bibliography**.

3 Scroll as necessary to view the entire list of three references, and then click anywhere in the inserted text.

The bibliography entries that you created display as a field, which is indicated by the gray shading. This field links to the Source Manager for the citations. The references display alphabetically by the author's last name.

4 In the bibliography, point to the left of the first entry—beginning *Glaser, John P.*—to display the ⬈ pointer. Drag down to select all three references in the field.

5 On the **HOME tab**, in the **Paragraph group**, change the **Line spacing** to **2.0**, and then on the **PAGE LAYOUT tab**, in the **Paragraph group**, change the **Spacing After** to **0 pt**.

The entries display according to MLA guidelines; the text is double-spaced, the extra space between paragraphs has been removed, and each entry uses a *hanging indent*—the first line of each entry extends 0.5 inch to the left of the remaining lines of the entry.

6 At the top of **Page 4**, click anywhere in the title text *Works Cited*, and then press Ctrl + E to center the title. Compare your screen with Figure 3.15, and then **Save** 🖫 your document.

In MLA style, the *Works Cited* title is centered.

FIGURE 3.15

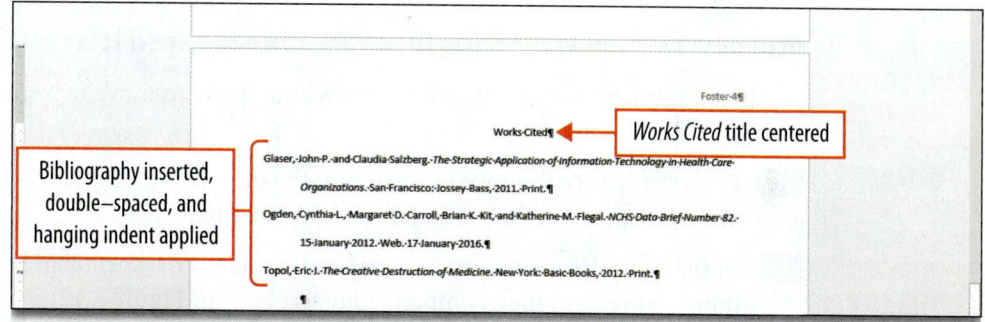

Works Cited title centered

Bibliography inserted, double–spaced, and hanging indent applied

Activity 3.10 | Managing and Modifying Sources for a Document

Use the Source Manager to organize the sources cited in your document. For example, in the Source Manager dialog box, you can copy sources from the master list to the current list, delete a source, edit a source, or search for a source. You can also display a preview of how your citations will appear in your document.

1 On the **REFERENCES tab**, in the **Citations & Bibliography group**, click **Manage Sources**.

2 On the left, in the **Master List**, click the entry for *Sopol, Eric J.* and then between the **Master List** and the **Current List**, click **Edit**.

The name of this source should be *Topol* instead of *Sopol*.

3 In the **Edit Source** dialog box, in the **Author** box, delete *S* and type **T**

4 Click **OK**. When the message box indicates *This source exists in your master list and current document. Do you want to update both lists with these changes?* click **Yes**. Compare your screen with Figure 3.16.

In the lower portion of the Source Manager dialog box, a preview of the corrected entry displays.

FIGURE 3.16

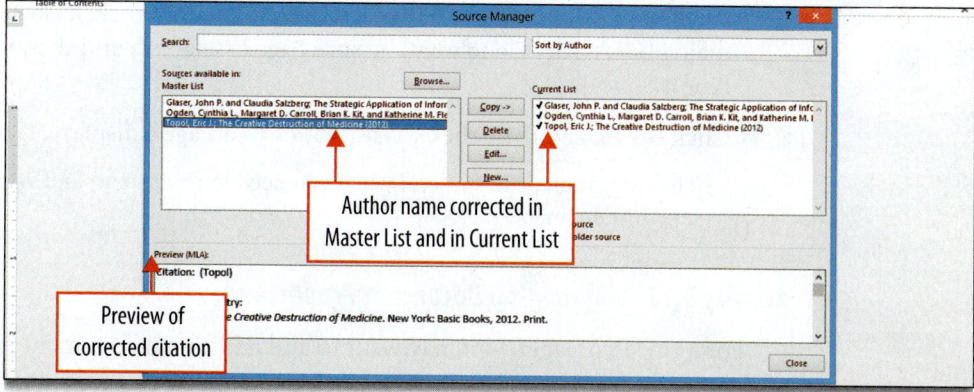

Author name corrected in Master List and in Current List

Preview of corrected citation

5 In the lower right corner, click **Close**. On your **Works Cited page**, notice that the author name is *not* corrected. Scroll to view the lower portion of **Page 2**, and notice that the author name *is* corrected and the citation is selected.

6 On the selected citation *(Topol 5)*, click the **Citation Options arrow**, and then click **Update Citations and Bibliography**. Press Ctrl + End, and notice that this action updates the **Works Cited page** with the corrected name.

> Editing a source in Source Manager updates only the sources in the document; to update the Works Cited page, use the Update Citations and Bibliography command on the citation.

7 Drag to select all the lines for the three references. On the **HOME tab**, in the **Paragraph group**, click **Line and Paragraph Spacing** ⬚▾, and then click **2.0**. Click **Save** 🖫.

Activity 3.11 | Using the Navigation Pane to Go to a Specific Page

In a multipage document, use the navigation pane to move to a specific page or to find specific objects in the document.

1 Press Ctrl + Home to move to the top of the document. Click the **VIEW tab**, and then in the **Show group**, select the **navigation pane** check box.

2 In the **navigation pane**, on the right end of the **Search document** box, click the **Search for more things arrow**, and then compare your screen with Figure 3.17.

FIGURE 3.17

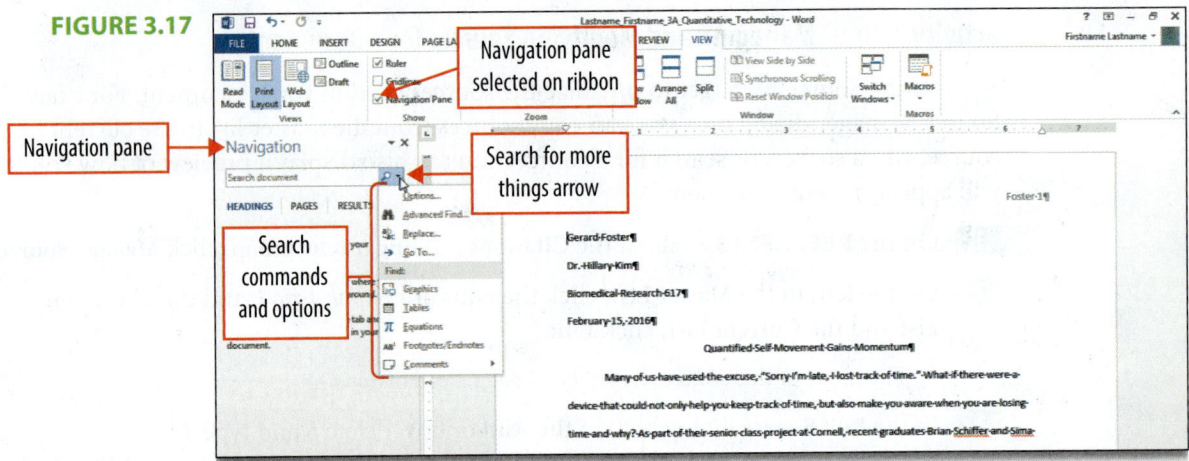

3 Under **Find**, click **Footnotes/Endnotes**. Notice that the first numbered footnote is selected.

4 In the **navigation pane**, to the right of *Result 1 of 2*, click the down arrow to move to the next numbered footnote.

5 Click the **Search for more things arrow** again, and then click **Go To**. In the **Find and Replace** dialog box, under **Go to what**, be sure **Page** is selected, and then in the **Enter page number** box, type **4**

6 Click **Go To**, and then click **Close**. Notice that **Page 4** displays. **Close** ✕ the **navigation pane**.

> The navigation pane is useful when you need to navigate to find various elements, especially in a lengthy document.

Activity 3.12 | Managing Document Properties

For a research paper, you may want to add additional document properties.

1 Press Ctrl + Home to return to the top of your document. Click the **FILE tab** to display **Backstage** view, and then in the lower right corner of the screen, click **Show All Properties**.

2 As the document **Title**, type **Quantified Self Movement Gains Momentum** and then as the **Tags**, type **quantified self, physiologic monitoring, research paper**

3 Click in the **Comments** box and type **Draft copy of a research report that will be distributed to class members** and then in the **Categories** box, type **Biomedical Research**

4 In the **Subject** box, type your course name and section number. In the **Company** box, select and delete any existing text, and then type **University Medical Center**

5 Click in the **Manager** box and type **Dr. Hillary Kim** Be sure your name displays as the **Author** and edit if necessary.

6 At the top of the **Properties** list, click the text *Properties*, and then click **Advanced Properties**. In the dialog box, click the **Summary tab**, and then compare your screen with Figure 3.18.

In the Advanced Properties dialog box, you can view and modify additional document properties.

FIGURE 3.18

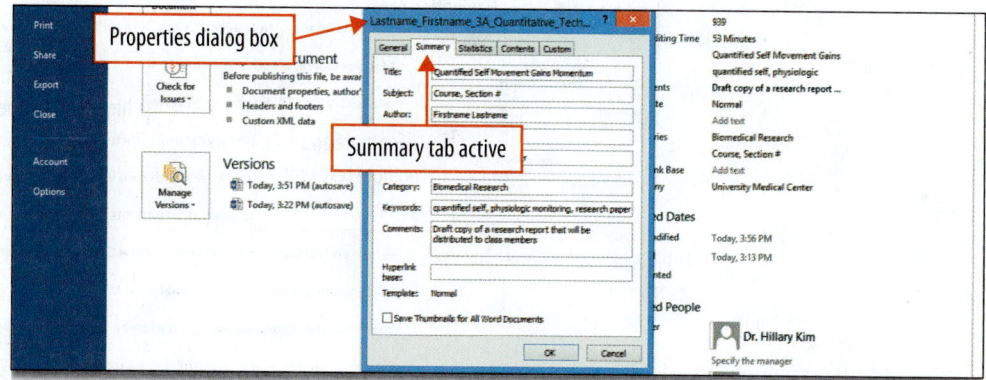

7 Click the **Statistics tab**.

The document statistics show the number of revisions made to the document, the last time the document was edited, and the number of paragraphs, lines, words, and characters in the document. Additional information categories are available by clicking the Custom tab.

8 **Close** ✖ the dialog box, and then on the left, click **Save** to save and return to your document.

Objective 4   Use Read Mode and PDF Reflow

Video W3-4

Read Mode optimizes the view of the Word screen for the times when you are *reading* Word documents on the screen and not creating or editing them. Microsoft's research indicates that two-thirds of user sessions in Word contain no editing—meaning that people are simply reading the Word document on the screen. The Column Layout feature of Read Mode reflows the document to fit the size of the device you are reading so that the text is as easy to read on a tablet device as on a 24-inch screen. The Object Zoom feature of Read Mode resizes graphics to fit the screen you are using, but you can click or tap to zoom in on the graphic.

PDF Reflow provides the ability to import PDF files into Word so that you can transform a PDF back into a fully editable Word document. This is useful if you have lost the original Word file or if someone sends you a PDF that you would like to modify. PDF Reflow is not intended to act as a viewer for PDF files—for that you will still want to use the desktop app known as Adobe Reader or the *Windows Reader app*, with which you can open a PDF or XPS file, zoom, find words or phrases, take notes, save changes, and then print or share the file.

Activity 3.13   Using Read Mode

1 If necessary, press Ctrl + Home to move to the top of your document. On the **VIEW tab**, in the **Views group**, click **Read Mode**, and notice that **Read Mode** keeps footnotes displayed on the page associated with the footnote.

 **ANOTHER WAY**   On the right side of the status bar, click the Read Mode button 📖.

2 In the upper left corner, click **TOOLS**.

You can use these tools to find something within the document or jump out to Bing to conduct an Internet search.

3 Click **Find**, and then in the **Search** box, type **Topol** Notice that Word displays the first page where the search term displays and highlights the term in yellow. Compare your screen with Figure 3.19.

FIGURE 3.19

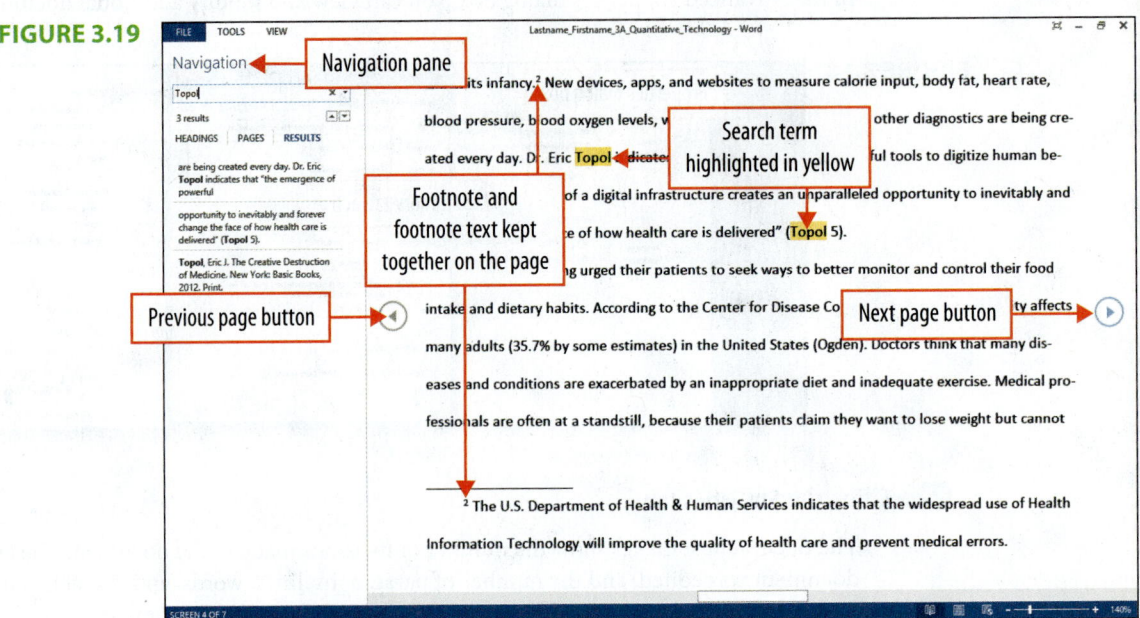

4 In the upper left corner, click **VIEW**, and then take a moment to study the table in Figure 3.20.

FIGURE 3.20

VIEW COMMANDS IN READ MODE	
VIEW COMMAND	**ACTION**
Edit Document	Return to Print Layout view to continue editing the document.
Navigation Pane	Search for specific text or click a heading or page to move to that location.
Show Comments	See comments, if any, within the document.
Column Width	Change the display of the document to fit more or less text on each line.
Page Color	Change the colors used to show the document to make it easier to read. Some readers prefer a sepia (brownish-gray) shading as the background or a black background with white text.
Layout	Read in different layouts. Select Column Layout, which is the default, or Paper Layout, which mimics the 8.5 × 11 format but without the ribbon.

5 On the VIEW menu, click **Edit Document** to return to **Print Layout** view. **Close** ☒ the **navigation pane**.

 **ANOTHER WAY**   On the status bar on the right, click the Print Layout button 📄.

Activity 3.14 | Using PDF Reflow

1 Save 💾 your document. Click the **FILE tab**, and then on the left, click **Close** to close your document but leave Word open.

2 Press `Ctrl` + `F12` to display the **Open** dialog box, navigate to your student data files, and then click **w03A_PDF**. In the lower right corner, click **Open**. If a message indicates that *Word will now convert the PDF to an editable Word document...*, click **OK**.

3 If necessary, on the right side of the status bar, click **Print Layout** 📄.

4 In the newsletter heading, change the **Volume** number to **3** Insert a footer, and then, using your own name, type **Lastname_Firstname_3A_PDF_Reflow** as shown in Figure 3.21.

FIGURE 3.21

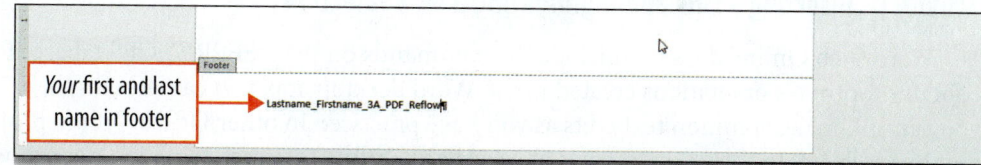

Your first and last name in footer → Lastname_Firstname_3A_PDF_Reflow

5 Close the footer area. Press `F12` to display the **Save As** dialog box, and then navigate to your **Word Chapter 3** folder. In the lower portion of the dialog box, click the **Save as type arrow**, and then click **PDF**.

6 In the **File name** box, type **Lastname_Firstname_3A_PDF_Reflow** and then in the lower right corner, click **Save** or press `Enter`.

This action re-saves the document as a PDF file.

🔄 **ANOTHER WAY**   Click the FILE tab, on the left click Export, click Create PDF/XPS, navigate to the desired folder, and then click Publish.

7 **Close** the **w03A_PDF** document without saving. **Close** ❎ Word. Print or submit electronically the two files that are the result of this project.

More Knowledge   **Inserting Watermarks**

You can add ghost text such as *Draft* or *Confidential* behind the content of a page. To do so, on the DESIGN tab, in the Page Background group, click Watermark, and select or create the watermark you want to use.

END | You have completed Project 3A

GO! with Office Online (formerly Web Apps)

Objective   Insert a Link and Highlight Text in a Word Online Document

You can use Word Online to insert a link to a website.

ALERT!   **Working with Web-Based Applications and Services**

Computer programs and services on the web receive continuous updates and improvements, so the steps to complete this web-based activity may differ from the ones shown. You can often look at the screens and the information presented to determine how to complete the activity.

Activity | Inserting a Link and Highlighting a Text Selection

Word Web Online does not include the commands on the REFERENCES tab, so if you open a report that contains footnotes or citations created in the Word desktop app, you cannot edit them in Word Online. However, you can still make common text edits as you have practiced in other Office Online projects. You can also insert a link to a website. In this activity, you will use Word Online to insert a link in a report, which you might want to do before sharing the report electronically for review by others.

1 From the desktop, start Internet Explorer. Navigate to **http://onedrive.com**, and then sign in to your Microsoft account. Open your **GO! Web Projects** folder; or create this folder if you have not done so.

2 In the OneDrive menu bar, click **Upload**. Navigate to your student data files, click **w03_3A_Web**, and then click **Open**.

3 Point to the uploaded file **w03_3A_Web**, and then right-click. On the shortcut menu, scroll as necessary, and then click **Rename**. Using your own last name and first name, type **Lastname_Firstname_WD_3A_Web** and then press Enter to rename the file.

4 Click the file that you just renamed, and then click **EDIT DOCUMENT**. On the list, click **Edit in Word Online**.

5 In the paragraph that begins *The implications*, drag to select *Tic-Toc-Trac*, and then on the **HOME tab**, in the

Font group, click **Text Highlight Color** 🎨▾. Click the **Yellow** block to highlight this text in yellow.

6 Press Ctrl + End to move to the end of the document, and then press Enter.

7 On the **INSERT tab**, in the **Links group**, click **Link**. In the **Display text** box, type **See how Tic-Toc-Trac works!**

8 In the **Address** box, type **www.tictoctrac.com** and then click **Insert**. Compare your screen with Figure A.

9 To test the link, point to it, hold down Ctrl and then click one time. The site opens on a new tab.

10 In your browser, close the **TicTocTrac** tab.

11 Submit as directed by your instructor. Sign out of your OneDrive.

FIGURE A

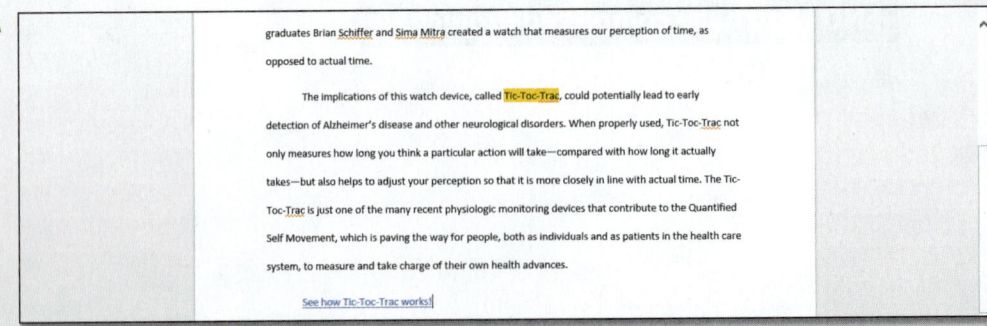

Newsletter with Mailing Labels

PROJECT ACTIVITIES

In Activities 3.15 through 3.29, you will edit a newsletter that University Medical Center is sending to the board of directors and create the necessary mailing labels. Your completed documents will look similar to Figure 3.22.

PROJECT FILES

For Project 3B, you will need the following files:

New blank Word document
w03B_Environment_Newsletter
w03B_Addresses
w03B_Recycling

You will save your documents as:

Lastname_Firstname_3B_Mailing_Labels
Lastname_Firstname_3B_Addresses
Lastname_Firstname_3B_Environment_Newsletter

PROJECT RESULTS

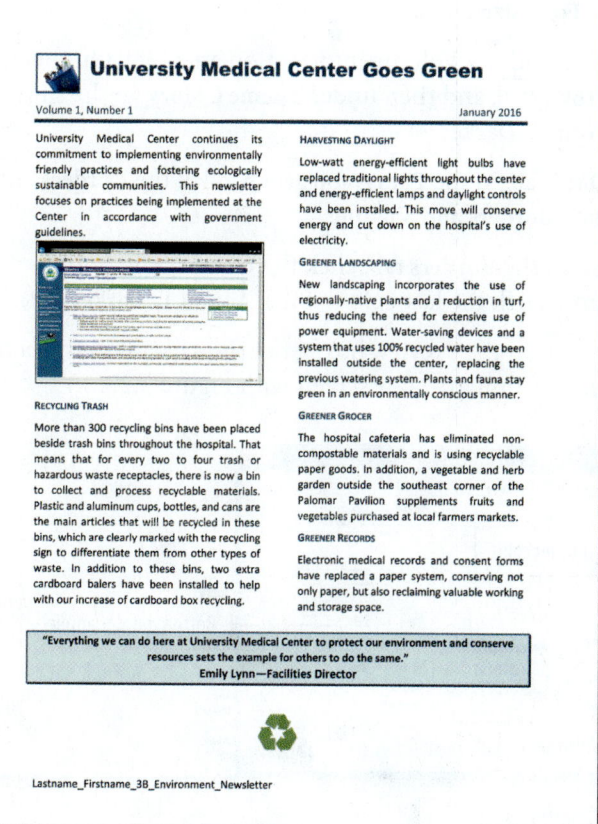

FIGURE 3.22 Project 3B Newsletter with Mailing Labels

Video W3-5

A *newsletter* is a periodical that communicates news and information to a specific group. Newsletters, as well as all newspapers and most magazines, use multiple columns for articles because text in narrower columns is easier to read than text that stretches across a page. You can create a newsletter in Word by changing a single column of text into two or more columns. If a column does not end where you want it to, you can end the column at a location of your choice by inserting a *manual column break*—an artificial end to a column to balance columns or to provide space for the insertion of other objects.

Activity 3.15 | Changing One Column of Text to Two Columns

Newsletters are usually two or three columns wide. When using 8.5 × 11-inch paper in portrait orientation, avoid creating four or more columns because they are so narrow that word spacing looks awkward, often resulting in one long word on a line by itself.

1 Start Word. On Word's opening screen, in the lower left, click **Open Other Documents**. Navigate to your student files, and then locate and open the document **w03B_Environment_Newsletter**. If necessary, display the formatting marks and rulers. **Save** the file in your **Word Chapter 3** folder as **Lastname_Firstname_3B_Environment_Newsletter** and then add the file name to the footer.

2 Select the first paragraph of text—*University Medical Center Goes Green*. On the mini toolbar, change the **Font** to **Arial Black** and the **Font Size** to **18**.

3 Select the first two paragraphs—the title and the Volume information and date. On the mini toolbar, click the **Font Color button arrow** ![A] , and then under **Theme Colors**, in the fifth column, click the last color—**Blue, Accent 1, Darker 50%**.

4 With the text still selected, on the **HOME tab**, in the **Paragraph group**, click the **Borders button arrow** ![borders] , and then at the bottom, click **Borders and Shading**.

5 In the **Borders and Shading** dialog box, on the **Borders tab**, click the **Color arrow**, and then under **Theme Colors**, in the fifth column, click the last color—**Blue, Accent 1, Darker 50%**.

6 Click the **Width arrow**, and then click **3 pt**. In the **Preview** box at the right, point to the *bottom* border of the preview and click one time. Compare your screen with Figure 3.23.

FIGURE 3.23

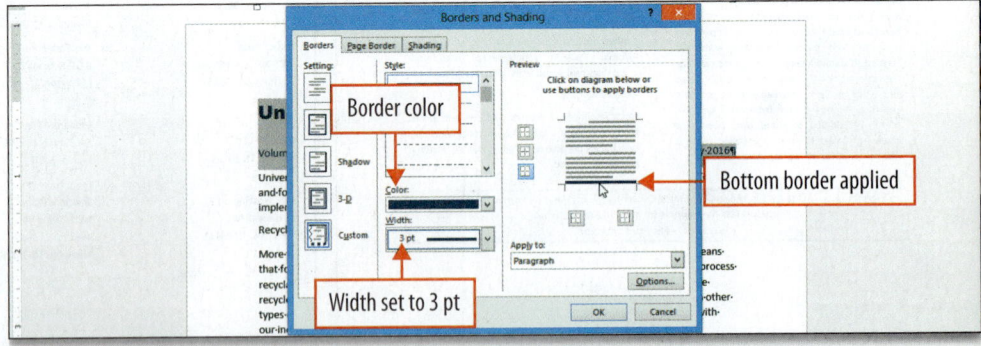

 **ANOTHER WAY** In the Preview area, click the Bottom Border button ![button].

7 In the **Borders and Shading** dialog box, click **OK**.

The line visually defines the newsletter's *nameplate*—the banner on the front page of a newsletter that identifies the publication.

8 Below the Volume information, click at the beginning of the paragraph that begins *University Medical Center continues*. By using the vertical scroll box, scroll to view the lower portion of the document, hold down Shift, and then click after the paragraph mark at the end of the paragraph that begins *Electronic medical records* to select all of the text between the insertion point and the sentence ending with the word *space*. Be sure that the paragraph mark is included in the selection. Compare your screen with Figure 3.24.

Use Shift to define a selection that may be difficult to select by dragging.

FIGURE 3.24

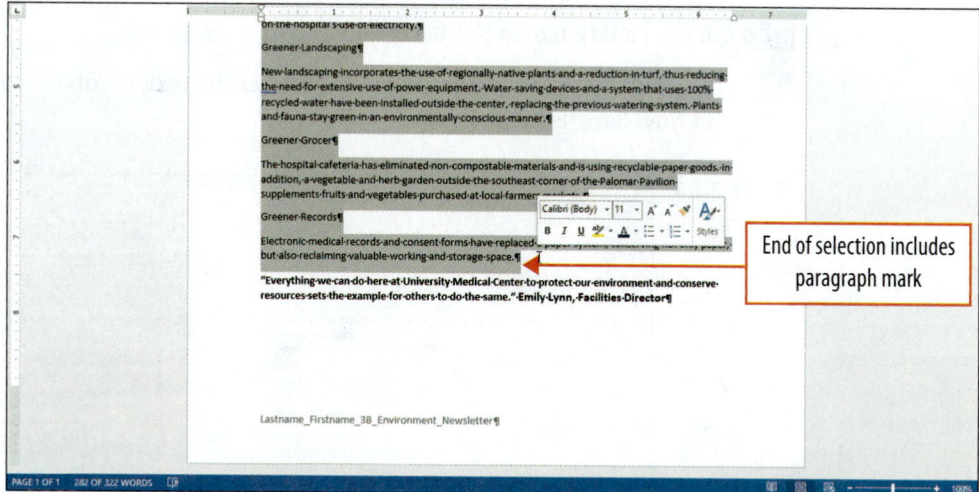

End of selection includes paragraph mark

9 On the **PAGE LAYOUT tab**, in the **Page Setup group**, click **Columns**, and then click **Two**. Compare your screen with Figure 3.25, and then **Save** 💾 your newsletter.

Word divides the text into two columns and inserts a *section break* at the end of the selection, dividing the one-column section of the document from the two-column section of the document. A *section* is a portion of a document that can be formatted differently from the rest of the document. A section break marks the end of one section and the beginning of another section.

FIGURE 3.25

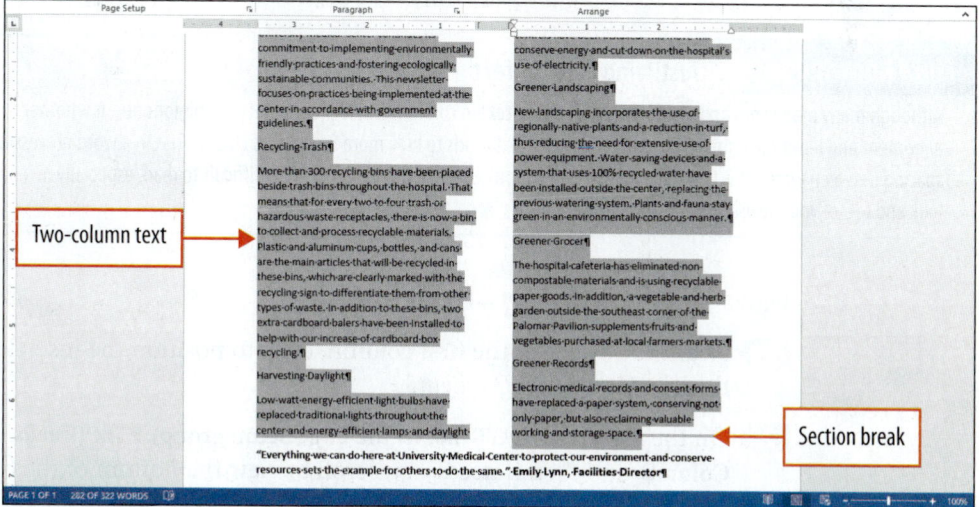

Two-column text

Section break

Activity 3.16 | Formatting Multiple Columns

The uneven right margin of a single page-width column is easy to read. When you create narrow columns, justified text is sometimes preferable. Depending on the design and layout of your newsletter, you might decide to reduce extra space between paragraphs and between columns to improve the readability of the document.

1 With the two columns of text still selected, on the **PAGE LAYOUT tab**, in the **Paragraph group**, click the **Spacing After down spin arrow** one time to change the spacing after to **6 pt**.

2 On the **HOME tab**, in the **Paragraph group**, click **Justify** ▤.

3 Click anywhere in the document to deselect the text, compare your screen with Figure 3.26, and then **Save** 🖫.

FIGURE 3.26

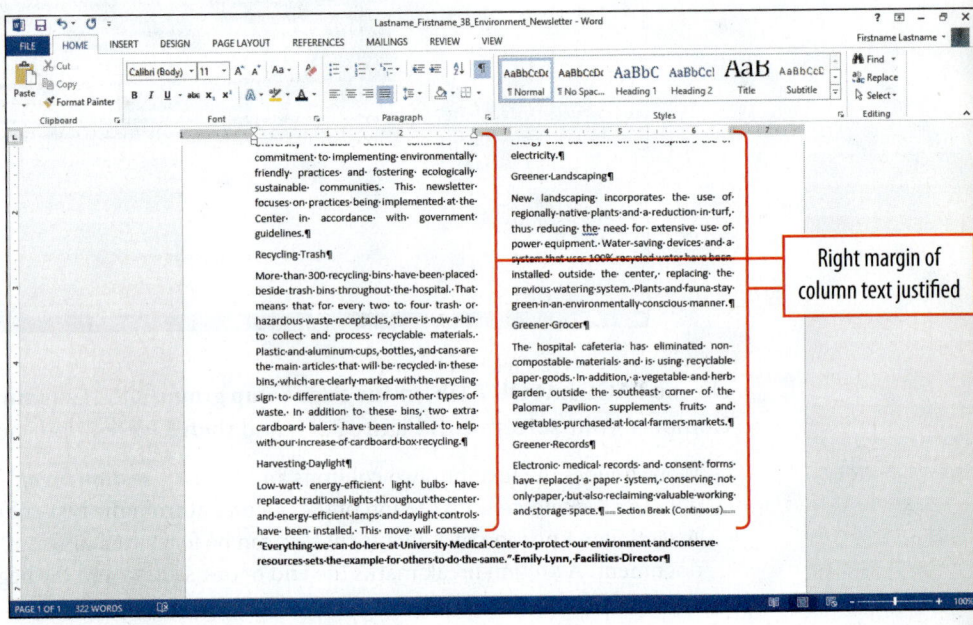

Right margin of column text justified

More Knowledge   **Justifying Column Text**

Although many magazines and newspapers still justify text in columns, there are a variety of opinions about whether to justify the columns, or to use left alignment and leave the right edge uneven. Justified text tends to look more formal and cleaner, but in a word processing document, it also results in uneven spacing between words. It is the opinion of some authorities that justified text is more difficult to read, especially in a page-width document. Let the overall look and feel of your newsletter be your guide.

Activity 3.17 | Inserting a Column Break

1 Near the bottom of the first column, click to position the insertion point at the beginning of the line *Harvesting Daylight*.

2 On the **PAGE LAYOUT tab**, in the **Page Setup group**, click **Breaks**. Under **Page Breaks**, click **Column**, and then if necessary, scroll to view the bottom of the first column.

A column break displays at the bottom of the first column; text to the right of the column break moves to the top of the next column.

3 Compare your screen with Figure 3.27, and then **Save** 🖫.

A *column break indicator*—a dotted line containing the words *Column Break*—displays at the bottom of the column.

FIGURE 3.27

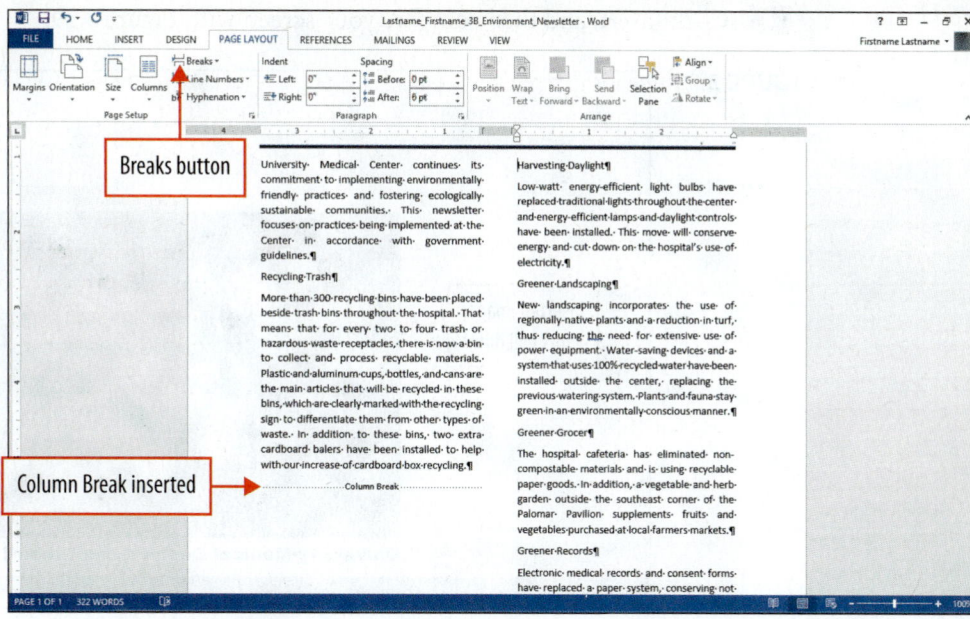

Breaks button

Column Break inserted

Activity 3.18 | Inserting an Online Picture

You can search for and insert online pictures in your document without saving the images to your computer. Pictures can make your document visually appealing and more interesting.

1 Press Ctrl + Home. On the **INSERT tab**, in the **Illustrations group**, click **Online Pictures**.

2 In the **Bing Image Search** box, type **recycling bottles** so that Word can search for images that contain the keywords *recycling* and *bottles*. Press Enter.

3 Click the image of the recycle bin on a black background. If the image does not display, select a similar picture. Compare your screen with Figure 3.28.

FIGURE 3.28

Selected image

4 Click **Insert**, and then compare your screen with Figure 3.29.

FIGURE 3.29

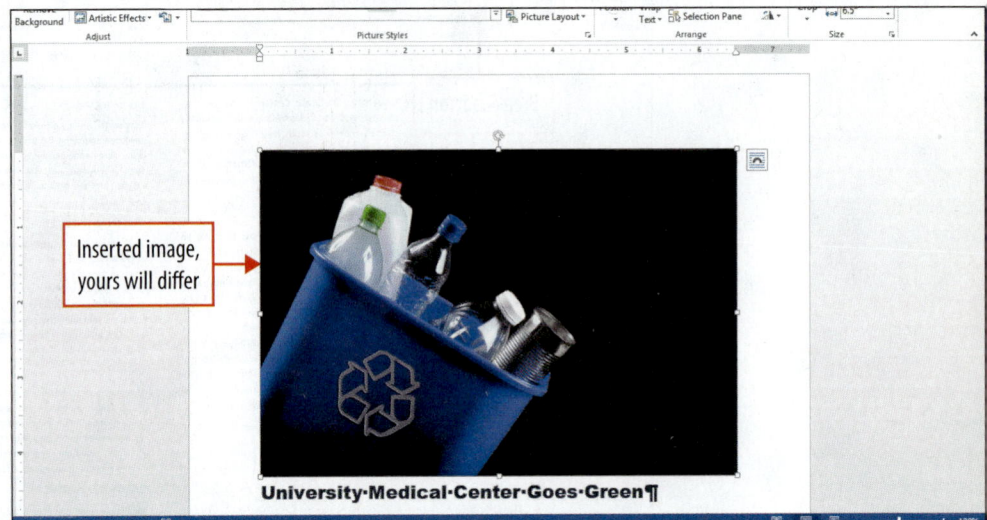

Inserted image, yours will differ

University·Medical·Center·Goes·Green¶

5 Press Ctrl + End to move to the end of the document. On the **INSERT tab**, in the **Illustrations group**, click **Online Pictures**. In the **Bing Image Search** box, type **green recycling symbol** and then press Enter.

6 Click the first recycling symbol and then compare your screen with Figure 3.30. If the picture is not available, choose a similar picture.

FIGURE 3.30

Selected image, yours may differ

7 Click **Insert**. With the picture selected, on the **FORMAT tab**, in the **Size group**, click in the **Height** box. Type **0.5** and then press Enter. To the right of the picture, click **Layout Options**, and then click **Square**. At the bottom of the **Layout Options gallery**, click **See more**.

8 On the **Position tab**, under **Horizontal**, click the **Alignment** option button. Click the **Alignment arrow**, and then click **Centered**. Click the **relative to arrow** and then click **Page**. Under **Vertical**, click the **Alignment** option button. Click the **Alignment arrow**, and then click **Bottom**. Click the **relative to arrow**, and then click **Margin**. Compare your screen with Figure 3.31.

FIGURE 3.31

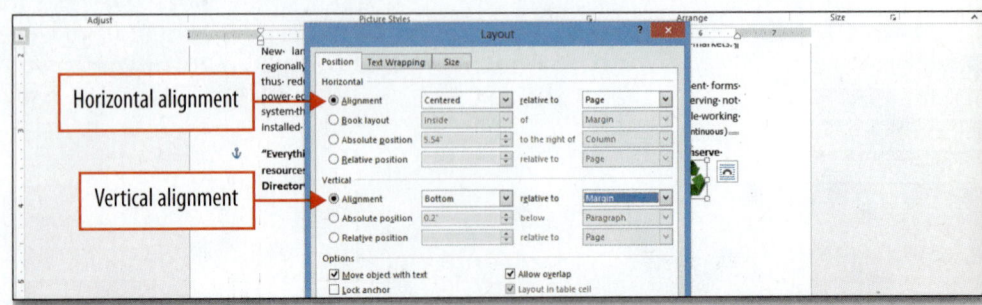

Horizontal alignment

Vertical alignment

9 ▸ Click **OK**, scroll to the bottom of the page, and then notice that the recycle image displays at the bottom of the second page. **Save** 🔲 the document.

 **ANOTHER WAY**   Drag the image to visually position the image.

Activity 3.19 │ Cropping a Picture and Resizing a Picture by Scaling

In this activity, you will edit the recycle bin image by cropping and scaling the picture. When you *crop* a picture, you remove unwanted or unnecessary areas of the picture. When you *scale* a picture, you resize it to a percentage of its size.

1 ▸ Press ⌈Ctrl⌉ + ⌈Home⌉ to move to the top of the document, and then click the recycle bin picture to select it. On the **FORMAT tab**, in the **Size group**, click the upper portion of the **Crop** button to display crop handles around the picture. Compare your screen with Figure 3.32.

Crop handles are used like sizing handles to define unwanted areas of the picture.

FIGURE 3.32

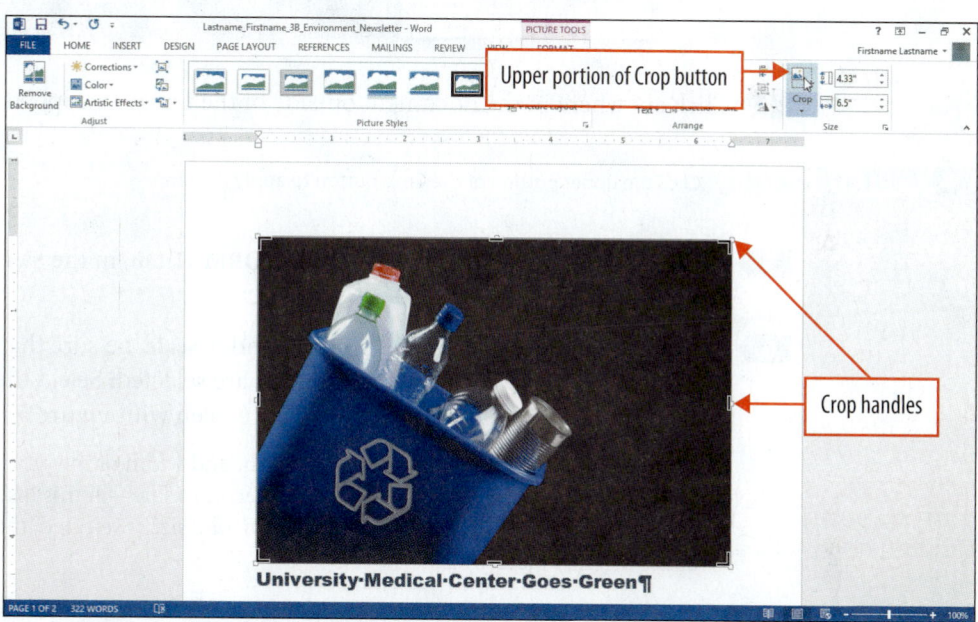

2 ▸ Point to the center right crop handle to display the ⌈✛⌉ pointer. Compare your screen with Figure 3.33.

Use the *crop pointer* to crop areas of a picture.

FIGURE 3.33

3 With the crop pointer displayed, hold down the left mouse button and drag to the left to approximately **5 inches on the horizontal ruler**, and then release the mouse button. Compare your screen with Figure 3.34.

The portion of the image to be removed displays in gray.

FIGURE 3.34
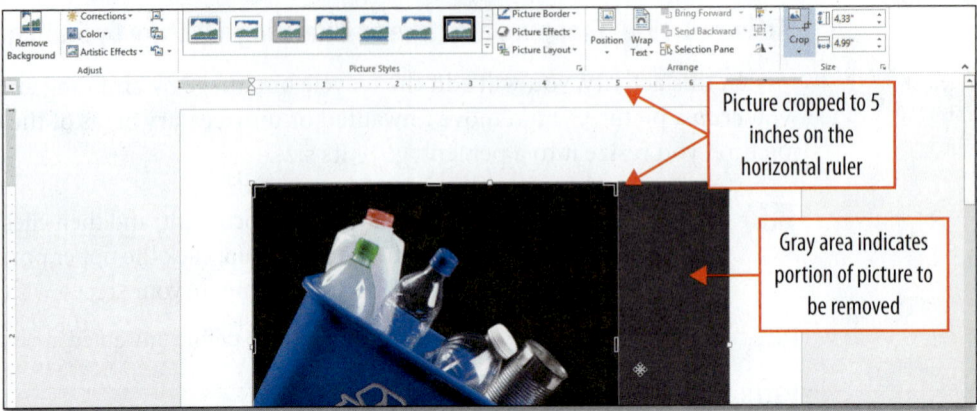

Picture cropped to 5 inches on the horizontal ruler

Gray area indicates portion of picture to be removed

4 Click anywhere in the document outside of the image to apply the crop.

↻ ANOTHER WAY Click the upper portion of the Crop button to apply the crop.

5 Click to select the picture again. On the **FORMAT tab**, in the **Size group**, click the **Dialog Box Launcher** button .

6 In the **Layout dialog box**, on the **Size tab**, under **Scale**, be sure that the **Lock aspect ratio** and **Relative to original picture size** check boxes are selected. Select the number in the **Height box**, type **10** and then press Tab. Compare your screen with Figure 3.35.

When *Lock aspect ratio* is selected, the height and width of the picture are sized proportionately and only one scale value is necessary. The second value—in this instance Width—adjusts proportionately. When *Relative to original picture size* is selected, the scale is applied as a percentage of the original picture size.

FIGURE 3.35
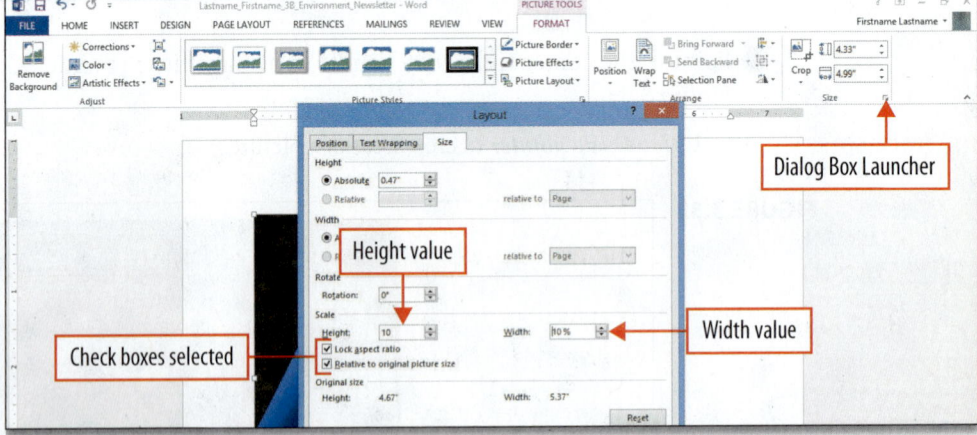

Dialog Box Launcher

Height value

Width value

Check boxes selected

7 In the **Layout** dialog box, click the **Text Wrapping tab**. Under **Wrapping style**, click **Square**.

8 Click the **Position tab**, and then under **Horizontal**, click the **Alignment** option button. Be sure that the **Alignment** indicates **Left** and **relative to Column**. Under **Vertical**, click the **Alignment** option button, and then change the alignment to **Top relative to Margin**. Click **OK**, and then compare your screen with Figure 3.36.

FIGURE 3.36

3
WORD

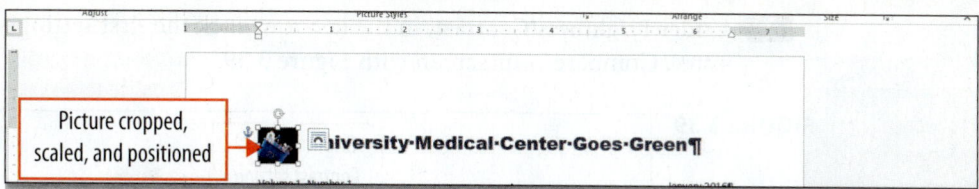

Activity 3.20 | Setting Transparent Color and Recoloring a Picture

You can make one color in a picture transparent using the Set Transparent Color command. When you *recolor* a picture, you change all the colors in the picture to shades of a single color.

1 On the **VIEW tab**, in the **Zoom group**, click **Zoom**, and then click **200%**. Click **OK**. Drag the scroll bars as necessary so that you can view the recycle bin picture at the top of the document.

2 If necessary, select the recycle bin picture. On the **FORMAT tab**, in the **Adjust group**, click **Color**, and then below the gallery, click **Set Transparent Color**. Move the pointer into the document to display the ✎ pointer.

3 Point anywhere in the black background of the recycle bin picture, and then click to apply the transparent color to the background. Compare your screen with Figure 3.37.

FIGURE 3.37

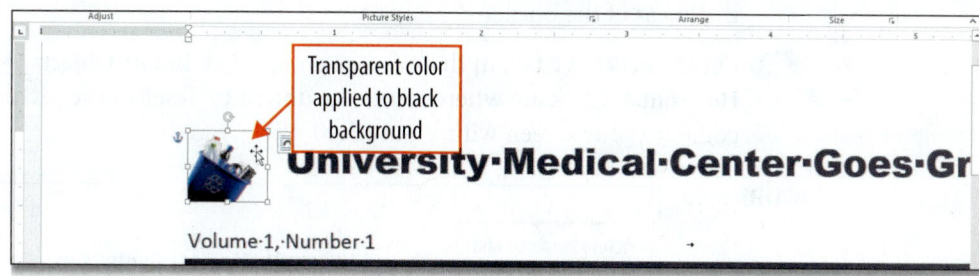

4 Press Ctrl + End to move to the end of your document, and then select the picture of the recycle symbol. On the **FORMAT tab**, in the **Adjust group**, click **Color** to display a gallery of recoloring options. Under **Recolor**, in the last row, click the fourth option— **Olive Green, Accent color 3 Light**. Compare your screen with Figure 3.38, and then **Save** 🖫 the document.

FIGURE 3.38

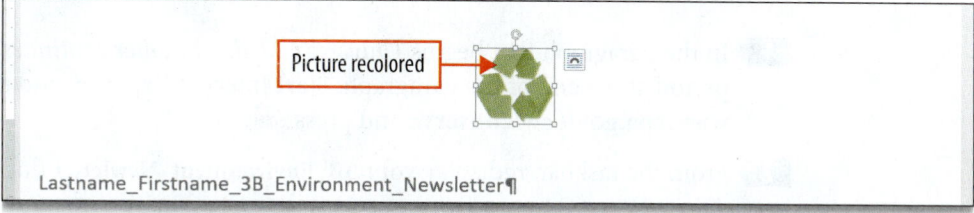

Activity 3.21 | Adjusting the Brightness and Contrast of a Picture

Brightness is the relative lightness of a picture. **Contrast** is the difference between the darkest and lightest area of a picture.

1 If necessary, select the recycle symbol. On the **FORMAT tab**, in the **Adjust group**, click **Corrections**. Under **Brightness/Contrast**, point to several of the options to view the effect that the settings have on the picture.

2 Under **Brightness/Contrast**, in the last row, click the first setting—**Brightness: –40% Contrast: +40%**. Compare your screen with Figure 3.39.

FIGURE 3.39

Brightness and Contrast setting applied to picture

Lastname_Firstname_3B_Environment_Newsletter¶

3 On the **VIEW tab**, in the **Zoom group**, click **100%**, and then **Save** 🖫 the document.

Activity 3.22 | Applying a Border to a Picture and Flipping a Picture

The *flip* commands create a reverse image of a picture or object.

1 Press Ctrl + Home to move to the top of the document, and then select the picture of the recycle bin. On the **FORMAT tab**, in the **Picture Styles group**, click the **Picture Border button arrow**. Under **Theme Colors**, in the fourth column, click the first color—**Dark Blue, Text 2**.

2 Click the **Picture Border arrow** again, and then point to **Weight**. Click **1 1/2 pt** to change the thickness of the border.

3 On the **FORMAT tab**, in the **Arrange group**, click **Rotate Objects** 🔄, and then click **Flip Horizontal**. Click anywhere in the document to deselect the picture. **Save** 🖫, and then compare your screen with Figure 3.40.

FIGURE 3.40

Picture bordered and flipped

University·Medical·Center·Goes·Green¶

Volume·1,·Number·1   →   January·2016¶

Activity 3.23 | Inserting a Screenshot

A *screenshot* is an image of an active window on your computer that you can paste into a document. Screenshots are especially useful when you want to insert an image of a website into your Word document. You can insert a screenshot of any open window on your computer.

1 In the paragraph that begins *University Medical Center continues*, click after the period at the end of the paragraph. Start Internet Explorer, and then navigate to **www.epa.gov/osw/conserve** and press Enter.

2 From the taskbar, redisplay your **3B_Environment_Newletter** document.

3 With the insertion point positioned at the end of the paragraph, on the **INSERT tab**, in the **Illustrations group**, click **Screenshot**.

All of your open windows display in the Available Windows gallery and are available to paste into the document.

4 In the **Screenshot** gallery, click the browser window that contains the EPA site to insert the screenshot at the insertion point. If a message box displays asking if you want to hyperlink the screenshot, click No, and then notice that the image is inserted and is sized to fit between the margins of the first column. Compare your screen with Figure 3.41.

By selecting No in the message box, you are inserting a screenshot without links to the actual website. Choose Yes, if you want to link the image to the website.

FIGURE 3.41

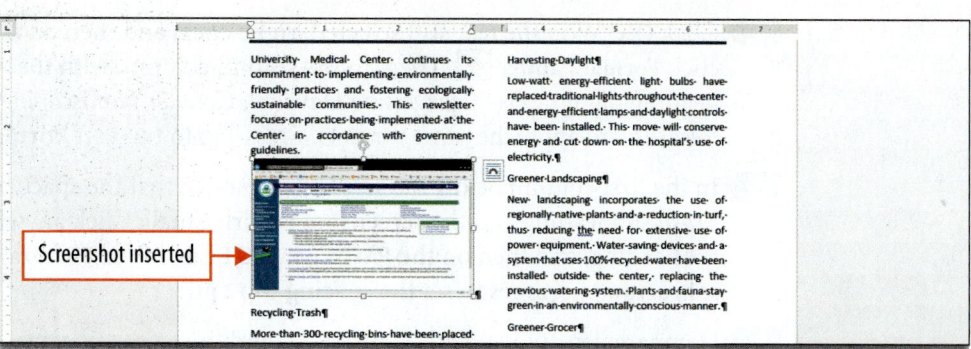

Screenshot inserted

5 With the inserted screenshot selected, on the **FORMAT tab**, in the **Picture Styles group**, click the **Picture Border button arrow**, and then under **Theme Colors**, in the second column, click the first color—**Black, Text 1**.

6 Save 🖫 the document.

Objective 6 Use Special Character and Paragraph Formatting

Video W3-6

Special text and paragraph formatting is useful to emphasize text, and it makes your newsletter look more professional. For example, you can place a border around one or more paragraphs or add shading to a paragraph. When adding shading, use light colors; dark shading can make the text difficult to read.

Activity 3.24 | Applying the Small Caps Font Effect

For headlines and titles, *small caps* is an attractive font effect. The effect changes lowercase letters to uppercase letters, but with the height of lowercase letters.

1 Under the screenshot, select the paragraph *Recycling Trash* including the paragraph mark.

2 Right-click the selected text, and then on the shortcut menu, click **Font** to display the **Font** dialog box. Click the **Font color arrow**, and then change the color to **Blue, Accent 1, Darker 50%**—in the fifth column, the last color.

3 Under **Font style**, click **Bold**. Under **Effects**, select the **Small caps** check box. Compare your screen with Figure 3.42.

The Font dialog box provides more options than are available on the ribbon and enables you to make several changes at the same time. In the Preview box, the text displays with the selected formatting options applied.

FIGURE 3.42

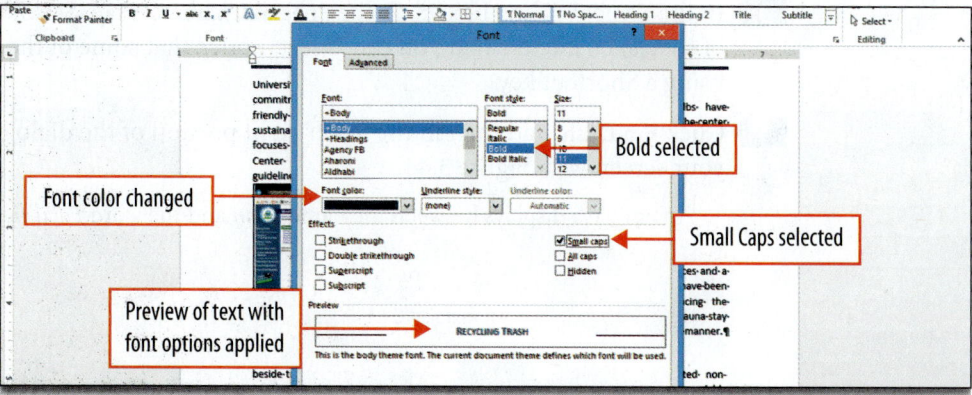

Font color changed

Bold selected

Small Caps selected

Preview of text with font options applied

4 ▶ Click **OK**. With the text still selected, right-click, and then on the mini toolbar, double-click **Format Painter** 💉. Then, in the second column, with the 📑 pointer, select each of the heading paragraphs—*Harvesting Daylight, Greener Landscaping, Greener Grocer,* and *Greener Records*—to apply the same formats. Press Esc to turn off **Format Painter**.

5 ▶ In the first column below the screenshot, notice that the space between the *Recycling Trash* subheading and the screenshot is fairly small. Click anywhere in the *Recycling Trash* subheading, and then on the **PAGE LAYOUT tab**, in the **Paragraph group**, click the **Before up spin arrow** two times to set the spacing to **12 pt**.

6 ▶ Compare your screen with Figure 3.43, and then **Save** 💾 your document.

FIGURE 3.43

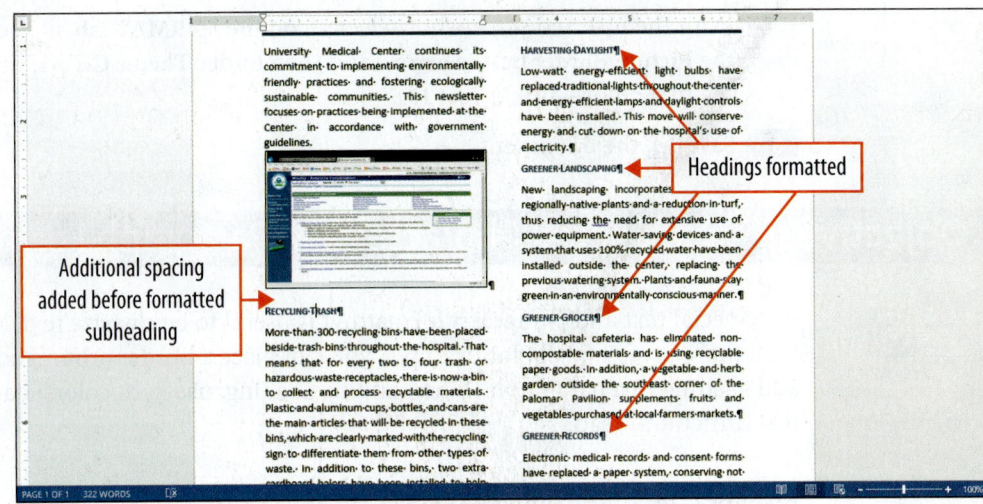

Activity 3.25 | Inserting Symbols and Special Characters

You can insert symbols and special characters in a Word document, including copyright symbols, trademark symbols, and em dashes. An ***em dash*** is a punctuation symbol used to indicate an explanation or emphasis.

1 ▶ Press Ctrl + End to move to the end of the document, and then after the name *Emily Lynn* delete the comma and the space that separates her name from her job title—*Facilities Director*.

2 ▶ With the insertion point positioned before the *F* in *Facilities*, on the **INSERT tab**, in the **Symbols group**, click **Symbol**. Below the gallery, click **More Symbols** to display the **Symbol** dialog box.

Here you can choose the symbol that you want to insert in your document.

3 ▶ In the **Symbol** dialog box, click the **Special Characters tab**. Scroll the list to view the types of special characters that you can insert; notice that some of the characters can be inserted using a Shortcut key.

4 ▶ Click **Em Dash**, and then in the lower right portion of the dialog box, click **Insert**. Compare your screen with Figure 3.44.

An em dash displays between the name *Lynn* and the word *Facilities*.

FIGURE 3.44

3
WORD

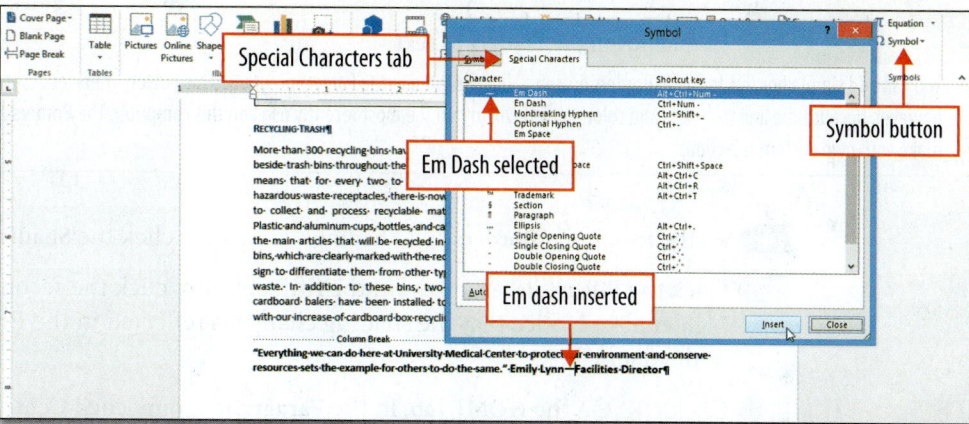

5 ▶ In the **Symbol** dialog box, click **Close**, and then **Save** 🖫 your document.

Activity 3.26 | Adding Borders and Shading to a Paragraph and Inserting a Manual Line Break

Paragraph borders provide strong visual cues to the reader. You can use paragraph shading with or without borders; however, combined with a border, light shading can be very effective in drawing the reader's eye to the text.

1 ▶ At the end of the document, select the two lines of bold text that begin *"Everything we can do.*

The recycle picture may also be selected because it is anchored to the paragraph.

2 ▶ On the **HOME tab**, in the **Paragraph group**, click the **Borders button arrow** ⊞ ▾, and then click **Borders and Shading**.

3 ▶ In the **Borders and Shading** dialog box, be sure the **Borders tab** is selected. Under **Setting**, click **Shadow**. Click the **Color arrow**, and then in the fifth column, click the last color—**Blue, Accent 1, Darker 50%**. Click the **Width arrow**, and then click **1 pt**. Compare your screen with Figure 3.45.

In the lower right portion of the Borders and Shading dialog box, the *Apply to* box indicates *Paragraph*. The *Apply to* box directs where the border will be applied—in this instance, the border will be applied only to the selected paragraph.

FIGURE 3.45

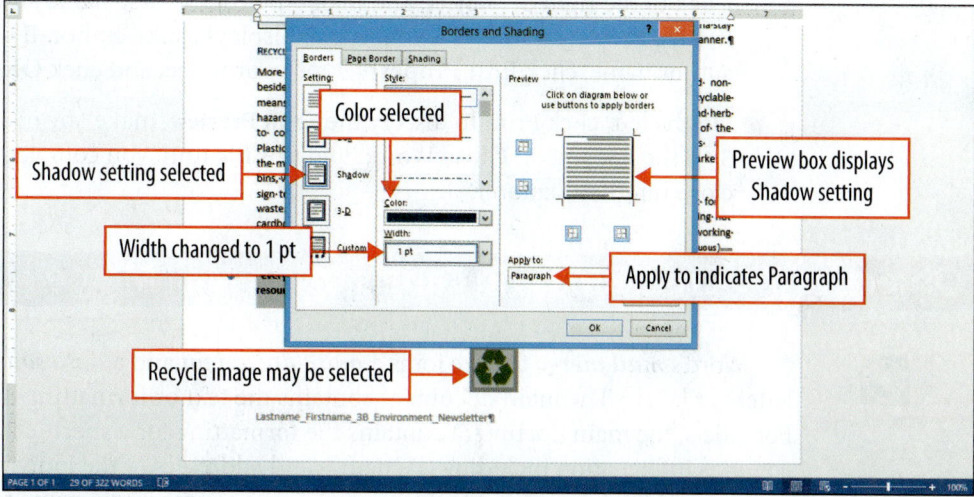

4 At the top of the **Borders and Shading** dialog box, click the **Shading tab**.

5 Click the **Fill arrow**, and then in the fifth column, click the second color—**Blue, Accent 1, Lighter 80%**. Notice that the shading change is reflected in the **Preview area** on the right side of the dialog box.

6 Click **OK**. On the **HOME tab**, in the **Paragraph group**, click **Center** 📄.

7 Click anywhere in the document to deselect, and then compare your screen with Figure 3.46.

FIGURE 3.46

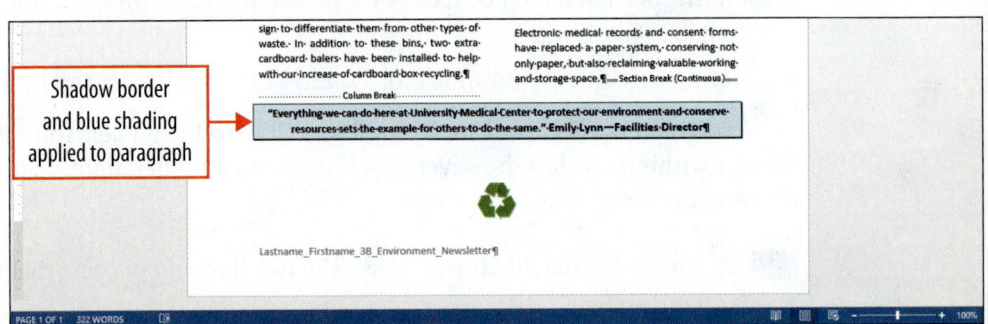

Shadow border and blue shading applied to paragraph

8 In the shaded paragraph, in the second line, click in front of the *E* in the name *Emily*. Hold down Shift and then press Enter.

Holding down Shift while pressing Enter inserts a ***manual line break***, which moves the text to the right of the insertion point to a new line while keeping the text in the same paragraph. A ***line break indicator***, in the shape of a bent arrow, indicates a manual line break.

9 Press Ctrl + Home to move the insertion point to the top of the document. Click the **FILE tab** to display **Backstage** view. On the right, at the bottom of the **Properties** list, click **Show All Properties**.

10 On the list of **Properties**, click to the right of **Tags**, and then type **newsletter, January**

11 Click to the right of **Subject**, and then type your course name and section number. Under **Related People**, be sure that your name displays as the author. If necessary, right-click the author name, click **Edit Property**, type your name, and click **OK**.

12 On the left, click **Print** to display the **Print Preview**, make any necessary corrections, and then **Save** the document. **Close** Word; hold this file until you complete this project. If necessary, close Internet Explorer.

Objective 7   Create Mailing Labels Using Mail Merge

Video W3-7

Word's ***mail merge*** feature joins a ***main document*** and a ***data source*** to create customized letters or labels. The main document contains the text or formatting that remains constant. For labels, the main document contains the formatting for a specific label size. The data source contains information including the names and addresses of the individuals for whom the labels are being created. Names and addresses in a data source might come from a Word table, an Excel worksheet, or an Access database.

The easiest way to perform a mail merge is to use the Mail Merge Wizard, which asks you questions and, based on your answers, walks you step by step through the mail merge process.

Activity 3.27 | Starting the Mail Merge Wizard Template

In this activity, you will open the data source for the mail merge, which is a Word table containing names and addresses.

1 Start Word and display a new blank document. Display formatting marks and rulers. **Save** the document in your **Word Chapter 3** folder as **Lastname_Firstname_3B_Mailing_Labels**

2 With your new document open on the screen, from your student files, **Open** the file **w03B_Addresses. Save** the address file in your **Word Chapter 3** folder as **Lastname_Firstname_3B_Addresses** and then add the file name to the footer.

This document contains a table of addresses. The first row contains the column names. The remaining rows contain the names and addresses.

3 Click to position the insertion point in the last cell in the table, and then press [Tab] to create a new row. Enter the following information, and then compare your table with Figure 3.47.

FIRST NAME	LAST NAME	ADDRESS 1	UNIT	CITY	STATE	ZIP CODE
Monica	Warren	5626 Summer Road	#234	Lakeland	TN	38002

FIGURE 3.47

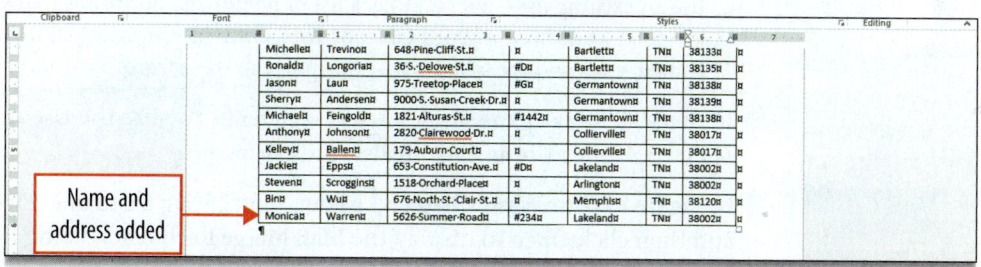

4 Save, and then **Close** the table of addresses. Be sure that your blank **Lastname_Firstname_3B_Mailing_Labels** document displays.

5 Click the **MAILINGS tab**. In the **Start Mail Merge group**, click **Start Mail Merge**, and then click **Step-by-Step Mail Merge Wizard** to display the **Mail Merge** pane on the right.

6 In the **Mail Merge** pane, under **Select document type**, click **Labels**. At the bottom of the **Mail Merge** pane, click **Next: Starting document** to display Step 2 of 6.

7 Under **Select starting document**, be sure **Change document layout** is selected, and then under **Change document layout**, click **Label options**.

8 In the **Label Options** dialog box, under **Printer information**, click the **Tray arrow**, and then if necessary, click **Default tray** (Automatically Select)—the exact wording may vary depending on your printer, but select the *Default* or *Automatic* option so that you can print the labels on regular paper rather than manually inserting labels in the printer.

9 Under **Label information**, click the **Label vendors arrow**, and then click **Avery US Letter**. Under **Product number**, scroll about halfway down the list, and then click **5160 Easy Peel Address Labels**. Compare your screen with Figure 3.48.

The Avery 5160 address label is a commonly used label. The precut sheets contain three columns of 10 labels each—for a total of 30 labels per sheet.

FIGURE 3.48

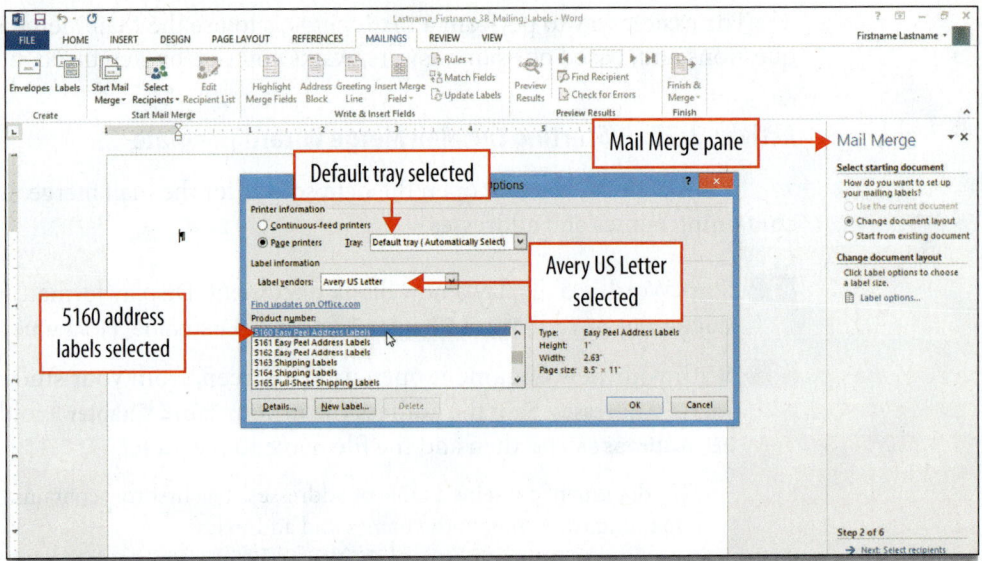

10 At the bottom of the **Label Options** dialog box, click **OK**. If a message box displays, click **OK** to set up the labels. If the gridlines do not display, on the **Layout tab**, in the **Table** group, click **View Gridlines**. At the bottom of the **Mail Merge** pane, click **Next: Select recipients**.

The label page is set up with three columns and ten rows. Here, in Step 3 of the Mail Merge Wizard, you must identify the recipients—the data source. For your recipient data source, you can choose to use an existing list—for example, a list of names and addresses that you have in an Access database, an Excel worksheet, a Word table, or your Outlook contacts list. If you do not have an existing data source, you can type a new list at this point in the wizard.

11 In the **Mail Merge** pane, under **Select recipients**, be sure the **Use an existing list** option button is selected. Under **Use an existing list**, click **Browse**.

12 Navigate to your **Word Chapter 3** folder, select your **Lastname_Firstname_3B_Addresses** file, and then click **Open** to display the **Mail Merge Recipients** dialog box. Compare your screen with Figure 3.49.

In the Mail Merge Recipients dialog box, the column headings are formed from the text in the first row of your Word table of addresses. Each row of information that contains data for one person is referred to as a *record*. The column headings—for example, *Last_Name* and *First_Name*—are referred to as *fields*. An underscore replaces the spaces between words in the field name headings.

FIGURE 3.49

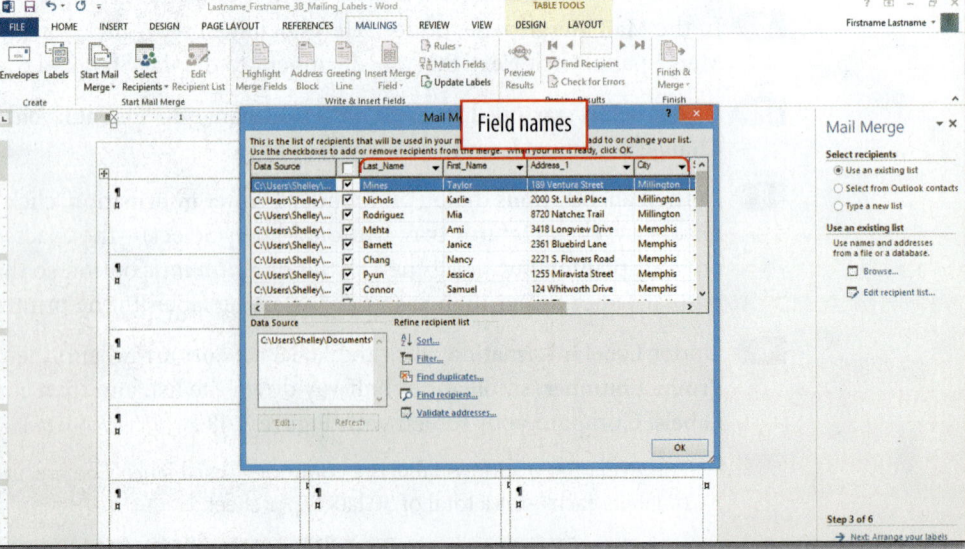

13 In the lower left portion of the **Mail Merge Recipients** dialog box, in the **Data Source** box, click the path that contains your file name. Then, at the bottom of the **Mail Merge Recipients** dialog box, click **Edit**.

14 In the upper right corner of the **Data Form** dialog box, click **Add New**. In the blank record, type the following, pressing `Tab` to move from field to field, and then compare your **Data Form** dialog box with Figure 3.50.

FIRST_NAME	LAST_NAME	ADDRESS_1	UNIT	CITY	STATE	ZIP CODE
Sharon	Williams	1251 Parker Road	#843	Memphis	TN	38123

FIGURE 3.50

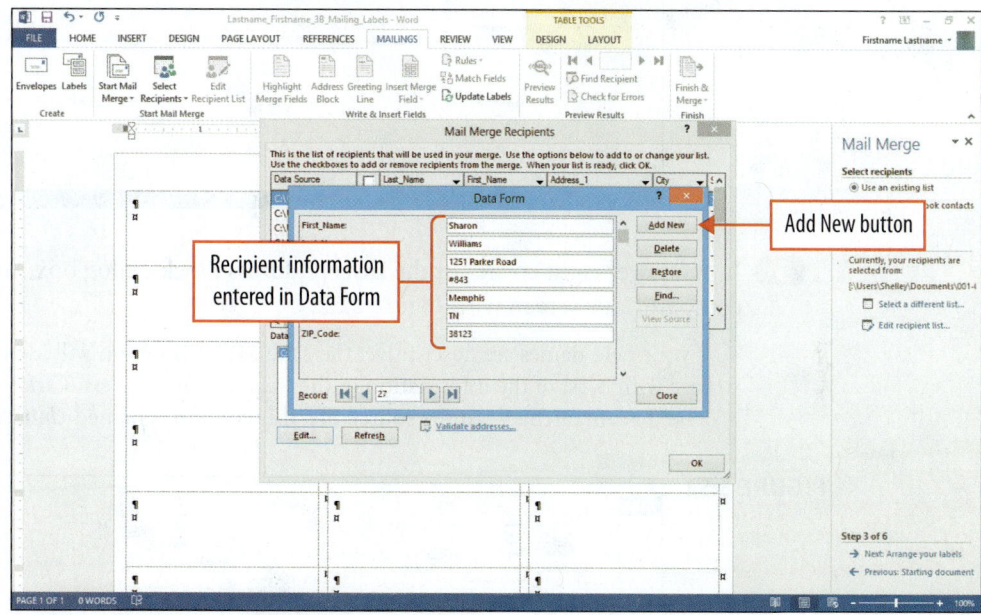

15 In the lower right corner of the **Data Form** dialog box, click **Close**. Scroll to the end of the recipient list to confirm that the record for *Sharon Williams* that you just added is in the list. At the bottom of the **Mail Merge Recipients** dialog box, click **OK**.

Activity 3.28 | Completing the Mail Merge Wizard

You can add or edit names and addresses while completing the Mail Merge. You can also match your column names with preset names used in Mail Merge.

1 At the bottom of the **Mail Merge** pane, click **Next: Arrange your labels**.

2 Under **Arrange your labels**, click **Address block**. In the **Insert Address Block** dialog box, under **Specify address elements**, examine the various formats for names. If necessary, under *Insert recipient's name in this format*, select the *Joshua Randall Jr.* format. Compare your dialog box with Figure 3.51.

FIGURE 3.51

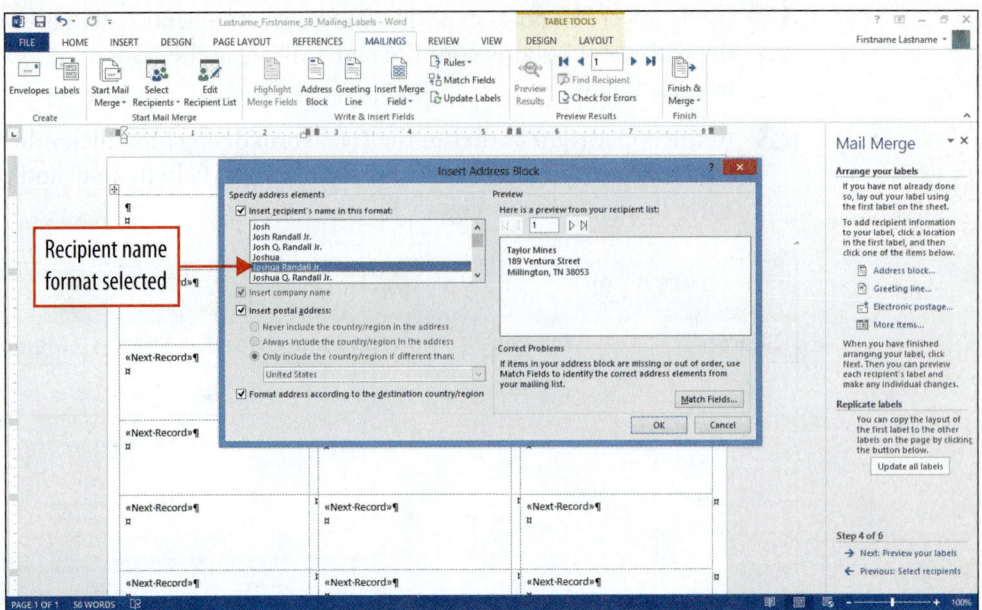

Recipient name format selected

3 In the lower right corner of the **Insert Address Block** dialog box, click **Match Fields**, and then compare your screen with Figure 3.52.

If your field names are descriptive, the Mail Merge program will identify them correctly, as is the case with most of the information in the *Required for Address Block* section. However, the Address 2 field is unmatched—in the source file, this column is named *Unit*.

FIGURE 3.52

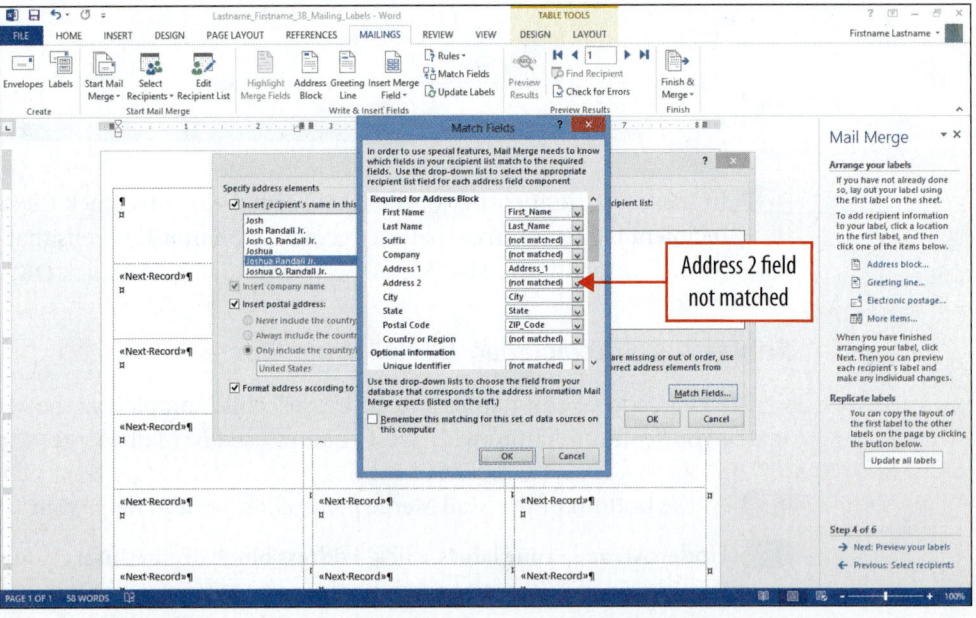

Address 2 field not matched

4 Click the **Address 2 arrow**, and then from the list of available fields, click **Unit** to match the Mail Merge field with the field in your data source.

5 At the bottom of the **Match Fields** dialog box, click **OK**. At the bottom of the **Insert Address Block** dialog box, click **OK**.

Word inserts the Address block in the first label space surrounded by double angle brackets. The *AddressBlock* field name displays, which represents the address block you saw in the Preview area of the Insert Address Block dialog box.

6 In the **Mail Merge** pane, under **Replicate labels**, click **Update all labels** to insert an address block in each label space for each subsequent record.

7 At the bottom of the **Mail Merge** pane, click **Next: Preview your labels**. Notice that for addresses with four lines, the last line of the address is cut off.

8 Press Ctrl + A to select all of the label text, click the **PAGE LAYOUT tab**, and then in the **Paragraph group**, click in the **Spacing Before** box. Type **3** and press Enter.

9 Click in any label to deselect, and notice that 4-line addresses are no longer cut off. Compare your screen with Figure 3.53.

FIGURE 3.53

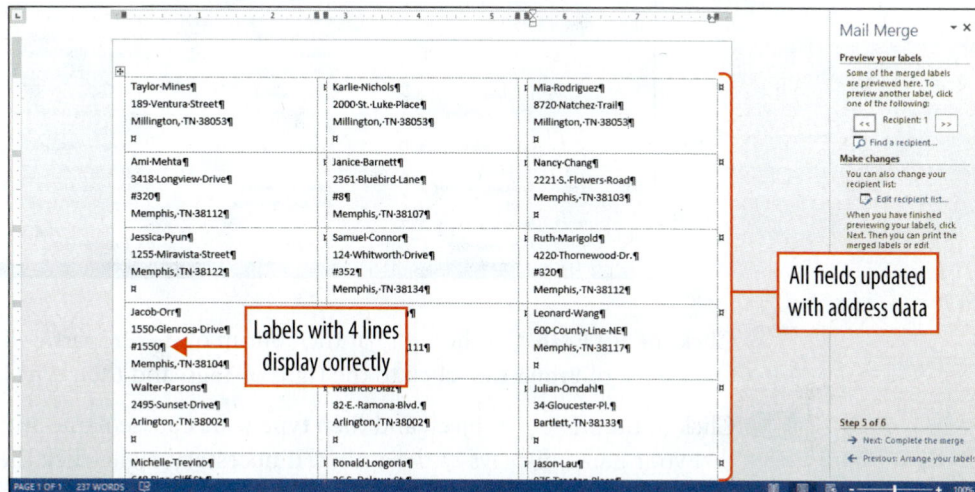

10 At the bottom of the **Mail Merge** pane, click **Next: Complete the merge**.

Step 6 of the Mail Merge displays. At this point you can print or edit your labels, although this is done more easily in the document window.

11 Save 🖫 your labels, and then on the right, **Close** ☒ the **Mail Merge** pane.

Activity 3.29 | Sorting Mail Merge Results

If you discover that you need to make further changes to your labels, you can still make them even though the Mail Merge task pane is closed.

1 Add the file name to the footer, close the footer area, and then move to the top of Page 2. Click anywhere in the empty table row, and then click the **LAYOUT tab**. In the **Rows & Columns group**, click **Delete**, and then click **Delete Rows**.

Adding footer text to a label sheet replaces the last row of labels on a page with the footer text, and moves the last row of labels to the top of the next page. In this instance, a blank second page is created, which you can delete by deleting the blank row.

2 Notice that the labels do not display in alphabetical order. Click the **MAILINGS tab**, and then in the **Start Mail Merge group**, click **Edit Recipient List** to display the list of names and addresses.

3 In the **Mail Merge Recipients** dialog box, click the **Last_Name** field heading, and notice that the names are sorted alphabetically by the recipient's last name.

Mailing labels are often sorted by either last name or by ZIP Code.

4 Click the **Last_Name** field heading again, and notice that the last names are sorted in descending order. Click the **Last_Name** field one more time to return to ascending order, and then click **OK**. Press Ctrl + Home, and then compare your screen with Figure 3.54.

FIGURE 3.54

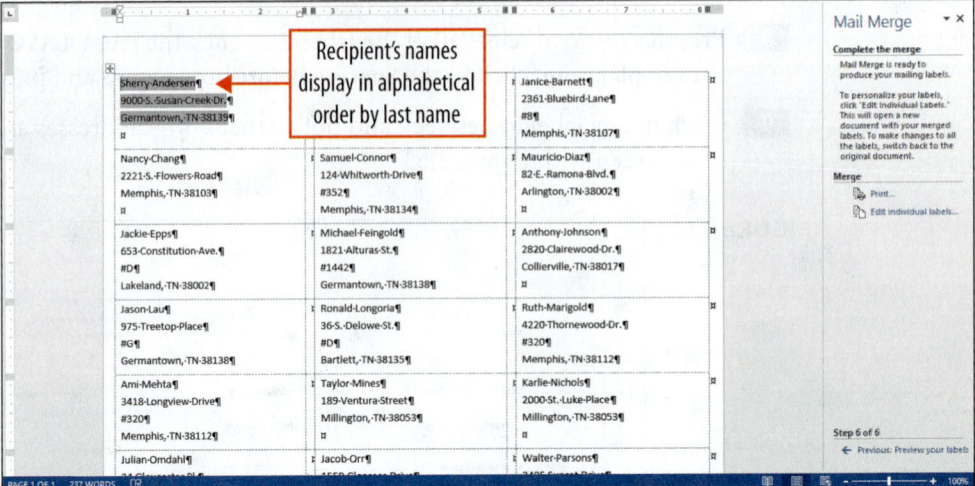

5 Click the **FILE tab**. On the right, at the bottom of the **Properties** list, click **Show All Properties**. On the list of **Properties**, click to the right of **Tags**, and then type **labels**

6 Click to the right of **Subject**, and then type your course name and section number. Be sure that your name displays as the author. If necessary, right-click the author name, click **Edit Property**, type your name, and click **OK**. **Save** 🔲 the file. **Close** the document, and click **Yes** to save the data source.

7 As directed by your instructor, print or submit electronically.

If you print, the labels will print on whatever paper is in the printer; unless you have preformatted labels available, the labels will print on a sheet of paper. Printing the labels on plain paper enables you to proofread the labels before you print them on more expensive label sheets.

8 In addition to your labels and address document, print or submit your **Lastname_Firstname_3B_Environment_Newsletter** document as directed. **Close** Word.

END | You have completed Project 3B

Objective | Format a Single-Column Newsletter in Word Online

You can use Word Online to insert clip art and to format text. You can change fonts and font color, and modify paragraph spacing.

> **A L E R T !** **Working with Web-Based Applications and Services**
>
> Computer programs and services on the web receive continuous updates and improvements, so the steps to complete this web-based activity may differ from the ones shown. You can often look at the screens and the information presented to determine how to complete the activity.

Activity | Formatting a Single-Column Newsletter

In this activity, you will use Word Online to edit a single-column newsletter similar to the one you edited in Project 3B.

1 From the desktop, start Internet Explorer. Navigate to **http://onedrive.com**, and then sign in to your Microsoft account. Open your **GO! Web Projects** folder; or create this folder if necessary.

2 In the OneDrive menu bar, click **Upload**. Navigate to your student data files, click **w03_3B_Web**, and then click **Open**.

3 Point to the uploaded file **w03_3B_Web**, and then right-click. On the shortcut menu, scroll as necessary, and then click **Rename**. Using your own last name and first name, type **Lastname_Firstname_WD_3B_Web** and then press Enter to rename the file.

4 Click the file that you just renamed, and then click **EDIT DOCUMENT**. On the list, click **Edit in Word Online**.

5 Drag to select the newsletter title—*University Medical Center Goes Green*. On the **HOME tab**, in the **Font group**, locate and click the **Grow Font button** two times to change the font size to **18**. With the newsletter title still selected, on the **HOME tab**, in the **Font group**, click **Font Color**, and then in the fifth column, click the

last color—**Blue Gray, Accent 1, Darker 50%**. Apply the same **Font Color** to the five subheadings—*Recycling Trash*, *Harvesting Daylight*, *Greener Landscaping*, *Greener Grocer*, and *Greener Records*.

6 Drag to select the first subheading—*Recycling Trash*. On the **PAGE LAYOUT tab**, in the **Paragraph group**, click in the **After box**. Type **12** and then press Enter—or click the arrow as necessary. Apply the same **Spacing After** to the remaining four subheadings—*Harvesting Daylight*, *Greener Landscaping*, *Greener Grocer*, and *Greener Records*. Click anywhere in the document, and then press Ctrl + Home to move to the top of the document. Compare your screen with Figure A.

7 Be sure the insertion point is positioned at the top of the document. On the **PAGE LAYOUT tab**, in the **Page Setup group**, click **Margins**, and then click **Custom Margins**. Click in the **Top** box and type **0.5** and then click in the **Bottom** box. Type **0.5** and then click **OK**.

8 On the **INSERT tab**, in the **Pictures group**, click **Picture**. Navigate to your student data files, and then click **w03B_Recycling**. Click **Insert**.

FIGURE A

(GO! with Office Online (formerly Web Apps) continues on the next page)

7 Be sure the insertion point is positioned at the top of the document. On the **PAGE LAYOUT tab**, in the **Page Setup group**, click **Margins**, and then click **Custom Margins**. Click in the **Top** box and type **0.5** and then click in the **Bottom** box. Type **0.5** and then click **OK**.

8 On the **INSERT tab**, in the **Pictures group**, click **Clip Art**. In the **Search** box, type **recycling bottles** and then press [Enter]. Click the image of the recycle bin filled with plastic bottles on a black background. If the image is not available, choose a similar picture. Click **Insert**.

9 On the **FORMAT tab**, in the **Image Size group**, click in the **Scale** box. Type **10** to replace the existing number, and then press [Enter]. On the **FORMAT tab**, in the **Picture Styles group**, use the ScreenTips to locate and then click **Reflected Rounded Rectangle**.

10 Press [Ctrl] + [End] to move to the end of the document, and then press [Enter]. On the **INSERT tab**, in the **Pictures group**, click **Online Pictures**. In the **Bing Image**

Search box, type **green recycle symbol** and then press [Enter]. Click an image of a green recycling symbol. Click **Insert**.

11 Click the image to select it, click the **PICTURE TOOLS FORMAT** tab, and then, in the **Image Size group**, set the **Scale** to 5%. On the **HOME tab**, in the **Paragraph group**, click **Center**.

12 In the last paragraph of the newsletter, click to position the insertion point between the second quotation mark and the letter *E* in *Emily*. Hold down [Shift] and then press [Enter] to insert a manual line break. On the **HOME tab**, in the **Paragraph group**, click **Center** to center the three lines of text in the last paragraph. Compare your screen with Figure B.

13 **Save** your file and submit as directed by your instructor. Then, on the ribbon, click the **FILE tab**, and then click **Exit**. Sign out of your SkyDrive.

FIGURE B

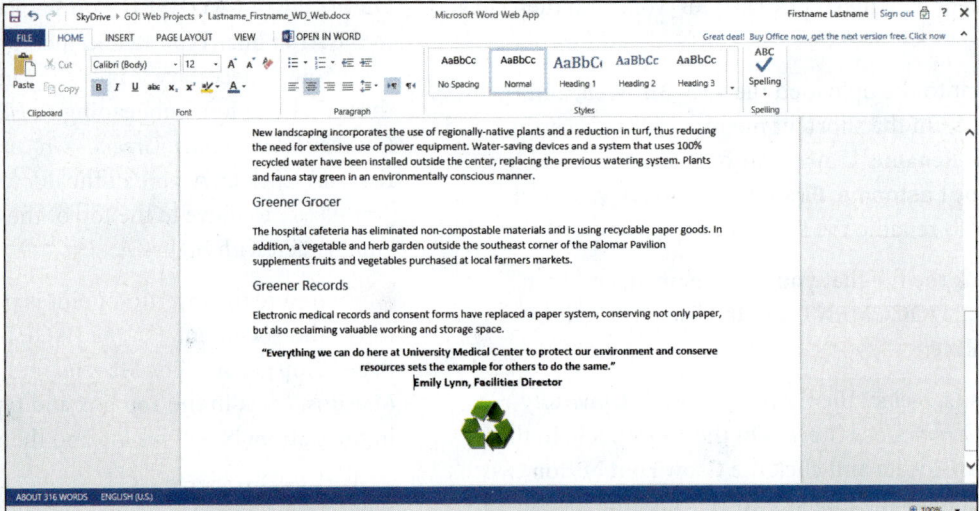

Andrew Rodriguez / Fotolia; FotolEdhar/ Fotolia; apops/ Fotolia; Yuri Arcurs/ Fotolia

The advantage of using Office 365 is that your organization does not have to purchase and install server hardware and software for sophisticated business applications and does not need a full-time IT person or staff just to manage the technology your teams need.

By using Office 365, you are able to have business-class services for your employees without investing in expensive hardware, software, and personnel. However, at least one person in an organization must be designated as the *Office 365 Administrator*—the person who creates and manages the account, adds new users, sets up the services your organization wants to use, sets permission levels, and manages the SharePoint team sites. You can have more than one Administrator if you want to share these tasks with others.

Microsoft provides easy-to-use instructions and videos to get you started, and you might also have contact with a Microsoft representative. You will probably find, however, that subscribing to and setting up the account, adding users, and activating services is a straightforward process that requires little or no assistance.

After purchasing the required number of licenses, you will add each team member as a user that includes his or her email address.

The Admin Overview page, as shown in the Figure below, assists the Office 365 Administrator. On the left, there are links to manage the users and domains in your Office 365 account. This is where you can add new users, delete users, set permission levels, enter and change passwords, and update the user properties and the licenses.

In the center, you can see the various services available to you in Office 365. In the site shown in Figure A, Outlook, Lync, SharePoint (team sites), and a public-facing website are all part of the services.

Activity | Using a Team Site to Collaborate

This group project relates to the **Bell Orchid Hotels**. If your instructor assigns this project to your class, you can expect to use a SharePoint team site in **Office 365** to collaborate on the following tasks for this chapter:

- If you are in the **Accounting Group**, you and your teammates will finalize the report to shareholders, merge the letter with the labels, and post the final report on the SharePoint team site.

- If you are in the **Engineering Group**, you and your teammates will finalize the report to the three insurance companies, merge the letter with the labels, and post the final report on the SharePoint team site.

- If you are in the **Food and Beverage Group**, you and your teammates will finalize the letter to customers planning a banquet, merge the letter with the labels, and post the final letter on the SharePoint team site.

- If you are in the **Human Resources Group**, you and your teammates will finalize the memo to employees, merge the memo with the labels, and post the final memo on the SharePoint team site.

- If you are in the **Operations Group**, you and your teammates will finalize the letter to job applicants, merge the letter with the labels, and post the final letter on the SharePoint team site.

- If you are in the **Sales and Marketing Group**, you and your teammates will finalize the letter to the 20 professional associations, merge the letter with the labels, and post the final letter on the SharePoint team site.

FIGURE A

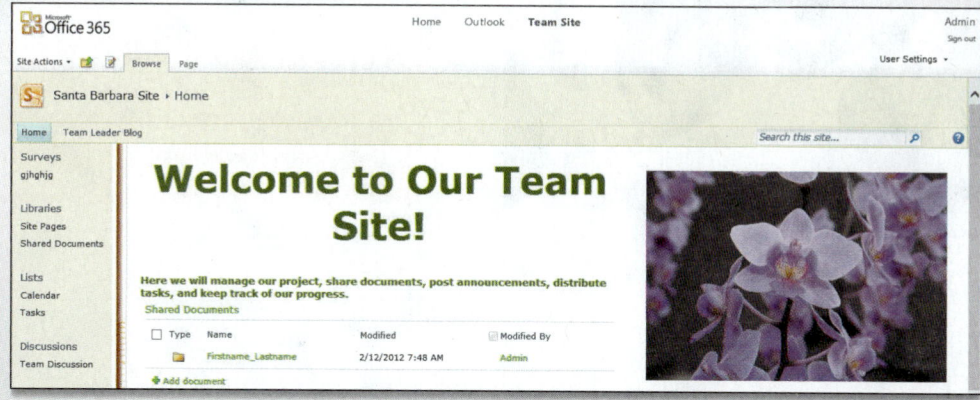

END OF CHAPTER

SUMMARY

Word assists you in formatting a research paper for college or business by providing built-in styles and applies the most commonly used footnote and citation styles for research papers—MLA and APA.

Word helps you create the bibliography for your research paper by recording all of your citations in the Source Manager, and then generating the bibliography—in MLA, called Works Cited—for you.

Newsletters are often used by organizations to communicate information to a specific group. A newsletter can be formatted in two columns with a nameplate at the top that identifies the publication.

The Mail Merge Wizard enables you to easily merge a main document and a data source to create customized letters or labels. The data source can be a Word table, Excel spreadsheet, or Access database.

GO! LEARN IT ONLINE

Review the concepts and key terms in this chapter by completing these online challenges, which you can find at **www.pearsonhighered.com/go**.

Matching and Multiple Choice: Answer matching and multiple choice questions to test what you learned in this chapter. MyITLab®

Crossword Puzzle: Spell out the words that match the numbered clues, and put them in the puzzle squares.

Flipboard: Flip through the definitions of the key terms in this chapter and match them with the correct term.

GO! FOR JOB SUCCESS

Video: Email Etiquette

Your instructor may assign this video to your class, and then ask you to think about, or discuss with your classmates, these questions:

FotolEdhar / Fotolia

Why do you think it is important to follow specific etiquette when composing email?

Why is it important to include a greeting and sign every email that you send?

What are the differences between sending a business email and a personal email, and what are three specific things you should never do in a business email?

END OF CHAPTER

REVIEW AND ASSESSMENT GUIDE FOR WORD CHAPTER 3

Your instructor may assign one or more of these projects to help you review the chapter and assess your mastery and understanding of the chapter.

Review and Assessment Guide for Word Chapter 3			
Project	**Apply Skills from These Chapter Objectives**	**Project Type**	**Project Location**
3C	Objectives 1-4 from Project 3A	**3C Skills Review** A guided review of the skills from Project 3A.	On the following pages
3D	Objectives 5-7 from Project 3B	**3D Skills Review** A guided review of the skills from Project 3B.	On the following pages
3E	Objectives 1-4 from Project 3A	**3E Mastery (Grader Project)** A demonstration of your mastery of the skills in Project 3A with extensive decision making.	In MyITLab and on the following pages
3F	Objectives 5-7 from Project 3B	**3F Mastery (Grader Project)** A demonstration of your mastery of the skills in Project 3B with extensive decision making.	In MyITLab and on the following pages
3G	Objectives 1-7 from Projects 3A and 3B	**3G Mastery (Grader Project)** A demonstration of your mastery of the skills in Projects 3A and 3B with extensive decision making.	In MyITLab and on the following pages
3H	Combination of Objectives from Projects 3A and 3B	**3H GO! Fix It** A demonstration of your mastery of the skills in Projects 3A and 3B by creating a correct result from a document that contains errors you must find.	Online
3I	Combination of Objectives from Projects 3A and 3B	**3I GO! Make It** A demonstration of your mastery of the skills in Projects 3A and 3B by creating a result from a supplied picture.	Online
3J	Combination of Objectives from Projects 3A and 3B	**3J GO! Solve It** A demonstration of your mastery of the skills in Projects 3A and 3B, your decision-making skills, and your critical thinking skills. A task-specific rubric helps you self-assess your result.	Online
3K	Combination of Objectives from Projects 3A and 3B	**3K GO! Solve It** A demonstration of your mastery of the skills in Projects 3A and 3B, your decision-making skills, and your critical thinking skills. A task-specific rubric helps you self-assess your result.	On the following pages
3L	Combination of Objectives from Projects 3A and 3B	**3L GO! Think** A demonstration of your understanding of the chapter concepts applied in a manner that you would outside of college. An analytic rubric helps you and your instructor grade the quality of your work by comparing it to the work an expert in the discipline would create.	On the following pages
3M	Combination of Objectives from Projects 3A and 3B	**3M GO! Think** A demonstration of your understanding of the chapter concepts applied in a manner that you would outside of college. An analytic rubric helps you and your instructor grade the quality of your work by comparing it to the work an expert in the discipline would create.	Online
3N	Combination of Objectives from Projects 3A and 3B	**3N You and GO!** A demonstration of your understanding of the chapter concepts applied in a manner that you would in a personal situation. An analytic rubric helps you and your instructor grade the quality of your work.	Online
3O	Combination of Objectives from Projects 3A and 3B	**3O Cumulative Group Project for Word Chapter 3** A demonstration of your understanding of concepts and your ability to work collaboratively in a group role-playing assessment, requiring both collaboration and self-management.	Online
Capstone Project for Word Chapters 1-3	Combination of Objectives from Projects 1A, 1B, 2A, 2B, 3A, and 3B	A demonstration of your mastery of the skills in Chapters 1-3 with extensive decision making. **(Grader Project)**	In MyITLab and online

GLOSSARY

GLOSSARY OF CHAPTER KEY TERMS

American Psychological Association (APA) One of two commonly used style guides for formatting research papers.

Bibliography A list of cited works in a report or research paper; also referred to as Works Cited, Sources, or References, depending upon the report style.

Brightness The relative lightness of a picture.

Citation A note inserted into the text of a research paper that refers the reader to a source in the bibliography.

Column break indicator A dotted line containing the words *Column Break* that displays at the bottom of the column.

Contrast The difference between the darkest and lightest area of a picture.

Crop A command that removes unwanted or unnecessary areas of a picture.

Crop handles Handles used to define unwanted areas of a picture.

Crop pointer The pointer used to crop areas of a picture.

Data source A document that contains a list of variable information, such as names and addresses, that is merged with a main document to create customized form letters or labels.

Em dash A punctuation symbol used to indicate an explanation or emphasis.

Endnote In a research paper, a note placed at the end of a document or chapter.

Fields In a mail merge, the column headings in the data source.

Flip A command that creates a reverse image of a picture or object.

Footnote In a research paper, a note placed at the bottom of the page.

Hanging indent An indent style in which the first line of a paragraph extends to the left of the remaining lines and that is commonly used for bibliographic entries.

Line break indicator A non-printing character in the shape of a bent arrow that indicates a manual line break.

Mail merge A feature that joins a main document and a data source to create customized letters or labels.

Main document In a mail merge, the document that contains the text or formatting that remains constant.

Manual column break An artificial end to a column to balance columns or to provide space for the insertion of other objects.

Manual line break A break that moves text to the right of the insertion point to a new line while keeping the text in the same paragraph.

Manual page break The action of forcing a page to end and placing subsequent text at the top of the next page.

Modern Language Association (MLA) One of two commonly used style guides for formatting research papers.

Nameplate The banner on the front page of a newsletter that identifies the publication.

Newsletter A periodical that communicates news and information to a specific group.

Note In a research paper, information that expands on the topic, but that does not fit well in the document text.

Office 365 Administrator—the person who creates and manages the account, adds new users, sets up the services your organization wants to use, sets permission levels, and manages the SharePoint team sites.

Page break indicator A dotted line with the text *Page Break* that indicates where a manual page break was inserted.

Parenthetical references References that include the last name of the author or authors, and the page number in the referenced source.

PDF Reflow The ability to import PDF files into Word so that you can transform a PDF back into a fully editable Word document.

Read Mode A view in Word that optimizes the Word screen for the times when you are reading Word documents on the screen and not creating or editing them.

Recolor A feature that enables you to change all colors in the picture to shades of a single color.

Record Each row of information that contains data for one person.

Scale A command that resizes a picture to a percentage of its size.

Screenshot An image of an active window on your computer that you can paste into a document.

Section A portion of a document that can be formatted differently from the rest of the document.

Section break A double dotted line that indicates the end of one section and the beginning of another section.

Small caps A font effect that changes lowercase letters to uppercase letters, but with the height of lowercase letters.

Style A group of formatting commands, such as font, font size, font color, paragraph alignment, and line spacing that can be applied to a paragraph with one command.

Style guide A manual that contains standards for the design and writing of documents.

Suppress A Word feature that hides header and footer information, including the page number, on the first page of a document.

Windows Reader app A Windows Store app with which you can open a PDF or XPS file, zoom, find words or phrases, take notes, save changes, and then print or share the file.

Works Cited In the MLA style, a list of cited works placed at the end of a research paper or report.

CHAPTER REVIEW

Skills Review · Project 3C Diet and Exercise Report

In the following Skills Review, you will edit and format a research paper that contains information about the effects of diet and exercise. This paper was created by Rachel Holder, a medical intern at University Medical Center, for distribution to her classmates studying physiology. Your completed document will look similar to the one shown in Figure 3.55.

PROJECT FILES

For Project 3C, you will need the following file:

w03C_Diet_Exercise

You will save your document as:

Lastname_Firstname_3C_Diet_Exercise

PROJECT RESULTS

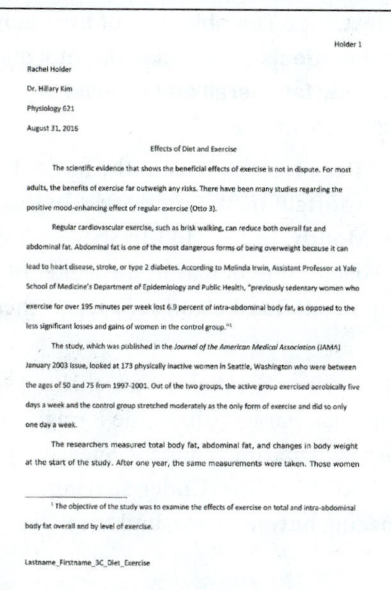

FIGURE 3.55

(Project 3C Diet and Exercise Report continues on the next page)

CHAPTER REVIEW

1 Start Word. From your student files, locate and open the document **w03C_Diet_Exercise**. Display the formatting marks and rulers. **Save** the file in your **Word Chapter 3** folder as **Lastname_Firstname_3C_Diet_Exercise**

a. Press Ctrl + A to select all the text. On the **HOME tab**, in the **Paragraph group**, click **Line and Paragraph Spacing**, and then change the line spacing to **2.0**. On the **PAGE LAYOUT tab**, change the **Spacing After** to **0 pt**.

b. Press Ctrl + Home, press Enter to create a blank line at the top of the document, and then click to position the insertion point in the new blank line. Type **Rachel Holder** and press Enter. Type **Dr. Hillary Kim** and press Enter. Type **Physiology 621** and press Enter. Type **August 31, 2016** and press Enter.

c. Type **Effects of Diet and Exercise** and then press Ctrl + E to center the title you just typed.

2 On the **INSERT tab**, in the **Header & Footer group**, click **Header**, and then at the bottom of the list, click **Edit Header**. Type **Holder** and then press Spacebar.

a. Under **HEADER & FOOTER TOOLS**, on the **DESIGN tab**, in the **Header & Footer group**, click **Page Number**, and then point to **Current Position**. Under **Simple**, click **Plain Number**.

b. On the **HOME tab**, in the **Paragraph group**, click **Align Right**. Double-click anywhere in the document to close the Header area.

c. Near the top of **Page 1**, locate the paragraph beginning *The scientific evidence*, and then click to position the insertion point at the beginning of that paragraph. Scroll to the end of the document, hold down Shift, and then click to the right of the last paragraph mark to select all of the text from the insertion point to the end of the document.

d. On the **HOME tab**, in the **Paragraph group**, click the **Dialog Box Launcher** button. In the **Paragraph** dialog box, on the **Indents and Spacing tab**, under **Indentation**, click the **Special arrow**, and then click **First line**. Click **OK**.

e. On the **INSERT tab**, in the **Header & Footer group**, click **Footer**, and then click **Edit Footer**. In the **Insert group**, click **Document Info**, and then click **File Name**. Click **Close Header and Footer**.

3 Scroll to view the top of **Page 2**, locate the paragraph that begins *Exercise also has*, and then at the end of that paragraph, click to position the insertion point to the right of the period following *Irwin*. On the **REFERENCES tab**, in the **Footnotes group**, click **Insert Footnote**.

a. As the footnote text, type **Physical activity may provide a low-risk method of preventing weight gain. Unlike diet-induced weight loss, exercise-induced weight loss increases cardiorespiratory fitness levels.**

b. In the upper portion of **Page 1**, locate the paragraph that begins *Regular cardiovascular exercise*. Click to position the insertion point at the end of the paragraph and insert a footnote.

c. As the footnote text, type **The objective of the study was to examine the effects of exercise on total and intra-abdominal body fat overall and by level of exercise. Save** your document.

4 At the bottom of **Page 1**, right-click in the footnote you just typed. On the shortcut menu, click **Style**. In the **Style** dialog box, click **Modify**. In the **Modify Style** dialog box, locate the small Formatting toolbar in the center of the dialog box, click the **Font Size button arrow**, and then click **11**.

a. In the lower left corner of the dialog box, click **Format**, and then click **Paragraph**. In the **Paragraph** dialog box, under **Indentation**, click the **Special arrow**, and then click **First line**. Under **Spacing**, click the **Line spacing button arrow**, and then click **Double**.

b. Click **OK** to close the **Paragraph** dialog box, click **OK** to close the **Modify Style** dialog box, and then click **Apply** to apply the new style. **Save** your document.

5 Scroll to view the top of **Page 1**, and then in the paragraph that begins *The scientific evidence*, click to position the insertion point to the left of the period at the end of the paragraph.

a. On the **REFERENCES tab**, in the **Citations & Bibliography group**, click the **Style button arrow**, and then click **MLA** to insert a reference using MLA style. Click **Insert Citation**, and then click **Add New Source**. Click the **Type of Source arrow**, scroll as

(Project 3C Diet and Exercise Report continues on the next page)

necessary to locate and click **Book**, and then add the following information:

Author	Otto, Michael and Jasper A. J. Smits
Title	Exercise for Mood and Anxiety: Proven Strategies for Overcoming Depression and Enhancing Well-Being
Year	2011
City	New York
Publisher	Oxford University Press, USA
Medium	Print

b.   Click **OK** to insert the citation. In the paragraph, click to select the citation, click the **Citation Options arrow**, and then click **Edit Citation**. In the **Edit Citation** dialog box, under **Add**, in the **Pages** box, type **3** and then click **OK**.

c.   On the upper portion of **Page 2**, in the paragraph that begins *Other positive effects*, in the third line, click to position the insertion point to the left of the period following *substantially*. In the **Citations & Bibliography group**, click **Insert Citation**, and then click **Add New Source**. Click the **Type of Source arrow**, click **Book**, and then add the following information:

Author	Lohrman, David and Lois Heller
Title	Cardiovascular Physiology, Seventh Edition
Year	2010
City	New York
Publisher	McGraw-Hill Professional
Medium	Print

d.   Click **OK**. Click to select the citation in the paragraph, click the **Citation Options arrow**, and then click **Edit Citation**. In the **Edit Citation** dialog box, under **Add**, in the **Pages** box, type **195** and then click **OK**.

6 ▶ Press Ctrl + End to move to the end of the last paragraph in the document. Click to the left of the period following *loss*. In the **Citations & Bibliography group**,

click **Insert Citation**, and then click **Add New Source**. Click the **Type of Source arrow**, click **Web site**, and then select the **Corporate Author** check box. Add the following information:

Corporate Author	U.S. Department of Health and Human Services
Name of Web Page	NIH News
Year	2012
Month	October
Day	15
Year Accessed	2016
Month Accessed	July
Day Accessed	21
Medium	Web

a.   Click **OK**. Press Ctrl + End to move the insertion point to the end of the document. Press Ctrl + Enter to insert a manual page break. On the **HOME tab**, in the **Paragraph group**, click the **Dialog Box Launcher** button. In the **Paragraph** dialog box, on the **Indents and Spacing tab**, under **Indentation**, click the **Special arrow**, and then click **(none)**. Click **OK**.

b.   Type **Works Cited** and then press Enter. On the **REFERENCES tab**, in the **Citations & Bibliography group**, be sure **MLA** displays in the **Style** box. In the **Citations & Bibliography group**, click **Bibliography**, and then at the bottom, click **Insert Bibliography**.

c.   Click anywhere in the *Works Cited* title, and then press Ctrl + E to center the title. **Save** your document.

7 ▶ On the **REFERENCES tab**, in the **Citations & Bibliography group**, click **Manage Sources**. On the left, on the **Master List**, click the entry for *Lohrman, David*, and then click **Edit**. In the **Edit Source** dialog box, in the **Author** box, change the *L* in *Lohrman* to **M** Click **OK**, click **Yes**, and then click **Close**.

a.   On **Page 2**, in the paragraph that begins *Other positive effects*, in the third line, on the selected citation, click the **Citation Options arrow**, and then click **Update Citations and Bibliography**.

(Project 3C Diet and Exercise Report continues on the next page)

CHAPTER REVIEW

b. In the bibliography, move the pointer to the left of the first entry—beginning *Mohrman*—to display the ⬚ pointer. Drag down to select all three references in the field. On the **HOME tab**, in the **Paragraph group**, set the **Line spacing** to **2.0**. On the **PAGE LAYOUT tab**, set the **Spacing After** to **0 pt**.

c. Click the **FILE tab**, and then in the lower right corner, click **Show All Properties**. Add the following information:

Title	Diet and Exercise
Tags	weight loss, exercise, diet
Comments	Draft copy of report for class
Categories	biomedical research
Company	University Medical Center
Manager	Dr. Hillary Kim

END | You have completed Project 3C

d. In the **Subject** box, type your course name and section number. Be sure that your name displays as the Author and edit if necessary. On the left, click **Save** to redisplay your document. On the **VIEW tab**, in the **Views group**, click **Read Mode**. In the upper left, click **TOOLS**, click **Find**, and then in the search box, type **Yale** and notice that the text you searched for is highlighted in the document.

e. In the upper left, click **VIEW**, and then click **Edit Document** to return to **Print Layout** view. **Close** the **navigation pane**. **Save** your document, view the **Print Preview**, and then print or submit electronically as directed by your instructor. **Close** Word.

CHAPTER REVIEW

Apply 3B skills from these Objectives:

5 Format a Multiple-Column Newsletter

6 Use Special Character and Paragraph Formatting

7 Create Mailing Labels Using Mail Merge

Skills Review Project 3D Career Newsletter

In the following Skills Review, you will format a newsletter regarding professional development opportunities offered by University Medical Center, and you will create mailing labels for staff interested in these opportunities. Your completed document will look similar to Figure 3.56.

PROJECT FILES

For Project 3D, you will need the following files:

New blank Word document
w03D_Career_Newsletter
w03D_Addresses

You will save your documents as:

Lastname_Firstname_3D_Career_Newsletter
Lastname_Firstname_3D_Addresses
Lastname_Firstname_3D_Mailing_Labels

PROJECT RESULTS

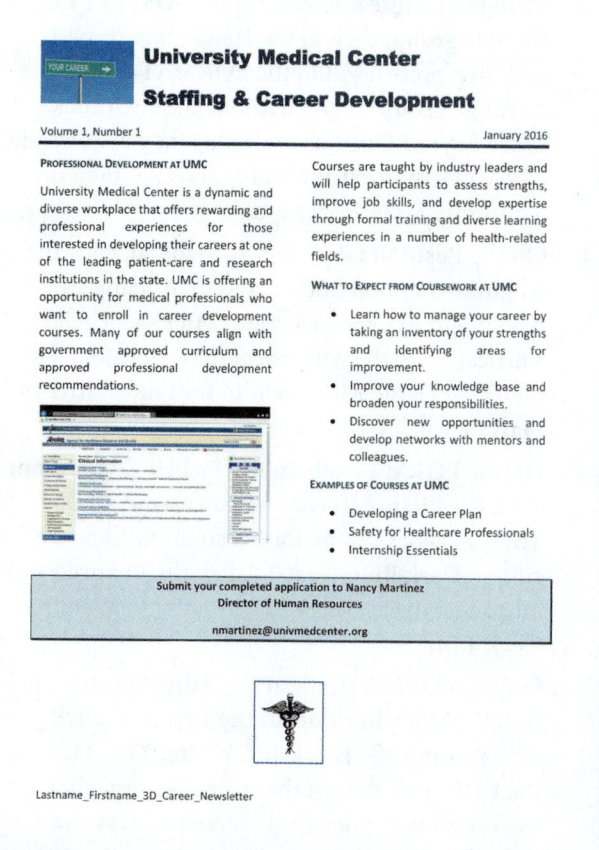

Lastname_Firstname_3D_Career_Newsletter

Lastname_Firstname_3D_Mailing_Labels

FIGURE 3.56

(Project 3D Career Newsletter continues on the next page)

CHAPTER REVIEW

1 ▶ Start Word. On Word's opening screen, in the lower left, click **Open Other Documents**. Navigate to your student files, and then locate and open **w03D_Career_Newsletter**. **Save** the file in your **Word Chapter 3** folder as **Lastname_Firstname_3D_Career_Newsletter** and then add the file name to the footer.

  a. Select the first two lines of the document. On the mini toolbar, change the **Font** to **Arial Black** and the **Font Size** to **18**. Select the first three lines of the document. Click the **Font Color button arrow**, and then under **Theme Colors**, in the fifth column, click the last color—**Blue, Accent 1, Darker 50%**.

  b. With the text still selected, on the **HOME tab**, in the **Paragraph group**, click the **Borders button arrow**, and then at the bottom, click **Borders and Shading**. In the **Borders and Shading** dialog box, on the **Borders tab**, click the **Color arrow**, and then under **Theme Colors**, in the fifth column, click the last color—**Blue, Accent 1, Darker 50%**.

  c. Click the **Width arrow**, and then click **3 pt**. In the **Preview** box, click the bottom border. Click **OK**.

  d. Click at the beginning of the paragraph that begins *Professional Development*. Scroll the document, hold down Shift, and then click after the paragraph mark at the end of the *Internship Essentials* line. On the **PAGE LAYOUT tab**, in the **Page Setup group**, click **Columns**, and then click **Two**. With the two columns of text selected, on the **HOME tab**, in the **Paragraph group**, click **Justify**.

  e. In the first column, click at the beginning of the paragraph that begins *Courses are taught*. On the **PAGE LAYOUT tab**, in the **Page Setup group**, click **Breaks**. Under **Page Breaks**, click **Column**.

2 ▶ Press Ctrl + Home. On the **INSERT tab**, in the **Illustrations group**, click **Online Pictures**. In the **Office.com Clip Art** search box, type **career** and then press Enter. Click the image of the sign with the text *Your Career*. If the image does not display, select a similar picture. Click **Insert**.

  a. On the **FORMAT tab**, in the **Size group**, click the **Dialog Box Launcher** button. In the **Layout** dialog box, on the **Size tab**, under **Scale**, be sure the **Lock aspect ratio** and **Relative to original picture size** check boxes are selected. Select the number in the **Height** box, type **10** and then press Tab.

  b. In the **Layout** dialog box, click the **Text Wrapping tab**. Under **Wrapping style**, click **Square**.

  c. Click the **Position tab**, and then under **Horizontal**, click the **Alignment** option button. Be sure that the **Alignment** indicates **Left** and **relative to Column**. Under **Vertical**, click the **Alignment** option button, and then change the alignment to **Top relative to Margin**. Click **OK**. **Save** your newsletter.

3 ▶ Press Ctrl + End to move to the end of the document. On the **INSERT tab**, in the **Illustrations group**, click **Online Pictures**. In the **Bing Image Search** box, search for **caducei healthcare symbol** and then insert one of the first displayed images of a single symbol.

  a. With the picture selected, on the **FORMAT tab**, in the **Size group**, click in the **Height** box. Type **1** and then press Enter. On the **FORMAT tab**, in the **Arrange group**, click **Position**, and then click **More Layout Options** to display the **Layout** dialog box. Click the **Text Wrapping tab**, and then under **Wrapping Style**, click **Square**.

  b. On the **Position tab**, under **Horizontal**, click the **Alignment** option button, and then change the **Alignment** to **Centered relative to Page**. Under **Vertical**, click the **Alignment** option button, and then change the **Alignment** to **Bottom relative to Margin**. Click **OK**.

  c. On the **FORMAT tab**, in the **Picture Styles group**, click the **Picture Border button arrow**. Under **Theme Colors**, in the fourth column, click the first color—**Dark Blue, Text 2**. Click the **Picture Border button arrow** again, and then point to **Weight**. Click **1 pt**.

  d. On the **FORMAT tab**, in the **Adjust group**, click **Color**. Under **Recolor**, in the first row, click the last option—**Black and White, 75%**. On the **FORMAT tab**, in the **Adjust group**, click **Corrections**. Under **Brightness/Contrast**, in the second row, click the fourth setting—**Brightness: +20% Contrast: –20%**.

(Project 3D Career Newsletter continues on the next page)

CHAPTER REVIEW

4 In the paragraph that begins *University Medical Center is a dynamic*, click after the period at the end of the paragraph, and then press Enter. Start Internet Explorer, maximize the window, and then navigate to **www.ahrq.gov/clinic/**

a. Redisplay your **3D_Career_Newletter** document. With the insertion point positioned in the blank line above the column break, on the **INSERT tab**, in the **Illustrations group**, click **Screenshot**. In the **Screenshot** gallery, click the browser window that contains the website; click **No** in the message that displays.

b. Select the subheading *Professional Development at UMC* including the paragraph mark. Right-click the selected text, and then on the shortcut menu, click **Font**. In the **Font** dialog box, click the **Font color arrow**, and then in the fifth column, click the last color—**Blue, Accent 1, Darker 50%**. Under **Font style**, click **Bold**, and then under **Effects**, select **Small caps**. Click **OK**.

c. With the text still selected, right-click, and then on the mini toolbar, double-click **Format Painter**. In the second column, with the pointer, select each of the subheadings—*What to Expect from Coursework at UMC* and *Example of Courses at UMC*. Press Esc to turn off **Format Painter**.

5 Press Ctrl + End to move to the end of the document, and then select the two lines of bold text—the graphic will also be selected. On the **HOME tab**, in the **Paragraph group**, click the **Borders button arrow**, and then click **Borders and Shading**.

a. In the **Borders and Shading** dialog box, on the **Borders tab**, under **Setting**, click **Shadow**. Click the **Color arrow**, and then in the fifth column, click the last color—**Blue, Accent 1, Darker 50%**. Click the **Width arrow**, and then click **1 pt**.

b. In the **Borders and Shading** dialog box, click the **Shading tab**. Click the **Fill arrow**, and then in the fifth column, click the second color—**Blue, Accent 1, Lighter 80%**. Click **OK**. On the **HOME tab**, in the **Paragraph group**, click **Center**. In the shaded paragraph, click in front of the *D* in the word *Director*. Hold down Shift and then press Enter.

c. Press Ctrl + Home, and then click the **FILE tab**. At the bottom of the **Properties** list, click **Show All Properties**. Click to the right of **Tags**, and then type **newsletter, careers** Click to the right of **Subject**, and then type your course name and section number. Under **Related People**, if necessary, type your name in the Author box. Display the **Print Preview** and make any necessary corrections. **Save** the document; close Word and close Internet Explorer.

6 Start Word and display a new blank document. **Save** the document in your **Word Chapter 3** folder as **Lastname_Firstname_3D_Mailing_Labels** With your new document open on the screen, from your student files, **Open** the file **w03D_Addresses**. **Save** the address file in your **Word Chapter 3** folder as **Lastname_Firstname_3D_Addresses** and then add the file name to the footer. **Save** and then **Close** the file. Be sure that your **Lastname_Firstname_3D_Mailing_Labels** document displays.

a. Click the **MAILINGS tab**. In the **Start Mail Merge group**, click **Start Mail Merge**, and then click **Step-by-Step Mail Merge Wizard**. In the **Mail Merge** pane, under **Select document type**, click **Labels**. At the bottom of the **Mail Merge** pane, click **Next: Starting document**.

b. Under **Select starting document**, under **Change document layout**, click **Label options**. In the **Label Options** dialog box, under **Printer information**, be sure that the **Default tray** is selected.

c. Under **Label information**, click the **Label vendors arrow**, and then click **Avery US Letter**. Under **Product number**, scroll about halfway down the list, and then click **5160 Easy Peel Address Labels**. At the bottom of the **Label Options** dialog box, click **OK**. At the bottom of the **Mail Merge** pane, click **Next: Select recipients**.

d. In the **Mail Merge** pane, under **Select recipients**, under **Use an existing list**, click **Browse**. Navigate to your **Word Chapter 3** folder, select your **Lastname_Firstname_3D_Addresses** file, and then click **Open**.

7 In the lower left portion of the **Mail Merge Recipients** dialog box, in the **Data Source** box, click the path that contains your file name. Then, at the bottom of the **Mail Merge Recipients** dialog box, click **Edit**. In the

(Project 3D Career Newsletter continues on the next page)

CHAPTER REVIEW

upper right corner of the **Data Form** dialog box, click **Add New**. In the blank record, type the following, pressing ⎆ Tab to move from field to field:

First_Name:	Mia
Last_Name:	Orr
Address_1:	1378 Lima Ave.
Unit:	#82
City:	Memphis
State:	TN
ZIP_Code:	38123

a. In the lower right corner of the **Data Form** dialog box, click **Close**. At the bottom of the **Mail Merge Recipients** dialog box, click **OK**.

b. At the bottom of the **Mail Merge** pane, click **Next: Arrange your labels**. Under **Arrange your labels**, click **Address block**. In the lower right corner of the **Insert Address Block** dialog box, click **Match Fields**.

c. Click the **Address 2 arrow**, and then from the list of available fields, click **Unit**. Click **OK** two times.

d. In the **Mail Merge** pane, under **Replicate labels**, click **Update all labels**. At the bottom of the **Mail Merge** pane, click **Next: Preview your labels**. Press

⎈ Ctrl + A to select all of the label text, click the **PAGE LAYOUT tab**, and then in the **Paragraph group**, click in the **Spacing Before** box. Type **3** and press ⎆ Enter. At the bottom of the **Mail Merge** pane, click **Next: Complete the merge**.

e. Click the **MAILINGS tab**, and then in the **Start Mail Merge group**, click **Edit Recipient List** to display the list of names and addresses. In the **Mail Merge Recipients** dialog box, click the **Last_Name** field heading to sort the names. Click **OK**. **Close** the **Mail Merge** pane.

f. Scroll the document and then click anywhere in the empty table row at the bottom. Click the **LAYOUT tab**. In the **Rows & Columns group**, click **Delete**, and then click **Delete Rows**. Add the file name to the footer, close the footer area, and then click the **FILE tab**. Click **Show All Properties**. As the **Tags**, type **labels** and as the **Subject**, type your course name and section number. Be sure your name displays as the **Author**, and then **Save** your file.

g. As directed by your instructor, print or submit electronically. **Close** the document, click **Yes** to save the data source, and then if necessary, click **Save** to save the labels. In addition to your labels and address document, submit your **3D_Career_Newsletter** document as directed. **Close** Word.

END | You have completed Project 3D

CONTENT-BASED ASSESSMENTS

Mastering Word   Project 3E Skin Protection Report

ply 3A skills from these bjectives:

1 Create a Research Paper

2 Insert Footnotes in a Research Paper

3 Create Citations and a Bibliography in a Research Paper

4 Use Read Mode and PDF Reflow

   In the following Mastering Word project, you will edit and format a research paper that contains information about skin protection and the use of sunblocks and sunscreens. This paper was created by Rachel Holder, a medical intern at University Medical Center, for distribution to her classmates studying dermatology. Your completed document will look similar to the one shown in Figure 3.57.

PROJECT FILES

For Project 3E, you will need the following file:

w03E_Skin_Protection

You will save your document as:

Lastname_Firstname_3E_Skin_Protection

PROJECT RESULTS

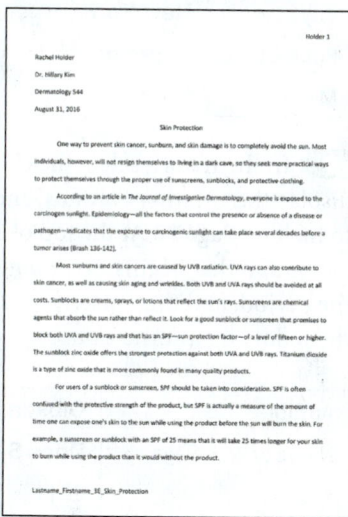
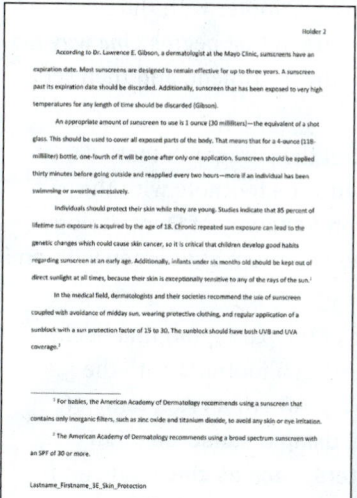
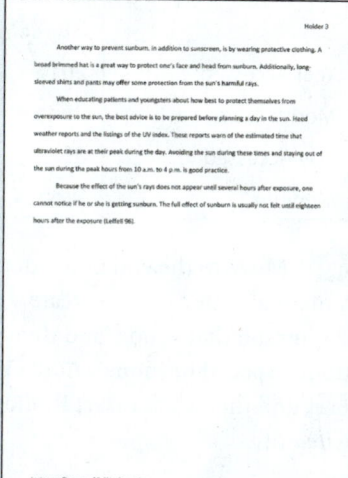

FIGURE 3.57

(Project 3E Skin Protection Report continues on the next page)

CONTENT-BASED ASSESSMENTS

1 Start Word. From your student files, locate and open the document **w03E_Skin_Protection**. Display formatting marks and rulers. Save the file in your **Word Chapter 3** folder as **Lastname_Firstname_3E_Skin_Protection**

2 Select all the text, change the **Line Spacing** to **2.0**, and then change the **Spacing After** to **0 pt**. At the top of the document, insert a new blank paragraph, and then in the new paragraph, type **Rachel Holder** Press Enter. Type **Dr. Hillary Kim** and press Enter. Type **Dermatology 544** and press Enter. Type **August 31, 2016** and press Enter. Type **Skin Protection** and then press Ctrl + E to center the title you just typed.

3 Insert a header, type **Holder** and then press Spacebar. Display the **Page Number gallery**, and then in the **Current Position**, add the **Plain Number** style. Apply **Align Right** formatting to the header. Insert a footer with the file name. Starting with the paragraph that begins *One way to prevent*, select all the text in the document, and then set a **First line** indent of **0.5"**.

4 On **Page 2**, at the end of the paragraph that begins *In the medical field*, insert a footnote with the following text: **The American Academy of Dermatology recommends using a broad spectrum sunscreen with an SPF of 30 or more.**

5 On **Page 2**, at the end of the paragraph that begins *Individuals should protect*, insert a footnote with the following text: **For babies, the American Academy of Dermatology recommends using a sunscreen that contains only inorganic filters, such as zinc oxide and titanium dioxide, to avoid any skin or eye irritation.**

6 Modify the **Footnote Text** style so that the **Font Size** is **11**, there is a **First line indent** of **0.5"**, and the spacing is **Double**, and then apply the style.

7 On **Page 1**, at the end of the paragraph that begins *According to an article*, click to the left of the period, and then using **MLA** format, insert a citation for a **Journal Article** with the following information:

Author	Frash, D. E., A. S. Jonason, and J. A. Simon
Title	Sunlight and Sunburn in Human Skin Cancer
Journal Name	The Journal of Investigative Dermatology

Year	1996
Pages	136-142
Medium	Print

8 In the report, select the citation you just created, display the **Citation Options**, and then edit the citation to include **Pages 136-142** At the end of the last paragraph of the report, click to the left of the period, and then insert a citation for a **Book** with the following information:

Author	Leffell, David
Title	Total Skin: The Definitive Guide to Whole Skin Care for Life
Year	2000
City	New York
Publisher	Hyperion
Medium	Print

9 In the report, select the citation you just created, display the **Citation Options**, and then edit the citation to include **Page 96** At the top of **Page 2**, at the end of the paragraph that begins *According to Dr.*, click to the left of the period, and then insert a citation for a **Web site** with the following information:

Author	Gibson, Lawrence E.
Name of Web Page	Does Sunscreen Expire?
Year	2011
Month	April
Day	01
Year Accessed	2016
Month Accessed	June
Day Accessed	30
Medium	Web

10 Move to the end of the document, and then insert a manual page break to create a new page. Display the **Paragraph** dialog box, and then change the **Indentation** under **Special** to **(none)**. Add a **Works Cited** title, press Enter, and then click **Insert Bibliography**. **Center** the *Works Cited* title.

(Project 3E Skin Protection Report continues on the next page

CONTENT-BASED ASSESSMENTS

11 By using the **Manage Sources** command, display the **Source Manager**. On the **Master List**, select the entry for **Frash, D. E.**, and then **Edit** this source—the last name should be **Brash** instead of *Frash*. In the message that displays, update both lists. Locate the citation in the text of the report, display the **Citation Options**, and then **Update Citations and Bibliography**. On the Works Cited page, select the references, apply **Double** line spacing, and then set the **Spacing After** paragraphs to **0 pt**.

12 Update the **Document Properties** with the following information:

Title	**Skin Protection**
Tags	**sunscreen, sun exposure**
Comments	**Draft copy of report for class**
Categories	**Dermatology**
Company	**University Medical Center**
Manager	**Dr. Hillary Kim**

13 In the **Subject** box, type your course name and section number. Be sure that your name displays as the **Author** and edit if necessary. On the left, click **Print** to view the **Print Preview**, and then click **Save** to redisplay your document. Print or submit electronically as directed by your instructor. **Close** Word.

END | You have completed Project 3E

CONTENT-BASED ASSESSMENTS

Mastering Word Project 3F Dogs Newsletter and Mailing Labels

Apply 3B skills from these Objectives:

5 Format a Multiple-Column Newsletter

6 Use Special Character and Paragraph Formatting

7 Create Mailing Labels Using Mail Merge

In the following Mastering Word project, you will format a newsletter with information about the therapy dogs handled by volunteers at the University Medical Center. You will also create mailing labels so that the newsletter can be sent to the volunteer staff. Your completed documents will look similar to Figure 3.58.

PROJECT FILES

For Project 3F, you will need the following files:

New blank Word document
w03F_Dogs_Newsletter
w03F_Addresses

You will save your documents as:

Lastname_Firstname_3F_Dogs_Newsletter
Lastname_Firstname_3F_Addresses
Lastname_Firstname_3F_Mailing_Labels

PROJECT RESULTS

University Medical Center
Health Improvement Newsletter

Volume 3   Spring 2016

DOGS FOR HEALING

At University Medical Center, therapy dogs have been a welcomed asset to patient care and recovery since 2004. UMC works with several non-profit organizations to bring dedicated volunteers and their canine teams into the hospital to visit children, adults, and seniors. Information regarding service dog regulations, training, and laws is available on the ADA website.

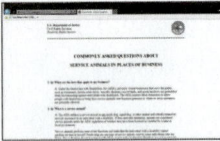

BENEFITS TO PATIENTS

Medical research shows that petting a dog or other domestic animal relaxes patients and helps ease symptoms of stress from illness or from the hospital setting. Studies have shown that such therapies contribute to decreased blood pressure and heart rate, and can help with patient respiratory rate.

CUDDLES

Cuddles, a 4 year-old Labrador, is one of our most popular therapy dogs and is loved by both young and senior patients. You'll see Cuddles in the Children's wing on Mondays with his owner, Jason, who trained him since he was a tiny pup.

BRANDY

Brandy is a 6 year-old Beagle who brings smiles and giggles to everyone she meets. Over the past several years, Brandy has received accolades and awards for her service as a therapy dog. Brandy is owned by Melinda Sparks, a 17-year veteran employee of University Medical Center. Brandy and Melinda can be seen making the rounds on Wednesdays in the Children's wing and on Mondays and Fridays throughout the hospital.

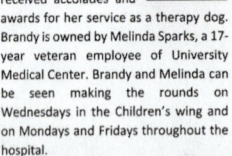

Your picture may differ.

To request a visit from a therapy dog, or to learn how to become involved with therapy dog training, call Carole Yates at extension 2365.

Lastname_Firstname_3F_Dogs_Newsletter

Mary Ackerman
82 E. Roxie Blvd.
Arlington, TN 38002

Jacqueline Epps
653 Vista Ave.
#D
Lakeland, TN 38002

Emily Gold
888 Packard Court
Lakeland, TN 38002

Bin Lee
676 Silver St.
Memphis, TN 38120

Leland Marcus
600 Garfield Ave.
Memphis, TN 38117

Thai Nguyen
179 Sierra Court
Collierville, TN 38017

Erica Scott
124 Susan Drive
#352
Memphis, TN 38134

Simone Thompson
648 Michaela St.
Bartlett, TN 38133

Miranda Yanos
1256 Loma Ave.
#34
Memphis, TN 38123

Anthony Borman
2820 Lincoln Ave.
Collierville, TN 38017

Renee Farnsworth
36 S. Levin St.
#D
Bartlett, TN 38135

Abel Heaphy
55 Amigo Lane
#4
Collierville, TN 38017

Anh Ly
1255 Chestnut Street
Memphis, TN 38122

Walter McKidd
2495 Holly Drive
Arlington, TN 38002

Thomas Norris
492 Mahogany Street
Bartlett, TN 38135

Andrew Sharma
1550 Beverly Drive
#1550
Memphis, TN 38104

David Turnbull
1821 Chelsea St.
#1442
Germantown, TN 38138

Jerry Camden
543 Verde Way
Memphis, TN 38120

Anita Figueroa
9000 S. Masters Dr.
Germantown, TN 38139

Katie Hughes
34 Sadler Pl.
Bartlett, TN 38133

Priya Malik
975 Ricardo Place
#G
Germantown, TN 38138

Sharon Moreno
1330 Golden Ave.
Memphis, TN 38120

Daniel Scofield
1518 Price Place
Arlington, TN 38002

Sara Thompson
4220 Glendora Dr.
#320
Memphis, TN 38112

Jackson Williams
15 Atlantic Rd.
Memphis, TN 38111

Lastname_Firstname_3F_Mailing_Labels

FIGURE 3.58

(Project 3F Dogs Newsletter and Mailing Labels continues on the next page)

CONTENT-BASED ASSESSMENTS

1 Start Word. From your student files, open **w03F_Dogs_Newsletter**. **Save** the file in your **Word Chapter 3** folder as **Lastname_Firstname_3F_Dogs_Newsletter** and then add the file name to the footer. Select the first three lines of the document, and then change the **Font Color** to **Olive Green, Accent 3, Darker 25%**—in the seventh column, the fifth color. With the text selected, display the **Borders and Shading** dialog box. Apply a **3 pt** bottom border in **Black, Text 1**.

2 Click at the beginning of the newsletter title *University Medical Center*. Insert an online picture of your choice from **Bing Image Search** by searching for **physician symbols**. Change the **Brightness/Contrast** to **Brightness: 0% (Normal) Contrast: +40%**.

3 Change the picture **Width** to **1"** and then change the **Text Wrapping** to **Square**. Change the **Horizontal Alignment** to **Left relative** to **Margin** and the **Vertical Alignment** to **Top relative** to **Margin**.

4 Starting with the paragraph that begins *Dogs for Healing*, select all of the text from that point to the end of the document. Change the **Spacing After** to **10 pt**, format the text in two columns, and apply **Justify** alignment. Insert a **Column break** before the subheading *Cuddles*.

5 Click at the beginning of the sentence that begins with *Brandy is a 6 year-old Beagle*. From your student data files, insert the picture **w03F_Dog**. Rotate the picture using **Flip Horizontal**. Change the picture **Height** to **1.5** and then apply the **Square** layout option. Change the **Horizontal Alignment** to **Right relative** to **Margin** and the **Vertical Alignment** to **Top relative** to **Line**. Apply a **Black, Text 1 Picture Border** and change the **Weight** to **2 1/4 pt.**

6 Start Internet Explorer, navigate to **www.ada.gov/qasrvc.htm** and then maximize your browser window. In your **3F_Dogs_Newsletter** file, click at the end of the paragraph below the *Dogs for Healing* subheading, and then press Enter. In the blank line, insert a **Screenshot** of the website; do not link to the URL. Apply a **Black, Text 1 Picture Border** and change the **Weight** to **1 pt**.

7 Select the subheading *Dogs for Healing* including the paragraph mark. By using the **Font** dialog box, change the **Size** to **16**, apply **Bold**, apply the **Small caps** effect, and change the **Font color** to **Olive Green, Accent 3, Darker 50%**—in the seventh column, the last color. Apply the same formatting to the subheadings *Benefits to Patients*, *Cuddles*, and *Brandy*.

8 Select the last paragraph in the newsletter, and then apply a **1 pt Shadow** border, in **Black, Text 1**. Shade the paragraph with a **Fill** color of **Olive Green, Accent 3, Lighter 80%**—in the seventh column, the second color. Click the **FILE tab**, and then click **Show All Properties**. As the **Tags**, type **dogs, newsletter** As the **Subject**, type your course name and section number. Under **Related People**, if necessary, type your name in the **Author box**. **Print Preview** the document and make any necessary corrections. **Save** the document and **close** Word.

9 Start Word and display a new blank document. **Save** the document in your **Word Chapter 3** folder as **Lastname_Firstname_3F_Mailing_Labels** From your student files, **Open** the file **w03F_Addresses**. **Save** the address file in your **Word Chapter 3** folder as **Lastname_Firstname_3F_Addresses** and then add the file name to the footer. **Save** and **Close** the file. Be sure that your **Lastname_Firstname_3F_Mailing_Labels** document displays.

10 Start the **Step-by-Step Mail Merge Wizard** to create **Labels**. Be sure that the **Default tray** is selected and that the label vendor is **Avery US Letter**. The **Product number** is **5160 Easy Peel Address Labels**. Select the **Use an existing list** option, and then from your **Word Chapter 3** folder, open your **Lastname_Firstname_3F_Addresses** file. Add the following record to your file:

First Name	Miranda
Last Name	Yanos
Address 1	1256 Loma Ave.
Unit	#34
City	Memphis
State	TN
ZIP Code	38123

(Project 3F Dogs Newsletter and Mailing Labels continues on the next page)

CONTENT-BASED ASSESSMENTS

11 Insert an **Address block** and match the fields. Match the **Address 2** field to the **Unit** field, and then update the labels. Preview the labels, and then select the entire document. Change the **Spacing Before** to **3** and then **Complete the merge**. Delete the last row from the bottom of the table, and then add the file name to the footer.

12 Display the document properties. As the **Tags** type **labels** and as the **Subject** type your course name and section number. Be sure your name displays in the **Author box**, and then **Save** your file. As directed by your instructor, print or submit electronically. In addition to your labels and address document, submit your **3F_Dogs_Newsletter** document as directed. **Close** Word and Internet Explorer.

END | You have completed Project 3F

CONTENT-BASED ASSESSMENTS

Mastering Word Project 3G Research Paper, Newsletter, and Mailing Labels

In the following Mastering Word project, you will edit and format a research paper and a newsletter, and you will create mailing labels. Your completed documents will look similar to Figure 3.59.

Apply 3A and 3B skills from these Objectives:

1 Create a Research Paper
2 Insert Footnotes in a Research Paper
3 Create Citations and a Bibliography in a Research Paper
4 Use Read Mode and PDF Reflow
5 Format a Multiple-Column Newsletter
6 Use Special Character and Paragraph Formatting
7 Create Mailing Labels Using Mail Merge

PROJECT FILES

For Project 3G, you will need the following files:

New blank Word document
w03G_Electronic_Records
w03G_Newsletter
w03G_Addresses

You will save your documents as:

Lastname_Firstname_3G_Electronic_Records
Lastname_Firstname_3G_Newsletter
Lastname_Firstname_3G_Mailing_Labels
Lastname_Firstname_3G_Addresses

PROJECT RESULTS

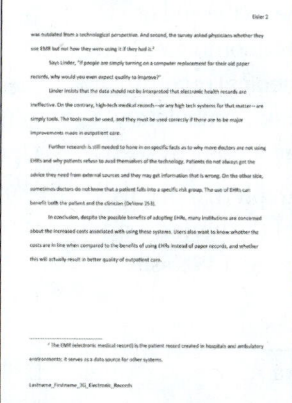
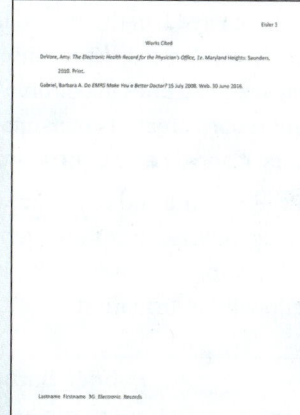
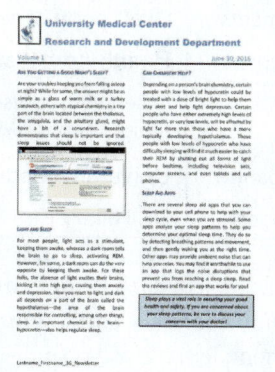

FIGURE 3.59

(Project 3G Research Paper, Newsletter, and Mailing Labels continues on the next page)

CONTENT-BASED ASSESSMENTS

1 ▶ Start Word. From your student files, locate and open the document **w03G_Electronic_Records**, and then **Save** it in your **Word Chapter 3** folder as **Lastname_Firstname_3G_Electronic_Records** Display the header area, type **Eisler** and then press [Spacebar]. From the **Header & Footer group**, add a **Plain Number** page number from the **Current Position** gallery. Apply **Align Right** formatting to the header. Move to the footer area and add the file name to the footer.

Select all the text in the document, change the **Line Spacing** to **2.0**, and then change the **Spacing After** to **0 pt**. **Center** the title *Electronic Health Records*. Beginning with text below the centered title, select the text from that point to the end of the document, and then set a **First line** indent of **0.5"**.

2 ▶ At the top of **Page 1**, at the end of the paragraph that begins *There is often*, insert a footnote with the following text: **Electronic Health Records is an evolving concept that shares records in digital format across different health care settings and might include medical history, test results, and x-rays.**

At the top of **Page 2**, in the second line, at the end of the sentence that ends *if they had it*, insert a footnote with the following text: **The EMR (electronic medical record) is the patient record created in hospitals and ambulatory environments; it serves as a data source for other systems.**

3 ▶ On **Page 1**, at the end of the paragraph that begins *Those clinical practices*, click to the left of the period, and then using **MLA** format, insert a citation for a **Web site** with the following information:

Author	Sabriel, Barbara A.
Name of Web Page	Do EMRS Make You a Better Doctor?
Year	2008
Month	July
Day	15
Year Accessed	2016
Month Accessed	June
Day Accessed	30
Medium	Web

On **Page 2**, at the end of the paragraph that begins *Further research*, click to the left of the period, and then

using **MLA** format, insert a citation for a **Book** with the following information:

Author	DeVore, Amy
Title	The Electronic Health Record for the Physician's Office, 1e
Year	2010
City	Maryland Heights
Publisher	Saunders
Medium	Print

In the report, select the citation you just created, display the **Citation Options**, and then edit the citation to include **Pages 253**

4 ▶ Insert a manual page break at the end of the document. On the new **Page 3**, display the **Paragraph** dialog box, and then change the **Special** indentation to **(none)**. Type **Works Cited** and then press [Enter]. On the **REFERENCES tab**, click **Bibliography**, and then click **Insert Bibliography**. **Center** the *Works Cited* title.

Use the **Source Manager** to change the name of the reference *Sabriel* to **Gabriel** and update both lists. Then in the selected citation in the report, display the **Citation Options** and click **Update Citations and Bibliography**. On the Works Cited page, select the references, apply **Double** line spacing, and then set the **Spacing After** paragraphs to **0 pt**.

Update the **Document Properties** with the following information:

Title	Electronic Records
Tags	EMR, health records
Comments	Draft copy of report for class
Categories	Health Administration
Subject	(insert your course name and section number)
Company	University Medical Center
Manager	Dr. Hillary Kim

On the left, click **Print** to display the **Print Preview**, make any necessary corrections, **save** and **close** the document; leave Word open. Hold this file until you complete this project.

(Project 3G Research Paper, Newsletter, and Mailing Labels continues on the next page)

CONTENT-BASED ASSESSMENTS

Mastering Word | Project 3G Research Paper, Newsletter, and Mailing Labels (continued)

5 From your student files, open **w03G_ Newsletter**. **Save** the file in your **Word Chapter 3** folder as **Lastname_ Firstname_3G_Newsletter** and then add the file name to the footer. Select the first three lines of the document and apply a **3 pt** bottom border in **Black, Text 1**.

Click at the beginning of the newsletter title *University Medical Center*. Insert an online picture from **Bing Image Search** by searching for **microscope** Insert a picture of a black and white microscope. **Recolor** the picture by applying **Blue, Accent color 1 Light**. Apply a **Black, Text 1 Picture Border** and change the **Weight** to **2 1/4 pt**.

Change the picture **Height** to **0.7**, and then change the **Text Wrapping** to **Square**. Change the **Horizontal Alignment** to **Left relative to Margin** and the **Vertical Alignment** to **Top relative to Margin**.

6 Starting with the paragraph that begins *Are You Getting a Good Night's Sleep?*, select all of the text from that point to the end of the document. Format the text in two columns, and apply **Justify** alignment. Insert a **Column break** before the subheading *Can Chemistry Help?*

Start and maximize Internet Explorer, and then navigate to **www.nhlbi.nih.gov/health** and then in the middle of the page, click **Sleep Disorders**. In your **3G_Newsletter** file, click at the end of the paragraph below the *Are You Getting a Good Night's Sleep* subheading, and then press Enter. In the blank line, insert a **Screenshot** of the website; do not link to the URL. Apply a **Black, Text 1 Picture Border** and change the **Weight** to **1 pt**.

Select the subheading *Are You Getting a Good Night's Sleep?* including the paragraph mark. From the **Font** dialog box, apply **Bold** and **Small Caps** and change the **Font color** to **Dark Blue, Text 2**—in the fourth column, the first color. Apply the same formatting to the subheadings *Light and Sleep, Can Chemistry Help?* and *Sleep Aid Apps*.

7 Select the last paragraph in the newsletter, and then apply a **1 pt Shadow** border using **Black, Text 1**. Shade the paragraph with the **Fill color Dark Blue, Text 2, Lighter 80%**—in the fourth column, the second color. **Center** the text.

Click the **FILE tab**, and then click **Show All Properties**. As the **Tags**, type **sleep, newsletter** As the **Subject**, type your course name and section number. Under **Related People**, if necessary, type your name in the **Author box**. On the left, click **Print** to display the

Print Preview. Make any necessary corrections. **Save** the document and **Exit** Word.

8 Start Word and display a new blank document. **Save** the document in your **Word Chapter 3** folder as **Lastname_Firstname_3G_Mailing_Labels** From your student files, **Open** the file **w03G_Addresses**. **Save** the address file in your **Word Chapter 3** folder as **Lastname_ Firstname_3G_Addresses** and then add the file name to the footer. **Save** and **Close** the file. Be sure that your **Lastname_Firstname_3G_Mailing_Labels** document displays.

9 Start the **Step-by-Step Mail Merge Wizard** to create **Labels**. Be sure that the **Default tray** is selected and that the label vendor is **Avery US Letter**. The **Product number** is **5160 Easy Peel Address Labels**. Select the **Use an existing list option**, and then from your **Word Chapter 3** folder, **Open** your **Lastname_Firstname_3G_Addresses** file. Add the following record to your file:

First Name	Mason
Last Name	Zepeda
Address 1	134 Atlantic Ave.
Unit	#21
City	Memphis
State	TN
ZIP Code	38123

10 Insert an **Address block** and match the fields. Match the **Address 2** field to the **Unit** field, and then update the labels. Preview the labels, and then select the entire document. Change the **Spacing Before** to **3** and then **Complete the merge**. Delete the last row from the bottom of the table, and then add the file name to the footer.

Display the document properties. As the **Tags** type **labels** and as the **Subject** type your course name and section number. Be sure your name displays in the **Author box**, and then **Save** your file. As directed by your instructor, print or submit your work electronically. In addition to your labels and address document, submit your **3G_Newsletter** and **3G_Electronic_Records** documents as directed. **Close** Word and Internet Explorer.

END | You have completed Project 3G

CONTENT-BASED ASSESSMENTS

Apply a combination of the 3A and 3B skills.

GO! Fix It   Project 3H Hospital Materials   Online

GO! Make It   Project 3I Health Newsletter   Online

Build from Scratch

GO! Solve It   Project 3J Colds and Flu   Online

GO! Solve It   Project 3K Cycling Newsletter

PROJECT FILES

For Project 3K, you will need the following file:

w03K_Cycling_Newsletter

You will save your document as:

Lastname_Firstname_3K_Cycling_Newsletter

The UMC Emergency Department publishes a newsletter focusing on safety and injury prevention. The topic for the current newsletter is bicycle safety. From your student data files, open w03K_Cycling_Newsletter, add the file name to the footer, and then save the file in your Word Chapter 3 folder as **Lastname_Firstname_3K_Cycling_Newsletter**.

Using the techniques that you practiced in this chapter, format the document in two-column, newsletter format. Format the nameplate so that it is clearly separate from the body of the newsletter. Insert column breaks as necessary and apply appropriate formatting to subheadings. Insert and format at least one appropriate online picture and insert a screenshot of a relevant website. Apply a border and shading to the last paragraph.

Add your name, your course name and section number, and the keywords **safety, newsletter** to the Properties area. Submit as directed.

CONTENT-BASED ASSESSMENTS

Performance Level

Performance Criteria	Exemplary: You consistently applied the relevant skills	Proficient: You sometimes, but not always, applied the relevant skills	Developing: You rarely or never applied the relevant skills
Format nameplate	The nameplate is formatted attractively and in a manner that clearly indicates that it is the nameplate.	The nameplate includes some formatting but is not clearly separated from the body of the newsletter.	The newsletter does not include a nameplate.
Insert and format at least one online picture	An sized and positioned online picture image is included.	An online picture is inserted but is either inappropriate, or is formatted or positioned poorly.	No online picture is included.
Border and shading added to a paragraph	The last paragraph displays an attractive border with shading.	An appropriate border or shading is displayed but not both.	No border or shading is applied.
Insert a screenshot	A relevant screenshot is inserted in one of the columns.	A screenshot is inserted in the document but does not relate to the content of the article.	No screenshot is inserted.

END | You have completed Project 3K

OUTCOMES-BASED ASSESSMENTS

RUBRIC

The following outcomes-based assessments are *open-ended assessments*. That is, there is no specific correct result; your result will depend on your approach to the information provided. Make *Professional Quality* your goal. Use the following scoring rubric to guide you in *how* to approach the problem and then to evaluate *how well* your approach solves the problem.

The *criteria*—Software Mastery, Content, Format and Layout, and Process—represent the knowledge and skills you have gained that you can apply to solving the problem. The *levels of performance*—Professional Quality, Approaching Professional Quality, or Needs Quality Improvements—help you and your instructor evaluate your result.

	Your completed project is of Professional Quality if you:	Your completed project is Approaching Professional Quality if you:	Your completed project Needs Quality Improvements if you:
1-Software Mastery	Choose and apply the most appropriate skills, tools, and features and identify efficient methods to solve the problem.	Choose and apply some appropriate skills, tools, and features, but not in the most efficient manner.	Choose inappropriate skills, tools, or features, or are inefficient in solving the problem.
2-Content	Construct a solution that is clear and well organized, contains content that is accurate, appropriate to the audience and purpose, and is complete. Provide a solution that contains no errors in spelling, grammar, or style.	Construct a solution in which some components are unclear, poorly organized, inconsistent, or incomplete. Misjudge the needs of the audience. Have some errors in spelling, grammar, or style, but the errors do not detract from comprehension.	Construct a solution that is unclear, incomplete, or poorly organized; contains some inaccurate or inappropriate content; and contains many errors in spelling, grammar, or style. Do not solve the problem.
3-Format & Layout	Format and arrange all elements to communicate information and ideas, clarify function, illustrate relationships, and indicate relative importance.	Apply appropriate format and layout features to some elements, but not others. Overuse features, causing minor distraction.	Apply format and layout that does not communicate information or ideas clearly. Do not use format and layout features to clarify function, illustrate relationships, or indicate relative importance. Use available features excessively, causing distraction.
4-Process	Use an organized approach that integrates planning, development, self-assessment, revision, and reflection.	Demonstrate an organized approach in some areas, but not others; or, use an insufficient process of organization throughout.	Do not use an organized approach to solve the problem.

Apply a combination of the
3A and 3B skills.

Build from
Scratch

OUTCOMES-BASED ASSESSMENTS

GO! Think   Project 3L Influenza Report

PROJECT FILES

For Project 3L, you will need the following file:

New blank Word document

You will save your document as:

Lastname_Firstname_3L_Influenza

As part of the ongoing research conducted by University Medical Center in the area of community health and contagious diseases, Dr. Hillary Kim has asked Sarah Stanger to create a report on influenza—how it spreads, and how it can be prevented in the community.

Create a new file and save it as **Lastname_Firstname_3L_Influenza** Create the report in MLA format. The report should include at least two footnotes, at least two citations, and should include a *Works Cited* page.

The report should contain an introduction, and then information about what influenza is, how it spreads, and how it can be prevented. A good place to start is at http://health.nih.gov/topic/influenza.

Add the file name to the footer. Add appropriate information to the Document Properties and submit it as directed.

END | You have completed Project 3L

OUTCOMES-BASED ASSESSMENTS

Build from Scratch

| GO! Think | Project 3M Volunteer Newsletter | Online |

Build from Scratch

| You and GO! | Project 3N College Newsletter | Online |

| GO! Cumulative Group Project | Project 3O Bell Orchid Hotels | Online |

Using Styles and Creating Multilevel Lists and Charts

GO! to Work
Video W4

PROJECT 4A

OUTCOMES
Edit a handout using styles and arrange text into an organized list.

OBJECTIVES

1. Apply and Modify Styles
2. Create New Styles
3. Manage Styles
4. Create a Multilevel List

PROJECT 4B

OUTCOMES
Change a style set and create and format a chart.

OBJECTIVES

5. Change the Style Set of a Document and Apply a Template
6. Insert a Chart and Enter Data into a Chart
7. Change a Chart Type
8. Format a Chart and Save a Chart as a Template

In This Chapter

In this chapter, you will apply styles, create multilevel lists, attach a template to a document, display numerical data in charts, and save a chart as a template. The theme and style set features provide a simple way to coordinate colors, fonts, and effects used in a document. For example, if you publish a monthly newsletter, you can apply styles to article headings and modify lists to ensure that all editions of the newsletter maintain a consistent and professional look. Charts display numerical data in a visual format. Formatting chart elements adds interest and assists the reader in interpreting the displayed data.

The projects in this chapter relate to **Costa Rican Treks**, a tour company named for the small country in Central America with a diverse ecosystem. Costa Rican Treks offers exciting but affordable adventure tours for individuals and groups. Travelers go off the beaten path to explore amazing remote places in this scenic country. If you prefer to experience the heart of Costa Rica on the water, try scuba diving or rafting tours. Costa Rican Treks also offers hiking and Jeep tours. Whatever you prefer—mountain, sea, volcano—our trained guides are experts in the history, geography, culture, and flora and fauna of Costa Rica.

Customer Handout

PROJECT ACTIVITIES

In Activities 4.01 through 4.11, you will create a handout for Costa Rican Treks customers who are interested in scuba diving tours. You will use styles and multilevel list formats so that the document is attractive and easy to read. Your completed document will look similar to Figure 4.1.

PROJECT FILES

For Project 4A, you will need the following file:

w04A_Customer_Handout

You will save your file as:

Lastname_Firstname_4A_Customer_Handout

PROJECT RESULTS

> ## Costa Rican Treks
> ### REQUIREMENTS FOR SCUBA DIVING TRIPS
>
> *Costa Rican Treks offers several tours that include scuba diving. For any tours where equipment will be rented, facilitators must ensure that several pieces of safety equipment are available for each participant.*
>
> *Please notify us when you book a tour if you would like us to supply any of the following scuba gear for you. We are happy to do so at a reasonable price.*
>
> #### Equipment
> 1. Air Tank
>   - The air tank holds high-pressure breathing gas. Typically, each diver needs just one air tank. Contrary to common perception, the air tank does not hold pure oxygen; rather, it is filled with compressed air that is about 21 percent oxygen and 79 percent nitrogen.
>   + Examples: Aluminum, steel, pony
> 2. Buoyancy Compensator
>   - The buoyancy compensator controls the overall buoyancy of the diver so that descending and ascending can be controlled.
>   + Examples: Wings, stab jacket, life jacket
> 3. Regulator
>   - A regulator controls the pressure of the breathing gas supplied to the diver to make it safe and comfortable to inhale.
>   + Examples: Constant flow, twin-hose
> 4. Weights
>   - Weights add just enough weight to help the diver descend rather than float. The right amount of weight will not cause the diver to sink.
>   + Examples: Weight belt, integrated weight systems
>
> #### Attire
> 1. Dry Suits
>   - A dry suit is intended to insulate and protect the diver's skin. Dry suits are different from wet suits in that they prevent water from entering the suits.
>   + Examples: Membrane, neoprene, hybrid
> 2. Wet Suits
>   - A wet suit insulates and protects, whether in cool or warm water. Wet suits differ from dry suits in that a small amount of water gets between the suit and the diver's skin.
>   + Examples: Two millimeter, 5 millimeter, 7 millimeter, Titanium
>
> Lastname_Firstname_4A_Customer_Handout

FIGURE 4.1 Project 4A Customer Handout

Objective 1   Apply and Modify Styles

Video W4-1

A *style* is a group of formatting commands, such as font, font size, font color, paragraph alignment, and line spacing. You can retrieve a style by name and apply it to text with one click.

Using styles to format text has several advantages over using *direct formatting*—the process of applying each format separately; for example, bold, then font size, then font color, and so on. Styles are faster to apply, result in a consistent look, and can be automatically updated in all instances in a document, which can be especially useful in long documents.

Activity 4.01 │ Applying Styles to Text

Styles that are grouped together comprise a *style set*. A style set is a group of styles that are designed to work together. Specific styles—for example, *Title* or *Heading 1*—that display in the Styles gallery on the ribbon can be applied to any selected text.

1 Start Word, and then click **Open Other Documents**.. Under **Places**, double-click **Computer**. From your student files, locate and open the document **w04A_Customer_Handout**.

2 Press F12 to display the **Save As** dialog box. In the **Save As** dialog box, navigate to the location where you are saving your files for this chapter. Create a new folder named **Word Chapter 4 Save** the document as **Lastname_Firstname_4A_Customer_Handout**

3 Scroll to the bottom of **Page 1**, right-click in the footer area, and then click **Edit Footer**. On the ribbon, under **HEADER & FOOTER TOOLS**, on the **DESIGN tab**, in the **Insert group**, click **Document Info**, and then click **File Name**. **Close** the footer area. If necessary, display the rulers and formatting marks.

4 Press Ctrl + Home to move to the top of the document.

5 On the **HOME tab**, in the **Styles group**, notice that the **Normal** style is selected—outlined in blue. Compare your screen with Figure 4.2.

The *Normal* style is the default style in Word for a new document. Normal style formatting includes the Calibri font, 11 point font size, line spacing at 1.08, and 8 pt spacing after a paragraph.

FIGURE 4.2

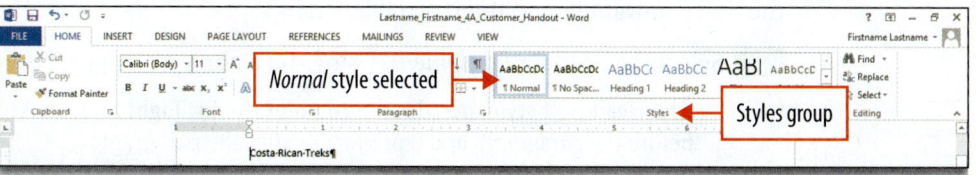

6 Including the paragraph mark, select the first paragraph, which forms the title of the document. On the **HOME tab**, in the **Styles group**, click **More** ⏷ to display the **Styles gallery**. Point to the style named **Title**, and then compare your screen with Figure 4.3.

Live Preview displays how the text will look with the Title style applied.

FIGURE 4.3

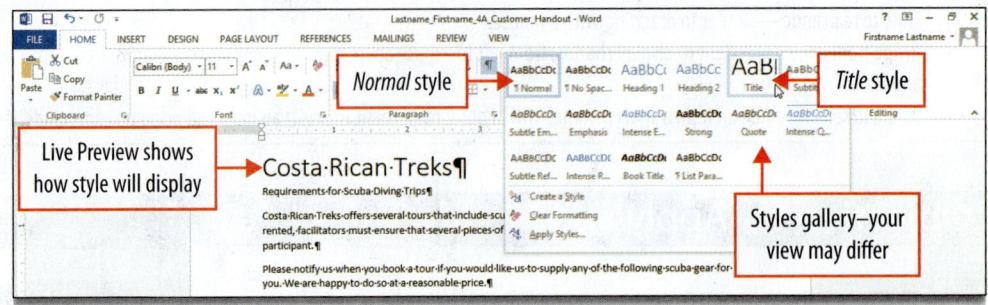

7 Click **Title**, and then click anywhere in the document to deselect the title.

The Title style includes the 28 point Calibri Light font, single line spacing, and 0 pt spacing after the paragraph.

8 Select the second paragraph, which begins *Requirements for*, and is the subtitle of the document. In the **Styles group**, click **More** ⏷, and then in the gallery, click **Subtitle**.

The Subtitle style includes a Text 1 font color and expands the text by 0.75 pt.

9 Select the third and fourth paragraphs, beginning with *Costa Rican Treks offers* and ending with the text *at a reasonable price*. In the **Styles group**, click **More** ⏷, and then in the gallery, click **Emphasis**. Click anywhere to deselect the text, and then compare your screen with Figure 4.4.

FIGURE 4.4

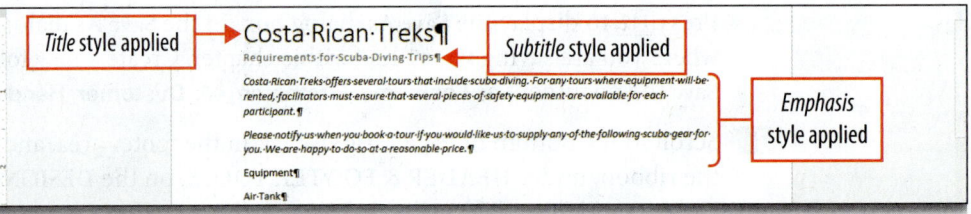

10 Save 💾 your document.

Activity 4.02 | Modifying Existing Style Attributes

You are not limited to the exact formatting of a style—you can change it to suit your needs. For example, you might like the effect of a style with the exception of the font size. If you plan to use a customized style repeatedly in a document, it's a good idea to modify the style to look exactly the way you want it, and then save it as a *new* style.

1 Select the heading *Equipment*. Using the technique you practiced, apply the **Heading 1** style.

The Heading 1 style includes the 16 point Calibri Light font, an Accent 1 font color, 12 pt spacing before the paragraph, and 0 pt spacing after the paragraph.

A small black square displays to the left of the paragraph indicating that the Heading 1 style also includes the *Keep with next* and *Keep lines together* formatting—Word commands that keep a heading with its first paragraph of text on the next page, or prevent a single line from displaying by itself at the bottom of a page or at the top of a page.

2 With the paragraph selected, on the mini toolbar, change the **Font Size** to **18**, and then click **Styles**. In the **Styles** gallery, right-click **Heading 1**, and then compare your screen with Figure 4.5.

ANOTHER WAY   On the HOME tab, display the Styles gallery, and then right-click the Heading 1 style.

FIGURE 4.5

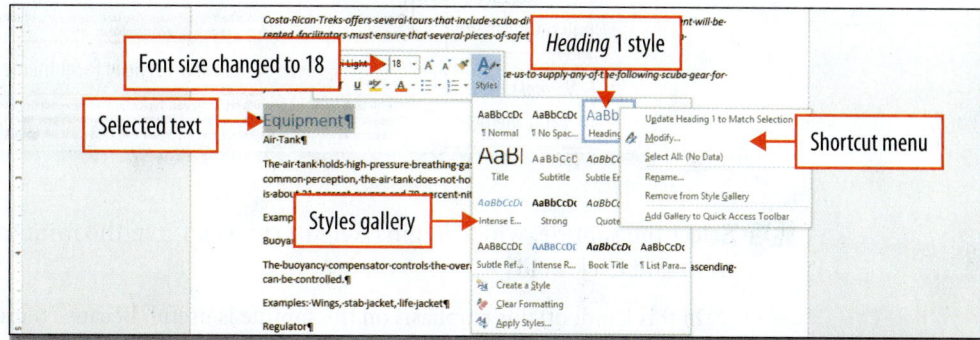

3 From the shortcut menu, click **Update Heading 1 to Match Selection**, and then click anywhere to deselect the text.

By updating the heading style, you ensure that the next time you apply the Heading 1 style in *this* document, it will retain these new formats. In this manner, you can customize a style. The changes to the Heading 1 style are stored *only* in this document and will not affect the Heading 1 style in any other documents.

4 Scroll down to view the lower portion of **Page 1**, and then select the heading *Attire*. On the **HOME tab**, in the **Styles** group, click **Heading 1**, and notice that the *modified* **Heading 1** style is applied to the paragraph. Click anywhere in the document to deselect the text. **Save** 🖫 your document.

Activity 4.03 | Changing the Document Theme

Recall that a theme is a predefined combination of colors, fonts, and effects; the *Office* theme is the default setting. Styles use the font scheme, color scheme, and effects associated with the current theme. If you change the theme, the styles adopt the fonts, colors, and effects of the new theme.

1 Press Ctrl + Home. Click the **DESIGN tab**, and then in the **Document Formatting group**, click **Themes**. In the gallery, point to the various themes and notice the changes in your document.

Live Preview enables you to see the effects that a theme has on text with styles applied.

2 Click **Facet**, and then compare your screen with Figure 4.6.

The Facet theme's fonts, colors, and effects display in the document. All the styles will now use the Facet theme.

FIGURE 4.6

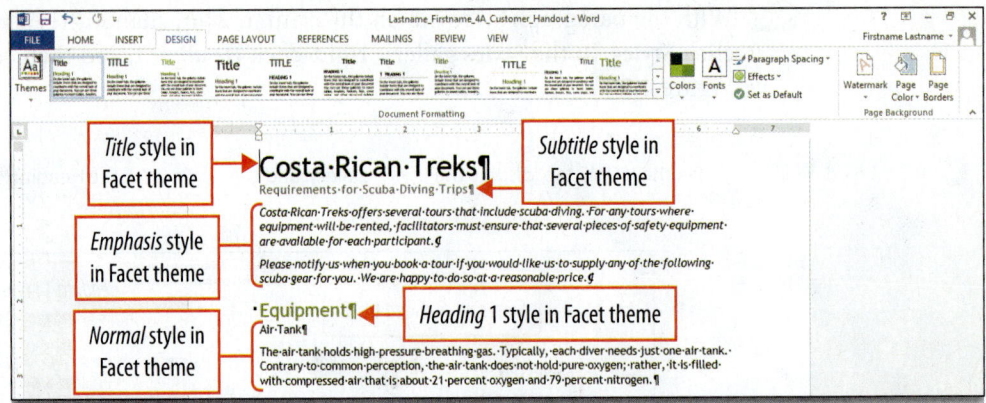

3 ▶ Select the subtitle, which begins *Requirements for*. On the mini toolbar, change the **Font Size** to **14** and click **Bold** [B].

In this handout, this emphasis on the subtitle is useful. Because there are no other subtitles and you will not be applying this style again in this document, it is not necessary to modify the actual style.

4 ▶ With the subtitle still selected, click the **HOME tab**. In the **Font group**, click **Change Case** [Aa ▾], and then from the list, click **UPPERCASE**.

The ***Change Case*** feature allows you to quickly change the capitalization of characters. In the selection, all characters now display in uppercase letters.

5 ▶ Select the third and fourth paragraphs, beginning with *Costa Rican Treks offers* and ending with the text *at a reasonable price*. On the mini toolbar, change the **Font Size** to **12**, and then click **Styles**. In the **Styles** gallery, right-click **Emphasis**, and then click **Update Emphasis to Match Selection**. Click anywhere to deselect the text. **Save** [💾] your document.

Objective 2 │ Create New Styles

Video W4-2

You can create a new style based on formats that you specify. For example, if you frequently use a 12 point Verdana font with bold emphasis and double spacing, you can create a style to apply those settings to a paragraph with a single click, instead of using multiple steps each time you want that specific formatting. Any new styles that you create are stored with the document and are available any time that the document is open.

Activity 4.04 │ Creating Custom Styles and Assigning Shortcut Keys

You can assign a shortcut key to a style, which allows you to apply the style using the keyboard instead of clicking the style in the Styles gallery.

1 ▶ Select the paragraph that begins *Examples: Aluminum*, and then on the mini toolbar, change the **Font Size** to **12**, click **Bold** [B], and then click **Italic** [I].

2 ▶ With the paragraph still selected, on the **HOME tab**, in the **Styles group**, click **More** [▾]. In the lower portion of the gallery, click **Create a Style**.

 **ANOTHER WAY**   On the mini toolbar, click Styles, and then click Create a Style.

3 In the **Create New Style from Formatting** dialog box, in the **Name** box, type **Examples** Compare your screen with Figure 4.7.

Select a name for your new style that will remind you of the type of text to which the style applies. A preview of the style displays in the Paragraph style preview box.

FIGURE 4.7

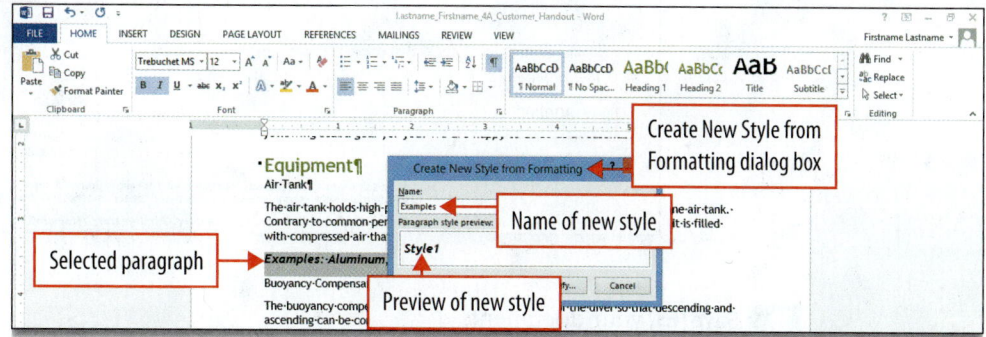

4 At the bottom of the dialog box, click **Modify**.

5 In the **Create New Style from Formatting** dialog box, at the bottom left, click **Format**, and then click **Shortcut key**.

6 In the **Customize Keyboard** dialog box, with the insertion point in the **Press new shortcut key** box, press Alt + E. Compare your screen with Figure 4.8.

The Command box indicates that the shortcut key will be assigned to the Examples style. The text *Alt+E* indicates the keys that have been pressed. A message indicates that the shortcut key is currently unassigned.

FIGURE 4.8

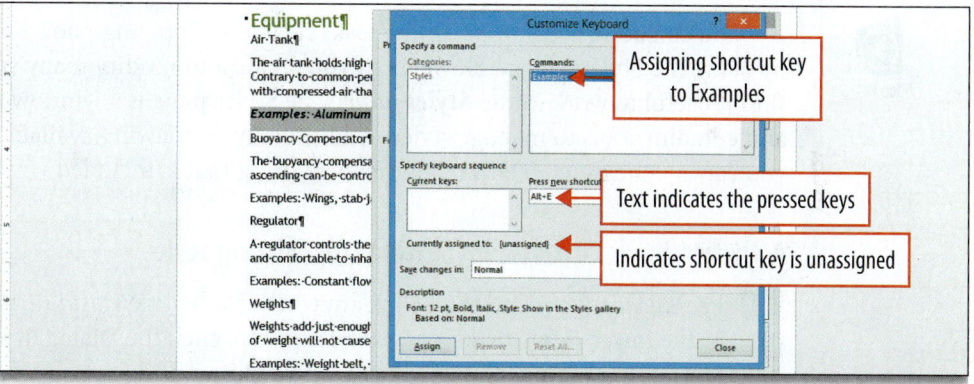

7 In the **Customize Keyboard** dialog box, click **Close**, and then in the **Create New Style from Formatting** dialog box, click **OK**.

The *Examples* style is added to the available styles for this document and displays in the Styles gallery. The shortcut key Alt + E is assigned to the *Examples* style.

8 Scroll down as necessary and select the paragraph that begins *Examples: Wings*. Press Alt + E to apply the new style *Examples*.

9 Using the technique you just practiced, select the four remaining paragraphs that begin *Examples:*, and then apply the **Examples** style. Click anywhere to deselect the text, and then compare your screen with Figure 4.9.

FIGURE 4.9

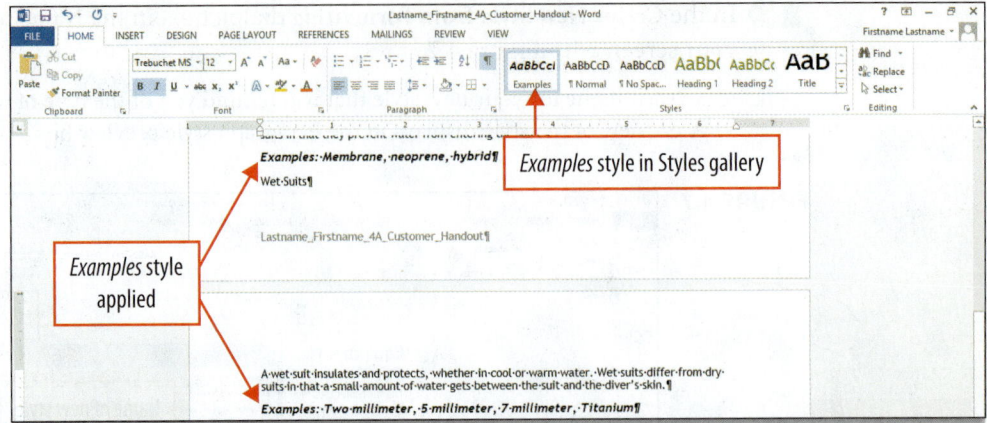

Examples style in Styles gallery

Examples style applied

10 Save 💾 your document.

More Knowledge | **Saving a Style Set**

If you modify existing styles or create new styles, you can save the revised style set as a template in order to apply the style set to other documents. On the DESIGN tab, in the Document Formatting group, display the Style Set gallery, and then click Save as a New Style Set. In the Save as a New Style Set dialog box, navigate to the location where you wish to save the file—the default location is the QuickStyles folder on your hard drive. Assign an appropriate file name, and then click Save. The file is saved as a Word template with the file extension .dotx. Alternatively, you can save the template to your OneDrive and share it with coworkers.

Objective 3 | Manage Styles

Video W4-3

You can accomplish most of the tasks related to applying, modifying, and creating styles easily by using the Styles gallery. However, if you create and modify many styles in a document, you will find it useful to work in the ***Styles pane***. The Styles pane is a window that displays a list of styles and contains tools to manage styles. Additionally, by viewing available styles in the Styles pane, you can see the exact details of all the formatting that is included with each style.

Activity 4.05 | Customizing Settings for Existing Styles

1 Press Ctrl + Home, and then click anywhere in the title *Costa Rican Treks*. On the **HOME tab**, in the lower right corner of the **Styles** group, click the **Dialog Box Launcher** 🔲 to display the **Styles** pane. Compare your screen with Figure 4.10.

The Styles pane displays the same group of available styles found in the Styles gallery, including the new *Examples* style that you created.

FIGURE 4.10

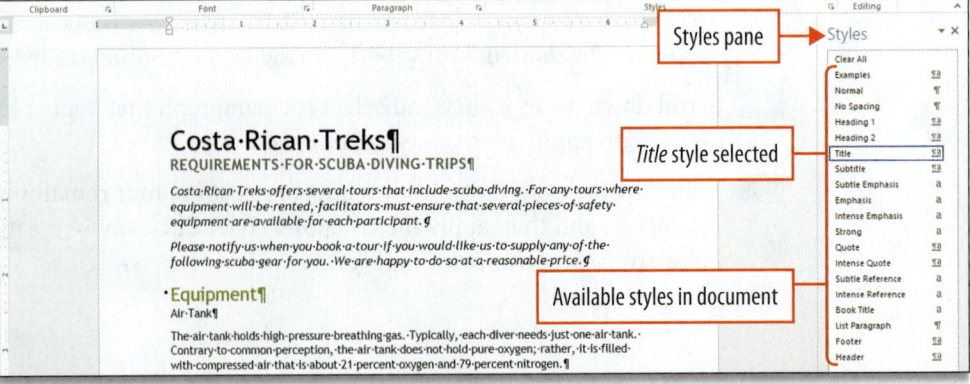

Styles pane

Title style selected

Available styles in document

2 In the **Styles** pane, point to **Title** to display a ScreenTip with the details of the formats associated with the style. In the **ScreenTip**, under **Style**, notice that *Style Linked* is indicated.

3 Move your mouse pointer ⟦🔲⟧ into the document to close the ScreenTip. In the **Styles** pane, examine the symbols to the right of each style, as shown in Figure 4.11.

A *character style*, indicated by the symbol **a**, contains formatting characteristics that you apply to text—for example, font name, font size, font color, bold emphasis, and so on.

A *paragraph style*, indicated by the symbol ¶, includes everything that a character style contains, plus all aspects of a paragraph's appearance—for example, text alignment, tab stops, line spacing, and borders.

A *linked style*, indicated by the symbol ¶**a**, behaves as either a character style or a paragraph style, depending on what you select.

List styles, which apply formats to a list, and *table styles*, which apply a consistent look to the borders, shading, and so on of a table, are also available but do not display here.

FIGURE 4.11

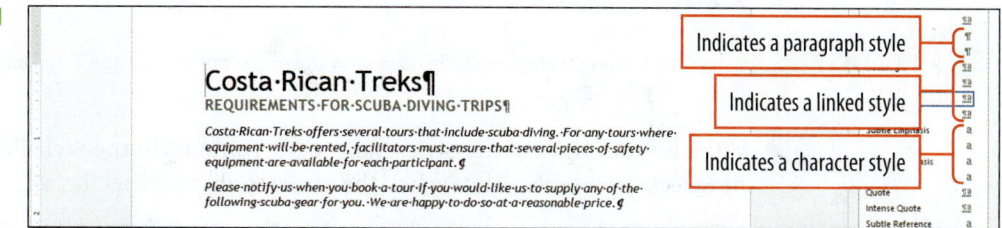

4 In the **Styles** pane, point to **Heading 1**, and then click the arrow to display a list of commands. Compare your screen with Figure 4.12.

🔄 **ANOTHER WAY**   In the Styles gallery, right-click Heading 1.

FIGURE 4.12

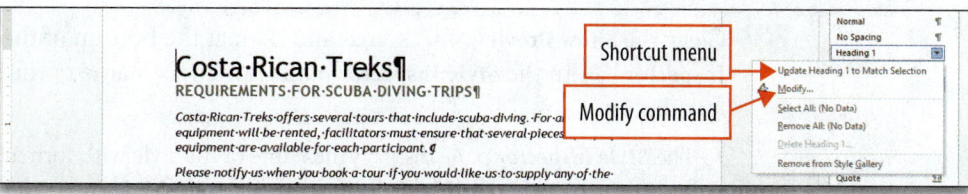

5 From the displayed list, click **Modify**. In the **Modify Style** dialog box, under **Formatting**, click **Underline** ⟦U⟧. Click the **Font Color arrow**, and then in the eighth column, click the fifth color—**Orange, Accent 4, Darker 25%**. Compare your screen to Figure 4.13.

The Modify command allows you to make changes to the selected style In this case, the font color is changed and underline formatting is added to the style.

FIGURE 4.13

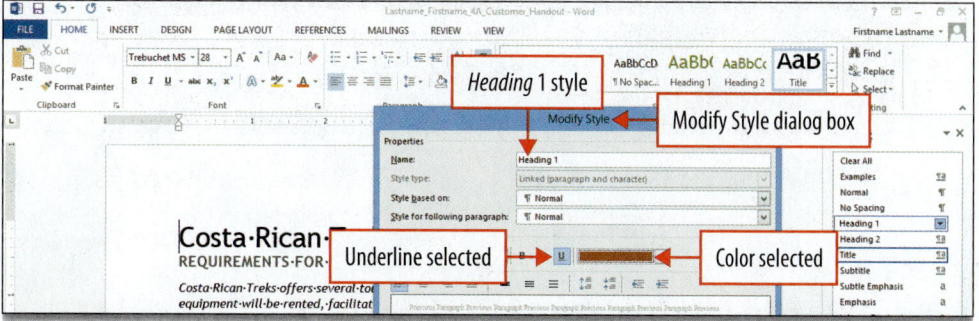

6 Click **OK** to close the **Modify Styles** dialog box. Scroll as necessary, and then notice that both headings—*Equipment* and *Attire*—are underlined and display as an orange font color. **Save** 💾 your document.

More Knowledge	**Using Styles in Other Documents**

By default, styles that you create are stored in the current document only. However, you can make the style available in other documents. To do so, in the Modify Styles dialog box, select the New documents based on this template option button, which deselects the Only in the document option button.

Activity 4.06 | Viewing Style Formats

You can examine existing styles in several ways—for example, when you want to review the formatting characteristics of selected text.

1 Scroll to view the upper portion of **Page 1**, and then select the heading *Equipment*. Notice that in the **Styles** pane *Heading 1* is selected.

🔄 **BY TOUCH**   Tap the document and then slide up to view the upper portion of Page 1. Tap and drag the heading *Equipment*.

---

2 At the bottom right of the **Styles** pane, click **Options**. In the **Style Pane Options** dialog box, in the **Select styles to show** box, click the **arrow** to display specific selection styles.

The selected option—in this case, the default option *Recommended*—determines the styles that display in the Styles pane. The Recommended option causes the most commonly used styles to display.

3 At the bottom of the **Style Pane Options** dialog box, click **Cancel** to close the dialog box.

4 Near the bottom of the **Styles** pane, select the **Show Preview** check box.

The *Show Preview* feature causes a visual representation of each style to display in the Styles window.

5 Clear the **Show Preview** check box, and then at the bottom of the **Styles** pane, click **Style Inspector** 📝. In the **Style Inspector** pane, notice the name of the style applied to the selected text displays.

The *Style Inspector* pane displays the name of the style with formats applied and contains paragraph-level and text-level formatting options that allow you to modify the style or reset to default formats.

6 At the bottom of the **Style Inspector** pane, click **Reveal Formatting** 🔍 to display the **Reveal Formatting** pane. If necessary, drag the **Styles** pane to the left until it is docked. Compare your screen with Figure 4.14. Note: Your view may differ.

The *Reveal Formatting* pane displays the formatted selection—in this case, *Equipment*—and displays a complete description of the formats applied to the selection.

FIGURE 4.14

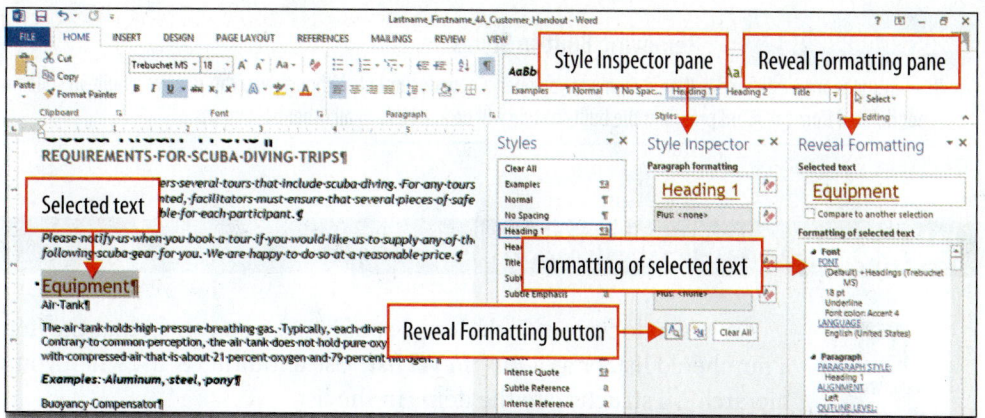

7 ▸ Close **X** the **Style Inspector** pane, the **Reveal Formatting** pane, and the **Styles** pane. Save 🖫 your document.

Activity 4.07 | Clearing Existing Formats

There may be instances where you wish to remove all formatting from existing text—for example, when you create a multilevel list.

1 ▸ Scroll to view the upper portion of **Page 1**, and then select the paragraph that begins *Examples: Aluminum*. On the **HOME tab**, in the **Font group**, click **Clear All Formatting** 🗛. Compare your screen with Figure 4.15.

The Clear All Formatting command removes all formatting of the applied style from the selected text. Text returns to the *Normal* style formatting for the current theme.

FIGURE 4.15

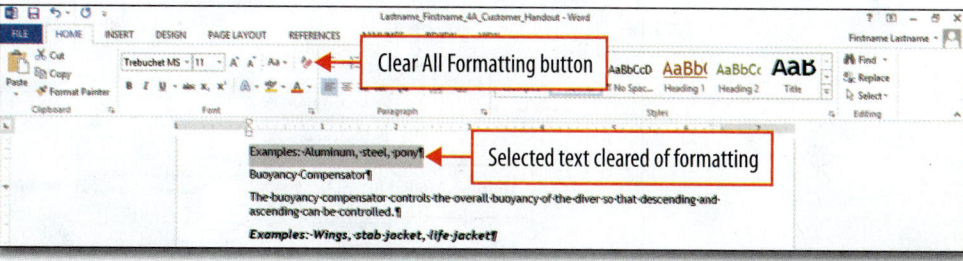

🔄 **ANOTHER WAY** Select the desired text, and then at the top of the Styles pane, click the Clear All command.

2 ▸ With the text still selected, in the **Styles group**, right-click **Examples**, and then click **Update Examples to Match Selection**.

All instances of text formatted with the Examples style now display with the Normal style formatting.

3 ▸ Save 🖫 your document.

Activity 4.08 | Removing a Style

If a style that you created is no longer needed, you can remove it from the Styles gallery.

1 ▸ In the **Styles group**, right-click **Examples**, and then click **Remove from Style Gallery**.

The Examples style is removed from the Styles gallery. The style is no longer needed because all the paragraphs that are examples of scuba gear will be included in a multilevel list. Although the Examples style is removed from the Styles gallery, it is not deleted from the document.

2 ▸ Save 🖫 your document.

Objective 4 | Create a Multilevel List

Video W4-4

When a document includes a list of items, you can format the items as a bulleted list, as a numbered list, or as a *multilevel list*. Use a multilevel list when you want to add a visual hierarchical structure to the items in the list.

Activity 4.09 | Creating a Multilevel List with Bullets and Modifying List Indentation

1 On **Page 1**, scroll to position the heading *Equipment* near the top of your screen. Beginning with the paragraph *Air Tank*, select the 12 paragraphs between the headings *Equipment* and *Attire*.

2 On the **HOME tab**, in the **Paragraph group**, click **Multilevel List** to display the gallery. Under **List Library**, locate the ❖, ➤, • (bullet) style, which is the multilevel bullet list style. Compare your screen with Figure 4.16.

Word provides several built-in styles for multilevel lists. You can customize any style.

FIGURE 4.16

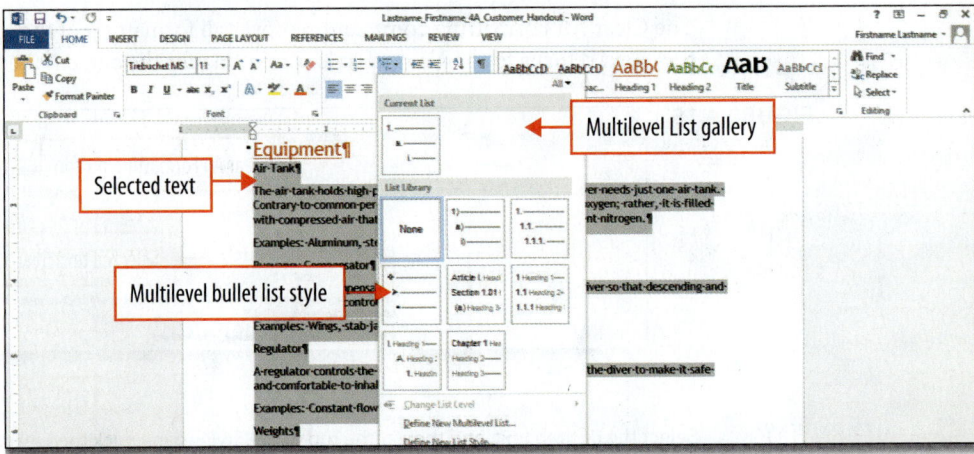

3 Click the **multilevel bullet list** style. Compare your screen with Figure 4.17.

All the items in the list display at the top level; the items are not visually indented to show different levels.

FIGURE 4.17

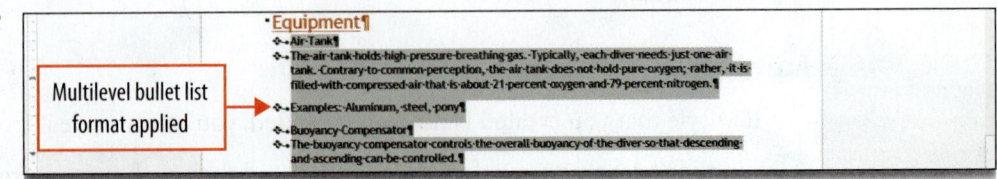

4 Click anywhere in the second list item, which begins *The air tank*. In the **Paragraph group**, click **Increase Indent** , and then compare your screen with Figure 4.18.

The list item displays at the second level which uses the ➤ symbol. The Increase Indent command demotes an item to a lower level; the Decrease Indent command promotes an item to a higher level. To change the list level using the Increase Indent command or Decrease Indent command, it is not necessary to select the entire paragraph.

FIGURE 4.18

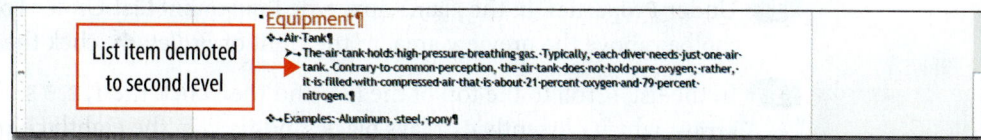

List item demoted to second level

↻ ANOTHER WAY   Select the item, and press [Tab] to demote the item or press [Shift] + [Tab] to promote it.

5 Click in the third item in the list, which begins *Examples: Aluminum*. In the **Paragraph group**, click **Increase Indent** two times, and then compare your screen with Figure 4.19.

The list item displays at the third level, which uses the ■ symbol.

FIGURE 4.19

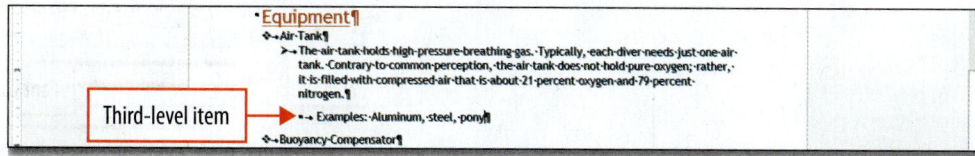

Third-level item

6 Using the technique you just practiced, continue setting levels for the remainder of the multilevel list as follows: Apply the second-level indent for the descriptive paragraphs that begin *The buoyancy*, *A regulator*, and *Weights add*. Apply the third-level indent for the paragraphs that begin *Examples*.

7 Compare your screen with Figure 4.20. If necessary, adjust your list by clicking **Increase Indent or Decrease Indent** so that your list matches the one shown in Figure 4.20.

FIGURE 4.20

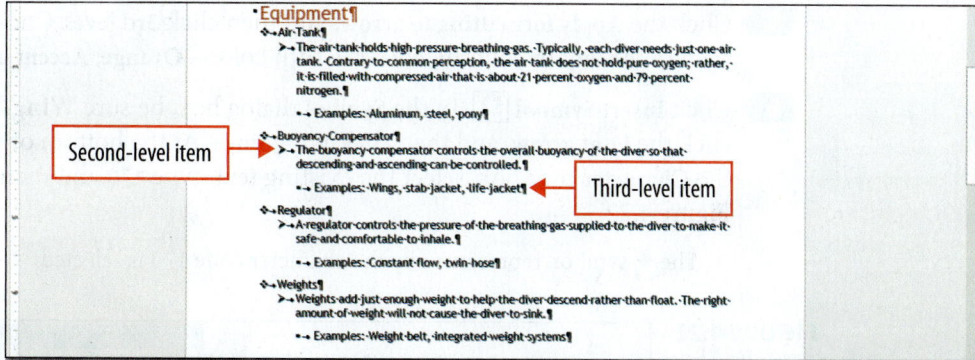

Second-level item

Third-level item

8 Save your document.

More Knowledge   **Selecting List Items**

To select several items in a document that are ***contiguous***—adjacent to one another—to the left of the first item, click in the margin, hold down [Shift], and then to the left of the last item, click in the margin. To select several items that are ***noncontiguous***—not adjacent to one another—hold down [Ctrl], and then click in the margin to the left of each item. After items are selected, you can format all the selected items at one time.

Activity 4.10 | Modifying the Numbering and Formatting in a Multilevel List Style

1 Select the entire multilevel list. Click **Multilevel List** [icon]. At the bottom of the gallery, click **Define New List Style**.

In the Define New List Style dialog box, you can select formatting options for each level in your list. By default, the dialog box displays formatting options starting with the *1st level*.

2 Under **Properties**, in the **Name** box, type **Equipment List** Under **Formatting**, in the small toolbar above the preview area, to the right of *Bullet:* ❖, click the **Numbering Style arrow**.

3 In the list, scroll to the top of the list, and then click the **1, 2, 3** style. Click the **Font Color arrow**, which currently displays black, and then in the eighth column, click the fifth color—**Orange, Accent 4, Darker 25%**. Compare your screen with Figure 4.21.

The numbering style and font color change will be applied only to first-level items. The style changes are visible in the preview area.

FIGURE 4.21

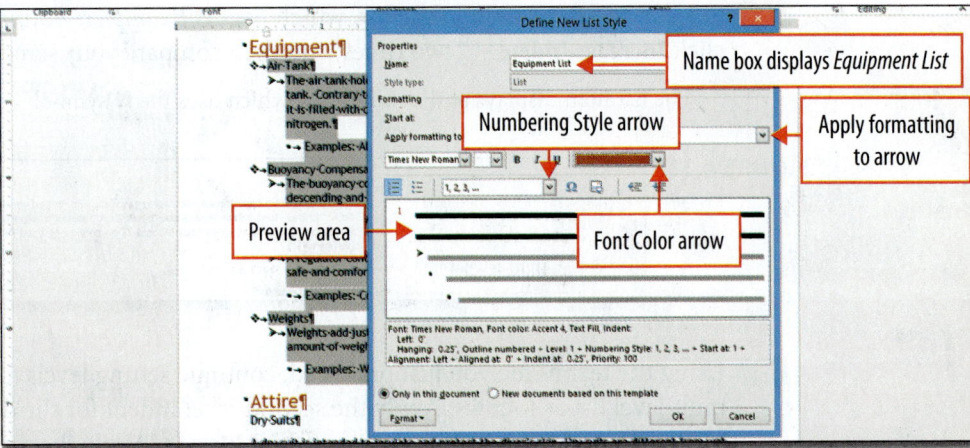

4 Under **Formatting**, click the **Apply formatting to arrow**, and then click **2nd level**. Click the **Font Color arrow**, and then in the eighth column, click the first color—**Orange, Accent 4**—to change the bullet color for the second-level items.

5 Click the **Apply formatting to arrow**, and then click **3rd level**. Click the **Font Color arrow**, and then in the eighth column, click the fifth color—**Orange, Accent 4, Darker 25%**.

6 Click **Insert Symbol** [Ω]. In the **Symbol** dialog box, be sure **Wingdings** displays. If necessary, click the **Font arrow**, and then click **Wingdings**. At the bottom of the **Symbol** dialog box, in the **Character code** box, select the existing text, type **170** and then compare your screen with Figure 4.22.

The ◆ symbol, represented by the character code 170 is selected.

FIGURE 4.22

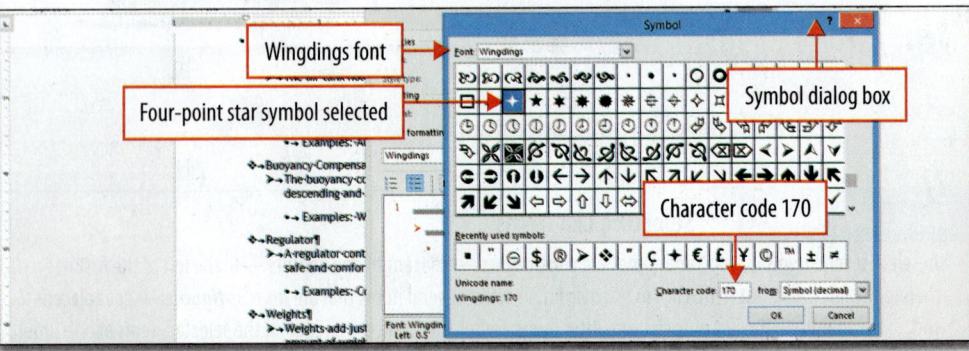

7 Click **OK** to apply the selected symbol and close the **Symbol** dialog box.

Third-level items will display with the ◆ symbol and orange font color.

8 In the **Define New List Style** dialog box, notice the preview of your changes, and then click **OK** to close the dialog box. Click anywhere to deselect the text, and then compare your screen with Figure 4.23.

FIGURE 4.23

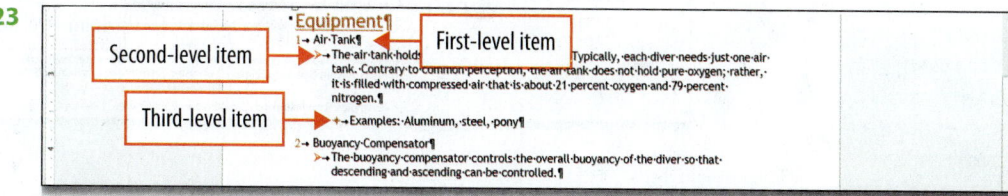

9 Select the entire list. With all 12 paragraphs selected, click the **PAGE LAYOUT tab**, and then in the **Paragraph group**, click the **Spacing After spin box down arrow** to **6 pt**. **Save** 🖫 your changes.

Activity 4.11 | Applying the Current List Style and Changing the List Levels

After you define a new list style, you can apply the style to other similar items in your document.

1 Scroll to display the heading *Attire* and all remaining paragraphs in the document. Beginning with the paragraph *Dry Suits*, select the remaining paragraphs of the document.

2 Click the **HOME tab**, and then in the **Paragraph group**, click **Multilevel List** ⸬. In the gallery, under **List Styles**, click the displayed style. Compare your screen with Figure 4.24.

The current list style formats each paragraph as first-level items.

FIGURE 4.24

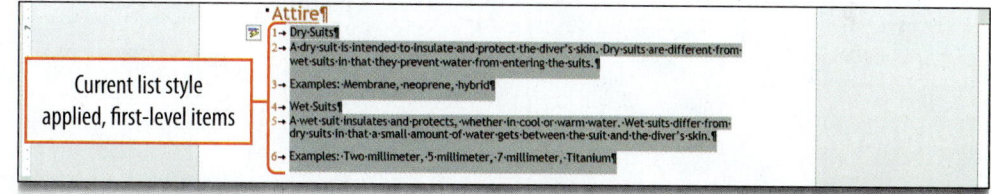

3 Under the *Attire* heading, select the two descriptive paragraphs that begin *A dry suit* and *A wet suit*. Click **Multilevel List** ⸬, and then click **Change List Level**. Compare your screen with Figure 4.25.

All available list levels display for the selected paragraphs. You can increase or decrease the list level for selected items in a list by assigning the desired level.

FIGURE 4.25

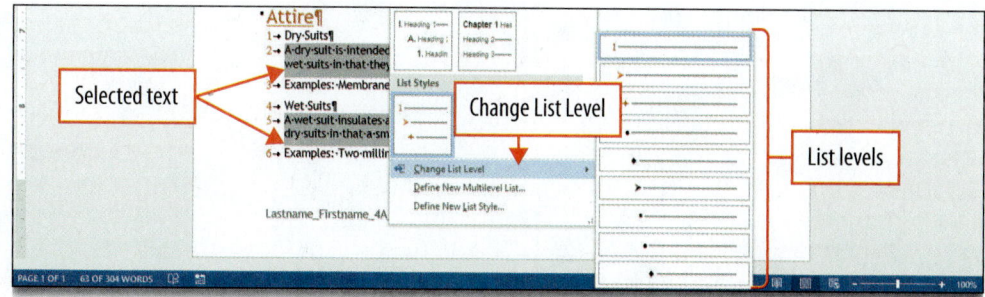

4 From the levels list, select the second list level that displays the symbol ➤—**Level 2**.

5 Select the two paragraphs that begin *Examples*, and then using the technique you just practiced, assign the third list level that displays the symbol ◆—**Level 3**.

6 Select the entire list. With all six paragraphs selected, click the **PAGE LAYOUT tab**, and then in the **Paragraph group**, click the **Spacing After spin box down arrow** to **6 pt**. Deselect the text, and then compare your screen with Figure 4.26.

FIGURE 4.26

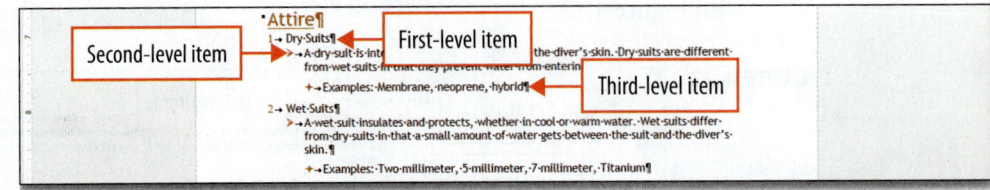

7 Click the **FILE tab** to display **Backstage** view. On the right, at the bottom of the **Properties** list, click **Show All Properties**. In the **Tags** box, type **scuba diving, trip handout** and then in the **Subject** box, type your course name and section number. If necessary, edit the author name to display your name.

8 In **Backstage** view, click **Print** to display the **Print Preview**. Examine the **Print Preview**, make any necessary adjustments, and then **Save** your document.

9 Print your document or submit it electronically as directed by your instructor. **Close** ☒ Word.

END | You have completed Project 4A

Planning Memo with a Chart

PROJECT ACTIVITIES

In Activities 4.12 through 4.23, you will edit a memo to all the company tour guides regarding the planning session. The Tour Operations Manager of Costa Rican Treks is preparing for a planning session in which he and other key decision makers will discuss the types of tours the company will offer in the coming year. They want to use information gathered from customer research to provide an appropriate mix of tour types that will appeal to a wide audience. You will add a chart to illustrate plans for tour types in the coming year. Your completed documents will look similar to Figure 4.27.

PROJECT FILES

For Project 4B, you will need the following files:

w04B_Planning_Memo
w04B_Custom_Styles

You will save your files as:

Lastname_Firstname_4B_Planning_Memo
Lastname_Firstname_4B_Planning_Revised
Lastname_Firstname_4B_Chart_Template—not shown in figure

PROJECT RESULTS

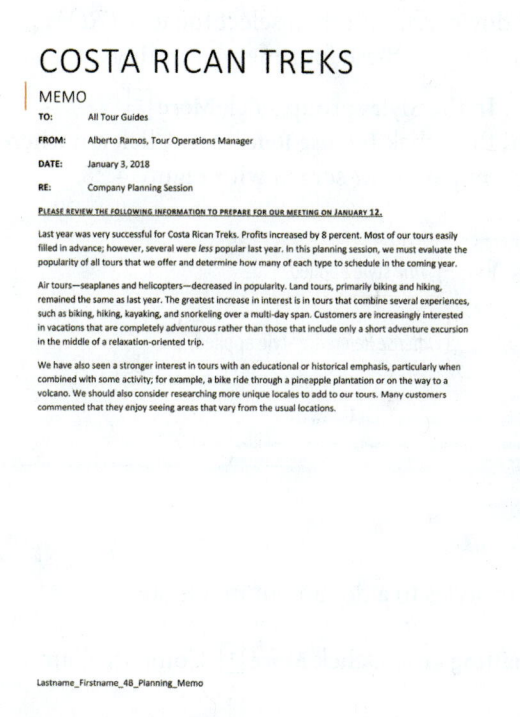

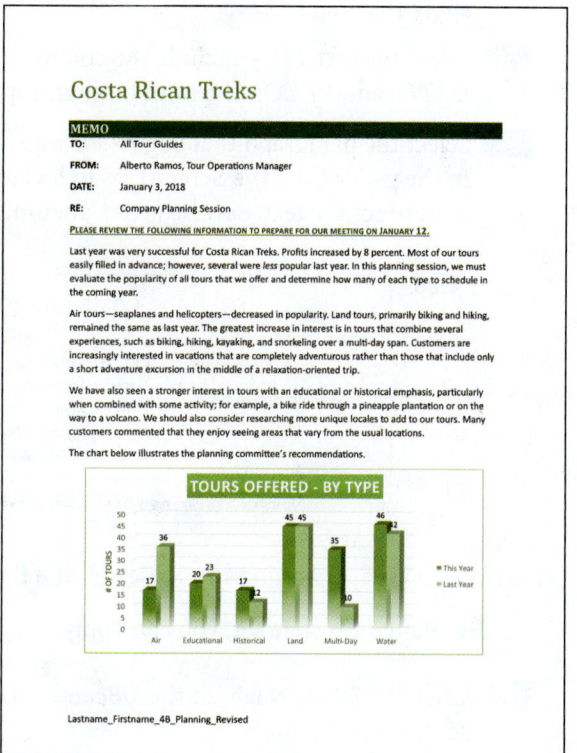

FIGURE 4.27 Project 4B Planning Memo

Video W4-5

Recall that a style set is a group of styles that is designed to work together. A style set is useful when you want to change the look of all the styles in a document in one step rather than modifying individual styles. You can modify the document using a built-in style set or by attaching a template.

Activity 4.12 | Formatting a Memo

A *memo*, also referred to as a *memorandum*, is a written message to someone working in the same organization. Among organizations, memo formats vary, and there are many acceptable memo formats. Always consult trusted references or the preferences set by your organization when deciding on the proper formats for your professional memos.

1 **Start** Word. From your student files, locate and open the file **w04B_Planning_Memo**.

2 Save the document in your **Word Chapter 4** folder as **Lastname_Firstname_4B_Planning_Memo** Scroll to the bottom of the page, right-click in the footer area, and then click **Edit Footer**. On the ribbon, under **HEADER & FOOTER TOOLS**, on the **DESIGN tab**, in the **Insert group**, click **Document Info**, and then click **File Name**. **Close** the footer area. If necessary, display the rulers and formatting marks.

3 Select the first paragraph of the document—*Costa Rican Treks*. On the **HOME tab**, in the **Styles group**, click **More** ⊽, and then in the gallery, click **Title**.

4 Select the second paragraph, the heading *MEMO*, click **More** ⊽, and then in the gallery, apply **Heading 1**.

5 Select the text *TO:*—include the colon—hold down Ctrl, and then select the text *FROM:*, *DATE:*, and *RE:*. On the mini toolbar, apply **Bold** B to these four memo headings.

6 Select the paragraph that begins *Please review*. In the **Styles** group, click **More** ⊽. In the gallery, use the ScreenTips to locate and then click **Intense Reference**. Click anywhere to deselect the text. **Save** 🖫 your document. Compare your screen with Figure 4.28.

FIGURE 4.28

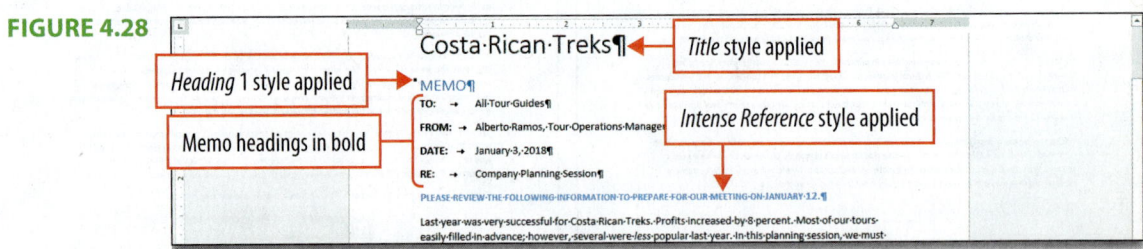

Activity 4.13 | Changing the Style Set of a Document

By changing a style set, you can apply a group of styles to a document in one step.

1 Click the **DESIGN tab**. In the **Document Formatting group**, click **More** ⊽. Compare your screen with Figure 4.29.

> All available style sets display in the Style Set gallery; there are seventeen built-in style sets. The default style set is Word 2013. The style set currently applied to a document displays under This Document.

FIGURE 4.29

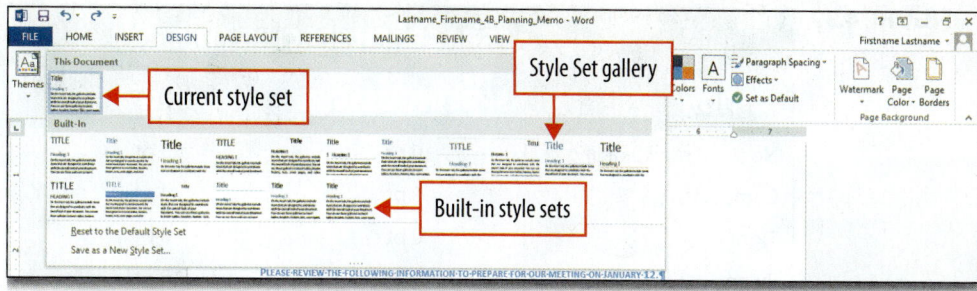

2 In the gallery, under **Built-In**, in the second row, click the first style—**Minimalist**. Compare your screen with Figure 4.30, and then **Save** 🔲 your document.

> *Minimalist* is the name of a particular style set. Applying the *Minimalist* style set, which includes a default font size of 10.5, causes styles—such as Title, Heading 1, and Intense Reference—to display a different format.

FIGURE 4.30

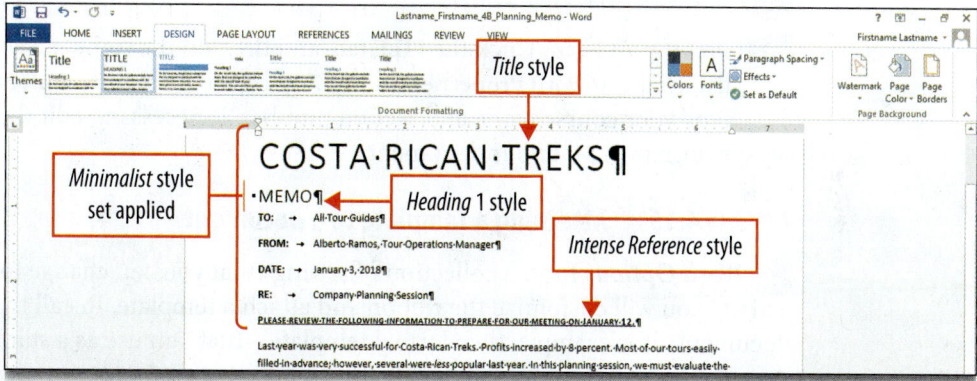

Activity 4.14 | Changing the Paragraph Spacing of a Document

Each style set reflects the font scheme and color scheme of the current theme, including the paragraph spacing formats. Built-in paragraph spacing formats allow you to change the paragraph spacing and line spacing for an entire document in one step.

1 On the **DESIGN tab**, in the **Document Formatting group**, click **Paragraph Spacing**. Compare your screen with Figure 4.31, and then take a moment to study the table shown in Figure 4.32.

> Word provides six built-in styles for paragraph spacing. The *Minimalist* style set uses custom paragraph spacing that includes line spacing of 1.3, 0 pt spacing before, and 8 pt spacing after a paragraph.

FIGURE 4.31

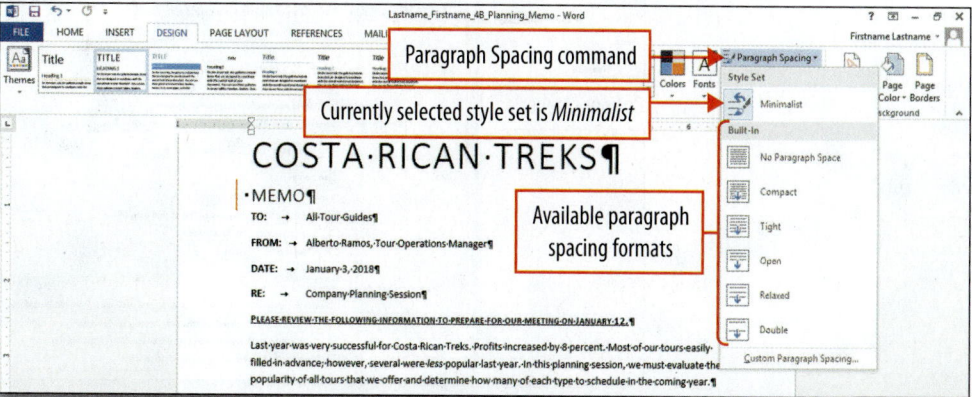

FIGURE 4.32

PARAGRAPH SPACING FORMATS			
OPTION	**SPACING BEFORE**	**SPACING AFTER**	**LINE SPACING**
No paragraph spacing	0 pt	0 pt	1
Compact	0 pt	4 pt	1
Tight	0 pt	6 pt	1.15
Open	0 pt	10 pt	1.15
Relaxed	0 pt	6 pt	1.5
Double	0 pt	8 pt	2

2 In the gallery, point to **Double**. Notice that the ScreenTip describes the paragraph spacing format and that Live Preview displays how the document would look with this paragraph spacing format applied.

3 In the gallery, click **Open**.

4 Press Ctrl + Home. Click the **FILE tab**, and then on the right, at the bottom of the **Properties** list, click **Show All Properties**. In the **Tags** box, type **memo, draft** and then in the **Subject** box, type your course name and section number. If necessary, edit the author name to display your name. **Save** your document.

Activity 4.15 | Attaching a Template to a Document

Word Options form a collection of settings that you can change to customize Word. In this activity you will customize the ribbon and attach a template. Recall that a template is an existing document—for example, the Normal template—that you use as a starting point for a new document. You can apply a template to an existing document to change the appearance of the document.

1 Press F12 to display the **Save As** dialog box. Navigate to your **Word Chapter 4** folder, and then **Save** the document as **Lastname_Firstname_4B_Planning_Revised** Right-click in the footer area, and then click **Edit Footer**. In the footer, right-click the existing file name, and then click **Update Field**. **Close** the footer area.

2 Press Ctrl + Home. Click the **FILE tab**, and then on the left, click **Options** to display the **Word Options** dialog box. Compare your screen with Figure 4.33, and then take a few moments to study the table in Figure 4.34.

In an organizational environment such as a college or business, you may not have access or permission to change some or all of the settings.

FIGURE 4.33

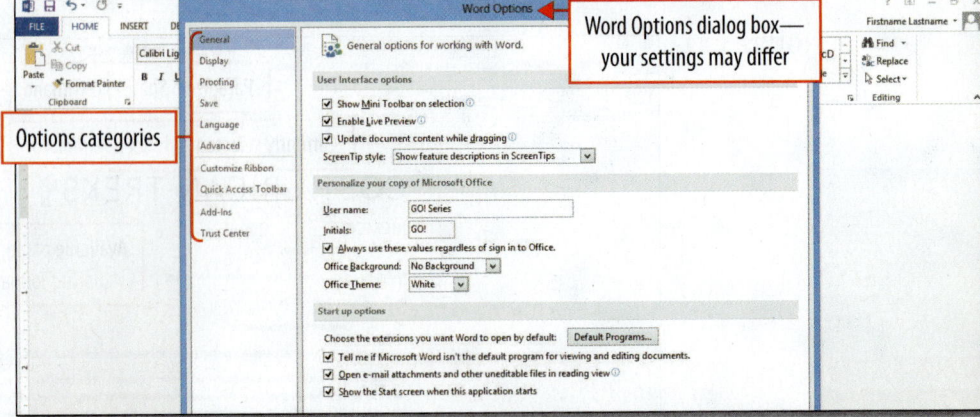

FIGURE 4.34

WORD OPTIONS	
CATEGORY	**OPTIONS TO:**
General	Set up Word for your personal way of working—for example, changing the Office Background—and personalize Word with your name and initials.
Display	Control the way content displays pages on the screen and when it prints.
Proofing	Control how Word corrects and formats your text—for example, how AutoCorrect and spell checker perform.
Save	Specify where you want to save your Word documents by default and set the AutoRecover time for saving information.
Language	Set the default language and add additional languages for editing documents.
Advanced	Control advanced features, including editing and printing options.
Customize Ribbon	Add commands to existing tabs, create new tabs, and set up your own keyboard shortcuts.
Quick Access Toolbar	Customize the Quick Access Toolbar by adding commands.
Add-Ins	View and manage add-in programs that come with the Word software or ones that you add to Word.
Trust Center	Control privacy and security when working with files from other sources or when you share files with others.

3 In the **Word Options** dialog box, on the left, click **Customize Ribbon**.

> The Word Options dialog box displays a list of popular commands on the left and main tabs display on the right. Under Main Tabs, the checkmarks to the left of the tab names indicate tabs that are currently available on the ribbon.

4 In the **Word Options** dialog box, in the **Main Tabs** list, select the **Developer** check box. Compare your screen with Figure 4.35.

> The Developer tab extends the capabilities of Word—including commands for using existing templates.

FIGURE 4.35

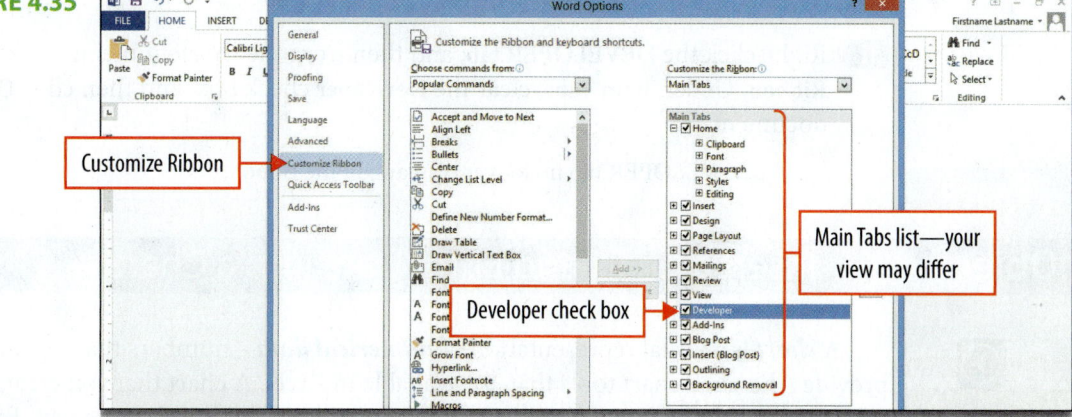

5 Click **OK** to close the **Word Options** dialog box.

> The DEVELOPER tab displays on the ribbon to the right of the VIEW tab.

6 Click the **DEVELOPER tab**, and then in the **Templates group**, click **Document Template**.

7 In the **Templates and Add-ins** dialog box, to the right of the **Document template** box, click **Attach** to display the **Attach Template** dialog box.

8 In the **Attach Template** dialog box, navigate to the location of your student files, click **w04B_Custom_Styles**, and then click **Open**.

The file w04B_Custom_Styles is a Word template that contains styles created by the marketing director to be used in all Costa Rican Treks documents.

9 In the **Templates and Add-ins** dialog box, to the left of **Automatically update document styles**, select the check box, and then compare your screen with Figure 4.36.

FIGURE 4.36

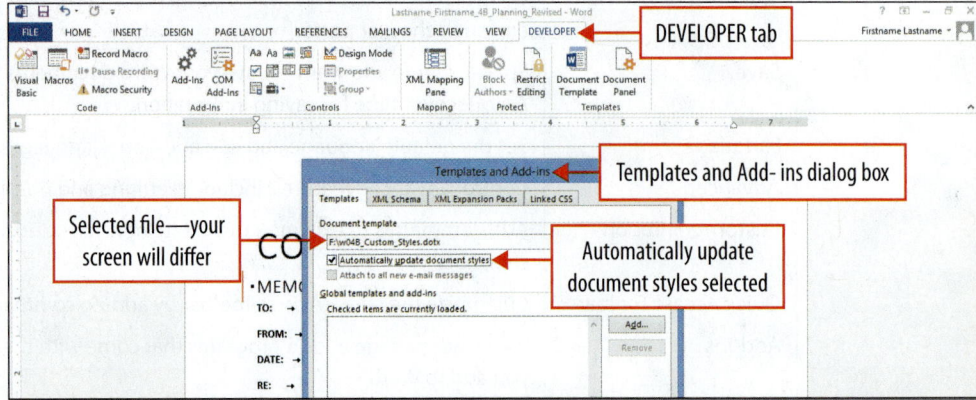

10 In the **Templates and Add-ins** dialog box, click **OK**. Compare your screen with Figure 4.37.

All styles contained in the w04B_Custom_Styles template are applied to your Lastname_Firstname_4B_Planning_Revised document.

FIGURE 4.37

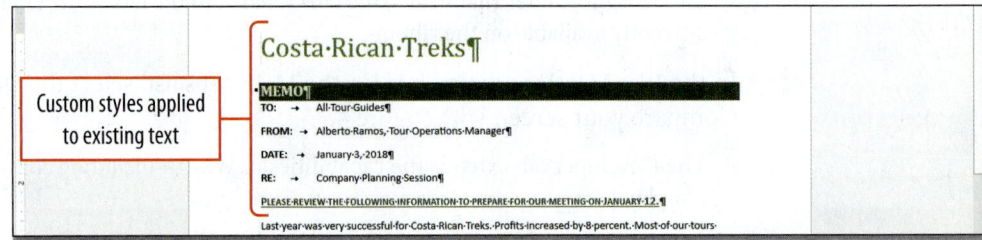

11 Right-click the **DEVELOPER tab**, and then from the shortcut menu, click **Customize the Ribbon**. Under **Main Tabs**, clear the **Developer** check box, and then click **OK**. **Save** 🔲 your document.

The DEVELOPER tab no longer displays on the ribbon.

Objective 6 | Insert a Chart and Enter Data into a Chart

Video W4-6

A *chart* is a visual representation of *numerical data*—numbers that represent facts. Word provides the same chart tools that are available in Excel. A chart that you create in Word is stored in an Excel worksheet, and the worksheet is saved with the Word document. Excel, which is part of Microsoft Office 2013, is a spreadsheet application that makes calculations on numbers. An Excel worksheet is a set of cells, identified by row and column headings, that is part of a worksheet. Charts make numbers easier for the reader to understand.

Activity 4.16 | Selecting a Chart Type

1 Press Ctrl + End. Press Enter, and then type **The chart below illustrates the planning committee's recommendations.** Press Enter.

2 Click the **INSERT tab**, and then in the **Illustrations group**, click **Chart** to display the **Insert Chart** dialog box. Take a moment to examine the chart types described in the table shown in Figure 4.38.

Ten chart types display on the left side of the Insert Chart dialog box. The most commonly used chart types are column, bar, pie, line, and area.

FIGURE 4.38

COMMONLY USED CHART TYPES AVAILABLE IN WORD	
CHART TYPE	**PURPOSE OF CHART**
Column, Bar	Show comparison among related data
Pie	Show proportion of parts to a whole
Line, Area	Show trends over time

3 On the left side of the **Insert Chart** dialog box, click **Bar**. In the right pane, at the top, click the fourth style—**3-D Clustered Bar**. Compare your screen with Figure 4.39.

A bar chart is a good choice because this data will *compare* the number of tours offered in two different years.

FIGURE 4.39

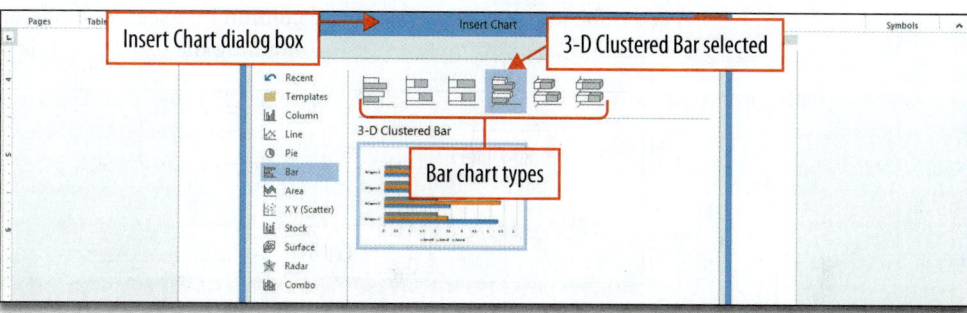

4 Click **OK** to insert the chart in your document and open the related Chart in Microsoft Word worksheet, which is an Excel worksheet. Compare your screen with Figure 4.40.

The chart displays on Page 2 of your Word document. Sample data displays in the worksheet.

The process of inserting a chart in your document in this manner is referred to as *embedding*—the object, in this case a chart, becomes part of the Word document. When you edit the data in the worksheet, the chart in your Word document updates automatically.

FIGURE 4.40

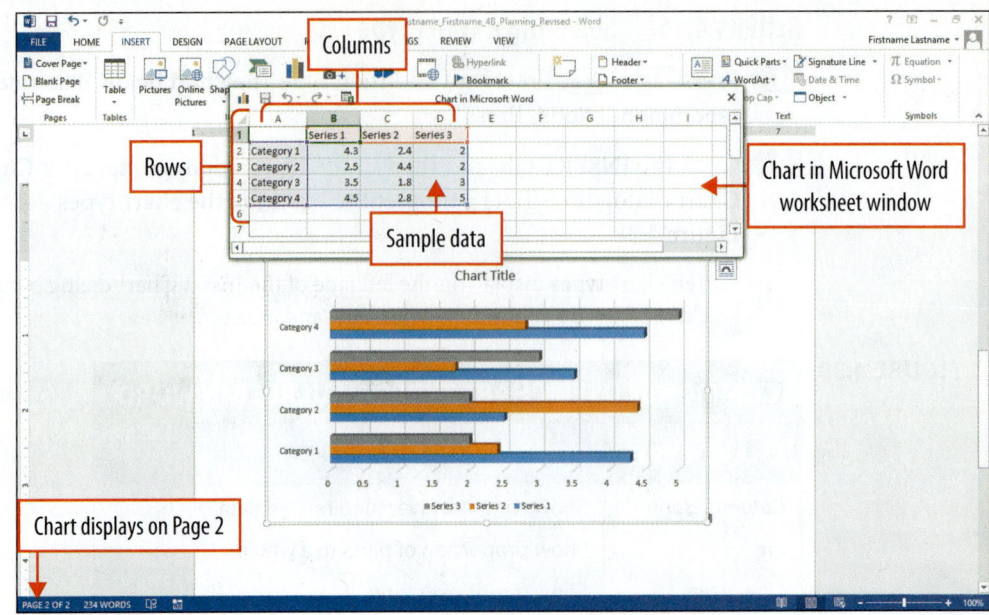

Activity 4.17 | Entering Chart Data

You can replace the sample data in the worksheet with specific tour data for your chart.

1 In the **Chart in Microsoft Word** worksheet, point to the small box where **column B** and **row 1** intersect—referred to as cell **B1**—and click. Compare your screen with Figure 4.41.

A **cell** is the location where a row and column intersect. The cells are named by their column and row headings. For example, cell B1, containing the text *Series 1*, is in column B and row 1.

FIGURE 4.41

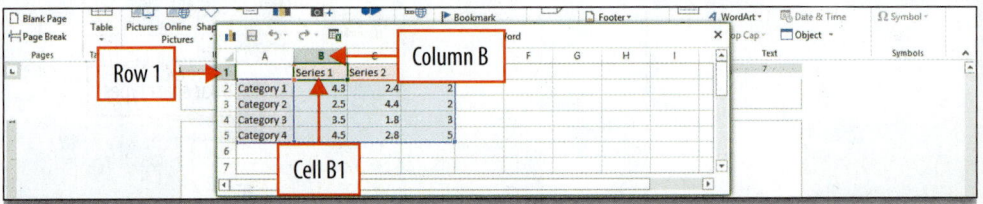

2 With cell **B1** selected, type **This Year** and then press (Tab). With cell **C1** selected, type **Last Year** and then click cell **A2**—which displays the text *Category 1*.

3 With cell **A2** selected, type **Air** and then press (Tab) to move to cell **B2**. Type **17** and then press (Tab). In cell **C2** type **36** and then press (Tab) two times to move to **row 3**.

As you enter data in the worksheet, the chart is automatically updated in the Word document. When entering a large amount of data in a cell, it may not fully display. If necessary, the data worksheet or chart can be modified to display the data completely.

4 Without changing any values in **column D**, type the following data—after typing *42* in C7, press (Tab) to select cell D7.

	THIS YEAR	LAST YEAR	SERIES 3
Air	17	36	2
Educational	13	9	2
Historical	17	12	3
Land	45	45	5
Multi-Day	35	10	
Water	46	42	

5 Compare your screen with Figure 4.42. If necessary, position the ⬚ pointer at the top of the worksheet window, and then drag up to fully display your data.

> The red lines and shading for cells B1 through D1 indicate data headings. The purple lines and shading for cells A2 through A7 indicate category headings. The blue line—the *data range border*—surrounds the cells containing numerical data that display in the chart. The group of cells with red, purple, and blue shading is referred to as the *chart data range*—the range of data that will be used to create the chart.

FIGURE 4.42

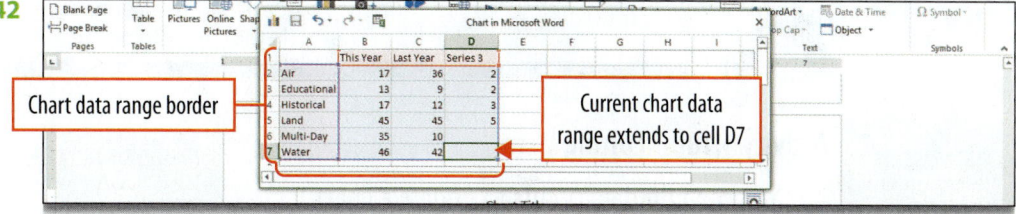

Chart data range border

Current chart data range extends to cell D7

6 In the **Chart in Microsoft Word** worksheet, point to the lower right corner of the blue border to display the ⬚ pointer, and then drag to the left to select only cells **A1** through **C7**. Compare your screen with Figure 4.43.

FIGURE 4.43

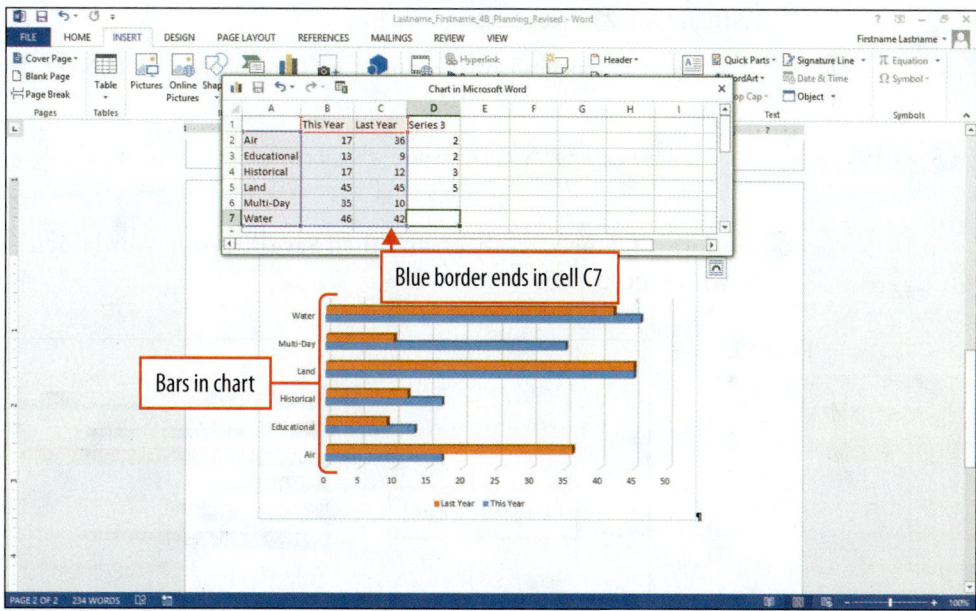

Blue border ends in cell C7

Bars in chart

7 In the upper right corner of the worksheet window, click **Close** ⟨ **x** ⟩. Click the chart border to select the chart. If necessary, point to the top border of the chart until the ⬚ pointer displays, and then drag the chart upward so that it displays near the top of **Page 2** of your document. **Save** 🖫 your Word document, and then compare your screen with Figure 4.44.

> The *chart area* refers to the entire chart and all its elements. The categories—the tour type names—display along the left side of the chart on the *vertical axis*, which is also referred to as the *Y-axis*. The scale—based on the numerical data—displays along the lower edge of the chart on the *horizontal axis*, which is also referred to as the *X-axis*.

> *Data markers*, the bars in your chart, are the shapes representing each of the cells that contain data, referred to as the *data points*. A *data series* consists of related data points represented by a unique color. For example, this chart has two data series—*This Year* and *Last Year*. The *legend* identifies the colors assigned to each data series or category.

> With the chart selected, the CHART TOOLS display on the ribbon and include two additional tabs— DESIGN and FORMAT—to provide commands with which you can modify and format chart elements.

FIGURE 4.44

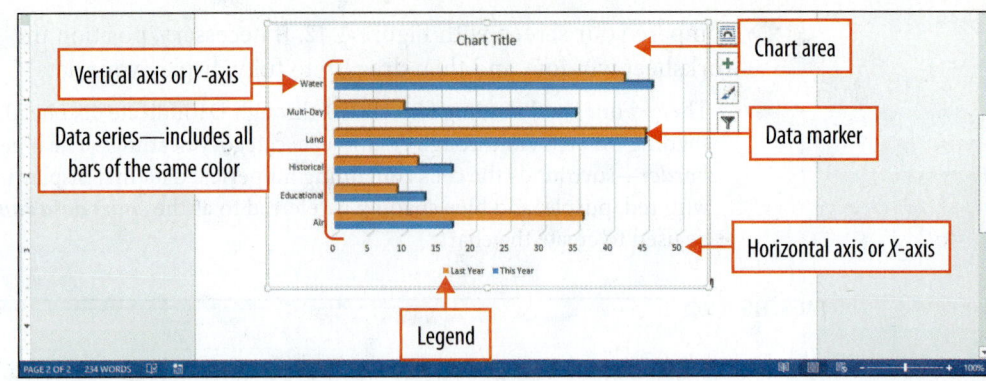

Activity 4.18 | Editing Data

You can edit data points to update a chart.

1 Be sure your chart is selected; if necessary, click the chart border to select it. On the ribbon, under **CHART TOOLS**, click the **DESIGN tab**, and then in the **Data group**, click **Edit Data** to redisplay the embedded Chart in Microsoft Word worksheet.

2 In the **Chart in Microsoft Word** worksheet, click cell **B3**, and then type **20** Click cell **C3**, and then type **23** Press Enter.

Word automatically updates the chart to reflect these data point changes.

BY TOUCH   Double-tap a cell, and then type the number.

3 **Close** [x] the worksheet, and then **Save** [disk icon] your Word document. Compare your screen with Figure 4.45.

FIGURE 4.45

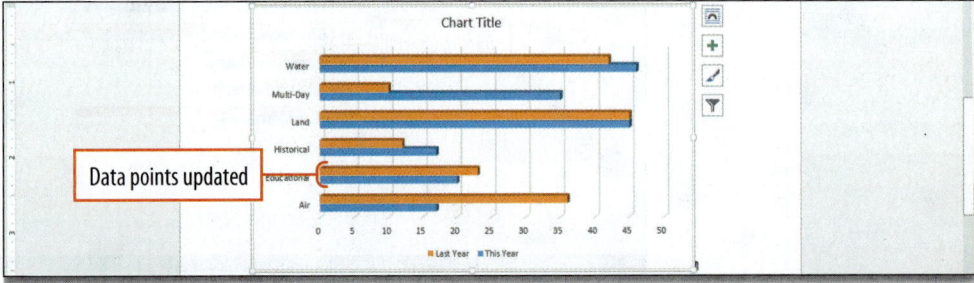

Objective 7   Change a Chart Type

Video W4-7

A chart commonly shows one of three types of relationships—a comparison among data, the proportion of parts to a whole, or trends over time. You may decide to alter the chart type—for example, change a bar chart to a column chart—so that the chart displays more attractively in the document. You can modify, add, or delete chart elements such as the chart title, data labels, and text boxes.

Activity 4.19 | Changing the Chart Type

The data in the tour types chart compares tour numbers for two years and is appropriately represented by a bar chart. A column chart is also appropriate to compare data.

1 With the chart selected, on the ribbon, under **CHART TOOLS**, on the **DESIGN tab**, in the **Type group**, click **Change Chart Type**.

2 In the **Change Chart Type** dialog box, on the left, click **Column**, and then in the right pane, at the top, click the fourth chart type—**3-D Clustered Column**. Click **OK**, and then compare your screen with Figure 4.46.

> The category names display in alphabetical order on the horizontal axis; the number scale displays on the vertical axis.

FIGURE 4.46

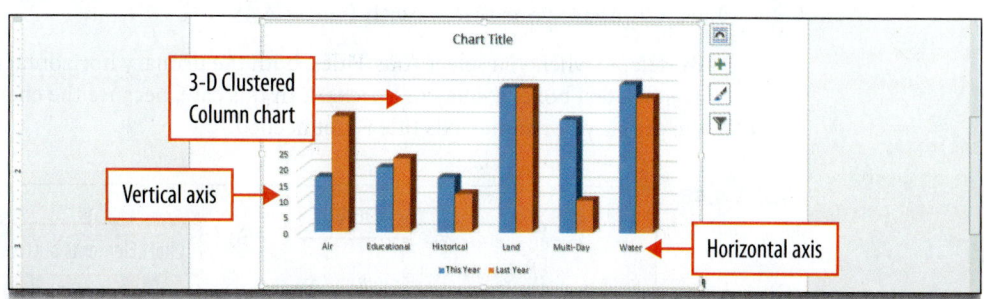

3 Save your document.

Activity 4.20 | Adding Chart Elements

Add chart elements to help the reader understand the data in your chart. For example, you can add a title to the chart and to individual axes, or add *data labels*, which display the value represented by each data marker.

1 Four buttons—*Layout Options*, *Chart Elements*, *Chart Styles*, and *Chart Filters*—display to the right of the selected chart. Take a moment to read the descriptions of each button in the table in Figure 4.47.

FIGURE 4.47

AVAILABLE CHART BUTTONS		
CHART BUTTON	**ICON**	**PURPOSE**
Layout Options	▣	To set how a chart interacts with the text around it
Chart Elements	➕	To add, remove, or change chart elements—such as a chart title, legend, gridlines, and data labels
Chart Styles	🖌	To apply a style and color scheme to a chart
Chart Filters	▽	To define what data points and names display on a chart

2 To the right of the chart, click **Chart Elements** ➕. In the list, point to **Gridlines**, and then with the **Gridlines** check box selected, click the **arrow**. Notice that *Primary Major Horizontal* is selected.

> Gridlines assist the reader in identifying specific values. The major gridlines in this chart extend horizontally from the vertical axis to the right of the last data marker. Use the Gridlines command to display or hide vertical or horizontal gridlines—either major or minor—based on the complexity of the chart.

 **ANOTHER WAY**   Under CHART TOOLS, on the DESIGN tab, in the Chart Layouts group, click Add Chart Element, and then point to Gridlines.

3 In the **Chart Elements** list, point to **Axes**, and then click the **arrow**. Notice that both *Primary Horizontal* and *Primary Vertical* are selected.

4 Press (Esc) to close the **Chart Elements** list. Above the chart, click in the text box that displays *Chart Title*, delete the existing text, and then type **Tours Offered – By Type**

5 If necessary, click in an empty corner of the chart to display the buttons at the right. Click **Chart Elements** ➕, and then select the **Axis Titles** check box. Click the **arrow**, and then clear the **Primary Horizontal** check box to remove the primary horizontal title text box from the chart. Compare your screen with Figure 4.48.

> By default, when you select Axis Titles, both the primary horizontal axis title and primary vertical axis title text boxes display in the chart. In this case, because the chart title identifies the categories, the primary horizontal axis title is not needed.

FIGURE 4.48

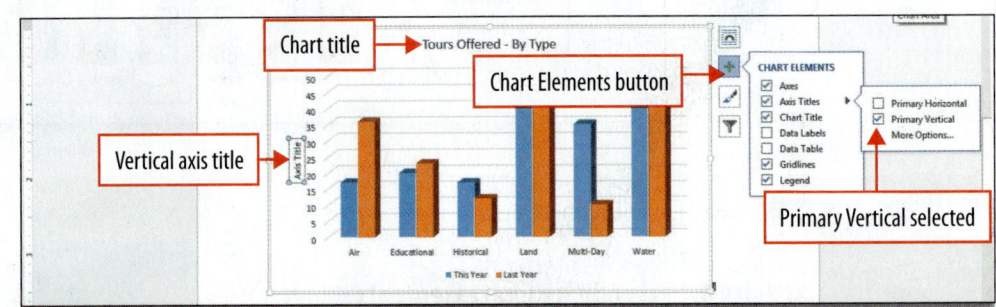

6 To the left of the vertical axis, select the text **Axis Title**, and then type **# of Tours** Notice that the text displays vertically in the text box.

7 Click in an empty corner of the chart to deselect the text box. Click **Chart Elements** ➕, and then select the **Data Labels** check box. **Save** 💾 your document.

> The data point values display above each data marker column in the chart. In addition to the scale on the vertical axis, data labels are helpful for the reader to understand the values represented in the columns.

Objective 8   Format a Chart and Save a Chart as a Template

Video W4-8

You can format a chart to change the appearance of chart elements. After formatting a chart, you can save the chart as a template. If a document contains several charts, using a chart template provides consistency in style and formatting.

Activity 4.21 | Changing the Chart Style and Formatting Chart Elements

A *chart style* refers to the overall visual look of a chart in terms of its graphic effects, colors, and backgrounds. For example, you can have flat or beveled columns, colors that are solid or transparent, and backgrounds that are dark or light. Individual chart elements can also be formatted to enhance the appearance of the chart.

1 To the right of the chart, click **Chart Styles** 🖌. With **STYLE** selected, scroll down and click the eighth style—**Style 8**. At the top of the **Chart Styles** list, click **COLOR**. Under **Monochromatic**, in the sixth row, click the green color scheme—**Color 10**. Compare your screen with Figure 4.49.

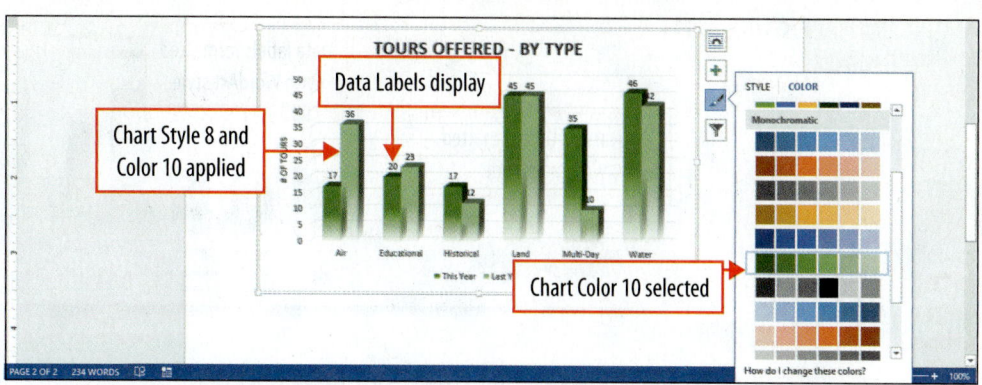

FIGURE 4.49

🔄 **ANOTHER WAY**   Under CHART TOOLS, on the DESIGN tab, in the Chart Styles group, click the More button to display the Chart Styles gallery and click the Change Colors button to display the Color Gallery.

2 Click in the document to close the Chart Styles list. Select the chart title. On the ribbon, under **CHART TOOLS**, click the **FORMAT tab**, and then in the **Shape Styles group**, click **More** ⏷. In the gallery, in the fifth row, click the last style—**Moderate Effect – Green, Accent 6**. Click in an empty corner of the chart to deselect the chart title, and then compare your screen with Figure 4.50.

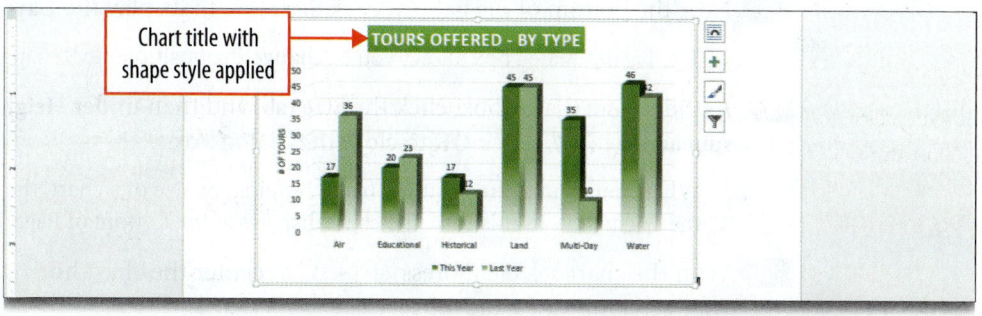

FIGURE 4.50

3 To the left of the vertical axis, select the text *# of Tours*. On the mini toolbar, click the **Font Color arrow** 🅰⏷, and then in the last column, click the last color—**Green, Accent 6, Darker 50%**.

4 Above the **Air** columns, click **17** to select the data labels for each data marker in the *This Year* data series.

5 On the **FORMAT tab**, in the **WordArt Styles group**, click **More** ⏷. In the gallery, click the first style—**Fill – Black, Text 1, Shadow**.

All the data labels in the *This Year* data series display with the WordArt style applied.

6 Using the technique you just practiced, apply the **Fill – Black, Text 1, Shadow** WordArt style to the data labels in the *Last Year* data series.

7 Click the border of the chart. On the **FORMAT tab**, in the **Shape Styles group**, click **Shape Outline** ☑, and then in the last column, click the first color—**Green, Accent 6**. Deselect the chart, and then compare your screen with Figure 4.51.

A border surrounds the entire chart.

FIGURE 4.51

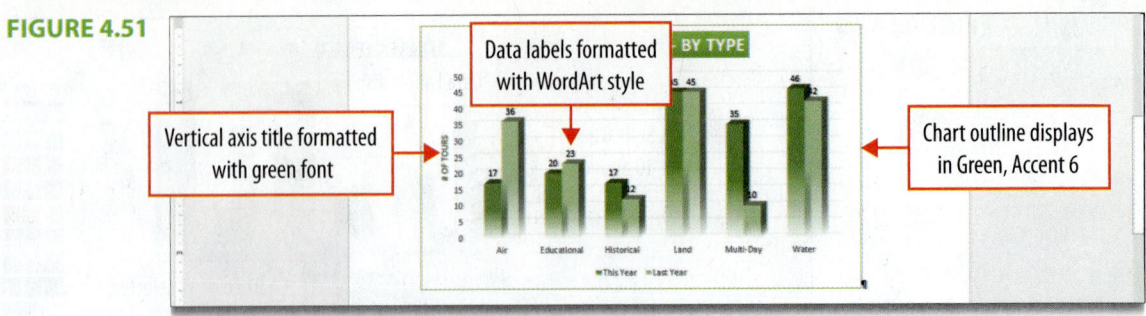

Activity 4.22 | **Resizing and Positioning a Chart**

You can resize and position both the chart and individual chart elements. You can also position the chart on the page relative to the left and right margins.

1 Click in the chart. To the right of the chart, click **Chart Elements** ➕, and then point to **Legend**. With *Legend* selected, click the **arrow,** and then click **Right**.

The legend displays on the right side of the chart.

2 To the right of the chart, click **Layout Options** 🔼.

When you insert a chart, the default text wrapping setting is In Line with Text.

3 Near the bottom of the gallery, click **See more** to display the **Layout** dialog box.

The Layout dialog box allows you to change the position, text wrapping, and size of a chart.

4 In the **Layout** dialog box, click the **Size tab**, and then under **Height**, click the **Absolute down spin arrow** to **2.7**. Click **OK** to close the dialog box.

When you change the position, text wrapping, or size of a chart, the chart may display differently in the document. In this case, the chart displays at the bottom of Page 1.

5 With the chart selected, press Ctrl + E to center the chart horizontally on the page. Compare your screen with Figure 4.52.

FIGURE 4.52

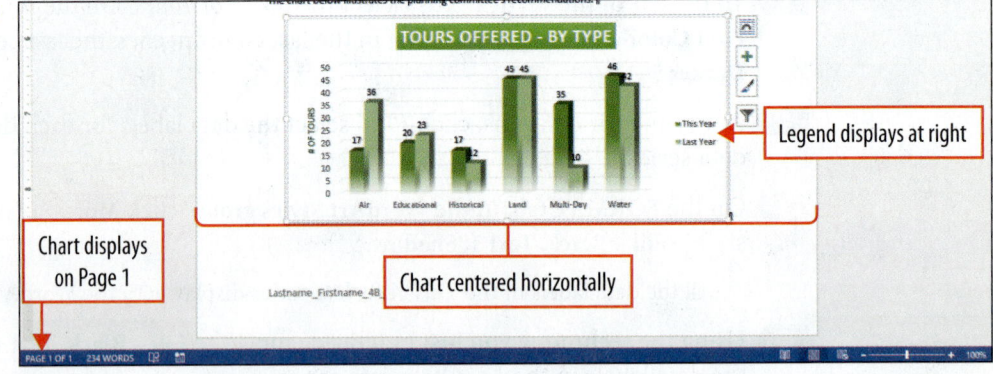

ANOTHER WAY   On the FORMAT tab, in the Arrange group, you can modify the text wrapping and alignment of the chart; and in the Size group, you can change the size.

6 Save 💾 your document.

Activity 4.23 | Saving a Chart as a Template

After formatting the chart and chart elements, you can save the chart as a template. If a document contains several charts, using a chart template provides consistency in style and formatting.

1 Right-click the border of the chart, and then from the shortcut menu, click **Save as Template**.

2 In the **Save Chart Template** dialog box, navigate to your **Word Chapter 4** folder, and then save the chart as **Lastname_Firstname_4B_Chart_Template**

> The chart template is saved with the file extension .crtx.

3 Press Ctrl + Home. Click the **FILE tab** to display **Backstage** view. On the right, at the bottom of the **Properties** list, click **Show All Properties**, if necessary. In the **Tags** box, delete any text, and then type **planning memo, tours data**

4 In **Backstage** view, click **Print**. Examine the **Print Preview**, and make any necessary adjustments. **Save** your document.

5 Print your two documents or submit all three files electronically as directed by your instructor. **Close** ⌐ × ⌐ Word.

More Knowledge Saving a Chart Template to Your OneDrive

If you save the template to your OneDrive and share it with coworkers, all charts created within the department or organization can have a consistent appearance.

END | You have completed Project 4B

END OF CHAPTER

SUMMARY

Use built-in and customized theme and style features to coordinate colors, fonts, effects, and other formatting elements. Apply themes and styles to maintain a consistent and professional appearance in documents.

A multilevel list displays information in an organized, hierarchical structure. You can create and save a custom multilevel list style, and apply it to other lists within the same document or in other documents.

A custom theme that is saved as a Word template can be attached to other documents. This is a quick and easy method to change the appearance of an existing document and provide consistency among related documents.

Because a chart displays numbers in a visual format, readers can easily understand the data. Add and format chart elements to enhance the chart's appearance. Save the chart as a template for use in other documents.

GO! LEARN IT ONLINE

Review the concepts and key terms in this chapter by completing these online challenges, which you can find at **www.pearsonhighered.com/go**.

Matching and Multiple Choice:
Answer matching and multiple choice questions to test what you learned in this chapter. MyITLab®

Crossword Puzzle:
Spell out the words that match the numbered clues, and put them in the puzzle squares.

Flipboard:
Flip through the definitions of the key terms in this chapter and match them with the correct term.

END OF CHAPTER

REVIEW AND ASSESSMENT GUIDE FOR WORD CHAPTER 4

Your instructor may assign one or more of these projects to help you review the chapter and assess your mastery and understanding of the chapter.

		Review and Assessment Guide for Word Chapter 4	
Project	**Apply Skills from These Chapter Objectives**	**Project Type**	**Project Location**
4C	Objectives 1-4 from Project 4A	**4C Skills Review** A guided review of the skills from Project 4A.	On the following pages
4D	Objectives 5-8 from Project 4B	**4D Skills Review** A guided review of the skills from Project 4B.	On the following pages
4E	Objectives 1-4 from Project 4A	**4E Mastery (Grader Project)** A demonstration of your mastery of the skills in Project 4A with extensive decision making.	In MyITLab and on the following pages
4F	Objectives 5-8 from Project 4B	**4F Mastery (Grader Project)** A demonstration of your mastery of the skills in Project 4B with extensive decision making.	In MyITLab and on the following pages
4G	Objectives 1-8 from Projects 4A and 4B	**4G Mastery (Grader Project)** A demonstration of your mastery of the skills in Projects 4A and 4B with extensive decision making.	In MyITLab and on the following pages
4H	Combination of Objectives from Projects 4A and 4B	**4H GO! Fix It** A demonstration of your mastery of the skills in Projects 4A and 4B by creating a correct result from a document that contains errors you must find.	Online
4I	Combination of Objectives from Projects 4A and 4B	**4I GO! Make It** A demonstration of your mastery of the skills in Projects 4A and 4B by creating a result from a supplied picture.	Online
4J	Combination of Objectives from Projects 4A and 4B	**4J GO! Solve It** A demonstration of your mastery of the skills in Projects 4A and 4B, your decision-making skills, and your critical thinking skills. A task-specific rubric helps you self-assess your result.	Online
4K	Combination of Objectives from Projects 4A and 4B	**4K GO! Solve It** A demonstration of your mastery of the skills in Projects 4A and 4B, your decision-making skills, and your critical thinking skills. A task-specific rubric helps you self-assess your result.	On the following pages
4L	Combination of Objectives from Projects 4A and 4B	**4L GO! Think** A demonstration of your understanding of the chapter concepts applied in a manner that you would outside of college. An analytic rubric helps you and your instructor grade the quality of your work by comparing it to the work an expert in the discipline would create.	On the following pages
4M	Combination of Objectives from Projects 4A and 4B	**4M GO! Think** A demonstration of your understanding of the chapter concepts applied in a manner that you would outside of college. An analytic rubric helps you and your instructor grade the quality of your work by comparing it to the work an expert in the discipline would create.	Online
4N	Combination of Objectives from Projects 4A and 4B	**4N You and GO!** A demonstration of your understanding of the chapter concepts applied in a manner that you would in a personal situation. An analytic rubric helps you and your instructor grade the quality of your work.	Online

GLOSSARY

GLOSSARY OF CHAPTER KEY TERMS

Area chart A chart type that shows trends over time.

Bar chart A chart type that shows a comparison among related data.

Cell The intersection of a column and row.

Change Case A formatting command that allows you to quickly change the capitalization of selected text.

Character style A style, indicated by the symbol **a**, that contains formatting characteristics that you apply to text, such as font name, font size, font color, bold emphasis, and so on.

Chart A visual representation of numerical data.

Chart area The entire chart and all its elements.

Chart data range The group of cells with red, purple, and blue shading that is used to create a chart.

Chart Elements A Word feature that displays commands to add, remove, or change chart elements, such as the legend, gridlines, and data labels.

Chart Filters A Word feature that displays commands to define what data points and names display on a chart.

Chart style The overall visual look of a chart in terms of its graphic effects, colors, and backgrounds.

Chart Styles A Word feature that displays commands to apply a style and color scheme to a chart.

Column chart A chart type that shows a comparison among related data.

Contiguous Items that are adjacent to one another.

Data labels The part of a chart that displays the value represented by each data marker.

Data markers The shapes in a chart representing each of the cells that contain data.

Data points The cells that contain numerical data used in a chart.

Data range border The blue line that surrounds the cells containing numerical data that display in in the chart.

Data series In a chart, related data points represented by a unique color.

Direct formatting The process of applying each format separately, for example bold, then font size, then font color, and so on.

Embedding The process of inserting an object, such as a chart, into a Word document so that it becomes part of the document.

Horizontal axis (*X*-axis) The axis that displays along the lower edge of a chart.

Keep lines together A formatting feature that prevents a single line from displaying by itself at the bottom of a page or at the top of a page.

Keep with next A formatting feature that keeps a heading with its first paragraph of text on the same page.

Layout Options A Word feature that displays commands to control the manner in which text wraps around a chart or other object.

Legend The part of a chart that identifies the colors assigned to each data series or category.

Line chart A chart type that shows trends over time.

Linked style A style, indicated by the symbol **¶a**, that behaves as either a character style or a paragraph style, depending on what you select.

List style A style that applies a format to a list.

Memorandum (Memo) A written message sent to someone working in the same organization.

Multilevel list A list in which the items display in a visual hierarchical structure.

Noncontiguous Items that are not adjacent to one another.

Normal The default style in Word for new documents and which includes default styles and customizations that determine the basic look of a document; for example, it includes the Calibri font, 11 point font size, line spacing at 1.08, and 8 pt spacing after a paragraph.

Numerical data Numbers that represent facts.

Paragraph style A style, indicated by ¶, that includes everything that a character style contains, plus all aspects of a paragraph's appearance; for example text alignment, tab stops, line spacing, and borders.

Pie chart A chart type that shows the proportion of parts to a whole.

Reveal Formatting A pane that displays the formatted selection and includes a complete description of formats applied.

Show Preview A formatting feature that displays a visual representation of each style in the Styles window.

Style A group of formatting commands, such as font, font size, font color, paragraph alignment, and line spacing, which can be applied to selected text with one command.

Style Inspector A pane that displays the name of the selected style with formats applied and contains paragraph- and text-level formatting options.

Style set A group of styles that are designed to work together.

Styles pane A window that displays a list of styles and contains tools to manage styles.

Table style A style that applies a consistent look to borders, shading, and so on of a table.

Vertical axis (*Y*-axis) The axis that displays along the left side of a chart.

Word Options A collection of settings that you can change to customize Word.

CHAPTER REVIEW

Apply **4A** skills from these Objectives:

1. Apply and Modify Styles
2. Create New Styles
3. Manage Styles
4. Create a Multilevel List

Skills Review Project 4C Training Classes

In the following Skills Review, you will add styles and a multilevel list format to a document that describes training classes for Costa Rican Treks tour guides. Your completed document will look similar to Figure 4.53.

PROJECT FILES

For Project 4C, you will need the following file:

w04C_Training_Classes

You will save your file as:

Lastname_Firstname_4C_Training_Classes

PROJECT RESULTS

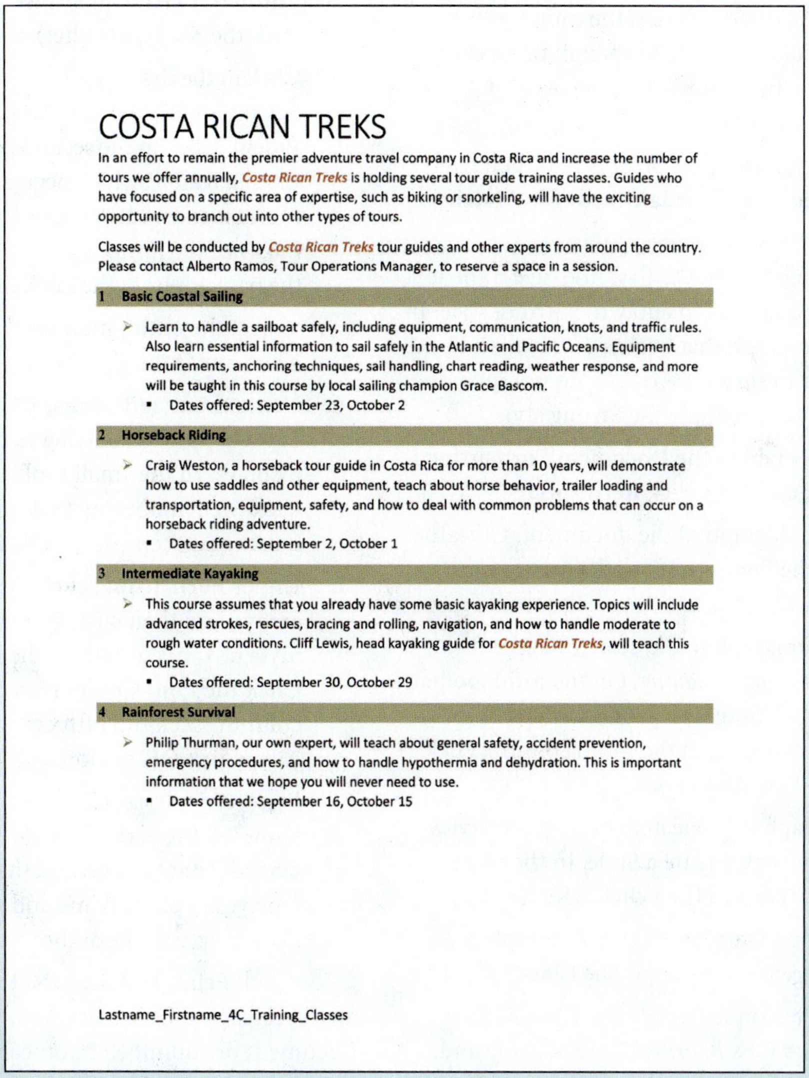

COSTA RICAN TREKS

In an effort to remain the premier adventure travel company in Costa Rica and increase the number of tours we offer annually, *Costa Rican Treks* is holding several tour guide training classes. Guides who have focused on a specific area of expertise, such as biking or snorkeling, will have the exciting opportunity to branch out into other types of tours.

Classes will be conducted by *Costa Rican Treks* tour guides and other experts from around the country. Please contact Alberto Ramos, Tour Operations Manager, to reserve a space in a session.

1 **Basic Coastal Sailing**

- Learn to handle a sailboat safely, including equipment, communication, knots, and traffic rules. Also learn essential information to sail safely in the Atlantic and Pacific Oceans. Equipment requirements, anchoring techniques, sail handling, chart reading, weather response, and more will be taught in this course by local sailing champion Grace Bascom.
  - Dates offered: September 23, October 2

2 **Horseback Riding**

- Craig Weston, a horseback tour guide in Costa Rica for more than 10 years, will demonstrate how to use saddles and other equipment, teach about horse behavior, trailer loading and transportation, equipment, safety, and how to deal with common problems that can occur on a horseback riding adventure.
  - Dates offered: September 2, October 1

3 **Intermediate Kayaking**

- This course assumes that you already have some basic kayaking experience. Topics will include advanced strokes, rescues, bracing and rolling, navigation, and how to handle moderate to rough water conditions. Cliff Lewis, head kayaking guide for *Costa Rican Treks*, will teach this course.
  - Dates offered: September 30, October 29

4 **Rainforest Survival**

- Philip Thurman, our own expert, will teach about general safety, accident prevention, emergency procedures, and how to handle hypothermia and dehydration. This is important information that we hope you will never need to use.
  - Dates offered: September 16, October 15

Lastname_Firstname_4C_Training_Classes

FIGURE 4.53

(Project 4C Training Classes continues on the next page)

CHAPTER REVIEW

1 Start Word. From your student files, open the file **w04C_Training_Classes**. **Save** the document in your **Word Chapter 4** folder as **Lastname_Firstname_4C_Training_Classes** Scroll to the bottom of the page, right-click in the footer area, and then click **Edit Footer**. On the ribbon, in the **Insert group**, click **Document Info**, and then click **File Name**. **Close** the footer area.

a. Select the first paragraph. On the **HOME tab**, in the **Styles group**, click **More**, and then in the gallery, click **Title**.

b. In the second paragraph, in the second line, select the text *Costa Rican Treks*. Display the **Styles** gallery, and then click **Strong**.

c. Right-click the selected text. On the mini toolbar, click the **Font Color arrow**, and then in the sixth column, click the first color—**Orange, Accent 2**.

d. With the text *Costa Rican Treks* still selected, display the **Styles** gallery, right-click **Strong**, and then from the shortcut menu, click **Update Strong to Match Selection**.

e. In the third paragraph, in the first line, select the text *Costa Rican Treks*, and then apply the **Strong** style. In the eleventh paragraph that begins *This course*, in the third line, select *Costa Rican Treks*—do not include the comma—and then apply the **Strong** style.

2 On the **DESIGN tab**, in the **Document Formatting group**, click **Themes**, and then click **Retrospect**.

a. Select the first paragraph of the document. Click the **HOME tab**. In the **Font group**, click **Change Case**, and then click **UPPERCASE**.

b. Including the paragraph mark, select the fourth paragraph *Basic Coastal Sailing*. On the mini toolbar, apply **Bold**. In the **Paragraph group**, click the **Shading arrow**, and then in the ninth column, click the first color—**Tan, Accent 5**.

c. With the paragraph still selected, display the **Styles** gallery, and then click **Create a Style**. In the **Name** box, type **Class Title** and then click **OK**.

d. Scroll down as necessary, select the paragraph *Horseback Riding*, and then apply the **Class Title** style.

e. Using the same technique, apply the **Class Title** style to the paragraphs *Intermediate Kayaking* and *Rainforest Survival*.

3 Press Ctrl + Home. In the **Styles group**, click the **Dialog Box Launcher**.

a. In the **Styles** pane, point to **Strong**, click the **arrow**, and then click **Modify**.

b. In the **Modify Style** dialog box, under **Formatting**, click **Italic**. Click **OK** to close the dialog box and update all instances of the *Strong* style. **Close** the **Styles** pane.

4 Click to position the insertion point to the left of the paragraph *Basic Coastal Sailing*, and then from this point, select all remaining text in the document.

a. On the **HOME tab**, in the **Paragraph group**, click **Multilevel List**. Under **List Library**, locate and then click the ❖, ➤, • (bullet) style.

b. Click in the first paragraph following *Basic Coastal Sailing*, and then in the **Paragraph group**, click **Increase Indent**. Click in the second paragraph following *Basic Coastal Sailing*, which begins *Dates*, and then click **Increase Indent** two times. Under *Horseback Riding*, *Intermediate Kayaking*, and *Rainforest Survival*, format the paragraphs in the same manner.

5 Select the entire multilevel list. Click **Multilevel List**. At the bottom of the gallery, click **Define New List Style**.

a. Name the style **Training Class** Under **Formatting**, in the **Apply formatting to** box, be sure *1st level* displays. In the small toolbar above the preview area, click the **Numbering Style arrow**, in the list, scroll to locate and then click the **1, 2, 3** style.

b. Under **Formatting**, click the **Apply formatting to arrow**, and then click **2nd level**. In the **Numbering Style** box, make certain the **Bullet:** ➤ style displays. Click the **Font Color arrow**, and then in the ninth column, click the fifth color—**Tan, Accent 5, Darker 25%**. Click **OK** to close the dialog box.

c. Press Ctrl + Home. Click the **FILE tab**, and then click **Show All Properties**. In the **Tags** box, type **training classes, description** and then in the **Subject** box, type your course name and section number. If necessary, edit the author name to display your name.

6 Click **Print**. Examine the **Print Preview**, and make any necessary adjustments. **Save** your changes. Print your document or submit electronically as directed by your instructor. **Close** Word.

END | You have completed Project 4C

CHAPTER REVIEW

Apply **4B** skills from these Objectives:

5 Change the Style Set of a Document and Apply a Template

6 Insert a Chart and Enter Data into a Chart

7 Change a Chart Type

8 Format a Chart and Save a Chart as a Template

Skills Review | Project 4D Strategy Session

In the following Skills Review, you will create a memo for Maria Tornio, President of Costa Rican Treks, which details the company's financial performance and provides strategies for the upcoming year. Your completed documents will look similar to Figure 4.54.

PROJECT FILES

For Project 4D, you will need the following files:

w04D_Strategy_Session
w04D_Memo_Styles

You will save your files as:

Lastname_Firstname_4D_Strategy_Session
Lastname_Firstname_4D_Revised_Strategy
Lastname_Firstname_4D_Tour_Chart – not shown in figure

PROJECT RESULTS

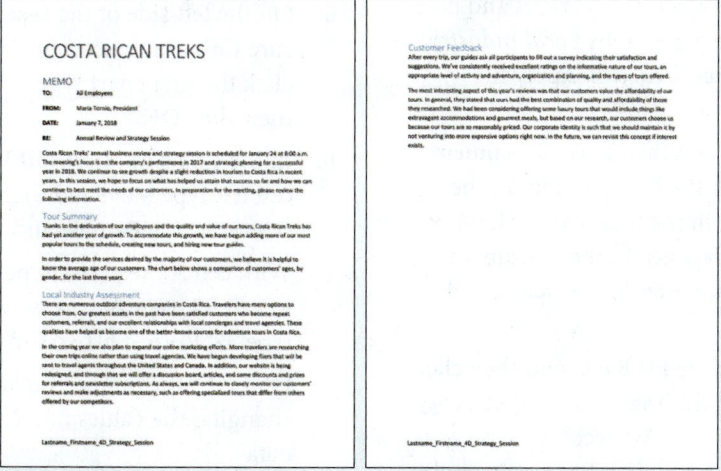
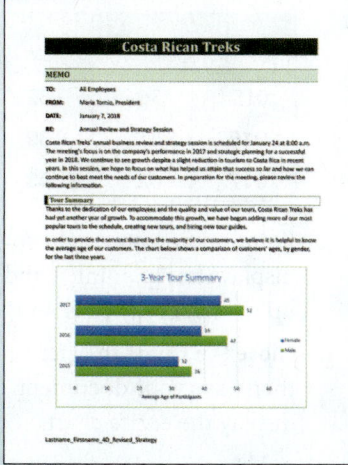
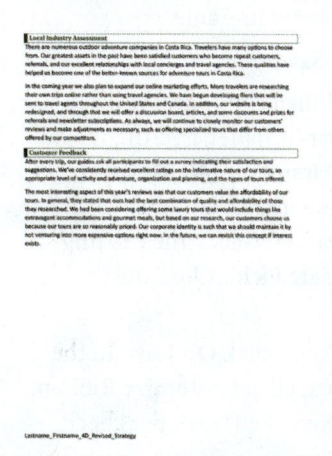

FIGURE 4.54

(Project 4D Strategy Session continues on the next page)

CHAPTER REVIEW

1 ▶ Start Word. From your student files, locate and then open the file **w04D_Strategy_Session**. **Save** the document in your **Word Chapter 4** folder as **Lastname_Firstname_4D_Strategy_Session** Scroll to the bottom of **Page 1**, right-click in the footer area, and then click **Edit Footer**. On the ribbon, in the **Insert group**, click **Document Info**, and then click **File Name**. **Close** the footer area.

a. Select the first paragraph—*Costa Rican Treks*. On the **HOME tab**, in the **Styles** group, click the **More** button, and then click **Title**. Select the second paragraph—*MEMO*, display the **Styles** gallery, and then click **Heading 1**.

b. Select the memo heading TO:—include the colon—hold down Ctrl and then select the memo headings FROM:, DATE:, and RE:. On the mini toolbar, click **Bold**.

c. Select the paragraph *Tour Summary*, press and hold Ctrl, and then select the paragraphs *Local Industry Assessment* and *Customer Feedback*. Apply the **Heading 2** style.

d. Click the **DESIGN tab**, and then in the **Document Formatting group**, click the **More** button. In the gallery, under **Built-In**, in the first row, click the first style set—**Basic (Elegant)**. In the **Document Formatting group**, click **Paragraph Spacing**, and then click **Open**.

e. Press Ctrl + Home. Click the **FILE tab**, and then click **Show All Properties**. In the **Tags** box, type **strategy memo, draft** and then in the **Subject** box, type your course name and section number. If necessary, edit the author name to display your name.

f. In **Backstage** view, click **Save**.

2 ▶ Click the **FILE tab**, and then click **Save As**. Navigate to your **Word Chapter 4** folder, and then save the document as **Lastname_Firstname_4D_Revised_Strategy** Right-click in the footer area, and then click **Edit Footer**. In the footer area, right-click the existing file name, and then click **Update Field**. **Close** the footer area.

a. Click the **FILE tab**, and then click **Options**. In the **Word Options** dialog box, click **Customize Ribbon**. In the **Main Tabs** list, select the **Developer** check box, and then click **OK**.

b. On the **DEVELOPER tab**, in the **Templates group**, click **Document Template**. In the **Templates and Add-ins** dialog box, click **Attach**. In the **Attach Template** dialog box, navigate to your student files, click **w04D_Memo_Styles**, and then click **Open**. Select the **Automatically update document styles** check box, and then click **OK**.

c. Click the **FILE tab**, and then click **Options**. In the **Word Options** dialog box, click **Customize Ribbon**. In the **Main Tabs** list, click to deselect the **Developer** check box, and then click **OK**.

d. On **Page 1**, below *Tour Summary*, locate the paragraph that begins *In order to provide*. Position the insertion point at the end of the paragraph, and then press Enter.

3 ▶ Click the **INSERT tab**, and then in the **Illustrations group**, click **Chart**.

a. On the left side of the **Insert Chart** dialog box, be sure **Column** is selected. At the top of the right pane, click the first chart type—**Clustered Column**—and then click **OK**.

b. In the **Chart in Microsoft Word** worksheet, click cell **B1**, type **Male** and then press Tab. With cell **C1** selected, type **Female** and then click cell **A2**.

c. With cell **A2** selected, type **2015** and then press Tab. In cell **B2**, type **36**, press Tab, and then in cell **C2**, type **32**. Press Tab two times to move to **row 3**.

d. Using the technique you just practiced, and without changing the values in **column D**, enter the following data:

	Male	Female	Series 3
2015	36	32	2
2016	47	39	2
2017	52	43	3

e. Point to the lower right corner of the blue border to display the ◣ pointer, and then drag to the left and up to select only cells **A1** through **C4**.

f. **Close** the **Chart** in Microsoft Word worksheet, and then **Save** your document. Scroll as necessary to display the entire chart.

(Project 4D Strategy Session continues on the next page)

CHAPTER REVIEW

4 If necessary, click in an empty area of the chart to select it. Under **CHART TOOLS**, on the **DESIGN tab**, in the **Data group**, click **Edit Data** to redisplay the worksheet.

a. In the worksheet, click cell **C4**, type **45** press Enter, and then **Close** the worksheet.

b. With the chart selected, under **CHART TOOLS**, on the **DESIGN tab**, in the **Type group**, click **Change Chart Type**.

c. In the **Change Chart Type** dialog box, on the left, click **Bar**, and then on the right, at the top, click the first chart type—**Clustered Bar**. Click **OK**.

5 Select the text *Chart Title*, and then type **3-Year Tour Summary**

a. Click in an empty area of the chart, and then to the right of the chart, click **Chart Elements**. Select the **Axis Titles** check box, click the arrow, and then clear the **Primary Vertical** check box. Below the horizontal axis, select the text *Axis Title*, and then type **Average Age of Participants**

b. Click in an empty area of the chart, and then to the right of the chart, click **Chart Elements**. Select the **Data Labels** check box.

c. Click **Chart Styles**. Scroll down, and then click the fifth style—**Style 5**. At the top of the list, click **COLOR**, and then under **Colorful**, in the fourth row, click the color scheme **Color 4** to display the chart with blue and green data markers.

d. Select the chart title. Click the **FORMAT tab**, and then in the **WordArt Styles group**, click **More**. In the gallery, in the second row, click the second style—**Gradient Fill – Blue, Accent 1, Reflection**. Click in an empty corner area of the chart. On the **FORMAT tab**, in the **Shape Styles group**, click **Shape Outline**, and then in the last column, click the first color—**Green, Accent 6**.

e. Click **Chart Elements**, point to **Legend**, click the arrow, and then click **Right**. Click in an empty corner of the chart so that the entire chart is selected.

f. Click **Layout Options**, and then click **See more**. In the **Layout** dialog box, Click the **Size tab** and under **Height**, change the **Absolute down spin arrow** to **3.3"** Click **OK** to close the dialog box. Press Ctrl + E.

6 Right-click in an empty area of the chart, and then from the shortcut menu, click **Save as Template**. Save the chart in your **Word Chapter 4** folder as **Lastname_Firstname_4D_Tour_Chart**

a. Click the **FILE tab**, and then click **Show All Properties**. In the **Tags** box, delete the existing text, and then type **strategy session, memo**

7 In **Backstage** view, click **Save**. Print your two documents or submit your three files electronically as directed by your instructor. **Close** Word.

END You have completed Project 4D

CONTENT-BASED ASSESSMENTS

Mastering Word Project 4E Trip Tips

Apply 4A skills from these Objectives:

1 Apply and Modify Styles
2 Create New Styles
3 Manage Styles
4 Create a Multilevel List

In the following Mastering Word project, you will create a handout that details tips for tour participants for Alberto Ramos, Tour Operations Manager of Costa Rican Treks. Your completed document will look similar to Figure 4.55.

PROJECT FILES

For Project 4E, you will need the following file:

w04E_Trip_Tips

You will save your file as:

Lastname_Firstname_4E_Trip_Tips

PROJECT RESULTS

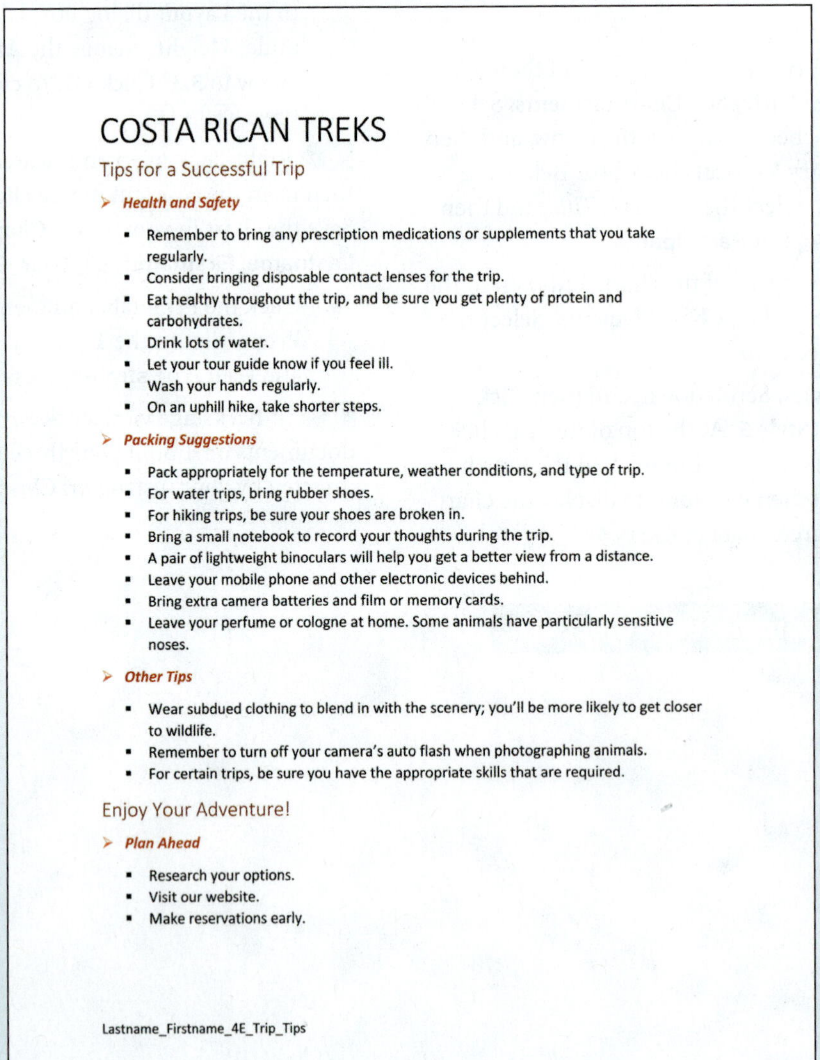

COSTA RICAN TREKS

Tips for a Successful Trip

➢ *Health and Safety*

- Remember to bring any prescription medications or supplements that you take regularly.
- Consider bringing disposable contact lenses for the trip.
- Eat healthy throughout the trip, and be sure you get plenty of protein and carbohydrates.
- Drink lots of water.
- Let your tour guide know if you feel ill.
- Wash your hands regularly.
- On an uphill hike, take shorter steps.

➢ *Packing Suggestions*

- Pack appropriately for the temperature, weather conditions, and type of trip.
- For water trips, bring rubber shoes.
- For hiking trips, be sure your shoes are broken in.
- Bring a small notebook to record your thoughts during the trip.
- A pair of lightweight binoculars will help you get a better view from a distance.
- Leave your mobile phone and other electronic devices behind.
- Bring extra camera batteries and film or memory cards.
- Leave your perfume or cologne at home. Some animals have particularly sensitive noses.

➢ *Other Tips*

- Wear subdued clothing to blend in with the scenery; you'll be more likely to get closer to wildlife.
- Remember to turn off your camera's auto flash when photographing animals.
- For certain trips, be sure you have the appropriate skills that are required.

Enjoy Your Adventure!

➢ *Plan Ahead*

- Research your options.
- Visit our website.
- Make reservations early.

Lastname_Firstname_4E_Trip_Tips

FIGURE 4.55

(Project 4E Trip Tips continues on the next page)

CONTENT-BASED ASSESSMENTS

1 Start Word. From your student files, open the document **w04E_Trip_Tips**. Save the file in your **Word Chapter 4** folder as **Lastname_Firstname_4E_Trip_Tips** Insert the file name in the footer.

2 Select the first paragraph—*Costa Rican Treks*. Apply the **Title** style, and then **Change Case** to **UPPERCASE**. Select the second paragraph that begins *Tips for*, apply the **Heading 2** style. Change the **Font Size** to **16**, change the **Font Color** to **Green, Accent 6, Darker 50%**—in the last column, the last color, and then change the **Spacing After** to **6 pt**. Display the **Styles** gallery, right-click **Heading 2**, and then click **Update Heading 2 to Match Selection**.

3 Near the bottom of **Page 1**, select the paragraph *Enjoy Your Adventure!* Apply the **Heading 2** style. Change the document **Theme** to **Celestial**.

4 Near the top of **Page 1**, select the third paragraph, *Health and Safety*. Apply **Italic** emphasis, and then change the **Font Color** to **Red, Accent 6, Darker 25%**—in the last column, the fifth color. With the text selected, display the **Styles** gallery. Click **Create a Style**, and then name the new style **Tip Heading** Apply the **Tip Heading** style to the paragraphs *Packing Suggestions*, *Other Tips*, and *Plan Ahead*. **Modify** the **Tip Heading** style by applying **Bold** emphasis.

5 Select the block of text beginning with *Health and Safety* and ending with *that are required* near the bottom of **Page 1**. Apply a **Multilevel List** with the ❖, ➤, • style. Select the paragraphs below each *Tip Heading* paragraph, and then **Increase Indent** one time.

6 Select the entire list, and then display the **Define New List Style** dialog box. Name the style **Tips List** Change the **1st level** to **Bullet:** ➤ and set the color to **Red, Accent 6**—in the last column, the first color. Set the **2nd level** to **Bullet:** ■. Be sure the bullet ■ displays in black. Click **OK**.

7 At the bottom of **Page 1**, beginning with *Plan Ahead*, select the last four paragraphs. Apply the **Tips List** multilevel list style. Select the last three paragraphs, and then **Increase Indent** one time.

8 Click the **FILE tab**, and then click **Show All Properties**. In the **Tags** box, type **trip tips list** and then in the **Subject** box, type your course name and section number. If necessary, edit the author name to display your name.

9 Check your document in **Print Preview**, and then make any necessary corrections. **Save** the document, and then print the document or submit electronically as directed by your instructor. **Close** Word.

END | You have completed Project 4E

CONTENT-BASED ASSESSMENTS

Apply 4B skills from these Objectives:

5 Change the Style Set of a Document and Apply a Template

6 Insert a Chart and Enter Data into a Chart

7 Change a Chart Type

8 Format a Chart and Save a Chart as a Template

In the following Mastering Word project, you will create a document that provides frequently asked questions and includes a chart about hiking trips offered by Costa Rican Treks. Your completed documents will look similar to Figure 4.56.

PROJECT FILES

For Project 4F, you will need the following files:

w04F_Hiking_FAQ

w04F_Hiking_Styles

You will save your files as:

Lastname_Firstname_4F_Hiking_FAQ

Lastname_Firstname_4F_FAQ_Revised

Lastname_Firstname_4F_Rainfall_Chart– not shown in figure

PROJECT RESULTS

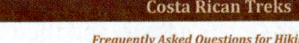

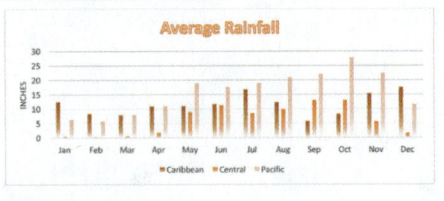

FIGURE 4.56

(Project 4F Hiking FAQ continues on the next page)

CONTENT-BASED ASSESSMENTS

1 ▶ Start Word. From your student files, open the file **w04F_Hiking_FAQ**, and then **Save** the document in your **Word Chapter 4** folder as **Lastname_Firstname_4F_Hiking_FAQ** Insert the file name in the footer.

2 ▶ Format the first paragraph *Costa Rican Treks* with the **Heading 1** style, and then change the **Font Size** to **18**. Select the second paragraph, and then apply the **Heading 2** style. Select the paragraph *Costa Rica's Climate*, and then apply the **Subtitle** style. Change the **Style Set** to **Basic (Stylish)**. Change the **Paragraph Spacing** style to **Compact**. Select all the numbered paragraphs, and then apply **Bold**. For each single paragraph following a numbered paragraph, click **Increase Indent** one time.

3 ▶ **Show All Properties**, add the tags **FAQ, hiking** Insert your course name and section number, and display your name as the author. **Save** your document.

4 ▶ Click the **FILE tab**, and then click **Save As**. **Save** the document to your **Word Chapter 4** folder as **Lastname_Firstname_4F_FAQ_Revised** In the footer, **Update Field**.

5 ▶ Display the **Word Options** dialog box, and then click **Customize Ribbon**. Display the **DEVELOPER tab**. Display the **Templates and Add-ins** dialog box, and then click **Attach**. From your student files, **Open** the file **w04F_Hiking_Styles**, and then **Automatically update document styles**. Hide the **DEVELOPER tab**.

6 ▶ Move the insertion point to the end of the document, and then press Enter. **Insert** a **Clustered Column** chart, and then beginning in cell **B1**, type the following data, pressing Tab to move from one cell to the next.

	Caribbean	Central	Pacific
Jan	12.5	0.4	6.3
Feb	8.3	0.2	5.7
Mar	8	0.5	8
Apr	10.9	1.7	11
May	11	8.9	18.9
Jun	11.7	11.3	17.5
Jul	16.8	8.5	18.9
Aug	12.3	9.8	20.9
Sep	5.7	13	22
Oct	8.2	13	27.7
Nov	15.4	5.6	22.3
Dec	17.5	1.6	11.6

7 ▶ With the chart range **A1** through **D13** selected, **Close** the worksheet. Select the text *Chart Title*, and then type **Average Rainfall** Display a **Primary Vertical Axis Title** with the title **Inches**

8 ▶ Change the **Chart Style** to **Style 9**, and then change the chart **Color** scheme to **Color 6**—under **Monochromatic**, in the second row, the orange color scheme. Format the chart title with the **WordArt** style **Fill – Orange, Accent 2, Outline – Accent 2**.

9 ▶ Display the **Layout** dialog box, and then change the **Absolute Height** of the chart **2.4"**. **Center** the chart horizontally on the page. **Save** the chart as a **chart template** in your **Word Chapter 4** folder as **Lastname_Firstname_4F_Rainfall_Chart**

10 ▶ **Show All Properties**, and then change the tags to **FAQ, final Save** your document. Print both documents or submit all three files electronically as directed by your instructor. **Close** Word.

END | You have completed Project 4F

CONTENT-BASED ASSESSMENTS

Mastering Word Project 4G Expense Reduction

In the following Mastering Word project, you will create a memo that includes ideas for reducing expenses for Paulo Alvarez, Vice President of Finance for Costa Rican Treks. Your completed document will look similar to Figure 4.57.

PROJECT FILES

For Project 4G, you will need the following file:

w04G_Expense_Reduction

You will save your files as:

Lastname_Firstname_4G_Expense_Reduction
Lastname_Firstname_4G_Pie_Chart – not shown in figure

PROJECT RESULTS

COSTA RICAN TREKS
MEMO

TO: Maria Tornio, President; Alberto Ramos, Tour Operations Manager

FROM: Paulo Alvarez, Vice President Finance

DATE: August 12, 2018

SUBJECT: Company Cost Savings

I have examined company expenses and have several recommendations for cutting costs. Please review the attachment, which covers operating, marketing, and employee-related costs. Briefly, I recommend that we look across all areas of our budget in terms of making cuts. Some of my suggestions include eliminating paper communication as much as possible and relying mostly on email, faxes, and our website to communicate with vendors and customers. Shopping around for better local and long-distance phone service should yield a better rate. We should also analyze the effectiveness of our advertising strategy and determine which efforts are yielding the best results. Finally, I recommend that we switch employees' mobile phone accounts to smaller, emergency-oriented plans.

I have scheduled a meeting on August 18 at 2 p.m. in Conference Room B so that we can discuss our plan. Please let me know what other members of our team you think should be invited.

Lastname_Firstname_4G_Expense_Reduction

1. Employee Related Cost Savings
   A. Mobile phone plans reduced to smaller plans with focus on emergency-only calls
   B. Reduction in vehicle allowance
2. Operations Related Cost Savings
   A. Focus on electronic communications instead of paper communications
   B. Research less expensive local and long-distance phone services
3. Marketing Related Cost Savings
   A. Evaluate current marketing strategies and advertisements, evaluate effectiveness, and focus on most successful ventures
   B. Utilize Web site, electronic newsletter, and other electronic formats as much as possible

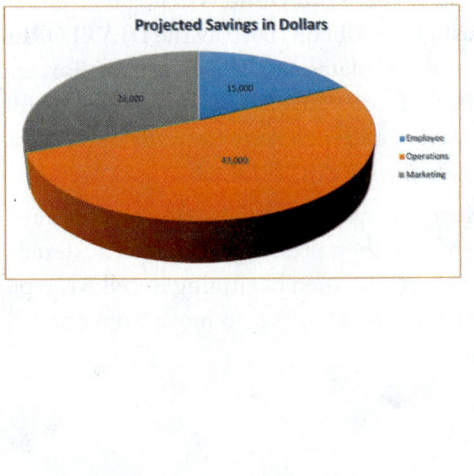

Lastname_Firstname_4G_Expense_Reduction

FIGURE 4.57

(Project 4G Expense Reduction continues on the next page)

1 Start Word. From your student files, open the file **w04G_Expense_Reduction**, and then save the document in your **Word Chapter 4** folder as **Lastname_Firstname_4G_Expense_Reduction** Insert the file name in the footer.

2 Apply the **Title** style to the first paragraph. Apply the **Strong** style to the second paragraph *Memo*, With *Memo* selected, change the **Font Size** to **26**, and then change the text to **UPPERCASE**. Select the text *TO:*—include the colon—and then apply **Bold** and change the **Font Color** to **Orange, Accent 2, Darker 25%**. Save the selection as a new style with the name **Memo Heading** Apply the **Memo Heading** style to the memo headings *FROM:*, *DATE:*, and *SUBJECT:*.

3 Change the **Style Set** to **Basic (Elegant)**, and then change the **Paragraph Spacing** style to **Relaxed**. On **Page 1**, beginning with the heading *TO:*, change the **Font Size** of all the remaining text in the document to **12**. Select the text on **Page 2**, and then apply a **Multilevel List** with the format **1., a., i.** For the paragraphs beginning *Mobile phone*, *Reduction*, *Focus*, *Research*, *Evaluate*, and *Utilize*, **Increase Indent** one time.

4 Select the entire list, and then display the **Define New List Style** dialog box. Name the style **Reduction List** Change the **2nd level** letter style to **A, B, C.**

5 Position the insertion point at the end of the document. Insert a **3-D Pie** chart. Type the following chart data:

	Projected Savings in Dollars
Employee	15,000
Operations	43,000
Marketing	26,000

6 Select the chart data range **A1** through **B4**, and then **Close** the worksheet. Apply the **Style 5** chart style. Display **Data Labels** in the **Center** position. Format the chart **Shape Outline** as **Orange, Accent 2, Darker 25%**. Display the **Legend** to the **Right** of the chart. **Center** the chart horizontally on the page.

7 **Save** the chart as a **Chart Template** in your **Word Chapter 4** folder as **Lastname_Firstname_4G_Pie_Chart**

8 **Show All Properties**. Add the tags **expenses, reduction** Add your course name and section number, and make sure your name displays as the author. Check your document in **Print Preview**, and then make any necessary corrections. **Save** your document. Print your document or submit both files as directed by your instructor. **Close** Word.

END | You have completed Project 4G

CONTENT-BASED ASSESSMENTS

GO! Fix It	Project 4H New Tours	Online
GO! Make It	Project 4I Newsletter	Online
GO! Solve It	Project 4J Fall Newsletter	Online
GO! Solve It	Project 4K Custom Adventure	

Apply a combination of the **4A** and **4B** skills.

PROJECT FILES

For Project 4K, you will need the following file:

w04K_Custom_Adventure

You will save your file as:

Lastname_Firstname_4K_Custom_Adventure

Open the file **w04K_Custom_Adventures** and save it in your **Word Chapter 4** folder as **Lastname_Firstname_4K_Custom_Adventure** Change the theme, and apply existing styles to the first two and last two paragraphs of the document. Create a new style for *Choose a Region*, and apply the style to *Choose Your Favorite Activities* and *Develop Your Skills*. Define a new multilevel list style and apply the style to all lists in the document. Adjust paragraph and text formats to display the information appropriately in a one-page document. Include the file name in the footer, add appropriate document properties, and print your document or submit electronically as directed by your instructor.

Performance Level

Performance Criteria		Exemplary: You consistently applied the relevant skills	Proficient: You sometimes, but not always, applied the relevant skills	Developing: You rarely or never applied the relevant skills
	Change theme and apply existing styles	All existing styles are applied correctly using an appropriate theme.	Existing styles are applied correctly but an appropriate theme is not used.	One or more styles are not applied correctly.
	Create a new style	A new style is created and applied correctly.	A new style is created but not applied correctly.	A new style is not created.
	Create a multilevel list	A multilevel list style is created and applied correctly.	A multilevel list style is applied correctly but the default style is used.	A multilevel list style is not applied correctly.
	Format attractively and appropriately	Document formatting is attractive and appropriate.	The document is adequately formatted but is unattractive or difficult to read.	The document is formatted inadequately.

END | You have completed Project 4K

OUTCOMES-BASED ASSESSMENTS

RUBRIC

The following outcomes-based assessments are *open-ended assessments*. That is, there is no specific correct result; your result will depend on your approach to the information provided. Make *Professional Quality* your goal. Use the following scoring rubric to guide you in *how* to approach the problem and then to evaluate *how well* your approach solves the problem.

The *criteria*—Software Mastery, Content, Format and Layout, and Process—represent the knowledge and skills you have gained that you can apply to solving the problem. The *levels of performance*—Professional Quality, Approaching Professional Quality, or Needs Quality Improvements—help you and your instructor evaluate your result.

	Your completed project is of Professional Quality if you:	Your completed project is Approaching Professional Quality if you:	Your completed project Needs Quality Improvements if you:
1-Software Mastery	Choose and apply the most appropriate skills, tools, and features and identify efficient methods to solve the problem.	Choose and apply some appropriate skills, tools, and features, but not in the most efficient manner.	Choose inappropriate skills, tools, or features, or are inefficient in solving the problem.
2-Content	Construct a solution that is clear and well organized, contains content that is accurate, appropriate to the audience and purpose, and is complete. Provide a solution that contains no errors in spelling, grammar, or style.	Construct a solution in which some components are unclear, poorly organized, inconsistent, or incomplete. Misjudge the needs of the audience. Have some errors in spelling, grammar, or style, but the errors do not detract from comprehension.	Construct a solution that is unclear, incomplete, or poorly organized; contains some inaccurate or inappropriate content; and contains many errors in spelling, grammar, or style. Do not solve the problem.
3-Format & Layout	Format and arrange all elements to communicate information and ideas, clarify function, illustrate relationships, and indicate relative importance.	Apply appropriate format and layout features to some elements, but not others. Overuse features, causing minor distraction.	Apply format and layout that does not communicate information or ideas clearly. Do not use format and layout features to clarify function, illustrate relationships, or indicate relative importance. Use available features excessively, causing distraction.
4-Process	Use an organized approach that integrates planning, development, self-assessment, revision, and reflection.	Demonstrate an organized approach in some areas, but not others; or, use an insufficient process of organization throughout.	Do not use an organized approach to solve the problem.

OUTCOMES-BASED ASSESSMENTS

Apply a combination of the **4A** and **4B** skills.

Build from
Scratch

GO! Think   Project 4L Training Memo

PROJECT FILES

For Project 4L, you will need the following file:

New blank Word document

You will save your files as:

Lastname_Firstname_4L_Training_Chart
Lastname_Firstname_4L_Training_Memo

Alberto Ramos, Tour Operations Manager, wants to send a memo to all tour guides concerning upcoming training opportunities.

Date	Training	Location	Length
June 6	Horseback Riding	Barbille Stables	4 hours
June 17	Orienteering	Manuel Antonio Park	8 hours
June 29	Basic Coastal Sailing	Playa Hermosa	6 hours
July 7	White Water Rafting	Pacuare River	5 hours

Using this information, create the memo. Include a custom multilevel list for the four training sessions. Insert a chart to compare class length. Format the entire memo in a manner that is professional and easy to read and understand. Save the chart template as **Lastname_Firstname_4L_Training_Chart** Save the document as **Lastname_Firstname_4L_Training_Memo** Insert the file name in the footer and add appropriate document properties. Print your document or submit both files electronically as directed by your instructor.

END | You have completed Project 4L

Build from
Scratch

GO! Think   Project 4M Waterfalls Handout   **Online**

Build from
Scratch

You and GO!   Project 4N Cover Letter   **Online**

Using Advanced Table Features

GO! to Work
Video W5

PROJECT 5A	OUTCOMES
	Use advanced table features such as custom table styles, sort, and properties.

OBJECTIVES

1. Create and Apply a Custom Table Style
2. Format Cells
3. Use Advanced Table Features
4. Modify Table Properties

PROJECT 5B	OUTCOMES
	Create a custom table that includes a nested table and an Excel spreadsheet.

OBJECTIVES

5. Draw a Freeform Table
6. Use Nested Tables
7. Insert an Excel Spreadsheet

JackF/Fotolia

In This Chapter

A table provides a convenient way to organize text. In addition to using the Table command, there are other methods for inserting a table in a document. For example, you can draw a table, convert existing text into a table format, or insert Excel spreadsheets. You can insert formulas in a table to perform calculations on numerical data. Formatting a table makes data easier to read and provides a professional appearance. You can create and apply custom table styles, merge and split cells, and change the way text displays within the cells. The Organizer allows you to copy custom styles from one document to another.

The projects in this chapter relate to **Chesterfield Creations**, a manufacturer of high-quality leather and fabric accessories for men and women. Products include wallets, belts, handbags, key chains, backpacks, business cases, laptop sleeves, and travel bags. The Toronto-based company distributes its products to department stores and specialty shops throughout the United States and Canada. Chesterfield Creations also has a website from which over 60 percent of its products are sold. The company pays shipping costs for both delivery and returns, and bases its operating philosophy on exceptional customer service.

PROJECT
5A
Product Summary

MyITLab®
Project 5A Training

PROJECT ACTIVITIES

In Activities 5.01 through 5.12, you will create, modify, and format tables containing new product information to produce a document that will be distributed to the Chesterfield Creations sales team. Chesterfield Creations is introducing new products for the spring season. Charles Ferguson, Marketing Vice President, has asked you to create a document that summarizes the new product lines. Your completed document will look similar to Figure 5.1.

PROJECT FILES

For Project 5A, you will need the following files: You will save your file as:

w05A_Product_Summary   **Lastname_Firstname_5A_Product_Summary**
w05A_Custom_Styles

PROJECT RESULTS

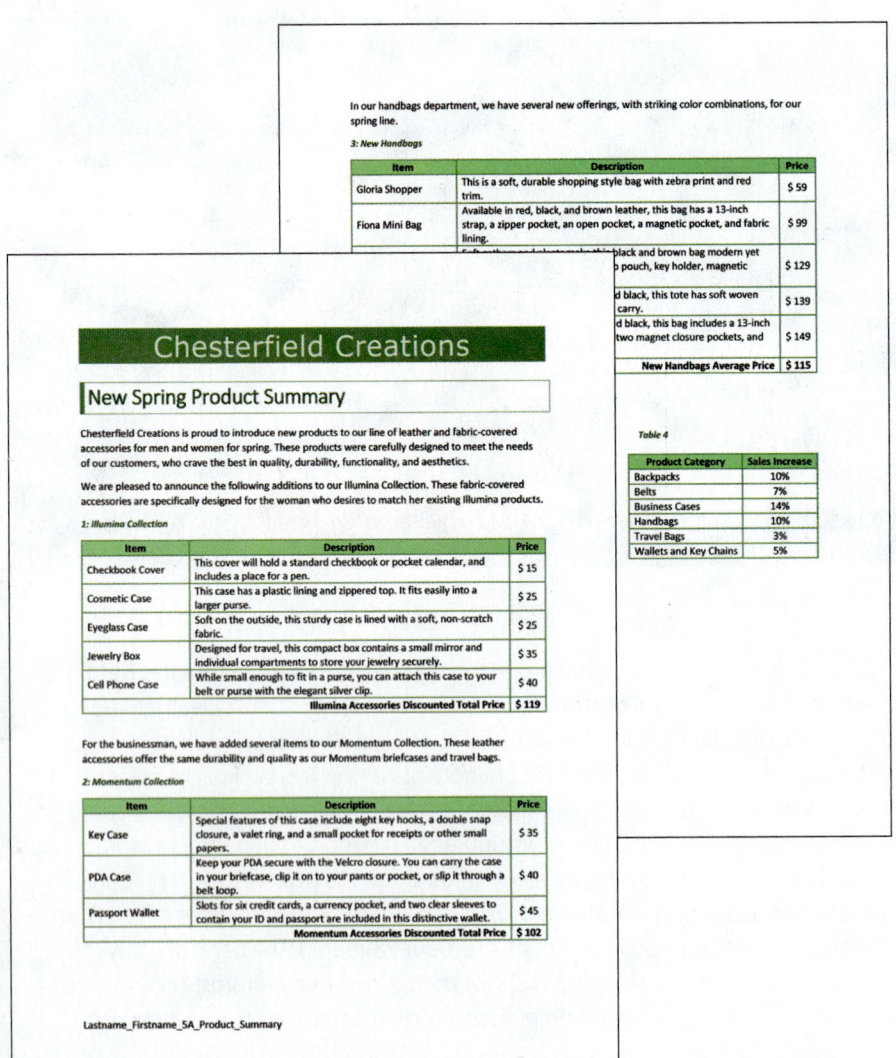

FIGURE 5.1 Project 5A Product Summary

Objective 1   Create and Apply a Custom Table Style

Video W5-1

Recall that a *style* is a group of formatting commands—such as font, font size, and font color—that can be applied with a single command. Styles in an existing document can be copied to another document. You can create a *table style* and apply it repeatedly to give your tables a consistent format. A table style can include formatting for the entire table and specific table elements, such as rows and columns. You can use the *Split Table* feature to divide an existing table into two tables in which the selected row—where the insertion point is located—becomes the first row of the second table.

Activity 5.01 | Using the Organizer to Manage Styles

You can copy styles using the *Organizer*—a dialog box where you can modify a document by using styles stored in another document or template.

1 Start Word. From your student files, locate and open the file **w05A_Product_Summary**. If necessary, display the rulers and formatting marks. If any words are flagged as spelling or grammar errors, right-click, and then click **Ignore All**.

2 Press F12 to display the **Save As** dialog box. Navigate to the location where you are saving your files for this chapter. Create a new folder named **Word Chapter 5** and then **Save** the document as **Lastname_Firstname_5A_Product_Summary** Right-click in the footer area, and then click **Edit Footer**. Under **HEADER & FOOTER TOOLS**, on the **DESIGN tab**, in the **Insert group**, click **Document Info**, and then click **File Name**. **Close** the footer area.

3 Press Ctrl + Home. Click the **FILE tab** to display **Backstage** view, and then click **Options**. In the **Word Options** dialog box, click **Add-Ins**.

4 At the bottom of the **Word Options** dialog box, click the **Manage box arrow**, and then click **Templates**. Compare your screen with Figure 5.2.

FIGURE 5.2

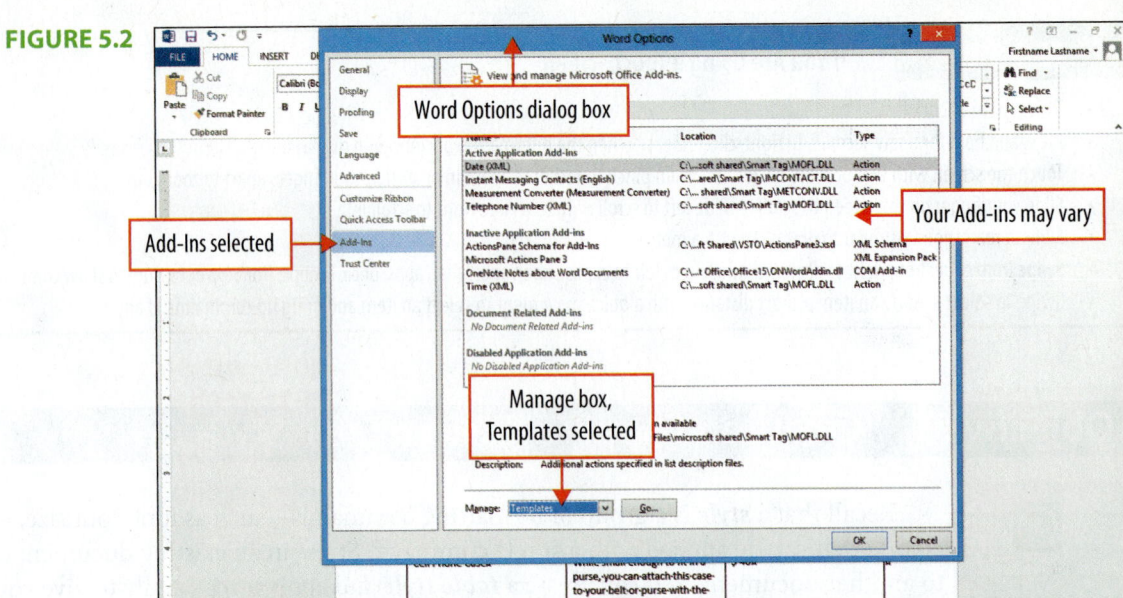

Word Options dialog box

Add-Ins selected

Your Add-ins may vary

Manage box, Templates selected

5 To the right of the **Manage** box, click **Go**.

6 In the **Templates and Add-ins** dialog box, at the bottom left, click **Organizer**.

7 On the left side of the **Organizer** dialog box, be sure that *Lastname_Firstname_5A_Product_ Summary (Document)* displays in the **Styles available in** box. On the right side of the dialog box, click **Close File**. Notice the button changes to an **Open File** button.

8 Click **Open File**, navigate to your student files, select the file **w05A_Custom_Styles**, and then click **Open**. Compare your screen with Figure 5.3.

The styles stored in the *w05A_Custom_Styles (Template)* display on the right side of the dialog box.

FIGURE 5.3

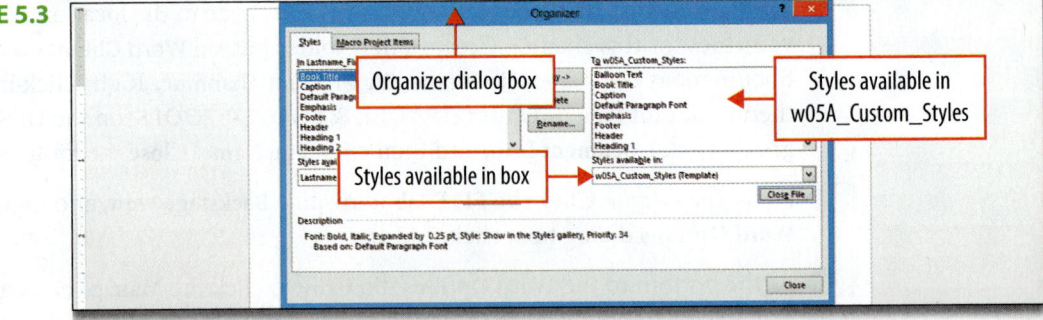

Organizer dialog box

Styles available in w05A_Custom_Styles

Styles available in box

9 In the top right box, scroll down, and then click **Heading 2**. Press and hold Ctrl, scroll down, and then click **Title**.

You can select one or more styles that you want to copy to another document. In this case, two styles are selected.

10 In the center of the **Organizer** dialog box, click **Copy**. If a message box displays asking if you want to overwrite the existing style entry **Heading 2**, click **Yes to All**. Click **Close** to close the dialog box. Compare your screen with Figure 5.4.

The Heading 2 and Title styles are copied to your *Lastname_Firstname_5A_Product_Summary* document.

FIGURE 5.4

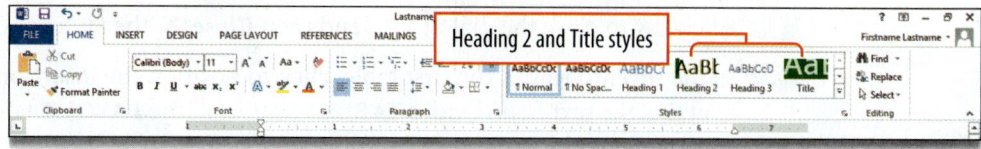

Heading 2 and Title styles

Activity 5.02 | Creating a Table Style and Splitting a Table

When you create a table style, you can apply formats, such as borders, to the entire table and add special formats to individual parts of the table, such as bold emphasis and shading to specific cells. Creating a table style saves time when formatting multiple tables and provides a uniform appearance.

1 Select the first paragraph of the document—the company name *Chesterfield Creations*. On the **HOME tab**, in the **Styles group**, click **Title**.

2 Select the second paragraph that begins *New Spring*, and then in the **Styles group**, click **Heading 2**. Click anywhere in the third paragraph, and then compare your screen with Figure 5.5.

FIGURE 5.5

Title and Heading 2 styles applied

3 On the **HOME tab**, in the **Styles group**, click the **Dialog Box Launcher** to display the **Styles** pane.

4 At the bottom of the **Styles** pane, click the **New Style** button. In the **Create New Style from Formatting** dialog box, under **Properties**, in the **Name** box, type **Chesterfield Creations** Click the **Style type arrow**, and then click **Table**.

> A sample table displays in the preview area. You can create a new style to apply a set of formats to a table by using the Create New Style from Formatting dialog box.

5 Under **Formatting**, click the **Border button arrow**, and then click **All Borders**. Click the **Line Weight arrow**, and then click **1 pt**. Click the **Border Color arrow**, and then under **Theme Colors**, in the last column, click the fifth color—**Green, Accent 6, Darker 25%**. Compare your screen with Figure 5.6.

> Notice that under *Formatting*, in the *Apply formatting to* box, the formatting will be applied to the whole table. By default, notice at the bottom of the dialog box that this style is available only in this document.

FIGURE 5.6

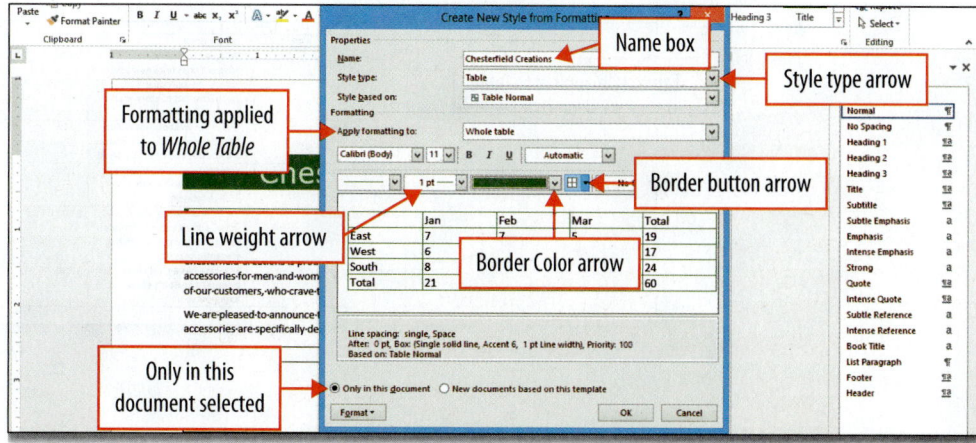

6 Click **OK** to close the dialog box, and then **Close** ✖ the **Styles** pane.

7 In the seventh row of the first table, click to position the insertion point in the first cell that contains the text *Item*. Under **TABLE TOOLS**, on the **LAYOUT tab**, in the **Merge group**, click **Split Table**.

> The original table is divided into two separate tables and a new, blank paragraph is inserted above the second table.

8 If necessary, position the insertion point in the blank paragraph above the second table, and then press Enter. Type **For the businessman, we have added several items to our Momentum Collection. These leather accessories offer the same durability and quality as our Momentum briefcases and travel bags.**

 **BY TOUCH**   Tap in the blank paragraph, and then on the taskbar, tap the Touch Keyboard button. Tap the appropriate keys to type the text, and then on the Touch Keyboard, tap the X button.

9 Save 🖫 your changes.

More Knowledge   **Creating a Custom Table Style from the Table Styles Gallery**

If the insertion point is in an existing table, you can create a custom table style from the Table Styles gallery. Under TABLE TOOLS, on the DESIGN tab, in the Table Styles group, click More, and then click New Table Style to display the Create New Style from Formatting dialog box.

Activity 5.03 | **Applying and Modifying a Table Style**

You can apply a table style to an existing table. Additionally, you can modify an existing style or make formatting changes after a style has been applied to a table.

1 Display the first table in the document, and then click in the top left cell that contains the text *Item*.

> You can apply a table style when the insertion point is positioned anywhere within a table.

2 Under **TABLE TOOLS**, on the **DESIGN tab**, in the **Table Styles group**, click **More** ⊡.

3 In the **Table Styles** gallery, under **Custom**, point to the style. Notice that the ScreenTip— *Chesterfield Creations*—displays.

4 Click the **Chesterfield Creations** style to apply the table style to the table. Compare your screen with Figure 5.7.

FIGURE 5.7

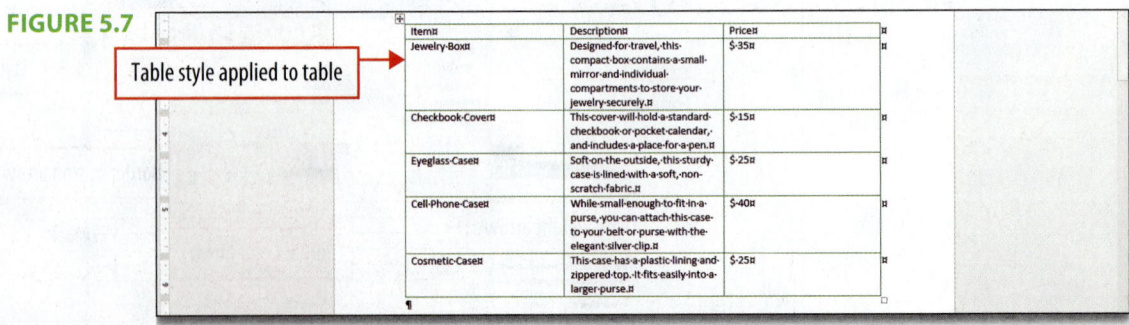

Table style applied to table

5 Scroll as necessary, and then click to position the insertion point anywhere in the second table of the document—the table is split, displaying across two pages. Under **TABLE TOOLS**, on the **DESIGN tab**, in the **Table Styles group**, click **More** ⌄, and then under **Custom**, click **Chesterfield Creations**.

In the Table Styles group, at the extreme left, the *Chesterfield Creations* table style displays.

6 In the **Table Styles** group, right-click the **Chesterfield Creations** style. A shortcut menu displays several options for working with styles as described in the table in Figure 5.8.

FIGURE 5.8

TABLE STYLE OPTIONS	
STYLE OPTION	**DESCRIPTION**
Apply (and Clear Formatting)	Table style applied; text formatting reverts to Normal style
Apply and Maintain Formatting	Table style applied, including text formatting
New Table Style	Option to create a new, custom table style
Modify Table Style	Option to edit the table style
Delete Table Style	Removes the style from the Table Styles gallery
Set as Default	Style is used as the default for all tables created in the document
Add Gallery to Quick Access Toolbar	Table Styles gallery is added to the Quick Access Toolbar

7 From the shortcut menu, click **Modify Table Style**. In the **Modify Style** dialog box, under **Formatting**, click the **Apply formatting to arrow**, and then click **Header row**.

You can apply formatting to specific table elements. In the *Chesterfield Creations* style, you want to change formats that only apply to the *header row*—the first row of a table containing column titles.

8 Click **Bold** B , and then click the **Fill Color arrow** No Color ⌄. Under **Theme Colors**, in the last column, click the fourth color—**Green, Accent 6, Lighter 40%**. Compare your screen with Figure 5.9.

FIGURE 5.9

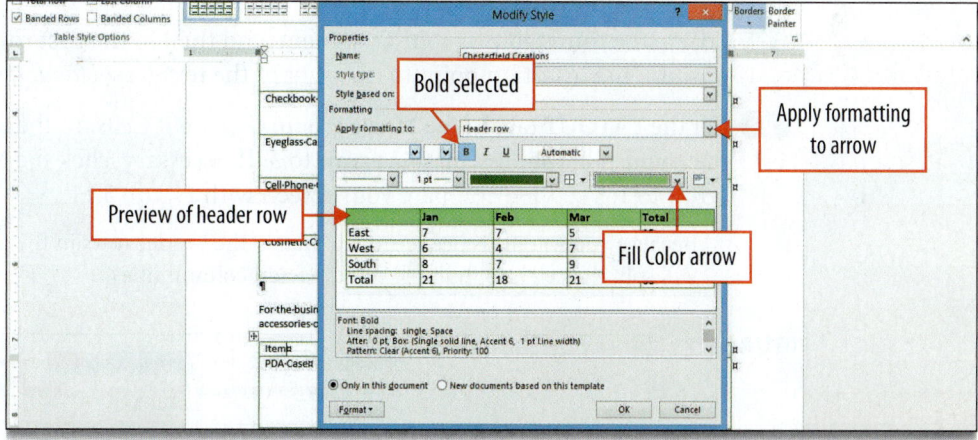

9 Click **OK** to close the dialog box, and then press Ctrl + Home. On the **VIEW tab**, in the **Zoom group**, click **Multiple Pages**. Compare your screen with Figure 5.10.

The additional formatting has been applied to the header rows in the first and second tables.

FIGURE 5.10

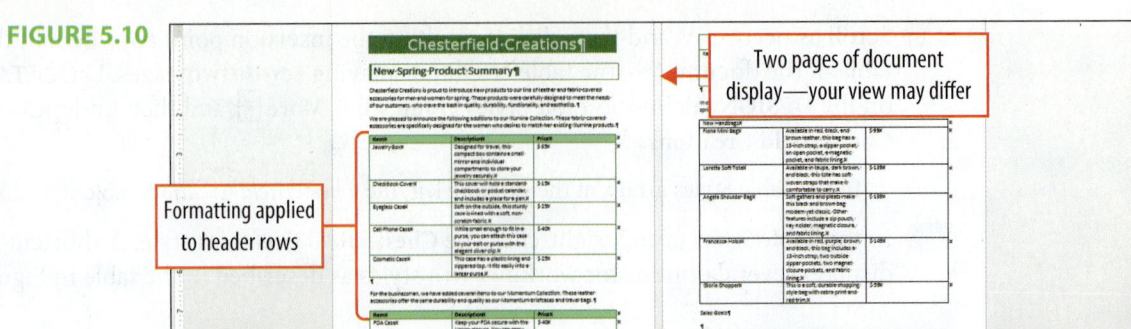

Two pages of document display—your view may differ

Formatting applied to header rows

> **10** ▶ On the **VIEW tab**, in the **Zoom group**, click **100%**, and then **Save** 🖫 your changes.

More **Knowledge** | **Repeating Header Rows**

When a table is large enough to cause part of the table to display on a second page, the header row of the table can be repeated on the second page. With the insertion point in the header row, on the LAYOUT tab, in the Table group, click Properties. In the Table Properties dialog box, click the Row tab, and then under Options, click *Repeat as header row at the top of each page*.

Objective 2 | Format Cells

Video W5-2

Special formatting features that are unavailable for use with paragraph text are available in tables. For example, you can combine or divide cells and adjust the positioning of text.

Activity 5.04 | Merging and Splitting Cells

You can *merge* or *split* cells to change the structure of a table. Merging is the process of combining two or more adjacent cells into one cell so that the text spans across multiple columns or rows. Splitting divides selected cells into multiple cells with a specified number of rows and columns. In this activity, you will split cells to add column titles to a header row.

> **1** ▶ Locate the third table of your document, and then in the first row, in the first cell, click to position the insertion point to the right of the text *New Handbags*.

> **2** ▶ On the **LAYOUT tab**, in the **Merge group**, click **Split Cells**. In the **Split Cells** dialog box, click the **Number of columns up spin arrow** to **3**. If necessary, click the **Number of rows down spin arrow** to **1**, and then compare your screen with Figure 5.11.

> Because you want this header row to match the header rows in the other two product tables, you will split the cell into multiple cells and add column titles.

FIGURE 5.11

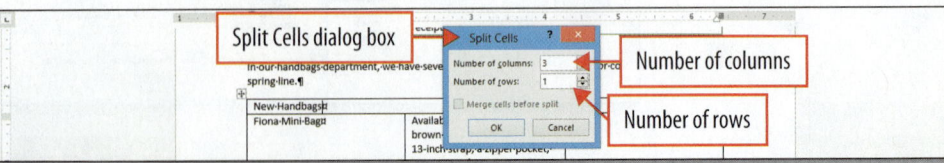

Split Cells dialog box

Number of columns

Number of rows

> **3** ▶ Click **OK** to close the dialog box. Notice that the selected cell has been split into three cells.

> When splitting a cell that contains text, the text is automatically moved to the top left cell created by the division. When you change the structure of a table, some formatting features may be removed.

4 In the first cell of the header row, select the existing text *New Handbags*, and then type **Item** Press `Tab` to move to the second cell of the header row, and then type **Description** Press `Tab`, and then in the last cell of the header row type **Price** Under **TABLE TOOLS**, on the **DESIGN tab**, in the **Table Styles group**, click **More** ⬇. In the **Table Styles** gallery, under **Custom**, click **Chesterfield Creations**. **Save** 🖫 your changes, and then compare your screen with Figure 5.12.

FIGURE 5.12

> Table style applied
>
> Header row

More Knowledge | **Splitting Multiple Cells**

You can modify the number of rows or columns for any group of adjacent cells in a table. Select the cells you want to modify, and then on the LAYOUT tab, in the Merge group, click Split Cells. In the Split Cells dialog box, change the number of columns or rows to the desired values.

Activity 5.05 | Positioning Text within Cells

You can align text horizontally—left, center, or right—and vertically—top, center, or bottom—within cells. The default setting is to align text at the top left of a cell. Changing cell alignments creates a table with a professional appearance.

1 Locate the first table in your document, and then select the **header row**. On the **LAYOUT tab**, in the **Alignment group**, click **Align Center** 🔲.

All text in the header row is centered horizontally and vertically within the cell.

2 Below the header row, select all the cells in the first and second columns, and then in the **Alignment group**, click **Align Center Left** 🔲.

The selected text is left aligned and centered vertically within the cells.

3 Below the header row, select all the cells in the third column, and then in the **Alignment group**, click **Align Center** 🔲. Deselect the text, and then compare your screen with Figure 5.13.

FIGURE 5.13

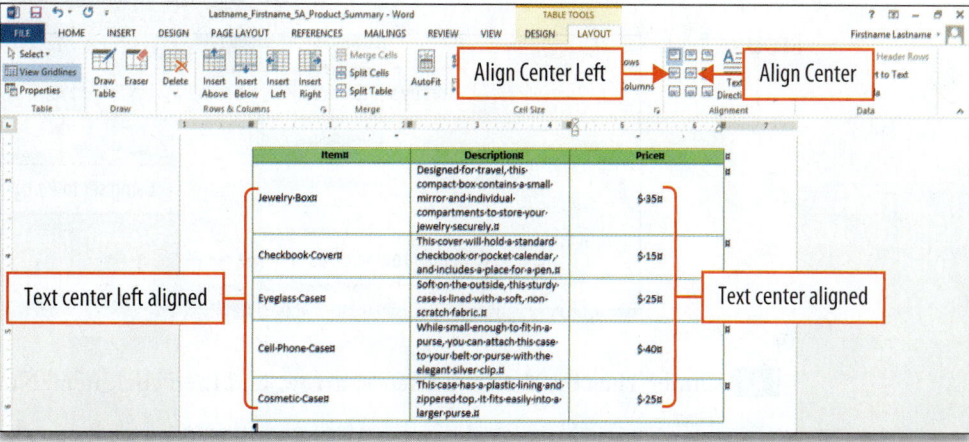

> Align Center Left
>
> Align Center
>
> Text center left aligned
>
> Text center aligned

4 Using the technique you just practiced, format the **header row** in the second and third tables to match the formatting of the header row in the first table—**Align Center** 🔲. In the second and third tables, **Align Center Left** 🔲 the first and second columns below the header row, and then **Align Center** 🔲 the text in the third column below the header row. Deselect the text, and then **Save** 🖫 your changes.

Video W5-3

Objective 3 | Use Advanced Table Features

Word tables have some capabilities similar to those in an Excel spreadsheet—for example, sorting data and performing simple calculations. Additionally, you can convert existing text to a table format and resize tables in several ways.

Activity 5.06 | Sorting Tables by Category

In this activity, you will sort the data in the three product tables by price and item to make it easier for the sales team to reference specific items.

1 Scroll as necessary to display the entire contents of the first table in the document, and then position the insertion point anywhere in the table.

> Recall that data in a table can be sorted in ascending—from the smallest to the largest number or from A to Z order—or descending order—from the largest to the smallest number or from Z to A order. Regardless of the columns that are selected in the sort, all cells in each row are moved to keep the data intact.

2 On the **LAYOUT tab**, in the **Data group**, click **Sort**.

> The Sort dialog box allows you to sort text alphabetically, by number, or by date. The Sort feature can be applied to entire tables, selected data within tables, paragraphs, or body text that is separated by characters, such as tabs or commas. You can sort information using a maximum of three columns.

3 In the **Sort** dialog box, under **Sort by**, click the **Sort by arrow**, and then click **Price**. Compare your screen with Figure 5.14.

> You are sorting the data in the table by the product's price. When a table has a header row, Word displays each column's header text in the Sort by list. By default, the Header row option is selected at the bottom left of the Sort dialog box. If a table does not have a header row, select the No header row option button. Without a header row, the sort options for a table will display as *Column 1, Column 2*, and so on.
>
> Because the Price column contains numbers, the Type box displays *Number*. When working in tables, the Using box displays the default *Paragraphs*.

FIGURE 5.14

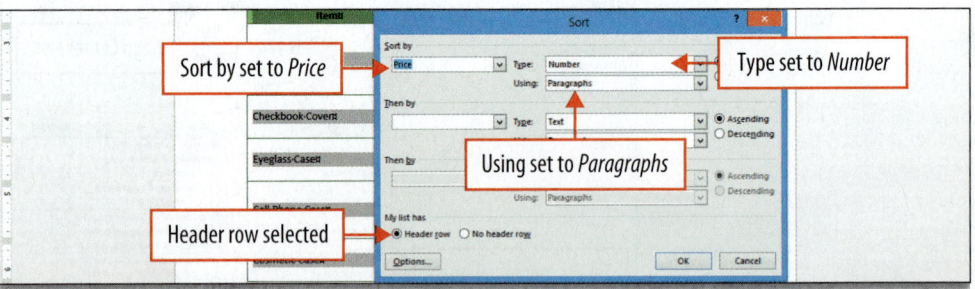

Sort by set to *Price*

Type set to *Number*

Using set to *Paragraphs*

Header row selected

4 Under **Then by**, click the **Then by arrow**, and then click **Item**. Notice that the **Type** box displays *Text*.

> It is important to designate the columns in the order that you want them sorted. Word will first sort the data by price in ascending order. If two or more items have the same price, Word will arrange those items in alphabetical order.

5 Click **OK** to close the dialog box and notice that the two items with the same price of **$ 25** are listed in alphabetical order. Deselect the table, and then compare your screen with Figure 5.15.

FIGURE 5.15

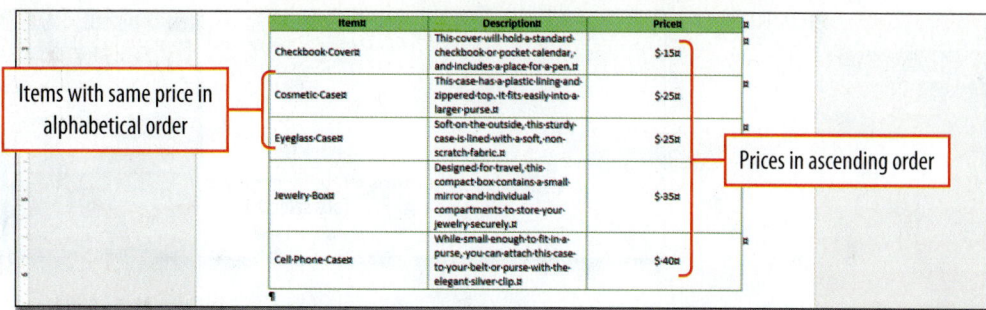

Items with same price in alphabetical order

Prices in ascending order

6 ▶ Click to position the insertion point anywhere in the second table of the document. On the **LAYOUT tab**, click **Sort**.

The Sort by box displays *Price*, and the Then by box displays *Item*. In the Sort dialog box, Word retains the last sort options used in a document.

7 ▶ Click **OK**, and notice that the table is sorted similarly to the first table.

8 ▶ Click to position the insertion point anywhere in the third table of the document. On the **LAYOUT tab**, click **Sort**, and then click **OK**. Notice that the table is sorted in the same manner as the previous tables.

9 ▶ Deselect the table, and then **Save** 🖫 your changes.

Activity 5.07 | Converting Text to a Table and Modifying Fonts within a Table

To improve the appearance of a document, you can convert existing text, such as a list of information, to a table. In this activity, you will convert text to a table so that you can apply the same table style used for the other tables of the document.

1 ▶ Scroll as necessary, and then immediately below the third table, select the paragraph *Sales Goals*. On the mini toolbar, change the **Font Size** to 14, apply **Bold** B , and then change the **Font Color** A ⁻ to **Green, Accent 6, Darker 25%**—in the last column, the fifth color. Press Ctrl + E to center the paragraph.

2 ▶ Beginning with the paragraph that begins *Product Category*, drag down to select all the remaining text in the document. Be sure to include the text on *Page 3*—you should have seven paragraphs selected.

3 ▶ On the **INSERT tab**, in the **Tables group**, click **Table**, and then click **Convert Text to Table** to display the **Convert Text to Table** dialog box. Compare your screen with Figure 5.16.

Word uses characters such as tabs, commas, or hyphens to determine the number of columns. The selected text consists of seven paragraphs—or rows—with each paragraph containing a single tab. By default, Word uses the tab formatting mark to separate each paragraph into two parts—forming the two columns of the table. Under the Separate text at section of the dialog box, you can define the character Word uses to separate the text into columns. You can also change the number of columns or rows, based on the text you are converting.

FIGURE 5.16

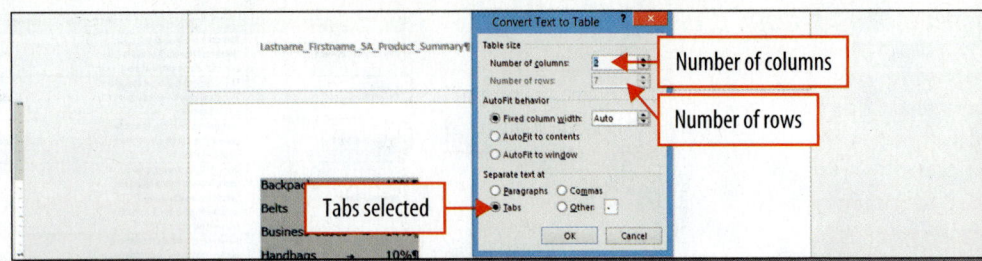

4 Click **OK** to close the dialog box.

Word creates a table that contains two columns and seven rows. The table is split, displaying across two pages.

5 With the table selected, on the **HOME tab**, in the **Font group**, click the **Font arrow** Calibri (Body), and then click **Calibri (Body)**.

6 Save 🖫 your changes.

More Knowledge | **Converting a Table to Text**

To convert an existing table to text, on the LAYOUT tab, in the Data group, click Convert to Text, and then in the Convert Table to Text dialog box, select the type of text separator you want to use.

Activity 5.08 | Defining the Dimensions of a Table and Setting AutoFit Options

Word provides several methods for resizing a table. The *AutoFit* feature automatically adjusts column widths or the width of the entire table. *AutoFit Contents* resizes the column widths to accommodate the maximum field size. You can change a row height or column width by dragging a border, or designating specific width and height settings. To improve the overall appearance of the document, you will modify column widths.

1 In the first table in the document, point to the top border of the first column—*Item*—and when the ↓ pointer displays, click to select the entire column. On the **LAYOUT tab**, in the **Cell Size group**, click the **Width down spin arrow** to **1.5"**. Select the second column in the table—*Description*—and then in the **Cell Size group**, click the **Width up spin arrow** to **4.5"**. Select the last column in the table—*Price*—and then in the **Cell Size group**, click the **Width down spin arrow** to **0.5"**. Deselect the column, and then compare your screen with Figure 5.17.

FIGURE 5.17

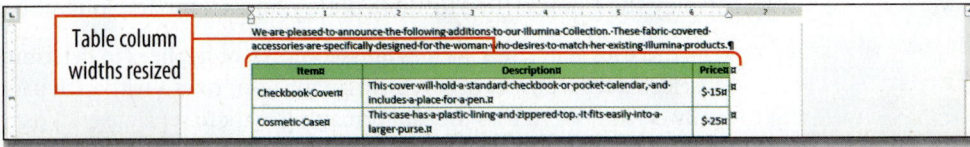

2 In the second and third tables of the document, using the technique you just practiced, change the **Width** of the first column to **1.5"**, the **Width** of the second column to **4.5"**, and the **Width** of the third column to **0.5"**.

All product tables have the same structure—the first, second, and third column widths in all tables are identical.

3 Below the second table, click to position the insertion point to the left of the paragraph that begins *In our handbags department*, and then press Ctrl + Enter to insert a page break.

4 Click to position your insertion point anywhere in the last table of the document. On the **LAYOUT tab**, in the **Cell Size group**, click **AutoFit**, and then click **AutoFit Contents**. Compare your screen with Figure 5.18.

> AutoFit Contents resizes a table by changing the column widths to fit the existing data. In this table, the widths of both columns were decreased.

FIGURE 5.18

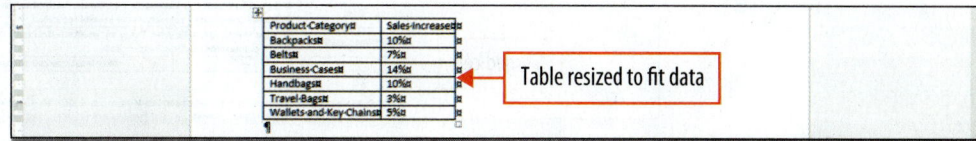

Table resized to fit data

5 Click to position the insertion point anywhere in the table, and then under **TABLE TOOLS**, on the **DESIGN tab**, in the **Table Styles group**, click **More** ▾. In the **Table Styles** gallery, under **Custom**, click **Chesterfield Creations**.

6 Select the **header row**, and then on the **LAYOUT tab**, in the **Alignment group**, click **Align Center** ▤. Select the remaining cells in the second column, and then click **Align Center** ▤. **Save** ▤ your changes.

More Knowledge | **Using the Sizing Handle**

At the lower right of a table, drag the sizing handle to change the entire table to the desired size.

Activity 5.09 | Using Formulas in Tables and Creating Custom Field Formats

To perform simple calculations, you can insert a *formula* in a table. A formula is a mathematical expression that contains *functions*, operators, constants, and properties, and returns a value to a cell. A function is a predefined formula that performs calculations by using specific values in a particular order. Word includes a limited number of built-in functions—for example, SUM and AVERAGE.

1 Click anywhere in the first table of the document, and then point to the bottom left corner of the table to display the **One-Click Row/Column Insertion** button ⊕. Compare your screen with Figure 5.19.

> The One-Click Row/Column Insertion button provides a quick method to insert a row or column in a table.

FIGURE 5.19

One-Click Row/Column Insertion button

2 Click the **One-Click Row/Column Insertion** button ⊕ to insert a new row at the bottom of the table.

 **ANOTHER WAY** On the LAYOUT tab, in the Rows & Columns group, click Insert Below.

---

3 In the new row, select the first two cells, and then on the **LAYOUT tab**, in the **Merge group**, click **Merge Cells**. In the merged cell, type **Illumina Accessories Total Price** Select the text, and then on the mini toolbar, apply **Bold** [B]. On the **LAYOUT tab**, in the **Alignment group**, click **Align Center Right** [≣]. Press [Tab] to move to the last cell in the table. Compare your screen with Figure 5.20.

FIGURE 5.20

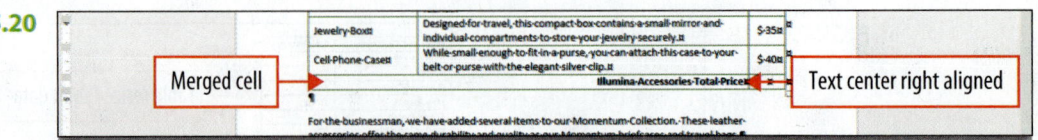

4 On the **LAYOUT tab**, in the **Data group**, click **Formula**. In the **Formula** dialog box, under **Number format**, click the **Number format arrow**, and then click **#,##0**. Click to position the insertion point to the left of the Number format text, and then type **$** Compare your screen with Figure 5.21.

> The Formula dialog box contains the default formula =SUM(ABOVE). All formulas begin with an equal sign [=]. This formula includes the SUM function and calculates the total of the numbers in all of the cells above the current cell—up to the first empty cell or a cell that contains text—and places the result in the current cell. You can specify a special number format—in this case a whole number preceded by a dollar sign.

FIGURE 5.21

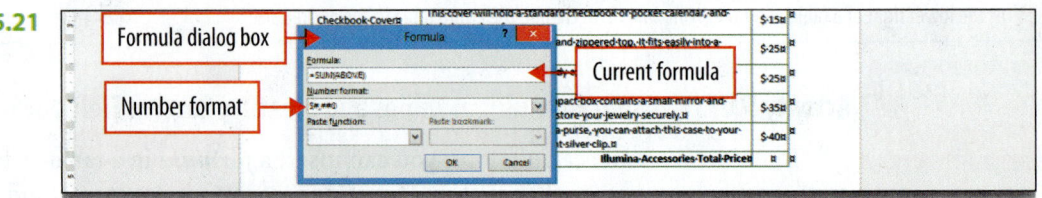

5 Click **OK** to close the dialog box. Notice that *$ 140*—the sum of the prices for the Illumina accessories—displays in the active cell.

> A formula is a type of *field*—a placeholder for data. The displayed number is a formula field representing the value calculated by the formula.

6 Select the inserted text, and then on the mini toolbar, apply **Bold** [B].

7 Position the insertion point anywhere in the second table. Point to the lower left border of the table, and then click the **One-Click Row/Column Insertion** button [⊕]. In the new row, select the first two cells, right-click and then from the shortcut menu, click **Merge Cells**. In the merged cell, type **Momentum Accessories Total Price** and then apply **Bold** [B] and **Align Center Right** [≣]. Press [Tab].

8 On the **LAYOUT tab**, in the **Data group**, click **Formula**. In the **Formula** dialog box, under **Number format**, click the **Number format arrow**, and then click **#,##0**. Click to position the insertion point to the left of the Number format text, and then type **$** Click **OK**. Compare your screen with Figure 5.22.

> The sum of the prices for the Momentum accessories—*$ 120*—displays in the active cell.

FIGURE 5.22

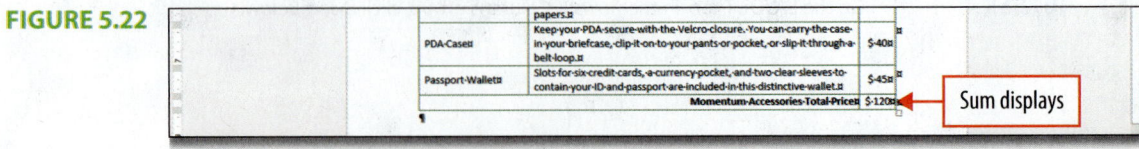

9 Select the inserted text, and then on the mini toolbar, apply **Bold** B.

10 In the third table of the document, use the technique you practiced to insert a new row at the bottom of the table. In the new row, select the first two cells, and then using any technique you practiced, **Merge Cells**. In the merged cell, type **New Handbags Average Price** and then apply **Bold** B and **Align Center Right** 🔲.

11 Press Tab to position the insertion point in the last cell of the table, and then click **Formula**. In the **Formula** dialog box, in the **Formula** box, delete the existing text, and then type **=** Under **Paste function**, click the **Paste function arrow**, and then click **AVERAGE**. In the **Formula** box, notice that *=AVERAGE* displays followed by (). With the insertion point between the left and right parentheses, type **ABOVE**

> You can use the Paste function box to specify a built-in function—such as AVERAGE, PRODUCT, MIN, the minimum value in a list, or MAX, the maximum value in a list. By typing *ABOVE*, the calculation includes all of the values listed above the current cell in the table. You are using the AVERAGE function to calculate the average price of the new handbags.

12 In the **Formula** dialog box, under **Number format**, click the **Number format arrow**, and then click **#,##0**. Click to position the insertion point to the left of the Number format text, and then type **$** Compare your screen with Figure 5.23.

FIGURE 5.23

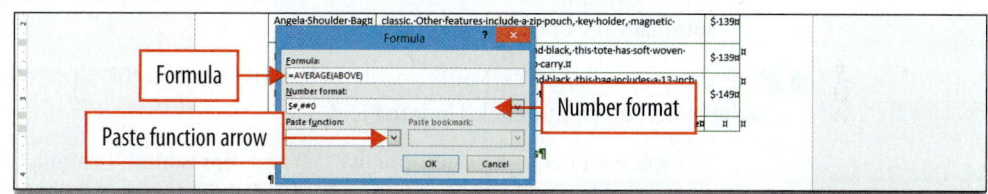

13 Click **OK** to close the **Formula** dialog box. Select the inserted text, and then apply **Bold** B. **Save** 💾 your changes.

> The average price of the five handbags—*$ 117*—displays in the active cell.

More Knowledge | **Inserting Rows and Columns in a Table**

To insert a new row in an existing table, point to the left of the border between two existing rows, and then click the One-Click Row/Column Insertion button. To insert a new column, point above the border between two existing columns, and then click the One-Click Row/Column Insertion button. To insert a column at the extreme right of the table, point to the top right corner of the table, and then click the One-Click Row/Column Insertion button.

Activity 5.10 | Updating Formula Fields in Tables

You can edit an existing formula in a table. Additionally, if a value is changed in a table, it is necessary to manually update the field containing the formula.

1 In the first table, in the last row, click to position the insertion point to the left of *Total*, type **Discounted** and then press Spacebar. Press Tab, right-click the selection, and then from the shortcut menu, click **Edit Field**. In the **Field** dialog box, under **Field properties**, click **Formula**.

2 In the **Formula** dialog box, in the **Formula** box, be sure the insertion point displays to the right of the formula *=SUM(ABOVE)*, and then type ***.85** Compare your screen with Figure 5.24.

> Formulas are not restricted to the built-in functions. You can also create your own. Customers purchasing the entire accessories collection receive a 15 percent discount. The modified formula reflects this discounted price. The total price is multiplied by 85 percent (.85), representing 100 percent minus the 15 percent discount.

FIGURE 5.24

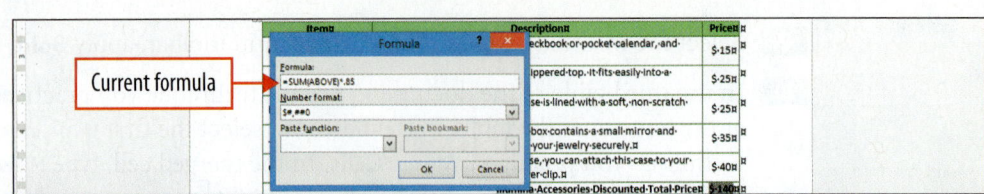

Current formula

3 ▶ Click **OK**, and notice that a new, lower value—*$ 119*—displays in the active cell.

4 ▶ In the second table, in the last row, click to position the insertion point to the left of *Total*, type **Discounted** and then press Spacebar. Press Tab, right-click the selection, and then from the shortcut menu, click **Edit Field**. In the **Field** dialog box, under **Field properties**, click **Formula**.

5 ▶ In the **Formula** dialog box, in the **Formula** box, click to position the insertion point to the right of the displayed formula *=SUM(ABOVE)*, if necessary, and then type ***.85** Click **OK**.

The discounted total for the Momentum accessories—*$ 102*—displays in the active cell.

6 ▶ In the third table, in the last column, below the header row, click in the third cell—the price of the Angela Shoulder Bag. Select only the number *139*, and then type **129**

Unlike Excel, when you change a value that is used in a formula, the resulting calculation is not automatically updated.

7 ▶ In the bottom right cell of the table, select the text. Right-click the selection, and then from the shortcut menu, click **Update Field**.

The value *$ 115* displays in the active cell and represents a formula field. If a number used in the calculation is changed, you must use the Update Field command to recalculate the value.

8 ▶ **Save** 🖫 your changes.

NOTE   **Summing Rows**

The default formula is =SUM(ABOVE), assuming the cell above the selected cell contains a number. If there is a number in the cell to the left of the selected cell and no number in the cell above, the default is =SUM(LEFT). If you want to sum the entire range, be sure to avoid leaving a cell empty within a range. If there is no value, then enter a 0.

Activity 5.11 | Adding Captions, Excluding Labels from Captions, and Setting Caption Positions

Captions are titles that can be added to Word objects; Word numbers them sequentially as they are added to the document. You can add a caption to each table in a document to make it easier to refer to specific tables in the body text.

1 ▶ Click to position the insertion point anywhere in the first table. On the **REFERENCES tab**, in the **Captions group**, click **Insert Caption**.

Because the object selected is a table, in the Caption box, the default caption *Table 1* displays. Word automatically numbers objects sequentially. If the selected object is not a table, you can change the object type by clicking the Label arrow in the Caption dialog box.

2 ▶ In the **Caption** dialog box, select the **Exclude label from caption** check box.

The label *Table* is removed, and only the number *1* displays in the Caption box.

3 ▶ In the **Caption** box, to the right of *1,* type **:** and press Spacebar, and then type **Illumina Collection** If necessary, under **Options**, click the **Position arrow**, and then click **Above selected item**. Compare your screen with Figure 5.25.

You can adjust the position of a caption to display above or below the document element. In this case, the caption is set to display above the table.

FIGURE 5.25

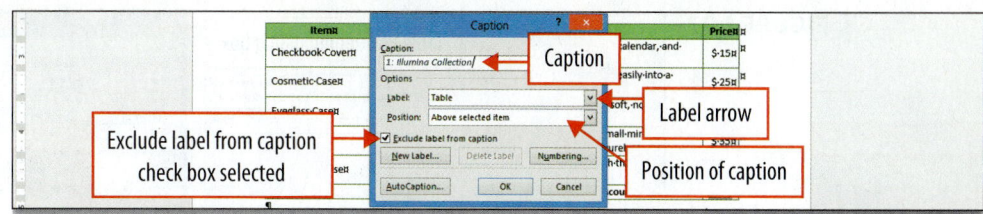

4 Click **OK** to close the **Caption** dialog box. Notice that the caption displays above the table.

5 Using the technique you just practiced, add captions to the second and third tables. For the second table caption, insert the caption **2: Momentum Collection** above the table, and then for the third table, insert the caption **3: New Handbags** above the table.

6 Save the your changes.

Objective 4 | Modify Table Properties

Video W5-4

Tables, like all other Word objects, have properties that can be altered. For example, you can change how text wraps around tables and define cell spacing. Modifying table properties can improve the overall appearance of your document.

Activity 5.12 | Wrapping Text around Tables and Changing Caption Formats

If you have a long document with several tables and body text, you can apply text wrapping to have the text flow around the table. This can create a shorter document and improve the overall appearance of the document.

1 In the last table of the document, click anywhere in the table, and then point to the upper left corner of the table to display the **table move handle** . Drag the table until the top border is aligned with the top of the paragraph that begins *Spring is*, and the right border is at approximately **6.5 inches on the horizontal ruler**. Deselect the table, and then compare your screen with Figure 5.26. If your table position does not match the figure, click **Undo** and begin again.

FIGURE 5.26

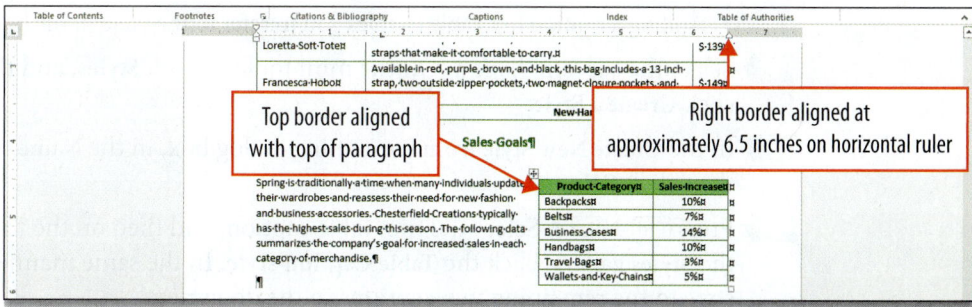

2 Click to position the insertion point anywhere in the table. On the **LAYOUT tab**, in the **Table group**, click **Properties**. In the **Table Properties** dialog box, on the **Table tab**, under **Text wrapping**, be sure **Around** is selected, and then click **Positioning**. In the **Table Positioning** dialog box, under **Distance from surrounding text**, click the **Left up spin arrow** to **0.5"**. Compare your screen with Figure 5.27.

You can define how close existing text displays in relation to the top, bottom, left, or right of a table. By changing the Left box value to 0.5", the text will display one-half inch from the left border of the table.

FIGURE 5.27

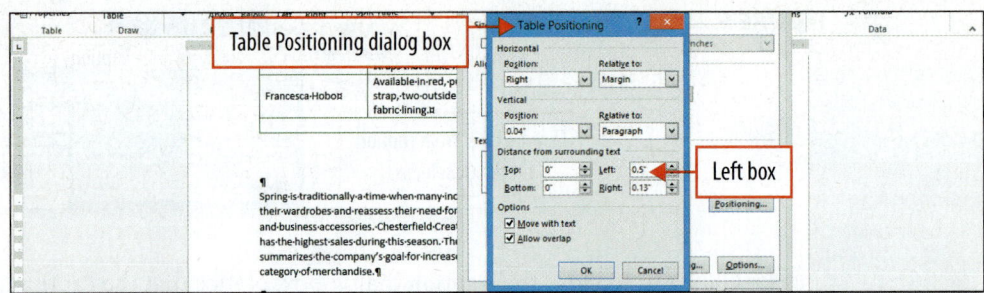

3 ▶ Click **OK** two times to close the dialog boxes.

4 ▶ With the insertion point in the table, on the **REFERENCES tab**, in the **Captions group**, click **Insert Caption**. In the **Caption** dialog box, clear the **Exclude label from caption** check box. With *Table 4* displayed in the **Caption** box and *Above selected item* displayed in the **Position** box, click **OK** to close the dialog box and insert the caption at the left margin.

5 ▶ Select the caption. On the mini toolbar, change the **Font Size** to **10**, apply **Bold** B , and then change the **Font Color** A ⏷ to **Green, Accent 6, Darker 50%**—in the last column, the last color. At the left end of the horizontal ruler, if necessary, click the **Tab Alignment** button to display the **Left tab** button L . To set a left tab stop, on the horizontal ruler, click at **4.0 inches on the horizontal ruler**. Click to the left of the caption, and then press Tab . Compare your screen with Figure 5.28.

> You can format a caption, just as you would format body text. In this case, you format the caption to display above the table and coordinate with the color scheme of the table.

FIGURE 5.28

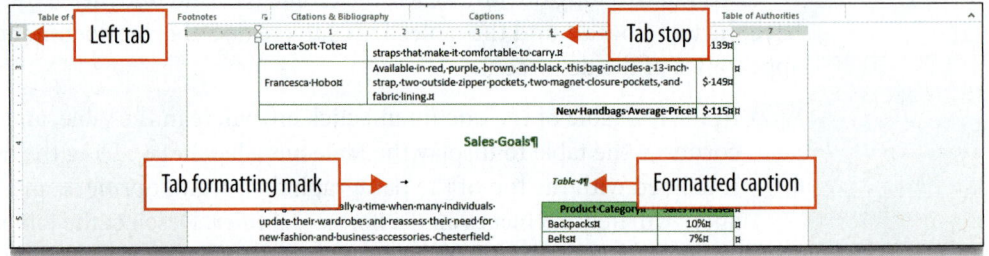

6 ▶ In the last sentence of the document, select the text *The following data*, and then type **Table 4**

> Adding a caption to a table enables you to refer to the table in the body text.

7 ▶ Select the caption *Table 4*. On the mini toolbar, click **Styles**, and then in the **Styles** gallery, click **Create a Style**.

8 ▶ In the **Create New Style from Formatting** dialog box, in the **Name** box, type **Table Caption** and then click **OK**.

9 ▶ Press Ctrl + Home . Select the first table caption, and then on the mini toolbar, click **Styles**. In the **Styles** gallery, click the **Table Caption** style. In the same manner, apply the **Table Caption** style to the remaining two captions in the document.

10 ▶ Press Ctrl + Home . Click the **FILE tab** to display **Backstage** view. On the right, at the bottom of the **Properties** list, click **Show All Properties**. In the **Tags** box, type **product summary, tables** In the **Subject** box, type your course name and section number. If necessary, edit the author name to display your name.

11 ▶ **Save** 🖫 your document. Print your document or submit electronically as directed by your instructor. **Close** ✕ Word.

END | You have completed Project 5A

Expense Form

PROJECT ACTIVITIES

In Activities 5.13 through 5.22, you will create an expense form by drawing a table, use nested tables to display expense codes, and insert an Excel spreadsheet. Rachel Anders, Chief Financial Officer for Chesterfield Creations, has asked you to design an expense reimbursement form to be used by the company's sales representatives. Your completed document will look similar to Figure 5.29.

PROJECT FILES

For Project 5B, you will need the following files:

New blank Word document
w05B_Logo

You will save your file as:

Lastname_Firstname_5B_Expense_Form

PROJECT RESULTS

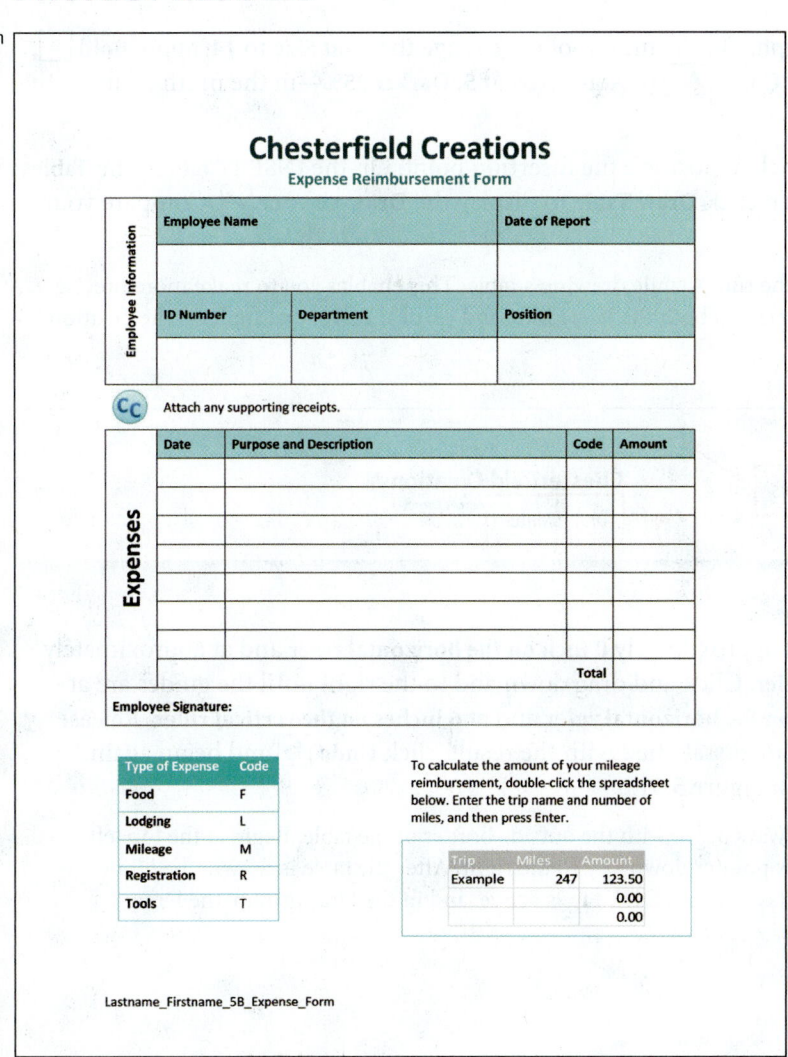

FIGURE 5.29 Project 5B Expense Form

Video W5-5

When a table is inserted into a Word document, the result is a table structure that consists of rows and columns of a uniform size. Sometimes you must modify the table structure to create rows and columns of varying sizes, such as on a purchase order or employee expense form. Word provides tools that work like an electronic pencil and eraser to draw the table objects. After the table is drawn, you can use the features on the DESIGN and LAYOUT tabs to refine the table format.

Activity 5.13 | Drawing a Freeform Table

1 Start Word, and then open a new blank document. **Save** the document in your **Word Chapter 5** folder as **Lastname_Firstname_5B_Expense_Form** Insert the file name in the footer. If necessary, change the zoom level to 100%. Display the rulers and formatting marks.

2 On the **DESIGN tab**, in the **Document Formatting group**, click **Colors**, and then click **Green**.

3 On the **HOME tab**, in the **Styles group**, click the second style—**No Spacing**. Type **Chesterfield Creations** Press Enter, type **Expense Reimbursement Form** and then press Enter.

4 Select the first paragraph. On the mini toolbar, change the **Font Size** to **26**, apply **Bold** B and then change the **Font Color** A ⁻ to **Aqua, Accent 5, Darker 50%**—in the ninth column, the last color. Press Ctrl + E.

5 Select the second paragraph. On the mini toolbar, change the **Font Size** to **14**, apply **Bold** B, and then change the **Font Color** A ⁻ to **Aqua, Accent 5, Darker 25%**—in the ninth column, the fifth color. Press Ctrl + E.

6 In the third paragraph, click to position the insertion point. On the **INSERT tab**, in the **Tables group**, click **Table**, and then click **Draw Table** to display the **Draw** pointer. Compare your screen with Figure 5.30.

It is a good idea to view the rulers while drawing a table. This enables you to make more precise measurements. Lines display on both the horizontal and vertical rulers that indicate the position of the Draw pointer.

FIGURE 5.30

7 Position the pointer at approximately **0 inch on the horizontal ruler** and at approximately **0.75 inch on the vertical ruler**. Click and drag down and to the right until the guides are at approximately **6.5 inches on the horizontal ruler** and at **6 inches on the vertical ruler**. Release the mouse button. If you are dissatisfied with the result, click **Undo** and begin again. Compare your screen with Figure 5.31.

When drawing a table, always begin with the outside border of the table. Begin at the top left corner and drag the Draw pointer down and to the right. After the table is drawn, the Draw pointer continues to display, the LAYOUT tab is active, and in the Draw group, the Draw Table button is turned on.

FIGURE 5.31

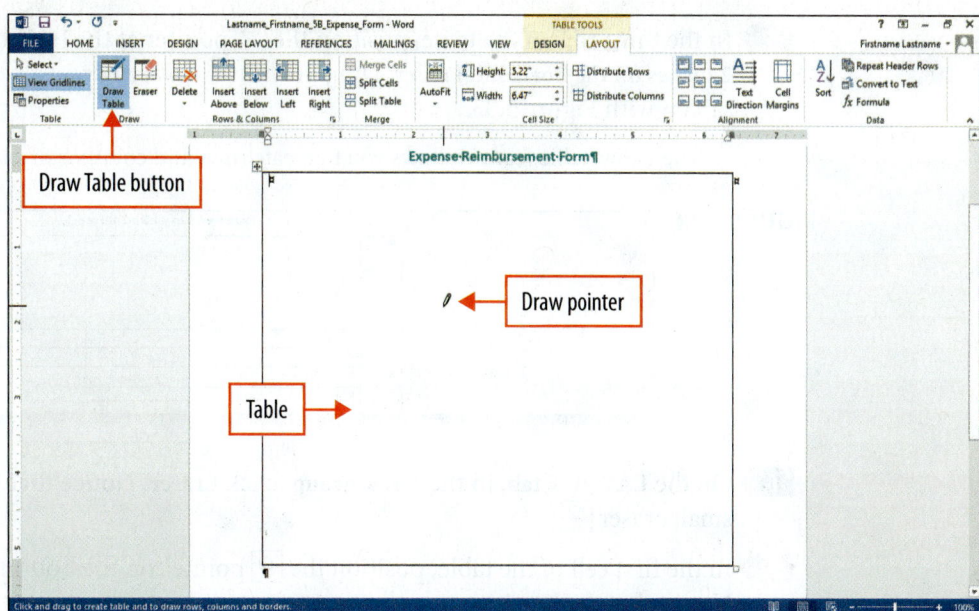

8 ▶ **Save** 🖫 your changes.

More **Knowledge** | **Wrapping Text When Drawing a Table**

To cause existing text to flow around the table you are drawing, click the Draw Table command, and then press and hold Ctrl as you draw the table.

Activity 5.14 | Adding and Removing Columns and Rows

You can draw horizontal and vertical lines inside the table to create cells of various sizes. Your table requires a section for entering employee information and another section for listing expenses incurred. Each section requires cells that vary in size.

1 ▶ On the **LAYOUT tab**, in the **Draw group**, click **Draw Table**. Position the tip of the ✏ pointer on the top border of the table at **0.5 inch on the horizontal ruler**. Drag down, and then, when you see the dotted vertical line extending to the bottom table border, release the mouse button.

By drawing a vertical dividing line, you have created an inside border forming two columns in the table.

2 ▶ Position the ✏ pointer on the left border of the table at **1.25 inches on the vertical ruler**. Drag to the right, and when you see the line extending to the right table border, release the mouse button to create the first row of the table. Compare your screen with Figure 5.32.

By drawing a horizontal line, you have created an inside border forming two rows in the table.

FIGURE 5.32

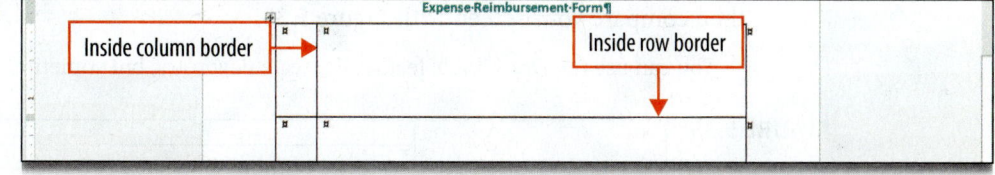

3 ▶ Draw three more horizontal lines—one beginning at **1.5 inches on the vertical ruler**, one beginning at **1.75 inches on the vertical ruler**, and one beginning at **2 inches on the vertical ruler**.

4 ▶ In the first row of the table, position the ✏ pointer at the top border at **4.25 inches on the horizontal ruler**. Drag down four rows to draw a vertical line.

5 In the third row of the table, position the 🖉 pointer at the top border of the second cell at **2 inches on the horizontal ruler**. Drag down two rows to draw a vertical line. Compare your screen with Figure 5.33.

The Draw Table feature allows you to create rows and columns of various sizes.

FIGURE 5.33

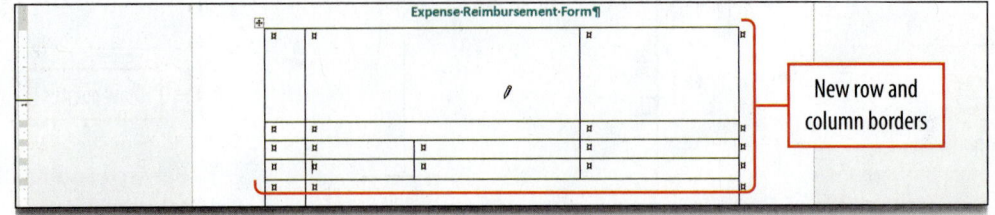

6 On the **LAYOUT tab**, in the **Draw group**, click **Eraser**. Notice that the pointer displays as a small eraser 🖉.

7 In the first cell of the table, position the 🖉 pointer on the bottom cell border, and click. Notice that the line is removed.

8 In the newly merged cell, position the 🖉 pointer on the bottom cell border, and then click to remove the line. Position the 🖉 pointer on the bottom cell border, click to remove the line, and then compare your screen with Figure 5.34.

FIGURE 5.34

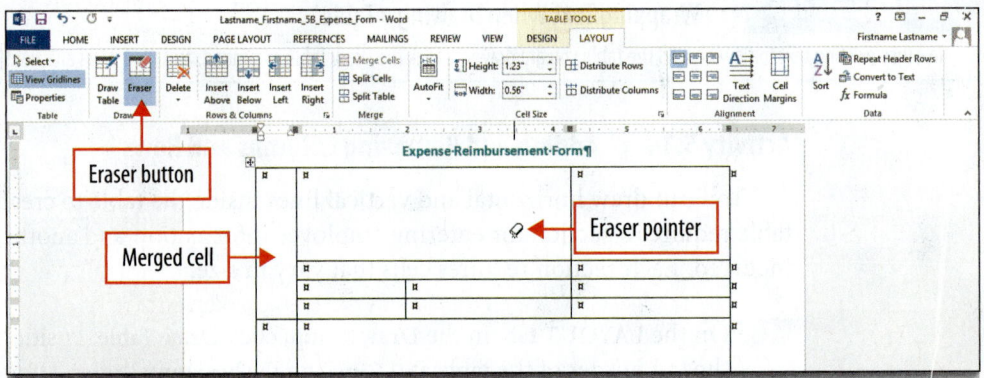

9 On the **LAYOUT tab**, in the **Draw group**, click **Draw Table**. In the last row of the table, in the first cell, position the 🖉 pointer at the left border of the cell at **2.5 inches on the vertical ruler**. Drag across to draw a horizontal line extending to the right border of the table.

10 On the **LAYOUT tab**, in the **Draw group**, click **Draw Table** to turn off the feature. Click in the last table cell. On the **LAYOUT tab**, in the **Merge group**, click **Split Cells**. In the **Split Cells** dialog box, click the **Number of columns down spin arrow** to **1**, and then click the **Number of rows up spin arrow** to **9**. Click **OK**. Click in the paragraph immediately above the table, and then compare your screen with Figure 5.35.

You can use the Draw Table feature to create new rows, but sometimes it is faster to use Split Cells.

FIGURE 5.35

11 Click anywhere in the table. On the **LAYOUT tab**, in the **Draw group**, click **Draw Table**. In the sixth row of the table—the top row of the rows you just inserted—position the ✏ pointer at the top border of the row at **1.25 inches on the horizontal ruler**. Drag down to draw a vertical line extending to the bottom border of the table.

12 In the same row, draw two more vertical lines—one beginning at **5 inches on the horizontal ruler** and one beginning at **5.5 inches on the horizontal ruler**. On the **LAYOUT tab**, in the **Draw group**, click **Draw Table** to turn it off. **Save** 💾 your changes, and then compare your screen with Figure 5.36.

FIGURE 5.36

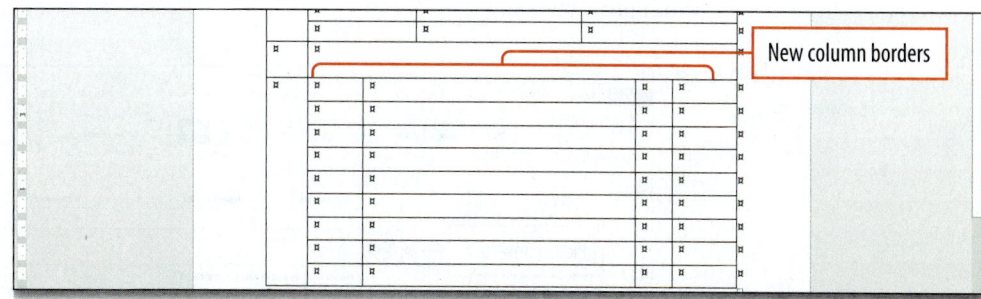

New column borders

Activity 5.15 | **Inserting Text and Graphics**

You can insert text and objects, such as pictures and WordArt, into table cells.

1 In the first row of the table, position the insertion point in the second cell, and then type **Employee Name** Press ⁤Tab⁤, and type **Date of Report**

2 Press ⁤Tab⁤ five times to move to the second cell in the third row of the table, and type **ID Number** Press ⁤Tab⁤, type **Department** press ⁤Tab⁤, and then type **Position**

3 In the sixth row, position the insertion point in the second cell, and then type **Date** Press ⁤Tab⁤, and then type **Purpose and Description** Press ⁤Tab⁤, type **Code** press ⁤Tab⁤, and then type **Amount**

4 Select the first six rows of the table, and then on the **LAYOUT tab**, in the **Alignment group**, click **Align Center Left** ▤.

5 In the first row, select the text *Employee Name*, and on the mini toolbar, apply **Bold** ⁤B⁤. Using the same technique, apply **Bold** ⁤B⁤ to all the remaining text in the table, being careful not to apply Bold to empty cells. Compare your screen with Figure 5.37.

FIGURE 5.37

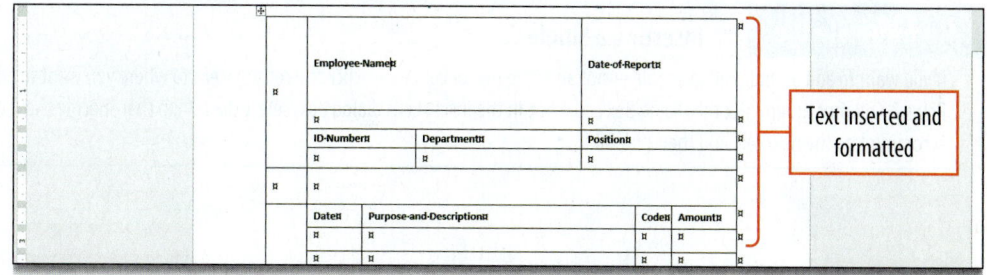

Text inserted and formatted

6 In the first column, position your insertion point in the second cell. On the **INSERT tab**, in the **Illustrations group**, click **Pictures**. Navigate to the location where your student data files are stored, select the file **w05B_Logo**, and then click **Insert**. Notice that the picture—the company logo—is inserted in the cell.

The size of the graphic causes the column width and row height to increase.

7 With the graphic selected, on the **FORMAT tab**, in the **Size group**, click the **Shape Width down spin arrow** ⊞ Width: 6.49" ⬍ to **0.4"**. Compare your screen with Figure 5.38.

Using this method to reduce the size of the image automatically reduces the row height and column width proportionally.

FIGURE 5.38

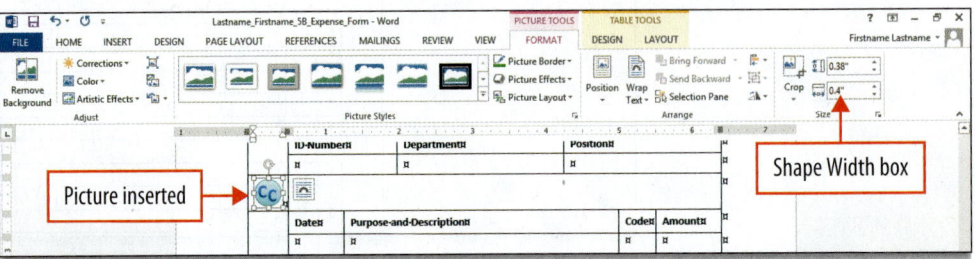

8 In the fifth row, to the right of the graphic, click in the second cell, and then type **Attach any supporting receipts.**

9 In the last row of the table, select the second, third, and fourth cells. On the **LAYOUT tab**, in the **Merge group**, click **Merge Cells**. In the **Alignment group**, click **Align Center Right** ▤.

10 Click in the merged cell, and type **Total** Select the text. On the mini toolbar, apply **Bold** ▣, click **Insert**, and then click **Insert Below**.

The mini toolbar contains buttons to insert or delete rows and columns—in this case, to insert a row.

11 In the last row of the table, with all the cells selected, on the **LAYOUT tab**, in the **Merge group**, click **Merge Cells**. In the **Alignment group**, click **Align Center Left** ▤. If necessary, in the **Cell Size group**, change the **Height** to **0.4"**.

12 With the insertion point in the last row of the table, type **Employee Signature:** Select the text, and on the mini toolbar, apply **Bold** ▣. Deselect the text, **Save** ▤ your changes, and then compare your screen with Figure 5.39.

FIGURE 5.39

More Knowledge | **Inserting a Single Cell**

If you want to add a single cell to a table—not an entire row or column—click the cell adjacent to where you want to add the cell. On the LAYOUT tab, in the Rows & Columns group, click the Dialog Box Launcher. In the Insert Cells dialog box, select the option that specifies how adjacent cells should be moved to accommodate the new cell, and then click OK.

Activity 5.16 | Changing Text Direction

Word tables include a feature that enables you to change the text direction. This is effective for column titles that do not fit at the top of narrow columns or for row headings that cover multiple rows.

1 Click to position the insertion point in the first cell of the table. On the **LAYOUT tab**, in the **Alignment group**, click **Text Direction** two times. Notice that the insertion point displays horizontally in the cell.

> Use the Text Direction button to change the positioning of text within a cell. The appearance of the Text Direction button changes to indicate the direction of the text within the currently selected cell.

2 Type **Employee Information** On the **LAYOUT tab**, in the **Alignment group**, click **Align Center** . Select the text, and then on the mini toolbar, apply **Bold** B . Deselect the text, and then compare your screen with Figure 5.40.

FIGURE 5.40

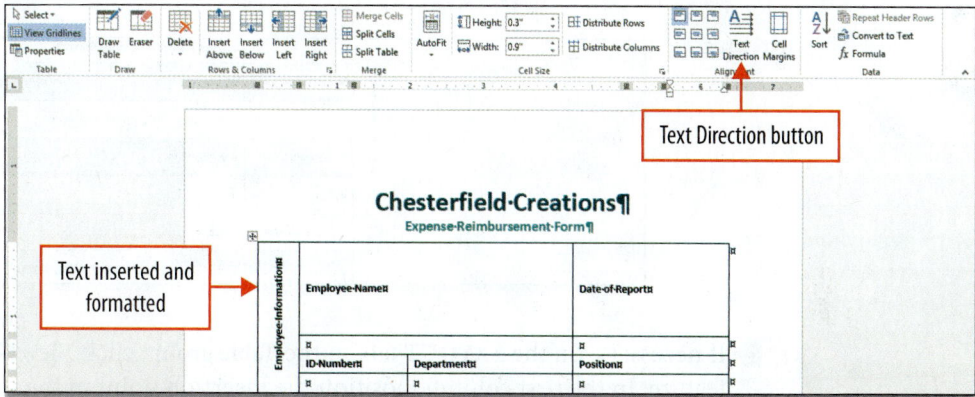

3 In the first column, click to position the insertion point in the third cell. On the **LAYOUT tab**, in the **Alignment group**, click **Text Direction** two times. Notice that the insertion point displays horizontally in the cell.

4 Type **Expenses** On the **LAYOUT tab**, in the **Alignment group**, click **Align Center** . Select the text, and then on the mini toolbar, change the **Font Size** to **20** and apply **Bold** B . **Save** your changes.

Activity 5.17 | Distributing Rows and Columns

When you draw a freeform table, you may have rows that you want to be exactly the same height or columns that you want to be the same width. The *Distribute Columns* command adjusts the width of the selected columns so that they are equal. Similarly, the *Distribute Rows* command causes the height of the selected rows to be equal.

1 In the first four rows of the table, select all of the cells to the right of the first column. On the **LAYOUT tab**, in the **Cell Size group**, click **Distribute Rows** . Deselect the cells, and then compare your screen with Figure 5.41.

> The four rows are equal in height.

FIGURE 5.41

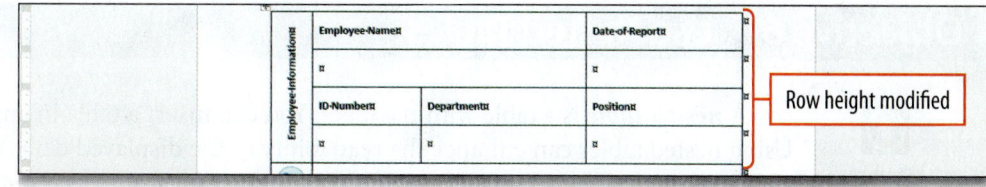

2 **Save** your changes.

Activity 5.18 | Formatting a Table

Table cells can be formatted to enhance the appearance of a table. You will add shading to cells and modify the borders of the table.

1 In the first row, select the second and third cells. Under **TABLE TOOLS**, on the **DESIGN tab**, in the **Table Styles group**, click the **Shading button arrow**, and then under **Theme Colors**, in the ninth column, click the third color—**Aqua, Accent 5, Lighter 60%**.

2 In the third row, select the second, third, and fourth cells, and then in the **Table Styles group**, click the **Shading** button—not the **Shading button arrow**. In the sixth row, select cells two through five, and in the **Table Styles group**, click **Shading**. Deselect the cells, and then compare your screen with Figure 5.42.

> The Shading button retains the color that was last selected. By clicking the Shading button, the current color is applied to the selected cells.

FIGURE 5.42

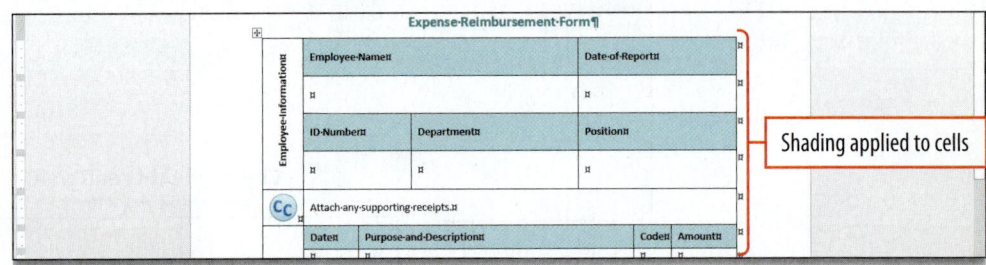

3 If necessary, on the **LAYOUT tab**, in the **Table group**, click **View Gridlines** to turn on the feature. In the first column, position the insertion point in the second cell that contains the graphic. Be careful not to select the graphic. Under **TABLE TOOLS**, on the **DESIGN tab**, in the **Borders group**, click the **Borders button arrow**, and then click **Left Border**. Click the **Borders button arrow**, and then click **Right Border**. Notice that the left and right borders of the cell no longer display; instead they are replaced by the dashed lines as shown in Figure 5.43.

> *Gridlines*—the dashed lines—are nonprinting cell borders that can be used as a guide for viewing table cells. They are useful when positioning content in a table when you are not using a table border. Removing borders can improve the appearance of certain content—for example, the graphic in this table.

FIGURE 5.43

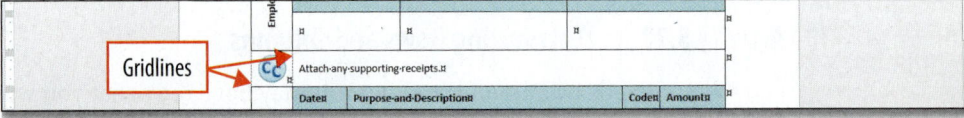

4 Press Tab. In the **Borders group**, click **Borders**—not the **Borders button arrow**.

> The Border button retains the last setting—in this case, Right Border. A gridline displays at the right of the cell.

5 On the **LAYOUT tab**, in the **Table group**, click **View Gridlines** to turn it off. **Save** 🖫 your changes.

> Hiding the gridlines allows you to see how a table will display in print.

Objective 6   Use Nested Tables

Video W5-6

A *nested table* is a table within a table. You can insert a table in any cell of an existing table. Using nested tables can enhance the readability of the displayed data. You can also improve the appearance of data within tables by changing *cell margins* and *cell spacing*. Cell margins are the amount of space between a cell's content and the left, right, top, and bottom borders of the cell. Cell spacing is the distance between the individual cells of a table.

Activity 5.19 | Changing Cell Margins and Cell Spacing and Using the Border Painter

To create a nested table, you must first have an existing table.

1 Press [Ctrl] + [End] to move to the end of the document. Press [Enter].

2 On the **INSERT tab**, in the **Tables group**, click **Table**, and then under **Insert Table**, in the **Table** grid, in the second row, click the second square to insert a 2 × 2 table.

> A table with two rows and two columns displays at the insertion point location, and the insertion point displays in the upper left cell.

3 On the **LAYOUT tab**, in the **Alignment group**, click **Cell Margins**.

> The Table Options dialog box allows you to set the cell margins and cell spacing for a table.

4 In the **Table Options** dialog box, under **Default cell margins**, click the **Top up spin arrow** to **0.1"**. Using the same technique, change the **Bottom**, **Left**, and **Right** cell margins to **0.1"**.

> Contents of each cell within the table will be displayed 0.1" from each cell border.

5 Under **Default cell spacing**, click to select the **Allow spacing between cells** check box, and then click the **Allow spacing between cells up spin arrow** to **0.05"**. Compare your screen with Figure 5.44.

> All cells in the table will be separated by 0.05" of space.

FIGURE 5.44

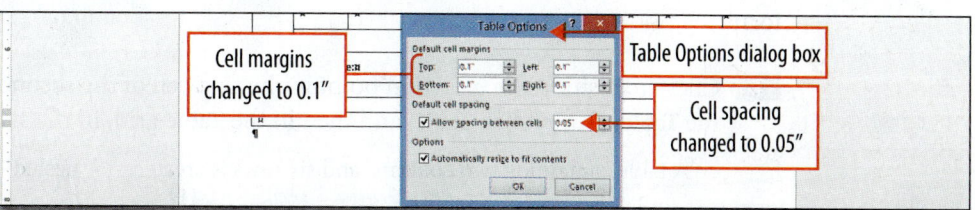

6 Click **OK**. In the table, select the two cells in the first column, and then on the **LAYOUT tab**, in the **Merge group**, click **Merge Cells**. Compare your screen with Figure 5.45.

FIGURE 5.45

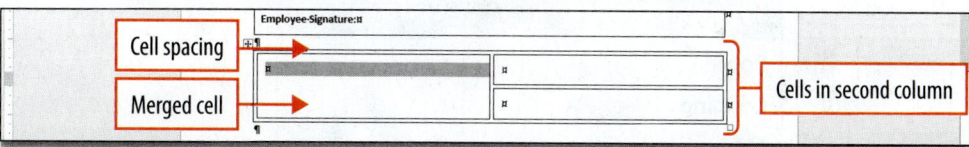

7 Point slightly outside of the upper left corner of the table to display the **table move handle** ⊞. With the 🐭 pointer displayed, click the **table move handle** ⊞ to select the entire table.

8 On the **LAYOUT tab**, in the **Table group**, click **View Gridlines** to turn on the feature. Under **TABLE TOOLS**, on the **DESIGN tab**, in the **Borders group**, click the **Borders button arrow**, and then click **No Border**.

9 In the second column, position the insertion point in the second cell. Under **TABLE TOOLS**, on the **DESIGN tab**, in the **Borders group**, click **Pen Color**, and then under **Theme Colors**, in the ninth column, click the first color—**Aqua, Accent 5**.

> By default, in the Borders group, when you change the Border Style, Pen Color, or Line Weight, the ***Border Painter*** feature becomes active. The Border Painter applies selected formatting to specific borders of a table. When the Border Painter is turned on, the pointer takes the shape of a small brush.

10 In the second column, above the second cell, click the border. Notice that the border color changes to the selected color.

11 In a similar manner, use the **Border Painter** to change the color of the left, right, and bottom borders of the cell. Compare your screen with Figure 5.46.

FIGURE 5.46

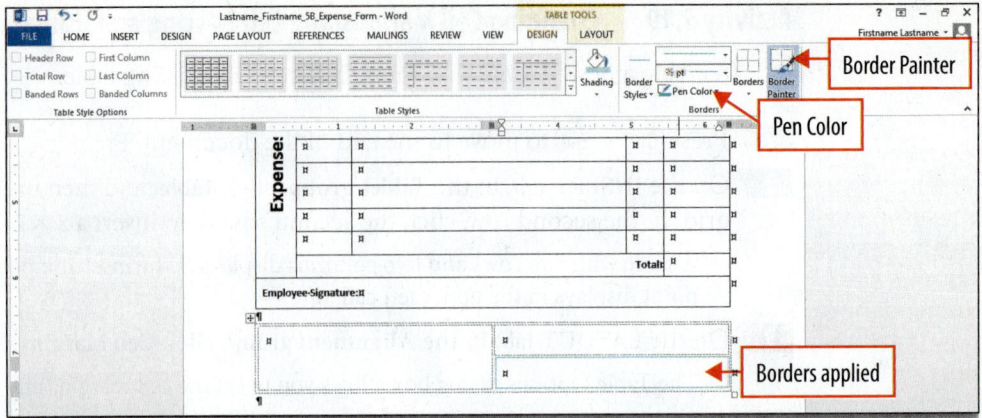

12 ▶ In the **Borders group**, click the **Pen Color arrow**, and then click **Automatic**. Click the **Border Painter** to turn off the feature. **Save** 🔲 your changes.

Activity 5.20 | Inserting a Nested Table and Setting a Table Title by Adding Alternative Text

In this activity, you will create a nested table to display the codes that are used on the expense form.

1 ▶ Click to position the insertion point in the first cell of the second table. On the **INSERT tab**, in the **Tables group**, click **Table**, and then in the **Table** grid, in the sixth row, click the second cell.

A table containing two columns and six rows is created—or nested—within the first cell of the table.

2 ▶ In the first cell of the nested table, type **Type of Expense** Press (Tab), and then type **Code**

3 ▶ In the same manner, enter the following data in the remaining cells of the table:

Type Of Expense	Code
Food	F
Lodging	L
Mileage	M
Registration	R
Tools	T

4 ▶ If necessary, click to position the insertion point in the nested table. On the **LAYOUT tab**, in the **Cell Size group**, click **AutoFit**, and then click **AutoFit Contents** to resize the nested table to fit the existing text.

5 ▶ Under **TABLE TOOLS**, on the **DESIGN tab**, in the **Table Styles group**, click **More** 🔽. In the **Table Styles** gallery, scroll down, and then under **List Tables**, in the third row, click the sixth style—**List Table 3 – Accent 5**. Compare your screen with Figure 5.47.

FIGURE 5.47

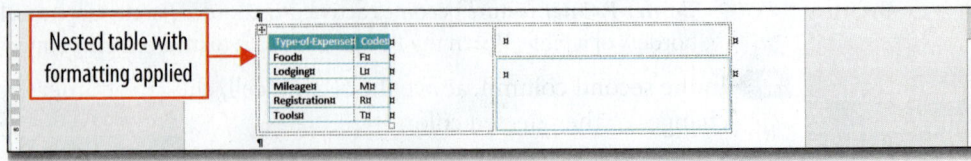

Nested table with formatting applied

6 ▶ With the insertion point in the table, on the **LAYOUT tab**, in the **Table group**, click **Properties**.

7 In the **Table Properties** dialog box, click the **Alt Text tab**.

Alternative text can be added to the properties of an object—for example, a table, chart, or picture. This is useful for a person with vision or cognitive impairments who may not be able to view or understand the object as it displays in the document. The title of the object—in this case, the table—can be read to the person with the disability. If applicable, the description can also be read to provide more information.

8 In the **Title** box, type **Expense Codes** In the **Description** box, type **The table contains the codes to be used when completing the expense form.**

9 Click **OK** to close the dialog box, and then **Save** 🖫 your changes.

Objective 7   Insert an Excel Spreadsheet

Video W5-7

You can insert an Excel spreadsheet in a document to provide a table that performs calculations.

Activity 5.21 | Inserting an Excel Spreadsheet

In this activity, you will insert an Excel spreadsheet to assist employees with calculating mileage reimbursements.

1 On the right side of the status bar, on the **Zoom Slider**, click **Zoom In** ➕ two times to change the zoom level to 120%.

Each click of the Zoom In button causes the zoom level to increase in 10 percent increments.

🔁 **BY TOUCH**   On the status bar, tap the Zoom In button to increase the zoom level in 10 percent increments.

2 In the original table that contains the nested table, in the second column, position the insertion point in the top cell. Type **To calculate the amount of your mileage reimbursement, double-click the spreadsheet below. Enter the trip name and number of miles, and then press Enter.**

3 Click to position the insertion point in the remaining empty cell. On the **INSERT tab**, in the **Tables group**, click **Table**, and then click **Excel Spreadsheet**.

An Excel spreadsheet and part of the table display on **Page 2** of the document.

4 In cell **A1**, type **Trip** and then press `Tab`. In cell **B1**, type **Miles** and then press `Tab`. In cell **C1**, type **Amount** Compare your screen with Figure 5.48.

FIGURE 5.48

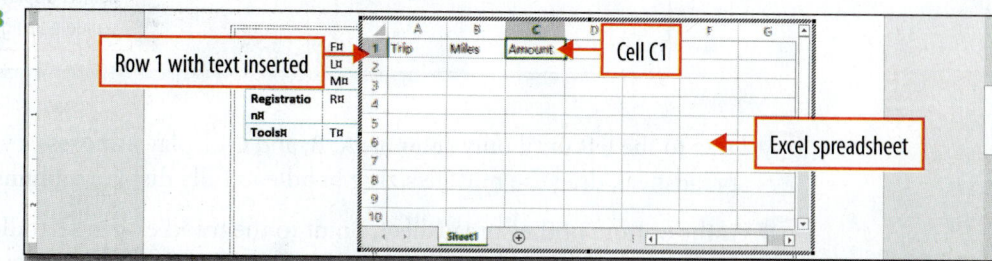

5 Click in cell **A2**, type **Example** and then press `Tab`. In cell **B2**, type **247** and then press `Tab`. In cell **C2**, type **=B2*0.5**

The formula is based on a mileage reimbursement rate of 50 cents per mile.

6 Press Ctrl + Enter, and notice that the value *123.5* displays in cell **C2**.

Calculations can be performed in the spreadsheet with the full capability of Excel. In Excel, all formulas are preceded by the = symbol. In this case, the formula prompts the program to multiply the number in cell B2 by 0.50, the company's mileage reimbursement rate. The calculated value displays in cell C2.

7 With cell **C2** selected, on the **HOME tab**, in the **Number group**, click **Increase Decimal**.

8 With cell **C2** selected, in the lower right corner of the cell, point to the **fill handle**—the small square—until the ⊞ pointer displays, as shown in Figure 5.49.

FIGURE 5.49

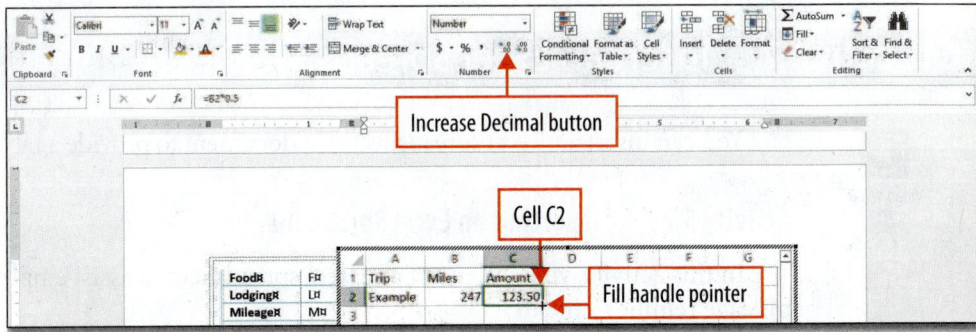

9 With the ⊞ pointer displayed, drag down to cell **C8**. Notice that the number *0.00* displays in cells **C3** through **C8**.

Dragging the fill handle copies the formula in C2 to the cells below. Excel changes the cell references in the formula to match the row number—for example, in cell C3 the formula is copied as =B3*0.5. Because you haven't entered any data in rows 3 through 8, the Amount column displays a value of 0 for those rows. You have copied the formula so that the person using the form can calculate the reimbursement amount for several trips without having to delete any data in the spreadsheet.

10 Select cells **A1** through **C1**. On the **HOME tab**, in the **Styles group**, click **Cell Styles**. In the **Cell Styles** gallery, under **Themed Cell Styles**, in the fourth row, click the third style—**Accent 3**.

11 On the right edge of the spreadsheet, point to the middle sizing handle until the ↔ pointer displays. Compare your screen with Figure 5.50.

FIGURE 5.50

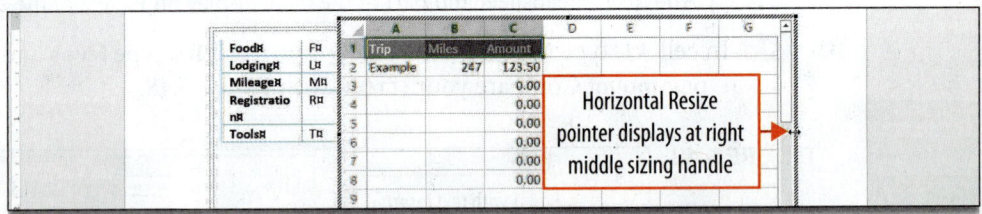

12 Drag to the left until only **columns A, B,** and **C** display. If necessary, on the right side of the spreadsheet, drag the middle sizing handle to fully display **columns A, B,** and **C.**

13 At the bottom of the spreadsheet, point to the middle sizing handle until the ↕ pointer displays. Drag upward until only **rows 1** through **4** display. If necessary, at the bottom of the spreadsheet, drag the middle sizing handle up or down to fully display **rows 1** through **4.** Compare your screen with Figure 5.51.

FIGURE 5.51

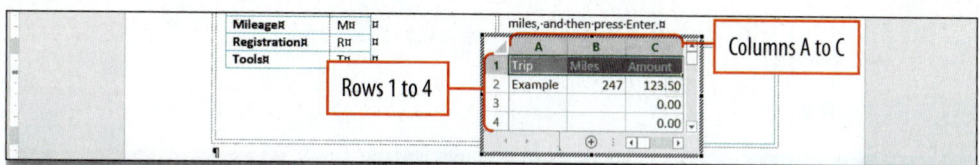

14 To close the Excel spreadsheet, click in a blank area of the document. Click in a blank area of the cell containing the Excel table, and then on the **LAYOUT tab**, in the **Alignment group**, click **Align Center** .

15 In the **Table group**, click **View Gridlines** to turn off the feature. **Save** your changes.

Activity 5.22 | Modifying the Dimensions of a Table

1 On the status bar, click **Zoom Out** two times to restore the document view to 100%.

2 At the bottom of the page, position the insertion point in the table containing the expense codes. At the lower right corner of the table, point to the corner sizing handle. With the pointer displayed, drag down until the bottom border of the table is aligned with the 8.5-inch mark on the vertical ruler. Compare your screen with Figure 5.52.

Use the corner sizing handle to quickly change the dimensions of a table.

FIGURE 5.52

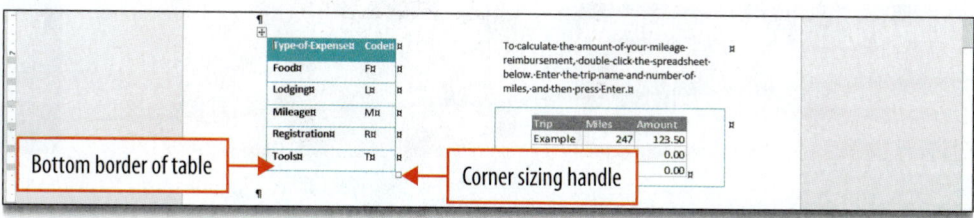

3 Press Ctrl + Home. Click the **FILE tab** to display **Backstage** view. In the **Tags** box, type **expense form, nested table** In the **Subject** box, type your course name and section number. If necessary, edit the author name to display your name.

4 **Save** your changes. Print your document, or submit electronically, as directed by your instructor. **Close** Word.

END | You have completed Project 5B

END OF CHAPTER

SUMMARY

Creating and applying a table style standardizes the appearance of multiple tables in a document. The style can include formatting for the entire table and for specific elements—such as rows and columns.

Word has advanced tools that enable you to present table data efficiently and attractively—such as changing alignment within cells, merging and splitting cells, sorting data, and changing text direction.

The Draw Table and Table Eraser features function as an electronic pencil and eraser. By drawing and erasing borders, you can create a table with rows and columns of varying sizes—for example, in a form.

Insert a nested table or modify the cell margins and cell spacing to improve readability of data within a table. To perform simple or complex calculations within a document, insert an Excel spreadsheet.

GO! LEARN IT ONLINE

Review the concepts and key terms in this chapter by completing these online challenges, which you can find at **www.pearsonhighered.com/go**.

Matching and Multiple Choice: Answer matching and multiple choice questions to test what you learned in this chapter. MyITLab®

Crossword Puzzle: Spell out the words that match the numbered clues, and put them in the puzzle squares.

Flipboard: Flip through the definitions of the key terms in this chapter and match them with the correct term.

END OF CHAPTER

REVIEW AND ASSESSMENT GUIDE FOR WORD CHAPTER 5

Your instructor may assign one or more of these projects to help you review the chapter and assess your mastery and understanding of the chapter.

		Review and Assessment Guide for Word Chapter 5	
Project	**Apply Skills from These Chapter Objectives**	**Project Type**	**Project Location**
5C	Objectives 1–4 from Project 5A	**5C Skills Review** A guided review of the skills from Project 5A.	On the following pages
5D	Objectives 5–7 from Project 5B	**5D Skills Review** A guided review of the skills from Project 5B.	On the following pages
5E	Objectives 1–4 from Project 5A	**5E Mastery (Grader Project)** A demonstration of your mastery of the skills in Project 5A with extensive decision making.	In MyITLab and on the following pages
5F	Objectives 5–7 from Project 5B	**5F Mastery (Grader Project)** A demonstration of your mastery of the skills in Project 5B with extensive decision making.	In MyITLab and on the following pages
5G	Objectives 1–7 from Projects 5A and 5B	**5G Mastery (Grader Project)** A demonstration of your mastery of the skills in Projects 5A and 5B with extensive decision making.	In MyITLab and on the following pages
5H	Combination of Objectives from Projects 5A and 5B	**5H GO! Fix It** A demonstration of your mastery of the skills in Projects 5A and 5B by creating a correct result from a document that contains errors you must find.	Online
5I	Combination of Objectives from Projects 5A and 5B	**5I GO! Make It** A demonstration of your mastery of the skills in Projects 5A and 5B by creating a result from a supplied picture.	Online
5J	Combination of Objectives from Projects 5A and 5B	**5J GO! Solve It** A demonstration of your mastery of the skills in Projects 5A and 5B, your decision-making skills, and your critical thinking skills. A task-specific rubric helps you self-assess your result.	Online
5K	Combination of Objectives from Projects 5A and 5B	**5K GO! Solve It** A demonstration of your mastery of the skills in Projects 5A and 5B, your decision-making skills, and your critical thinking skills. A task-specific rubric helps you self-assess your result.	On the following pages
5L	Combination of Objectives from Projects 5A and 5B	**5L GO! Think** A demonstration of your understanding of the chapter concepts applied in a manner that you would outside of college. An analytic rubric helps you and your instructor grade the quality of your work by comparing it to the work an expert in the discipline would create.	On the following pages
5M	Combination of Objectives from Projects 5A and 5B	**5M GO! Think** A demonstration of your understanding of the chapter concepts applied in a manner that you would outside of college. An analytic rubric helps you and your instructor grade the quality of your work by comparing it to the work an expert in the discipline would create.	Online
5N	Combination of Objectives from Projects 5A and 5B	**5N You and GO!** A demonstration of your understanding of the chapter concepts applied in a manner that you would in a personal situation. An analytic rubric helps you and your instructor grade the quality of your work.	Online

GLOSSARY

AutoFit A table feature that automatically adjusts column widths or the width of the entire table.

AutoFit Contents A table feature that resizes the column widths to accommodate the maximum field size.

Border Painter: A table feature that applies selected formatting to specific borders of a table.

Caption A title that is added to a Word object and numbered sequentially.

Cell margins The amount of space between a cell's content and the left, right, top, and bottom borders of the cell.

Cell spacing The distance between the individual cells in a table.

Distribute Columns A command that adjusts the width of the selected columns so that they are equal.

Distribute Rows A command that causes the height of the selected rows to be equal.

Field A placeholder for data.

Formula A mathematical expression that contains functions, operators, constants, and properties, and returns a value to a cell.

Function A predefined formula that performs calculations by using specific values in a particular order.

Gridlines Nonprinting lines that indicate cell borders.

Header row The first row of a table containing column titles.

Merge A table feature that combines two or more adjacent cells into one cell so that the text spans across multiple columns or rows.

Nested table A table inserted in a cell of an existing table.

Organizer A dialog box where you can modify a document by using styles stored in another document or template.

Split A table feature that divides selected cells into multiple cells with a specified number of rows and columns.

Split Table A table feature that divides an existing table into two tables in which the selected row—where the insertion point is located—becomes the first row of the second table.

Style A group of formatting commands— such as font, font size, and font color— that can be applied with a single command.

Table style A style that includes formatting for the entire table and specific table elements, such as rows and columns.

CHAPTER REVIEW

Skills Review Project 5C Sales Conference

Apply 5A skills from these Objectives:

1 Create and Apply a Custom Table Style
2 Format Cells
3 Use Advanced Table Features
4 Modify Table Properties

In the following Skills Review, you will format tables and insert formulas to create a memo regarding a conference for Sales Managers at Chesterfield Creations. Your completed document will look similar to Figure 5.53.

PROJECT FILES

For Project 5C, you will need the following files:

w05C_Sales_Conference
w05C_Sales_Styles

You will save your file as:

Lastname_Firstname_5C_Sales_Conference

PROJECT RESULTS

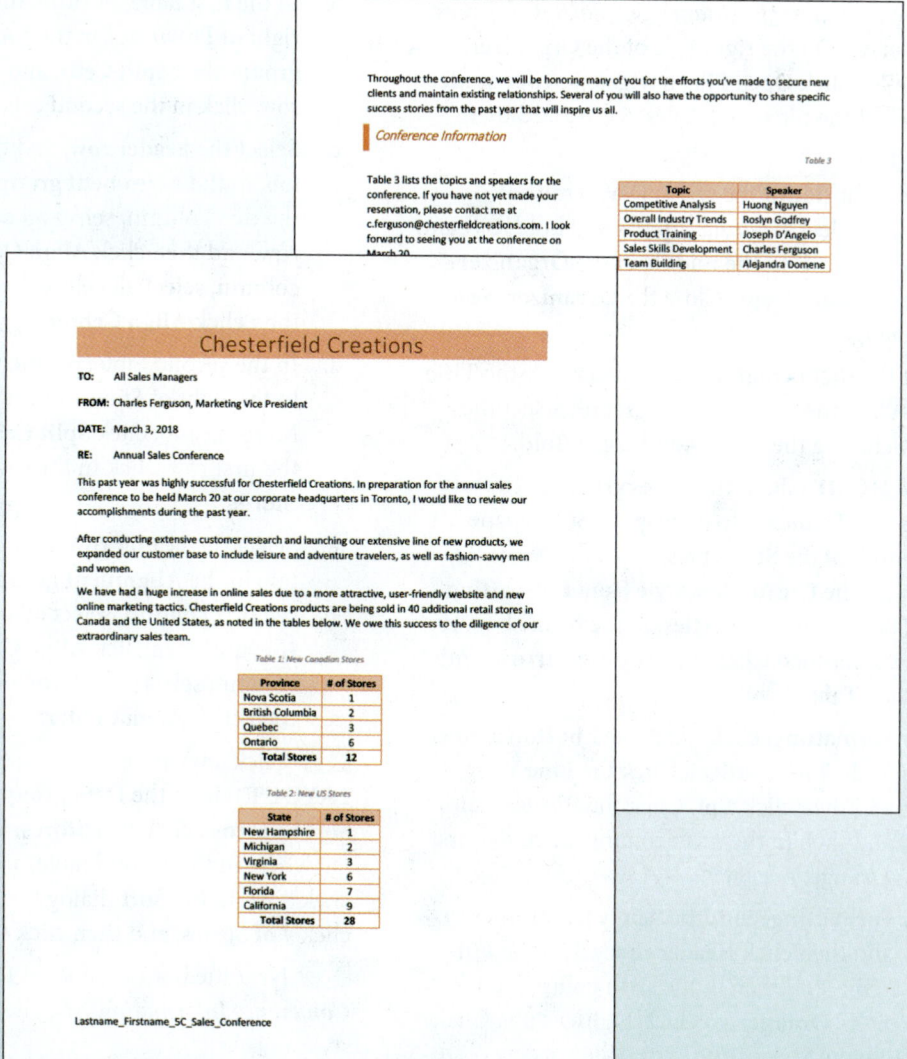

FIGURE 5.53

(Project 5C Sales Conference continues on the next page)

CHAPTER REVIEW

1 Start Word. Navigate to your student files and open the file **w05C_Sales_Conference. Save** the document in your **Word Chapter 5** folder as **Lastname_Firstname_5C_Sales_Conference** Insert the file name in the footer. Display the rulers and formatting marks. If any words are flagged as spelling errors, click **Ignore All**.

a. Click the **FILE tab**, and then click **Options**. In the **Word Options** dialog box, click **Add-Ins**.

b. At the bottom of the **Word Options** dialog box, click the **Manage box arrow**, click **Templates**, and then click **Go**.

c. In the **Templates and Add-ins** dialog box, click **Organizer**.

d. On the left side of the **Organizer** dialog box, be sure that the *Lastname_Firstname_5C_Sales_Conference* file displays. On the right side of the **Organizer**, click **Close File**. Click **Open File**, navigate to your student files, select the file **w05C_Sales_Styles**, and then click **Open**.

e. On the right side of the **Organizer**, scroll as necessary, select **Heading 2**, press and hold Ctrl, and then select **Title**. In the middle of the **Organizer** dialog box, click **Copy**. **Close** the **Organizer**. **Save** your changes.

2 Select the first paragraph, and then apply the **Title** style. For each of the next four paragraphs, select the heading—including the colon—and apply **Bold**.

a. On the **HOME tab**, in the **Styles group**, click the **Dialog Box Launcher** to display the **Styles** pane. At the bottom of the **Styles** pane, click the **New Style** button. In the **Create New Style from Formatting** dialog box, under **Properties**, in the **Name** box, type **Sales Conference** Click the **Style type arrow**, and then click **Table**.

b. Under **Formatting**, click the **Border button arrow**, and then click **All Borders**. Click the **Line Weight arrow**, and then click **1 pt**. Click the **Border Color arrow**, and then in the sixth column, click the first color—**Orange, Accent 2**.

c. Under **Formatting**, click the **Apply formatting to arrow**, and then click **Header row**. Click the **Fill Color arrow**, and then in the sixth column, click the third color—**Orange, Accent 2, Lighter 60%**. Click **OK. Close** the **Styles** pane.

d. In the sixth row of the table, click in the first cell that contains the text *State*. On the **LAYOUT tab**, in the **Merge group**, click **Split Table**.

3 In the first table in the document, click in the first cell. Under **TABLE TOOLS**, on the **DESIGN tab**, in the **Table Styles group**, click the **Sales Conference** table style. In a similar manner, click in the first cell in the second table of the document, and then apply the **Sales Conference** table style.

a. Under **TABLE TOOLS**, on the **DESIGN tab**, in the **Table Styles group**, right-click the **Sales Conference** table style, and then click **Modify Table Style**. Click the **Apply formatting to arrow**, and then click **Header row**. Apply **Bold**, and then click **OK**.

b. In the first table, position the insertion point to the right of *Province*. On the **LAYOUT tab**, in the **Merge group**, click **Split Cells**, and then click **OK**. In the first row, click in the second cell, and type **# of Stores**

c. Select the **header row**, and then on the **LAYOUT tab**, in the **Alignment group**, click **Align Center**. In the first column, select all cells below the header row, and then click **Align Center Left**. In the second column, select all cells below the header row, and then click **Align Center**.

d. In the second table, position the insertion point to the right of *State*. On the **LAYOUT tab**, in the **Merge group**, click **Split Cells**, and then click **OK**. In the first row, click in the second cell, and type **# of Stores**

e. Select the **header row**, and then on the **LAYOUT tab**, in the **Alignment group**, click **Align Center**. In the first column, select all cells below the header row, and then click **Align Center Left**. In the second column, select all cells below the header row, and then click **Align Center**.

4 Click anywhere in the first table, and then on the **LAYOUT tab**, in the **Data group**, click **Sort**. Click the **Sort by arrow**, click **# of Stores**, and then click **OK**. Click anywhere in the second table, and then in the **Data group**, click **Sort**. In the **Sort** dialog box, click the **Sort by arrow**, click **# of Stores**, and then click **OK**.

5 Near the bottom of **Page 1**, select the paragraph *Conference Information*, and then apply the **Heading 2** style.

(Project 5C Sales Conference continues on the next page)

CHAPTER REVIEW

a. Locate the paragraph that begins *Topic*, and then drag to select all the remaining text in the document—a total of six paragraphs.

b. On the **INSERT tab**, in the **Tables group**, click **Table**, and then click **Convert Text to Table**. Click **OK** to close the dialog box.

6 Click to position your insertion point anywhere in the table you inserted. Under **TABLE TOOLS**, on the **DESIGN tab**, in the **Table Styles group**, click the **Sales Conference** table style.

a. On the **LAYOUT tab**, in the **Cell Size group**, click **AutoFit**, and then click **AutoFit Contents**.

b. Select the **header row**, and then in the **Alignment group**, click **Align Center**. Select the remaining cells in the table, and then click **Align Center Left**.

7 In the first table, click to position the insertion point in the first cell of the last row. On the **LAYOUT tab**, in the **Cell Size group**, click **AutoFit**, and then click **AutoFit Contents**. Point to the bottom left corner of the table, and then click the **One-Click Row/Column Insertion** button.

a. In the new last row of the table, click in the first cell, and then type **Total Stores** Select the text, and apply **Bold**. In the **Alignment group**, click **Align Center Right**. Press `Tab`, and then in the **Data group**, click **Formula**.

b. In the **Formula** dialog box, with *=SUM(ABOVE)* displayed, click the **Number format arrow**, and then click **0**. Click **OK**. Select the inserted text, and apply **Bold**.

8 In the second table, click to position the insertion point in the first cell of the last row. On the **LAYOUT tab**, in the **Cell Size group**, click **AutoFit**, and then click **AutoFit Contents**. Point to the bottom left corner of the table, and then click the **One-Click Row/Column Insertion** button.

a. In the new last row, click in the first cell, and then type **Total Stores** Select the text, and apply **Bold**. In the **Alignment group**, click **Align Center Right**. Press `Tab`, and then in the **Data group**, click **Formula**.

b. In the **Formula** dialog box, with *=SUM(ABOVE)* displayed, click the **Number format arrow**, and then click **0**. Click **OK**. Select the inserted text, and apply **Bold**.

c. In the first table, in the second column, click in the fifth cell. Select *5*, and then type **6** In the last cell of the table, select *11*, right-click the selection, and then click **Update Field**.

d. In the second table, in the second column, click in the sixth cell. Select *8*, and then type **7** In the last cell of the table, select *29*, right-click the selection, and then click **Update Field**.

9 Click to position the insertion point anywhere in the first table. On the **REFERENCES tab**, in the **Captions group**, click **Insert Caption**. In the **Caption** dialog box, with the insertion point to the right of *Table 1,* type **:** Press `Spacebar`, and then type **New Canadian Stores** If necessary, under **Options**, click the **Position arrow**, and then click **Above selected item**. Click **OK**.

a. Click to position the insertion point anywhere in the second table. In the **Captions group**, click **Insert Caption**. In the **Caption** dialog box, with the insertion point to the right of *Table 2*, type **:** Press `Spacebar`, and then type **New US Stores** If necessary, under **Options**, click the **Position arrow**, and then click **Above selected item**. Click **OK**.

b. Click to position the insertion point anywhere in the last table. On the **LAYOUT tab**, in the **Table group**, click the **Properties** button. In the **Table Properties** dialog box, if necessary, under **Text wrapping**, click **Around**, and then click **Positioning**.

c. In the **Table Positioning** dialog box, under **Distance from surrounding text**, click the **Left up spin arrow** to 0.5". Click **OK** two times to close the dialog boxes. Display the **Table Move Handle**, and drag the table up and to the right until the top border is even with the first line of the last paragraph and the right border is aligned with the right margin.

d. Click anywhere in the table. On the **REFERENCES tab**, in the **Captions group**, click **Insert Caption**. In the **Caption** dialog box, with *Table 3* displayed, click **OK**. Select the caption, and then on the **HOME tab**, in the **Paragraph group**, click **Align Right**. In the last paragraph of the document, select the text *Listed below are*, and then type **Table 3 lists**

(Project 5C Sales Conference continues on the next page)

CHAPTER REVIEW

10 Click to position the insertion point anywhere in the first table. On the **LAYOUT tab**, in the **Table group**, click **Properties**. In the **Table Properties** dialog box, under **Alignment**, click **Center**, and then click **OK**. Click to position the insertion point anywhere in the second table. In the **Table group**, click **Properties**. In the **Table Properties** dialog box, under **Alignment**, click **Center**, and then click **OK**. Select the captions for *Table 1* and *Table 2*, and then press Ctrl + E.

11 Press Ctrl + Home. Click the **FILE tab**, and then click **Show All Properties**. In the **Tags** box, type **sales conference** In the **Subject** box, type your course name and section number. If necessary, edit the author name to display your name. **Save** your document.

12 Print your document or submit electronically as directed by your instructor. **Close** Word.

END | You have completed Project 5C

CHAPTER REVIEW

Apply 5B skills from these Objectives:

5 Draw a Freeform Table

6 Use Nested Tables

7 Insert an Excel Spreadsheet

Skills Review | Project 5D Registration Form

In the following Skills Review, you will create a registration form for the Employee Charity Bowling Tournament sponsored by Chesterfield Creations. Your completed document will look similar to Figure 5.54.

PROJECT FILES

For Project 5D, you will need the following file:

w05D_Registration_Form

You will save your file as:

Lastname_Firstname_5D_Registration_Form

PROJECT RESULTS

Chesterfield Creations

Annual Employee Charity Bowling Tournament

The administrative team of Chesterfield Creations hosts a bowling tournament each year for its employees. Proceeds from the tournament are given to the Greater Toronto Food Bank. This year the tournament will be held at the Regency Bowling Lanes in Toronto on May 14 and 15. Various prizes are awarded to individuals and teams of four. In addition to the three games of bowling each day, continental breakfast and lunch are available for an additional fee. Consider joining us this year for fun and fellowship with your coworkers.

Registration Form

Employee Information	Name:	Department:
	Phone:	Email:
	Home Address:	

Use the Excel spreadsheet below to calculate the total amount due.

Day	Item	Charge	Your Cost
	Entry Fee	$150	
Friday	Breakfast	$10	
Friday	Lunch	$20	
Saturday	Breakfast	$10	
Saturday	Lunch	$20	
	Total	$210	0

Amount Enclosed: $

Please send your check and a copy of the completed registration form to Rachel Anders, Chief Financial Officer, at our Toronto address. Make checks payable to Chesterfield Creations Bowling Tournament.

Lastname_Firstname_5D_Registration_Form

FIGURE 5.54

(Project 5D Registration Form continues on the next page)

1 Start Word. Navigate to your student files and open the file **w05D_Registration_Form**. **Save** the document in your **Word Chapter 5** folder as **Lastname_Firstname_5D_Registration_Form** Insert the file name in the footer. Display the rulers and formatting marks.

a. Select the first two paragraphs. Change the **Font Size** to **18**, apply **Bold**, and then change the **Font Color** to **Orange, Accent 2, Darker 25%**. Press Ctrl + E. Select the fourth paragraph—*Registration Form*. Change the **Font Size** to **16**, apply **Bold**, and then change the **Font Color** to **Orange, Accent 2, Darker 50%**. Press Ctrl + E.

2 Click to position the insertion point in the fifth paragraph, which is blank. On the **INSERT tab**, in the **Tables group**, click **Table**, and then click **Draw Table**.

a. Position the pointer at the left margin and at approximately **2.75 inches on the vertical ruler**. Drag down and to the right until the guides are at approximately **6.5 inches on the horizontal ruler** and at **8 inches on the vertical ruler**. Release the mouse button. If necessary, under **TABLE TOOLS**, on the **DESIGN tab**, in the **Borders group**, change the **Line Weight** to **½ pt** and the **Pen Color** to **Automatic**.

b. With the insertion point in the table, on the **HOME tab**, in the **Styles group**, click the **No Spacing** style, and then change the **Font Size** to **12**.

c. On the **LAYOUT tab**, in the **Draw group**, click **Draw Table**. Position the pointer on the left border of the table at approximately **0.75 inch on the vertical ruler**, and drag to the right table border. In a similar manner, draw horizontal lines at **1.25 inches, 2 inches, and 4.5 inches on the vertical ruler**.

d. Position the pointer on the top border of the table at **0.5 inch on the horizontal ruler**, and drag down three rows. Position the pointer on the top border at approximately **3.25 inches on the horizontal ruler**, and drag down to the bottom of the table. Click **Draw Table** to turn off the feature.

e. On the **LAYOUT tab**, in the **Draw group**, click **Eraser**. In the first cell of the table, position the pointer on the bottom cell border and click. In the newly merged cell, position the pointer on the bottom cell border and click. In the fourth row, in the first cell, position the pointer on the right cell border and click. Click **Eraser** to turn it off.

3 Starting in the second column, select the first three rows of the table. On the **LAYOUT tab**, in the **Cell Size group**, click **Distribute Rows**. Click in the fourth row. Under **TABLE TOOLS**, on the **DESIGN tab**, in the **Borders group**, click the **Borders button arrow**, and then click **Left Border**. Click the **Borders button arrow**, and then click **Right Border**. Select the last row, click the **Borders button arrow**, and then click **No Border**. If necessary, on the **LAYOUT tab**, in the **Table group**, click the **View Gridlines** button to display the gridlines.

a. In the first row of the table, in the second cell, type **Name:** Press Tab, and then type **Department:** In the second row, in the cell below *Name*, type **Phone:** Press Tab, and then type **Email:** In the third row, in the cell below *Phone*, type **Home Address:** Select the text in the three rows, and then on the **LAYOUT tab**, in the **Alignment group**, click **Align Center Left**.

b. In the third row of the table, select the second and third cells, and then on the **LAYOUT tab**, in the **Merge group**, click **Merge Cells**. Position the insertion point in the first cell of the table, and then on the **LAYOUT tab**, in the **Alignment group**, click **Text Direction** two times. Type **Employee Information** In the **Alignment group**, click **Align Center**, and then apply **Bold**.

c. In the last row of the table, click in the first cell, and then in the **Alignment group**, click **Align Center Right**. Type **Amount Enclosed:** Press Tab, and then type **$** In the **Alignment group**, click **Align Center Left**. In the last row, select both cells, and then apply **Bold**.

4 Click to position the insertion point in the fourth row of the table. On the **LAYOUT tab**, in the **Alignment group**, click **Align Center**.

a. With the insertion point in the fourth row, on the **INSERT tab**, in the **Tables group**, click the **Table** button, and then under **Insert Table**, in the **Table** grid, in the second row, click the second square to insert a 2 × 2 table.

b. On the **LAYOUT tab**, in the **Alignment group**, click **Cell Margins**. In the **Table Options** dialog box, under **Default cell margins**, change the **Top** and **Bottom** margins to **0.01"**, and then change the **Left** and **Right** margins to **0.4"**.

(Project 5D Registration Form continues on the next page)

c. Under **Default cell spacing**, select the **Allow spacing between cells** check box, and then change the cell spacing to **0.1"**. Click **OK**.

d. In the nested table, select the two cells in the first column, and then on the **LAYOUT tab**, in the **Merge group**, click **Merge Cells**. Select the nested table. Under **TABLE TOOLS**, on the **DESIGN tab**, in the **Borders group**, click the **Borders button arrow**, and then click **No Border**.

5 Click to position the insertion point in the first cell of the nested table. On the **LAYOUT tab**, in the **Alignment group**, click **Align Center**. On the **INSERT tab**, in the **Illustrations group**, click **Online Pictures**. In the **Insert Pictures** dialog box, in the **Search Bing** box, type **bowling** and then press Enter. Click the image shown in Figure 5.54, or select a similar graphic, and then click **Insert**.

a. Click in the top right cell of the nested table, and then type **Use the Excel spreadsheet below to calculate the total amount due.** Click to position the insertion point in the bottom right cell of the nested table. On the **INSERT tab**, in the **Tables group**, click **Table**, and then click **Excel Spreadsheet**.

b. Click to position the insertion point in cell **A1**, if necessary, and then type **Day** Press Tab, and then in cell **B1**, type **Item** Press Tab, and then in cell **C1**, type **Charge** Press Tab, and then in cell **D1**, type **Your Cost** Type the following text in the appropriate cells under the headings you typed:

	A	B	C
1	Day	Item	Charge
2		**Entry Fee**	**$150**
3	**Friday**	**Breakfast**	**$10**
4	**Friday**	**Lunch**	**$20**
5	**Saturday**	**Breakfast**	**$10**
6	**Saturday**	**Lunch**	**$20**
7		**Total**	

c. Click in cell **C7**, type **=SUM(C2:C6)** and then press Tab. In cell **D7**, type **=SUM(D2:D6)** and then press Enter. Select cells **A1** through **D7**. On the **HOME tab**, in the **Styles group**, click the **Cell Styles** button. In the **Cell Styles** gallery, under **Themed Cell Styles**, click **40% –Accent 4**.

d. On the right edge of the spreadsheet, point to the middle sizing handle, and drag to the left until only **columns A** through **D** display. At the bottom of the spreadsheet, point to the middle sizing handle, and drag upward until only **rows 1** through **7** display. To close the Excel spreadsheet, click in a blank area of the document. On the **LAYOUT tab**, in the **Table group**, click **View Gridlines** to turn it off.

6 Press Ctrl + Home. Click the **FILE tab**, and then click **Show All Properties**. In the **Tags** box, type **registration, bowling tournament** In the **Subject** box, type your course name and section number. If necessary, change the author name to display your name. **Save** your document. Print your document or submit electronically as directed by your instructor. **Close** Word.

END | You have completed Project 5D

CONTENT-BASED ASSESSMENTS

In the following Mastering Word project, you will create a memo to all Chesterfield Creations Sales Managers announcing the Flair Collection of travel bags. Your completed document will look similar to Figure 5.55.

Apply 5A skills from these Objectives:

1 Create and Apply a Custom Table Style

2 Format Cells

3 Use Advanced Table Features

4 Modify Table Properties

PROJECT FILES

For Project 5E, you will need the following file:

w05E_Travel_Bags

You will save your file as:

Lastname_Firstname_5E_Travel_Bags

PROJECT RESULTS

Memo

TO: All Sales Managers

FROM: Charles Ferguson, Marketing Vice President

DATE: September 20, 2018

RE: Flair Collection

Chesterfield Creations is proud to add the Flair Collection to our travel bag line of leather and fabric accessories for men and women. Designed for the active traveler, these products were carefully crafted to meet the needs of our customers, who crave the best in quality, durability, functionality, and aesthetics. Please familiarize yourself with these items as they will be available for distribution to stores next month.

Table 1: Flair Collection

Day Pack	This is a comfortable, roomy yet lightweight bag that can hold a wallet, sunglasses, camera, maps, and a guide book.	$ 59
Laptop Case	A classic style, this case includes a pocket ideal for storing a PDA, cell phone, cables, cords, and more. The sturdy frame holds your laptop securely. The shoulder strap has a shoulder pad to make carrying more comfortable.	$ 79
Tote Bag	This soft yet durable leather bag is perfect for shopping trips. It also includes a pocket for travel documents and other papers.	$ 79
Messenger Bag	This casual day bag carries all the essentials and includes many pockets to keep it all organized. The material is soft yet durable. The shoulder strap has a shoulder pad to make carrying more comfortable.	$ 99
Large Backpack	This backpack safely stores a laptop computer while providing plenty of extra room for electronic accessories, a change of clothes, personal items, and more. The backpack straps have been developed to be supportive and comfortable.	$ 129
Rolling Garment Bag	This bag includes individual shoe pockets, a hook for hanging garments, and foam padding to protect clothes and minimize wrinkling. It is ideal for a short trip.	$ 349
	Average Price	**$ 132**

Lastname_Firstname_5E_Travel_Bags

FIGURE 5.55

(Project 5E Travel Bags continues on the next page)

CONTENT-BASED ASSESSMENTS

1 Start Word. Navigate to your student files, and open the file **w05E_Travel_Bags**. **Save** the document in your **Word Chapter 5** folder as **Lastname_Firstname_5E_Travel_Bags** Insert the file name in the footer, and display the rulers and formatting marks.

2 Select the first paragraph and apply the **Title** style. For each of the next four paragraphs, select the heading—including the colon—and apply the **Strong** style.

3 Display the **Styles** pane, and then click the **New Style** button. In the **Create New Style from Formatting** dialog box, for the **Name**, type **Flair Collection** Change the **Style type** to **Table**. Apply the border style to **All Borders**. Change the **Line Weight** to **1 ½ pt**. Change the **Border Color** to **Gold, Accent 4, Darker 25%**. Change the **Fill Color** to **Gold, Accent 4, Lighter 80%**, and then click **OK**. **Close** the **Styles** pane.

4 Locate the paragraph that begins *Rolling Garment Bag*, drag to select the remaining six paragraphs of the document, and then **Convert Text to Table**. With the insertion point anywhere in the table, **Sort** the table by **Column 3** in **Ascending** order. Apply the **Flair Collection** table style. Select the first two columns of the table, and change the alignment to **Align Center Left**. Select the third column, and change the alignment to **Align Center**. Resize the table to **AutoFit Contents**. In the second column, select all six cells, and then change the **Width** to **4.5"**.

5 At the bottom of the table, insert a new row. In the last row, select the first and second cells, and then **Merge Cells**. Change the alignment to **Align Center Right**, type **Average Price** and then apply **Bold**. In the last cell of the table, click **Formula**, change the **Formula** to **=AVERAGE(ABOVE)** Change the **Number format** to **#,##0**, and then to the left of the number format, type **$** Click **OK**. Select the displayed value, and apply **Bold**.

6 Display the **Table Properties** dialog box, and then change the table alignment to **Center**.

7 Display the **Caption** dialog box, and then modify the text as necessary to display above the table as *Table 1: Flair Collection*. Select the caption, change the **Font Size** to **12**, and then change the **Font Color** to **Gold, Accent 4, Darker 25%**.

8 Press Ctrl + Home. Click the **FILE tab**, and then click **Show All Properties**. In the **Tags** box, type **travel bags, Flair** In the **Subject** box, type your course name and section number. If necessary, change the author name to display your name. **Save** your document.

9 Print your document or submit electronically as directed by your instructor. **Close** Word.

END | You have completed Project 5E

CONTENT-BASED ASSESSMENTS

Mastering Word Project 5F Buyer Program

In the following Mastering Word project, you will create a flyer explaining the Frequent Buyer Program to Chesterfield Creations customers. Your completed document will look similar to Figure 5.56.

PROJECT FILES

For Project 5F, you will need the following file:

w05F_Buyer_Program

You will save your file as:

Lastname_Firstname_5F_Buyer_Program

PROJECT RESULTS

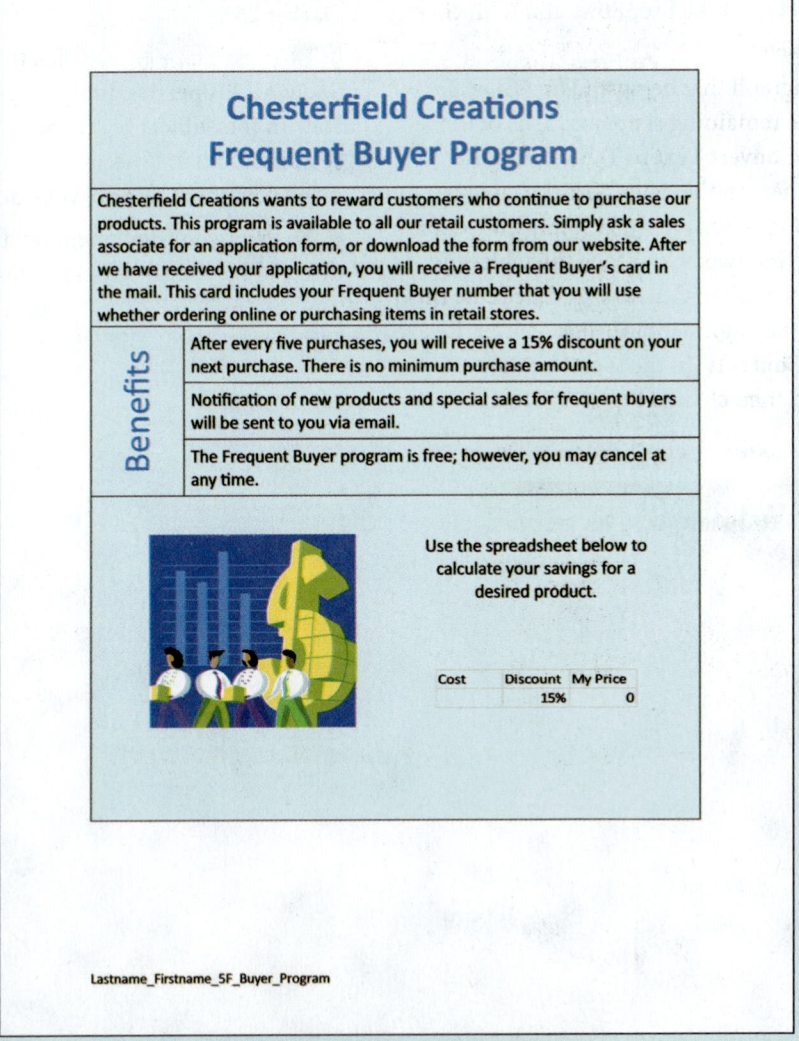

FIGURE 5.56

(Project 5F Buyer Program continues on the next page)

CONTENT-BASED ASSESSMENTS

1 Start Word. Navigate to your student files, and open the file **w05F_Buyer_Program**. **Save** the document in your **Word Chapter 5** folder as **Lastname_Firstname_5F_Buyer_Program** Insert the file name in the footer, and display rulers and formatting marks.

2 Select the first cell of the table, and change the **Width** to 1". Select the second cell, and change the **Width** to 5.5".

3 On the **LAYOUT tab**, in the **Rows & Columns group**, click **Insert Above**. Click anywhere in the second row, and then click **Insert Below**. In the last row, change the **Height** to 4.8". In the first row, change the **Height** to 1.2".

4 In the **Draw group**, click **Draw Table**. Begin at the left border of the table and at **5.5 inches on the vertical ruler**, and draw a horizontal line extending to the right border of the table. Begin at the right border of the first column and at **4.5 inches on the vertical ruler**, and draw a horizontal line extending to the right table border. In a similar manner, draw a horizontal line positioned at **5 inches on the vertical ruler**. In the first row, use the **Eraser** to remove the border between the two cells. In a similar manner, use the **Eraser** to remove the inside border in the second and sixth rows. Turn off the **Eraser**.

5 In the first row of the table, type **Chesterfield Creations** Press Enter, and then type **Frequent Buyer Program** Select the text, change the **Font Size** to **28 pt**, apply **Bold**, and then change the **Font Color** to **Blue, Accent 1, Darker 25%**. Click **Align Center**.

6 In the third row, select the first cell, change the **Height** to 0.75", click **Align Center**, and then click **Text Direction** two times. Type **Benefits** Select the text, change the **Font Size** to **28 pt**, and then change the **Font Color** to **Blue, Accent 1, Darker 25%**.

7 In the second row, select the last sentence that begins *The Frequent*, and drag to move the text to the second cell in the fifth row. In a similar manner, move the sentence that begins *Notification* to the fourth row, and then move the two sentences beginning with *After every five* and ending with *amount* to the third row. Select all three cells to the right of *Benefits*, click **Align Center Left**, and then click **Distribute Rows**. Remove any unnecessary spaces that display at the end of the paragraphs in **rows 2** through **5**.

8 Select the entire main table, and then change the **Shading** to **Blue, Accent 1, Lighter 80%**.

9 In the last row of the table, insert a nested table that contains two rows and two columns. Select the entire nested table, and apply **No Border**. If necessary, turn on **View Gridlines**. Change all **Default cell margins** to 0.1", change **Default cell spacing** to 0.3", and then click **Align Center**. Select the first column, and then **Merge Cells**. In the nested table, click in the first cell. Insert an online picture from **Bing Image Search**—search for **dollars** and then select the image shown in Figure 5.56 or a similar graphic. Change the **Shape Height** to 2".

10 In the nested table, in the first cell of the second column, type **Use the spreadsheet below to calculate your savings for a desired product.** In the second cell of the second column, insert an **Excel Spreadsheet**. In cell **A1**, type **Cost** In cell **B1**, type **Discount** and then in cell **C1**, type **My Price** In cell **B2**, type **15%** and then in cell **C2**, type **=A2*.85** Press Enter. Resize the spreadsheet to display only **columns A** through **C** and **rows 1** and **2**, and then click in a blank area of the document.

11 Press Ctrl + Home. Click the **FILE tab**, and then click **Show All Properties**. In the **Tags** box, type **frequent buyer program** In the **Subject** box, type your course name and section number. If necessary, change the author name to display your name. **Save** your document. Print your document or submit electronically as directed by your instructor. **Close** Word.

END | You have completed Project 5F

CONTENT-BASED ASSESSMENTS

Mastering Word Project 5G Holiday Special

MyITLab® grader

Apply 5A and 5B skills from these Objectives:

1 Create and Apply a Custom Table Style
2 Format Cells
3 Use Advanced Table Features
4 Modify Table Properties
5 Draw a Freeform Table
6 Use Nested Tables
7 Insert an Excel Spreadsheet

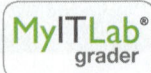

In the following Mastering Word project, you will create a flyer that provides descriptions of new products available for holiday shopping at Chesterfield Creations. Your completed document will look similar to Figure 5.57.

PROJECT FILES

For Project 5G, you will need the following file:

w05G_Holiday_Special

You will save your file as:

Lastname_Firstname_5G_Holiday_Special

PROJECT RESULTS

NEW PRODUCTS FOR THE BUSINESSWOMAN

Just in time for the holiday shopping season, Chesterfield Creations is pleased to add three computer bags to our Mainline Collection designed for the professional woman. These bags offer the same durability and quality as our other business bags but with an extra dose of style and sophistication for today's fashionable woman.

Item	Description	Price
Compact Bag	Special features include a pocket for items such as tickets and other travel information, and the most comfortable shoulder strap on the market. The computer sleeve has extra padding for the ultimate protection.	$ 149
Streamlined Tote	Available in a choice of five colors, the front pocket provides ample storage for tickets and other documents, metal feet protect the bag from dirty surfaces, extra padding in the computer sleeve stores your laptop securely, and the removable pouch can hold personal items.	$ 199
Large Tote	Similar to our other computer totes, this item has plenty of extra room for notebooks, pens, presentation information, personal items, and electronic accessories.	$ 209
	Average Price	**$ 186**

As a sales incentive during December, these items will be available at a 25% discount.

Retail Price	
Discount	25%
Sale Price	0

Lastname_Firstname_5G_Holiday_Special

FIGURE 5.57

(Project 5G Holiday Special continues on the next page)

CONTENT-BASED ASSESSMENTS

1 Start Word, and then open the file **w05G_Holiday_Special**. **Save** the document in your **Word Chapter 5** folder as **Lastname_Firstname_5G_Holiday_Special** Insert the file name in the footer, and display rulers and formatting marks.

2 Select the first paragraph, and then apply the **Heading 1** style. Select the second paragraph, and then change the **Font Size** to **12**. Select the remaining three paragraphs of the document, change the **Font Size** to **14**, and then with the text still selected, **Convert Text to Table**.

3 Display the **Styles** pane, and then click the **New Style** button. In the **Create New Style from Formatting** dialog box, create a new style named **Holiday** Set the **Style type** to **Table**. Apply the style to **All Borders**. Set the **Line Weight** to **1 ½ pt**, and then set the **Border Color** to **Green, Accent 6, Darker 25%**. Change the **Fill Color** to **Green, Accent 6, Lighter 80%**. Apply the **Holiday** style to the entire table.

4 Select the first column, and then change the column **Width** to **1.2"**. Change the second column **Width** to **4.5"**, and the third column **Width** to **0.7"**. Position the insertion point anywhere in the first row, and then click **Insert Above**. In the first cell of the table, type **Item** and then press `Tab`. Type **Description** Press `Tab` and then type **Price** Select the **header row**, apply **Bold**, and then click **Align Center**. Change the **Height** of **rows 2, 3,** and **4** to **1.5", 1.8",** and **1.4"**, respectively.

5 In the first column, select all the cells below the header row. Apply **Bold**, click **Align Center**, and then click **Text Direction** two times. In the second column, select all the cells below the header row, and then click **Align Center Left**. In the last column, select all the cells below the header row, and click **Align Center**.

6 Point to the bottom left corner of the table, and then click the **One-Click Row/Column Insertion** button. In the last row, change the **Height** to **0.4"**. Select the first and second cells, and then **Merge Cells**. Click **Text Direction**, and then click **Align Center Right**. Type **Average Price** and then apply **Bold**. In the last cell of the table, insert the **Formula: =AVERAGE(ABOVE)** Change the **Number format** to **#,##0**, and to the left of the number format, type **$** and then click **OK**. Select the displayed text, and then apply **Bold**.

7 Point to the bottom left corner of the table, and then click the **One-Click Row/Column Insertion** button. Select both cells in the last row, and then **Merge Cells**. Insert a nested table containing one row and two columns. Select both cells, and then apply **No Border**. Change all **Cell Margins** to **0.1"**, set **Allow spacing between cells** to **0.02"**. Click **Align Center**.

8 In the first cell of the nested table, type **As a sales incentive during December, these items will be available at a 25% discount.** In the second cell of the nested table, insert an **Excel Spreadsheet**. In cell **A1**, type **Retail Price** and then in cell **A2**, type **Discount** In cell **A3**, type **Sale Price** In cell **B2**, type **25%** and then in cell **B3**, type **=B1*.75** Press `Enter`. Resize the spreadsheet to display only **columns A** and **B** and **rows 1** through **3**, and then click in a blank area of the document.

9 Press `Ctrl` + `Home`. Click the **FILE tab**, and then click **Show All Properties**. In the **Tags** box, type **holiday special, Mainline** In the **Subject** box, type your course name and section number. If necessary, edit the author name to display your name. **Save** your document. Print the document or submit electronically as directed by your instructor. **Close** Word.

END | You have completed Project 5G

CONTENT-BASED ASSESSMENTS

Apply a combination of the 5A and 5B skills.

GO! Fix It	Project 5H Safety Program	Online
GO! Make It	Project 5I Product Flyer	Online
GO! Solve It	Project 5J Planning Committee	Online
GO! Solve It	Project 5K Wallet Collection	

PROJECT FILES

For Project 5K, you will need the following file:

w05K_Wallet_Collection

You will save your file as:

Lastname_Firstname_5K_Wallet_Collection

Open the file **w05K_Wallet_Collection** and save it to your **Word Chapter 5** folder as **Lastname_Firstname_5K_Wallet_Collection** Using the information for the specific wallets, convert the text to a table. Insert a header row, add appropriate column headings, and then sort the table by price and item name. Create a formula to display the average price of the items. Create and apply a table style. Adjust paragraph, text, table, and cell formats to display attractively in a one-page document. Insert the file name in the footer and add appropriate document properties. Print your document or submit electronically as directed by your instructor.

Performance Level

Performance Criteria	Exemplary: You consistently applied the relevant skills	Proficient: You sometimes, but not always, applied the relevant skills	Developing: You rarely or never applied the relevant skills
Convert text to table	All appropriate text is displayed in a table.	At least one item of text is not displayed in a table.	No text is displayed in a table.
Sort the table	The data in the table is sorted by both price and item name.	The data in the table is sorted only by price or item name.	The data in the table is not sorted.
Create a formula	The average price is calculated using a formula and displays in a new row.	The average price displays in a new row, but a formula is not used.	The average price does not display in a new row.
Create and apply a table style	A new table style is created and applied to the table.	A table style is applied to the table, but it is a built-in style—not new.	No table style is applied to the table.
Format the document	All items in the document are formatted appropriately.	At least one item in the document is not formatted appropriately.	No items in the document are formatted.

END | You have completed Project 5K

OUTCOMES-BASED ASSESSMENTS

RUBRIC

The following outcomes-based assessments are open-ended assessments. That is, there is no specific correct result; your result will depend on your approach to the information provided. Make *Professional Quality* your goal. Use the following scoring rubric to guide you in *how* to approach the problem and then to evaluate *how well* your approach solves the problem.

The *criteria*—Software Mastery, Content, Format and Layout, and Process—represent the knowledge and skills you have gained that you can apply to solving the problem. The *levels of performance*—Professional Quality, Approaching Professional Quality, or Needs Quality Improvements—help you and your instructor evaluate your result.

	Your completed project is of Professional Quality if you:	Your completed project is Approaching Professional Quality if you:	Your completed project Needs Quality Improvements if you:
1-Software Mastery	Choose and apply the most appropriate skills, tools, and features and identify efficient methods to solve the problem.	Choose and apply some appropriate skills, tools, and features, but not in the most efficient manner.	Choose inappropriate skills, tools, or features, or are inefficient in solving the problem.
2-Content	Construct a solution that is clear and well organized, contains content that is accurate, appropriate to the audience and purpose, and is complete. Provide a solution that contains no errors in spelling, grammar, or style.	Construct a solution in which some components are unclear, poorly organized, inconsistent, or incomplete. Misjudge the needs of the audience. Have some errors in spelling, grammar, or style, but the errors do not detract from comprehension.	Construct a solution that is unclear, incomplete, or poorly organized; contains some inaccurate or inappropriate content; and contains many errors in spelling, grammar, or style. Do not solve the problem.
3-Format & Layout	Format and arrange all elements to communicate information and ideas, clarify function, illustrate relationships, and indicate relative importance.	Apply appropriate format and layout features to some elements, but not others. Overuse features, causing minor distraction.	Apply format and layout that does not communicate information or ideas clearly. Do not use format and layout features to clarify function, illustrate relationships, or indicate relative importance. Use available features excessively, causing distraction.
4-Process	Use an organized approach that integrates planning, development, self-assessment, revision, and reflection.	Demonstrate an organized approach in some areas, but not others; or, use an insufficient process of organization throughout.	Do not use an organized approach to solve the problem.

OUTCOMES-BASED ASSESSMENTS

Build from
Scratch

GO! Think | Project 5L Company Picnic

PROJECT FILES

For Project 5L, you will need the following file:

New blank Word document

You will save your file as:

Lastname_Firstname_5L_Company_Picnic

Every year, Chesterfield Creations holds a picnic for employees and their families. This year the picnic will be held on June 16 from 10 a.m. to 4 p.m. at High Park in Toronto. Lunch and snacks are provided. There will be music and an assortment of games for young and old. In addition, other park activities are available for a fee—such as pony rides and miniature golf.

Using this information, create a flyer to distribute to employees as an email attachment. Create a document that explains the picnic and lists the schedule of events in a table format. Insert a second table that lists fees for specific activities. Use a formula to provide the total cost for these events. Create a table style and apply it to both tables. Format the flyer, including table and cell properties, so that it is attractive and easy to read. Save the file as **Lastname_Firstname_5L_Company_Picnic** Insert the file name in the footer and add appropriate document properties. Print the document or submit as directed by your instructor.

END | You have completed Project 5L

Build from
Scratch

GO! Think | Project 5M Employee Newsletter | Online

Build from
Scratch

You and GO! | Project 5N Personal Budget | Online

Building Documents from Reusable Content and Using Markup Tools

GO! to Work
Video W6

6
WORD 2013

PROJECT 6A

OUTCOMES
Create reusable content and construct a document with building blocks and theme templates.

PROJECT 6B

OUTCOMES
Collaborate with others to edit, review, and finalize a document.

OBJECTIVES

1. Create Custom Building Blocks
2. Create and Save a Theme Template
3. Create a Document by Using Building Blocks

OBJECTIVES

4. Use Comments in a Document
5. Track Changes in a Document
6. View Side by Side, Compare, and Combine Documents

Blend Images/Fotolia

In This Chapter

In this chapter you will work with building blocks—objects that can be reused in multiple documents. You will customize predefined building blocks and create your own reusable content. You will create a theme—by defining the colors, fonts, and effects—to give documents a customized appearance. You will build a new document from the custom building blocks and theme. Word includes features to review revisions and comments made in a document. This makes it easy to work with a team to collaborate on documents. You will insert comments, track changes, review changes made by others, and then accept or reject those changes.

The projects in this chapter relate to **Mountain View Public Library**, which serves the Claremont, Tennessee community at three locations—the Main library, the East Branch, and the West Branch. The library's extensive collection includes books, audio books, music CDs, video DVDs, magazines, and newspapers—for all ages. The Mountain View Public Library also provides sophisticated online and technology services, youth programs, and frequent appearances by both local and nationally known authors. The citizens of Claremont support the Mountain View Public Library with local taxes, donations, and special events fees.

Newsletter with Reusable Content and Custom Theme

PROJECT ACTIVITIES

In Activities 6.01 through 6.09, you will assist Benedetta Herman, Director of Operations at Mountain View Public Library, in designing a custom look for documents that the library produces by creating a custom theme and building blocks for content that can be reused. Your completed documents will look similar to Figure 6.1.

PROJECT FILES

Build from Scratch

For Project 6A, you will need the following files:

Three new blank Word documents
w06A_February_Articles
w06A_Classes

You will save your files as:

Lastname_Firstname_6A_Building_Blocks
Lastname_Firstname_6A_February_Newsletter
Lastname_Firstname_6A_Library_Theme—not shown in figure

PROJECT RESULTS

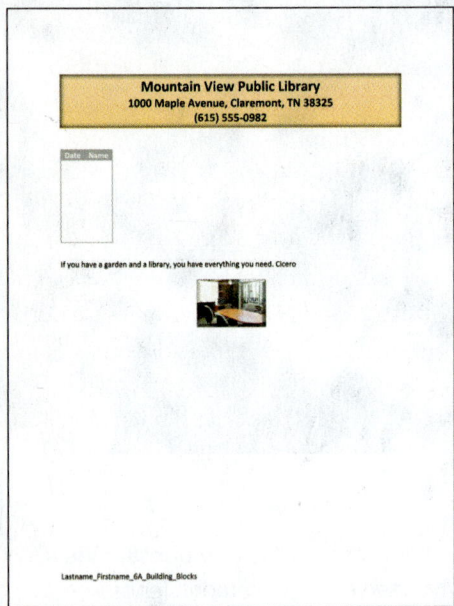

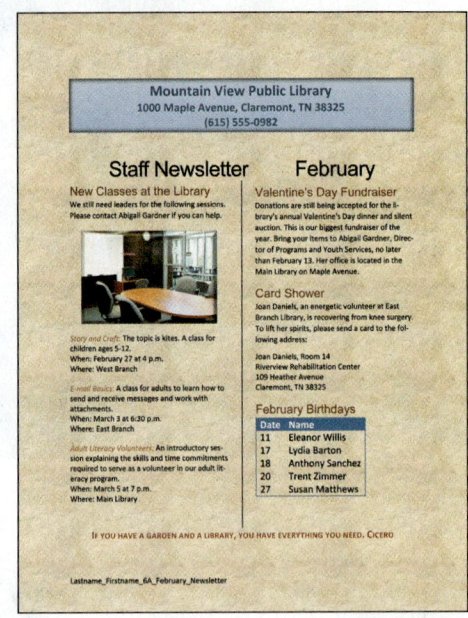

FIGURE 6.1 Project 6A February Newsletter

Objective 1 | Create Custom Building Blocks

Video W6-1

Building blocks are reusable pieces of content or other document parts—for example, headers, footers, page number formats—that are stored in galleries. The Headers gallery, the Footers gallery, the Page Numbers gallery, and the Bibliographies gallery, some of which you have already used, are all examples of building block galleries. You can also create your own building blocks for content that you use frequently.

Activity 6.01 | Inserting a Text Box and Creating a Custom Building Block

Recall that a *text box* is a movable, resizable container for text or graphics. In this activity, you will create a distinctive text box that the library can use for any documents requiring the library's contact information.

1 Start Word, and then click **Blank document**. Press F12. In the **Save As** dialog box, navigate to the location where you are saving your files for this chapter, and then create a folder named **Word Chapter 6** Save the document as **Lastname_Firstname_6A_Building_Blocks** At the bottom of the document, right-click in the footer area, and then click **Edit Footer**. On the ribbon, in the **Insert group**, click **Document Info**, and then click **File Name**. **Close** the footer area. If necessary, display the rulers and formatting marks.

2 Press Enter two times, and then position the insertion point in the first blank paragraph.

3 On the **INSERT tab**, in the **Text group**, click **Text Box**. Notice that predesigned, built-in building blocks display in the **Text Box** gallery. Click the first text box—**Simple Text Box**.

> A text box containing placeholder text displays at the top of your document. Text boxes can be formatted like other graphic elements in Word and saved as building blocks.

4 On the **FORMAT tab**, in the **Shape Styles group**, click **More** ⬇. In the **Shape Styles** gallery, in the fourth row, click the fifth style—**Subtle Effect – Gold, Accent 4**.

5 On the **FORMAT tab**, if the **Size group** is visible, change the **Shape Width** ⬚ Width: 6.49" ⬍ to **6.5"**; otherwise, to the right of the **Arrange group**, click **Size**, and then change the **Shape Width** ⬚ Width: 6.49" ⬍ to **6.5"**. Compare your screen with Figure 6.2.

> Depending on the resolution setting of your monitor, either the Size group or the Size button will display.

FIGURE 6.2

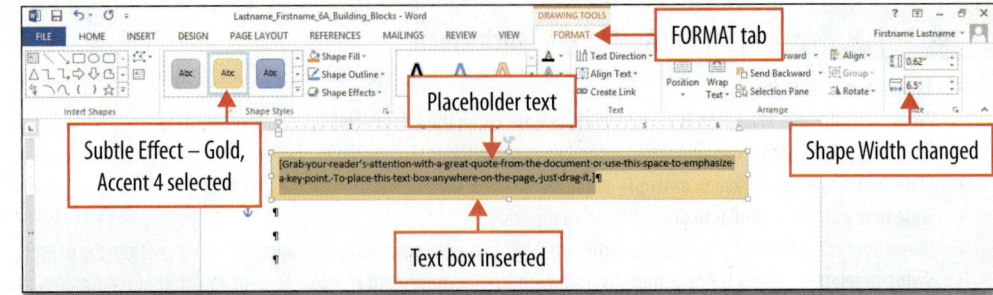

---

6 ▶ On the **FORMAT tab**, in the **Shape Styles group**, click **Shape Effects**. Point to **Shadow**, and then under **Inner**, in the second row, click the second style—**Inside Center**.

7 ▶ In the text box, type the following text to replace the placeholder text: **Mountain View Public Library** Press Enter, and then type **1000 Maple Avenue, Claremont, TN 38325** Press Enter, and then type **(615) 555-0982**

8 ▶ Select all three paragraphs. On the mini toolbar, click **Styles**, and then in the **Styles** gallery, click **No Spacing**. With the three paragraphs selected, press Ctrl + E to center the paragraphs. Select the first paragraph, change the **Font Size** to **20**, and then apply **Bold** B . Select the second and third paragraphs, change the **Font Size** to **16**, and then apply **Bold** B . Notice that the height of the text box automatically adjusts to accommodate the text.

9 ▶ Click in the first paragraph to deselect the text. Click the outer edge of the text box so that none of the text is selected, but that the text box itself is selected and displays sizing handles. Compare your screen with Figure 6.3.

FIGURE 6.3

10 ▶ On the **INSERT tab**, in the **Text group**, click **Text Box**, and then click **Save Selection to Text Box Gallery**. In the **Create New Building Block** dialog box, in the **Name** box, type **Library Information** Notice that the **Gallery** box displays *Text Boxes*.

By selecting the Text Boxes gallery, this building block will display in the gallery of other text box building blocks.

11 ▶ In the **Description** box, type **Use as the library contact information in newsletters, flyers, public meeting agendas, and other publications** Compare your screen with Figure 6.4.

FIGURE 6.4

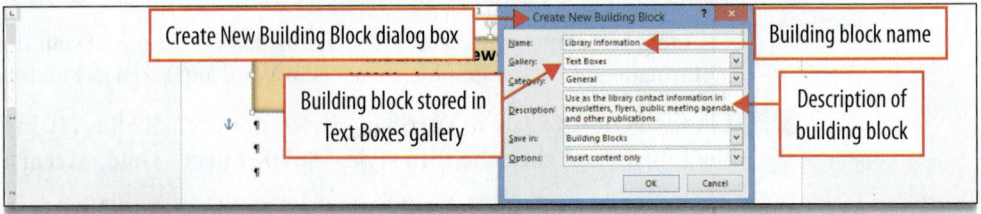

12 ▶ Click **OK** to close the dialog box and save the building block. **Save** 🖫 your document.

ALERT! **Saving Building Blocks**

Building blocks that you create in a gallery are saved in the Word software on the computer at which you are working. The document you are creating here is only for the purpose of submitting it to your instructor or to distribute to someone else who would like to use the building blocks on his or her computer.

Activity 6.02 | Using the Building Blocks Organizer to View, Edit, and Move Building Blocks

The ***Building Blocks Organizer*** enables you to view—in a single location—all of the available building blocks from all the different galleries.

1 On the **INSERT tab**, in the **Text group**, click **Quick Parts**.

Quick Parts refers to all of the reusable pieces of content that are available to insert into a document, including building blocks, document properties, and fields.

2 From the list, click **Building Blocks Organizer**. In the **Building Blocks Organizer** dialog box, in the upper left corner, click **Name** to sort the building blocks alphabetically by name.

Here you can view all of the building blocks available in Word. In this dialog box, you can also delete a building block, edit its properties—for example, change the name, description, or gallery location—or select and insert it into a document.

3 By using the scroll bar in the center of the **Building Blocks Organizer** dialog box, scroll down until you see your building block that begins *Library*, and then click to select it. Compare your screen with Figure 6.5.

You can see that Word provides numerous building blocks. In the preview area on the right, notice that under the preview of the building block, the name and description that you entered displays.

FIGURE 6.5

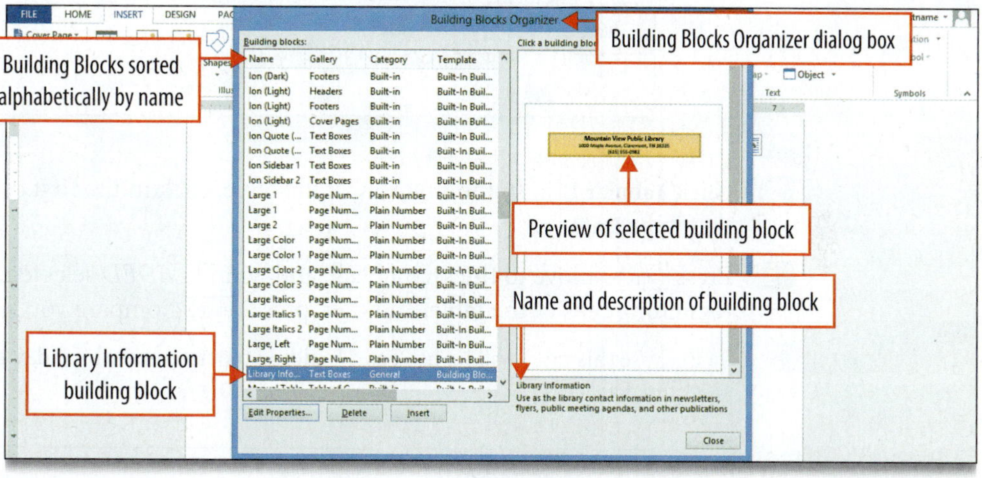

4 In the **Building Blocks Organizer** dialog box, click **Edit Properties**. In the **Modify Building Block** dialog box, click the **Save in box arrow**. In the displayed list, notice that *Building Blocks* is selected.

By default, the text box building block you created is saved in a folder that contains all predefined building blocks. You can move a building block to a document template by selecting the name of the file from the list. In this case, only the Normal template displays in the list.

5 Be sure *Building Blocks* is selected in the list, and then in the **Modify Building Block** dialog box, click in the **Description** box.

6 In the **Description** box, select the text *public*, and then press Delete.

You can edit building block properties in the Modify Building Block dialog box. In this case, you are changing the description of the text box building block.

7 In the **Modify Building Block** dialog box, click **OK**. In the **Microsoft Word** message box, when asked if you want to redefine the building block entry, click **Yes**. In the lower right corner of the **Building Blocks Organizer** dialog box, click **Close**.

Activity 6.03 | Saving a Custom Building Block as a Quick Table

Quick Tables are tables that are stored as building blocks. Word includes many predesigned Quick Tables, and you can also create your own tables and save them as Quick Tables in the Quick Tables gallery. In this activity you will modify an existing Quick Table and then save it as a new building block. Benedetta Herman will use this table to announce staff birthdays in the quarterly newsletter and in the monthly staff bulletin.

1 Below the text box, position the insertion point in the second blank paragraph. On the **INSERT tab**, in the **Tables group**, click **Table**, and then at the bottom of the list, point to **Quick Tables**. In the **Quick Tables** gallery, scroll down to locate **Tabular List**, as shown in Figure 6.6.

FIGURE 6.6

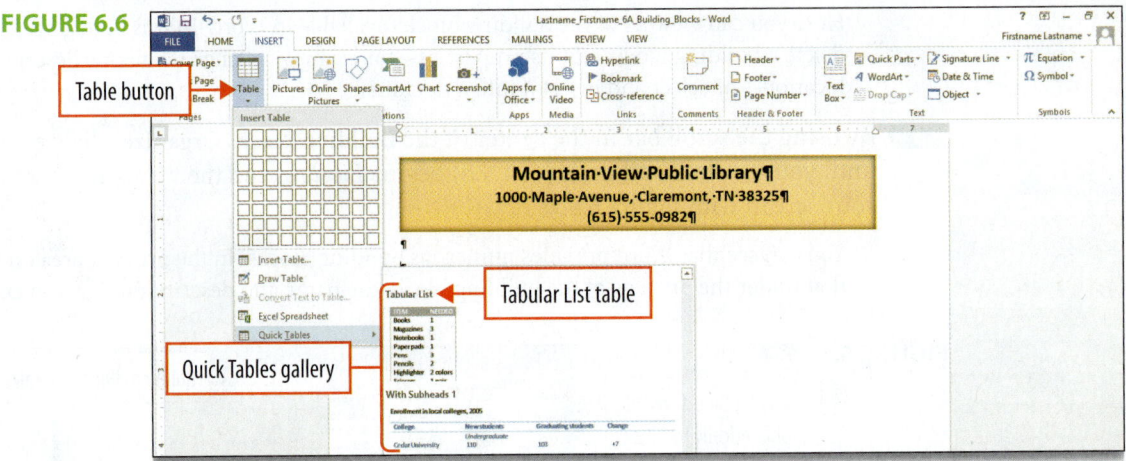

2 Click **Tabular List**. In the first row of the table, click in the first cell, select the text *ITEM*, and then type **Date**

3 Press Tab to move to the second cell, and with *NEEDED* selected, type **Name** Select all the remaining cells of the table, and then press Delete. Compare your screen with Figure 6.7.

Because this table will be used as a building block to enter birthday information, the sample text is not needed.

FIGURE 6.7

ALERT!   **Viewing Gridline**

If the table borders do not display, under TABLE TOOLS, click the LAYOUT tab, and then in the Table group, click View Gridlines.

---

4 Click in the table, point slightly outside of the upper left corner of the table, and then click the **table move handle** to select the entire table.

5 With the table selected, on the **INSERT tab**, in the **Tables group**, click **Table**. In the displayed list, point to **Quick Tables**, and then at the bottom of the list, click **Save Selection to Quick Tables Gallery**.

6 In the **Create New Building Block** dialog box, in the **Name** box, type **Birthday Table** In the **Description** box, type **Use for staff birthdays in newsletters and bulletins** Compare your screen with Figure 6.8.

FIGURE 6.8

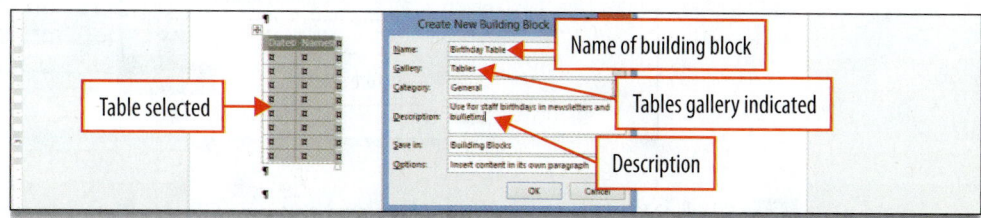

7 Click **OK** to save the table in the **Quick Tables** gallery. **Save** 💾 your document.

Activity 6.04 | Saving a Picture and an AutoText Entry as Quick Parts

In this activity, you will modify an image and save it as a building block so that Benedetta Herman can use it in any document that includes information about library classes.

1 Click in the second blank paragraph below the table. On the same line, point to display the ⊥ pointer at approximately **3.25 inches on the horizontal ruler** as shown in Figure 6.9.

> The *click and type pointer* is the text select—I-beam—pointer with various attached shapes that indicate which formatting—left-aligned, centered, or right-aligned—will be applied when you double-click in a blank area of the document. In this case, if you double-click, the paragraph will be formatted with center alignment.

FIGURE 6.9

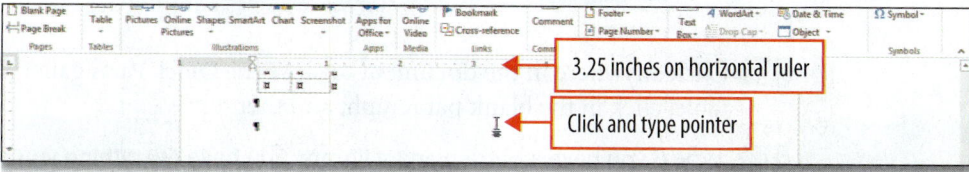

2 At the **3.25 inches mark on the horizontal ruler**, double-click to change the blank paragraph formatting to center alignment. On the **INSERT tab**, in the **Illustrations group**, click **Pictures**.

3 In the **Insert Picture** dialog box, navigate to your student files, select the file **w06A_Classes**, and then click **Insert**.

4 With the picture selected, on the **FORMAT tab**, in the **Picture Styles group**, click **Picture Effects**. Point to **Bevel**, and then under **Bevel**, in the first row, click the fourth bevel—**Cool Slant**.

5 On the **FORMAT tab**, in the **Size group**, change the **Shape Width** to **1.3"**.

 **BY TOUCH**   Tap the picture, and then press and drag the picture's resize handle.

6 With the picture selected, on the **INSERT tab**, in the **Text group**, click **Quick Parts**. From the list, click **Save Selection to Quick Part Gallery**.

> By choosing the Save Selection to Quick Part Gallery command, building blocks that you create are saved in the Quick Parts gallery and assigned to the General category. However, you can save the building block in any of the other relevant galleries or create your own custom gallery. You can also create your own category if you want to do so.

7 In the **Create New Building Block** dialog box, in the **Name** box, type **Classes Picture** and then in the **Description** box, type **Use this picture in documents containing information about the library classes** Compare your screen with Figure 6.10.

You can create and then select any content and save it as a building block in this manner.

FIGURE 6.10

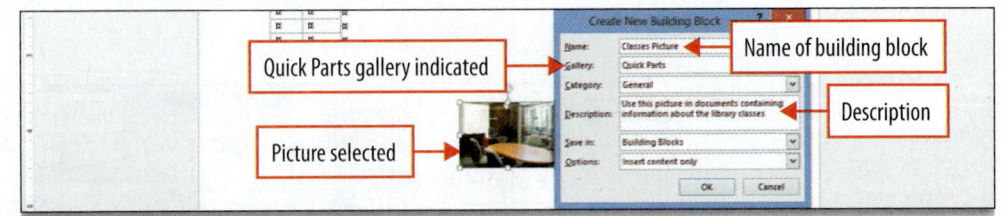

8 Click **OK** to close the dialog box and save the **Classes Picture** building block.

Your new building block is saved; you can insert it in a document by selecting it from the Quick Parts gallery.

9 On the **INSERT tab**, in the **Text group**, click **Quick Parts**, and then point to **Classes Picture**. Compare your screen with Figure 6.11.

Your picture displays under General in the Quick Parts gallery.

FIGURE 6.11

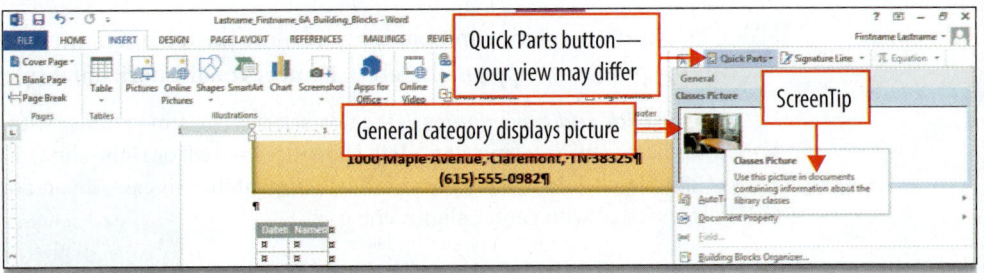

10 Click anywhere in the document to close the **Quick Parts** gallery. Immediately below the table, click in the blank paragraph, and then press Enter.

11 Type **If you have a garden and a library, you have everything you need. Cicero**

12 Select the text you just typed. Be careful not to select the paragraph mark. On the **INSERT tab**, in the **Text group**, click **Quick Parts**. From the list, click **AutoText**, and then click **Save Selection to AutoText Gallery**.

13 In the **Create New Building Block** dialog box, in the **Name** box, type **Library Quote** and then in the **Description** box, type **Quote for newsletter** Click the **Save in box arrow**, and then click **Building Blocks**. Compare your screen with Figure 6.12.

FIGURE 6.12

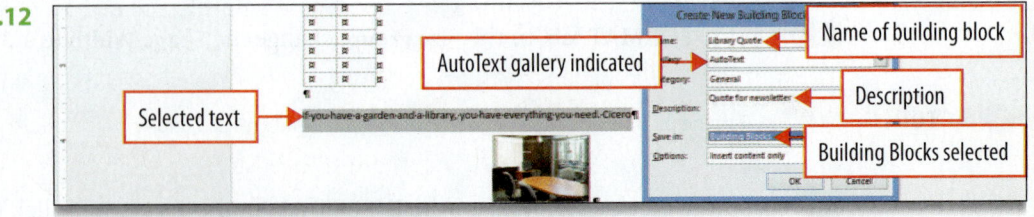

14 Click **OK** to close the dialog box, and then press ⌃ Ctrl + ⌂ Home. Click the **FILE tab**, click the **Info tab**, and then click **Show All Properties**. In the **Tags** box, type **library newsletter, building blocks** In the **Subject** box, type your course name and section number. If necessary, edit the author name to display your name.

15 From **Backstage** view, click **Save**. Press ⌃ Ctrl + ⌂ W to close the document and leave Word open for the next activity.

The purpose of this document is to submit a copy of your building blocks to your instructor. After the building blocks are stored in a gallery, they are saved on your system and no document is required unless you want to distribute your building blocks to someone else who would like to use the building blocks on his or her computer.

 **ANOTHER WAY**   Click the FILE tab, and then click Close to close a document and leave Word open.

ALERT! | **What Happens If I Accidentally Close Word?**

If you accidentally close Word, in the dialog box regarding changes to building blocks, click Save to accept the changes.

Objective 2   Create and Save a Theme Template

Video W6-2

Recall that a ***theme*** is a predefined combination of colors, fonts, and line and fill effects that look good together and is applied to an entire document by a single selection. Word comes with a group of predefined themes—the default theme is named *Office*. You can also create your own theme by selecting any combination of colors, fonts, and effects, which, when saved, creates a ***theme template***. A theme template, which stores a set of colors, fonts, and effects—lines and fill effects—can be shared with other Office programs, such as Excel and PowerPoint.

Activity 6.05 | Creating Custom Theme Colors and Theme Fonts

In this activity, you will create a custom theme.

1 Press ⌃ Ctrl + ⌂ N to display a new blank document.

2 On the **DESIGN tab**, in the **Document Formatting group**, click **Themes**. In the **Themes** gallery, click **Organic**.

3 On the **DESIGN tab**, in the **Document Formatting group**, click **Colors** . In the **Theme Colors** gallery, take a moment to examine the various color schemes, scrolling as necessary, and then at the bottom of the list, click **Customize Colors**.

4 In the **Create New Theme Colors** dialog box, click the **Text/Background – Dark 1 arrow**, and then under **Theme Colors**, in the seventh column, click the fifth color—**Blue-Gray, Accent 3, Darker 25%**. Using the same technique, change **Accent 1** to **Red, Accent 4**—in the eighth column, the first color, and then change **Accent 4** to **Blue-Gray, Accent 3, Lighter 40%**—in the seventh column, the fourth color. In the **Name** box, delete the existing text, and then type **Newsletter Colors** Compare your screen with Figure 6.13.

A set of theme colors contains four text and background colors, six accent colors, and two hyperlink colors. You can select a new color for any category and save the combination of colors with a new name. In this case, you are changing the colors for the Text/Background – Dark 1, Accent 1, and Accent 4 categories, and saving the color combination with the name Newsletter Colors. The Sample box displays the modified theme color scheme.

FIGURE 6.13

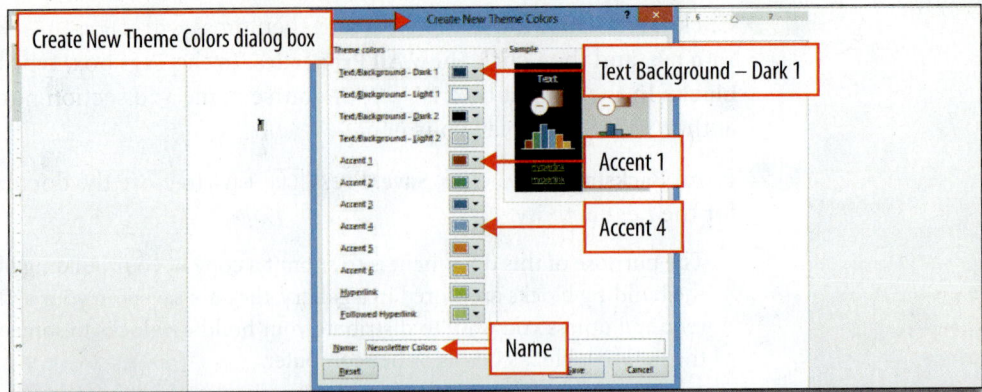

Create New Theme Colors dialog box

Text Background – Dark 1

Accent 1

Accent 4

Name

5 ▶ Click **Save** to close the **Create New Theme Colors** dialog box. In the **Document Formatting group**, click **Fonts** A , and then at the bottom of the list, click **Customize Fonts**.

Theme fonts contain a heading font—the upper font—and a body text font—the lower font. You can use an existing set of built-in fonts for your new theme, or define new sets of fonts.

6 ▶ In the **Create New Theme Fonts** dialog box, click the **Heading font arrow**, scroll as necessary to locate and then click **Arial**. Click the **Body font arrow**, scroll as necessary, and then click **Calibri**. In the **Name** box, delete the existing text, and then type **Newsletter Fonts**

The custom Theme Fonts—Newsletter Fonts—includes the Arial heading font and the Calibri body text font.

7 ▶ Click **Save** to close the **Create New Theme Fonts** dialog box. In the **Document Formatting group**, click **Effects** .

Theme effects are sets of lines and fill effects. Here you can see the lines and fill effects for each predefined theme. You cannot create your own set of theme effects, but you can choose any set of effects to combine with other theme colors and theme fonts.

8 ▶ In the **Theme Effects** gallery, click **Office**.

9 ▶ Leave Word open—you will save your custom theme in the next activity.

Activity 6.06 | Creating a Custom Theme Template

To use your custom theme in other Microsoft Office files, you can save it as a theme template.

1 ▶ In the **Document Formatting group**, click **Themes**, and then at the bottom of the **Themes** gallery, click **Save Current Theme** to display the **Save Current Theme** dialog box. Compare your screen with Figure 6.14.

By default, saving a new theme displays the Templates folder, which includes the Document Themes folder, containing separate folders for Theme Colors, Theme Effects, and Theme Fonts. The Save as type box specifies the file type *Office Theme*.

If you save your theme in the Templates folder, it is available to the Office programs on the computer at which you are working. In a college or organization, you may not have permission to update this folder, but on your own computer, you can save your themes here if you want to do so.

FIGURE 6.14

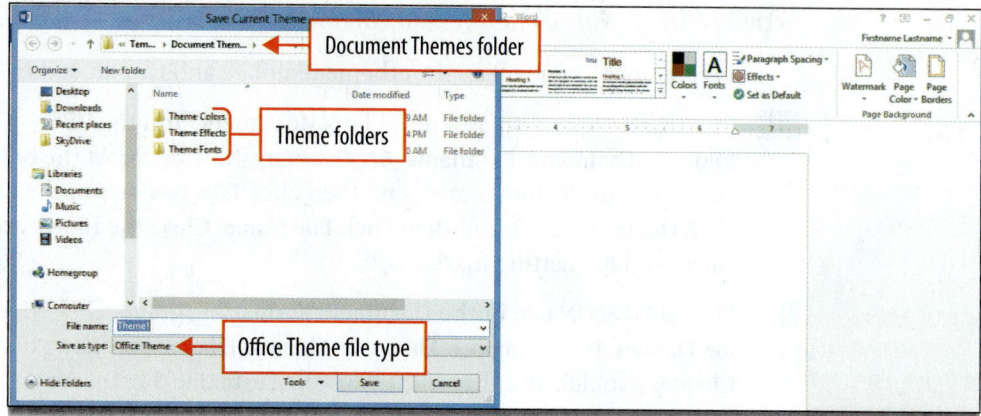

2 In the **Save Current Theme** dialog box, navigate to your **Word Chapter 6** folder. In the **File name** box, type **Lastname_Firstname_6A_Library_Theme** and then click **Save**.

For the purpose of this instruction, you are saving the theme to your Word Chapter 6 folder.

3 In the **Document Formatting group**, click **Themes**, and then click **Browse for Themes**. In the **Choose Theme or Themed Document** dialog box, navigate to your **Word Chapter 6** folder, right-click your file **Lastname_Firstname_6A_Library_Theme**, and then click **Properties**. Compare your screen with Figure 6.15.

The Properties dialog box for the Theme displays. A Microsoft Office theme is saved with the file extension .thmx. By default, a theme template is set to open with PowerPoint; however, the theme can also be applied in Word or Excel.

FIGURE 6.15

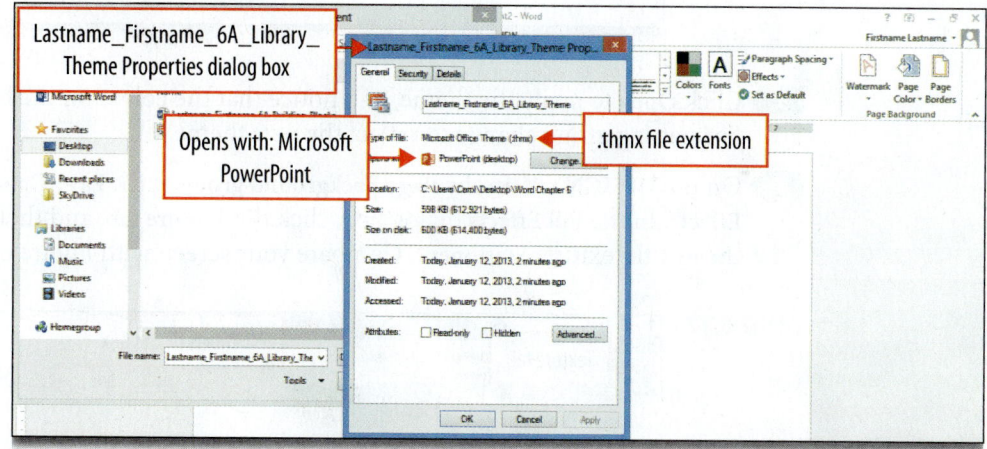

4 Click **OK** to close the **Properties** dialog box, and then **Close** ✕ the **Choose Theme or Themed Document** dialog box. Click the **FILE tab**, and then **Close** the blank document without saving changes. Keep Word open for the next activity.

Objective 3 Create a Document by Using Building Blocks

Video W6-3

One of the benefits of creating building blocks and theme templates is that they can be used repeatedly to create individual documents. The building blocks ensure consistency in format and structure, and the theme template provides consistency in colors, fonts, and effects.

Activity 6.07 | Formatting Text in Columns

In this activity, you will apply a theme template and format text in columns.

1 Press ⌈Ctrl⌉ + ⌈N⌉ to display a new blank document, and then Save it in your **Word Chapter 6** folder as **Lastname_Firstname_6A_February_Newsletter** At the bottom of the document, right-click in the footer area, and then click **Edit Footer**. On the ribbon, in the **Insert group**, click **Document Info**, and then click **File Name**. **Close** the footer area. If necessary, display the rulers and formatting marks.

2 On the **DESIGN tab**, in the **Document Formatting group**, click **Themes**, and then click **Browse for Themes**. In the **Choose Theme or Themed Document** dialog box, navigate to your **Word Chapter 6** folder, and then click your file **Lastname_Firstname_6A_Library_Theme**. Compare your screen with Figure 6.16.

FIGURE 6.16

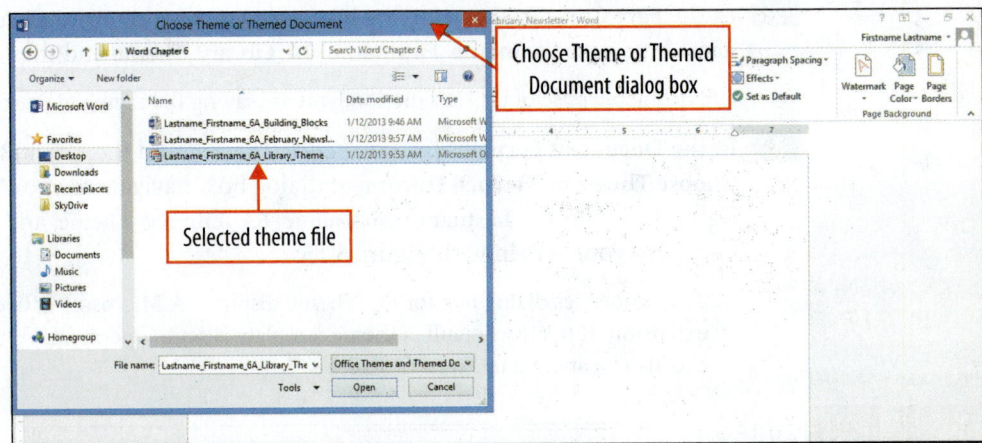

3 Click **Open** to apply the theme, and notice that the colors on the buttons in the Document Formatting group change to reflect the new theme.

4 On the **DESIGN tab**, in the **Page Background group**, click **Page Color**, and then click **Fill Effects**. In the **Fill Effects** dialog box, click the **Texture tab**, and then in the fourth row, click the fourth texture–**Stationery**. Compare your screen with Figure 6.17.

FIGURE 6.17

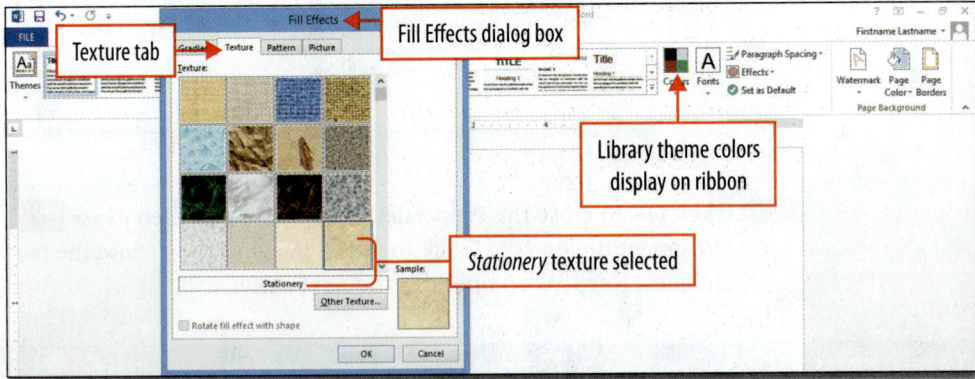

5 Click **OK** to apply the textured background.

6 Press ⌈Enter⌉ two times. Type **Staff Newsletter** press ⌈Tab⌉ two times, type **February** and then press ⌈Enter⌉. Select the paragraph you just typed, on the mini toolbar, click **Styles**, and then click **Title**. Press ⌈Ctrl⌉ + ⌈E⌉ to center the paragraph.

7 Above the title, select the two blank paragraphs, and then on the **HOME tab**, in the **Styles group**, click **No Spacing**. Below the title, position the insertion point in the blank paragraph. On the **HOME tab**, in the **Styles group**, click **Normal**. Select the paragraph mark, and then compare your screen with Figure 6.18.

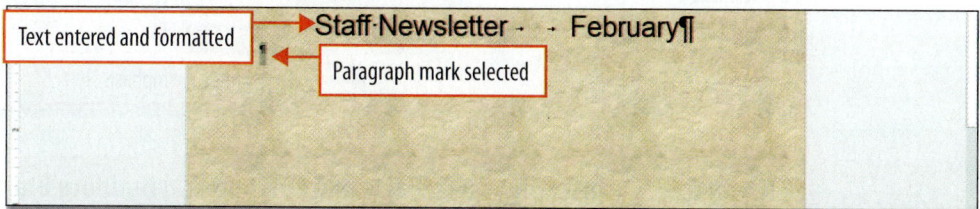

FIGURE 6.18

Text entered and formatted

Staff·Newsletter · · February¶

Paragraph mark selected

8 With the paragraph mark selected, on the **PAGE LAYOUT tab**, in the **Page Setup group**, click **Columns**, and then click **Two**. Click to the left of the paragraph mark, and then compare your screen with Figure 6.19.

A continuous section break is inserted at the end of the previous paragraph. The remainder of the document will be formatted in two columns.

FIGURE 6.19

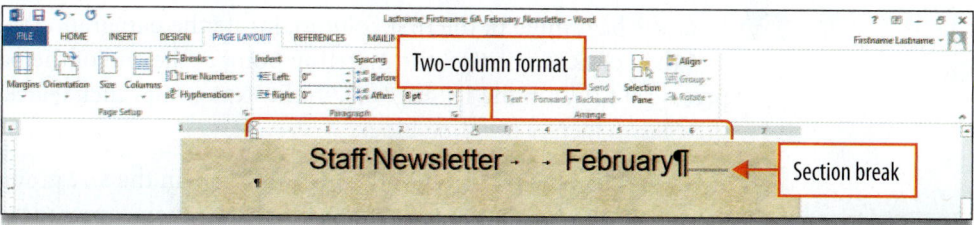

Two-column format

Staff·Newsletter · · February¶

Section break

9 On the **INSERT tab**, in the **Text group**, click the **Object arrow**, and then click **Text from File**. In the **Insert File** dialog box, navigate to your student files, click **w06A_February_Articles**, and then click **Insert**.

Word inserts the text in the first column.

10 On the **PAGE LAYOUT tab**, in the **Page Setup group**, click the **Columns arrow**, and then click **More Columns** to display the **Columns** dialog box.

You can modify column formats in the Columns dialog box. For example, you can change the number of columns, the width of the columns, the spacing after columns, and insert a line to separate the columns.

11 In the **Columns** dialog box, select the **Line between** check box, and then click **OK**. Compare your screen with Figure 6.20.

A line displays between the two columns.

FIGURE 6.20

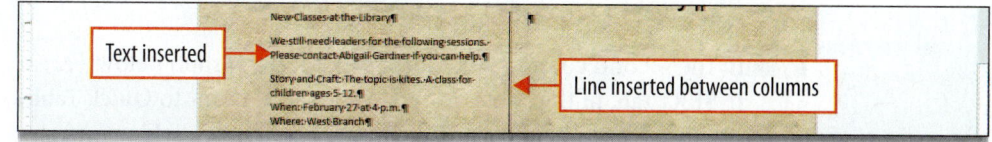

Text inserted

New·Classes·at·the·Library¶

We·still·need·leaders·for·the·following·sessions.· Please·contact·Abigail·Gardner·if·you·can·help.¶

Story·and·Craft:·The·topic·is·kites.·A·class·for· children·ages·5-12.¶
When:·February·27·at·4·p.m.¶
Where:·West·Branch¶

Line inserted between columns

12 Select the paragraph *New Classes at the Library*. Press and hold Ctrl, and then select the paragraphs *Valentine's Day Fundraiser* and *Card Shower*. On the mini toolbar, click **Styles**, and then click **Heading 1**.

13 In the *New Classes* section, select the headings *Story and Craft:*, *E-mail Basics:*, and *Adult Literacy Volunteers:*—be sure to include each colon. Display the **Styles** gallery, and then click **Intense Emphasis**.

14 At the top of the second column, click in the blank paragraph.

 **15** Type **February Birthdays** and then press Enter. Select the text you just typed, display the **Styles** gallery, and then click **Heading 1**. Compare your screen with Figure 6.21, and then **Save** 🔲 your document.

FIGURE 6.21

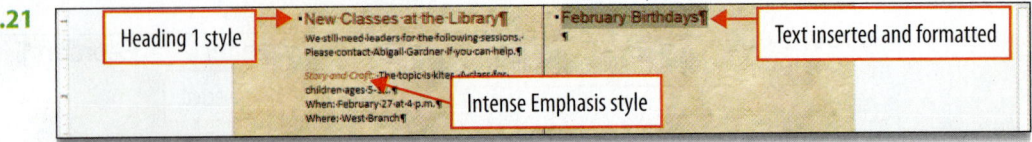

Activity 6.08 | Inserting Quick Parts and Customizing Building Blocks, and Manually Hyphenating a Document

In this activity, you will complete the newsletter by using the building blocks that you created.

1 Press Ctrl + Home. On the **INSERT tab**, in the **Text group**, click **Text Box**. Scroll to the bottom of the **Text Box** gallery, and then under **General**, click the **Library Information** building block.

> The theme colors of your custom theme are applied to the building block and the text in the columns is redistributed.

2 Near the beginning of the first column, locate the paragraph that begins *We still need leaders*, and then click to position the insertion point at the end of the paragraph. Press Enter, and then press Ctrl + E. On the **INSERT tab**, in the **Text group**, click **Quick Parts**. Under **General**, click the **Classes Picture** building block.

3 Click to select the picture. On the **FORMAT tab**, in the **Size group**, change the **Shape Height** 📏 Height: 0.19" to **1.7"**. Deselect the picture, and then compare your screen with Figure 6.22.

FIGURE 6.22

4 At the bottom of the first column, position the insertion point to the left of the heading *Valentine's Day Fundraiser*. On the **PAGE LAYOUT tab**, in the **Page Setup group**, click **Breaks**, and then under **Page Breaks**, click **Column**.

> You can insert a manual column break to define the point where text should flow to the next column. In this case, the heading is moved to the beginning of the second column.

5 With the insertion point to the left of *Valentine's*, on the **PAGE LAYOUT tab**, in the **Paragraph group**, change the **Spacing Before** to **18 pt**.

6 In the second column, click in the blank paragraph below *February Birthdays*. On the **INSERT tab**, in the **Tables group**, click **Table**, point to **Quick Tables**, scroll toward the bottom of the list, and then under **General**, click **Birthday Table**.

7 In the second row of the table, position the insertion point in the first cell, and then type **11** Press Tab, and then type **Eleanor Willis** Press Tab. Use the same technique to type the following text in the table.

17	Lydia Barton
18	Anthony Sanchez
20	Trent Zimmer
27	Susan Matthews

8 Select the last three empty rows of the table. On the mini toolbar, click **Delete**, and then click **Delete Rows**. Click the **table move handle** 🔀, and then on the mini toolbar, change the **Font Size** to **14**.

9 At the bottom of the second column, select the blank paragraph mark. With the paragraph mark selected, on the **PAGE LAYOUT tab**, in the **Page Setup group**, click **Columns**, and then click **One**.

> The existing text remains formatted in two columns; however, the bottom of the document returns to one column—full page width.

10 With the paragraph mark selected, on the **INSERT tab**, in the **Text group**, click **Quick Parts**, click **AutoText**, and then click **Library Quote**. Select the inserted text. On the mini toolbar, click **Styles**, click **Intense Reference**, and then change the **Font Size** to **14**. Press Ctrl + E, and then deselect the text. Compare your screen with Figure 6.23.

> The Library Quote AutoText is inserted and centered between the left and right margins.

FIGURE 6.23

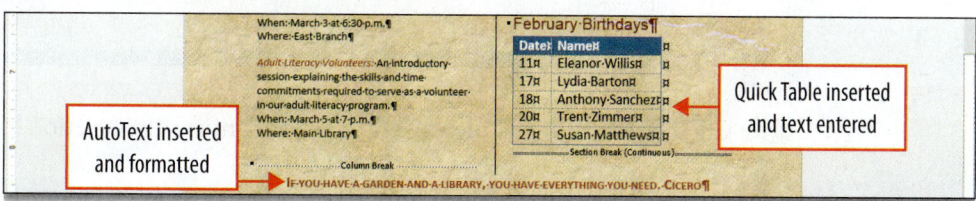

11 **Save** 💾 your document.

12 Press Ctrl + Home. On the **PAGE LAYOUT tab**, in the **Page Setup group**, click **Hyphenation**, and then click **Manual** to display the **Manual Hyphenation: English (United States)** dialog box.

> *Hyphenation* is a tool in Word that controls how words are split between two lines. By selecting Manual, you can control which words are hyphenated.

13 In the **Manual Hyphenation: English (United States)** dialog box, in the **Hyphenate at** box, with *at-tach-ments* displayed, click **No** to reject hyphenating the word. In the **Hyphenate at** box, with *ses-sion* displayed, click **Yes** to accept the hyphenated word. Using the same technique, click **Yes** to accept all remaining hyphenated words.

14 When a message displays indicating that the hyphenation is complete, click **OK**. **Save** 💾 your document.

Activity 6.09 | Deleting Custom Building Blocks, Theme Colors, and Theme Fonts

You can delete user-created building blocks, theme colors, and theme fonts if they are no longer needed. If you are sharing a computer with others, you must restore Word to its default settings. In this activity, you will delete the building blocks, theme colors, and theme fonts that you created.

1 On the **INSERT tab**, in the **Text group**, click **Quick Parts**. Right-click the **Classes Picture** building block, and then click **Organize and Delete**. Compare your screen with Figure 6.24.

> The Classes Picture building block is selected in the Building Blocks Organizer dialog box. A preview of the building block displays on the right. The name and description of the building block displays below the preview.

FIGURE 6.24

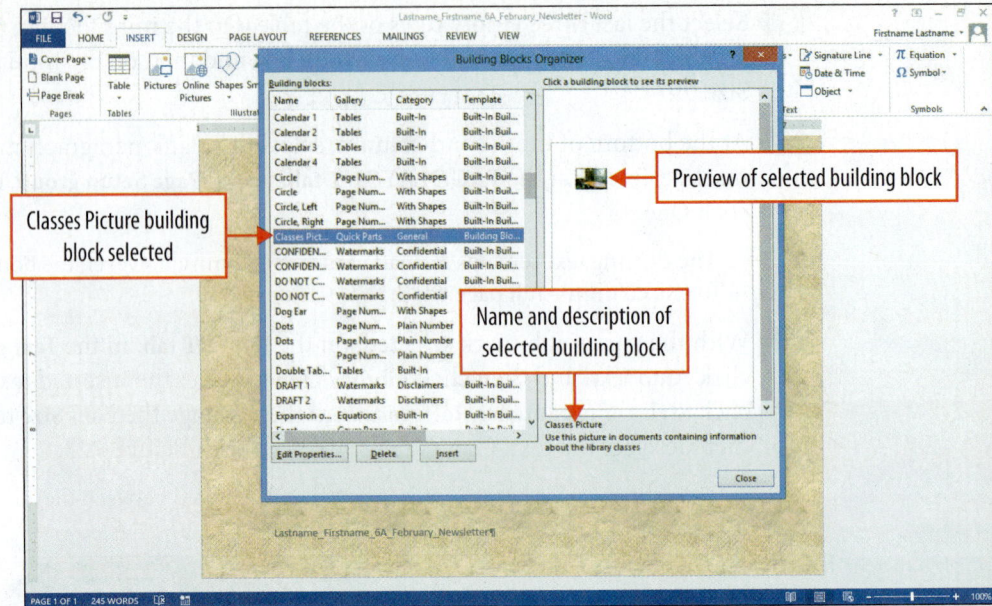

Classes Picture building block selected

Preview of selected building block

Name and description of selected building block

2 Click **Delete**. When a message displays to confirm the deletion, click **Yes**.

---

3 In the **Building Blocks Organizer** dialog box, in the upper left corner, click **Name** to sort the building blocks alphabetically by name.

4 By using the scroll bar in the center of the **Building Blocks Organizer** dialog box, scroll down until you see your building block that begins *Birthday*, and then click to select it. Click **Delete**, and then click **Yes** to confirm the deletion.

5 Using the same technique, scroll to locate your building block *Library Information*, and then delete it. Delete the **Library Quote** building block. **Close** the **Building Blocks Organizer** dialog box.

6 On the **DESIGN tab**, in the **Document Formatting group**, click **Colors**. At the top of the **Theme Colors** gallery, right-click **Newsletter Colors**, and then click **Delete**. When a message displays to confirm the deletion, click **Yes**. Using the same technique, display the **Theme Fonts** gallery, and then delete the **Newsletter Fonts**.

Because the theme—including the custom theme colors and theme fonts—has been saved, you no longer need the Newsletter Colors and Newsletter Fonts to display in the respective lists.

7 Click the **FILE tab**, click the **Info tab**, and then click **Show All Properties**. In the **Tags** box, type **library newsletter, February** In the **Subject** box, type your course name and section number. If necessary, edit the author name to display your name.

8 Save your document. Print your two Word documents—you cannot print the theme file— or submit all three files electronically as directed by your instructor. **Close** Word. When a message displays regarding changes to building blocks, click **Save** to accept the changes.

END | You have completed Project 6A

Events Schedule with Tracked Changes

PROJECT ACTIVITIES

In Activities 6.10 through 6.19, you will assist Abigail Gardner, Director of Programs and Youth Services, in using the markup tools in Word to add comments and make changes to a schedule of events. You will accept or reject each change, and then compare and combine your document with another draft version to create a final document. Your completed documents will look similar to Figure 6.25.

PROJECT FILES

For Project 6B, you will need the following files: You will save your files as:

w06B_Events_Schedule
w06B_Schedule_Revisions

Lastname_Firstname_6B_Events_Schedule
Lastname_Firstname_6B_Schedule_Revisions
Lastname_Firstname_6B_Schedule_Combined

PROJECT RESULTS

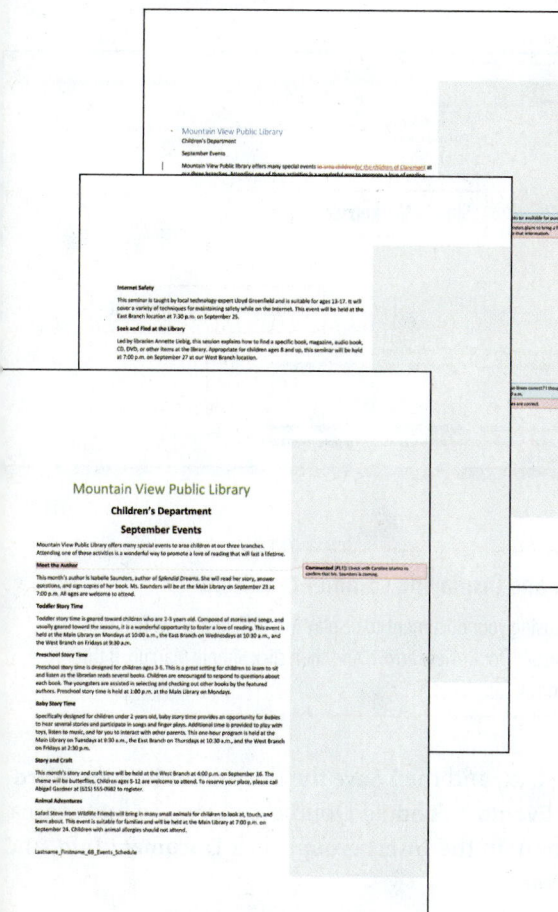
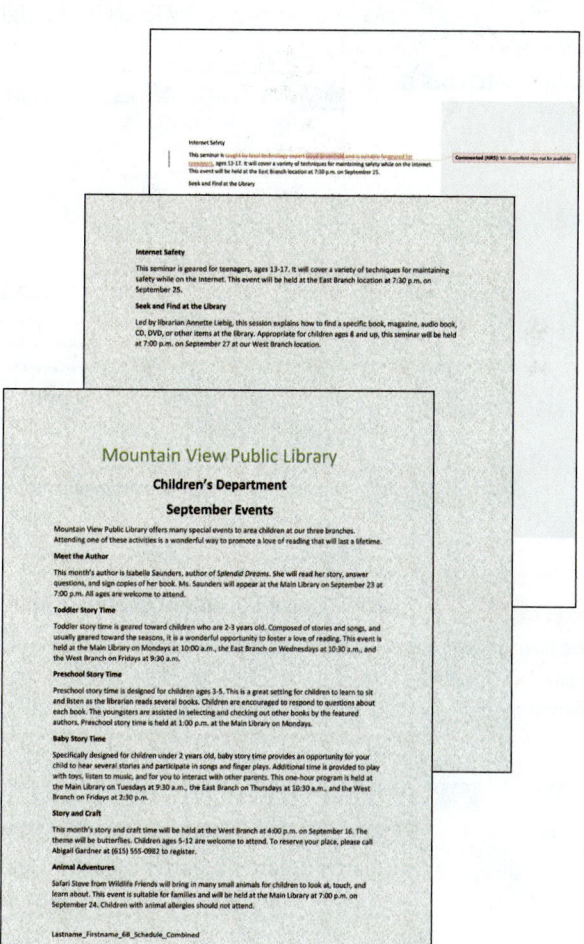

FIGURE 6.25 Project 6B Events Schedule

Video W6-4

Building a final document often involves more than one person. One person usually drafts the original and becomes the document **author**—or *owner*—and then others add their portions of text and comment on, or propose changes to, the text of others. A **reviewer** is someone who reviews and marks changes on a document.

A **comment** is a note that an author or reviewer adds to a document. Comments are a good way to communicate when more than one person is involved with the writing, reviewing, and editing process. Comments are like sticky notes attached to the document—they can be viewed and read by others but are not part of the document text.

Activity 6.10 | Inserting Comments

For the library's monthly schedule of events, Abigail Gardner has created a draft document; edits and comments have been added by others. In this activity, you will insert a comment to suggest confirming a scheduled guest.

1 Start Word. From your student files, locate and open the file **w06B_Events_Schedule**. If necessary, display the rulers and formatting marks. Compare your screen with Figure 6.26.

The document displays in **Simple Markup** view, in which **revisions**—changes made to a document—are indicated by vertical red lines in the left margin, and comments that have been made are indicated by icons in the right margin.

FIGURE 6.26

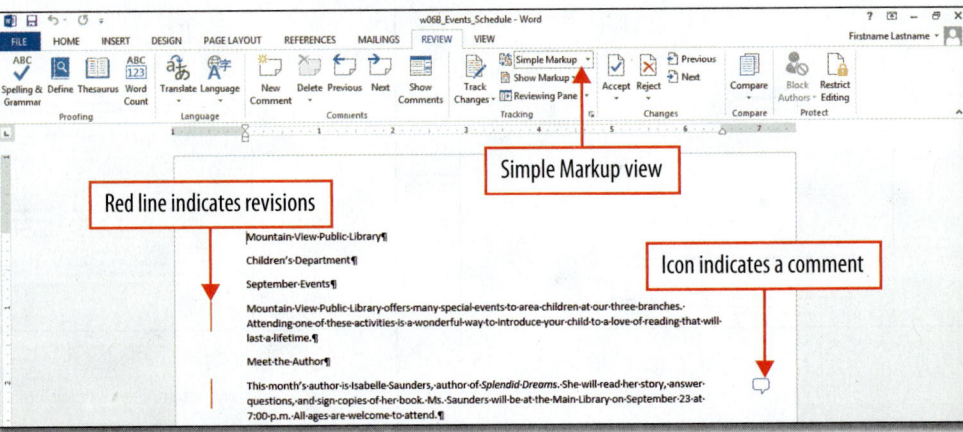

ALERT!   **Displaying a Document in Simple Markup View and Displaying Comments as Icons**

If you are sharing a computer, tracking changes features may have been used previously, causing your document to display in a different view. To display the document in Simple Markup view, on the REVIEW tab, in the Tracking group, click the Display for Review arrow, and then click Simple Markup. If the comments do not display as icons, in the Comments group, click Show Comments to turn off the command.

---

2 Click the **FILE tab**, display the **Save As** dialog box, and then **Save** the document in your **Word Chapter 6** folder as **Lastname_Firstname_6B_Events_Schedule** Double-click in the footer area, and then delete the existing text. On the ribbon, in the **Insert group**, click **Document Info**, and then click **File Name. Close** the footer area.

3 Press Ctrl + Home. On the **REVIEW tab**, in the **Comments group**, click **Show Comments**. Compare your screen with Figure 6.27.

The comments display in *balloons* in the nonprinting *markup area*. A balloon is the outline shape in which a comment or formatting change displays. The markup area is the space to the right or left of the document where comments and also formatting changes—for example, applying italic—display. Each comment includes the name of the reviewer who made the comment. Each reviewer's comments are identified by a distinct color. An image will also display if the reviewer is signed in with a Microsoft personal account or an Active Directory at work and has a picture associated with the profile.

FIGURE 6.27

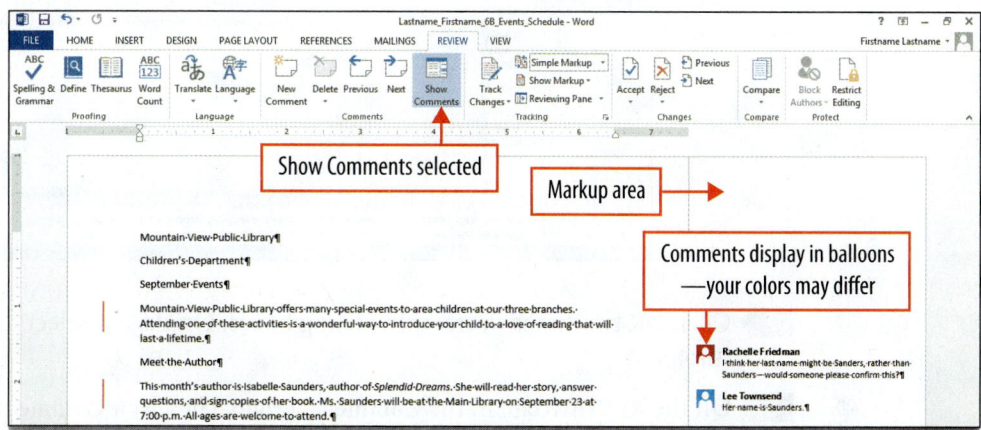

4 On the **REVIEW tab**, in the **Tracking group**, click the **Dialog Box Launcher**. In the **Track Changes Options** dialog box, click **Change User Name**.

5 In the **Word Options** dialog box, under **Personalize your copy of Microsoft Office**, on a piece of paper, make a note of the user name and initials—if you are using your own computer, your own name and initials may display.

The user name identifies the person who makes comments and changes in a document.

ALERT! | **Changing the User Name and Initials**

In a school lab or organization, you may not be able to change the user name and initials, so make a note of the name and initials currently displayed so that you can identify your revisions in this document.

---

6 If you are able to do so, in the **User name** box, delete any existing text, and then type your own first and last names. In the **Initials** box, delete any existing text, and then type your initials. Below the **Initials** box, select the **Always use these values regardless of sign in to Office** check box. Compare your screen with Figure 6.28. If you are unable to make this change, move to Step 7.

FIGURE 6.28

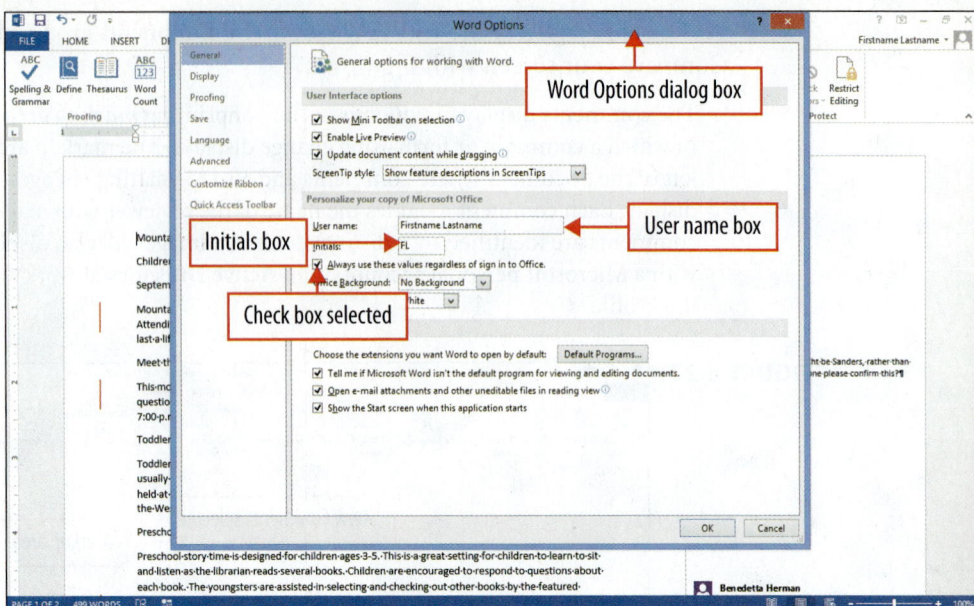

7 Click **OK** two times to close the dialog boxes. On **Page 1**, select the fifth paragraph *Meet the Author*.

8 On the **REVIEW tab**, in the **Comments group**, click **New Comment**, and notice that the comment balloon displays in the markup area with the user name. Type **Check with Barry Smith to confirm that Ms. Saunders is coming.** Click anywhere outside of the comment, and then compare your screen with Figure 6.29.

> You can insert a comment at a specific location in a document or to selected text, such as an entire paragraph. Your name—or the name configured for the computer at which you are working—displays at the beginning of the comment.

FIGURE 6.29

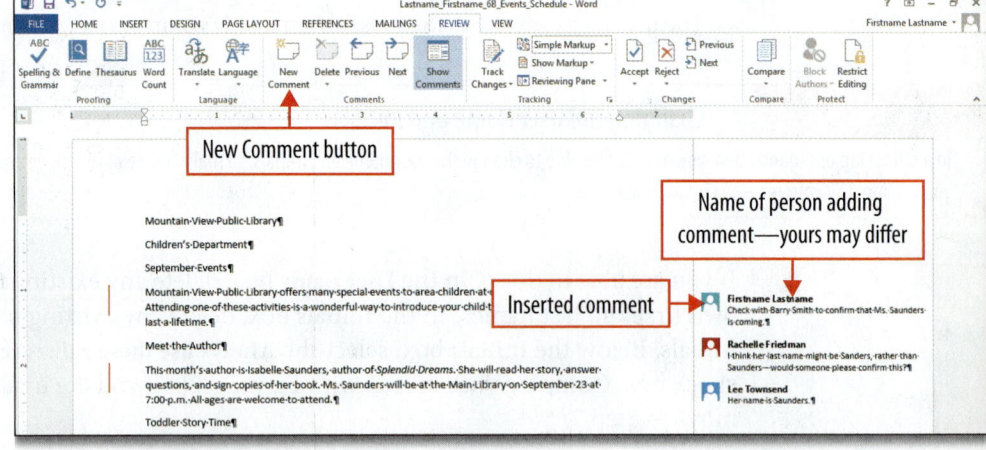

ANOTHER WAY   On the INSERT tab, in the Comments group, click New Comment.

9 Near the bottom of **Page 1**, locate the comment by Rachelle Friedman that begins *Should we mention*. Point to the balloon containing the comment and notice that shaded text displays in the document indicating where the comment was inserted.

10 In the top right corner of the balloon, click **Reply** 🔲. Compare your screen with Figure 6.30.

> Your name is inserted in the balloon. It is indented, indicating that this is a *reply* to Rachelle Friedman's comment. The insertion point displays below your name.

FIGURE 6.30

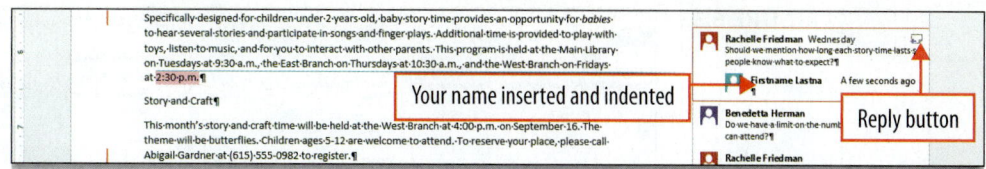

11 With the insertion point in the balloon, type **The program is scheduled for approximately one hour.** Click anywhere outside the comment, and then compare your screen with Figure 6.31.

FIGURE 6.31

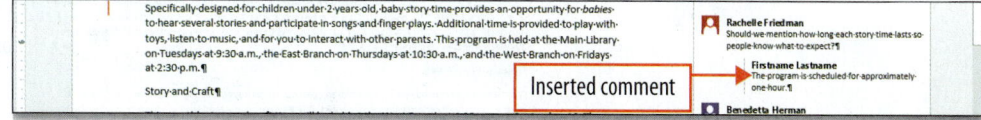

12 Save 💾 your document.

Activity 6.11 | Editing and Deleting Comments

Typically, comments are temporary. One person inserts a comment, another person answers the question or clarifies the text based on the comment—and then the comments are removed before the document is final. In this activity, you will replace text in your comment and delete comments.

1 Locate the comment you inserted referencing *Barry Smith*—the first comment in the document. Select the text *Barry Smith*, and then type **Caroline Marina** If necessary, press Spacebar.

In this manner, you can edit your comments.

2 Immediately below your comment, locate the comment created by Rachelle Friedman, which begins *I think her last name*, and the following comment created by *Lee Townsend*. Compare your screen with Figure 6.32.

Because the question asked by Rachelle Friedman has been answered by Lee Townsend, both comments can be deleted.

FIGURE 6.32

3 Click anywhere in the comment by *Rachelle Friedman*, and then in the **Comments group**, click **Delete**.

4 Point to the comment by *Lee Townsend*, right-click, and then from the shortcut menu, click **Delete Comment**.

Use either technique to delete a comment.

5 In the **Comments group**, click **Next**. In the markup area, notice that the balloon containing a comment by *Benedetta Herman* is selected. Compare your screen with Figure 6.33.

In the Comments group, you can use the Next and Previous buttons in this manner to navigate through the comments in a document.

FIGURE 6.33

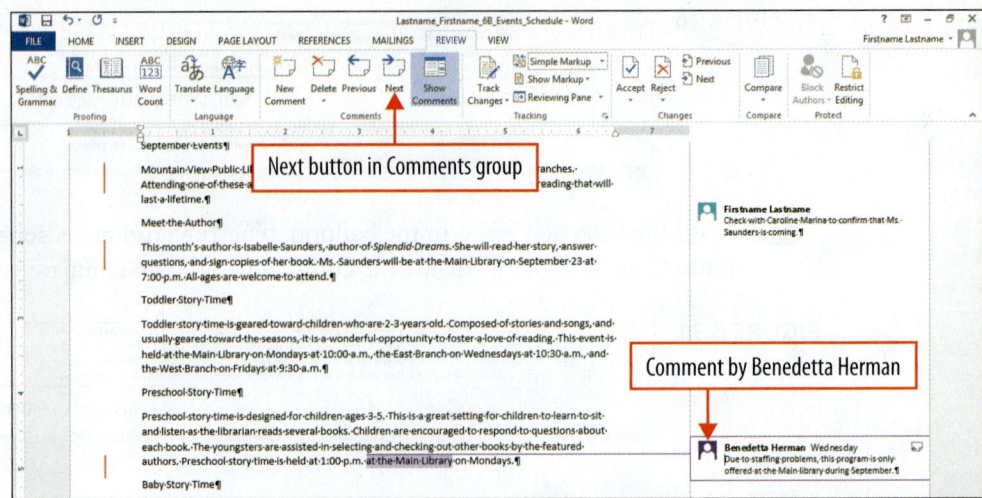

Next button in Comments group

Comment by Benedetta Herman

6 With the comment that begins *Due to staffing problems* selected, right-click, and then click **Delete Comment**.

7 In the **Comments group**, click **Next** three times to select the comment by Benedetta Herman that begins *Do we have*, and then use any technique you have practiced to delete the comment.

8 Scroll as necessary, and delete the two comments by Rachelle Friedman that begin *No, the room* and *We considered*. **Save** 💾 your document.

Four comments remain in the document.

More Knowledge | **Printing Comments**

To print the comments in a document, click the FILE tab, and then click Print. Under Settings, click the Print All Pages arrow, and then under Document Info, click List of Markup.

Objective 5 Track Changes in a Document

Video W6-5

When you turn on the *Track Changes* feature, it makes a record of—*tracks*—the changes made to a document. As you revise the document with your changes, Word uses markup to visually indicate insertions, deletions, comments, formatting changes, and content that has moved.

Each reviewer's revisions and comments display in a different color. This is useful if, for example, you want to quickly scan only for edits made by your supervisor or only for edits made by a coworker. After the document has been reviewed by the appropriate individuals, you can locate the changes and accept or reject the revisions on a case-by-case basis or globally in the entire document.

Activity 6.12 | Viewing All Changes in a Document

After one or more reviewers have made revisions and inserted comments, you can view the revisions in various ways. You can display the document in its original or final form, showing or hiding revisions and comments. Additionally, you can choose to view the revisions and comments by only some reviewers or view only a particular type of revision—for example, only formatting changes.

1 Press Ctrl + Home. On the **REVIEW tab**, in the **Tracking group**, locate the **Display for Review** box that displays the text *Simple Markup*. Click the **Display for Review arrow** to display a list. Compare your screen with Figure 6.34.

> Recall that *Simple Markup* view is a view for tracking changes; revisions are indicated by a vertical red bar in the left margin and comments are indicated by an icon in the right margin.
>
> *All Markup* view displays the document with all revisions and comments visible.
>
> *No Markup* view displays the document in its final form—with all proposed changes included and comments hidden.
>
> *Original* view displays the original, unchanged document with all revisions and comments hidden.

FIGURE 6.34

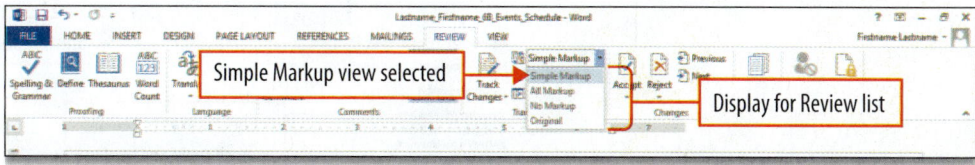

2 On the list, click **No Markup**. Notice that all comments and indicated changes are hidden. The document displays with all proposed changes included.

> When you are editing a document in which you are proposing changes, this view is useful because the revisions of others or the markup of your own revisions is not distracting.

3 In the **Tracking group**, click the **Display for Review arrow**, and then from the list, click **All Markup**. Compare your screen with Figure 6.35.

> At the stage where you, the document owner, must decide which revisions to accept or reject, you will find this view to be the most useful. The document displays with revisions—changes are shown as *markup*. Markup refers to the formatting Word uses to denote the revisions visually. For example, when a reviewer changes text, the original text displays with strikethrough formatting by default. When a reviewer inserts new text, the new text is underlined. A *vertical change bar* displays in the left margin next to each line of text that contains a revision. In All Markup view, the vertical change bar displays in gray; in Simple Markup view, it displays in red.
>
> In All Markup view, shaded text indicates where a comment has been inserted.

FIGURE 6.35

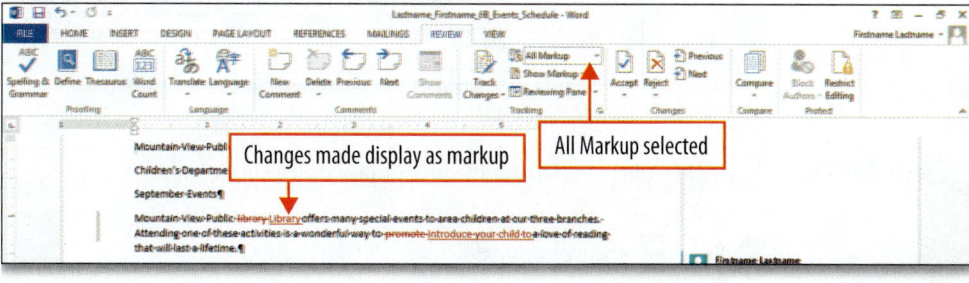

🔄 **ANOTHER WAY**   Click any vertical change bar to toggle between Simple Markup view and All Markup view.

🔄 **BY TOUCH**   Tap any vertical change bar to toggle between Simple Markup view and All Markup view.

---

4 In the **Tracking group**, click **Show Markup**, and then point to **Balloons**.

> The default setting *Show Only Comments and Formatting in Balloons* is selected. In this default setting, insertions and deletions *do not* display in balloons. Rather, insertions and deletions display directly in the text with insertions underlined and deletions struck out with a line. Comments and formatting *do* display in balloons.

5 Display the **Show Markup** list, if necessary, and then point to **Specific People** to see the name of each individual who proposed changes to this document. Compare your screen with Figure 6.36.

> Here you can turn off the display of revisions by one or more reviewers. For example, you might want to view only the revisions proposed by a supervisor—before you consider the revisions proposed by others—by clearing the check box for all reviewers except the supervisor.
>
> In the Show Markup list, you can also determine which changes display by deselecting one or more of the options. *Ink* refers to marks made directly on a document by using a stylus on a Tablet PC.

FIGURE 6.36

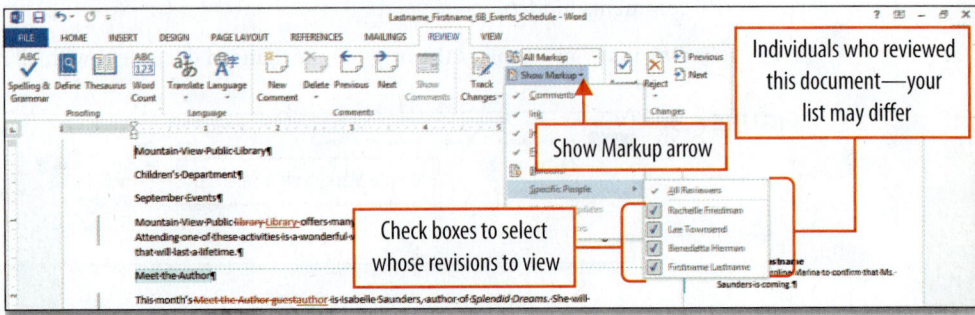

6 Click anywhere in the document to close the **Show Markup** list and leave all revision types by all reviewers displayed.

7 In the fifth paragraph, point to the shaded text *Meet the Author*, where you inserted a comment. Notice that the comment displays as a ScreenTip—indicating the date and time that the comment was created.

8 Near the bottom of **Page 1**, locate the comment by Rachelle Friedman that begins *Should we mention*, and then point to the image. Compare your screen with Figure 6.37.

> A *Person Card* related to the reviewer displays. The Person Card allows you to communicate with a reviewer—using email, instant messaging, phone, or video—directly from the comment. Users must be signed in with a Microsoft account or an Active Directory account at work. In this instruction, because no reviewers are signed in, the commands are inactive.

FIGURE 6.37

🔄 **BY TOUCH**   In a comment, tap the image to display the Person Card.

9 Save 🖫 your changes.

Activity 6.13 | Setting Tracking and Markup Options

In this activity, you will change the way the markup area displays in the document.

1 Press Ctrl + Home to move to the top of the document. In the **Tracking group**, click the **Dialog Box Launcher**.

2 In the **Track Changes Options** dialog box, click **Advanced Options** to display the **Advanced Track Changes Options** dialog box. Take a moment to study Figure 6.38 and the table shown in Figure 6.39.

> Here you can change how markup, moved text, table revisions, and balloons display.

FIGURE 6.38

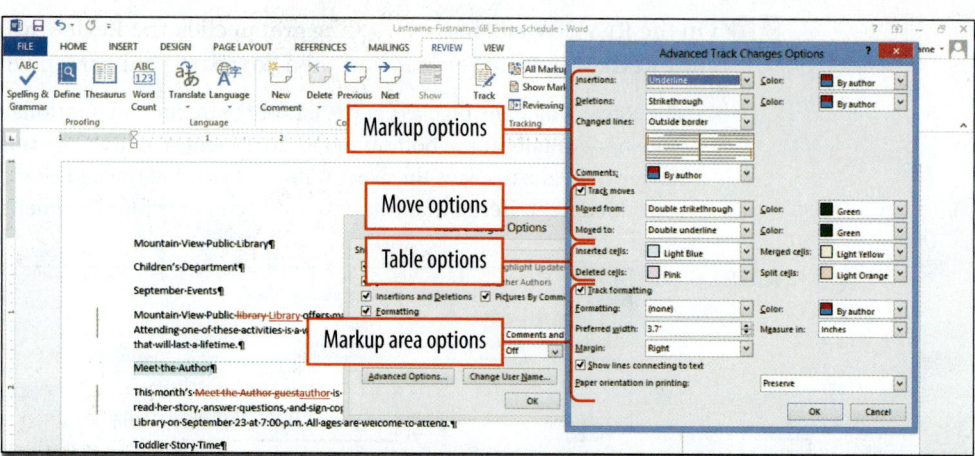

FIGURE 6.39

SETTINGS IN THE ADVANCED TRACK CHANGES OPTIONS DIALOG BOX	
OPTION	**SETTINGS YOU CAN ADJUST**
Markup	Specify the format and color of inserted text, deleted text, and changed lines. By default, inserted text is underlined, deleted text displays with strikethrough formatting, and the vertical change bar indicating changed lines displays on the outside border—left margin. Click an arrow to select a different format, and click the Color arrow to select a different color. By author, the default, indicates that Word will assign a different color to each person who inserts comments or tracks changes.
Move	Specify the format of moved text. The default is green with double strikethrough in the moved content and a double underline below the content in its new location. To turn off this feature, clear the Track moves check box.
Table	Specify the color that will display in a table if cells are inserted, deleted, merged, or split.
Markup area	Specify the location and width of the markup area. By default the location is at the right margin and the preferred width for balloons is set to 3.7". You can also control the display of connecting lines to text.

3 In the **Advanced Track Changes Options** dialog box, locate and verify that the **Track formatting** check box is selected. Below the check box, click the **Preferred width spin box down arrow to 3"**.

This action will cause the markup area to display with a width of 3".

4 Click **OK** two times, and then **Save** 🖫 your document.

Use the Advanced Track Changes Options dialog box in this manner to set Track Changes to display the way that works best for you.

Activity 6.14 | Using the Reviewing Pane

The **Reviewing Pane**, which displays in a separate scrollable window, shows all of the changes and comments that currently display in your document. In this activity you will use the Reviewing Pane to view a summary of all changes and comments in the document.

1 On the **REVIEW tab**, in the **Tracking group**, click the **Reviewing Pane arrow**. From the list, click **Reviewing Pane Vertical**, and then compare your screen with Figure 6.40.

The Reviewing Pane displays at the left of the document. Optionally, you can display the Reviewing Pane horizontally at the bottom of the document window. The summary section at the top of the Reviewing Pane displays the exact number of visible tracked changes and comments that remain in your document. Recall that this document contains four comments.

FIGURE 6.40

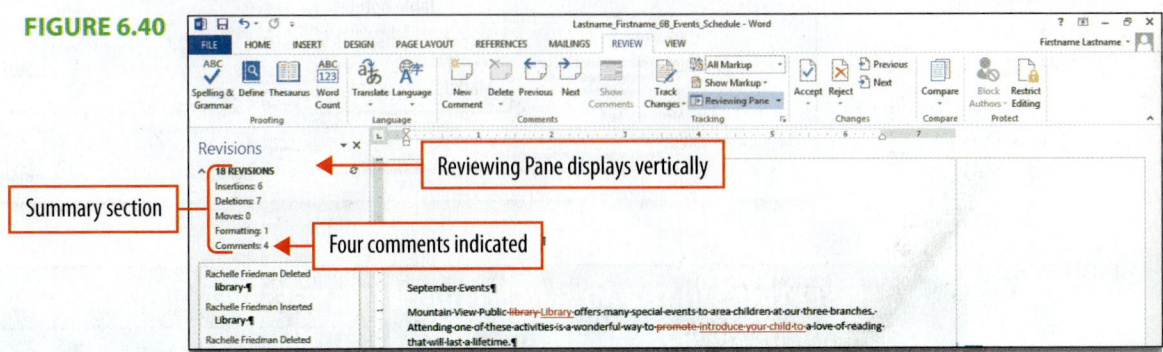

2 Take a moment to read the entries in the **Reviewing Pane**.

In the Reviewing Pane, you can view each type of revision, view the name of the reviewer associated with each item, and read long comments that do not fit within a comment balloon. The Reviewing Pane is also useful for ensuring that all tracked changes have been *removed* from your document when it is ready for final distribution.

3 At the top of the **Reviewing Pane**, click **Close** ☒.

> **ALERT!** **Completing the Remainder of This Project in One Working Session**
>
> Plan to complete the remaining activities of this project in one working session. For purposes of instruction, some revisions in documents must be made within a restricted time frame. If you must take a break, save the document, and then close Word. When you return to complete the project, reopen your file Lastname_Firstname_6B_Events_Schedule. If you are sharing a computer, be sure the user name and initials are the same as in the previous activities.

Activity 6.15 | Tracking Changes and Locking Tracking to Restrict Editing

The Track Changes feature is turned off by default; you must turn on the feature each time you want to begin tracking changes in a document.

1 Press Ctrl + Home, if necessary, to move to the top of the document. In the **Tracking group**, click the upper portion of the **Track Changes** button to enable tracking. Notice that the button displays in blue to indicate that the feature is turned on.

2 In the **Tracking group**, click the **Track Changes arrow**, and then click **Lock Tracking**.

The *Lock Tracking* feature prevents reviewers from turning off Track Changes and making changes that are not visible in markup.

3 In the **Lock Tracking** dialog box, in the **Enter password (optional)** box, type **1721** In the **Reenter to confirm** box, type **1721** Compare your screen with Figure 6.41.

The Track Changes feature will remain turned on, regardless of who edits the document—the author or reviewers. The password only applies to tracking changes; it does not protect the document.

FIGURE 6.41

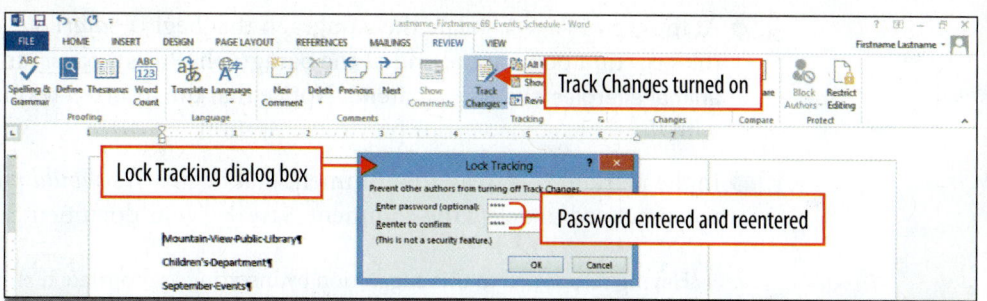

4 Click **OK** to close the **Lock Tracking** dialog box. Notice that the **Track Changes** button no longer displays in blue.

5 Select the first paragraph—*Mountain View Public Library*. Be sure to include the paragraph mark. On the mini toolbar, change the **Font Size** to 28, change the **Font Color** [A ▾] to **Green, Accent 6, Darker 25%**—in the last column, the fifth color. With the paragraph selected, press [Ctrl] + [E]. Click anywhere to deselect the text, and then compare your screen with Figure 6.42.

As you make each change, the markup displays in the markup area, and the vertical change bar displays to the left of the paragraph. The types of changes—formatted text and center alignment— are indicated in balloons, and lines point to the location of the revisions.

FIGURE 6.42

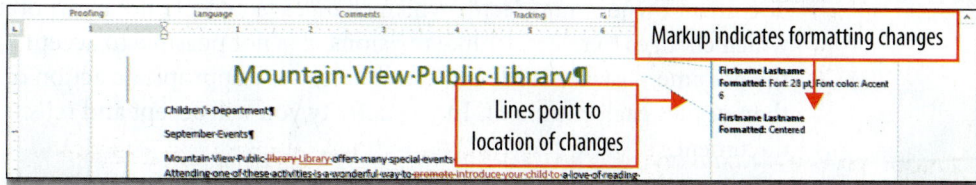

6 Select the second and third paragraphs, change the **Font Size** to 20, apply **Bold** [B], and then press [Ctrl] + [E].

7 Select the paragraph heading *Meet the Author*, hold down [Ctrl], and then by using the **vertical scrollbar down arrow** [▾], move through the document and select the remaining paragraph headings—*Toddler Story Time, Preschool Story Time, Baby Story Time, Story and Craft, Animal Adventures, Internet Safety*, and *Seek and Find at the Library*. Apply **Bold** [B] to the selected headings.

8 Scrolling as necessary, locate the paragraph below *Baby Story Time* that begins *Specifically designed*. In the third line, click to position the insertion point to the left of *program*, type **one-hour** and then press [Spacebar].

The inserted text is underlined and displays with your designated color.

9 Point to the inserted text, and then compare your screen with Figure 6.43.

A ScreenTip displays, showing the revision that was made, which reviewer made the change, and the date and time of the change.

FIGURE 6.43

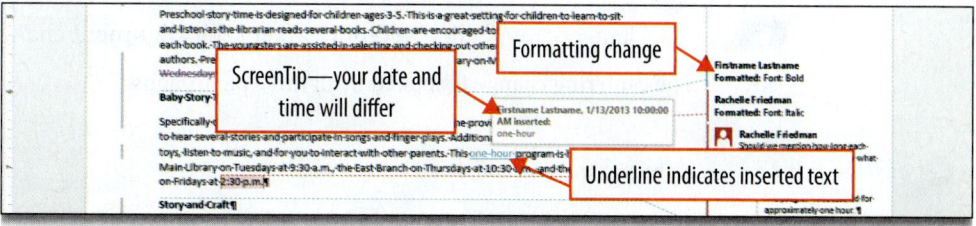

10 At the top of **Page 2**, locate the paragraph that begins *Safari Steve*, and then click to position the insertion point at the end of the paragraph. Press Spacebar, and then type **Children with animal allergies should not attend.** Notice that the inserted text is underlined and displays with the same color as your previous insertion.

11 In the markup area, read the comment that begins *We should mention.* Use any technique you practiced to delete the comment. **Save** 🔲 your document.

> Having responded to this suggestion by inserting appropriate text, you can delete the comment. When developing important documents, having others review the document can improve its content and appearance.

More Knowledge   **Sharing a Document Using OneDrive**

Use the Share command to allow reviewers to insert comments or edit a document that has been saved to the OneDrive. To share a saved document, open the document. Click the FILE tab, click Share, and then click Invite People. Under Invite People, enter the names or email addresses of the individuals you want to review the document. Click Can Edit to allow your coworkers to change the file, and then click Share.

Activity 6.16 | Accepting or Rejecting Changes in a Document

After all reviewers have made their proposed revisions and added their comments, the document owner must decide which changes to accept and incorporate into the document and which changes to reject. Unlike revisions, it is not possible to accept or reject comments; instead, the document owner reads the comments, takes appropriate action or makes a decision, and then deletes each comment. In this activity you will accept and reject changes to create a final document.

1 Press Ctrl + Home.

> When reviewing comments and changes in a document, it is good practice to start at the beginning of the document to be sure you do not miss any comments or revisions.

2 On the **REVIEW tab**, in the **Tracking group**, click the **Track Changes arrow**, and then click **Lock Tracking**. In the **Unlock Tracking** dialog box, in the **Password** box, type **1721** and then click **OK**.

> Because you are finalizing the changes in a document, it is necessary to unlock tracking. After entering the password, you have unlocked tracking. In the Tracking group, the Track Changes button displays in blue, which indicates that the feature is turned on.

3 On the **REVIEW tab**, in the **Changes group**, click **Next**—be careful to select **Next** in the **Changes group**, *not* the **Comments group**. Notice that the first paragraph is selected.

> In the Changes group, the Next button and the Previous button enable you to navigate from one revision or comment to the next or previous one, respectively.

4 In the **Changes group**, click the upper portion of the **Accept** button.

> The text formatting is accepted for the first paragraph, the related balloon no longer displays in the markup area, and the next change—center alignment for the first three paragraphs—is selected. When reviewing a document, changes can be accepted or rejected individually, or all at one time.

5 In the **Changes group**, click **Accept** to accept the alignment change.

> The centering change is applied to all three paragraphs.

🔄 **ANOTHER WAY**   Right-click the selection, and then click Accept.

---

6 In the **Changes group**, click **Accept** to accept the text formatting for the second and third paragraphs.

7 In the next paragraph, point to the strikethrough text *library* and notice that the ScreenTip indicates that Rachelle Friedman deleted *library*. Then, point to the underline directly below *Library* to display a ScreenTip. Compare your screen with Figure 6.44.

When a reviewer replaces text—for example, when Rachelle replaced *library* with *Library*—the inserted text displays with an underline and in the color designated for the reviewer. The original text displays with strikethrough formatting.

FIGURE 6.44

8 In the **Changes group**, click **Accept** two times to accept the deletion of *library* and the insertion of *Library*.

The next change, the deletion of *promote* is selected.

9 In the **Changes group**, click **Reject**, and then point to the selected text *introduce your child to*, to display a ScreenTip. Compare your screen with Figure 6.45.

The original text *promote* is reinserted in the sentence. As the document owner, you decide which proposed revisions to accept; you are not required to accept every change in a document.

FIGURE 6.45

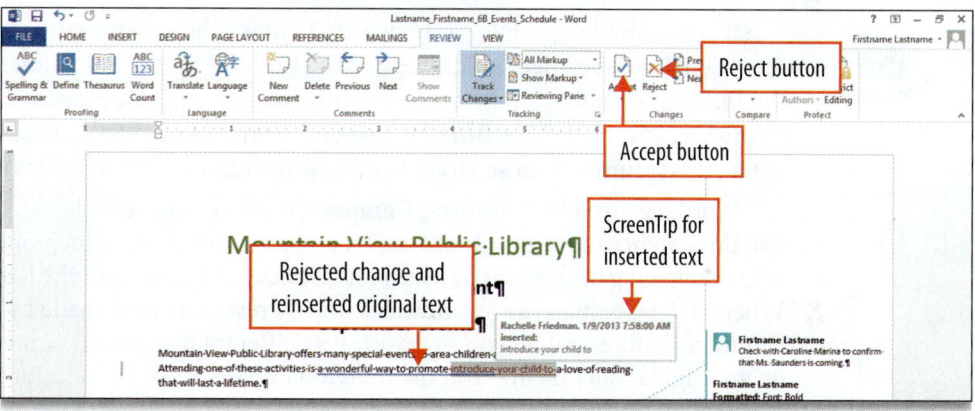

10 Click **Reject** again to reject the insertion of *introduce your child to* and to select the next change.

11 On the **REVIEW tab**, in the **Comments group**, click **Next** two times to select the comment by Rachelle Friedman—be careful to select **Next** in the **Comments group**, *not* in the **Changes group**. Read the comment, and then delete the comment.

Because you replied to Rachelle Friedman's comment, your comment is also deleted. Recall that you cannot accept or reject comments. Rather, you can take appropriate action, and then delete the comment when it is no longer relevant. Because you entered text indicating the program length, you can delete the comment.

12 In the **Changes group**, click the **Accept arrow**. From the list, click **Accept All Changes and Stop Tracking**.

All remaining changes in the document are accepted and Track Changes is turned off.

13 In the **Tracking group**, click the **Dialog Box Launcher** , and then click **Advanced Options**. In the **Advanced Track Changes Options** dialog box, below the **Track formatting** check box, click the **Preferred width spin box up arrow** to **3.7"**. Click **OK** two times to close the dialog boxes.

> This action restores the system to the default settings. One comment remains, and the markup area is still visible.

14 Press Ctrl + Home, verify that the remaining comment displays, and then compare your screen with Figure 6.46.

FIGURE 6.46

15 Click the **FILE tab**, click the **Info tab**, and then click **Show All Properties**. In the **Tags** box, type **events schedule, reviewed** In the **Subject** box, type your course name and section number. If necessary, edit the author name to display your name.

16 **Save** your document; leave it open for the next activity.

Objective 6 View Side by Side, Compare, and Combine Documents

Video W6-6

It is not always possible for reviewers to make their comments and edits on a single Word file. Each reviewer might edit a copy of the file, and then the document owner must gather all of the files and combine all the revisions into a single final document. One method to examine the changes is to use the ***View Side by Side*** command. Using the View Side by Side command displays two open documents, in separate windows, next to each other on your screen.

Word has two other features, ***Compare*** and ***Combine***, which enable you to view revisions in two documents and determine which changes to accept and which ones to reject. Compare is useful when reviewing differences between an original document and the latest version of the document. When using Compare, Word indicates that all revisions were made by the same individual. The Combine feature enables you to review two different documents containing revisions—both based on an original document—and the individuals who made the revisions are identified.

Activity 6.17 │ Using View Side by Side

Abigail Garner has received another copy of the original file, which contains revisions and comments from two additional reviewers—Angie Harper and Natalia Ricci. In this activity, you will use View Side by Side to compare the new document with the version you finalized in the previous activity.

1 With your file **Lastname_Firstname_6B_Events_Schedule** open and the insertion point at the top of the document, navigate to your student files, and then open the file **w06B_Schedule_Revisions**.

2 On the **VIEW tab**, in the **Window group**, click **View Side by Side** to display both documents.

> This view enables you to see whether there have been any major changes to the original document that should be discussed by the reviewers before making revisions. Both documents contain the same basic text.

3 In the **w06B_Schedule_Revisions** document, if necessary, drag the horizontal scroll bar to the right so that you can see the markup area. Notice that both documents scroll. Compare your screen with Figure 6.47. Depending on your screen resolution, your view may differ.

Edits and comments made by Angie Harper and Natalia Ricci display in the w06B_Schedule_Revisions file. When View Side by Side is active, *synchronous scrolling*—both documents scroll simultaneously—is turned on by default.

FIGURE 6.47

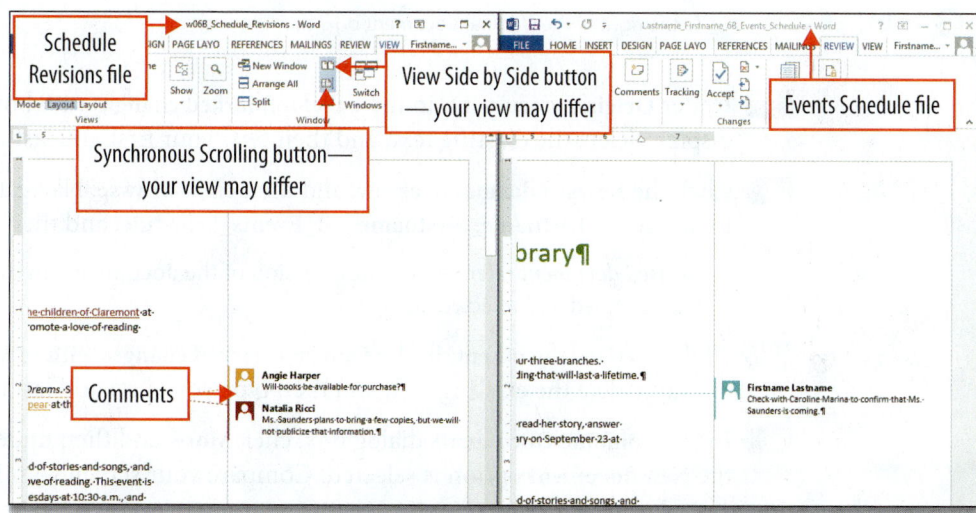

4 In the **w06B_Schedule_Revisions** document, in the **Window group**, click **View Side by Side** to restore program windows to their original size.

5 In the **w06B_Schedule_Revisions** document, select the first paragraph, and then on the mini toolbar, click **Styles**. In the **Styles** gallery, click **Heading 1**.

For purposes of instruction, you are making a formatting change to the same paragraph that you modified in your Lastname_Firstname_6B_Events_Schedule document. A reviewer usually makes revisions in only one version of a document.

6 Display the **Save As** dialog box, and then **Save** the file in your **Word Chapter 6 folder** as **Lastname_Firstname_6B_Schedule_Revisions**

7 **Close** ☒ the **Lastname_Firstname_6B_Schedule_Revisions** document. Notice your **Lastname_Firstname_6B_Events_Schedule** document displays.

8 Press Ctrl + W to close your **Lastname_Firstname_6B_Events_Schedule**, without closing Word.

Activity 6.18 | Combining Documents and Resolving Multi-Document Style Conflicts

In this activity, you will combine the document containing revisions and comments by Angie Harper and Natalia Ricci with your finalized version of the events schedule. Then, you will accept or reject the additional revisions to create a final document ready for distribution to the public.

1 On the **REVIEW tab**, in the **Compare group**, click **Compare**. From the list, click **Combine** to display the **Combine Documents** dialog box.

When using the Combine feature, it is not necessary to have an open document.

2 In the **Combine Documents** dialog box, click the **Original document arrow**, and then click **Browse**. In the **Open** dialog box, navigate to your **Word Chapter 6** folder, select the file **Lastname_Firstname_6B_Schedule_Revisions**, and then click **Open**.

Recall that this file includes revisions and comments from two additional reviewers. *Original document* usually refers to a document without revisions or, in this case, the document that you have not yet reviewed. The file also includes the formatting change you made to the first paragraph.

↻ ANOTHER WAY   To the right of the Original document box, click Browse.

3 Under **Original document**, in the **Label unmarked changes with** box, if your name does not display, delete the existing text, and then type your first and last names.

4 Click the **Revised document arrow**, and then click **Browse**. Navigate to your **Word Chapter 6** folder, select **Lastname_Firstname_6B_Events_Schedule**, and then click **Open**.

Revised document refers to the latest version of the document—in this case, the document where you accepted and rejected changes.

5 Under **Revised document**, in the **Label unmarked changes with** box, if your name does not display, delete the existing text, and then type your first and last names.

6 In the **Combine Documents** dialog box, click **More**, and then under **Show changes in**, be sure the **New document** option is selected. Compare your screen with Figure 6.48.

The More button expands the dialog box to display additional settings. By selecting the New document option, all changes in both files display in a new document.

FIGURE 6.48

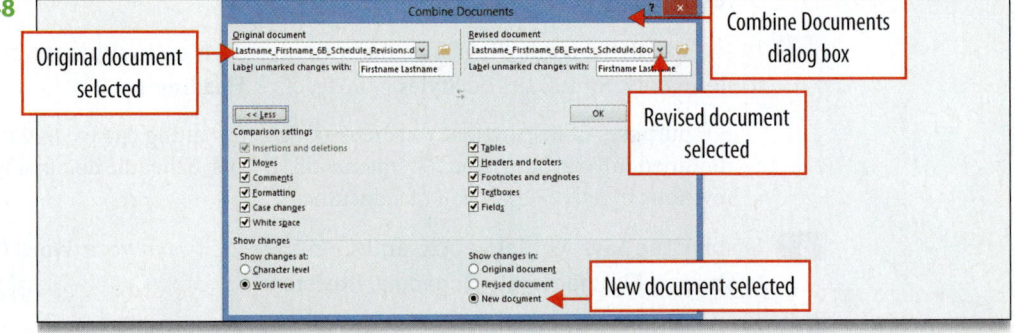

7 ▶ In the **Combine Documents** dialog box, click **Less**, and then click **OK**. In the message box indicating that Word can only store one style of formatting changes in the final merged document, under **Keep formatting changes from**, select **The other document (Lastname_Firstname_6B_Events_Schedule)** option button. Note: If the message box does not display, proceed to Step 8, the second sentence—compare your screen with Figure 6.49.

When combining two documents, style conflicts can exist when formatting changes are made to the same text in different versions of the document in the same time frame. In this case, the conflict exists because both files contain a formatting change applied to the first paragraph. The message box allows you to select the document that contains the formatting change you want to display in the combined document.

8 ▶ In the message box, click **Continue with Merge**. Compare your screen with Figure 6.49.

The tri-pane Review Panel displays with the combined document in the left pane, the original document in the top right pane, and the revised document in the bottom right pane. The Reviewing Pane displays to the left of your screen, indicating all accepted changes in your Lastname_Firstname_6B_Events_Schedule file with your user name.

FIGURE 6.49

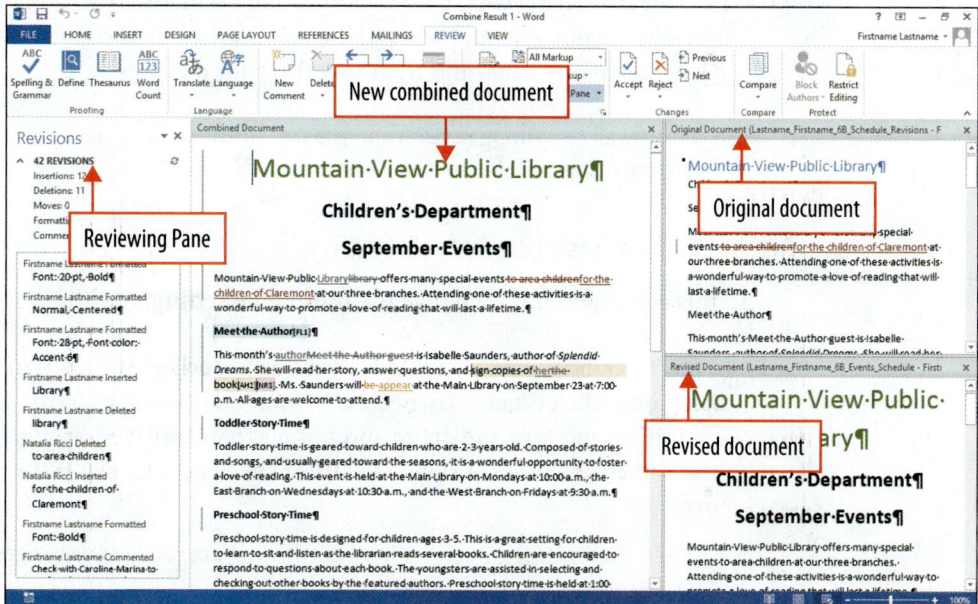

ALERT!   **Should Both Documents Display?**

If only the combined document displays, in the Compare group, click Compare, click Show Source Documents, and then click Show Both. If the Reviewing Pane does not display, in the Tracking group, click the Reviewing Pane arrow, and then click Reviewing Pane Vertical.

9 ▶ If necessary, click to position the insertion point at the beginning of the **Combined Document**. **Save** the document in your **Word Chapter 6** folder as **Lastname_Firstname_6B_Schedule_Combined**

10 ▶ At the top of the **Reviewing Pane**, locate the summary and notice that there are six comments in the combined document. Take a moment to read each comment.

11 ▶ On the **REVIEW tab**, in the **Comments group**, click the **Delete arrow**, and then click **Delete All Comments in Document**. If necessary, press [Ctrl] + [Home].

All comments have been reviewed and are no longer needed.

12 ▶ In the **Changes group**, click **Next**, and then click **Accept** to accept the first change. Continue to click **Accept** until the revision *to area children* is selected. Compare your screen with Figure 6.50.

FIGURE 6.50

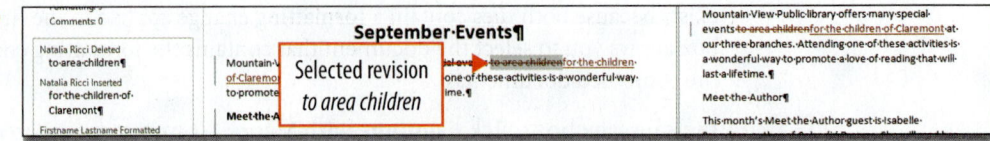

September·Events¶

Selected revision *to area children*

13 ▶ On the **REVIEW tab**, in the **Changes group**, with the revision *to area children* selected, click **Reject** two times.

14 ▶ In the **Changes group**, click the **Accept arrow**, and then click **Accept All Changes and Stop Tracking**. In the **Reviewing Pane**, notice that no further revisions or comments remain. On the right of your screen, **Close** ☒ the two panes—the original and revised documents. **Close** ☒ the **Reviewing Pane**, and then **Save** 🖫 your changes.

Because all remaining revisions in the document are accepted, there is no longer a need to view the original or revised documents.

Activity 6.19 | Restoring Default Settings

In this activity, you will change the user name settings and finalize the document.

1 ▶ In the **Tracking group**, click the **Dialog Box Launcher**, and then in the **Track Changes Options** dialog box, click **Change User Name**. If you made changes to the user name, delete your name and initials and type the name and initials that displayed originally. Clear the **Always use these values regardless of sign in to Office** check box. Click **OK** two times to close the dialog boxes.

When sharing a computer with others, if you have made any changes, it is good practice to restore the settings when you are finished.

2 ▶ Press [Ctrl] + [Home]. On the **DESIGN tab**, in the **Page Background group**, click **Page Color**, and then click **Fill Effects**. In the **Fill Effects** dialog box, click the **Texture tab**, and then in the fourth row, click the first texture—**Newsprint**. Click **OK**.

The page background is added to improve the final appearance of the document. Because you have been assigned the task of preparing the final document for distribution, it is appropriate to make this formatting change.

> **N O T E** **Printing Page Backgrounds**
>
> Page backgrounds do not display in Print Preview and do not print by default.

3 ▶ At the bottom of **Page 1**, right-click in the footer area, and then click **Edit Footer**. Right-click the file name, and then click **Update Field**. **Close** the footer area.

4 ▶ Click the **FILE tab**, click the **Info tab**, and then click **Show All Properties**. In the **Tags** box, type **events schedule, reviewed, combined** In the **Subject** box, type your course name and section number. If necessary, edit the author name to display your name.

5 From **Backstage** view, click **Print** to display the **Print Preview**. Examine the **Print Preview**, check for any spelling or grammatical errors, and then **Save** 🖫 your document. Print all three documents or submit electronically as directed by your instructor. **Close** ✕ Word.

More **Knowledge** | **Printing Page Backgrounds**

To print the background color or fill effect of a document, display the Word Options dialog box, select Display, and under Printing Options, select the Print background colors and images check box. Click OK.

END | You have completed Project 6B

END OF CHAPTER

SUMMARY

Inserting building blocks—such as text boxes, pictures, Quick Tables, and AutoText—can save time and provide consistency in your documents. Use built-in document elements or create your own building blocks.

A theme template, defined by colors, fonts, and effects, enhances the appearance of a document. Attach a theme template to multiple documents to create documents that have a coordinated appearance.

The Track Changes feature enables a group of individuals to work together on a document. Reviewers can insert comments; reply to comments made by others; insert, edit, delete, and move text; and format documents.

The author of the document can accept or reject revisions. The author can compare two different versions of a document that has been revised using the Track Changes feature or combine them in a new document.

GO! LEARN IT ONLINE

Review the concepts and key terms in this chapter by completing these online challenges, which you can find at **www.pearsonhighered.com/go**.

Matching and Multiple Choice:
Answer matching and multiple choice questions to test what you learned in this chapter. MyITLab°

Crossword Puzzle:
Spell out the words that match the numbered clues and put them in the puzzle squares.

Flipboard:
Flip through the definitions of the key terms in this chapter and match them with the correct term.

END OF CHAPTER

REVIEW AND ASSESSMENT GUIDE FOR WORD CHAPTER 6

Your instructor may assign one or more of these projects to help you review the chapter and assess your mastery and understanding of the chapter.

Review and Assessment Guide for Word Chapter 6			
Project	**Apply Skills from These Chapter Objectives**	**Project Type**	**Project Location**
6C	Objectives 1–3 from Project 6A	**6C Skills Review** A guided review of the skills from Project 6A.	On the following pages
6D	Objectives 4–6 from Project 6B	**6D Skills Review** A guided review of the skills from Project 6B.	On the following pages
6E	Objectives 1–3 from Project 6A	**6E Mastery (Grader Project)** A demonstration of your mastery of the skills in Project 6A with extensive decision making.	In MyITLab and on the following pages
6F	Objectives 4–6 from Project 6B	**6F Mastery (Grader Project)** A demonstration of your mastery of the skills in Project 6B with extensive decision making.	In MyITLab and on the following pages
6G	Objectives 1–6 from Projects 6A and 6B	**6G Mastery (Grader Project)** A demonstration of your mastery of the skills in Projects 6A and 6B with extensive decision making.	In MyITLab and on the following pages
6H	Combination of Objectives from Projects 6A and 6B	**6H GO! Fix It** A demonstration of your mastery of the skills in Projects 6A and 6B by creating a correct result from a document that contains errors you must find.	Online
6I	Combination of Objectives from Projects 6A and 6B	**6I GO! Make It** A demonstration of your mastery of the skills in Projects 6A and 6B by creating a result from a supplied picture.	Online
6J	Combination of Objectives from Projects 6A and 6B	**6J GO! Solve It** A demonstration of your mastery of the skills in Projects 6A and 6B, your decision-making skills, and your critical thinking skills. A task-specific rubric helps you self-assess your result.	Online
6K	Combination of Objectives from Projects 6A and 6B	**6K GO! Solve It** A demonstration of your mastery of the skills in Projects 6A and 6B, your decision-making skills, and your critical thinking skills. A task-specific rubric helps you self-assess your result.	On the following pages
6L	Combination of Objectives from Projects 6A and 6B	**6L GO! Think** A demonstration of your understanding of the chapter concepts applied in a manner that you would outside of college. An analytic rubric helps you and your instructor grade the quality of your work by comparing it to the work an expert in the discipline would create.	On the following pages
6M	Combination of Objectives from Projects 6A and 6B	**6M GO! Think** A demonstration of your understanding of the chapter concepts applied in a manner that you would outside of college. An analytic rubric helps you and your instructor grade the quality of your work by comparing it to the work an expert in the discipline would create.	Online
6N	Combination of Objectives from Projects 6A and 6B	**6N You and GO!** A demonstration of your understanding of the chapter concepts applied in a manner that you would in a personal situation. An analytic rubric helps you and your instructor grade the quality of your work.	Online

GLOSSARY

All Markup A Track Changes view that displays the document with all revisions and comments visible.

Author The owner, or creator, of the original document.

Balloon The outline shape in which a comment or formatting change displays.

Building blocks Reusable pieces of content or other document parts—for example, headers, footers, and page number formats—that are stored in galleries.

Building Blocks Organizer A feature that enables you to view—in a single location—all of the available building blocks from all the different galleries.

Click and type pointer The text select—I-beam—pointer with various attached shapes that indicate which formatting—left-aligned, centered, or right-aligned—will be applied when you double-click in a blank area of a document.

Combine A Track Changes feature that allows you to review two different documents containing revisions, both based on an original document.

Comment A note that an author or reviewer adds to a document.

Compare A Track Changes feature that enables you to review differences between an original document and the latest version of the document.

Hyphenation A tool in Word that controls how words are split between two lines.

Ink Revision marks made directly on a document by using a stylus on a Tablet PC.

Lock Tracking A feature that prevents reviewers from turning off Track Changes and making changes that are not visible in markup.

Markup The formatting Word uses to denote a document's revisions visually.

Markup area The space to the right or left of a document where comments and formatting changes display in balloons.

No Markup A Track Changes view that displays the document in its final form—with all proposed changes included and comments hidden.

Original A Track Changes view that displays the original, unchanged document with all revisions and comments hidden.

Person Card A feature that allows you to communicate with a reviewer—using email, instant messaging, phone, or video—directly from a comment.

Quick Parts All of the reusable pieces of content that are available to insert into a document, including building blocks, document properties, and fields.

Quick Tables Tables that are stored as building blocks.

Reviewer An individual who reviews and marks changes on a document.

Reviewing Pane A separate scrollable window that shows all of the changes and comments that currently display in a document.

Revisions Changes made to a document.

Simple Markup The default Track Changes view that indicates revisions by vertical red lines in the left margin and indicates comments by icons in the right margin.

Synchronous scrolling The setting that causes two documents to scroll simultaneously.

Text box A movable, resizable container for text or graphics.

Theme A predesigned set of colors, fonts, and line and fill effects that look good together and is applied to an entire document by a single selection.

Theme template A stored, user-defined set of colors, fonts, and effects that can be shared with other Office programs.

Track Changes A feature that makes a record of the changes made to a document.

Vertical change bar A line that displays in the left margin next to each line of text that contains a revision.

View Side by Side A view that displays two open documents in separate windows, next to each other on the screen.

CHAPTER REVIEW

Build from Scratch

Skills Review | Project 6C Literacy Program

In the following Skills Review, you will create and save building blocks and create a theme to be used in a flyer seeking volunteers for Mountain View Public Library's Adult Literacy Program. Your completed documents will look similar to Figure 6.51.

PROJECT FILES

For Project 6C, you will need the following files:

Two new blank Word documents
w06C_Literacy_Information
w06C_Literacy_Image

You will save your files as:

Lastname_Firstname_6C_Literacy_Blocks
Lastname_Firstname_6C_Literacy_Program
Lastname_Firstname_6C_Literacy_Theme—not shown in the figure

PROJECT RESULTS

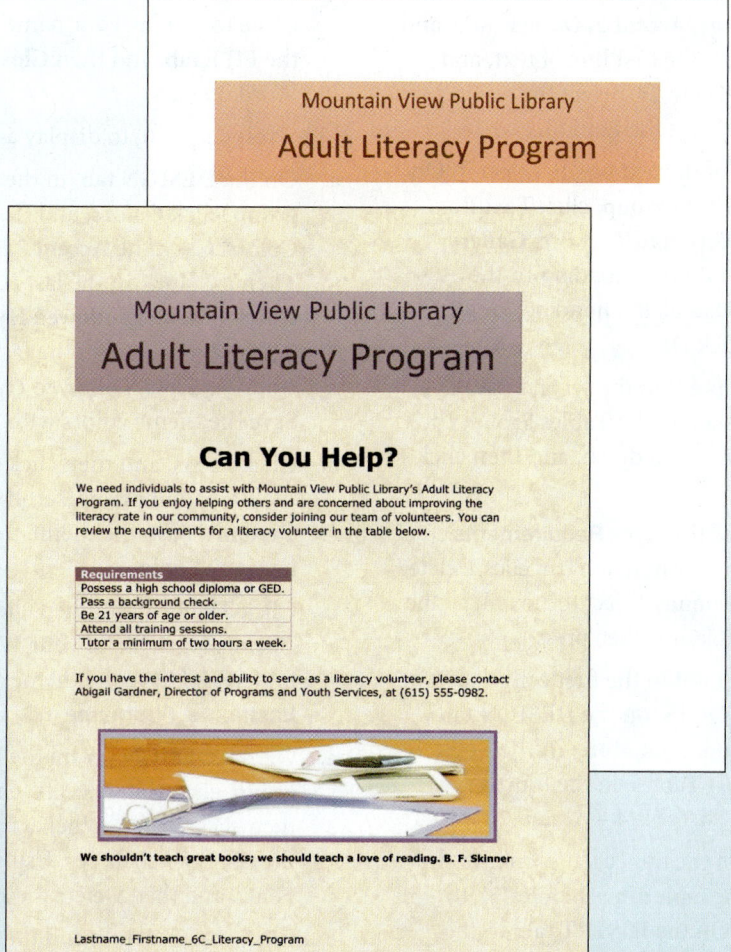

FIGURE 6.51

(Project 6C Literacy Program continues on the next page)

CHAPTER REVIEW

1 Start Word to display a new blank document. If necessary, display the rulers and formatting marks. Click the **FILE tab**, display the **Save As** dialog box, navigate to your **Word Chapter 6** folder, and then **Save** the document as **Lastname_Firstname_6C_Literacy_Blocks** Insert the file name in the footer.

a. Press Enter three times, and then position the insertion point in the first blank paragraph. On the **INSERT tab**, in the **Text group**, click **Text Box**, and then locate and click **Simple Text Box**. On the **FORMAT tab**, in the **Shape Styles group**, click **More**. In the fourth row, click the third style—**Subtle Effect – Orange, Accent 2**. In the **Size group**, change the **Shape Width** to 6.5".

b. Replace the placeholder text by typing **Mountain View Public Library** Press Enter, and then type **Adult Literacy Program** Select both lines of text, change the **Font Color** to **Orange, Accent 2, Darker 50%**, and then apply **Center**. Select the first line of text, and then change the **Font Size** to **24**. Select the second line of text, and then change the **Font Size** to **36**.

c. Click the outside edge of the text box to select it. On the **INSERT tab**, in the **Text group**, click **Text Box**, and then click **Save Selection to Text Box Gallery**. In the **Name** box, type **Literacy Heading** In the **Description** box, type **Use as the heading for all literacy documents** Click **OK**.

2 Position the insertion point in the second blank paragraph. On the **INSERT tab**, in the **Tables group**, click **Table**, point to **Quick Tables**, scroll down, and then click **Tabular List**.

a. Select the text *ITEM*, and then type **Requirements** Press Tab. Right-click, on the mini toolbar, click **Delete**, and then click **Delete Columns**. Select the text in all the remaining cells of the table, and then press Delete.

b. Position the insertion point in the first cell of the table. Under **TABLE TOOLS**, on the **DESIGN tab**, in the **Table Styles group**, click **More**. In the **Table Styles** gallery, under **List Tables**, in the fourth row, click the third style—**List Table 4 – Accent 2**.

c. Point slightly outside of the upper left corner of the table, and then click the **table move handle** ⊞ to select the entire table. On the **INSERT tab**, in the **Tables group**, click **Table**. Point to **Quick Tables**, and then at the bottom of the gallery, click **Save Selection**

to **Quick Tables Gallery**. In the **Name** box, type **Job Information** In the **Description** box, type **Use for listing job requirements** Click **OK**.

d. Press Ctrl + End. Type **We shouldn't teach great books; we should teach a love of reading. B. F. Skinner** and then select the text you just typed. On the **INSERT tab**, in the **Text group**, click **Quick Parts**, click **AutoText**, and then click **Save Selection to AutoText Gallery**. In the **Create New Building Block** dialog box, in the **Name** box, type **Literacy Quote** and then in the **Description** box, type **Quote for program** Click the **Save in arrow**, and then click **Building Blocks**. Click **OK**.

e. Click the **FILE tab**, and then click **Show All Properties**. In the **Tags** box, type **literacy, building blocks** In the **Subject** box, type your course name and section number. If necessary, edit the author name to display your name. **Save** your changes. Click the **FILE tab**, and then **Close** the document but leave Word open.

3 Press Ctrl + N to display a new blank document.

a. On the **DESIGN tab**, in the **Document Formatting group**, click **Colors**, and then click **Customize Colors**. Click the **Accent 2 arrow**, and then under **Theme Colors**, in the last column, click the first color—**Purple, Followed Hyperlink**. Click the **Accent 3 arrow**, and then in the last column, click the fifth color—**Purple, Followed Hyperlink, Darker 25%**. Save the theme colors with the name **Literacy Colors**

b. Click **Fonts**, and then click **Customize Fonts**. Click the **Body font arrow**, scroll down, and then click **Verdana. Save** the theme fonts with the name **Literacy Fonts**

c. Click **Themes**, and then click **Save Current Theme**. Navigate to your **Word Chapter 6** folder, and **Save** the theme as **Lastname_Firstname_6C_Literacy_Theme**

d. On the **DESIGN tab**, in the **Document Formatting group**, click **Colors**, right-click **Literacy Colors**, and then click **Delete**. When a message displays to confirm the deletion, click **Yes**. Using the same technique, click **Fonts**, and then **Delete** the **Literacy Fonts**.

e. Click the **FILE tab**, and then **Close** the document without saving changes, but leave Word open.

(Project 6C Literacy Program continues on the next page)

CHAPTER REVIEW

4 Press Ctrl + N. **Save** the document in your **Word Chapter 6** folder as **Lastname_Firstname_6C_Literacy_Program** Insert the file name in the footer, and display rulers and formatting marks, if necessary.

a. On the **DESIGN tab**, in the **Document Formatting group**, click **Themes**, and then click **Browse for Themes**. Navigate to your **Word Chapter 6** folder, select your **Lastname_Firstname_6C_Literacy_Theme**, and then click **Open**. In the **Page Background group**, click **Page Color**, and then click **Fill Effects**. In the **Fill Effects** dialog box, click the **Texture tab**, and then in the fourth row, click the third texture—**Parchment**. Click **OK**.

b. Press Enter two times, and then position the insertion point in the first blank paragraph. On the **INSERT tab**, in the **Text group**, click **Text Box**. Scroll to the bottom of the gallery, and then under **General**, click your **Literacy Heading** building block. Press Ctrl + End.

c. On the **INSERT tab**, in the **Text group**, click the **Object arrow**, and then click **Text from File**. Navigate to your student files, click **w06C_Literacy_Information**, and then click **Insert**. At the end of the paragraph that ends *in the table below*, position the insertion point after the period, and then press Enter two times.

5 On the **INSERT tab**, in the **Tables group**, click **Table**, point to **Quick Tables**, scroll toward the bottom of the gallery, and then under **General**, click **Job Information**.

a. Position the insertion point in the second row of the table. Type the following text in the table, pressing Tab after each line:

Possess a high school diploma or GED.

Pass a background check.

Be 21 years of age or older.

Attend all training sessions.

Tutor a minimum of two hours a week.

b. Select the last three empty rows of the table. On the mini toolbar, click **Delete**, and then click **Delete Rows**.

6 Press Ctrl + End, press Enter, and then press Ctrl + E. On the **INSERT tab**, in the **Illustrations group**, click **Pictures**. In the **Insert Picture** dialog box, navigate to your student data files, select the file **w06C_Literacy_Image**, and then click **Insert**. On the **FORMAT tab**, change the **Shape Height** to 1.6".

a. Position the insertion point to the right of the picture, and then press Enter. On the **INSERT tab**, in the **Text group**, click **Quick Parts**, click **AutoText**, and then click **Literacy Quote**. Select the inserted text, change the **Font Size** to **10**, and then apply **Bold**. If necessary, at the end of the document, delete the blank paragraph.

b. Press Ctrl + Home. Click the **FILE tab**, and then click **Show All Properties**. In the **Tags** box, type **literacy program, volunteers** In the **Subject** box, type your course name and section number. If necessary, edit the author name to display your name.

c. On the **INSERT tab**, in the **Text group**, click **Quick Parts**, and then click **Building Blocks Organizer**. In the **Building Blocks Organizer** dialog box, in the upper left corner, click **Name** to sort the building blocks alphabetically by name. Locate your building block **Job Information**, click to select it, click **Delete**, and then click **Yes** to confirm the deletion. Using the same technique, scroll to locate and then delete your building blocks **Literacy Heading** and **Literacy Quote**. **Close** the dialog box, and then **Save** the document.

7 Print your two documents—you cannot print your theme—or submit all three files electronically as directed by your instructor. **Close** Word. When a message displays regarding changes to building blocks, click **Save** to accept the changes.

END | You have completed Project 6C

CHAPTER REVIEW

Apply 6B skills from these Objectives:

4 Use Comments in a Document

5 Track Changes in a Document

6 View Side by Side, Compare, and Combine Documents

Skills Review Project 6D User Guide

In the following Skills Review, you will edit a user guide for Mountain View Public Library by creating and deleting comments, inserting text, applying formatting, and accepting changes made by others. Your completed documents will look similar to Figure 6.52.

PROJECT FILES

For Project 6D, you will need the following files:

w06D_User_Guide

w06D_Reviewed_Guide

You will save your files as:

Lastname_Firstname_6D_User_Guide

Lastname_Firstname_6D_Combined_Guide

PROJECT RESULTS

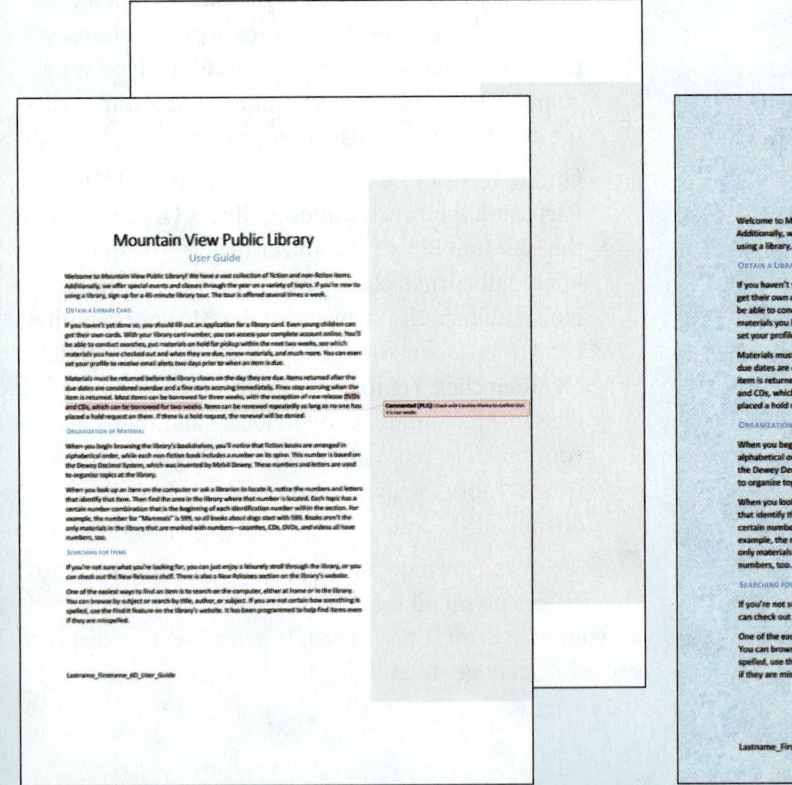

FIGURE 6.52

(Project 6D User Guide continues on the next page)

CHAPTER REVIEW

1 ▶ Start Word. Navigate to your student files and open the file **w06D_User_Guide**. **Save** the document in your **Word Chapter 6** folder as **Lastname_Firstname_6D_User_ Guide** In the footer, delete any existing text, and then insert the file name.

a. On the **REVIEW tab**, in the **Tracking group**, click the **Dialog Box Launcher**. In the **Track Changes Options** dialog box, click **Change User Name**. Under **Personalize your copy of Microsoft Office**, on a piece of paper, make a note of the user name and initials. In the **User name** box, type your own first and last names, and then in the **Initials** box, type your initials, if necessary. Immediately below the **Initials** box, be sure the check box is selected. Click **OK** two times.

b. On the **REVIEW tab**, in the **Tracking group**, click the **Display for Review arrow**, and then click **All Markup**, if necessary. In the paragraph beginning *Materials must be*, select the text *DVDs and CDs, which can be borrowed for two weeks*. On the **REVIEW tab**, in the **Comments group**, click **New Comment**. In the comment, type **Check with Angie Harper to confirm that it is two weeks.**

c. Press [Ctrl] + [Home]. Click to position the insertion point in the text for the *Benedetta Herman* comment that begins *I thought*, and then in the **Comments group**, click **Delete**. Using the same technique, delete the *Caroline Marina* comment that begins *We offer*.

d. Locate your comment, and then replace *Angie Harper* with **Caroline Marina**

2 ▶ To enable tracking, in the **Tracking group**, click **Track Changes** so that it displays in blue. Select the first paragraph—the title—and then apply **Center**. Select the second paragraph, change the **Font Size** to **18**, change the **Font Color** to **Blue, Accent 1**—in the fifth column, the first color—and then apply **Center**.

a. In the paragraph that begins *When you begin browsing*, in the third line, replace the text *Melville* with **Melvil** and then delete the related *Benedetta Herman* comment. On **Page 2**, in the paragraph that begins *The branches of*, in the second line, delete the sentence *We have many comfortable desks and chairs*.

b. Press [Ctrl] + [End]. Press [Enter], and then type **To find out more information about any library services, please contact us at (615) 555-0982.** Select the text you just

typed, change the **Font Size** to **12**, and apply **Italic**. Delete the *Benedetta Herman* comment that begins *Please add*.

c. Press [Ctrl] + [Home]. On the **REVIEW tab**, in the **Changes group**, click the **Accept arrow**, and then click **Accept All Changes and Stop Tracking**.

d. In the **Tracking group**, click the **Dialog Box Launcher**. In the **Track Changes Options** dialog box, click **Change User Name**. If you made changes to the user name, delete your name and initials and type those that displayed originally. Click **OK** two times.

e. Click the **FILE tab**, and then click **Show All Properties**. In the **Tags** box, type **user guide, edited** In the **Subject** box, type your course name and section number. If necessary, edit the author name to display your name. **Save** your document. Click the **FILE tab**, and then **Close** the document but leave Word open.

3 ▶ On the **REVIEW tab**, in the **Compare group**, click **Compare**, and then click **Combine**. In the **Combine Documents** dialog box, click the **Original document arrow**, and then click **Browse**. Navigate to your student files, select the file **w06D_Reviewed_Guide**, and then click **Open**.

a. Click the **Revised document arrow**, and then click **Browse**. Navigate to your **Word Chapter 6** folder, select the file **Lastname_Firstname_6D_User_Guide**, and then click **Open**.

b. In the **Combine Documents** dialog box, click **More**, and then under **Show changes in**, select the **New document** option, if necessary. Click **Less**, and then click **OK**. If necessary, on the right of your screen, **Close** the **Original Document Pane** and the **Revised Document Pane**, and then on the left, **Close** the **Reviewing Pane**, if necessary.

c. If necessary, position the insertion point at the beginning of the **Combined Document**. Click **Save**, and then **Save** the document in your **Word Chapter 6** folder as **Lastname_Firstname_6D_Combined_Guide**

4 ▶ On the **REVIEW tab**, in the **Changes group**, click the **Accept arrow**, and then click **Accept All Changes and Stop Tracking**.

a. On **Page 2**, locate the *Angie Harper* comment. Select the two sentences that begins *Be aware*, and ends *wireless device*. delete the two sentences.

b. On the **REVIEW tab**, in the **Comments group**, click the **Delete arrow**, and then click **Delete All Comments in Document**.

(Project 6D User Guide continues on the next page)

CHAPTER REVIEW

5 Right-click in the footer area, and then click **Edit Footer**. Right-click the existing text, and then from the shortcut menu, click **Update Field**. **Close** the footer area.

a. On the **DESIGN tab**, in the **Page Background group**, click **Page Color**, and then click **Fill Effects**. In the **Fill Effects** dialog box, click the **Texture tab**, scroll as necessary, and then in the next to last row, click the first texture—**Blue tissue paper**. Click **OK**.

b. Press Ctrl + Home. Click the **FILE tab**, and then click **Show All Properties**. In the **Tags** box, type **user guide, reviewed, combined** In the **Subject** box, type your course name and section number. If necessary, edit the author name to display your name.

c. **Save** your document.

6 Print both documents or submit them electronically as directed by your instructor. **Close** Word.

END | You have completed Project 6D

CONTENT-BASED ASSESSMENTS

MyITLab®
grader

Apply **6A** skills from these Objectives:

1 Create Custom Building Blocks

2 Create and Save a Theme Template

3 Create a Document by Using Building Blocks

Build from Scratch

In the following Mastering Word project, you will create and save building blocks and create a theme for an agenda for Mountain View Public Library's seminar on Public Libraries and the Internet. Your completed documents will look similar to Figure 6.53.

PROJECT FILES

For Project 6E, you will need the following files:

New blank Word document
w06E_Seminar_Agenda

You will save your files as:

Lastname_Firstname_6E_Seminar_Blocks
Lastname_Firstname_6E_Seminar_Agenda
Lastname_Firstname_6E_Seminar_Theme—not shown in the figure

PROJECT RESULTS

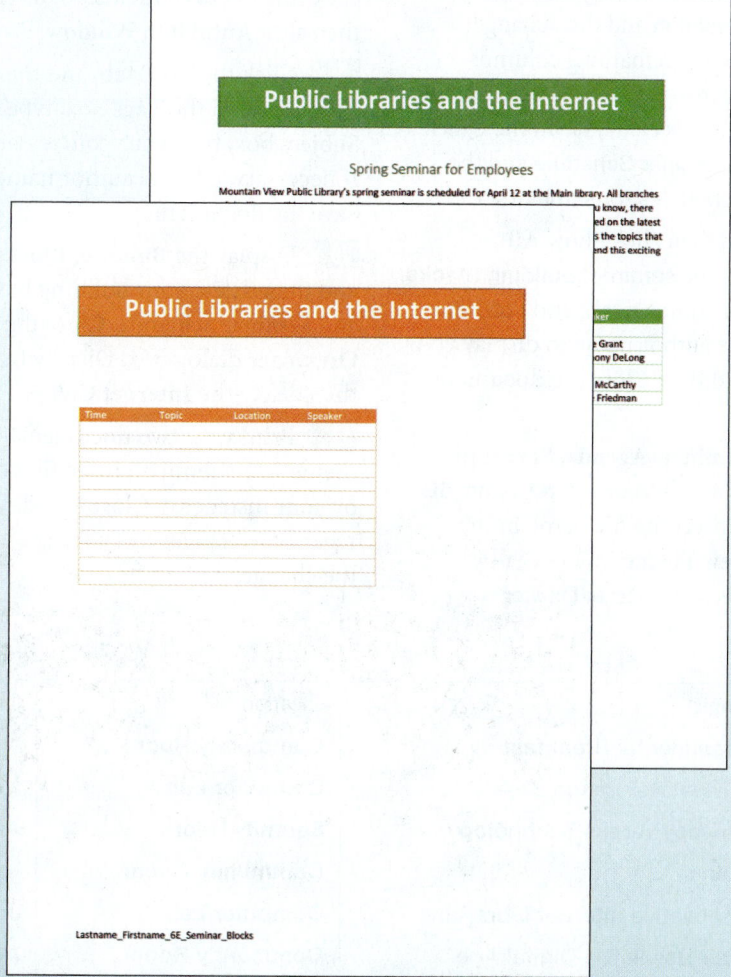

FIGURE 6.53

(Project 6E Seminar Agenda continues on the next page)

CONTENT-BASED ASSESSMENTS

1 Start Word. Display a blank document. Be sure rulers and formatting marks display. **Save** the document in your **Word Chapter 6** folder as **Lastname_Firstname_6E_Seminar_Blocks** Insert the file name in the footer.

2 Press Enter three times. In the first blank paragraph, **Insert** a **Simple Text Box**, change the **Shape Height** to **0.7"**, and then change the **Shape Width** to **6.5"**. Apply the shape style **Colored Fill – Orange, Accent 2**. In the text box, type **Public Libraries and the Internet** Select the text you typed, change the **Font Size** to **28** and then apply **Bold** and **Center**. Select and then **Save** the text box in the **Text Box** gallery with the name **Internet Seminar** and the **Description Use in all Internet Seminar documents**

3 In the third blank paragraph, display the **Quick Tables** gallery, and then insert a **Double Table**. Above the table, delete the text *The Greek Alphabet*. Replace the text *Letter name* with **Time** and then press Tab. Change *Uppercase* to **Topic** Change *Lowercase* to **Location** and then change *Letter name* to **Speaker** Delete the remaining columns, and then delete the remaining text. Apply the table style **List Table 4 – Accent 2**. **Save** the selected table in the **Quick Tables** gallery with the name **Seminar Schedule** and the **Description Use to display schedules for seminars**

4 Click the **FILE tab**, and then click **Show All Properties**. In the **Tags** box, type **seminar, building blocks** In the **Subject** box, type your course name and section number. If necessary, edit the author name to display your name. **Save** your changes, and then **Close** the document but leave Word open.

5 Open the file **w06E_Seminar_Agenda**, **Save** it in your **Word Chapter 6** folder as **Lastname_Firstname_6E_Seminar_Agenda** and then insert the file name in the footer. Display the **Create New Theme Colors** dialog box. Change **Accent 1** to **Green, Accent 6, Darker**

25%, and then change **Accent 2** to **Green, Accent 6**. **Save** the Theme Colors as **Internet Colors Save** the current theme in your **Word Chapter 6** folder as **Lastname_Firstname_6E_Seminar_Theme**

6 In the first blank paragraph, display the **Text Box** gallery, and then insert your **Internet Seminar** text box.

7 Select the text *Spring Seminar for Employees*, apply the **Heading 1** style, and then apply **Center**. On the **PAGE LAYOUT tab**, in the **Paragraph group**, change the **Spacing After** to **6 pt**. Select the text *AGENDA*, apply the **Heading 2** style, apply **Center**, and then change the **Spacing After** to **12 pt**. Position the insertion point in the blank paragraph following *AGENDA*, display the **Quick Tables** gallery, and then insert your **Seminar Schedule**. In the table, enter the text shown in Table 1 below. Delete empty rows as necessary.

8 Select the table, right-click, point to **AutoFit**, and then click **AutoFit to Contents**. Right-click, point to **AutoFit**, and then click **AutoFit to Window**. Press Ctrl + Home.

9 Click the **FILE tab**, and then click **Show All Properties**. In the **Tags** box, type **seminar, agenda** In the **Subject** box, type your course name and section number. If necessary, edit the author name to display your name. **Save** the document.

10 Display the **Building Blocks Organizer** dialog box, and then delete your building blocks **Internet Seminar** and **Seminar Schedule**. **Close** the **Building Blocks Organizer** dialog box. Display the **Theme Colors** list, and then delete the **Internet Colors**.

11 Print your two documents—you cannot print your theme—or submit all three files electronically as directed by your instructor. **Close** Word. When a message displays regarding changes to building blocks, click **Save** to accept the changes.

TABLE 1

Time	Topic	Location	Speaker
8 a.m. – 9 a.m.	Continental Breakfast	Community Room	
9 a.m. – 10 a.m.	Virtual Reference Desks	Computer Lab A	Irene Grant
10 a.m. – Noon	Privacy versus Technology	Serenity Room	Anthony DeLong
Noon – 1 p.m.	Lunch	Community Room	
1 p.m. – 3 p.m.	Innovative Internet Librarians	Computer Lab A	Josh McCarthy
3 p.m. – 5 p.m.	Fair Use in the Digital Age	Community Room	Alice Friedman

END | You have completed Project 6E

(Return to Step 8)

CONTENT-BASED ASSESSMENTS

MyITLab® grader

Mastering Word Project 6F Library Classes

In the following Mastering Word project, you will edit a user guide for Mountain View Public Library by creating and deleting comments, inserting text, applying formatting, and accepting changes made by others. Your completed documents will look similar to Figure 6.54.

Apply 6B skills from these objectives:

4 Use Comments in a Document

5 Track Changes in a Document

6 View Side by Side, Compare, and Combine Documents

PROJECT FILES

For Project 6F, you will need the following files:

w06F_Library_Classes

w06F_Classes_Reviewed

You will save your files as:

Lastname_Firstname_6F_Library_Classes

Lastname_Firstname_6F_Classes_Combined

PROJECT RESULTS

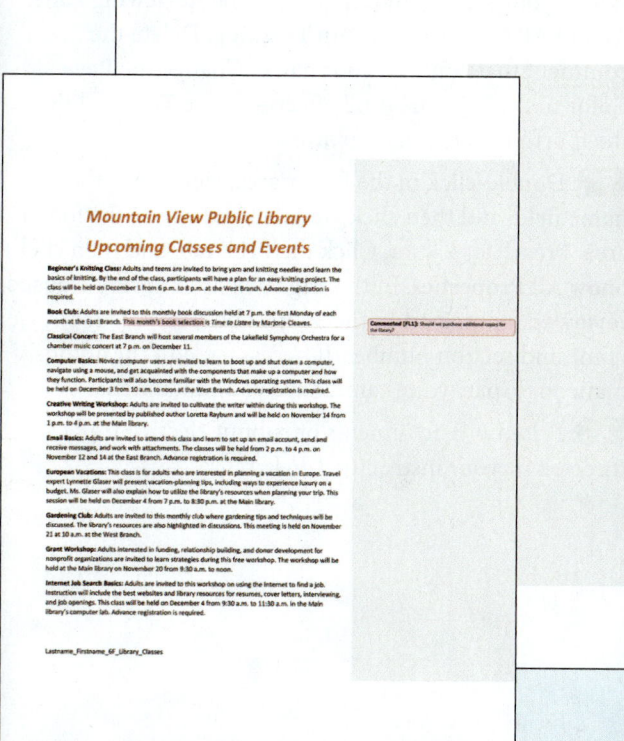

FIGURE 6.54

(Project 6F Library Classes continues on the next page)

CONTENT-BASED ASSESSMENTS

1 Start Word, and then open the file **w06F_Library_Classes**. **Save** the document in your **Word Chapter 6** folder as **Lastname_Firstname_6F_Library_Classes** In the footer, delete the existing text, and then insert the file name. On the **REVIEW tab**, in the **Tracking group**, display the **Track Changes Options** dialog box, and then click **Change User Name**. Note the existing user name and initials. Under **Personalize your copy of Microsoft Office**, type your name in the **User name** box, and then type your initials in the **Initials** box, if necessary. Immediately below Initials, be sure the check box is selected. In the **Tracking group**, change **Display for Review** to **All Markup**, if necessary.

2 In the fourth paragraph, select the text *This month's book selection*. Insert a new comment, and then type **Should we purchase additional copies for the library?** Delete the *Abigail Gardner* comment and the *Caroline Marina* comment.

3 Turn on **Track Changes**. Select the first two paragraphs, and then apply the **Book Title** style. Change the **Font Size** to **28**, change the **Font Color** to **Orange, Accent 2, Darker 25%**, and then apply **Center**. On **Page 2**, locate the paragraph that begins *Microsoft Word*. Delete the text *101*, and then press Ctrl + End. Press Enter, and then type **To register for a class or to obtain more information, contact Abigail Gardner at (615) 555-0982.** Select the sentence you just typed, and then apply **Italic** and **Center**.

4 Press Ctrl + Home, and then **Accept All Changes and Stop Tracking**. Display the **Track Changes Options** dialog box, and then click **Change User Name**. If necessary, delete your name in the **User Name** box, delete your

initials in the **Initials** box, and then restore the original text and settings. Click the **FILE tab**, and then click **Show All Properties**. In the **Tags** box, type **library classes, edited** In the **Subject** box, type your course name and section number. If necessary, edit the author name to display your name. **Save** your document, click the **FILE tab**, and then **Close** the document but leave Word open.

5 Display the **Combine Documents** dialog box. For the **Original document**, in your student data files, select the file **w06F_Classes_Reviewed**. For the **Revised document**, in your **Word Chapter 6** folder, select the file **Lastname_Firstname_6F_Library_Classes**. Click **More**, and then select the **New document** option. Click **Less**, and then click **OK**.

6 **Save** the document in your **Word Chapter 6** folder as **Lastname_Firstname_6F_Classes_Combined** If necessary, **Close** the two document panes on the right side of your screen, and then **Close** the **Reviewing Pane**. **Accept All Changes and Stop Tracking**. Delete the comment that contains your name. Change the **Page Color** to the **Newsprint** fill effect—on the **Texture tab**, in the fourth row, the first texture.

7 Double-click in the footer area, right-click the file name field, and then click **Update Field**. **Close** the footer area. Press Ctrl + Home. Click the **FILE tab**, and then click **Show All Properties**. In the **Tags** box, type **library classes, reviewed, combined** In the **Subject** box, type your course name and section number. If necessary, edit the author name to display your name. **Save** your document.

8 Print both documents or submit electronically as directed by your instructor. **Close** Word.

END | You have completed Project 6F

CONTENT-BASED ASSESSMENTS

Mastering Word   Project 6G Website Flyer

Apply 6A and 6B skills from these Objectives:

1 Create Custom Building Blocks

2 Create and Save a Theme Template

3 Create a Document by Using Building Blocks

4 Use Comments in a Document

5 Track Changes in a Document

6 View Side by Side, Compare, and Combine Documents

In the following Mastering Word project, you will create a document to announce the launch of Mountain View Public Library's new website by creating and inserting building blocks, creating a custom theme, inserting text, applying formatting, and accepting changes made by others. Your completed documents will look similar to Figure 6.55.

PROJECT FILES

For Project 6G, you will need the following files:

New blank Word document
w06G_Website_Flyer

You will save your files as:

Lastname_Firstname_6G_Website_Blocks
Lastname_Firstname_6G_Website_Flyer
Lastname_Firstname_6G_Website_Theme—not shown in the figure

Build from Scratch

PROJECT RESULTS

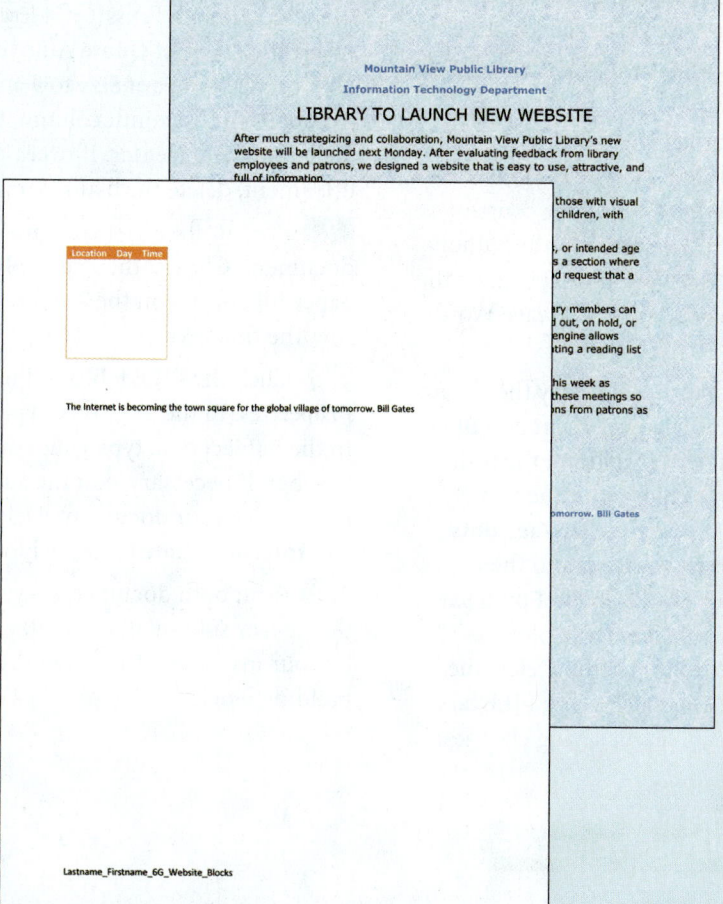

FIGURE 6.55

(Project 6G Website Flyer continues on the next page)

CONTENT-BASED ASSESSMENTS

1 Start Word, and then display a new document. **Save** the document in your **Word Chapter 6** folder as **Lastname_Firstname_6G_Website_Blocks** Insert the file name in the footer. Be sure rulers and formatting marks display.

2 Display the **Quick Tables** gallery, and insert a **Tabular List**. In the first cell, replace the text *ITEM* with **Location** In the second cell, replace the text *NEEDED* with **Day** Right-click to display the mini toolbar, click **Insert**, and then click **Insert Right** to create a third column. In the first cell of the third column, type **Time** Delete all remaining text in the table, and then apply the **List Table 3 – Accent 2** table style. **Save** the table in the **Quick Tables** gallery with the name **Training Schedule** and the **Description Use to display schedules for training**

3 Press Ctrl + End. Press Enter two times, and then type **The Internet is becoming the town square for the global village of tomorrow. Bill Gates** Select the text, and then **Save** the selection in the **AutoText** gallery with the name **Internet Quote** and the **Description Use in website documents**

4 Press Ctrl + Home. Click the **FILE tab**, and then click **Show All Properties**. In the **Tags** box, type **IT Department, building blocks** In the **Subject** box, type your course name and section number. If necessary, edit the author name to display your name. **Save** your changes. Click the **FILE tab**, and then **Close** the document but leave Word open.

5 Display a new blank document. Display the **Create New Theme Colors** dialog box, change **Accent 2** to **Blue, Accent 5, Darker 25%**—in the ninth column, the fifth color; and then **Save** the theme colors with the name **Website Colors** Display the **Create New Theme Fonts** dialog box, change **Body font** to **Verdana**, and then save the theme fonts with the name **Website Fonts Save** the current theme in your **Word Chapter 6** folder as **Lastname_Firstname_6G_Website_Theme** Delete the **Website Colors** and **Website Fonts**. Click the **FILE tab**, and then **Close** the document, without saving changes, but leave Word open.

6 Open the file **w06G_Website_Flyer**, and then **Save** it in your **Word Chapter 6** folder as **Lastname_Firstname_6G_Website_Flyer** In the footer, delete the existing text, and then insert the file name. Apply your custom theme—**Lastname_Firstname_6G_Website_Theme**.

7 Select the first two paragraphs of the document. Change the **Font Color** to **Blue, Accent 5**, and then apply **Bold** and **Center**. Press Ctrl + End, and then insert the **Training Schedule** Quick Table. Beginning in the first cell of the second row, type the following text in the table.

East Branch	Tuesday	2 p.m.
Main Library	Monday	9 a.m.
West Branch	Friday	3 p.m.

8 Delete all empty rows in the table. Select the table, and then **AutoFit Contents**. **Center** the table horizontally in the document. Press Ctrl + End, and then press Enter. Insert the **Internet Quote** AutoText. Select the inserted text, change the **Font Size** to **9** and the **Font Color** to **Blue, Accent 5**—in the ninth column, the first color; and then apply **Bold** and **Center**. If necessary, at the end of the document, delete the blank paragraph.

9 Press Ctrl + Home. **Accept All Changes** in the document. Change the **Page Color** to the **Blue tissue paper** fill effect—on the **Texture tab**, in the next to last row, the first texture.

10 Click the **FILE tab**, and then click **Show All Properties**. In the **Tags** box, type **website flyer, reviewed** In the **Subject** box, type your course name and section number. If necessary, edit the author name to display your name. **Save** your document. Delete the **Training Schedule** and **Internet Quote** building blocks.

11 Print both documents—you cannot print the theme—or submit all three files electronically as directed by your instructor. **Close** Word, and **Save** changes to building blocks.

END | You have completed Project 6G

CONTENT-BASED ASSESSMENTS

Apply a combination of the 6A and 6B skills.

GO! Fix It	Project 6H Internship Memo	Online

GO! Make It	Project 6I Request Form	Online

Build from Scratch

GO! Solve It	Project 6J Employee Newsletter	Online

Build from Scratch

GO! Solve It	Project 6K Library Rules

PROJECT FILES

For Project 6K, you will need the following files:

New blank Word document
w06K_Library_Rules

You will save your files as:

Lastname_Firstname_6K_Rules_Blocks
Lastname_Firstname_6K_Library_Rules

Display a new blank document and save it in your **Word Chapter 6** folder as **Lastname_Firstname_6K_Rules_Blocks** Insert a graphic related to a library and save it as a building block. Save a text box as a building block that includes the text **Library Rules** Insert the file name in the footer and add appropriate document properties.

From your student files, open the document **w06K_Library_Rules**. Accept all changes. Save the file to your **Word Chapter 6** folder as **Lastname_Firstname_6K_Library_Rules** Modify the theme colors and format the text to improve readability. Insert the building blocks you created. Adjust the building blocks and text to create an attractive, one-page document. Insert the file name in the footer and add appropriate document properties. Print both documents or submit electronically as directed by your instructor.

Performance Element

Performance Criteria		Exemplary: You consistently applied the relevant skills	Proficient: You sometimes, but not always, applied the relevant skills	Developing: You rarely or never applied the relevant skills
	Create a graphic building block	An appropriate graphic is saved as a building block.	A graphic is saved as a building block but is not related to the topic.	No graphic is saved as a building block.
	Create a text box building block	A text box containing the correct information is saved as a building block.	A text box is saved as a building block but contains incorrect information.	No text box is saved as a building block.
	Accept changes	All changes are accepted.	Some changes are accepted but others are not.	No changes are accepted.
	Modify theme colors and format text	The theme colors are modified and the text is formatted attractively.	The theme colors are not modified or the text is not formatted attractively.	The theme colors are not modified and the text is not formatted.
	Insert building blocks	Both building blocks are inserted and positioned appropriately.	One building block is not inserted or is positioned inappropriately.	Both building blocks are not inserted or are positioned inappropriately.

END | You have completed Project 6K

OUTCOMES-BASED ASSESSMENTS

RUBRIC

The following outcomes-based assessments are *open-ended assessments*. That is, there is no specific correct result; your result will depend on your approach to the information provided. Make *Professional Quality* your goal. Use the following scoring rubric to guide you in *how* to approach the problem and then to evaluate *how well* your approach solves the problem.

The *criteria*—Software Mastery, Content, Format and Layout, and Process—represent the knowledge and skills you have gained that you can apply to solving the problem. The *levels of performance*—Professional Quality, Approaching Professional Quality, or Needs Quality Improvements—help you and your instructor evaluate your result.

	Your completed project is of Professional Quality if you:	Your completed project is Approaching Professional Quality if you:	Your completed project Needs Quality Improvements if you:
1-Software Mastery	Choose and apply the most appropriate skills, tools, and features and identify efficient methods to solve the problem.	Choose and apply some appropriate skills, tools, and features, but not in the most efficient manner.	Choose inappropriate skills, tools, or features, or are inefficient in solving the problem.
2-Content	Construct a solution that is clear and well organized, contains content that is accurate, appropriate to the audience and purpose, and is complete. Provide a solution that contains no errors in spelling, grammar, or style.	Construct a solution in which some components are unclear, poorly organized, inconsistent, or incomplete. Misjudge the needs of the audience. Have some errors in spelling, grammar, or style, but the errors do not detract from comprehension.	Construct a solution that is unclear, incomplete, or poorly organized; contains some inaccurate or inappropriate content; and contains many errors in spelling, grammar, or style. Do not solve the problem.
3-Format & Layout	Format and arrange all elements to communicate information and ideas, clarify function, illustrate relationships, and indicate relative importance.	Apply appropriate format and layout features to some elements, but not others. Overuse features, causing minor distraction.	Apply format and layout that does not communicate information or ideas clearly. Do not use format and layout features to clarify function, illustrate relationships, or indicate relative importance. Use available features excessively, causing distraction.
4-Process	Use an organized approach that integrates planning, development, self-assessment, revision, and reflection.	Demonstrate an organized approach in some areas, but not others; or, use an insufficient process of organization throughout.	Do not use an organized approach to solve the problem.

OUTCOMES-BASED ASSESSMENTS

Apply a combination of the 6A and 6B skills.

Build from
Scratch

GO! Think   Project 6L Fundraising Flyer

PROJECT FILES

For Project 6L, you will need the following file:

New blank Word document

You will save your files as:

Lastname_Firstname_6L_Fundraising_Blocks
Lastname_Firstname_6L_Fundraising_Flyer

The Mountain View Public Library is conducting a fundraising campaign with a goal of $200,000 needed to upgrade the computer lab at the Main library and fund library programs. Donations can be sent to 1000 Maple Avenue, Claremont, TN 38325. Benedetta Herman, Director of Operations, is chairing the fundraising committee and can be reached at (615) 555-0982. Donor levels include:

Type of Recognition	Amount of Gift
Bronze Book Club	$ 100 or more
Silver Book Club	$ 500 or more
Gold Book Club	$ 1,000 or more

Create a document that includes a text box containing the name and address of the library, an appropriate image, and an appropriate quotation. Save all three objects as building blocks. Save the document as **Lastname_Firstname_6L_Fundraising_Blocks** Create a flyer explaining the campaign and how donors will be acknowledged. Customize the theme, add appropriate text, and insert your building blocks. Include a Quick Table to display the recognition types. Format the flyer in a professional manner. Save the file as **Lastname_Firstname_6L_Fundraising_Flyer** For both documents, insert the file name in the footer and add document properties. Submit both documents as directed by your instructor.

END | You have completed Project 6L

OUTCOMES-BASED ASSESSMENTS

Build from
Scratch

GO! Think	Project 6M Reading Certificate	**Online**
You and GO!	Project 6N Personal Calendar	**Online**

Build from
Scratch

Creating Web Content and Using Advanced Editing Tools

GO! to Work
Video W7

WORD 2013

7

PROJECT
7A

OUTCOMES
Manage web content in Word.

PROJECT
7B

OUTCOMES
Use editing tools and save a document in RTF format.

OBJECTIVES

1. Create a Webpage from a Word Document
2. Insert and Modify Hyperlinks in a Word Document
3. Create a Blog Post

OBJECTIVES

4. Manage Document Versions
5. Collect and Paste Images and Text
6. Locate Supporting Information and Insert Equations
7. Use Advanced Find and Replace Options
8. Save in Other File Formats

aurehar/Fotolia

In This Chapter

In this chapter you will use text, graphic, and document formatting features in Word to create documents saved as attractive, professional-looking webpages that include hyperlinks. You will also create blog posts, which can contain text, images, and links to related blogs or webpages. You will modify Word option settings to create document versions that are automatically saved. You will use Word's research features and the Clipboard to collect and organize information in documents. You will also insert equations in documents and use Find and Replace to edit text. Finally, you will save documents in other useful formats.

The projects in this chapter relate to **Oregon Wireless Specialties**, a supplier of accessories and software for all major brands of cell phones, smartphones, tablet computers, MP3 players, and laptop computers. The company sells distinctive products in its stores, which are located throughout Oregon and the northwestern United States. Items are also available on its website. For online orders, the company offers its retail and wholesale customers low shipping costs and full credit on returns. Oregon Wireless Specialties takes pride in offering unique categories of accessories such as waterproof and ruggedized gear.

385

PROJECT 7A

Customer Webpage

MyITLab®
Project 7A Training

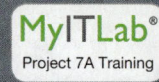

PROJECT ACTIVITIES

In Activities 7.01 through 7.13, you will assist Nanci Scholtz, Vice President of Marketing for Oregon Wireless Specialties, in creating a new home page for the online store and a new blog post for the company's customer service blog. Your completed documents will look similar to Figure 7.1.

PROJECT FILES

For Project 7A, you will need the following files:

w07A_Home_Page
w07A_Features_Guide

You will save your files as:

Lastname_Firstname_7A_Home_Page
Lastname_Firstname_7A_Features_Guide
Lastname_Firstname_7A_Blog_Post

PROJECT RESULTS

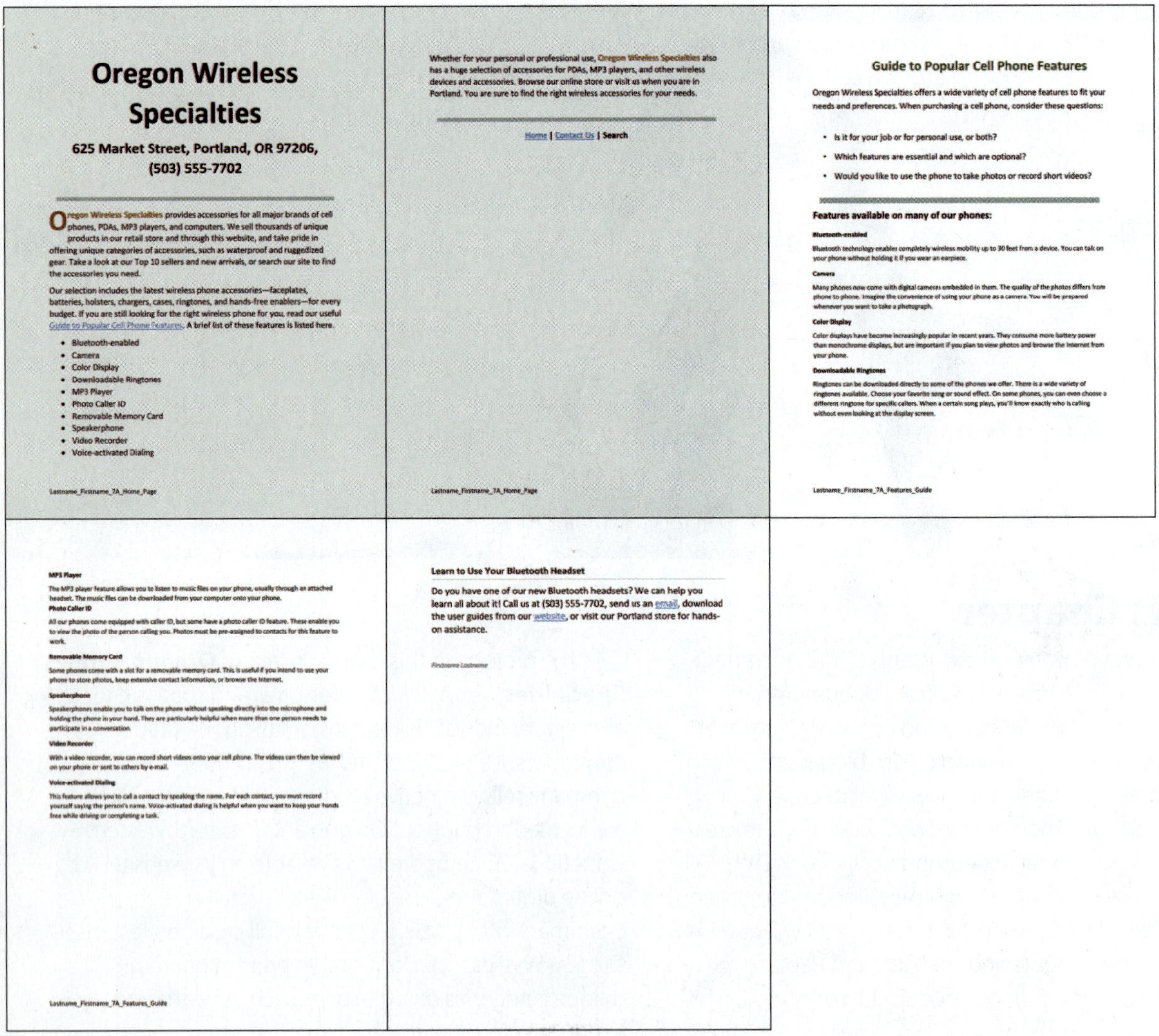

FIGURE 7.1 Project 7A Customer Webpage

Objective 1   Create a Webpage from a Word Document

Video W7-1

You can create a *webpage* from a Word document. A webpage is a file coded in *HyperText Markup Language*—referred to as *HTML*—that can be viewed on the Internet by using a *web browser*. A web browser—also referred to as simply a *browser*—is software that interprets HTML files, formats them into webpages, and then displays them. HTML is a markup language that communicates color and graphics in a format that all computers can understand.

Activity 7.01 | Saving a Document as a Webpage and Changing Document Views

For a Word document to display in a browser, you must save it in HTML. In this activity, you will save a Word document in the Web Page format so it can be added to the company's website.

1 Start Word. From your student files, locate and open the file **w07A_Home_Page**. If necessary, display formatting marks and rulers.

2 Click the **FILE tab**, and then click **Save As**. In the **Save As** dialog box, navigate to the location where you are saving your files for this chapter. Create a new folder named **Word Chapter 7** In the lower portion of the **Save As** dialog box, click the **Save as type arrow**, and then from the list, click **Web Page**.

In this project, you will use the *Web Page format*, a file type that saves a Word document as an HTML file, with some elements of the webpage saved in a folder, separate from the webpage. The format is useful if you want to access individual elements, such as pictures, separately.

3 Near the bottom of the dialog box, click **Change Title**, and then in the **Enter Text** dialog box, in the **Page title** box, type **Oregon Wireless Specialties** Compare your screen with Figure 7.2.

By creating this title, when the document is viewed as a webpage with a browser, *Oregon Wireless Specialties* will display on the title bar. Because Internet search engines locate the content of webpages by title, it is important to create a title that describes the content of the webpage.

FIGURE 7.2

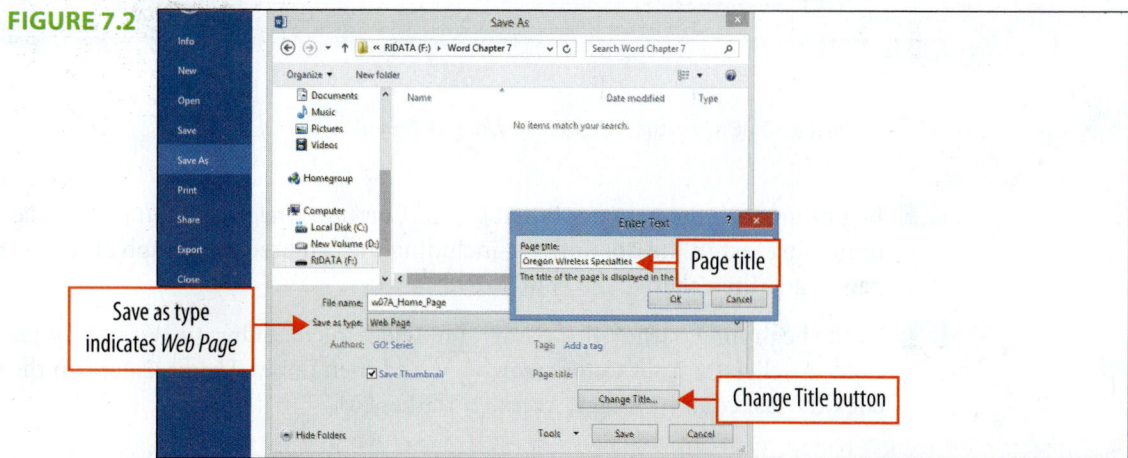

4 Click **OK**. In the **Save As** dialog box, in the **File name** box, type **Lastname_Firstname_7A_Home_Page** and then click **Save**. Compare your screen with Figure 7.3.

Because you saved the document as a webpage, the document displays in Web Layout view, and on the status bar, the Web Layout button is active. The Zoom level may change to display text according to the size of your screen.

FIGURE 7.3

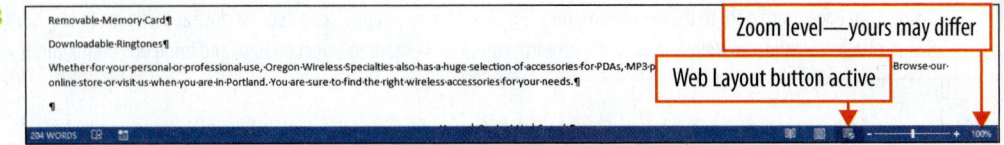

5 Click the **INSERT tab**, and then in the **Header & Footer group**, click **Footer**. At the bottom of the list, click **Edit Footer**. On the ribbon, in the **Insert group**, click **Document Info**, and then click **File Name**. **Close** the footer area.

In Web Layout view, headers and footers do not display on the screen.

6 On the status bar, click **Print Layout**. Scroll to the bottom of the page, if necessary, and then notice that the file name displays in the footer in this view.

7 Press Ctrl + Home, and then on the status bar, click **Web Layout** to return to **Web Layout** view. **Save** your document.

Activity 7.02 | Applying Background Color

In this activity, you will format text and change the background color of the document so that when it is viewed as a webpage, an attractive background color displays.

1 Select the first paragraph of the document—the company name *Oregon Wireless Specialties*. On the mini toolbar, apply **Bold** B, and then change the **Font Size** to **48**.

2 Select the second paragraph—the company address and telephone number. On the mini toolbar, apply **Bold** B, and then change the **Font Size** to **24**.

3 Select the first and second paragraphs, and then press Ctrl + E to center the paragraphs. Click anywhere to deselect the text, and then compare your screen with Figure 7.4.

FIGURE 7.4

🔄 **ANOTHER WAY**   On the HOME tab, in the Paragraph group, click Center.

4 Beginning with the paragraph that begins *Oregon Wireless Specialties provides*, select all the remaining text in the document—including the centered paragraph at the bottom of the page—and then change the **Font Size** to **14**.

5 At the beginning of the third paragraph, select the text *Oregon Wireless Specialties*. Apply **Bold** B, click the **Font Color arrow** A, and then under **Theme Colors**, in the sixth column, click the last color—**Orange, Accent 2, Darker 50%**.

6 Press [Ctrl] + [End]. In the paragraph that begins *Whether*, select the text *Oregon Wireless Specialties*. Apply **Bold** [B], and then click **Font Color** [A ▾].

7 Select the last paragraph, apply **Bold** [B], and then deselect the text.

8 Press [Ctrl] + [Home]. Click the **DESIGN tab**. In the **Page Background group**, click **Page Color**, and then in the third column, click the first color—**Gray – 25%, Background 2**. **Save** [💾] your document, and then compare your screen with Figure 7.5.

FIGURE 7.5

Activity 7.03 | Inserting a Drop Cap

A **drop cap** is a large capital letter at the beginning of a paragraph that formats text in a visually distinctive manner.

1 At the beginning of the third paragraph in the document, select the orange letter *O*. Click the **INSERT tab**. In the **Text group**, click **Drop Cap**, and then click **Drop Cap Options**. Compare your screen with Figure 7.6.

> Here you can select either the **Dropped** position, which enlarges the letter and drops it into the text, or the **In margin** position, which drops the enlarged letter into the left margin. The Drop Cap dialog box provides a visual example of each position.

FIGURE 7.6

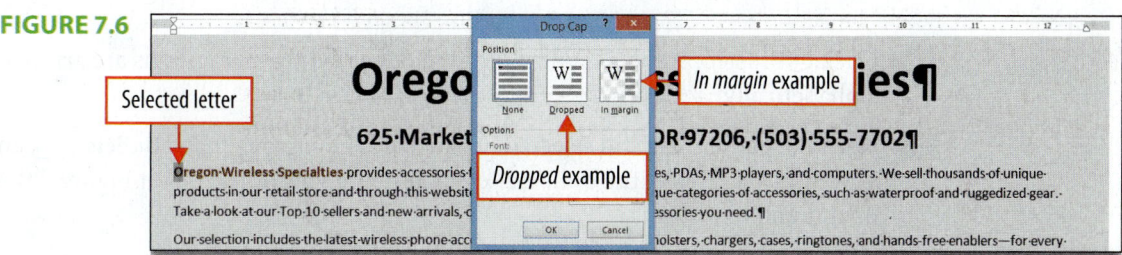

2 In the **Drop Cap** dialog box, under **Position**, click **Dropped**. Under **Options**, click the **Lines to drop down spin arrow** one time to change the number of lines by which to drop to **2** lines. Compare your screen with Figure 7.7.

FIGURE 7.7

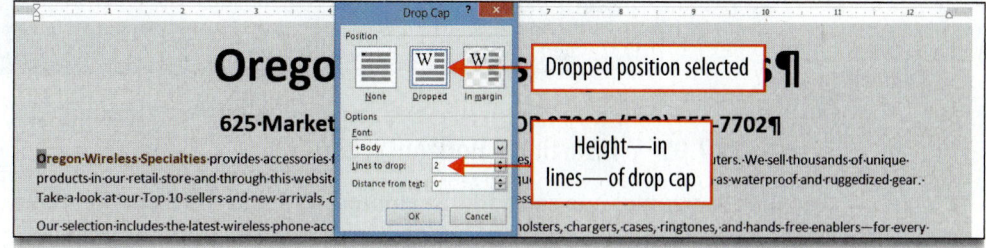

3 In the **Drop Cap** dialog box, click **OK**.

> Sizing handles display around the border of the dropped letter indicating that it is selected.

4 Click anywhere in the document to deselect the drop cap, and then **Save** [💾] your document.

Activity 7.04 | Sorting Paragraphs

Sorting is the action of ordering data, usually in alphabetical or numeric order. *Ascending* refers to sorting alphabetically from A to Z or ordering numerically from the smallest to the largest. *Descending* refers to sorting alphabetically from Z to A or ordering numerically from the largest to the smallest.

1 Scroll to display the ten paragraphs that comprise the cell phone features—begin with *Speakerphone* and end with *Downloadable Ringtones*. Click to position the insertion point to the left of *Speakerphone*, and then select the ten paragraphs.

 **BY TOUCH**   Tap Speakerphone, and then drag the selection handle to the end of the last paragraph Downloadable Ringtones.

2 On the **HOME tab**, in the **Paragraph group**, click **Sort** to display the **Sort Text** dialog box. Compare your screen with Figure 7.8.

Here you can select what you want to sort by, which in this instance is *Paragraphs*; the type of data to sort, which in this instance is *Text*; and the type of sort—ascending or descending.

FIGURE 7.8

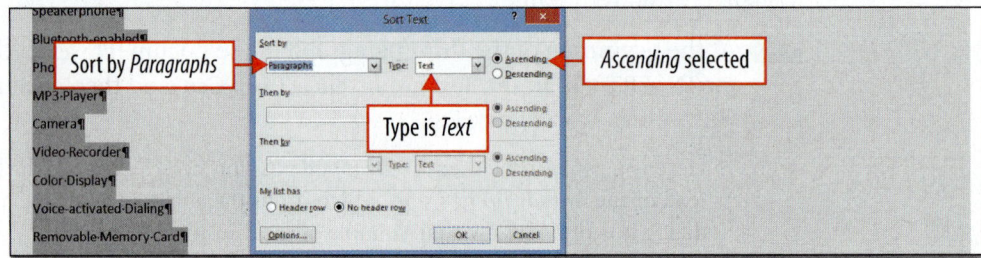

3 Click **OK** to accept the default settings. Notice that the paragraphs are arranged alphabetically.

4 With the paragraphs still selected, in the **Paragraph group**, click **Bullets**, and then click anywhere to deselect the bulleted text. Compare your screen with Figure 7.9. **Save** your document.

FIGURE 7.9

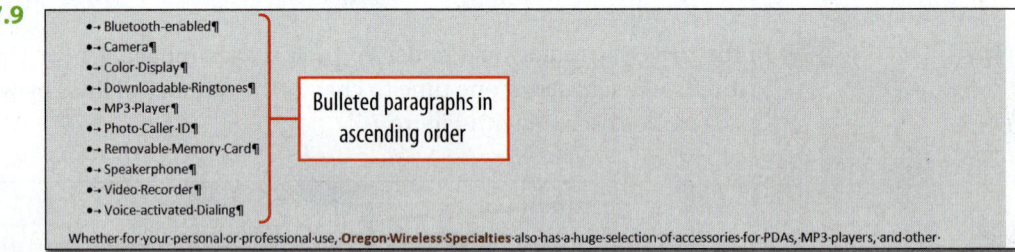

Activity 7.05 | Inserting a Horizontal Line

A horizontal line can add visual interest to and differentiate sections of a webpage.

1 Press Ctrl + Home. In the second paragraph, click to position the insertion point to the right of the telephone number.

2 Press Enter. On the **HOME tab**, in the **Paragraph group**, click the **Borders button arrow**, and then click **Horizontal Line**. Notice a horizontal line is inserted in the document.

ANOTHER WAY   On the INSERT tab, in the Illustrations group, click Shapes, and then under Lines, click the first shape—Line.

3 Right-click the horizontal line, and then from the shortcut menu, click **Format Horizontal Line**.

4 In the **Format Horizontal Line** dialog box, click the **Width spin box down arrow** to **95%** and then click the **Height spin box up arrow** to **6 pt**. Under **Color**, select the **Use solid color (no shade)** check box. Compare your screen with Figure 7.10.

FIGURE 7.10

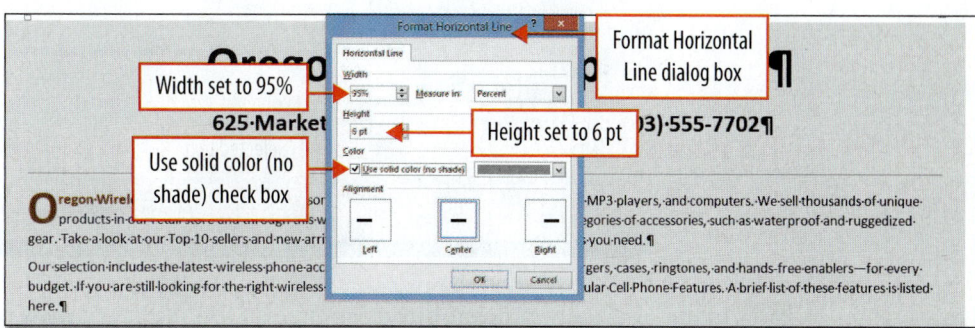

5 Click **OK**. Point to the line, right-click, and then click **Copy**.

6 In the blank paragraph immediately above the last paragraph of the document that begins *Home*, click to position the insertion point. Right-click, and then under **Paste Options**, click the first option—**Keep Source Formatting**—to insert a copy of the horizontal line with the same formatting. **Save** your document.

Objective 2 | Insert and Modify Hyperlinks in a Word Document

Video W7-2

Hyperlinks are text, buttons, pictures, or other objects in a document that, when clicked, access other sections of the active document or another file. A web browser—for example, *Internet Explorer* developed by Microsoft—enables you to transfer files, play sound or video files that are embedded in webpages, and follow hyperlinks to other webpages and files.

Activity 7.06 | Inserting a Hyperlink

By inserting hyperlinks, individuals who view your webpage can move to other webpages inside your *website* or to pages in another website. A website is a group of related webpages published to a specific location on the Internet. The most common type of hyperlink is a *text link*—a link applied to a selected word or phrase. Text links usually display as blue underlined text.

1 Press Ctrl + End, and notice that the last paragraph consists of a series of words and phrases.

Websites commonly have a *navigation bar*—a series of text links across the top or bottom of a webpage that, when clicked, will link to another webpage in the same website.

2 Select the first word in the paragraph—*Home*—and then on the **INSERT tab**, in the **Links group**, click **Hyperlink**. Under **Link to**, click **Existing File or Web Page**, if necessary. Compare your screen with Figure 7.11.

In the Insert Hyperlink dialog box, the Text to display box indicates the selected word *Home*.

ANOTHER WAY   Right-click the selected text, and then from the shortcut menu, click Hyperlink.

FIGURE 7.11

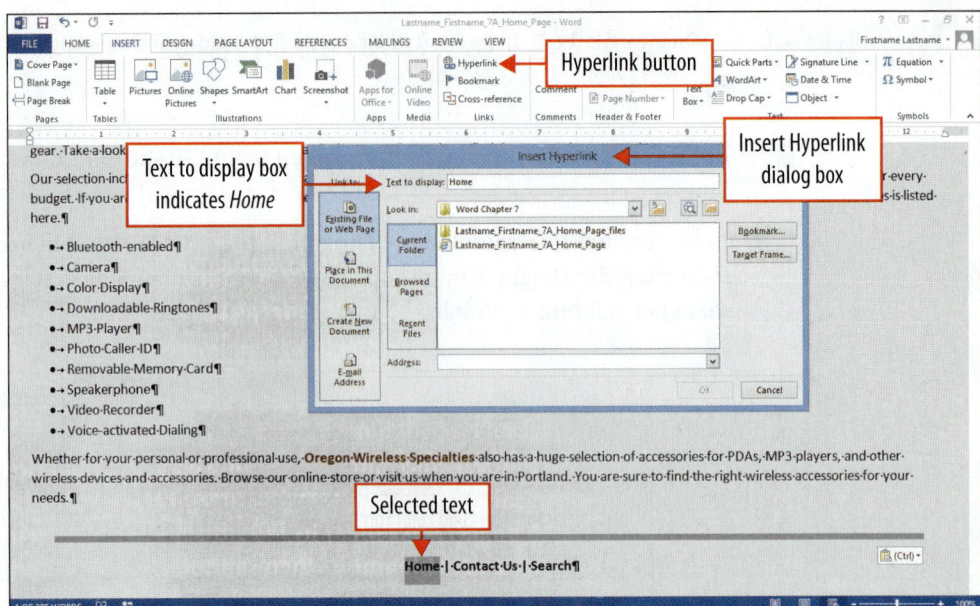

3 In the **Address** box, delete any existing text, and then type **www.owspecialties.com** As you begin typing the Internet address, notice that the text *http://* is automatically inserted at the left of the box. If another address displays while you are typing, continue typing to replace it. When you are finished typing, if any other characters display, delete them.

> If another address displays as you type, it is a result of the AutoComplete feature, which displays the most recently used web address from your computer.

4 In the upper right corner of the dialog box, click **ScreenTip**. In the **Set Hyperlink ScreenTip** dialog box, in the **ScreenTip text** box, type **Oregon Wireless Specialties** Compare your screen with Figure 7.12.

> Text that you type here will display as a ScreenTip when an individual viewing your site points to this hyperlink.

FIGURE 7.12

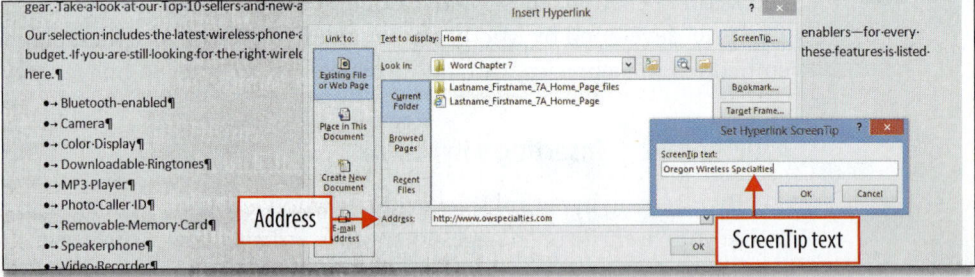

5 In the **Set Hyperlink ScreenTip** dialog box, click **OK**. In the **Insert Hyperlink** dialog box, click **OK**.

> The hyperlink is recorded, and the selected text is blue and underlined.

6 In the same paragraph, select the word *Search*. Using the techniques you practiced, display the **Insert Hyperlink** dialog box, and then in the **Address** box, type **www.owspecialties.com /search** As the **ScreenTip text**, type **Search OWS**

7 Click **OK** two times to close the dialog boxes, and then compare your screen with Figure 7.13.

FIGURE 7.13

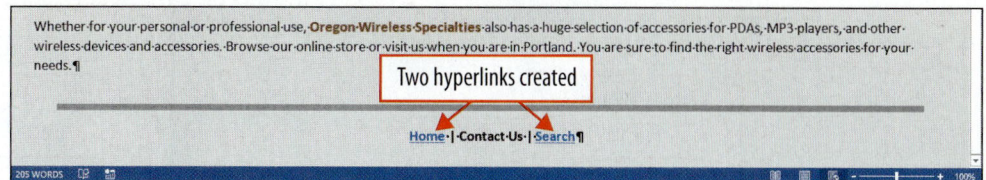

8 Save 💾 the document.

Activity 7.07 | Inserting a Hyperlink That Opens a New Email Message

Another common type of hyperlink is an *email address link*, which opens a new message window so that an individual viewing your site can send an email message.

1 At the end of the document, select the text *Contact Us*, and then display the **Insert Hyperlink** dialog box. Under **Link to**, click **E-mail Address**.

2 In the **E-mail address** box, type **jlovrick@owspecialties.com** As the **ScreenTip text**, type **Operations Manager** and then compare your screen with Figure 7.14.

> As you type an email address, Word automatically inserts *mailto:*. Other email addresses may display in the Recently used e-mail addresses box.

FIGURE 7.14

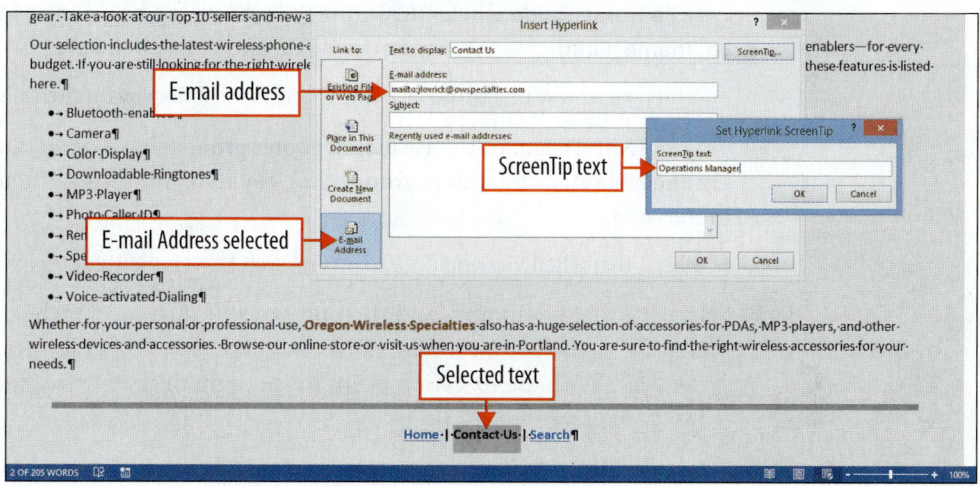

3 Click **OK** two times to close the dialog boxes, and then click **Save** 💾.

> The hyperlink is recorded, and the selected text changes to blue and is underlined.

Activity 7.08 | Using PDF Reflow to Edit a File in Word and Creating a Webpage for an Internal Link

An *internal link* is a hyperlink that connects to another page in the same website. In this activity, you will use PDF Reflow to import a PDF file into Word, and then create a second webpage for the website and create a link to this page from the home page.

1 Without closing your **Lastname_Firstname_7A_Home_Page** document, click the **FILE tab**, on the left click **Open**, and then navigate to your student files. In the **Open** dialog box, select the PDF file **w07A_Features_Guide**. Compare your screen with Figure 7.15.

> The icon indicates that the document is saved as a *PDF* file. Recall that PDF stands for *Portable Document Format*, a technology that creates an image that preserves the look of your file but that cannot be easily changed or edited. You can open and edit a PDF file in Word.

FIGURE 7.15

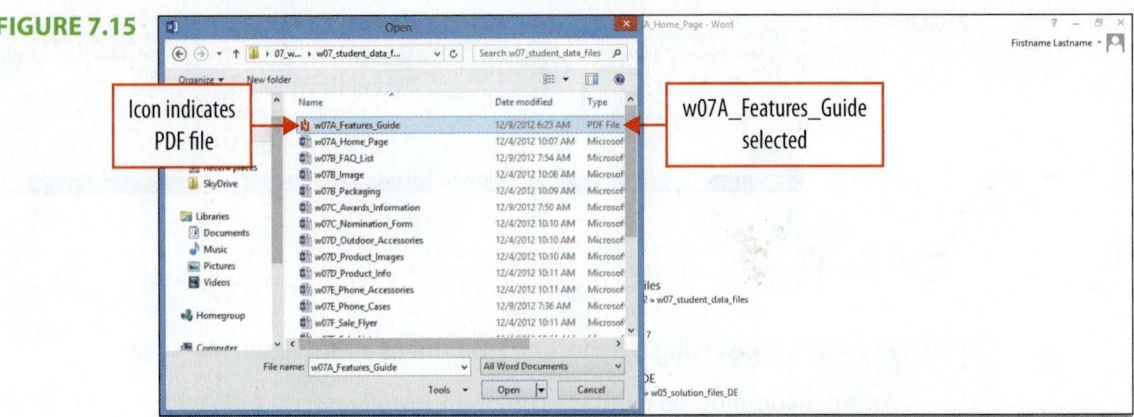

> 2 ▶ In the **Open** dialog box, with the file **w07A_Features_Guide** selected, click **Open**. If necessary, in the **Microsoft Word** message box, click **OK** to convert the PDF file to a Word document.

Because you are currently working in Web Layout view, the document opens in Web Layout view.

> 3 ▶ Click the **FILE tab**, and then click **Save As**. Navigate to your **Word Chapter 7** folder. Click the **Save as type arrow**, and then click **Web Page**.

> 4 ▶ Click **Change Title** to display the **Enter Text** dialog box, and then in the **Page title** box, type **Features Guide** Click **OK**. In the **Save As** dialog box, in the **File name** box, type **Lastname_Firstname_7A_Features_Guide** and then click **Save**.

When viewed with a browser, *Features Guide* will display on the title bar.

> 5 ▶ On the **INSERT tab**, in the **Header & Footer group**, click **Footer**, and then click **Edit Footer**. On the ribbon, in the **Insert group**, click **Document Info**, and then click **File Name**. **Close** the footer area.

Recall that when viewing documents in Web Layout view, footers do not display.

> 6 ▶ Select the first paragraph, and then press `Ctrl` + `E` to center the paragraph. Below the bulleted list, to the right of the horizontal line, select the tab formatting mark, and then press `Delete`. With the insertion point to the right of the horizontal line, press `Ctrl` + `E`. Press `Ctrl` + `Home`.

> 7 ▶ Click the **FILE tab**, if necessary, click **Info**, and then click **Show All Properties**. In the **Tags** box, type **website, features** In the **Subject** box, type your course name and section number. If necessary, edit the author name to display your name. Click **Save**, and then **Close** your **Lastname_Firstname_7A_Features_Guide** document.

> 8 ▶ With your **Lastname_Firstname_7A_Home_Page** document displayed, in the paragraph that begins *Our selection includes*, select the text *Guide to Popular Cell Phone Features*. On the **INSERT tab**, in the **Links group**, click **Hyperlink**.

> 9 ▶ Under **Link to**, click **Existing File or Web Page**. In the **Look in** box, be sure that the name of your **Word Chapter 7** folder displays, and then from the list below, click your *file*—not the folder—named **Lastname_Firstname_7A_Features_Guide**. Compare your screen with Figure 7.16.

FIGURE 7.16

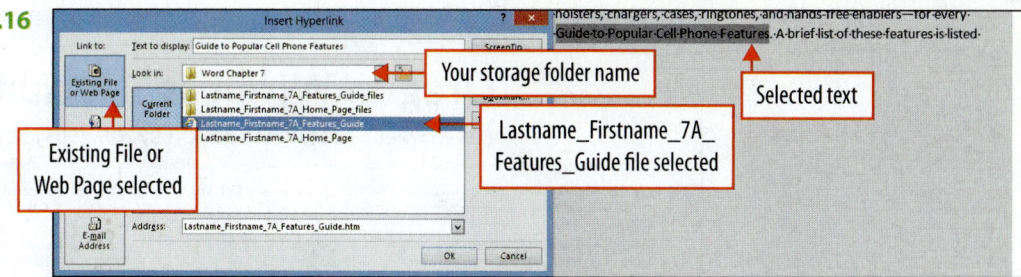

10 ▶ Click **ScreenTip**, type **Features Guide** and then click **OK** two times to close the dialog boxes.

The selected text displays in blue and is underlined.

11 ▶ Click the **FILE tab**, if necessary, click **Info**, and then click **Show All Properties**. In the **Tags** box, type **website, home page** In the **Subject** box, type your course name and section number. If necessary, edit the author name to display your name.

12 ▶ On the left, click **Print** to display the **Print commands** and the **Print Preview**. Examine the **Print Preview**, which displays as a two-page document in **Print Layout** view without a background color. Click **Back** ⊙, make any necessary adjustments, and then **Save** 🖫 your document.

13 ▶ **Close** ✕ Word. In the **Microsoft Word** message box, when asked if you want a picture to be available, click **No**.

Activity 7.09 | Testing Webpages in a Browser

In this activity, you will display and test your webpages in your browser.

A L E R T !	Are You Connected to the Internet?

If the system on which you are working is not connected to the Internet, skip this activity and move to Activity 7.10.

1 ▶ If necessary, display the Desktop. From the taskbar, start **File Explorer**. Navigate to your **Word Chapter 7** folder, and then select your **Lastname_Firstname_7A_Home_Page** HTML document. Compare your screen with Figure 7.17.

FIGURE 7.17

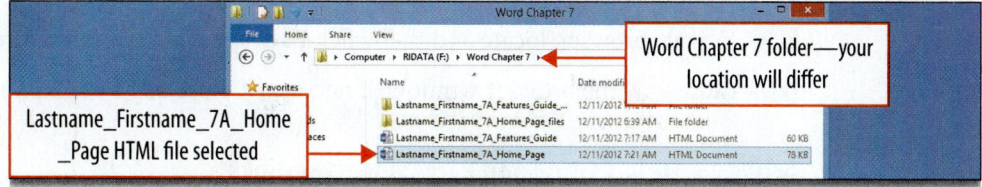

2 ▶ Double-click the file to open it in your browser.

3 ▶ If necessary, scroll to the bottom of the webpage, and then point to the text *Home* to display the 🖑 pointer, and the ScreenTip that you created. Compare your screen with Figure 7.18.

At the bottom left of your screen, the web address assigned to the hyperlink displays as another ScreenTip.

FIGURE 7.18

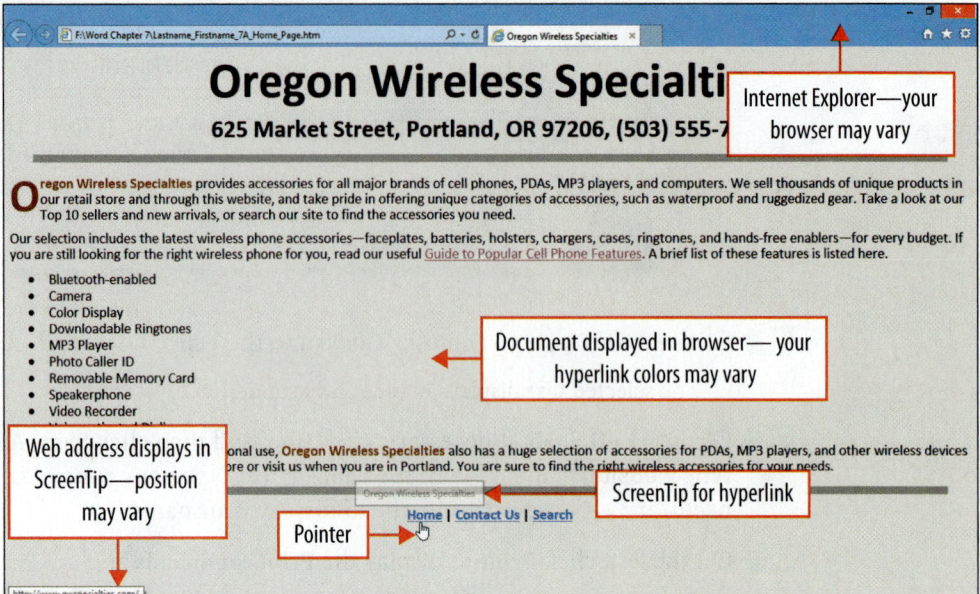

4 ▶ On the same line, point to the text *Contact Us* and *Search* to display the **ScreenTips**.

5 ▶ Locate and then click the **Guide to Popular Cell Phone Features** link to display the linked page. Compare your screen with Figure 7.19.

> The browser displays the Features Guide webpage.

 **BY TOUCH**   Tap the Guide to Popular Cell Phone Features link.

FIGURE 7.19

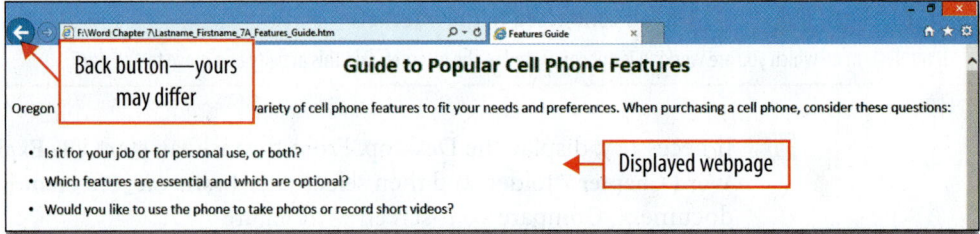

6 ▶ In your browser, locate and then click **Back** ⬅ to return to the previously displayed page.

7 ▶ **Close** ✖ the browser window. If necessary, close any File Explorer windows.

Activity 7.10 | Editing and Removing Hyperlinks

You can modify the hyperlinks in your webpage—for example, to change an address or ScreenTip—and you can also remove a hyperlink.

1 ▶ Start Word. On the left, under **Recent Documents**, click **Lastname_Firstname_7A_Home_Page**.

2 ▶ Press Ctrl + End. In the navigation bar, right-click the **Contact Us** link, and then click **Edit Hyperlink**.

3 ▶ In the upper right corner of the **Edit Hyperlink** dialog box, click **ScreenTip**, and then edit the **ScreenTip** text to indicate **Click here to send a message to our Operations Manager** Compare your screen with Figure 7.20.

FIGURE 7.20

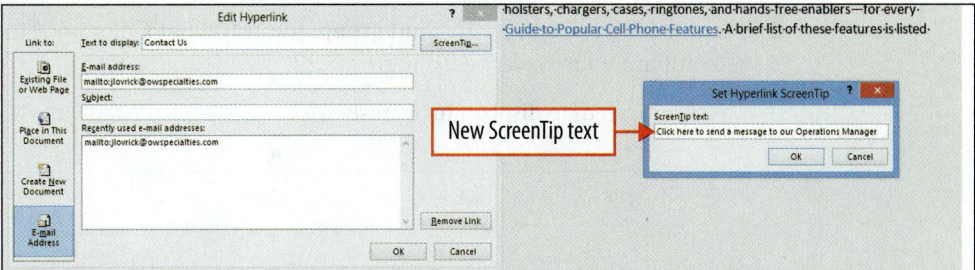

4 Click **OK** two times to close the dialog boxes.

5 In the navigation bar, right-click the **Search** link, and then click **Remove Hyperlink**.

The link is removed, but the link can be added again at a later time when Oregon Wireless Specialties decides how customers will be able to search the website.

6 **Save** 💾 your document.

Activity 7.11 | Configuring Language Options in a Document

When working with a multilingual team, you may want to change the language used to edit a document and view ScreenTips. In this activity you will explore the language options in Word.

1 Click the **FILE tab** to display **Backstage** view. On the left, click **Options** to display the **Word Options** dialog box.

2 On the left side of the **Word Options** dialog box, click **Language**. Compare your screen with Figure 7.21.

The Word Options dialog box displays three sections for configuring the language options—Choose Editing Languages, Choose Display and Help Languages, and Choose ScreenTip Language. You can install additional languages from Office.com.

FIGURE 7.21

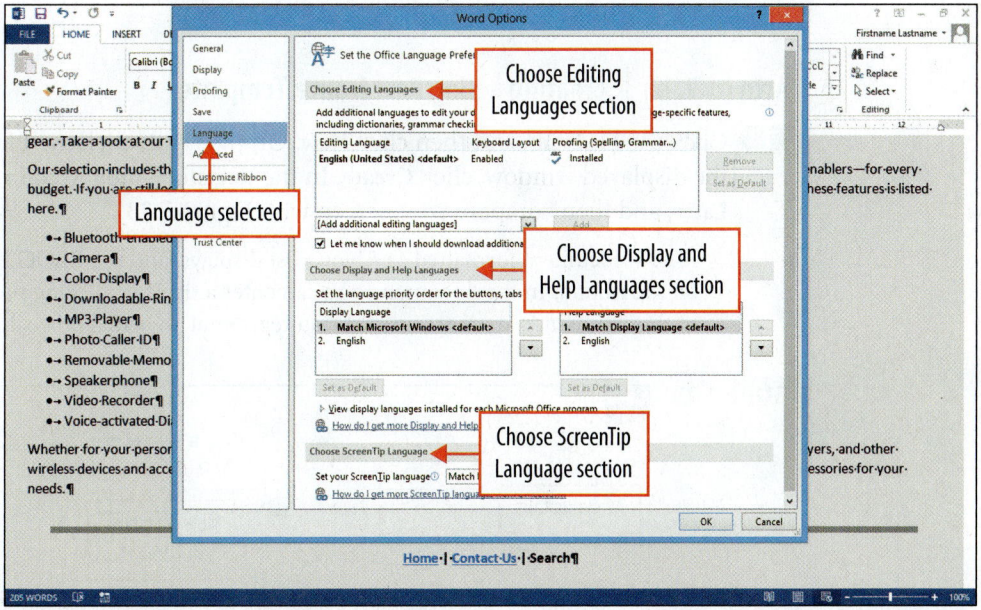

3 In the **Word Options** dialog box, under **Choose ScreenTip Language**, click the **Set your ScreenTip language box arrow**, and then click **Spanish (Spain) [español]**.

4 Click **OK** to close the **Word Options** dialog box.

5 On the **HOME tab**, in the **Font group**, point to **Font Color** to display the **ScreenTip**. Compare your screen with Figure 7.22.

The ScreenTip displays in Spanish.

FIGURE 7.22

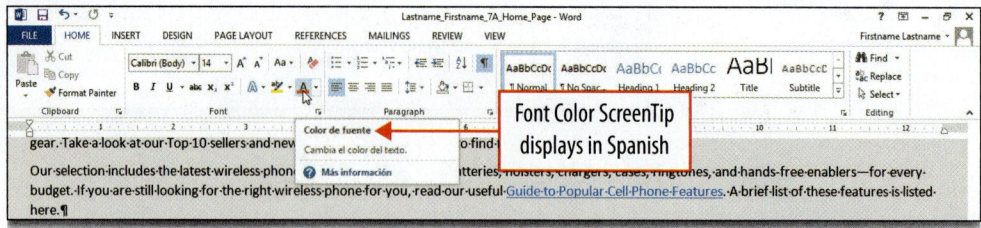

6 Click the **FILE tab**, and then click **Options** to display the **Word Options** dialog box.

7 On the left side of the **Word Options** dialog box, click **Language**.

8 In the **Word Options** dialog box, under **Choose ScreenTip Language**, click the **Set your ScreenTip language box arrow**, and then click **Match Display Language** to reset the **ScreenTip language** to the default language used on the computer where you are working.

9 Click **OK** to close the **Word Options** dialog box, and then **Save** your document.

10 Click the **FILE tab**, and then click **Close** to close the document but leave Word open for the next activity.

Objective 3 | Create a Blog Post

Video W7-3

A **blog**, short for *Web log*, is a website that displays dated entries. Blogs are fast-changing websites and usually contain many hyperlinks—links to other blogs, to resource sites about the topic, or to photos and videos. A **blog post** is an individual article entered in a blog with a time and date stamp.

Activity 7.12 | Creating a Blog Post from a Template

1 Click the **FILE tab**, and then click **New**. On the right, click the **Blog post** template, and then in the displayed window, click **Create**. In the **Register a Blog Account** dialog box, click **Register Later**, and then compare your screen with Figure 7.23.

A new document formatted as a blog post displays, and the BLOG POST and INSERT tabs display on the ribbon. In the document, you can enter a title for the blog post and then type the text. Some of the commands are inactive until you register at an actual blog site.

FIGURE 7.23

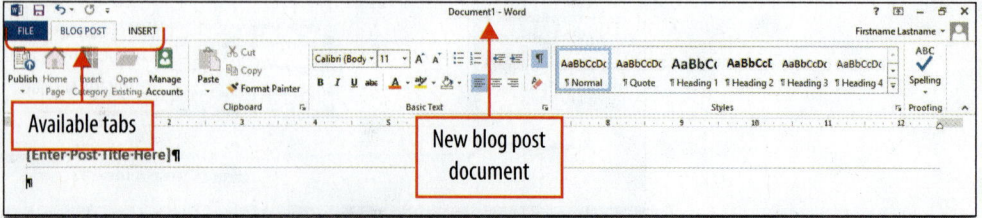

2 Press F12 to display the **Save As** dialog box, and then navigate to your **Word Chapter 7** folder. In the **File name** box, type **Lastname_Firstname_7A_Blog_Post** and then click **Save**.

The file, which displays in Web Layout view, is saved as a Word document, not an HTML file.

3 At the top of the document, click anywhere in the text **Enter Post Title Here** field to select the placeholder text, and then type **Learn to Use Your Bluetooth Headset**

4 Under the line, click in the body text area, and then type the following text:

> **Do you have one of our new Bluetooth headsets? We can help you learn all about it! Call us at (503) 555-7702, send us an email, download the user guides from our website, or visit our Portland store for hands-on assistance.**

5 Select all the text you typed in the previous step, and then on the mini toolbar, change the **Font** to **Verdana** and the **Font Size** to **16**. **Save** ⊟ your blog post.

> Although it is not required to do so, you can use Word's formatting tools to change the font, size, color, or alignment of text.

Activity 7.13 | Inserting Hyperlinks in a Blog Post

Blog posts are not limited to text. You can link to pictures, graphics, other websites, and email addresses.

1 In the last sentence, select the text *email*. Click the **INSERT tab**, and then in the **Links group**, click **Hyperlink**.

ANOTHER WAY   Right-click the selected text, and then on the shortcut menu, click Hyperlink.

2 In the **Insert Hyperlink** dialog box, under **Link to**, click **E-mail Address**, if necessary. In the **E-mail address** box, type **jlovrick@owspecialties.com** Compare your screen with Figure 7.24.

> Recall that when you create an email hyperlink, Word automatically inserts *mailto:*. Because this is the same email address you typed previously, it may display in the Recently used e-mail addresses: box.

FIGURE 7.24

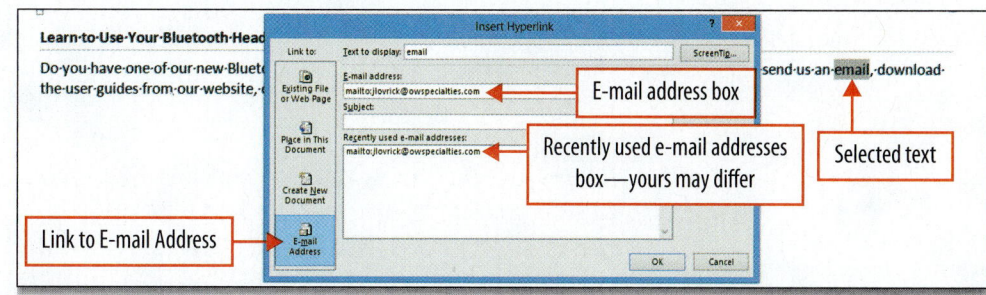

3 Click **OK**. Notice that the text *email* displays with hyperlink formatting.

4 In the last sentence, select the text *website*, and then using the technique you practiced, create a hyperlink to an existing webpage. As the **Address**, type **www.owspecialties.com** With *http://* and your typed text displayed, if any other characters display, delete them. As the **ScreenTip**, type **Oregon Wireless Specialties** Click **OK** two times to close the dialog boxes.

5 Click to position the insertion point at the end of the paragraph, press Enter two times, and then type your first and last name.

6 Select your name that you just typed. On the **BLOG POST tab**, in the **Styles group**, click **More** ⊽, and then apply the **Heading 5** style. Click anywhere in the document to deselect the text, and then compare your screen with Figure 7.25.

FIGURE 7.25

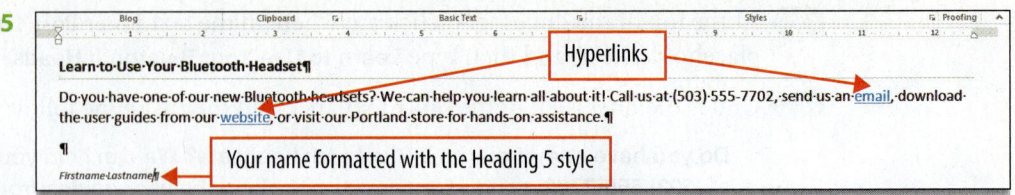

7 Click the **FILE tab**, if necessary, click **Info**, and then click **Show All Properties**. In the **Tags** box, type **webpage, blog, Bluetooth** In the **Subject** box, type your course name and section number. If necessary, edit the author name to display your name.

8 **Save** 💾 your document.

9 On the status bar, click **Print Layout** 📄.

10 Print or submit electronically your two HTML files and your blog post as directed by your instructor. **Close** ❌ Word.

END | You have completed Project 7A

FAQ List

PROJECT ACTIVITIES

In Activities 7.14 through 7.26, you will examine Word settings, gather supporting information, insert an equation, and use find and replace options to create a draft version of an FAQ list. Additionally, you will save the file in a different format. Nanci Scholtz, Vice President of Marketing for Oregon Wireless Specialties, is compiling a list of Frequently Asked Questions, or FAQs, from customers who shop from the online site. She plans to include the information in a separate webpage on the company's website. Your completed documents will look similar to Figure 7.26.

PROJECT FILES

For Project 7B, you will need the following files:

w07B_FAQ_List
w07B_Image
w07B_Packaging

You will save your files as:

Lastname_Firstname_7B_FAQ_List
Lastname_Firstname_7B_FAQ_RTF

PROJECT RESULTS

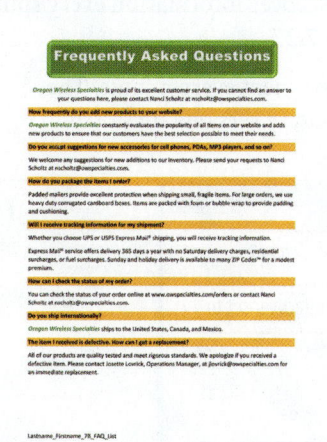
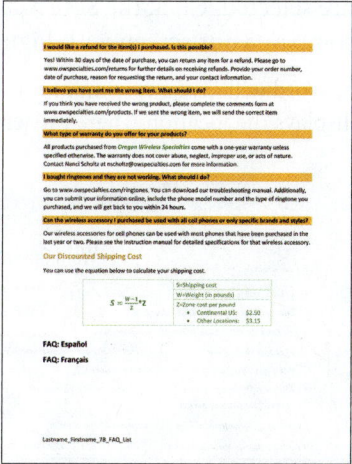

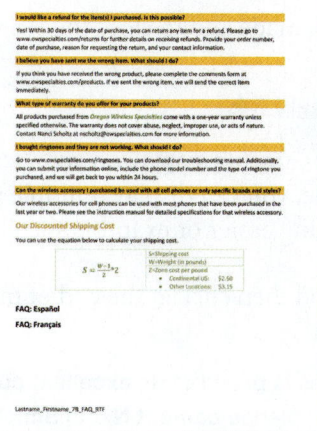

FIGURE 7.26 Project 7B FAQ List

Video W7-4

When you install Microsoft Office, default settings are created for many features. For example, when working on an unsaved document, Word saves a temporary version every ten minutes. This time can be adjusted to suit your needs. Recall that Word settings are modified in the Word Options dialog box.

Activity 7.14 | Changing the AutoSave Frequency

In this activity, you will change the save frequency for the *AutoRecover* option. The AutoRecover feature helps prevent losing unsaved changes by automatically creating a backup version of the current document.

1 Start Word. From your student files, locate and then open the file **w07B_FAQ_List**. If necessary, display the rulers and formatting marks.

2 Be sure your document displays in **Print Layout** view. Press F12, and then **Save** the document in your **Word Chapter 7** folder as **Lastname_Firstname_7B_FAQ_List** At the bottom of **Page 1**, right-click in the footer area, and then click **Edit Footer**. On the ribbon, in the **Insert group**, click **Document Info**, and then click **File Name**. **Close** the footer area.

3 Click the **FILE tab**, and then click **Options** to display the **Word Options** dialog box.

4 In the **Word Options** dialog box, on the left, click **Save**. Under **Save documents**, verify that the *Save AutoRecover information every* check box and the *Keep the last autosaved version if I close without saving* check box are selected. Click the **Save AutoRecover information every spin box down arrow** to **1**, and then compare your screen with Figure 7.27.

> For purposes of this instruction, Word will save a version of this document every minute. The AutoRecover file location box displays the location where the temporary versions are stored.

FIGURE 7.27

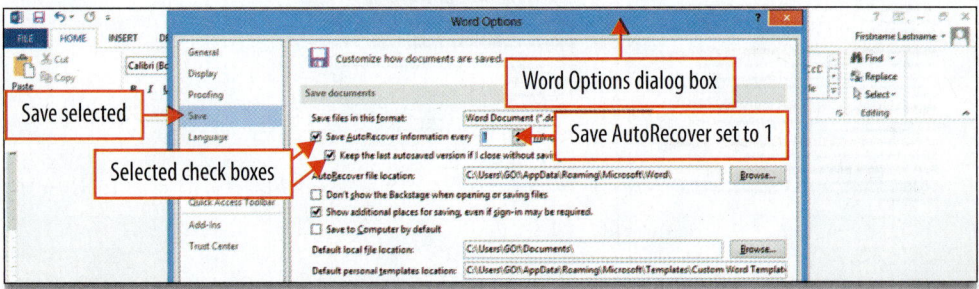

5 Click **OK** to save the change you made and to close the **Word Options** dialog box.

Activity 7.15 | Zooming from the VIEW Tab

By changing the way in which documents display on your screen, you make your editing tasks easier and more efficient. For example, you can display multiple pages of a long document or increase the zoom level to make reading easier or examine specific text more closely.

1 Press Ctrl + Home if necessary, and then click at the end of the first paragraph—*FAQ*. Press Enter to insert a new blank paragraph.

2 Type **Oregon Wireless Specialties is proud of its excellent customer service. If you cannot find an answer to your question here, please contact Nanci Scholtz at nscholtz@owspecialties.com.**

3 Click the **VIEW tab**, and then in the **Zoom group**, click **Zoom**. In the **Zoom** dialog box, under **Zoom to**, click the **200%** option button, and then compare your screen with Figure 7.28.

In the Zoom dialog box, you can select from among several pre-set zoom levels, select a specific number of pages to view at one time, or use the Percent box to indicate a specific zoom level.

FIGURE 7.28

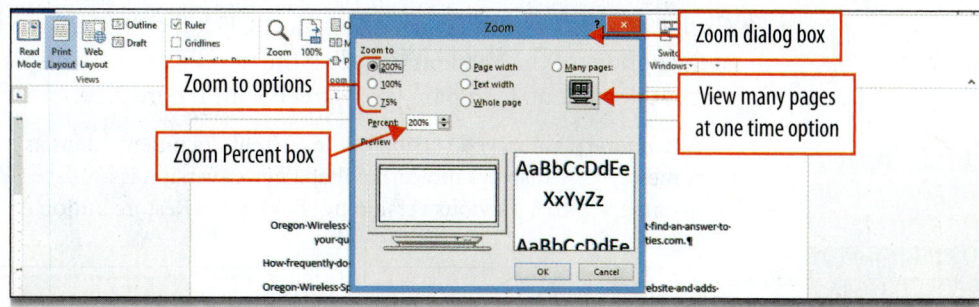

4 Click **OK**, and notice that the document displays in a magnified view.

5 Scroll as necessary, and in the paragraph that begins *We welcome*, notice that the email address has an extra character to the right of the letter *l*—the text should display as *owspecialties*. Click to position the insertion point to the right of *l*, and then press Delete to delete the *i*.

A magnified view is useful when you must make a close inspection of characters—for example, when typing email addresses or scientific formulas.

6 On the **VIEW tab**, in the **Zoom group**, click **Multiple Pages** to display both **Page 1** and **Page 2** on your screen.

The *Multiple Pages* zoom setting decreases the magnification. Although the displayed text is smaller, you have an overall view of the page arrangement.

7 On the **VIEW tab**, in the **Zoom group**, click **100%** to return to the default zoom setting.

Activity 7.16 | Managing Document Versions

You may want to examine an older version of your current document that was automatically saved—for example, to check the wording of a paragraph.

1 Click the **FILE tab**, and then click **Info**, if necessary. To the right of the **Manage Versions** box, take a moment to review the **Versions** list.

The Versions list displays the most recently saved versions of the current document. Recall that you changed the AutoSave frequency to 1 minute. Several versions may display depending on the amount of time it has taken you to reach this step in the project.

2 Click **Manage Versions**, and then click **Recover Unsaved Documents** to display the **Open** dialog box.

In the Open dialog box, the *UnsavedFiles* folder displays the file names of all old documents that have never been saved. From this dialog box, you can select the file you want to display. Note: This folder may be empty on your computer.

3 Click **Cancel** to close the **Open** dialog box. Click the **FILE tab**. To the right of **Manage Versions**, at the bottom of the **Versions** list, click the last file name to display the oldest version of the current document. Compare your screen with Figure 7.29.

A temporary, autosaved version of the current document opens as a Read-Only document. A message bar displays indicating that a newer version is available. You can replace a current document with a previous version by clicking the Restore button on the message bar.

FIGURE 7.29

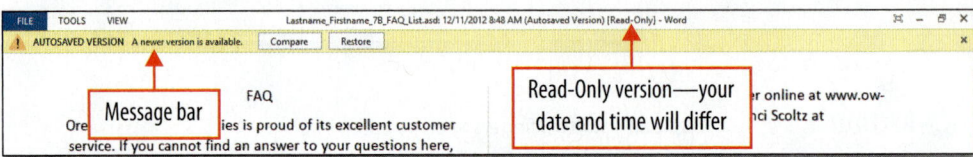

4 Close ⊠ the document. In the **Microsoft Word** message box, click **Don't Save**.

All recent versions of the current document display in the Versions list.

5 At the bottom of the **Versions** list, right-click the last file name, and then from the shortcut menu, click **Delete This Version**. In the message box, click **Yes** to confirm the deletion.

The oldest version of the current document is deleted.

6 Click **Options**, and then in the **Word Options** dialog box, on the left click **Save**. Click the **Save AutoRecover information every up spin arrow** to **10**, and then click **OK** to close the **Word Options** dialog box and restore the default setting. **Save** 🔲 your document.

Objective 5   Collect and Paste Images and Text

Video W7-5

As you are writing, you may want to gather material—for example, text or pictures related to your topic. This supporting information may be located in another document or on the Internet. Recall that you can use the Clipboard to collect a group of graphics or selected text blocks and then paste them into a document.

Activity 7.17 | Collecting Images and Text from Multiple Documents

In this activity, you will copy images and text from two different documents and then paste them into your current document.

1 Press [Ctrl] + [Home]. On the **HOME tab**, in the lower right corner of the **Clipboard group**, click the **Dialog Box Launcher** 🔲 to display the **Clipboard** pane. If necessary, at the top of the pane, click **Clear All** to delete anything currently on the Clipboard.

2 Be sure that only your **Lastname_Firstname_7B_FAQ_List** document and the **Clipboard** display; if necessary, close any other open windows. Then, from your student files, locate and open the file **w07B_Image**. If necessary, in the **Clipboard group**, click the **Dialog Box Launcher** 🔳 to display the pane.

3 With the **w07B_Image** document displayed, select the **Frequently Asked Questions** graphic. Right-click the graphic, and then click **Copy**. Compare your screen with Figure 7.30.

The image in your w07B_Image document displays on the Clipboard pane.

FIGURE 7.30

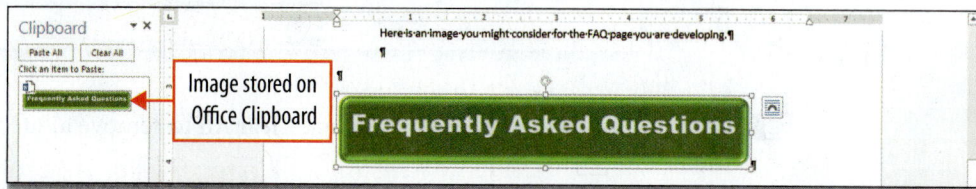

4 Close ✖ the **w07B_Image** file.

5 From your student files, open the file **w07B_Packaging**. If necessary, on the **HOME tab**, in the **Clipboard group**, click the **Dialog Box Launcher** 🔳 to display the **Clipboard** pane. Without selecting the paragraph mark at the end, select the entire paragraph that begins *Padded mailers*, and then **Copy** the selection to the Clipboard. Compare your screen with Figure 7.31.

The first few lines of the copied text display on the Clipboard. When copying multiple items to the Clipboard, the most recently copied item displays at the top of the list.

FIGURE 7.31

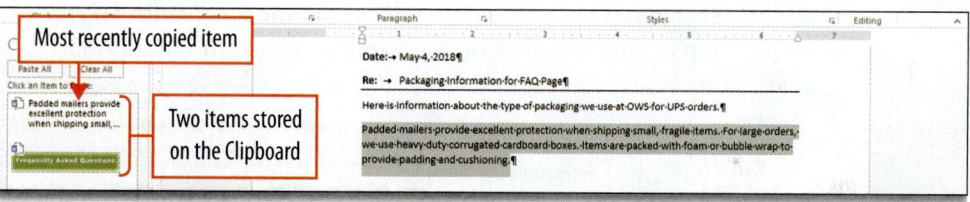

6 Close ✖ the **w07B_Packaging** document.

Activity 7.18 | Pasting Information from the Clipboard Pane

After you have collected text items or images on the Clipboard, you can paste them into a document in any order.

1 Press Ctrl + Home. Without selecting the paragraph mark, select only the text *FAQ*, and then press Delete. In the **Clipboard** pane, click the graphic *Frequently Asked Questions*.

The graphic is inserted in the blank paragraph.

2 Locate the sixth text paragraph of the document, which begins *Will I receive*. Click to position the insertion point to the left of the paragraph, press Enter, and then press ⬆. In the new paragraph, type **How do you package the items I order?** and then press Enter.

3 In the **Clipboard** pane, click the text entry that begins *Padded mailers* to paste the entire block of text at the insertion point. Compare your screen with Figure 7.32.

FIGURE 7.32

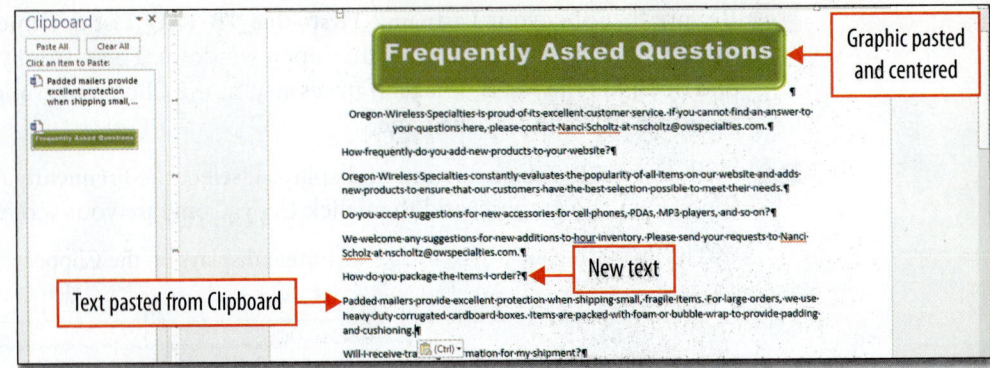

At the top of the **Clipboard** pane, click **Clear All** to remove all items from the **Clipboard**, and then **Close** ❌ the **Clipboard** pane.

4

Press Ctrl + Home. Locate the paragraph that begins *How frequently*, and then select the entire paragraph, including the paragraph mark. Press and hold Ctrl, and then select the next question—the paragraph that begins *Do you accept*.

5

Continue to hold down Ctrl, and then select all the remaining paragraphs that end in a question mark, scrolling down with the scroll bar or the **Vertical Scrollbar down arrow** ✓ as necessary to move through the document.

6

With all the questions selected, apply **Bold** B. On the **HOME tab**, in the **Paragraph group**, click the **Shading arrow** 🎨, and then in the eighth column, click the first color—**Gold, Accent 4**.

7

Click anywhere to deselect the text, scroll through the document to be sure you have shaded each question, and then scroll so that the *Frequently Asked Questions* graphic displays at the top of your screen. Compare your screen with Figure 7.33.

8

FIGURE 7.33

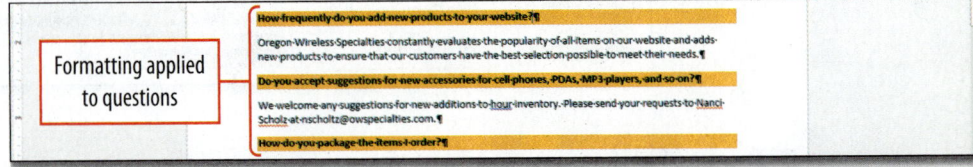

Save 💾 your document.

9

Objective 6   Locate Supporting Information and Insert Equations

Video W7-6

While composing a document, you can use the Research pane to locate additional information about your topic. For example, you can look up additional facts on the Internet, replace words with synonyms to improve readability, or translate a phrase into another language. Additionally, Word provides tools to enter simple or complex equations in a document.

Activity 7.19 | Using the research Pane to Locate Information

In this activity, you will use the Research Sites feature in the Research pane to search for additional information and make changes to the FAQ list.

1 In the middle of **Page 1**, locate the paragraph that begins *Whether you choose*, and then click to position the insertion point at the end of the paragraph. Press Enter to insert a blank paragraph.

2 With the insertion point in the blank paragraph, press and hold Alt and click the left mouse button to display the Research pane.

The Research pane displays at the right of your screen.

3 In the **Research** pane, in the **Search for** box, type **usps express mail** Under the **Search for** box, in the second box—the **Search location** box—click the **arrow**, point to **Bing**, and then compare your screen with Figure 7.34.

In the Search location box, you can specify the type of reference source from which you want to locate information. For example, you might want to use the Microsoft search engine Bing as a reference source.

ALert! **What If Bing Does Not Display?**

If Bing does not display, you may be running an older version of Windows. Consult your instructor.

Figure 7.34

4 Click **Bing**, and then to the right of the **Search for** box, click **Start Searching** 🔍. On the list of results, locate the item titled *USPS – Priority Mail Express*, and then click the related link that begins *https://www.usps.com*. Compare your screen with Figure 7.35.

The webpage with the address *https://www.usps.com/ship/priority-mail-express* displays in your browser.

Figure 7.35

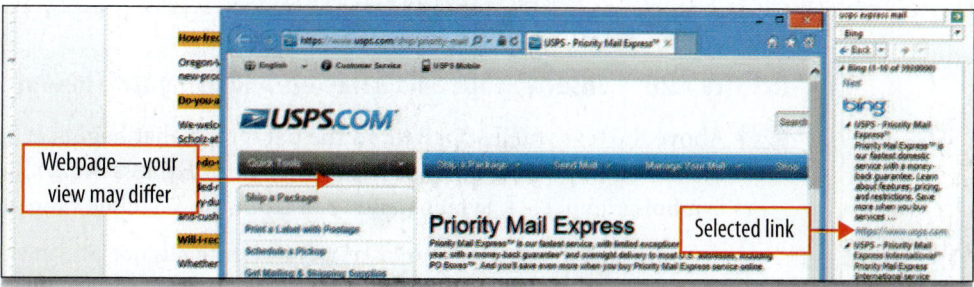

Copyright© 2013 USPS.

5 Maximize ⬜ the browser window. On the webpage, select the first paragraph *Priority Mail Express*. Compare your screen with Figure 7.36.

A blue arrow, called an *accelerator*, displays when you select text in Internet Explorer. The accelerator allows you to perform different actions with selected text. Because webpages change frequently, your results may not look similar to Figure 7.36.

FigUre 7.36

Copyright© 2013 USPS.

6 Close ❌ the browser.

For purposes of instruction, you will not copy text from the webpage.

7 In your **Lastname_Firstname_7B_FAQ_List** document, be sure the insertion point is in the blank line below the paragraph that begins *Whether you choose*. Type the following text: **Express Mail service offers delivery 365 days a year with no Saturday delivery charges, residential surcharges, or fuel surcharges. Sunday and holiday delivery is available to many ZIP Codes for a modest premium.** Compare your screen with Figure 7.37.

FigUre 7.37

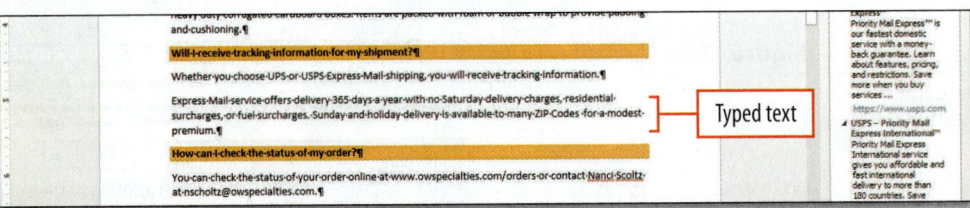

8 Close ✖ the **Research** pane, and then **Save** 💾 your document.

> **NOTE** **Be Careful of Copyright Issues**
>
> Nearly everything you find on the Internet is protected by copyright law, which protects authors of original works, including text, art, photographs, and music. If you want to use text or graphics that you find online, you must get permission. One of the exceptions to the law is the use of small amounts of information for educational purposes, which falls under Fair Use guidelines. As a general rule, however, if you want to use someone else's material, always get permission first.

Activity 7.20 | Inserting Special Characters and Using the Thesaurus

1 Above the text you just pasted, in the paragraph that begins *Whether you choose*, position the insertion point immediately to the right of *Express Mail*. Click the **INSERT tab**. In the **Symbols group**, click **Symbol**, and then from the list, click **More Symbols**.

Sometimes it is necessary to insert a character that is not available on your keyboard.

2 In the **Symbol** dialog box, click the **Special Characters tab**, and then click the symbol ®—**Registered**. Notice the keyboard shortcut—Alt+Ctrl+R—displays to the right of the symbol.

> The *federal registration symbol*—®—indicates that a patent or trademark has been registered with the United States Patent and Trademark Office. In this case, the symbol applies to the term *Express Mail*.

3 Click **Insert** to insert the symbol to the right of *Mail*, and then click **Close**. Compare your screen with Figure 7.38.

Figure 7.38

4 In the next paragraph that begins *Express Mail*, position the insertion point to the right of *Mail*, and then press Alt + Ctrl + R to insert the registered symbol. To insert a trademark symbol, in the same paragraph, click to the right of *Codes*, and then press Alt + Ctrl + T.

5 In the lower portion of **Page 1**, in the paragraph that begins *All of our products*, in the first line, point to and then right-click the word *stringent*. From the shortcut menu, point to **Synonyms**, and then click **Thesaurus** to display the **Thesaurus** pane. Compare your screen with Figure 7.39.

> In the Thesaurus pane, *stringent* displays in the Search for box, and synonyms for the word *stringent* display under Thesaurus.

AnoTher WAy To display the Thesaurus pane, on the REVIEW tab, in the Proofing group, click Thesaurus.

Figure 7.39

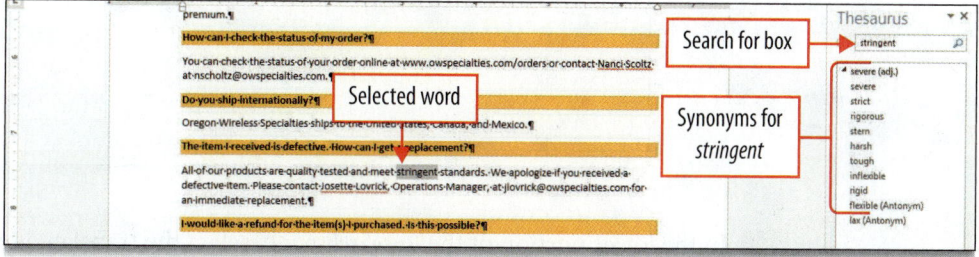

6 In the **Thesaurus** pane, point to *rigorous*, click the **arrow**, and then click **Insert** to replace *stringent* with *rigorous*.

7 **Close** ☒ the **Thesaurus** pane. At the bottom of **Page 1**, click to position the insertion point to the left of the paragraph that begins *I would like*. Press Ctrl+Enter, which is the keyboard shortcut to insert a **page break**. **Save** 🖫 your document.

> Because the document contains questions and answers, it is good document design to keep the question and answer together on the same page.

AnoTher WAy On the PAGE LAYOUT tab, in the Page Setup group, click Breaks, and then under Page Breaks, click Page.

More Knowledge | **Installing a Dictionary**

To use the Define command, which enables you to search for definitions of selected words or phrases, you must install a robust dictionary—a free add-in. On the ribbon, on the REVIEW tab, click Define. In the Dictionaries pane, below any one of the displayed dictionaries, click Download. After a dictionary has been installed, click Define to display the Dictionaries pane and search for definitions.

Activity 7.21 | Translating Text from the Research Pane

You can translate a word or phrase into a different language from the Research pane. Because Oregon Wireless Specialties has customers outside of the United States, the FAQ will include text for Spanish-speaking and French-speaking customers that can eventually be linked to FAQ pages written in those languages. In this activity, you will add Spanish and French text to the FAQ list.

1 Press Ctrl + End, press Enter, and then type **FAQ: Spanish**

2 Select the text *Spanish*. Click the **REVIEW tab**. In the **Language group**, click **Translate**, and then click **Translate Selected Text**.

> The Research pane displays on the right.

3 In the **Research** pane, verify that *Spanish* displays in the **Search for** box, and that *Translation* displays in the **Search location** box.

> In the Search for box you can type a word or phrase that you want to translate. In the Search location box you can select the type of reference you want to search—including online references.

4 If necessary, under **Translation**, click the **From arrow**, and then click **English (United States)**. Click the **To arrow**, and then click **Spanish (Spain)**. Compare your screen with Figure 7.40.

> The translated text—español—displays in the Translation area of the pane.

FIGURE 7.40

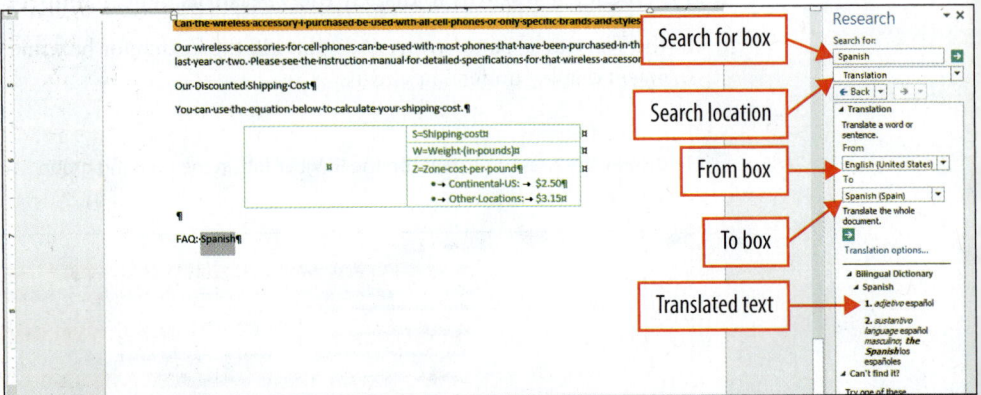

5 In the lower portion of the **Research** pane, select the translated text *español*, right-click, and then click **Copy**. In your document, right-click the selected text *Spanish*, and then under **Paste Options**, click **Keep Text Only** [A]. In the pasted text, select the first letter *e*, type **E** and then compare your screen with Figure 7.41.

> Word uses a machine translation service—not a human being—to translate text, which can result in slight discrepancies in the translated phrases. The main idea is captured, but an accurate translation may differ slightly.

FIGURE 7.41

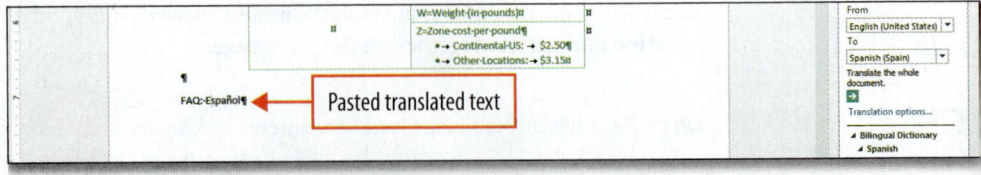

6 Position the insertion point at the end of the paragraph. Press Enter, type **FAQ:** and then press Spacebar.

7 In the **Research** pane, in the **Search for** box, type **French** Click the **To arrow**, and then click **French (France)**.

8 ▸ Using the technique you just practiced, insert the French text *français* at the insertion point location in your document. Select the first letter *f*, and then type **F**

9 ▸ Select both paragraphs that begin *FAQ*, and then on the mini toolbar, change the **Font Size** to **14**, and apply **Bold** B .

Ms. Scholtz will develop specific FAQs in both languages here.

10 ▸ **Close** ☒ the **Research** pane, and then **Save** 🖫 your document.

Activity 7.22 | Inserting Equations

In this activity, you will insert an equation to help customers calculate shipping costs.

1 ▸ On **Page 2**, select the paragraph *Our Discounted Shipping Cost*. On the mini toolbar, change the **Font Size** to **14**, and apply **Bold** B . Click the **Font Color arrow** A ▾, and in the eighth column, click the fifth color—**Gold, Accent 4, Darker 25%**.

2 ▸ Click in the first cell of the table. Click the **INSERT tab**, and then in the **Symbols group**, click the **Equation arrow**. In the list, take a moment to view the **Built-In** equations, and then at the bottom of the list, click **Insert New Equation**.

An equation placeholder displays in the table cell. On the ribbon, under EQUATION TOOLS, the DESIGN tab displays. The DESIGN tab includes built-in formulas and components you can modify to meet your needs.

3 ▸ With the equation placeholder selected, type **S=** On the ribbon, under **EQUATION TOOLS**, on the **DESIGN tab**, in the **Structures group**, click **Fraction**. From the **Fraction** gallery, under **Fraction**, click the first format—**Stacked Fraction**.

A fraction with a top and bottom placeholder is inserted to the right of the text you just typed.

4 ▸ In the fraction, click the top placeholder, and then type **W-1** Click the bottom placeholder, and then type **2** Click to the right of the fraction, and then type ***Z** Compare your screen with Figure 7.42.

The *variables*—letters that represent values—in the equation are described in the second cell of the table. In this equation, the customer will pay a reduced shipping cost based on the weight and destination; and, if the weight is one pound or less, the customer pays no shipping cost.

FIGURE 7.42

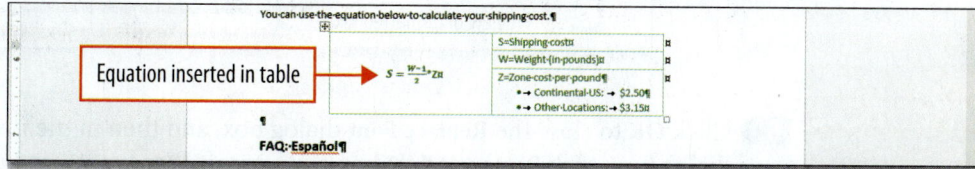

5 ▸ Select the entire equation, and then on the **HOME tab**, change the **Font Size** to **14**. **Save** 🖫 your document.

Video W7-7

From the Find and Replace dialog box, you can locate occurrences of words that sound the same although spelled differently, find phrases that are capitalized in exactly the same way, and find different forms of a word—such as *work*, *worked*, and *working*.

Activity 7.23 | Using Find and Replace to Change Text Formatting

You can change the formatting of a word or phrase that is repeated throughout a document quickly by using the Find and Replace dialog box. In this activity, you will change the formatting of the company name that appears numerous times in the FAQ list.

1 Press [Ctrl] + [Home]. On the **HOME tab**, in the **Editing group**, click **Replace** to display the **Find and Replace** dialog box.

2 In the **Find what** box, type **Oregon Wireless Specialties** and then in the **Replace with** box, type the exact same text **Oregon Wireless Specialties**

3 Below the **Replace with** box, click **More** to expand this dialog box.

The More button exposes advanced settings with which you can refine this command. At the bottom of the expanded dialog box, the Format button provides additional options for text, paragraph, tab, and style formats. The Special button provides options for location or replacing special characters.

4 Near the bottom of the **Find and Replace** dialog box, under **Replace**, click **Format**, and then from the list, click **Font**.

5 In the **Replace Font** dialog box, under **Font style**, click **Bold Italic**. Click the **Font color arrow**, and then in the last column, click the fifth color—**Green, Accent 6, Darker 25%**. Compare your screen with Figure 7.43.

FIGURE 7.43

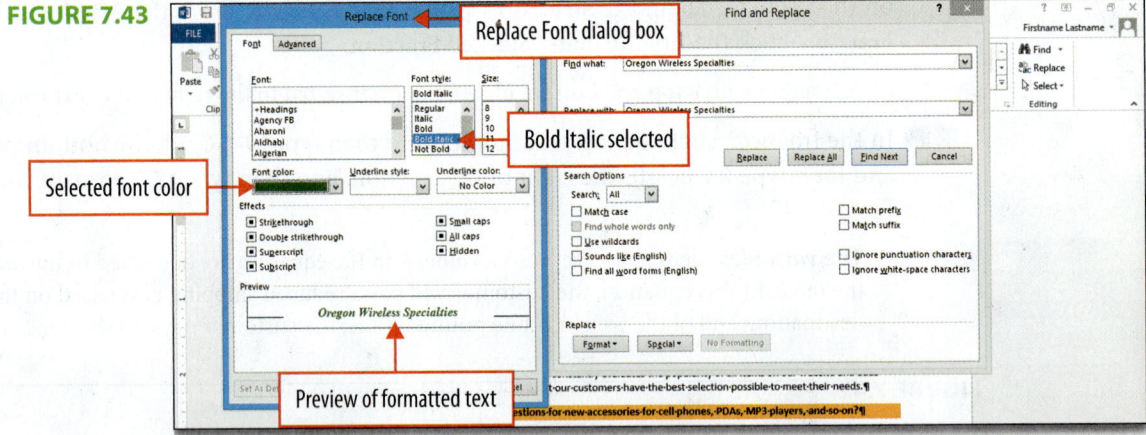

6 Click **OK** to close the **Replace Font** dialog box, and then in the middle of the **Find and Replace** dialog box, click **Replace All**. When a Microsoft Word message box displays indicating that you have made *4* replacements, click **OK**. Leave the expanded dialog box displayed.

This action finds each instance of the text *Oregon Wireless Specialties*, and then replaces the font format with bold italic in the green color that you selected.

Activity 7.24 | Using Wildcards to Find and Replace Text

Use a *wildcard* in the Find and Replace dialog box when you are not certain of the exact term you want to find. A wildcard is a special character such as * or ? that can be inserted with a Find what term. For example, searching a document for the term b*k could find *blink*, *book*, *brick*, or any other word in the document that begins with b and ends with k. Using a wildcard can save time when you do not know the specific characters in the search term. In this activity, you will use a wildcard to search for names that may be spelled incorrectly.

1 In the **Find and Replace** dialog box, in the **Find what** box, delete the existing text, and then type **Sc*z**

2 Press Tab to move to and select the text in the **Replace with** box, and then type **Scholtz** At the bottom of the **Find and Replace** dialog box, click **No Formatting** to remove the formatting settings from the previous activity.

3 Under **Search Options**, select the **Use wildcards** check box. Compare your screen with Figure 7.44.

The name Scholtz may have been spelled incorrectly. By using the Find command to locate each instance that begins with *S* and ends with *z*, you can find, and then verify, the correct spelling of the name in every instance.

FIGURE 7.44

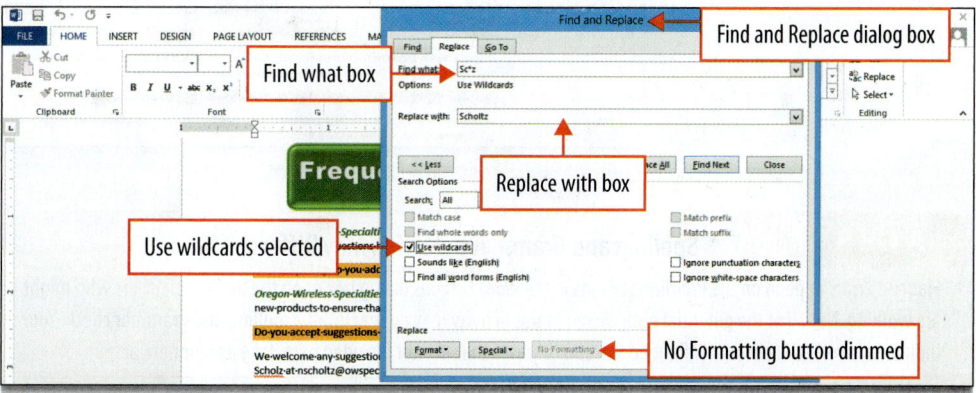

4 In the **Find and Replace** dialog box, click **Less** so that the dialog box is smaller. Click **Find Next**. Notice that the text *Scholtz* is selected in the document. If necessary, move the Find and Replace dialog box to view the selection.

This instance is spelled correctly—no changes are required.

5 In the **Find and Replace** dialog box, click **Find Next** again, and notice that this occurrence—*Scholz*—is not spelled correctly.

6 Click **Replace**, and then compare your screen with Figure 7.45.

The text *Scholtz* is spelled correctly, and Word selects the next occurrence of text that begins with *Sc* and ends with *z*.

FIGURE 7.45

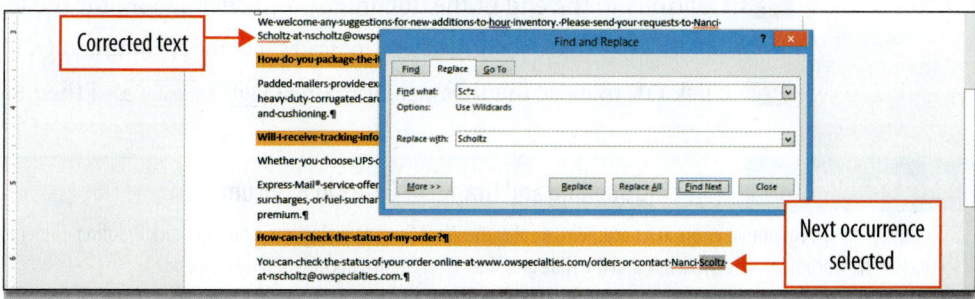

7 The selected text *Scoltz* is incorrect; click **Replace** to correct the error and move to the next occurrence.

8 The selected text *Scholtz* is spelled correctly. Click **Find Next** to move to the next occurrence.

A Microsoft Word message box indicates that you have searched the entire document.

9 In the message box, click **OK**. In the **Find and Replace** dialog box, click **More**, clear the **Use wildcards** check box, and then click **Less** to restore the dialog box to its default settings. Close ✕ the **Find and Replace** dialog box, and then **Save** 🖫 the document.

Activity 7.25 | Checking Spelling and Grammar in the Document

1 Press Ctrl + Home. On the **REVIEW tab**, in the **Proofing group**, click **Spelling & Grammar**. Compare your screen with Figure 7.46.

The Spelling pane displays on the right, indicating the first suggested error—Nanci. It is good practice to position the insertion point at the beginning of the document when checking the entire document for errors in spelling and grammar.

FIGURE 7.46

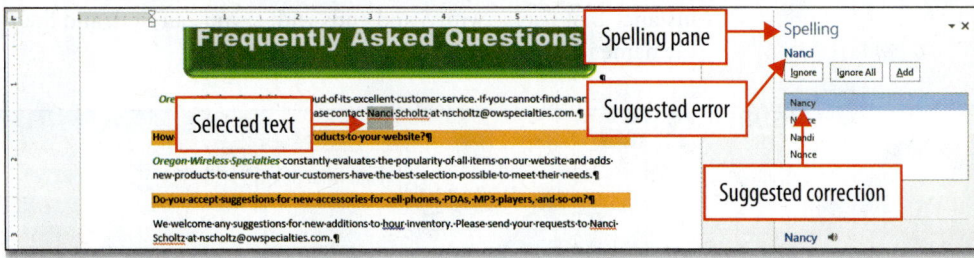

ALERT!   **Spelling and Grammar Selection May Differ**

Flagged errors depend on the Proofing settings in the Word Options dialog box or on the actions of others who might have used the computer at which you are working. Not all of the potential errors listed in this activity may appear in your spelling and grammar check. Your document may also display errors not indicated here. If you encounter flagged words or phrases that are not included here, take appropriate action.

---

2 If *Nanci* is indicated as a spelling error, in the **Spelling** pane, click **Ignore All**.

All occurrences of *Nanci* are ignored, and the word *Scholtz* displays with a red underline as a potential spelling error.

3 If *Scholtz* is indicated as a spelling error, click **Ignore All**.

All occurrences of *Scholtz* are ignored, and the next potential error—hour—is selected. Because this is a possible contextual error, the pane displays as a *Grammar* pane.

4 In the **Grammar** pane, if *hour* is highlighted, with *our* selected, click **Change**. If *hour* is not identified as an error, proceed to Step 5.

In this case, Word identified *hour* as a word that is spelled correctly but used in the wrong context.

5 Click **Ignore All** as necessary to ignore the proper names *Josette* and *Lovrick*.

6 Continue to the end of the document, and click **Ignore** for the foreign words.

A Microsoft Word message box indicates that the spelling and grammar check is complete.

7 Click **OK** to close the message box. Press Ctrl + Home, and then **Save** 🖫 the document.

More Knowledge   **Hiding Spelling and Grammar Errors in a Document**

To hide spelling or grammar errors in a document, display the Word Options dialog box, and then click Proofing. Under Exceptions for, select the Hide spelling errors in this document only check box and the Hide grammar errors in this document only check box.

Video W7-8

If you send a Word document to someone who uses a word processing program other than Microsoft Word, he or she may not be able to read the document. If you expect that your document must be read or edited in another word processing program, save your Word document in *Rich Text Format*, or *RTF*. Rich Text Format is a universal document format that can be read by nearly all word processing programs and retains most text and paragraph formatting. Saving a document as an RTF file adds the .rtf extension to the document file name. An RTF file that you might receive can be easily converted to the Word document file format.

Activity 7.26 | Saving a Document in RTF Format

When you save a Word document as an RTF file, all but the most complex formatting is translated into a format usable by most word processing programs. Nanci Scholtz is sending the FAQ list to her sales managers for review before saving it as a webpage. In this activity, you will save the FAQ list as an RTF file to ensure that all the managers can review the document.

1 Click the **FILE tab**, if necessary, click **Info**, and then click **Show All Properties**. In the **Tags** box, type **faq list** In the **Subject** box, type your course name and section number. If necessary, edit the author name to display your name.

> Recall that your document is saved with the default Word file format with the .docx file extension.

2 On the left, click **Save**.

3 Press F12. In the **Save As** dialog box, if necessary, navigate to your **Word Chapter 7** folder. In the lower portion of the **Save As** dialog box, click the **Save as type arrow**, and then on the list, click **Rich Text Format**.

4 In the **File name** box, type **Lastname_Firstname_7B_FAQ_RTF** Compare your screen with Figure 7.47.

FIGURE 7.47

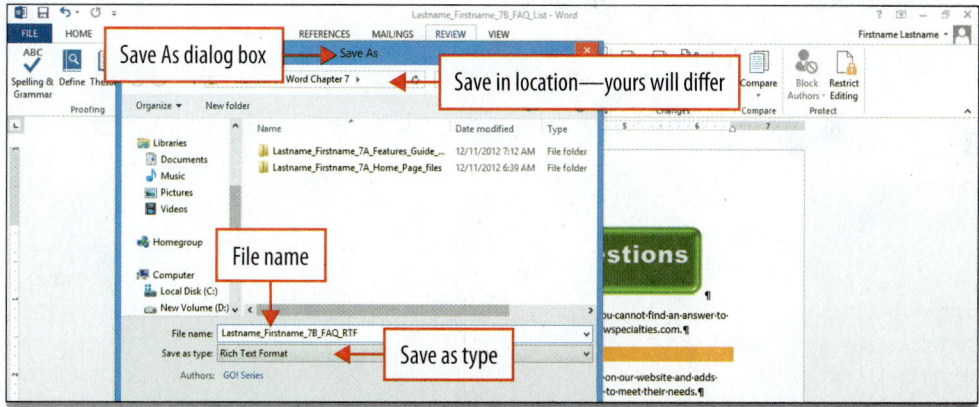

5 Click **Save**. Scroll to the bottom of **Page 1**, and then double-click the footer. Right-click the file name, and then from the shortcut menu, click **Update Field** to update the file name and format, and then **Close** the footer area.

6 Click the **FILE tab**, if necessary, click **Info**, and then click **Show All Properties**. In the **Tags** box, delete the existing text, type **faq, rtf** and then **Save** 🖫 your document.

7 Print your two files or submit electronically as directed by your instructor. **Close** ✖ Word.

More Knowledge | **Saving in PDF or XPS Formats**

In Microsoft Word, you can save documents in other formats such as PDF—Portable Document Format—and XPS—XML Paper Specification. Click the FILE tab, click Export, and then click the Create a PDF/XPS button. In the Publish as PDF or XPS dialog box, click the Save as type arrow, click PDF or XPS Document, and then click Publish.

END | You have completed Project 7B

END OF CHAPTER

SUMMARY

Documents saved in Web Page format—enhanced with elements such as drop caps, horizontal lines, and hyperlinks—can be viewed in a browser. A Blog post template provides a simple format to create a message.

The AutoRecover feature automatically creates backup versions of the current document, which helps prevent losing unsaved changes. Setting the AutoSave frequency determines how often a document is saved.

The Clipboard, the Research pane, and the Translation pane are Word features you use to gather information from a variety of sources—including other documents and websites using a search engine, such as Bing.

The Find and Replace feature includes advanced options for formatting text and searching for specific text using wildcards. Saving a file in Rich Text Format allows persons without Word to read the document.

GO! LEARN IT ONLINE

Review the concepts and key terms in this chapter by completing these online challenges, which you can find at **www.pearsonhighered.com/go**.

Matching and Multiple Choice: Answer matching and multiple choice questions to test what you learned in this chapter. MyITLab®

Crossword Puzzle: Spell out the words that match the numbered clues and put them in the puzzle squares.

Flipboard: Flip through the definitions of the key terms in this chapter and match them with the correct term.

END OF CHAPTER

REVIEW AND ASSESSMENT GUIDE FOR WORD CHAPTER 7

Your instructor may assign one or more of these projects to help you review the chapter and assess your mastery and understanding of the chapter.

Project	Apply Skills from These Chapter Objectives	Project Type	Project Location
7C	Objectives 1-3 from Project 7A	**7C Skills Review** A guided review of the skills from Project 7A.	On the following pages
7D	Objectives 4-8 from Project 7B	**7D Skills Review** A guided review of the skills from Project 7B.	On the following pages
7E	Objectives 1-3 from Project 7A	**7E Mastery (Grader Project)** A demonstration of your mastery of the skills in Project 7A with extensive decision making.	In MyITLab and on the following pages
7F	Objectives 4-8 from Project 7B	**7F Mastery (Grader Project)** A demonstration of your mastery of the skills in Project 7B with extensive decision making.	In MyITLab and on the following pages
7G	Objectives 1-8 from Projects 7A and 7B	**7G Mastery (Grader Project)** A demonstration of your mastery of the skills in Projects 7A and 7B with extensive decision making.	In MyITLab and on the following pages
7H	Combination of Objectives from Projects 7A and 7B	**7H GO! Fix It** A demonstration of your mastery of the skills in Projects 7A and 7B by creating a correct result from a document that contains errors you must find.	Online
7I	Combination of Objectives from Projects 7A and 7B	**7I GO! Make It** A demonstration of your mastery of the skills in Projects 7A and 7B by creating a result from a supplied picture.	Online
7J	Combination of Objectives from Projects 7A and 7B	**7J GO! Solve It** A demonstration of your mastery of the skills in Projects 7A and 7B, your decision-making skills, and your critical thinking skills. A task-specific rubric helps you self-assess your result.	Online
7K	Combination of Objectives from Projects 7A and 7B	**7K GO! Solve It** A demonstration of your mastery of the skills in Projects 7A and 7B, your decision-making skills, and your critical thinking skills. A task-specific rubric helps you self-assess your result.	On the following pages
7L	Combination of Objectives from Projects 7A and 7B	**7L GO! Think** A demonstration of your understanding of the chapter concepts applied in a manner that you would outside of college. An analytic rubric helps you and your instructor grade the quality of your work by comparing it to the work an expert in the discipline would create.	On the following pages
7M	Combination of Objectives from Projects 7A and 7B	**7M GO! Think** A demonstration of your understanding of the chapter concepts applied in a manner that you would outside of college. An analytic rubric helps you and your instructor grade the quality of your work by comparing it to the work an expert in the discipline would create.	Online
7N	Combination of Objectives from Projects 7A and 7B	**7N You and GO!** A demonstration of your understanding of the chapter concepts applied in a manner that you would in a personal situation. An analytic rubric helps you and your instructor grade the quality of your work.	Online

GLOSSARY

GLOSSARY OF CHAPTER KEY TERMS

Ascending The order of text sorted alphabetically from A to Z or numbers sorted from the smallest to the largest.

AutoRecover A feature that helps prevent losing unsaved changes by automatically creating a backup version of the current document.

Blog A website that displays dated entries, short for *Web log*.

Blog post An individual article entered in a blog with a time and date stamp.

Descending The order of text sorted alphabetically from Z to A or numbers sorted from the largest to the smallest.

Drop cap A large capital letter at the beginning of a paragraph that formats text in a visually distinctive manner.

Dropped The position of a drop cap when it is within the text of the paragraph.

Email address link A hyperlink that opens a new message window so that an individual viewing a website can send an email message.

Federal registration symbol The symbol ® that indicates that a patent or trademark is registered with the United States Patent and Trademark Office.

Hyperlinks Text, buttons, pictures, or other objects that, when clicked, access other sections of the active document or another file.

Hypertext Markup Language (HTML) The markup language that communicates color and graphics in a format that all computers can understand.

In margin The position of a drop cap when it is in the left margin of a paragraph.

Internal link A hyperlink that connects to another page in the same website.

Internet Explorer A web browser developed by Microsoft.

Multiple Pages A zoom setting that decreases the magnification to display several pages of a document.

Navigation bar A series of text links across the top or bottom of a webpage that, when clicked, will link to another webpage on the same website.

Portable Document Format (PDF) A technology that creates an image that preserves the look of your file but that cannot be easily changed or edited.

Rich Text Format (RTF) A universal file format, using the .rtf file extension, that can be read by many word processing programs.

Sorting The action of ordering data, usually in alphabetical or numeric order.

Text link A hyperlink applied to a selected word or phrase.

Variable In an equation, a letter that represents a value.

Web browser (Browser) Software that interprets HTML files, formats them into webpages, and then displays them.

Web Page format A file type that saves a Word document as an HTML file, with some elements of the webpage saved in a folder, separate from the webpage itself.

Webpage A file coded in HTML that can be viewed on the Internet using a web browser.

Website A group of related webpages published to a specific location on the Internet.

Wildcard A special character such as * or ? that is used to search for an unknown term.

CHAPTER REVIEW

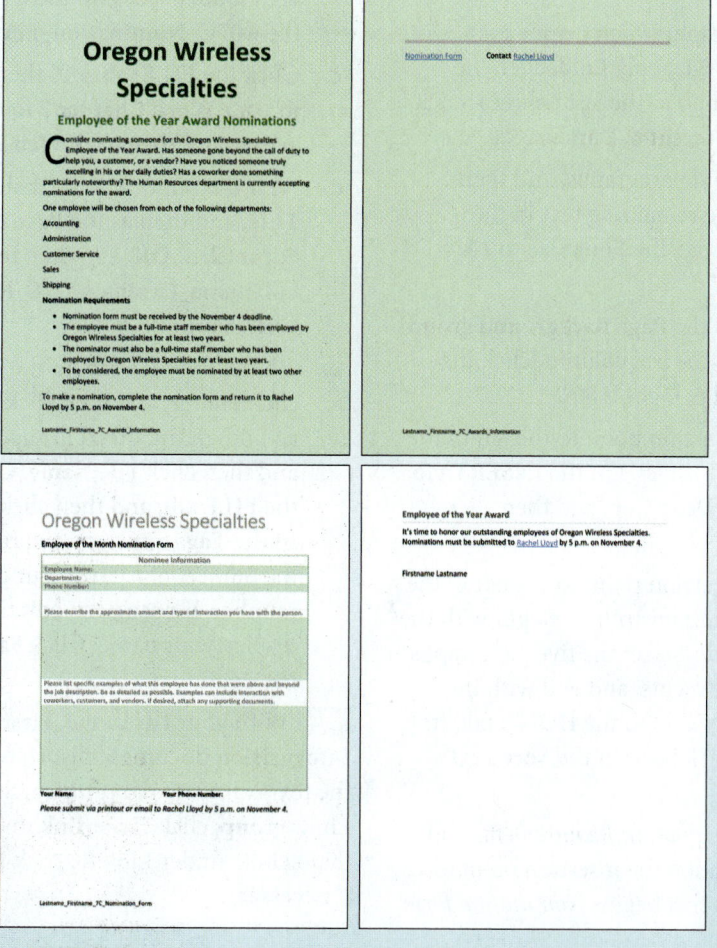

Apply 7A skills from these objectives:

1 Create a Webpage from a Word Document

2 Insert and Modify Hyperlinks in a Word Document

3 Create a Blog Post

Skills Review | Project 7C Awards Information

In the following Skills Review, you will modify and add hyperlinks to the webpage containing nomination information for the Employee of the Year Award that is given to outstanding individuals at Oregon Wireless Specialties. You will also create a blog post related to the nomination process. Your completed documents will look similar to Figure 7.48, although your text wrapping may vary.

PROJECT FILES

For Project 7C, you will need the following files:

w07C_Awards_Information

w07C_Nomination_Form

You will save your files as:

Lastname_Firstname_7C_Awards_Information

Lastname_Firstname_7C_Nomination_Form

Lastname_Firstname_7C_Awards_Blog

PROJECT RESULTS

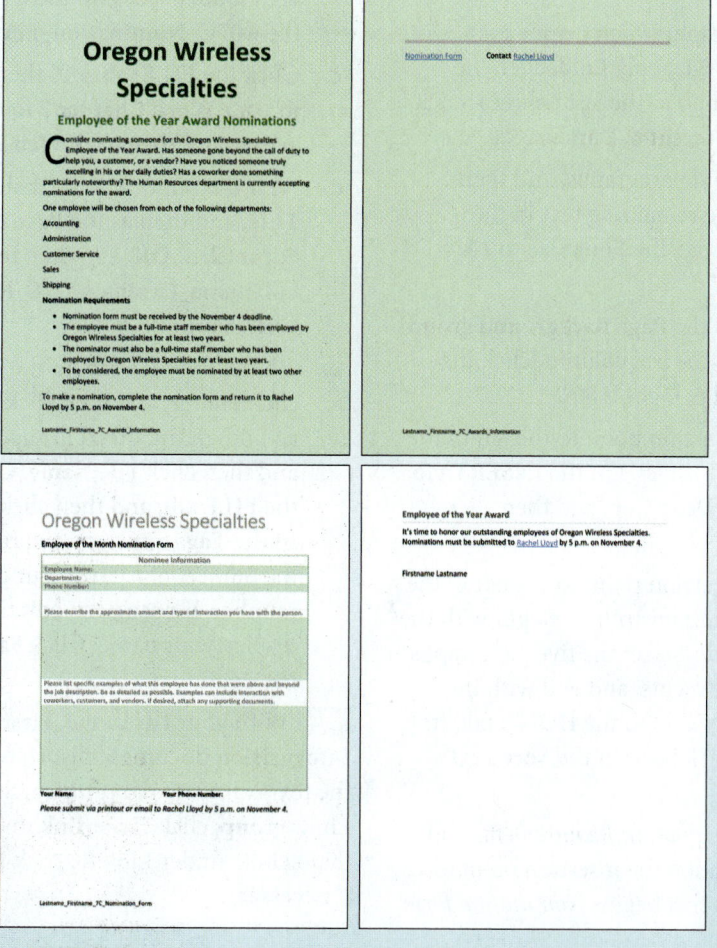

FIGURE 7.48

(Project 7C Awards Information continues on the next page)

CHAPTER REVIEW

1 ▶ Start Word. From your student files, locate and then open the file **w07C_Awards_Information**. Click the **FILE tab**, display the **Save As** dialog box, navigate to your **Word Chapter 7** folder, and then in the lower portion of the dialog box, click the **Save as type arrow**. On the list, click **Web Page**. Near the bottom of the dialog box, click **Change Title**, and then in the **Enter Text** dialog box, in the **Page title** box, type **Awards Information** Click **OK**. In the **File name** box, using your own name, type **Lastname_Firstname_7C_Awards_Information** and then press Enter.

a. On the **INSERT tab**, in the **Header & Footer group**, click **Footer**, and then click **Edit Footer**. On the ribbon, in the **Insert group**, click **Document Info**, and then click **File Name**. **Close** the footer area.

b. Select the first paragraph—*Oregon Wireless Specialties*. On the mini toolbar, change the **Font Size** to **48**, apply **Bold**, click the **Font Color arrow**, and then in the last column, click the last color—**Green, Accent 6, Darker 50%**.

c. Select the second paragraph, which begins *Employee*. Change the **Font Size** to **24**, apply **Bold**, click the **Font Color arrow**, and then in the last column, click the fifth color—**Green, Accent 6, Darker 25%**.

d. Select the first and second paragraphs, and then press Ctrl + E. Select the remaining text in the document, and then change the **Font Size** to **14**. Deselect the text.

2 ▶ On the **DESIGN tab**, in the **Page Background group**, click **Page Color**, and then in the last column, click the second color—**Green, Accent 6, Lighter 80%**.

a. Click to position the insertion point to the left of the paragraph that begins *Consider*. On the **INSERT tab**, in the **Text group**, click **Drop Cap**, and then click **Dropped**.

b. Click to position the insertion point to the left of the paragraph that begins *Administration*. Begin with the paragraph *Administration*, select the five paragraphs that comprise the departments, and end with the paragraph *Customer Service*. On the **HOME tab**, in the **Paragraph group**, click **Sort**. In the **Sort Text** dialog box, click **OK**.

c. Select the paragraph *Nomination Requirements* and apply **Bold**. Click to position the insertion point to the left of the paragraph that begins *Nomination form*

must be. Beginning with the paragraph *Nomination form*, select the four paragraphs that comprise the requirements, and end with the paragraph that begins *To be considered*. On the **HOME tab**, in the **Paragraph group**, click **Bullets**, and then click anywhere to deselect the text. **Save** your changes.

3 ▶ In the paragraph that begins *To make a nomination*, click to position the insertion point to the right of the period at the end of the sentence, and then press Enter. On the **HOME tab**, in the **Paragraph group**, click the **Border arrow**, and then click **Horizontal Line**.

a. Point to the inserted line, right-click, and then click **Format Horizontal Line**. In the **Format Horizontal Line** dialog box, change the **Height** to **6 pt**, and then under **Color**, select the **Use solid color (no shade)** check box. Click **OK**, and then click anywhere to deselect the line.

b. Click the **FILE tab**, click **Open**, and then navigate to your student files. In the Open dialog box, select the file **w07C_Nomination_Form**, and then click **Open**.

c. Click the **FILE tab**, and then click **Save As**. Navigate to your **Word Chapter 7** folder. Click the **Save as type arrow**, and then click **Web Page**.

d. Near the bottom of the dialog box, click **Change Title**, and then as the **Page title**, type **Nomination Form** Click **OK**, and then in the **File name** box, type **Lastname_Firstname_7C_Nomination_Form** Click **Save**.

e. On the **INSERT tab**, in the **Header & Footer group**, click **Footer**, and then click **Edit Footer**. On the ribbon, in the **Insert group**, click **Document Info**, and then click **File Name**. **Close** the footer area. Click the **FILE tab**, and then click **Show All Properties**. In the **Tags** box, type **awards, nomination form** In the **Subject** box, type your course name and section number. If necessary, edit the author name to display your name. Click **Save**, and then **Close** the document.

4 ▶ With your **Lastname_Firstname_7C_Awards_Information** document displayed, press Ctrl + End. Select the text *Nomination Form*. On the **INSERT tab**, in the **Links group**, click **Hyperlink**. In the **Insert Hyperlink** dialog box, under **Link to**, click **Existing File or Web Page**, if necessary.

(Project 7C Awards Information continues on the next page)

CHAPTER REVIEW

a. In the **Look in** box, if necessary, navigate to your **Word Chapter 7** folder, click your **Lastname_Firstname_7C_Nomination_Form** document, and then click **ScreenTip**. In the **ScreenTip text** box, type **Nomination Form** and then click **OK** two times.

b. Select the text *Rachel Lloyd*, and then display the **Insert Hyperlink** dialog box. Under **Link to**, click **E-mail Address**. In the **E-mail address** box, type **rlloyd@owspecialties.com** As the **ScreenTip text**, type **Human Relations Director** and then click **OK** two times.

c. At the bottom of the webpage, point to *Rachel Lloyd* to display the ScreenTip. Right-click the **Rachel Lloyd** hyperlink, and then click **Edit Hyperlink**. Click **ScreenTip**, and then edit the **ScreenTip text** to indicate **Click here to send an email message** Click **OK** two times, and then point to the *Rachel Lloyd* link to display the ScreenTip.

d. Press Ctrl + Home. Click the **FILE tab**, and then click **Show All Properties**. In the **Tags** box, type **awards information, webpage** In the **Subject** box, type your course name and section number. If necessary, edit the author name to display your name.

e. **Save** your changes. Click the **FILE tab**, and then click **Close**.

5 Click the **FILE tab**, and then click **New**. On the right, click the **Blog post** template, and then in the displayed window, click **Create**. In the **Register a Blog Account** dialog box, click **Register Later**.

a. Press F12. In the **Save As** dialog box, navigate to your **Word Chapter 7** folder, and then **Save** the file as **Lastname_Firstname_7C_Awards_Blog**

b. Click anywhere in the **Enter Post Title Here** field to select the placeholder text, and then type **Employee of the Year Award** Click under the line in the body text area, and then type **It's time to honor our outstanding employees of Oregon Wireless Specialties. Nominations must be submitted to Rachel Lloyd by 5 p.m. on November 4.**

c. Select all the body text, and then change the **Font Size** to **14**. In the second sentence, select the text *Rachel Lloyd*. Click the **INSERT tab**, and then in the **Links group**, click **Hyperlink**. Under **Link to**, click **E-mail Address**, and then in the **E-mail address** box, type **rlloyd@owspecialties.com** Click **OK**.

d. Click to position the insertion point at the end of the paragraph, press Enter two times, and then type your first and last names.

e. Press Ctrl + Home. Click the **FILE tab**, and then click **Show All Properties**. In the **Tags** box, type **awards nomination, blog** In the **Subject** box, type your course name and section number. If necessary, edit the author name to display your name. **Save** your document, and then on the status bar, change the document view to **Print Layout**. **Close** Word.

6 Print, or submit electronically, the three files— the blog post and two webpages—as directed by your instructor.

END | You have completed Project 7C

CHAPTER REVIEW

Apply 7B skills from these Objectives:

4 Manage Document Versions

5 Collect and Paste Images and Text

6 Locate Supporting Information and Insert Equations

7 Use Advanced Find and Replace Options

8 Save in Other File Formats

Skills Review   Project 7D Outdoor Accessories

In the following Skills Review, you will create a document for Nanci Scholtz, Marketing Vice President of Oregon Wireless Specialties, which details the waterproof and ruggedized accessories sold by the company. Your completed documents will look similar to Figure 7.49.

PROJECT FILES

For Project 7D, you will need the following files:

w07D_Outdoor_Accessories

w07D_Product_Info

w07D_Product_Images

You will save your files as:

Lastname_Firstname_7D_Outdoor_Accessories

Lastname_Firstname_7D_Accessories_RTF

PROJECT RESULTS

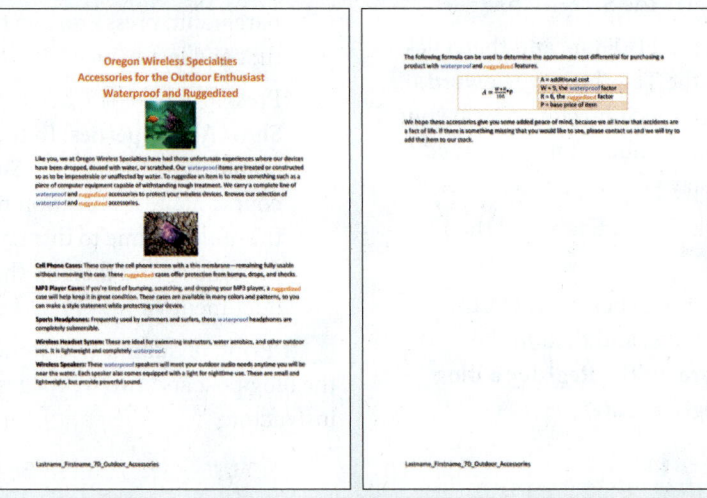

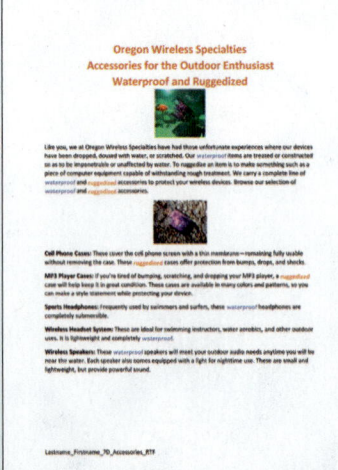

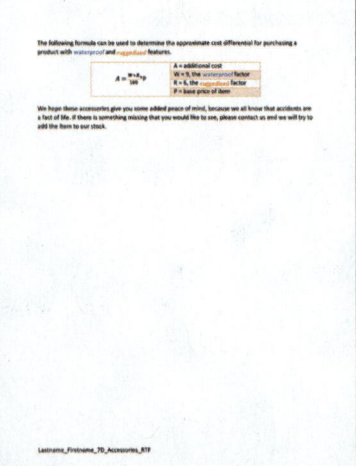

FIGURE 7.49

(Project 7D Outdoor Accessories continues on the next page)

CHAPTER REVIEW

1 Start Word. From your student files, locate and then open the file **w07D_Outdoor_Accessories**. Click the **FILE tab**, click **Save As**, navigate to your **Word Chapter 7** folder, and then save the document as **Lastname_Firstname_7D_Outdoor_Accessories**

a. Right-click in the footer area, and then click **Edit Footer**. On the ribbon, in the **Insert group**, click **Document Info**, and then click **File Name**. **Close** the footer area.

b. Click the **VIEW tab**. In the **Zoom group**, click **Zoom**. In the **Zoom** dialog box, under **Zoom to**, click **200%**, and then click **OK**. In the first row of the table, click to position the insertion point to the left of *cost*, and then press [Backspace] to remove the extra space. On the **VIEW tab**, in the **Zoom group**, click **100%**.

c. Select the first three paragraphs. On the mini toolbar, change the **Font Size** to **20**, apply **Bold**, click the **Font Color arrow**, and then in the sixth column, click the fifth color—**Orange, Accent 2, Darker 25%**. Press [Ctrl] + [E].

d. Click the **HOME tab**, and then in the **Clipboard group**, click the **Dialog Box Launcher** to display the **Clipboard** pane. If necessary, at the top of the pane, click **Clear All** to delete anything on the **Clipboard**.

e. From your student files, open **w07D_Product_Images**. If necessary, display the **Clipboard** pane. Point to the first graphic—a cell phone in water—right-click, and then click **Copy**. Using the same technique, **Copy** the rock graphic. **Close** the **w07D_Product_Images** file.

f. From your student files, open **w07D_Product_Info**. Press [Ctrl] + [A] to select all of the text, right-click the selected text, click **Copy**, and then **Close** the **w07D_Product_Info** file.

2 Above the paragraph that begins *Like you*, position the insertion point in the blank paragraph. In the **Clipboard** pane, click the *water* graphic, and then press [Ctrl] + [E].

a. Click to position the insertion point at the end of the paragraph that begins *Like you*, and then press [Enter]. In the **Clipboard** pane, click the *rock* graphic, and then press [Ctrl] + [E].

b. Click to position the insertion point to the left of the paragraph that begins *The following formula*. In the

Clipboard pane, click the text entry that begins *Cell Phone Cases* to paste the entire block of text at the insertion point. In the **Clipboard** pane, click **Clear All**, and then **Close** the **Clipboard** pane.

c. In the paragraph that begins *Cell Phone Cases*, click to position the insertion point to the right of *membrane*. Click the **INSERT tab**. In the **Symbols group**, click **Symbol**, and then click **More Symbols**. In the **Symbol** dialog box, click the **Special Characters tab**, and then click the first character— **Em Dash**. Click **Insert**, and then **Close** the **Symbol** dialog box. Type **remaining** and then **Save** the document.

3 In the paragraph that begins *Like you*, position the insertion point at the end of the first sentence—following the period after *scratched*. Press [Spacebar], and then type **Our waterproof items are** Press and hold [Alt] and then press the left mouse button.

a. In the **Research** pane, in the **Search for** box, delete any existing text, and then type **waterproof** In the **Search location** box, click the **arrow**. From the list, click **Encarta Dictionary: English (North America)**. Under **Encarta Dictionary**, locate the text *impervious to water*. Indented and immediately below the definition, select the text that begins *treated or constructed* and ends with *by water*. Right-click the selection, and then from the shortcut menu click **Copy**.

b. Click in your document at the point you stopped typing—after *are*, right-click, and then from the shortcut menu, under **Paste Options**, click **Keep Text Only** to insert the copied text in the document. Type a period, and then press [Spacebar]. Type **To ruggedize an item is**

c. In the **Research** pane, in the **Search for** box, replace *waterproof* with **ruggedize** and then press [Enter]. Under **Encarta Dictionary**, locate and then select the entire definition that begins *to make something* and ends with *rough treatment*. Right-click the selection, and then click **Copy**.

d. Click in the document at the point you stopped typing, right-click, and then under **Paste Options**, click **Keep Text Only**. Type a period. **Close** the **Research** pane.

(Project 7D Outdoor Accessories continues on the next page)

CHAPTER REVIEW

e. Near the bottom of **Page 1**, click to the left of the paragraph that begins *The following formula*, and then press Ctrl + Enter. On **Page 2**, click in the first cell of the table, and then on the **INSERT tab**, in the **Symbols group**, click **Equation**. In the inserted equation placeholder, type **A=** Under **EQUATION TOOLS**, on the **DESIGN tab**, in the **Structures group**, click **Fraction**, and then click the first format—**Stacked Fraction**.

f. In the fraction, click in the top placeholder, and then type **W+R** Click in the bottom placeholder, and then type **100** Click to the right of the fraction, and then type ***P Save** your document.

4 Press Ctrl + Home. Click the **HOME tab**, and then in the **Editing group**, click **Replace**. In the **Find and Replace** dialog box, in the **Find what** box, type **waterproof** and then in the **Replace with** box, type the same text **waterproof**

a. Below the **Replace with** box, click **More**. Under **Search Options**, select the **Match case** check box. At the bottom, under **Replace**, click **Format**, and then from the list, click **Font**.

b. In the **Replace Font** dialog box, under **Font style**, click **Bold**. Click the **Font color arrow**, and then in the ninth column, click the first color—**Blue, Accent 5**.

c. Click **OK** to close the **Replace Font** dialog box, and then in the **Find and Replace** dialog box, click **Replace All**. When a **Microsoft Word** message box displays indicating that you have made 8 replacements, click **OK**.

d. Using the same technique, replace all instances of *ruggedized* and select **Match case**. For the replaced text, change the **Font style** to **Bold** and change the **Font color** to **Orange, Accent 2**—in the sixth column, the first color. When a **Microsoft Word** message box displays indicating that you have made 6 replacements, click **OK**.

e. In the **Find and Replace** dialog box, **Delete** the text in the **Find what** box, and then clear the **Match case** check box. **Delete** the text in the **Replace with** box, click **No Formatting**, and then click **Less**. **Close** the **Find and Replace** dialog box.

5 Press Ctrl + Home. Click the **REVIEW tab**, and then in the **Proofing group**, click **Spelling & Grammar**.

a. For any grammar errors, select the suggestion if necessary, and then click **Change**. Click **Ignore Once** for all other errors. When a message indicates that the spelling and grammar check is complete, click **OK** to close the dialog box. Note: If Word does not identify *their* as a grammar error, change the word to *there*.

b. Click the **FILE tab**, and then click **Show All Properties**. In the **Tags** box, type **waterproof, ruggedized** In the **Subject** box, type your course name and section number. If necessary, edit the author name to display your name. **Save** your document.

c. Click the **FILE tab**, and then click **Save As**. If necessary, navigate to your **Word Chapter 7** folder. In the lower portion of the **Save As** dialog box, click the **Save as type arrow**, and then from the list, click **Rich Text Format**. In the **File name** box, type **Lastname_Firstname_7D_Accessories_RTF** and then click **Save**. If a dialog box displays, click **Continue**.

d. Scroll to the bottom of the document, and then double-click in the footer area. Right-click the file name, and then from the shortcut menu, click **Update Field**. **Close** the footer area.

e. Click the **FILE tab**, and then click **Show All Properties**. In the **Tags** box, position the insertion point to the right of the existing text, type **, rtf** and then **Save** your document.

6 Print or submit electronically the two files—the Word document and the RTF file—as directed by your instructor. **Close** Word.

END | You have completed Project 7D

CONTENT-BASED ASSESSMENTS

Mastering Word | Project 7E Phone Accessories

Apply 7A skills from these Objectives:

1 Create a Webpage from a Word Document
2 Insert and Modify Hyperlinks in a Word Document
3 Create a Blog Post

In the following Mastering Word project, you will create a webpage for Nanci Scholtz, Marketing Vice President of Oregon Wireless Specialties, which describes the types of cell phone accessories available for purchase. You will also create a blog post announcing savings on purchases. Your completed documents will look similar to Figure 7.50, although text wrapping may vary.

PROJECT FILES

For Project 7E, you will need the following files:

w07E_Phone_Accessories
w07E_Phone_Cases

You will save your files as:

Lastname_Firstname_7E_Phone_Accessories
Lastname_Firstname_7E_Phone_Cases
Lastname_Firstname_7E_Newsletter_Offer

PROJECT RESULTS

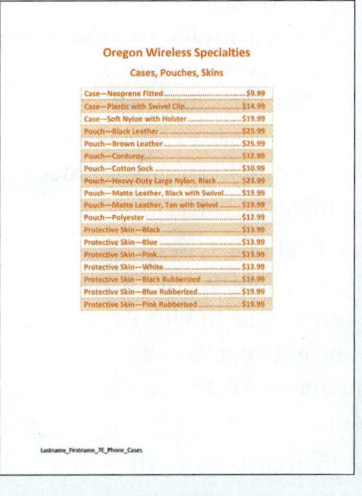

FIGURE 7.50

(Project 7E Phone Accessories continues on the next page)

CONTENT-BASED ASSESSMENTS

1 Start Word, open the document **w07E_Phone_Accessories**, display the **Save As** dialog box, and then navigate to your **Word Chapter 7** folder. Change the **Save as type** to **Web Page**, change the **Page title** to **Cell Phone Accessories** and then save the file as **Lastname_Firstname_7E_Phone_Accessories** Insert the file name in the footer.

2 Select the first paragraph, change the **Font Size** to **28**, apply **Bold**, and then change the **Font Color** to **Blue, Accent 5, Darker 25%**. Select the second paragraph, change the **Font Size** to **20**, apply **Bold**, and then change the **Font Color** to **Blue, Accent 5, Darker 50%**. Select the first and second paragraphs, and then press Ctrl + E. Click to the left of the fourth paragraph that begins *Are you looking*. Insert a **Drop Cap**, click **Dropped**, and then change **Lines to drop** to **2**. Change the **Font Color** of the dropped cap to **Blue, Accent 5**.

3 Click in the third paragraph, which is blank. On the **HOME tab**, display the **Borders** list, and then insert a **Horizontal Line**. Change the **Width** of the line to **95%**, change the **Height** to **6 pt**, and then under **Color**, select the **Use Solid color (no shade)** check box. Click to the left of the paragraph *Cases and Pouches*. Select the next 12 paragraphs, ending with *Memory Cards*. **Sort** the list in ascending order, and then apply **Bullets**. **Save** your document.

4 Open the document **w07E_Phone_Cases**, display the **Save As** dialog box, navigate to your **Word Chapter 7** folder, and then change the **Save as type** to **Web Page**. Change the **Page title** to **Cases and Pouches** and then save the file as **Lastname_Firstname_7E_Phone_Cases** Insert the file name in the footer.

5 Click the **FILE tab**, and then click **Show All Properties**. In the **Tags** box, type **cases, webpage** In the **Subject** box, type your course name and section number. If necessary, edit the author name to display your name. **Save** your changes, and then **Close** the document.

6 In your **Lastname_Firstname_7E_Phone_Accessories** document, in the bulleted list, select the text *Cases and Pouches*. Insert a hyperlink to the existing file in your **Word Chapter 7** folder named **Lastname_Firstname_7E_Phone_Cases**. In the last paragraph of the document, select the text *customer service department*, and then insert a hyperlink to the email address **service@owspecialties.com** In the last sentence, select the text *Sign up*, and then insert a hyperlink to the email address **newsletter@owspecialties.com**

7 Click the **FILE tab**, and then click **Show All Properties**. In the **Tags** box, type **accessories, webpage** In the **Subject** box, type your course name and section number. If necessary, edit the author name to display your name. **Save** your changes, click the **FILE tab**, and then click **Close**.

8 Create a new **Blog post**, and then click **Register Later**. **Save** the document in your **Word Chapter 7** folder as **Lastname_Firstname_7E_Newsletter_Offer** In the **Enter Post Title Here** field, type **Newsletter Offer** In the body text area, type **Sign up for our newsletter to receive a coupon for 15% off your next order.** Select the text *Sign up*, and then insert a hyperlink to the email address **newsletter@owspecialties.com** At the end of the paragraph, press Enter two times, and then type your first and last names.

9 Click the **FILE tab**, and then click **Show All Properties**. In the **Tags** box, type **newsletter, blog** In the **Subject** box, type your course name and section number. If necessary, edit the author name to display your name. **Save** the blog post. On the status bar, change the document view to Print Layout.

10 Print or submit electronically the three files—the blog post and two webpages—as directed by your instructor. **Close** Word.

END | You have completed Project 7E

CONTENT-BASED ASSESSMENTS

Mastering Word Project 7F Sale Flyer

In the following Mastering Word project, you will create an RTF document for Nanci Scholtz, Marketing Vice President of Oregon Wireless Specialties, which announces an upcoming sale. Your completed document will look similar to Figure 7.51.

Apply 7B skills from these Objectives:

4 Manage Document Versions

5 Collect and Paste Images and Text

6 Locate Supporting Information and Insert Equations

7 Use Advanced Find and Replace Options

8 Save in Other File Formats

PROJECT FILES

For Project 7F, you will need the following files:

w07F_Sale_Flyer
w07F_Sale_List

You will save your file as:

Lastname_Firstname_7F_Sale_Flyer

PROJECT RESULTS

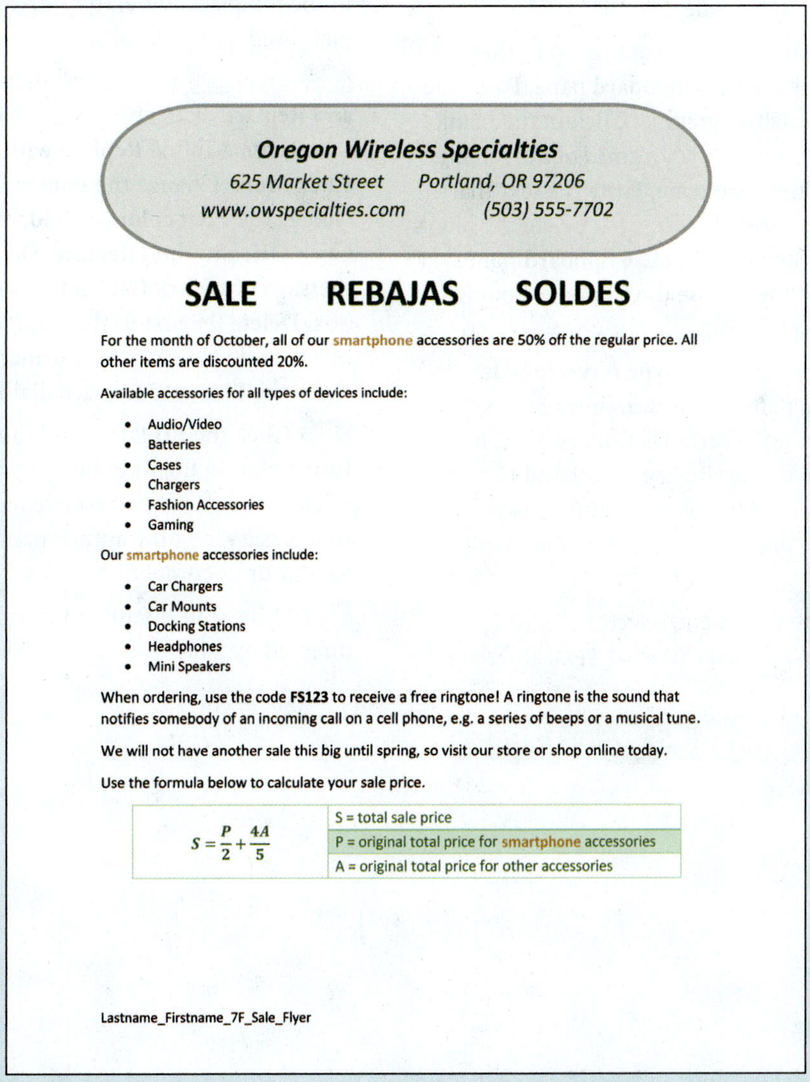

Oregon Wireless Specialties

625 Market Street   Portland, OR 97206
www.owspecialties.com   (503) 555-7702

SALE   REBAJAS   SOLDES

For the month of October, all of our smartphone accessories are 50% off the regular price. All other items are discounted 20%.

Available accessories for all types of devices include:

- Audio/Video
- Batteries
- Cases
- Chargers
- Fashion Accessories
- Gaming

Our smartphone accessories include:

- Car Chargers
- Car Mounts
- Docking Stations
- Headphones
- Mini Speakers

When ordering, use the code **FS123** to receive a free ringtone! A ringtone is the sound that notifies somebody of an incoming call on a cell phone, e.g. a series of beeps or a musical tune.

We will not have another sale this big until spring, so visit our store or shop online today.

Use the formula below to calculate your sale price.

$$S = \frac{P}{2} + \frac{4A}{5}$$

S = total sale price
P = original total price for smartphone accessories
A = original total price for other accessories

Lastname_Firstname_7F_Sale_Flyer

FIGURE 7.51

(Project 7F Sale Flyer continues on the next page)

1 Start Word, open the file **w07F_Sale_Flyer**, and then save it in your **Word Chapter 7** folder as a **Rich Text Format** file with the name **Lastname_Firstname_7F_ Sale_Flyer** If a dialog box displays, click **Continue**. Insert the file name in the footer.

2 Increase the **Zoom** to **200%**. In the first row of the table, position the insertion point to the left of the equal sign, and then press Backspace. Change the **Zoom** to **100%**.

3 Display the **Clipboard** pane, and then if any items display, click **Clear All**. Open the document **w07F_Sale_ List**. If necessary, display the **Clipboard** pane. **Copy** the **Oregon Wireless Specialties** graphic to the **Clipboard**. Beginning with the text *Available accessories*, select the remaining text in the document, and then **Copy** it to the **Clipboard**. **Close** the **w07F_Sale_List** file.

4 Click in the blank paragraph at the top of the document, and then from the **Clipboard** pane, **Paste** the **Oregon Wireless Specialties** graphic. Click in the blank line following the paragraph that begins *For the month*, and then from the **Clipboard** pane, **Paste** the text that begins *Available accessories*. If necessary, delete the blank line following the pasted text. In the **Clipboard** pane, **Clear All** entries, and then **Close** the **Clipboard** pane.

5 Click at the end of the paragraph that begins *When ordering*, press Spacebar, and then type **A ringtone is** Display the **Research** pane, in the **Search for** box, type **ringtone** and then using **Encarta Dictionary**, search for the definition. In the **Research** pane, select and **Copy** the text that begins *the sound that notifies*, and ends with *a musical tune*. **Paste** the text in the document. Type a period.

6 At the top of the document, select the text *SALE*. Click **Translate**, click **Translate Selected Text**, and then

translate the text to **Spanish**. **Copy** the word following the first occurrence of *reduced prices*. In the document, click to the right of *SALE*, press Tab two times, and then **Paste** the translated text. Format the text as **UPPERCASE**, and then with the insertion point to the right of the text, press Tab two times. Using the same technique, translate the text to **French**. Copy and paste the translated text, and then format the text as **UPPERCASE**. **Close** the **Research** pane.

7 Click in the first cell of the table, and then insert an **Equation** placeholder. In the placeholder, type **S=** Display the **Fractions** gallery, insert a **Stacked Fraction**, type **+** and then insert a second **Stacked Fraction**. In the first fraction, in the top placeholder, type **P** and then in the bottom placeholder, type **2** In the second fraction, in the top placeholder, type **4A** and then in the bottom placeholder, type **5**

8 Press Ctrl + Home, and then display the **Find and Replace** dialog box. In the **Find what** box, type **smartphone** In the **Replace with** box, type **smartphone** Click **More**. Change the **Font style** to **Bold**, and then change the **Font color** to **Gold, Accent 4, Darker 25%**. Click **OK**, and then **Replace All**. In the **Microsoft Word** message box, click **OK**. In the **Find and Replace** dialog box, **Delete** the text in the **Find what** and **Replace with** boxes, and then click **No Formatting**. Click **Less**, and then **Close** the **Find and Replace** dialog box.

9 Click the **FILE tab**, and then click **Show All Properties**. In the **Tags** box, type **sale flyer, rtf** In the **Subject** box, type your course name and section number. If necessary, edit the author name to display your name. **Save** your document.

10 Print your document or submit electronically as directed by your instructor. **Close** Word.

END | You have completed Project 7F

CONTENT-BASED ASSESSMENTS

Mastering Word | Project 7G Returns Policy

In the following Mastering Word project, you will create a webpage and blog post for Josette Lovrick, Operations Manager of Oregon Wireless Specialties, which explains the return and exchange policy for the company. Your completed documents will look similar to Figure 7.52.

Apply 7A and 7B skills from these Objectives:

1 Create a Webpage from a Word Document
2 Insert and Modify Hyperlinks in a Word Document
3 Create a Blog Post
4 Manage Document Versions
5 Collect and Paste Images and Text
6 Locate Supporting Information and Insert Equations
7 Use Advanced Find and Replace Options
8 Save in Other File Formats

PROJECT FILES

For Project 7G, you will need the following files:

w07G_Returns_Policy
w07G_Returns_Image
w07G_Shipping_Policy

You will save your files as:

Lastname_Firstname_7G_Returns_Policy
Lastname_Firstname_7G_Shipping_Policy
Lastname_Firstname_7G_Returns_Blog

PROJECT RESULTS

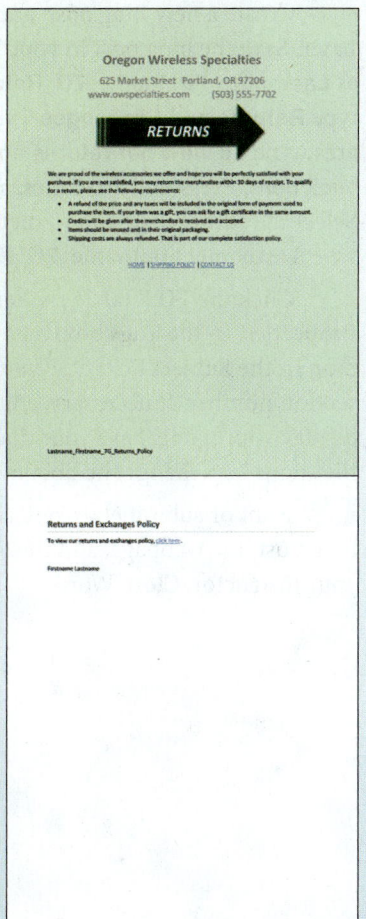

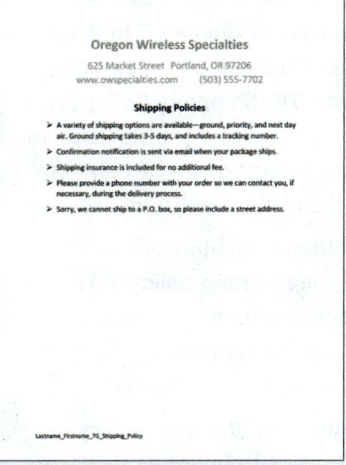

FIGURE 7.52

(Project 7G Returns Policy continues on the next page)

CONTENT-BASED ASSESSMENTS

1 Start Word, open the document **w07G_Returns_Policy**, display the **Save As** dialog box, navigate to your **Word Chapter 7** folder, and then change the file type to **Web Page**. Change the page title to **Returns and Exchanges** and then save the file as **Lastname_Firstname_7G_Returns_Policy** Insert the file name in the footer.

2 Change the **Zoom** to **200%**. In the paragraph that begins *We are proud*, position the insertion point to the left of *30*, and then press Backspace. Change the **Zoom** to **100%**.

3 Change the **Page Color** to **Green, Accent 6, Lighter 80%**. Position the insertion point to the left of the paragraph that begins *Items*, and then select the next four paragraphs. **Sort** the list alphabetically, and then apply **Bullets**. Display the **Clipboard** pane, and clear it if necessary.

4 Open the file **w07G_Returns_Image**. **Copy** the image to the **Clipboard**, and then **Close** the document. Open the file **w07G_Shipping_Policy**. Display the **Save As** dialog box, navigate to your **Word Chapter 7** folder, change the file type to **Rich Text Format**, and then save the file as **Lastname_Firstname_7G_Shipping_Policy** If a dialog box displays, click **Continue**. Insert the file name in the footer. Select the first three paragraphs—the company information, and then **Copy** the text to the **Clipboard**.

5 Click the **FILE tab**, and then click **Show All Properties**. In the **Tags** box, type **shipping policy, RTF** In the **Subject** box, type your course name and section number. If necessary, edit the author name to display your name. **Save** and **Close** the document.

6 With **Lastname_Firstname_7G_Returns_Policy** displayed, press Ctrl + Home. In the **Clipboard** pane, **Paste** the text in the document. Below the pasted text, click in the blank paragraph, **Paste** the image, and then press Ctrl + E. **Clear All** items from the **Clipboard** pane, and

then **Close** the pane. At the bottom of the document, select *HOME*, and then insert a hyperlink to **www.owspecialties.com** In the same paragraph, select the text *SHIPPING POLICY*, and then insert a hyperlink to the file in your **Word Chapter 7** folder named **Lastname_Firstname_7G_Shipping_Policy**. Select the text *CONTACT US*, and then insert a hyperlink to the email address **service@owspecialties.com**

7 In the second bulleted paragraph, replace the word *approved* with the synonym *accepted*. Click the **Spelling & Grammar** button, and then take appropriate action to correct any errors.

8 Click the **FILE tab**, and then click **Show All Properties**. In the **Tags** box, type **returns, exchanges** In the **Subject** box, type your course name and section number. If necessary, edit the author name to display your name. **Save** the document. Click the **FILE tab**, and then **Close** the document.

9 Create a new **Blog post**, and then click **Register Later**. **Save** the blog post in your **Word Chapter 7** folder as **Lastname_Firstname_7G_Returns_Blog** As the title, type **Returns and Exchanges Policy** In the body text area, type **To view our returns and exchanges policy, click here.** Press Enter two times, and then type your name. Select the text *click here*, and then insert a hyperlink to your **Lastname_Firstname_7G_Returns_Policy** file.

10 Click the **FILE tab**, and then click **Show All Properties**. In the **Tags** box, type **returns, exchanges, blog** In the **Subject** box, type your course name and section number. If necessary, edit the author name to display your name. **Save** your document. If necessary, on the status bar, change the document view to Print Layout.

11 Print or submit electronically your three files—the blog post, the webpage, and the RTF file—as directed by your instructor. **Close** Word.

END | You have completed Project 7G

CONTENT-BASED ASSESSMENTS

GO! Fix It	Project 7H Company Overview	Online
GO! Make It	Project 7I Screen Protectors	Online
GO! Solve It	Project 7J Wholesalers	Online
GO! Solve It	Project 7K Staff Increase	

Build from Scratch

Apply a combination of the 7A and 7B skills.

Build from Scratch

PROJECT FILES

For Project 7K, you will need the following files:

New blank Word document
w07K_Staff_Increase

You will save your files as:

Lastname_Firstname_7K_Staff_Schedule
Lastname_Firstname_7K_Staff_Increase

Open a new blank document, and then save it in your **Word Chapter 7** folder as an RTF file with the file name **Lastname_Firstname_7K_Staff_Schedule** Use the following information to create an attractive document.

The document should include an *Employee Schedule for December*. Four additional sales associates must be scheduled at the Portland store during the holiday season for the following times: Monday through Friday 9 a.m. to 3 p.m. and 3 p.m. to 9 p.m., Saturday 10 a.m. to 6 p.m., and Sunday 11 a.m. to 5 p.m. Employees will work the same hours throughout December. No employee can be scheduled for two different time periods. Using fictitious employee names, arrange the time periods in an alphabetical list that includes the employee names as bulleted items. Add appropriate document properties including the tags **schedule, December**

Sales Manager Yolanda Richards is sending a memo to President Roslyn Thomas with the *Employee Schedule for December* included as a hyperlink. Open the file **w07K_Staff_Increase** and save it as **Lastname_Firstname_7K_Staff_Increase** Using the existing text, add appropriate hyperlinks to the schedule you created and to contact Ms. Reynolds at yreynolds@owspecialties.com Add appropriate properties including the tags **staff, increase** Proofread the document, correcting any errors. Insert the file names in the footers. Print both files—the RTF file and the memo—or submit electronically as directed by your instructor.

(Project 7K Staff Increase continues on the next page)

CONTENT-BASED ASSESSMENTS

Performance Level

Performance Criteria	Exemplary: You consistently applied the relevant skills	Proficient: You sometimes, but not always, applied the relevant skills	Developing: You rarely or never applied the relevant skills
Save in RTF format	The schedule is saved in RTF format with the appropriate file name.	The schedule is saved in RTF format but has an incorrect file name.	The schedule is saved in the wrong format.
Insert lists	Sorted, bulleted lists are inserted in the schedule.	Lists are inserted in the schedule but they are not sorted.	No lists are inserted in the schedule.
Insert hyperlinks	Hyperlinks are inserted in the memo for the schedule and contact information, using existing text.	Hyperlinks are inserted in the memo but at the wrong locations or include incorrect text.	No hyperlinks are inserted in the memo.
Insert and format text	The schedule contains the correct information and is formatted attractively.	The schedule contains the correct information but the format is not consistent or attractive.	The schedule does not contain the correct information.
Correct errors	Both documents have no spelling or grammar errors.	One document contains spelling or grammar errors.	Both documents contain spelling or grammar errors.

END | You have completed Project 7K

OUTCOMES-BASED ASSESSMENTS

RUBRIC

The following outcomes-based assessments are *open-ended assessments*. That is, there is no specific correct result; your result will depend on your approach to the information provided. Make *Professional Quality* your goal. Use the following scoring rubric to guide you in *how* to approach the problem and then to evaluate *how well* your approach solves the problem.

The *criteria*—Software Mastery, Content, Format and Layout, and Process—represent the knowledge and skills you have gained that you can apply to solving the problem. The *levels of performance*—Professional Quality, Approaching Professional Quality, or Needs Quality Improvements—help you and your instructor evaluate your result.

	Your completed project is of Professional Quality if you:	Your completed project is Approaching Professional Quality if you:	Your completed project Needs Quality Improvements if you:
1-Software Mastery	Choose and apply the most appropriate skills, tools, and features and identify efficient methods to solve the problem.	Choose and apply some appropriate skills, tools, and features, but not in the most efficient manner.	Choose inappropriate skills, tools, or features, or are inefficient in solving the problem.
2-Content	Construct a solution that is clear and well organized, contains content that is accurate, appropriate to the audience and purpose, and is complete. Provide a solution that contains no errors in spelling, grammar, or style.	Construct a solution in which some components are unclear, poorly organized, inconsistent, or incomplete. Misjudge the needs of the audience. Have some errors in spelling, grammar, or style, but the errors do not detract from comprehension.	Construct a solution that is unclear, incomplete, or poorly organized; contains some inaccurate or inappropriate content; and contains many errors in spelling, grammar, or style. Do not solve the problem.
3-Format & Layout	Format and arrange all elements to communicate information and ideas, clarify function, illustrate relationships, and indicate relative importance.	Apply appropriate format and layout features to some elements, but not others. Overuse features, causing minor distraction.	Apply format and layout that does not communicate information or ideas clearly. Do not use format and layout features to clarify function, illustrate relationships, or indicate relative importance. Use available features excessively, causing distraction.
4-Process	Use an organized approach that integrates planning, development, self-assessment, revision, and reflection.	Demonstrate an organized approach in some areas, but not others; or, use an insufficient process of organization throughout.	Do not use an organized approach to solve the problem.

OUTCOMES-BASED ASSESSMENTS

Apply a combination of the 7A and 7B skills.

Build from Scratch

GO! Think   Project 7L Phone Jewelry

PROJECT FILES

For Project 7L, you will need the following file:

New blank Word document

You will save your file as:

Lastname_Firstname_7L_Phone_Jewelry

The marketing director at Oregon Wireless Specialties wants to create a flyer to advertise its latest product line—cell phone bling, a variety of jewelry accessories. The categories include butterfly, tiger, seashore, carnation, and mountain. This document will be reviewed by others because it includes Spanish and French translations of the styles.

Create a flyer with basic information about the new product line. Include a brief paragraph describing cell phone bling and accessories. Use the Research pane to locate descriptive information, adding a hyperlink to the website where you obtained the data. Display the individual styles in an organized list. Use Word's translate feature to create two additional style lists—in Spanish and French. Be sure the document has an attractive design and is easy to read. Correct all spelling and grammar errors, excluding the translated text.

Save the file in Rich Text Format, with the file name **Lastname_Firstname_7L_Phone_Jewelry** Add appropriate information in the Properties area and insert the file name in the footer. Print your file or submit electronically as directed by your instructor.

END | You have completed Project 7L

GO! Think   Project 7M Memory Cards   Online

Build from Scratch

You and GO!   Project 7N Personal Webpage   Online

Build from Scratch

Creating Mass Mailings

PROJECT 8A

OUTCOMES
Filter records and create envelopes.

OBJECTIVES

1. Merge a Data Source and a Main Document
2. Use Mail Merge to Create Envelopes

PROJECT 8B

OUTCOMES
Create and modify a data source and create a directory.

OBJECTIVES

3. Edit and Sort a Data Source
4. Match Fields and Apply Rules
5. Create a Data Source and a Directory

goodluz/Fotolia

In This Chapter

In this chapter, you will use data sources with mail merge to create letters, envelopes, postcards, and a directory. Mail merge provides a time-saving and convenient way to produce personalized mass mailings, such as customized letters and envelopes. You can construct your own table of data or use an existing file. You can also sort and filter the data to specify what information will be used. For example, you might want to send individual letters to customers who purchased a specific cruise. You can also use a data source with mail merge to generate a directory—for example, a list of company employees and their phone extensions.

The projects in this chapter relate to **Caribbean Customized**, which specializes in exciting cruises in the Caribbean, including excursions to islands and the mainland in North and Central America. With its tropical beauty and cultural diversity, the Caribbean region offers lush jungles, freshwater caves, miles of white sand beaches, ancient ruins, and charming cities. Ships are innovative and include rock-climbing walls and extensive spa facilities. A variety of accommodations are available on each ship to meet the needs and budgets of a wide array of travelers. The food and entertainment are rated as exceptional by all.

Customer Letters

PROJECT ACTIVITIES

Caribbean Customized is launching a new rewards program for its valued customers. Lucinda Parsons, the president of the company, has asked you to create a document describing the Emerald Program that can be sent to all customers who previously booked multiple cruises. In Activities 8.01 through 8.07, you will create a customized form letter and envelope. This will enable the company to send a personalized letter to the targeted group of customers. Your completed documents will look similar to Figure 8.1.

PROJECT FILES

For Project 8A, you will need the following files:

Two new blank Word documents
w08A_Customers

You will save your files as:

Lastname_Firstname_8A_Letters_Main
Lastname_Firstname_8A_Letters_Merged
Lastname_Firstname_8A_Envelopes_Main
Lastname_Firstname_8A_Envelopes_Merged
Lastname_Firstname_8A_Customers—not shown in figure

PROJECT RESULTS

Build from
Scratch

FIGURE 8.1 Project 8A Customer Letters

Objective 1   Merge a Data Source and a Main Document

Video W8-1

Recall that *mail merge* is a Word feature that joins a *data source* with a *main document* to create a customized document, such as mailing labels. The data source, containing categories of information such as names and addresses, can be stored in a variety of formats—a Word table, an Excel worksheet, an Access table or query, an Outlook contact list, or any text file that has text separated by *delimiters*. Delimiters are characters—such as commas and tabs—used to separate text into groups. Placeholders for the customized information from the data source are inserted in the main document. You can use mail merge to create personalized letters, envelopes, labels, or directories.

Activity 8.01 | Using an Excel Spreadsheet as a Data Source

Previously you used a Word table as a data source to create mailing labels. An Excel worksheet can also be used as a data source. In this activity, you will examine an Excel worksheet containing information that will be used to create personalized letters to loyal customers explaining the Emerald Program.

1 Start Excel. Near the lower left of the screen, click **Open Other Workbooks**, and then double-click **Computer**. In the **Open** dialog box, navigate to your student data files, and then locate and open the file **w08A_Customers**. Compare your screen with Figure 8.2. Take a moment to study the data that includes names and addresses for current and potential customers.

Row 1 of the worksheet contains headers describing each field—column of data. The name of the worksheet—*Customer Information*—displays on the tab at the bottom of the worksheet. It is important to know the name of the worksheet you are using as a data source because an Excel file may contain several worksheets.

FIGURE 8.2

2 Press F12 to display the **Save As** dialog box. Navigate to the location where you are saving your files for this chapter, and then create a new folder named **Word Chapter 8** Using your own name, save the file to your **Word Chapter 8** folder as **Lastname_Firstname_8A_Customers**

3 Close [✕] Excel.

When performing a mail merge, it is not necessary to have a data source file—in this case, the Excel file—open.

Activity 8.02 | Using the MAILINGS Tab Commands to Begin Mail Merge

The MAILINGS tab contains commands for features that are inaccessible when using the Mail Merge Wizard—for example, creating rules using fields and automatically checking for errors. In this activity, you will use the commands on the MAILINGS tab to define the main document and data source that will be used to create the letter to customers.

1 Start Word and display a new document. Using your own name, save the document to your **Word Chapter 8** folder as **Lastname_Firstname_8A_Letters_Main** If necessary display the rulers and formatting marks.

2 Click the **MAILINGS tab**. In the **Start Mail Merge group**, click **Start Mail Merge**, and then click **Letters**.

3 On the **MAILINGS tab**, in the **Start Mail Merge group**, click **Select Recipients**, and then click **Use an Existing List**.

4 In the **Select Data Source** dialog box, navigate to your **Word Chapter 8** folder, locate and select the file **Lastname_Firstname_8A_Customers**, and then click **Open**.

5 In the **Select Table** dialog box, if necessary, select **'Customer Information$'**. At the lower left of the dialog box, if necessary, select the **First row of data contains column headers** check box. Compare your screen with Figure 8.3.

Recall that you are using the Excel worksheet named Customer Information as your data source. The worksheet contains column headers in row 1.

FIGURE 8.3

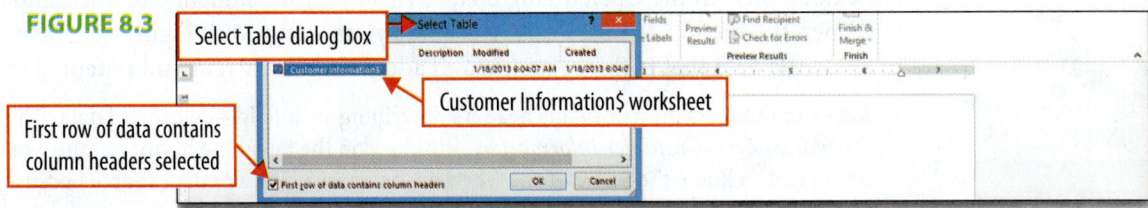

Select Table dialog box

Customer Information$ worksheet

First row of data contains column headers selected

6 Click **OK**. Leave Word open for the next activity.

Although visually nothing appears to happen, when you designate a data source, the file—in this case, the Excel file—is linked to the main document based on the current locations of both files.

More Knowledge **Using Outlook as a Data Source**

You can use an Outlook Contacts list as a data source. To use the Contacts list, on the MAILINGS tab, in the Start Mail Merge group, click Select Recipients. Then, from the list, click Choose from Outlook Contacts. In the Choose Profile dialog box, select the folder where your Outlook Contacts list is stored, and then click OK.

Activity 8.03 | Filtering Records and Creating a Character Style

A data source is comprised of *fields*, categories—or columns—of data, and *records*. A record is a row of information that contains the data for one entity—for example, information about one customer. When using a data source, you can *filter* the data source. A filter is a set of criteria applied to fields to display specific records—for example, information only for customers who live in a particular state. Because the Emerald Program is available only to individuals who have previously toured with Caribbean Customized, you will filter the data source to display only existing customers.

1 On the **MAILINGS tab**, in the **Start Mail Merge group**, click **Edit Recipient List**. In the **Mail Merge Recipients** dialog box, under **Refine recipient list**, click **Filter**.

2 In the **Filter and Sort** dialog box, on the **Filter Records tab**, click the **Field arrow**, scroll as necessary, and then click **Booked Cruise**. Click the **Comparison arrow**, and then if necessary, click **Equal to**. In the **Compare to** box, type **Yes** and then compare your screen with Figure 8.4.

> The data source will be filtered to display only those records where the Booked Cruise field is equal to Yes.

FIGURE 8.4

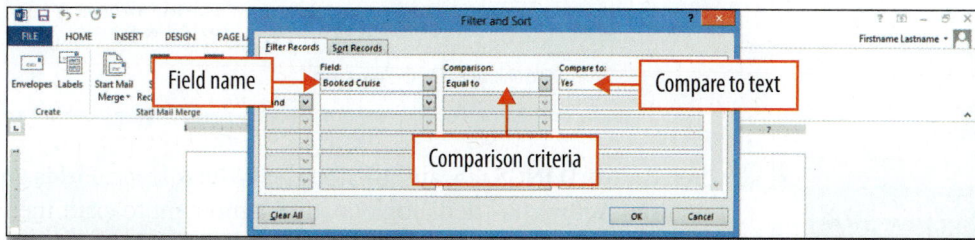

3 Click **OK**. In the **Mail Merge Recipients** dialog box, scroll horizontally and vertically as necessary, and notice that in the **Booked Cruise** field only eight records with *Yes* display.

4 Click **OK** to close the **Mail Merge Recipients** dialog box.

5 Click the **HOME tab**, and then in the **Styles group**, click the **Dialog Box Launcher** to display the **Styles** pane.

6 At the bottom of the **Styles** pane, click the **New Style** button. In the **Create New Style from Formatting** dialog box, under **Properties**, in the **Name** box, type **Parsons** Click the **Style type arrow**, and then click **Character**.

> Recall that a character style contains formatting characteristics that you apply to text—for example, font name, font size, font color, and bold emphasis.

7 Under **Formatting**, if necessary, change the **Font** to **Calibri**, change the **Font Size** to **12**, and then apply **Bold** B . Click the **Font Color arrow** A , and then in the last column, click the last color—**Green, Accent 6, Darker 50%**. Click **OK** to close the dialog box, and then **Close** X the **Styles** pane.

> The Parsons style displays on the HOME tab, in the Styles group. You will apply the style in the next activity.

Activity 8.04 | Inserting Merge Fields

You are creating a *form letter*—a letter with standardized wording that can be sent to many different people. Each letter can be customized by inserting *merge fields*—placeholders that represent specific information in the data source. In this activity, you will type the form letter and insert appropriate merge fields.

1 With the insertion point positioned at the beginning of the document, on the **HOME tab**, in the **Styles group**, double-click **No Spacing**.

> It is necessary to double-click the style to turn off the effects of the *Parsons* style. Recall that Word, by default, has formatting associated with the Normal template, such as Before and After paragraph spacing. By choosing No Spacing, this spacing is removed.

2 ▶ Type **Caribbean Customized** and then press Enter. Type **1300 Bay View Drive** and then press Enter. Type **Coral Gables, FL 33124** and then press Enter.

3 ▶ Select the first line of text, and then on the mini toolbar, change the **Font Size** to **28**. Select the second and third paragraphs, and then on the mini toolbar, change the **Font Size** to **16**.

4 ▶ Select the first three paragraphs, and then on the mini toolbar, apply **Bold** B , click the **Font Color arrow** A ▾, and then in the last column, click the fifth color—**Green, Accent 6, Darker 25%**. Press Ctrl + E to center the three paragraphs.

5 ▶ Position the insertion point in the blank paragraph, and then press Enter two times. Type **January 3, 2018** press Enter four times, and then compare your screen with Figure 8.5.

Because you are using a letter style as a main document, you created a letterhead for Caribbean Customized and included the date of the letter.

FIGURE 8.5

6 ▶ Click the **MAILINGS tab**, and then in the **Write & Insert Fields group**, click **Address Block**. In the **Insert Address Block** dialog box, take a moment to examine the various settings associated with this dialog box, and then click **OK**. In the document, notice that the **Address Block** merge field is inserted.

A standard feature of a business letter is the *inside address*—the name and address of the recipient of the letter. The *Address Block* is a predefined merge field that includes the recipient's name, street address, city, state, and postal code. The Insert Address Block dialog box provides options for changing the way the inside address displays. You are inserting the Address Block merge field as a placeholder for the inside address. Each merge field in a main document is surrounded by double angle brackets—characters used to distinguish where data will be populated.

7 ▶ Press Enter two times, and then in the **Write & Insert Fields group**, click **Greeting Line**. In the **Insert Greeting Line** dialog box, under **Greeting line format**, in the box on the right—the **Punctuation** box, click the **Punctuation arrow**, and then click **:** (the colon). Compare your screen with Figure 8.6.

Another standard feature of a business letter is the *salutation*—or greeting line. The *Greeting Line* is a predefined merge field that includes an introductory word, such as *Dear*, and the recipient's name. When using a business letter format, a colon usually follows the salutation. The Insert Greeting Line dialog box allows you to choose the introductory word and punctuation that displays in the salutation.

FIGURE 8.6

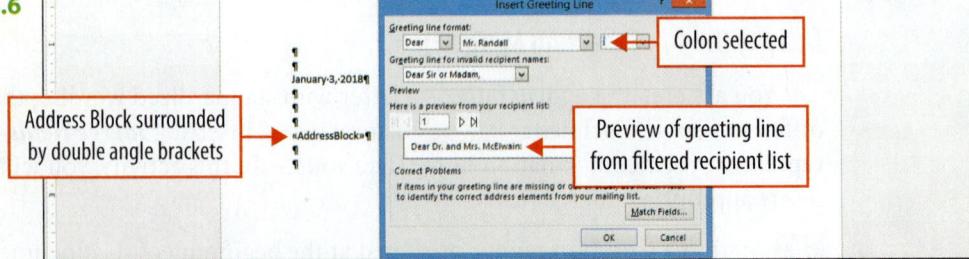

8 ▶ Click **OK**. Notice that the **Greeting Line** merge field is inserted in the document.

The Greeting Line merge field is used as a placeholder for the salutation.

9 ▶ Press Enter two times, and then type the following:

> **Caribbean Customized values our loyal customers. Because you have booked a cruise with us in the past, we would like to inform you of our new Emerald Program.**

10 ▶ Press Enter two times, and then type the following:

> **As a reward for frequent bookings, you can take advantage of this program at no additional cost. The Emerald Program provides the following benefits:**

11 ▶ Press Enter, and then type the following text, pressing Enter after each line:

> **A subscription to our quarterly magazine**
>
> **Special savings coupons to be used in our restaurants and entertainment areas**
>
> **The services of an Emerald representative, available on every cruise**
>
> **A members-only onboard event**

12 ▶ Select the four lines of text you just typed, click the **HOME tab**, and then in the **Paragraph group**, click the **Bullets** button ▒ ▾.

13 ▶ Position the insertion point in the blank line below the bulleted text, and then press Enter. Click the **MAILINGS tab**, and then in the **Write & Insert Fields group**, click **Insert Merge Field**. Be careful to click the button, not the arrow.

14 ▶ In the **Insert Merge Field** dialog box, under **Fields**, click **Title**, and then click **Insert**. Click the **Last Name** field, click **Insert**, and then compare your screen with Figure 8.7.

FIGURE 8.7

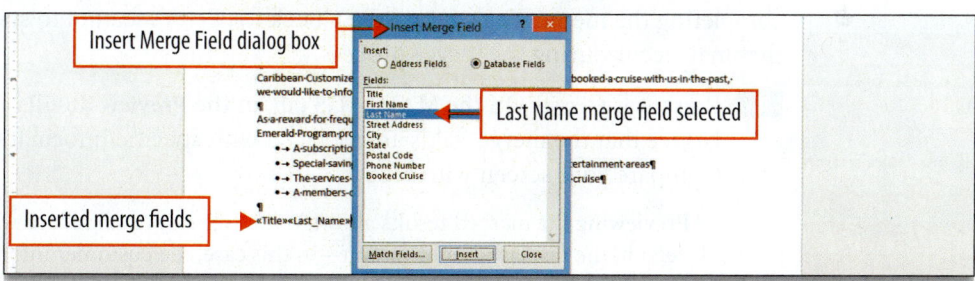

15 ▶ **Close** ✕ the **Insert Merge Field** dialog box.

> The Title and Last_Name merge fields are inserted within the paragraph. When creating a main document, merge fields can be inserted at any location.

16 ▶ Position the insertion point between the **Title** field and the **Last_Name** field—one merge field may be shaded. Press Spacebar. To the right of the **Last_Name** field, type **,** (a comma). Compare your screen with Figure 8.8.

> When inserting merge fields as part of a sentence, it is important to add spaces or punctuation as required.

FIGURE 8.8

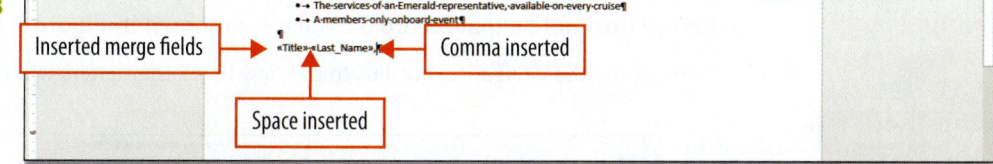

17 ▶ Press Spacebar, and then type the following:

> **please contact us at (305) 555-0768 if you are interested in enrolling in our Emerald Program. Caribbean Customized appreciates our faithful guests and hopes you continue to sail with us.**

18 Press Enter two times, and then type **Sincerely,**

A *complimentary closing*—such as *Sincerely* or *Yours truly*—is a phrase used to end a business letter. The complimentary closing is always followed by a comma.

19 Press Enter four times, and then type **Lucinda Parsons, President**

Extra line spacing is created between the complimentary closing and the signature line to allow for a handwritten signature by the writer of the letter.

20 Select the text you just typed, on the mini toolbar, click **Styles**, and then in the **Styles** gallery, click **Parsons**. Deselect the text, and then compare your screen with Figure 8.9. **Save** 🖫 your changes.

FIGURE 8.9

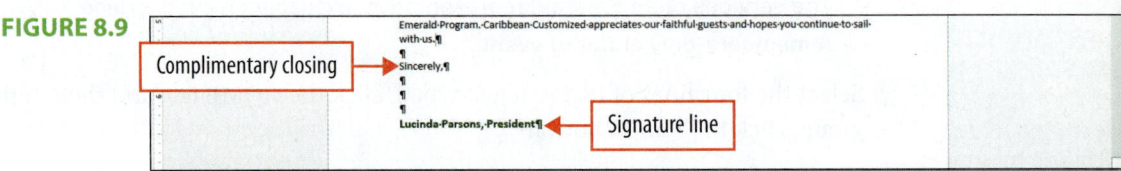

Activity 8.05 | Previewing Results and Validating Merged Data

After the merge fields are added to the form letter, you can preview the letters one at a time. Before you complete the merge process, it is a good idea to scan the letters to check for spelling, punctuation, and spacing errors. If you find an error, correct it in the main document before completing the merge. You can use the Check for Errors feature to specify how to handle errors that may occur during the merge process.

1 Press Ctrl + Home. On the **MAILINGS tab**, in the **Preview Results group**, click **Preview Results**. Notice that the merge fields are replaced with specific information from the data source. Compare your screen with Figure 8.10.

Previewing the merged results allows you to see how each record will display in the letter. By default, the displayed information—in this case, the customer information—is from record 1, as indicated in the Go to Record box.

FIGURE 8.10

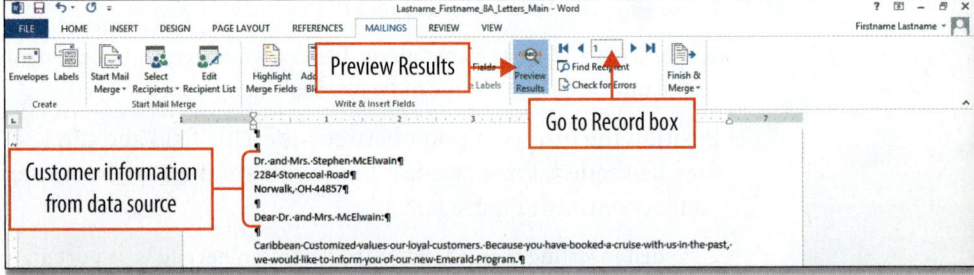

2 On the **MAILINGS tab**, in the **Preview Results group**, click **Next Record** ▶ two times. In the **Go to Record** box, notice that record **3** displays, as shown in Figure 8.11.

You can use the navigation buttons to preview how other letters will display after the merge.

FIGURE 8.11

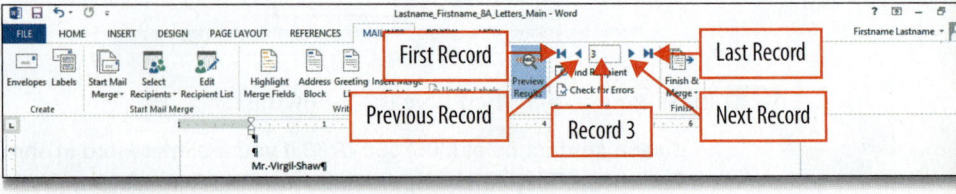

3 On the **MAILINGS tab**, in the **Preview Results group**, click **Last Record** ▶|. In the **Go to Record** box, notice that record **8** displays and the record's information from the data source displays in the inside address, salutation, and last paragraph of the letter.

4 On the **MAILINGS tab**, in the **Preview Results group**, click **First Record** |◀. In the **Go to Record** box, notice that record **1** displays.

5 On the **MAILINGS tab**, in the **Preview Results group**, click **Preview Results** to turn off the preview and display the merge fields in the letter.

6 On the **MAILINGS tab**, in the **Preview Results group**, click **Check for Errors**.

7 In the **Checking and Reporting Errors** dialog box, click to select the first option that begins **Simulate the merge**, and then click **OK**.

> By simulating the merge, you can designate how to handle errors that might occur during the final merge process. If there are any errors, the *Invalid Merge Field* dialog box displays with the options to *Remove Field* or to *Choose a matching field from the Fields in Data Source list*. In this case, there are no errors reported.

8 Click **OK** to close the **Microsoft Word** message box.

Activity 8.06 | Merging to a New Document

Recall that your form letter is the main document containing the merge fields. You can print the letters directly from the main document or merge all of the letters into one Word document that you can edit. You will finish the merge process by merging the data source and the main document to a new, single document that contains the individual letters. This new document will no longer be connected to the data source.

1 On the **MAILINGS tab**, in the **Finish group**, click **Finish & Merge**, and then click **Edit Individual Documents**. The **Merge to New Document** dialog box displays, as shown in Figure 8.12.

> Although *All* is selected by default, you can use the Merge to New Document dialog box to specify which records you want to merge to a new document.

FIGURE 8.12

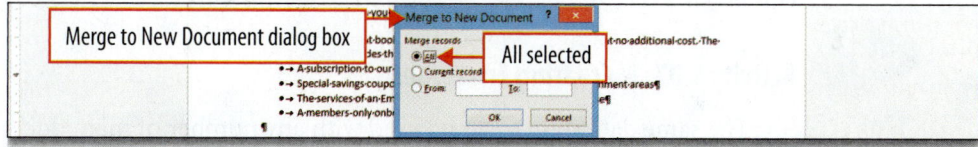

Merge to New Document dialog box

All selected

2 In the **Merge to New Document** dialog box, click **OK**.

> Notice that a new merged document displays with *Letters1 – Microsoft Word* in the title bar.

3 Scroll to examine the document. Notice that the document consists of eight individual letters.

> You can edit individual letters in a merged document, if necessary.

4 Press Ctrl + Home, and then scroll to the bottom of **Page 1**. Compare your screen with Figure 8.13.

> The status bar indicates that there are eight pages—the individual letters. Each page, or letter, is separated by a Next Page section break.

FIGURE 8.13

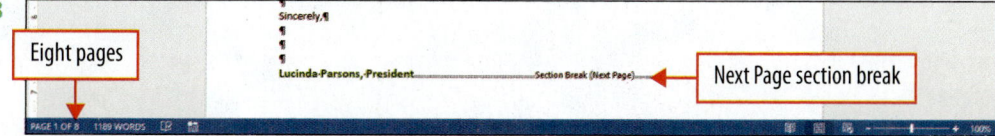

Eight pages

Next Page section break

5 Press F12. In the **Save As** dialog box, navigate to your **Word Chapter 8** folder, and then **Save** the document as **Lastname_Firstname_8A_Letters_Merged** At the bottom of **Page 1**, right-click in the footer area, click **Edit Footer**, and then insert the file name. **Close** the footer area.

6 Click the **FILE tab**, and then click **Show All Properties**. In the **Tags** box, type **customer letters, merged** and then in the **Subject** box, type your course name and section number. If necessary, edit the author name to display your name.

7 **Save** 💾 your changes, and then press Ctrl + W to close the document.

8 In the displayed document—the main document—scroll to the bottom of the page, and then insert the file name in the footer.

9 Click the **FILE tab**, and then click **Show All Properties**. In the **Tags** box, type **customer letters, main** and then in the **Subject** box, type your course name and section number. If necessary, edit the author name to display your name.

10 **Save** 💾 your document. Press Ctrl + W to close the document but leave Word open.

More Knowledge **Using a Main Document to Send Email Messages**

You can use a main document as the text of an email message. On the MAILINGS tab, in the Start Mail Merge group, click Start Mail Merge, and then click E-mail Messages. Click Select Recipients, and then click Choose from Outlook Contacts. In the Choose Profile dialog box, select the Outlook profile you are using. Compose your message, inserting merge fields as required. In the Finish group, click Finish & Merge, and then click Send E-mail messages. In the Merge to E-mail dialog box, in the Subject line box, type the subject for the email message, and then click OK.

Objective 2 Use Mail Merge to Create Envelopes

Video W8-2

Word provides two options for creating envelopes. You can create a single envelope by selecting a recipient's name and address in an existing document. The mail merge process allows you to create multiple envelopes. You can specify the envelope size and text formatting. Additionally you can include electronic postage, if the appropriate software is installed on your computer.

Activity 8.07 | Creating Envelopes

The same data source can be used with any number of main documents of different types. In this activity, you will use mail merge to create envelopes for the form letters using the same filtered data source.

1 Press Ctrl + N to open a new document. Click the **MAILINGS tab**. In the **Start Mail Merge group**, click **Start Mail Merge**, and then click **Envelopes**.

2 In the **Envelope Options** dialog box, on the **Envelope Options tab**, under **Envelope size**, click the **Envelope size arrow**, and then if necessary, click **Size 10 (4 1/8 × 9 1/2 in)**. Compare your screen with Figure 8.14.

The Envelope Options dialog box allows you to select an envelope size. You can also change the font formatting for the delivery address and return address by clicking the appropriate Font button.

FIGURE 8.14

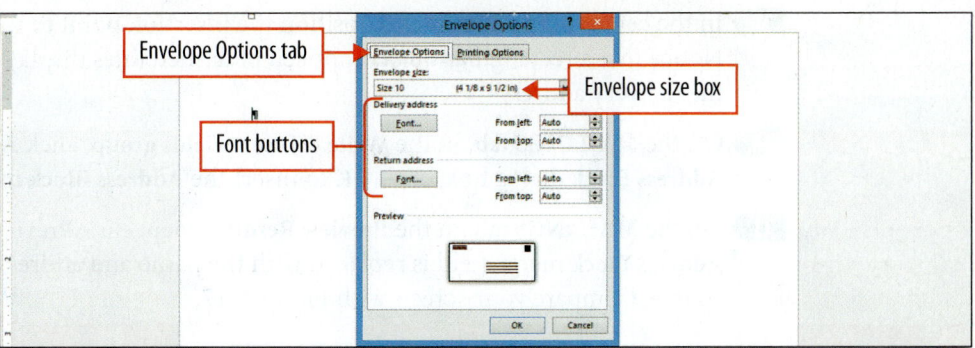

3 ▸ Click **OK**. Press F12, navigate to your **Word Chapter 8** folder, and then save the document as **Lastname_Firstname_8A_Envelopes_Main** If necessary, change the zoom level to 100%.

4 ▸ On the **MAILINGS tab**, in the **Start Mail Merge group**, click **Select Recipients**, and then click **Use an Existing List**.

5 ▸ In the **Select Data Source** dialog box, navigate to your **Word Chapter 8** folder, select the file **Lastname_Firstname_8A_Customers**, and then click **Open**.

6 ▸ In the **Select Table** dialog box, if necessary, select **'Customer Information$'**. At the lower left of the dialog box, if necessary, select the **First row of data contains column headers** check box. Click **OK**.

7 ▸ On the **MAILINGS tab**, in the **Start Mail Merge group**, click **Edit Recipient List**. In the **Mail Merge Recipients** dialog box, under **Refine recipient list**, click **Filter**.

8 ▸ In the **Filter and Sort** dialog box, on the **Filter Records tab**, click the **Field arrow**, scroll as necessary, and then click **Booked Cruise**. Click the **Comparison arrow**, and then click **Equal to**. In the **Compare to** box, type **Yes** Compare your screen with Figure 8.15.

The data source will be filtered to display only those records where the Booked Cruise field is equal to Yes.

FIGURE 8.15

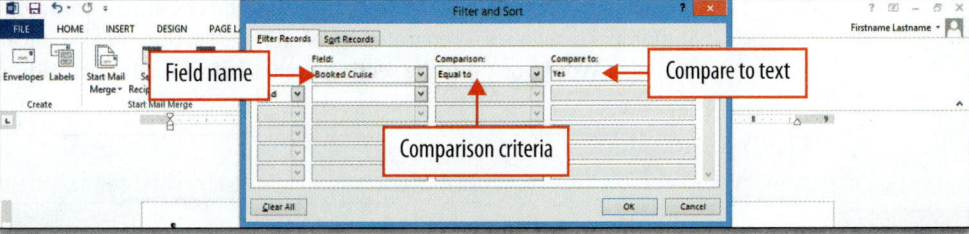

9 ▸ Click **OK** two times to close the dialog boxes.

10 ▸ If necessary, press Ctrl + Home. If a return address displays, delete the existing text. Type the following return address, pressing Enter after the first and second lines. Compare your screen with Figure 8.16.

Caribbean Customized
1300 Bay View Drive
Coral Gables, FL 33124

FIGURE 8.16

11 In the center of the document, position the insertion point to the left of the paragraph mark. Notice that a rectangular box comprised of dashed lines displays to indicate the position of the delivery address.

12 On the **MAILINGS tab**, in the **Write & Insert Fields group**, click **Address Block**. In the **Insert Address Block** dialog box, click **OK** to insert the **Address Block** merge field in the document.

13 On the **MAILINGS tab**, in the **Preview Results group**, click **Preview Results**. Notice that the **Address Block** merge field is replaced with the name and address for record 1 in the data source. Compare your screen with Figure 8.17.

FIGURE 8.17

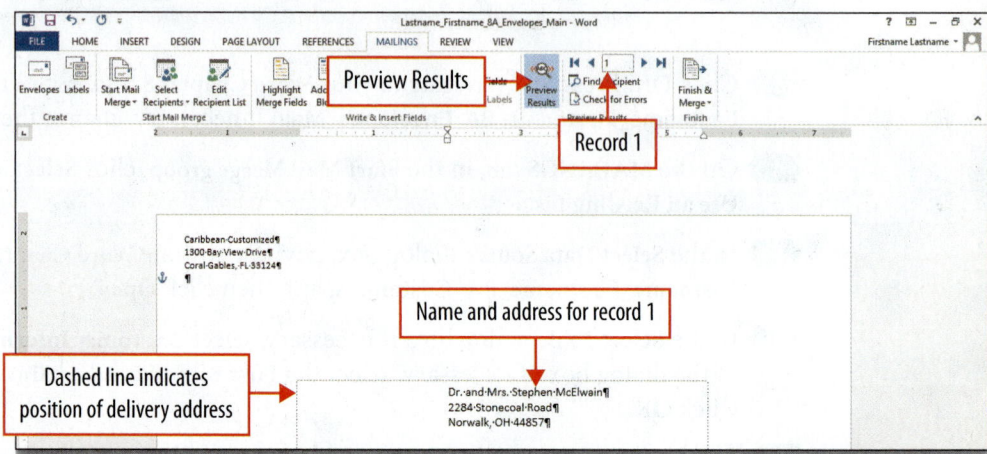

14 On the **MAILINGS tab**, in the **Preview Results group**, click **Preview Results** to turn off the preview.

15 On the **MAILINGS tab**, in the **Preview Results group**, click **Check for Errors**.

16 In the **Checking and Reporting Errors** dialog box, click to select the third option that begins **Complete the merge without pausing**, and then click **OK**. Compare your screen with Figure 8.18.

By selecting this option, the merge is completed and any errors are reported in a new document. In this case, there are no errors. Notice that the document contains eight pages—consisting of individual envelopes—separated by Next Page section breaks. Because the delivery address is in a text box, Word positions the section breaks below the return address.

FIGURE 8.18

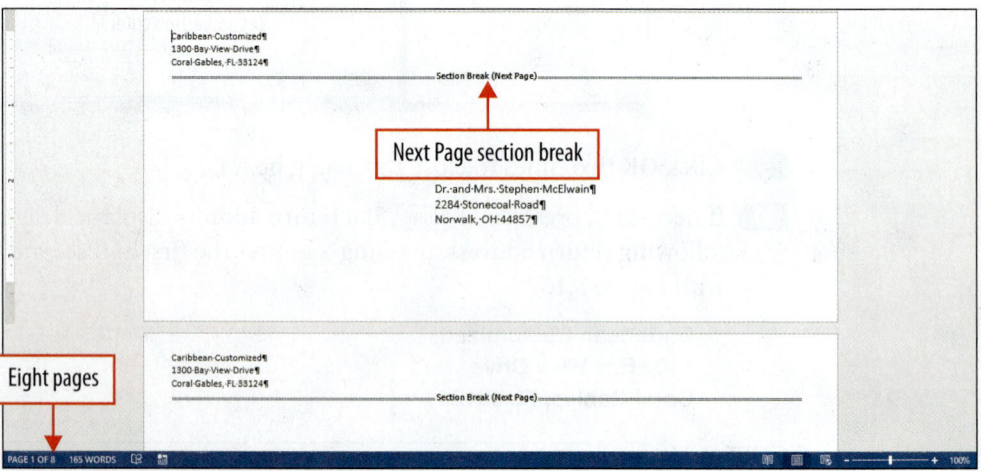

17 Press F12, navigate to your **Word Chapter 8** folder, and then save the document as **Lastname_Firstname_8A_Envelopes_Merged** Insert the file name in the footer. Click the **FILE tab**, and then click **Show All Properties**. In the **Tags** box, type **customer envelopes, merged** and then in the **Subject** box, type your course name and section number. If necessary, edit the author name to display your name. **Save** 🖫 your document, and then press Ctrl + W to close the document.

18 In the main document, insert the file name in the footer. Click the **FILE tab**, and then click **Show All Properties**. In the **Tags** box, type **customer envelopes, main** and then in the **Subject** box, type your course name and section number. If necessary, edit the author name to display your name. **Save** 🖫 your document.

19 Print your four documents—it is not necessary to print the data source—or submit all five files electronically as directed by your instructor. **Close** ❌ Word.

More **Knowledge**   **Printing an Envelope or Label from Selected Data**

To print a single envelope or label from selected data, in any document, select the name and address you want to use. On the MAILINGS tab, in the Create group, click Envelopes for an envelope or Labels for a label. In the Envelopes and Labels dialog box, you can edit the delivery address and make other changes, and then click Print.

END | You have completed Project 8A

Cruise Postcards

PROJECT ACTIVITIES

Caribbean Customized is offering a special cruise to loyal customers. Maria Ramirez, Cruise Consultant, has asked you to create postcards to advertise the cruise. In Activities 8.08 through 8.17, you will use mail merge to create the postcards. You will also create a contact list for customers who are going on the cruise. Your completed files will look similar to Figure 8.19.

PROJECT FILES

Build from Scratch

For Project 8B, you will need the following files:

Two new blank Word documents
w08B_Cruise_Clients
w08B_Ancient_Ruin
w08B_Appreciation_Cruise

You will save your files as:

Lastname_Firstname_8B_Postcards_Main
Lastname_Firstname_8B_Postcards_Merged
Lastname_Firstname_8B_List_Main
Lastname_Firstname_8B_List_Merged
Lastname_Firstname_8B_Cruise_Clients— not shown in figure
Lastname_Firstname_8B_Cruise_Contacts— not shown in figure

PROJECT RESULTS

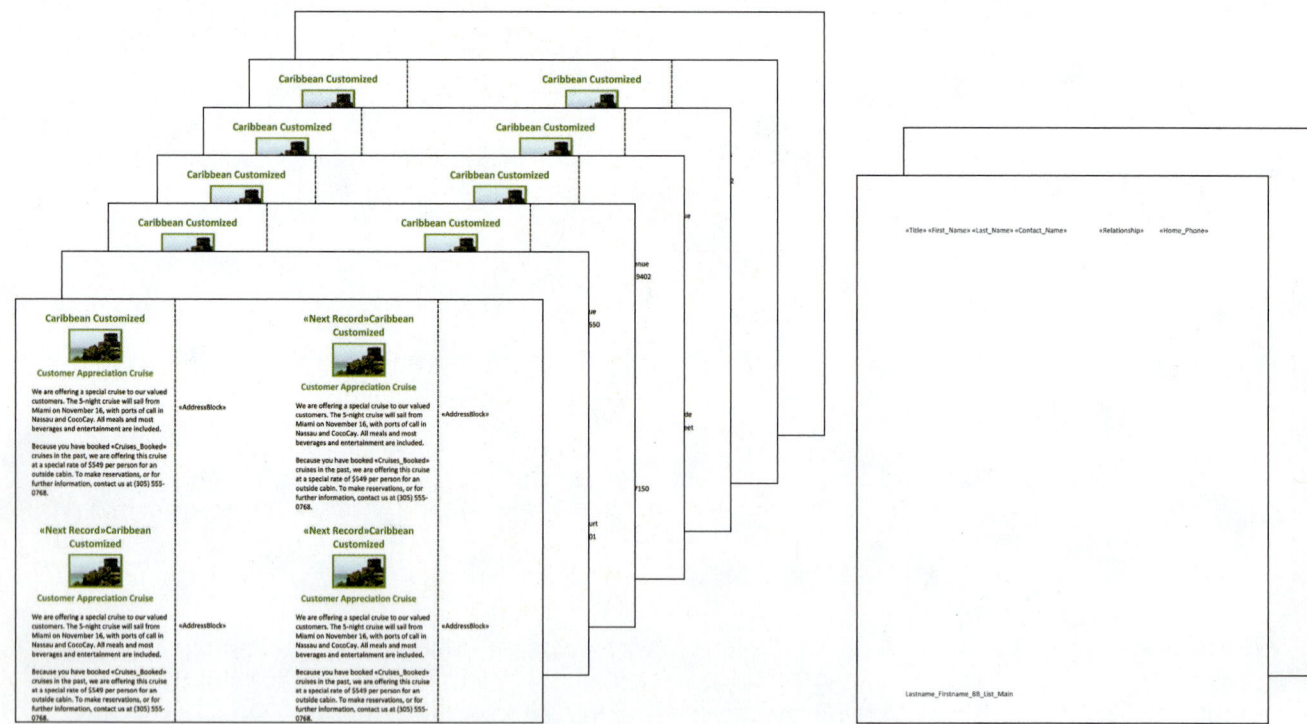

FIGURE 8.19 Project 8B Cruise Postcards

Video W8-3

During the merge process you can modify information in the data source and arrange the records in a particular order. For example, you may want to add new records or display the records in alphabetical or numerical order based on a specific field.

Activity 8.08 | Managing a Recipient List by Editing a Data Source

Devon Marshall, Database Coordinator for Caribbean Customized, has asked you to edit the customer data source—a table in an Access *database*. A database is an organized collection of facts about people, events, things, or ideas related to a particular topic or purpose. In this activity, you will select a postcard template from available label options. Then you will add two customer records and delete a customer record from the data source.

1 Start Access. Near the lower left of the screen, click **Open Other Files**, and then under **Places**, double-click **Computer**. In the **Open** dialog box, navigate to your student files, and then open the Access file **w08B_Cruise_Clients**. Click the **FILE tab**, and then click **Save As**. On the **Save As** screen, with **Save Database As** selected, click **Save As**.

2 In the **Save As** dialog box, navigate to your **Word Chapter 8** folder, and then save the file as **Lastname_Firstname_8B_Cruise_Clients Close**  any open windows.

3 Start Word and display a new blank document. If necessary, display the rulers and formatting marks. On the **MAILINGS tab**, in the **Start Mail Merge group**, click **Start Mail Merge**, and then click **Labels**.

4 In the **Label Options** dialog box, under **Label information**, click the **Label vendors arrow**, and then click **Avery US Letter**. Under **Product number**, scroll as necessary, and then click **3263 Postcards**. Compare your screen with Figure 8.20.

A description of the selected label displays under Label information on the right side of the Label Options dialog box. In addition to labels, some product numbers are designated as business cards, name tags, or—in this case—postcards.

FIGURE 8.20

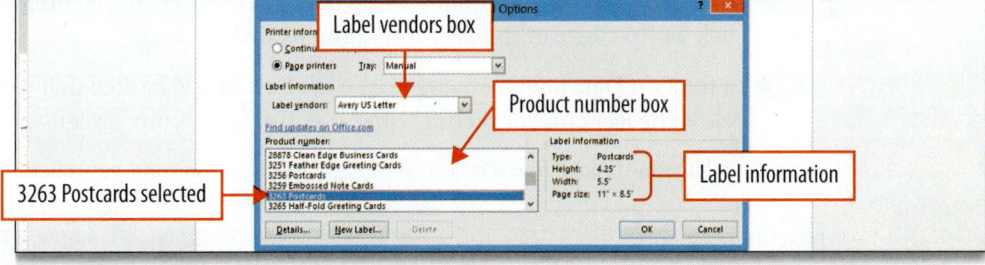

ALERT!   The Product Number Does Not Display

If the Avery US Letter 3263 label option does not display, in the Label Options dialog box, click the New Label button to create a custom postcard template. Set the Top Margin and Side Margin to 0. Set the Label Height to 4.25 and the Label Width to 5.5. Set the Vertical Pitch to 4.25 and the Horizontal Pitch to 5.5. Set the Number Across and Number Down to 2. Set the Page Size to Letter Landscape (11 × 8 ½).

5 In the **Label Options** dialog box, click **OK**. Verify that the gridlines—dashed lines—display in the document. If necessary, click the **LAYOUT tab**, and then in the **Table group**, click **View Gridlines** to display the gridlines.

The postcard template is a table consisting of four cells.

6 Press F12 to display the **Save As** dialog box. Navigate to your **Word Chapter 8** folder, and then save the document as **Lastname_Firstname_8B_Postcards_Main**

7 On the **MAILINGS tab**, in the **Start Mail Merge group**, click **Select Recipients**, and then click **Use an Existing List**. In the **Select Data Source** dialog box, navigate to your **Word Chapter 8** folder, select **Lastname_Firstname_8B_Cruise_Clients**, and then click **Open**. In the second, third, and fourth cells, notice that the <<Next Record>> field displays.

> When you are using a label template, the <<Next Record>> field allows the contents of the first label to be propagated to the remaining cells of the table during the mail merge process.

8 On the **MAILINGS tab**, in the **Start Mail Merge group**, click **Edit Recipient List**. In the **Mail Merge Recipients** dialog box, under **Data Source**, click **Lastname_Firstname_8B_Cruise_Clients**, and then click **Edit**.

> You can edit a data source during the merge process by changing existing data or by adding or deleting records.

9 In the **ID** field, scroll as necessary, and locate the cell containing *7*. To the left of the cell in the **ID** field, click the **row selector** box—the small square to the left of the row. Compare your screen with Figure 8.21.

> Clicking the row selector box selects an entire record. This is useful if you want to delete a record.

FIGURE 8.21

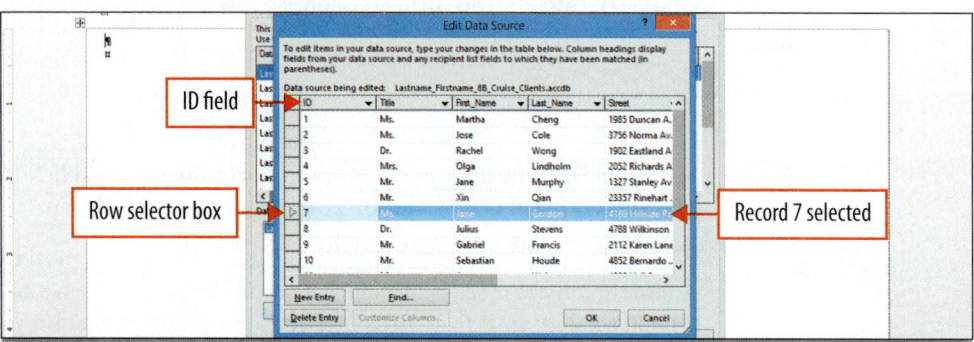

10 In the **Edit Data Source** dialog box, click **Delete Entry**. In the **Microsoft Word** message box, click **Yes** to confirm the deletion of the record.

11 In the **Edit Data Source** dialog box, click **New Entry**. Notice that a new record line displays below the last current record with ID *0*. Compare your screen with Figure 8.22.

> The new record line enables you to add information for a new client to the data source.

FIGURE 8.22

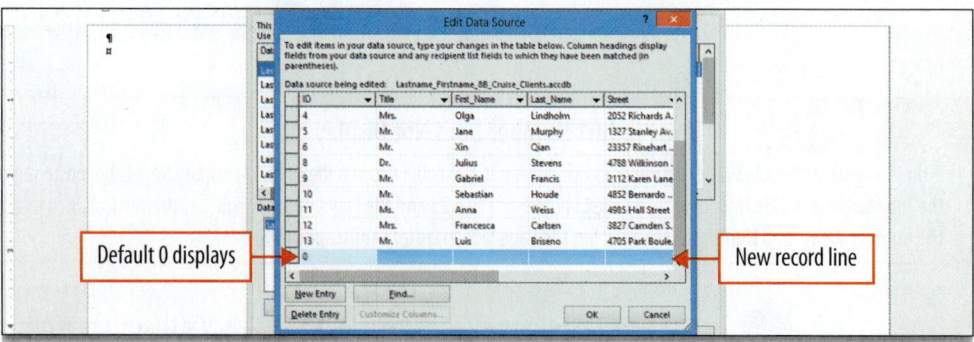

12 In the new record line, in the **ID** field, position the insertion point to the right of **0**, if necessary. Type **14** and then press Tab. In the **ID** field, notice that *14* displays, without the default *0*.

> It is not necessary to delete the default 0 when entering data in cells containing numbers. In this case, the ID, Postal_Code, and Cruises_Booked fields all contain numbers and will display with the default 0.

13 In the cell in the **Title** field, type **Dr.** and then press Tab. Using the technique you practiced, type the following text in the remaining cells of the row, pressing Tab after each entry.

First_Name	Last_Name	Street	City	State	Postal_Code	Cruises_Booked
Delilah	Robinson	2696 Park Lane	Mason City	IA	50401	3

> The data for a new customer has been entered, and a new line displays to add a new record.

14 In the same manner, type the following text in the cells for record 15, pressing Tab after each entry except the last entry.

ID	Title	First_Name	Last_Name	Street	City	State	Postal Code	Cruises_Booked
15	Mrs.	Michael	DeMarco	4372 Nixon Avenue	Ansonia	OH	45303	2

15 Press Enter. Scroll to the left as necessary to display the **ID** field. Compare your screen with Figure 8.23.

> Data for a second additional customer has been entered as a new record.

FIGURE 8.23

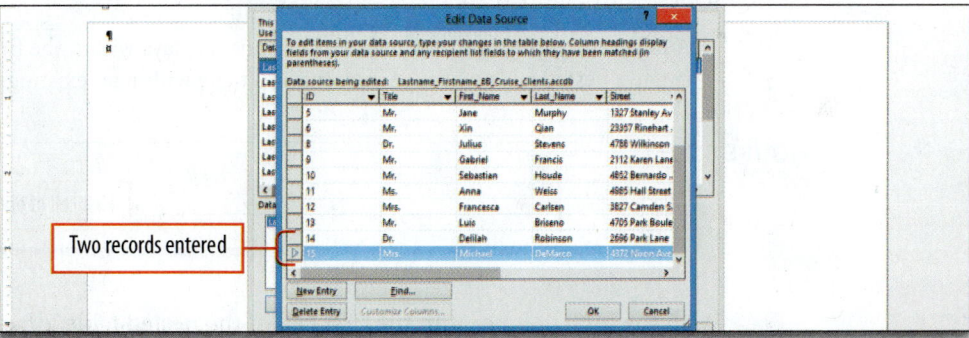

Two records entered

16 Click **OK**. In the **Microsoft Word** message box, click **Yes** to update your recipient list and save the changes to **Lastname_Firstname_8B_Cruise_Clients**. Leave the **Mail Merge Recipients** dialog box open for the next activity.

Activity 8.09 | Sorting a Recipient List

Sorting a data source by postal code can be useful if you want a mailing to qualify as *bulk mail*. Bulk mail is a large mailing, sorted by postal code, which is eligible for reduced postage rates, available from the United States Postal Service.

 In the **Mail Merge Recipients** dialog box, scroll to display the **Postal_Code** field. To the right of **Postal_Code** click the **arrow**, and then click **Sort Ascending**. Compare your screen with Figure 8.24.

By sorting the records, when the merge process is complete, the individual postcards will display in order by postal code.

FIGURE 8.24

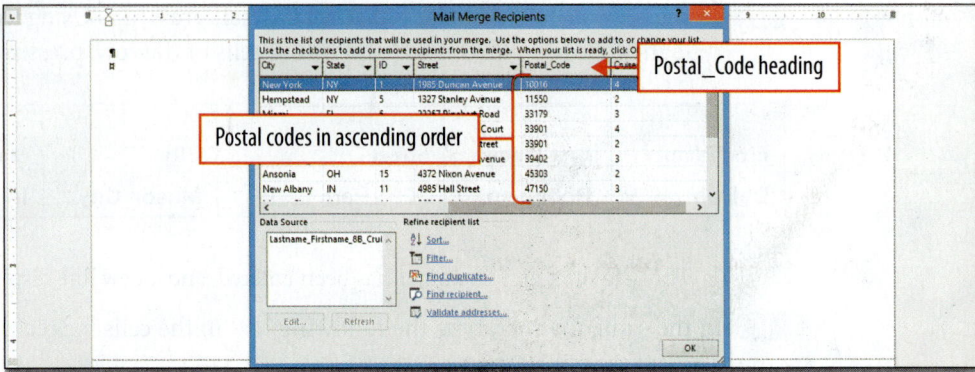

Postal_Code heading

Postal codes in ascending order

2 Click **OK**, and then **Save** 💾 your changes.

Activity 8.10 | Using Nested Tables and Formatting the Main Document

In Word documents, recall that you can create a **nested table**—a table inserted in a cell of an existing table. In this activity, you will create a nested table to simplify formatting the postcard, and then add text and merge fields.

1 Press ⌃Ctrl + Home. Click the **INSERT tab**, and then in the **Tables group**, click **Table**. Under **Insert Table**, click the cell in the first row and second column to create a 2 × 1 table. Compare your screen with Figure 8.25.

A table containing one row and two columns displays within the first cell of the original table. You create a nested table whenever you insert a table within an existing cell.

FIGURE 8.25

Nested table

First cell of original table

2 With the insertion point in the first cell of the nested table, drag to the right to select both cells in the new nested table. Under **TABLE TOOLS**, on the **DESIGN tab**, in the **Borders group**, click the **Borders button arrow**, and then click **No Border**.

3 With the cells still selected, click the **LAYOUT tab**, and then in the **Cell Size group**, change the **Table Row Height** ↕ Height: 0.19" to **4.25"**. Compare your screen with Figure 8.26.

FIGURE 8.26

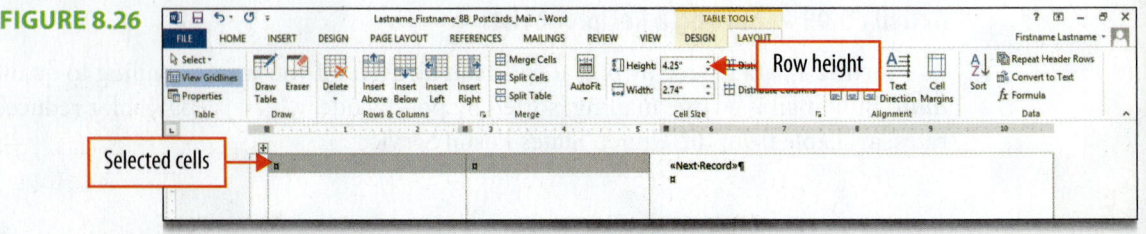

Row height

Selected cells

4 Position the insertion point in the second cell of the nested table. Under **TABLE TOOLS**, click the **DESIGN tab**. In the **Borders group**, click the **Line Style arrow** , and then click the third line style. Click the **Line Weight arrow**, and then click **1 ½ pt**. Click the **Pen Color button arrow**, and then under **Theme Colors**, in the last column, click the last color— **Green, Accent 6, Darker 50%**. In the **Borders group**, click the **Borders button arrow**, and then click **Left Border**.

5 Point to the left border of the second cell of the nested table, and then drag to the right until the border aligns at approximately **3 inches on the horizontal ruler**. Compare your screen with Figure 8.27.

This border will visually separate the message from the delivery address in the completed postcards.

FIGURE 8.27

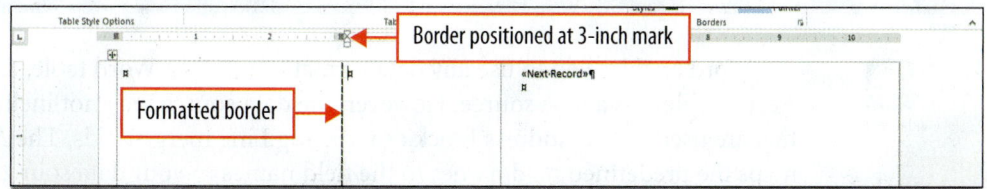

Border positioned at 3-inch mark

Formatted border

6 In the first cell of the nested table, click to position the insertion point. Type **Caribbean Customized** and then press Enter three times. Select the text in the first paragraph. On the mini toolbar, change the **Font Size** to **16**, apply **Bold** B, and then change the **Font Color** A to **Green, Accent 6, Darker 25%**—in the last column, the fifth color. Press Ctrl + E to center the first paragraph. Click the **PAGE LAYOUT tab**, and then in the **Paragraph group**, change the **Spacing Before** to **18 pt**.

7 In the second paragraph, click to position the insertion point. Click the **INSERT tab**, and then in the **Illustrations group**, click **Pictures**. From your student files, locate and insert **w08B_Ancient_Ruin**. With the graphic selected, press Ctrl + E.

8 In the third paragraph, click to position the insertion point, and then type **Customer Appreciation Cruise** Select the text. On the mini toolbar, change the **Font Size** to **14**, apply **Bold** B and then click **Font Color** A. Press Ctrl + E. Deselect the text, and then compare your screen with Figure 8.28.

FIGURE 8.28

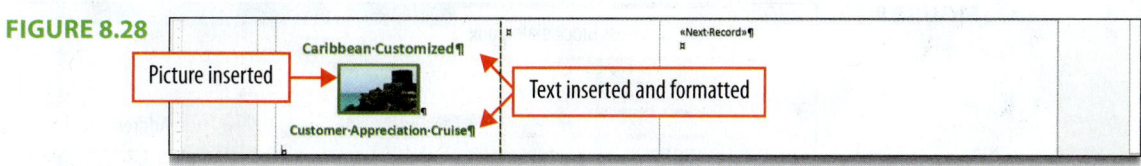

Picture inserted

Text inserted and formatted

9 Position the insertion point in the last line of the cell—to the left of the cell marker. Click the **INSERT tab**. In the **Text group**, click the **Object button arrow**, and then click **Text from File**. Navigate to your student files, select the file **w08B_Appreciation_Cruise**, and then click **Insert**.

10 Position the insertion point anywhere in the paragraph that begins *We are offering*. Click the **PAGE LAYOUT tab**. In the **Paragraph group**, click the **Spacing Before spin box up arrow** to **12 pt**, and then click the **Spacing After spin box up arrow** to **12 pt**.

11 Locate the paragraph that begins *Because you have booked*. Click to position the insertion point to the right of *booked*, and then press Spacebar. Click the **MAILINGS tab**. In the **Write & Insert Fields group**, click the **Insert Merge Field button arrow**, and then click **Cruises_Booked**. Compare your screen with Figure 8.29.

The Cruises_Booked field contains the number of cruises previously booked by each customer. By inserting this merge field, you can personalize the postcards.

FIGURE 8.29

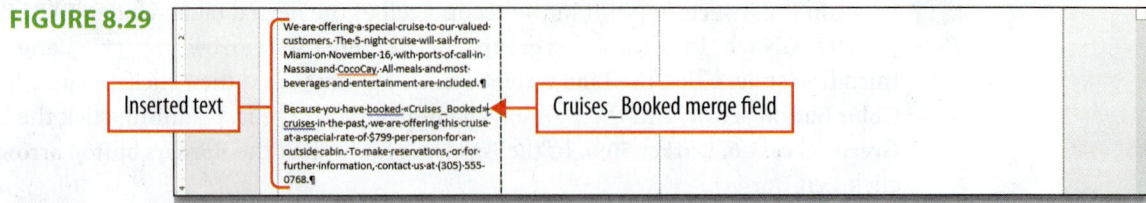

Inserted text

Cruises_Booked merge field

---

12 ▶ **Save** 💾 your changes.

Objective 4 | Match Fields and Apply Rules

Video W8-4

Word enables you to use any data format—such as a Word table, an Excel worksheet, or an Access table—as a data source. However, the data source may not include the same field names that are used in the Address Block or Greeting Line merge fields. The *Match Fields* feature maps the predefined field names to the field names in your data source. You can apply *rules*—conditional Word fields—that allow you to determine how the merge process is completed. This allows you to personalize the final document in additional ways—for example, inserting a specific date in a letter based on the department field in a data source with employee information.

Activity 8.11 | Matching Fields to a Data Source

The Address Block and Greeting Line merge fields include specific field names—such as Last Name, Address 1, and Postal Code. Word enables you to match the fields in your data source with the fields used in the Address Block and Greeting Line dialog boxes. In this activity, you will use the Match Fields feature to map the Address Block fields to your data source fields to display the delivery address correctly.

1 ▶ In the nested table, click in the second cell to position the insertion point. On the **MAILINGS tab**, in the **Write & Insert Fields group**, click **Address Block**. Compare your screen with Figure 8.30.

In the Preview box only the name, city, and state of the customer display.

FIGURE 8.30

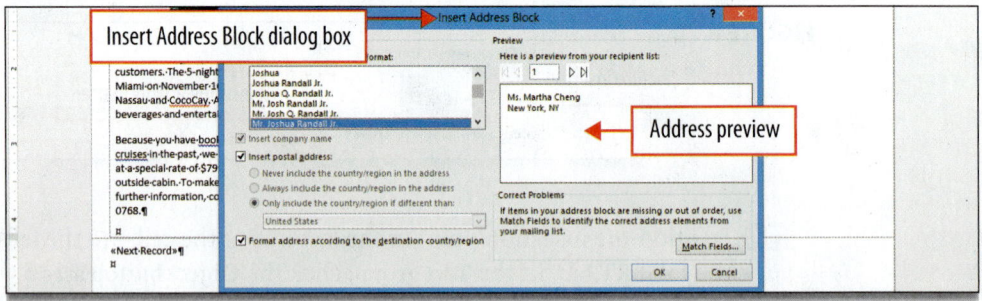

Insert Address Block dialog box

Address preview

2 ▶ In the **Insert Address Block** dialog box, under **Correct Problems**, click **Match Fields**. In the **Match Fields** dialog box, click the **Address 1 arrow**, and then from the displayed list, click **Street**.

3 ▶ Click the **Postal Code arrow**, and then click **Postal_Code**. Compare your screen with Figure 8.31.

Word did not recognize the Street and Postal_Code fields in the data source, so it was necessary to associate them with the predefined Address 1 and Postal Code fields, respectively. When you are working with a data source, it is important to remember that *every* character is interpreted by Word. For example, the underscore in Postal_Code caused the field not to be recognized as the predefined Postal Code field.

FIGURE 8.31

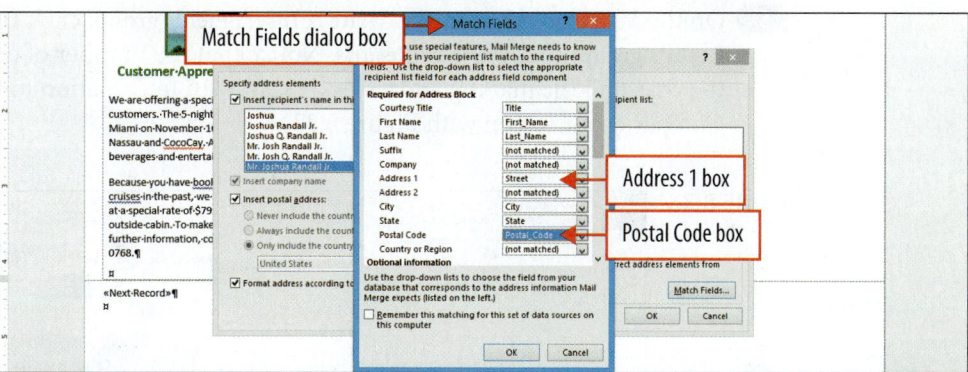

Match Fields dialog box

Address 1 box

Postal Code box

4 Click **OK**. In the **Microsoft Word** message box, when asked if you want to match this field to Unique Identifier, click **Yes**. Notice that the **Preview** box displays the complete mailing address.

5 Click **OK** to insert the **Address Block** merge field in the document.

6 If necessary, move the insertion point to the second cell of the nested table, and then under **TABLE TOOLS**, click the **LAYOUT tab**. In the **Alignment group**, click **Align Center Left** . Save your changes.

Activity 8.12 | Applying Rules to a Merge

You can apply rules to add a decision-making element to the mail merge process. In this activity, you will add a rule that will place different cruise prices in the individual postcards, based on the number of cruises the customer has booked.

1 In the first cell of the nested table, in the last paragraph, select the text *$799*, being careful not to select the space formatting marks, and then press Delete.

2 On the **MAILINGS tab**, in the **Write & Insert Fields group**, click **Rules**, and then click **If…Then…Else**.

3 In the **Insert Word Field: IF** dialog box, under **IF**, click the **Field name arrow**, scroll as necessary, and then click **Cruises_Booked**. Click the **Comparison arrow**, and then click **Greater than or equal**. In the **Compare to** box, type **3** In the **Insert this text** box, type **$549** In the **Otherwise insert this text** box, type **$699** Compare your screen with Figure 8.32.

> The If…Then…Else rule allows you to set a condition so that specific text is inserted if the condition is met, and different text is inserted if the condition is not satisfied. In this case, if the number of cruises booked is greater than or equal to 3, during the merge process, Word will insert the text $549. Otherwise, Word will insert the text $699.

FIGURE 8.32

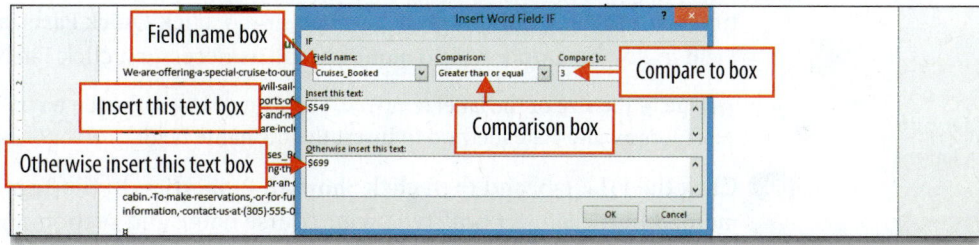

Field name box

Compare to box

Insert this text box

Comparison box

Otherwise insert this text box

4 Click **OK**. Notice that $549 is inserted as the default value for the rule.

5 On the **MAILINGS tab**, in the **Write & Insert Fields group**, click **Update Labels**. In the **Preview Results group**, click **Preview Results**. Notice that the number of cruises booked, the text for the rule, and the mailing addresses display, with information for record 1 in the first cell. Compare your screen with Figure 8.33.

FIGURE 8.33

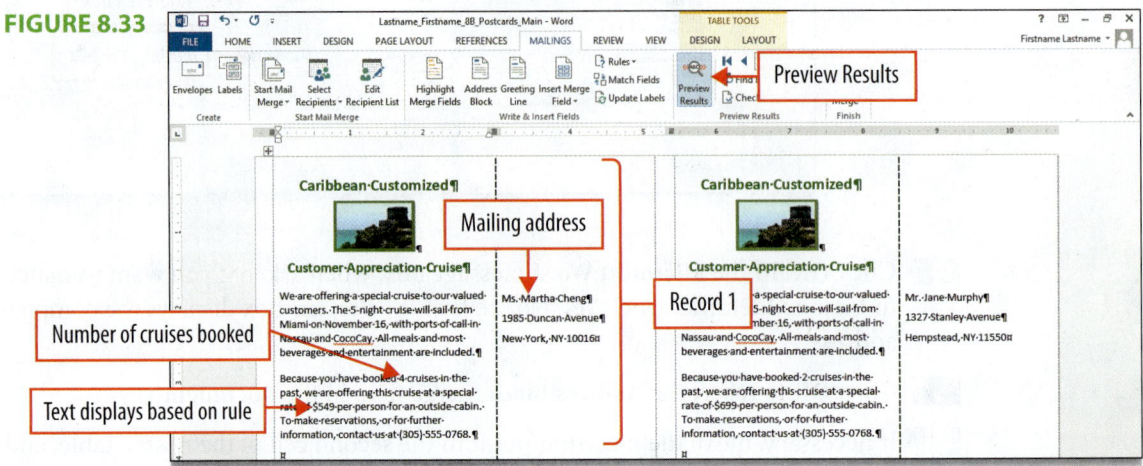

6 On the **MAILINGS tab**, in the **Preview Results group**, click **Preview Results** to turn off the preview.

7 In the **Finish group**, click **Finish & Merge**, and then click **Edit Individual Documents**. In the **Merge to New Document** dialog box, click **OK**. If any words are flagged as spelling errors, **Ignore All**. Compare your screen with Figure 8.34.

   The new document contains the postcards with the merged data. Notice that the rule text—cruise price—agrees with the number of cruises booked. By default, a blank page is included at the end of the document.

FIGURE 8.34

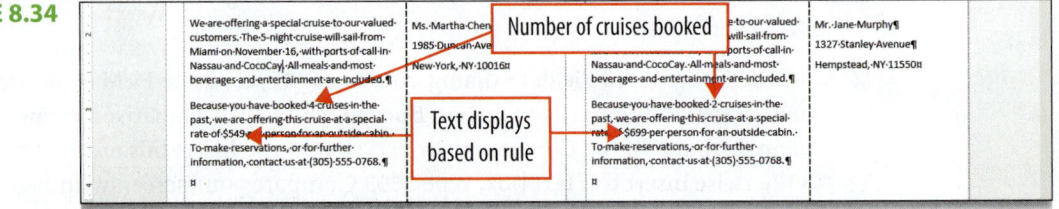

8 Press **F12** to display the **Save As** dialog box. Navigate to your **Word Chapter 8** folder, and then save the document as **Lastname_Firstname_8B_Postcards_Merged**

9 At the top of **Page 5**, position the insertion point in the blank line, and then press **Enter** two times. Click the **INSERT tab**. In the **Text group**, click **Quick Parts**, and then click **Field**. In the **Field** dialog box, under **Field names**, scroll as necessary, click **FileName**, and then click **OK**.

   Due to the size of the label template, you cannot insert the file name in the footer of the document. This is an alternate method to insert the file name field.

10 Click the **FILE tab**, and then click **Show All Properties**. In the **Tags** box, type **cruise postcards, merged** In the **Subject** box, type your course name and section number, and then if necessary, edit the author name to display your name. Save your document, and then press **Ctrl** + **W**.

11 In the main document, at the top of **Page 2**, position the insertion point in the blank line, and then press **Enter** two times. Click the **INSERT tab**. In the **Text group**, click **Quick Parts**, and then click **Field**. In the **Field** dialog box, under **Field names**, scroll as necessary, click **FileName**, and then click **OK**.

12 ▶ Click the **FILE tab**, and then click **Show All Properties**. In the **Tags** box, type **cruise postcards, main** In the **Subject** box, type your course name and section number, and then if necessary, edit the author name to display your name. **Save** your document, and then press $\boxed{\text{Ctrl}}$ + $\boxed{\text{W}}$ to close the document but leave Word open. If you want to take a break before completing the next activity, **Close** $\boxed{\times}$ Word.

Objective 5 ▏ Create a Data Source and a Directory

Video W8-5

Previously in this chapter, you used mail merge to create documents that contain individual components—such as letters, envelopes, and postcards. You can also use mail merge to create a *directory*—a single list of selected data records using specified fields from a data source. For example, a directory might contain the names, departments, and phone numbers for company employees.

Activity 8.13 ▏ Creating a Data Source

Maria Ramirez, Cruise Consultant, has asked you to create a directory that lists emergency contact information, which is recorded on paper forms, for customers booked on the Customer Appreciation Cruise. In this activity, you will create the data source as part of the mail merge process.

1 ▶ Press $\boxed{\text{Ctrl}}$ + $\boxed{\text{N}}$ to display a new document, or if necessary, start Word and open a new blank document. Click the **MAILINGS tab**. In the **Start Mail Merge group**, click **Start Mail Merge**, and then click **Directory**.

2 ▶ Press $\boxed{\text{F12}}$ to display the **Save As** dialog box, navigate to your **Word Chapter 8** folder, and save the document as **Lastname_Firstname_8B_List_Main**

3 ▶ On the **MAILINGS tab**, in the **Start Mail Merge group**, click **Select Recipients**, and then click **Type a New List**. Compare your screen with Figure 8.35.

Because an electronic data source containing the necessary information does not exist, you must create one. The New Address List dialog box allows you to customize the columns used in the data source.

FIGURE 8.35

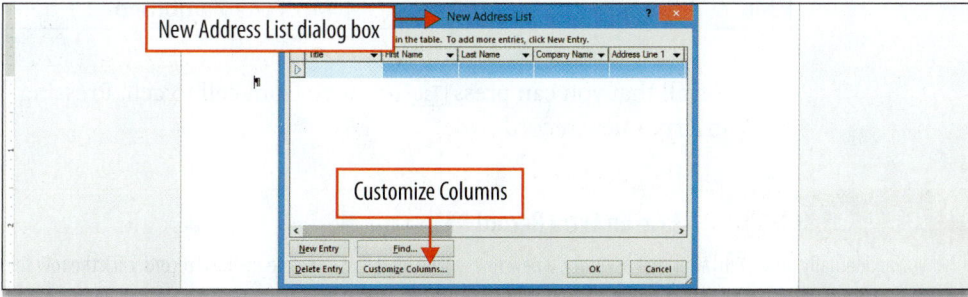

4 ▶ In the **New Address List** dialog box, click **Customize Columns**.

In your data source, you will customize the fields to include the customer's name, the name of the person to contact in case of an emergency, the contact's relationship to the customer, and the contact's phone number.

5 ▶ In the **Customize Address List** dialog box, under **Field Names**, click **Company Name**, and then click **Rename**. In the **Rename Field** dialog box, in the **To** box, type **Contact Name** and then click **OK**.

> You can add new fields or rename existing fields. Solely for the purpose of this instruction you are renaming the *Company Name* field.

6 ▶ In the **Customize Address List** dialog box, click **Address Line 1**, and then click **Delete**. In the **Microsoft Word** message box, click **Yes** to confirm the deletion.

7 ▶ In the same manner, delete the following fields: **Address Line 2**, **City**, **State**, **ZIP Code**, **Country or Region**, **Work Phone**, and **E-mail Address**.

8 ▶ On the right side of the **Customize Address List** dialog box, click **Add**, and then in the **Add Field** dialog box, in the **Type a name for your field** box, type **Relationship** Click **OK**.

9 ▶ With **Relationship** selected, click **Move Up**, and then compare your screen with Figure 8.36.

FIGURE 8.36

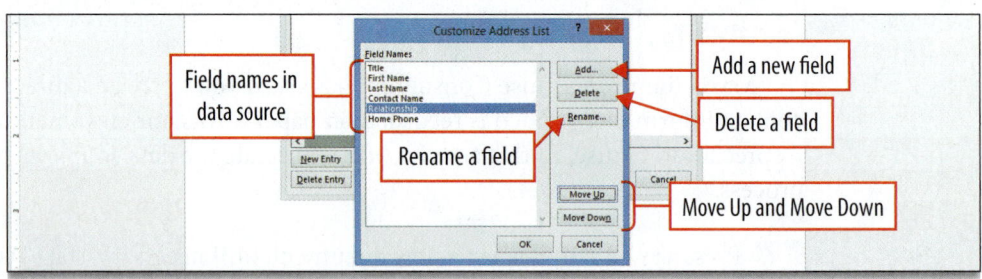

10 ▶ Click **OK**. In the **New Address List** dialog box, click to position the insertion point in the **Title** field. Type the following data, pressing Tab after each entry except the last entry—(310) 555-8643.

Title	First Name	Last Name	Contact Name	Relationship	Home Phone
Mrs.	Nema	Eros	Ms. Maria Salva	sister	(773) 555-9244
Mr.	Charles	Guernon	Mrs. Janet Deimler	daughter	(410) 555-7163
Mrs.	Bridget	Reinhard	Mr. Herman Reinhard	husband	(218) 555-2279
Dr.	Ursula	Tezuka	Dr. Julius Tezuka	brother	(208) 555-7128
Mr.	Ernest	Zambrano	Mr. Tony Zambrano	son	(310) 555-8643

> Recall that you can press Tab to move from cell to cell. Pressing Tab at the end of a row inserts a new record (row).

ALERT! **I Have an Extra Record**

If you accidentally press Tab after that list entry, a new row will be inserted. To delete the new record, click the row selector box to select the row, click Delete Entry, and then click Yes to delete the entry.

---

11 ▶ In the **New Address List** dialog box, click **OK**. The **Save Address List** dialog box displays.

> When you create a new data source, it must be saved.

12 ▶ In the **Save Address List** dialog box, navigate to your **Word Chapter 8** folder, in the **File name** box type **Lastname_Firstname_8B_Cruise_Contacts** Notice that **Save as type** is set to **Microsoft Office Address Lists**. Click **Save**.

> A data source that is created in Word is saved as an Access file with the .mdb file extension. It is not necessary to have Access installed on your computer to create data source files in Word.

Activity 8.14 | Creating the Main Document

In this activity, you will create the main document by inserting designated merge fields and setting tabs to align the content in those fields.

1 If necessary, press Ctrl + Home. At the left end of the horizontal ruler, if necessary, click to display the **Left Tab** button ⌐. To set a left tab stop, click at approximately **2.25 inches on the horizontal ruler**. To set two additional left tab stops, click at approximately **4 inches** and then at **5.25 inches on the horizontal ruler**.

2 On the **MAILINGS tab**, in the **Write & Insert Fields group**, click **Insert Merge Field**. In the **Insert Merge Field** dialog box, under **Fields**, click **Title**, and then click **Insert**.

3 Using the same technique, insert the **First Name**, **Last Name**, **Contact Name**, **Relationship**, and **Home Phone** fields. **Close** ✕ the **Insert Merge Field** dialog box, and then compare your screen with Figure 8.37.

> All of the merge fields from the data source are inserted on the first line of the document. Recall that each merge field in the main document is surrounded by double angle brackets. When the directory is created, all the information for one record—a customer—will display on a single line.

FIGURE 8.37

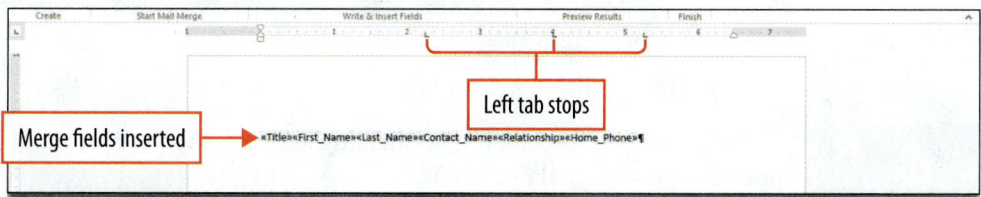

4 Position the insertion point between the **Title** field and the **First_Name** field. Press Spacebar. Use the same technique to insert a space between the **First_Name** and **Last_Name** fields.

> It is necessary to add spacing between merge fields in the same manner that you do with text.

5 Position the insertion point between the **Last_Name** field and **Contact_Name** field. Press Tab—because of the length of the field names, the tab formatting mark may not display. Using the same technique, insert a tab formatting mark between the **Contact_Name** and **Relationship** fields and between the **Relationship** and **Home_Phone** fields.

> The tabs will allow the data in each field to display in columns, creating a professional appearance.

6 Position the insertion point to the right of the **Home_Phone** field, and press Enter. Compare your screen with Figure 8.38, and then **Save** 🖫 your changes.

> By adding a new paragraph to the document, when the data is merged, each record will display on a new line.

FIGURE 8.38

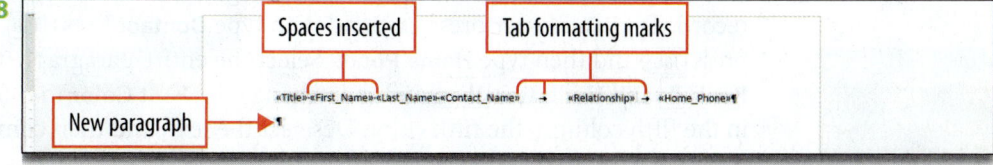

Activity 8.15 | Merging Files to Create a Directory

When completing the merge process for a directory, all of the data represented by the merge fields is displayed in a single document.

1 On the **MAILINGS tab**, in the **Preview Results group**, click **Preview Results**.

Because you are creating a directory, only one record—the first record—displays.

2 To view the second record, in the **Preview Results group**, click **Next Record** ▶. In the same manner, view the other three records, and then click **Preview Results**.

3 On the **MAILINGS tab**, in the **Finish group**, click **Finish & Merge**, and then click **Edit Individual Documents**. In the **Merge to New Document** dialog box, click **OK**. Compare your screen with Figure 8.39.

FIGURE 8.39

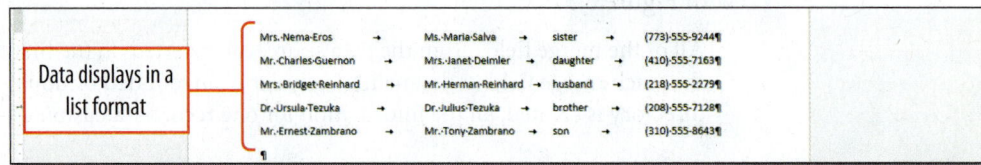

Data displays in a list format

Mrs.·Nema·Eros	→	Ms.·Maria·Salva	→	sister	→	(773)-555-9244¶
Mr.·Charles·Guernon	→	Mrs.·Janet·Delmler	→	daughter	→	(410)-555-7163¶
Mrs.·Bridget·Reinhard	→	Mr.·Herman·Reinhard	→	husband	→	(218)-555-2279¶
Dr.·Ursula·Tezuka	→	Dr.·Julius·Tezuka	→	brother	→	(208)-555-7128¶
Mr.·Ernest·Zambrano	→	Mr.·Tony·Zambrano	→	son	→	(310)-555-8643¶

Activity 8.16 | Editing a Directory

In the merged directory, you can add elements, such as a title and headings, to improve the appearance of the final document.

1 With the insertion point at the beginning of the document, press Enter, and then press ↑.

2 Type the following text, pressing Enter after each line.

Caribbean Customized
Customer Appreciation Cruise
Emergency Contact List

When creating a directory, a title and other specific elements must be added after the merge process is completed.

3 Select the first paragraph, and on the mini toolbar, change the **Font Size** to **28**. With the text selected, click the **HOME tab**. In the **Font group**, click **Text Effects** Ⓐ▾, and in the first row, click the second effect—**Fill – Blue, Accent 1, Shadow**. In the **Paragraph group**, apply **Center** ☰.

4 Select the second and third paragraphs. On the mini toolbar, change the **Font Size** to **16**, apply **Bold** Ⓑ, and then change the **Font Color** to **Blue, Accent 1, Darker 25%**—in the fifth column, the fifth color. Press Ctrl + E.

5 Position the insertion point in the blank paragraph immediately above the first customer record. Type **Customer** press Tab, and then type **Contact** Press Tab, type **Relationship** press Tab, and then type **Home Phone** Select the entire paragraph. On the mini toolbar, apply **Bold** Ⓑ and **Underline** Ⓤ▾, and then change the **Font Color** to **Blue, Accent 1, Darker 25%**—in the fifth column, the fifth color. Deselect the text, and then compare your screen with Figure 8.40.

FIGURE 8.40

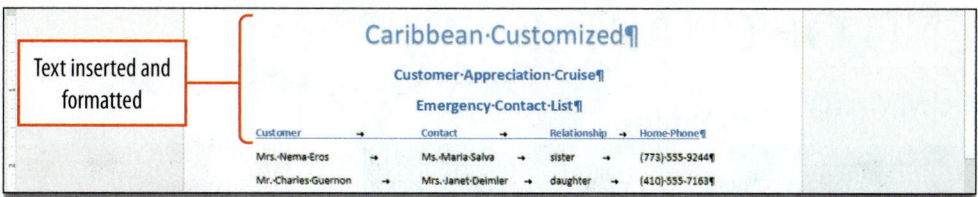

Text inserted and formatted

Caribbean·Customized¶

Customer·Appreciation·Cruise¶

Emergency·Contact·List·¶

Customer		Contact		Relationship		Home·Phone¶
Mrs.·Nema·Eros	→	Ms.·Maria·Salva	→	sister	→	(773)·555·9244¶
Mr.·Charles·Guernon	→	Mrs.·Janet·Deimler	→	daughter	→	(410)·555·7163¶

6 Press F12, and then save the document in your **Word Chapter 8** folder as
Lastname_Firstname_8B_List_Merged

Activity 8.17 | Inserting a Watermark

A *watermark* is a text or graphic element that displays behind document text. You add a watermark to identify the status of a document or to create a visual impact. In this activity, you will add a watermark to indicate that the directory information is confidential.

1 Click the **DESIGN tab**, and then in the **Page Background group**, click **Watermark**. In the **Watermark** gallery, under **Confidential**, click the first style—**CONFIDENTIAL 1**. Notice that the word *CONFIDENTIAL* displays in the background of the document. Compare your screen with Figure 8.41.

Inserting the Confidential watermark helps ensure the privacy of customers when the document is distributed.

FIGURE 8.41

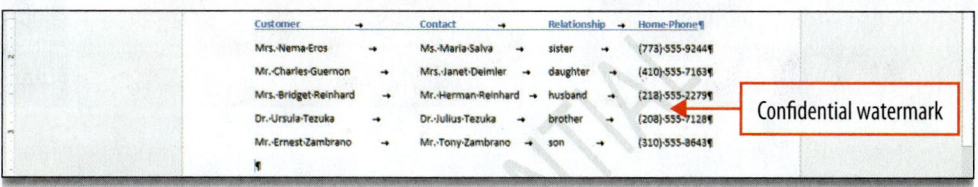

Customer		Contact		Relationship		Home·Phone¶
Mrs.·Nema·Eros	→	Ms.·Maria·Salva	→	sister	→	(773)·555·9244¶
Mr.·Charles·Guernon	→	Mrs.·Janet·Deimler	→	daughter	→	(410)·555·7163¶
Mrs.·Bridget·Reinhard	→	Mr.·Herman·Reinhard	→	husband	→	(218)·555·2279¶
Dr.·Ursula·Tezuka	→	Dr.·Julius·Tezuka	→	brother	→	(208)·555·7128¶
Mr.·Ernest·Zambrano	→	Mr.·Tony·Zambrano	→	son	→	(310)·555·8643¶

Confidential watermark

2 Insert the file name in the footer. Click the **FILE tab**, and then click **Show All Properties**. In the **Tags** box, type **contact list, merged** In the **Subject** box, type your course name and section number. If necessary, edit the author name to display your name. **Save** your document, and then press Ctrl + W.

3 In the displayed document—the main document—insert the file name in the footer. Click the **FILE tab**, and then click **Show All Properties**. In the **Tags** box, type **contact list, main** In the **Subject** box, type your course name and section number. If necessary, edit the author name to display your name. **Save** your document.

4 Print the four Word documents—it is not necessary to print the data sources—or submit all six files electronically as directed by your instructor, and then **Close** **X** Word.

More Knowledge | **Inserting a Picture as a Watermark**

To insert a picture as a watermark, on the DESIGN tab, in the Page Background group, click Watermark. In the Watermark gallery, click Custom Watermark. In the Printed Watermark dialog box, select Picture watermark, and then click Select Picture. In the Insert Pictures dialog box, navigate to the location of the image, and then click Insert. Change the Scale and Washout options as desired, and then click OK.

END | You have completed Project 8B

END OF CHAPTER

SUMMARY

The mail merge feature joins a main document with a data source—for example, an Excel spreadsheet or an Access table—to create personalized documents such as letters, envelopes, mailing labels, and directories.

Filter the data source to display specific records or sort the data source to display records in a specific order. Predefined merge fields or individual merge fields determine the placement of data in the document.

Match Fields maps predefined field names to the field names in the data source. Apply a rule to check criteria—for example, to insert a specific date based on a particular field—when completing the merge process.

When performing a mail merge, Word provides a feature to create a new data source, customize the field names, and enter data. A directory is a single list of records using specified fields from a data source.

GO! LEARN IT ONLINE

Review the concepts and key terms in this chapter by completing these online challenges, which you can find at **www.pearsonhighered.com/go**.

Matching and Multiple Choice:
Answer matching and multiple choice questions to test what you learned in this chapter. **MyITLab®**

Crossword Puzzle:
Spell out the words that match the numbered clues, and put them in the puzzle squares.

Flipboard:
Flip through the definitions of the key terms in this chapter and match them with the correct term.

END OF CHAPTER

REVIEW AND ASSESSMENT GUIDE FOR WORD CHAPTER 8

Your instructor may assign one or more of these projects to help you review the chapter and assess your mastery and understanding of the chapter.

	Review and Assessment Guide for Word Chapter 8		
Project	**Apply Skills from These Chapter Objectives**	**Project Type**	**Project Location**
8C	Objectives 1–2 from Project 8A	**8C Skills Review** A guided review of the skills from Project 8A.	On the following pages
8D	Objectives 3–5 from Project 8B	**8D Skills Review** A guided review of the skills from Project 8B.	On the following pages
8E	Objectives 1–2 from Project 8A	**8E Mastery (Grader Project)** A demonstration of your mastery of the skills in Project 8A with extensive decision making.	In MyITLab and on the following pages
8F	Objectives 3–5 from Project 8B	**8F Mastery (Grader Project)** A demonstration of your mastery of the skills in Project 8B with extensive decision making.	In MyITLab and on the following pages
8G	Objectives 1–5 from Projects 8A and 8B	**8G Mastery (Grader Project)** A demonstration of your mastery of the skills in Projects 8A and 8B with extensive decision making.	In MyITLab and on the following pages
8H	Combination of Objectives from Projects 8A and 8B	**8H GO! Fix It** A demonstration of your mastery of the skills in Projects 8A and 8B by creating a correct result from a document that contains errors you must find.	Online
8I	Combination of Objectives from Projects 8A and 8B	**8I GO! Make It** A demonstration of your mastery of the skills in Projects 8A and 8B by creating a result from a supplied picture.	Online
8J	Combination of Objectives from Projects 8A and 8B	**8J GO! Solve It** A demonstration of your mastery of the skills in Projects 8A and 8B, your decision-making skills, and your critical thinking skills. A task-specific rubric helps you self-assess your result.	Online
8K	Combination of Objectives from Projects 8A and 8B	**8K GO! Solve It** A demonstration of your mastery of the skills in Projects 8A and 8B, your decision-making skills, and your critical thinking skills. A task-specific rubric helps you self-assess your result.	On the following pages
8L	Combination of Objectives from Projects 8A and 8B	**8L GO! Think** A demonstration of your understanding of the chapter concepts applied in a manner that you would outside of college. An analytic rubric helps you and your instructor grade the quality of your work by comparing it to the work an expert in the discipline would create.	On the following pages
8M	Combination of Objectives from Projects 8A and 8B	**8M GO! Think** A demonstration of your understanding of the chapter concepts applied in a manner that you would outside of college. An analytic rubric helps you and your instructor grade the quality of your work by comparing it to the work an expert in the discipline would create.	Online
8N	Combination of Objectives from Projects 8A and 8B	**8N You and GO!** A demonstration of your understanding of the chapter concepts applied in a manner that you would in a personal situation. An analytic rubric helps you and your instructor grade the quality of your work.	Online

GLOSSARY

GLOSSARY OF CHAPTER KEY TERMS

Address Block A predefined merge field that includes the recipient's name and address.

Bulk mail A large mailing, sorted by postal code, which is eligible for reduced postage rates, available from the United States Postal Service.

Complimentary closing A phrase—such as *Sincerely* or *Yours truly*—that is used to end a business letter.

Data source A list of variable information, such as names and addresses, that is merged with a main document to create customized form letters or labels.

Database An organized collection of facts about people, events, things, or ideas related to a particular topic or purpose.

Delimiters Characters—such as commas and tabs—that are used to separate text into groups.

Directory A single list of records using specified fields from a data source.

Fields In a mail merge, a category—or column—of data.

Filter A set of criteria applied to fields in a data source to display specific records.

Form letter A letter with standardized wording that can be sent to many different people.

Greeting Line A predefined merge field that includes an introductory word, such as *Dear*, and the recipient's name.

Inside address The name and address of the person receiving the letter; positioned below the date line.

Mail merge A Word feature that joins a main document and a data source to create customized letters or labels.

Main document In a mail merge, the document that contains the text or formatting that remains constant.

Match Fields A Word feature that maps predefined field names to the field names in a data source.

Merge field In a mail merge, a placeholder that represents specific information in the data source.

Nested table A table inserted in a cell of an existing table.

Record All of the categories of data pertaining to one person, place, thing, event, or idea, and which is formatted as a row in a database table.

Rules Conditional Word fields that allow you to determine how the merge process is completed.

Salutation The greeting line of a business letter, such as *Dear Sir*.

Watermark A text or graphic element that displays behind document text.

CHAPTER REVIEW

Skills Review Project 8C Eastern Cruise

Apply **8A** skills from these Objectives:

1 Merge a Data Source and a Main Document

2 Use Mail Merge to Create Envelopes

In the following Skills Review, you will create a form letter, customized for current customers, that announces a new cruise offered by Caribbean Customized. You will also create envelopes to accompany the merged letters. Your completed documents will look similar to Figure 8.42.

PROJECT FILES

For Project 8C, you will need the following files:

New blank Word document
w08C_Eastern_Letter
w08C_Eastern_Customers

You will save your files as:

Lastname_Firstname_8C_Eastern_Main
Lastname_Firstname_8C_Eastern_Merged
Lastname_Firstname_8C_EasternEnv_Main
Lastname_Firstname_8C_EasternEnv_Merged
Lastname_Firstname_8C_Eastern_Customers—not shown in figure

PROJECT RESULTS

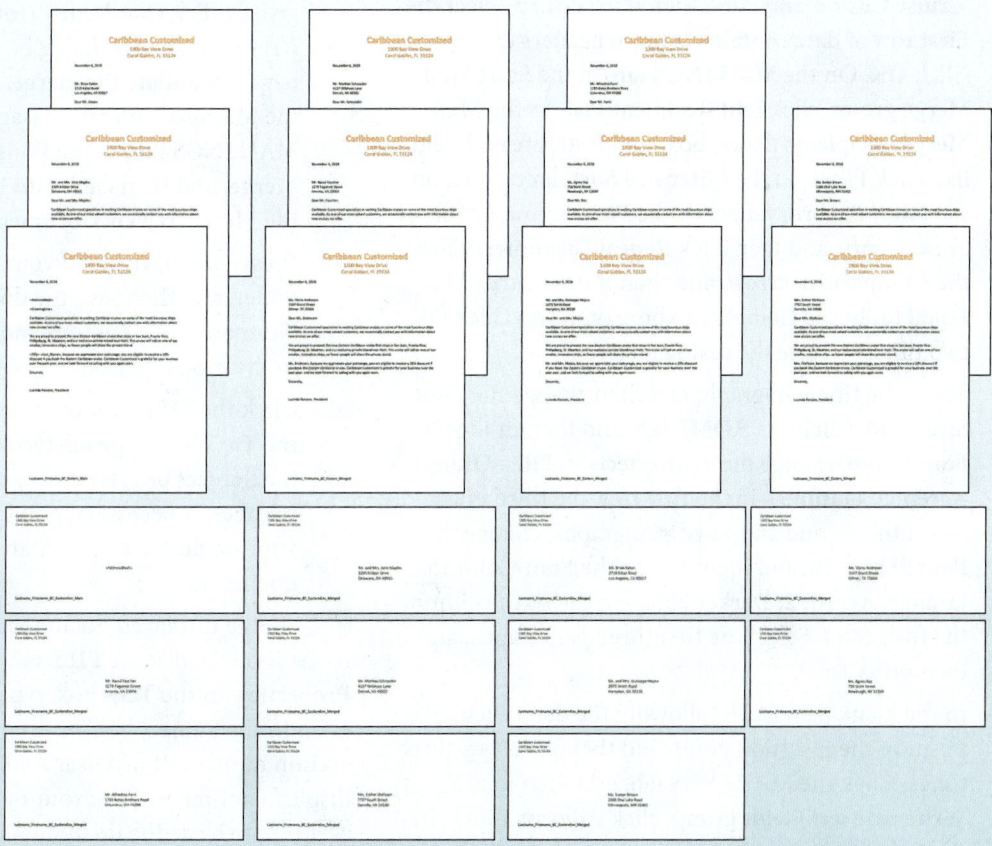

FIGURE 8.42

(Project 8C Eastern Cruise continues on the next page)

CHAPTER REVIEW

1 Start Excel. Navigate to your student files, and open the file **w08C_Eastern_Customers**. Press F12, navigate to your **Word Chapter 8** folder, and then save the file as **Lastname_ Firstname_8C_Eastern_Customers** Close Excel.

a. Start Word. Navigate to your student files, open the file **w08C_Eastern_Letter**, and then **Save** the document to your **Word Chapter 8** folder as **Lastname_Firstname_8C_Eastern_Main** If necessary display the rulers and formatting marks. For any words flagged as a spelling error, click **Ignore All**.

b. Click the **MAILINGS tab**. In the **Start Mail Merge group**, click **Start Mail Merge**, and then click **Letters**. In the **Start Mail Merge group**, click **Select Recipients**, and then click **Use an Existing List**. In the **Select Data Source** dialog box, navigate to your **Word Chapter 8** folder, select the file **Lastname_Firstname_8C_Eastern_Customers**, and then click **Open**.

c. In the **Select Table** dialog box, if necessary, select **'Cruise Customers$'**, and then if necessary, select the **First row of data contains column headers** check box. Click **OK**. On the **MAILINGS tab**, in the **Start Mail Merge group**, click **Edit Recipient List**. In the **Mail Merge Recipients** dialog box, under **Refine recipient list**, click **Filter**. In the **Filter and Sort** dialog box, on the **Filter Records tab**, click the **Field arrow**, scroll as necessary, and then click **Repeat Customer**. Click the **Comparison arrow**, and then if necessary, click **Equal to**. In the **Compare to** box, type **Yes** Click **OK** two times to close the dialog boxes.

d. Select the first paragraph, and then change the **Font Size** to **28**. Click the **HOME tab**, and then in the **Font group**, change the **Text Effects** to **Fill – Orange, Accent 2, Outline**—in the first row, the third effect. Select the second and third paragraphs, change the **Font Size** to **16**, and then change the **Font Color** to **Orange, Accent 2, Darker 25%**—in the sixth column, the fifth color. Select the first three paragraphs, and then press Ctrl + E.

e. In the blank paragraph following the date, click to position the insertion point, and then press Enter three times. Click the **MAILINGS tab**, and then in the **Write & Insert Fields group**, click **Address Block**. In the **Insert Address Block** dialog box, click **OK**. Press

Enter two times, and then in the **Write & Insert Fields group**, click **Greeting Line**. In the **Insert Greeting Line** dialog box, under **Greeting line format**, in the box on the right—the **Punctuation** box, click the **Punctuation arrow**, and then click **:** (the colon). Click **OK**, and then press Enter.

2 Position the insertion point to the left of the paragraph that begins *Because*. Select the word *Because*, and then press Delete. On the **MAILINGS tab**, in the **Write & Insert Fields group**, click **Insert Merge Field**. In the **Insert Merge Field** dialog box, under **Fields**, click **Title** and then click **Insert**. Click the **Last Name** field, click **Insert**, and then **Close** the **Insert Merge Field** dialog box.

a. Click to position the insertion point between the **Title** field and the **Last Name** field, and then press Spacebar. Click to position the insertion point to the right of the **Last Name** field, and then beginning with a comma type **, because** Press Spacebar and then **Save** your changes.

b. On the **MAILINGS tab**, in the **Preview Results group**, click **Check for Errors**. In the **Checking and Reporting Errors** dialog box, select the option that begins **Simulate the merge**, and then click **OK**. In the **Microsoft Word** message box, click **OK**. On the **MAILINGS tab**, in the **Finish group**, click **Finish & Merge**, and then click **Edit Individual Documents**. In the **Merge to New Document** dialog box, click **OK**.

c. Press F12. Navigate to your **Word Chapter 8** folder, and then save the document as **Lastname_ Firstname_8C_Eastern_Merged** Insert the file name in the footer.

d. Click the **FILE tab**, and then **Show All Properties**. In the **Tags** box, type **eastern cruise letters, merged** In the **Subject** box, type your course name and section number. If necessary, edit the author name to display your name. Save your changes, and then close the document.

3 In the displayed document, insert the file name in the footer. Click the **FILE tab**, and then **Show All Properties**. In the **Tags** box, type **eastern cruise letters, main** In the **Subject** box, type your course name and section number. If necessary, edit the author name to display your name. Save your document, and then press Ctrl + W to close the document but leave Word open.

(Project 8C Eastern Cruise continues on the next page)

CHAPTER REVIEW

4 Press Ctrl + N to open a new document. Click the **MAILINGS tab**. In the **Start Mail Merge group**, click **Start Mail Merge**, and then click **Envelopes**. In the **Envelope Options** dialog box, on the **Envelope Options tab**, under **Envelope size**, click **Size 10 (4 1/8 × 9 1/2 in)**. Click **OK**. Navigate to your **Word Chapter 8** folder, and then save the document as **Lastname_Firstname_8C_EasternEnv_Main**

a. On the **MAILINGS tab**, in the **Start Mail Merge group**, click **Select Recipients**, and then click **Use an Existing List**. In the **Select Data Source** dialog box, navigate to your **Word Chapter 8** folder, locate and select the file **Lastname_Firstname_8C_Eastern_Customers**, and then click **Open**. In the **Select Table** dialog box, if necessary, select '**Cruise Customers$**', and then if necessary, select the **First row of data contains column headers** check box. Click **OK**.

b. On the **MAILINGS tab**, in the **Start Mail Merge group**, click **Edit Recipient List**. In the **Mail Merge Recipients** dialog box, click **Filter**. In the **Filter and Sort** dialog box, on the **Filter Records tab**, click the **Field arrow**, scroll as necessary, and then click **Repeat Customer**. Click the **Comparison arrow**, and then if necessary, click **Equal to**. In the **Compare to** box, type **Yes** Click **OK** two times to close the dialog boxes.

c. Type the following return address, pressing Enter after the first and second lines.

Caribbean Customized
1300 Bay View Drive
Coral Gables, FL 33124

d. In the center of the document, position the insertion point to the left of the paragraph mark. On the **MAILINGS tab**, in the **Write & Insert Fields group**, click **Address Block**. In the **Insert Address Block** dialog box, click **OK**. On the **MAILINGS tab**, in the **Preview Results group**, click **Check for Errors**. In the **Checking and Reporting Errors** dialog box, select the third option that begins **Complete the merge without pausing**, and then click **OK**.

5 Navigate to your **Word Chapter 8** folder, and save the document as **Lastname_Firstname_8C_EasternEnv_Merged** Insert the file name in the footer. Click the **FILE tab**, and then **Show All Properties**. In the **Tags** box, type **customer envelopes, merged** In the **Subject** box, type your course name and section number. If necessary, edit the author name to display your name. Save your document, and then press Ctrl + W.

6 In the main document, insert the file name in the footer. Click the **FILE tab**, and then **Show All Properties**. In the **Tags** box, type **customer envelopes, main** In the **Subject** box, type your course name and section number. If necessary, edit the author name to display your name. Save your document.

7 Print your four files—it is not necessary to print the data source—or submit all five files electronically as directed by your instructor. Close Word.

END | You have completed Project 8C

CHAPTER REVIEW

Build from Scratch

Skills Review | Project 8D Name Tags

In the following Skills Review, you will use mail merge to create name tags for customers taking the Western Caribbean cruise by selecting a label option, editing records, and sorting the data source. You will create a new data source and match fields to create a list of Southern Caribbean cruise employees and their addresses. Your completed documents will look similar to the ones shown in Figure 8.43.

PROJECT FILES

For Project 8D, you will need the following files:

Two new blank Word documents
w08D_Cruise_Customers

You will save your files as:

Lastname_Firstname_8D_NameTags_Main
Lastname_Firstname_8D_NameTags_Merged
Lastname_Firstname_8D_Employee_List
Lastname_Firstname_8D_Cruise_Customers—not shown in figure
Lastname_Firstname_8D_Southern_Employees—not shown in figure

PROJECT RESULTS

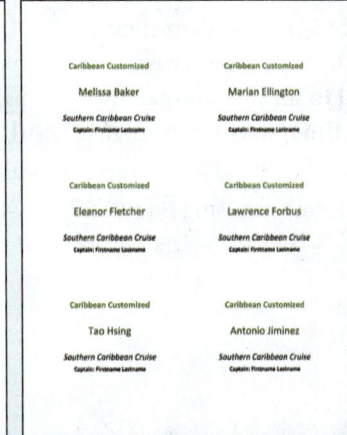

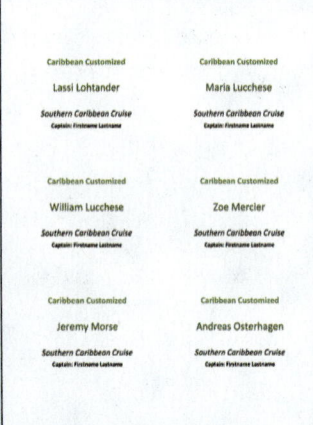

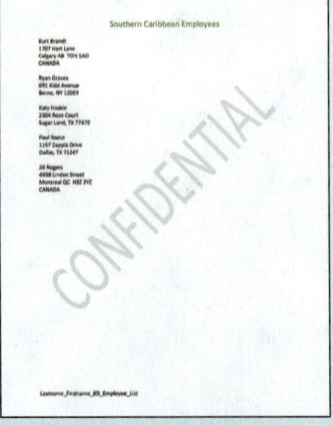

FIGURE 8.43

(Project 8D Name Tags continues on the next page)

CHAPTER REVIEW

Skills Review   Project 8D Name Tags (continued)

1 Start Access. Near the lower left of the screen, click **Open Other Files**, and then under **Places**, double-click **Computer**. Navigate to your student data files, and then open file **w08D_Cruise_Customers**. Click the **FILE tab**, and then click **Save As**. **Save** the file to your **Word Chapter 8** folder, as **Lastname_Firstname_8D_Cruise_Customers** Close any open windows. Start Word. Open a new blank document. If necessary, display the rulers and formatting marks.

a. Click the **MAILINGS tab**, in the **Start Mail Merge group**, click **Start Mail Merge**, and then click **Labels**. In the **Label Options** dialog box, under **Label information**, click the **Label vendors arrow** and select **Avery US Letter**, and then in the **Product number** box, scroll as necessary and click **5392 Name Badges Insert Refills**. Click **OK**. Click the **LAYOUT tab**, and then in the **Table group**, if necessary, click **View Gridlines** to display gridlines. Navigate to your **Word Chapter 8** folder, and then Save the document as **Lastname_Firstname_8D_NameTags_Main**

b. Click the **MAILINGS tab**, in the **Start Mail Merge group**, click **Select Recipients**, and then click **Use an Existing List**. In the **Select Data Source** dialog box, navigate to your **Word Chapter 8** folder, select **Lastname_Firstname_8D_Cruise_Customers**, and then click **Open**.

c. On the **MAILINGS tab**, in the **Start Mail Merge group**, click **Edit Recipient List**. In the **Mail Merge Recipients** dialog box, at the lower left, under **Data Source**, click **Lastname_Firstname_8D_Cruise_Customers**, and then click **Edit**. In the **Edit Data Source** dialog box, click **New Entry**. In the new record line, in the **First_Name** field, type **Lawrence** and then press **Tab**. In the **Last_Name** field, type **Forbus** and then press **Tab**. In the **Country** field, type **USA** and then press **Tab**.

d. In the new line, in the **First_Name** field, type **Melissa** and then press **Tab**. In the **Last_Name** field, type **Baker** and then press **Tab**. In the **Country** field, type **CANADA** Click **OK**. In the **Microsoft Word** message box, click **Yes** to update your recipient list.

e. In the **Mail Merge Recipients** dialog box, immediately to the right of **Last_Name**, click the **arrow**, and then click **Sort Ascending**. Click **OK**.

2 Select the entire table, click the **LAYOUT tab**, and then in the **Alignment group**, click **Align Center**.

a. In the first cell of the table, click to position the insertion point. Type **Caribbean Customized** and then press **Enter** two times. Select the text you just typed, change the **Font Size** to **16**, apply **Bold**, and then change the **Font Color** to **Green, Accent 6, Darker 25%**—in the last column, the fifth color.

b. In the third blank paragraph, click to position the insertion point. Click the **MAILINGS tab**. In the **Write & Insert Fields group**, click the **Insert Merge Field button arrow**, and then click **First_Name**. Press **Spacebar**, click the **Insert Merge Field button arrow**, and then click **Last_Name**. Press **Enter** three times. Select the merge fields you just inserted, change the **Font Size** to **20**, and then change the **Font Color** to **Green, Accent 6, Darker 50%**.

c. In the fifth paragraph, click to position the insertion point. Type **Southern Caribbean Cruise** select the text, change the **Font Size** to **16**, and then apply **Italic**. In the sixth paragraph, type **Captain:** press **Spacebar**, type your own first name, press **Spacebar**, and then type your own last name. Select the text you just typed, and then apply **Bold**.

d. On the **MAILINGS tab**, in the **Write & Insert Fields group**, click **Update Labels**. In the **Finish group**, click **Finish & Merge**, and then click **Edit Individual Documents**. In the **Merge to New Document** dialog box, click **OK**. Navigate to your **Word Chapter 8** folder, and then save the document as **Lastname_Firstname_8D_NameTags_Merged** Click the **FILE tab**, and then click **Show All Properties**. In the **Tags** box, type **name tags, merged** In the **Subject** box, type your course name and section number. If necessary, edit the author name to display your name. Save your document, and then press **Ctrl** + **W**.

3 In the main document, click **Show All Properties**. In the **Tags** box, type **name tags, main** In the **Subject** box, type your course name and section number. If necessary, edit the author name to display your name. Save your document. Close the document but leave Word open.

(Project 8D Name Tags continues on the next page)

CHAPTER REVIEW

4 Press Ctrl + N to display a new document. On the **HOME tab**, in the **Styles group**, change the style to **No Spacing**.

a. Click the **MAILINGS tab**, in the **Start Mail Merge group**, click **Start Mail Merge**, and then click **Directory**. On the **MAILINGS tab**, in the **Start Mail Merge group**, click **Select Recipients**, and then click **Type a New List**.

b. In the **New Address List** dialog box, click **Customize Columns**. In the **Customize Address List** dialog box, under **Field Names**, click the **State** field, and then click **Rename**. In the **Rename Field** dialog box, in the **To** box, type **State/Province** and then click **OK**. In the **Customize Address List** dialog box, under **Field Names**, click **Title**, click **Delete**, and then click **Yes**. In a similar manner delete the **Company Name**, **Address Line 2**, **Home Phone**, **Work Phone**, and **E-mail Address** fields. Click **OK**.

c. In the **New Address List** dialog box, under **First Name**, position the insertion point in the first cell. Type the following data, shown in **Table 1**, pressing Tab after each entry except the last entry—**CANADA**.

d. In the **New Address List** dialog box, click **OK**. In the **Save Address List** dialog box, navigate to your **Word Chapter 8** folder. Save the file as **Lastname_Firstname_8D_Southern_Employees** On the **MAILINGS tab**, in the **Write & Insert Fields group**, click **Address Block**. In the **Insert Address Block** dialog box, under **Correct Problems**, click **Match Fields**. In the **Match Fields** dialog box, click the **State arrow**, and then from the displayed list, click **State/Province**. Click **OK** two times to close the dialog boxes.

e. Position the insertion point to the right of the **Address Block** merge field, if necessary, and then press Enter two times. On the **MAILINGS tab**, in the **Finish group**, click **Finish & Merge**, and then click **Edit Individual Documents**. In the **Merge to New Document** dialog box, click **OK**.

5 With the insertion point at the beginning of the document, press Enter two times. In the first paragraph, type **Southern Caribbean Employees** Select the paragraph, change the **Font Size** to **16**, change the **Font Color** to **Green, Accent 6, Darker 25%**—in the last column, the fifth color—and then press Ctrl + E.

a. Click the **DESIGN tab**, and then in the **Page Background group**, click **Watermark**. In the **Watermark** gallery, under **Confidential**, click **CONFIDENTIAL 1**.

b. Press F12. Navigate to your **Word Chapter 8** folder, and save the document as **Lastname_Firstname_8D_Employee_List** Insert the file name in the footer.

c. Click the **FILE tab**, and then click **Show All Properties**. In the **Tags** box, type **employee list, addresses** In the **Subject** box, type your course name and section number. If necessary, edit the author name to display your name. Save your document, and then close the document. Close Word without saving the main document.

6 Print your three documents—it is not necessary to print the data sources—or submit all five files electronically as directed by your instructor.

TABLE 1

First Name	Last Name	Address Line 1	City	State/Province	ZIP Code	Country or Region
Kurt	Brandt	1707 Hart Lane	Calgary	AB	TOH 1AO	CANADA
Ryan	Graves	691 Kidd Avenue	Berne	NY	12059	USA
Katy	Hoskie	2304 Rose Court	Sugar Land	TX	77479	USA
Paul	Reese	1157 Zappia Drive	Dallas	TX	75247	USA
Jill	Rogers	4938 Linden Street	Montreal	QC	H3Z 2YZ	CANADA

(Return to Step 4)

END | You have completed Project 8D

CONTENT-BASED ASSESSMENTS

Mastering Word | Project 8E Hospitality Team

In the following Mastering Word project, you will use mail merge to filter a data source and customize a form letter to employees who have been selected for the hospitality team for the Ultimate Southern cruise. Your completed documents will look similar to the ones shown in Figure 8.44.

Apply 8A skills from these Objectives:

1 Merge a Data Source and a Main Document
2 Use Mail Merge to Create Envelopes

PROJECT FILES

For Project 8E, you will need the following files:

New blank Word document
w08E_Hospitality_Team
w08E_Hospitality_Letter

You will save your files as:

Lastname_Firstname_8E_Hospitality_Main
Lastname_Firstname_8E_Hospitality_Merged
Lastname_Firstname_8E_HospitalityEnv_Main
Lastname_Firstname_8E_HospitalityEnv_Merged
Lastname_Firstname_8E_Hospitality_Team—not shown in figure

PROJECT RESULTS

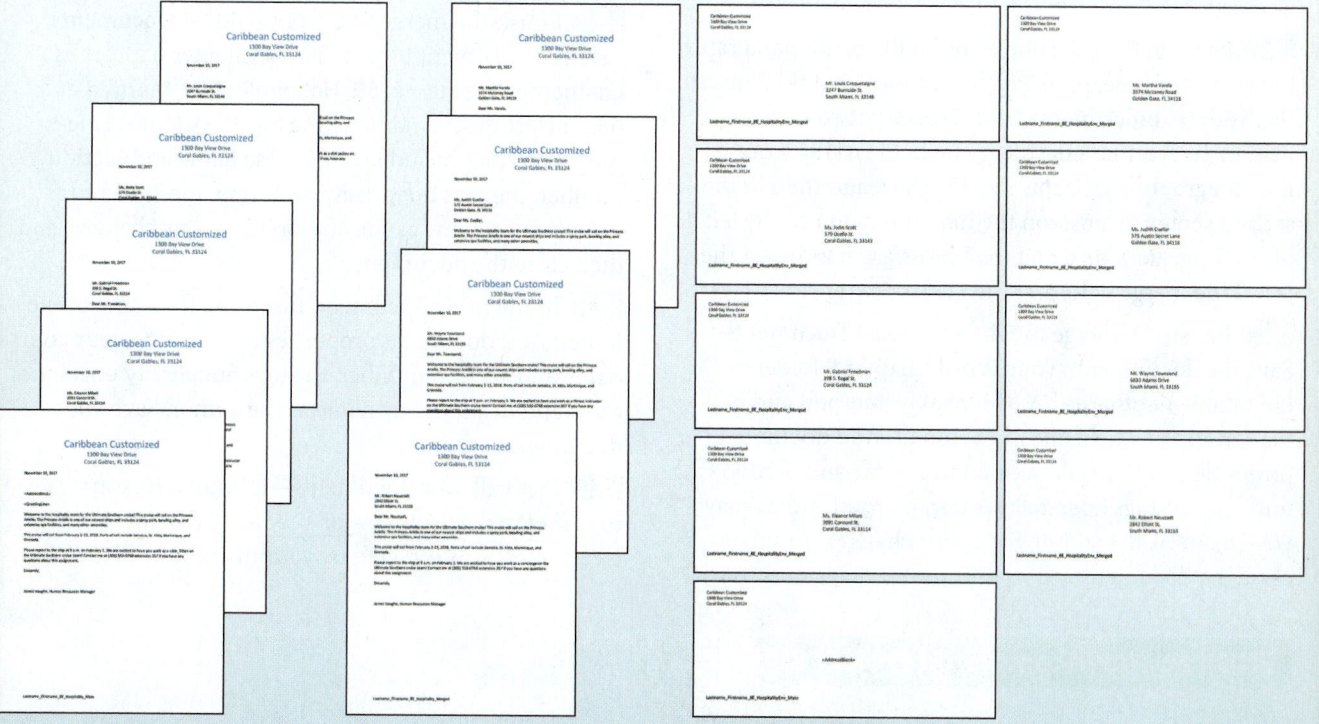

FIGURE 8.44

(Project 8E Hospitality Team continues on the next page)

CONTENT-BASED ASSESSMENTS

1 Start Excel. Navigate to your student files, and open the file **w08E_Hospitality_Team**. Save the file to your **Word Chapter 8** folder as **Lastname_Firstname_8E_Hospitality_Team** Close Excel.

2 Start Word. Navigate to your student files, and open the file **w08E_Hospitality_Letter**. Save the document to your **Word Chapter 8** folder as **Lastname_Firstname_8E_Hospitality_Main** If necessary, display the rulers and formatting marks.

3 **Start Mail Merge**, and select **Letters**. As the data source, from your **Word Chapter 8** folder, select the file **Lastname_Firstname_8E_Hospitality_Team**, and then select the worksheet 'Employee Information$'. **Filter** the data source so that the **Job Title** field is **Not equal to lounge manager**

4 Select the first paragraph, change the **Font Size** to **28**, change the **Font Color** to **Blue, Accent 1, Darker 25%**, and then apply **Center**. Select the second and third paragraphs, change the **Font Size** to **16**, change the **Font Color** to **Blue, Accent 1, Darker 50%**, and then apply **Center**.

5 Position the insertion point in the blank paragraph following the date, press Enter three times, and then insert the **Address Block** merge field. Press Enter two times, insert the **Greeting Line** merge field. Press Enter. Locate the paragraph that begins *Please report*, and then in the second sentence, position the insertion point to the left of *on*. Type **work as a** and then press Spacebar. Insert the **Job_Title** merge field, and then press Spacebar.

6 Finish the merge to **Edit Individual Documents**. Save the document in your **Word Chapter 8** folder as **Lastname_Firstname_8E_Hospitality_Merged** and then insert the file name in the footer. Add document properties that include your course name and section number, the tags **hospitality letter, merged** and display your name as the author. Save your changes, and then close the document.

7 In the main document, insert the file name in the footer. Add document properties that include your course name and section number, the tags **hospitality letter, main** and display your name as the author. Save your document, and then close the document, but leave Word open.

8 In a new document, click **Start Mail Merge**, select **Envelopes**, and then select **Size 10 (4 1/8 × 9 1/2 in)**. Save the document to your **Word Chapter 8** folder as **Lastname_Firstname_8E_HospitalityEnv_Main** As the data source, from your **Word Chapter 8** folder, select the file **Lastname_Firstname_8E_Hospitality_Team**, and then select the worksheet 'Employee Information$'. **Filter** the data source so that the **Job Title** field is **Not equal to lounge manager** In the center of the document, insert the **Address Block** merge field. Press Ctrl + Home, and then using three lines, type the return address:

Caribbean Customized

1300 Bay View Drive

Coral Gables, FL 33124

9 Finish the merge to **Edit Individual Documents**. Save the document to your **Word Chapter 8** folder as **Lastname_Firstname_8E_HospitalityEnv_Merged** and then insert the file name in the footer. Add document properties that include your course name and section number, the tags **hospitality envelope, merged** and display your name as the author. Save your changes, and then close the document.

10 In the main document, insert the file name in the footer. Add document properties that include your course name and section number, the tags **hospitality envelope, main** and display your name as the author. Save your document.

11 Print all four documents—it is not necessary to print the data source—or submit all five files electronically as directed by your instructor. Close Word.

END | You have completed Project 8E

CONTENT-BASED ASSESSMENTS

Mastering Word · Project 8F Cruise Ships

Apply 8B skills from these Objectives:

3 Edit and Sort a Data Source

4 Match Fields and Apply Rules

5 Create a Data Source and a Directory

Build from Scratch

In the following Mastering Word project, you will use mail merge and sort a data source to create jewel case labels for DVDs containing information about Caribbean Customized cruises and ships. Additionally, you will create a directory listing customer information. Your completed files will look similar to the ones shown in Figure 8.45.

PROJECT FILES

For Project 8F, you will need the following files:

Two new blank Word documents

w08F_Ships_Data

You will save your files as:

Lastname_Firstname_8F_Ships_Data—not shown in figure

Lastname_Firstname_8F_Ships_Main

Lastname_Firstname_8F_Ships_Merged

Lastname_Firstname_8F_Eastern_Data—not shown in figure

Lastname_Firstname_8F_Cruise_Roster

PROJECT RESULTS

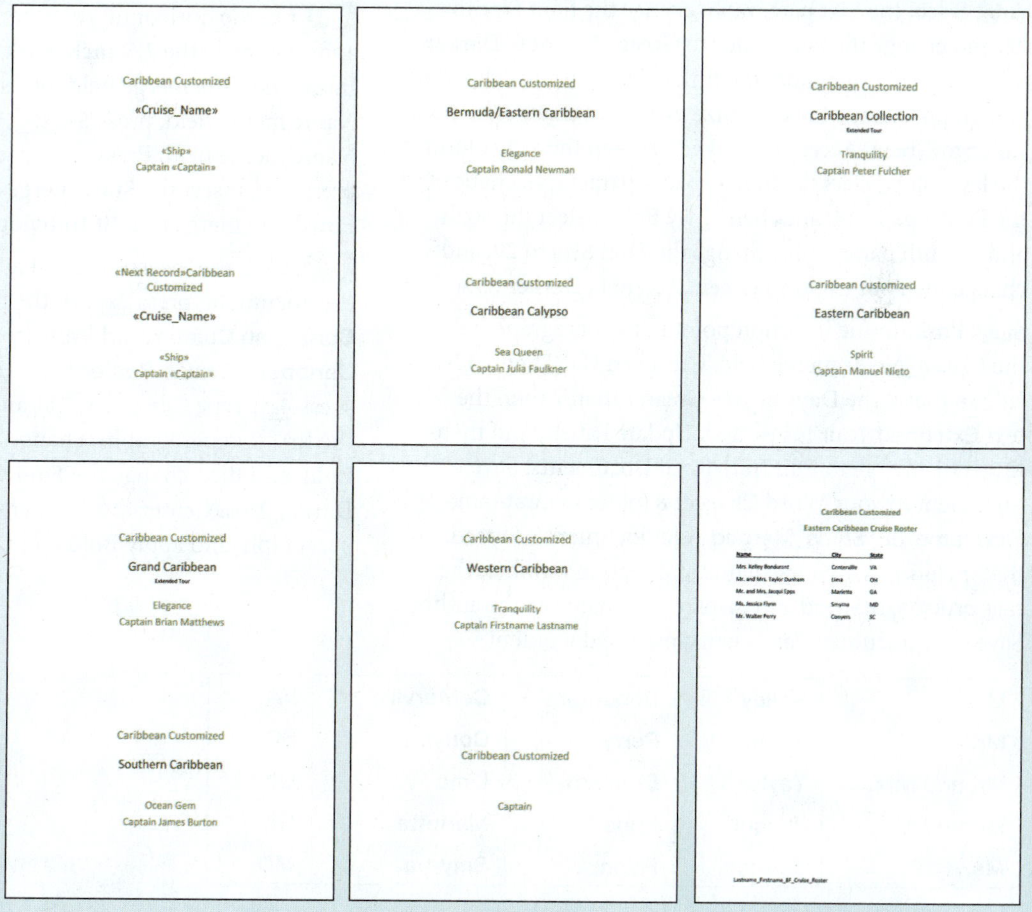

Caribbean Customized «Cruise_Name» «Ship» Captain «Captain» «Next Record»Caribbean Customized «Cruise_Name» «Ship» Captain «Captain»	Caribbean Customized Bermuda/Eastern Caribbean Elegance Captain Ronald Newman Caribbean Customized Caribbean Calypso Sea Queen Captain Julia Faulkner	Caribbean Customized Caribbean Collection Extended Tour Tranquility Captain Peter Fulcher Caribbean Customized Eastern Caribbean Spirit Captain Manuel Nieto
Caribbean Customized Grand Caribbean Extended Tour Elegance Captain Brian Matthews Caribbean Customized Southern Caribbean Ocean Gem Captain James Burton	Caribbean Customized Western Caribbean Tranquility Captain Firstname Lastname Caribbean Customized Captain	Caribbean Customized Eastern Caribbean Cruise Roster [roster table] Lastname_Firstname_8F_Cruise_Roster

The roster table (top-right of last page):

Name	City	State
Mrs. Ashby Bondurant	Centerville	VA
Mr. and Mrs. Taylor Durham	Lima	OH
Mr. and Mrs. Jacqui Epps	Marietta	GA
Ms. Jessica Flynn	Smyrna	MD
Mr. Walter Perry	Conyers	SC

FIGURE 8.45

(Project 8F Cruise Ships continues on the next page)

CONTENT-BASED ASSESSMENTS

1 Start Access. From your student files, open the file **w08F_Ships_Data**. Save the file to your **Word Chapter 8** folder as **Lastname_Firstname_8F_Ships_Data** Close any open windows.

2 Start Word and open a new blank document. **Start Mail Merge**, and select **Labels**. Change the **Label vendors** to **Avery US Letter**, and then change the **Product number** to **8962 DVD Labels. Save** the document to your **Word Chapter 8** folder as **Lastname_Firstname_8F_Ships_Main** Select the file **Lastname_Firstname_8F_Ships_Data** as the data source. Edit the data source, in the **Captain** field, by replacing **Stewart Johnson** with your first and last names. Sort the data source to display the **Cruise_Name** field in ascending order.

3 Select the entire table. Change the alignment to **Align Center**. In the first cell, type **Caribbean Customized** and then press Enter two times. Insert the **Cruise_Name** merge field, and then press Enter three times. Insert the **Ship** merge field, and then press Enter. Type **Captain:** press Spacebar and then insert the **Captain** merge field.

4 Select the first paragraph, change the **Font Size** to **22**, and change the **Font Color** to **Green, Accent 6, Darker 25%**—in the last column, the fifth color. Select the third paragraph, change the **Font Size** to **24**, and change the **Font Color** to **Green, Accent 6, Darker 50%**—in the last column, the last color. Select the fourth, blank paragraph, change the **Font Size** to **14**, and then apply **Bold**. Select the sixth and seventh paragraphs, change the **Font Size** to **20**, and change the **Font Color** to **Green, Accent 6, Darker 25%**.

5 Position the insertion point in the paragraph below the *Cruise_Name* merge field. Create an **If…Then…Else** rule so that if the **Days** field is **Greater than 7** then the text **Extended Tour** is inserted. **Update Labels**, and then finish the merge to **Edit Individual Documents**. Save the document to your **Word Chapter 8** folder as **Lastname_Firstname_8F_Ships_Merged** Add document properties that include your course name and section number, the tags **cruises, merged** and display your name as the author. Save your document, and then close the document.

6 In the main document, add document properties that include your course name and section number, the tags **cruises, main** and display your name as the author. Save your document, and then close the document but leave Word open.

7 In a new document, **Start Mail Merge**, and then select **Directory**. To **Select Recipients**, **Type a New List**. Display the **Customize Address List** dialog box, **Move Up** the **City** and **State** field names to display directly below **Last Name**. Beginning with **Company Name**, delete all remaining field names.

8 In the **New Address List** dialog box, under **Title**, position the insertion point in the first cell, and then type the following data in the appropriate cells.

9 In the **Save Address List** dialog box, navigate to your **Word Chapter 8** folder, and save the file as **Lastname_Firstname_8F_Eastern_Data** as the data source. Sort the data source to display the **Last Name** field in ascending order.

10 On the horizontal ruler, set left tabs at approximately the **2.5-inch mark** and **3.5-inch mark**. Insert the **Title** merge field, press Spacebar, insert the **First Name** merge field, press Spacebar, and then insert the **Last Name** merge field. Press Tab, insert the **City** merge field, press Tab, insert the **State** merge field, and then press Enter. Finish the merge to **Edit Individual Documents**.

11 With the insertion point at the beginning of the document, press Enter. In the first paragraph, type **Caribbean Customized** Press Enter, and then type **Eastern Caribbean Cruise Roster** Press Enter two times, type **Name** press Tab, type **City** press Tab, and then type **State** Select the first two paragraphs, change the **Font Size** to **16**, apply **Bold**, and then change the **Font Color** to **Green, Accent 6, Darker 25%**. **Center** the two paragraphs. Select the fourth paragraph, and apply **Bold** and **Underline**.

Mrs.	Kelley	Bondurant	Centerville	VA
Mr.	Walter	Perry	Conyers	SC
Mr. and Mrs.	Taylor	Dunham	Lima	OH
Mr. and Mrs.	Jacqui	Epps	Marietta	GA
Ms.	Jessica	Flynn	Smyrna	MD

‹- -► (Return to Step 9)

(Project 8F Cruise Ships continues on the next page)

12 Save the document to your **Word Chapter 8** folder as **Lastname_Firstname_8F_Cruise_Roster** and then insert the file name in the footer. Add document properties that include your course name and section number, the tags **customers, roster** and display your name as the author. Save your document, and then close the document. Close Word without saving the main document.

13 Print your three documents—it is not necessary to print the data sources—or submit all five files electronically as directed by your instructor.

END | You have completed Project 8F

CONTENT-BASED ASSESSMENTS

Apply 8A and 8B skills from these Objectives:

1 Merge a Data Source and a Main Document
2 Use Mail Merge to Create Envelopes
3 Edit and Sort a Data Source
4 Match Fields and Apply Rules
5 Create a Data Source and a Directory

Build from Scratch

In the following Mastering Word project, you will create a letter to solicit entertainers for next year's Caribbean Customized cruises. You will filter the data source, match fields, and insert merge fields to modify the form letter. Your completed documents will look similar to the ones shown in Figure 8.46.

PROJECT FILES

For Project 8G, you will need the following files:

Two new blank Word documents
w08G_Entertainers
w08G_Entertainers_Letter

You will save your files as:

Lastname_Firstname_8G_Entertainers_Main
Lastname_Firstname_8G_Entertainers_Merged
Lastname_Firstname_8G_EntertainersEnv_Main
Lastname_Firstname_8G_EntertainersEnv_Merged
Lastname_Firstname_8G_Entertainers_Directory
Lastname_Firstname_8G_Entertainers—not shown in figure

PROJECT RESULTS

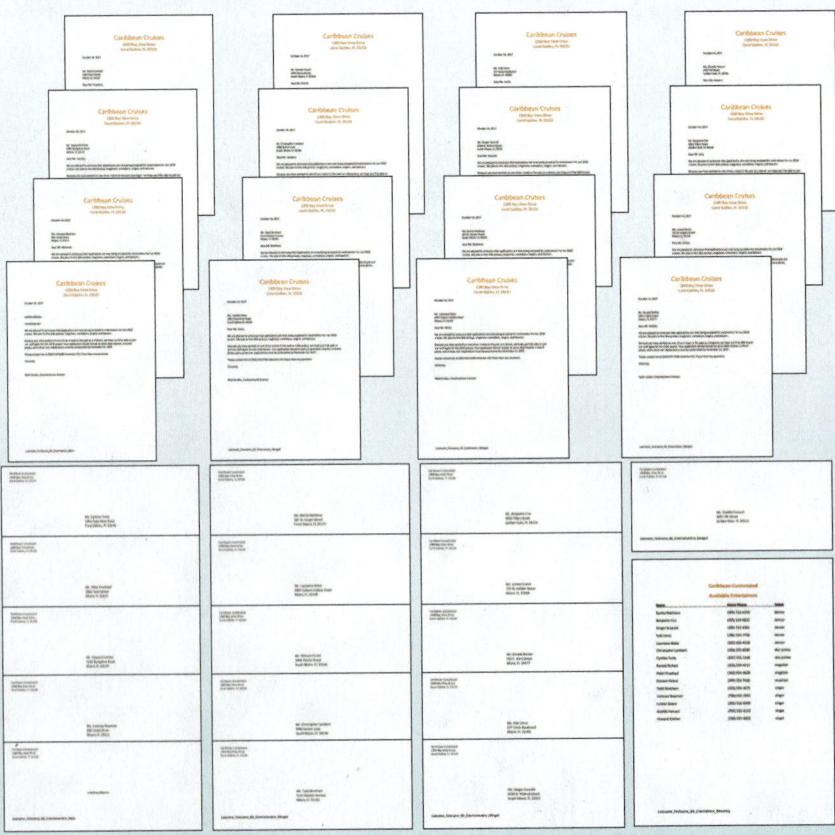

FIGURE 8.46

(Project 8G Entertainers continues on the next page)

CONTENT-BASED ASSESSMENTS

Mastering Word   Project 8G Entertainers (continued)

1 Start Excel. Navigate to your student files, and open the file **w08G_Entertainers**. Save the file to your **Word Chapter 8** folder as **Lastname_Firstname_8G_ Entertainers** Close Excel. Start Word. Navigate to your student files, and open the file **w08G_Entertainers_Letter**. Save the document to your **Word Chapter 8** folder as **Lastname_Firstname_8G_Entertainers_Main** If necessary, display the rulers and formatting marks.

2 Click **Start Mail Merge**, and select **Letters**. As the data source, from your **Word Chapter 8** folder, select the file **Lastname_Firstname_8G_Entertainers**, and then select **'Entertainer Information$'**. Edit the data source by changing the **Postal Code** for *Howard Fulcher* to **33114** Sort the data source to display the **Postal Code** field in ascending order.

3 Select the first paragraph, change the **Font Size** to **28**, and then change the **Font Color** to **Orange, Accent 2**. Select the second and third paragraphs, change the **Font Size** to **16**, and change the **Font Color** to **Orange, Accent 2, Darker 25%**. Center the first three paragraphs.

4 Position the insertion point in the blank paragraph following the date, and press Enter three times. Insert the **Address Block** merge field, matching the field **Street** with the **Address 1** field. Press Enter two times, insert the **Greeting Line** merge field, and then press Enter. Locate the paragraph that begins *Because you have*, and then position the insertion point to the right of *past*, before the comma. Press Spacebar, type **as a** and then press Spacebar. Insert the **Talent** merge field.

5 Finish the merge to **Edit Individual Documents**. Save the document in your **Word Chapter 8** folder as **Lastname_Firstname_8G_Entertainers_Merged** and then insert the file name in the footer. Add document properties that include your course name and section number, the tags **entertainers, letter, merged** and display your name as the author. Save your changes, and then close the document.

6 In the main document, insert the file name in the footer. Add document properties that include your course name and section number, the tags **entertainers, letter, main** and display your name as the author. Save your document, and then close the document, but leave Word open.

7 In a new document, click **Start Mail Merge**, select **Envelopes**, and then select **Size 10 (4 1/8 × 9 1/2 in)**. Save the document to your **Word Chapter 8** folder as **Lastname_Firstname_8G_EntertainersEnv_Main** As the data source, from your **Word Chapter 8** folder, select the file **Lastname_Firstname_8G_Entertainers**. Sort the data source to display the **Postal Code** field in ascending order. In the center of the document, insert the **Address Block** merge field, matching the field **Street** with the **Address 1** field. Press Ctrl + Home, and then using three lines, type the return address:

Caribbean Customized

1300 Bay View Drive

Coral Gables, FL 33124

8 Finish the merge to **Edit Individual Documents**. Save the document to your **Word Chapter 8** folder as **Lastname_Firstname_8G_EntertainersEnv_Merged** and then insert the file name in the footer. Add document properties that include your course name and section number, the tags **entertainers, envelope, merged** and display your name as the author. Save your changes, and then close the document.

9 In the main document, insert the file name in the footer. Add document properties that include your course name and section number, the tags **entertainers, envelope, main** and display your name as the author. Save your document. close the document without closing Word.

10 In a new document click **Start Mail Merge**, and select **Directory**. Select the file **Lastname_Firstname_8G_ Entertainers** as the data source. Sort the data source to display the **Talent** field in ascending order.

11 On the horizontal ruler, set left tabs at the **3-inch mark** and the **5-inch mark**. Insert the **First Name** merge field, press Spacebar, and then insert the **Last Name** merge field. Press Tab, insert the **Home Phone** merge field, press Tab, and then insert the **Talent** merge field. Press Enter. Finish the merge to **Edit Individual Documents**.

12 Press Ctrl + Home, press Enter, and then press ↑. Type **Caribbean Customized** Press Enter, type **Available Entertainers** and then press Enter. Type **Name** press Tab, type **Home Phone** press Tab, and then type **Talent** Select the first two paragraphs, change the **Font Size** to **16**, apply **Bold** and then change the **Font Color** to **Orange, Accent 2, Darker 25%**. Center the paragraphs. Select the third paragraph, and apply **Bold** and **Underline**.

(Project 8G Entertainers continues on the next page)

CONTENT-BASED ASSESSMENTS

13 Save the document to your **Word Chapter 8** folder as **Lastname_Firstname_8G_Entertainers_Directory** and then insert the file name in the footer. Add document properties that include your course name and section number, the tags **entertainers, directory, merged** and display your name as the author. Save your changes, and then close the document. Close Word without saving the main document.

14 Print all five documents—it is not necessary to print the data source—or submit all six files electronically as directed by your instructor.

END | You have completed Project 8G

CONTENT-BASED ASSESSMENTS

GO! Fix It	Project 8H Marketing Plan	Online
GO! Make It	Project 8I Business Cards	Online
GO! Solve It	Project 8J Planning Session	Online
GO! Solve It	Project 8K Shipping Information	

Build from
Scratch

Apply a combination of the
8A and **8B** skills.

Build from
Scratch

PROJECT FILES

For Project 8K, you will need the following files:

Two new blank Word documents
w08K_Shipping_Information

You will save your files as:

Lastname_Firstname_8K_Shipping_Information
Lastname_Firstname_8K_Shipping_Main
Lastname_Firstname_8K_Shipping_Merged
Lastname_Firstname_8K_Southern_Directory

From your student files, open the file **w08K_Shipping_Information**. Save it to your **Word Chapter 8** folder as **Lastname_Firstname_8K_Shipping_Information** Using mail merge, select a label option for a mailing label with a height of 2" and a width of 4". Save the document to your **Word Chapter 8** folder as **Lastname_Firstname_8K_Shipping_Main** Use **Lastname_Firstname_8K_Shipping_Information** as the data source, sort the data by Postal Code, and apply a filter to display only individuals on the Southern cruise. Include the Address Block merge field—match fields as necessary—and the Cruise merge field and any related text on the label. Format the document. Save the merged document to your **Word Chapter 8** folder as **Lastname_Firstname_8K_Shipping_Merged** Save the main document. Create a directory that includes the name, city, state, and phone numbers for all individuals on the Southern cruise. Add appropriate text and format the document to create a professional appearance. Save the merged directory to your **Word Chapter 8** folder as **Lastname_Firstname_8K_Southern_Directory** Insert the file name in the footer. For all saved files, add appropriate document properties. Print your three documents or submit all four files electronically as directed by your instructor.

(Project 8K Shipping Information continues on the next page)

CONTENT-BASED ASSESSMENTS

Performance Level

Performance Criteria	Performance Element	Exemplary: You consistently applied the relevant skills	Proficient: You sometimes, but not always, applied the relevant skills	Developing: You rarely or never applied the relevant skills
	Select a mailing label	A mailing label template is used and the labels are the correct size.	A mailing label template is used, but the labels are not the correct size.	No label template is used.
	Sort and filter the data source	The data source is sorted and filtered.	The data source is not sorted or it is not filtered.	The data source is neither sorted nor filtered.
	Match fields in the Address Block	All fields are matched and display correctly in the Address Block.	Some fields are not matched and do not display in the Address Block.	No fields are matched.
	Insert text and merge fields in labels	Text and merge fields are inserted and formatted appropriately.	At least one item is not inserted or is not formatted appropriately.	No items are inserted or formatted appropriately.
	Create a directory	All text and merge fields are inserted and formatted appropriately.	At least one item is not inserted or is not formatted appropriately.	No items are inserted or formatted appropriately.

END | You have completed Project 8K

OUTCOMES-BASED ASSESSMENTS

RUBRIC

The following outcomes-based assessments are *open-ended assessments*. That is, there is no specific correct result; your result will depend on your approach to the information provided. Make *Professional Quality* your goal. Use the following scoring rubric to guide you in *how* to approach the problem and then to evaluate *how well* your approach solves the problem.

The *criteria*—Software Mastery, Content, Format and Layout, and Process—represent the knowledge and skills you have gained that you can apply to solving the problem. The *levels of performance*—Professional Quality, Approaching Professional Quality, or Needs Quality Improvements—help you and your instructor evaluate your result.

	Your completed project is of Professional Quality if you:	Your completed project is Approaching Professional Quality if you:	Your completed project Needs Quality Improvements if you:
1-Software Mastery	Choose and apply the most appropriate skills, tools, and features and identify efficient methods to solve the problem.	Choose and apply some appropriate skills, tools, and features, but not in the most efficient manner.	Choose inappropriate skills, tools, or features, or are inefficient in solving the problem.
2-Content	Construct a solution that is clear and well organized, contains content that is accurate, appropriate to the audience and purpose, and is complete. Provide a solution that contains no errors in spelling, grammar, or style.	Construct a solution in which some components are unclear, poorly organized, inconsistent, or incomplete. Misjudge the needs of the audience. Have some errors in spelling, grammar, or style, but the errors do not detract from comprehension.	Construct a solution that is unclear, incomplete, or poorly organized; contains some inaccurate or inappropriate content; and contains many errors in spelling, grammar, or style. Do not solve the problem.
3-Format & Layout	Format and arrange all elements to communicate information and ideas, clarify function, illustrate relationships, and indicate relative importance.	Apply appropriate format and layout features to some elements, but not others. Overuse features, causing minor distraction.	Apply format and layout that does not communicate information or ideas clearly. Do not use format and layout features to clarify function, illustrate relationships, or indicate relative importance. Use available features excessively, causing distraction.
4-Process	Use an organized approach that integrates planning, development, self-assessment, revision, and reflection.	Demonstrate an organized approach in some areas, but not others; or, use an insufficient process of organization throughout.	Do not use an organized approach to solve the problem.

OUTCOMES-BASED ASSESSMENTS

Apply a combination of the **8A** and **8B** skills.

Build from
Scratch

GO! Think   Project 8L Health Insurance

PROJECT FILES

For Project 8L, you will need the following file:

New blank Word document

You will save your files as:

Lastname_Firstname_8L_Insurance_Main
Lastname_Firstname_8L_Insurance_Data
Lastname_Firstname_8L_Insurance_Merged

Caribbean Customized is changing to a new health insurance provider—MediCertain—at the beginning of the year. MediCertain offers more coverage at a lower rate and a variety of plans for employees. James Vaughn, Human Resources Manager, is conducting information sessions for employees during November in Conference Room D at 9:30 a.m. The Administrative department will meet on November 1; all other departments will meet on November 3. The enrollment period begins November 10 and ends November 30.

Create a memo to department managers, from Mr. Vaughn, informing them of the new provider and the scheduled time for the department's information session. Save the main document as **Lastname_Firstname_8L_Insurance_Main** Create a data source that includes the name of each department and department manager; you should include at least five departments, including the Administrative department. Save the data source as **Lastname_Firstname_8L_Insurance_Data** Insert appropriate merge fields in the memo, and create a rule to display the date of the session based on department. Format the memo in a professional manner. Save the merged document as **Lastname_Firstname_8L_Insurance_Merged** For each document you save, insert the file name in the footer and add appropriate document properties. Print your documents or submit all three files electronically as directed by your instructor.

> **END | You have completed Project 8L**

Build from
Scratch

GO! Think   Project 8M Training Sessions   Online

You and GO!   Project 8N Graduation Invitation   Online

Build from
Scratch

Creating Standardized Forms and Managing Documents

GO! to Work
Video W9

OBJECTIVES

1. Create a Customized Form
2. Modify and Lock a Form
3. Use a Template to Complete a Form

PROJECT 9B	OUTCOMES
	Format illustrations, insert signature lines, and add protection to documents.

OBJECTIVES

4. Customize the Ribbon
5. Format Pictures and Text Boxes
6. Add a Digital Signature to a Document
7. Prepare a Document for Distribution

In This Chapter

A form is a structured document that includes fields—such as check boxes—that assist the user with entering information. A form can be saved as a template, protected from unauthorized changes, and then made available to others for completion in Word. You can also customize the ribbon to improve productivity. Using advanced graphic features—for example, stacking and grouping—you can enhance the appearance of a document. When a document that requires a signature is sent electronically, the recipient can digitally sign the file. Removing document properties and personal information prepares a document for distribution.

The projects in this chapter relate to **Myristicanna Spices**. After ten years as an Executive Chef, Anna Carter started her own business in Tampa, Florida. The company sells quality products in retail stores and online for cooking, eating, and entertaining. In addition to fresh and dried herbs and spices, Myristicanna Spices offers a wide variety of condiments, confections, jams, sauces, oils, and vinegars. Later this year, Chef Carter will add a line of tools, cookbooks, and gift baskets. The company name is a combination of Anna's first name and the name of an order of plants related to nutmeg.

PROJECT ACTIVITIES

In Activities 9.01 through 9.14, you will create a form that will be used to measure customer satisfaction. Juan Morales, Marketing Vice President, wants to get feedback from customers regarding the quality of products and services offered by Myristicanna Spices. You will customize the form and save it as a template so that it can be completed by individual users. To test the form prior to distribution, you will enter customer information in the survey form. Your completed documents will look similar to Figure 9.1.

PROJECT FILES

Build from Scratch

For Project 9A, you will need the following files:

New blank Word document
w09A_Customer_Survey

You will save your files as:

Lastname_Firstname_9A_Survey_Template
Lastname_Firstname_9A_Survey_Completed

PROJECT RESULTS

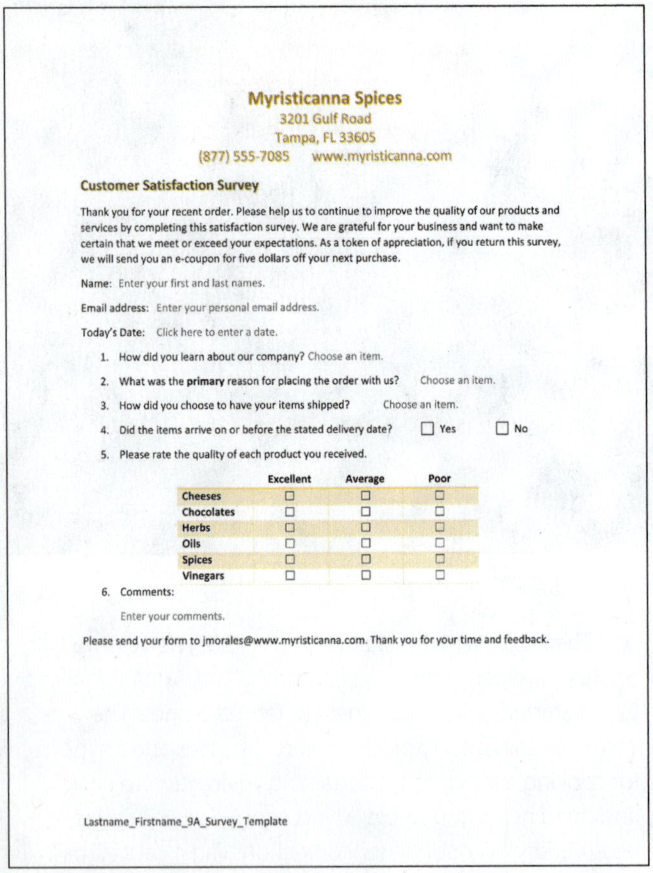

Myristicanna Spices
3201 Gulf Road
Tampa, FL 33605
(877) 555-7085   www.myristicanna.com

Customer Satisfaction Survey

Thank you for your recent order. Please help us to continue to improve the quality of our products and services by completing this satisfaction survey. We are grateful for your business and want to make certain that we meet or exceed your expectations. As a token of appreciation, if you return this survey, we will send you an e-coupon for five dollars off your next purchase.

Name: Enter your first and last names.

Email address: Enter your personal email address.

Today's Date: Click here to enter a date.

1. How did you learn about our company? Choose an item.
2. What was the **primary** reason for placing the order with us?   Choose an item.
3. How did you choose to have your items shipped?   Choose an item.
4. Did the items arrive on or before the stated delivery date?   ☐ Yes   ☐ No
5. Please rate the quality of each product you received.

	Excellent	Average	Poor
Cheeses	☐	☐	☐
Chocolates	☐	☐	☐
Herbs	☐	☐	☐
Oils	☐	☐	☐
Spices	☐	☐	☐
Vinegars	☐	☐	☐

6. Comments:

Enter your comments.

Please send your form to jmorales@www.myristicanna.com. Thank you for your time and feedback.

Lastname_Firstname_9A_Survey_Template

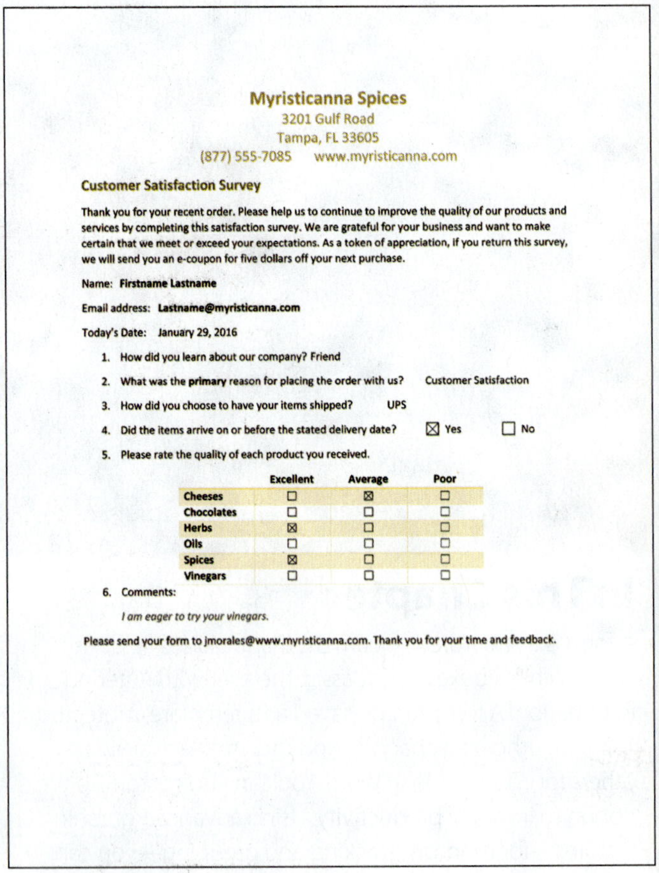

Myristicanna Spices
3201 Gulf Road
Tampa, FL 33605
(877) 555-7085   www.myristicanna.com

Customer Satisfaction Survey

Thank you for your recent order. Please help us to continue to improve the quality of our products and services by completing this satisfaction survey. We are grateful for your business and want to make certain that we meet or exceed your expectations. As a token of appreciation, if you return this survey, we will send you an e-coupon for five dollars off your next purchase.

Name: Firstname Lastname

Email address: Lastname@myristicanna.com

Today's Date: January 29, 2016

1. How did you learn about our company? Friend
2. What was the **primary** reason for placing the order with us?   Customer Satisfaction
3. How did you choose to have your items shipped?   UPS
4. Did the items arrive on or before the stated delivery date?   ☒ Yes   ☐ No
5. Please rate the quality of each product you received.

	Excellent	Average	Poor
Cheeses	☐	☒	☐
Chocolates	☐	☐	☐
Herbs	☒	☐	☐
Oils	☐	☐	☐
Spices	☒	☐	☐
Vinegars	☐	☐	☐

6. Comments:

I am eager to try your vinegars.

Please send your form to jmorales@www.myristicanna.com. Thank you for your time and feedback.

FIGURE 9.1 Project 9A Survey Form

Objective 1 Create a Customized Form

Video W9-1

A *form* is a structured document that has *static text*—descriptive text such as headings and labels—and reserved spaces, or *content controls*, for information to be entered by the user. A content control is a data entry field in a form in which a particular type of information, such as a name or date, is supplied by the user. For example, you can create a survey form that provides a place for the user to enter text or choose a specific entry from a list. You can also protect the form to restrict changes made by a user.

Activity 9.01 | Saving the Form as a Template

A form is usually stored as a *template* so that it can be used repeatedly without changing the original document. A template is a predefined structure that contains basic document settings, such as fonts, margins, and available styles, and can also store elements such as building blocks and content controls. Recall that Microsoft Office provides built-in templates; however, in this activity, you will create your own document template.

1 Start Word. Open a new blank document, and then press F12. In the **Save As** dialog box, click the **Save as type arrow**, and then click **Word Template**. Navigate to the location where you are saving the files for this chapter, and then create a new folder named **Word Chapter 9** Using your own name for the file name, type **Lastname_Firstname_9A_Survey_Template** and then compare your screen with Figure 9.2.

Because you will submit your file to your instructor, and others do not require access to it, you will save the template in your Word Chapter 9 folder instead of the default Templates folder. Document templates are saved with a .dotx file extension.

FIGURE 9.2

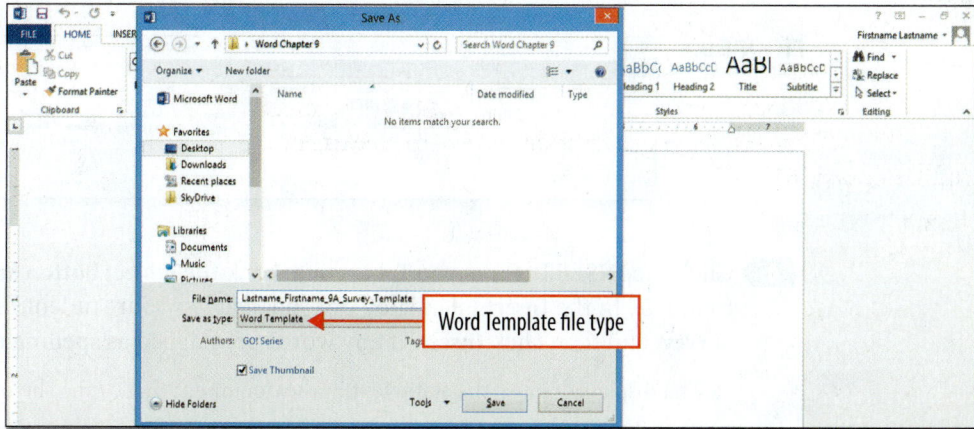

Word Template file type

2 Click **Save**. If necessary, display the rulers and formatting marks.

Activity 9.02 | Displaying the DEVELOPER Tab

Content controls are inserted in forms that will be filled in electronically. Content controls are accessed from the DEVELOPER tab; and by default, the DEVELOPER tab does not display on the ribbon.

1 Click the **FILE tab**, and then click **Options**. In the **Word Options** dialog box, click **Customize Ribbon**.

2 In the **Main Tabs** list, locate and then click to select the **Developer** check box. Compare your screen with Figure 9.3.

Main tabs that display on the ribbon are indicated with a check mark.

FIGURE 9.3

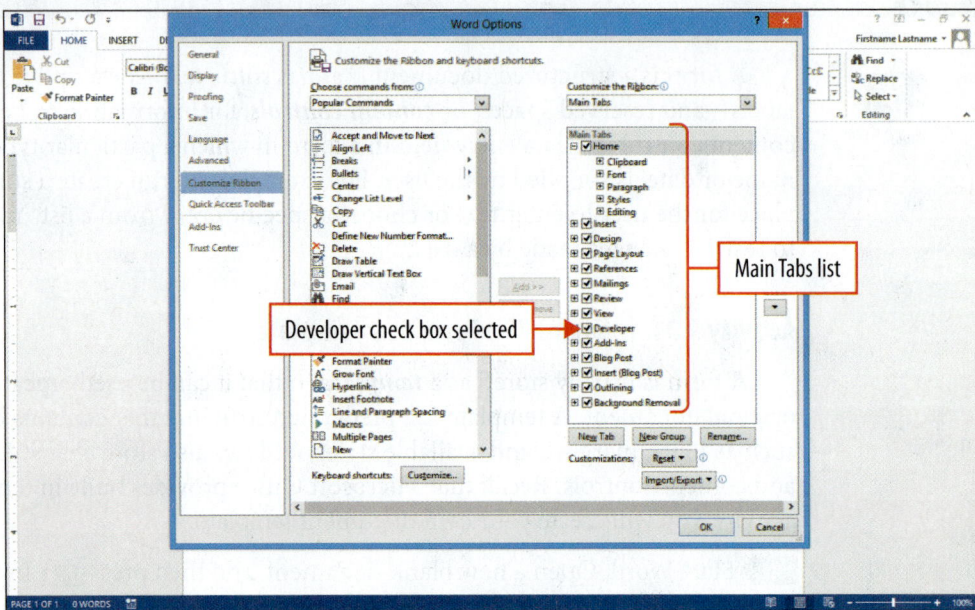

3 Click **OK** to close the **Word Options** dialog box. On the ribbon, locate and then click the **DEVELOPER tab**. Compare your screen with Figure 9.4.

The DEVELOPER tab enables you to extend the capabilities of Word. For example, a form can be created, and then distributed and completed by users. Content controls can be integrated with other applications to store the information that users have entered in the completed form. Content control commands are located in the Controls group.

FIGURE 9.4

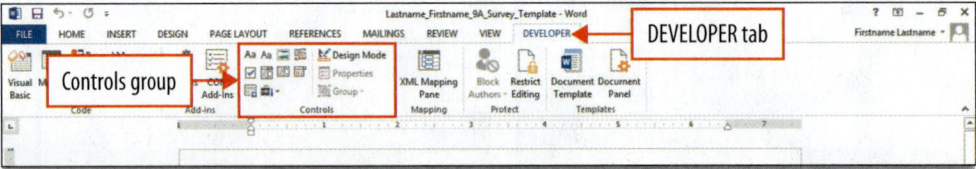

4 Click the **INSERT tab**, in the **Text group**, click the **Object button arrow**, and then click **Text from File**. In the **Insert File** dialog box, navigate to your student files, click **w09A_Customer_Survey**, and then click **Insert**. If any words are flagged as spelling errors, click **Ignore All**.

The displayed text is the static text in the document that cannot be modified when the form is filled in by a user.

5 Select the first three paragraphs of the document, click the **HOME tab**, and then in the **Styles group**, click **No Spacing**.

6 Select the first paragraph of the document. On the mini toolbar, change the **Font Size** [11 ▾] to **18**, apply **Bold** [B], click the **Font Color button arrow** [A ▾], and then in the eighth column, click the fifth color—**Gold, Accent 4, Darker 25%**. Press [Ctrl] + [E].

7 Select the next three paragraphs. On the mini toolbar, change the **Font Size** [11 ▾] to **14**, and then click **Font Color** [A ▾]. Press [Ctrl] + [E].

8 Select the fifth paragraph. On the mini toolbar, change the **Font Size** [11 ▾] to **14**, apply **Bold** [B], click the **Font Color button arrow** [A ▾], and then in the eighth column, click the last color—**Gold, Accent 4, Darker 50%**. **Save** [💾] your changes.

Activity 9.03 │ Inserting a Plain Text Content Control

The *Plain Text content control* inserts a field in the form that enables the user to insert *unformatted text*—plain text—in the document. You will add several Plain Text content controls to the form so that the user can provide personal information and comments.

1 Locate the paragraph *Name*, and then scroll as necessary so that the paragraph displays near the top of your screen. Click to position the insertion point to the right of *Name*—after the colon, and then press [Tab].

2 Click the **DEVELOPER tab**, in the **Controls group**, click **Design Mode**.

Turning on *Design Mode* enables you to edit content controls that are inserted in a document.

3 In the **Controls group**, click **Plain Text content control** [Aa]. At the insertion point, notice that a field with the default text *Click here to enter text.* displays. Compare your screen with Figure 9.5.

The default text is used as a placeholder so that the person filling in the form knows what to do.

FIGURE 9.5

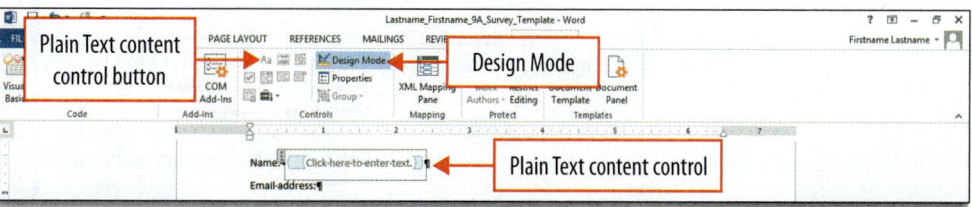

4 Locate the paragraph *Email address*. Click to position the insertion point to the right of the colon, press [Tab], and then in the **Controls group**, click **Plain Text content control** [Aa].

5 Press [Ctrl]+[End] to move to the end of the document. Delete the blank paragraph at the end of the document, and then click to position the insertion point in the blank paragraph above the last paragraph that begins *Please send*.

6 Press [Tab] two times, and then in the **Controls group**, click **Plain Text content control** [Aa]. Click in a blank area of the document to deselect the content control, and then compare your screen with Figure 9.6.

FIGURE 9.6

7 **Save** [💾] your changes.

Activity 9.04 | Inserting a Date Picker Content Control

The *Date Picker content control* allows the user to select a date from a calendar. In this activity, you will insert the Date Picker content control and then specify the format for displaying the date.

1 ▶ Locate the paragraph *Today's Date*. Click to position the insertion point to the right of the colon, and then press Tab.

2 ▶ On the **DEVELOPER tab**, in the **Controls group**, click the **Date Picker content control** button. Notice that the default text *Click here to enter a date.* displays in the content control.

3 ▶ With the **Date Picker content control** selected, in the **Controls group**, click **Properties**. In the **Content Control Properties** dialog box, under **Date Picker Properties**, in the **Display the date like this** box, click the third style—your date will differ. Compare your screen with Figure 9.7.

The Content Control Properties dialog box is used to modify settings for a content control—in this case, the date format MMMM d, yyyy. The date selected by a user will display in the format you specify.

FIGURE 9.7

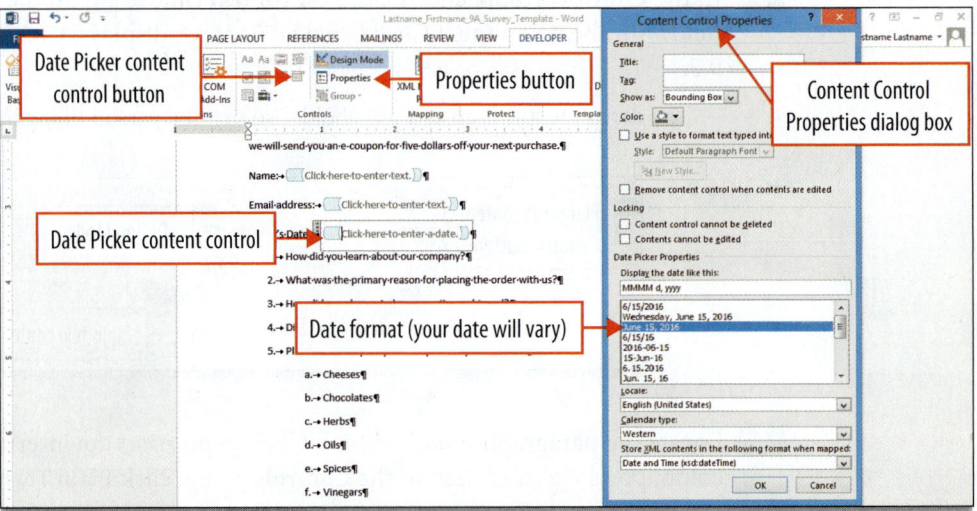

4 ▶ Click **OK** to close the **Content Control Properties** dialog box, and then **Save** your changes.

Activity 9.05 | Inserting a Drop-Down List Content Control

The *Drop-Down List content control* allows the user to select a specific item from a list, created by the designer of the form. By providing a list, you limit the choices for the user and ensure acceptable responses. You will use the Drop-Down List content control to solicit information regarding company awareness and shipping options.

1 ▶ Locate the paragraph that begins *1. How did you learn*. Click to position the insertion point to the right of the question mark, and then press Tab.

2 ▶ In the **Controls group**, click **Drop-Down List content control**. With the **Drop-Down List content control** selected, in the **Controls group**, click **Properties**.

3 In the **Content Control Properties** dialog box, under **Drop-Down List Properties**, click **Add**. In the **Add Choice** dialog box, in the **Display Name** box, type **Internet** Notice that as you type, the text in the **Value** box changes to match what you type in the *Display Name* box. Compare your screen with Figure 9.8.

The Add button enables you to specify the items that will be included in the Drop-Down List content control. Each item in the list is identified by a name and a value. The display name is the text that will display to users when they view the list.

FIGURE 9.8

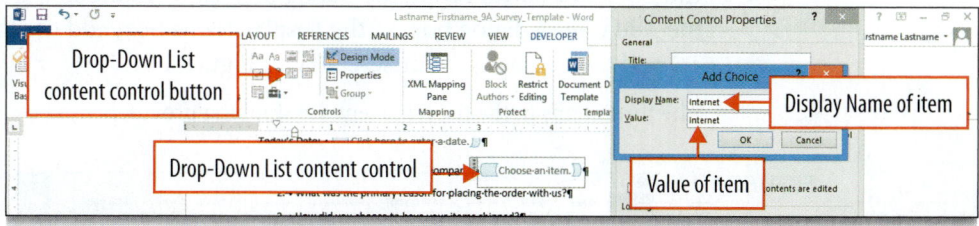

4 Click **OK**. In the **Content Control Properties** dialog box, click **Add**. In the **Add Choice** dialog box, in the **Display Name** box, type **Magazine** and then click **OK**.

5 Using the technique you just practiced, **Add** the choices **Television** and **Friend**

6 In the **Content Control Properties** dialog box, under **Drop-Down List Properties**, click **Friend**, and then click **Move Up** three times. Compare your screen with Figure 9.9.

It is helpful for the user if the items in the list are in alphabetical order. You can use the Move Up and Move Down buttons to modify the order of the items.

FIGURE 9.9

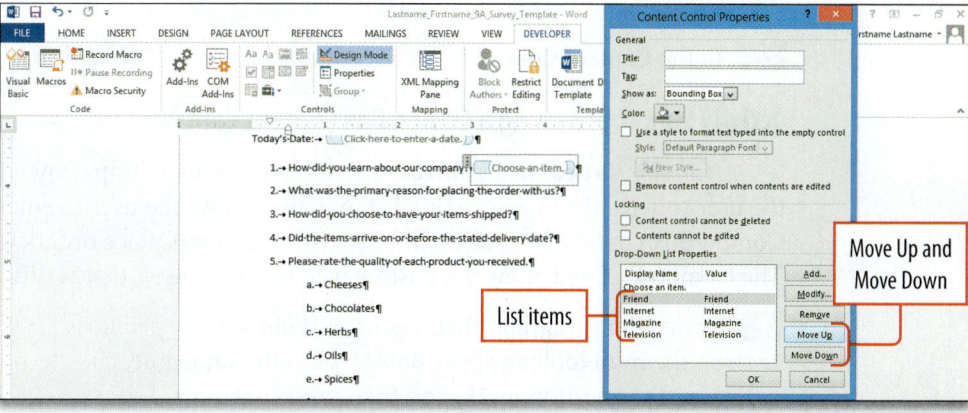

7 Click **OK**, and then on the **DEVELOPER tab**, in the **Controls group**, click **Design Mode** to turn off **Design Mode**. In the inserted **Drop-Down List content control**, click the **Drop-Down List arrow**, and then compare your screen with Figure 9.10.

The listed items are the various ways that a customer might have learned about the company. When Design Mode is turned off, you can view the document as it will be seen by the person filling in the form. The phrase *Choose an item.* displays by default.

FIGURE 9.10

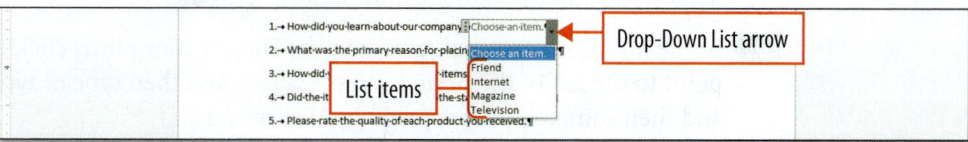

8 ▸ Click in an empty area of the document to deselect the **Drop-Down List content control**. On the **DEVELOPER tab**, in the **Controls group**, click **Design Mode** to turn on **Design Mode**.

9 ▸ Locate the paragraph that begins *3. How did you choose*. Click to position the insertion point to the right of the question mark, and then press Tab.

10 ▸ In the **Controls group**, click **Drop-Down List content control** ▣, and then in the **Controls group**, click **Properties**.

11 ▸ In the **Content Control Properties** dialog box, click **Add**. Using the technique you practiced, in the **Add Choice** dialog box, in the **Display Name** box, add the three terms **FedEx UPS** and **USPS** and then compare your screen with Figure 9.11.

The three items in the list represent the shipping providers used by Myristicanna Spices.

FIGURE 9.11

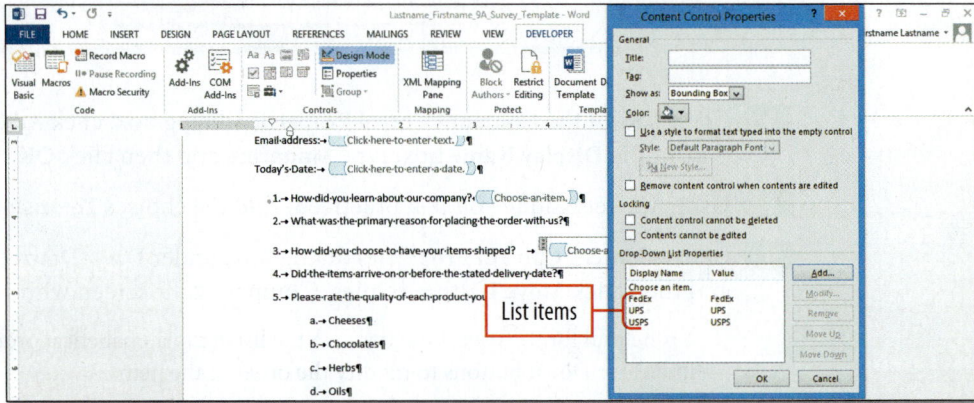

12 ▸ In the **Content Control Properties** dialog box, click **OK**, and then **Save** 🖫 your changes.

Activity 9.06 | Inserting a Combo Box Content Control

A **Combo Box content control**, which is similar to a Drop-Down List content control, allows the user to select from an existing list, but also allows the user to enter new text. You will add a Combo Box content control to find out why customers place orders with Myristicanna Spices. The Combo Box will allow the customer to enter a reason that is different from the listed items.

1 ▸ Locate the paragraph that begins *2. What was the primary*. Select the word **primary**, and then on the mini toolbar, apply **Bold** B . On the same line, click to position the insertion point after the question mark, and then press Tab.

2 ▸ On the **DEVELOPER tab**, in the **Controls group**, click **Combo Box content control** ▣, and then in the **Controls group**, click **Properties**.

3 ▸ In the **Content Control Properties** dialog box, under **Drop-Down List Properties**, click **Add**. In the **Add Choice** dialog box, in the **Display Name** box, type **Price** and then click **OK**.

4 ▸ In a similar manner, **Add** the choices **Quality** and **Selection**

5 ▸ In the **Content Control Properties** dialog box, under **Drop-Down List Properties**, click the default text *Choose an item.* and then click **Modify**.

6 ▸ In the **Modify Choice** dialog box, in the **Display Name** box, click to position the insertion point to the left of the period, press Spacebar, and then type **or type another reason** Click **OK**, and then compare your screen with Figure 9.12.

Recall that a Combo Box content control allows the user to insert new text. In this case, you want to provide the customer with the option to enter a reason—that is not already listed—for choosing Myristicanna Spices.

FIGURE 9.12

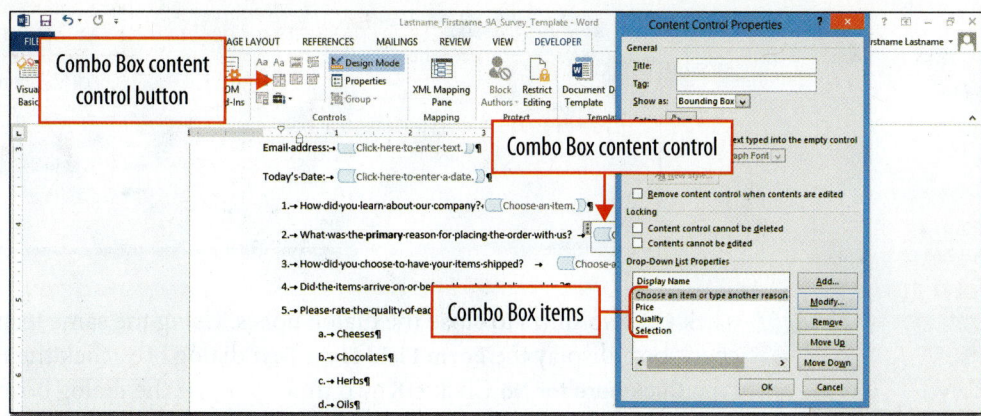

7 ▶ In the **Content Control Properties** dialog box, click **OK**, and then **Save** 🔲 your changes.

Activity 9.07 │ Inserting and Modifying a Check Box Form Field

A **Check Box form field** is a legacy control that allows the user to select, or not select, a specific option. **Legacy controls** are fields used in designing a form for persons who possess older versions of Word. For purposes of this instruction, you are adding content controls and legacy controls in the same form. In this activity, you will add two check box form fields and then modify their properties.

1 ▶ Locate the paragraph that begins *4. Did the items arrive.* Click to position the insertion point to the right of the question mark, and then press Tab.

2 ▶ On the **DEVELOPER tab**, in the **Controls group**, click **Legacy Tools** 🖼, and then under **Legacy Forms**, point to **Check Box Form Field** ☑. Compare your screen with Figure 9.13.

FIGURE 9.13

3 ▶ Click **Check Box Form Field** ☑. With the insertion point to the right of the inserted check box, press Spacebar two times, and then type **Yes**

4 ▶ With the insertion point to the right of *Yes*, press Tab two times. In the **Controls group**, click **Legacy Tools** 🖼, and then under **Legacy Forms**, click **Check Box Form Field** ☑. With the insertion point to the right of the check box, press Spacebar two times, and then type **No**

A check box can be selected or deselected when the person using the form clicks the field.

5 ▶ Click the first check box, and then in the **Controls group**, click **Properties**. In the **Check Box Form Field Options** dialog box, at the bottom left, click **Add Help Text**.

6 ▶ In the **Form Field Help Text** dialog box, click the **Help Key (F1) tab**, click in the **Type your own** box, and then type **Click here for Yes** Compare your screen with Figure 9.14.

As the user completes the form, the text for the check box form field will display in a Help message box when the F1 key is pressed.

FIGURE 9.14

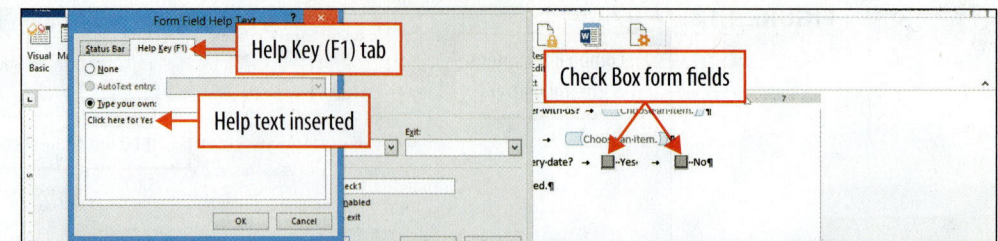

7 ▸ Click **OK** two times to close the dialog boxes. Using the same technique, select the second check box, display the **Form Field Help Text** dialog box, click the **Help Key (F1) tab**, and then type **Click here for No** Click **OK** two times to close the dialog boxes. Save 🔲 your changes.

Deleting Form Fields and Content Controls

To delete a form field or content control, select the field you want to remove, and then press Delete.

Activity 9.08 | Converting Text to a Table

1 ▸ Select the six paragraphs formatted with lowercase letters—beginning with *a. Cheeses* and ending with *f. Vinegars*. Click the **HOME tab**, in the **Paragraph group**, click **Numbering** 📋 ▾ to turn off the numbered format. Click the **INSERT tab**, in the **Tables group**, click **Table**, and then click **Convert Text to Table**.

2 ▸ In the **Convert Text to Table** dialog box, under **Separate text at**, be sure the **Paragraphs** option button is selected. Click **OK**, and then compare your screen with Figure 9.15.

Recall that a table can be used to display information in an organized manner.

FIGURE 9.15

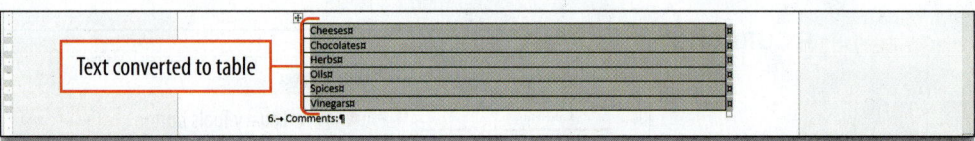

3 ▸ In the first cell of the table, click to position the insertion point to the right of *Cheeses*. Point slightly above the top right corner of the cell, and then click the **One-Click Row/Column Insertion** button ⊕ three times to insert three additional table columns.

4 ▸ Click in the first cell of the table, and then under **TABLE TOOLS**, click the **LAYOUT tab**, in the **Rows & Columns group**, click **Insert Above** to insert a new row at the top of the table.

5 ▸ In the first row of the table, click to position the insertion point in the second cell. Type **Excellent** press ⟨Tab⟩, type **Average** press ⟨Tab⟩, and then type **Poor**

6 ▸ Under **TABLE TOOLS**, click the **DESIGN tab**, in the **Table Styles group**, click **More** ▾. In the **Table Styles** gallery, under **Grid Tables**, in the second row, click the fifth style—**Grid Table 2 – Accent 4**. If necessary, on the LAYOUT tab, in the Table group, select the View Gridlines check box.

7 ▸ Slightly outside the upper left corner of the table, point to the table move handle ⊞. With the ⟨🖞⟩ pointer, click one time to select the entire table. On the **LAYOUT tab**, in the **Cell Size group**, in the **Height** box, type **0.2** In the **Cell Size group**, in the **Width** box, type **1** and then press ⟨Enter⟩.

8 ▶ On the **LAYOUT tab**, in the **Table group**, click **Properties**. In the **Table Properties** dialog box, on the **Table tab**, under **Alignment**, click **Center**. Click **OK**, deselect the table, and then compare your screen with Figure 9.16.

FIGURE 9.16

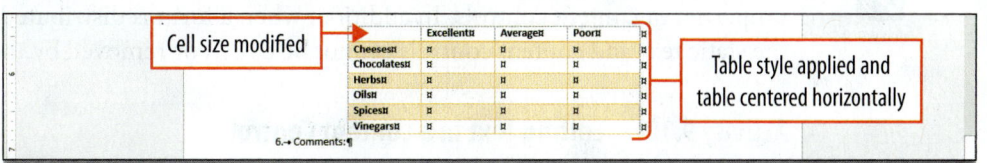

9 ▶ Save 🖫 your changes.

Activity 9.09 │ Inserting a Check Box Content Control

A *Check Box content control* is a field that allows the user to select, or not select, a specific option. In this activity, you will add several check boxes to the form.

1 ▶ In the second row of the table, click to position the insertion point in the second cell. Click the **DEVELOPER tab**, in the **Controls group**, click **Check Box content control** ☑. Compare your screen with Figure 9.17

FIGURE 9.17

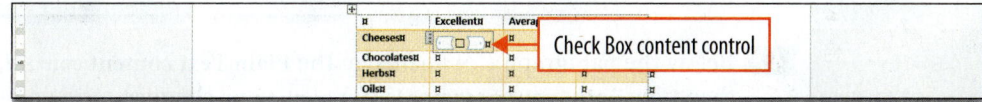

2 ▶ In the current cell, with the insertion point to the left of the check box, on the content control, click **Select Field** ⊞ to select the **Check Box content control**. Right-click the selection, and then click **Copy**. In the second row, click in the third cell, and then press Ctrl+V to paste the **Check Box content control** in the cell. Press Tab, and then press Ctrl+V to paste the **Check Box content control**.

You can copy and paste content controls in the same manner as text and graphics.

3 ▶ In a similar manner, paste the **Check Box content control** in the remaining empty cells of the table.

4 ▶ Select the second, third, and fourth columns of the table. On the **LAYOUT tab**, in the **Alignment group**, click **Align Center** ▤. Press Ctrl + End, and then compare your screen with Figure 9.18. **Save** 🖫 your changes.

FIGURE 9.18

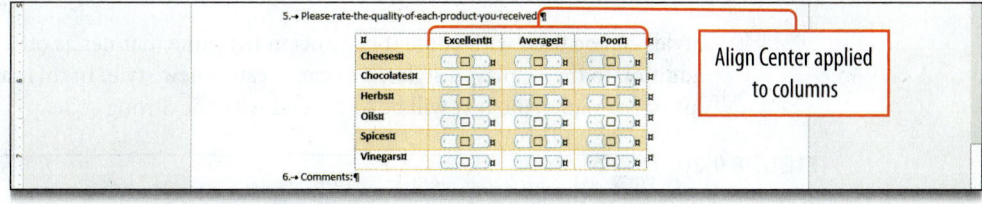

More Knowledge │ **Inserting Other Controls**

The Picture content control allows the user to insert an image—for example, a photo for identification. Use the Building Block Gallery content control to insert a building block in a content control—allowing the user to add specific text. The Repeating Section content control contains other controls and repeats the contents as needed.

Video W9-2

You can manage the information provided by the person filling in the form by modifying the properties of content controls. In addition, when a form is distributed, you can protect it so that the static text and content controls cannot be edited or removed by the user.

Activity 9.10 | Editing Text in a Content Control

You can customize the placeholder text that displays in content controls.

1 Locate the paragraph that begins *Name*, and then in the same paragraph, click the **Plain Text content control** to select it.

2 In the **Plain Text content control**, select the existing text, and then type **Enter your first and last names.**

3 To the right of the text *Email address*, in the **Plain Text content control**, select the existing text, and then type **Enter your personal email address.** Deselect the content control, and then compare your screen with Figure 9.19.

FIGURE 9.19

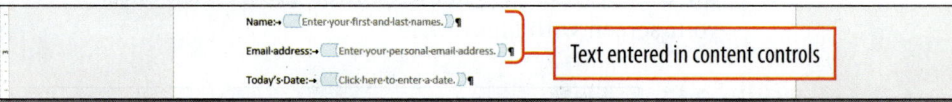
Text entered in content controls

4 Below the paragraph *Comments*, in the **Plain Text content control**, select the existing text, and then type **Enter your comments. Save** 🖫 your changes.

Activity 9.11 | Modifying Content Control Properties

You can designate the characteristics of a content control by modifying its properties. In this activity, you will assign a title and style to Plain Text content controls.

1 Locate the paragraph that begins *Name*, and then in the same paragraph, click the **Plain Text content control** to select it.

2 Click the **DEVELOPER tab**, in the **Controls group**, click **Properties**.

3 In the **Content Control Properties** dialog box, in the **Title** box, type **Name**

Assigning a title that displays on the content control makes it easier for the user to identify it.

4 In the **Content Control Properties** dialog box, under **General**, select the **Use a style to format text typed into the empty control** check box. Click the **Style arrow**, and then click **Strong**. Compare your screen with Figure 9.20.

Styles can be used with content controls in the same manner as other text in the document. In addition to the displayed styles, you can create a new style. In this case, when the customer types his or her name, the text will be formatted with the Strong style.

FIGURE 9.20

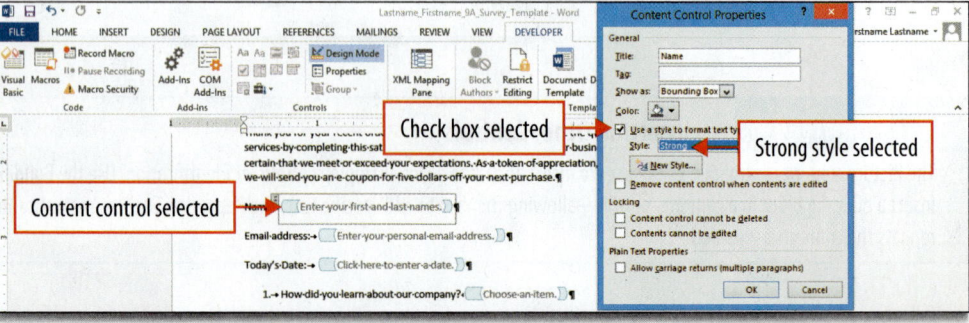
Check box selected
Strong style selected
Content control selected

5 Click **OK**. Notice that the title *Name* displays on the **Plain Text content control**.

6 Locate the paragraph that begins *Email address*, and then in the same paragraph, click the **Plain Text content control** to select it.

7 In the **Controls group**, click **Properties**. In the **Content Control Properties** dialog box, in the **Title** box, type **Email Address** and then under **General**, click to select the **Use a style to format text typed into the empty control** check box. Click the **Style arrow**, click **Strong**, and then click **OK**.

8 Press Ctrl + End. Above the last paragraph of the document, click the **Plain Text content control** to select it.

9 In the **Controls group**, click **Properties**. In the **Content Control Properties** dialog box, in the **Title** box, type **Comments** and then under **General**, click to select the **Use a style to format text typed into the empty control** check box. Click the **Style arrow**, click **Quote**, and then click **OK**.

> The customer's comments will be formatted with the Quote style.

10 Save 🖫 your changes.

Activity 9.12 | Using a Password to Protect a Document

Individuals using a form should be able to enter data in the content controls only—without editing other text or modifying any formats in the document. You can protect a form to restrict its use to allow the user to enter data only in the control fields. In this activity, you will apply restrictions and add a password to safeguard the form.

1 On the **DEVELOPER tab**, in the **Controls group**, click **Design Mode** to turn off **Design Mode**.

> When you finish designing a form, you must turn off Design Mode before it can be restricted and distributed for use.

2 On the **DEVELOPER tab**, in the **Protect group**, click **Restrict Editing** to display the **Restrict Editing** pane.

> By restricting the formatting and editing, you can control the changes that a user makes in a document. Select the first option to restrict only formatting changes. Select the second option to define how the document can be edited.

3 In the **Restrict Editing** pane, under **2. Editing restrictions**, click to select the **Allow only this type of editing in the document** check box.

4 Click the **Allow only this type of editing in the document arrow**, and then click **Filling in forms**. Compare your screen with Figure 9.21.

> This option restricts the use of the document so that a user can only fill in the content controls in the document.

FIGURE 9.21

5 In the **Restrict Editing** pane, under **3. Start enforcement**, click **Yes, Start Enforcing Protection**.

Before you begin enforcing protection, you should always confirm that all elements of the document display correctly.

6 In the **Start Enforcing Protection** dialog box, in the **Enter new password (optional)** box, type **survey15** Notice that as you type, the characters are replaced with bullets.

A *password* is a code that is used to gain access to a file—in this case, the customer survey document.

7 In the **Reenter password to confirm** box, type **survey15** and then compare your screen with Figure 9.22.

FIGURE 9.22

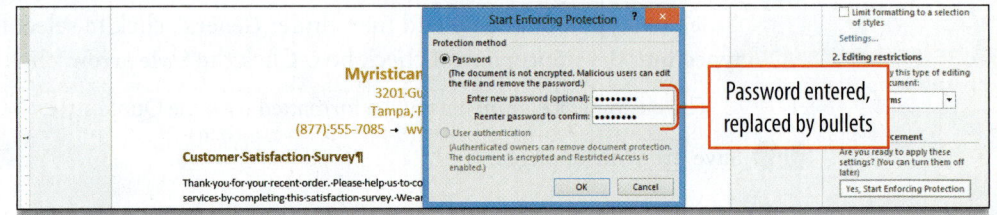

8 Click **OK**, and notice that a content control is selected.

By restricting the editing to filling in forms, only the content controls are accessible in the document.

9 **Close** ☒ the **Restrict Editing** pane, and then **Save** 🖫 your changes. **Close** ☒ Word.

> **More Knowledge** **Adding a Password to Any Document**
>
> You can add a password to any document to prevent unauthorized persons from making changes. At the bottom of the Save As dialog box, click Tools, and then click General Options. In the General Options dialog box, in the Password to open or Password to modify box, type a password. Click OK to close the General Options dialog box. In the Confirm Password dialog box, type the password again, and then click OK. Save the document.

Objective 3 | Use a Template to Complete a Form

Video W9-3

After the form is protected, it can be distributed to others by sending it as an email attachment. The user can complete the form in Word.

Activity 9.13 | Filling in the Form

In this activity, you will complete the customer satisfaction survey.

1 On the taskbar, click **File Explorer** 📁. Navigate to your **Word Chapter 9** folder, and then double-click the file **Lastname_Firstname_9A_Survey_Template**. Notice that the **customer satisfaction survey** form displays, as shown in Figure 9.23.

Because you are using the template to create a new document, the form displays with the default file name *Document1*—your number may vary. The first content control is selected because the form has been restricted to filling in forms.

FIGURE 9.23

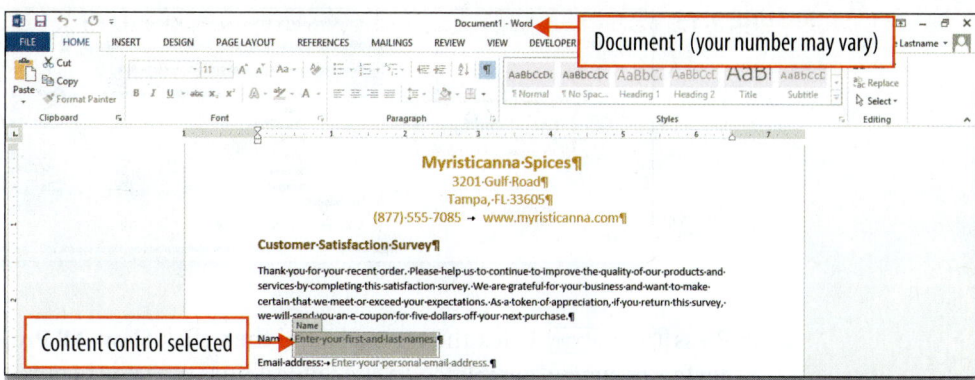

2 Press **F12**, and then navigate to your **Word Chapter 9** folder. Using your own name, type the file name **Lastname_Firstname_9A_Survey_Completed** and then click **Save**.

3 In the paragraph that begins *Name*, with the **Plain Text content control** selected, using your own name, type **Firstname Lastname**

Your name is formatted with the Strong style—the style you selected in the Content Control Properties dialog box.

4 Press **Tab**, and then in the paragraph that begins *Email address*, in the **Plain Text content control**, using your own last name, type **Lastname@myristicanna.com**

Because the form is protected—only filling in information is allowed—you can move from one content control to the next by pressing **Tab**.

5 Press **Tab**, click the **Date Picker content control arrow** to display the calendar, and then at the bottom of the calendar, click **Today**.

The date displays with the format you selected in the Content Control Properties dialog box. In the Date Picker content control, you can navigate in the calendar to select any date.

6 Press **Tab**. To the right of the paragraph that begins with *1*, click the **Drop-Down List content control arrow**, and then click **Friend**.

7 Press **Tab**. To the right of the paragraph that begins *2*, click the **Combo Box content control arrow**, click **Choose an item or type another reason.** and then type **Customer Satisfaction**

Recall that you modified the default text in the list to read *Choose an item or type another reason.* The user of the form can type a response that differs from the listed items.

8 Press **Tab**. To the right of the paragraph that begins *3*, click the **Drop-Down List content control arrow**, and then click **UPS**.

9 Locate the paragraph that begins *4*, and then to the left of **Yes**, click the **Check Box form field**. Press **F1** to display the **Help** dialog box. Take a moment to read the help text, and then click **OK** to close the **Help** dialog box.

10 In the table, in the **Cheeses** row, in the **Average** column, click the check box. In the **Herbs** row, in the **Excellent** column, click the check box. In the **Spices** row, in the **Excellent** column, click the check box.

11 Below the paragraph that begins *6. Comments*, click the **Plain Text content control**, and then type **I am eager to try your vinegars.** Deselect the content control, and then compare your screen with Figure 9.24.

The text is formatted with the Quote style—the style you selected in the Content Control Properties dialog box.

FIGURE 9.24

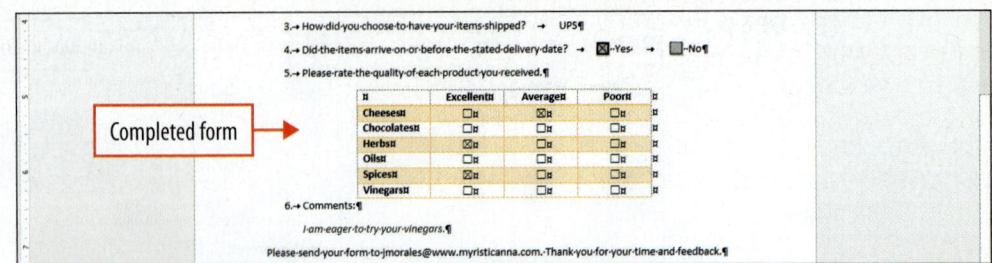

Completed form

3.→ How-did-you-choose-to-have-your-items-shipped? → UPS¶

4.→ Did-the-items-arrive-on-or-before-the-stated-delivery-date? → ☒-Yes· → ☐·-No¶

5.→ Please-rate-the-quality-of-each-product-you-received.¶

¤	Excellent¤	Average¤	Poor¤	¤
Cheeses¤	☐¤	☒¤	☐¤	¤
Chocolates¤	☐¤	☐¤	☐¤	¤
Herbs¤	☒¤	☐¤	☐¤	¤
Oils¤	☐¤	☐¤	☐¤	¤
Spices¤	☒¤	☐¤	☐¤	¤
Vinegars¤	☐¤	☐¤	☐¤	¤

6.→ Comments:¶

I-am-eager-to-try-your-vinegars.¶

Please-send-your-form-to-jmorales@www.myristicanna.com.·Thank-you-for-your-time-and-feedback.¶

12 Press Ctrl + Home. Click the **FILE tab**, and then click **Show All Properties**. In the **Tags** box, type **customer survey, completed** In the **Subject** box, type your course name and section number. If necessary, edit the author name to display your name. **Save** 🖫 your changes, and then press Ctrl + W to close the document and keep Word open.

More Knowledge | **Linking a Form to a Database**

To link data that is entered in a form to a database, the best option is to use a form in a Microsoft Access database. To link a form designed in Word to a database requires extensive programming skills.

Activity 9.14 | Unlocking a Form

1 Click the **FILE tab**, click **Open**, and then under **Recent Documents**, click **Lastname_Firstname_9A_Survey_Template**.

2 Click the **DEVELOPER tab**, in the **Protect group**, click **Restrict Editing** to display the **Restrict Editing** pane. At the bottom of the **Restrict Editing** pane, click **Stop Protection**. In the **Unprotect Document** dialog box, in the **Password** box, type **survey15** and then click **OK**.

Recall that the form is protected with a password. You must know the password to unlock the form.

3 **Close** ⊠ the **Restrict Editing** pane, and then insert the file name in the footer.

4 Click the **FILE tab**, and then click **Show All Properties**. In the **Tags** box, type **customer survey, template** In the **Subject** box, type your course name and section number. If necessary, edit the author name to display your name.

5 From **Backstage** view, click **Options**. In the **Word Options** dialog box, click **Customize Ribbon**. In the **Main Tabs** list, locate and then clear the **Developer** check box. Click **OK**, and notice that the **DEVELOPER tab** no longer displays on the ribbon.

6 **Save** 🖫 your changes, and then print both files or submit electronically as directed by your instructor. **Close** ⊠ Word.

END | You have completed Project 9A

Moving Agreement

PROJECT ACTIVITIES

In Activities 9.15 through 9.24, you will create a document pertaining to an upcoming office move. Myristicanna Spices is relocating its administrative offices. To help ensure that no items are lost or damaged, Rachel Enders, who is in charge of the move, has asked each employee to sign an agreement indicating that everything has been properly packed, is labeled, and is ready to be moved. The completed document is to be returned through interoffice mail. You will customize the ribbon to increase your efficiency in creating the agreement. You will use a combination of graphic elements to create a company heading on the document and insert a signature line. Your completed document will look similar to Figure 9.25.

PROJECT FILES

For Project 9B, you will need the following files:

w09B_Nutmeg
w09B_Moving_Agreement

You will save your files as:

Lastname_Firstname_9B_Moving_Agreement
Lastname_Firstname_9B_
    Agreement_Compatibility

PROJECT RESULTS

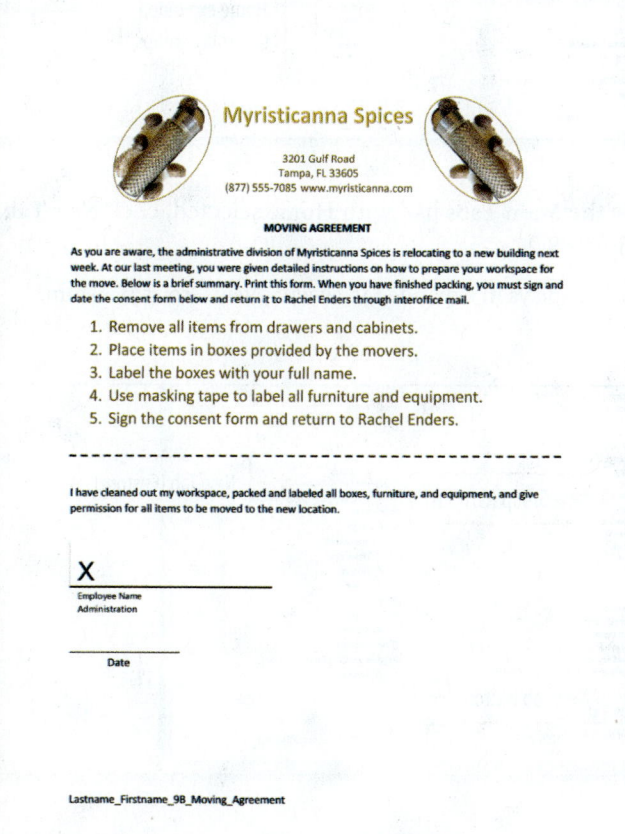

FIGURE 9.25   Project 9B Moving Agreement

Video W9-4

The ribbon contains groups of commands on various tabs that are organized in a logical way. You can personalize Word and improve your efficiency by adding frequently used commands to an existing tab or by creating a new custom tab.

Activity 9.15 | Creating a Custom Tab

1 Start Word. Click **Open Other Documents**. Navigate to your student files, and then open the file **w09B_Moving_Agreement**.

2 Click the **FILE tab**, and then click **Options**.

3 In the **Word Options** dialog box, click **Customize Ribbon**, and then compare your screen with Figure 9.26.

The Word Options dialog box displays a list of popular commands on the left and main tabs on the right. Under Main Tabs, recall that the check marks to the left of tab names indicate tabs that are currently available on the ribbon. You can expand or collapse the view of tabs and groups by clicking + or − respectively. By default, Home is selected and expanded to display the groups on the HOME tab.

FIGURE 9.26

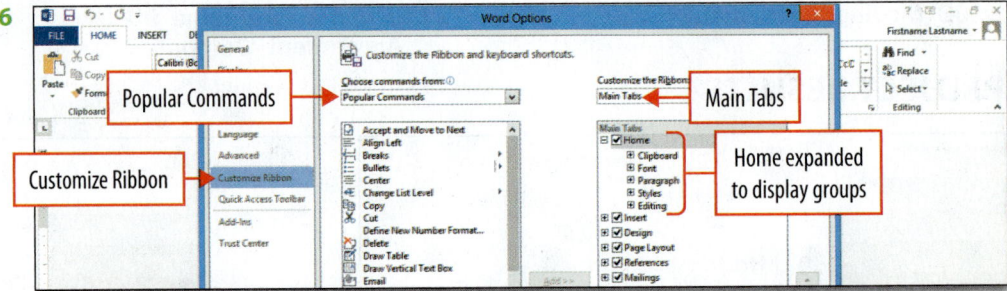

4 In the **Word Options** dialog box, below the **Main Tabs** list, with **Home** selected, click **New Tab**, and then compare your screen with Figure 9.27.

In the Main Tabs list, New Tab (Custom) displays in expanded view with New Group (Custom) indented and selected.

FIGURE 9.27

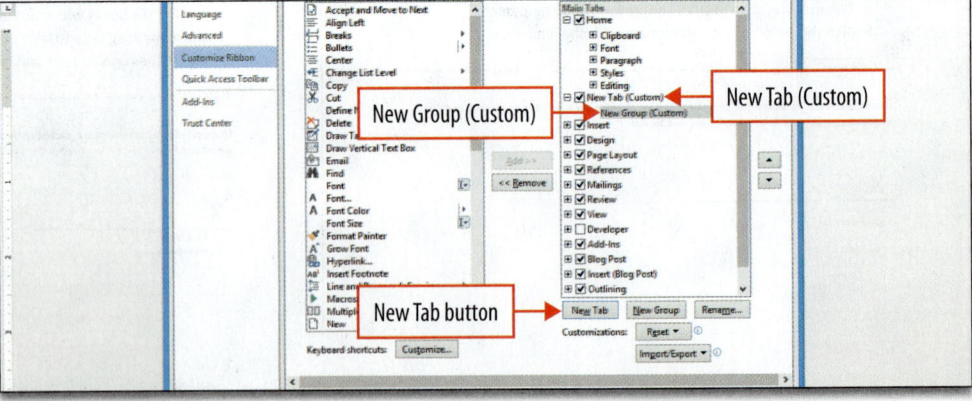

5 Click **New Tab (Custom)** to select it, and then at the bottom right of the **Word Options** dialog box, click **Rename**. In the **Rename** dialog box, in the **Display name** box, type your initials using uppercase letters, and then click **OK**.

6 Click **New Group (Custom)** to select it, and then at the bottom right of the **Word Options** dialog box, click **Rename**. In the **Rename** dialog box, in the **Display name** box, type **Common Tasks** and then click **OK**. Leave the **Word Options** dialog box open for the next activity.

Activity 9.16 | Adding Commands to a Tab

Commands are usually arranged within groups on a tab. You can add any command directly to a tab, but it is good practice to add related commands to a group.

1 In the **Word Options** dialog box, near the top, locate the **Choose commands from** box, and notice that **Popular Commands** displays.

2 In the scroll box under **Popular Commands**, scroll as necessary, click **Print Preview and Print**, and then click **Add**. In the **Main Tabs** list, notice that **Print Preview and Print** displays below the **Common Tasks (Custom) group** you created. Compare your screen with Figure 9.28.

FIGURE 9.28

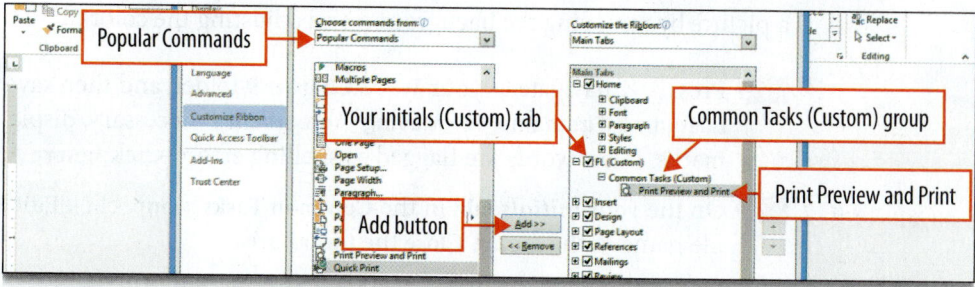

3 In the **Word Options** dialog box, click the **Choose commands from arrow**, and then click **All Commands**.

In the *Choose commands from* box, you can select a different group of available commands.

4 Under **All Commands**, scroll as necessary, click **Edit Footer**, and then click **Add**. In the **Main Tabs** list, notice that in the **Common Tasks (Custom) group**, **Edit Footer** displays below **Print Preview and Print**.

5 Click the **Choose commands from arrow**, and then click **File Tab**.

6 In the **File Tab** list, click **Close**, and then click **Add**.

The Close command closes a document and keeps Word open.

7 In the **Main Tabs** list, with **Close** selected, to the right of the **Main Tabs** list, click **Move Up** two times. Click **Edit Footer**, click **Move Up**, and then compare your screen with Figure 9.29.

The commands are displayed in alphabetical order. You can use the Move Up and Move Down buttons to arrange tabs, groups, and commands in any order.

FIGURE 9.29

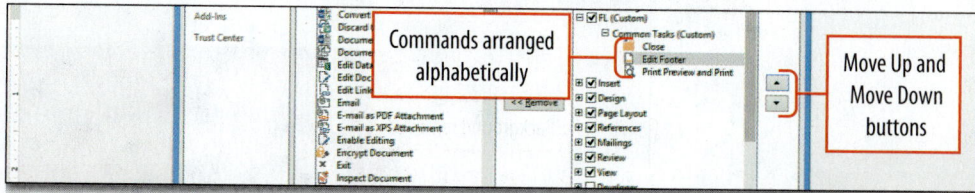

8 Click **OK** to close the **Word Options** dialog box, and notice that your custom tab with your initials displays to the right of the **HOME tab** on the ribbon.

9 Click the *your initials* tab. Notice that the **Common Tasks group** displays on the left and includes the three commands you added.

Objective 5 | Format Pictures and Text Boxes

Video W9-5

You can format objects—such as clip art, pictures, and text boxes—in a variety of ways. Making color adjustments, removing backgrounds, and changing the size and orientation can enhance the appearance of an illustration. Multiple graphics can be grouped to form one object.

Activity 9.17 | Removing the Background and Correcting Colors in a Picture

Just as you customized the ribbon to improve productivity, you can improve the appearance of a picture by removing the background and adjusting the colors.

1 Press F12, navigate to your **Word Chapter 9** folder, and then save the document as **Lastname_Firstname_9B_Moving_Agreement** If necessary, display the rulers and formatting marks. If any words are flagged as spelling errors, click **Ignore All**.

2 On the *your initials* tab, in the **Common Tasks group**, click **Edit Footer**, and then insert the file name in the footer. **Close** the footer area.

3 Press Ctrl + Home. Click the **INSERT tab**, in the **Illustrations group**, click **Pictures**. In the **Insert Picture** dialog box, navigate to your student files, select the file **w09B_Nutmeg**, and then click **Insert**.

4 On the **PICTURE TOOLS FORMAT tab**, in the **Arrange group**, click **Wrap Text**, and then click **Top and Bottom**.

5 On the **PICTURE TOOLS FORMAT tab**, in the **Adjust group**, click **Compress Pictures**  to display the **Compress Pictures** dialog box. In the **Compress Pictures** dialog box, click **OK**.

You can *compress* a graphic—reduce the file size—when you plan to transmit a document electronically. By default, the image is reduced to the resolution of the document.

6 On the **PICTURE TOOLS FORMAT tab**, in the **Adjust group**, click **Remove Background**. Compare your screen with Figure 9.30.

The BACKGROUND REMOVAL tab contains commands to remove the color surrounding the main portion of a picture. The removed portion of the picture displays in dark pink.

FIGURE 9.30

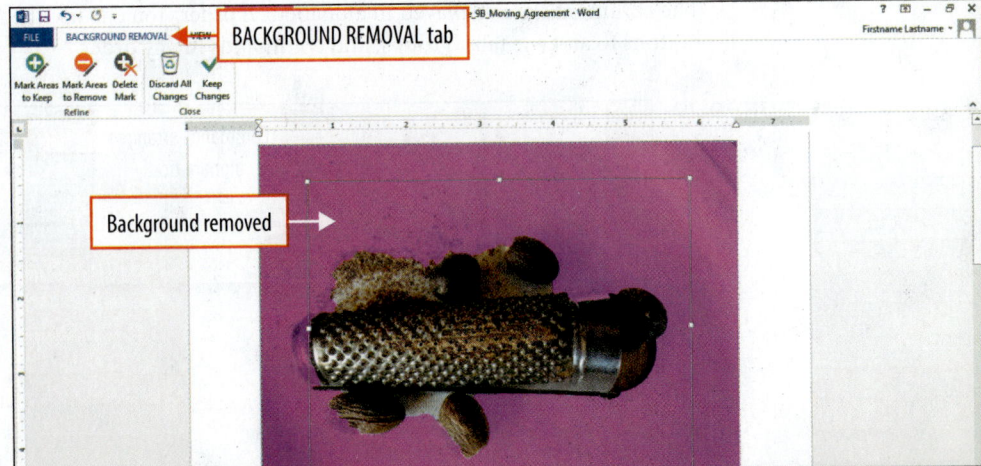

7 On the **BACKGROUND REMOVAL tab**, in the **Close group**, click **Keep Changes**.

8 If necessary, select the graphic, and then on the **PICTURE TOOLS FORMAT tab**, in the **Adjust group**, click **Corrections**. In the **Corrections** gallery, point to several options and notice how the colors change in the picture.

9 In the **Corrections** gallery, under **Brightness and Contrast**, in the third row, click the fourth option—**Brightness: +20% Contrast: 0% (Normal)**. Notice that the picture is brighter and more distinct.

> *Brightness* is the relative lightness of a picture. Increasing the value creates a brighter image. *Contrast* is the difference between the darkest and lightest areas of a picture. Increasing the contrast value creates more distinct colors in the graphic. In this case, to improve the appearance of the picture, you are changing the brightness and contrast.

10 Save 🖫 your changes.

Activity 9.18 | Cropping, Rotating, and Aligning Pictures

In this activity, you will *crop* a picture to focus the attention on a particular portion of the picture. Cropping is the process of removing any unwanted parts from the edges of a picture. You will also rotate the picture and create a mirror image.

1 With the picture selected, on the **FORMAT tab**, in the **Picture Styles group**, click the **Picture Border button arrow**, and then in the eighth column, click the fifth color—**Gold, Accent 4, Darker 25%**.

> Because the picture is selected, the border color may not display on all edges.

2 On the **FORMAT tab**, in the **Size group**, click **Crop**, which causes black crop handles to display around the image.

3 On the left border of the graphic, point to the middle crop handle. When the ⊣ pointer displays, drag to the right to approximately **0.5 inch on the horizontal ruler**. Compare your screen with Figure 9.31.

> The cropped portions of a picture are not deleted, just hidden. You can redisplay cropped portions of an image by using the crop handles.

FIGURE 9.31

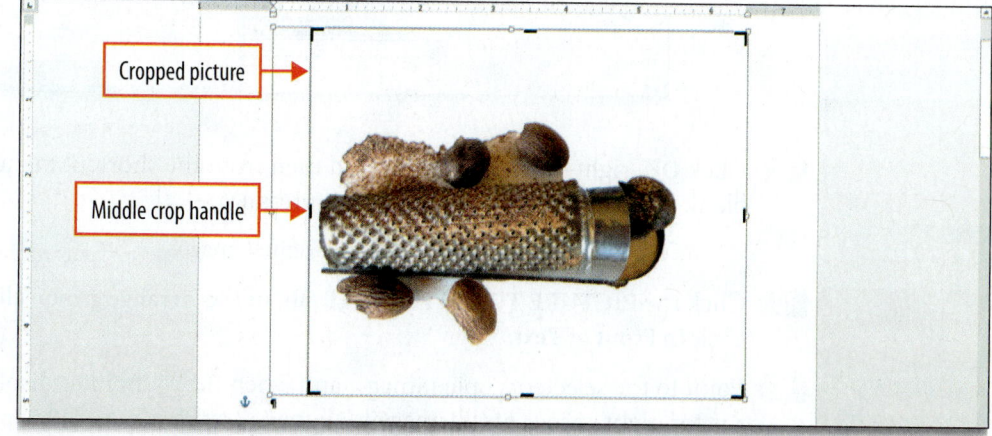

4 Using the same technique, on the top border, drag the middle crop handle down to approximately **1 inch on the vertical ruler**. In a similar manner, crop the right border to display at **5.5 inches on the horizontal ruler**, and then crop the bottom border to display at **4.25 inches on the vertical ruler**.

5 In the **Size group**, click the **Crop button arrow**, click **Crop to Shape**, and then under **Basic Shapes**, click the first shape—**Oval**.

In addition to cropping the edges of a graphic, you can also display the graphic within a shape.

6 In the **Size group**, change the **Shape Height** ‡☐ Height: 0.19" ↕ to **1"**, and then compare your screen with Figure 9.32.

FIGURE 9.32

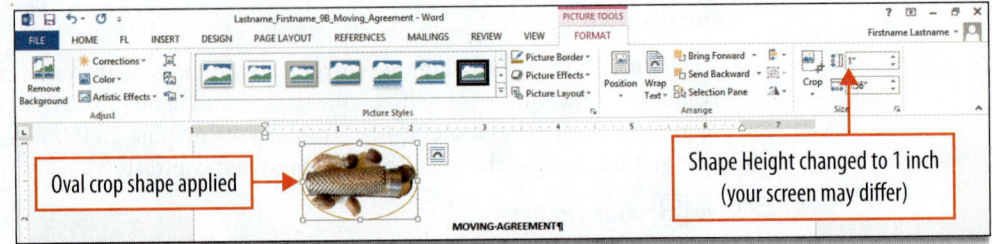

Oval crop shape applied

Shape Height changed to 1 inch (your screen may differ)

7 In the **Arrange group**, click **Rotate Objects** ◢, and then click **More Rotation Options**.

8 In the **Layout** dialog box, on the **Size tab**, under **Rotate**, click the **Rotation spin box down arrow** to **−65°**. Compare your screen with Figure 9.33.

To specify an exact degree of rotation for an image, use the Layout dialog box.

More Knowledge | **Rotating an Image**

If a precise angle is not required, above the top middle sizing handle, point to the rotate button, and then drag to rotate the image.

FIGURE 9.33

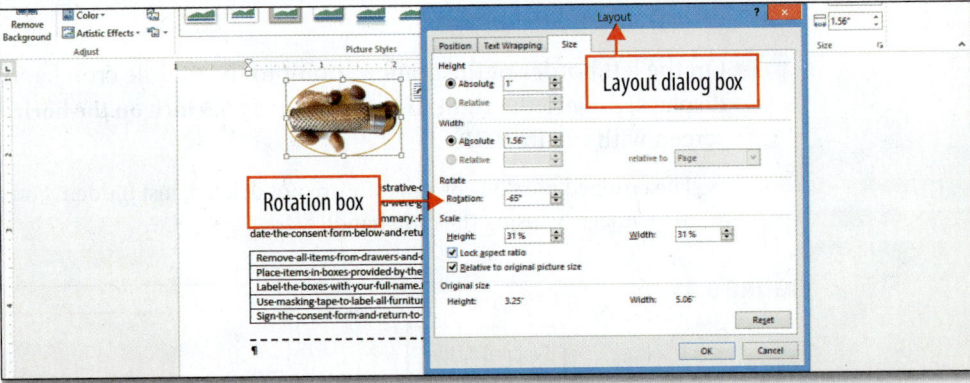

Layout dialog box

Rotation box

9 Click **OK**, right-click the picture, and then from the shortcut menu, click **Copy**. Click in a blank area of the document, and then press Ctrl + V.

The copied image is pasted above the original image.

10 Click the **PICTURE TOOLS FORMAT tab**, in the **Arrange group**, click **Wrap Text**, and then click **In Front of Text**.

11 Point to the selected, copied image, and when the ⊹ pointer displays, drag to the right until the top right corner of the image is aligned at approximately **0.5 inch on the vertical ruler** and at approximately **5.5 inches on the horizontal ruler**.

12 With the image on the right selected, press and hold down ⌃Ctrl, click the image on the left, and then release ⌃Ctrl. With both images selected, in the **Arrange group**, click **Align Objects** ⊨, and then click **Align Top**. Compare your screen with Figure 9.34.

> Use the Align feature to position objects in a consistent manner. You can align—line up—the top, bottom, sides, or middle of multiple graphic elements. In this case, you are ensuring that the top points of both images are aligned.

FIGURE 9.34

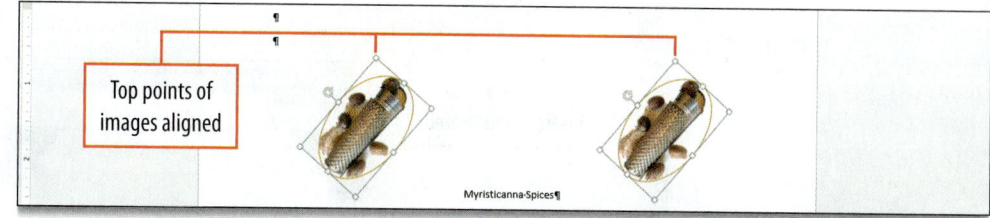

Top points of images aligned

13 Click the image on the right, and then click the **PICTURE TOOLS FORMAT tab**. In the **Arrange group**, click **Rotate Objects** ⬧, and then click **Flip Horizontal**. Compare your screen with Figure 9.35.

> *Flipping* a graphic reverses the direction of a graphic either vertically or horizontally.

FIGURE 9.35

Image flipped horizontally

14 Save 🖫 your changes.

Activity 9.19 | **Stacking and Grouping Objects and Converting Text to WordArt**

You will insert and format two additional objects—a text box and *WordArt*—in the document. WordArt is a feature that applies combinations of decorative formatting to text, including shadows, reflections, and 3-D effects, as well as changing the line and fill color of the text. When multiple objects—such as pictures, shapes, and text boxes—are inserted in a document, they are automatically *stacked*—placed in individual layers. You can modify the stacking order to allow the objects to overlap. Additionally, you can group individual objects to form a single object—in this case, the company heading.

1 In the first blank paragraph above the images, click to position the insertion point. Click the **INSERT tab**. In the **Text group**, click **Text Box**, and then click **Simple Text Box**.

2 With the text box selected, on the **DRAWING TOOLS FORMAT tab**, in the **Size group**, change the **Shape Height** [⊞ Height: 0.19"] to **0.9"**, and then change the **Shape Width** [⊞ Width: 6.49"] to **5"**. Compare your screen with Figure 9.36, and then, if necessary, move your text box and realign the two images so that all objects are positioned as shown in the figure.

Adding the text box to the document creates a third layer. The original image and the second pasted image represent the other two layers. When you add a visual object to a document, by default that object becomes the top layer in the stacking order.

FIGURE 9.36

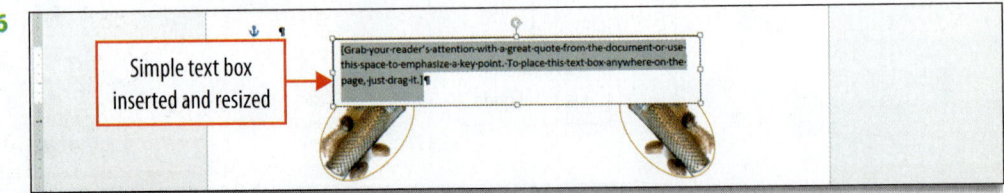

Simple text box inserted and resized

3 With the text selected, click the **HOME tab**, and then in the **Styles group**, click **No Spacing**. Press [Enter], and then type **3201 Gulf Road** Press [Enter], and then type **Tampa, FL 33605** Press [Enter], type **(877) 555-7085** press [Tab], and then type **www.myristicanna.com** If **www.myristicanna.com** displays as a hyperlink, point to the text, right-click, and then from the shortcut menu, click **Remove Hyperlink**.

4 Select the three lines of text. On the mini toolbar, change the **Font Color** [A ▾] to **Gold, Accent 4, Darker 50%**—in the eighth column, the last color. Press [Ctrl] + [E].

5 Click the **DRAWING TOOLS FORMAT tab**. In the **Shape Styles group**, click the **Shape Outline button arrow** [⊿], and then click **No Outline**.

The outline for the text box changes to a dashed line.

6 In the **Arrange group**, click the **Send Backward button arrow** [⊡], and then click **Send to Back**.

The Send to Back command causes the text box to become the bottom layer in the stacking order. This allows the two images to display completely.

7 Point to the border of the text box to display the [⊹] pointer. Drag the text box down so that the bottom border of the text box is aligned with the bottom of the two pictures. Compare your screen with Figure 9.37. If necessary, adjust your images to display as shown in Figure 9.37.

FIGURE 9.37

Send to Back applied to text box

8 Click on the border of the text box to display a solid outline and sizing handles. With the text box selected, press and hold [Ctrl]. On the left side of the document, above the text box, click the image to select it. Continue to hold down [Ctrl], and then on the right side of the document, above the text box, click the other image. Release [Ctrl], and notice all three graphics are selected. Compare your screen with Figure 9.38.

Pressing [Ctrl] allows you to select several graphics at the same time.

FIGURE 9.38

All three graphics selected

9 With all three graphics selected, click the **DRAWING TOOLS FORMAT tab**. In the **Arrange group**, click **Group** 🖼, and then from the displayed list, click **Group**. Notice that only sizing handles for the entire grouped object display, and the object moves into the text area of the document.

> *Grouping* is the process of combining multiple elements into a single object. You can move or resize the entire group, ensuring that the individual elements remain together in the same position and stacking order.

10 On the **DRAWING TOOLS FORMAT tab**, in the **Arrange group**, click **Wrap Text**, and then click **Top and Bottom**. Deselect the grouped object.

11 Below the grouped object, select the paragraph *Myristicanna Spices*. Click the **INSERT tab**. In the **Text group**, click **WordArt**, and then in the **WordArt** gallery, in the first row, click the last style—**Fill – Gold, Accent 4, Soft Bevel**. Select the text, and then on the mini toolbar, change the **Font Size** to **22**.

12 On the **FORMAT tab**, in the **Arrange group**, click **Wrap Text**, and then click **Top and Bottom**.

13 Point to the border of the **WordArt** text box, and when the 🔭 pointer displays, drag the **WordArt** text box so that it is centered above the grouped graphic as shown in Figure 9.39.

FIGURE 9.39

WordArt centered

14 If necessary, select the **WordArt** text box so that the border displays as a solid outline. Press and hold down Shift, point to the grouped graphic, and when the 🔭 pointer displays, click the grouped graphic. With both objects selected, on the **DRAWING TOOLS FORMAT tab**, in the **Arrange group**, click **Group** 🖼, and then from the displayed list, click **Group**.

15 With the entire grouped object selected, on the **DRAWING TOOLS FORMAT tab**, in the **Arrange group**, click **Wrap Text**, and then click **In Line with Text**. Select the entire graphic including the paragraph mark, and then press Ctrl + E.

16 Save 🖫 your changes.

More Knowledge | **Using the Drawing Canvas**

The Drawing Canvas is useful for positioning, stacking, and grouping numerous objects. To display the Drawing Canvas, on the INSERT tab, in the Illustrations group, click the Shapes button, and then at the bottom of the list, click New Drawing Canvas.

Video W9-6

When a document is sent electronically, the recipient must be able to confirm the source of the file. With a paper document, a signature and notarization are legal tools used to identify the validity of the signature and file source. When a document is transmitted electronically, a *digital signature* can be applied. A digital signature is an electronic stamp that is added to a document to verify the document's authenticity. To use a digital signature, you must create a *digital certificate*. A digital certificate, or *digital ID*, is a file that contains information about a person and is used to electronically sign a document. A digital signature is based on the digital identification and verifies that the document is valid and has not been changed since the signature was added.

Activity 9.20 | Converting a Table to Text

You can change the appearance of a document by converting text in a table to display in a paragraph format.

1 Click anywhere in the table. Click the **LAYOUT tab**, and then in the **Data group**, click **Convert to Text**.

2 In the **Convert Table to Text** dialog box, under **Separate text with**, if necessary, click the **Paragraph marks** option button, and then compare your screen with Figure 9.40.

You can choose how the content of the table cells will be separated—by paragraph marks, tabs, commas, or any other single character.

FIGURE 9.40

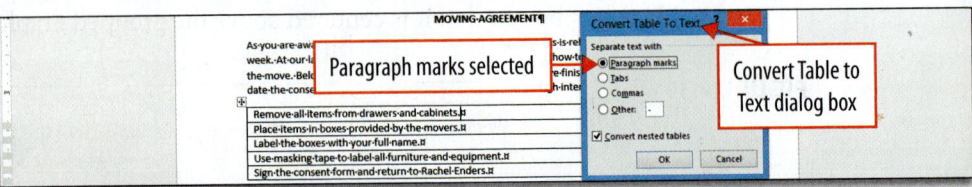

3 In the **Convert Table to Text** dialog box, click **OK**. Notice that the table is replaced with five paragraphs.

4 With all five paragraphs selected, on the mini toolbar, change the **Font Size** [11] to **16**, and then change the **Font Color** [A] to **Gold, Accent 4, Darker 50%**—in the eighth column, the last color. On the **HOME tab**, in the **Paragraph group**, click **Numbering** [≡]. Deselect the text, and then compare your screen with Figure 9.41.

FIGURE 9.41

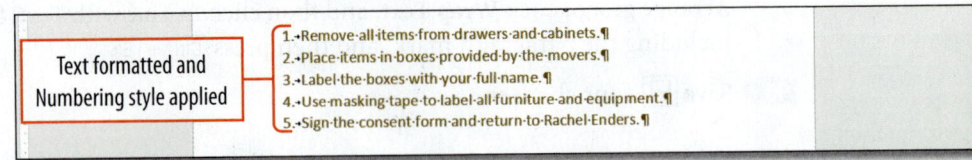

5 Save [💾] your document.

Activity 9.21 | Adding a Signature Line to a Document

A *signature line* is an element added to a document that specifies who should sign the document. In this activity, you will add a signature line, indicating that an employee signature is required to confirm that items are ready to be moved.

1 Below the paragraph that begins *I have cleaned*, click to position the insertion point in the empty paragraph. Click the **INSERT tab**. In the **Text group**, click the **Signature Line button arrow**, and then click **Microsoft Office Signature Line**.

2 In the **Signature Setup** dialog box, in the **Suggested signer** box, type **Employee Name** In the **Suggested signer's title** box, type **Administration**

3 Click **OK** to insert the signature line in the document. Compare your screen with Figure 9.42.

The signer can sign a hard copy—a printed copy—or sign the document electronically by inserting an image of a signature or by using a *stylus*—a pen-like device—with a *tablet PC*—a computer with a monitor that allows you to write on the screen.

More Knowledge | **Inserting a Digital ID**

You can also sign a document electronically by inserting a digital ID. Digital IDs can be purchased from a certification authority.

FIGURE 9.42

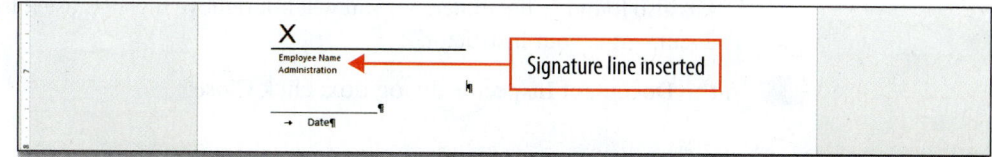

Signature line inserted

---

4 Click the *your initials* tab, and then in the **Common Tasks group**, click **Print Preview and Print**. Click **Back** ⊖, return to your document, correct any spelling errors, and then **Save** 🖫 your document.

ALERT! | **What Is the Banner That Displays below the Ribbon?**

If you open a file that contains a signature line, but the document has not been digitally signed, a banner may display below the ribbon stating that the document needs to be signed. For purposes of this instruction, you can ignore the banner.

Objective 7 Prepare a Document for Distribution

Video W9-7

Before a document is distributed to others, it should be inspected to make sure it does not contain unwanted personal information or *metadata*—details about a file that describe or identify it. In addition, the document should be identified as being in final form.

Activity 9.22 | Inspecting a Document and Removing Document Metadata

In this activity, you will remove all personal information from your document.

1 Press Ctrl + Home. Click the **FILE tab**, and then, if necessary, click **Info**. In the **Inspect Document** section, click **Check for Issues**, and then click **Inspect Document**.

2 In the **Document Inspector** dialog box, be sure all eight check boxes are selected, and then click **Inspect**. Notice the results of the inspection display in the **Document Inspector** dialog box. Compare your screen with Figure 9.43.

The document is inspected for many types of data, including comments and revisions, document properties and personal information, custom XML data, and hidden text.

FIGURE 9.43

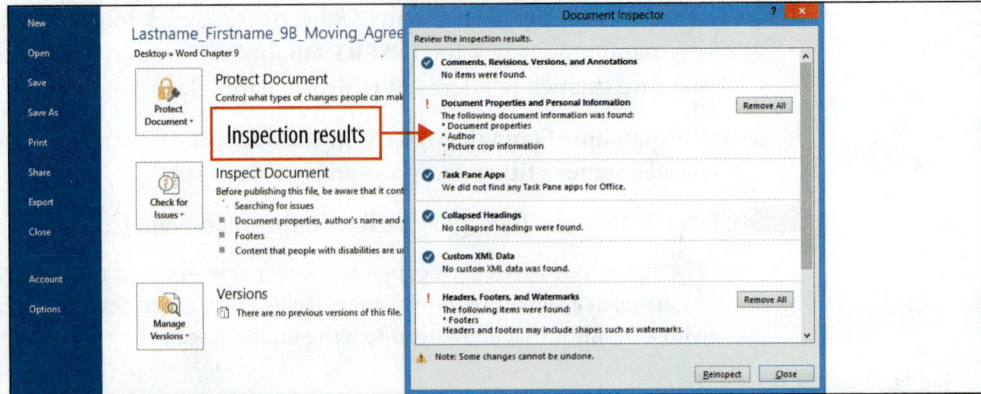

3 To the right of **Document Properties and Personal Information**, click **Remove All**.

This will remove all personal information found in the document properties. Personal information was also found in the footer, but you will not remove this because it is needed to identify your document to your instructor.

4 In the **Document Inspector** dialog box, click **Close**.

Activity 9.23 | Marking a Document as Final

After all changes have been made, a document can be identified as a final version—making it a *read-only file*. A read-only file can be viewed but not changed.

1 From **Backstage** view, click **Show All Properties**. In the **Tags** box, type **moving agreement, graphics** In the **Subject** box, type your course name and section number. In the **Author** box, type your first and last names.

Although you removed the document properties in the previous activity, as a part of this instruction, you will include the properties to identify your document to your instructor.

2 From **Backstage** view, with the **Info tab** selected, in the **Protect Document** section, click **Protect Document**, and then click **Mark as Final**.

3 In the **Microsoft Word** dialog box, click **OK** to confirm that the document will be marked as final.

4 In the **Microsoft Word** message box indicating that the document has been marked as final and saved, click **OK**.

5 Click **Back** ⊖, and then compare your screen with Figure 9.44.

The title bar indicates that this is a read-only file. A MARKED AS FINAL banner displays above the document, the commands on the ribbon are hidden, and a Marked as Final icon displays on the status bar. The viewer will be able to read the document but not make any changes.

FIGURE 9.44

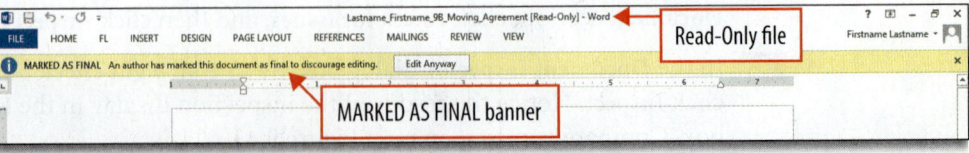

6 Click the **HOME tab** to display the commands. Notice that most of the buttons on the ribbon are unavailable.

7 ▸ Click the *your initials* tab, and then in the **Common Tasks group**, click **Close** to close your document.

8 ▸ Click the **FILE tab**, and then under **Recent Documents**, click the first document—**Lastname_Firstname_9B_Moving_Agreement**.

The document displays in Read Mode.

9 ▸ On the **MARKED AS FINAL** banner, click **Edit Anyway** to remove the read-only characteristics. **Save** 🖫 your changes.

Activity 9.24 | Maintaining Backward Compatibility

There may be times when you want a document to be available to persons using versions of Word older than Word 2007. To make a document backward compatible, you must save it as a Word 97–2003 document with the file extension .doc.

1 ▸ Press F12. In the **Save As** dialog box, navigate to your **Word Chapter 9** folder. Click the **Save As type box arrow**, and then click **Word 97–2003 Document**. In the **File name** box, type **Lastname_Firstname_9B_Agreement_Compatibility** and then click **Save**. Compare your screen with Figure 9.45. Note: If the dialog box does not display, study the figure, and then proceed to Step 3.

The Microsoft Word Compatibility Checker dialog box indicates that some features in the current document are not supported in an older version of Word. The Summary box indicates the elements of the document that may be modified.

FIGURE 9.45

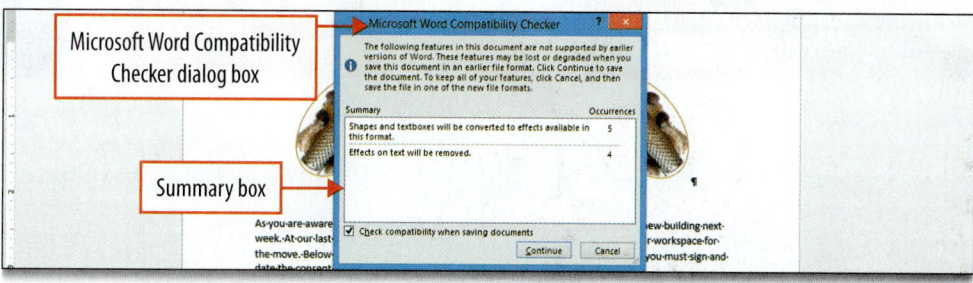

2 ▸ In the **Microsoft Word Compatibility Checker** dialog box, click **Continue**. Notice the WordArt formatting is removed from *Myristicanna Spices*, and the borders of the images have changed from an oval shape to a rectangular shape.

3 ▸ Click the *your initials* tab, and then click **Edit Footer**. Right-click the file name, and then click **Update Field**. Close the footer area.

4 ▸ Click the **FILE tab**, and then click **Show All Properties**. In the **Tags** box, delete the text *graphics*, and then type **converted** In the **Subject** box, type your course name and section number. In the **Author** box, type your first and last names. **Save** 🖫 your document.

5 ▸ Right-click the *your initials* tab, and then click **Customize the Ribbon**. In the **Word Options** dialog box, in the **Main Tabs** list, right-click *your initials* (**Custom**), and then from the shortcut menu, click **Remove**. Click **OK** to close the dialog box, and notice that your custom tab no longer displays on the ribbon.

6 ▸ Print your two documents or submit electronically as directed by your instructor.

7 ▸ **Close** ☒ Word. In the **Microsoft Word** message box, click **No**.

END | You have completed Project 9B

END OF CHAPTER

SUMMARY

Adding content controls and protecting the document makes it easy for the user to complete a form. By saving the document as a template, the form can be used repeatedly without changing the original file.

Add titles in content controls to clarify the purpose for the user. Add items to Drop-Down Lists and Combo Boxes to provide choices for the user to select. Format static text to improve the form's appearance.

Personalize the ribbon to improve efficiency. In the Word Options dialog box, display the DEVELOPER tab, add frequently used commands to existing tabs and groups, or create your own custom tabs and groups.

Word provides numerous options for formatting pictures, text boxes, and other graphics. You can convert existing text to WordArt. You can also insert a signature line so that a document can be signed electronically.

GO! LEARN IT ONLINE

Review the concepts and key terms in this chapter by completing these online challenges, which you can find at **www.pearsonhighered.com/go**.

Matching and Multiple Choice: Answer matching and multiple choice questions to test what you learned in this chapter. MyITLab®

Crossword Puzzle: Spell out the words that match the numbered clues and put them in the puzzle squares.

Flipboard: Flip through the definitions of the key terms in this chapter and match them with the correct term.

END OF CHAPTER

REVIEW AND ASSESSMENT GUIDE FOR WORD CHAPTER 9

Your instructor may assign one or more of these projects to help you review the chapter and assess your mastery and understanding of the chapter.

Project	Apply Skills from These Chapter Objectives	Project Type	Project Location
9C	Objectives 1–3 from Project 9A	**9C Skills Review** A guided review of the skills from Project 9A.	On the following pages
9D	Objectives 4–7 from Project 9B	**9D Skills Review** A guided review of the skills from Project 9B.	On the following pages
9E	Objectives 1–3 from Project 9A	**9E Mastery (Grader project)** A demonstration of your mastery of the skills in Project 9A with extensive decision making.	In MyITLab and on the following pages
9F	Objectives 4–7 from Project 9B	**9F Mastery (Grader project)** A demonstration of your mastery of the skills in Project 9B with extensive decision making.	In MyITLab and on the following pages
9G	Objectives 1–7 from Projects 9A and 9B	**9G Mastery (Grader project)** A demonstration of your mastery of the skills in Projects 9A and 9B with extensive decision making.	In MyITLab and on the following pages
9H	Combination of Objectives from Projects 9A and 9B	**9H GO! Fix It** A demonstration of your mastery of the skills in Projects 9A and 9B by creating a correct result from a document that contains errors you must find.	Online
9I	Combination of Objectives from Projects 9A and 9B	**9I GO! Make It** A demonstration of your mastery of the skills in Projects 9A and 9B by creating a result from a supplied picture.	Online
9J	Combination of Objectives from Projects 9A and 9B	**9J GO! Solve It** A demonstration of your mastery of the skills in Projects 9A and 9B, your decision-making skills, and your critical thinking skills. A task-specific rubric helps you self-assess your result.	Online
9K	Combination of Objectives from Projects 9A and 9B	**9K GO! Solve It** A demonstration of your mastery of the skills in Projects 9A and 9B, your decision-making skills, and your critical thinking skills. A task-specific rubric helps you self-assess your result.	On the following pages
9L	Combination of Objectives from Projects 9A and 9B	**9L GO! Think** A demonstration of your understanding of the chapter concepts applied in a manner that you would outside of college. An analytic rubric helps you and your instructor grade the quality of your work by comparing it to the work an expert in the discipline would create.	On the following pages
9M	Combination of Objectives from Projects 9A and 9B	**9M GO! Think** A demonstration of your understanding of the chapter concepts applied in a manner that you would outside of college. An analytic rubric helps you and your instructor grade the quality of your work by comparing it to the work an expert in the discipline would create.	Online
9N	Combination of Objectives from Projects 9A and 9B	**9N You and GO!** A demonstration of your understanding of the chapter concepts applied in a manner that you would in a personal situation. An analytic rubric helps you and your instructor grade the quality of your work.	Online

GLOSSARY

GLOSSARY OF CHAPTER KEY TERMS

Brightness The light to dark ratio of an image.

Check Box content control A content control that allows the user to select, or not select, a specific option.

Check Box form field A legacy control that allows the user to select, or not select, a specific option.

Combo Box content control A content control that allows the user to select an item from a list or enter new text.

Compress The process of reducing the size of a file.

Content control A data entry field where the particular type of information is supplied by the user.

Contrast The difference between the darkest and lightest areas of a picture.

Cropping The process of removing unwanted parts from the edges of a picture.

Date Picker content control A content control that allows the user to select a date from a calendar.

Design Mode A command that enables the user to edit content controls that are inserted in a document.

Digital certificate (Digital ID) A file that contains information about a person and is used to electronically sign a document.

Digital signature An electronic stamp that is added to a document to verify the document's authenticity.

Drop-Down List content control A content control that allows the user to select a specific item from a list.

Flipping The process of reversing the direction of an object either vertically or horizontally.

Form A structured document that has static text and reserved spaces for information to be entered by the user.

Grouping The process of combining multiple elements into a single object.

Legacy control A field used in designing a form for persons who possess older versions of Word.

Metadata Details about a file that describe or identify it.

Password A code that is used to gain access to a file.

Plain Text content control A content control that enables the user to enter unformatted text.

Read-only file A file that can be viewed but not changed.

Rich Text content control A content control that enables the user to enter text and apply formatting.

Signature line An element added to a document that specifies who should sign the document.

Stacking The process of placing objects in individual layers of the document.

Static text Descriptive text such as labels or headings.

Stylus A pen-like device used for writing on an electronic document.

Tablet PC A computer with a monitor that allows you to write on the screen.

Template A predefined structure that contains basic document settings, such as fonts, margins, and available styles, and can also store elements such as building blocks and content controls.

Unformatted text Plain text without any special formatting applied.

WordArt A feature that applies combinations of decorative formatting to text, including shadows, reflections, and 3-D effects, as well as changing the line and fill color of text.

CHAPTER REVIEW

Apply 9A skills from these Objectives:

1 Create a Customized Form
2 Modify and Lock a Form
3 Use a Template to Complete a Form

Skills Review | Project 9C Meeting Reservation

In the following Skills Review, you will add content controls to create a form for reserving space for meetings at Myristicanna Spices. After the form is protected and saved as a template, you will fill in the form. Your completed documents will look similar to Figure 9.46.

Build from Scratch

PROJECT FILES

For Project 9C, you will need the following files:

New blank Word document
w09C_Meeting_Reservation

You will save your files as:

Lastname_Firstname_9C_Meeting_Reservation
Lastname_Firstname_9C_Reservation_Completed

PROJECT RESULTS

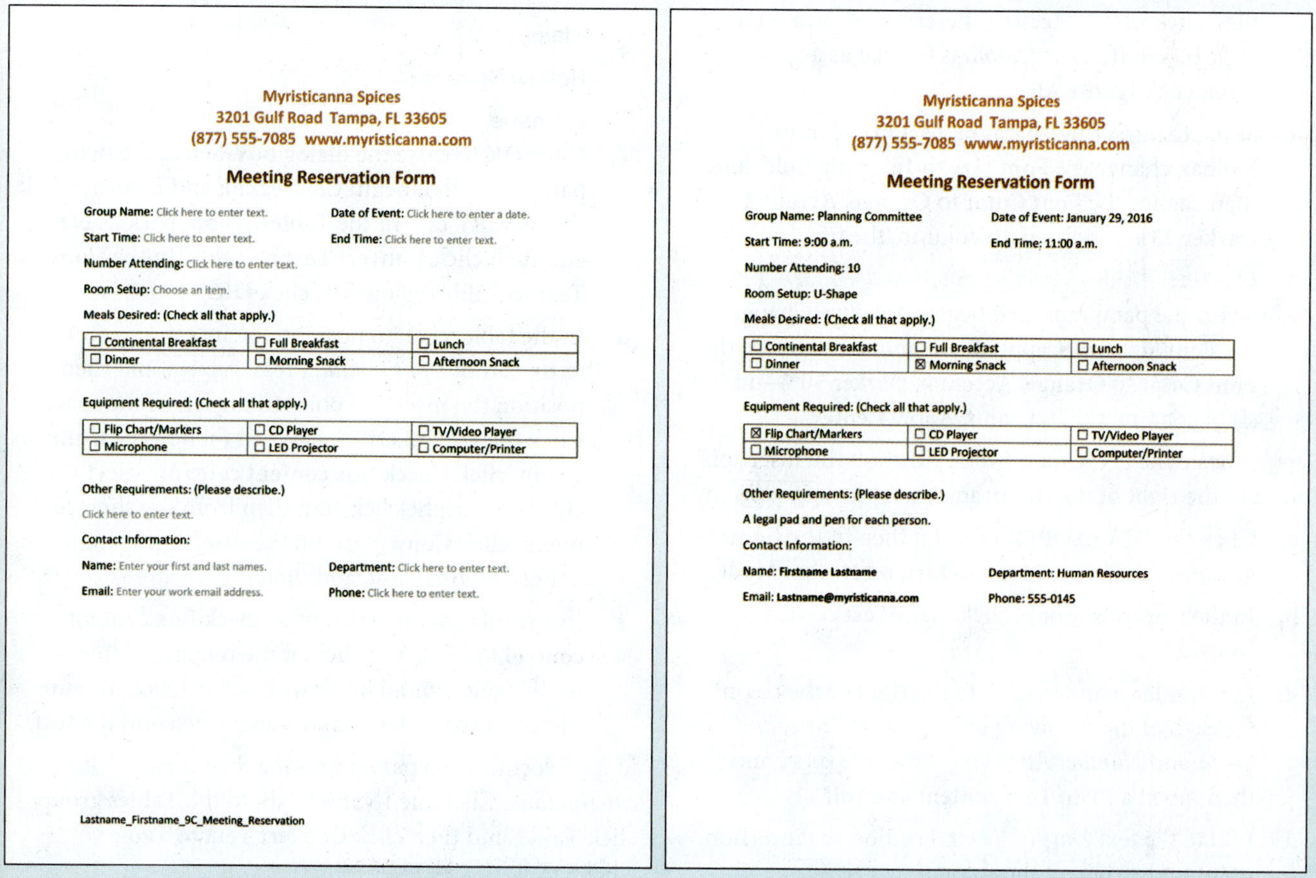

Myristicanna Spices
3201 Gulf Road Tampa, FL 33605
(877) 555-7085 www.myristicanna.com

Meeting Reservation Form

Group Name: Click here to enter text.   **Date of Event:** Click here to enter a date.

Start Time: Click here to enter text.   **End Time:** Click here to enter text.

Number Attending: Click here to enter text.

Room Setup: Choose an item.

Meals Desired: (Check all that apply.)

| ☐ Continental Breakfast | ☐ Full Breakfast | ☐ Lunch |
| ☐ Dinner | ☐ Morning Snack | ☐ Afternoon Snack |

Equipment Required: (Check all that apply.)

| ☐ Flip Chart/Markers | ☐ CD Player | ☐ TV/Video Player |
| ☐ Microphone | ☐ LED Projector | ☐ Computer/Printer |

Other Requirements: (Please describe.)
Click here to enter text.

Contact Information:

Name: Enter your first and last names.   **Department:** Click here to enter text.

Email: Enter your work email address.   **Phone:** Click here to enter text.

Lastname_Firstname_9C_Meeting_Reservation

Myristicanna Spices
3201 Gulf Road Tampa, FL 33605
(877) 555-7085 www.myristicanna.com

Meeting Reservation Form

Group Name: Planning Committee   **Date of Event:** January 29, 2016

Start Time: 9:00 a.m.   **End Time:** 11:00 a.m.

Number Attending: 10

Room Setup: U-Shape

Meals Desired: (Check all that apply.)

| ☐ Continental Breakfast | ☐ Full Breakfast | ☐ Lunch |
| ☐ Dinner | ☒ Morning Snack | ☐ Afternoon Snack |

Equipment Required: (Check all that apply.)

| ☒ Flip Chart/Markers | ☐ CD Player | ☐ TV/Video Player |
| ☐ Microphone | ☐ LED Projector | ☐ Computer/Printer |

Other Requirements: (Please describe.)
A legal pad and pen for each person.

Contact Information:

Name: Firstname Lastname   **Department:** Human Resources

Email: Lastname@myristicanna.com   **Phone:** 555-0145

FIGURE 9.46

(Project 9C Meeting Reservation continues on the next page)

CHAPTER REVIEW

1 Start Word. Open a blank document, and then press F12. In the **Save As** dialog box, click the **Save As type arrow**, and then click **Word Template**. Navigate to your **Word Chapter 9** folder. Using your own name, save the document as **Lastname_Firstname_9C_Meeting_ Reservation** and then click **Save**. If necessary, display the rulers and formatting marks.

a. Click the **FILE tab**, and then click **Options**. On the left side of the **Word Options** dialog box, click **Customize Ribbon**.

b. In the **Main Tabs** list, locate and then click to select the **Developer** check box. Click **OK** to close the **Word Options** dialog box.

c. Click the **INSERT tab**. In the **Text group**, click the **Object button arrow**, and then click **Text from File**. In the **Insert File** dialog box, navigate to your student files, click **w09C_Meeting_Reservation**, and then click **Insert**. If *Myristicanna* is flagged as a spelling error, click **Ignore All**.

d. Select the first three paragraphs. On the mini toolbar, change the **Font Size** to **16**, apply **Bold**, and then change the **Font Color** to **Orange, Accent 2, Darker 25%**—in the sixth column, the fifth color. Press Ctrl + E.

e. Select the paragraph that begins *Meeting*. Change the **Font Size** to **18**, apply **Bold**, and then change the **Font Color** to **Orange, Accent 2, Darker 50%**—in the sixth column, the last color. Apply **Center**.

2 Locate the text *Group Name*. Position the insertion point to the right of the colon, and then press Spacebar.

a. Click the **DEVELOPER tab**, and then in the **Controls group**, click **Design Mode** to turn on **Design Mode**.

b. In the **Controls group**, click **Plain Text content control**.

c. In a similar manner, click to the right of the colon for each of the following terms—*Start Time*, *End Time*, and *Number Attending*—press Spacebar, and then insert a **Plain Text content control**.

d. Locate the text *Date of Event*. Position the insertion point to the right of the colon, press Spacebar, and then in the **Controls group**, click **Date Picker content control**.

e. With the **Date Picker content control** selected, in the **Controls group**, click **Properties**. In the **Content**

Control Properties dialog box, under **Date Picker Properties**, in the **Display the date like this** box, click the third style—October 9, 2016—your date will differ. Click **OK**.

3 Locate the text *Room Setup*. Position the insertion point to the right of the colon, press Spacebar, and then in the **Controls group**, click **Drop-Down List content control**.

a. With the **Drop-Down List content control** selected, in the **Controls group**, click **Properties**. In the **Content Control Properties** dialog box, under **Drop-Down List Properties**, click **Add**. In the **Add Choice** dialog box, in the **Display Name** box, type **Banquet** Click **OK**.

b. Using the same technique, add the following choices to the **Drop-Down List content control**:

Classroom

Hollow Square

U-Shape

c. Click **OK** to close the dialog box. Select the two paragraphs that begin *Continental* and *Dinner*. Click the **INSERT tab**. In the **Tables group**, click **Table**, and then click **Convert Text to Table**. In the **Convert Text to Table** dialog box, click **OK**.

d. In the table, click to position the insertion point to the left of *Continental*. Press Spacebar, and then position the insertion point to the left of the space. Click the **DEVELOPER tab**, and then in the **Controls group**, click **Check Box content control**. Select the check box, right-click, and then from the shortcut menu, click **Copy**. Position the insertion point to the left of *Full Breakfast*, and then press Ctrl + V.

e. In a similar manner, insert a **Check Box content control** to the left of each of the remaining items in the table. For all items with a check box, be sure there is a space between the check box and the text.

4 Select the two paragraphs that begin *Flip Chart* and *Microphone*. Click the **INSERT tab**. In the **Tables group**, click **Table**, and then click **Convert Text to Table**. Click **OK**.

a. Using the technique you just practiced, insert a **Check Box content control** to the left of all the items in the table.

(Project 9C Meeting Reservation continues on the next page)

b. Click to position the insertion point in the blank paragraph above *Contact Information*. Click the **DEVELOPER tab**, and then in the **Controls group**, click **Plain Text content control**.

c. Below *Contact Information*, locate the text *Name*. Click to position the insertion point to the right of the colon, and then press Spacebar.

d. In the **Controls group**, click **Plain Text content control**.

e. In a similar manner, to the right of the colon for each of the following items—*Department*, *Email*, and *Phone*—press Spacebar, and then insert a **Plain Text content control**.

5 To the right of the paragraph that begins *Name*, in the **Plain Text content control**, select the text, and then type **Enter your first and last names.**

a. To the right of the paragraph that begins *Email*, in the **Plain Text content control**, select the text, and then type **Enter your work email address.**

b. To the right of *Name*, click in the **Plain Text content control**. On the **DEVELOPER tab**, in the **Controls group**, click **Properties**. In the **Content Control Properties** dialog box, in the **Title** box, type **Name** Select the **Use a style to format text typed into the empty control** check box. Click the **Style arrow**, click **Strong**, and then click **OK**.

c. To the right of *Email*, click in the **Plain Text content control**. On the **DEVELOPER tab**, in the **Controls group**, click **Properties**. In the **Content Control Properties** dialog box, in the **Title** box, type **Email Address** Select the **Use a style to format text typed into the empty control** check box. Click the **Style arrow**, click **Strong**, and then click **OK**. At the bottom of the document, delete the blank paragraph.

6 Press Ctrl + Home. On the **DEVELOPER tab**, in the **Controls group**, click **Design Mode** to turn off **Design Mode**.

a. On the **DEVELOPER tab**, in the **Protect group**, click **Restrict Editing**.

b. In the **Restrict Editing** pane, under **2. Editing restrictions**, select the **Allow only this type of editing in the document** check box. Click the **Allow only this type of editing in the document arrow**, and then click **Filling in forms**.

c. In the **Restrict Editing** pane, under **3. Start enforcement**, click **Yes, Start Enforcing Protection**.

d. In the **Start Enforcing Protection** dialog box, click **OK**. Close the **Restrict Editing** pane, save your changes, and then close Word.

7 On the taskbar, click **File Explorer**. Navigate to your **Word Chapter 9** folder, and then double-click the file **Lastname_Firstname_9C_Meeting_Reservation**. Press F12, and then navigate to your **Word Chapter 9** folder. Using your own name, type the file name **Lastname_Firstname_9C_Reservation_Completed** and then click **Save**.

a. In the content control following *Group Name*, type **Planning Committee** Press Tab, click the **Date Picker content control arrow**, and then click **Today**. Continue filling in the form using the information shown below:

Start Time	9:00 a.m.
End Time	11:00 a.m.
Number Attending	10
Room Setup	U-Shape
Meals Desired	Morning Snack
Equipment Required	Flip Chart/Markers
Other Requirements	**A legal pad and pen for each person.**
Name	*Use your firstname and lastname*
Department	**Human Resources**
Email	*YourLastname@ myristicanna.com*
Phone	**555-0145**

b. Click the **FILE tab**, and then click **Show All Properties**. In the **Tags** box, type **meeting reservation, completed** In the **Subject** box, type your course name and section number. If necessary, edit the author name to display your name. Save your changes, and then press Ctrl + W to close the document.

c. Click the **FILE tab**, and then click **Open**. Navigate to your **Word Chapter 9** folder, and then open the file **Lastname_Firstname_9C_Meeting_Reservation**.

(Project 9C Meeting Reservation continues on the next page)

CHAPTER REVIEW

d. Click the **DEVELOPER tab**, and then in the **Protect group**, click **Restrict Editing**. At the bottom of the **Restrict Editing** pane, click **Stop Protection**. **Close the Restrict Editing** pane. Press Ctrl + End, and then insert the file name in the footer.

e. Click the **FILE tab**, and then click **Show All Properties**. In the **Tags** box, type **meeting reservation, template** In the **Subject** box, type your course name and section number. If necessary, edit the author name to display your name. Save your changes.

END | You have completed Project 9C

8 Click the **FILE tab**, and then click **Options**. In the **Word Options** dialog box, click **Customize Ribbon**. In the **Main Tabs** list, locate and then clear the **Developer** check box. Click **OK**, and notice that the **DEVELOPER tab** no longer displays on the ribbon.

9 Print both documents or submit electronically as directed by your instructor. Close Word.

CHAPTER REVIEW

Apply **9B** skills from these Objectives:

4 Customize the Ribbon

5 Format Pictures and Text Boxes

6 Add a Digital Signature to a Document

7 Prepare a Document for Distribution

Build from Scratch

Skills Review Project 9D Privacy Policy

In the following Skills Review, you will finalize a document that explains the privacy policy of Myristicanna Spices. This will require creating a grouped object, inserting a signature line, and formatting the document. Your completed document will look similar to Figure 9.47.

PROJECT FILES

For Project 9D, you will need the following files:

New blank Word document
w09D_Security
w09D_Privacy
w09D_Privacy_Policy

You will save your file as:

Lastname_Firstname_9D_Privacy_Policy

PROJECT RESULTS

Myristicanna Spices Privacy Policy

Myristicanna Spices believes in protecting the privacy of our online visitors. This policy applies only to our website and to emails you may send us; it does not apply to telephone calls you make to us or postal mail you may send.

Information We Collect

In certain locations on our website we may request that you provide personal information—for example, when filling in order forms or registering for our monthly newsletter. We may request your name, email address, mailing address, and telephone number. Only information we believe we need to fulfill our obligation to you will be marked *required*. You may choose not to provide particular information; however, this may result in not being able to utilize all of our website's services.

We may also collect certain non-personal information which cannot be used to identify or contact you. This technical information may include your IP address, the type of browser your system uses, and the websites you visit before and after Myristicanna Spices site.

How Collected Information Is Used

The personal information we gather will usually be in response to a service you are requesting. We will use that information to fulfill your online orders, enter you in a contest, provide information you requested, and compile data you have provided in surveys and polls. We combine the non-personal information we gather to better understand the demographics of our users and determine how our site is being used. This data allows us to refine our website content and improve our product offerings.

If you send us email or fill out an online form, we may use your personal information to contact you with a response to a question or concern. We may also keep information for future data compilation. We do not share your personal information with any non-affiliated third party without your consent. We may, however, disclose the statistical data gathered through non-personal information with our third-party affiliates.

Any questions regarding our Privacy Policy should be directed to privacy@myristicanna.com.

X _____

Anna Carter
President

Lastname_Firstname_9D_Privacy_Policy

FIGURE 9.47

(Project 9D Privacy Policy continues on the next page)

1 ▶ Start Word, and display a blank document. Click the **FILE tab**, and then click **Options**. In the **Word Options** dialog box, click **Customize Ribbon**.

a. Below the **Main Tabs** list, with **Home** selected, click **New Tab**. Click **New Tab (Custom)**, and then click **Rename**. In the **Rename** dialog box, in the **Display name** box, type *your initials*, and then click **OK**.

b. Click **New Group (Custom)**, and then click **Rename**. In the **Rename** dialog box, in the **Display name** box, type **Frequent Tasks** and then click **OK**.

c. With **Frequent Tasks (Custom)** selected, in the **Word Options** dialog box, click the **Choose commands from arrow**, and then click **All Commands**. Under **All Commands**, scroll as necessary, click **Edit Footer**, and then click **Add**. Click **OK** to close the **Word Options** dialog box.

2 ▶ Press F12, navigate to your **Word Chapter 9** folder, and then save the document as **Lastname_Firstname_ 9D_Privacy_Policy** If necessary, display the rulers and formatting marks.

a. Click the *your initials* tab. In the **Frequent Tasks** group, click **Edit Footer**, and then insert the file name in the footer. Close the footer area.

b. Click the **INSERT tab**, and then in the **Illustrations** group, click **Pictures**. In the **Insert Picture** dialog box, navigate to your student files, select the file **w09D_Security**, and then click **Insert**.

c. On the **PICTURE TOOLS FORMAT tab**, in the **Arrange group**, click **Wrap Text**, and then click **Square**. In the **Adjust group**, click **Corrections**. In the **Corrections** gallery, under **Brightness and Contrast**, in the third row, click the fourth option— **Brightness: +20% Contrast: 0% (Normal)**.

d. In the **Picture Styles group**, click **Picture Effects**, point to **Soft Edges**, and then click **10 Point**.

e. In the **Size group**, change the **Shape Height** to 2". Click to the right of the picture to deselect it.

3 ▶ Click the **INSERT tab**, and then in the **Illustrations** group, click **Pictures**. In the **Insert Picture** dialog box, navigate to your student files, select the file **w09D_Privacy**, and then click **Insert**. In the **Size group**, change the **Shape Width** to 4". In the **Arrange group**, click **Wrap Text**, and then click **In Front of Text**.

a. In the **Size group**, click **Crop**. On the left border, drag the middle crop handle to the right to approximately **2.75 inches on the horizontal ruler** until the border is slightly to the left of the text **www.myristicanna.com**.

b. Using the same technique, on the right border, drag the middle crop handle to the left to approximately **5.75 inches on the horizontal ruler** until the border is slightly to the right of the text. In the **Size group**, click **Crop**.

c. In the **Arrange group**, click **Rotate Objects**, and then click **More Rotation Options**. In the **Layout** dialog box, on the **Size tab**, under **Rotate**, click the **Rotation spin box down arrow** to −65. Click **OK**.

4 ▶ Drag the picture to the left and position it as shown in Figure 9.47. If necessary, in the **Arrange group**, click **Rotate Objects**, click **More Rotation Options**, and then change the **Rotation** box so that the privacy picture is rotated as shown in Figure 9.47.

a. With the privacy picture selected, press and hold Ctrl, and then click the security picture. Release Ctrl. With both images selected, on the **PICTURE TOOLS FORMAT tab**, in the **Arrange group**, click **Group**, and then click **Group**.

b. Click the **DRAWING TOOLS FORMAT tab**. In the **Arrange group**, click **Wrap Text**, and then click **Square**. Click **Wrap Text** again, and then click **Move with Text**. Click to deselect the group.

c. Click the **INSERT tab**. In the **Text group**, click the **Object button arrow**, and then click **Text from File**. Navigate to your student files, select the file **w09D_Privacy_Policy**, and then click **Insert**. If any words are flagged as spelling or grammar errors, click **Ignore All**.

d. Select the first paragraph. Change the **Font Size** to 16, and apply **Bold**.

e. Select the paragraph *Information We Collect*, change the **Font Size** to 12, and apply **Bold**. Select the paragraph that begins *How Collected*, change the **Font Size** to 12, and then apply **Bold**.

5 ▶ Press Ctrl + End. On the **INSERT tab**, in the **Text group**, click the **Signature Line button arrow**, and then click **Microsoft Office Signature Line**.

(Project 9D Privacy Policy continues on the next page)

a. In the **Signature Setup** dialog box, in the **Suggested signer** box, type **Anna Carter** In the **Suggested signer's title** box, type **President** and then click **OK**.

b. Save your changes.

6 Press Ctrl + Home. Click the **FILE tab**, and then, if necessary, click **Info**. In the **Inspect Document** section, click **Check for Issues**, and then click **Inspect Document**.

a. In the **Document Inspector** dialog box, be sure all eight check boxes are selected, and then click **Inspect**.

b. To the right of **Document Properties and Personal Information**, click **Remove All**.

c. In the **Document Inspector** dialog box, click **Close**.

7 From **Backstage** view, click **Show All Properties**. In the **Tags** box, type **privacy policy, grouped object** In the **Subject** box, type your course name and section number. In the **Author** box, type your own name.

END | You have completed Project 9D

a. From **Backstage** view, in the **Protect Document** section, click **Protect Document**, and then click **Mark as Final**.

b. In the **Microsoft Word** message box, click **OK**. In the second **Microsoft Word** message box, click **OK**.

8 Print your document or submit electronically as directed by your instructor. Press Ctrl + W to close your document without closing Word.

a. Click the **FILE tab**, and then click **Options**. In the **Word Options** dialog box, click **Customize Ribbon**. In the **Main Tabs** list, right-click *your initials* **(Custom)**, and then from the shortcut menu, click **Remove**. Click **OK**, and then close Word.

CONTENT-BASED ASSESSMENTS

Mastering Word Project 9E Ergonomic Study

Apply 9A skills from these Objectives:

1 Create a Customized Form
2 Modify and Lock a Form
3 Use a Template to Complete a Form

In the following Mastering Word project, you will create a form for the IT Department at Myristicanna Spices. The department plans to survey employees regarding health issues related to their workstations. You will insert content controls, restrict editing, and save the document as a template. Using the template, you will fill in the form. Your completed document will look similar to Figure 9.48.

PROJECT FILES

For Project 9E, you will need the following file:

w09E_Ergonomic_Study

You will save your files as:

Lastname_Firstname_9E_Ergonomic_Study
Lastname_Firstname_9E_Study_Completed

PROJECT RESULTS

Myristicanna Spices - IT Department

The IT department in conjunction with the Human Resources department is conducting an ergonomics study to assess the current status of our equipment as it relates to your workstation and health issues. Please send the completed form to technology@myristicanna.com.

Name: Click here to enter text.   **Date:** Click here to enter a date.

Job Task
For each job function listed below, indicate the hours per day on average that you devote to each task.

Computer Use	Choose an item.
Phone Use	Choose an item.
Paperwork / Reading	Choose an item.
Copying / Collating	Choose an item.
Filing / Storing	Choose an item.

Input Devices	Yes	No
1. Does your keyboard have all the features that your job tasks require?	☐	☐
2. Do all of the keys on your keyboard work reliably?	☐	☐
3. Do you regularly use your numeric keypad to enter data?	☐	☐
4. Does your mouse work reliably?	☐	☐
5. Does your mouse provide the features your job requires?	☐	☐

Monitor	Yes	No
1. Is the top of your monitor at or slightly below eye level?	☐	☐
2. Is your monitor located about an arm's reach away?	☐	☐
3. Can your monitor tilt and swivel?	☐	☐
4. Is your monitor easy to read, clear, and free from blurry areas?	☐	☐
5. Is your monitor free from glare?	☐	☐

Special Conditions	Yes	No
1. If you use a wrist rest, is it free from sharp edges and positioned at the same height as your keyboard?	☐	☐
2. If you use a footrest, is it easy to position and adjust in height and angle?	☐	☐
3. If you wear eyeglasses, are the lenses specifically adjusted for computer use?	☐	☐
4. If you wear bifocals, can you view your monitor without backward neck bending?	☐	☐
5. If you share a workstation, is all the equipment adjustable to accommodate you and your job tasks?	☐	☐
6. If you answered NO to Question 5, please explain what is causing the glare. Click here to enter text.		

Lastname_Firstname_9E_Ergonomic_Study

Myristicanna Spices - IT Department

The IT department in conjunction with the Human Resources department is conducting an ergonomics study to assess the current status of our equipment as it relates to your workstation and health issues. Please send the completed form to technology@myristicanna.com.

Name: Firstname Lastname   **Date:** 1/27/2016

Job Task
For each job function listed below, indicate the hours per day on average that you devote to each task.

Computer Use	5
Phone Use	Choose an item.
Paperwork / Reading	Choose an item.
Copying / Collating	Choose an item.
Filing / Storing	Choose an item.

Input Devices	Yes	No
1. Does your keyboard have all the features that your job tasks require?	☐	☐
2. Do all of the keys on your keyboard work reliably?	☐	☐
3. Do you regularly use your numeric keypad to enter data?	☐	☐
4. Does your mouse work reliably?	☐	☐
5. Does your mouse provide the features your job requires?	☐	☐

Monitor	Yes	No
1. Is the top of your monitor at or slightly below eye level?	☐	☐
2. Is your monitor located about an arm's reach away?	☐	☐
3. Can your monitor tilt and swivel?	☐	☐
4. Is your monitor easy to read, clear, and free from blurry areas?	☐	☐
5. Is your monitor free from glare?	☐	☐

Special Conditions	Yes	No
1. If you use a wrist rest, is it free from sharp edges and positioned at the same height as your keyboard?	☐	☐
2. If you use a footrest, is it easy to position and adjust in height and angle?	☐	☐
3. If you wear eyeglasses, are the lenses specifically adjusted for computer use?	☐	☐
4. If you wear bifocals, can you view your monitor without backward neck bending?	☐	☐
5. If you share a workstation, is all the equipment adjustable to accommodate you and your job tasks?	☐	☐
6. If you answered NO to Question 5, please explain what is causing the glare. Click here to enter text.		

FIGURE 9.48

(Project 9E Ergonomic Study continues on the next page)

CONTENT-BASED ASSESSMENTS

1 Start Word. Navigate to your student files, and then open the document **w09E_Ergonomic_Study**. Save the document as a **Word Template** in your **Word Chapter 9** folder with the file name **Lastname_Firstname_9E_Ergonomic_Study** If necessary, display the rulers and formatting marks. On the ribbon, display the **DEVELOPER tab**. If any words are flagged as spelling errors, click **Ignore All**.

2 Select the first paragraph. Change the **Font Size** to **16**, apply **Bold**, and then change the **Font Color** to **Green, Accent 6, Darker 50%**. **Center** the paragraph. Select the paragraph *Job Task*, change the **Font Size** to **14**, apply **Bold,** and then change the **Font Color** to **Green, Accent 6, Darker 25%**. Select the paragraph that begins *For each*, and then apply **Italic**. Apply the table style **Grid Table 4 – Accent 6** to all four tables.

3 Turn on **Design Mode**. In the document, locate the text *Name*, position the insertion point to the right of the colon, press Spacebar, and then insert a **Plain Text content control**. Locate the text *Date*, position the insertion point to the right of the colon, press Spacebar, and then insert a **Date Picker content control**.

4 In the first table, in the first row, click in the second cell, and then insert a **Drop-Down List content control**. Display the **Content Control Properties** dialog box, and then click **Add**. In the **Add Choice** dialog box, in the **Display Name** box, type **1** In a similar manner, add the numbers **2** through **8** to the list. Copy the content control to the remaining empty cells in the first table. Select the second column, and then **Align Center**.

5 In the second table, position the insertion point in the first empty cell below *Yes*, and then insert a **Check Box content control**. Copy the content control to the remaining empty cells in all three tables. For the second, third, and fourth tables, select the second and third columns, and then **Align Center**.

6 In the fourth table, in the last row, position the insertion point in the first cell. Click the **LAYOUT tab**, and then in the **Rows & Columns group**, click **Insert Below**. With all three cells selected, **Merge Cells**. In the **Alignment group**, click **Align Center Left**.

7 Click in the merged cell, and then type **6**. Press Spacebar two times, and then type **If you answered NO to Question 5, please explain what is causing the glare.** Press Enter, and then insert a **Plain Text content control**.

8 Press Ctrl + Home, and then turn off **Design Mode**. Display the **Restrict Editing** pane, and then under **2. Editing restrictions**, select the **Allow only this type of editing in the document** check box. Click the **Allow only this type of editing in the document arrow**, and then click **Filling in forms**. Under **3. Start enforcement**, click **Yes, Start Enforcing Protection**. In the **Start Enforcing Protection** dialog box, click **OK**. Close the **Restrict Editing** pane.

9 Click the **FILE tab**, and then click **Show All Properties**. In the **Tags** box, type **ergonomic study, template** In the **Subject** box, type your course name and section number. If necessary, edit the author name to display your name. Save your changes. Close Word.

10 Navigate to your **Word Chapter 9** folder, and then double-click **Lastname_Firstname_9E_Ergonomic_Study**. Save the file to your **Word Chapter 9** folder as **Lastname_Firstname_9E_Study_Completed**

11 In the content control following *Name*, using your own name, type **Firstname Lastname** Press Tab, click the **Date Picker content control arrow**, and then click **Today**. Press Tab. To the right of *Computer Use*, click the **Drop-Down List content control arrow**, and then click **5**.

12 Click **Show All Properties**. In the **Tags** box, delete the text *template*, and then type **completed** If necessary, edit the author name to display your name. Save your changes. Press Ctrl + W.

13 Open the file **Lastname_Firstname_9E_Ergonomic_Study**. Display the **Restrict Editing** pane, and then click **Stop Protection**. Close the **Restrict Editing** pane. Insert the file name in the footer, and then Save your changes.

14 In the **Word Options** dialog box, turn off the display of the **DEVELOPER tab**.

15 Print your documents or submit electronically as directed by your instructor. Close Word.

END | You have completed Project 9E

CONTENT-BASED ASSESSMENTS

Apply **9B** skills from these Objectives:

4 Customize the Ribbon

5 Format Pictures and Text Boxes

6 Attach a Digital Signature to a Document

7 Prepare a Document for Distribution

In the following Mastering Word project, you will create a memo from George Tillman, Director of Human Resources, explaining staffing needs for next year at Myristicanna Spices. The document will require you to group objects to create a letterhead, insert a signature line, and mark the document as final. Your completed document will look similar to Figure 9.49.

PROJECT FILES

For Project 9F, you will need the following files:

New blank Word document

w09F_Staff

w09F_Staffing_Needs

You will save your file as:

Lastname_Firstname_9F_Staffing_Needs

PROJECT RESULTS

Build from Scratch

Myristicanna Spices Human Resources

TO: Anna Carter, President

FROM: George Tillman, Director of Human Resources

DATE: September 8

RE: Next Year's Staffing Needs

In accordance with this year's budget, staffing requirements will remain even with last year. We anticipate a turnover of approximately ten percent based on past years. With no planned changes in product lines or major increases in production requirements, Myristicanna Spices should be able to maintain its high quality merchandise and excellent customer service.

Several job descriptions have been changed and current employees will be invited to apply for those new positions. We believe that current employees will be able to fill the new positions, and we do not anticipate any layoffs based on these changes. We have the resources available to provide new or additional training where necessary. Our staff has always been willing to accept new responsibilities and adapt to change.

In accordance with Myristicanna Spices policies and internal guidelines, we will continue to strive for an employee base that is diverse—actively recruiting minorities, veterans, and people with physical challenges.

_____

George Tillman
Director of Human Resources

Lastname_Firstname_9F_Staffing_Needs

FIGURE 9.49

(Project 9F Staffing Needs continues on the next page)

CONTENT-BASED ASSESSMENTS

1 Start Word, and open a blank document. Navigate to your **Word Chapter 9** folder, and save the document as **Lastname_Firstname_9F_Staffing_Needs** Insert the file name in the footer. If necessary, display the rulers and formatting marks.

2 Insert a **Simple Text Box**, and then change the **Shape Width** to **6.5"**. Change **Wrap Text** to **Top and Bottom**, and then change the **Shape Outline** to **No Outline**.

3 In the text box, type **Myristicanna Spices** Press Enter, and then type **Human Resources** Select both paragraphs, change the **Font** to **Arial**, and then change the **Font Size** to **28**. Apply **Bold**, and then change the **Font Color** to **Orange, Accent 2, Darker 25%**—in the sixth column, the fifth color. **Center** the paragraphs. Deselect the text box.

4 Display the **Insert Picture** dialog box, navigate to your student files, and then **Insert** the file **w09F_Staff**. Change **Wrap Text** to **In Front of Text**, and then change the **Shape Width** to **1.2"**. Position the picture so that the top left corner is at the top and left margins as shown in Figure 9.49. **Copy** the picture, click in a blank area of the document, and then press Ctrl+V. Position the picture so that the top right corner is at the top and right margins. With the pasted picture selected, click **Flip Horizontal**. Select both pictures, and then click **Align Top**.

5 Select both pictures and the text box, and then **Group** the items. Change **Wrap Text** to **In Line with Text**. Press Enter to position the insertion point below the graphic.

6 Insert **Text from File**—from your student files, select the file **w09F_Staffing_Needs**. If any names are flagged as spelling errors, click **Ignore All**.

7 Press Ctrl + End, and then insert a **Microsoft Office Signature Line**. As the **Suggested signer**, type **George Tillman** As the **Suggested signer's title**, type **Director of Human Resources** Save your changes.

8 Press Ctrl + Home. Display the **Document Inspector** dialog box, and then with all check boxes selected, inspect the document. To the right of **Document Properties and Personal Information**, click **Remove All**, and then close the **Document Inspector** dialog box.

9 Click **Show All Properties**. In the **Tags** box, type **staffing needs, memo** In the **Subject** box, type your course name and section number. If necessary, edit the author name to display your name.

10 With the **Info tab** selected, click **Protect Document**, and then click **Mark as Final**. In the **Microsoft Word** message box, click **OK**. In the second **Microsoft Word** message box, click **OK**.

11 Print your document or submit electronically as directed by your instructor. Close Word. When prompted regarding content on the Clipboard, click **No**.

END | You have completed Project 9F

CONTENT-BASED ASSESSMENTS

Mastering Word Project 9G Seminar Evaluation

In the following Mastering Word project, you will create a custom form that will be used by employees to evaluate training seminars at Myristicanna Spices. As part of the document, you will format and group objects to create a heading. Your completed document will look similar to Figure 9.50.

Apply 9A and 9B skills from these Objectives:

1 Create a Customized Form
2 Modify and Lock a Form
3 Use a Template to Complete a Form
4 Customize the Ribbon
5 Format Pictures and Text Boxes
6 Add a Digital Signature to a Document
7 Prepare a Document for Distribution

PROJECT FILES

For Project 9G, you will need the following files:

w09G_Seminar_Evaluation
w09G_Training
w09G_Seminar

You will save your file as:

Lastname_Firstname_9G_Seminar_Evaluation

PROJECT RESULTS

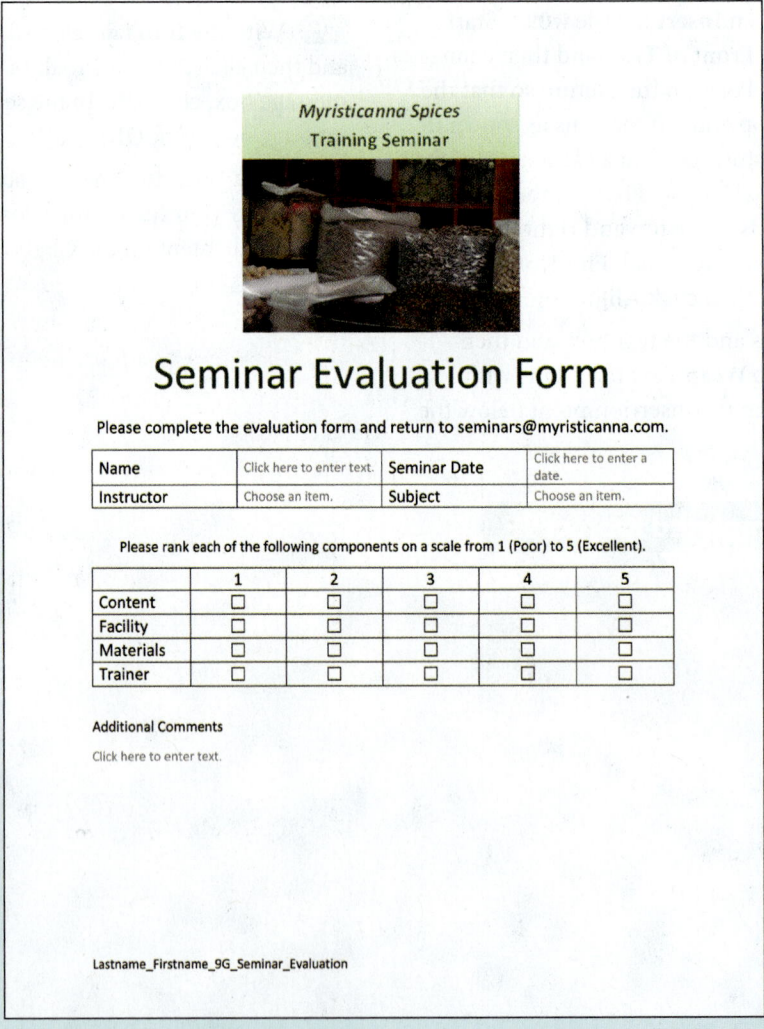

FIGURE 9.50

(Project 9G Seminar Evaluation continues on the next page)

Mastering Word Project 9G Seminar Evaluation (continued)

1 Start Word. From your student files, open the file **w09G_Seminar_Evaluation**. In your **Word Chapter 9** folder, save the document as a **Word Template** with the name **Lastname_Firstname_9G_Seminar_Evaluation** Insert the file name in the footer. If necessary, display rulers and formatting marks. Display the **DEVELOPER tab**.

2 Press Ctrl + Home. From your student files, insert the picture **w09G_Training**. Change **Wrap Text** to **Square**, and then change the **Shape Width** to **3.1"**. Deselect the picture, and then from your student files, insert the picture **w09G_Seminar**. Change **Wrap Text** to **In Front of Text**.

3 Drag the **w09G_Seminar** picture so that the top left corner is aligned with the top left corner of the **w09G_Training** picture as shown in Figure 9.50.

4 Group the two pictures, and then change **Wrap Text** to **In Line with Text**. Select the grouped object, including the paragraph mark next to it, and then apply **Center**.

5 Position the insertion point in the empty paragraph immediately below the grouped object. Type **Seminar Evaluation Form** and then press Enter. Select the text you just typed, change the **Font Size** to **36**, and then change the **Font Color** to **Green, Accent 6, Darker 50%**. Apply **Center**.

6 Position the insertion point in the empty paragraph above the first table, and then type **Please complete the evaluation form and return to seminars@myristicanna .com.** Select the text you just typed, and then change the **Font Size** to **14** and apply **Center**. If necessary, remove the hyperlink. Position the insertion point in the empty paragraph above the second table, and then type **Please rank each of the following components on a scale from 1 (Poor) to 5 (Excellent).** Select the text you just typed, and then change the **Font Size** to **12** and apply **Center**.

7 Turn on **Design Mode**. In the first table, in the cell to the right of *Name*, insert a **Plain Text content control**. In the cell to the right of *Seminar Date*, insert a **Date Picker content control**, and then change the format to **M/d/yy**. In the cell following *Instructor*, insert a **Drop-Down List content control**, and then add the following names:

Alvin Barnes

Charles Corbin

Susan Parrish

8 In the last cell of the first table, insert a **Drop-Down List content control**, and then add the following topics:

Customer Service

Employee Benefits

Microsoft Office

Safety Issues

9 In the second table, insert a **Check Box content control** in each of the empty cells. Press Ctrl + End, and then insert a **Plain Text content control**. Turn off **Design Mode**.

10 Click the **FILE tab**, and then click **Show All Properties**. In the **Tags** box, type **seminar evaluation form** In the **Subject** box, type your course name and section number. If necessary, edit the author name to display your name. Save your changes.

11 Press Ctrl + Home. Display the **Restrict Editing** pane. Under **2. Editing restrictions**, select the **Allow only this type of editing in the document** check box. Click the **Allow only this type of editing in the document arrow**, and then click **Filling in forms**. Under **3. Start enforcement**, click **Yes, Start Enforcing Protection**. In the **Start Enforcing Protection** dialog box, click **OK**. Close the **Restrict Editing** pane.

12 From the **Word Options** dialog box, turn off the display of the **DEVELOPER tab**, and then save your changes.

13 Print your document or submit electronically as directed by your instructor. Close Word.

END | You have completed Project 9G

CONTENT-BASED ASSESSMENTS

Apply a combination of the **9A** and **9B** skills.

Build from Scratch

Build from Scratch

Build from Scratch

GO! Fix It	Project 9H Complaint Form	Online
GO! Make It	Project 9I Phone Request	Online
GO! Solve It	Project 9J Accident Report	Online
GO! Solve It	Project 9K Staff Promotion	

PROJECT FILES

For Project 9K, you will need the following files:

New blank Word document
w09K_Promotion_Data

You will save your file as:

Lastname_Firstname_9K_Staff_Promotion

Anna Carter, President of Myristicanna Spices, needs to fill the position of Executive Assistant. She would like to promote an individual from within the company. She has identified ten candidates; however, she wants the department managers to identify the strengths and weaknesses of the individuals. Create a memorandum from Ms. Carter to department managers, including the current date and an appropriate subject line. In the body of the memo, design a form that includes appropriate content controls to select the name of the individual being evaluated and rate the candidate on a variety of skills using a five-point scale ranging from Poor to Excellent. Information regarding candidates' names and required skills can be found in the student file **w09K_Promotion_Data**. Save the document as a Word template with the file name **Lastname_Firstname_9K_Staff_Promotion** Insert the file name in the footer and add appropriate document properties. Restrict editing to filling in the form. Print your document or submit electronically as directed by your instructor.

Performance Level

Performance Element		Exemplary: You consistently applied the relevant skills	Proficient: You sometimes, but not always, applied the relevant skills	Developing: You rarely or never applied the relevant skills
	Insert and format text	All required information is included and the document is formatted as a memo.	Some information is missing or the document is not formatted as a memo.	No specific information is included and the document is not formatted as a memo.
	Insert content controls	Appropriate content controls are used and required items are added.	Some content controls are inappropriate or some required items are missing.	No content controls are inserted.
	Insert 5-point rating scale	The scale allows for 5 ratings and displays appropriately with skills and content controls.	The scale does not contain 5 ratings or does not display appropriately with skills and content controls.	There is no scale.
	Save as template and restrict editing	The document is saved as a template and is restricted to filling in forms.	The document is not saved as a template or is not restricted to filling in forms.	The document is not saved as a template and the form is not restricted.

END | You have completed Project 9K

OUTCOMES-BASED ASSESSMENTS

RUBRIC

The following outcomes-based assessments are *open-ended assessments*. That is, there is no specific correct result; your result will depend on your approach to the information provided. Make *Professional Quality* your goal. Use the following scoring rubric to guide you in *how* to approach the problem and then to evaluate *how well* your approach solves the problem.

The *criteria*—Software Mastery, Content, Format and Layout, and Process—represent the knowledge and skills you have gained that you can apply to solving the problem. The *levels of performance*—Professional Quality, Approaching Professional Quality, or Needs Quality Improvements—help you and your instructor evaluate your result.

	Your completed project is of Professional Quality if you:	Your completed project is Approaching Professional Quality if you:	Your completed project Needs Quality Improvements if you:
1-Software Mastery	Choose and apply the most appropriate skills, tools, and features and identify efficient methods to solve the problem.	Choose and apply some appropriate skills, tools, and features, but not in the most efficient manner.	Choose inappropriate skills, tools, or features, or are inefficient in solving the problem.
2-Content	Construct a solution that is clear and well organized, contains content that is accurate, appropriate to the audience and purpose, and is complete. Provide a solution that contains no errors in spelling, grammar, or style.	Construct a solution in which some components are unclear, poorly organized, inconsistent, or incomplete. Misjudge the needs of the audience. Have some errors in spelling, grammar, or style, but the errors do not detract from comprehension.	Construct a solution that is unclear, incomplete, or poorly organized; contains some inaccurate or inappropriate content; and contains many errors in spelling, grammar, or style. Do not solve the problem.
3-Format & Layout	Format and arrange all elements to communicate information and ideas, clarify function, illustrate relationships, and indicate relative importance.	Apply appropriate format and layout features to some elements, but not others. Overuse features, causing minor distraction.	Apply format and layout that does not communicate information or ideas clearly. Do not use format and layout features to clarify function, illustrate relationships, or indicate relative importance. Use available features excessively, causing distraction.
4-Process	Use an organized approach that integrates planning, development, self-assessment, revision, and reflection.	Demonstrate an organized approach in some areas, but not others; or, use an insufficient process of organization throughout.	Do not use an organized approach to solve the problem.

OUTCOMES-BASED ASSESSMENTS

Apply a combination of the **9A** and **9B** skills.

Build from Scratch

GO! Think | Project 9L Computer Equipment

PROJECT FILES

For Project 9L, you will need the following file:

New blank Word document

You will save your files as:

Lastname_Firstname_9L_Computer_Equipment
Lastname_Firstname_9L_Computer_Request

Every three years, the IT department of Myristicanna Spices updates computer equipment and software for the administrative staff. Employees may choose either a desktop or laptop computer. Other options include, but are not limited to, a choice of printers or a scanner. In conjunction with the new computer rollout, the IT department wants to prioritize training needs by asking employees to select a topic—File Management, Microsoft Office, or Website Development—that would be most helpful to them.

Create a questionnaire that can be sent to the administrative staff. Include appropriate text and content controls for the employee's name, the current date, and types of computer equipment and training. Restrict editing the document to filling in forms. Save the document as a Word template with the file name **Lastname_Firstname_9L_Computer_Equipment** Using the template, create a new document and complete the form, using your name as the employee. Save the document as **Lastname_Firstname_9L_Computer_Request** Add appropriate document properties, and mark the document as final. In your template, stop protection, insert the file name in the footer, and add appropriate document properties. Print both documents or submit electronically as directed by your instructor.

END | You have completed Project 9L

Build from Scratch

GO! Think | Project 9M Vacation Compensation   **Online**

Build from Scratch

You and GO! | Project 9N Cover Page   **Online**

Working with Long Documents

GO! to Work
Video W10

PROJECT 10A

OUTCOMES
Create, navigate, and inspect a master document and subdocuments, and modify footers.

OBJECTIVES

1. Create a Master Document and Subdocuments
2. Manage a Master Document and Subdocuments
3. Navigate and Inspect the Master Document
4. Create and Modify Headers and Footers

PROJECT 10B

OUTCOMES
Work with and format long documents and create an index, table of contents, and table of figures.

OBJECTIVES

5. Create an Index
6. Create a Table of Contents
7. Create a Table of Figures
8. Control the Flow and Formatting of Pages and Text

keller/Fotolia

In This Chapter

When several people work on a document, keeping track of the different versions can be difficult. In this chapter, you will create a master document and subdocuments from a multipage file to allow parts of the document to be edited while maintaining the integrity of the complete document. The navigation features in Word allow you to view and edit the final master document. Additionally, you will create navigational and reference aids for a long document, including a table of contents, a table of figures, and an index. Defining the flow of text on the pages of the document will improve readability.

The projects in this chapter relate to the **City of Tawny Creek**, a growing community located between Los Angeles and San Diego, about 20 miles from the Pacific shore. Just 10 years ago, the population was under 100,000; today it has grown to almost 300,000. Community leaders have always focused on quality of life and economic development in decisions on housing, open space, education, and infrastructure, making the city a model for other communities its size around the United States. The city provides many recreational and cultural opportunities with a large park system and thriving arts community.

Autumn Schedule

PROJECT ACTIVITIES

In Activities 10.01 through 10.12, you will create a master document with four subdocuments. The finished document will be a description of the autumn activities offered by the City of Tawny Creek. Your completed documents will look similar to Figure 10.1.

PROJECT FILES

For Project 10A, you will need the following files:

w10A_Autumn_Schedule
w10A_Teens

You will save your files as:

Lastname_Firstname_10A_Autumn_Schedule
Lastname_Firstname_10A_Teens

PROJECT RESULTS

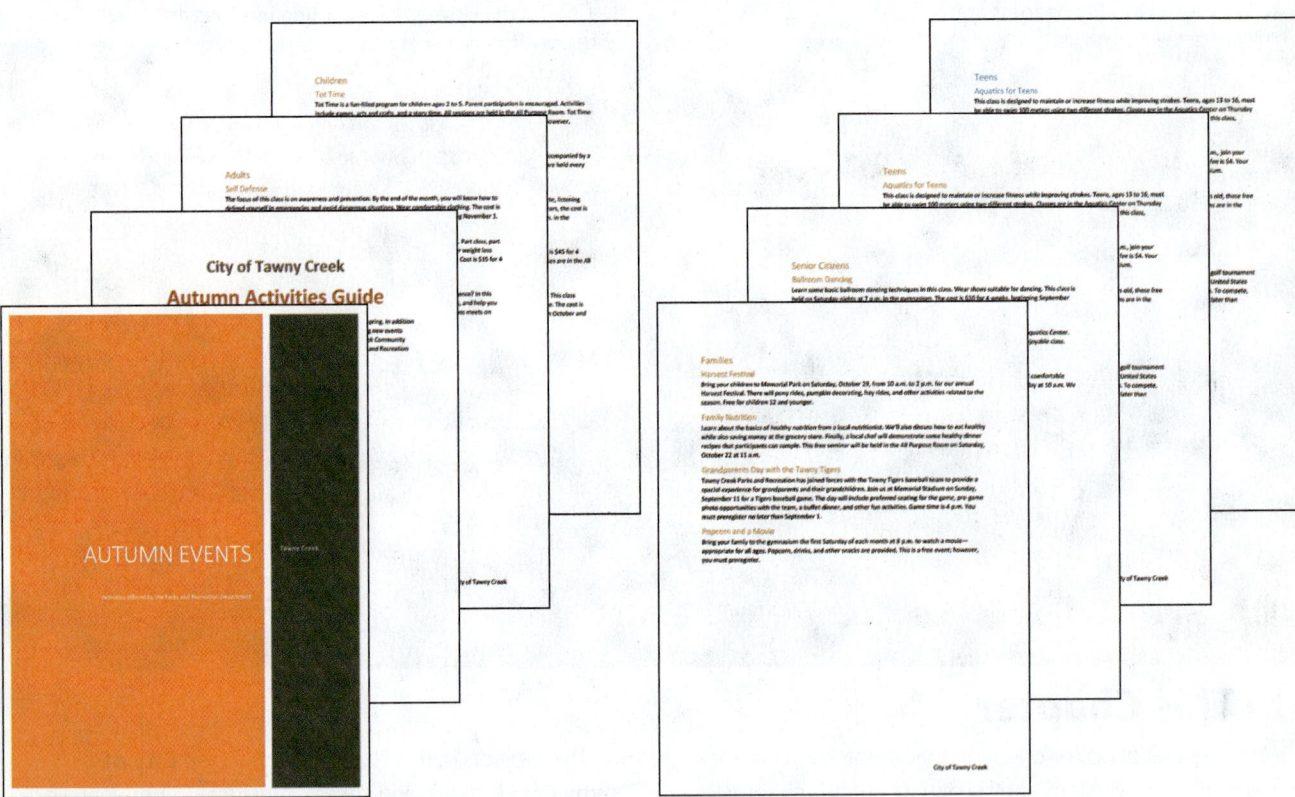

FIGURE 10.1 Project 10A Autumn Schedule

Objective 1   Create a Master Document and Subdocuments

Video W10-1

You can organize a long document into sections—a *master document* and *subdocuments*—to make it easier to work with different parts of the document. A master document is a Word document that serves as a container for the different parts of a document. A subdocument is a section of the document that is linked to the master document. Changes made in the subdocument are reflected in the master document. Using subdocuments enables the individuals collaborating on a project to edit the various sections of the document without altering the entire long document. Each individual can work on a specific section, and then the sections can be integrated into the final document.

Using a master document allows you to maintain consistent formatting and styles across all of the subdocuments even though different people are working on the sections. *Outline view* displays the overall organization, or hierarchy, of parts of a document, including headings, subheadings, and subordinate text.

Activity 10.01 | Creating a Master Document from an Existing Document

1 ▷ Start Word. Navigate to your student files, locate and open the file **w10A_Autumn_Schedule**. Press F12. In the **Save As** dialog box, navigate to the location where you are saving your files for this chapter, and create a folder named **Word Chapter 10** Open the **Word Chapter 10** folder, and then create a folder named **Project 10A** Save the document to your **Project 10A** folder as **Lastname_Firstname_10A_Autumn_Schedule** If necessary, display the rulers and formatting marks.

2 ▷ Click the **DESIGN tab**. In the **Document Formatting group**, click **Themes**, and then in the **Themes** gallery, click **Retrospect**. Click the **HOME tab**, and then compare your screen with Figure 10.2.

> Recall that changing the theme affects the default fonts, colors, and styles. In this case, the theme colors—and some styles—change to a brown color scheme. The *body text*—text that does not have a heading style applied—is not changed.

FIGURE 10.2

3 ▷ Select the first paragraph of the document. On the mini toolbar, change the **Font Size** to **28**. On the **HOME tab**, in the **Font group**, click **Text Effects** 🅰️ ⋅, and then in the **Text Effects** gallery, in the first row, select the fifth effect—**Fill – Brown, Accent 4, Soft Bevel**. Press Ctrl + E.

4 Select the second paragraph. On the mini toolbar, change the **Font Size** to **36**, apply **Bold** [B], and then click the **Font Color button arrow** [A ▾] and change the color to **Orange, Accent 1, Darker 25%**—in the fifth column, the fifth color. Press [Ctrl] + [E].

5 Select the fourth paragraph, *Children*. On the **HOME tab**, in the **Styles group**, click the third style—**Heading 1**. In a similar manner, apply the **Heading 1** style to the paragraphs *Adults*, *Families*, *Senior Citizens*, and *Ballroom Dancing*. Deselect the text.

6 On the **VIEW tab**, in the **Views group**, click **Outline**, and then press [Ctrl] + [Home]. If necessary, change the **Zoom** level to **100%**. Compare your screen with Figure 10.3.

> Outline view makes it easy to view the different levels in a document. The paragraphs formatted with the Heading 1 style are designated as Level 1 headings and display with a gray bullet containing a plus sign—indicating that subordinate levels display below those paragraphs. All other paragraphs are indented and display with a smaller gray bullet to indicate body text. Outline view does not display paragraph alignments—in this case, the first two paragraphs do not display as centered.

FIGURE 10.3

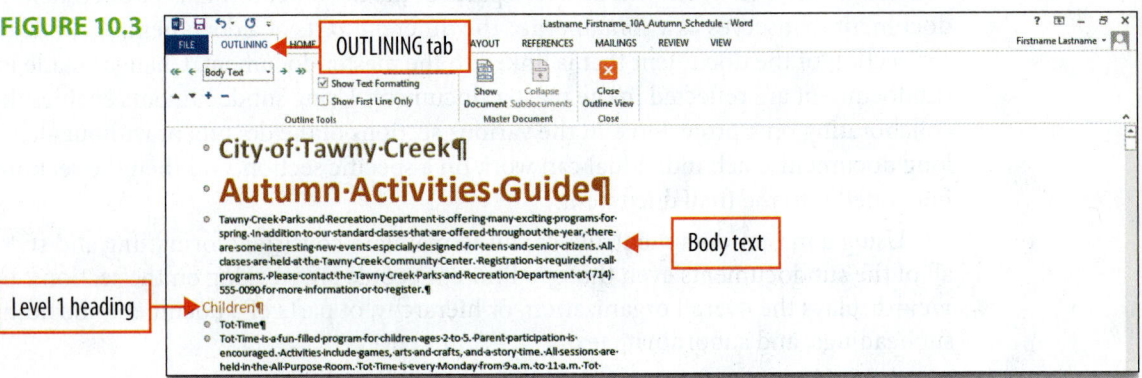

7 Click to position the insertion point to the left of the paragraph *Children*. Compare your screen with Figure 10.4.

> On the OUTLINING tab, in the Outline Tools group, the Outline Level box displays Level 1. Paragraphs formatted with Heading 1 are the top-level paragraphs in the document.

FIGURE 10.4

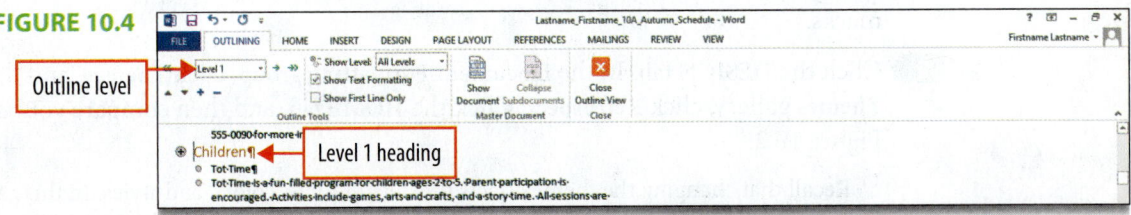

8 Immediately below the paragraph *Children*, click to position the insertion point to the left of the paragraph *Tot Time*. On the **OUTLINING tab**, in the **Outline Tools group**, click the **Outline Level arrow** [Body Text ▾], and then click **Level 2**. Notice that a gray bullet containing a plus sign displays to the left of *Tot Time* and the text formatting is changed.

> You can set levels for specific paragraphs by using Outline view. The *Tot Time* paragraph is assigned a Level 2 heading and the Heading 2 style is automatically applied.

9 ▸ Click to position the insertion point to the left of the paragraph *Toddler Aquatics*. On the **OUTLINING tab**, in the **Outline Tools group**, click **Promote** [←]. Notice that this paragraph displays as a *Level 2* paragraph—the same level and format as the *Tot Time* paragraph. Compare your screen with Figure 10.5.

> The Promote button allows you to move a selected paragraph to a higher level.

FIGURE 10.5

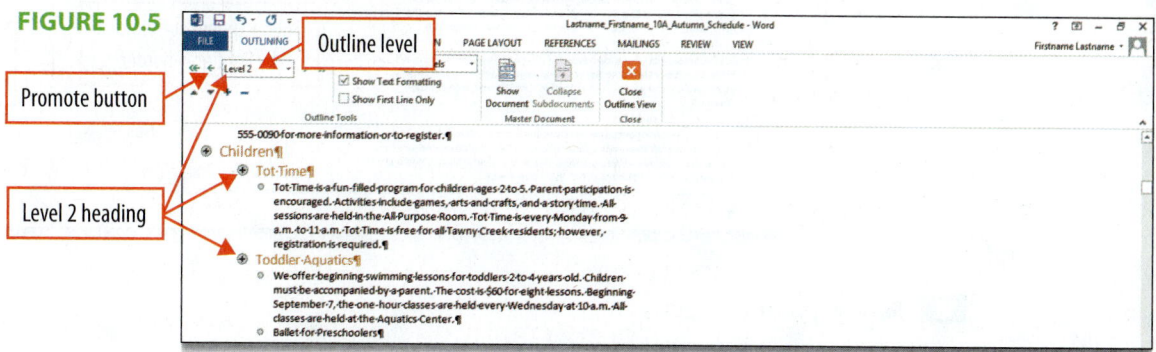

10 ▸ Using the same technique, **Promote** [←] the paragraphs *Ballet for Preschoolers*, *Tap Dance*, and *Beginning Karate*.

11 ▸ Under *Adults*, select the paragraph heading *Self Defense*. Press and hold down (Ctrl), and then select the paragraph headings *Losing Weight Healthfully* and *Flower Arranging for the Novice*. With the three paragraph headings selected, on the **OUTLINING tab**, in the **Outline Tools group**, click the **Outline Level arrow** [Body Text ▾], and then click **Level 2**.

12 ▸ Using the same technique, under *Families*, select the four paragraph headings, and then apply a **Level 2** outline level.

13 ▸ Under *Senior Citizens*, click to position the insertion point to the left of the paragraph *Ballroom Dancing*. On the **OUTLINING tab**, in the **Outline Tools group**, click **Demote** [→].

> The Demote button allows you to move a selected paragraph to a lower level. In this case, the paragraph is changed to Level 2 and the Heading 2 style is automatically applied.

14 ▸ Select the two remaining paragraph headings—*Water Aerobics* and *Walking for Fun and Fitness*, and then apply a **Level 2** outline level.

15 ▸ Press (Ctrl) + (Home). Click to position the insertion point to the left of *Children*. Drag down to select all remaining paragraphs in the document. On the **OUTLINING tab**, in the **Master Document group**, click **Show Document** to turn it on, and then click the **Create** button. Compare your screen with Figure 10.6.

> The first heading level in the selection determines where each subdocument is created. In this instance, the Level 1 headings of the document are used to create subdocuments. A light gray border displays around each subdocument, and a subdocument icon displays to the left of the first line of each new subdocument. All of the text that was not selected remains as body text within the master document.

> **Continuous section breaks** define the beginning and end of each subdocument. Recall that a **section break** is a mark that stores the section formatting information, such as the margins, page orientation, headers and footers, and sequence of page numbers. A continuous section break indicates that the section will begin on the same page of the document.

FIGURE 10.6

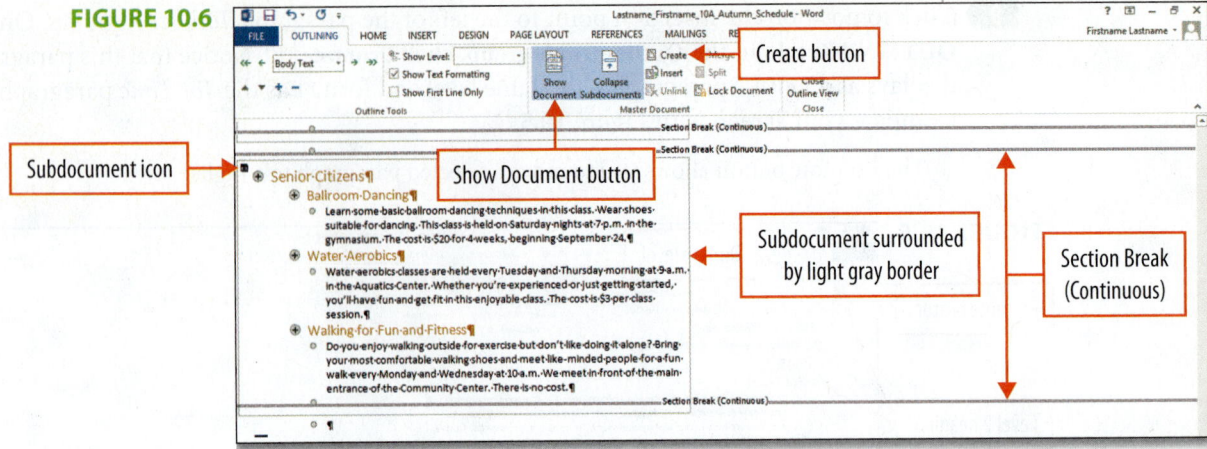

16 ▶ **Save** 💾 your changes.

Activity 10.02 | Collapsing and Rearranging Subdocuments

When a master document is created, the subdocuments display in expanded form—all text in the document is visible. You can collapse one or more subdocuments to hide a portion of the text. Collapsing all subdocuments is useful if you want to change the position of a subdocument in the master document.

1 ▶ On the **OUTLINING tab**, in the **Master Document group**, click **Collapse Subdocuments**. Compare your screen with Figure 10.7.

The subdocuments are collapsed and display as hyperlinks. Each subdocument is saved as a separate document in the same location as the master document—in this case, your Project 10A folder. The file name of the subdocument is created automatically by using the heading text of the subdocument. All files for a master document and its subdocuments are usually stored in the same folder.

When the master document is collapsed, the Lock icon displays next to the links for all subdocuments. When a subdocument is locked, no one else can make changes to it.

FIGURE 10.7

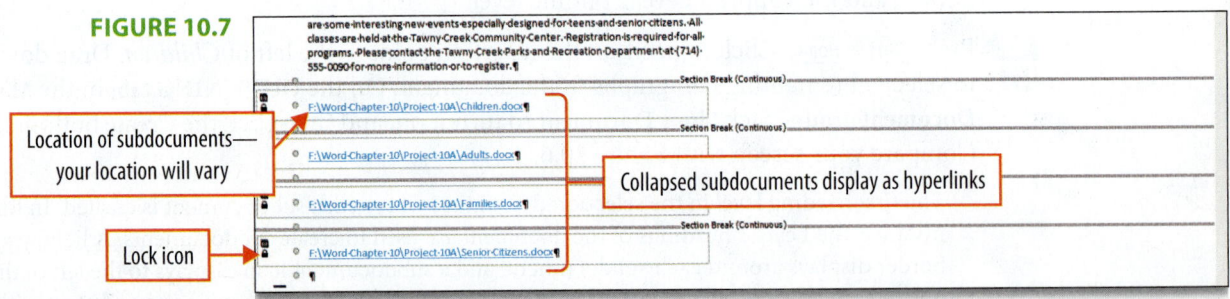

More Knowledge   **Locking a Subdocument**

If you want to lock a specific subdocument, position the insertion point in the subdocument, and then on the OUTLINING tab, in the Master Document group, click the Lock Document button.

---

2 ▶ Point to the **Word Chapter 10\Project 10A\Children.docx** hyperlink, press and hold down Ctrl, and then click to open the link—in this case, the *Children* subdocument. Notice that the subdocument displays in a new window with the default Office theme applied.

3 **Close** ✖ the **Children** document.

> Because you opened the *Children* subdocument by clicking the hyperlink, the color of the hyperlink changes in the master document.

4 Click in the **Lastname_Firstname_10A_Autumn_Schedule** document to make it active. To the left of the *Children* subdocument, click the **Subdocument** icon ▦, and then with the ↕ pointer displayed, drag down until the *Children* **Subdocument** icon displays above the **Section Break (Continuous)** that begins the *Families* subdocument. When a gray line indicates the location as shown in Figure 10.8, release the mouse button.

FIGURE 10.8

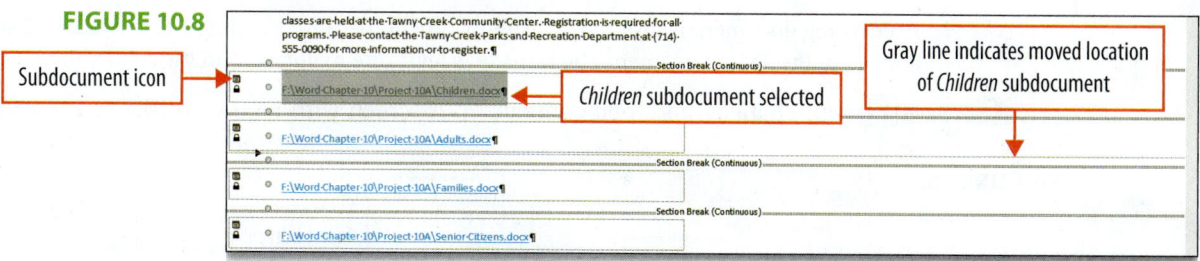

5 Deselect the text, and then **Save** 🖫 your changes.

Activity 10.03 | Inserting an Existing File as a Subdocument

Any existing document can be inserted as a subdocument in a master document. It is necessary to expand the subdocuments when inserting a new document.

1 On the **OUTLINING tab**, in the **Master Document group**, click **Expand Subdocuments**. Click the **FILE tab**, navigate to your student files, and then open the file **w10A_Teens**.

> The first paragraph is formatted with the Heading 1 style, and the four paragraph headings are formatted with the Heading 2 style.

2 Press [F12]. In the **Save As** dialog box, navigate to your **Project 10A** folder, and then compare your screen with Figure 10.9.

> The four subdocuments that were saved when you created the master document display in your Project 10A folder along with your master document.

FIGURE 10.9

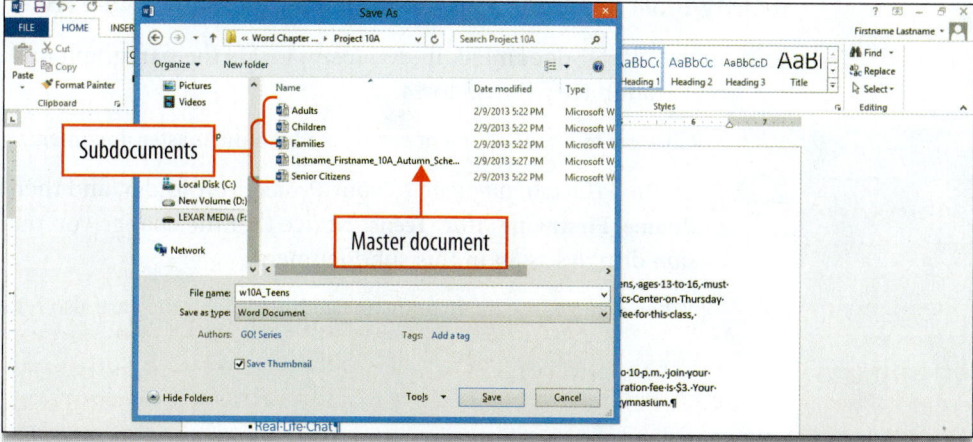

3 Save the file in your **Project 10A** folder as **Lastname_Firstname_10A_Teens** Click the **FILE tab**, and then **Show All Properties**. In the **Tags** box, type **subdocument, teens** In the **Subject** box, type your course name and section number. If necessary, edit the author name to display your name. **Save** your changes, and then **Close** ❌ the *Teens* document.

4 Click in the **Lastname_Firstname_10A_Autumn_Schedule** document to make it active. Press Ctrl + End. On the **OUTLINING tab**, in the **Master Document group**, if necessary, click **Show Document** to turn it on, and then click **Insert**. In the **Insert Subdocument** dialog box, if necessary, navigate to your **Project 10A** folder, select **Lastname_Firstname_10A_Teens**, and then click **Open**.

An existing document is inserted as a subdocument. Because Heading 1 and Heading 2 styles were applied in the *Teens* document, the respective levels are maintained in the subdocument.

5 Save 🖫 your changes, and then compare your screen with Figure 10.10.

FIGURE 10.10

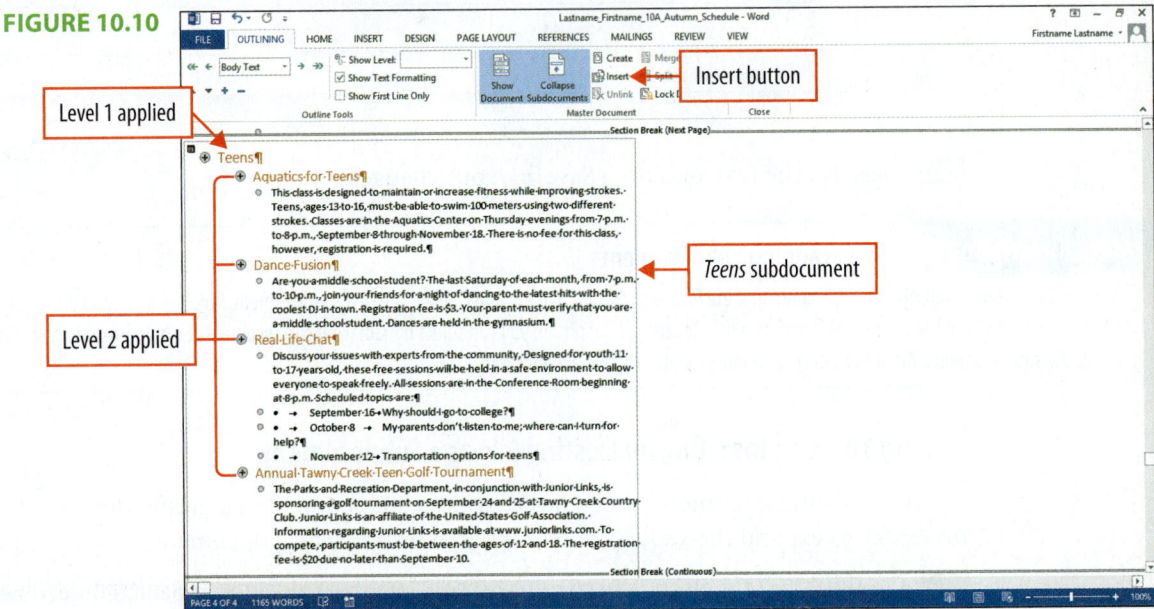

Objective 2 | Manage a Master Document and Subdocuments

Video W10-2

The main reason to work with a master document is to allow different people to edit subdocuments without affecting the master document. There are two ways to edit a subdocument—by editing the master document or by editing the subdocument.

Activity 10.04 | Editing a Master Document and Subdocuments

1 In the master document, under *Teens*, locate the paragraph under *Dance Fusion*. Change the registration fee from *$3* to **$4**

Changes to a subdocument can be made in the master document.

2 Click the **FILE tab**, navigate to your **Project 10A** folder, and then open the document named **Lastname_Firstname_10A_Teens**. Notice that the change you made to the cost for *Dance Fusion* displays as *$4* in this subdocument.

When changes are made to the master document, they are also reflected in the subdocument.

3 In the **Lastname_Firstname_10A_Teens** document, locate the paragraph below *Real Life Chat*. In the second sentence, change the ages from *11 to 17* to **13 to 16** Compare your screen with Figure 10.11.

FIGURE 10.11

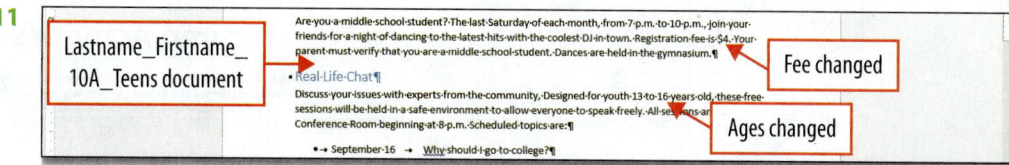

Lastname_Firstname_10A_Teens document

Fee changed

Ages changed

4 Save 🖫 your changes.

5 On the taskbar, point to the **Word** icon 📄, and then click the **Lastname_Firstname_10A_Autumn_Schedule** document to make it active.

🔄 **ANOTHER WAY** Click the VIEW tab. In the Window group, click Switch Windows, and then click Lastname_Firstname_10A_Autumn_Schedule.

6 Click in the **Lastname_Firstname_10A_Autumn_Schedule** document, and then under *Teens*, locate the paragraph below *Real Life Chat*. Notice that the change has been made for ages *13 to 16*.

7 On the taskbar, point to the **Word** icon 📄, and then **Close** ❌ the **Lastname_Firstname_10A_Teens** document.

8 If necessary, click in the **Lastname_Firstname_10A_Autumn_Schedule** document to make it active. On the **OUTLINING tab**, in the **Close group**, click the **Close Outline View** button. Save 🖫 your changes.

Objective 3 Navigate and Inspect the Master Document

Video W10-3

After all subdocuments have been edited, it is important to view the master document and, if necessary, make any final revisions. Word provides several features for examining a document—such as browsing the document by pages or locating a specific item. In a long document, these features allow you to navigate quickly to the sections you want to review.

Activity 10.05 │ Using the Navigation Pane to View a Document

1 Press Ctrl + Home. Click the **VIEW tab**, and then in the **Show group**, select the **Navigation Pane** check box. Notice that the **Navigation** pane displays to the left of your document. Near the top of the **Navigation** pane, click **PAGES**. Compare your screen with Figure 10.12.

The Navigation pane contains three ways to browse your document—by headings, by pages, or by using the results of a search. The Navigation pane displays *thumbnails*—graphical representations of pages—for all the pages in your document. In this case, the current page—where the insertion point is located—displays and is selected in the Navigation pane.

FIGURE 10.12

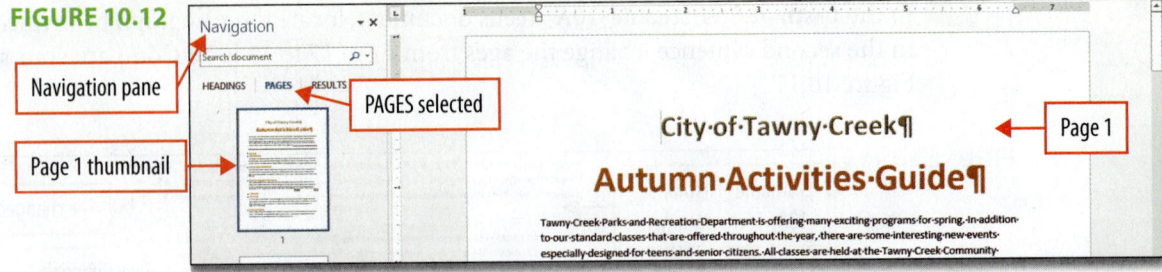

2 In the **Navigation** pane, click the thumbnail for page **3**. Notice that the top of **Page 3** displays.

3 Near the top of the **Navigation** pane, click **HEADINGS**. Compare your screen with Figure 10.13.

Because HEADINGS is active, the individual headings in your document display.

FIGURE 10.13

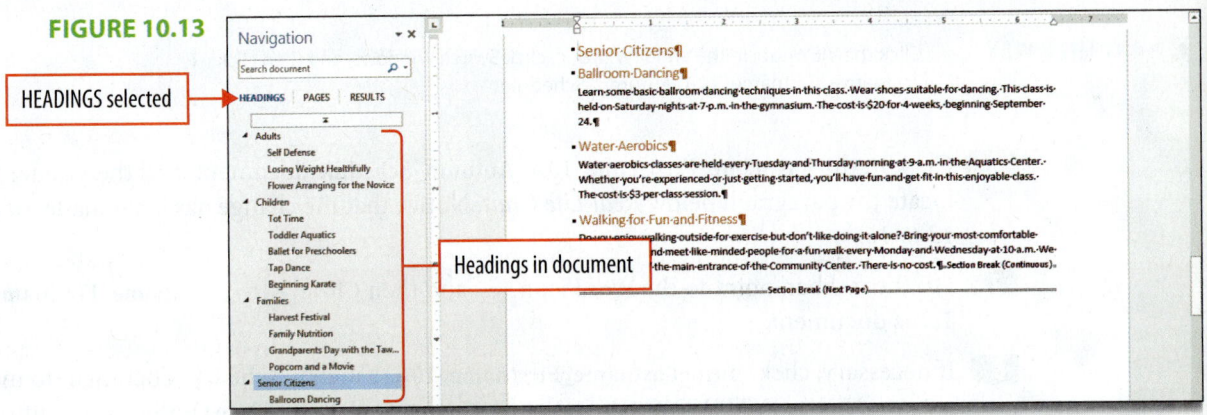

4 In the **Navigation** pane, under **Children**, click the heading **Beginning Karate**. Notice that the *Beginning Karate* heading displays at the top of your screen. Leave the **Navigation** pane open for the next activity.

More Knowledge	**Rearranging the Content in a Document**

You can drag and drop a tab in the Browse Headings list to move a heading or subheading and all related paragraphs to a new location in the document.

Activity 10.06 | Creating Bookmarks

A *bookmark* identifies the exact location of text, a table, or other object that you name for future reference. You can use bookmarks to locate specific parts of a document quickly.

1 In the **Navigation** pane, click the heading **Adults**. In the document, select the text for the heading *Adults*, being careful not to select the paragraph mark.

2 Click the **INSERT tab**, and then in the **Links group**, click **Bookmark**.

3 In the **Bookmark** dialog box, in the **Bookmark name** box, type **Adults** Compare your screen with Figure 10.14.

FIGURE 10.14

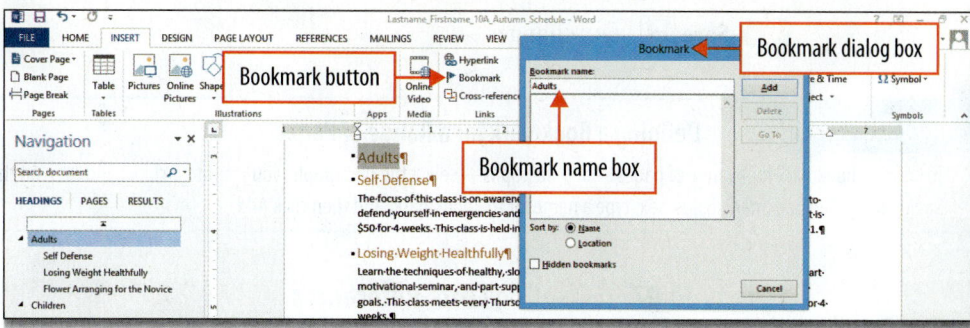

4 ▶ Click **Add**.

5 ▶ In the **Navigation** pane, click the heading **Children**. In the document, select the text for the heading *Children*, being careful not to select the paragraph mark. In the **Links group**, click **Bookmark**. In the **Bookmark** dialog box, in the **Bookmark name** box, type **Children** and then click **Add**.

6 ▶ In a similar manner, insert a bookmark for the *Families* heading, using the **Bookmark name** **Families**

When bookmarks are added to a document, by default they are listed in alphabetical order by name.

7 ▶ In a similar manner, insert a bookmark for the *Teens* heading, using the **Bookmark name** **Teens**

8 ▶ In the document, select the heading text *Senior Citizens*. In the **Links group**, click **Bookmark**. In the **Bookmark** dialog box, in the **Bookmark name** box, type **Senior_Citizens** and then click **Add**.

Bookmark names cannot include spaces; however, you can insert an underscore between the two words in a bookmark name.

9 ▶ Press Ctrl + Home. In the **Navigation** pane, click the **Search document arrow**, and then click **Go To**.

🔄 **ANOTHER WAY**   On the HOME tab, in the Editing group, click the Find button arrow, and then click Go To.

10 ▶ In the **Find and Replace** dialog box, with the **Go To tab** selected, in the **Go to what** box, scroll as necessary and then click **Bookmark**. Click the **Enter bookmark name arrow**, and then compare your screen with Figure 10.15.

All five bookmarks display in alphabetical order.

FIGURE 10.15

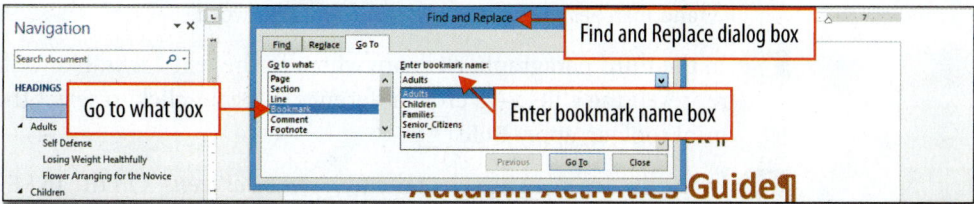

11 ▶ From the list, click **Children**, and then click **Go To**. Close ❌ the **Find and Replace** dialog box, and then **Close** ❌ the **Navigation** pane.

The section of the document that begins with the bookmark *Children* displays.

12 Save ⊟ your changes.

Activity 10.07 | Creating Cross-References

A *cross-reference* is a text link to an item that displays in another location in the document, such as a heading, a caption of a figure, or a footnote. Cross-references function as internal hyperlinks that enable you to move quickly to specific locations in a document.

1 Press Ctrl + Home. In the third paragraph, in the second sentence, select the text *teens*, being careful not to select any spaces.

> When creating a cross-reference, either select text or place the insertion point where you want the cross-reference to display in your document. In this case, you want the cross-reference to display instead of the word *teens*.

2 On the **INSERT tab**, in the **Links group**, click **Cross-reference**.

ANOTHER WAY   On the REFERENCES tab, in the Captions group, click Cross-reference.

3 In the **Cross-reference** dialog box, click the **Reference type arrow**, and then click **Bookmark**. If necessary, click the **Insert reference to arrow** to display **Bookmark text**, and select the **Insert as hyperlink** check box.

4 Under **For which bookmark**, click **Teens**, and then compare your screen with Figure 10.16.

FIGURE 10.16

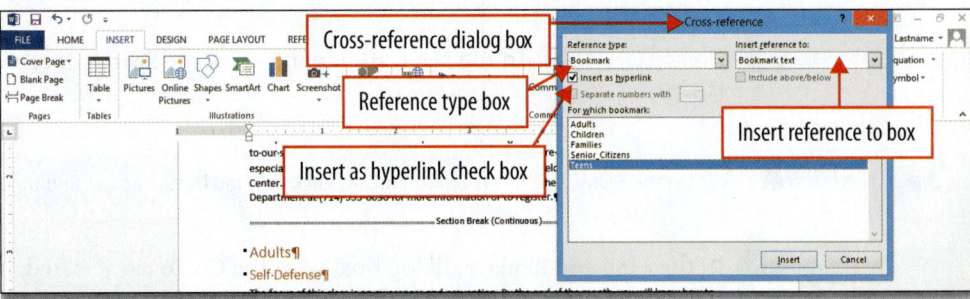

5 In the **Cross-reference** dialog box, click **Insert**, and then click **Close**.

> The text you selected when you created the bookmark replaces the existing text in the paragraph and matches the formatting of the replaced word.

6 In the third paragraph, click anywhere in the text *Teens*. Notice that it displays as a gray box representing a field—a cross-reference. Double-click to select the entire field *Teens*. On the mini toolbar, apply **Bold** B .

7 In the same sentence, select the text *senior citizens*. On the **INSERT tab**, in the **Links group**, click **Cross-reference**.

8 In the **Cross-reference** dialog box, if necessary, click the **Reference type arrow**, and then click **Bookmark**. Be sure the **Insert reference to** box displays **Bookmark text**, and the **Insert as hyperlink** check box is selected. Under **For which bookmark**, click **Senior_Citizens**. Click **Insert**, and then click **Close**.

> The formatting of the inserted bookmark text matches the rest of the paragraph, except the underscore is replaced with a space.

9 Select the *Senior Citizens* cross-reference text. On the mini toolbar, apply **Bold** $\boxed{B}$, and then deselect the text.

10 Click the **Teens** cross-reference. Compare your screen with Figure 10.17.

> A ScreenTip displays, indicating how to activate the hyperlink.

FIGURE 10.17

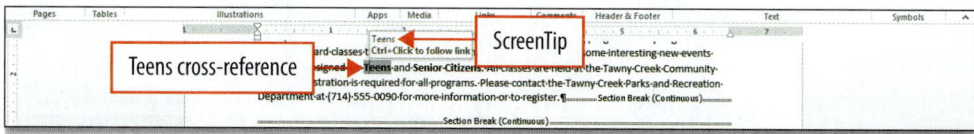

11 Hold down $\boxed{\text{Ctrl}}$, and when the 🖑 pointer displays, click **Teens**.

> The Teens section of the document displays at the bookmark location.

12 Press $\boxed{\text{Ctrl}}$ + $\boxed{\text{Home}}$. **Save** 🖫 your changes.

Activity 10.08 | Reviewing Word Count and Readability Statistics

The ***word count*** refers to the number of words in a document. The Word Counts dialog box displays the number of words, paragraphs, pages, and characters in a document. If the document will be distributed to a group of people, you may want to determine the ease of readability based on the average number of syllables per word and words per sentence by viewing the ***readability statistics***. Readability Statistics is a Spelling and Grammar tool that analyzes a document and determines the reading level of the text.

1 On the **REVIEW tab**, in the **Proofing group**, click **Word Count**. Compare your screen with Figure 10.18.

> The Word Count dialog box indicates how many words, paragraphs, pages, and characters are contained in the document. In addition, the word count displays on the status bar in Word.

FIGURE 10.18

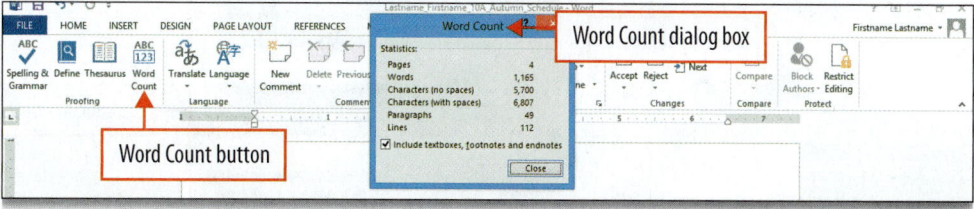

2 Click **Close** to close the **Word Count** dialog box.

3 Click the **FILE tab**, and then click **Options**. In the **Word Options** dialog box, click **Proofing**. Under **When correcting spelling and grammar in Word**, select the **Show readability statistics** check box to turn on the display of readability statistics. Click **OK**.

4 On the **REVIEW tab**, in the **Proofing group**, click **Spelling & Grammar**.

> You must complete a spelling and grammar check to review the readability statistics.

5 In the **Grammar** pane, click **Ignore** for all found errors. Compare your screen with Figure 10.19.

In the Readability Statistics dialog box, under Readability, three readability ratings display. The first rating is the percentage of passive sentences in the document. The Flesch Reading Ease score is based on a 100-point scale—the higher the score, the easier it is for the reader to understand the document. The Flesch-Kincaid Grade Level score displays the reading level based on U.S. grade levels. For example, 9.0 indicates that the document can be comprehended by a student reading at a ninth grade level.

FIGURE 10.19

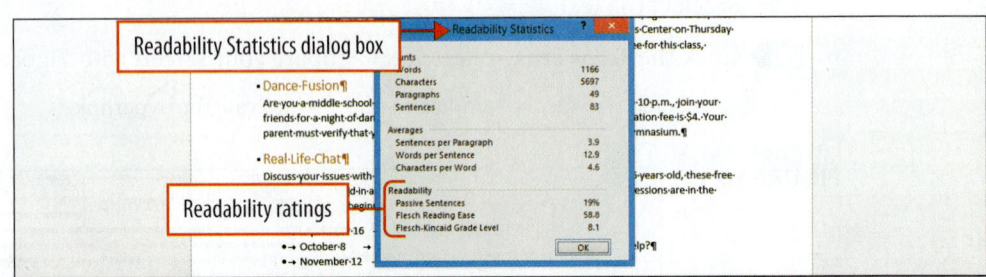

6 Click **OK** to close the **Readability Statistics** dialog box. Click the **FILE tab**, and then click **Options**. In the **Word Options** dialog box, click **Proofing**. Under **When correcting spelling and grammar in Word**, clear the **Show readability statistics** check box. Click **OK**.

Activity 10.09 | Finalizing a Master Document

To prepare a master document for distribution, you should remove the links to the subdocuments.

1 Press Ctrl + Home. On the **VIEW tab**, in the **Views group**, click **Outline**. On the **OUTLINING tab**, in the **Master Document group**, click **Show Document** to turn it on. If necessary, in the **Master Document group**, click **Expand Subdocuments**. If a **Microsoft Word** message box displays, click **OK** to save changes to the master document.

2 Scroll so that the paragraph *Adults* displays near the top of your screen. To the left of the paragraph *Adults*, click the **Subdocument** icon [icon] to select the entire *Adults* subdocument. Compare your screen with Figure 10.20.

FIGURE 10.20

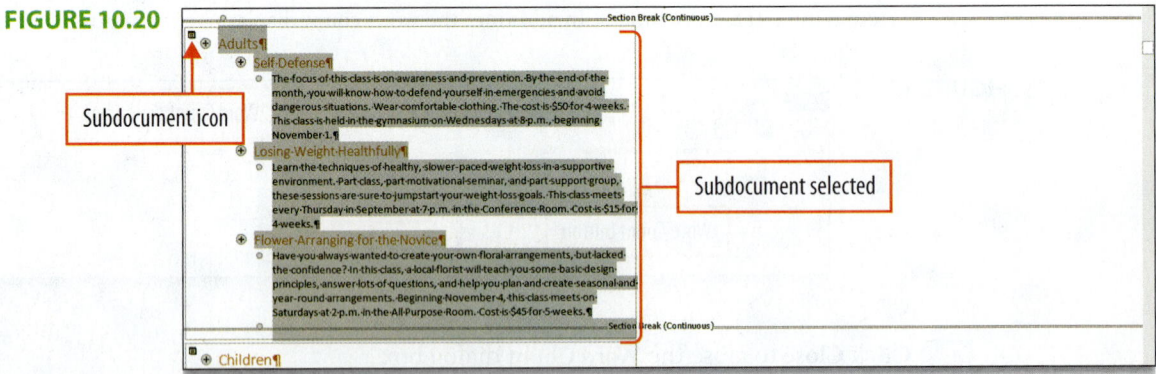

3 With the *Adults* subdocument selected, in the **Master Document group**, click **Unlink**.

The Adults paragraph and all subordinate paragraphs are no longer linked to a subdocument. The Subdocument icon and gray border surrounding the text no longer display.

4 To the left of the paragraph *Children*, click the **Subdocument** icon 🖾 to select the entire *Children* subdocument. In the **Master Document group**, click **Unlink**.

5 In a similar manner, **Unlink** the subdocuments *Families*, *Senior Citizens*, and *Teens*.

6 Above the paragraph *Adults*, click to position the insertion point to the right of the first bullet for *Section Break (Continuous)*. Compare your screen with Figure 10.21.

FIGURE 10.21

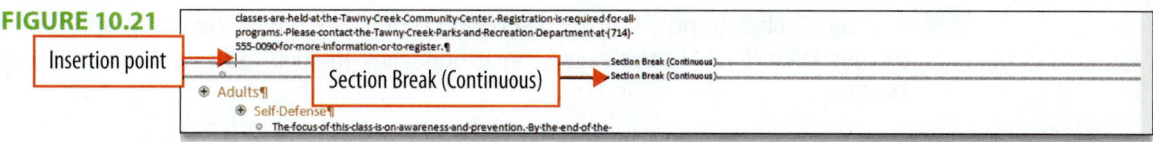

classes·are·held·at·the·Tawny·Creek·Community·Center.·Registration·is·required·for·all·
programs.·Please·contact·the·Tawny·Creek·Parks·and·Recreation·Department·at·(714)·
555-0090·for·more·information·or·to·register.¶

Insertion point → ⟶ ————————————————————— Section Break (Continuous)——
                          Section Break (Continuous) ⟶ ——— Section·Break·(Continuous)————

⊕ Adults¶
  ⊕ Self-Defense¶
    ○ The·focus·of·this·class·is·on·awareness·and·prevention.·By·the·end·of·the·

7 Press Delete to remove the **Section Break (Continuous)**. In a similar manner, delete all instances of **Section Break (Continuous)** and **Section Break (Next Page)**.

The section breaks are no longer needed because the subdocuments are no longer defined. The separate subdocument (.docx) files still exist in the Project 10A folder, but they are no longer linked to the main document.

8 On the **OUTLINING tab**, in the **Close group**, click **Close Outline View**.

9 Press Ctrl + Home, and then **Save** 🖫 your changes.

More **Knowledge** | **Opening a Master Document**

If you open a master document, the subdocuments are collapsed and display as hyperlinks. To view the entire document, on the VIEW tab, in the Views group, click Outline. On the OUTLINING tab, click the Expand Subdocuments button.

Objective 4 | Create and Modify Headers and Footers

Video W10-4

You can display different headers and footers on the first page, odd pages, and even pages in a document by inserting section breaks. Recall that sections are portions of a document that can be formatted differently.

Activity 10.10 | Inserting Odd and Even Page Breaks

1 On **Page 1**, click to position the insertion point to the left of the paragraph *Adults*. On the **PAGE LAYOUT tab**, in the **Page Setup group**, click **Breaks**, and then under **Section Breaks**, click **Even Page**.

The paragraph *Adults* displays at the top of Page 2.

2 Press Ctrl + Home, and then compare your screen with Figure 10.22.

An ***Even Page section break*** is inserted at the end of Page 1. An Even Page section break is a formatting mark that indicates the beginning of a new section on the next even-numbered page.

FIGURE 10.22

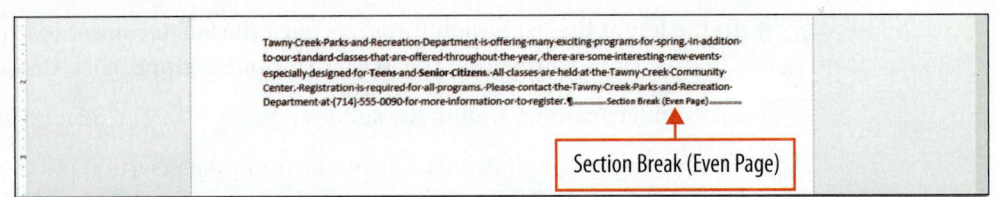

Section Break (Even Page)

3 ▶ On **Page 2**, click to position the insertion point to the left of the paragraph *Children*. On the **PAGE LAYOUT tab**, in the **Page Setup group**, click **Breaks**, and then under **Section Break**, click **Odd Page**.

The paragraph *Children* displays at the top of Page 3. An ***Odd Page section break*** is inserted on Page 2. An Odd Page section break is a formatting mark that indicates the beginning of a new section on the next odd-numbered page.

4 ▶ Using the same technique, insert an **Even Page** section break to the left of the paragraphs *Families* and *Teens*. Insert an **Odd Page** section break to the left of the paragraph *Senior Citizens*.

5 ▶ On **Page 2**, right-click in the footer area, and then click **Edit Footer**. On the **HEADER & FOOTER TOOLS DESIGN tab**, in the **Options group**, select the **Different Odd & Even Pages** check box. Scroll to display the bottom of **Page 2** and the top of **Page 3**. Compare your screen with Figure 10.23.

At the bottom of Page 2, the text *Even Page Footer – Section 2* displays on the footer tab. At the top of Page 3, the text *Odd Page Header – Section 3* displays on the header tab. By inserting section breaks and selecting different formatting options, you can insert different text or objects in the various sections of the document.

FIGURE 10.23

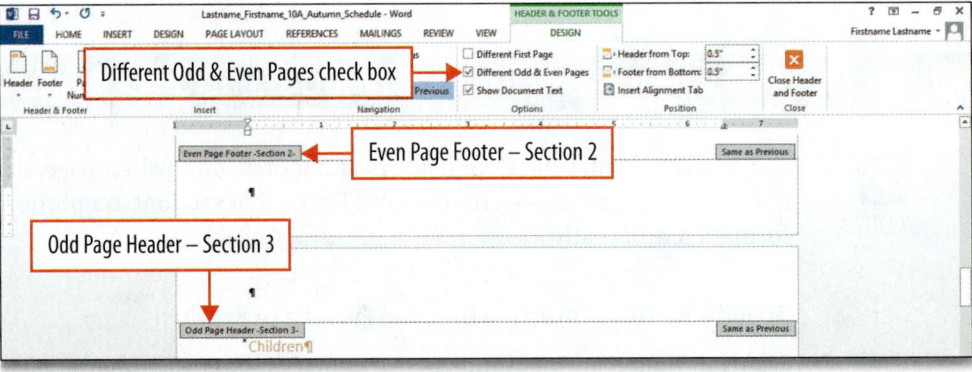

Different Odd & Even Pages check box

Even Page Footer – Section 2

Odd Page Header – Section 3

6 ▶ With the insertion point in the footer **Even Page Footer – Section 2**, press Tab two times, and then type **City of Tawny Creek**

7 ▶ On the **HEADER & FOOTER TOOLS DESIGN tab**, in the **Navigation group**, click **Next**. Notice that the insertion point displays in the footer *Odd Page Footer – Section 3*.

8 ▶ With the insertion point in the *Odd Page Footer – Section 3* footer, insert the file name.

9 ▶ In the **Navigation group**, click **Next**. Compare your screen with Figure 10.24.

The right-aligned text displays. Because this is an even page footer, the file name does not display.

FIGURE 10.24

| Even Page Footer -Section 4- | | | | Same as Previous |

Page 4

Even Page footer → City-of-Tawny-Creek¶

PAGE 4 OF 6   1165 WORDS

10 ▶ In the **Navigation group**, click **Previous** three times to display the footer **Odd Page Footer – Section 1**.

11 ▶ In the **Close group**, click **Close Header and Footer**. **Save** 🖫 your changes.

Activity 10.11 │ Inserting a Cover Page

A **cover page** is the first page of a document that provides introductory information—for example, the title, the author, a brief description, or a date.

1 ▶ Press Ctrl + Home. Click the **INSERT tab**, and then in the **Pages group**, click **Cover Page** to display the **Cover Page** gallery. Compare your screen with Figure 10.25.

The Cover Page gallery contains predesigned cover page styles.

FIGURE 10.25

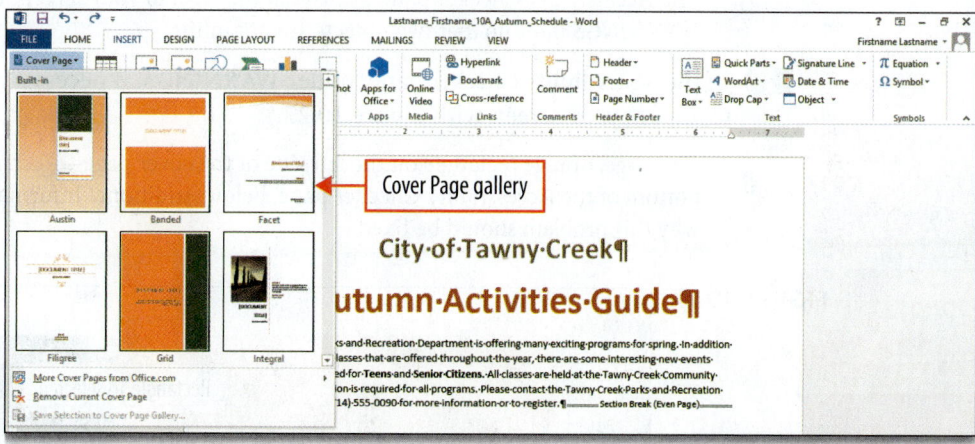

2 ▶ In the **Cover Page** gallery, in the second row, click the second style—**Grid**.

The cover page, which contains text placeholders, is inserted on a new first page of the document.

3 ▶ Click in the **Title** placeholder, and then type **autumn events** Below the title, click in the **Abstract** placeholder, and then type **Activities offered by the Parks and Recreation Department** Click in the **Subtitle** placeholder, and then type **Tawny Creek** Compare your screen with Figure 10.26.

FIGURE 10.26

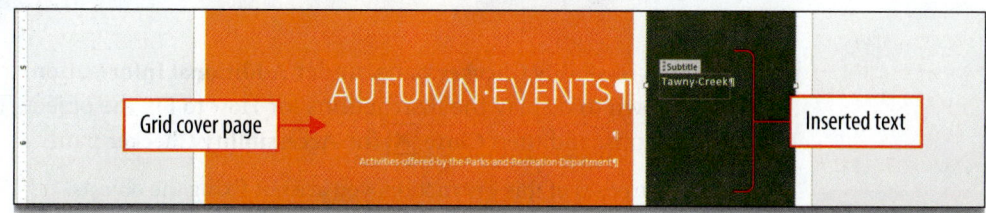

4 ▶ Press Ctrl + Home, and then **Save** 🖫 your document.

5 Click the **FILE tab**, and then **Show All Properties**.

The Title and Subtitle placeholders in the cover page are linked to the Title and Subject document properties, respectively. The text *autumn events* may display in the Title box and the text *Tawny Creek* may display in the Subject box.

6 In the **Tags** box, type **autumn schedule, master** and then in the **Categories** box, type your course name and section number. Edit the author name to display your name. **Save** 🔲 your document.

Because the Subtitle placeholder on the cover page is linked to the Subject document property, you are entering the course name and section number in the Categories box.

Activity 10.12 │ Creating Documents for Use with Accessibility Tools

The *Accessibility Checker* searches a document for content that people with disabilities might find difficult to read and suggests ways to modify the content.

1 Click the **FILE tab**. In the **Inspect Document** section, click **Check for Issues**, and then click **Check Accessibility**.

The Accessibility Checker pane displays at the right of your screen. Under *Inspection Results*, *WARNINGS* indicate that two objects are not inline.

2 In the **Accessibility Checker** pane, under **WARNINGS**, if necessary, click to select **Rectangle 16**. Compare your screen with Figure 10.27.

The large, orange rectangle on the left side of the cover page—Rectangle 16—is selected. At the bottom of the Accessibility Checker pane, below Additional Information, there is an explanation why this problem should be fixed.

FIGURE 10.27

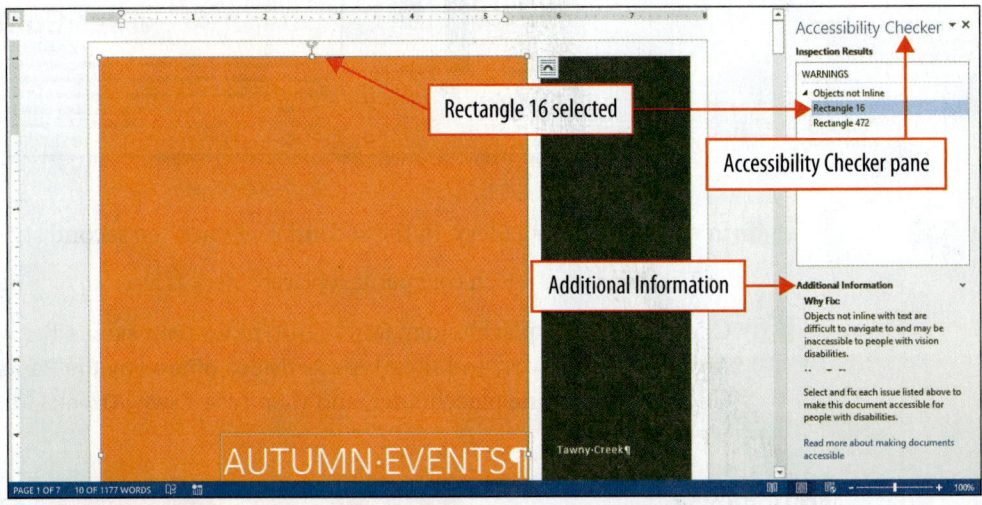

3 In the **Accessibility Checker** pane, under **Additional Information**, to the right of **Why Fix**, scroll down to display the instructions for **How to Fix** the object. Take a moment to read the instructions, and then **Close** ☒ the **Accessibility Checker** pane.

For purposes of this instruction, you are not fixing the objects.

4 Press Ctrl + Home. **Save** 🔲 your document, and then press Ctrl + W.

5 Click the **FILE tab**, click **Open**, navigate to your **Project 10A** folder, and then open the file **Lastname_Firstname_10A_Teens**.

6 At the bottom of **Page 1**, in the last paragraph, position the insertion point to the right of the period after the last sentence. Press Delete to delete the **Section Break (Next Page)**. Insert the file name in the footer, and then **Save** 🖫 the document.

7 Print both of your documents or submit your files electronically as directed by your instructor. **Close** ✖ Word.

END | You have completed Project 10A

PROJECT 10B Reference Guide

MyITLab® Project 10B Training

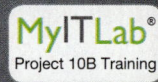

PROJECT ACTIVITIES

In Activities 10.13 through 10.23, you will add an index, a table of contents, and a table of figures to a document that describes the City of Tawny Creek. Your completed document will look similar to Figure 10.28.

PROJECT FILES

For Project 10B, you will need the following file:
w10B_Reference_Guide

You will save your file as:
Lastname_Firstname_10B_Reference_Guide

PROJECT RESULTS

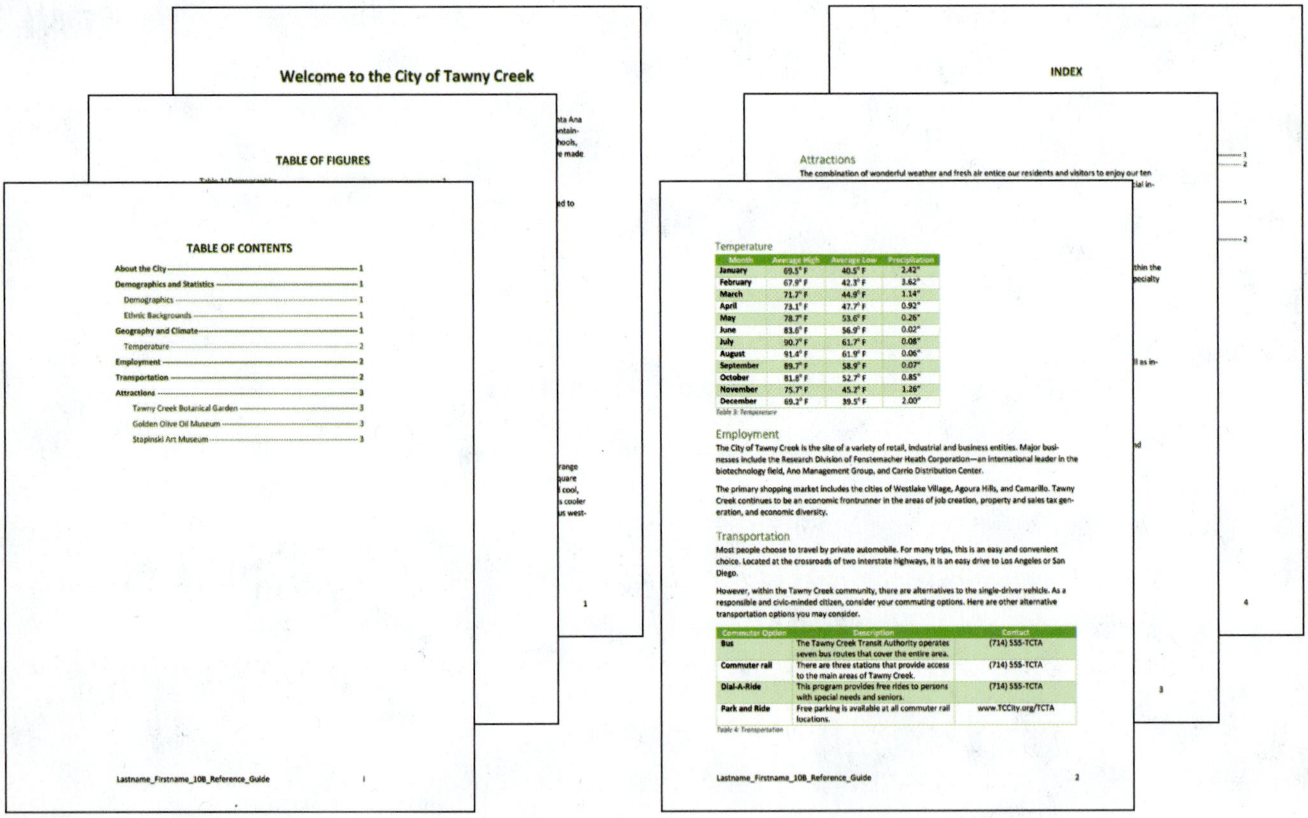

FIGURE 10.28 Project 10B Reference Guide

Video W10-5

An *index* is a compilation of topics, names, and terms accompanied by page numbers that displays at the end of a document. Each entry indicates where the *index entry* can be found. An index entry is a word or phrase that is listed in the index. To create an entry, you mark the words you want to include in the index as an index entry.

Activity 10.13 │ Formatting the Document

1 Start Word. From your student files, open the file **w10B_Reference_Guide**. **Save** the file in your **Word Chapter 10** folder as **Lastname_Firstname_10B_Reference_Guide** If necessary, display the rulers and formatting marks. **Ignore All** spelling errors.

2 Scroll to the bottom of **Page 1**, right-click in the footer area, and then click **Edit Footer**. Insert the file name in the footer. In the footer area, with the insertion point to the right of the file name, press Tab two times. On the **HEADER & FOOTER TOOLS DESIGN tab**, in the **Header & Footer group**, click **Page Number**, and then click **Current Position** to display the **Page Number** gallery. Compare your screen with Figure 10.29.

The page numbers in the document are used as a reference in the index. The Page Number gallery provides built-in formats for inserting page numbers.

FIGURE 10.29

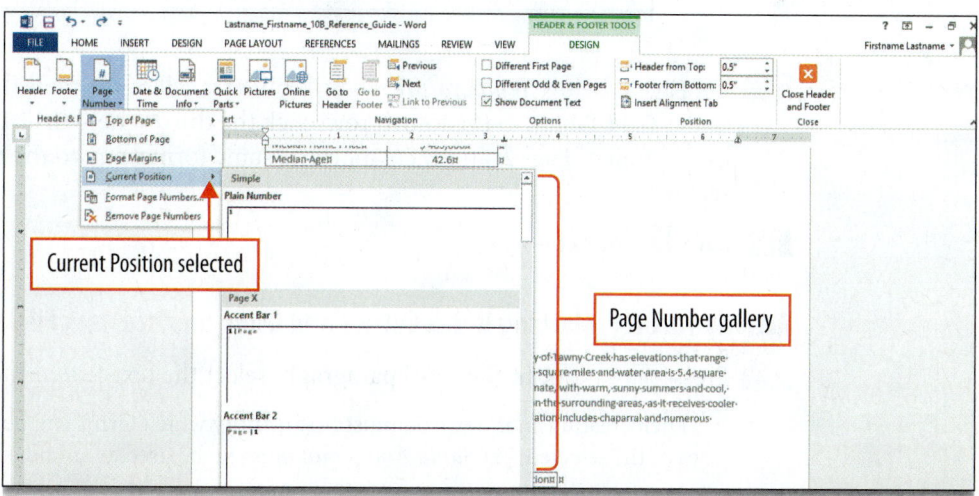

Current Position selected

Page Number gallery

3 In the **Page Number** gallery, under **Simple**, click the first style—**Plain Number**. Notice that the page number *1* is inserted in the footer at the right margin. In the **Close group**, click **Close Header and Footer**. Press Ctrl + Home.

4 Click the **DESIGN tab**. In the **Document Formatting group**, click **Colors**, and then click **Green**.

5 Select the first paragraph. On the mini toolbar, change the **Font Size** to 22, apply **Bold** B, and then change the **Font Color** A to **Lime, Accent 2, Darker 50%**—in the sixth column, the last color. Press Ctrl + E.

6 Select the second paragraph. Click the **HOME tab**, and then in the **Styles group**, click **Heading 1**. In a similar manner, apply the **Heading 1** style to the paragraphs *Demographics and Statistics, Geography and Climate, Employment, Transportation*, and *Attractions*.

7 On **Page 1**, select the paragraph *Demographics*, and in the **Styles group**, click **Heading 2**. In a similar manner, apply the **Heading 2** style to the paragraphs *Ethnic Backgrounds* and *Temperature*.

8 On **Page 3**, select the paragraph *Tawny Creek Botanical Garden*. On the mini toolbar, click **Font Color** [A ▾]. In a similar manner, for the paragraphs *Golden Olive Oil Museum* and *Stapinski Art Museum*, click **Font Color** [A ▾]. Recall that the most recently used font color remains active on the Font Color button.

9 Press [Ctrl] + [Home]. Locate the first table in the document—under *Demographics*. Click to position the insertion point in the first cell of the table. Click the **TABLE TOOLS DESIGN tab**. In the **Table Style Options group**, clear the **Header Row** check box. In the **Table Styles group**, click **More** [▾], and then under **Grid Tables**, in the second row, click the third style—**Grid Table 2 – Accent 2**. Click in the second table—under *Ethnic Backgrounds*. In the **Table Style Options group**, clear the **Header Row** check box. In the **Table Styles group**, under **Grid Tables**, in the second row, click the third style—**Grid Table 2 – Accent 2**. Compare your screen with Figure 10.30.

FIGURE 10.30

Header Row check box cleared

Grid Table 2 – Accent 2 style applied

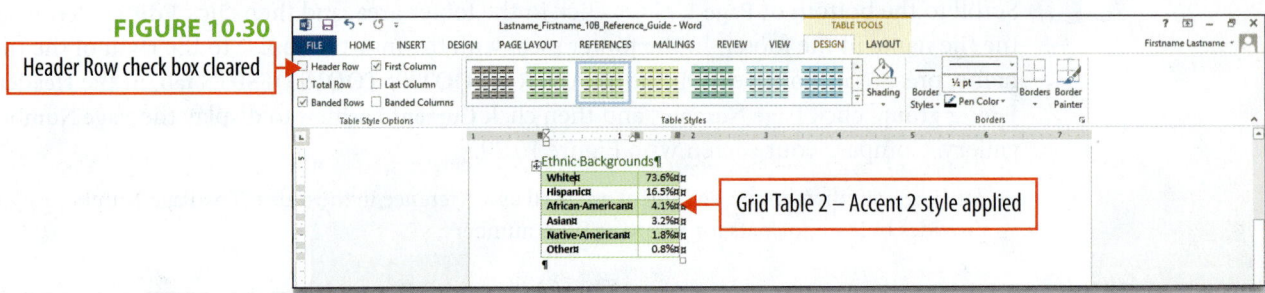

10 On **Page 1**, below *Temperature*, click in the first cell of the table. In the **Table Styles group**, under **Grid Tables**, in the fourth row, click the third style—**Grid Table 4 – Accent 2**. Scroll to the bottom of **Page 2**, and then apply the same formatting to the table in the *Transportation* section.

11 Save  your changes.

Activity 10.14 | Marking Index Entries and Using an AutoMark File

1 Press [Ctrl] + [Home]. In the third paragraph, select the text *Santa Ana Mountains*.

When creating an index, you must first identify which terms will be used for index entries—in this case, the selected text *Santa Ana Mountains* will be used as an index entry.

2 Click the **REFERENCES tab**, and then in the **Index group**, click **Mark Entry** to display the **Mark Index Entry** dialog box. Compare your screen with Figure 10.31, and then take a moment to read the description of the dialog box features in the table shown in Figure 10.32.

Santa Ana Mountains displays in the Main entry box. When text is selected, by default it displays in the Main entry box.

FIGURE 10.31

Mark Index Entry dialog box

Main entry box

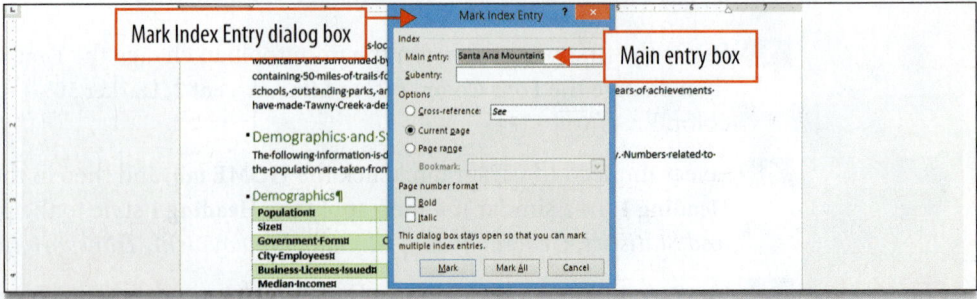

FIGURE 10.32

MARK INDEX ENTRY DIALOG BOX FEATURES	
FEATURE	**DESCRIPTION**
Main entry	The word, phrases, or selected text that will be used to identify the index entry.
Subentry	A more specific term that refers to the main entry. For example, the index entry *Transportation* could have subentries for *Automobiles*, *Buses*, and *Trains*.
Cross-reference	An entry that refers the reader to another topic that provides more information. For example, the main entry *England* might be listed in the index as *See United Kingdom*.
Current page	The index entry is marked with the current page number.
Page range	The index entry is marked with a range of page numbers.
Page number format	This option controls how the page number will display in the index.
Mark	Marks only the selected text.
Mark All	Marks all occurrences of the selected text in the document.

3 In the **Mark Index Entry** dialog box, click **Mark All**, and then **Close** the **Mark Index Entry** dialog box. Notice that the index entry displays to the right of the selected text. Compare your screen with Figure 10.33.

> After you mark text as an index entry, Word inserts an **index entry field**, to the right of the selected text. An index entry field is code containing the identifier *XE* and the term to be used in the index. The code is formatted as **hidden text**—nonprinting text. Because you clicked the Mark All button, the occurrence of *Santa Ana Mountains* at the bottom of Page 1 is also marked.

FIGURE 10.33

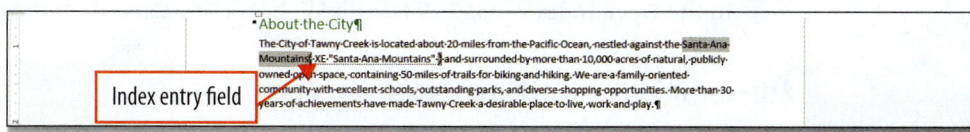

4 On **Page 1**, select the paragraph *Demographics and Statistics*. On the **REFERENCES tab**, in the **Index group**, click **Mark Entry**. In the **Mark Index Entry** dialog box, with *Demographics and Statistics* displayed in the **Main entry** box, click **Mark**, but do not close the **Mark Index Entry** dialog box.

> The text *Demographics and Statistics* is marked as an entry for the index.

5 Click in the document, and then select the paragraph *Geography and Climate*. If necessary, point to the **Mark Index Entry** dialog box title bar to display the pointer, and then drag the **Mark Index Entry** dialog box to the side of your screen. With the paragraph still selected, click in the **Main entry** box, and notice that *Geography and Climate* displays. Click **Mark**.

6 In a similar manner, **Mark** entries for the paragraphs *Employment*, *Transportation*, and *Attractions*.

7 Below *Attractions*, locate the text *Tawny Creek Botanical Garden*, and then position the insertion point to the right of *Garden*. In the **Mark Index Entry** dialog box, click in the **Main entry** box, and then type **Attractions** In the **Subentry** box, type **Tawny Creek Botanical Garden** Click **Mark**, and then compare your screen with Figure 10.34.

> The text *Tawny Creek Botanical Garden* is added as an index entry—as a subentry under *Attractions*. The index entry field displays the main entry text, a colon, and the subentry text.

FIGURE 10.34

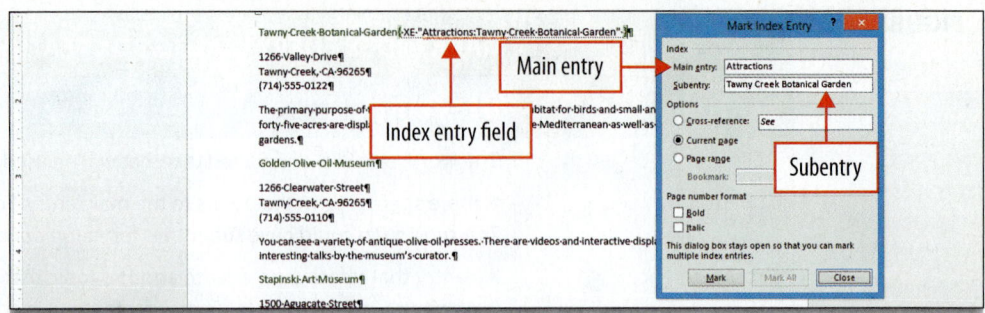

8 ▶ Position the insertion point to the right of the text *Golden Olive Oil Museum*. In the **Main entry** box, type **Attractions** In the **Subentry** box, type **Golden Olive Oil Museum** Click **Mark**.

9 ▶ With the **Mark Index Entry** dialog box still open, position the insertion point to the right of the text *Stapinski Art Museum*. In the **Main Entry** box, type **Attractions** In the **Subentry** box, type **Stapinski Art Museum** Click **Mark**, and then **Close** the **Mark Index Entry** dialog box.

10 ▶ **Save** 🖫 your changes.

11 ▶ In the **Index group**, click **Insert Index**. In the **Index** dialog box, click **AutoMark** to display the **Open Index AutoMark File** dialog box.

> If a document contains words that are frequently used as index entries, the words can be saved as an *AutoMark file*. An AutoMark file contains a two-column table that is used to mark words that will be used as index entries. The first column lists the terms to be searched for in the document. The second column lists the corresponding entries. In the Open Index AutoMark File dialog box, you can select an AutoMark file to automatically insert index entries in a document.

12 ▶ In the **Open Index AutoMark File** dialog box, click **Cancel**.

Activity 10.15 | Inserting an Index

After text or phrases have been marked as index entries, the next step is to insert the index. Generally, an index is inserted on a separate page at the end of a document.

1 ▶ Press Ctrl + End, and then press Ctrl + Enter to insert a manual page break.

2 ▶ With the insertion point at the top of the new page, type **INDEX** and then press Enter two times.

3 ▶ Select the *INDEX* paragraph you just typed. On the mini toolbar, change the **Font Size** to **16**, apply **Bold** B , and then click **Font Color** A ▾ . Press Ctrl + E .

4 ▶ Click to position the insertion point in the last paragraph of the document. On the **REFERENCES tab**, in the **Index group**, click **Insert Index** to display the **Index** dialog box.

5 ▶ In the **Index** dialog box, on the **Index tab**, click the **Formats arrow**, and then click **Classic**. Click the **Right align page numbers** check box. Compare your screen with Figure 10.35.

> The Index dialog box allows you to select your own options, including predefined index formats, and then preview the selection. You can also create your own index format using a template.

FIGURE 10.35

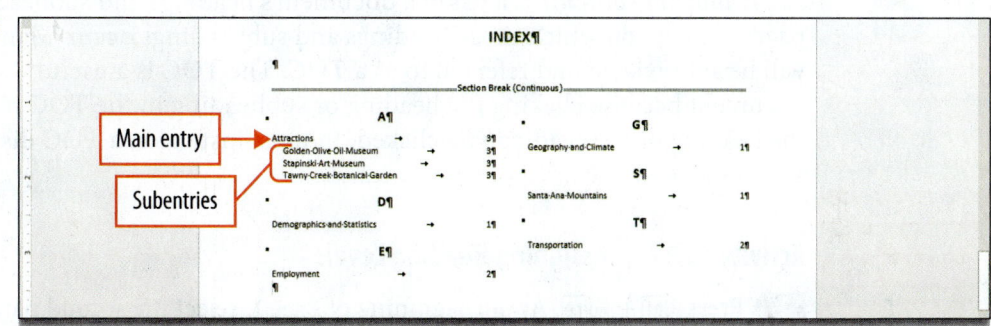

6 Click **OK**, and then compare your screen with Figure 10.36.

The index is inserted in a two-column format. Word distributes the text evenly between the two columns.

FIGURE 10.36

7 Save 💾 your changes.

Activity 10.16 | Updating an Index

After an index has been inserted into a document, the index can be updated if you want to include additional words in the index or if the page numbers in the document change.

1 Scroll to the bottom of **Page 1**, and position the insertion point to the right of *Temperature*.

2 On the **REFERENCES tab**, in the **Index group**, click **Mark Entry**. In the **Mark Index Entry** dialog box, in the **Main entry** box, type **Geography and Climate** In the **Subentry** box, type **Temperature** Click **Mark**, and then **Close** the **Mark Index Entry** dialog box.

3 Press Ctrl + End. Position the insertion point anywhere in the index entries, and notice that under the *Geography and Climate* main entry, the newly marked subentry—*Temperature*— does not display in the existing index.

Because the index is a field, it displays as shaded text.

4 On the **REFERENCES tab**, in the **Index group**, click **Update Index**. Compare your screen with Figure 10.37.

The index is updated to include the additional entry *Temperature*.

 **ANOTHER WAY**   Right-click the Index field, and then from the shortcut menu, click Update Field.

FIGURE 10.37

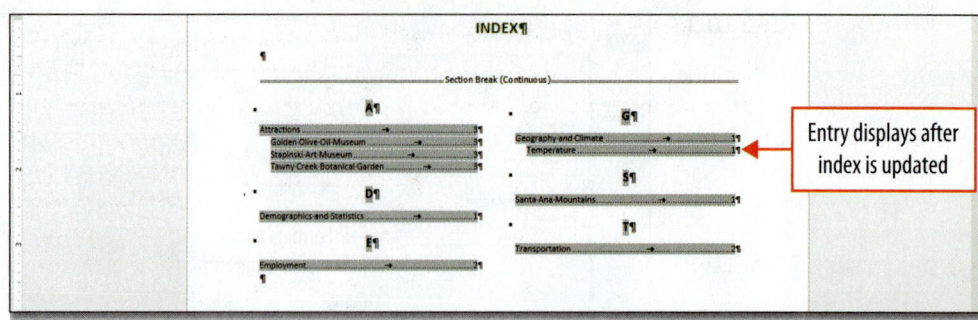

5 ▸ **Save** 🖫 your changes.

Objective 6 | Create a Table of Contents

Video W10-6

A ***table of contents*** is a list of a document's headings and subheadings, marked with the page numbers on which those headings and subheadings occur. Many times a table of contents will be abbreviated and referred to as a ***TOC***. The TOC is a useful way to navigate a long document because clicking the heading or subheading in the TOC moves you to the page of the heading or subheading you clicked. In most instances, a TOC displays at the beginning of a document.

Activity 10.17 | Assigning Heading Levels

1 ▸ Press Ctrl + Home. At the beginning of **Page 1**, select the second paragraph *About the City*.

2 ▸ On the **REFERENCES tab**, in the **Table of Contents group**, click **Add Text**. Notice that *Level 1* is selected.

The Add Text button is used to identify the entries that will be included in the TOC. Each entry in the TOC is identified by a heading level—Level 1 being the highest. When text is formatted with a heading style, Word matches the heading style number with the corresponding level number and automatically adds it to the TOC. In this case, Level 1 is selected because the text is formatted with the Heading 1 style. You can change the level for selected text or add unformatted text to the TOC by assigning the appropriate level.

3 ▸ Above the first table, select the paragraph *Demographics*. In the **Table of Contents group**, click **Add Text**. Notice that *Level 2* is already selected. Compare your screen with Figure 10.38.

Level 2 is selected because the text *Demographics* is formatted with the Heading 2 style.

FIGURE 10.38

Add Text button

Level 2 selected

Selected paragraph

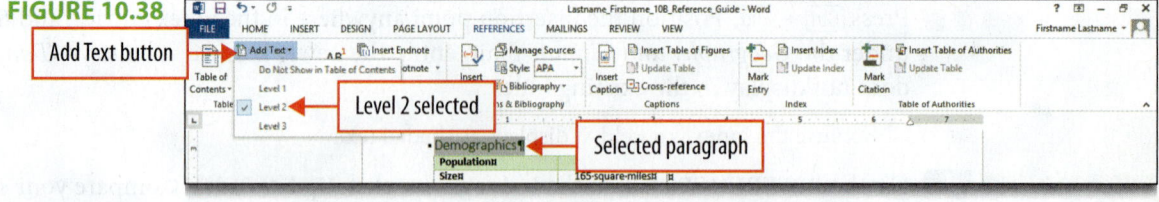

4 On **Page 3**, select the paragraph *Tawny Creek Botanical Garden*. In the **Table of Contents group**, click the **Add Text** button, and then click **Level 3**. In a similar manner, assign **Level 3** to the paragraphs *Golden Olive Oil Museum* and *Stapinski Art Museum*.

> Because these paragraphs were not formatted with a Heading style, you must assign a level for the terms to display in the TOC. By selecting *Level 3*, the paragraphs are formatted with the *Heading 3* style.

5 Press Ctrl + Home, and then **Save** your changes.

Activity 10.18 | Creating and Formatting a Table of Contents

A TOC can be customized to include formatting. Any formatting added to the TOC will not affect the rest of the document. It is a good idea to format the TOC to make it stand out from the rest of the document.

1 With the insertion point at the beginning of the document, click the **PAGE LAYOUT tab**. In the **Page Setup group**, click **Breaks**, and then under **Section Breaks**, click **Next Page**.

> A TOC is typically displayed as a separate, first page of a document.

2 Press Ctrl + Home to move to the beginning of the document. Click the **HOME tab**, and then in the **Styles group**, click **Normal**.

3 Type **TABLE OF CONTENTS** and then press Enter two times.

4 Select the paragraph you just typed. On the mini toolbar, change the **Font Size** to **16**, apply **Bold** B, and then click **Font Color** A ·. Press Ctrl + E.

5 On **Page 1**, position the insertion point in the blank paragraph to the left of the section break. Click the **REFERENCES tab**, and then in the **Table of Contents group**, click **Table of Contents**. Notice that the **Table of Contents** gallery displays. Compare your screen with Figure 10.39.

> You can insert a built-in TOC by clicking the style you want, or you can click Custom Table of Contents to create your own TOC style.

FIGURE 10.39

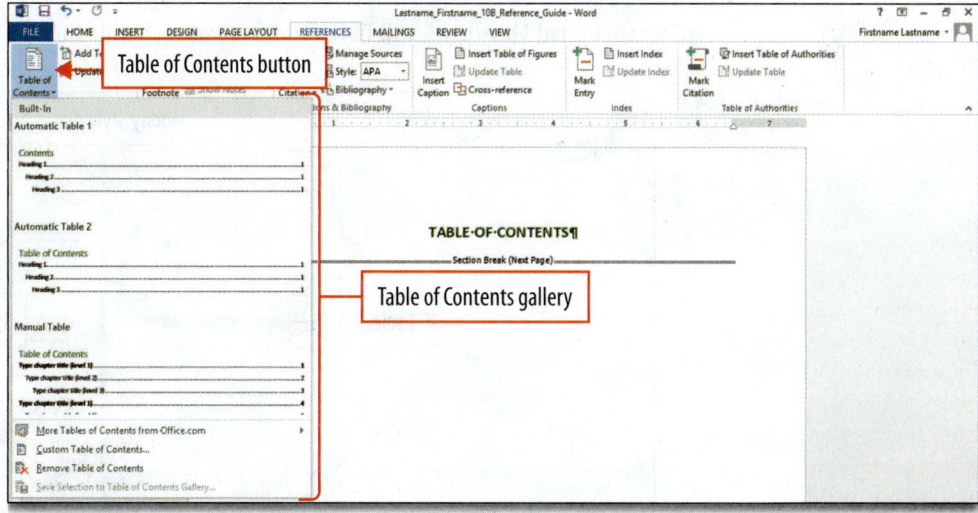

6 ▶ In the **Table of Contents** gallery, click **Custom Table of Contents**.

7 ▶ In the **Table of Contents** dialog box, under **Web Preview**, if necessary, select the **Use hyperlinks instead of page numbers** check box. Notice that the **Print Preview** box displays the TOC format with Heading 2 and Heading 3 indented. Compare your screen with Figure 10.40.

A hyperlink will enable a reader of a document to click a page number in the TOC and move to that part of the document. The Show levels box displays *3*—representing the three heading levels assigned to specific text in the document. By using the Formats arrow, you can select a formatting style for the TOC. The Options button allows you to indicate the heading levels that will be used in the TOC. The Modify button allows you to change the formatting of the TOC—for example, fonts, paragraphs, and tabs.

FIGURE 10.40

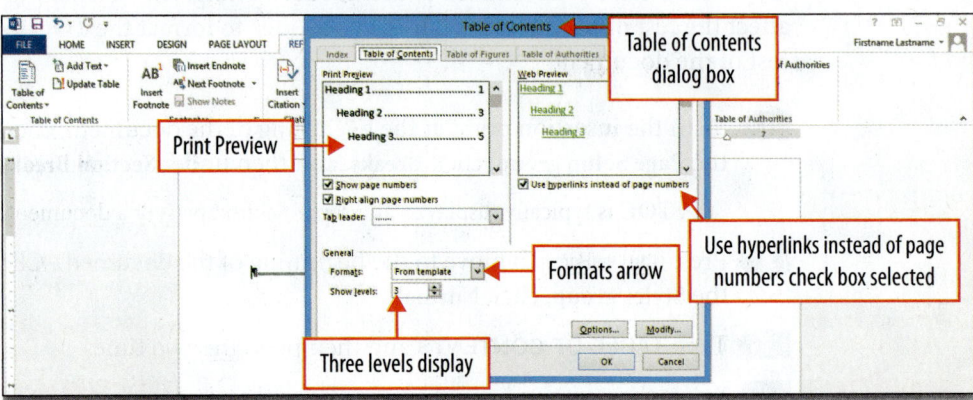

8 ▶ In the **Table of Contents** dialog box, click **Modify**. In the displayed **Style** dialog box, under **Styles**, if necessary, click to select **TOC 1**.

Under Preview, the current format for Heading 1 displays along with a description of the specific format elements.

9 ▶ In the **Style** dialog box, click **Modify**. In the **Modify Style** dialog box, under **Formatting**, click **Bold** B . Compare your screen with Figure 10.41.

All text assigned Heading 1 will have bold formatting applied in the TOC.

FIGURE 10.41

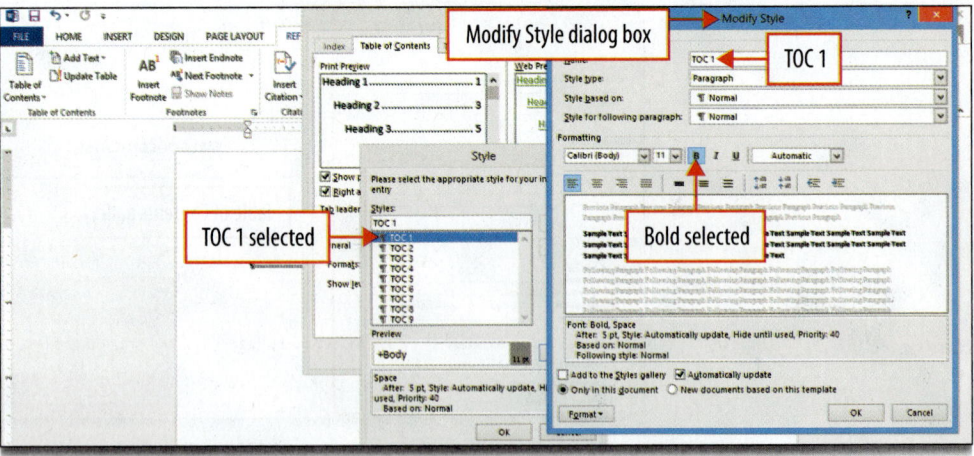

10 Click **OK** two times. On the left side of the **Table of Contents** dialog box, click the **Tab leader arrow**, and then click the second line style—a dashed line.

> A tab leader is a dotted, dashed, or solid line used to connect related information and improve the readability of a line.

11 Click **OK** to insert the TOC. Select the entire TOC. Click the **HOME tab**, and then in the **Font group**, click **Font Color** [A ▾]. Click in a blank area of the page, and then compare your screen with Figure 10.42.

> All document headings display with the related page number. If a document is edited and page numbers change, you can update the TOC to reflect the changes.

FIGURE 10.42

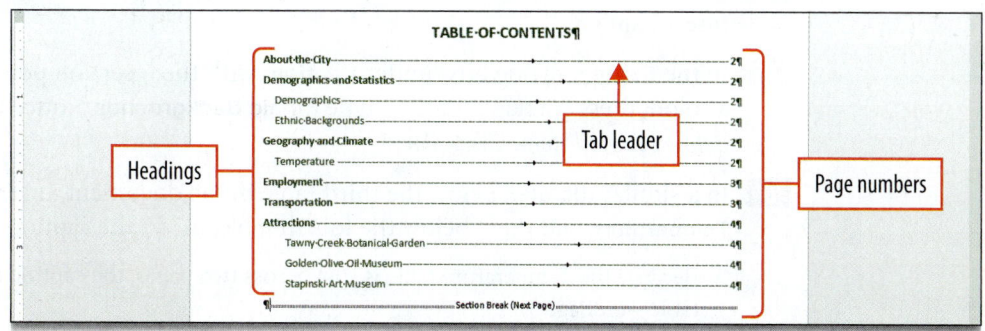

12 Point to the *Attractions* entry in the TOC to display the ScreenTip, which indicates the entry is a hyperlink. Press and hold Ctrl and click **Attractions**.

> The insertion point moves to Page 4 where the related text begins and is positioned to the left of the *Attractions* heading.

13 **Save** [💾] your changes.

Objective 7 | Create a Table of Figures

Video W10-7

A *table of figures* is a list of the figure captions in a document. In most instances, a table of figures displays at the beginning of a document, on a separate page following the TOC.

Activity 10.19 | Creating a Table of Figures

In this activity, you will add captions to the four tables in the document, and then create the table of figures.

1 On **Page 2**, in the first table—below the heading *Demographics*, click in the first cell. Click the **REFERENCES tab**, and then in the **Captions group**, click **Insert Caption**.

2 In the **Caption** dialog box, in the **Caption** box, with the insertion point to the right of *Table 1*, type a colon, press Spacebar, and then type **Demographics** Click the **Position arrow**, and then click **Below selected item**. Compare your screen with Figure 10.43.

FIGURE 10.43

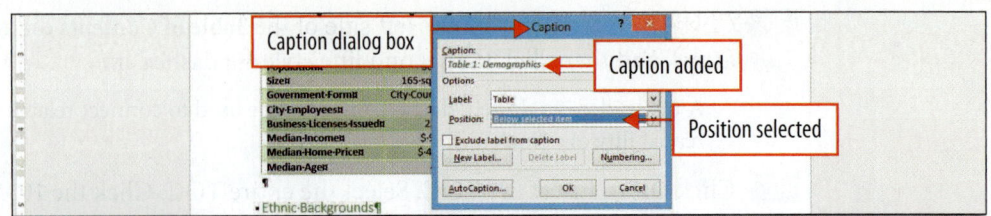

3 Click **OK**. Notice that the caption displays below the table.

Recall that a caption is a title that is added to a Word object and numbered sequentially.

4 At the bottom of **Page 2**, in the second table, click in the first cell. In the **Captions group**, click **Insert Caption**.

5 In the **Caption** dialog box, under **Caption**, with the insertion point to the right of *Table 2*, type a colon, press [Spacebar], and then type **Ethnic Backgrounds** Notice that the **Position** box displays *Below selected item*. Click **OK**.

6 In a similar manner, below the third table in the document, insert the caption **Table 3: Temperature** and then, below the fourth table, insert the caption **Table 4: Transportation**

Because the Temperature table is split across two pages, the caption displays at the bottom of the table—on Page 3.

7 Press [Ctrl] + [Home]. Click to position the insertion point in the last paragraph of **Page 1**—to the left of the section break. Press [Ctrl] + [Enter] to insert a manual page break. Notice that the insertion point moves to the first paragraph on the new, second page.

8 Type **TABLE OF FIGURES** and then press [Enter]. Select the paragraph you just typed. On the mini toolbar, change the **Font Size** to **16**, apply **Bold** [B], and then press [Ctrl] + [E].

9 Click to position the insertion point in the blank paragraph to the left of the section break. On the **REFERENCES tab**, in the **Captions group**, click **Insert Table of Figures**. In the **Table of Figures** dialog box, click the **Tab leader arrow**, and then click the second line style—the dashed line.

The Table of Figures dialog box is similar to the Table of Contents dialog box and provides many of the same options.

10 Click **OK** to insert the table of figures. Select the entire table of figures, including the title, and then on the **HOME tab**, in the **Font group**, click **Font Color** [A ▾]. Click in a blank area of the page, and then compare your screen with Figure 10.44.

The captions and their respective page numbers display, separated by the dashed line tab leader.

FIGURE 10.44

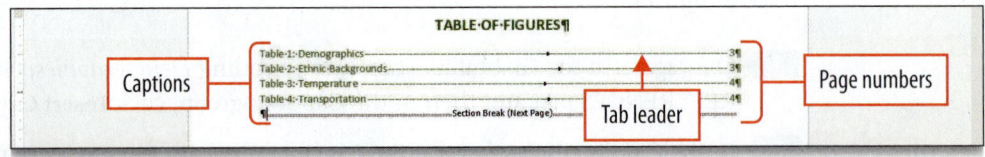

11 Point to the *Temperature* entry in the table of figures to display a ScreenTip, which indicates the entry is a hyperlink. Press and hold [Ctrl], and then click the **Temperature** entry.

The insertion point moves to Page 4 and is positioned to the left of the *Table 3: Temperature* caption.

12 **Save** [💾] your changes.

Video W10-8

Recall that page breaks and section breaks allow you to control how text, tables, page numbers, and other objects display in your document. It is important that text flows smoothly and page numbers display properly. The process of arranging and numbering the pages in a document is called **pagination**.

Activity 10.20 | Hiding White Space and Applying Hyphenation

In Print Layout view, to maximize your view of the document, you can hide the white spaces at the top and bottom of each page as well as the gray space between the pages. Recall that Word's hyphenation feature allows you to control how words are split between two lines, resulting in a less ragged edge at the right margin.

1 Scroll up to display the bottom of **Page 3** and the top of **Page 4**. Position the mouse pointer between the pages until it changes to the **Double-click to hide white space** pointer 茸, and then double-click. Compare your screen with Figure 10.45.

> The white space, including the footer, at the top and bottom of the pages and the gray space between the pages no longer display. You must be in Print Layout view to use the Hide White Space feature.

FIGURE 10.45

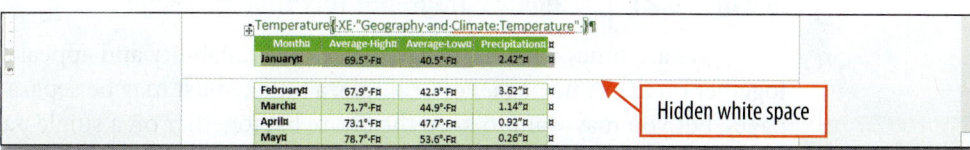
Hidden white space

2 Click the **PAGE LAYOUT tab**, and then in the **Page Setup group**, click **Hyphenation**. Compare your screen with Figure 10.46.

> *None* is selected because the hyphenation feature is turned off by default. Selecting *Automatic* will cause Word to automatically hyphenate the entire document. If you modify the document, as you work Word will change the hyphenation as necessary. Selecting *Manual* allows you to decide how specific words should be hyphenated. You can select *Hyphenation Options* to modify hyphenation settings for either automatic or manual hyphenation.

FIGURE 10.46

Hyphenation button

Hyphenation list

3 Click **Hyphenation Options**. In the **Hyphenation** dialog box, select the **Automatically hyphenate document** check box, and then click the **Limit consecutive hyphens to spin box up arrow** to **2**.

> Word will automatically hyphenate the document. If several consecutive lines of text contain words that could be hyphenated, then Word will apply hyphens on only two lines.

4 Click **OK** to close the **Hyphenation** dialog box. Click the **HOME tab**, and then hide the formatting marks.

> To view how hyphenation will be applied in the final document, it is useful to hide the formatting marks for the Mark Entry references.

5 Scroll to **Page 3**, and then in the paragraph below the *About the City* heading, in the second line, notice *containing* is hyphenated.

ALERT   **Different Words Are Hyphenated**

Depending on the width of your screen, word wrapping may cause your text to display differently. The hyphenated word may display on a different line, or the word may display without any hyphenation.

---

6 Scroll to the bottom of **Page 3**, and then in the last paragraph, notice that *western* is hyphenated.

7 Scroll to display the bottom of **Page 3** and the top of **Page 4**. Point to the gray border separating the two pages, and then when the **Double-click to show white space** pointer displays, double-click. Notice that the white space at the top and bottom of the page and the gray space between the pages display.

8 **Save** your changes.

Activity 10.21 | Keeping Paragraphs Together on a Page

There are times when it may enhance the readability and appeal of text to keep paragraphs together on the same page. For example, a bulleted list may be separated and displayed on two pages, but you may want to keep the entire list together on a single page.

1 Scroll until the bottom of **Page 3** and the top of **Page 4** are visible. Notice the table is split across two pages.

> To edit split text, you should hide formatting marks and always work from the beginning to the end of the document.

2 At the bottom of **Page 3**, above the table, select the paragraph *Temperature,* and then continue the selection to include the entire table including the caption.

3 Click the **HOME tab**, and then in the **Paragraph group**, click the **Dialog Box Launcher** to display the **Paragraph** dialog box.

4 In the **Paragraph** dialog box, click the **Line and Page Breaks tab**, and then under **Pagination**, select the **Keep with next** check box. Compare your screen with Figure 10.47, and then take a moment to study the table in Figure 10.48.

> In this case, Word will keep the entire selection—the paragraph and the table—together on the same page.

> The **Keep with next** command causes two elements, such as paragraphs, to display together on the same page. For example, this could be used to keep a heading together with the paragraph of text that follows it.

FIGURE 10.47

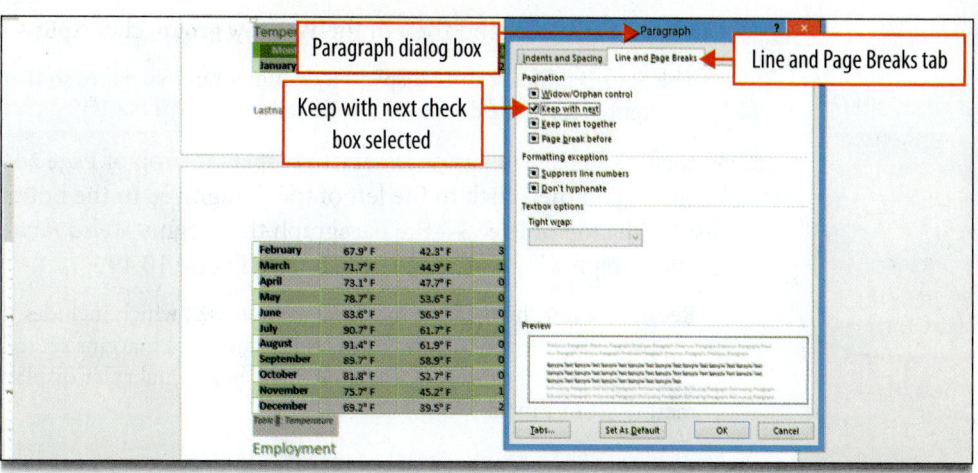

Paragraph dialog box

Line and Page Breaks tab

Keep with next check box selected

FIGURE 10.48

PAGINATION COMMANDS	
COMMAND	**DESCRIPTION**
Widow/Orphan control	Prevents a paragraph from splitting to display a single line at the top—widow—or bottom—orphan—of a page.
Keep with next	Causes two elements, such as paragraphs, to display together on the same page. For example, a heading will display on the same page as the paragraph of text that follows it.
Keep lines together	Prevents a page break from occurring within a paragraph.
Page break before	Forces a page break to occur before a paragraph.

5 ▶ Click **OK**. Deselect the text, and notice that the paragraph *Temperature* is at the top of the page, above the table.

The heading paragraph *Temperature* refers to the information in the table. Keeping the paragraph and table together on the same page improves the readability.

6 ▶ Display formatting marks, and then **Save** 🖫 your changes.

Because Mark Entry formatting marks are displayed in some paragraphs, the hyphenation of the document changes when formatting marks are displayed.

Activity 10.22 | Changing Page Settings, Splitting the Window, and Modifying Page Numbers

When a document contains section breaks, you can change the page settings—such as orientation or margins—and page numbering formats for different sections. In this activity, you will change the page margins for the TOC and table of figures, modify the page numbering for the document, and then update the TOC, table of figures, and index to reflect the changes you made.

1 ▶ Press Ctrl + Home. Click the **PAGE LAYOUT tab**. In the **Page Setup group**, click **Margins**, and then click **Wide**.

The left and right margins in Section 1 of the document—Page 1 and Page 2—are changed to 2 inches.

2 ▶ Click the **VIEW tab**, and then in the **Window group**, click **Split**.

The *Split Window* feature displays a document in two panes so that you can view or work on different parts of the document at the same time.

3 ▶ In the top pane, scroll as necessary to display the top of **Page 2**—the paragraph *Table of Figures*—and then click to the left of the paragraph. In the bottom pane, scroll as necessary to display the top of **Page 3**—the paragraph that begins *Welcome to*—and then click to the left of the paragraph. Compare your screen with Figure 10.49.

Recall that you changed the margins for *Section 1*, which includes the *Table of Figures* page. In the top pane, the horizontal ruler displays left and right margins set to 2 inches. In the bottom pane that displays the beginning of *Section 2*, the horizontal ruler displays the default left and right margin set to 1 inch.

FIGURE 10.49

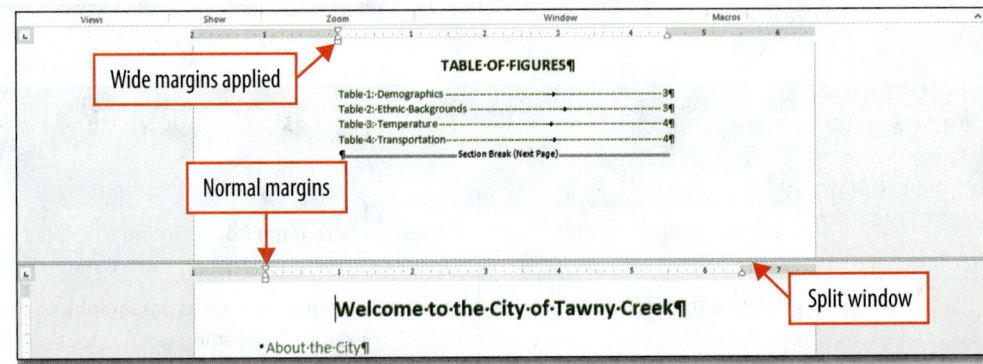

4 ▶ In the **Window group**, click **Remove Split** to return the document to a single full screen.

5 ▶ Press Ctrl + Home, and then scroll to the bottom of **Page 1**. Right-click in the footer area, and then click **Edit Footer**.

6 ▶ In the footer, select the page number *1*. On the **HEADER & FOOTER TOOLS DESIGN tab**, in the **Header & Footer group**, click **Page Number**, and then click **Format Page Numbers**.

In the Page Number Format dialog box, you can modify page number styles.

7 ▶ In the **Page Number Format** dialog box, click the **Number format arrow**, and then click the fifth numbering style—**i, ii, iii**. Compare your screen with Figure 10.50.

FIGURE 10.50

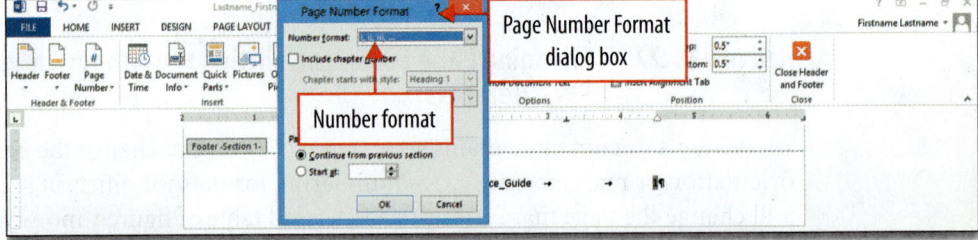

8 ▶ Click **OK**, and notice that the page number changes to *i*.

9 ▶ Scroll to the bottom of **Page 3**. Notice that the page number retains the original numbering style—*3*. Click to position the insertion point anywhere in the footer area.

At the top left of the footer area, the *Footer - Section 2* tab displays. Page 3 begins Section 2. When you created the TOC page, you inserted a Next Page section break. The TOC and table of figures are in Section 1 of the document. At the top right of the footer area, the *Same as Previous* tab displays.

10 In the **Navigation group**, click **Link to Previous** to turn it off. Notice that the *Same as Previous* tab no longer displays at the top right of the footer area on **Page 3**. Compare your screen with Figure 10.51.

By clicking the Link to Previous button, the footer for Section 2—the rest of the document—is no longer linked to the footer for Section 1—the first two pages. The Section 2 footer can be modified without affecting the Section 1 footer.

FIGURE 10.51

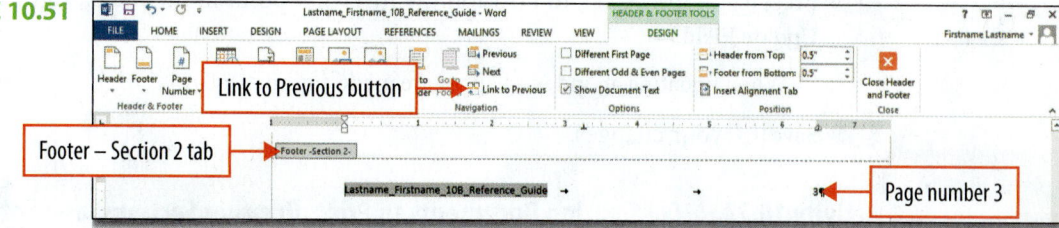

11 In the footer, select the page number *3*, right-click, and then from the shortcut menu, click **Format Page Numbers**. In the **Page Number Format** dialog box, under **Page numbering**, click the **Start at** option button, and then compare your screen with Figure 10.52.

The Start at option allows you to select the first page number that should display in a new section of a document. By default, the number *1* displays in the Start at box.

FIGURE 10.52

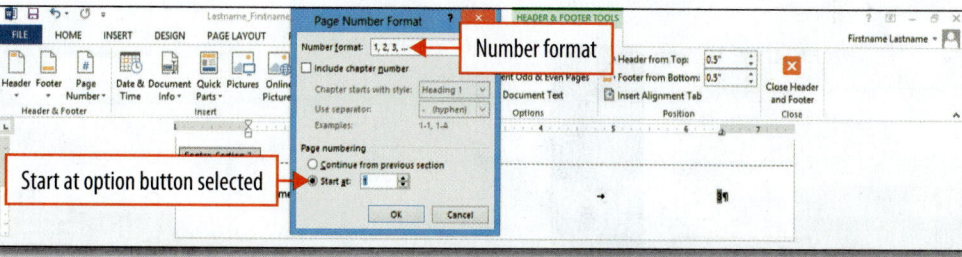

12 Click **OK**. Notice that the page number *1* displays in the footer on the third page of the document. In the **Close group**, click **Close Header and Footer**.

13 Press **Ctrl** + **Home**. Click to position the insertion point in the TOC, right-click, and then click **Update Field**. In the **Update Table of Contents** dialog box, with the **Update page numbers only** option button selected, click **OK** to update the page numbers in the TOC. Click in the blank paragraph below the TOC, and then compare your screen with Figure 10.53.

Because you inserted breaks and changed page numbering styles, it is necessary to update the page numbers for the TOC, table of figures, and the index.

ANOTHER WAY   On the REFERENCES tab, in the Table of Contents group, click the Update Table button.

FIGURE 10.53

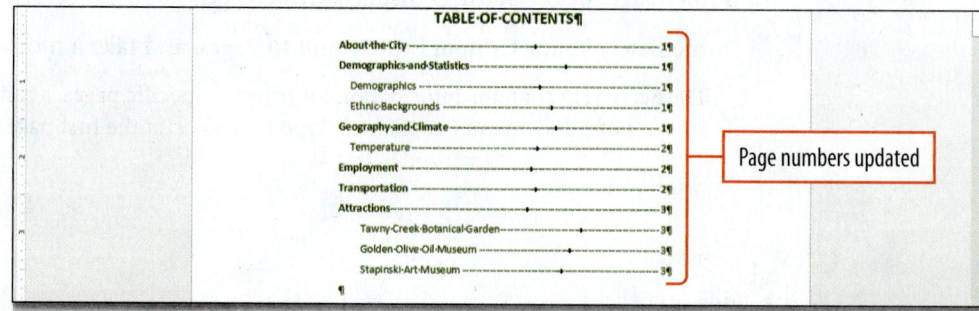

14 On the second page of the document—*Page ii*, click to position the insertion point in the table of figures. Right-click, and then click **Update Field**. In the **Update Table of Figures** dialog box, with the **Update page numbers only** option button selected, click **OK**.

ANOTHER WAY   On the REFERENCES tab, in the Captions group, click the Update Table button.

15 Press Ctrl + End. Click to position the insertion point in the index, right-click, and then click **Update Field**.

When updating an index, changes are made automatically.

16 Save your changes.

Activity 10.23 | Configuring Documents to Print, Printing Sections, and Setting Print Scaling

You can modify print settings to suit your needs. For example, you may want to print a range of pages or scale the printout for a specific paper size.

1 Press Ctrl + Home. Click the **FILE tab**, and then at the left of your screen, click Print.

2 Under **Settings**, click **Print All Pages**. Compare your screen with Figure 10.54.

A list of *Document* and *Document Info* settings displays. You can print specific pages, selected portions of a document, or information related to the document.

FIGURE 10.54

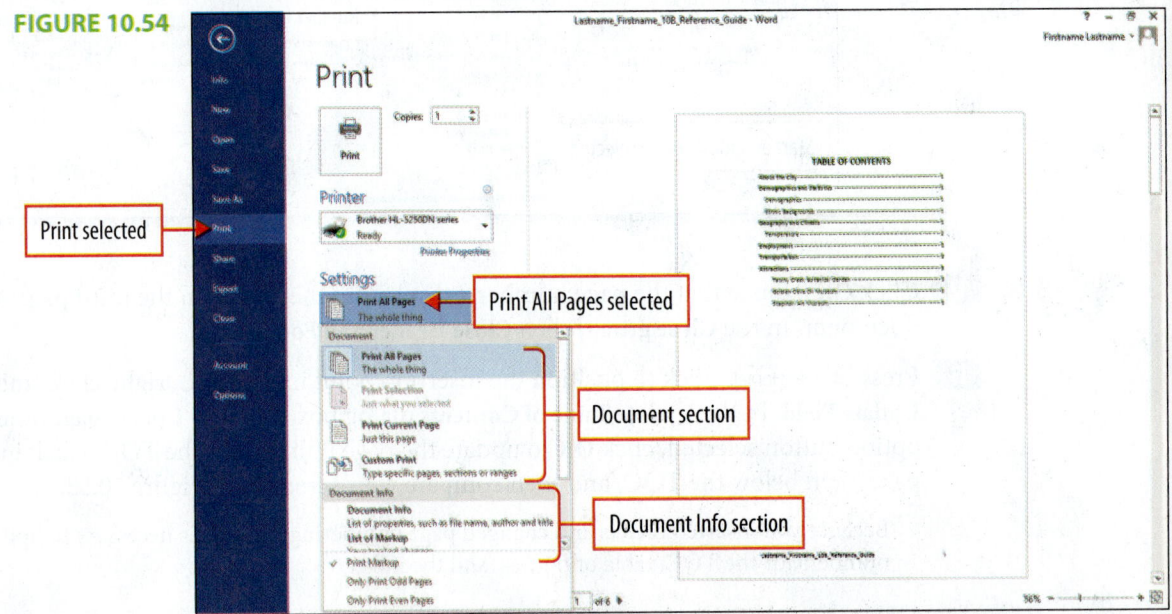

3 In the list, scroll as necessary, and then click **Custom Print**. Notice that the button immediately below Settings displays *Custom Print* and the insertion point is in the *Pages* box.

4 Immediately below **Custom Print**, point to **Pages**, and take a moment to read the ScreenTip.

The ScreenTip contains information for printing specific pages, a range of pages, or specific sections of a document. For example type *p1s1* to print the first page in Section 1.

5 Under **Settings**, click **1 Page Per Sheet**, and then point to **Scale to Paper Size**.

In the main list, you can select the number of pages on which you want to print your document. In the secondary list, you can select the paper size for the printed document.

6 From **Backstage** view, click **Info**, and then **Show All Properties**. In the **Tags** box, type **reference guide, TOC, index** In the **Subject** box, type your course name and section number. If necessary, edit the author name to display your name.

7 **Save** 🖫 your changes.

8 Print your document or submit electronically as directed by your instructor. **Close** Word.

END | You have completed Project 10B

END OF CHAPTER

SUMMARY

When a document is created or edited by several people, one efficient way of assembling or editing the document is to create a master document and subdocuments. Unlink the subdocuments to create a final document.

To navigate to specific locations in a document, use bookmarks, cross-references, and the Navigation pane. Insert section breaks to create different footers on odd and even pages. Include a cover page for interest.

An index indicates where specific text is located in the document. A table of contents helps the reader go directly to specific topics. The reader can use a table of figures to navigate to graphic elements.

Apply hyphenation and pagination options to improve readability. Modify page numbers to differentiate introductory pages—for example, a table of contents—from the main pages of the document.

GO! LEARN IT ONLINE

Review the concepts and key terms in this chapter by completing these online challenges, which you can find at **www.pearsonhighered.com/go**.

Matching and Multiple Choice: Answer matching and multiple choice questions to test what you learned in this chapter. **MyITLab®**

Crossword Puzzle: Spell out the words that match the numbered clues and put them in the puzzle squares.

Flipboard: Flip through the definitions of the key terms in this chapter and match them with the correct term.

END OF CHAPTER

REVIEW AND ASSESSMENT GUIDE FOR WORD CHAPTER 10

Your instructor may assign one or more of these projects to help you review the chapter and assess your mastery and understanding of the chapter.

		Review and Assessment Guide for Word Chapter 10	
Project	**Apply Skills from These Chapter Objectives**	**Project Type**	**Project Location**
10C	Objectives 1–4 from Project 10A	**10C Skills Review** A guided review of the skills from Project 10A.	On the following pages
10D	Objectives 5–8 from Project 10B	**10D Skills Review** A guided review of the skills from Project 10B.	On the following pages
10E	Objectives 1–4 from Project 10A	**10E Mastery (Grader Project)** A demonstration of your mastery of the skills in Project 10A with extensive decision making.	In MyITLab and on the following pages
10F	Objectives 5–8 from Project 10B	**10F Mastery (Grader Project)** A demonstration of your mastery of the skills in Project 10B with extensive decision making.	In MyITLab and on the following pages
10G	Objectives 1–8 from Projects 10A and 10B	**10G Mastery (Grader Project)** A demonstration of your mastery of the skills in Projects 10A and 10B with extensive decision making.	In MyITLab and on the following pages
10H	Combination of Objectives from Projects 10A and 10B	**10H GO! Fix It** A demonstration of your mastery of the skills in Projects 10A and 10B by creating a correct result from a document that contains errors you must find.	Online
10I	Combination of Objectives from Projects 10A and 10B	**10I GO! Make It** A demonstration of your mastery of the skills in Projects 10A and 10B by creating a result from a supplied picture.	Online
10J	Combination of Objectives from Projects 10A and 10B	**10J GO! Solve It** A demonstration of your mastery of the skills in Projects 10A and 10B, your decision-making skills, and your critical thinking skills. A task-specific rubric helps you self-assess your result.	Online
10K	Combination of Objectives from Projects 10A and10B	**10K GO! Solve It** A demonstration of your mastery of the skills in Projects 10A and 10B, your decision-making skills, and your critical thinking skills. A task-specific rubric helps you self-assess your result.	On the following pages
10L	Combination of Objectives from Projects 10A and 10B	**10L GO! Think** A demonstration of your understanding of the chapter concepts applied in a manner that you would outside of college. An analytic rubric helps you and your instructor grade the quality of your work by comparing it to the work an expert in the discipline would create.	On the following pages
10M	Combination of Objectives from Projects 10A and 10B	**10M GO! Think** A demonstration of your understanding of the chapter concepts applied in a manner that you would outside of college. An analytic rubric helps you and your instructor grade the quality of your work by comparing it to the work an expert in the discipline would create.	Online
10N	Combination of Objectives from Projects 10A and 10B	**10N You and GO!** A demonstration of your understanding of the chapter concepts applied in a manner that you would in a personal situation. An analytic rubric helps you and your instructor grade the quality of your work.	Online

GLOSSARY

GLOSSARY OF CHAPTER KEY TERMS

Accessibility Checker A Word feature that searches a document for content that people with disabilities might find difficult to read and suggest ways to modify the content.

AutoMark file A Word document that contains a two-column table that is used to mark words as index entries.

Body text Text that does not have a heading style applied.

Bookmark A link that identifies the exact location of text, a table, or other object.

Continuous section break When working with subdocuments, a mark that defines the beginning and end of each subdocument.

Cover page The first page of a document that provides introductory information.

Cross-reference A text link to an item that appears in another location in the document, such as a heading, a caption, or a footnote.

Even Page section break A formatting mark that indicates the beginning of a new section on the next even-numbered page.

Hidden text Nonprinting text—for example, an index entry field.

Index A compilation of topics, names, and terms accompanied by page numbers that displays at the end of a document.

Index entry A word or phrase that is listed in the index.

Index entry field Code, formatted as hidden text and displaying to the right of an index entry, containing the identifier XE and the term to be included in the index.

Keep with next A formatting feature that causes two elements, such as paragraphs, to display together on the same page.

Master document A Word document that serves as a container for the different parts of a document.

Odd Page section break A formatting mark that indicates the beginning of a new section on the next odd-numbered page.

Outline view A document view that displays the overall organization, or hierarchy, of the document's parts, including headings, subheadings, and subordinate text.

Pagination The process of arranging and numbering the pages in a document.

Readability statistics A Spelling and Grammar tool that analyzes a document and determines the reading level of the text.

Section break A mark that stores the formatting information for a section of a document.

Split Window A Word feature that displays a document in two panes so that you can view or work on different parts of the document at the same time.

Subdocument A section of a document that is linked to the master document.

Table of contents (TOC) A list of a document's headings and subheadings, marked with the page numbers where those headings and subheadings occur.

Table of figures A list of the figure captions in a document.

Thumbnail A graphical representation of a page.

Word count The number of words in a document.

XE Code identifying an index entry.

CHAPTER REVIEW

Skills Review   Project 10C Summer Calendar

Apply **10A** skills from these
Objectives:

1 Create a Master
Document and
Subdocuments

2 Manage a Master
Document and
Subdocuments

3 Navigate and Inspect the
Master Document

4 Create and Modify
Headers and Footers

In the following Skills Review, you will create a master document and subdocuments for events happening during the summer in the City of Tawny Creek. Your completed documents will look similar to Figure 10.55.

PROJECT FILES

For Project 10C, you will need the following files:

w10C_Summer_Calendar
w10C_Shakespeare_Festival

You will save your files as:

Lastname_Firstname_10C_Summer_Calendar
Lastname_Firstname_10C_Shakespeare_Festival

PROJECT RESULTS

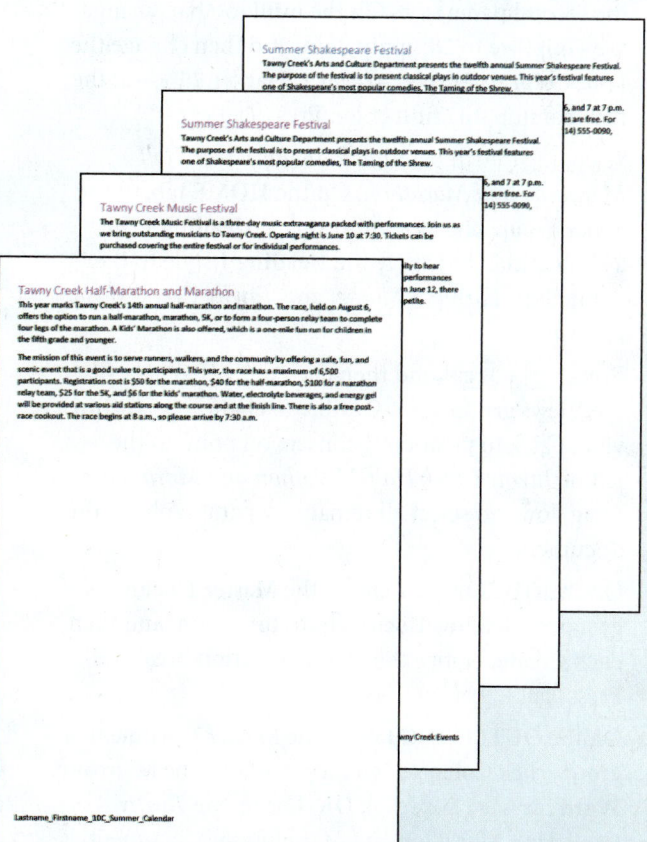

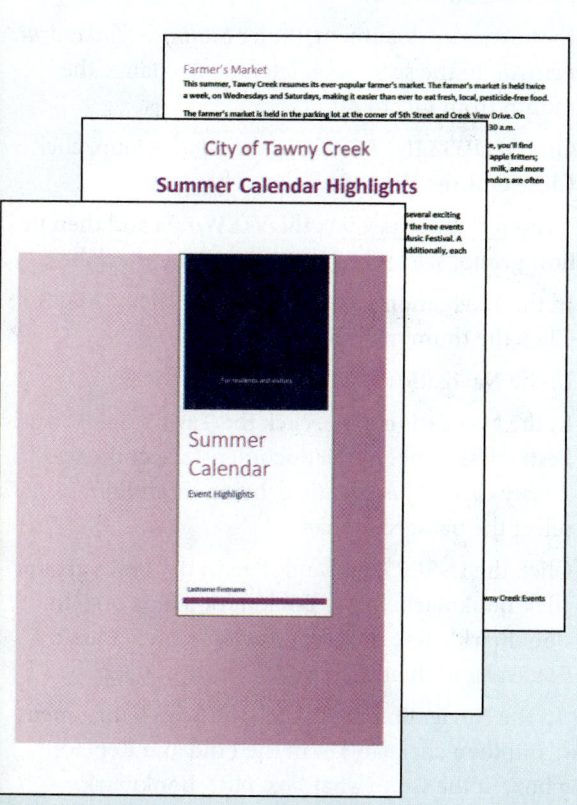

FIGURE 10.55

(Project 10C Summer Calendar continues on the next page)

CHAPTER REVIEW

1 ▶ Start Word. From your student files, locate and open the file **w10C_Summer_Calendar**. Press F12 to display the **Save As** dialog box, navigate to your **Word Chapter 10** folder, and then create a folder named **Project 10C Save** the document to your **Project 10C** folder as **Lastname_Firstname_10C_Summer_Calendar** If necessary, display the rulers and formatting marks.

a. Click the **DESIGN tab**. In the **Document Formatting group**, click **Themes**, and then click **Celestial**.

b. Select the first paragraph. On the mini toolbar, change the **Font Size** to **26**. With the text selected, click the **HOME tab**. In the **Font group**, click the **Text Effects** button, and then in the **Text Effects** gallery, in the first row, select the second effect—**Fill – Purple, Accent 1, Shadow**. Apply **Center**. Select the second paragraph. On the mini toolbar, change the **Font Size** to **28**, apply **Bold,** and then change the **Font Color** to **Purple, Accent 1, Darker 25%**—in the fifth column, the fifth color. Press Ctrl + E.

c. Select the fourth paragraph *Tawny Creek Half-Marathon and Marathon*. On the **HOME tab**, in the **Styles group**, click the third style—**Heading 1**. In a similar manner, apply the **Heading 1** style to the paragraphs *Farmer's Market* and *Tawny Creek Music Festival*.

d. Press Ctrl + Home, and then click the **VIEW tab**. In the **Views group**, click **Outline** to change to **Outline** view. Click to position the insertion point to the left of *Tawny Creek Half-Marathon and Marathon*. Drag down to select all remaining paragraphs in the document.

e. On the **OUTLINING tab**, in the **Master Document group**, click **Show Document** to turn it on, and then click **Create**. Notice the inserted section breaks. Press Ctrl + Home.

f. On the **OUTLINING tab**, in the **Master Document group**, click **Collapse Subdocuments**. In the **Microsoft Word** message box, click **OK**. Locate the *Tawny Creek Half-Marathon and Marathon* subdocument, and then to the left of the subdocument, click the **Subdocument** icon. Drag down until the **Subdocument** icon is above the *Section Break (Continuous)* for the *Tawny Creek Music Festival* subdocument. Deselect the text, and then **Save** your changes. On the **OUTLINING tab**, in the **Master Document group**, click **Expand Subdocuments**.

2 ▶ From your student files, locate and open the file **w10C_Shakespeare_Festival**.

a. Press F12 to display the **Save As** dialog box. **Save** the file in your **Project 10C** folder as **Lastname_Firstname_10C_Shakespeare_Festival** Click the **FILE tab**, and then click **Show All Properties**. In the **Tags** box type **subdocument, Shakespeare** In the **Subject** box, type your course name and section number. If necessary, edit the author name to display your name. **Save** your changes, and then **Close** the *Shakespeare Festival* document.

b. In the master document, press Ctrl + End to move to the end of the document. In the **Master Document group**, click **Insert**. In the **Insert Subdocument** dialog box, navigate to your **Project 10C** folder, select **Lastname_Firstname_10C_Shakespeare_Festival**, and then click **Open**.

c. In the master document, under *Summer Shakespeare Festival*, in the second bulleted item, change the month from *July* to **August**

d. On the **OUTLINING tab**, in the **Close group**, click **Close Outline View**. **Save** your changes.

3 ▶ Press Ctrl + Home. Click the **VIEW tab**, and then in the **Show group**, select the **Navigation Pane** check box.

a. In the **Navigation** pane, if necessary, click **PAGES**. Click the thumbnail for **Page 3**.

b. In the **Navigation** pane, click **HEADINGS**.

c. In the **Navigation** pane, click the **Tawny Creek Music Festival** heading. In the document, select the text *Tawny Creek Music Festival*, being careful not to select the paragraph mark.

d. Click the **INSERT tab**, and then in the **Links group**, click **Bookmark**. In the **Bookmark** dialog box, in the **Bookmark name** box, type **Tawny_Creek_Music_Festival** and then click **Add**. Press Ctrl + Home.

4 ▶ In the **Navigation** pane, click the **Search document arrow**, and then click **Go To**. In the **Find and Replace** dialog box, in the **Go to what** box, click **Bookmark**.

a. Below the **Enter bookmark name** box, which displays *Tawny_Creek_Music_Festival*, click **Go To**. **Close** the **Find and Replace** dialog box, and then **Close** the **Navigation** pane.

(Project 10C Summer Calendar continues on the next page)

b. Press Ctrl + Home. In the third paragraph, in the second sentence, select the text *Music Festival*, being careful not to select the space to the left or the period on the right.

c. On the **INSERT tab**, in the **Links group**, click **Cross-reference**.

d. In the **Cross-reference** dialog box, click the **Reference type arrow**, and then click **Bookmark**. If necessary, click the **Insert reference to arrow** to display **Bookmark text**, and select the **Insert as hyperlink** check box.

e. Under **For which bookmark**, with *Tawny_Creek_ Music_Festival* selected, in the **Cross-reference** dialog box, click **Insert**, and then click **Close**.

5 Move your mouse pointer over the **Tawny Creek Music Festival** cross-reference. Press and hold Ctrl, and when the 🖑 pointer displays, click **Tawny Creek Music Festival**.

a. Press Ctrl + Home. Click the **FILE tab**, and then click **Options**. In the **Word Options** dialog box, click **Proofing**. Under **When correcting spelling and grammar in Word**, select the **Show readability statistics** check box to turn on the display of readability statistics. Click **OK**.

b. On the **REVIEW tab**, in the **Proofing group**, click **Spelling & Grammar**.

c. Click **OK** to close the **Readability Statistics** dialog box. Click the **FILE tab**, and then click **Options**. In the **Word Options** dialog box, click **Proofing**. Under **When correcting spelling and grammar in Word**, clear the **Show readability statistics** check box. Click **OK**.

6 Press Ctrl + Home. On the **VIEW tab**, in the **Views group**, click **Outline**. If necessary, on the **OUTLINING tab**, in the **Master Document group**, click **Show Document**.

a. To the left of the paragraph *Farmer's Market*, click the **Subdocument** icon to select the entire *Farmer's Market* subdocument. In the **Master Document group**, click **Unlink**.

b. In a similar manner, **Unlink** the subdocuments *Tawny Creek Half-Marathon and Marathon*, *Tawny Creek Music Festival*, and *Summer Shakespeare Festival*.

c. Above the paragraph *Farmer's Market*, click to position the insertion point to the right of the first bullet for **Section Break (Continuous)**, and then press Delete.

d. In a similar manner, delete all instances of **Section Break (Continuous)** and **Section Break (Next Page)** that display.

e. On the **OUTLINING tab**, in the **Close group**, click **Close Outline View**.

7 Position the insertion point to the left of the paragraph *Farmer's Market*. Click the **PAGE LAYOUT tab**. In the **Page Setup group**, click **Breaks**, and then under **Section Breaks**, click **Even Page**. To the left of the paragraph *Tawny Creek Music, Festival* insert an **Even Page** section break.

a. To the left of the paragraphs that begin *Tawny Creek Half-Marathon* and *Summer Shakespeare*, insert an **Odd Page** section break.

b. At the bottom of **Page 2**, right-click in the footer area, and then click **Edit Footer**. On the **HEADER & FOOTER TOOLS DESIGN tab**, in the **Options group**, select the **Different Odd & Even Pages** check box.

c. On **Page 2**, click in the **Even Page** footer, press Tab two times, and then type **Tawny Creek Events**

d. On **Page 3**, in the **Odd Page** footer, insert the file name.

e. In the **Close group**, click the **Close Header and Footer** button. **Save** your changes.

8 Press Ctrl + Home. Click the **INSERT tab**. In the **Pages group**, click **Cover Page**, and then click the **Austin** style.

a. Click in the **Title** placeholder, and then type **Summer Calendar**

b. Click in the **Subtitle** placeholder, and then type **Event Highlights**

c. Click in the **Abstract** placeholder, and then type **For residents and visitors**

d. In the **Author** placeholder, if necessary, delete the existing text, and then type your first and last names.

(Project 10C Summer Calendar continues on the next page)

CHAPTER REVIEW

9 Click the **FILE tab**, and then click **Show All Properties**. In the **Author** box, verify that your first and last names display. In the **Tags** box, type **summer calendar, master** and then in the **Categories** box, type your course name and section number.

a. **Save** your document, and then press Ctrl + W.

b. Click the **FILE tab**, and then click **Open**. Navigate to your **Project 10C** folder, and open the file

Lastname_Firstname_10C_Shakespeare_Festival. Position the insertion point at the end of the third paragraph. Press Delete to delete the **Section Break (Next Page)**. Right-click in the footer area, click **Edit Footer**, and then insert the file name. **Save** your changes.

10 Print both of your documents or submit your files electronically as directed by your instructor. **Close** Word.

END | You have completed Project 10C

CHAPTER REVIEW

Apply 10B skills from these Objectives:

5 Create an Index

6 Create a Table of Contents

7 Create a Table of Figures

8 Control the Flow and Formatting of Pages and Text

Skills Review Project 10D Job Descriptions

In the following Skills Review, you will add an index, a table of contents, and a table of figures to the listing of job descriptions for the City of Tawny Creek. Your completed document will look similar to Figure 10.56.

PROJECT FILES

For Project 10D, you will need the following file:

w10D_Job_Descriptions

You will save your file as:

Lastname_Firstname_10D_Job_Descriptions

PROJECT RESULTS

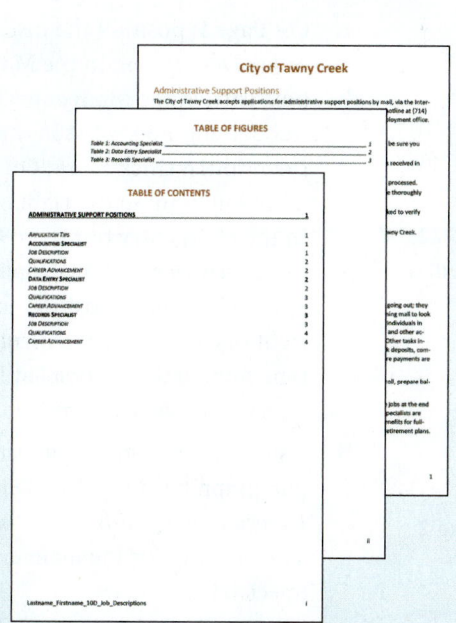
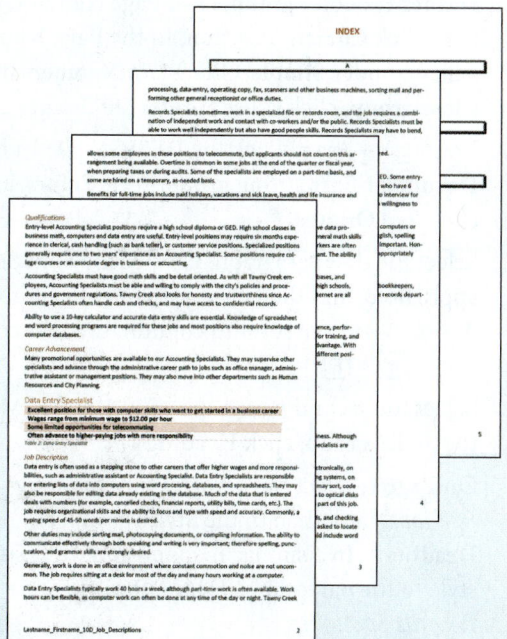

FIGURE 10.56

(Project 10D Job Descriptions continues on the next page)

CHAPTER REVIEW

1 Start Word. From your student files, open the file **w10D_Job_Descriptions**. **Save** the file in your **Word Chapter 10** folder as **Lastname_Firstname_10D_ Job_Descriptions** If necessary, display the rulers and formatting marks. If any words are flagged as spelling errors, right-click the first occurrence of each, and then click **Ignore All**.

a. Scroll to the bottom of **Page 1**, right-click in the footer area, click **Edit Footer**, and then insert the file name in the footer. With the footer area displayed, be sure the insertion point is to the right of the file name, and then press Tab two times. On the **HEADER & FOOTER TOOLS DESIGN tab**, in the **Header & Footer group**, click **Page Number**, and then click **Current Position**. In the **Page Number** gallery, under **Simple**, click **Plain Number**. In the **Close group**, click **Close Header and Footer**.

b. Press Ctrl + Home. Click the **DESIGN tab**. In the **Document Formatting group**, click **Colors**, and then click **Red Orange**.

c. Select the first paragraph. Change the **Font Size** to **22**, apply **Bold**, and then change the **Font Color** to **Red, Accent 3**—in the seventh column, the first color. Press Ctrl + E.

d. Select the second paragraph. Click the **HOME tab**, in the **Styles group**, click **Heading 1**.

e. On **Page 1**, select the paragraph *Accounting Specialist*, and then in the **Styles group**, click **Heading 2**. In a similar manner, apply the **Heading 2** style to the paragraphs *Data Entry Specialist* and *Records Specialist*.

f. Press Ctrl + Home. Locate the first table in the document—under *Accounting Specialist*. Click to position the insertion point in the first cell of the table. Click the **TABLE TOOLS DESIGN tab**, and then in the **Table Style Options group**, clear the **Header Row** check box. In the **Table Styles group**, click **More**, and then under **Grid Tables**, in the second row, click the fourth style—**Grid Table 2 – Accent 3**. In the remaining two tables, use the same technique to deselect the **Header Row** check box and apply the **Grid Table 2 – Accent 3** style.

g. Press Ctrl + Home, and then **Save** your changes.

2 In the fourth paragraph, select the text *Application Tips*. Click the **REFERENCES tab**, and then in the **Index group**, click **Mark Entry**. In the **Mark Index Entry** dialog box, click **Mark**.

a. Click in the document, and then select the paragraph *Accounting Specialist*. If necessary, point to the **Mark Index Entry** dialog box title bar, and then drag the **Mark Index Entry** dialog box to the side of your screen. With the paragraph selected, click in the **Mark Index Entry** dialog box, and notice that *Accounting Specialist* displays. Click **Mark**.

b. Without closing the **Mark Index Entry** dialog box, in a similar manner, **Mark** entries for *Data Entry Specialist* and *Records Specialist*.

c. On **Page 1**, position the insertion point to the right of *Job Description*. In the **Mark Index Entry** dialog box, click in the **Main entry** box, and then type **Accounting Specialist** In the **Subentry** box, type **Job Description** Click **Mark**. On **Page 2**, position the insertion point to the right of *Qualifications*. In the **Main entry** box, type **Accounting Specialist** In the **Subentry** box, type **Qualifications** and then click **Mark**. On **Page 2**, position the insertion point to the right of *Career Advancement*. In the **Main entry** box, type **Accounting Specialist** In the **Subentry** box, type **Career Advancement** and then click **Mark**.

d. Using the technique you just practiced, under the paragraph heading *Data Entry Specialist*, mark *Job Description*, *Qualifications*, and *Career Advancement* as subentries for the main entry **Data Entry Specialist**.

e. In a similar manner, under the paragraph heading *Records Specialist*, mark subentries for *Job Description*, *Qualifications*, and *Career Advancement* as subentries for the main entry **Records Specialist**.

f. **Close** the **Mark Index Entry** dialog box and then **Save** your changes.

3 Press Ctrl + End, and then press Ctrl + Enter to insert a manual page break. With the insertion point at the top of the new page, type **INDEX** and then press Enter. Select the text *INDEX*, including the paragraph mark, change the **Font Size** to **16**, apply **Bold**, and then click **Font Color**. Press Ctrl + E.

(Project 10D Job Descriptions continues on the next page)

a. Click to position the insertion point in the last paragraph of the document. On the **REFERENCES tab**, in the **Index group**, click **Insert Index** to display the **Index** dialog box.

b. In the **Index** dialog box, on the **Index tab**, click the **Formats arrow**, and then click **Fancy**. On the right side of the **Index** dialog box, click the **Columns spin box down arrow** to **1**. Click **OK**.

c. On **Page 1**, select the first paragraph with italic formatting—*Application Tips*. In the **Table of Contents group**, click **Add Text**, and then click **Level 3**. In a similar manner, assign **Level 3** to the remaining nine italicized paragraph headings. Press Ctrl + Home, and then **Save** your changes.

4 With the insertion point at the beginning of the document, click the **PAGE LAYOUT tab**. In the **Page Setup group**, click **Breaks**, and then under **Section Breaks**, click **Next Page**. Press Ctrl + Home to move to the beginning of the document. Click the **HOME tab**, and then in the **Styles group**, click **Normal**.

a. Type **TABLE OF CONTENTS** and then press Enter two times. Select the text you just typed, including the paragraph mark, change the **Font Size** to **16**, apply **Bold**, and then click **Font Color**. Press Ctrl + E.

b. Click to position the insertion point in the last paragraph on the page—to the left of the section break. Click the **REFERENCES tab**, and then in the **Table of Contents group**, click **Table of Contents**. In the **Table of Contents** gallery, click **Custom Table of Contents**. In the **Table of Contents** dialog box, if necessary, select the **Use hyperlinks instead of page numbers** check box.

c. Under **General**, click the **Formats arrow**, and then click **Fancy**. Click **OK**, and then **Save** your changes.

5 On **Page 2**, below the heading *Accounting Specialist*, in the first table, click in the first cell. On the **REFERENCES tab**, in the **Captions group**, click **Insert Caption**.

a. In the **Caption** dialog box, in the **Caption** box, with the insertion point to the right of *Table 1*, type a colon, press Spacebar, and then type **Accounting Specialist** Click the **Position arrow**, and then click **Below selected item**. Click **OK**.

b. On **Page 3**, click in the first cell of the table. In the **Captions group**, click **Insert Caption**. In the **Caption** dialog box, in the **Caption** box, with the insertion point to the right of *Table 2*, type a colon, press Spacebar, and then type **Data Entry Specialist** Click **OK**.

c. In a similar manner, insert the caption **Table 3: Records Specialist** below the third table in the document. Click **OK**.

6 Press Ctrl + Home. Click to position the insertion point in the last paragraph of the page—to the left of the section break. Press Ctrl + Enter to insert a manual page break.

a. Type **TABLE OF FIGURES** and then press Enter. Select the text you just typed, change the **Font Size** to **16**, apply **Bold**, and then click **Font Color**. Press Ctrl + E.

b. Click to position the insertion point in the last paragraph on **Page 2**—to the left of the section break. On the **REFERENCES tab**, in the **Captions group**, click **Insert Table of Figures**.

c. In the **Table of Figures** dialog box, under **General**, click the **Formats arrow**, and then click **Distinctive**. Click **OK**, and then **Save** your changes.

d. Click the **PAGE LAYOUT tab**. In the **Page Setup group**, click **Hyphenation**, and then click **Automatic**.

e. Below the paragraph that begins *The usual work week*, locate the paragraph heading *Qualifications*. Click to the left of the paragraph, and then press Ctrl + Enter.

7 Press Ctrl + Home, and then scroll to the bottom of **Page 1**. Right-click in the footer area, and then click **Edit Footer**. In the footer, select the page number.

a. On the **HEADER & FOOTER TOOLS DESIGN tab**, in the **Header & Footer group**, click **Page Number**, and then click **Format Page Numbers**.

b. In the **Page Number Format** dialog box, click the **Number format arrow**, and then click the fifth numbering style—**i, ii, iii**. Click **OK**.

c. On **Page 3**, in the footer, select the page number **3**. In the **Header & Footer group**, click **Page Number**, and then click **Format Page Numbers**. In the **Page Number Format** dialog box, under **Page numbering**, click the **Start at** option button. With *1* displayed in the **Start at** box, click **OK**. In the **Close group**, click **Close Header and Footer**.

(Project 10D Job Descriptions continues on the next page)

CHAPTER REVIEW

8 Click to position the insertion point in the TOC, right-click, and then click **Update Field**. In the **Update Table of Contents** dialog box, with the **Update page numbers only** option button selected, click **OK**.

a. On **Page 2**, click to position the insertion point in the table of figures. Right-click, and then click **Update Field**. In the **Update Table of Figures** dialog box, with the **Update page numbers only** option button selected, click **OK**.

b. Press Ctrl + End. Click to position the insertion point in the index, right-click, and then click **Update Field**.

c. Press Ctrl + Home. Click the **FILE tab**, and then **Show All Properties**. In the **Tags** box, type **jobs, TOC, index** In the **Subject** box, type your course name and section number. If necessary, edit the author name to display your name. **Save** your changes.

9 Print your document or submit electronically as directed by your instructor. **Close** Word.

END | You have completed Project 10D

Mastering Word | Project 10E Council Topics

Apply 10A skills from these Objectives:

1 Create a Master Document and Subdocuments

2 Manage a Master Document and Subdocuments

3 Navigate and Inspect the Master Document

4 Create and Modify Headers and Footers

In the following Mastering Word project, you will create a master document and subdocuments for a document that summarizes topics to be discussed at the February meeting of the Tawny Creek City Council. Your completed documents will look similar to Figure 10.57.

PROJECT FILES

For Project 10E, you will need the following files:

w10E_Council_Topics
w10E_Agenda_Item

You will save your files as:

Lastname_Firstname_10E_Council_Topics
Lastname_Firstname_10E_Agenda_Item

PROJECT RESULTS

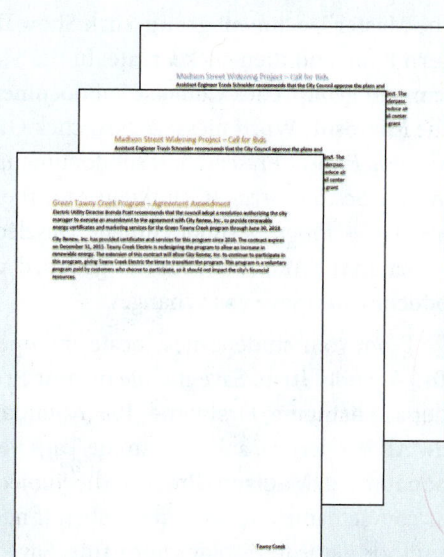

FIGURE 10.57

(Project 10E Council Topics continues on the next page)

CONTENT-BASED ASSESSMENTS

1 Start Word. From your student files, locate and open the file **w10E_Council_Topics**. Navigate to your **Word Chapter 10** folder, and create a folder named **Project 10E Save** the file in your **Project 10E** folder as **Lastname_Firstname_10E_Council_Topics** If necessary, display the rulers and formatting marks.

2 Apply the **Retrospect** theme. Select the first paragraph of the document, change the **Font Size** to **28**, apply **Center**, and then change the **Text Effects** to **Gradient Fill – Brown, Accent 4, Outline – Accent 4**. Select the second paragraph, change the **Font Size** to **28**, apply **Bold**, change the **Font Color** to **Brown, Accent 4, Darker 25%**, and then apply **Center**. Apply the **Heading 1** style to the paragraphs that begin *Repurpose, Comments,* and *Green.*

3 Change to **Outline** view. Beginning with the paragraph that begins *Repurpose,* select all the remaining paragraphs in the document. On the **OUTLINING tab**, in the **Master Document group**, click **Show Document** to turn it on, and then click **Create**. In the **Master Document group**, click **Collapse Subdocuments**, and then in the **Microsoft Word** message box, click **OK**. Move the *Repurpose Project Presentation* subdocument directly above the *Section Break (Continuous)* for the *Green Tawny Creek Program* subdocument. Deselect the text, and then in the **Master Document group**, click **Expand Subdocuments**. **Save** your changes.

4 From your student files, locate and open the file **w10E_Agenda_Item**. Save the file in your **Project 10E** folder as **Lastname_Firstname_10E_Agenda_Item** Click **Show All Properties**, and then in the **Tags** box, type **subdocument, Madison Street** In the **Subject** box, type your course name and section number. If necessary, edit the author name to display your name. **Save** your changes, and then **Close** the document.

5 Press [Ctrl] + [End]. Insert the **Lastname_Firstname_10E_Agenda_Item** document as a subdocument. In the master document, under *Madison Street Widening Project,* in the last sentence, change the cost from *$1.6* to **$1.8** Click **Close Outline View**, and then **Save** your changes.

6 Press [Ctrl] + [Home]. Select the entire heading that begins *Green Tawny Creek Program* being careful not to select the paragraph mark. Display the **Bookmark** dialog box, and for the **Bookmark name**, type **Agreement_Amendment** Click **Add**. In the third paragraph, select the text *Green Tawny Creek Program*. **Insert** a cross-reference that is linked to the *Agreement_Amendment* bookmark.

7 Press [Ctrl] + [Home]. Change to **Outline** view. On the **OUTLINING tab**, in the **Master Document group**, click **Show Document** to turn it on. **Unlink** the subdocuments *Comments from the Public, Repurpose Project Presentation, Green Tawny Creek Program,* and *Madison Street Widening Project*. Delete all instances of **Section Break (Continuous)** and **Section Break (Next Page)** from the document, and then **Close Outline View**.

8 Insert **Even Page** section breaks to the left of the paragraphs that begin *Comments* and *Green*. Insert **Odd Page** section breaks to the left of the paragraphs that begin *Repurpose* and *Madison*. On **Page 2**, display the footer, on the **HEADER & FOOTER TOOLS DESIGN tab**, select the **Different Odd & Even Pages** check box. On **Page 2**, in the **Even Page** footer, press [Tab] two times, and then type **Tawny Creek** On **Page 3**, in the **Odd Page** footer, insert the file name. **Close** the footer area.

9 Press [Ctrl] + [Home], and then insert the **Grid** cover page. In the **Title** placeholder, type **Agenda Topics** In the **Subtitle** placeholder, type **City Council** In the **Abstract** placeholder, type **Items to be discussed at the next meeting**

10 Click **Show All Properties**, and then in the **Tags** box, type **council topics, master** In the **Categories** box, type your course name and section number. If necessary, edit the author name to display your name. **Save** your changes. **Open** the file **Lastname_Firstname_10E_Agenda_Item**. Delete the **Section Break (Next Page)**. Insert the file name in the footer, and then **Save** your changes.

11 Print both of your documents or submit your files electronically as directed by your instructor. **Close** Word.

END | You have completed Project 10E

CONTENT-BASED ASSESSMENTS

Mastering Word   Project 10F Business FAQ

In the following Mastering Word project, you will add an index, a table of contents, and a table of figures to a document containing frequently asked questions and answers related to doing business with the City of Tawny Creek. Your completed document will look similar to Figure 10.58.

Apply 10B skills from these Objectives:

5 Create an Index

6 Create a Table of Contents

7 Create a Table of Figures

8 Control the Flow and Formatting of Pages and Text

PROJECT FILES

For Project 10F, you will need the following file:

w10F_Business_FAQ

You will save your file as:

Lastname_Firstname_10F_Business_FAQ

PROJECT RESULTS

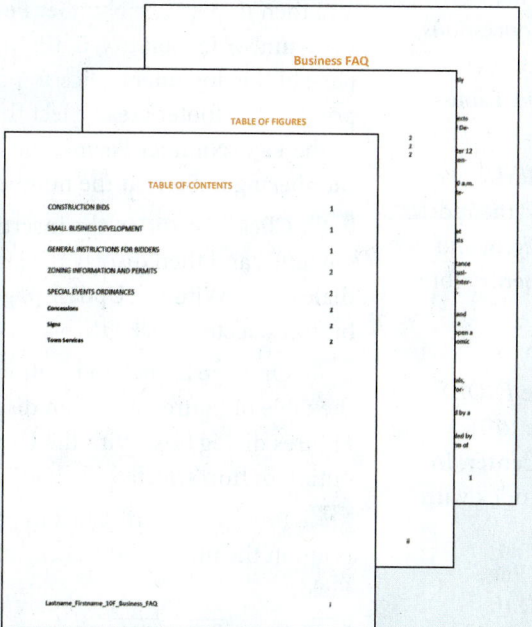
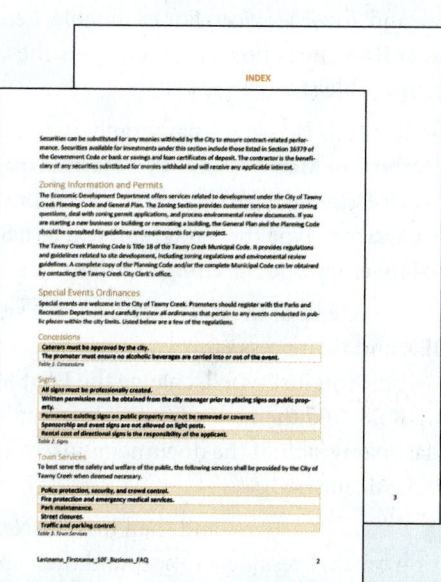

FIGURE 10.58

(Project 10F Business FAQ continues on the next page)

CONTENT-BASED ASSESSMENTS

1 Start Word. From your student files, open the file **w10F_Business_FAQ**. **Save** the file in your **Word Chapter 10** folder as **Lastname_Firstname_10F_Business_FAQ** If necessary, display the rulers and formatting marks. If any words are flagged as spelling errors, right-click the first occurrence of each, and click **Ignore All**. Insert the file name in the footer, and then press Tab two times. Click **Page Number**, click **Current Position**, and then click **Plain Number**. **Close** the footer.

2 Change the **Theme Colors** to **Aspect**. Select the first paragraph, change the **Font Size** to **22**, apply **Bold**, and then change the **Font Color** to **Orange, Accent 1**. Apply **Center**. Apply the **Heading 1** style to the paragraph headings that begin *Construction, Small Business, General Instructions, Zoning,* and *Special Events*. Apply the **Heading 2** style to the paragraphs that begin *Concessions, Signs,* and *Town Services*. For each table, deselect the **Header Row** check box, and then apply the **Grid Table 4 – Accent 1** table style.

3 For each *Heading 1* paragraph, use the **Mark Entry** dialog box, to **Mark** the text as a **Main entry** for the index. For each *Heading 2* paragraph—*Concessions, Signs,* and *Town Services*, type the paragraph text as a **Subentry** for the **Main entry Special Events Ordinances**

4 At the end of the document, press Enter. Type **INDEX** and then press Enter two times. Select the *INDEX* paragraph you just typed, change the **Font Size** to **16**, apply **Bold**, and then click **Font Color**. Apply **Center**. In the last paragraph of the document, insert an index with the **Classic** format.

5 Press Ctrl + Home, and then insert a **Next Page** section break. Press Ctrl + Home, and then apply the **Normal** style. Type **TABLE OF CONTENTS** and then press Enter two times. Select the text you typed, change the **Font Size** to **16**, apply **Bold**, and then click **Font Color**. Apply **Center**. In the last paragraph on the page, insert a table of contents with the **Classic** format. **Save** your changes.

6 Click anywhere in the first table in the document. Click **Insert Caption**, and then change the **Caption** to **Table 1: Concessions** Change the **Position** to **Below**

selected item. In a similar manner, for the second and third tables, change the captions to **Table 2: Signs** and **Table 3: Town Services**

7 Press Ctrl + Home. Click to position the insertion point in the last paragraph of the page—to the left of the section break. Press Ctrl + Enter, type **TABLE OF FIGURES** and then press Enter. Select the text you typed, change the **Font Size** to **16**, apply **Bold**, and then click **Font Color**. Apply **Center**. In the last paragraph on the page, insert a table of figures with the **Classic** format. **Save** your changes.

8 Press Ctrl + Home. Change the **Hyphenation** to **Automatic**.

9 On **Page 1**, in the footer, select the page number, and then in the **Page Number Format** dialog box, change the **Number format** to **i, ii, iii**. Click **OK**. On the third page of the document, click to position the insertion point in the footer area. Select the page number, and then in the **Page Number Format** dialog box, change the **Page numbering** to **Start at** the number **1**.

10 Click to position the insertion point in the table of contents, and then display the **Update Table of Contents** dialog box. With the **Update page numbers only** option button selected, click **OK**.

11 On **Page 2**, click to position the insertion point in the table of figures, and then display the **Update Table of Figures** dialog box. With the **Update page numbers only** option button selected, click **OK**.

12 Press Ctrl + End. Click to position the insertion point in the index, right-click, and then click **Update Field**.

13 Press Ctrl + Home, and then click **Show All Properties**. In the **Tags** box, type **business FAQ, TOC, index** In the **Subject** box, type your course name and section number. If necessary, edit the author name to display your name. **Save** your changes.

14 Print your document or submit electronically as directed by your instructor. **Close** Word.

END | You have completed Project 10F

CONTENT-BASED ASSESSMENTS

Mastering Word Project 10G Chamber Programs

In the following Mastering Word project, you will create a master document and subdocuments related to the programs offered by Tawny Creek's Chamber of Commerce. The final document will include an index, a table of contents, and a table of figures. Your completed documents will look similar to Figure 10.59.

Apply 10A and 10B skills from these Objectives:

1 Create a Master Document and Subdocuments
2 Manage a Master Document and Subdocuments
3 Navigate and Inspect the Master Document
4 Create and Modify Headers and Footers
5 Create an Index
6 Create a Table of Contents
7 Create a Table of Figures
8 Control the Flow and Formatting of Pages and Text

PROJECT FILES

For Project 10G, you will need the following files:

w10G_Chamber_Programs
w10G_Ambassadors_Club

You will save your files as:

Lastname_Firstname_10G_Chamber_Programs
Lastname_Firstname_10G_Ambassadors_Club

PROJECT RESULTS

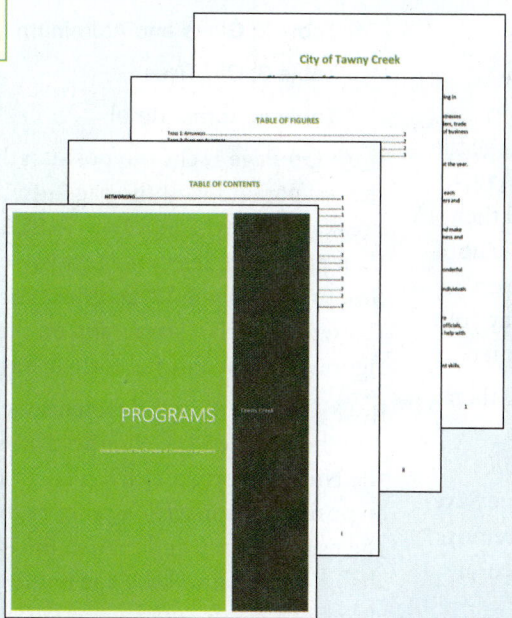
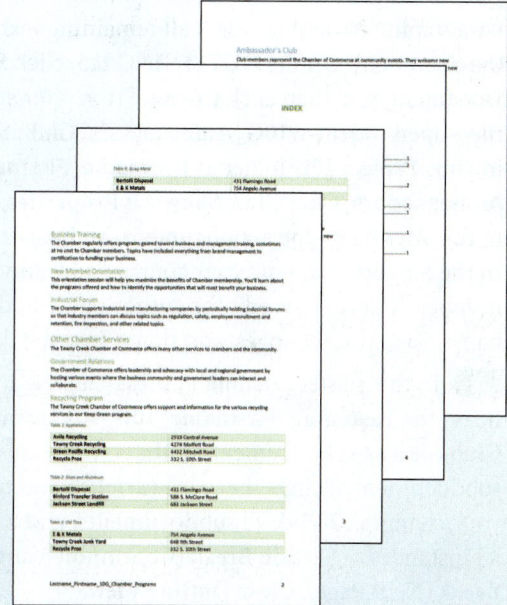

FIGURE 10.59

(Project 10G Chamber Programs continues on the next page)

CONTENT-BASED ASSESSMENTS

1 Start Word. From your student files, locate and open the file **w10G_Chamber_Programs**. Navigate to your **Word Chapter 10** folder, and then create a folder named **Project 10G Save** the document in your **Project 10G** folder as **Lastname_Firstname_10G_Chamber_Programs**

2 Change the **Theme Colors** to **Green Yellow**. Select the first two paragraphs, change the **Font Size** to 24, apply **Bold**, and then change the **Font Color** to **Lime, Accent 1, Darker 25%**. Apply **Center**. Apply the **Heading 1** style to the paragraphs that begin *Networking, Special Events, Workshops and Seminars*, and *Other Chamber Services*. Apply the **Heading 2** style to the paragraphs that begin *Morning, Lunches, Ribbon, Business Training, New Member, Industrial, Government*, and *Recycling*. For each table, deselect the **Header Row** check box, and then apply the **Grid Table 4 – Accent 1** table style.

3 Change to **Outline** view. Beginning with the paragraph *Networking*, select all remaining text in the document. On the **OUTLINING tab**, click **Show Document**, and then click **Create**. From your student files, open the file **w10G_Ambassadors_Club**. **Save** the file in your **Project 10G** folder as **Lastname_Firstname_10G_Ambassadors_Club** Click **Show All Properties**, and then in the **Tags** box, type **subdocument, ambassadors club** In the **Subject** box, type your course name and section number. If necessary, edit the author name to display your name. **Save** your changes, and then **Close** the document.

4 In the master document, press Ctrl + End, and then Insert the **Lastname_Firstname_10G_Ambassadors_Club** file as a subdocument. In the *Ambassadors Club* subdocument, change the word *various* to **numerous Save** your changes. **Unlink** all subdocuments, and then remove all instances of **Section Break (Continuous)** and **Section Break (Next Page)**. **Close Outline View.**

5 On **Page 1**, in the footer, insert the file name, and then press Tab two times. Click **Page Number**, click **Current Position**, and then click **Plain Number**. **Close** the footer.

6 Beginning on **Page 1**, for each *Heading 1* paragraph—*Networking, Special Events, Workshops and Seminars, Other Chamber Services*, and *Ambassador's Club*, use the **Mark Entry** dialog box to **Mark** the text as a **Main entry**. Below each *Heading 1* paragraph, mark each *Heading 2* paragraph as a **Subentry** using the appropriate *Heading 1* text for the **Main entry**. At the end of the

document, press Ctrl + Enter, type **INDEX** and then press Enter two times. Select the text you typed, change the **Font Size** to 16, apply **Bold**, and then click **Font Color**. Apply **Center**. In the last paragraph, insert an index with the **Formal** format.

7 Press Ctrl + Home, and then insert a **Next Page** section break. Press Ctrl + Home, and then apply the **Normal** style. Type **TABLE OF CONTENTS** and then press Enter two times. Select the text you typed, change the **Font Size** to 16, apply **Bold**, and then click **Font Color**. Apply **Center**. In the last paragraph on the page, insert a table of contents with the **Formal** format. **Save** your changes.

8 For each of the four tables, click **Insert Caption**, and then if necessary, change the **Position** to display **Above selected item**. Change the captions to display as follows:

    Table 1: Appliances

    Table 2: Glass and Aluminum

    Table 3: Old Tires

    Table 4: Scrap Metal

9 On **Page 1**, click to position the insertion point in the last paragraph of the page—to the left of the section break. Press Ctrl + Enter, type **TABLE OF FIGURES** and then press Enter. Select the text you typed, change the **Font Size** to 16, apply **Bold**, and then click **Font Color**. Apply **Center**. In the last paragraph on the page, insert a table of figures with the **Formal** format. **Save** your changes.

10 On **Page 1**, in the footer, select the page number, and then in the **Page Number Format** dialog box, change the **Number format** to i, ii, iii. Click **OK**. On **Page 3**, click to position the insertion point in the footer area. Select the page number, and then in the **Page Number Format** dialog box, change the **Page numbering** to **Start at** the number **1**.

11 Click to position the insertion point in the table of contents, and then display the **Update Table of Contents** dialog box. With the **Update page numbers only** option button selected, click **OK**. On **Page 2**, click to position the insertion point in the table of figures, and then display the **Update Table of Figures** dialog box. With the **Update page numbers only** option button selected, click **OK**. Press Ctrl + End. Right-click the index, and then click **Update Field**.

(Project 10G Chamber Programs continues on the next page)

CONTENT-BASED ASSESSMENTS

12 Press [Ctrl] + [Home]. Display the **Cover Page** gallery, and then insert the **Grid** cover page. In the **Title** placeholder, type **programs** In the **Subtitle** placeholder, type **Tawny Creek** and then in the **Abstract** placeholder, type **Descriptions of the Chamber of Commerce programs**

13 Click **Show All Properties**. In the **Tags** box, type **chamber programs, TOC, index** In the **Categories** box, type your course name and section number. If necessary, edit the author name to display your name. **Save** your changes. Open the **Lastname_Firstname_10G_Ambassadors Club** document. Delete the section break. Insert the file name in the footer, and then **Save** your changes.

14 Print both documents or submit electronically as directed by your instructor. **Close** Word.

END | You have completed Project 10G

CONTENT-BASED ASSESSMENTS

Apply a combination of the 10A and 10B skills.

GO! Fix It   Project 10H Boards Summary   **Online**

GO! Make It   Project 10I Internship Program   **Online**

GO! Solve It   Project 10J Health Department   **Online**

GO! Solve It   Project 10K Volunteer Program

PROJECT FILES

For Project 10K, you will need the following file:

w10K_Volunteer_Program

You will save your file as:

Lastname_Firstname_10K_Volunteer_Program

Open the file **w10K_Volunteer_Program** and save it to your **Word Chapter 10** folder as **Lastname_Firstname_10K_Volunteer_Program** Using fields, insert the file name and page number in the footer. Format the title paragraphs and apply styles to paragraph headings. Format the tables attractively and insert captions. Create a table of contents and table of figures on separate pages. Create an index that displays main headings as well as specific names for departments and organizations. Hyphenate and paginate the document. Modify the page numbering so that the first two pages have a different format and the third page starts at 1. Add appropriate document properties. Print your document or submit electronically as directed by your instructor.

Performance Level

Performance Element	Exemplary: You consistently applied the relevant skills	Proficient: You sometimes, but not always, applied the relevant skills	Developing: You rarely or never applied the relevant skills
Format tables and insert captions	All tables are formatted attractively and appropriate captions are inserted.	At least one table is not formatted or an appropriate caption is not inserted.	No tables are formatted and no captions are inserted.
Create table of contents and table of figures	The table of contents and table of figures are created correctly.	The table of contents or table of figures is not created correctly.	The table of contents and table of figures are not created.
Create index	The index is created and includes appropriate entries.	The index is created but some entries are missing.	The index is not created.
Hyphenate and paginate	The document is hyphenated and paginated appropriately.	The document is not hyphenated or is not paginated appropriately.	The document is not hyphenated and is not paginated appropriately.
Insert and format page numbers	Page numbers are inserted in the footer and formatted correctly.	Page numbers are inserted in the footer but not formatted correctly.	Page numbers are not inserted in the footer.

END | You have completed Project 10K

OUTCOMES-BASED ASSESSMENTS

RUBRIC

The following outcomes-based assessments are *open-ended assessments*. That is, there is no specific correct result; your result will depend on your approach to the information provided. Make *Professional Quality* your goal. Use the following scoring rubric to guide you in *how* to approach the problem and then to evaluate *how well* your approach solves the problem.

The *criteria*—Software Mastery, Content, Format and Layout, and Process—represent the knowledge and skills you have gained that you can apply to solving the problem. The *levels of performance*—Professional Quality, Approaching Professional Quality, or Needs Quality Improvements—help you and your instructor evaluate your result.

	Your completed project is of Professional Quality if you:	Your completed project is Approaching Professional Quality if you:	Your completed project Needs Quality Improvements if you:
1-Software Mastery	Choose and apply the most appropriate skills, tools, and features and identify efficient methods to solve the problem.	Choose and apply some appropriate skills, tools, and features, but not in the most efficient manner.	Choose inappropriate skills, tools, or features, or are inefficient in solving the problem.
2-Content	Construct a solution that is clear and well organized, contains content that is accurate, appropriate to the audience and purpose, and is complete. Provide a solution that contains no errors in spelling, grammar, or style.	Construct a solution in which some components are unclear, poorly organized, inconsistent, or incomplete. Misjudge the needs of the audience. Have some errors in spelling, grammar, or style, but the errors do not detract from comprehension.	Construct a solution that is unclear, incomplete, or poorly organized; contains some inaccurate or inappropriate content; and contains many errors in spelling, grammar, or style. Do not solve the problem.
3-Format & Layout	Format and arrange all elements to communicate information and ideas, clarify function, illustrate relationships, and indicate relative importance.	Apply appropriate format and layout features to some elements, but not others. Overuse features, causing minor distraction.	Apply format and layout that does not communicate information or ideas clearly. Do not use format and layout features to clarify function, illustrate relationships, or indicate relative importance. Use available features excessively, causing distraction.
4-Process	Use an organized approach that integrates planning, development, self-assessment, revision, and reflection.	Demonstrate an organized approach in some areas, but not others; or, use an insufficient process of organization throughout.	Do not use an organized approach to solve the problem.

OUTCOMES-BASED ASSESSMENTS

GO! Think   Project 10L Technology Plan

PROJECT FILES

For Project 10L, you will need the following files:

Build from Scratch

Two new blank Word documents

You will save your files as:

Lastname_Firstname_10L_Technology_Plan
Lastname_Firstname_10L_Maintenance

The City of Tawny Creek is developing a new technology plan. Search the Internet for information related to technology plans for government. Save a new document as **Lastname_Firstname_10L_Technology_Plan** Using the data you find, in your own words, create a report—including headings and subheadings—that explains the steps required to develop a plan. These steps should include the following topics: a vision statement, the goals, a needs assessment, design and purchase, and implementation. Note: You are defining what each step means; you are not entering specific technology data. Create a master document with subdocuments for each step. Save a second, new document as **Lastname_Firstname_10L_Maintenance** Create information defining maintenance—the final step in a technology plan. Insert this file as a subdocument in the master document. Unlink the subdocuments. Insert at least one bookmark and related cross-reference. For each document, insert the file name in the footer and add appropriate document properties. Print both documents or submit electronically as directed by your instructor.

END | You have completed Project 10L

Build from Scratch

GO! Think   Project 10M City Parks   **Online**

Build from Scratch

You and GO!   Project 10N Personal Journal   **Online**

Embedding and Linking Objects and Using Macros

GO! to Work
Video W11

PROJECT 11A

OUTCOMES
Embed and link objects.

OBJECTIVES
1. Embed Objects in a Word Document
2. Link Objects to a Word Document

PROJECT 11B

OUTCOMES
Create, edit, and run macros.

OBJECTIVES
3. Create Macros
4. Use Macros
5. Write a Procedure in VBA

NAN/Fotolia

In This Chapter

In this chapter, you will add objects to an existing document from files created with other Office applications. Because Microsoft Office 2013 is an integrated program suite, you can make use of the features of other programs within your Word document. In addition to copying and pasting objects and text, you can embed and link data from other Office applications—for example, an Access table, an Excel chart, or a PowerPoint slide. Using Word features and the Visual Basic Editor, you will also create macros. A macro allows you to improve your efficiency by performing a series of tasks in a single action.

The projects in this chapter relate to the **Greater Baltimore Job Fair**. Each year the organization holds a number of targeted job fairs. In addition, the annual Greater Baltimore Job Fair event draws over 200 employers in more than 40 industries and registers more than 8000 candidates. Candidate registration is free; employers pay a nominal fee for a booth to display and present at the fair. Candidate resumes and employer postings are managed by a computerized state-of-the-art database system, allowing participants quick and accurate access to job data and candidate qualifications.

PROJECT ACTIVITIES

In Activities 11.01 through 11.05, you will insert various objects—Excel charts, an Access table, a PowerPoint presentation, and a Word document—in a memo that discusses a publicity plan for the annual Greater Baltimore Job Fair. Related files are based on survey responses from employers and job seekers. Your completed documents will look similar to Figure 11.1.

PROJECT FILES

For Project 11A, you will need the following files:

w11A_Survey_Memo
w11A_Fair_Growth
w11A_Fair_Participants
w11A_Publicity_Strategy
w11A_Survey_Results
w11A_Participant_Survey

You will save your files as:

Lastname_Firstname_11A_Survey_Memo
Lastname_Firstname_11A_Survey_Results
Lastname_Firstname_11A_Participant_Survey

PROJECT RESULTS

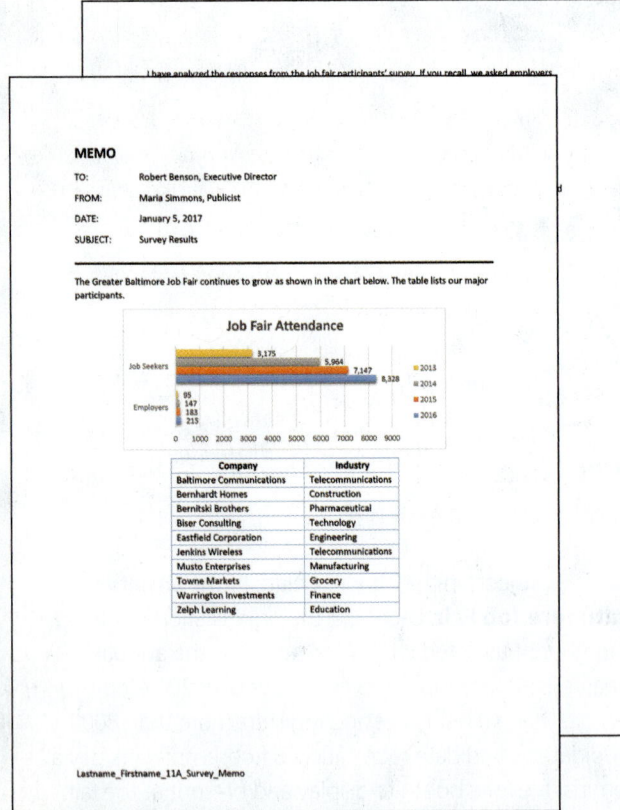

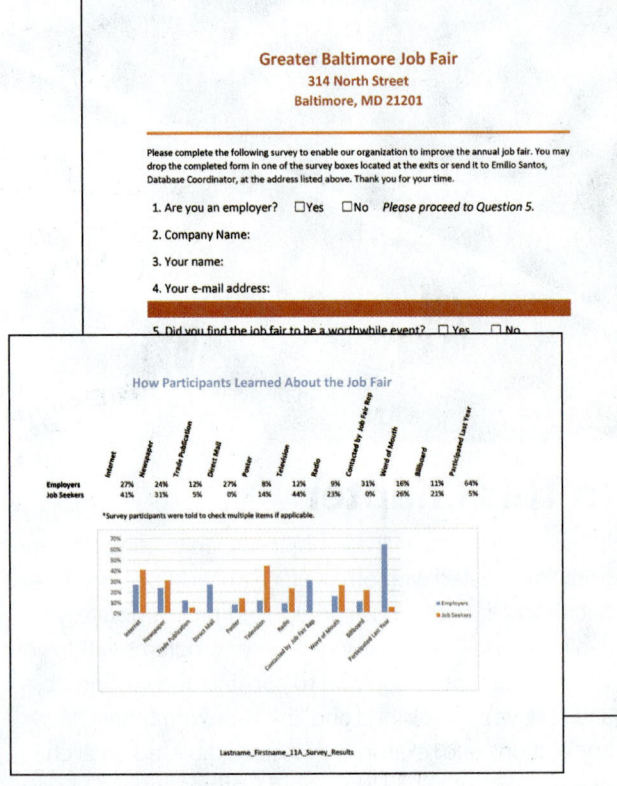

FIGURE 11.1 Project 11A Survey Memo

Objective 1   Embed Objects in a Word Document

Video W11-1

All Microsoft Office programs support **OLE**, which stands for *Object Linking and Embedding*. OLE is a program-integration technology for sharing information between Office programs. An *object* such as a table, chart, file, or other form of information created in one Office program—the *source file*—can be inserted in a file created with a different Office program—the *destination file*. *Embedding* is the process of inserting information from a source file, using a format that you specify, into a destination file. An *embedded object* maintains the structure of the original application but is not connected to the source file.

Activity 11.01   Using Paste Special to Embed an Excel Chart

When working with numerical data and creating charts, it makes sense to use Excel. Embedding an Excel chart in a Word document allows the reader to review the data in a visual format without viewing an entire spreadsheet.

1 Start Word. From your student files, locate and open the file **w11A_Survey_Memo**. Press F12, navigate to the location where you are saving your files for this chapter, and create a new folder named **Word Chapter 11** Save the document as **Lastname_Firstname_11A_Survey_Memo** Insert the file name in the footer. If necessary, display the rulers and formatting marks.

2 On the taskbar, click **File Explorer** 📁, navigate to your student files, and then locate and open the Excel file **w11A_Fair_Growth**. Compare your screen with Figure 11.2.

FIGURE 11.2

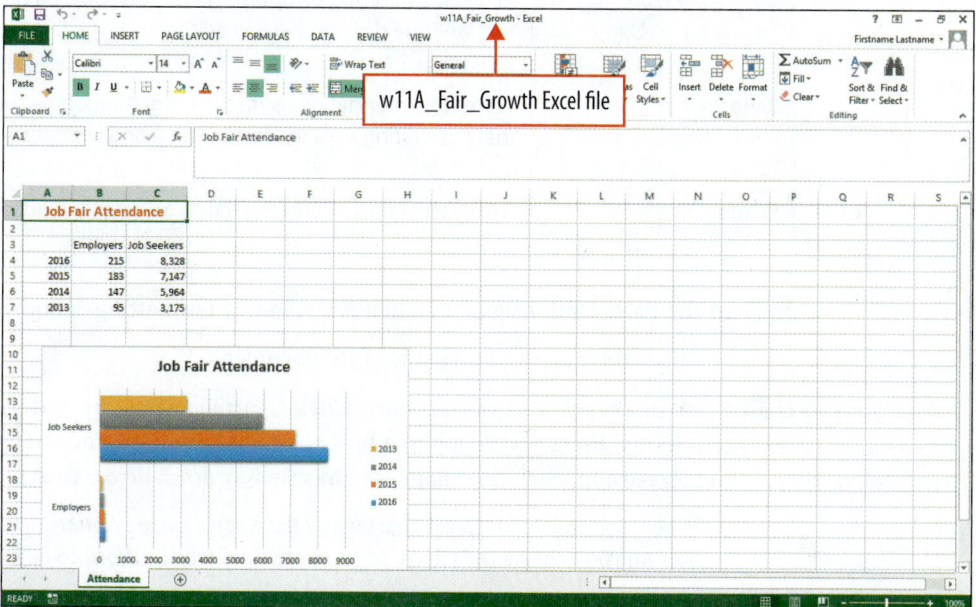

3 Right-click in a blank area of the *Job Fair Attendance* chart, and then from the shortcut menu, click **Copy** to copy the Excel chart to the Clipboard.

4 On the taskbar, click the **Word** icon 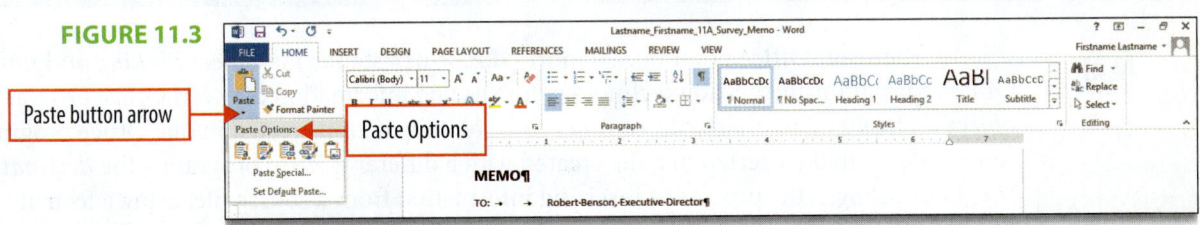 to make the *Lastname_Firstname_11A_Survey_Memo* document active. Immediately below the horizontal line, locate the paragraph that begins *The Greater Baltimore.* Click to position the insertion point at the end of the paragraph, and then press Enter.

5 On the **HOME tab**, in the **Clipboard group**, click the **Paste button arrow** to display the **Paste Options** gallery. Compare your screen with Figure 11.3.

There are different ways to paste an Excel chart into a Word document. The options vary according to the type of object you are pasting in the document.

FIGURE 11.3

Paste button arrow

Paste Options

6 In the **Paste Options** gallery, point to each of the buttons, and then read the ScreenTip. Take a moment to study the table shown in Figure 11.4, which describes the various pasting options.

FIGURE 11.4

PASTE OPTIONS	
COMMAND NAME	**DESCRIPTION**
Use Destination Theme & Embed Workbook	Pastes the information applying formatting based on the destination file's theme and enables you to edit the object using Word's features without changing the source file.
Keep Source Formatting & Embed Workbook	Pastes the information using the formatting in the source file and enables you to edit the object using Word's features without changing the source file.
Use Destination Theme & Link Data	Pastes the information applying formatting based on the destination file's theme and links the data so that any editing uses the features of—and changes—the source file.
Keep Source Formatting & Link Data	Pastes the information using the formatting of the source file and links the data so that any editing uses the features of—and changes—the source file.
Picture	Pastes the information as a picture object in the document.

7 In the **Paste Options** gallery, click **Keep Source Formatting & Embed Workbook (K)**.

The Excel chart displays in the Word document.

8 Click in a blank area of the chart. Click Chart Elements ⊞, and then select the **Data Labels** check box. Press Esc. Click in a blank area of the chart, and then click the **FORMAT tab**. In the **Size group**, click the **Shape Height spin box down arrow** to 2.1".

When you embed an Excel chart using the *Keep Source Formatting & Embed Workbook* paste option, you can use the Chart Tools contextual tabs in Word to edit the chart.

9 Click a border of the chart, and then press Ctrl + E. Compare your screen with Figure 11.5.

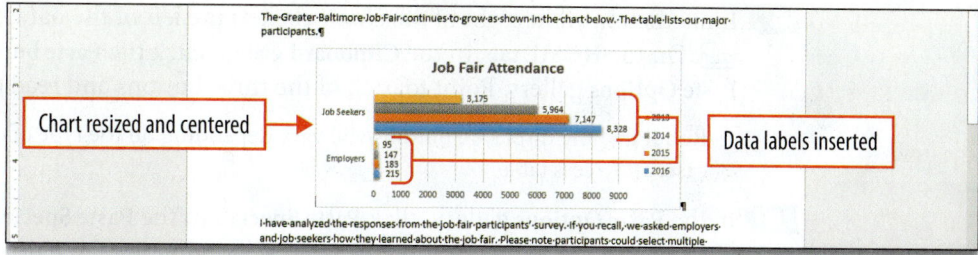

FIGURE 11.5

Chart resized and centered

Data labels inserted

> **10** Save 💾 your changes.

> **11** On the taskbar, click the **Excel** icon 📊 to make the **w11A_Fair_Growth** file active.

Because you embedded the chart, the changes you made in your Word document are not reflected in the Excel workbook—the source file.

> **12** Close ❎ Excel without saving changes.

Activity 11.02 | Using Paste Special to Embed an Access Table

Recall that Access is a database application. You can copy an Access table, or query results, and paste it in a Word document in a tabular format. The embedded table can be modified in Word without opening or changing the Access file.

> **1** On the taskbar, click **File Explorer** 📁, navigate to your student files, and then locate and open the Access file **w11A_Fair_Participants**. Immediately below the ribbon, if the *Security Warning* banner displays, click **Enable Content**.

ALERT! **What If I Don't Have Access?**

If you don't have Microsoft Access installed on your computer, consult your instructor.

> **2** On the left side of the Access window, under **Tables**, double-click the table **Major_Participants**. Compare your screen with Figure 11.6.

FIGURE 11.6

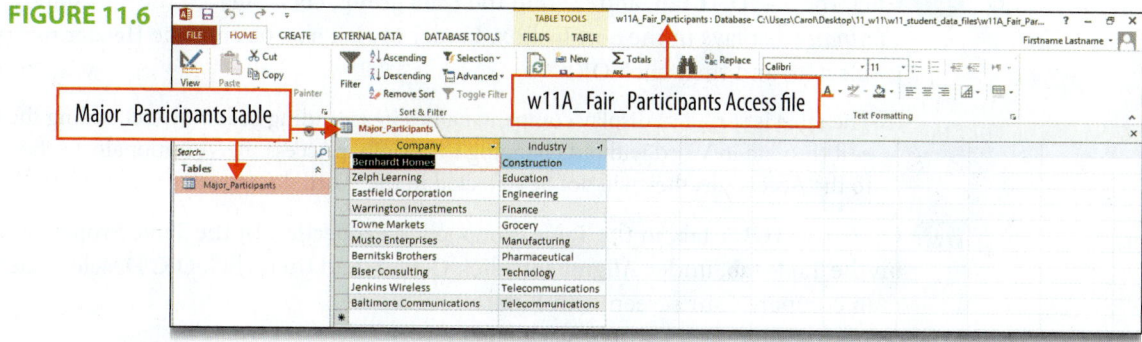

Major_Participants table

w11A_Fair_Participants Access file

> **3** Press Ctrl + A to select the entire table. On the **HOME tab**, in the **Clipboard group**, click **Copy**. **Close** ❎ Access, and then click in your Word document.

4 Immediately to the right of the chart, click to the left of the paragraph mark, and then press Enter. On the **HOME tab**, in the **Clipboard group**, click the **Paste button arrow** to display the **Paste Options** gallery. Point to each of the three buttons and read the ScreenTip.

Recall that the displayed buttons will vary depending on the type of object you are pasting—in this case, an Access table.

5 In the **Paste Options** gallery, click **Paste Special**. In the **Paste Special** dialog box, under **As**, click each option, and then under **Result**, for each option, read the description of how the Access data will be pasted in the document.

The Paste Special feature enables the user to insert data from the Access table in various formats.

6 In the **Paste Special** dialog box, under **As**, click **Formatted Text (RTF)**. Compare your screen with Figure 11.7

Selecting the Formatted Text (RTF) option inserts the data in a table format. By default, the Paste option button is selected.

FIGURE 11.7

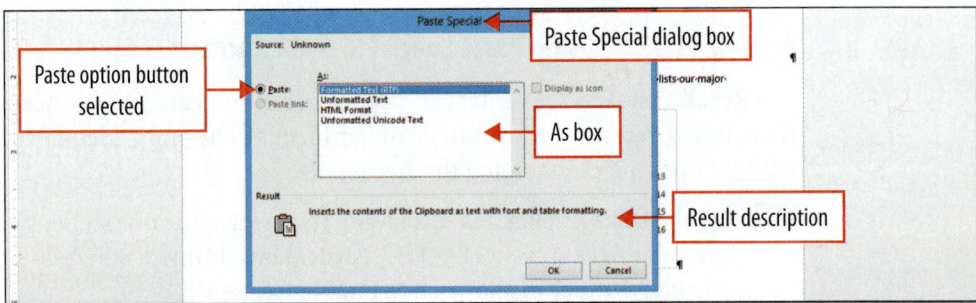

Paste option button selected

Paste Special dialog box

As box

Result description

7 In the **Paste Special** dialog box, click **OK**.

8 In the table, click in the first cell—*Company*. Click the **TABLE TOOLS DESIGN tab**, and then in the **Table Styles group**, click **More** ⬇. In the **Table Styles** gallery, scroll as necessary, and then under **List Tables**, in the third row, select the second table style—**List Table 3 – Accent 1**.

The Access table is embedded into the Word document. Because the data was inserted in a tabular format, you can use Table Tools contextual tabs in Word to modify the table.

9 Click the **LAYOUT tab**, and then in the **Data group**, click **Sort**. In the **Sort** dialog box, be sure *Company* displays in the **Sort by** box. Under **My list has**, be sure the **Header row** option button is selected, and then click **OK**.

The table is sorted to display company names in ascending order. By embedding the table, you can edit the data in Word without changing the original Access file. Additionally, if changes are made to the Access file, they will not be reflected in the Word document.

10 On the **LAYOUT tab**, in the **Table group**, click **Properties**. In the **Table Properties** dialog box, on the **Table tab**, under **Alignment**, click **Center**, and then click **OK**. Deselect the table, and then compare your screen with Figure 11.8.

FIGURE 11.8

Company names in ascending order

Table style applied and table centered

11 In the table, **Ignore All** spelling errors. **Save** 💾 your changes.

Activity 11.03 | Embedding a PowerPoint File

1️⃣ On the taskbar, click **File Explorer** 📁, navigate to your student files, and then locate and open the file **w11A_Publicity_Strategy**. Click the **DESIGN tab**, and then compare your screen with Figure 11.9.

> PowerPoint is used to create slide show presentations. A PowerPoint presentation contains individual slides that may include text, graphic elements, and other objects. This file contains six slides and is formatted with the *Ion Boardroom* theme. You can embed an entire PowerPoint presentation within a Word document.

FIGURE 11.9

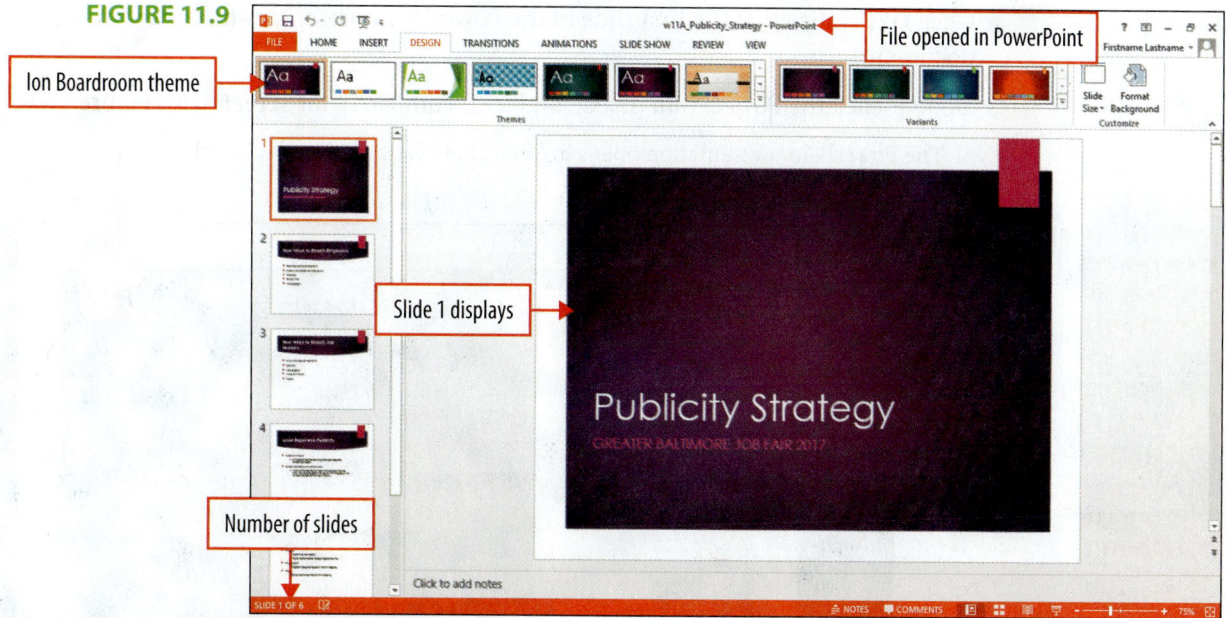

2️⃣ **Close** ⊠ PowerPoint.

> It is good practice to view a file before embedding it to ascertain that the file contains the correct information.

3️⃣ Click in your Word document. Locate the paragraph that begins *Based on the results*, and then position the insertion point at the end of the paragraph—on Page 2. Press Enter. Click the **INSERT tab**, and then in the **Text group**, click **Object**.

> The Object dialog box enables you to choose what type of object to insert in the document. By default, the Create New tab displays—allowing you to create a new object in a variety of formats.

4️⃣ In the **Object** dialog box, click the **Create from File tab**. Click **Browse**, navigate to your student files, click **w11A_Publicity_Strategy**, and then click **Insert**. Compare your screen with Figure 11.10.

> Select the Create from File tab to embed an existing object—in this case, a PowerPoint file. The file name displays in the File name box.

FIGURE 11.10

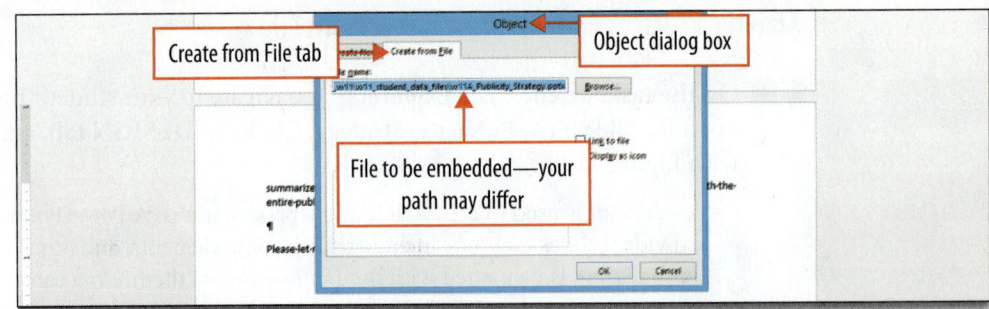

5 ▶ Click **OK**. Notice that the first slide of the PowerPoint presentation displays in the Word document.

6 ▶ Double-click the PowerPoint object, and then compare your screen with Figure 11.11.

The PowerPoint presentation opens in Slide Show view and displays the first slide.

FIGURE 11.11

7 ▶ Click the mouse button to advance to the next slide. In the same manner, view the remaining slides in the presentation. Notice that after the last click, you return to the Word document.

8 ▶ In the Word document, right-click the PowerPoint object. From the shortcut menu, point to **Presentation Object**, and then click **Edit** to switch to Edit mode.

Although you remain in Word, the ribbon changes to PowerPoint features. You can modify the embedded presentation without changing the original source file.

9 ▶ On the ribbon, click the **DESIGN tab**. In the **Themes group**, click **More** ⊡. Under **Office**, click **Slice**—the eighth theme. Compare your screen with Figure 11.12.

In the same manner as Word, themes can be changed in PowerPoint presentations.

FIGURE 11.12

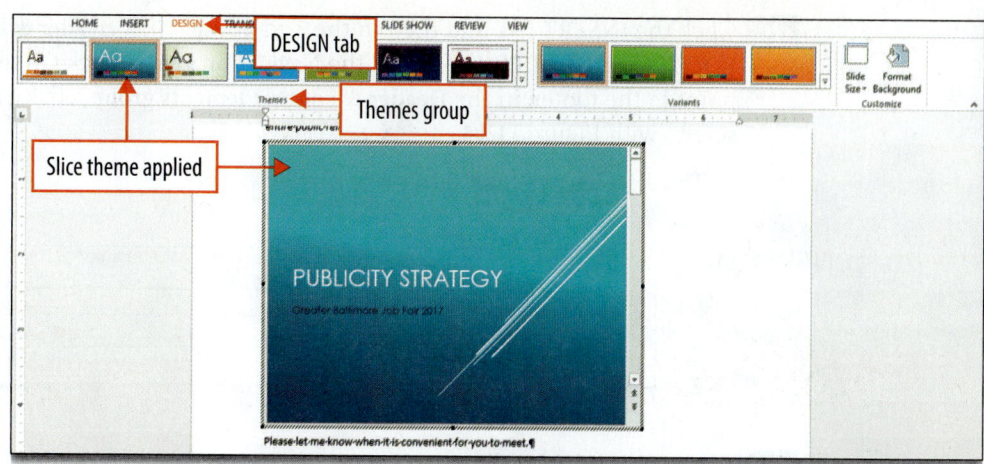

FIGURE 11.12

10 ▶ In the Word document, click outside the PowerPoint object to exit Edit mode. Click the slide to select the object, click the **HOME tab**, and then in the **Paragraph group**, apply **Center** ▤.

11 ▶ Press Ctrl + Home. **Save** 🖫 your changes.

Objective 2   Link Objects to a Word Document

Video W11-2

You can modify embedded objects without changing the source files. If you want to make changes to an object in a document and have those changes reflected in the original file, then *linking* the object, rather than embedding it, is what you want to do. Linking is the process of inserting information from a source file into a destination file while maintaining a connection between the two.

Activity 11.04   Linking to an Excel File

A *linked object* is an object that maintains a direct connection to the source file. Linked data is stored in the source file—for example an Excel workbook; the linked data is not stored in the destination file—in this case, a Word document.

1 ▶ From the taskbar, click **File Explorer** 🗔, navigate to your student files, and then locate and open the file **w11A_Survey_Results**. Press F12 to display the **Save As** dialog box. **Save** the file to your **Word Chapter 11** folder as **Lastname_Firstname_11A_Survey_Results** Compare your screen with Figure 11.13.

FIGURE 11.13

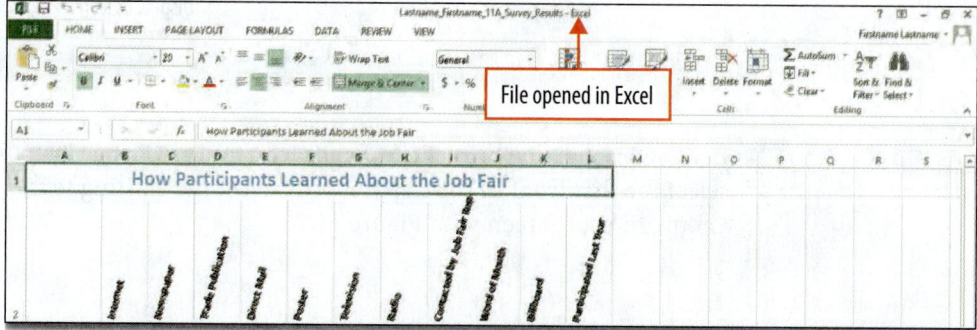

2 Click the **INSERT tab**, and then in the **Text group**, click **Header & Footer**. On the **HEADER & FOOTER TOOLS DESIGN tab**, in the **Navigation group**, click **Go to Footer**. With the insertion point in the footer, in the **Header & Footer Elements group**, click **File Name**. Compare your screen with Figure 11.14.

The default text *&[File]* displays.

FIGURE 11.14

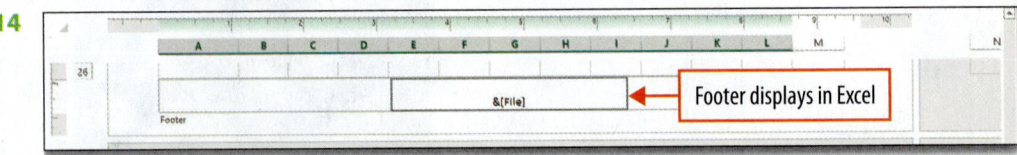

Footer displays in Excel

3 Click in any blank cell to deselect the footer. Notice that the file name displays in the footer.

4 Click the **VIEW tab**, and then in the **Workbook Views group**, click **Normal**. Press Ctrl + Home. **Save** 🖫 your changes, and then **Close** ✕ Excel.

5 Click in your Word document. At the bottom of **Page 1**, click to position the insertion point to the left of the paragraph that begins *I have analyzed*, and then press Ctrl + Enter to insert a page break. At the top of **Page 2**, click to position the insertion point at the end of the first paragraph, and press Enter.

6 Click the **INSERT tab**, and then in the **Text group**, click **Object**. In the **Object** dialog box, click the **Create from File tab**, which allows you to create a link to existing objects.

7 Click **Browse**, navigate to your **Word Chapter 11** folder, and then click **Lastname_ Firstname_11A_Survey_Results**. Click **Insert**.

8 On the right side of the **Object** dialog box, select the **Link to file** check box, and then select the **Display as icon** check box. Compare your screen with Figure 11.15.

A link will be established between the Word document and the Excel spreadsheet. When linking a file, you can choose to have the entire file display in your document or simply choose to display an icon representing the linked file. In this case, by selecting the *Display as icon* check box, your linked file will display as an icon in the Word document.

FIGURE 11.15

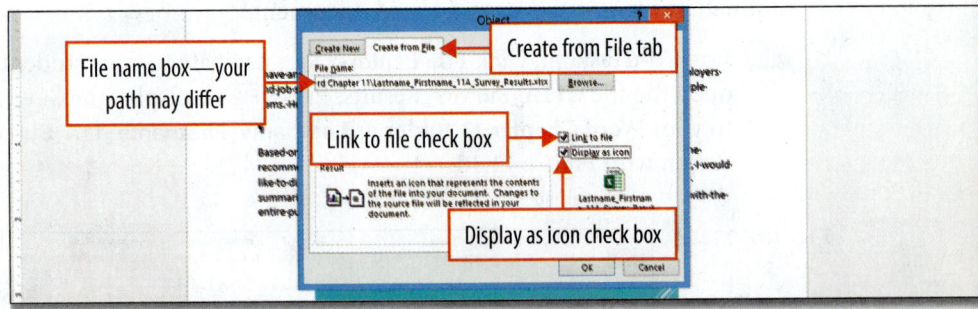

File name box—your path may differ

Create from File tab

Link to file check box

Display as icon check box

9 In the **Object** dialog box, click **Change Icon**. In the **Change Icon** dialog box, in the **Icon** box, select the first icon. In the **Caption** box, select the existing text, and then type **Survey Results** Compare your screen with Figure 11.16.

FIGURE 11.16

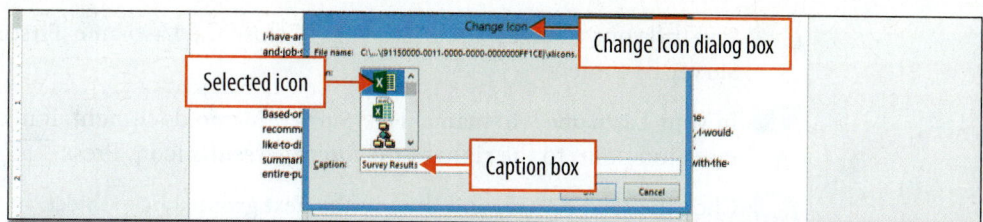

Change Icon dialog box

Selected icon

Caption box

10 Click **OK** two times.

An Excel file icon with the modified caption displays in the document. Changing the caption does not change the file name of the linked file.

11 Above *Survey Results,* double-click the icon. If necessary, maximize the Excel window.

Double-clicking the object icon causes the linked object to open in the native application. In this case, the Lastname_Firstname_11A_Survey_Results file opens in Excel.

ANOTHER WAY   Right-click the object icon, from the shortcut menu point to Linked Worksheet Object, and then click Open Link.

12 Click in cell **B4**—that contains the value *34%*. Type **41** and then press Enter. Notice the chart displays the revised *Job Seekers* value for *Internet*. Compare your screen with Figure 11.17.

FIGURE 11.17

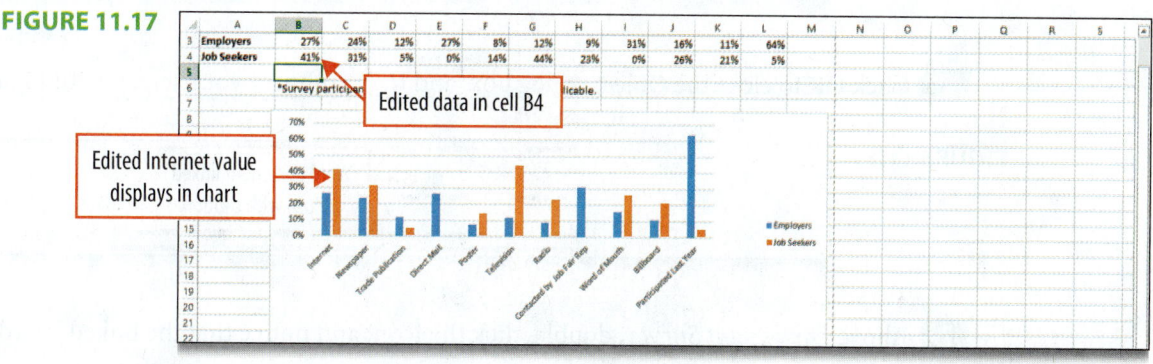

Edited data in cell B4

Edited Internet value displays in chart

13 Save 💾 your changes, and then **Close** ✖ Excel. In your Word document, **Save** 💾 your changes.

> **NOTE**   **Opening a Document Containing a Linked File**
>
> If you close a Word document that contains one or more linked files, when you reopen the document, a Microsoft Word message box will display. The message will prompt you to update the document with data from a linked file. Click Yes to maintain the link and update the information. Additionally, a link will not remain intact if the linked file is moved to a new location.

Activity 11.05 | Linking to Another Word Document

When linking objects in Word, you are not limited to using different Office application files. You can also link one Word document to another Word document.

1 In Word, from your student files, locate and open the file **w11A_Participant_Survey**. Press F12, and then **Save** the file to your **Word Chapter 11** folder as **Lastname_Firstname_11A_Participant_Survey** Insert the file name in the footer. **Close** the footer area.

2 Save 💾 your changes. Press Ctrl + W to close the **Lastname_Firstname_11A_Participant_ Survey** document.

3 In your **Lastname_Firstname_11A_Survey_Memo** document, if necessary, click to position the insertion point to the right of the *Survey Results* icon. Press Tab.

4 Click the **INSERT tab**, and then in the **Text group**, click **Object**. In the **Object** dialog box, click the **Create from File tab**. Click **Browse**, navigate to your **Word Chapter 11** folder, and then click **Lastname_Firstname_11A_Participant_Survey**. Click **Insert**.

5 On the right side of the **Object** dialog box, select the **Link to file** check box, and then select the **Display as icon** check box. In the **Object** dialog box, click **Change Icon**. In the **Change Icon** dialog box, in the **Caption box**, select the text, and then type **Participant Survey** Click **OK**. Compare your screen with Figure 11.18.

FIGURE 11.18

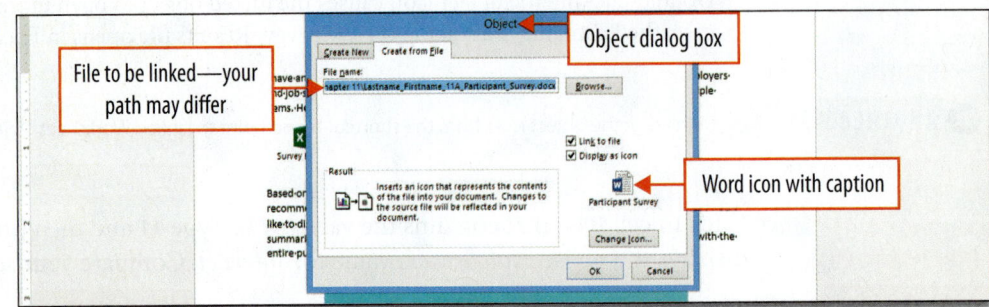

6 Click **OK** to close the **Object** dialog box, and then compare your screen with Figure 11.19.

FIGURE 11.19

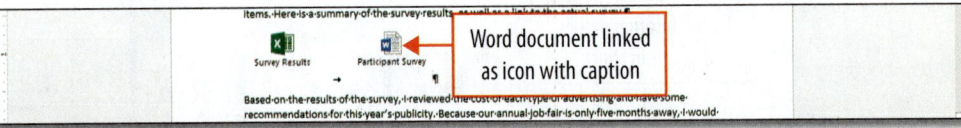

7 Above *Participant Survey*, double-click the icon, and notice that the linked Word file displays.

When linking an object, it is good practice to verify that the link is working.

8 In the **Lastname_Firstname_11A_Participant_Survey** document, in the first paragraph, click to position the insertion point to the left of *Fair*, type **Job** and then press Spacebar.

9 Save 💾 your changes. Press Ctrl + W to close the **Lastname_Firstname_11A_Participant_ Survey** document but leave Word open.

10 Select the paragraph containing the two linked files, and then press Ctrl + E to center the paragraph.

More Knowledge   **Editing a Linked File**

You can edit a linked file by directly opening the file and making changes. If the document containing the link is open, right-click the link, and then click Update Link. If the document containing the link is closed, you will be prompted to update the data the next time you open the document.

11 ▸ Press Ctrl + Home. Click the **FILE tab**, and then click **Show All Properties**. In the **Tags** box, type **survey memo, linked and embedded objects** In the **Subject** box, type your course name and section number. If necessary, edit the author name to display your name.

12 ▸ **Save** your changes. Print all three files—the two Word documents and the Excel *Survey Results* file—or submit electronically as directed by your instructor. **Close** [×] Word, and then **Close** [×] File Explorer.

END | You have completed Project 11A

Fair Flyer

MyITLab®
Project 11B Training

PROJECT ACTIVITIES

In Activities 11.06 through 11.17, you will assist Sharon Reynolds, Employer Coordinator for the Greater Baltimore Job Fair, in automating Word tasks by creating macros that will be executed with a single click or keyboard shortcut. These actions include inserting a specific footer, adding a formatted heading, inserting the current date and time in a header, adjusting indentation in a bulleted list, and placing quotation marks around selected text. Your completed documents will look similar to Figure 11.20.

PROJECT FILES

For Project 11B, you will need the following files:

w11B_Fair_Flyer
w11B_Fair_Memo

You will save your files as:

Lastname_Firstname_11B_Fair_Flyer
Lastname_Firstname_11B_Fair_Memo
Lastname_Firstname_11B_Screen_Captures

PROJECT RESULTS

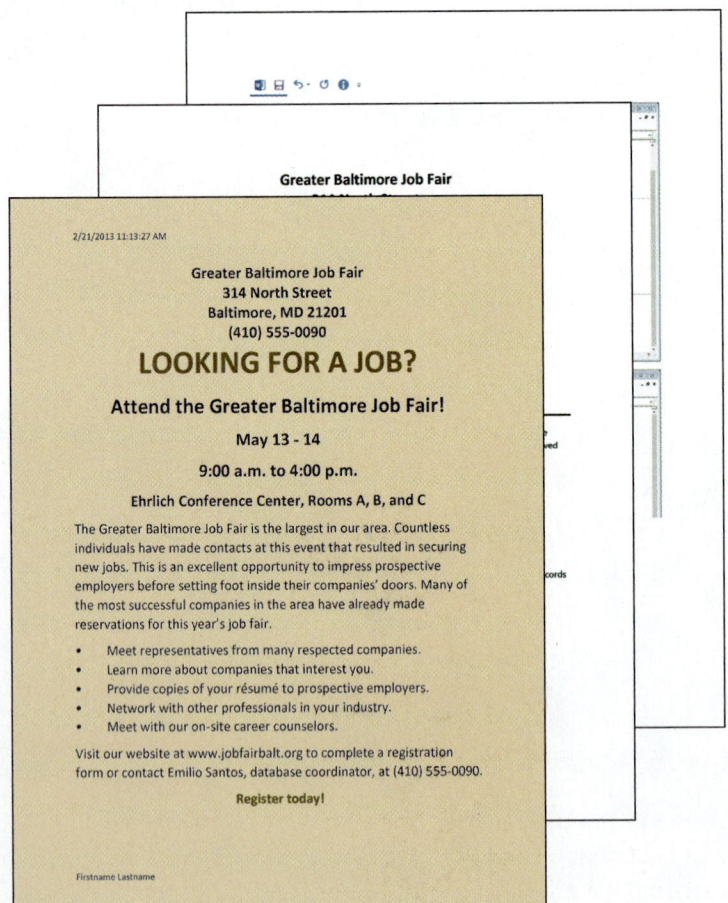

FIGURE 11.20 Project 11B Fair Flyer

Video W11-3

A *macro* is set of commands and instructions that can be grouped as a single command to accomplish a task automatically. When using Word, all macros are created in a programming language called *Visual Basic for Applications*, or *VBA*. You can use a macro to save time when performing routine editing and formatting, to combine several repetitive steps into one step, to make an option in a dialog box more accessible, or to automate a complex series of tasks. For example, you could create a macro that performs the steps to produce a customized header. The header could then be inserted into multiple documents without having to re-create the formatting steps for each document.

Activity 11.06 | Saving a Macro-Enabled Document

When you create, save, and use macros in a document, you must save the document as a Word Macro-Enabled Template (.dotm) or as a Word Macro-Enabled Document (.docm). Saving a document as either a Word document (.docx) or Word template (.dotx) will cause any macros to be removed.

1 Start Word. If necessary, display the rulers and formatting marks. Locate and open the file **w11B_Fair_Flyer**. Press F12 to display the **Save As** dialog box, and then navigate to your **Word Chapter 11** folder.

2 In the lower portion of the dialog box, click the **Save as type arrow**, and then from the list, click **Word Macro-Enabled Document**.

3 In the **File name** box, using your own name, type **Lastname_Firstname_11B_Fair_Flyer** and then compare your screen with Figure 11.21.

FIGURE 11.21

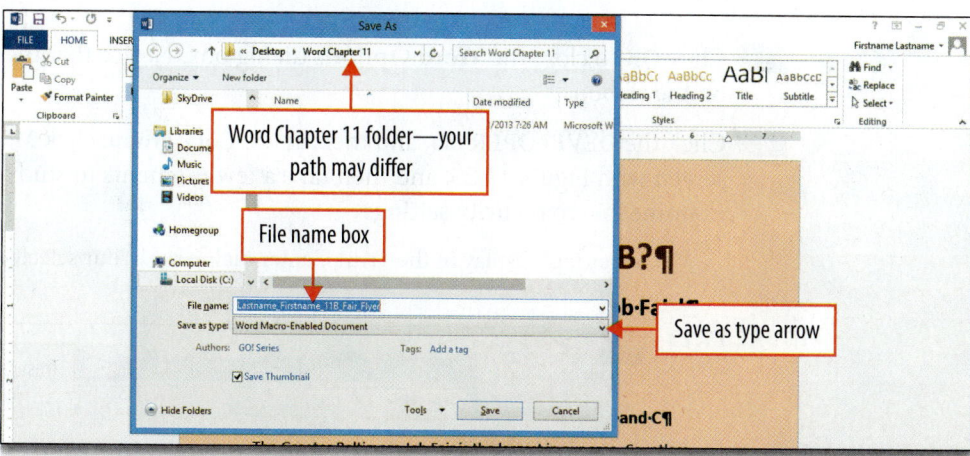

4 Click **Save**.

By saving your file as a macro-enabled document, new macros and changes to existing macros are automatically saved.

Activity 11.07 | Changing Macro Security Settings

When you create your own macros, you can trust the source. However, macros written by others may pose a potential security risk. Because a macro is written in programming language, files can be erased or damaged by inserting unauthorized code. This unauthorized code is called a *macro virus*. To protect systems from this type of virus, organizations commonly set their security programs to disable macros automatically or block any email attachment that contains a macro. Because the staff of the Greater Baltimore Job Fair uses macros to automate some of their tasks, you will adjust the security level in Word to allow macros to run.

1 ► Click the **FILE tab**, and then click **Options**. In the **Word Options** dialog box, on the left side, click **Customize Ribbon**.

Main tabs that display on the ribbon are indicated with a checkmark.

2 ► In the **Main Tabs** list, locate and then select the **Developer** check box. Compare your screen with Figure 11.22.

The DEVELOPER tab extends the capabilities of Word—including commands for inserting content controls and creating macros.

FIGURE 11.22

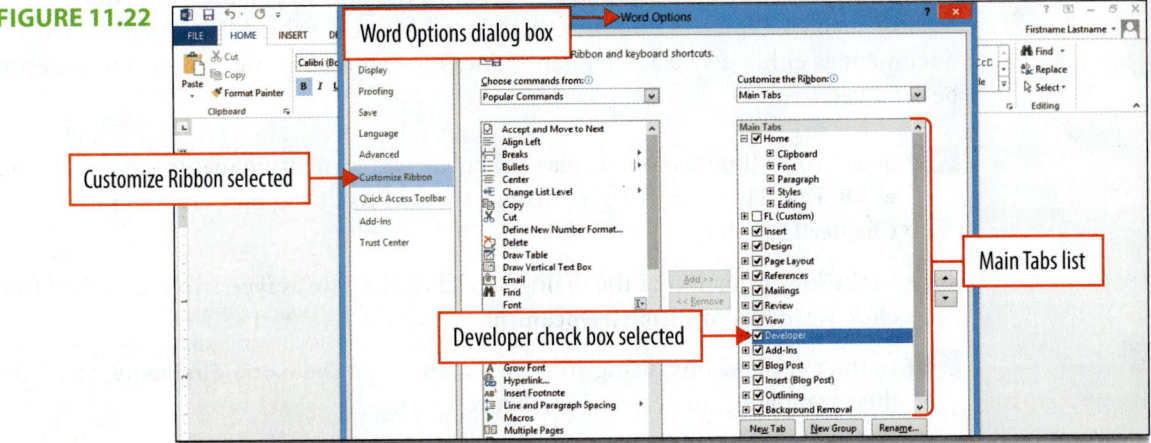

3 ► Click **OK** to close the **Word Options** dialog box. Notice that the **DEVELOPER tab** displays on the ribbon.

4 ► Click the **DEVELOPER tab**, and then in the **Code group**, click **Macro Security**. Compare your screen with Figure 11.23, and then take a few moments to study the table in Figure 11.24 to examine macro security settings.

Macro Settings display in the Trust Center dialog box. Your selected option may differ.

FIGURE 11.23

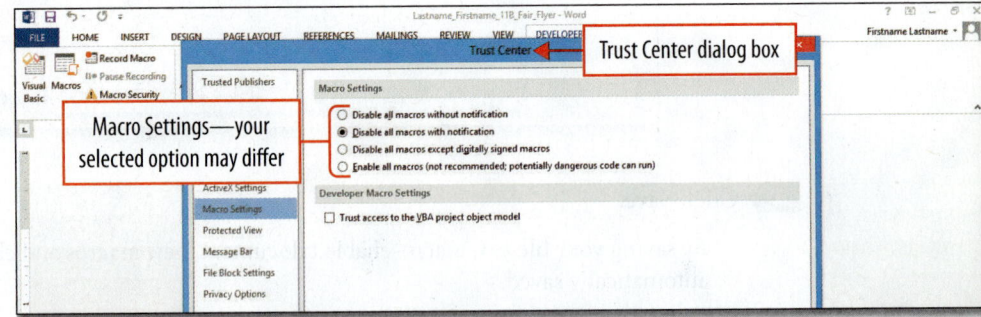

FIGURE 11.24

MACRO SECURITY SETTINGS	
SETTING	**DESCRIPTION**
Disable all macros without notification	Macros will not run in a document, and no notification message will display.
Disable all macros with notification	Macros will not run in a document, but a notification message will display with an option to run macros.
Disable all macros except digitally signed macros	Macros that have a valid digital signature and have been confirmed by Microsoft will be allowed to run.
Enable all macros	All macros will run. This option is a high security risk.

5 In the **Trust Center** dialog box, under **Macro Settings**, if necessary, click the **Disable all macros with notification** option button.

> By selecting this macro setting, opening a document that has a macro attached causes a security warning to display and gives you the option to disable the macro.

6 Click **OK** to close the **Trust Center** dialog box, and then **Save** 🖫 your changes.

Activity 11.08 | Recording a Keyboard-Activated Macro

The process of creating a macro while performing specific actions in a document is called *recording* a macro. Before you record a macro, the first thing you should do is plan the exact steps you will perform; and it is a good idea to write down those steps. For example, if you want to apply bold formatting and a specific Text Effect style during the recording of a macro, review the steps required to achieve this formatting before you begin recording the macro. You then can record the macro by completing all of the steps. In this activity, you will create a macro that will insert the file name in the footer.

1 On the **DEVELOPER tab**, in the **Code group**, click **Record Macro**.

2 In the **Record Macro** dialog box, in the **Macro name** box, type **Footer**

> Each macro must be given a unique name. It is a good idea to name the macro with a descriptive name to help you recall the function of the macro. If you reuse a name, the new macro will replace the original macro. Macro names cannot contain spaces; however, you can use underscores to improve readability.

3 Under **Store macro in**, if necessary, click the **Store macro in arrow**, and select **All Documents (Normal.dotm)**.

> By default, the macro will be saved in the Normal macro-enabled template so that it can be used in other documents.

4 In the **Description** box, click to position the insertion point, and then type **Inserts the author's name in a footer** Compare your screen with Figure 11.25.

FIGURE 11.25

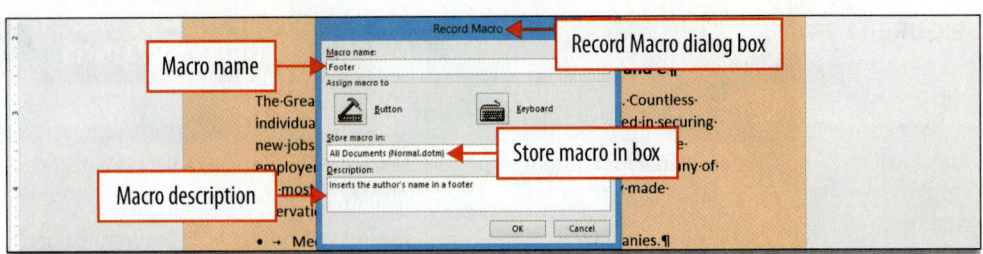

5 ▶ Under **Assign macro to**, click the **Keyboard** icon.

You can assign a button or a shortcut key to a macro. By clicking the *Keyboard* icon, you can assign a shortcut key that, when pressed, will cause the macro to run, or be executed.

6 ▶ In the **Customize Keyboard** dialog box, with the insertion point in the **Press new shortcut key** box, press and hold [Alt] and [Ctrl], and then press [B].

Alt+Ctrl+B displays in the *Press new shortcut key* box. If the shortcut key you choose is already in use, you should select another combination so that the original shortcut is not replaced. If the combination of keys is already in use, it will display next to *Currently assigned to*.

7 ▶ Near the bottom of the dialog box, click **Assign**. Compare your screen with Figure 11.26.

Alt+Ctrl+B displays in the *Current keys* box. This keyboard sequence is assigned to the macro that is selected in the *Commands* box—your *Footer* macro. The macro name displays as *Normal. NewMacros.Footer* to indicate that the macro is user-created and stored in the Normal template.

FIGURE 11.26

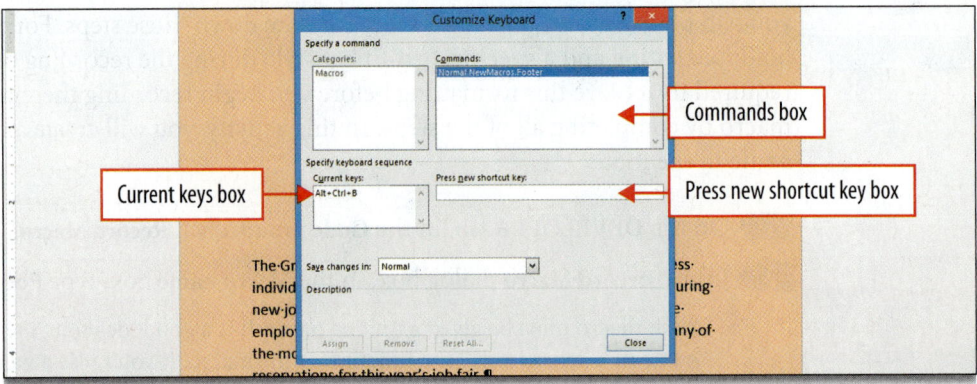

8 ▶ Near the bottom of the **Customize Keyboard** dialog box, click **Close**. Point anywhere in the document, and notice that the pointer changes to a ⌨ pointer. Compare your screen with Figure 11.27.

The ⌨ pointer indicates that you are now in recording mode. Any actions that you make will be recorded as part of the macro until you turn off the recording of the macro. It is important to take your time as you perform each action so that extra steps are not recorded as part of the macro.

FIGURE 11.27

9 Click the **INSERT tab**. In the **Header & Footer group**, click **Footer**, and then click **Edit Footer**.

10 With the insertion point in the footer, using your own name, type **Firstname Lastname** In the **Close group**, click **Close Header and Footer**.

11 Click the **DEVELOPER tab**, and then in the **Code group**, click **Stop Recording**.

All of the actions you performed in Steps 9 and 10 are recorded as part of the *Footer* macro. The same actions can be repeated by pressing Alt + Ctrl + B.

12 To test your macro, press Ctrl + N to display a new blank document. Press and hold Alt + Ctrl, and then press B. Scroll to the bottom of the page to view your name in the footer.

The macro runs—inserting your name in the footer.

ALERT!   **What If My Macro Doesn't Work?**

If your macro doesn't work properly, on the DEVELOPER tab, in the Code group, click Macros. In the Macros dialog box, click the name of your macro, and then click Delete. Close the dialog box, and then record the macro again.

---

13 Close ☒ the blank document without saving changes, and then **Save** 💾 your **Lastname_Firstname_11B_Fair_Flyer** document.

More Knowledge   **Pausing When Recording a Macro**

When recording a macro, you can temporarily suspend the recording if you need to perform other actions, and then resume the recording. To pause the recording, in the Code group, click Pause Recording. When you are ready to continue, click Resume Recorder.

Activity 11.09 | Recording a Button-Activated Macro

You can assign a macro to a command button that displays on the Quick Access Toolbar or on the ribbon. In this activity, you will create a macro to insert a heading and assign it to a button.

1 Press Ctrl + Home to position the insertion point at the beginning of the document. Press Enter, and then click to position the insertion point in the first paragraph of the document.

2 On the **DEVELOPER tab**, in the **Code group**, click **Record Macro**.

3 In the **Record Macro** dialog box, in the **Macro name box**, type **Heading** In the **Store macro in** box, be certain that **All Documents (Normal.dotm)** displays. In the **Description** box, type **Inserts the name, address, and phone number for the organization**

4 Under **Assign macro to**, click the **Button** icon. In the **Word Options** dialog box, with **Quick Access Toolbar** selected, under **Choose commands from**, click **Normal.NewMacros.Heading**—the name Word uses for your **Heading** macro.

5 In the middle of the dialog box, click **Add**. Compare your screen with Figure 11.28.

FIGURE 11.28

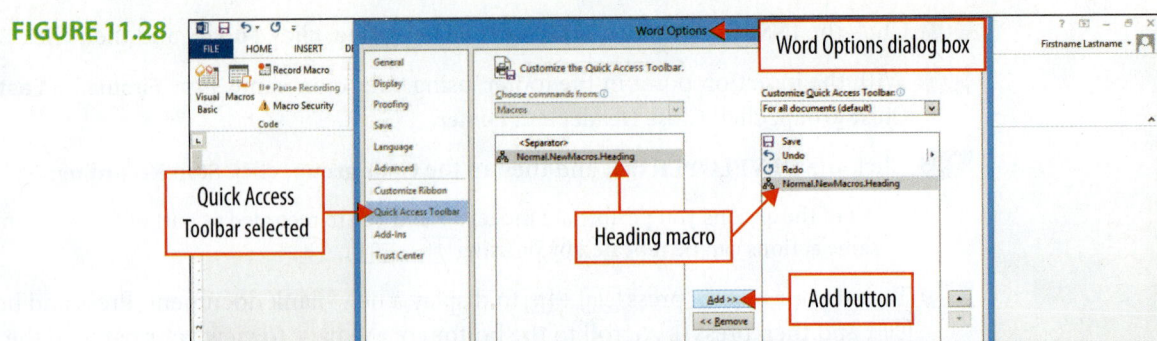

Word Options dialog box

Quick Access Toolbar selected

Heading macro

Add button

6 On the right side of the **Word Options** dialog box, click **Normal.NewMacros.Heading**. Below the list of commands, click **Modify**.

7 In the **Modify Button** dialog box, under **Symbol**, in the first row, click the third symbol—a blue circle containing a white i. In the **Display name** box, notice that the macro name displays. Compare your screen with Figure 11.29.

FIGURE 11.29

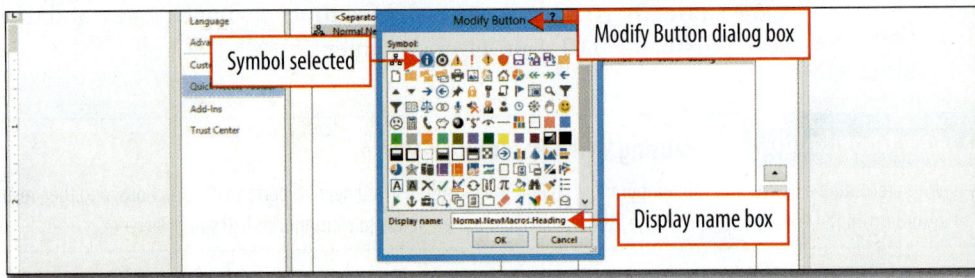

Modify Button dialog box

Symbol selected

Display name box

8 Click **OK**. In the list of **Quick Access Toolbar** commands, notice that the selected symbol displays to the left of *Normal.NewMacros.Heading*. Click **OK** to close the **Word Options** dialog box. Notice that the ⟨pointer⟩ pointer displays in the document and the **Heading** button displays on the **Quick Access Toolbar**.

9 Type the following text, pressing Enter after each of the first three lines.

Baltimore Job Fair

314 North Street

Baltimore, MD 21201

(410) 555-0090

10 With the insertion point to the right of the phone number, press Ctrl + Shift + Home to select all four lines.

When you are recording a macro, you must use the keyboard to select text—you cannot drag.

11 With all four lines selected, click the **HOME tab**. Change the style to **No Spacing**, change the **Font Size** to **18**, apply **Bold** B, and then click **Center** ≡.

12 Click the **DEVELOPER tab**, and then in the **Code group**, click **Stop Recording**. Compare your screen with Figure 11.30.

All of the text you typed and formatted is saved as part of the macro.

FIGURE 11.30

Inserted heading

Baltimore·Job·Fair¶
314·North·Street¶
Baltimore,·MD·21201¶
(410)·555-0090¶
LOOKING·FOR·A·JOB?¶

13 ▶ Press Ctrl + Home, and then **Save** 🖫 your changes.

Activity 11.10 | Creating a Macro That Runs Automatically

You can create a macro that runs automatically based on the occurrence of a specific event—for example, when you open a Word document or exit Word. In this activity, you will create a macro to insert the date and time in the header when you close a document.

1 ▶ On the **DEVELOPER tab**, in the **Code group**, click **Record Macro**.

2 ▶ In the **Record Macro** dialog box, in the **Macro name** box, type **AutoClose** Click the **Store macro in arrow**, and then click **Lastname_Firstname_11B_Fair_Flyer (document)**. Compare your screen with Figure 11.31 and then take a few moments to study the table in Figure 11.32 to examine the categories of automatic macros.

> *AutoClose* is a reserved word understood by Microsoft Word. When the term is used as a macro name, the macro will automatically run when the document is closed. Therefore, you do not need to assign a keystroke or button to the macro.

FIGURE 11.31

Macro name box

Record Macro dialog box

Store macro in arrow

FIGURE 11.32

AUTOMATIC MACROS	
MACRO	**DESCRIPTION**
AutoExec	Runs when Word starts.
AutoOpen	Runs each time a document is opened.
AutoNew	Runs each time a new document is created.
AutoClose	Runs each time a document is closed.
AutoExit	Runs whenever you exit Word.

ALERT!   **Should the Macro Be Saved in the Normal Template?**

Be careful to save this macro in your document rather than in the Normal.dotm template. If you save the macro in the Normal.dotm template on your computer, the macro will run every time any document is closed.

3 ▸ Click **OK** to start recording mode.

4 ▸ Click the **INSERT tab**. In the **Header & Footer group**, click **Header**, and then from the list, click **Edit Header**.

5 ▸ Press Ctrl + A, and then press Delete.

Any existing text is selected and then deleted. Because this macro will insert the current date and time whenever the document is closed, you want any existing content to be deleted.

6 ▸ On the **HEADER & FOOTER DESIGN tab**, in the **Insert group**, click **Date & Time**.

7 ▸ In the **Date and Time** dialog box, from the list, click the thirteenth format—with the date and time displayed in seconds. Compare your screen with Figure 11.33

FIGURE 11.33

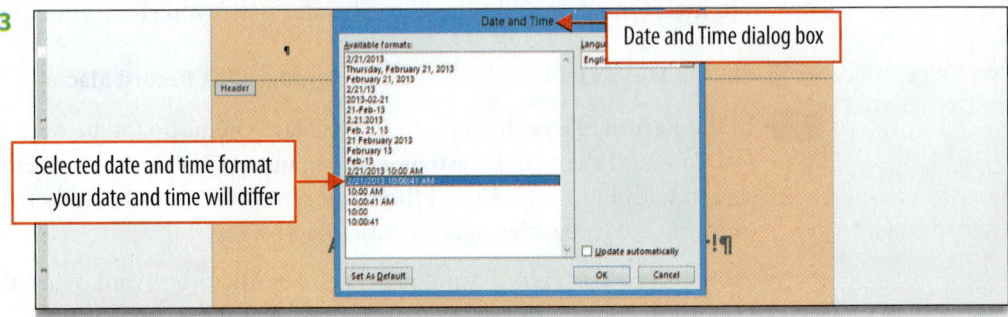

Date and Time dialog box

Selected date and time format —your date and time will differ

8 ▸ Click **OK** to close the **Date and Time** dialog box. In the **Close group**, click **Close Header and Footer**.

9 ▸ Click the **DEVELOPER tab**. In the **Code group**, click **Stop Recording**.

10 ▸ **Save** 🖫 your changes. Press Ctrl + W to close your document without closing Word. Compare your screen with Figure 11.34.

When you close your document, the *AutoClose* macro runs—inserting the current date and time in the header. Because this change is made while closing the document, a Microsoft Word message box displays, prompting you to save your changes.

FIGURE 11.34

Date and time inserted in header —your date and time will differ

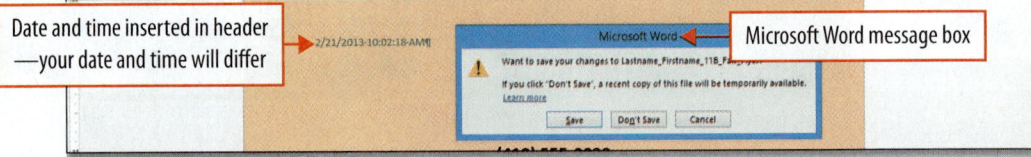

Microsoft Word message box

11 ▸ In the **Microsoft Word** message box, click **Save** to save your changes and **Close** the document.

Objective 4   Use Macros

Video W11-4

After a macro has been recorded, it can be reused so that you can work more efficiently.

Activity 11.11 | Running a Macro

1 ▸ Click the **FILE tab**, and then open the file **w11B_Fair_Memo**. Press F12 to display the **Save As** dialog box, and then navigate to your **Word Chapter 11** folder. In the lower portion of the dialog box, click the **Save as type arrow**, and then from the list, click **Word Macro-Enabled Document**.

2 In the **File name** box, using your own name, type **Lastname_Firstname_11B_Fair_Memo** and then click **Save**. If any words are flagged as spelling errors, right-click the word, and then click **Ignore All**.

3 Select the second paragraph *MEMO*. Click the **INSERT tab**, and then in the **Text group**, click the **WordArt button arrow** to display the **WordArt** gallery. In the **WordArt** gallery, in the second row, click the fifth style—**Fill – Gray – 50%, Accent 3, Sharp Bevel**.

4 On the **FORMAT tab**, in the **Arrange group**, click **Wrap Text**, and then click **In Line with Text**. Click the border of the WordArt graphic to display the FORMAT tab. In the **WordArt Styles group**, click **Text Effects** [A]. In the displayed list, point to **3-D Rotation**, and then under **Parallel**, in the second row, click the second effect—**Off Axis 1 Right**.

> You can format a WordArt object in numerous ways—for example, modifying the fill color, outline, or effect of the background or text. In this case, you are changing the text wrapping and rotation effect of the text.

5 Click to position the insertion point at the beginning of your document. On the **Quick Access Toolbar**, click the button assigned to your **Heading** macro—the blue circle containing a white i. Click anywhere in the document to cancel the selection, and then compare your screen with Figure 11.35.

> The Heading macro is executed and the heading information is inserted in your document. Recall that although you created the *Heading* macro in your *Lastname_Firstname_11B_Fair_Flyer* document, the macro was saved in the Normal template, allowing it to be available to other documents.

FIGURE 11.35

Heading inserted in document

Baltimore·Job·Fair¶
314·North·Street¶
Baltimore,·MD·21201¶
(410)·555-0090¶

MEMO¶ ← Text formatted as WordArt

6 Press and hold [Alt] + [Ctrl], and then press [B]. If necessary, scroll to the bottom of the page to view the footer.

> The *Footer* macro runs—inserting your name in the footer.

7 Press [Ctrl] + [Home], and then **Save** [💾] your changes.

Activity 11.12 | Editing a Macro in the Visual Basic Editor

One way to edit macros is by using the *Visual Basic Editor*. The Visual Basic Editor enables you to view the programming code for existing macros. You can use the Visual Basic Editor either to edit a macro or to create a new macro. The capability of VBA is extensive and can be used to create complex macros.

1 Locate the first paragraph of the document, and notice that it contains the text *Baltimore Job Fair*.

> Recall that the name of the organization is Greater Baltimore Job Fair.

2 Click the **DEVELOPER tab**, and then in the **Code group**, click **Macros**. In the **Macros** dialog box, select the **Heading** macro, and then click **Edit**. If necessary, maximize the *Normal – [NewMacros (Code)]* window. Compare your screen with Figure 11.36.

> The Visual Basic Editor displays the code associated with the *Footer* and *Heading* macros. A macro *procedure*—a block of programming code that performs one or more tasks—begins with the term *Sub* and ends with the term *End Sub*. The name following the word *Sub* indicates the name of the procedure. The description that you typed when you created the *Heading* macro displays as a **comment**. A comment is a line of text that is used solely for documentation—for example, the name of the individual who wrote the macro or the purpose of the macro. A comment is preceded by a single quotation mark, displays in green text, and is ignored when the macro runs.

FIGURE 11.36

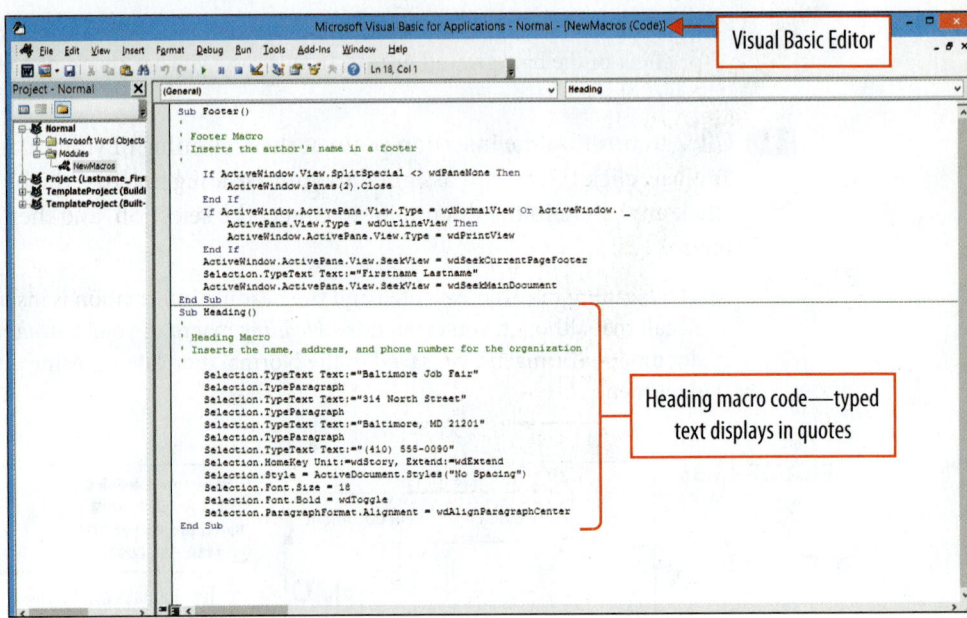

A L E R T !   **Why Does My Visual Basic Editor Display Differently?**

Depending on how the Visual Basic Editor was last used, different panes may be displayed. For purposes of this instruction, the only panes that are required are the Project pane on the left and the Code pane on the right.

---

3 In the pane on the right, locate the text *Baltimore Job Fair*. Click to position the insertion point to the left of *Baltimore*, type **Greater** and then press Spacebar. Compare your screen with Figure 11.37.

> You are editing the macro so that when it runs, the correct name of the organization displays.

FIGURE 11.37

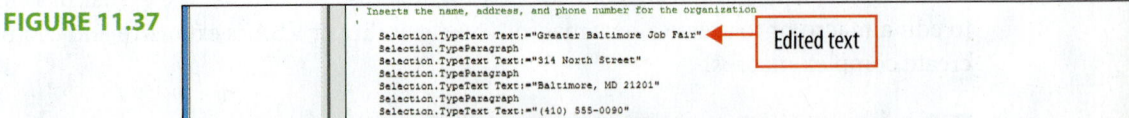

4 On the menu bar, click **File**, and then from the list, click **Close and Return to Microsoft Word**.

🔄 **ANOTHER WAY**   At the top right of the Visual Basic Editor window, click Close.

---

5 In the **Lastname_Firstname_11B_Fair_Memo** document, delete the heading—the first four paragraphs—leaving one blank paragraph above the word *MEMO*. On the **Quick Access Toolbar**, click the button assigned to your **Heading** macro, and then compare your screen with Figure 11.38.

The edited text displays in the heading.

FIGURE 11.38

6 Click anywhere in the document to cancel the selection, and then **Save** 🖫 your changes.

Activity 11.13 | Using a Built-in Word Macro

Word has many macros that are already built in and available in each document. In this activity, you will use a macro that allows you to adjust the size of the indents for a bulleted list.

1 Locate and select the four bulleted paragraphs.

2 On the **DEVELOPER tab**, in the **Code group**, click **Macros**. In the **Macros** dialog box, click the **Macros in arrow**, and then click **Word commands**. Under **Macro name**, scroll as necessary, and then from the list, click **AdjustListIndents**. Notice that the macro names are in alphabetical order.

A list of available Word commands (macros) displays. The Description area explains what a selected command will do. The *AdjustListIndents* built-in macro is used to modify the indenting of a bulleted or numbered list.

3 In the **Macros** dialog box, click **Run**. In the **Adjust List Indents** dialog box, click the **Bullet position up spin arrow** to **0.4"**. Click the **Text indent up spin arrow** to **0.6"**. Compare your screen with Figure 11.39.

FIGURE 11.39

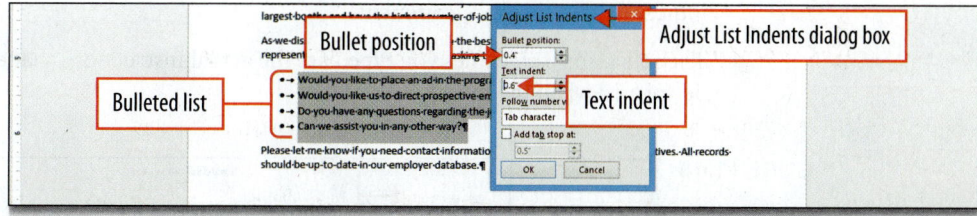

4 Click **OK**, and notice that the indentation of the bulleted list has changed.

5 Click anywhere in the document to cancel the selection, and then **Save** 🖫 your changes.

Video W11-5

You can use the Visual Basic Editor to write code in the Visual Basic for Applications language. To write effective procedures, you should take a formal course in VBA programming. However, you can learn the basic elements of a VBA code for a macro by entering a prewritten program.

Activity 11.14 | Writing a Procedure in VBA to Apply Quotation Marks

In this activity, you will write a procedure to apply quotation marks to selected text.

1 On the **DEVELOPER tab**, in the **Code group**, click **Visual Basic**. If necessary, maximize the *Normal – [NewMacros (Code)]* window.

The code for the *Footer* and *Heading* macros displays.

2 In the **Heading** macro, position the insertion point to the right of *End Sub*, and then press Enter. Using your own first and last names, type the following text, pressing Enter after each line—except the last line. Compare your screen with Figure 11.40.

Sub Quotes()
'
' Quotes Macro
' Macro created by Firstname Lastname
'

Quote$ = Chr$ (34)
Selection.InsertBefore Quote$
Selection.InsertAfter Quote$

The first line indicates that the following section of code is named *Quotes*. The name of the macro is followed by two parentheses with no space between them. When you type the *Sub* statement, an *End Sub* statement is added automatically.

The next four lines, formatted with a green font color, begin with a single quotation mark, indicating that these are comments.

The remaining three lines you typed are the actual instructions that determine what actions will be performed when the macro is executed.

FIGURE 11.40

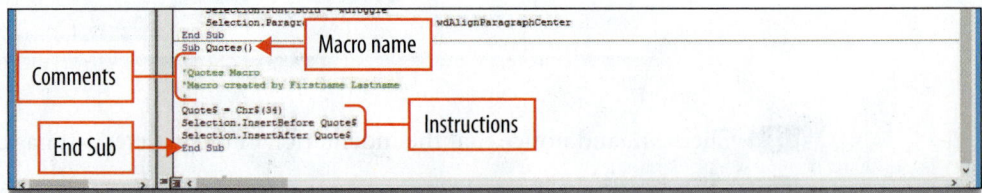

3 At the top of the **Microsoft Visual Basic for Applications** window, click **File**, and then from the list, click **Close and Return to Microsoft Word**.

4 In the paragraph immediately below the horizontal line, select the text *Gold Star*.

5 On the **DEVELOPER tab**, in the **Code group**, click **Macros**. In the **Macros** dialog box, click the **Macros in arrow**, and then click **All active templates and documents**. In the list of macro names, click **Quotes**. Compare your screen with Figure 11.41.

FIGURE 11.41

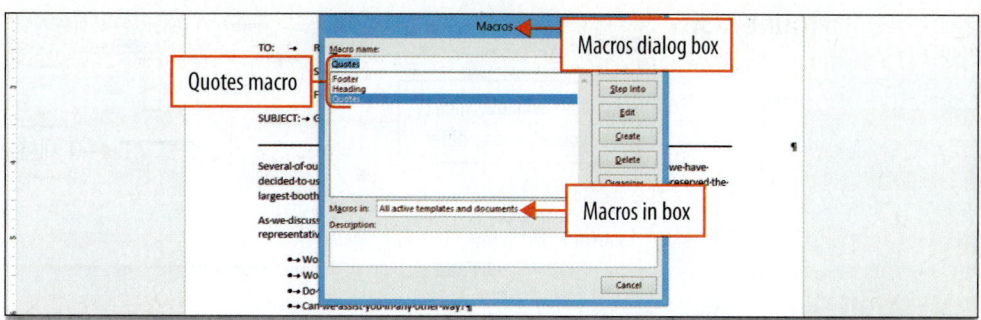

6 ▶ In the **Macros** dialog box, click **Run**. Notice that the quotation marks are inserted before and after the selected text.

ALERT! **Did You Receive an Error Message?**

Any typing error in the program code will cause a compilation error that prevents the macro from running properly. When this occurs, the Visual Basic Editor will open, and the line with the error will be highlighted. The usual cause of error is misspelling. For example, if you type *InsertBefore* as *Insert Before*, the program will not work. Also, if you type *End Sub* at the end of a macro, and the program has already inserted this command, the program will display a compile error. You can correct your mistake in the editor, and then close the editor.

7 ▶ Click anywhere in the document to cancel the selection, and then **Save** 🖫 your changes.

Activity 11.15 | Creating Screen Captures

There are several ways to capture images of your screen. In a Word document, you can create a ***screenshot***. A screenshot is an image of an active region or window on your computer that you can paste into a document. In this activity, you will capture images of your macro codes and the Quick Access Toolbar.

1 ▶ On the **DEVELOPER tab**, in the **Code group**, click **Visual Basic**. If necessary, scroll down to completely display the **Quotes** macro.

The Visual Basic code associated with all three macros in the document displays.

2 ▶ On the taskbar, point to the **Word** icon 🗐, and then click the **Lastname_Firstname_11B_Fair_Memo** document to make it active.

3 ▶ Press Ctrl+N to display a new document. **Save** the document in your **Word Chapter 11** folder as **Lastname_Firstname_11B_Screen_Captures** Press and hold Alt + Ctrl, and then press B to insert your name in the footer.

4 ▶ Click the **INSERT tab**, and then in the **Illustrations group**, click **Screenshot**. Compare your screen with Figure 11.42.

The Available Windows gallery displays thumbnails of all open windows that are not minimized. In this case, the *Lastname_Firstname_11B_Fair_Memo*, *Visual Basic Editor*, and *File Explorer* display. The Screen Clipping option allows you to select only a portion of an open window for the screen capture.

FIGURE 11.42

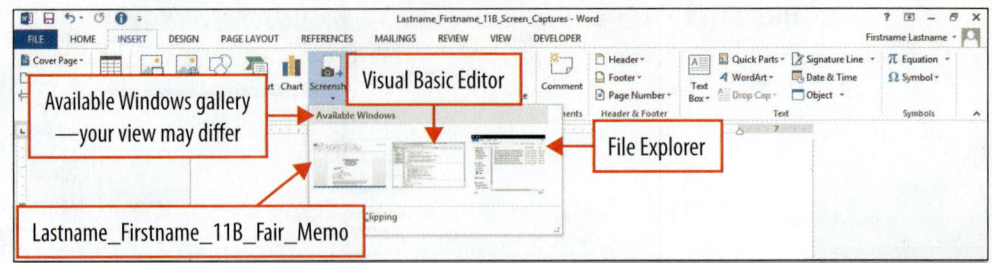

Visual Basic Editor

Available Windows gallery
—your view may differ

File Explorer

Lastname_Firstname_11B_Fair_Memo

5 ▶ In the **Available Windows** gallery, click **Screen Clipping**.

The *Lastname_Firstname_11B_Fair_Memo* document displays in a faded view and the pointer changes to a ➕ pointer.

6 ▶ Move the ➕ pointer to the top left corner of your screen, and then press and hold the left mouse button and drag to select only the *Quick Access Toolbar*. Release the mouse button. Compare your screen with Figure 11.43.

The image of the Quick Access Toolbar is pasted in your *Lastname_Firstname_11B_Screen_Captures* document.

FIGURE 11.43

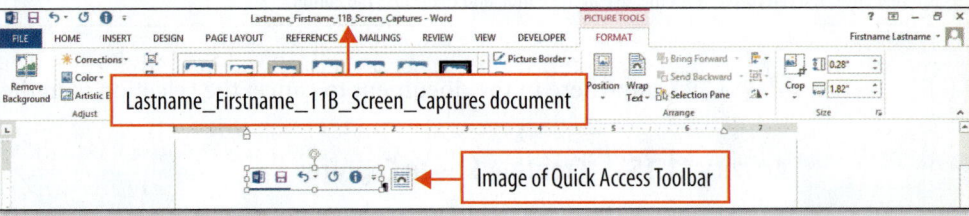

Lastname_Firstname_11B_Screen_Captures document

Image of Quick Access Toolbar

7 ▶ Click to the right of the image, and then press Enter. Click the **INSERT tab**, in the **Illustrations group**, click **Screenshot**, and then in the **Available Windows** gallery, click the thumbnail of the **Visual Basic Editor** window.

The image of the Visual Basic Editor window is pasted in your *Lastname_Firstname_11B_Screen_Captures* document.

8 ▶ Click to the right of the image, and then press Enter. **Save** 🖫 your changes.

9 ▶ On the taskbar, point to the **Word** icon 🇼, right-click the **Visual Basic Editor** window, and then click **Close**. On the taskbar, point to the **Word** icon 🇼, and then click the **Lastname_Firstname_11B_Fair_Memo** document to make it active.

10 ▶ In the **Lastname_Firstname_11B_Fair_Memo** document, press Ctrl + Home. Click the **FILE tab**, and then click **Show All Properties**. In the **Tags** box, type **job fair memo, with macros** In the **Subject** box, type your course name and section number. If necessary, edit the author name to display your name. **Save** your changes, and then **Close** ✖ the document.

11 ▶ With the **Lastname_Firstname_11B_Screen_Captures** document displayed, click the **FILE tab**, and then open the file **Lastname_Firstname_11B_Fair_Flyer**. On the **Security Warning** banner, click **Enable Content**.

12 ▶ Click the **DEVELOPER tab**, and then in the **Code group**, click **Visual Basic**.

13 ▶ In the **Visual Basic Editor**, on the left side of the screen, locate the **Project - Normal** pane. Position the pointer on the right side of the **Project** pane, until the ⊞ pointer displays. Drag to the right until the full name for the **Project (Lastname_Firstname_11B_Fair_Flyer)** folder displays. Under **Project (Lastname_Firstname_11B_Fair_Flyer)**, double-click the **Modules** folder, and then double-click **NewMacros**. Compare your screen with Figure 11.44.

The code for the *AutoClose* macro displays. Because this macro is stored only in this document (project), this code displays separately from the other macros codes that are stored in the Normal template.

FIGURE 11.44

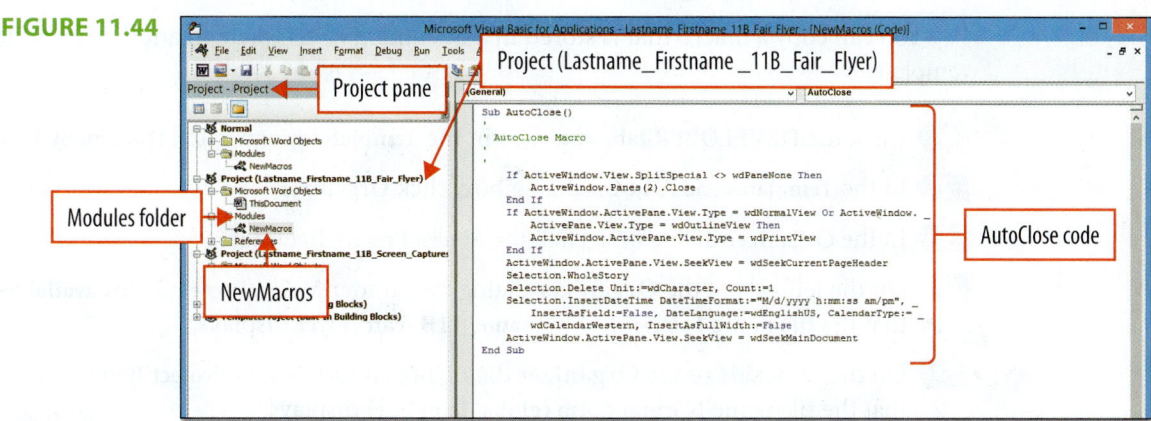

14 ▶ On the taskbar, point to the **Word** icon ⊞, and then click the **Lastname_Firstname_11B_Screen_Captures** document to make it active. Press Ctrl + End, and then press Enter.

15 ▶ Click the **INSERT tab**, in the **Illustrations group**, click **Screenshot**, and then in the **Available Windows** gallery, click the thumbnail of the **Visual Basic Editor** window.

The image of the entire Visual Basic Editor window is pasted in your *Lastname_Firstname_11B_Screen_Captures* document.

16 ▶ With the image selected, on the **FORMAT tab**, in the **Size group**, click **Crop**. Point to the bottom center crop handle, and drag upward until the bottom of the image is immediately below the last line of code—*End Sub*. Click in a blank area of the document to deselect the image. Compare your screen with Figure 11.45.

FIGURE 11.45

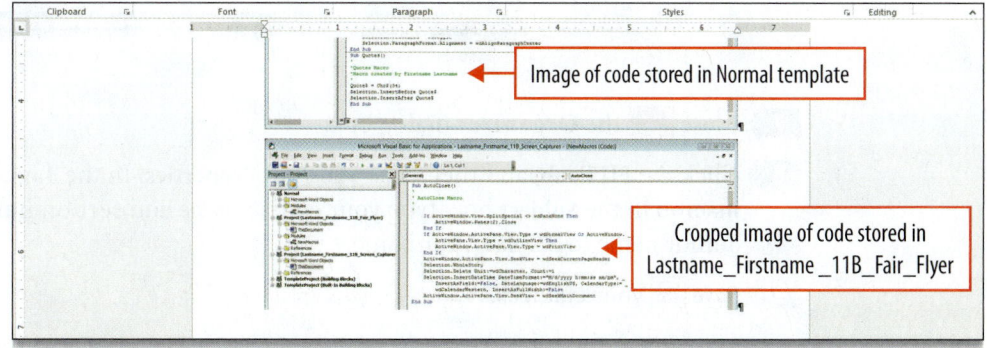

17 Save 🖫 your changes, and then **Close** ✕ the document. **Close** ✕ the Visual Basic Editor.

18 In the **Lastname_Firstname_11B_Fair_Flyer** document, delete the heading—the first four paragraphs, leaving one blank paragraph above the paragraph that begins *Looking*. On the **Quick Access Toolbar**, click the button for your **Heading** macro. Notice that the corrected heading displays. Press Ctrl + Home, and then **Save** 🖫 your changes.

Activity 11.16 | Copying a Macro from One Document to Another Document

You can copy a macro that is stored in a document or template to another document or template.

1 Click the **DEVELOPER tab**, and then in the **Templates group**, click **Document Template**.

2 In the **Templates and Add-ins** dialog box, click **Organizer**.

3 In the **Organizer** dialog box, click the **Macro Project Items tab**.

4 On the left side of the **Organizer** dialog box, under **Macro Project Items available in**, notice that the file name **Lastname_Firstname_11B_Fair_Flyer** displays.

5 On the right side of the **Organizer** dialog box, under **Macro Project Items available in**, notice that the file name **Normal.dotm (global template)** displays.

6 On the right side of the **Organizer** dialog box, under **In Normal**, click **NewMacros**. Compare your screen with Figure 11.46.

You can select any macro that displays in the Organizer, and then copy the macro to the other document. For purposes of this instruction, you will not copy any macros.

FIGURE 11.46

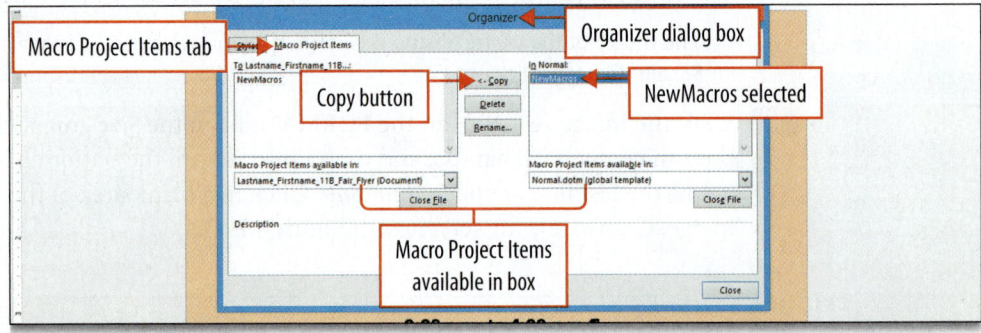

7 **Close** ✕ the **Organizer** dialog box.

8 Click the **FILE tab**, and then click **Show All Properties**. In the **Tags** box, type **job fair flyer, with macros** In the **Subject** box, type your course name and section number. If necessary, edit the author name to display your name.

9 **Save** 🖫 your changes.

Activity 11.17 | Restoring Default Settings

Because you will not need the macros you created in the Normal template after completing this project, you will delete them and restore the default settings you changed.

1 Click the **DEVELOPER tab**, and then in the **Code group**, click **Macros**. In the **Macros** dialog box, in the **Macros in** box, be sure **All active templates and documents** displays. Under **Macro name**, click **Footer**, and then click **Delete**. In the **Microsoft Word** dialog box, click **Yes** to confirm the deletion.

2 Using the same technique, delete the **Heading** and **Quotes** macros.

You are not deleting the *AutoClose* macro because it is stored only in this document.

3 Click **Close** to close the **Macros** dialog box.

4 Click the **FILE tab**, and then click **Options**. In the **Word Options** dialog box, click **Customize Ribbon**. Under **Main Tabs**, clear the **Developer** check box.

5 On the left side of the **Word Options** dialog box, click **Quick Access Toolbar**. On the right side, under **Customize Quick Access Toolbar**, click **Normal.NewMacros.Heading**. In the middle of the dialog box, click **Remove**, and then click **OK**.

6 **Close** [×] Word. In the **Microsoft Word** dialog box, click **Save** to save your changes. If asked if you want to keep the last item you copied, click **No**. If necessary, **Close** [×] File Explorer.

7 Print your three documents—the flyer, the memo, and the screen captures—or submit electronically as directed by your instructor.

END | You have completed Project 11B

END OF CHAPTER

SUMMARY

You can use the program-integration technology Object Linking & Embedding to link or embed an object that was created in another Office application—such as Access, Excel, or PowerPoint—in a Word document.

Paste Options provide different ways to insert an object in a document. When you edit an embedded object, changes are not reflected in the source file. When a linked object is modified, the source file is changed.

A macro—a set of commands and instructions that can be applied in a single action—helps you work more efficiently. You can use built-in macros or create your own macros by recording actions or typing code.

Visual Basic for Applications, or VBA, is a programming language used to create macros. In the Visual Basic Editor, you can edit the code in an existing macro or type your own procedure to create a new macro.

GO! LEARN IT ONLINE

Review the concepts and key terms in this chapter by completing these online challenges, which you can find at **www.pearsonhighered.com/go**.

Matching and Multiple Choice:
Answer matching and multiple choice questions to test what you learned in this chapter. **MyITLab®**

Crossword Puzzle:
Spell out the words that match the numbered clues, and put them in the puzzle squares.

Flipboard:
Flip through the definitions of the key terms in this chapter and match them with the correct term.

END OF CHAPTER

REVIEW AND ASSESSMENT GUIDE FOR WORD CHAPTER 11

Your instructor may assign one or more of these projects to help you review the chapter and assess your mastery and understanding of the chapter.

		Review and Assessment Guide for Word Chapter 11	
Project	**Apply Skills from These Chapter Objectives**	**Project Type**	**Project Location**
11C	Objectives 1 and 2 from Project 11A	**11C Skills Review** A guided review of the skills from Project 11A.	On the following pages
11D	Objectives 3–5 from Project 11B	**11D Skills Review** A guided review of the skills from Project 11B.	On the following pages
11E	Objectives 1 and 2 from Project 11A	**11E Mastery (Grader Project)** A demonstration of your mastery of the skills in Project 11A with extensive decision making.	In MyITLab and on the following pages
11F	Objectives 3–5 from Project 11B	**11F Mastery (Grader Project)** A demonstration of your mastery of the skills in Project 11B with extensive decision making.	In MyITLab and on the following pages
11G	Objectives 1–5 from Projects 11A and 11B	**11G Mastery (Grader Project)** A demonstration of your mastery of the skills in Projects 11A and 11B with extensive decision making.	In MyITLab and on the following pages
11H	Combination of Objectives from Projects 11A and 11B	**11H GO! Fix It** A demonstration of your mastery of the skills in Projects 11A and 11B by creating a correct result from a document that contains errors you must find.	Online
11I	Combination of Objectives from Projects 11A and 11B	**11I GO! Make It** A demonstration of your mastery of the skills in Projects 11A and 11B by creating a result from a supplied picture.	Online
11J	Combination of Objectives from Projects 11A and 11B	**11J GO! Solve It** A demonstration of your mastery of the skills in Projects 11A and 11B, your decision-making skills, and your critical thinking skills. A task-specific rubric helps you self-assess your result.	Online
11K	Combination of Objectives from Projects 11A and 11B	**11K GO! Solve It** A demonstration of your mastery of the skills in Projects 11A and 11B, your decision-making skills, and your critical thinking skills. A task-specific rubric helps you self-assess your result.	On the following pages
11L	Combination of Objectives from Projects 11A and 11B	**11L GO! Think** A demonstration of your understanding of the chapter concepts applied in a manner that you would outside of college. An analytic rubric helps you and your instructor grade the quality of your work by comparing it to the work an expert in the discipline would create.	On the following pages
11M	Combination of Objectives from Projects 11A and 11B	**11M GO! Think** A demonstration of your understanding of the chapter concepts applied in a manner that you would outside of college. An analytic rubric helps you and your instructor grade the quality of your work by comparing it to the work an expert in the discipline would create.	Online
11N	Combination of Objectives from Projects 11A and 11B	**11N You and GO!** A demonstration of your understanding of the chapter concepts applied in a manner that you would in a personal situation. An analytic rubric helps you and your instructor grade the quality of your work.	Online

GLOSSARY

AdjustListIndents A built-in macro used to modify the indenting of a bulleted or numbered list.

AutoClose A macro that will automatically run when closing a document.

Comment In a macro procedure, a line of text that is used solely for documentation.

Destination file The file where an object is embedded or linked.

Embedded object An object that maintains the structure of the original application, but is not connected to the source file.

Embedding The process of inserting an object, such as an Excel chart, into a Word document so that it becomes part of the document.

Linked object An object that maintains a direct connection to the source file.

Linking The process of inserting information from a source file into a destination file, while maintaining a connection between the two files.

Macro A set of commands and instructions that can be grouped as a single command to accomplish a task automatically.

Macro virus A macro that causes files to be erased or damaged by inserting unauthorized code.

Object A table, chart, graphic, file, or other form of information.

Object Linking and Embedding (OLE) A program-integration technology for sharing information between Office programs.

Procedure A block of programming code that performs one or more tasks.

Recording The process of creating a macro while performing specific actions in a document.

Screenshot An image of an active region or window on your computer that you can paste into a document.

Source file The file where an object is created.

Visual Basic Editor An editor that enables you to view and edit existing macro code or create a new macro.

Visual Basic for Applications (VBA) A programming language used to create macros.

CHAPTER REVIEW

Apply 11A skills from these Objectives:

1 Embed Objects in a Word Document
2 Link Objects to a Word Document

Skills Review Project 11C Sponsorship Program

In the following project, you will use OLE to include objects and files from other Office applications in a memo to Robert Benson, Executive Director of the Greater Baltimore Job Fair. The memo and related files explain the corporate sponsorship program. Your completed files will look similar to Figure 11.47.

PROJECT FILES

For Project 11C, you will need the following files:

w11C_Sponsorship_Memo
w11C_Sponsors_Chart
w11C_Sponsorship_Program
w11C_Top_Sponsors
w11C_Revenue
w11C_Agenda

You will save your files as:

Lastname_Firstname_11C_Sponsorship_Memo
Lastname_Firstname_11C_Revenue
Lastname_Firstname_11C_Agenda

PROJECT RESULTS

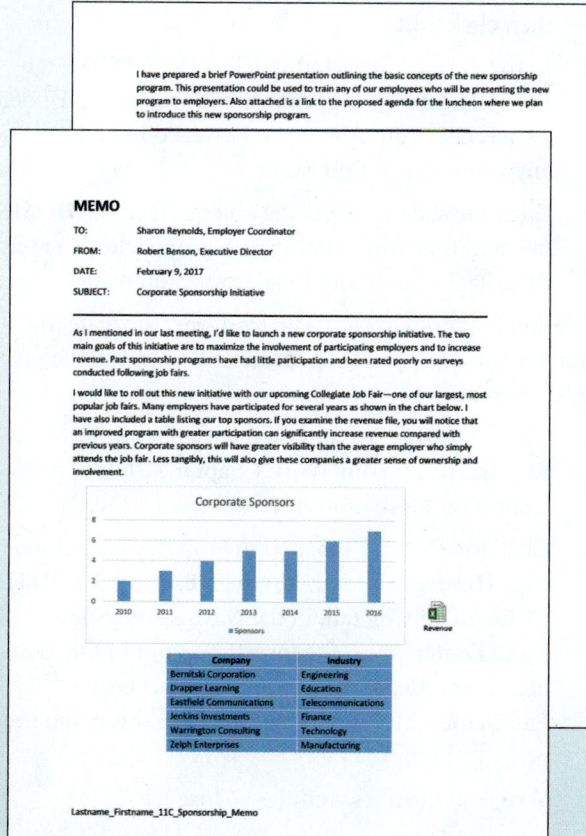

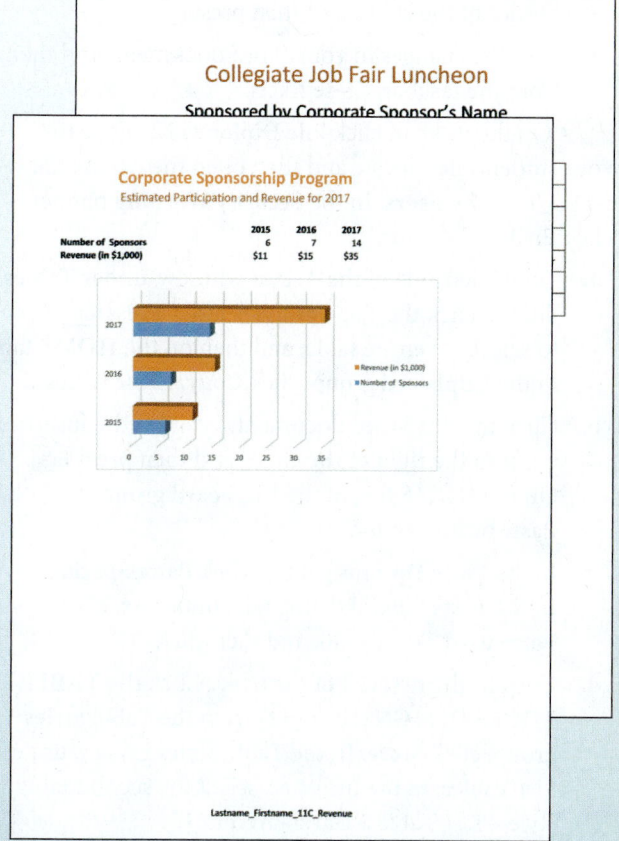

FIGURE 11.47

(Project 11C Sponsorship Program continues on the next page)

CHAPTER REVIEW

1 Start Word. From your student files, locate and open the file **w11C_Sponsorship_Memo**. **Save** it to your **Word Chapter 11** folder as **Lastname_Firstname_11C_Sponsorship_Memo** Insert the file name in the footer.

a. On the taskbar, click **File Explorer**. Navigate to your student files, and then open the Excel file **w11C_Sponsors_Chart**.

b. Right-click on a border of the chart, and then click **Copy**. On the taskbar, click the **Word** icon to make the **Lastname_Firstname_11C_Sponsorship_Memo** active. In your Word document, locate the paragraph that begins *I would like*, click to position the insertion point at the end of the paragraph, and then press Enter.

c. On the **HOME tab**, in the **Clipboard group**, click the **Paste button arrow**. From the **Paste Options** gallery, click **Keep Source Formatting & Embed Workbook (K)**.

d. Click in a blank area of the chart. Click the **Chart Elements** button, to the right of **Legend**, point to the arrow, and then click **Bottom**.

e. Click the **FORMAT tab**, and then in the **Size group**, click the **Height down spin arrow** to **2.4"**. Click on a border of the chart, and then press Ctrl + E.

f. **Save** the changes in your Word document, and then from the taskbar, **Close** Excel.

2 On the taskbar, click **File Explorer**. Navigate to your student files, locate and then open the Access file **w11C_Top_Sponsors**. In the **Security Warning** banner, click **Enable Content**.

a. On the left side of the Access window, under **Tables**, double-click the **Top Sponsors** table. Press Ctrl + A to select the entire table, and then on the **HOME tab**, in the **Clipboard group**, click **Copy**. **Close** Access.

b. Click in your Word document. Position the insertion point to the right of the chart, and then press Enter. On the **HOME tab**, in the **Clipboard group**, click the **Paste button arrow**.

c. In the **Paste Options** gallery, click **Paste Special**. In the **Paste Special** dialog box, under **As**, click **Formatted Text (RTF)**, and then click **OK**.

d. Click in the first cell of the table. Click the **TABLE TOOLS DESIGN tab**, and then in the **Table Styles group**, click **More**. In the **Table Styles** gallery, under **List Tables**, in the fifth row, select the second table style—**List Table 5 Dark – Accent 1**.

e. Click the **LAYOUT tab**, and then in the **Data group**, click **Sort**. In the **Sort** dialog box, be sure *Company* displays in the **Sort by** box and the **Header row** option button is selected, and then click **OK**.

f. On the **LAYOUT tab**, in the **Table group**, click **Properties**. In the **Table Properties** dialog box, on the **Table tab**, under **Alignment**, click **Center**, and then click **OK**. For each name in the table flagged as a spelling error, right-click, and then click **Ignore All**. **Save** your changes.

3 On **Page 2** of your Word document, click to position the insertion point at the end of the first paragraph, and then press Enter.

a. Click the **INSERT tab**, and then in the **Text group**, click the **Object** button.

b. In the **Object** dialog box, click the **Create from File tab**. Click **Browse**, navigate to your student files, click **w11C_Sponsorship_Program**, and then click **Insert**. Click **OK**.

c. Right-click the PowerPoint object, and then from the shortcut menu, point to **Presentation Object**, and then click **Edit**.

d. In the PowerPoint window, click the **DESIGN tab**. In the **Themes group**, click the **More** button. Under **Office**, click **Ion**. Above the PowerPoint object, click anywhere to exit Edit mode.

e. Click the slide to select the object. Click the **HOME tab**, and then in the **Paragraph group**, click **Center**. Press Ctrl + Home, and then **Save** your changes.

4 On the taskbar, click **File Explorer**. Navigate to your student files, and then locate and open the file **w11C_Revenue**.

a. Click the **FILE tab**, and then click **Save As**. **Save** the file to your **Word Chapter 11** folder as **Lastname_Firstname_11C_Revenue**

b. Click the **INSERT tab**, and then in the **Text group**, click **Header & Footer**. On the **HEADER & FOOTER TOOLS DESIGN tab**, in the **Navigation group**, click **Go to Footer**. With the insertion point in the footer box, in the **Header & Footer Elements group**, click **File Name**. Click any cell in the worksheet, and then press Ctrl + Home.

c. **Save** your changes, and then **Close** Excel.

(Project 11C Sponsorship Program continues on the next page)

5 Click in your Word document, and then position the insertion point to the right of the chart. Click the **INSERT tab**, and then in the **Text group**, click the **Object** button.

a. In the **Object** dialog box, click the **Create from File tab**. Click **Browse**, navigate to your **Word Chapter 11** folder, and then click **Lastname_Firstname_11C_ Revenue**. Click **Insert**.

b. On the right side of the **Object** dialog box, select the **Link to file** check box, and then select the **Display as icon** check box.

c. In the **Object** dialog box, click the **Change Icon** button, and then in the **Caption** box, delete the existing text, and then type **Revenue** Click **OK** two times.

d. Double-click the icon to open the Excel file. Maximize the Excel window.

e. Click in cell **D5**, which contains the value *12*. Type **14** and then press ⏎. **Save** your changes, and then **Close** Excel.

f. Press Ctrl + End. **Save** the changes in your Word document.

6 In Word, from your student files, open the file **w11C_Agenda**. Display the **Save As** dialog box, and then **Save** the file to your **Word Chapter 11** folder as **Lastname_Firstname_11C_Agenda** Insert the file name in the footer.

a. **Save** your changes. Press Ctrl + W to close the **Lastname_Firstname_11C_Agenda** document but leave Word open.

b. In your **Lastname_Firstname_11C_Sponsorship_ Memo**, on **Page 2**, click to position the insertion point to the right of the PowerPoint object. On the **INSERT tab**, in the **Text group**, click the **Object** button. In the **Object** dialog box, click the **Create from File tab**. Click **Browse**, navigate to your **Word Chapter 11** folder, click **Lastname_Firstname_11C_ Agenda**, and then click **Insert**.

c. On the right side of the **Object** dialog box, select the **Link to file** check box, and then select the **Display as icon** check box. Click the **Change Icon** button. In the **Caption** box, delete the existing text, and then type **Agenda** Click **OK** two times.

d. Double-click the **Agenda** icon. In the first paragraph, delete the text **Kick-Off**. **Save** your changes, and then **Close** the document.

e. Press Ctrl + Home. Click the **FILE tab**, and then click **Show All Properties**. In the **Tags** box, type **sponsorship, linked and embedded objects** In the **Subject** box, type your course name and section number. If necessary, edit the author name to display your name. **Save** your changes.

7 Print all three files—your two Word documents and the Excel file—or submit electronically as directed by your instructor. **Close** Word, and then **Close** File Explorer.

END | You have completed Project 11C

CHAPTER REVIEW

Skills Review Project 11D Fair Schedule

In the following project, you will create macros to improve your efficiency in editing a letter and press release that explain the scheduled job fairs conducted by the Greater Baltimore Job Fair. Your completed documents will look similar to Figure 11.48.

PROJECT FILES

For Project 11D, you will need the following files:

w11D_Fair_Schedule
w11D_Press_Release

You will save your files as:

Lastname_Firstname_11D_Fair_Schedule
Lastname_Firstname_11D_Press_Release
Lastname_Firstname_11D_Schedule_Code

PROJECT RESULTS

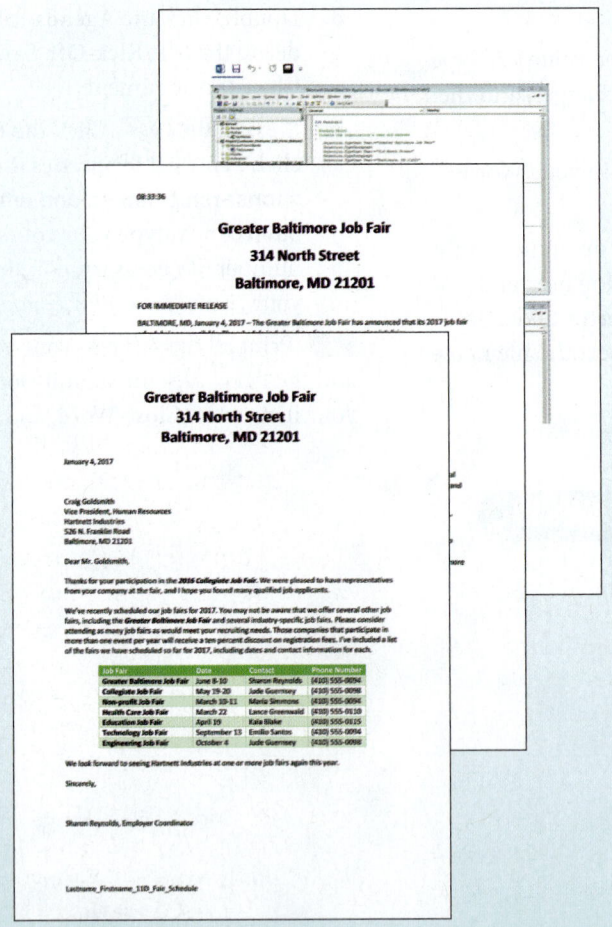

FIGURE 11.48

(Project 11D Fair Schedule continues on the next page)

CHAPTER REVIEW

1 Start Word. From your student files, locate and open the file **w11D_Fair_Schedule**. Display the **Save As** dialog box, and then navigate to your **Word Chapter 11** folder. In the lower portion of the dialog box, click the **Save as type arrow**, and then from the list, click **Word Macro-Enabled Document**. In the **File name** box, using your own name, type **Lastname_ Firstname_11D_Fair_Schedule** and then click **Save**.

a. Insert the file name in the footer.

b. Click the **FILE tab**, and then click **Options**. In the **Word Options** dialog box, on the left side, click **Customize Ribbon**.

c. In the **Main Tabs** list, locate and then select the **Developer** check box. Click **OK** to close the **Word Options** dialog box.

d. Click the **DEVELOPER tab**, and then in the **Code group**, click **Macro Security**. If necessary, in the **Trust Center** dialog box, under **Macro Settings**, select **Disable all macros with notification**. Click **OK** to close the dialog box. **Save** your changes.

2 Press Ctrl + Home. On the **DEVELOPER tab**, in the **Code group**, click **Record Macro**.

a. In the **Record Macro** dialog box, in the **Macro name** box, type **Heading** Be sure the **Store macro in** box displays **All Documents (Normal.dotm)**.

b. In the **Description** box, click to position the insertion point, and then type **Inserts the organization's name and address**

c. Under **Assign macro to**, click **Keyboard**. In the **Customize Keyboard** dialog box, with the insertion point in the **Press new shortcut key** box, press and hold Alt + Ctrl, and then press G. Click **Assign**, and then click **Close**.

d. In recording mode, with the insertion point at the beginning of the document, type the following text, pressing Enter after the first two lines.

Greater Baltimore Job Fair

314 North Street

Baltimore, MD 21203

e. With the insertion point to the right of the postal code, press and hold Ctrl + Shift + and then press ↑ three times to select all three lines. Click the **HOME tab**, change the **Font Size** to 22, and then apply **Bold** and **Center**. Click the **DEVELOPER tab**, and then in the **Code group**, click **Stop Recording**. **Save** your changes

3 In the first cell of the table, click to position the insertion point. On the **DEVELOPER tab**, in the **Code group**, click **Record Macro**. In the **Record Macro** dialog box, in the **Macro name** box, type **Table_Style** Be sure the **Store macro in** box displays **All Documents (Normal. dotm)**.

a. Under **Assign macro to**, click the **Button** icon. In the **Word Options** dialog box, with **Quick Access Toolbar** selected, under **Choose commands from**, click **Normal.NewMacros.Table_Style**. Click **Add**.

b. On the right side of the **Word Options** dialog box, click to select **Normal.NewMacros.Table_Style**. Below the list of commands, click **Modify**.

c. In the **Modify Button** dialog box, under **Symbol**, in the seventh row, click the first symbol—a box with a black border, and horizontal stripes of white, gray, and black. Click **OK** two times.

d. In recording mode, with the insertion point in the table, click the **TABLE TOOLS DESIGN tab**, and then in the **Table Styles group**, click **More**. In the **Table Styles** gallery, under **Grid Tables**, in the fourth row, click the last style—**Grid Table 4 – Accent 6**.

e. Click the **LAYOUT tab**, in the **Cell Size group**, click **AutoFit**, and then click **AutoFit Contents**. In the **Table group**, click **Properties**. In the **Table Properties** dialog box, under **Alignment**, click **Center**, and then click **OK**. Click the **DEVELOPER tab**, and then in the **Code group**, click **Stop Recording**. **Save** your changes.

4 From your student files, open the file **w11D_Press_ Release**. Press F12. In the **Save As** dialog box, navigate to your **Word Chapter 11** folder. In the lower portion of the dialog box, click the **Save as type arrow**, and then from the list, click **Word Macro-Enabled Document**. In the **File name** box, using your own name, type **Lastname_Firstname_11D_Press_Release** and then click **Save**.

a. Insert the file name in the footer, and then **Close** the footer. Click the **DEVELOPER tab**, and then in the **Code group**, click **Record Macro**. In the **Macro name** box, type **AutoClose** Click the **Store macro in arrow**, and then click **Lastname_Firstname_11D_Press_ Release (document)**. Click **OK**.

(Project 11D Fair Schedule continues on the next page)

CHAPTER REVIEW

b. Click the **INSERT tab**, in the **Header & Footer group**, click **Header**, and then from the displayed list, click **Edit Header**.

c. Press Ctrl + A, and then press Delete. On the **HEADER & FOOTER TOOLS DESIGN tab**, in the **Insert group**, click **Date and Time**. In the **Date and Time** dialog box, click the last option to display the time, and then click **OK**.

d. On the **HEADER & FOOTER TOOLS DESIGN tab**, in the **Close group**, click **Close Header and Footer**. Click the **DEVELOPER tab**, and then in the **Code group**, click **Stop Recording**.

5 In the first cell of the table, click to position the insertion point. On the **Quick Access Toolbar**, click the button with stripes of white, gray, and black to run the **Table_Style** macro and format the table.

a. On the **DEVELOPER tab**, in the **Code group**, click **Macros**. In the **Macros** dialog box, select the **Heading** macro, and then click **Edit**.

b. In the **Heading** macro, locate the postal code **21203**. Position the insertion point to the right of *3*, press Backspace, and then type **1**

c. Near the top of the **Visual Basic Editor** window, click **File**, and then click **Close and Return to Microsoft Word**.

d. Press Ctrl + Home, and then press Alt + Ctrl + G to run the **Heading** macro. Deselect the text.

e. Select the text *For Immediate Release*. On the **DEVELOPER tab**, in the **Code group**, click **Macros**. In the **Macros** dialog box, click the **Macros in arrow**, and then click **Word commands**. Under **Macro name**, locate and click **AllCaps**, and then click **Run** to change the text to all uppercase letters. Press Ctrl + Home, and then **Save** your changes.

6 From the taskbar, point to the **Word** icon, and then click your **Lastname_Firstname_11D_Fair_Schedule** document to make it active. Select the three heading paragraphs, being careful not to include the last paragraph mark following the zip code. Press Delete. Press Alt + Ctrl + G to run your edited **Heading** macro. **Save** your changes.

a. On the **DEVELOPER tab**, in the **Code group**, click **Visual Basic**. In the **Table_Style** macro, immediately below the line *End Sub*, click to position the

insertion point. Pressing Enter after each line, except the last line, and using your own first and last names, type the following text.

```
Sub Text_Format()
' Macro created by Firstname Lastname
Selection.Font.Bold = wdToggle
Selection.Font.Italic = wdToggle
```

b. At the top of the **Visual Basic Editor** window, click **File**, and then click **Close and Return to Microsoft Word**. In the first paragraph below the *Greeting* line, select the text *2016 Collegiate Job Fair*. On the **DEVELOPER tab**, in the **Code group**, click **Macros**.

c. In the **Macros** dialog box, click the **Macros in arrow**, and then click **All active templates and documents**. Click **Text_Format**, and then click **Run** to apply a bold and italic format to the selected text.

d. In the next paragraph, in a similar manner, select the text *Greater Baltimore Job Fair*, and run the **Text_Format** macro. Deselect the text, and then **Save** your changes.

e. Click the **FILE tab**, and then click **Show All Properties**. In the **Tags** box, type **schedule, macros** In the **Subject** box, type your course name and section number. If necessary, edit the author name to display your name. **Save** your changes, and then **Close** your **Lastname_Firstname_11D_Fair_Schedule** document.

f. On the **DEVELOPER tab**, in the **Code group**, click **Visual Basic**. On the taskbar, point to the **Word** icon, and then click the **Lastname_Firstname_11D_Press_Release** document to make it active.

7 Press Ctrl + N to display a new document. **Save** the document to your **Word Chapter 11** folder as **Lastname_Firstname_11D_Schedule_Code** Insert the file name in the footer.

a. Click the **INSERT tab**, and then in the **Illustrations group**, click **Screenshot**. In the **Available Windows** gallery, click **Screen Clipping**. Move the ✛ pointer to the top left corner of your screen, press and hold the left mouse button and drag to select only the **Quick Access Toolbar**. Release the mouse button to paste the selected image in your document.

b. Click to the right of the image, and then press Enter. Click the **INSERT tab**, in the **Illustrations group**,

(Project 11D Fair Schedule continues on the next page)

CHAPTER REVIEW

click **Screenshot**, and then in the **Available Windows** gallery, click the thumbnail of the **Visual Basic Editor** window. Click to the right of the image, and then press Enter. **Save** your changes.

c. On the taskbar, click the **Visual Basic Editor** icon to make the window active. On the left side of the screen, locate **Project (Lastname_Firstname_11D_Press_Release)**. Immediately below the project, double-click the **Modules** folder, and then double-click **New Macros**.

d. On the taskbar, make the **Lastname_Firstname_11D_Schedule_Code** document active. Click the **INSERT tab**, in the **Illustrations group**, click **Screenshot**, and then in the **Available Windows** gallery, click the thumbnail for **Visual Basic Editor**.

e. With the image selected, on the **FORMAT tab**, in the **Size group**, click **Crop**. Point to the bottom center cropping handle, and then drag upward until the bottom of the image is immediately below **End Sub**. Deselect the image.

8 Click the **FILE tab**, and then click **Show All Properties**. In the **Tags** box, type **schedule, code** In the **Subject** box, type

your course name and section number. If necessary, edit the author name to display your name. **Save** your changes, and then **Close** your document. **Close** the Visual Basic Editor.

a. In **Lastname_Firstname_11D_Press_Release**, click the **FILE tab**, and then click **Show All Properties**. In the **Tags** box, type **schedule, press release** In the **Subject** box, type your course name and section number. If necessary, edit the author name to display your name.

b. Display the **DEVELOPER tab**, and then in the **Code group**, click **Macros**. In the **Macros** dialog box, for each of the three macros—*Heading, Table_Style*, and *Text_Format*, select the macro, and then click **Delete**. In the message box, click **Yes** to confirm the deletion. Click the **FILE tab**, and then click **Options**. In the **Word Options** dialog box, click **Quick Access Toolbar**. On the right side of the window, click **Normal.NewMacros.Table_Style**, click **Remove**, and then click **OK**. **Close** Word, and then click **Save** to save your changes. **Close** File Explorer.

9 Print your three documents or submit electronically as directed by your instructor.

END | You have completed Project 11D

CONTENT-BASED ASSESSMENTS

Mastering Word Project 11E Counseling Program

In the following Mastering Word project, you will use OLE to include objects and files from other Office applications in a memo to Robert Benson, Executive Director of the Greater Baltimore Job Fair. The memo and related files support a proposal to provide career counseling services at job fairs. Your completed documents will look similar to Figure 11.49.

Apply 11A skills from these Objectives:

1 Embed Objects in a Word Document

2 Link Objects to a Word Document

PROJECT FILES

For Project 11E, you will need the following files:

w11E_Counseling_Memo
w11E_Counseling_Survey
w11E_Scheduled_Fairs
w11E_Career_Counseling
w11E_Counselors
w11E_Jobseeker_Survey

You will save your files as:

Lastname_Firstname_11E_Counseling_Memo
Lastname_Firstname_11E_Counselors
Lastname_Firstname_11E_Jobseeker_Survey

PROJECT RESULTS

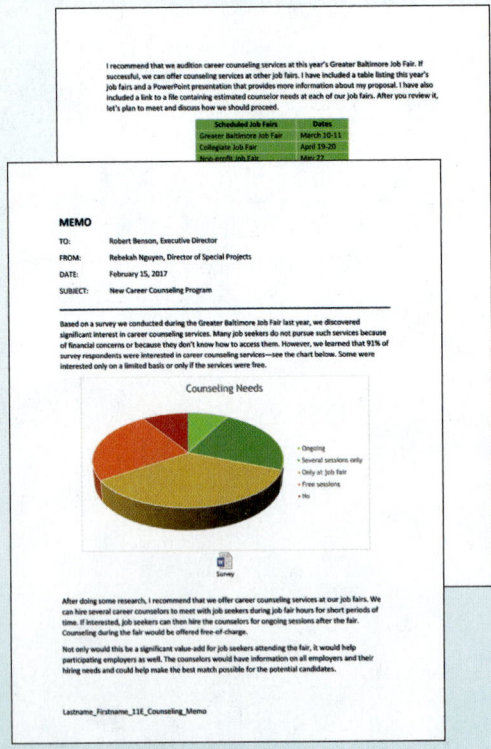

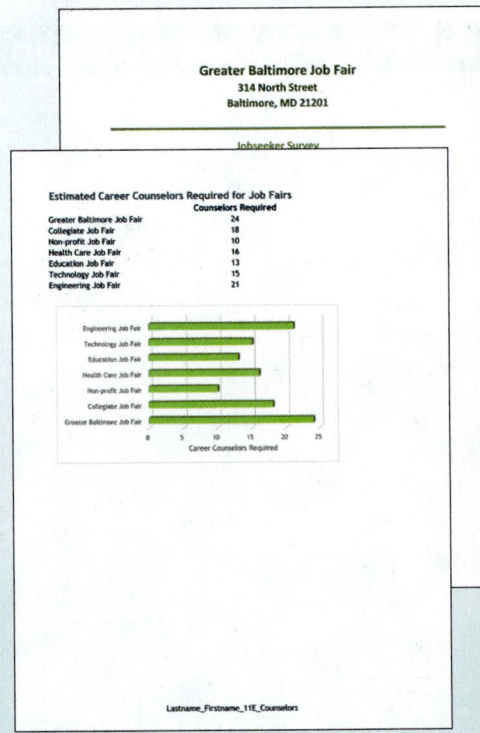

FIGURE 11.49

(Project 11E Counseling Program continues on the next page)

1 Start Word. Open the file **w11E_Counseling_Memo**, and then **Save** it to your **Word Chapter 11** folder as **Lastname_Firstname_11E_Counseling_Memo** Insert the file name in the footer. From your student files, open the Excel file **w11E_Counseling_Survey**. **Copy** the chart. Make your Word document active, place the insertion point at the end of the paragraph that begins *Based on*, and then press Enter. From the **Paste Options** gallery, click **Keep Source Formatting & Embed Workbook (K)**. **Center** the chart horizontally on the page. If necessary, change the Shape Height of the chart to 3.29 inches. **Save** your changes, and then **Close** Excel.

2 From your student files, open the Access file **w11E_Scheduled_Fairs**. In the **Security Warning** banner, click **Enable Content**. Open the **Job Fairs** table, press Ctrl + A to select the entire table, and then **Copy** the table. **Close** Access without saving changes. In your Word document, press Ctrl + End, and then press Enter. Paste the table as **Formatted Text (RTF)**. Apply the **List Table 5 Dark – Accent 6** table style—under **List Tables**, in the fifth row, the last style. Display the **Table Properties** dialog box, and then **Center** the table in the document. **Save** your changes.

3 In the paragraph below the table, click to position the insertion point, and then press Enter. Display the **Object** dialog box, click the **Create from File tab**, locate the PowerPoint file **w11E_Career_Counseling**, click **Insert**, and then click **OK**. Right-click the PowerPoint object, and then from the shortcut menu, point to **Presentation Object**, and then click **Edit**. Change the theme to **Facet**. **Center** the presentation object in the document, and then **Save** your changes.

4 From your student files, open the Excel file **w11E_Counselors**. **Save** the file to your **Word Chapter 11** folder as **Lastname_Firstname_11E_Counselors** Insert the file name in the footer. **Save** your changes, and then **Close** Excel.

5 In your Word document, to the right of the PowerPoint object, click to position the insertion point. **Insert** the **Lastname_Firstname_11E_Counselors** file as a linked file displayed as an icon with the modified caption **Counselor Needs** Double-click the inserted icon, click in cell B5, and then type **10** Press Enter, **Save** your changes, and then **Close** Excel. **Save** the changes in your Word document.

6 From your student files, open the Word file **w11E_Jobseeker_Survey**. **Save** the file to your **Word Chapter 11** folder as **Lastname_Firstname_11E_Jobseeker_Survey** Insert the file name in the footer. Click the **FILE tab**, and then click **Show All Properties**, In the **Tags** box, type **survey, linked** In the **Subject** box, type your course name and section number. If necessary, edit the author name to display your name. **Save** your changes, and then **Close** the document.

7 In your **Lastname_Firstname_11E_Counseling_Memo** document, on **Page 1**, click to position the insertion point to the right of the chart. Insert the file **Lastname_Firstname_11E_Jobseeker_Survey** as a linked file displayed as an icon with the modified caption **Survey** Below the chart, double-click the **Survey** icon. In the first paragraph, position the insertion point to the left of *Fair*, type **Job** and then press Spacebar. **Save** your changes, and then **Close** the *Survey* document.

8 Press Ctrl + Home. Click the **FILE tab**, and then click **Show All Properties**. In the **Tags** box, type **counseling, linked and embedded objects** In the **Subject** box, type your course name and section number. If necessary, edit the author name to display your name. **Save** your changes.

9 Print all three files—your two Word documents and the Excel file—or submit electronically as directed by your instructor. **Close** Word.

END | You have completed Project 11E

CONTENT-BASED ASSESSMENTS

Apply 11B skills from these Objectives:

3 Create Macros

4 Use Macros

5 Write a Procedure in VBA

In the following Mastering Word project, you will create macros to assist you with editing documents that will be sent to employers who are registered for the Collegiate Fair conducted by the Greater Baltimore Job Fair. Your completed documents will look similar to Figure 11.50.

PROJECT FILES

For Project 11F, you will need the following files:

New blank Word document
w11F_Collegiate_Fair
w11F_Recruiting_Tips

You will save your files as:

Lastname_Firstname_11F_Collegiate_Fair
Lastname_Firstname_11F_Recruiting_Tips
Lastname_Firstname_11F_Collegiate_Code

PROJECT RESULTS

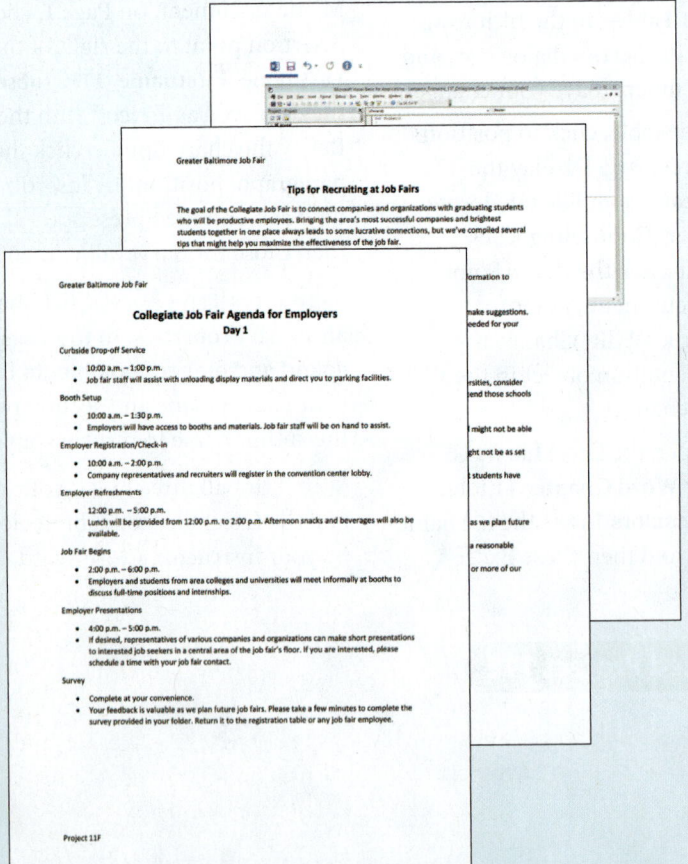

FIGURE 11.50

(Project 11F Collegiate Fair continues on the next page)

CONTENT-BASED ASSESSMENTS

1 Start Word. Locate and open the file **w11F_ Collegiate_Fair**. **Save** the file to your **Word Chapter 11** folder as a **Word Macro-Enabled Document** with the file name **Lastname_Firstname_11F_Collegiate_Fair** Display the **DEVELOPER tab**, and then change your **Macro Security** setting to **Disable all macros with notification**.

2 Display the **Record Macro** dialog box, and then in the **Macro name** box, type **Footer** Be sure the **Store macro in** box displays **All Documents (Normal.dotm)**. In the **Description** box, type **Inserts the project ID in the footer** Assign the **shortcut key** [Alt] + [Ctrl] + [J]. In recording mode, click the **INSERT tab**. In the **Header & Footer group**, click **Footer**, and then click **Edit Footer**. Press [Ctrl] + [A], press [Delete], and then type **Project 11F** Click **Close Header and Footer**, and then click **Stop Recording**. **Save** your changes.

3 Display the **Record Macro** dialog box, and then in the **Macro name** box, type **Header** Be sure the **Store macro in** box displays **All Documents (Normal.dotm)**. Click the **Button** icon, and then in the **Word Options** dialog box, **Add** the **Normal.NewMacros.Header** to the **Quick Access Toolbar**. Click **Modify**, and then under symbol, in the first row, click the third button—a blue circle containing a white i. In recording mode, click the **INSERT tab**, click **Header**, and then click **Edit Header**. Press [Ctrl] + [A], press [Delete], and then type **Greater Baltimore** Click **Close Header and Footer**. Click **Stop Recording**.

4 From your student files, open the file **w11F_ Recruiting_Tips**. **Save** the file to your **Word Chapter 11** folder as a **Word Macro-Enabled Document** with the file name **Lastname_Firstname_11F_Recruiting_Tips** Press [Ctrl] + [Alt] + [J]. Click the **FILE tab**, and then click **Show All Properties**. In the **Tags** box, type **tips, macro** In the **Subject** box, type your course name and section number. If necessary, edit the author name to display your name.

5 Display the **Macros** dialog box, select the **Header** macro, and then click **Edit**. Near the bottom of the **Header** macro code, position the insertion point to the right of *Baltimore*, press [Spacebar], and then type **Job Fair** Click **File**, and then click **Close and Return to Microsoft Word**. Press [Ctrl] + [Home]. On the **Quick Access Toolbar**, click the **Header** macro button. Select all the bulleted paragraphs, and then display the **Macros** dialog box. Click

the **Macros in arrow**, and then click **Word commands**. Under **Macro name**, locate and click **AdjustListIndents**, and then click **Run**. Change the **Bullet position** to **0.2"** and the **Text indent** to **0.4"**, and then click **OK**. **Save** your changes, and then **Close** the **Recruiting_Tips** document.

6 In your **Lastname_Firstname_11F_Collegiate_ Fair** document, on the **Quick Access Toolbar**, run the **Header** macro. **Save** your changes. Display the **Visual Basic Editor**. Display a new Word document. **Save** the document to your **Word Chapter 11** folder as **Lastname_ Firstname_11F_Collegiate_Code** Press [Alt] + [Ctrl] + [J] . Click the **FILE tab**, and then click **Show All Properties**. In the **Tags** box, type **collegiate fair, code** In the **Subject** box, type your course name and section number. If necessary, edit the author name to display your name. **Save** your changes.

7 Click the **INSERT tab**, and then in the **Illustrations group**, click **Screenshot**. In the **Available Windows** gallery, click **Screen Clipping**. Move the ⊞ pointer to the top left corner of your screen, select only the **Quick Access Toolbar**, and then paste the selected image in your document. Click to the right of the image, and then press [Enter]. Click the **INSERT tab**, in the **Illustrations group**, click **Screenshot**, and then in the **Available Windows** gallery, click the thumbnail of the **Visual Basic Editor** window. Press [Ctrl] + [Home]. **Save** your changes, and then **Close** the **Lastname_Firstname_11F_Collegiate_Code** document. **Close** the Visual Basic Editor.

8 In the **Lastname_Firstname_11F_Collegiate_Fair** document, click the **FILE tab**, and then click **Show All Properties**. In the **Tags** box, type **fair agenda, macros** In the **Subject** box, type your course name and section number. If necessary, edit the author name to display your name.

9 Display the **Macros** dialog box, click the **Macros in arrow**, and then click **All active templates and documents**. Delete the **Header** and **Footer** macros. From **Backstage** view, display the **Word Options** dialog box, click **Quick Access Toolbar**. On the right side of the window, click **Normal.NewMacros.Header**, click **Remove**, and then click **OK**. **Save** your changes, and then **Close** Word. If necessary, **Close** File Explorer.

10 Print your three documents or submit electronically as directed by your instructor.

END | You have completed Project 11F

CONTENT-BASED ASSESSMENTS

Mastering Word   Project 11G Catering

In the following Mastering Word project, you will use OLE to include objects in a letter to a caterer. The Greater Baltimore Job Fair provides luncheons and snacks to the employers attending the job fairs. You will create macros that will be used to increase your efficiency in creating documents to explain the job fair needs to the caterer. Your completed documents will look similar to Figure 11.51.

PROJECT FILES

For Project 11G, you will need the following files:

New blank Word document
w11G_Catering_Letter
w11G_Catering_Needs
w11G_Catering_Budget

You will save your files as:

Lastname_Firstname_11G_Catering_Letter
Lastname_Firstname_11G_Catering_Budget
Lastname_Firstname_11G_Catering_Code

PROJECT RESULTS

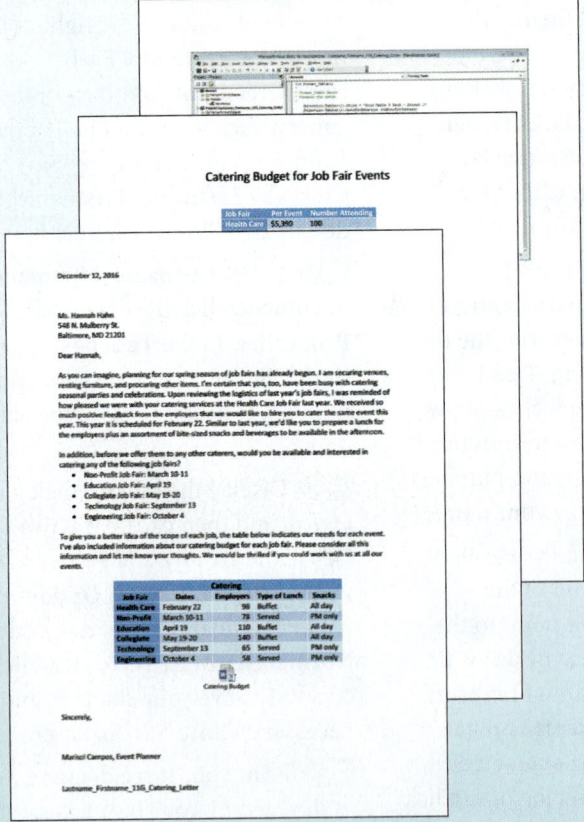

FIGURE 11.51

(Project 11G Catering continues on the next page)

Mastering Word Project 11G Catering (continued)

1 Start Word. Open the file **w11G_Catering_Letter**, and then **Save** it to your **Word Chapter 11** folder as a **Word Macro-Enabled Document** with the file name **Lastname_Firstname_11G_Catering_Letter** Insert the file name in the footer.

2 Open the Access file **w11G_Catering_Needs**, and click **Enable Content**. Open and then **Copy** the entire **Catering** table. **Close** Access. In your Word document, position the insertion point at the end of the paragraph that begins *To give you*, and then press Enter two times. **Paste** the table as **HTML Format**.

3 In the first cell of the table, click to position the insertion point. Display the **Record Macro** dialog box, and then in the **Macro name** box, type **Format_Table** Be sure the **Store macro in** box displays **All Documents (Normal.dotm)**. For the **Description**, type **Formats the table Assign** the shortcut key Alt + Ctrl + Q. **Close** the dialog box. In recording mode, with the insertion point in the table, click the **TABLE TOOLS DESIGN tab**, and then in the **Table Styles group**, click **More**. Under **Grid Tables**, click **Grid Table 5 Dark – Accent 1**—in the fifth row, the second style. Click the **LAYOUT tab**, in the **Cell Size group**, click **AutoFit**, and then click **AutoFit Contents**. In the **Table group**, click **Properties**. In the **Table Properties** dialog box, under **Alignment**, click **Center**, and then click **OK**. Click the **DEVELOPER tab**, and then in the **Code group**, click **Stop Recording**. **Save** your changes.

4 From your student files, open the file **w11G_Catering_Budget**. **Save** the file to your **Word Chapter 11** folder as a **Word Macro-Enabled Document** with the file name **Lastname_Firstname_11G_Catering_Budget** Insert the file name in the footer. Click the **FILE tab**, and then click **Show All Properties**. In the **Tags** box, type **budget, macro** In the **Subject** box, type your course name and section number. If necessary, edit the author name to display your name. Position the insertion point in the first cell of the table, and then run the **Format_Table** macro. **Save** your changes, and then **Close** the document.

5 In the **Lastname_Firstname_11G_Catering_Letter** document, below the table, position the insertion point in the first blank paragraph. **Insert** the **Lastname_Firstname_11G_Catering_Budget** file as a linked file displayed as an icon with the modified caption **Catering Budget** Select the icon and apply **Center**. Double-click the icon, and then change the **Number Attending** the *Health Care* Job Fair to **100** Press Ctrl + Home. **Save** your changes, and then **Close** the **Lastname_Firstname_11G_Catering_Budget** file.

6 Press Ctrl + Home. Display the **Visual Basic Editor**. Display a new Word document. **Save** the document to your **Word Chapter 11** folder as **Lastname_Firstname_11G_Catering_Code** Insert the file name in the footer. Click the **FILE tab**, and then click **Show All Properties**. In the **Tags** box, type **catering needs, code** In the **Subject** box, type your course name and section number. If necessary, edit the author name to display your name. **Save** your changes.

7 Click the **INSERT tab**, in the **Illustrations group**, click **Screenshot**, and then in the **Available Windows** gallery, click the thumbnail of the **Visual Basic Editor** window. Press Ctrl + Home. **Save** your changes, and then **Close** the **Lastname_Firstname_11G_Catering_Code** document. **Close** the Visual Basic Editor.

8 In the **Lastname_Firstname_11G_Catering_Letter** document, click the **FILE tab**, and then click **Show All Properties**. In the **Tags** box, type **letter, linked, macro** In the **Subject** box, type your course name and section number. If necessary, edit the author name to display your name. Display the **Macros** dialog box, and then delete the **Format_Table** macro. **Close** Word, and then if necessary, **Close** File Explorer.

9 Print your three documents or submit electronically as directed by your instructor.

END | You have completed Project 11G

CONTENT-BASED ASSESSMENTS

Apply a combination of the **11A** and **11B** skills.

GO! Fix It   Project 11H Employer Letter   **Online**

GO! Make It   Project 11I Engineering Fair   **Online**

GO! Solve It   Project 11J Job Support   **Online**

GO! Solve It   Project 11K Fair Attendance

PROJECT FILES

For Project 11K, you will need the following files:

New blank Word document
w11K_Attendance_Memo
w11K_Increased_Attendance
w11K_Attendance

You will save your files as:

Lastname_Firstname_11K_Attendance_Memo
Lastname_Firstname_11K_Attendance
Lastname_Firstname_11K_Attendance_Code

Open the Excel file **w11K_Attendance** and save it to your **Word Chapter 11** folder as **Lastname_Firstname_11K_Attendance** Insert the file name in the footer and add appropriate document properties. Open the file **w11K_Attendance_Memo** and save it to your **Word Chapter 11** folder as a macro-enabled document with the file name **Lastname_Firstname_11K_Attendance_Memo** Insert the file name in the footer. Create a macro that inserts the text **Greater Baltimore Job Fair** center-aligned in the header. Assign the macro to the Quick Access Toolbar as a button. Embed the **w11K_Increased_Attendance** PowerPoint file and link the **Lastname_Firstname_11K_Attendance** file as an icon at the appropriate places in the memo. In the Excel file, change the value for *2016 Attendance* to **8,732** Format the document to create a professional appearance. Create a new Word document and save it to your **Word Chapter 11** folder as **Lastname_Firstname_11K_Attendance_Code** Insert the file name in the footer and run the Header macro. Paste images of the Quick Access Toolbar and macro code in the document. Add appropriate document properties in both Word documents. Delete the macro you created, and then print both Word documents and the Excel file or submit all three files as directed by your instructor.

(Project 11K Fair Attendance continues on the next page)

GO! Solve It | Project 11K Fair Attendance (continued)

Performance Level

Performance Element	Exemplary: You consistently applied the relevant skills	Proficient: You sometimes, but not always, applied the relevant skills	Developing: You rarely or never applied the relevant skills
Create a macro	The macro is created and displays as a button on the Quick Access Toolbar.	The macro is created but does not display as a button on the Quick Access Toolbar.	A macro is not created.
Embed a file	The file is embedded at an appropriate location.	The file is embedded but is at an inappropriate location.	The file is not embedded.
Link and edit a file	The file is linked, displays as an icon, and is edited.	The file is linked but does not display as an icon or is not edited.	The file is not linked.
Format document	Formatting is attractive and appropriate.	Adequate formatting but difficult to read or unattractive.	Either there is no formatting or it is inadequate.
Paste images	Both images are pasted correctly.	Only one image is pasted correctly.	No images are pasted in the document.

END | You have completed Project 11K

OUTCOMES-BASED ASSESSMENTS

RUBRIC

The following outcomes-based assessments are *open-ended assessments*. That is, there is no specific correct result; your result will depend on your approach to the information provided. Make *Professional Quality* your goal. Use the following scoring rubric to guide you in *how* to approach the problem and then to evaluate *how well* your approach solves the problem.

The *criteria*—Software Mastery, Content, Format and Layout, and Process—represent the knowledge and skills you have gained that you can apply to solving the problem. The *levels of performance*—Professional Quality, Approaching Professional Quality, or Needs Quality Improvements—help you and your instructor evaluate your result.

	Your completed project is of Professional Quality if you:	Your completed project is Approaching Professional Quality if you:	Your completed project Needs Quality Improvements if you:
1-Software Mastery	Choose and apply the most appropriate skills, tools, and features and identify efficient methods to solve the problem.	Choose and apply some appropriate skills, tools, and features, but not in the most efficient manner.	Choose inappropriate skills, tools, or features, or are inefficient in solving the problem.
2-Content	Construct a solution that is clear and well organized, contains content that is accurate, appropriate to the audience and purpose, and is complete. Provide a solution that contains no errors in spelling, grammar, or style.	Construct a solution in which some components are unclear, poorly organized, inconsistent, or incomplete. Misjudge the needs of the audience. Have some errors in spelling, grammar, or style, but the errors do not detract from comprehension.	Construct a solution that is unclear, incomplete, or poorly organized; contains some inaccurate or inappropriate content; and contains many errors in spelling, grammar, or style. Do not solve the problem.
3-Format & Layout	Format and arrange all elements to communicate information and ideas, clarify function, illustrate relationships, and indicate relative importance.	Apply appropriate format and layout features to some elements, but not others. Overuse features, causing minor distraction.	Apply format and layout that does not communicate information or ideas clearly. Do not use format and layout features to clarify function, illustrate relationships, or indicate relative importance. Use available features excessively, causing distraction.
4-Process	Use an organized approach that integrates planning, development, self-assessment, revision, and reflection.	Demonstrate an organized approach in some areas, but not others; or, use an insufficient process of organization throughout.	Do not use an organized approach to solve the problem.

OUTCOMES-BASED ASSESSMENTS

Apply a combination of the 11A and 11B skills.

GO! Think   Project 11L Health Fair

PROJECT FILES

For Project 11L, you will need the following files:

Three new blank Word documents

You will save your files as:

Lastname_Firstname_11L_Health_Flyer
Lastname_Firstname_11L_Health_Letter
Lastname_Firstname_11L_Health_Code

Build from Scratch

The Greater Baltimore Job Fair conducts a health care job fair every year. The organization is located at 314 North Street, Baltimore, MD 21201. Search the Internet for the types of job opportunities that are available for health care careers. Save a new macro-enabled document as **Lastname_Firstname_11L_Health_Flyer** Create a flyer indicating the types of job recruiters that will be attending the fair. Use fictitious information for the date, time, and location. Create a macro for job fair contact information that will run in all documents. Create an AutoClose macro that will automatically insert the date and time in the header—only in this document. Format the document to create a professional appearance, insert the file name in the footer, and add appropriate document properties. Save a second, new macro-enabled document as **Lastname_Firstname_11L_Health_Letter** Create a letter to be sent to the local college—use fictitious information—asking that copies of the flyer be made available to students. Run the job fair's contact information macro in a letterhead and use your own name in the signature line. Insert a link to your flyer, displaying it as an icon. Insert the file name in the footer and add appropriate document properties. Save a third blank document as **Lastname_Firstname_11L_Health_Code** Insert images of the contact information and AutoClose macro codes, insert the file name in the footer, and add appropriate document properties. Delete the macros you created. Print all three documents or submit electronically as directed by your instructor.

END | You have completed Project 11L

OUTCOMES-BASED ASSESSMENTS

Build from Scratch

GO! Think   Project 11M Jobseeker Tips   **Online**

Build from Scratch

You and GO!   Project 11N Personal Letterhead   **Online**

Integrating Word with PowerPoint and Modifying Document Components

GO! to Work
Video W12

12

WORD 2013

PROJECT 12A

OUTCOMES
Integrate Word with PowerPoint.

OBJECTIVES

1. Integrate Word with PowerPoint
2. Modify a PowerPoint Presentation
3. Create a Table of Authorities

PROJECT 12B

OUTCOMES
Modify the document layout and format graphic and text elements.

OBJECTIVES

4. Modify the Document Layout
5. Format Graphic and Text Elements

In This Chapter

Microsoft Office 2013 is an integrated application suite. This integration enables you to use each application for its specified purpose and then combine components for a final result. For example, you can create a table in Access and then use that table to perform a mail merge in Word. You can create a table of authorities in a legal document by marking citations. You can customize Word in a variety of ways—for example, change the paper size, apply advanced formatting features to text, and modify graphic and text elements—to create a professional-looking document that meets your exact specifications.

The projects in this chapter relate to **Magical Park Corporation**, which operates 15 regional theme parks across the United States, Mexico, and Canada. Park types include traditional theme parks, water parks, and wildlife adventure parks. This year the company will launch three of its new "Imagination Parks" where attractions combine fun and the discovery of math and science information, and where teens and adults enjoy the free Friday night concerts. Magical Park Corporation also operates family-friendly resort hotels on many of their properties that include exceptional pools and championship golf courses.

PROJECT ACTIVITIES

In Activities 12.01 through 12.07, you will prepare an outline in Word to be used as a foundation for a PowerPoint presentation. After creating the presentation, you will create a handout in Word that includes thumbnails of each slide and a place for notes. At the next marketing meeting, Henry Nguyen, Marketing Vice President of Magical Park Corporation, would like to discuss the results of a survey of visitors to the company's animal parks. You will create a PowerPoint presentation and handouts for the meeting. Additionally, you add a table of authorities to a legal document that will be discussed at the meeting. Your completed files will look similar to Figure 12.1.

PROJECT FILES

For Project 12A, you will need the following files:

w12A_Planning_Outline
w12A_Frog
w12A_Monkey
w12A_Park_Brief

You will save your files as:

Lastname_Firstname_12A_Planning_Outline
Lastname_Firstname_12A_Planning_Presentation
Lastname_Firstname_12A_Planning_Handout
Lastname_Firstname_12A_Park_Brief

PROJECT RESULTS

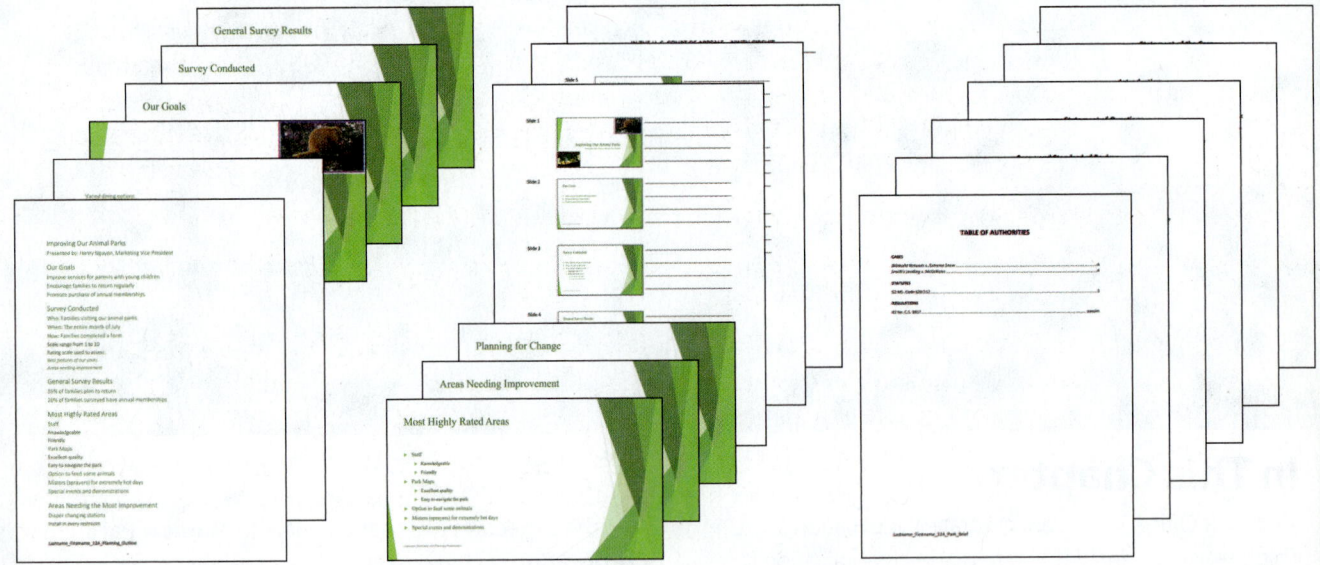

FIGURE 12.1 Project 12A Planning Presentation

- Tap an item to click it.
- Press and hold for a few seconds to right-click; release when the information or command displays.
- Touch the screen with two or more fingers and then pinch together to zoom in or stretch your fingers apart to zoom out.
- Slide your finger on the screen to scroll—slide left to scroll right and slide right to scroll left.
- Slide to rearrange—similar to dragging with a mouse.
- Swipe from edge: from right to display charms; from left to expose open apps, snap apps, or close apps; from top or bottom to show commands or close an app.
- Swipe to select—slide an item a short distance with a quick movement to select an item and bring up commands, if any.

Objective 1   Integrate Word with PowerPoint

Video W12-1

An *outline* provides a way to organize the contents of a document in a structured manner. Previously you used Outline view to create a master document and subdocuments. Outlines created in Word can also be used to create slides in PowerPoint. In Outline view, each paragraph is treated as a separate topic, or level, in the outline. Each topic is assigned either an *outline level* or is identified as body text. An outline level defines the position of the paragraph in relation to all topics in the document and is formatted with a corresponding heading style. You can assign up to nine levels in an outline.

Activity 12.01   Creating an Outline in Outline View

In this activity, you will apply outline levels to existing paragraphs and move paragraphs in order to create an outline.

1 Start Word. From your student files, open the file **w12A_Planning_Outline**. Navigate to the location where you are saving your files for this chapter, and then create a new folder named **Word Chapter 12** Using your own name, **Save** the document to your **Word Chapter 12** folder as **Lastname_Firstname_12A_Planning_Outline** Insert the file name in the footer and display rulers and formatting marks.

2 Click the **VIEW tab**, and then in the **Views group**, click the **Outline** button.

All paragraphs are preceded by an *outline symbol*—a small gray circle that identifies heading and body text paragraphs in an outline.

3 In the first paragraph, click the outline symbol to select the paragraph. On the **OUTLINING tab**, in the **Outline Tools group**, click the **Outline Level arrow** [Body Text ▾], and then click **Level 1**. Compare your screen with Figure 12.2.

The paragraph is designated as Level 1 and is formatted with the Heading 1 style—not visible in Outline view. A *plus outline symbol* displays to the left of the paragraph indicating there are subordinate heading or body text paragraphs.

FIGURE 12.2

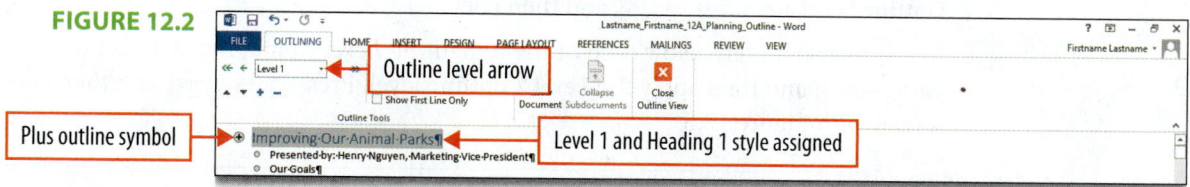

4 In the third paragraph, click the outline symbol to select the paragraph. On the **OUTLINING tab**, in the **Outline Tools group**, click **Promote to Heading 1** .

The paragraph is designated as Level 1and formatted with the Heading 1 style.

5 On the **OUTLINING tab**, in the **Close group**, click **Close Outline View**. Compare your screen with Figure 12.3.

The paragraphs designated as Level 1 display with the Heading 1 style. In Print Layout view, however, the outline symbols do not display.

ANOTHER WAY Click the Print Layout button on the status bar.

FIGURE 12.3

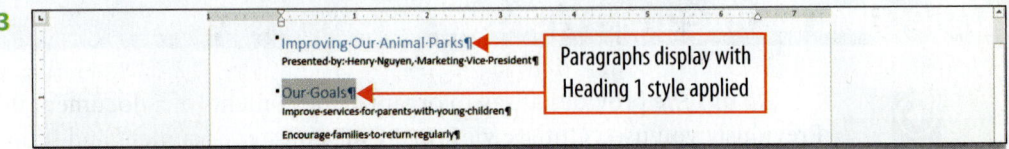

6 Click the **VIEW tab**, and then in the **Views group**, click **Outline**. Using the technique you practiced, assign **Level 1** to the paragraphs *Survey Conducted*, *Most Highly Rated Areas*, *Areas Needing the Most Improvement*, *Planning for Change*, and *General Survey Results*. Deselect the text, and then compare your screen with Figure 12.4.

FIGURE 12.4

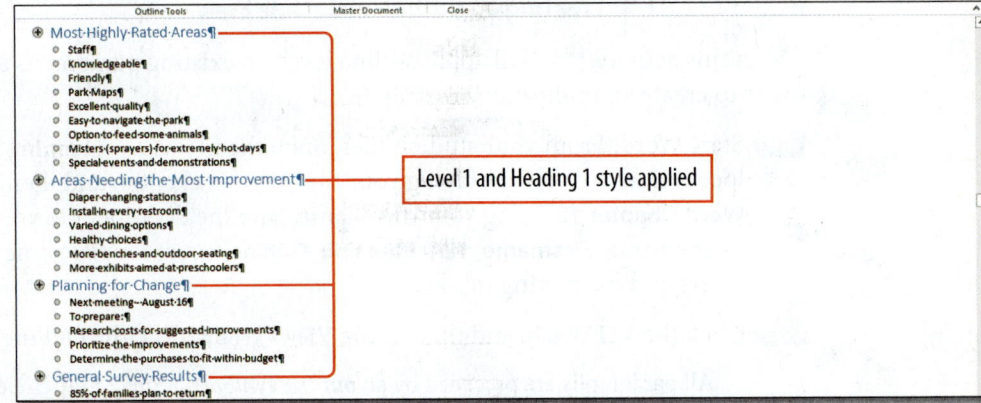

7 In the second paragraph, click the outline symbol, click the **Outline Level arrow** Body Text, and then click **Level 2**.

The paragraph is indented, designated as Level 2, and the Heading 2 style is applied. The *minus outline symbol* displays indicating there are no subordinate heading or body text paragraphs. Paragraphs are indented based on the assigned outline level.

8 Below the paragraph *Our Goals*, drag to select all three body text paragraphs. Click the **Outline Level arrow** Body Text, and then click **Level 2**.

9 In a similar manner, below each of the remaining *Level 1* paragraphs, select the body text paragraphs, and then apply the **Level 2** outline level. Press Ctrl + Home, and then compare your screen with Figure 12.5.

FIGURE 12.5

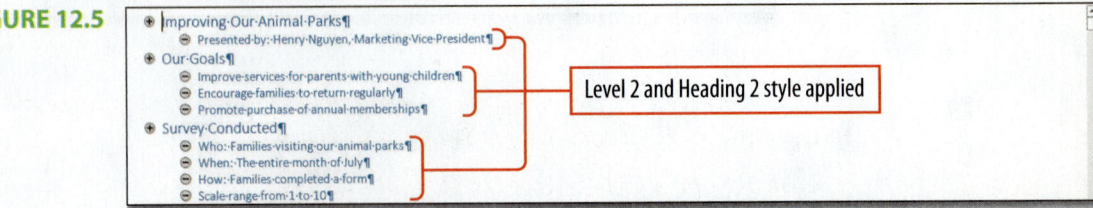

10 ▶ Below the *Survey Conducted* heading, select the two paragraphs that begin *Scale range* and *Rating scale*. On the **OUTLINING tab**, in the **Outline Tools group**, click **Demote** →. Compare your screen with Figure 12.6.

The Demote button assigns a paragraph to a lower level. In this case, the paragraphs are assigned a Level 3 outline level and the Heading 3 style is applied.

FIGURE 12.6

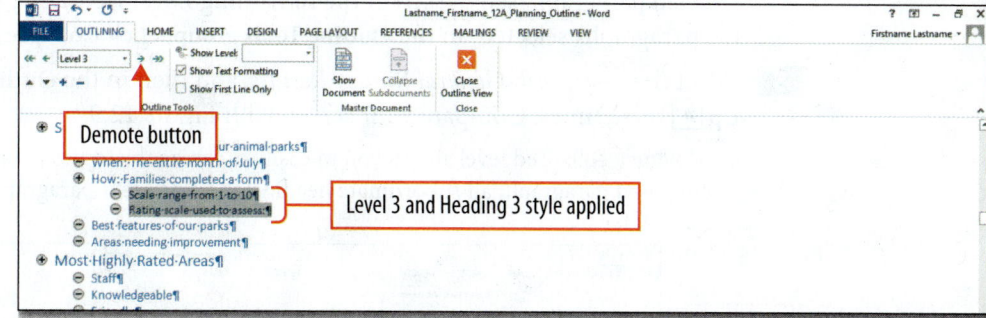

11 ▶ Below the paragraph that begins *Rating scale*, select the next two paragraphs, and then click **Demote** → two times.

The paragraphs are assigned a Level 4 outline level and the Heading 4 style is applied.

12 ▶ Below the paragraph *Staff*, select the next five paragraphs, and then click **Demote** →.

13 ▶ Select the paragraph *Park Maps*, and then in the **Outline Tools group**, click **Promote** ←. Compare your screen with Figure 12.7.

The Promote button assigns a paragraph to a higher level. In this case, the *Park Maps* paragraph is assigned a Level 2 outline level.

FIGURE 12.7

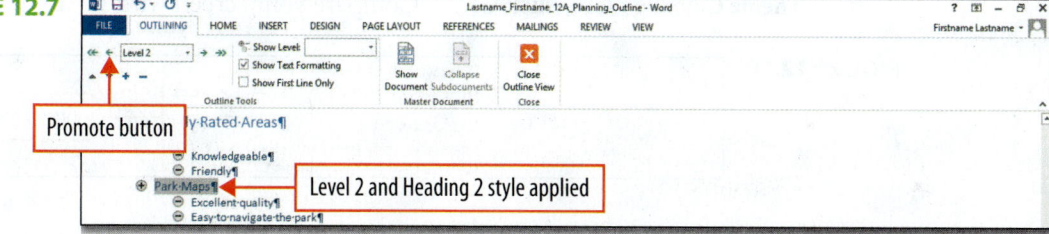

14 ▶ Assign a **Level 3** outline level to the paragraphs that begin *Install, Healthy, Research, Prioritize,* and *Determine*. **Save** 🖫 your changes.

Activity 12.02 | Collapsing and Expanding Outline Levels

1 ▶ In the **Outline Tools group**, above *Show Text Formatting*, click the **Show Level arrow**, and then click **Level 2**.

When you select a specific level, only text formatted with the designated level or a higher level displays. In this case, only text assigned Level 1 and Level 2 displays. All other text in the document is hidden.

2 ▶ In the **Outline Tools group**, click the **Show Level arrow**, and then click **All Levels** to display the entire document.

3 ▶ Locate the paragraph *Survey Conducted*, and then double-click the **plus outline symbol** to collapse the level. Compare your screen with Figure 12.8.

Collapsing an outline level hides all subordinate heading and body text paragraphs.

FIGURE 12.8

Improve·services·for·parents·with·young·children¶
Encourage·families·to·return·regularly¶
Promote·purchase·of·annual·me
Survey·Conducted¶ ← Collapsed paragraph
Most·Highly·Rated·Areas¶
  Staff¶

4 ▶ Drag to select the paragraph *Most Highly Rated Areas*, press and hold Ctrl, and then below the selected paragraph, select each of the remaining Level 1 paragraphs in the document. With the paragraphs selected, in the **Outline Tools group**, click **Collapse** [−].

5 ▶ Select the paragraph *General Survey Results*, and then in the **Outline Tools group**, click **Move Up** [▲] three times. Compare your screen with Figure 12.9.

> Moving a collapsed level allows you to easily organize the topics in an outline. When you move a collapsed paragraph, all subordinate heading and body text paragraphs are also moved.

FIGURE 12.9

Move Up button

Promote·purchase·of·annual·memberships¶
Survey·Conducted¶
General·Survey·Results¶ ← Paragraph moved
Most·Highly·Rated·Areas¶
Areas·Needing·the·Most·Improvement¶
Planning·for·Change¶

6 ▶ Deselect the paragraph, and then press Ctrl + Home. On the **OUTLINING tab**, in the **Close group**, click **Close Outline View**.

> Although paragraphs were collapsed in Outline view, all text displays in Print Layout view—the current view.

7 ▶ Click the **DESIGN tab**. In the **Document Formatting group**, click **Colors** [▦], and then in the **Theme Colors** gallery, click **Green**. Compare your screen with Figure 12.10.

FIGURE 12.10

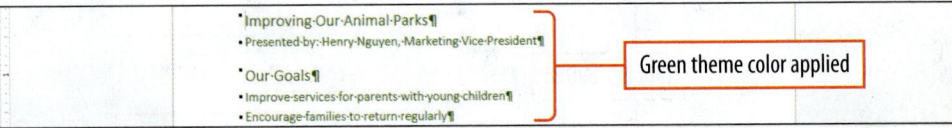

Improving·Our·Animal·Parks¶
Presented·by:·Henry·Nguyen,·Marketing·Vice·President¶

Our·Goals¶
Improve·services·for·parents·with·young·children¶
Encourage·families·to·return·regularly¶

Green theme color applied

8 ▶ Click the **FILE tab**, and then click **Show All Properties**. In the **Tags** box, type **planning presentation, outline** In the **Subject** box, type your course name and section number. If necessary, edit the author name to display your name.

9 ▶ Save [💾] your changes, and then **Close** Word.

Activity 12.03 | Using a Word Outline to Create a PowerPoint Presentation

Because Microsoft Office is an integrated suite of programs, you can open a Word outline in PowerPoint to automatically create slides based on the levels in the outline. The outline levels are used to determine the slide titles and bulleted items.

1 ▶ Start PowerPoint. Near the bottom left of your screen, click **Open Other Presentations**. Double-click **Computer** to display the **Open** dialog box. Navigate to your **Word Chapter 12** folder. At the bottom of the **Open** dialog box, click the **All PowerPoint Presentations arrow**, and then click **All Outlines**. Notice that your Lastname_Firstname_12A_Planning_Outline displays in the file list box. Compare your screen with Figure 12.11.

> By default, only existing PowerPoint files display in the Open dialog box. Because your outline is a Word document, it is necessary to change the setting to All Outlines.

FIGURE 12.11

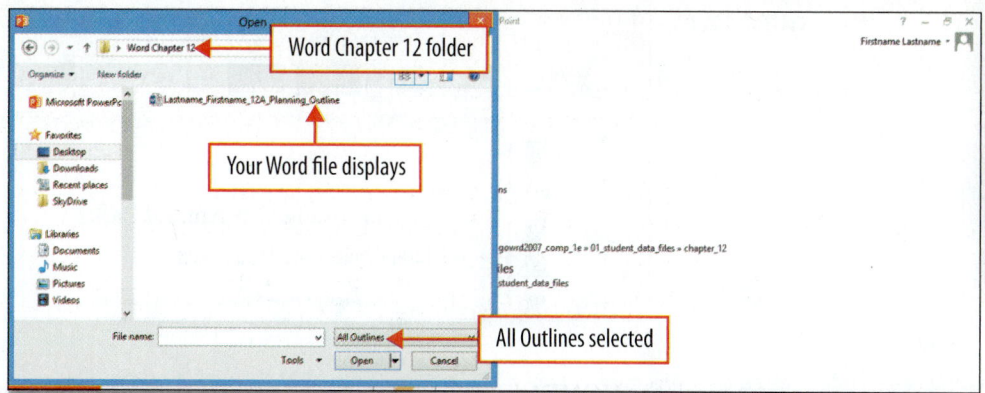

Word Chapter 12 folder

Your Word file displays

All Outlines selected

2 Click to select **Lastname_Firstname_12A_Planning_Outline**, and then click **Open.** Compare your screen with Figure 12.12.

Seven slides are created based on the outline levels in the outline. Heading 1 style paragraphs display as the title for each slide. Subordinate paragraphs display as bulleted items. The Slide pane displays a large image of the active slide. On the left, slide thumbnails display miniature images of each slide in the presentation.

FIGURE 12.12

Slide thumbnail

Improving Our Animal Parks

• Presented by: Henry Nguyen, Marketing Vice President

Slide pane

More Knowledge | **Using Body Text in an Outline**

When you use a Word outline to create slides in PowerPoint, heading styles must be applied to all paragraphs. Body text paragraphs will not display in the slides.

---

3 Press F12. In the **Save As** dialog box, navigate to your **Word Chapter 12** folder. Using your own name, **Save** the file as **Lastname_Firstname_12A_Planning_Presentation**

PowerPoint files are saved with the default file extension *.pptx*.

Objective 2 | Modify a PowerPoint Presentation

Video W12-2

Many features that you use to edit a Word document, such as deleting text and inserting pictures, can be used in a similar manner to modify a PowerPoint presentation.

Activity 12.04 | Modifying a PowerPoint Presentation

In this activity you will change the theme, change the slide *layout*, delete text, and insert pictures. The layout refers to the placement and arrangement of the text and graphic elements on a slide.

1 Click the **DESIGN tab**, and then in the **Themes group**, click **More**. In the **Themes** gallery, under **Office**, in the first row, click **Facet**. Compare your screen with Figure 12.13.

The themes available in Word also exist in other Microsoft Office applications. Recall that you changed the theme color to *Green* in your Word document. The slides are formatted with the *Facet* theme to coordinate the background, bullet styles, and title with the existing text.

FIGURE 12.13

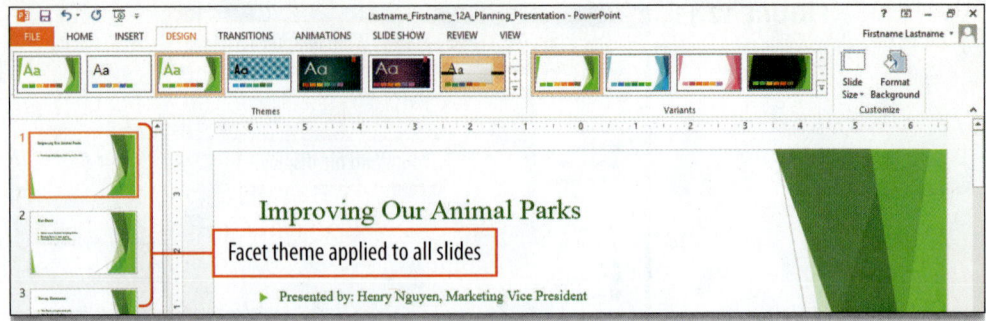

2 ► Click the **HOME tab**, and then in the **Slides group**, click the **Layout arrow** to display the **Slide Layout** gallery. Compare your screen with Figure 12.14.

> Fifteen slide arrangements display. By default, when you use a Word outline to create slides in PowerPoint, the Title and Text slide layout is applied to all slides.

FIGURE 12.14

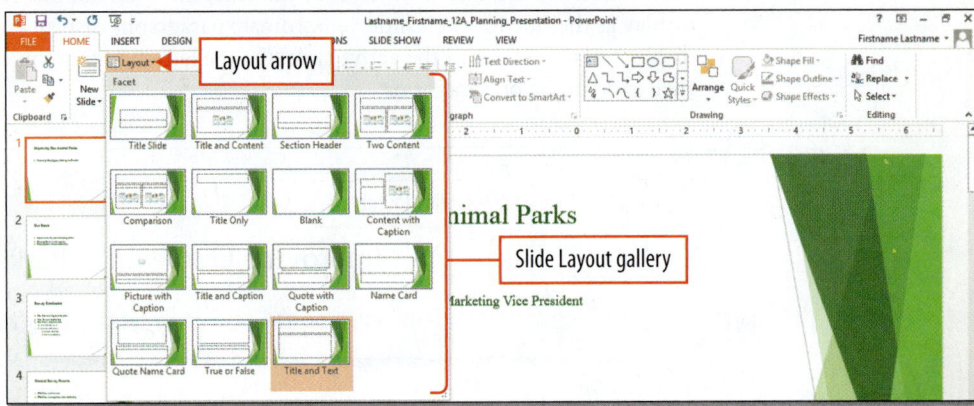

3 ► With **Slide 1** displayed in the **Slide** pane, in the **Slide Layout** gallery, click the first option—**Title Slide**. Compare your screen with Figure 12.15.

> It is good practice to begin each presentation with a title slide. The title slide for the Facet theme displays the main title—the Heading 1 style—near the middle of the slide, and the subtitle—the Heading 2 style—displays below the main title.

FIGURE 12.15

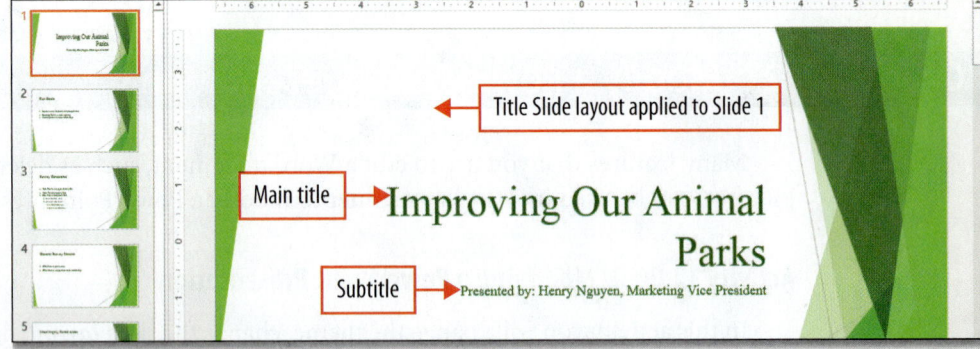

4 ► On **Slide 1**, select the text *Improving Our Animal Parks*. On the mini toolbar, change the **Font Size** to **44**. Compare your screen with Figure 12.16.

> Content placeholders are used to display all text on slides.

FIGURE 12.16

Content placeholder

Selected text

5 Click the thumbnail for **Slide 4**. In the **Slide** pane, with **Slide 4** displayed, double-click the text *surveyed*, and then press ⎯Delete⎯. In a similar manner, display **Slide 6**, and then in the title, delete the text *the Most*.

6 **Save** 🖫 your changes, and then compare your screen with Figure 12.17.

FIGURE 12.17

Title

7 Click the thumbnail for **Slide 1**. Click the **INSERT tab**, and then in the **Images group**, click **Pictures**.

8 In the **Insert Picture** dialog box, navigate to your student files for this chapter, click **w12A_Frog**, and then click **Insert**.

9 Click the **FORMAT tab**, and then in the **Size group**, change the **Shape Height** to **2.5"**. Position the picture so that the bottom left corner of the picture is aligned with the bottom left corner of the slide. Click in a blank area to deselect the picture, and then compare your screen with Figure 12.18.

FIGURE 12.18

Bottom left corner of Slide 1

Frog picture

10 Using the same technique, navigate to your student files, and then Insert the picture **w12A_Monkey**. On the **FORMAT tab**, in the **Size group**, change the **Shape Height** to **2.5"**. Position the picture so that the top right corner of the picture is aligned with the top right corner of the slide. Deselect the picture, and then compare your screen with Figure 12.19.

FIGURE 12.19

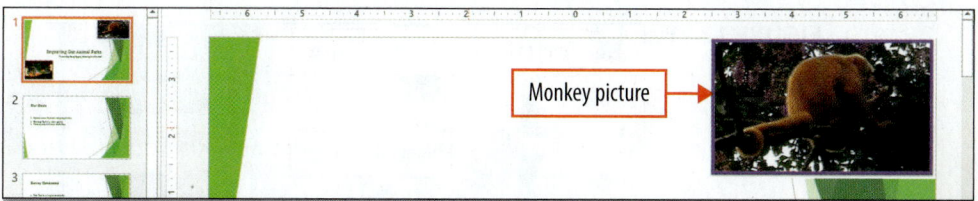

Monkey picture

11 ▶ Click the **INSERT tab**, and then in the **Text group**, click **Header & Footer**. In the **Header and Footer** dialog box, on the **Slide tab**, select the **Footer** check box. In the **Footer** box, type **Lastname_Firstname_12A_Planning_Presentation** Select the **Don't show on title slide** check box, and then click **Apply to All**.

> Unlike Word, PowerPoint does not provide the option to insert the file name using the Document Info command. The Header and Footer dialog box allows you to select the slides on which you want the footer to display. In this case, the footer will display on all slides except the title slide.

12 ▶ Click the thumbnail for **Slide 2**, and then compare your screen with Figure 12.20.

FIGURE 12.20

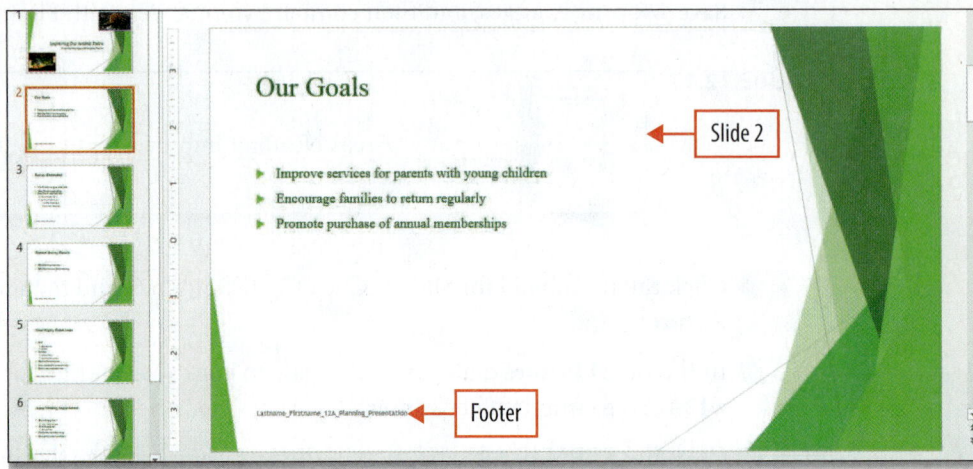

13 ▶ Click the thumbnail for **Slide 1**. Click the **FILE tab**, and then click **Show All Properties**. In the **Tags** box, type **presentation, planning** In the **Subject** box, type your course name and section number. If necessary, edit the author name to display your name. **Save** 🖫 your changes.

Activity 12.05 | Publishing a PowerPoint Presentation in Word

Any PowerPoint presentation can be used to create a corresponding *handout* in Word. A handout is a document that is given to an audience to accompany a lecture. The handout may include thumbnails of slides, a text-only outline, and an area displaying the presenter's notes or blank lines for the participant to enter notes.

1 ▶ Click the **FILE tab** to display **Backstage** view. Click **Export**, and then click **Create Handouts**.

2 ▶ Under **Create Handouts in Microsoft Word**, click **Create Handouts**, and then compare your screen with Figure 12.21.

> The Send to Microsoft Word dialog box displays, allowing the user to select the PowerPoint elements to include in the handout.

FIGURE 12.21

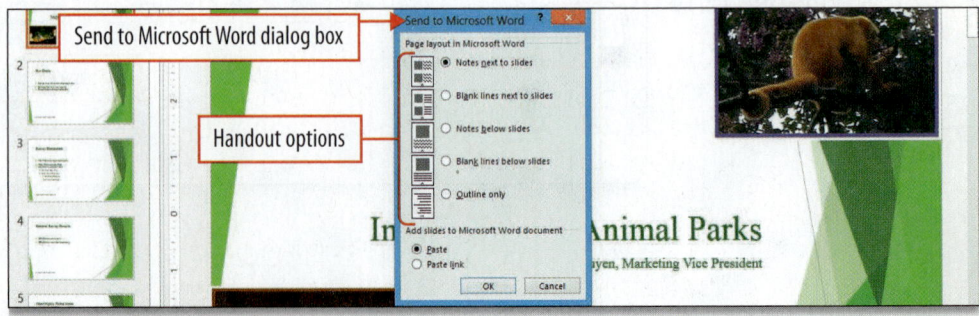

3 In the **Send to Microsoft Word** dialog box, under **Page layout in Microsoft Word**, click to select the **Blank lines next to slides** option, and then click **OK**.

4 On the taskbar, click the **Word** icon ![W] to display the newly created Word document, and then compare your screen with Figure 12.22. If necessary, on the **LAYOUT tab**, in the **Table group**, select the **View Gridlines** check box.

The Word document contains three pages and includes a table with three columns and seven rows. The first column displays the number of each slide in a separate cell. The second column displays a thumbnail of each slide, and the third column displays blank lines in each cell.

FIGURE 12.22

5 Press F12 to display the **Save As** dialog box. Navigate to your **Word Chapter 12** folder, and then using your own name, **Save** the file as **Lastname_Firstname_12A_Planning_Handout** Insert the file name in the footer.

6 In the first row of the table, in the third cell, select the first three lines, and then press Delete.

7 In a similar manner, in the third column, delete the first three lines from each of the remaining six cells.

8 On **Page 1**, point slightly outside of the upper left corner of the table to display the **Table Move Handle** ![⊞]. With the ![pointer] pointer displayed, click the **Table Move Handle** ![⊞] to select the entire table. Click the **LAYOUT tab**, and then in the **Cell Size group**, change the **Height** to **1.8"**. Compare your screen with Figure 12.23.

The handout can be modified to suit your purposes. In this case, you have deleted blank lines and reduced the row height to create a two-page handout.

FIGURE 12.23

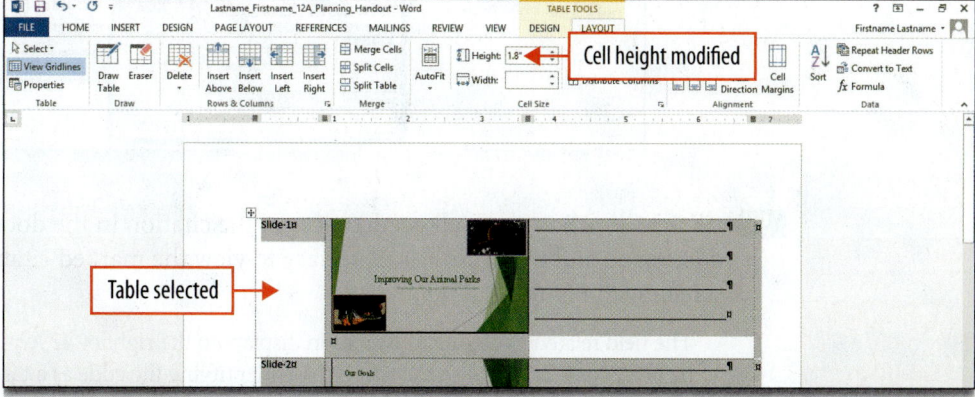

9 Press Ctrl + Home. Click the **FILE tab**, and then click **Show All Properties**. In the **Tags** box, type **planning presentation, handout** In the **Subject** box, type your course name and section number. If necessary, edit the author name to display your name. **Save** ![save] your changes, and then from **Backstage** view, **Close** the document but leave Word open.

10 On the taskbar, click the **PowerPoint** icon ![P]. With your PowerPoint presentation displayed, **Save** ![save] your changes, and then **Close** ![x] PowerPoint.

Video W12-3

A *table of authorities*, which is similar to a table of contents, is a list of all the references in a legal document and the page numbers where the references occur.

Activity 12.06 | Creating a Table of Authorities

In this activity you will create a table of authorities based on the *legal citations* in the document. A legal citation is a reference to an authoritative document, such as a regulation, a statute, or a case. For purposes of this instruction, you are using a document that is a partial example of a legal brief related to trademark infringement. All citations in the document are fictitious.

1 In Word, from your student files, open the file **w12A_Park_Brief**. Press F12, and then **Save** the document to your **Word Chapter 12** folder as **Lastname_Firstname_12A_Park_Brief** Insert the file name in the footer.

2 Scroll to the top of **Page 2**, and then take a moment to read the second paragraph.

The legal citation *42 Ne. C.S. §917* refers to a regulation. The legal citation *52 MS. Code §29.512* references a statute.

3 In the second paragraph, select the text *42 Ne. C.S. §917*. Be careful not to select the spaces before and after the text. Click the **REFERENCES tab**, and then in the **Table of Authorities group**, click **Mark Citation** to display the **Mark Citation** dialog box.

4 In the **Mark Citation** dialog box, under **Selected text**, notice that your selected text displays. Click the **Category arrow**, and then click **Regulations**. Compare your screen with Figure 12.24.

It is important to designate the type of citation you are marking so that the citation displays under the correct heading in the table of authorities.

FIGURE 12.24

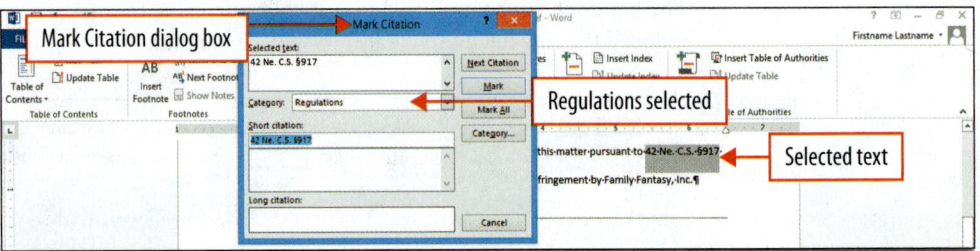

5 Click **Mark All** to mark all occurrences of the citation in the document. Click in the document, and then scroll as necessary to view the marked citation on **Page 2**. Compare your screen with Figure 12.25.

The field related to the marked citation displays to the right of *42 Ne. C.S. §917*. The field is surrounded by braces and begins with the letters *TA*—identifying the code as a table of authorities field.

FIGURE 12.25

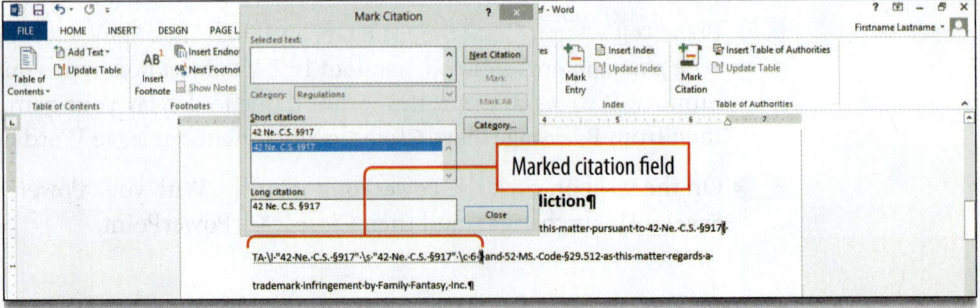

6 ▶ On **Page 3**, select the text *SkiWorld Network v. Extreme Snow.* Click in the **Mark Citation** dialog box, click the **Category arrow**, and then click **Cases**. Click **Mark**. Click in the document, select the text *Smith's Landing v. McCallister.* Click the **Mark Citation** dialog box, verify **Cases** is selected, and then click **Mark**. **Close** the **Mark Citation** dialog box.

7 ▶ At the bottom of **Page 1**, position the insertion point to the right of the date, and then press Ctrl + Enter two times. At the top of **Page 2**, click to position the insertion point to the left of the page break. Type **TABLE OF AUTHORITIES** and then press Enter two times. Select the text you just typed, and then on the mini toolbar, change the **Font Size** to 16 and apply **Bold**. Press Ctrl + E.

8 ▶ Click to position the insertion point to the left of the page break. On the **REFERENCES tab**, in the **Table of Authorities group**, click **Insert Table of Authorities**.

9 ▶ In the **Table of Authorities** dialog box, under **Category**, be sure *All* is selected. If necessary, select the **Use passim** check box. Click the **Formats arrow**, and then click **Classic**. Compare your screen with Figure 12.26.

> You can select a specific type of citation to display in the table of authorities. In this case, all types of citations will display. The term ***passim*** indicates that a citation occurs on five or more pages in a document. When the *Use passim* check box is selected, the term *passim* displays in a table of authorities instead of multiple page numbers for the citation.

FIGURE 12.26

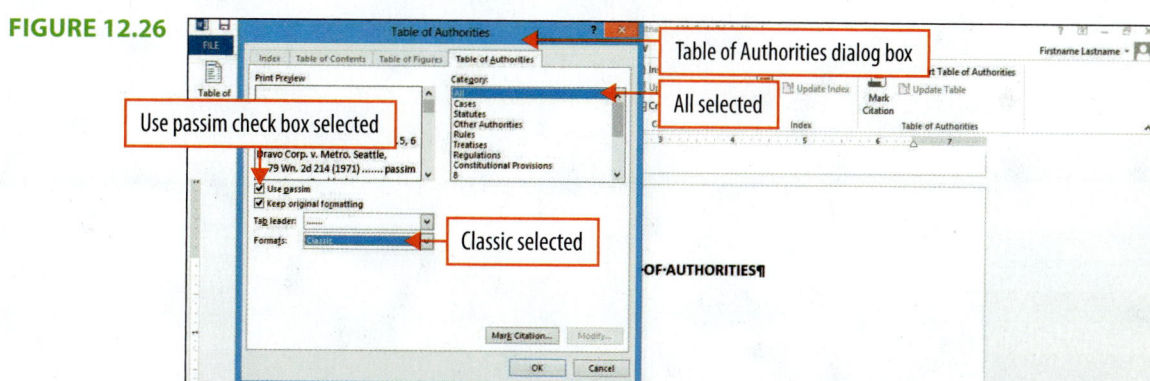

10 ▶ In the **Table of Authorities** dialog box, click **OK**.

> The table of authorities displays on Page 2 of your document. Based on the type of reference, citations display below the appropriate headings. Because the citation *42 Ne. C.S. §917* occurs on five pages in the document, the term *passim* displays instead of the page numbers.

11 ▶ **Save** 💾 your changes.

Activity 12.07 | Updating a Table of Authorities

1 ▶ Display **Page 3**, and then in the second paragraph, select the text *52 MS. Code §29.512.* On the **REFERENCES tab**, in the **Table of Authorities group**, click **Mark Citation**. Click the **Category arrow**, and then click **Statutes**. Click **Mark**, and then click **Close**.

2 ▶ Display **Page 2**, select the entire table of authorities—the *Cases* and *Regulations* fields. In the **Table of Authorities group**, click **Insert Table of Authorities**.

3 In the **Table of Authorities** dialog box, under **Category**, click **All**, and then click **OK**. In the **Microsoft Word** message box, when asked if you want to replace the selected category of the table of authorities, click **No**.

When changes to citations are made in the document—for example, marking a new citation—it is important to modify the table of authorities. If only page numbers are changed in the document, on the REFERENCES tab, in the Table of Authorities group, click Update Table.

4 Press Ctrl + Home. Click the **FILE tab**, and then **Show All Properties**. In the **Tags** box, type **legal brief, citations** In the **Subject** box, type your course name and section number. If necessary, edit the author name to display your name. **Save** 🖫 your changes, and then **Close** ✕ Word.

5 Print the three Word documents or submit all four files electronically as directed by your instructor.

END | You have completed Project 12A

Park Brochure

PROJECT ACTIVITIES

In Activities 12.08 through 12.15, you will create a brochure for visitors to the theme parks operated by Magical Park Corporation. To customize the document, you will change the paper size, modify how text displays, and edit graphics. Your completed file will look similar to Figure 12.27.

PROJECT FILES

For Project 12B, you will need the following files:

w12B_Park_Brochure
w12B_Carousel
w12B_Coaster
w12B_Comments
w12B_Brochure_Bullet

You will save your file as:

Lastname_Firstname_12B_Park_Brochure

PROJECT RESULTS

FIGURE 12.27 Project 12B Park Brochure

Video W12-4

Word provides many features to format and display text in an attractive manner, such as changing the spacing between characters and controlling the display of phrases where the individual components should not be split between two lines. Additionally, the paper size can be changed to produce the desired result—in this case, a small brochure.

Activity 12.08 │ Changing Paper Size

1 Start Word. From your student files, open the file **w12B_Park_Brochure**. **Save** the document to your **Word Chapter 12** folder as **Lastname_Firstname_12B_Park_Brochure** Insert the file name in the footer and display rulers and formatting marks. If any words are flagged as spelling errors, click **Ignore All**.

2 Click the **PAGE LAYOUT tab**. In the **Page Setup group**, click **Orientation**, and then click **Landscape**.

3 In the **Page Setup group**, click **Margins**, and then click **Narrow**. In the **Page Setup group**, click **Columns**, and then click **Three**.

4 On **Page 1**, in the first column, position the insertion point to the left of the paragraph *Entertainment*. In the **Page Setup group**, click **Breaks**, and then under **Page Breaks**, click **Column**. In the second column, position the insertion point to the left of the paragraph *Theme Park FAQ*. In the **Page Setup group**, click **Breaks**, and then under **Page Breaks**, click **Column**.

5 In the third column, position the insertion point to the left of the paragraph *Catering for Groups*, and then press [Ctrl] + [Enter]. Scroll up as necessary, and then notice that the column and page breaks display as shown in Figure 12.28.

FIGURE 12.28

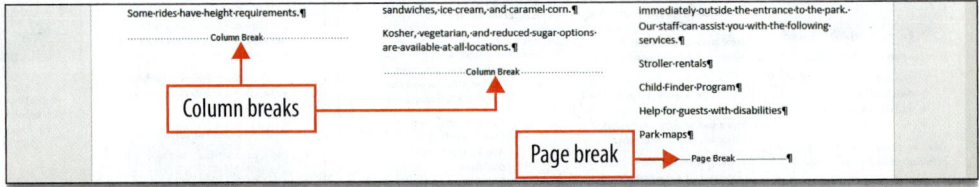

6 On **Page 2**, position the insertion point to the left of the paragraph *Magical Park Corporation*. In the **Page Setup group**, click **Breaks**, and then under **Page Breaks**, click **Column**. In the second column, position the insertion point in the last blank paragraph of the document, and then using the technique you practiced, insert a **Column** break.

7 Press [Ctrl] + [Home]. In the **Page Setup group**, click **Size**, and then at the bottom of the displayed list, click **More Paper Sizes**.

ANOTHER WAY   Click the dialog box launcher to display the Page Setup dialog box, and then click the Paper tab.

8 In the **Page Setup** dialog box, with the **Paper tab** displayed, under **Paper size,** click the **Paper size arrow**, which displays *Letter*, scroll as necessary, and then click **Custom size**. Click the **Width spin box down arrow** to 9". Click the **Height spin box down arrow** to 7". Compare your screen with Figure 12.29.

You can change the paper size to accommodate any type of document. In this case, the brochure requires a custom paper size.

FIGURE 12.29

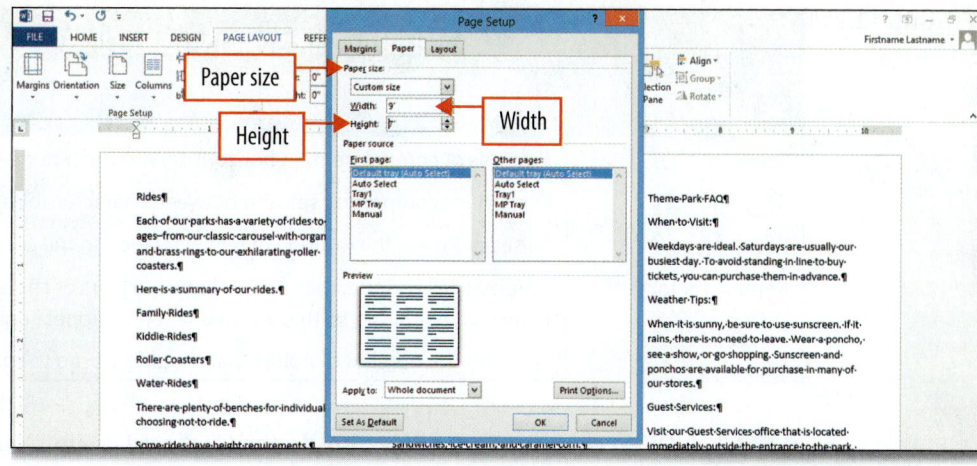

9 Click **OK** to close the **Page Setup** dialog box. Notice that changing the paper size caused some text to be moved to a second and third page; you will adjust this in subsequent steps.

10 **Save** 📁 your changes.

Activity 12.09 | Changing Character Spacing

You will format the text in the brochure by changing font sizes and applying styles. You will also change the ***character spacing*** for selected text to improve the appearance or readability of a document. Character spacing is a Word feature that allows you to change the default spacing constraints between characters. You can manually set spacing options or use ***kerning*** to have Word automatically modify space between characters in selected text. Kerning automatically adjusts the spacing between pairs of characters, with a specified minimum point size, so that words and letters appear equally spaced.

1 In the first column, select the first paragraph *Rides*. On the mini toolbar, change the **Font Size** to **14**, apply **Bold** 𝐁, click the **Font Color arrow** [A ▾], and then in the last column, click the last color—**Green, Accent 6, Darker 50%**. Press Ctrl + E.

2 With the paragraph *Rides* selected, click the **HOME tab**, and then in the **Font group**, click the **dialog box launcher** 🔽.

3 In the **Font** dialog box, click the **Advanced tab**. Under **Character Spacing**, click the **Spacing arrow**, and then click **Expanded**. Click the **By spin box up arrow** to **1.2 pt**. Compare your screen with Figure 12.30, and then take a moment to study the character spacing settings in Figure 12.31.

There are several different features that allow you to modify the character spacing. By changing the spacing to Expanded by 1.2 pt, the space between the characters is increased slightly. A preview of the character spacing displays in the Fonts dialog box.

FIGURE 12.30

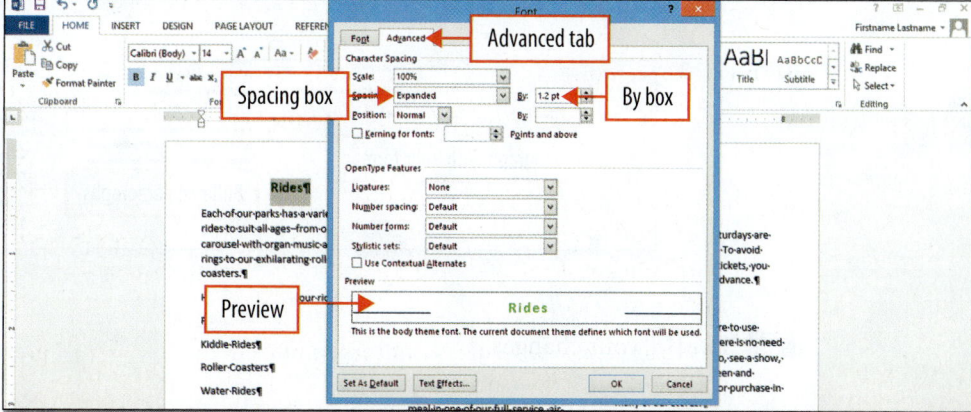

FIGURE 12.31

CHARACTER SPACING SETTINGS	
SETTING	**DESCRIPTION**
Scale	Expands or compresses text horizontally as a percentage of the current size.
Spacing	Expands or compresses spacing between characters by a specified number of points.
Position	Raises or lowers the location of text in relation to the current vertical location.
Kerning for fonts	Automatically adjusts the spacing between pairs of characters, with a specified minimum point size, so that words and letters appear equally spaced.
By	Specifies the number of points that should be used to space characters.

4. Click **OK** to close the **Font** dialog box. In the **Clipboard group**, double-click **Format Painter** to turn it on. Select each of the following paragraphs to apply the same formatting you applied to *Rides*: *Entertainment, Food, Theme Park FAQ,* and *Catering for Groups*. In the **Clipboard group**, click **Format Painter** to turn it off. Press Ctrl + Home and then compare your screen with Figure 12.32.

FIGURE 12.32

Formatted paragraphs

5. On **Page 1**, in the first column, select the four paragraphs beginning with *Family Rides* and ending with *Water Rides*. In the **Paragraph group**, click **Bullets**.

6. On **Page 1**, in the third column, select the paragraph *When to Visit*, being sure to include the colon. On the mini toolbar, apply **Bold** and **Underline**, click the **Font Color arrow**, and then in the last column, click the fifth color—**Green, Accent 6, Darker 25%**. In the **Paragraph group**, click **Line and Paragraph Spacing**, and then click **Remove Space After Paragraph**.

7. In the **Clipboard group**, double-click **Format Painter**, and then apply the formatting you applied to *When to Visit* to the paragraphs *Weather Tips, Guest Services, Food Options,* and *Bookings*. In the **Clipboard group**, click **Format Painter** to turn it off.

8. On **Page 1**, at the bottom of the third column, select the four paragraphs beginning with *Stroller rentals* and ending with *Park maps*. In the **Paragraph group**, click **Bullets**. Click to position the insertion point anywhere in the paragraph *Park maps*. In the **Paragraph group**, click **Line and Paragraph Spacing**, and then click **Remove Space After Paragraph**.

9. At the bottom of **Page 1**, in the first column, select the paragraph that begins *Some rides*. On the mini toolbar, change the **Font Size** to **10**, and then apply **Italic**. Deselect the text, and then compare your screen with Figure 12.33.

FIGURE 12.33

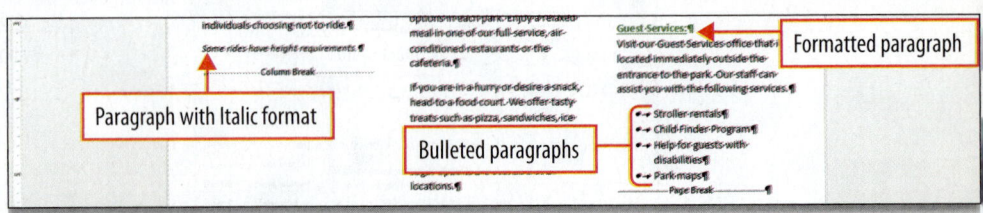

Paragraph with Italic format

Bulleted paragraphs

Formatted paragraph

10. **Save** your changes.

Activity 12.10 | Inserting Nonbreaking Hyphens and Nonbreaking Spaces

Recall that word wrap automatically moves text from the right edge of a paragraph to the beginning of the next line as is necessary to fit within the margins. You can insert a *nonbreaking hyphen* to prevent a hyphenated word or phrase from being displayed on two lines. Similarly, you can insert a *nonbreaking space* to keep two or more words together so that both words will wrap even if only the second word would normally wrap to the next line. For example, inserting nonbreaking spaces in a date will keep the entire date—month, day, and year—on the same line.

1 On **Page 1**, in the second column, in the fourth paragraph, locate the phrase *air-conditioned*. Select the hyphen, and then press [Ctrl] + [Shift] + [-] to insert a nonbreaking hyphen. Notice the entire term air-conditioned displays on the same line. Compare your screen with Figure 12.34.

You can improve the readability of a document by inserting a nonbreaking hyphen.

ANOTHER WAY On the INSERT tab, in the Symbols group, click Symbol, and then click More Symbols. In the Symbols dialog box, click the Special Characters tab, click Nonbreaking Hyphen, and then click Insert.

FIGURE 12.34

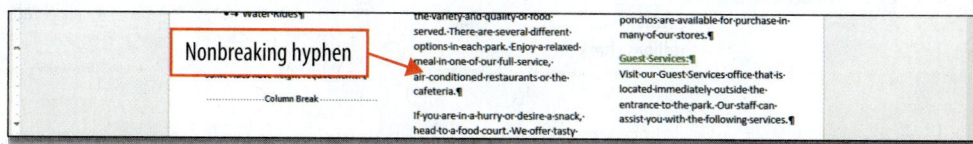

2 On **Page 2**, in the first column, in the fourth paragraph, locate the phrase *all-you-care-to-eat*. Select the hyphen between *all* and *you* and then press [Ctrl] + [Shift] + [-]. In a similar manner, insert nonbreaking hyphens to replace each of the remaining three hyphens in the phrase.

If you have a hyphenated term that contains multiple hyphens, it is good practice to replace all hyphens with nonbreaking hyphens. If preceding text or other elements are modified, this will ensure that the text will display on a single line.

3 On **Page 1**, in the second column, in the fifth paragraph, locate the term *ice cream*. Select the space following *ice*, and then press [Ctrl] + [Shift] + [Spacebar]. Compare your screen with Figure 12.35.

The term ice cream displays on one line. A small raised circle, the nonbreaking space formatting mark, displays between the two words.

FIGURE 12.35

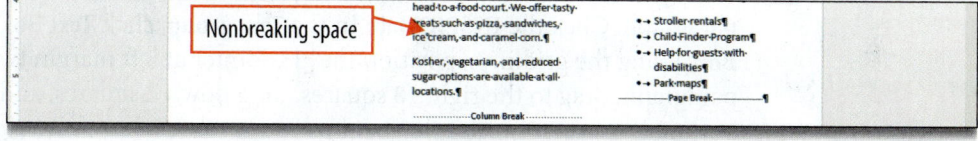

4 In the last line of the same paragraph, using the technique you just practiced, replace the space between *caramel* and *corn* with a nonbreaking space.

5 On **Page 2**, in the first column, in the last paragraph, locate the phone number. Using the technique you just practiced, replace the space with a nonbreaking space, and then replace the hyphen with a nonbreaking hyphen. Compare your screen with Figure 12.36.

FIGURE 12.36

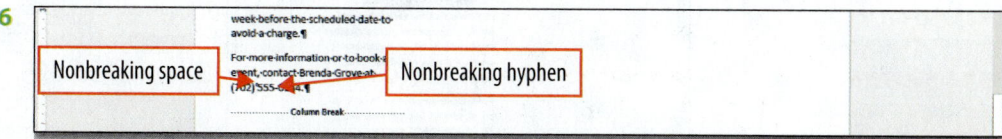

6 **Save** your changes.

Video W12-5

Inserting and formatting graphics and text can enhance the appearance of a document. Word provides many features to modify graphic and text elements. You have used some of these features in previous projects. In this project you will utilize additional features to modify text boxes, pictures, bullets, and text.

Activity 12.11 | Viewing Document Gridlines

Document gridlines—nonprinting horizontal and vertical lines—assist you in aligning graphics and other elements.

1 On **Page 2**, in the third column, click to position the insertion point in the blank paragraph. Click the **VIEW tab**, and then in the **Show group**, select the **Gridlines** check box. Compare your screen with Figure 12.37.

The gridlines display only within the margins of the document.

FIGURE 12.37

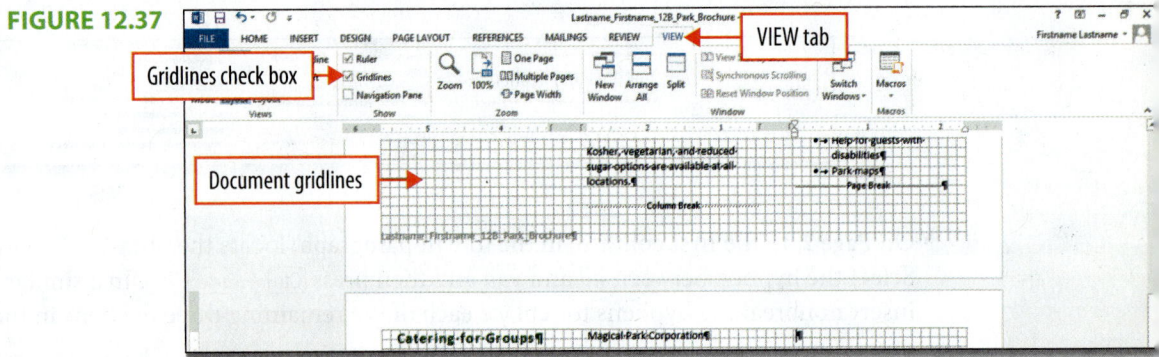

Activity 12.12 | Linking Text Boxes

Recall that text boxes are movable, resizable containers for text or graphics. Word includes a feature to link two or more text boxes. When text boxes are linked, if the first text box cannot hold all of the inserted text, the text will automatically flow into the next, linked text box. In this activity, you will use gridlines to help position text boxes, link two text boxes, and then insert text from an existing file.

1 On **Page 2**, in the first column, click to position the insertion point at the end of the last paragraph. Click the **INSERT tab**. In the **Text group**, click **Text Box**, and then click **Draw Text Box**. Using the gridlines, position the  pointer at left margin two gridlines below the last paragraph, drag to the right **18** squares, drag down **7** squares, and then release the mouse button. If necessary resize the text box so that the right border aligns at approximately 2 inches on the horizontal ruler and the bottom border aligns at approximately 0.75 inch on the lower portion of the vertical ruler. Compare your screen with Figure 12.38.

FIGURE 12.38

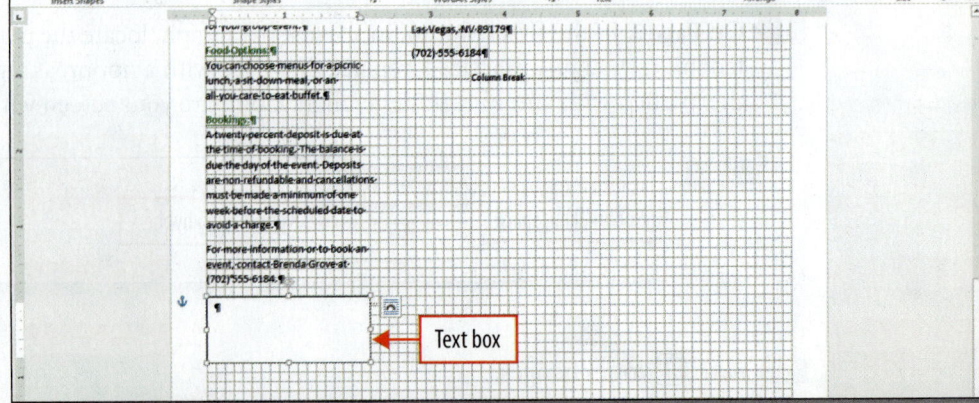

2 Deselect the text box. On **Page 2**, in the second column, select the four paragraphs, and then on the mini toolbar, apply **Bold** [B]. Press [Ctrl] + [E]. Click the **HOME tab**. In the **Paragraph group**, click **Line and Paragraph Spacing** [≡▾], and then click **Remove Space After Paragraph**.

3 In the second column, position the insertion point to the left of the first paragraph, and then press [Enter] two times.

4 In the second column, place the insertion point in the first blank paragraph. Click the **INSERT tab**. In the **Text group**, click **Text Box**, and then click **Draw Text Box**. Using the gridlines and existing text as a guide, position the [+] pointer at the top margin three gridlines to the left of *Magical*. Drag to the right **18** squares until the border is three gridlines to the right of *Corporation*, drag down until the bottom of the text box is aligned with the line below the text *avoid a charge* (in the first column), and then release the mouse button. If necessary, resize the text box so that the right border aligns at approximately 2 inches on the horizontal ruler and the bottom border aligns at approximately 3.25 inches on the vertical ruler.

5 With the text box selected, on the **FORMAT tab**, in the **Arrange group**, click **Wrap Text**, and then click **Top and Bottom**. Compare your screen with Figure 12.39.

> Top and Bottom text wrapping causes the four paragraphs of text and the two blank paragraphs above them to be moved below the text box.

FIGURE 12.39

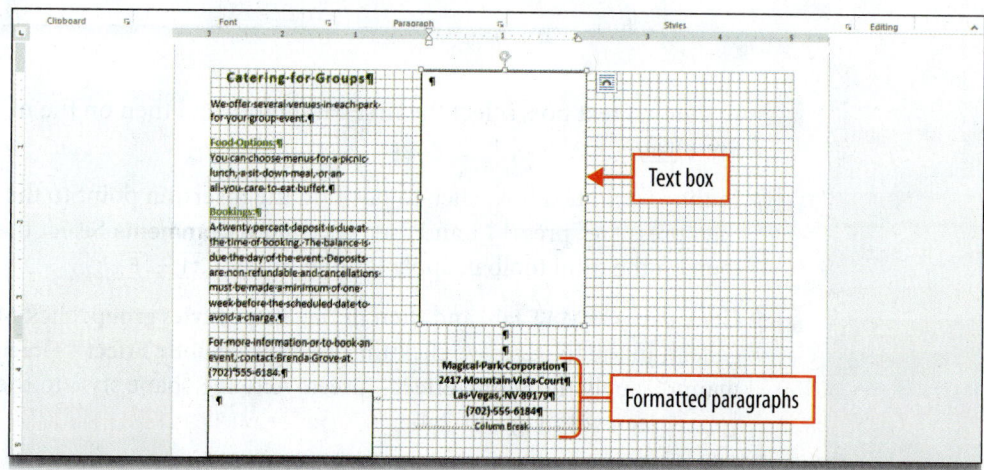

- Text box
- Formatted paragraphs

6 At the bottom of the first column, click in the text box to select it. On the **FORMAT tab**, in the **Text group**, click **Create Link**.

7 Move the pointer into a blank area of the document, and notice that the [🝪] pointer displays.

> The upright pitcher indicates that the first text box is ready to be linked to another text box.

8 Move your pointer into the text box in the second column, and notice that the [🝪] pointer displays. Compare your screen with Figure 12.40.

> The pouring pitcher indicates that this second text box can be linked to the first text box.

FIGURE 12.40

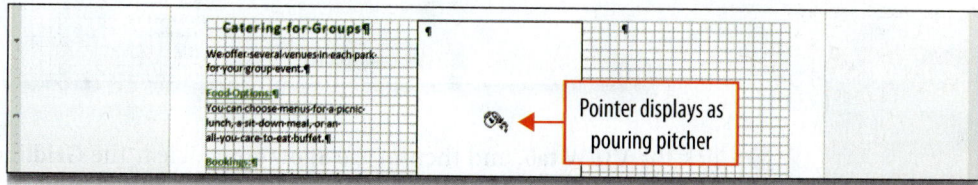

- Pointer displays as pouring pitcher

9 With the [🝪] pointer displayed, click in the second text box to create a link.

10 If necessary, click to position the insertion point in the first text box. Click the **INSERT tab**. In the **Text group**, click the **Object button arrow**, and then click **Text from File**. Navigate to the student files for this chapter, select the file **w12B_Comments**, and then click **Insert**. Compare your screen with Figure 12.41.

The first two paragraphs of text display in the first text box and the remaining text displays in the second text box.

FIGURE 12.41

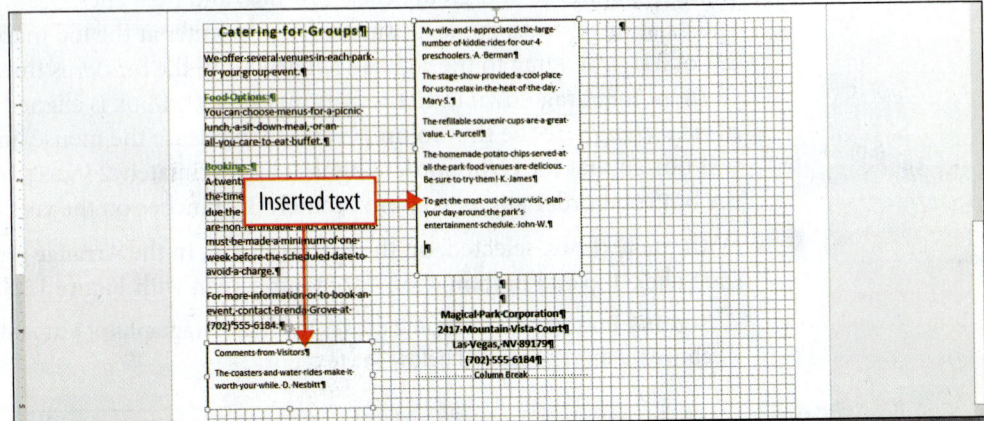

11 In the first text box, select the first paragraph, and then on the mini toolbar, apply **Bold** B . Press Ctrl + E .

12 In the second text box, click to position the insertion point to the left of the first paragraph, then press Enter, press ↑ , and then type **More Comments** Select the text you just typed, and then on the mini toolbar, apply **Bold** B . Press Ctrl + E .

13 Click the **FORMAT tab**, and then in the **Shape Styles group**, click **More** ▾ . In the **Shape Styles** gallery, in the fourth row, click the last style—**Subtle Effect – Green, Accent 6**. In a similar manner, apply the **Subtle Effect – Green, Accent 6** shape style to the other text box. Compare your screen with Figure 12.42.

FIGURE 12.42

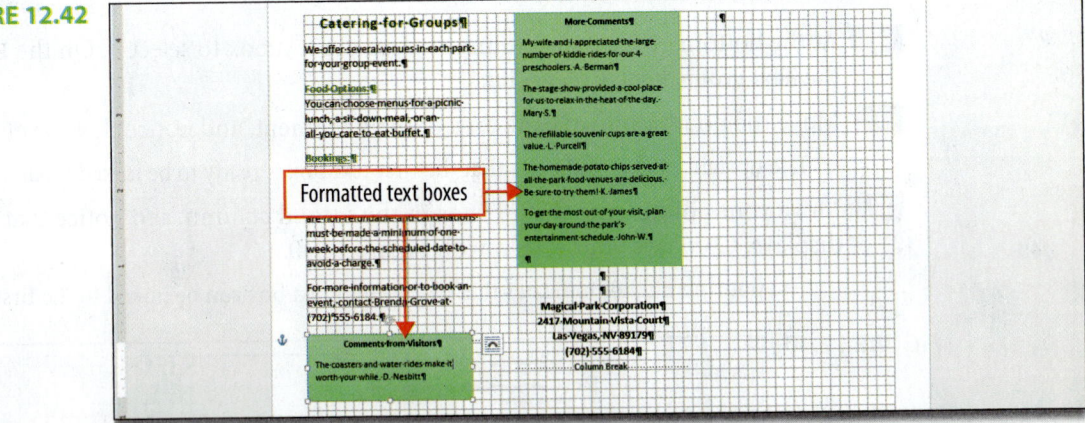

14 Click the **VIEW tab**, and then in the **Show group**, clear the **Gridlines** check box to hide the gridlines. **Save** 💾 your changes.

More Knowledge   **Unlinking Text Boxes**

To unlink text boxes, click in the first linked text box, and then on the FORMAT tab, in the Text group, click Break Link.

Activity 12.13 | Modifying Text Effects

You can modify the built-in text effects in Word in a variety of ways—for example, by changing the weight and color of the outline and by altering the type of reflection.

1 On **Page 2**, position the insertion point at the top of the third column, and then type **OUR THEME PARKS**

2 Press Enter two times, and then type **Fun for all ages!** Select the paragraph you just typed, and then on the mini toolbar, change the **Font Size** to **20**, and apply **Italic** [*I*]. Press Ctrl + E.

3 Click the **HOME tab**, and then in the **Font group**, click **Text Effects and Typography** [A ▾]. In the **Text Effects** gallery, in the first row, click the fifth effect—**Fill – Gold, Accent 4, Soft Bevel**. With the text still selected, click **Text Effects and Typography** [A ▾], point to **Outline**, and then under **Theme Colors**, in the last column, click the fifth color—**Green, Accent 6, Darker 25%**. In the **Font group**, click the **Font Color button arrow** [A ▾], and then in the last column, click the fourth color—**Green, Accent 6, Lighter 40%**. Deselect the text, and then compare your screen with Figure 12.43.

The theme allows you to choose a consistent color scheme to create a professional-looking document.

FIGURE 12.43

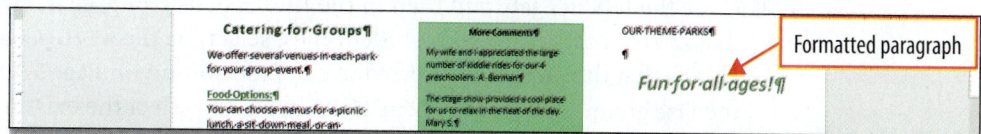

4 In the third column, select the first paragraph. On the mini toolbar, change the **Font Size** to **20**, and then apply **Bold** [B]. Press Ctrl + E. On the **HOME tab**, in the **Font Group**, click **Text Effects and Typography** [A ▾], and then in the second row, click the second effect—**Gradient Fill – Blue, Accent 1, Reflection**. Click **Text Effects and Typography** [A ▾], point to **Glow**, and then under **Glow Variations**, in the third row, click the last option—**Green, 11 pt glow, Accent color 6**. In the **Font group**, change the **Font Color** [A ▾] to **Green, Accent 6, Darker 25%**—in the last column, the fifth color. Deselect the text, and then compare your screen with Figure 12.44.

FIGURE 12.44

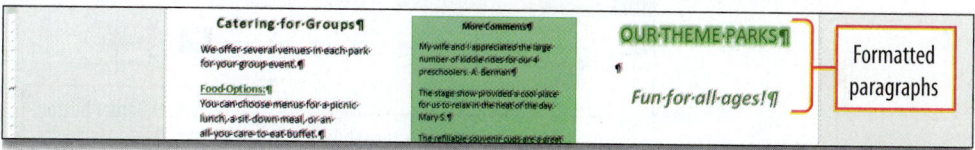

5 Save [💾] your changes.

Activity 12.14 | Applying Artistic Effects to Pictures

You can change the appearance of a picture by applying an *artistic effect*—a format applied to an image that makes the picture resemble a sketch or painting.

1 On **Page 1**, in the first column, position the insertion point at the end of the second paragraph, and then press Enter.

2 Click the **INSERT tab**, and then in the **Illustrations group**, click **Pictures**. In the **Insert Picture** dialog box, navigate to your student files, select the file **w12B_Carousel**, and then click **Insert**.

3 On the **FORMAT tab**, in the **Adjust group**, click **Artistic Effects**. Point to several options.

Live preview allows you to see how each option will modify the picture.

4 In the **Artistic Effects** gallery, in the fourth row, click the last option—**Plastic Wrap**. Compare your screen with Figure 12.45.

FIGURE 12.45

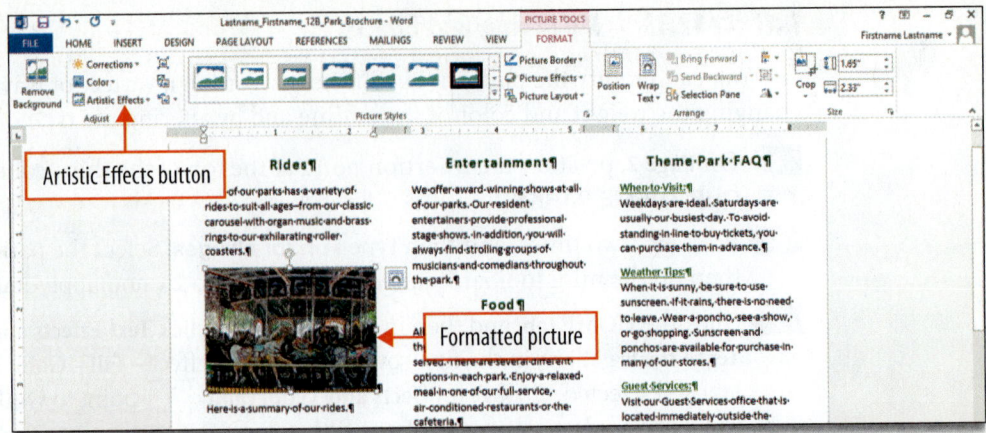

Artistic Effects button

Formatted picture

5. On **Page 2**, in the third column, position the insertion point in the second blank paragraph, and then press Ctrl + E.

6. Click the **INSERT tab**, and then in the **Illustrations group**, click **Pictures**. In the **Insert Picture** dialog box, navigate to your student files, select the file **w12B_Coaster**, and then click **Insert**. Notice that the picture is inserted in the first column on **Page 3**. On the **FORMAT tab**, in the **Size group**, click in the **Shape Height** box, select the existing text, type **4.2**, and then press Enter. Notice that the resized picture displays in the third column on **Page 2**.

7. In the **Adjust group**, click **Artistic Effects**, and then in the second row, click the fourth option—**Glow Diffused**.

8. On the **FORMAT tab**, in the **Picture Styles group**, click **More**, and then click the first option—**Simple Frame, White**. In the **Picture Styles group**, click the **Picture Border button arrow**, and then in the last column, click the fifth color—**Green, Accent 6, Darker 25%**. Compare your screen with Figure 12.46.

FIGURE 12.46

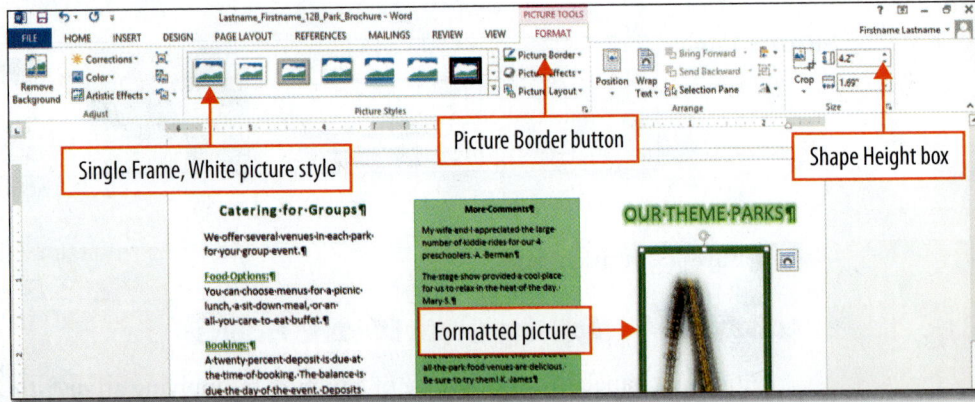

Single Frame, White picture style

Picture Border button

Shape Height box

Formatted picture

9. **Save** your changes.

Activity 12.15 | Using a Picture as a Bullet

In this activity, you will use a picture to replace the bullets in the document.

1. On **Page 1**, in the first column select the four bulleted paragraphs. Click the **HOME tab**, and then in the **Paragraph group**, click the **Bullets button arrow**, and then click **Define New Bullet**.

2. In the **Define New Bullet** dialog box, under **Bullet character**, click **Picture**.

3. In the **Insert Pictures** dialog box, to the right of **From a file**, click **Browse**.

4 ▶ In the **Insert Picture** dialog box, navigate to your student files, select the file **w12B_Brochure_ Bullet**, and then click **Insert**. Compare your screen with Figure 12.47.

The picture—a combination of yellow, blue, and green arrows—displays as a bullet in the Preview area of the Define New Bullet dialog box.

FIGURE 12.47

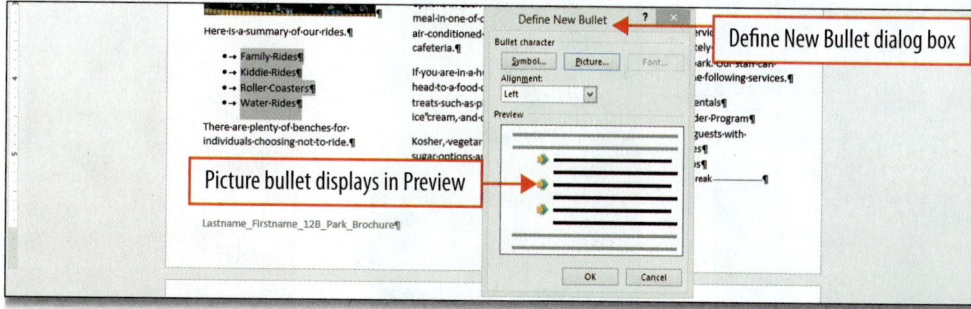

5 ▶ Click **OK**, and notice that the picture displays as bullets for the four paragraphs.

The new bullet is stored in the Bullet Library.

6 ▶ On **Page 1**, in the third column, select the four bulleted paragraphs. In the **Paragraph group**, click the **Bullets button arrow** ▤ ▾, and then compare your screen with Figure 12.48.

The new picture bullet displays under Recently Used Bullets, Bullet Library, and Document Bullets.

FIGURE 12.48

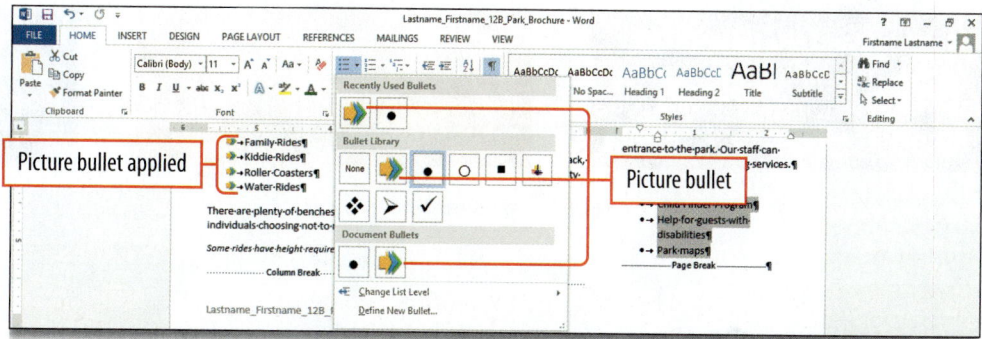

7 ▶ Under **Recently Used Bullets**, click the new picture bullet to apply the bullet to the selected paragraphs. Deselect the paragraphs, and then compare your screen with Figure 12.49.

FIGURE 12.49

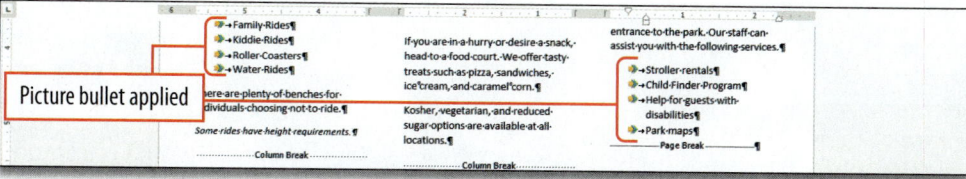

8 ▶ Press [Ctrl] + [Home]. Click the **FILE tab**, and then click **Show All Properties**. In the **Tags** box, type **brochure, graphics** In the **Subject** box, type your course name and section number. If necessary, edit the author name to display your name. **Save** 🖫 your changes.

9 ▶ On the **HOME tab**, in the **Paragraph group**, click the **Bullets button arrow**. In the **Bullets** gallery, under **Bullet Library**, right-click the picture bullet, and then from the shortcut menu, click **Remove**.

10 ▶ Print your document or submit electronically as directed by your instructor, and then **Close** ☒ Word.

END | You have completed Project 12B

END OF CHAPTER

SUMMARY

You can assign levels to paragraphs to create an outline in Word, and then use the outline to create a PowerPoint presentation. You can publish the presentation in Word as a handout, with an area for notes.

Legal citations are references to documents—for example, statutes, regulations, and cases. By marking the citations, you can create a table of authorities that provides a listing of all citations in the document.

Create specialized documents by changing the paper size and the margins. Modify how text displays by changing the character spacing, and using nonbreaking hyphens and nonbreaking spaces where appropriate.

Select a theme to maintain a consistent color scheme and create professional-looking documents. You can enhance a document by linking text boxes, applying artistic effects, and using a picture as a bullet.

GO! LEARN IT ONLINE

Review the concepts and key terms in this chapter by completing these online challenges, which you can find at **www.pearsonhighered.com/go**.

Matching and Multiple Choice: Answer matching and multiple choice questions to test what you learned in this chapter. **MyITLab®**

Crossword Puzzle: Spell out the words that match the numbered clues and put them in the puzzle squares.

Flipboard: Flip through the definitions of the key terms in this chapter and match them with the correct term.

END OF CHAPTER

REVIEW AND ASSESSMENT GUIDE FOR WORD CHAPTER 12

Your instructor may assign one or more of these projects to help you review the chapter and assess your mastery and understanding of the chapter.

		Review and Assessment Guide for Word Chapter 12	
Project	**Apply Skills from These Chapter Objectives**	**Project Type**	**Project Location**
12C	Objectives 1–3 from Project 12A	**12C Skills Review** A guided review of the skills from Project 12A.	On the following pages
12D	Objectives 4 and 5 from Project 12B	**12D Skills Review** A guided review of the skills from Project 12B.	On the following pages
12E	Objectives 1–3 from Project 12A	**12E Mastery (Grader Project)** A demonstration of your mastery of the skills in Project 12A with extensive decision making.	In MyITLab and on the following pages
12F	Objectives 4 and 5 from Project 12B	**12F Mastery (Grader Project)** A demonstration of your mastery of the skills in Project 12B with extensive decision making.	In MyITLab and on the following pages
12G	Objectives 1–5 from Projects 12A and 12B	**12G Mastery (Grader Project)** A demonstration of your mastery of the skills in Projects 12A and 12B with extensive decision making.	In MyITLab and on the following pages
12H	Combination of Objectives from Projects 12A and 12B	**12H GO! Fix It** A demonstration of your mastery of the skills in Projects 12A and 12B by creating a correct result from a document that contains errors you must find.	Online
12I	Combination of Objectives from Projects 12A and 12B	**12I GO! Make It** A demonstration of your mastery of the skills in Projects 12A and 12B by creating a result from a supplied picture.	Online
12J	Combination of Objectives from Projects 12A and 12B	**12J GO! Solve It** A demonstration of your mastery of the skills in Projects 12A and 12B, your decision-making skills, and your critical thinking skills. A task-specific rubric helps you self-assess your result.	Online
12K	Combination of Objectives from Projects 12A and 12B	**12K GO! Solve It** A demonstration of your mastery of the skills in Projects 12A and 12B, your decision-making skills, and your critical thinking skills. A task-specific rubric helps you self-assess your result.	On the following pages
12L	Combination of Objectives from Projects 12A and 12B	**12L GO! Think** A demonstration of your understanding of the chapter concepts applied in a manner that you would outside of college. An analytic rubric helps you and your instructor grade the quality of your work by comparing it to the work an expert in the discipline would create.	On the following pages
12M	Combination of Objectives from Projects 12A and 12B	**12M GO! Think** A demonstration of your understanding of the chapter concepts applied in a manner that you would outside of college. An analytic rubric helps you and your instructor grade the quality of your work by comparing it to the work an expert in the discipline would create.	Online
12N	Combination of Objectives from Projects 12A and 12B	**12N You and GO!** A demonstration of your understanding of the chapter concepts applied in a manner that you would in a personal situation. An analytic rubric helps you and your instructor grade the quality of your work.	Online

GLOSSARY

GLOSSARY OF CHAPTER KEY TERMS

.pptx The default file extension for a PowerPoint file.

Artistic effect Formats applied to images that make pictures resemble sketches or paintings.

Character spacing A Word feature that allows you to change the default spacing constraints between characters.

Document gridlines Nonprinting horizontal and vertical lines used to assist in aligning graphics and other elements in a document.

Handout A document that is given to an audience to accompany a lecture.

Kerning A character spacing option that automatically adjusts the spacing between pairs of characters, with a specified minimum point size, so that words and letters appear equally spaced.

Layout The placement and arrangement of the text and graphic elements on a slide.

Legal citation A reference to an authoritative document, such as a regulation, a statute, or a case.

Minus outline symbol A formatting mark that indicates there are no subordinate heading or body text paragraphs.

Nonbreaking hyphen A formatting mark that prevents a hyphenated word or phrase from being displayed on two lines.

Nonbreaking space A formatting mark that keeps two words together so that both words will wrap even if only the second word would normally wrap to the next line.

Outline A Word feature that allows you to organize the contents of a document in a structured manner.

Outline level A Word feature that defines the position of a paragraph in relation to all topics in a document and is formatted with a corresponding heading style.

Outline symbol A small gray circle that identifies heading and body text paragraphs.

Passim A term that indicates a citation occurs on five or more pages in a document.

Plus outline symbol A formatting mark that indicates there are subordinate heading or body text paragraphs.

Table of authorities A list of all references in a legal document and the page numbers where the references occur.

CHAPTER REVIEW

Skills Review | Project 12C Park Changes

Apply **12A** skills from these
Objectives:

1 Integrate Word with
PowerPoint

2 Modify a PowerPoint
Presentation

3 Create a Table of
Authorities

In the following Skills Review, you will create an outline and then use it to create a PowerPoint presentation explaining proposed changes for Magical Park Corporation's water parks for the upcoming season. You will create a handout for management based on the presentation. You will also modify a legal document to include a table of authorities for management review. Your completed files will look similar to Figure 12.50.

PROJECT FILES

For Project 12C, you will need the following files:

w12C_Changes_Outline
w12C_Water_Park
w12C_Logo_Brief

You will save your files as:

Lastname_Firstname_12C_Changes_Outline
Lastname_Firstname_12C_Changes_Presentation
Lastname_Firstname_12C_Changes_Handout
Lastname_Firstname_12C_Logo_Brief

PROJECT RESULTS

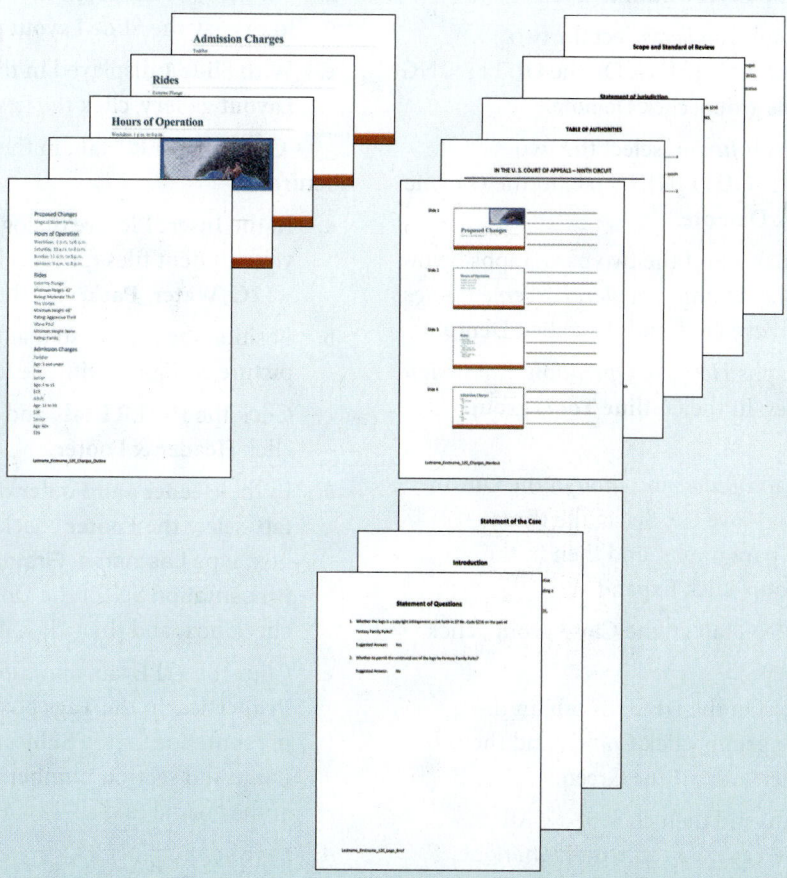

FIGURE 12.50

(Project 12C Park Changes continues on the next page)

CHAPTER REVIEW

1 ▶ Start Word. From your student files, open the file **w12C_Changes_Outline**. **Save** it to your **Word Chapter 12** folder as **Lastname_Firstname_12C_Changes_Outline** Insert the file name in the footer.

a. On the **VIEW tab**, in the **Views group**, click **Outline**.

b. Select the first paragraph. On the **OUTLINING tab**, in the **Outline Tools group**, click the **Outline Level arrow**, and then click **Level 1**.

c. For each of the three remaining paragraphs formatted with bold, on the **OUTLINING tab**, in the **Outline Tools group**, use the **Outline Level arrow** to assign the paragraphs to **Level 1**.

d. Select the second paragraph of the document, click the **Outline Level arrow**, and then click **Level 2**.

e. Below the paragraph *Hours of Operation*, select all four paragraphs, click the **Outline Level arrow**, and then click **Level 2**.

f. In a similar manner, below each of the remaining *Level 1* paragraphs, select the body text paragraphs, and then assign the **Level 2** outline level.

2 ▶ Below the paragraph *Toddler*, select the two paragraphs *Age: 3 and under* and *Free*. On the **OUTLINING tab**, in the **Outline Tools group**, click **Demote**.

a. Below the paragraph *Junior*, select the two paragraphs. On the **OUTLINING tab**, in the **Outline Tools group**, click **Demote**.

b. In a similar manner, select the two paragraphs below the *Level 2* paragraphs *Adult*, *Senior*, *Extreme Plunge*, *The Vortex*, and *Wave Pool*, and then click **Demote**.

c. Select the paragraphs *Hours of Operation*, *Admission Charges*, and *Rides*. In the **Outline Tools group**, click **Collapse**.

d. Select the paragraph *Rides*, and then in the **Outline Tools group**, click **Move Up**. Select the three collapsed **Level 1** paragraphs, and then in the **Outline Tools group**, click **Expand**.

e. On the **OUTLINING tab**, in the **Close group**, click **Close Outline View**.

3 ▶ Press [Ctrl] + [Home]. On the **DESIGN tab**, in the **Document Formatting group**, click **Colors**, and then in the **Theme Colors** gallery, click **Blue Green**.

a. Click the **FILE tab**, and then click **Show All Properties**. In the **Tags** box, type **park changes,**

outline In the **Subject** box, type your course name and section number. If necessary, edit the author name to display your name.

b. **Save** your changes, and then **Close** Word.

4 ▶ Start PowerPoint. At the bottom left of the screen, click **Open Other Presentations**, and then double-click **Computer**.

a. In the **Open** dialog box, navigate to your **Word Chapter 12** folder. At the bottom of the **Open** dialog box, click the **All PowerPoint Presentations arrow**, and then click **All Outlines**. Click to select **Lastname_Firstname_12C_Changes_Outline**, and then click **Open**.

b. Press [F12]. In the **Save As** dialog box, navigate to your **Word Chapter 12** folder, and then using your own name, **Save** the file as **Lastname_Firstname_12C_Changes_Presentation**

c. On the **DESIGN tab**, in the **Themes group**, click **More**. In the **Themes** gallery, click **Retrospect**.

d. On the **HOME tab**, in the **Slides group**, click **Layout** to display the **Slide Layout** gallery.

e. With **Slide 1** displayed in the **Slide pane**, in the **Slide Layout** gallery, click the first option—**Title Slide**.

5 ▶ On the **INSERT tab**, in the **Images group**, click **Pictures**.

a. In the **Insert Picture** dialog box, navigate to your student files for this chapter, click **w12C_Water_Park**, and then click **Insert**.

b. Position the picture so that the top right corner of the picture is aligned with the top right corner of the slide

c. Click the **INSERT tab**, and then in the **Text group**, click **Header & Footer**.

d. In the **Header and Footer** dialog box, on the **Slide** tab, select the **Footer** check box. In the **Footer** box, type **Lastname_Firstname_12C_Changes_Presentation** Select the **Don't show on title slide** check box, and then click **Apply to all**.

e. Click the **FILE tab**, and then click **Show All Properties**. In the **Tags** box, type **park changes, presentation** In the **Subject** box, type your course name and section number. If necessary, edit the author name to display your name.

f. **Save** your changes.

(Project 12C Park Changes continues on the next page)

6 Click the **FILE tab**, click **Export**, and then click **Create Handouts**.

a. Under **Create Handouts in Microsoft Word**, click **Create Handouts**. In the **Send to Microsoft Word** dialog box, under **Page layout in Microsoft Word**, click the **Blank lines next to slides** option. Click **OK**.

b. On the taskbar, click the **Word** icon. If necessary, on the **LAYOUT tab**, in the **Table group**, select **View Gridlines** check box.

c. Press **F12**. In the **Save As** dialog box, navigate to your **Word Chapter 12** folder, and then using your own name, **Save** the file as **Lastname_Firstname_12C_ Changes_Handout** Insert the file name in the footer.

d. In the first row of the table, in the third cell, select the first three lines, and then press **Delete**. In a similar manner, in the third column, delete the first three lines from each of the remaining three cells.

e. Point slightly outside of the upper left corner of the table to display the **Table Move Handle**. Click the **Table Move Handle** to select the entire table. On the **LAYOUT tab**, in the **Cell Size group**, change the **Shape Height** to 2.2".

f. Press **Ctrl** + **Home**. Click the **FILE tab**, and then click **Show All Properties**. In the **Tags** box, type **park changes, handout** In the **Subject** box, type your course name and section number. If necessary, edit the author name to display your name. **Save** your changes, and then from **Backstage** view, **Close** the document but leave Word open. On the taskbar, click the **PowerPoint** icon, **Save** your changes, and then **Close** PowerPoint.

7 In Word, from your student files, open the file **w12C_Logo_Brief**. **Save** it to your **Word Chapter 12** folder as **Lastname_Firstname_12C_Logo_Brief** Insert the file name in the footer.

a. On **Page 2**, in the second paragraph, select the text *37 Ne. Code §216*. Click the **REFERENCES tab**, and then in the **Table of Authorities group**, click **Mark Citation**. In the **Mark Citation** dialog box, click the **Category arrow**, and then click **Statutes**. Click **Mark All**.

b. Click in the document. On **Page 2**, select the text *64 MS. C.S. §57.226*. In the **Mark Citation** dialog box, click the **Category arrow**, and then click **Regulations**. Click **Mark**. On **Page 3**, select the text *Ramos Sports v. Algieres*. In the **Mark Citation** dialog box, click the **Category arrow**, and then click **Cases**. Click **Mark**, and then **Close** the **Mark Citation** dialog box.

c. At the bottom of **Page 1**, position the insertion point to the right of the date, and then press **Ctrl** + **Enter** two times. On **Page 2**, position the insertion point to the left of the page break, type **TABLE OF AUTHORITIES** and then press **Enter** two times. Select the text you typed, change the **Font Size** to **16**, and then apply **Bold** and **Center**.

d. Position the insertion point to the left of the page break, and then in the **Table of Authorities group**, click **Insert Table of Authorities**. In the **Table of Authorities** dialog box, under **Category**, click **All**. Click the **Formats arrow**, and then click **Formal**. If necessary, select the **Use passim** check box. Click **OK**.

e. Press **Ctrl** + **Home**. Click the **FILE tab**, and then click **Show All Properties**. In the **Tags** box, type **park brief, logo** In the **Subject** box, type your course name and section number. If necessary, edit the author name to display your name. **Save** your changes.

f. Print all three Word documents or submit all four files electronically as directed by your instructor. **Close** Word.

END | You have completed Project 12C

CHAPTER REVIEW

Apply 12B skills from these Objectives:

4 Modify the Document Layout

5 Format Graphic and Text Elements

Skills Review Project 12D Resort Facilities

In the following Skills Review, you will format a document, insert graphics, and link text boxes to create a brochure containing information about Magical Park Corporation's resorts. Your completed document will look similar to Figure 12.51.

PROJECT FILES

For Project 12D, you will need the following files:

w12D_Resort_Facilities
w12D_Resort_Reviews
w12D_Pools
w12D_Room
w12D_Resort_Bullet

You will save your file as:

Lastname_Firstname_12D_Resort_Facilities

PROJECT RESULTS

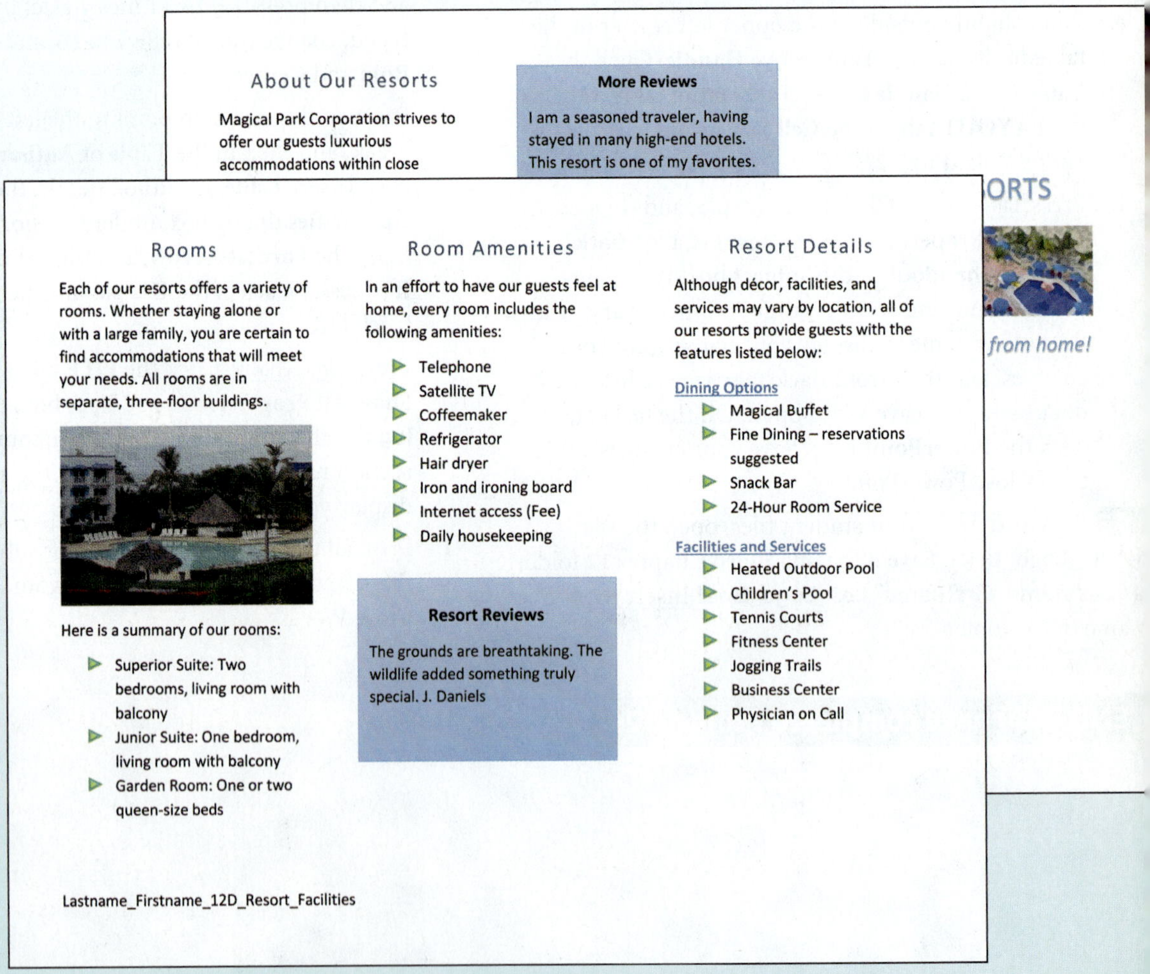

About Our Resorts

Magical Park Corporation strives to offer our guests luxurious accommodations within close

More Reviews

I am a seasoned traveler, having stayed in many high-end hotels. This resort is one of my favorites.

...ORTS

...from home!

Rooms

Each of our resorts offers a variety of rooms. Whether staying alone or with a large family, you are certain to find accommodations that will meet your needs. All rooms are in separate, three-floor buildings.

Here is a summary of our rooms:

- Superior Suite: Two bedrooms, living room with balcony
- Junior Suite: One bedroom, living room with balcony
- Garden Room: One or two queen-size beds

Room Amenities

In an effort to have our guests feel at home, every room includes the following amenities:

- Telephone
- Satellite TV
- Coffeemaker
- Refrigerator
- Hair dryer
- Iron and ironing board
- Internet access (Fee)
- Daily housekeeping

Resort Reviews

The grounds are breathtaking. The wildlife added something truly special. J. Daniels

Resort Details

Although décor, facilities, and services may vary by location, all of our resorts provide guests with the features listed below:

Dining Options
- Magical Buffet
- Fine Dining – reservations suggested
- Snack Bar
- 24-Hour Room Service

Facilities and Services
- Heated Outdoor Pool
- Children's Pool
- Tennis Courts
- Fitness Center
- Jogging Trails
- Business Center
- Physician on Call

Lastname_Firstname_12D_Resort_Facilities

FIGURE 12.51

(Project 12D Resort Facilities continues on the next page)

CHAPTER REVIEW

Skills Review Project 12D Resort Facilities (continued)

1 Start Word. From your student files, open the file **w12D_Resort_Facilities**. **Save** the document to your **Word Chapter 12** folder as **Lastname_Firstname_12D_Resort_Facilities** Insert the file name in the footer.

a. On the **PAGE LAYOUT tab**, in the **Page Setup group**, click **Orientation**, and then click **Landscape**. In the **Page Setup group**, click **Margins**, and then click **Narrow**. In the **Page Setup group**, click **Columns**, and then click **Three**.

b. On **Page 1**, in the first column, position the insertion point to the left of the paragraph *Room Amenities*. In the **Page Setup group**, click **Breaks**, and then under **Page Breaks**, click **Column**. In the second column, position the insertion point to the left of the paragraph *Resort Details*. Using the technique you just practiced, insert a **Column** break.

c. On **Page 2**, position the insertion point to the left of the paragraph *Resorts Division*, and then using the technique you practiced, insert a **Column** break. Press Ctrl + End, and then insert a **Column** break.

d. In the **Page Setup group**, click **Size**, and then at the bottom of the list, click **More Paper Sizes**. In the **Page Setup** dialog box, under **Paper Size**, click the **Paper Size arrow**, scroll down, and then click **Custom size**. Click the **Width spin box down arrow** to 9". Click the **Height spin box down arrow** to 7". Click **OK**, and then **Save** your changes.

2 On **Page 1**, in the first column, select the paragraph *Rooms*. On the mini toolbar, change the **Font Size** to 14, click the **Font Color button arrow**, and then click **Blue, Accent 1, Darker 50%**—in the fifth column, the last color. Press Ctrl + E.

a. With the paragraph still selected, on the **HOME tab**, in the **Font group**, click the **dialog box launcher**. In the **Font** dialog box, click the **Advanced tab**. Under **Character Spacing**, click the **Spacing arrow**, and then click **Expanded**. Click the **By spin box up arrow** to 1.2 pt. Click **OK**.

b. In the **Clipboard group**, double-click **Format Painter**. Select each of the following paragraphs to apply the format: *Room Amenities*, *Resort Details*, and *About Our Resorts*. Click **Format Painter** to turn it off.

c. On **Page 1**, in the first column, select the last three paragraphs beginning with *Superior Suite*. In the **Paragraph group**, click **Bullets**.

d. On **Page 1**, in the third column, select the paragraph *Dining Options*. On the mini toolbar, apply **Bold** and **Underline**, click the **Font Color button arrow**, and then click **Blue, Accent 1, Darker 25%**—in the fifth column, the fifth color.

e. In the **Paragraph group**, click **Line and Paragraph Spacing**, and then click **Remove Space After Paragraph**. In the **Clipboard group**, click **Format Painter**, and then in the third column, apply the format to the paragraph *Facilities and Services*.

f. In the second column, select the eight paragraphs beginning with *Telephone* and ending with *Daily Housekeeping*, and then in the **Paragraph group**, click **Bullets**. In a similar manner, apply bullets to the four paragraphs below *Dining Options*, and the seven paragraphs below *Facilities and Services*.

g. On **Page 2**, in the first column, in the last paragraph, locate the phone number. Select the space following *(702)*, and then press Ctrl + Shift + Spacebar to insert a nonbreaking space. Select the hyphen following *555*, and then press Ctrl + Shift + - to insert a nonbreaking hyphen. **Save** your changes.

3 Press Ctrl + Home. On the **VIEW tab**, in the **Show group**, select the **Gridlines** check box.

a. On the **INSERT tab**, in the **Text group**, click **Text Box**, and then click **Draw Text Box**. On **Page 1**, in the second column, position the ➕ pointer at the beginning of the column break formatting mark. Drag to the right until you are one gridline past the column break formatting mark, drag down 12 squares, and then release the mouse button. If necessary, resize the text box so that the right border aligns with the second gridline to the right of the 2.25 inches on the horizontal ruler and the bottom border aligns at approximately 1.5 inches on the lower portion of the vertical ruler.

b. On **Page 2**, in the second column, click to position the insertion point to the left of *Resorts Division*. On the **INSERT tab**, in the **Text group**, click **Text Box**, and then click **Draw Text Box**. In the second

(Project 12D Resort Facilities continues on the next page)

column, position the ✛ pointer at the top margin one gridline to the right of the beginning of the paragraph *Resorts*. Drag to the right **18** squares until the border is 3 squares to the right of *Corporation*, and then drag down until the bottom of the text box is aligned with the line below the text *Lodging Program for* (in the first column). Release the mouse button. If necessary, resize the text box so that the right border aligns at approximately 2.25 inches on the horizontal ruler and the bottom border aligns at approximately 3 inches on the vertical ruler.

c. On the **FORMAT tab**, in the **Arrange group**, click **Wrap Text**, and then click **Top and Bottom**. Scroll, if necessary, to display a portion of both text boxes simultaneously. On **Page 1**, in the second column, click the text box to select it. On the **FORMAT tab**, in the **Text group**, click **Create Link**. On **Page 2**, point to the text box, and then click to create a link.

d. If necessary, on **Page 1**, click to position the insertion point in the text box. On the **INSERT tab**, in the **Text group**, click the **Object button arrow**, and then click **Text from File**. From your student files, select the file **w12D_Resort_Reviews**, and then click **Insert**.

e. In the second text box, click to the left of the text *I am*, type **More Reviews** and then press Enter. Select the text you just typed, and on the mini toolbar, apply **Bold**. Press Ctrl + E.

f. With the second text box selected, on the **FORMAT tab**, in the **Shape Styles group**, click **More**. In the **Shape Styles** gallery, in the fourth row, click the second option—**Subtle Effect – Blue, Accent 1**. In a similar manner, apply the shape style to the first text box.

g. On the **VIEW tab**, in the **Show group**, clear the **Gridlines** check box to hide the gridlines. **Save** your changes.

4 On **Page 2**, in the second column, select the five paragraphs below the textbox. On the mini toolbar, apply **Bold**, and then press Ctrl + E. On the **HOME tab**, in the **Font group**, click **Text Effects and Typography**, and then in the second row, click the second text effect—**Gradient Fill – Blue, Accent 1, Reflection**.

a. On **Page 2**, position the insertion point at the beginning of the third column. Type **OUR RESORTS** Press Enter two times, and then type **Your home away from home!**

b. Select the paragraph you just typed, and then on the mini toolbar, change the **Font Size** to **14**, apply **Italic** and press Ctrl + E. On the **HOME tab**, in the **Font group**, click **Text Effects and Typography**. In the **Text Effects** gallery, in the first row, click the second effect—**Fill – Blue, Accent 1, Shadow**.

c. Select the first paragraph in the column. On the mini toolbar, change the **Font Size** to **20**, and then apply **Bold** and **Center**. On the **HOME tab**, in the **Font group**, click **Text Effects and Typography**, and then in the first row, click the second effect—**Fill – Blue, Accent 1, Shadow**. **Save** your changes.

5 On **Page 1**, in the first column, position the insertion point in the blank paragraph. On the **INSERT tab**, in the **Illustrations group**, click **Pictures**. In the **Insert Picture** dialog box, navigate to your student files, select the file **w12D_Room**, and then click **Insert**.

a. On the **FORMAT tab**, in the **Adjust group**, click **Artistic Effects**. In the **Artistic Effects** gallery, in the fourth row, click the second option—**Texturizer**.

b. On **Page 2**, in the third column, click in the blank paragraph. On the **INSERT tab**, in the **Illustrations group**, click **Pictures**. In the **Insert Picture** dialog box, navigate to your student files, select the file **w12D_Pools**, and then click **Insert**.

c. On the **FORMAT tab**, in the **Adjust group**, click **Artistic Effects**. In the **Artistic Effects** gallery, in the third row, click the second option—**Watercolor Sponge**.

d. Position the insertion point to the left of the paragraph *Our Resorts*, and then press Enter three times. **Save** your changes.

6 On **Page 1**, in the first column, select the three bulleted paragraphs. On the **HOME tab**, in the **Paragraph group**, click the **Bullet button arrow**, and then click **Define New Bullet**.

a. In the **Define New Bullet** dialog box, under **Bullet character**, click **Picture**. In the **Insert Pictures** dialog box, to the right of **From a file**, click **Browse**.

b. In the **Insert Picture** dialog box, navigate to your student files, select **w12D_Resort_Bullet**, and then click **Insert**. Click **OK**.

c. In the second column, select the bulleted list. In the **Paragraph group**, click the **Bullet button arrow**.

(Project 12D Resort Facilities continues on the next page)

CHAPTER REVIEW

Under **Recently Used Bullets**, click the *Resort Bullet*. In the same manner, apply the *Resort Bullet* to the two bulleted lists in the third column. Remove the picture bullet from the Bullet Library.

d. Press Ctrl + Home. Click the **FILE tab**, and then click **Show All Properties**. In the **Tags** box, type **facilities,** **graphics, reviews** In the **Subject** box, type your course name and section number. If necessary, edit the author name to display your name.

e. **Save** your changes. Print your document or submit electronically as directed by your instructor. **Close** Word.

END | You have completed Project 12D

CONTENT-BASED ASSESSMENTS

Mastering Word   Project 12E Summer Employment

Apply **12A** skills from these Objectives:

1 Integrate Word with PowerPoint

2 Modify a PowerPoint Presentation

3 Create a Table of Authorities

In the following Mastering Word project, you will create an outline and then use it to create a PowerPoint presentation that can be shown to individuals interested in summer employment at Magical Park Corporation theme park. You will create a handout for individuals based on the presentation. You will also modify a legal document for management review. Your completed files will look similar to Figure 12.52.

PROJECT FILES

For Project 12E, you will need the following files:

w12E_Employment_Outline
w12E_Vendor
w12E_Product_Brief

You will save your files as:

Lastname_Firstname_12E_Employment_Outline
Lastname_Firstname_12E_Employment_Presentation
Lastname_Firstname_12E_Employment_Handout
Lastname_Firstname_12E_Product_Brief

PROJECT RESULTS

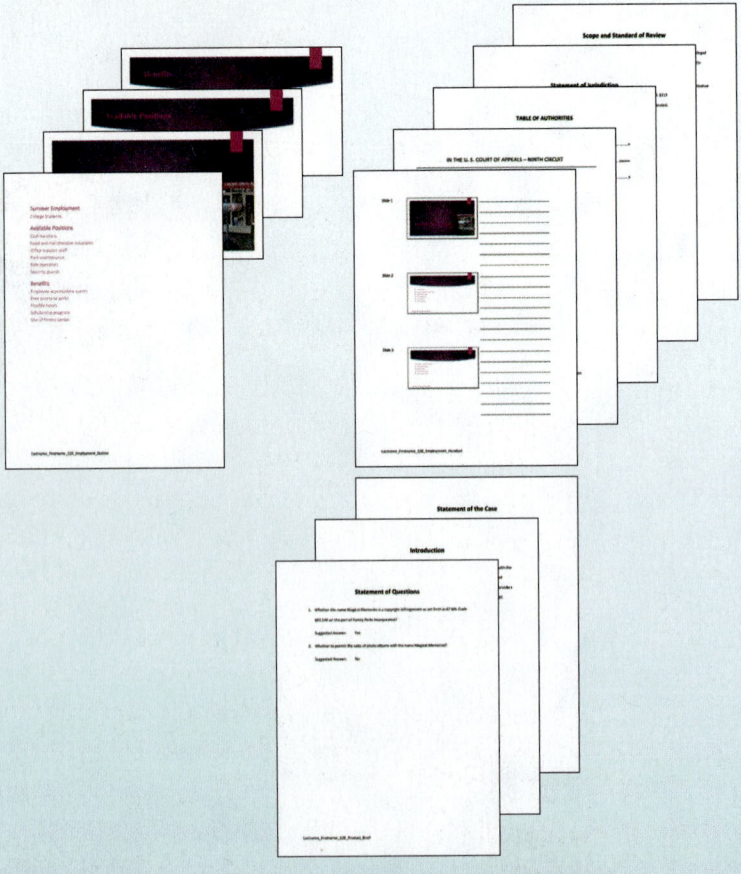

FIGURE 12.52

(Project 12E Summer Employment continues on the next page)

CONTENT-BASED ASSESSMENTS

1 Start Word. Navigate to your student files, and open the file **w12E_Employment_Outline**. **Save** the document to your **Word Chapter 12** folder as **Lastname_Firstname_12E_Employment_Outline** Insert the file name in the footer.

2 In **Outline** view, assign **Level 1** to all paragraphs formatted with bold, and then assign **Level 2** to all remaining paragraphs. **Collapse** the paragraphs *Benefits* and *Available Positions*. **Move Up** the *Available Positions* paragraph and subtext so that it displays above *Benefits*. **Expand** all *Level 1* paragraphs.

3 In **Print Layout** view, display the **Theme Colors** gallery, and then click **Red Violet**. Press Ctrl + Home. From **Backstage** view, click **Show All Properties**. In the **Tags** box, type **employment, outline** In the **Subject** box, type your course name and section number. If necessary, edit the author name to display your name. **Save** your changes, and then **Close** Word.

4 Start PowerPoint. Display the **Open** dialog box, change the types of files to **All Outlines**, and then from your **Word Chapter 12** folder, open your **Lastname_Firstname_12E_Employment_Outline** file. **Save** the PowerPoint file to your **Word Chapter 12** folder as **Lastname_Firstname_12E_Employment_Presentation** Display the **Themes** gallery, and click **Ion Boardroom**. Display the **Layout** gallery, and apply the **Title Slide** layout to **Slide 1**.

5 On **Slide 1**, from your student files, locate and then insert the picture file **w12E_Vendor**. Change the **Shape Height** to 4". Move the picture so that the bottom right corner of the picture is aligned with the bottom right corner of the slide, as shown in Figure 12.52. Display the **Header and Footer** dialog box. Select the **Footer** and **Don't show on title slide** check boxes, and then in the **Footer** box, type **Lastname_Firstname_12E_Employment_Presentation** Save your changes.

6 From **Backstage** view, click **Show All Properties**. In the **Tags** box, type **employment, presentation** In the **Subject** box, type your course name and section number. If necessary, edit the author name to display your name. **Save** your changes.

7 To create a handout, display the **Send to Microsoft Word** dialog box, and then select the **Blank lines** next to slides option. Click **OK**. In Word, **Save** the document to your **Word Chapter 12** folder as **Lastname_Firstname_12E_Employment_Handout** Insert the file name in the footer. From **Backstage** view, click **Show All Properties**. In the **Tags** box, type **employment, handout** In the **Subject** box, type your course name and section number. If necessary, edit the author name to display your name. **Save** your changes, and then from **Backstage** view, **Close** the document but leave Word open. In PowerPoint, **Save** your changes, and then **Close** PowerPoint.

8 In Word, from your student files, open the file **w12E_Product_Brief**. **Save** it to your **Word Chapter 12** folder as **Lastname_Firstname_12E_Product_Brief** Insert the file name in the footer.

9 On **Page 2**, in the second paragraph, select the text *98 Ne. C.S. §213*. Display the **Mark Citation** dialog box, select the category **Regulations**, and then click **Mark**. Select the text *67 MS. Code §83.144*. In the **Mark Citation** dialog box, select the category **Statutes**, and then click **Mark All**. On **Page 3**, select the text *Park World Network v. Extreme Rides*. In the **Mark Citation** dialog box, select the category **Cases**, and then click **Mark**. **Close** the **Mark Citation** dialog box.

10 At the bottom of **Page 1**, position the insertion point to the right of the date, and then press Ctrl + Enter two times. On **Page 2**, position the insertion point to the left of the page break, type **TABLE OF AUTHORITIES** and then press Enter two times. Select the text you typed, change the **Font Size** to 16, and then apply **Bold** and **Center**. Position the insertion point to the left of the page break, and then display the **Table of Authorities** dialog box. Under **Category**, click **All**, and then apply the **Classic** format. If necessary, select the **Use passim** check box. Click **OK**.

11 From **Backstage** view, click **Show All Properties**. In the **Tags** box, type **legal, product, copyright** In the **Subject** box, type your course name and section number. If necessary, edit the author name to display your name. **Save** your changes.

12 Print all three Word documents or submit all four files electronically as directed by your instructor. **Close** Word.

END | You have completed Project 12E

CONTENT-BASED ASSESSMENTS

MyITLab® grader

Mastering Word | Project 12F First Aid

Apply 12B skills from these Objectives:

4 Modify the Document Layout

5 Format Graphic and Text Elements

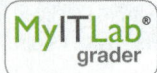

In the following Mastering Word project, you will format a document, insert graphics, and link text boxes to create a leaflet containing first aid information for Magical Park Corporation's employees. Your completed document will look similar to Figure 12.53.

PROJECT FILES

For Project 12F, you will need the following files:

w12F_First_Aid
w12F_Contact_Information
w12F_Medical
w12F_Medical_Bullet

You will save your document as:

Lastname_Firstname_12F_First_Aid

PROJECT RESULTS

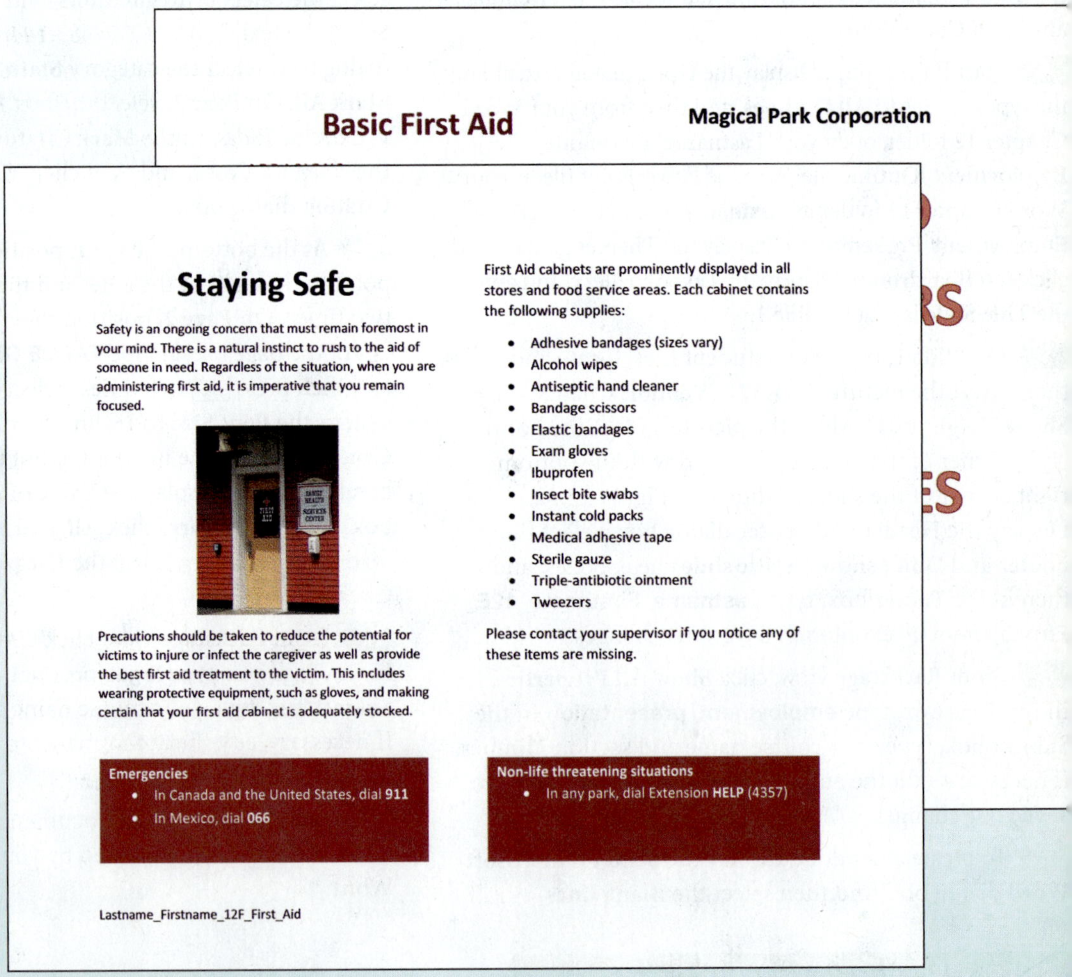

Basic First Aid

Magical Park Corporation

Staying Safe

Safety is an ongoing concern that must remain foremost in your mind. There is a natural instinct to rush to the aid of someone in need. Regardless of the situation, when you are administering first aid, it is imperative that you remain focused.

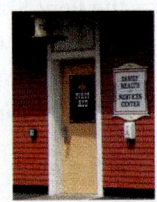

Precautions should be taken to reduce the potential for victims to injure or infect the caregiver as well as provide the best first aid treatment to the victim. This includes wearing protective equipment, such as gloves, and making certain that your first aid cabinet is adequately stocked.

Emergencies
- In Canada and the United States, dial **911**
- In Mexico, dial **066**

First Aid cabinets are prominently displayed in all stores and food service areas. Each cabinet contains the following supplies:

- Adhesive bandages (sizes vary)
- Alcohol wipes
- Antiseptic hand cleaner
- Bandage scissors
- Elastic bandages
- Exam gloves
- Ibuprofen
- Insect bite swabs
- Instant cold packs
- Medical adhesive tape
- Sterile gauze
- Triple-antibiotic ointment
- Tweezers

Please contact your supervisor if you notice any of these items are missing.

Non-life threatening situations
- In any park, dial Extension **HELP** (4357)

Lastname_Firstname_12F_First_Aid

FIGURE 12.53

(Project 12F First Aid continues on the next page)

1 Start Word. From your student files, open the file **w12F_First_Aid**. **Save** the document to your **Word Chapter 12** folder as **Lastname_Firstname_12F_First_Aid** Insert the file name in the footer.

2 On the **PAGE LAYOUT tab**, in the **Page Setup group**, change the **Orientation** to **Landscape**, and then change the **Columns** to **Two**. On **Page 1**, in the first column, position the insertion point to the left of the fourth paragraph that begins *First Aid*, and then insert a **Column** break. In the second column, position the insertion point to the left of the paragraph *Basic First Aid*, and then press Ctrl + Enter. On **Page 2**, position the insertion point to the left of *Magical Park Corporation*, and then insert a **Column** break. Display the **Page Setup** dialog box, change the **Paper Size** to **Custom size**, and then change the **Width** to **10"**. **Save** your changes.

3 Select the first paragraph *Staying Safe*. Change the **Font Size** to **28**, and then apply **Bold** and **Center**. In the second column, select the 13 paragraphs beginning with *Adhesive* and ending with *Tweezers*, and then apply **Bullets**. In the second column, select all the text, and then change the **Font Size** to **12**. On **Page 2**, select the first paragraph. Change the **Font Size** to **26**, apply **Bold** and **Center**, and then change the **Font Color** to **Red, Accent 2, Darker 25%**.

4 Select the paragraph *ABRASIONS*. Change the **Font Size** to **14**, and then change the **Font Color** to **Red, Accent 2**, and then set the **Spacing** to **Expanded** by **1.4 pt**. Turn on the **Format Painter**, and then apply the format to the paragraphs *SPRAINS* and *CHOKING*. Turn off the **Format Painter**. Select the four paragraphs below *ABRASIONS*, and apply **Bullets**. In a similar manner, apply **Bullets** to the paragraphs below *SPRAINS* and *CHOKING*.

5 On **Page 2**, in the second column, select the first paragraph, change the **Font Size** to **18**, and then apply **Bold** and **Center**. On **Page 1**, in the second paragraph, select the space to the right of *first*, and then insert a nonbreaking space. In a similar manner, in the third paragraph, in the first sentence, select the space to the right of *first*, and then insert a nonbreaking space. **Save** your changes.

6 Display the document **Gridlines**. Display the **Text Box** gallery, and then click **Draw Text Box**. On **Page 1**, at the bottom of the first column, begin at the left margin **4** gridlines below the last paragraph, drag down **9** squares, and then drag to the right until the border of the text box aligns with the end of the third paragraph mark. In the second column, draw a text box, beginning **6** gridlines below the left side of the page break, approximately the same size as the first text box. Change the **Shape Width** of both text boxes to **3.63"**.

7 Position the insertion point in the first text box, click **Create Link**, and then create a link to the second text box. On the **INSERT tab**, click the **Object button arrow**, and then click **Text from File**. From your student files, insert text from the file **w12F_Contact_Information**. Apply the **Light 1 Outline, Colored Fill – Red, Accent 2** shape style to both text boxes. Turn off the display of **Gridlines**. **Save** your changes.

8 On **Page 2**, in the second column, select the last four paragraphs. Change the **Font Size** to **48**, and then apply **Center**. Change the **Text Effects** to **Fill – Red, Accent 2, Outline – Accent 2**. Change the **Font Color** to **Red, Accent 2, Lighter 40%**.

9 On **Page 1**, position the insertion point at the end of the second paragraph that begins *Safety is*, and then press Enter. From your student files, insert the picture file **w12F_Medical**. Change the **Shape Height** to **2"**. Display the **Artistic Effects** gallery, and then apply the **Texturizer** effect. **Center** the picture.

10 On **Page 2**, select the first bulleted list. Define a new bullet using the file **w12F_Medical_Bullet**, and then apply it to the bulleted list. Apply the medical bullet to the remaining bulleted lists in the column.

11 From **Backstage** view, click **Show All Properties**. In the **Tags** box, type **first aid, leaflet** In the **Subject** box, type your course name and section number. If necessary, edit the author name to display your name. **Save** your changes. Remove the medical bullet from the Bullet Library.

12 Print your document or submit electronically as directed by your instructor. **Close** Word.

END | You have completed Project 12F

CONTENT-BASED ASSESSMENTS

In the following Mastering Word project, you will format an outline and then use it to create a PowerPoint presentation describing features of the new Imagination Parks operated by Magical Park Corporation. You will edit a letter by inserting graphics and modifying text. The company plans to send these files as email attachments to its newsletter subscribers. You will also modify a legal document for management review. Your completed documents will look similar to Figure 12.54.

Apply 12A and 12B skills from these Objectives:

1. Integrate Word with PowerPoint
2. Modify a PowerPoint Presentation
3. Create a Table of Authorities
4. Modify the Document Layout
5. Format Graphic and Text Elements

PROJECT FILES

For Project 12G, you will need the following files:

w12G_Imagination_Outline
w12G_Technology
w12G_Imagination_Brief
w12G_Park_Letter
w12G_Ride
w12G_Imagination_Bullet

You will save your files as:

Lastname_Firstname_12G_Imagination_Outline
Lastname_Firstname_12G_Imagination_Presentation
Lastname_Firstname_12G_Imagination_Handout
Lastname_Firstname_12G_Imagination_Brief
Lastname_Firstname_12G_Park_Letter

PROJECT RESULTS

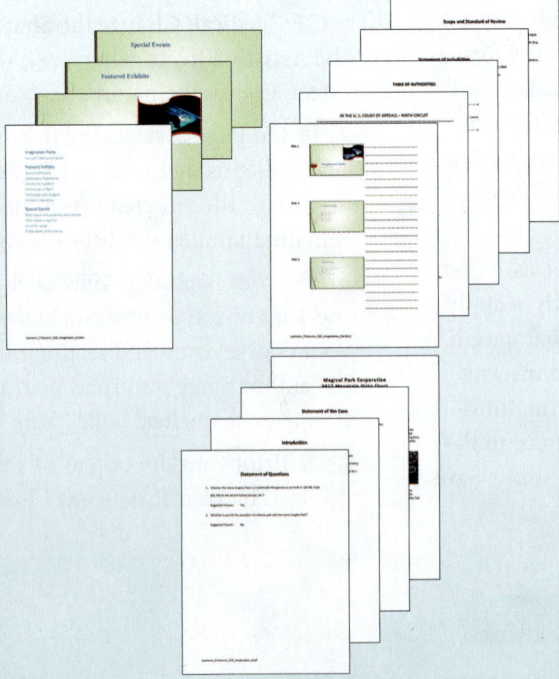

FIGURE 12.54

(Project 12G Imagination Parks continues on the next page)

1 Start Word. Navigate to your student files, and open the file **w12G_Imagination_Outline**. **Save** the document to your **Word Chapter 12** folder as **Lastname_Firstname_12G_Imagination_Outline** Insert the file name in a footer.

2 In **Outline** view, assign **Level 1** to all paragraphs formatted with bold, and then assign **Level 2** to all remaining paragraphs. In **Print Layout** view, display **Backstage** view, and then click **Show All Properties**. In the **Tags** box, type **imagination, outline** In the **Subject** box, type your course name and section number. **Save** your changes, and then **Close** Word.

3 Start PowerPoint. Display the **Open** dialog box, change the types of files to **All Outlines**, and then from your **Word Chapter 12** folder, open your **Lastname_Firstname_12G_Imagination_Outline** file. **Save** the PowerPoint file to your **Word Chapter 12** folder as **Lastname_Firstname_12G_Imagination_Presentation** Change the theme to **Wisp**. Display the **Layout** gallery, and apply the **Title Slide** layout to **Slide 1**.

4 Display the **Insert Picture** dialog box, and then from your student files, locate and open the file **w12G_Technology**. Position the picture so that the top right corner of the picture aligns with the top right corner of **Slide 1**. Display the **Header and Footer** dialog box. Select the **Footer** and **Don't show on title slide** check boxes, and then in the **Footer** box, type **Lastname_Firstname_12G_Imagination_Presentation** From **Backstage** view, click **Show All Properties**. In the **Tags** box, type **imagination, presentation** In the **Subject** box, type your course name and section number. If necessary, edit the author name to display your name.

5 To create a handout, display the **Send to Microsoft Word** dialog box, and then select the **Blank lines next to slides** option. Click **OK**. In Word, **Save** the document to your **Word Chapter 12** folder as **Lastname_Firstname_12G_Imagination_Handout** Insert the file name in the footer. From **Backstage** view, click **Show All Properties**. In the **Tags** box, type **imagination park, handout** In the **Subject** box, type your course name and section number. If necessary, edit the author name to display your name. **Save** your changes, and then from **Backstage** view, **Close** the document but leave Word open. In PowerPoint, **Save** your changes, and then **Close** PowerPoint.

6 In Word, from your student files, open the file **w12G_Imagination_Brief**. **Save** it to your **Word Chapter 12** folder as **Lastname_Firstname_12G_Imagination_Brief** Insert the file name in the footer.

7 On **Page 2**, in the second paragraph, select the text *92 Ne. C.S. §864*. Display the **Mark Citation** dialog box, select the category **Regulations**, and then click **Mark**. Select the text *129 MS. Code §51.789*. Display the **Mark Citation** dialog box, select the category **Statutes**, and then click **Mark All**. On **Page 3**, select the text *Port Santa Maria v. Williamson*. Display the **Mark Citation** dialog box, select the category **Cases**, and then click **Mark**. **Close** the **Mark Citation** dialog box.

8 At the bottom of **Page 1**, position the insertion point to the right of the date, and then press Ctrl + Enter two times. On **Page 2**, position the insertion point to the left of the page break, type **TABLE OF AUTHORITIES** and then press Enter two times. Select the text you typed, change the **Font Size** to **16**, and then apply **Bold** and **Center**. Position the insertion point to the left of the page break, and then display the **Table of Authorities** dialog box. Under **Category**, click **All**, and then apply the **Formal** format. If necessary, select the **Use Passim** check box. Click **OK**.

9 From **Backstage** view, click **Show All Properties**. In the **Tags** box, type **legal, park trademark** In the **Subject** box, type your course name and section number. If necessary, edit the author name to display your name. **Save** your changes. From **Backstage** view, **Close** the document but leave Word open.

10 In Word, from your student files, open the file **w12G_Park_Letter**. **Save** the document to your **Word Chapter 12** folder as **Lastname_Firstname_12G_Park_Letter** Insert the file name in the footer. If any words are flagged as spelling errors, click **Ignore All**. Select the first four paragraphs. Change the **Font Size** to **18**, and then apply **Bold** and **Center**. With all four paragraphs selected, change the **Spacing** to **Expanded** by **1.5 pt**.

11 Beginning with the paragraph that begins *The featured exhibit*, select the next seven paragraphs, and then change the **Font Size** to **14**. Select the six paragraphs below the paragraph that begins *The featured exhibit*, and then apply **Bullets**. In the paragraph that begins *Our parks*, locate the phone number, and then change

(Project 12G Imagination Parks continues on the next page)

CONTENT-BASED ASSESSMENTS

the space to a nonbreaking space, and then change the hyphen to a nonbreaking hyphen. **Save** your changes.

12 Position the insertion point to the right of the paragraph that begins *The featured exhibit*. From your student files, insert the picture file **w12G_Ride**. Change **Wrap Text** to **Square**, and then change the **Shape Height** to **1.6"**. Position the picture so that the top edge of the picture is aligned with the paragraph that begins *The featured exhibit*, and the right edge of the picture is aligned at the right margin. Display the **Artistic Effects** gallery, and then apply the **Glow Edges** effect.

13 Select the bulleted list. Define a new bullet using the file **w12G_Imagination_Bullet**, and then apply it to the bulleted list. Press Ctrl + Home. Remove the picture bullet from the Bullet Library.

14 From **Backstage** view, click **Show All Properties**. In the **Tags** box, type **letter, graphics, bullets** In the **Subject** box, type your course name and section number. If necessary, edit the author name to display your name. **Save** your changes.

15 Print your four Word documents or submit all five files electronically as directed by your instructor. **Close** Word.

END | You have completed Project 12G

CONTENT-BASED ASSESSMENTS

Apply a combination of the **12A** and **12B** skills.

GO! Fix It   Project 12H Grand Opening   Online

GO! Make It   Project 12I Season Pass   Online

GO! Solve It   Project 12J Employee Interviews   Online

GO! Solve It   Project 12K Appreciation Day

PROJECT FILES

For Project 12K, you will need the following files:

w12K_Appreciation_Day
w12K_Teacher_Quotes
w12K_School_Bullet

You will save your file as:

Lastname_Firstname_12K_Appreciation_Day

From your student files, open the file **w12K_Appreciation_Day** and save it to your **Word Chapter 12** folder as **Lastname_Firstname_12K_Appreciation_Day** Change the page orientation to Landscape and the paper size to a width of 7" and a height of 5". Format the text so that the first five paragraphs display on the first page and the remaining text is on a second page. Format the document attractively and apply character spacing and text effects to the appropriate text. On the second page, create a bulleted list for the five paragraphs describing benefits. Use the file **w12K_School_Bullet** to define and apply a picture bullet to the list. Draw text boxes at the bottom of both pages. Link the text boxes and insert text from the file **w12K_Teacher_Quotes**. Apply a shape style to both text boxes. Insert the file name in the footer and add appropriate document properties. Print your document or submit electronically as directed by your instructor.

(Project 12K Appreciation Day continues on the next page)

CONTENT-BASED ASSESSMENTS

Performance Level

	Exemplary: You consistently applied the relevant skills	Proficient: You sometimes, but not always, applied the relevant skills	Developing: You rarely or never applied the relevant skills
Change orientation and paper size	Page orientation and paper size are changed correctly.	The page orientation is not changed or the paper size is not changed.	No changes were made to the document layout.
Format text including character spacing and text effects	Text is formatted attractively and character spacing and text effects are applied.	Text is formatted attractively but either no character spacing or no text effect is applied.	Text is formatted but character spacing and text effects are not applied.
Define bullet and apply to list	A bullet is defined and applied to appropriate paragraphs.	A bulleted list is created but a picture bullet is not defined or applied.	No bulleted list is created.
Insert and link text boxes	Text boxes are inserted appropriately and linked.	Text boxes are inserted but do not display appropriately or are not linked.	No text boxes are inserted.
Insert text in text boxes and apply shape style	Text is inserted and a shape style is applied to both text boxes.	Text is not inserted or a shape style is not applied to both text boxes.	No text is inserted and a shape style is not applied.

Performance Element

END | You have completed Project 12K

OUTCOMES-BASED ASSESSMENTS

RUBRIC

The following outcomes-based assessments are *open-ended assessments*. That is, there is no specific correct result; your result will depend on your approach to the information provided. Make *Professional Quality* your goal. Use the following scoring rubric to guide you in *how* to approach the problem and then to evaluate *how well* your approach solves the problem.

The *criteria*—Software Mastery, Content, Format and Layout, and Process—represent the knowledge and skills you have gained that you can apply to solving the problem. The *levels of performance*—Professional Quality, Approaching Professional Quality, or Needs Quality Improvements—help you and your instructor evaluate your result.

	Your completed project is of Professional Quality if you:	Your completed project is Approaching Professional Quality if you:	Your completed project Needs Quality Improvements if you:
1-Software Mastery	Choose and apply the most appropriate skills, tools, and features and identify efficient methods to solve the problem.	Choose and apply some appropriate skills, tools, and features, but not in the most efficient manner.	Choose inappropriate skills, tools, or features, or are inefficient in solving the problem.
2-Content	Construct a solution that is clear and well organized, contains content that is accurate, appropriate to the audience and purpose, and is complete. Provide a solution that contains no errors in spelling, grammar, or style.	Construct a solution in which some components are unclear, poorly organized, inconsistent, or incomplete. Misjudge the needs of the audience. Have some errors in spelling, grammar, or style, but the errors do not detract from comprehension.	Construct a solution that is unclear, incomplete, or poorly organized; contains some inaccurate or inappropriate content; and contains many errors in spelling, grammar, or style. Do not solve the problem.
3-Format & Layout	Format and arrange all elements to communicate information and ideas, clarify function, illustrate relationships, and indicate relative importance.	Apply appropriate format and layout features to some elements, but not others. Overuse features, causing minor distraction.	Apply format and layout that does not communicate information or ideas clearly. Do not use format and layout features to clarify function, illustrate relationships, or indicate relative importance. Use available features excessively, causing distraction.
4-Process	Use an organized approach that integrates planning, development, self-assessment, revision, and reflection.	Demonstrate an organized approach in some areas, but not others; or, use an insufficient process of organization throughout.	Do not use an organized approach to solve the problem.

OUTCOMES-BASED ASSESSMENTS

Apply a combination of the 12A and 12B skills.

Build from Scratch

GO! Think | Project 12L Group Events

PROJECT FILES

For Project 12L, you will need the following file:

New blank Word document

You will save your files as:

Lastname_Firstname_12L_Group_Outline
Lastname_Firstname_12L_Group_Presentation
Lastname_Firstname_12L_Group_Handout

Magical Park Corporation offers special packages for a variety of groups. Types of groups include schools, family reunions, tour groups, service clubs, youth groups, and businesses. Benefits of a group program include reduced admission, catered meals, priority seating at shows, discounts at all concession stands, free parking, and the services of a park consultant.

Create an outline defining the group program. Save it as **Lastname_Firstname_12L_Group_Outline** Create a PowerPoint presentation from your outline file. Include a picture and apply an appropriate theme. Save the presentation as **Lastname_Firstname_12L_Group_Presentation** Create a one-page handout in Word. Save the document as **Lastname_Firstname_12L_Group_Handout** Insert the file name in the footer and add appropriate document properties to all three files. Print your documents or submit all three files electronically as directed by your instructor.

END | You have completed Project 12L

Build from Scratch

GO! Think | Project 12M Employment Opportunities | Online

Build from Scratch

You and GO! | Project 12N Personal Highlights | Online

Glossary

.pptx The default file extension for a PowerPoint file.

Accessibility Checker A Word feature that searches a document for content that people with disabilities might find difficult to read and suggest ways to modify the content.

Address bar (Internet Explorer) The area at the top of the Internet Explorer window that displays, and where you can type, a URL—Uniform Resource Locator—which is an address that uniquely identifies a location on the Internet.

Address bar (Windows) The bar at the top of a folder window with which you can navigate to a different folder or library, or go back to the previous one.

Address Block A predefined merge field that includes the recipient's name and address.

AdjustListIndents A built-in macro used to modify the indenting of a bulleted or numbered list.

Alignment The placement of paragraph text relative to the left and right margins.

Alignment guides Green vertical or horizontal lines that display when you are moving or sizing an object to assist you with object placement.

All Markup A Track Changes view that displays the document with all revisions and comments visible.

American Psychological Association (APA) One of two commonly used style guides for formatting research papers.

App The term that commonly refers to computer programs that run from the device software on a smartphone or a tablet computer—for example, iOS, Android, or Windows Phone—or computer programs that run from the browser software on a desktop PC or laptop PC—for example Internet Explorer, Safari, Firefox, or Chrome.

App for Office A webpage that works within one of the Office applications, such as Excel, and that you download from the Office Store.

Apps for Office 2013 and SharePoint 2013 A collection of downloadable apps that enable you to create and view information within your familiar Office programs.

Area chart A chart type that shows trends over time.

Artistic effects Formats applied to images that make pictures resemble sketches or paintings.

Ascending The order of text sorted alphabetically from A to Z or numbers sorted from the smallest to the largest.

Author The owner, or creator, of the original document.

AutoClose A macro that will automatically run when closing a document.

AutoCorrect A feature that corrects common typing and spelling errors as you type, for example changing *teh* to *the*.

AutoFit A table feature that automatically adjusts column widths or the width of the entire table.

AutoFit Contents A table feature that resizes the column widths to accommodate the maximum field size.

AutoMark file A Word document that contains a two-column table that is used to mark words as index entries.

AutoRecover A feature that helps prevent losing unsaved changes by automatically creating a backup version of the current document.

Backstage tabs The area along the left side of Backstage view with tabs to display screens with related groups of commands.

Backstage view A centralized space for file management tasks; for example, opening, saving, printing, publishing, or sharing a file. A navigation pane displays along the left side with tabs that group file-related tasks together.

Balloon The outline shape in which a comment or formatting change displays.

Bar chart A chart type that shows a comparison among related data.

Bibliography A list of cited works in a report or research paper; also referred to as Works Cited, Sources, or References, depending upon the report style.

Blog A website that displays dated entries, short for *Web log*.

Blog post An individual article entered in a blog with a time and date stamp.

Body The text of a letter.

Body text Text that does not have a heading style applied.

Bookmark A link that identifies the exact location of text, a table, or other object.

Border Painter A table feature that applies selected formatting to specific borders of a table.

Brightness The light to dark ratio of an image.

Building blocks Reusable pieces of content or other document parts—for example, headers, footers, and page number formats—that are stored in galleries.

Building Blocks Organizer A feature that enables you to view—in a single location—all of the available building blocks from all the different galleries.

Bulk mail A large mailing, sorted by postal code, which is eligible for reduced postage rates, available from the U.S. Postal Service.

Bulleted list A list of items with each item introduced by a symbol such as a small circle or check mark, and which is useful when the items in the list can be displayed in any order.

Bullets Text symbols such as small circles or check marks that precede each item in a bulleted list.

Caption A title that is added to a Word object and numbered sequentially.

Cell The box formed by the intersection of a column and row in a table or worksheet.

Cell margins The amount of space between a cell's content and the left, right, top, and bottom borders of the cell.

Cell spacing The distance between the individual cells in a table.

Center alignment The alignment of text or objects that is centered horizontally between the left and right margins.

Change Case A formatting command that allows you to quickly change the capitalization of selected text.

Character spacing A Word feature that allows you to change the default spacing constraints between characters.

Character style A style, indicated by the symbol α, that contains formatting characteristics that you apply to text, such as font name, font size, font color, bold emphasis, and so on.

Chart A visual representation of numerical data.

Chart area The entire chart and all its elements.

Chart data range The group of cells with red, purple, and blue shading that is used to create a chart.

Chart Elements A Word feature that displays commands to add, remove, or change chart elements, such as the legend, gridlines, and data labels.

Chart Filters A Word feature that displays commands to define what data points and names display on a chart.

Chart style The overall visual look of a chart in terms of its graphic effects, colors, and backgrounds.

Chart Styles A Word feature that displays commands to apply a style and color scheme to a chart.

Check Box content control A content control that allows the user to select, or not select, a specific option.

Check Box form field A legacy control that allows the user to select, or not select, a specific option.

Citation A note inserted into the text of a research paper that refers the reader to a source in the bibliography.

Click The action of pressing and releasing the left button on a mouse pointing device one time.

Click and type pointer The text select—I-beam—pointer with various attached shapes that indicate which formatting—left-aligned, centered, or right-aligned—will be applied when you double-click in a blank area of a document.

Clip art Downloadable predefined graphics available online from Office.com and other sites.

Clipboard A temporary storage area that holds text or graphics that you select and then cut or copy.

Cloud computing Refers to applications and services that are accessed over the Internet, rather than to applications that are installed on your local computer.

Cloud storage Online storage of data so that you can access your data from different places and devices.

Collaborate To work with others as a team in an intellectual endeavor to complete a shared task or to achieve a shared goal.

Collaboration The action of working together with others as a team in an intellectual endeavor to complete a shared task or achieve a shared goal.

Column break indicator A dotted line containing the words *Column Break* that displays at the bottom of the column.

Column chart A chart type that shows a comparison among related data.

Combine A Track Changes feature that allows you to review two different documents containing revisions, both based on an original document.

Combo Box content control A content control that allows the user to select an item from a list or enter new text.

Command An instruction to a computer program that causes an action to be carried out.

Comment (1) A note that an author or reviewer adds to a document. (2) In a macro procedure, a line of text that is used solely for documentation.

Common dialog boxes The set of dialog boxes that includes Open, Save, and Save As, which are provided by the Windows programming interface, and which display and operate in all of the Office programs in the same manner.

Compare A Track Changes feature that enables you to review differences between an original document and the latest version of the document.

Complimentary closing A parting phrase—such as *Sincerely* or *Yours truly*—that is used to end a business letter.

Compress The process of reducing the size of a file.

Compressed file A file that has been reduced in size and thus takes up less storage space and can be transferred to other computers quickly.

Compressed folder A folder that has been reduced in size and thus takes up less storage space and can be transferred to other computers quickly; also called a *zipped* folder.

Content control In a template, an area indicated by placeholder text that can be used to add text, pictures, dates, or lists.

Context menus Menus that display commands and options relevant to the selected text or object; also called *shortcut menus*.

Context-sensitive commands Commands that display on a shortcut menu that relate to the object or text that you right-clicked.

Contextual tabs Tabs that are added to the ribbon automatically when a specific object, such as a picture, is selected, and that contain commands relevant to the selected object.

Contiguous Items that are adjacent to one another.

Continuous section break A mark that defines the beginning and end of each subdocument.

Contrast The difference between the darkest and lightest areas of a picture.

Copy A command that duplicates a selection and places it on the Clipboard.

Cover letter A document that you send with your resume to provide additional information about your skills and experience.

Cover page The first page of a document that provides introductory information.

Crop A command that removes unwanted or unnecessary areas of a picture.

Crop handles Handles used to define unwanted areas of a picture.

Crop pointer The pointer used to crop areas of a picture.

Cropping The process of removing unwanted parts from the edges of a picture.

Cross-reference A text link to an item that appears in another location in the document, such as a heading, a caption, or a footnote.

Cut A command that removes a selection and places it on the Clipboard.

Data labels The part of a chart that displays the value represented by each data marker.

Data markers The shapes in a chart representing each of the cells that contain data.

Data points The cells that contain numerical data used in a chart.

Data range border The blue line that surrounds the cells containing numerical data that display in the chart.

Data series In a chart, related data points represented by a unique color.

Data source A document that contains a list of variable information, such as names and addresses, that is merged with a main document to create customized form letters or labels.

Database An organized collection of facts about people, events, things, or ideas related to a particular topic or purpose.

Date & Time A command with which you can automatically insert the current date and time into a document in a variety of formats.

Date Picker content control A content control that allows the user to select a date from a calendar.

Dateline The first line in a business letter that contains the current date and which is positioned just below the letterhead if a letterhead is used.

Decrease Indent A command that moves your paragraph closer to the margin.

Default The term that refers to the current selection or setting that is automatically used by a computer program unless you specify otherwise.

Delimiters Characters—such as commas and tabs—that are used to separate text into groups.

Descending The order of text sorted alphabetically from Z to A or numbers sorted from the largest to the smallest.

Deselect The action of canceling the selection of an object or block of text by clicking outside of the selection.

Design Mode A command that enables the user to edit content controls that are inserted in a document.

Desktop In Windows, the screen that simulates your work area.

Desktop app The term that commonly refers to a computer program that is installed on your computer and requires a computer operating system like Microsoft Windows or Apple OS to run.

Destination file The file where an object is embedded or linked.

Dialog box A small window that contains options for completing a task.

Dialog Box Launcher A small icon that displays to the right of some group names on the ribbon, and which opens a related dialog box or pane providing additional options and commands related to that group.

Digital certificate (Digital ID) A file that contains information about a person and is used to electronically sign a document.

Digital signature An electronic stamp that is added to a document to verify the document's authenticity.

Direct formatting The process of applying each format separately, for example bold, then font size, then font color, and so on.

Directory A single list of records using specified fields from a data source.

Distribute Columns A command that adjusts the width of the selected columns so that they are equal.

Distribute Rows A command that causes the height of the selected rows to be equal.

Document gridlines Nonprinting horizontal and vertical lines used to assist in aligning graphics and other elements in a document.

Document properties Details about a file that describe or identify it, including the title, author name, subject, and keywords that identify the document's topic or contents; also known as *metadata*.

Dot leader A series of dots preceding a tab that guides the eye across the line.

Drag The action of holding down the left mouse button while moving your mouse.

Drag-and-drop A technique by which you can move, by dragging, selected text from one location in a document to another.

Drawing objects Graphic objects, such as shapes, diagrams, lines, or circles.

Drop cap A large capital letter at the beginning of a paragraph that formats text in a visually distinctive manner.

Drop-Down List content control A content control that allows the user to select a specific item from a list.

Dropped The position of a drop cap when it is within the text of the paragraph.

Edit The process of making changes to text or graphics in an Office file.

Ellipsis A set of three dots indicating incompleteness; an ellipsis following a command name indicates that a dialog box will display if you click the command.

Em dash A punctuation symbol used to indicate an explanation or emphasis.

Email address link A hyperlink that opens a new message window so that an individual viewing a website can send an email message.

Embed code A code that creates a link to a video, picture, or other type of rich media content.

Embedded object An object that maintains the structure of the original application, but is not connected to the source file.

Embedding The process of inserting an object, such as an Excel chart, into a Word document so that it becomes part of the document.

Enclosures Additional documents included with a business letter.

Endnote In a research paper, a note placed at the end of a document or chapter.

Enhanced ScreenTip A ScreenTip that displays more descriptive text than a normal ScreenTip.

Even Page section break A formatting mark that indicates the beginning of a new section on the next even-numbered page.

Extract To decompress, or pull out, files from a compressed form.

Federal registration symbol The symbol ® that indicates that a patent or trademark is registered with the U.S. Patent and Trademark Office.

Field A placeholder for data.

Fields In a mail merge, the categories—or columns—in a data source.

File A collection of information stored on a computer under a single name, for example, a Word document or a PowerPoint presentation.

File Explorer The program that displays the files and folders on your computer, and which is at work anytime you are viewing the contents of files and folders in a window.

Fill The inside color of an object.

Filter A set of criteria applied to fields in a data source to display specific records.

Flip A command that creates a reverse image of a picture or object.

Flipping The process of reversing the direction of an object either vertically or horizontally.

Floating object A graphic that can be moved independently of the surrounding text characters.

Folder A container in which you store files.

Folder window In Windows, a window that displays the contents of the current folder, library, or device, and contains helpful parts so that you can navigate within the Windows file structure.

Font A set of characters with the same design and shape.

Font styles Formatting emphasis such as bold, italic, and underline.

Footer A reserved area for text or graphics that displays at the bottom of each page in a document.

Footnote In a research paper, a note placed at the bottom of the page.

Form A structured document that has static text and reserved spaces for information to be entered by the user.

Form letter A letter with standardized wording that can be sent to many different people.

Formatting The process of establishing the overall appearance of text, graphics, and pages in an Office file—for example, in a Word document.

Formatting marks Characters that display on the screen, but do not print, indicating where the Enter key, the Spacebar, and the Tab key were pressed; also called *nonprinting characters*.

Formula A mathematical expression that contains functions, operators, constants, and properties, and returns a value to a cell.

Function A predefined formula that performs calculations by using specific values in a particular order.

Gallery An Office feature that displays a list of potential results instead of just the command name.

Gradient fill A fill effect in which one color fades into another.

Graphics Pictures, charts, or drawing objects.

Greeting Line A predefined merge field that includes an introductory word, such as *Dear*, and the recipient's name.

Gridlines Nonprinting lines that indicate cell borders.

Grouping The process of combining multiple elements into a single object.

Groups On the Office ribbon, the sets of related commands that you might need for a specific type of task.

Handout A document that is given to an audience to accompany a lecture.

Hanging indent An indent style in which the first line of a paragraph extends to the left of the remaining lines and that is commonly used for bibliographic entries.

Header A reserved area for text or graphics that displays at the top of each page in a document.

Header row The first row of a table containing column titles.

Hidden text Nonprinting text—for example, an index entry field.

Horizontal axis (X-axis) The axis that displays along the lower edge of a chart.

Hyperlinks Text, buttons, pictures, or other objects that, when clicked, access other sections of the active document or another file.

Hypertext Markup Language (HTML) The markup language that communicates color and graphics in a format that all computers can understand.

Hyphenation A tool in Word that controls how words are split between two lines.

In margin The position of a drop cap when it is in the left margin of a paragraph.

Increase Indent A command moves your paragraph farther away from the margin.

Index A compilation of topics, names, and terms accompanied by page numbers that displays at the end of a document.

Index entry A word or phrase that is listed in the index.

Index entry field Code, formatted as hidden text and displaying to the right of an index entry, containing the identifier XE and the term to be included in the index.

Info tab The tab in Backstage view that displays information about the current file.

Ink Revision marks made directly on a document by using a stylus on a Tablet PC.

Inline Object An object or graphic inserted in a document that acts like a character in a sentence.

Insertion point A blinking vertical line that indicates where text or graphics will be inserted.

Inside address The name and address of the person receiving the letter and is positioned below the date line.

Interactive media Computer interaction that responds to your actions; for example by presenting text, graphics, animation, video, audio, or games. Also referred to as rich media.

Internal link A hyperlink that connects to another page in the same website.

Internet Explorer A web browser developed by Microsoft.

Justified alignment An arrangement of text in which the text aligns evenly on both the left and right margins.

Keep lines together A formatting feature that prevents a single line from displaying by itself at the bottom of a page or at the top of a page.

Keep with next A formatting feature that causes two elements, such as a heading and the paragraph that follows, to display together on the same page.

Kerning A character spacing option that automatically adjusts the spacing between pairs of characters, with a specified minimum point size, so that words and letters appear equally spaced.

Keyboard shortcut A combination of two or more keyboard keys, used to perform a task that would otherwise require a mouse.

KeyTip The letter that displays on a command in the ribbon and that indicates the key you can press to activate the command when keyboard control of the ribbon is activated.

Keywords Custom file properties in the form of words that you associate with a document to give an indication of the document's content; used to help find and organize files. Also called *tags*.

Landscape orientation A page orientation in which the paper is wider than it is tall.

Layout The placement and arrangement of the text and graphic elements on a slide.

Layout Options A Word feature that displays commands to control the manner in which text wraps around a chart or other object.

Leader character Characters that form a solid, dotted, or dashed line that fills the space preceding a tab stop.

Left alignment An arrangement of text in which the text aligns at the left margin, leaving the right margin uneven.

Legacy control A field used in designing a form for persons who possess older versions of Word.

Legal citation A reference to an authoritative document, such as a regulation, a statute, or a case.

Legend The part of a chart that identifies the colors assigned to each data series or category.

Letterhead The personal or company information that displays at the top of a letter.

Line break indicator A nonprinting character in the shape of a bent arrow that indicates a manual line break.

Line chart A chart type that shows trends over time.

Line spacing The distance between lines of text in a paragraph.

Linked object An object that maintains a direct connection to the source file.

Linked style A style, indicated by the symbol ¶a, that behaves as either a character style or a paragraph style, depending on what you select.

inking The process of inserting information from a source file into a destination file, while maintaining a connection between the two files.

ist style A style that applies a format to a list.

ive Layout A feature that reflows text as you move or size an object so that you can view the placement of surrounding text.

ive Preview A technology that shows the result of applying an editing or formatting change as you point to possible results—*before* you actually apply it.

ocation Any disk drive, folder, or other place in which you can store files and folders.

ock Tracking A feature that prevents reviewers from turning off Track Changes and making changes that are not visible in markup.

Macro A set of commands and instructions that can be grouped as a single command to accomplish a task automatically.

Macro virus A macro that causes files to be erased or damaged by inserting unauthorized code.

Mail merge A feature that joins a main document and a data source to create customized letters or labels.

Main document In a mail merge, the document that contains the text or formatting that remains constant.

Manual column break An artificial end to a column to balance columns or to provide space for the insertion of other objects.

Manual line break A break that moves text to the right of the insertion point to a new line while keeping the text in the same paragraph.

Manual page break The action of forcing a page to end and placing subsequent text at the top of the next page.

Margins The space between the text and the top, bottom, left, and right edges of the paper.

Markup The formatting Word uses to denote a document's revisions visually.

Markup area The space to the right or left of a document where comments and formatting changes display in balloons.

Master document A Word document that serves as a container for the different parts of a document.

Match Fields A Word feature that maps predefined field names to the field names in a data source.

Memorandum (Memo) A written message sent to someone working in the same organization.

Merge A table feature that combines two or more adjacent cells into one cell so that the text spans across multiple columns or rows.

Merge field In a mail merge, a placeholder that represents specific information in the data source.

Metadata Details about a file that describe or identify it, including the title, author name, subject, and keywords that identify the document's topic or contents; also known as *document properties*.

Microsoft Office 365 A set of secure online services that enable people in an organization to communicate and collaborate by using any Internet-connected device—a computer, a tablet, or a mobile phone.

Mini toolbar A small toolbar containing frequently used formatting commands that displays as a result of selecting text or objects.

Minus outline symbol A formatting mark that indicates there are no subordinate heading or body text paragraphs.

Modern Language Association (MLA) One of two commonly used style guides for formatting research papers.

MRU Acronym for *most recently used*, which refers to the state of some commands that retain the characteristic most recently applied; for example, the Font Color button retains the most recently used color until a new color is chosen.

Multilevel list A list in which the items display in a visual hierarchical structure.

Multiple Pages A zoom setting that decreases the magnification to display several pages of a document.

Nameplate The banner on the front page of a newsletter that identifies the publication.

Navigate The process of exploring within the organizing structure of Windows.

Navigation bar A series of text links across the top or bottom of a webpage that, when clicked, will link to another webpage on the same website.

Navigation pane In a folder window, the area on the left in which you can navigate to, open, and display favorites, libraries, folders, saved searches, and an expandable list of drives.

Nested table A table inserted in a cell of an existing table.

Newsletter A periodical that communicates news and information to a specific group.

No Markup A Track Changes view that displays the document in its final form—with all proposed changes included and comments hidden.

No Paragraph Style The built-in paragraph style—available from the Paragraph Spacing command—that inserts *no* extra space before or after a paragraph and uses line spacing of 1.

Nonbreaking hyphen A formatting mark that prevents a hyphenated word or phrase from being displayed on two lines.

Nonbreaking space A formatting mark that keeps two words together so that both words will wrap even if only the second word would normally wrap to the next line.

Noncontiguous Items that are not adjacent to one another.

Nonprinting characters Characters that display on the screen, but do not print, indicating where the Enter key, the Spacebar, and the Tab key were pressed; also called *formatting marks*.

Normal The default style in Word for new documents and which includes default styles and customizations that determine the basic look of a document; for example, it includes the Calibri font, 11 point font size, line spacing at 1.08, and 8 pt spacing after a paragraph.

Normal template The template that serves as a basis for all Word documents.

Note In a research paper, information that expands on the topic, but that does not fit well in the document text.

Notification bar An area at the bottom of an Internet Explorer window that displays information about pending downloads, security issues, add-ons, and other issues related to the operation of your computer.

Numbered list A list that uses consecutive numbers or letters to introduce each item in a list.

Numerical data Numbers that represent facts.

Object A table, chart, graphic, file, or other form of information.

Object anchor The symbol that indicates to which paragraph an object is attached.

Object Linking and Embedding (OLE) A program-integration technology for sharing information between Office programs.

Odd Page section break A formatting mark that indicates the beginning of a new section on the next odd-numbered page.

Office 365 Administrator The person who creates and manages the account, adds new users, sets up the services your organization wants to use, sets permission levels, and manages the SharePoint team sites.

Office Online (formerly Web Apps) The free online companions to Microsoft Word, Excel, PowerPoint, Access, and OneNote.

Office Presentation Service A Word feature to present your Word document to others who can watch in a web browser.

One-click Row/Column Insertion A Word table feature with which you can insert a new row or column by pointing to the desired location and then clicking.

OneDrive (formerly SkyDrive) A free file storage and file sharing service provided by Microsoft when you sign up for a Microsoft account.

Open dialog box A dialog box from which you can navigate to, and then open on your screen, an existing file that was created in that same program.

Option button In a dialog box, a round button that enables you to make one choice among two or more options.

Options dialog box A dialog box within each Office application where you can select program settings and other options and preferences.

Organizer A dialog box where you can modify a document by using styles stored in another document or template.

Original A Track Changes view that displays the original, unchanged document with all revisions and comments hidden.

Outline A Word feature that allows you to organize the contents of a document in a structured manner.

Outline level A Word feature that defines the position of a paragraph in relation to all topics in a document and is formatted with a corresponding heading style.

Outline symbol A small gray circle that identifies heading and body text paragraphs.

Outline view A document view that displays the overall organization, or hierarchy, of the document's parts, including headings, subheadings, and subordinate text.

Page break indicator A dotted line with the text *Page Break* that indicates where a manual page break was inserted.

Pagination The process of arranging and numbering the pages in a document.

Pane A separate area of a window.

Paragraph style A style, indicated by ¶, that includes everything that a character style contains, plus all aspects of a paragraph's appearance; for example text alignment, tab stops, line spacing, and borders.

Paragraph symbol The symbol (¶) that represents the end of a paragraph.

Parenthetical references References that include the last name of the author or authors, and the page number in the referenced source.

Passim A term that indicates a citation occurs on five or more pages in a document.

Password A code that is used to gain access to a file.

Paste The action of placing text or objects that have been copied or cut from one location to another location.

Paste Options gallery A gallery of buttons that provides a Live Preview of all the Paste options available in the current context.

Path A sequence of folders that leads to a specific file or folder.

PDF The acronym for Portable Document Format, which is a file format that creates an image that preserves the look of your file; this is a popular format for sending documents electronically because the document will display on most computers.

PDF Reflow The ability to import PDF files into Word so that you can transform a PDF back into a fully editable Word document.

Person Card A feature that allows you to communicate with a reviewer—using email, instant messaging, phone, or video—directly from a comment.

Picture Effects Formatting that enhances a picture with effects such as shadow, glow, reflection, or 3-D rotation.

Picture styles Frames, shapes, shadows, borders, and other special effects that can be added to an image to create an overall visual style for the image.

Pie chart A chart type that shows the proportion of parts to a whole.

Placeholder text The nonprinting text in a content control that indicates the type of information to be entered in a specific location.

Plain Text content control A content control that enables the user to enter unformatted text.

Plus outline symbol A formatting mark that indicates there are subordinate heading or body text paragraphs.

Point The action of moving your mouse pointer over something on your screen.

Pointer Any symbol that displays on your screen in response to moving your mouse.

Points A measurement of the size of a font; there are 72 points in an inch.

Portable Document Format (PDF) A file format that creates an image that preserves the look of your file, but that cannot be easily changed; a popular format for sending documents electronically, because the document will display on most computers.

Portrait orientation A page orientation in which the paper is taller than it is wide.

Print Preview A view of a document as it will appear when you print it.

Procedure A block of programming code that performs one or more tasks.

Progress bar In a dialog box or taskbar button, a bar that indicates visually the progress of a task such as a download or file transfer.

Protected View A security feature in Office 2013 that protects your computer from malicious files by opening them in a restricted environment until you enable them; you might encounter this feature if you open a file from an email or download files from the Internet.

pt The abbreviation for *point*; for example, when referring to a font size.

Quick Access Toolbar In an Office program window, the small row of buttons in the upper left corner of the screen from which you can perform frequently used commands.

Quick Parts All of the reusable pieces of content that are available to insert into a document, including building blocks, document properties, and fields.

Quick Tables Tables that are stored as building blocks.

Read Mode A view in Word that optimizes the Word screen when you are reading Word documents on the screen and not creating or editing them.

Readability statistics A Spelling and Grammar tool that analyzes a document and determines the reading level of the text.

Read-only A property assigned to a file that prevents the file from being modified or deleted; it indicates that you cannot save any changes to the displayed document unless you first save it with a new name.

Read-only file A file that can be viewed but not changed.

Recolor A feature that enables you to change all colors in the picture to shades of a single color.

Record All of the categories of data pertaining to one person, place, thing, event, or idea, and which is formatted as a row in a database table.

Recording The process of creating a macro while performing specific actions in a document.

Reveal Formatting A pane that displays the formatted selection and includes a complete description of formats applied.

Reviewer An individual who reviews and marks changes on a document.

Reviewing pane A separate scrollable window that shows all of the changes and comments that currently display in a document.

Revisions Changes made to a document.

Ribbon A user interface in both Office 2013 and File Explorer that groups the commands for performing related tasks on tabs across the upper portion of the program window.

Rich media Computer interaction that responds to your actions; for example by presenting text, graphics, animation, video, audio, or games. Also referred to as *interactive media*.

Rich Text content control A content control that enables the user to enter text and apply formatting.

Rich Text Format (RTF) A universal file format, using the .rtf file extension, that can be read by many word processing programs.

Right alignment An arrangement of text in which the text aligns at the right margin, leaving the left margin uneven.

Right-click The action of clicking the right mouse button one time.

Rotation handle A symbol with which you can rotate a graphic to any angle; displays above the top center sizing handle.

Rules Conditional Word fields that allow you to determine how the merge process is completed.

Salutation The greeting line of a business letter, such as *Dear Sir*.

Sans serif font A font design with no lines or extensions on the ends of characters.

Scale A command that resizes a picture to a percentage of its size.

Screenshot An image of an active region or window on your computer that you can paste into a document.

ScreenTip A small box that displays useful information when you perform various mouse actions such as pointing to screen elements or dragging.

Scroll bar A vertical or horizontal bar in a window or a pane to assist in bringing an area into view, and which contains a scroll box and scroll arrows.

Scroll box The box in the vertical and horizontal scroll bars that can be dragged to reposition the contents of a window or pane on the screen.

Section A portion of a document that can be formatted differently from the rest of the document.

Section break A double dotted line that indicates the end of one section and the beginning of another section.

Selecting Highlighting, by dragging with your mouse, areas of text or data or graphics, so that the selection can be edited, formatted, copied, or moved.

Serif font A font design that includes small line extensions on the ends of the letters to guide the eye in reading from left to right.

Shapes Lines, arrows, stars, banners, ovals, rectangles, and other basic shapes with which you can illustrate an idea, a process, or a workflow.

SharePoint Collaboration software with which people in an organization can set up team sites to share information, manage documents, and publish reports for others to see.

Shortcut menu A menu that displays commands and options relevant to the selected text or object; also called a *context menu*.

Show Preview A formatting feature that displays a visual representation of each style in the Styles window.

Signature line An element added to a document that specifies who should sign the document.

Simple Markup The default Track Changes view that indicates revisions by vertical red lines in the left margin and indicates comments by icons in the right margin.

Single spacing The common name for line spacing in which there is *no* extra space before or after a paragraph and that uses line spacing of 1.

Sizing handles Small squares that indicate a picture or object is selected.

SkyDrive see OneDrive.

Skype A Microsoft product with which you can make voice calls, make video calls, transfer files, or send messages—including instant message and text messages—over the Internet.

Small caps A font effect that changes lowercase letters to uppercase letters, but with the height of lowercase letters.

SmartArt A designer-quality visual representation of your information that you can create by choosing from among many different layouts to effectively communicate your message or ideas.

Sorting The action of ordering data, usually in alphabetical or numeric order.

Source file The file where an object is created.

Spin box A small box with an upward- and downward-pointing arrow that lets you move rapidly through a set of values by clicking.

Split A table feature that divides selected cells into multiple cells with a specified number of rows and columns.

Split button A button divided into two parts and in which clicking the main part of the button performs a command and clicking the arrow opens a menu with choices.

Split Table A table feature that divides an existing table into two tables in which the selected row—where the insertion point is located—becomes the first row of the second table.

Split Window A Word feature that displays a document in two panes so that you can view or work on different parts of the document at the same time.

Stacking The process of placing objects in individual layers of the document.

Start search The search feature in Windows 8 in which, from the Start screen, you can begin to type and by default, Windows 8 searches for apps; you can adjust the search to search for files or settings.

Static text Descriptive text such as labels or headings.

Status bar The area along the lower edge of an Office program window that displays file information on the left and buttons to control how the window looks on the right.

Style A group of formatting commands, such as font, font size, font color, paragraph alignment, and line spacing, that can be applied to a paragraph with one command.

Style guide A manual that contains standards for the design and writing of documents.

Style Inspector A pane that displays the name of the selected style with formats applied and contains paragraph- and text-level formatting options.

Style set A group of styles that are designed to work together.

Styles pane A window that displays a list of styles and contains tools to manage styles.

Stylus A pen-like device used for writing on an electronic document.

Subdocument A section of a document that is linked to the master document.

Subfolder A folder within a folder.

Subject line The optional line following the inside address in a business letter that states the purpose of the letter.

Suppress A Word feature that hides header and footer information, including the page number, on the first page of a document.

Synchronization The process of updating computer files that are in two or more locations according to specific rules—also called *syncing*.

Synchronous scrolling The setting that causes two documents to scroll simultaneously.

Syncing The process of updating computer files that are in two or more locations according to specific rules—also called *synchronization*.

Synonyms Words with the same or similar meaning.

Tab stop A specific location on a line of text, marked on the Word ruler, to which you can move the insertion point by pressing the Tab key, and which is used to align and indent text.

Table An arrangement of information organized into rows and columns.

Table of authorities A list of all references in a legal document and the page numbers where the references occur.

Table of contents (TOC) A list of a document's headings and subheadings, marked with the page numbers where those headings and subheadings occur.

Table of figures A list of the figure captions in a document.

Table style A style that applies a consistent look to a table and includes formatting for the entire table and specific table elements, such as rows and columns.

Tablet PC A computer with a monitor that allows you to write on the screen.

Tabs (ribbon) On the Office ribbon, the name of each activity area.

Tags Custom file properties in the form of words that you associate with a document to give an indication of the document's content; used to help find and organize files. Also called *keywords*.

Taskbar The area along the lower edge of the desktop that displays buttons representing programs.

Team A group of workers tasked with working together to solve a problem, make a decision, or create a work product.

Template An existing doucment that you use as a starting point for a new document; it contains basic document settings, such as fonts, margins, and available styles, and can also store elements such as building blocks and content controls.

Text box A movable, resizable container for text or graphics.

Text control A content control that accepts only a text entry.

Text effects Decorative formats, such as shadowed or mirrored text, text glow, 3-D effects, and colors that make text stand out.

Text link A hyperlink applied to a selected word or phrase.

Text wrapping The manner in which text displays around an object.

Theme A predesigned set of colors, fonts, and line and fill effects that look good together and is applied to an entire document by a single selection.

Theme template A stored, user-defined set of colors, fonts, and effects that can be shared with other Office programs.

Thesaurus A research tool that provides a list of synonyms.

Thumbnail A graphical representation of a page.

Title bar The bar at the top edge of the program window that indicates the name of the current file and the program name.

Toggle button A button that can be turned on by clicking it once, and then turned off by clicking it again.

Toolbar In a folder window, a row of buttons with which you can perform common tasks, such as changing the view of your files and folders or burning files to a CD.

Track Changes A feature that makes a record of the changes made to a document.

Triple-click The action of clicking the left mouse button three times in rapid succession.

Trusted Documents A security feature in Office that remembers which files you have already enabled; you might encounter this feature if you open a file from an email or download files from the Internet.

Unformatted text Plain text without any special formatting applied.

Uniform Resource Locator An address that uniquely identifies a location on the Internet.

URL The acronym for Uniform Resource Locator, which is an address that uniquely identifies a location on the Internet.

USB flash drive A small data storage device that plugs into a computer USB port.

Variable In an equation, a letter that represents a value.

Vertical axis (Y-axis) The axis that displays along the left side of a chart.

Vertical change bar A line that displays in the left margin next to each line of text that contains a revision.

View Side by Side A view that displays two open documents in separate windows, next to each other on the screen.

Visual Basic Editor An editor that enables you to view and edit existing macro code or create a new macro.

Visual Basic for Applications (VBA) A programming language used to create macros.

Watermark A text or graphic element that displays behind document text.

Web browser (Browser) Software that interprets HTML files, formats them into webpages, and then displays them.

Web Page format A file type that saves a Word document as an HTML file, with some elements of the webpage saved in a folder, separate from the webpage itself.

Webpage A file coded in HTML that can be viewed on the Internet using a web browser.

Website A group of related webpages published to a specific location on the Internet.

Wildcard A special character such as * or ? that is used to search for an unknown term.

Window A rectangular area on a computer screen in which programs and content appear, and which can be moved, resized, minimized, or closed.

Windows Reader app A Windows Store app with which you can open a PDF or XPS file, zoom, find words or phrases, take notes, save changes, and then print or share the file.

Word count The number of words in a document.

Word Options A collection of settings that you can change to customize Word.

WordArt A feature that applies combinations of decorative formatting to text, including shadows, reflections, and 3-D effects, as well as changing the line and fill color of text.

Wordwrap The feature that moves text from the right edge of a paragraph to the beginning of the next line as necessary to fit within the margins.

Works Cited In the MLA style, a list of cited works placed at the end of a research paper or report.

Writer's identification The name and title of the author of a letter, placed near the bottom of the letter under the complimentary closing—also referred to as the *writer's signature block*.

Writer's signature block The name and title of the author of a letter, placed near the bottom of the letter, under the complimentary closing—also referred to as the *writer's identification*.

XE Code identifying an index entry.

XML Paper Specification A Microsoft file format that creates an image of your document and that opens in the XPS viewer.

XPS The acronym for XML Paper Specification—a Microsoft file format that creates an image of your document and that opens in the XPS viewer.

Zipped folder A folder that has been reduced in size and thus takes up less storage space and can be transferred to other computers quickly; also called a *compressed* folder.

Zoom The action of increasing or decreasing the size of the viewing area on the screen.

Index